THE PAPERS OF
THOMAS JEFFERSON

BARBARA B. OBERG
GENERAL EDITOR

THE PAPERS OF
Thomas Jefferson

Volume 29
1 March 1796 to 31 December 1797

BARBARA B. OBERG, EDITOR

JAMES P. McCLURE AND ELAINE WEBER PASCU,
ASSOCIATE EDITORS

LINDA MONACO, EDITORIAL ASSISTANT

JOHN E. LITTLE, RESEARCH ASSOCIATE

PRINCETON AND OXFORD
PRINCETON UNIVERSITY PRESS
2002

As INDICATED in the first volume, this edition was made possible by a grant of $200,000 from The New York Times Company to Princeton University. Since this initial subvention, its continuance has been assured by additional contributions from The New York Times Company and The New York Times Company Foundation; by grants of the Ford Foundation, the National Historical Publications and Records Commission, and the National Endowment for the Humanities; by grants of the Andrew W. Mellon Foundation, the Packard Humanities Institute, the Pew Charitable Trusts, the John Ben Snow Memorial Trust, and the L. J. Skaggs and Mary C. Skaggs Foundation to Founding Fathers Papers, Inc.; by benefactions from the Barkley Fund and the Lyn and Norman Lear Foundation through the National Trust for the Humanities, the Florence Gould Foundation, the Charlotte Palmer Phillips Foundation, Time Inc., the Dyson Foundation, and the Lucius N. Littauer Foundation; and by gifts from Robert C. Baron, James Russell Wiggins, David K. E. Bruce, and B. Batmanghelidj. In common with other editions of historical documents, THE PAPERS OF THOMAS JEFFERSON is a beneficiary of the good offices of the National Historical Publications and Records Commission, tendered in many useful forms through its officers and dedicated staff. For these and other indispensable aids generously given by librarians, archivists, scholars, and collectors of manuscripts, the Editors record their sincere gratitude.

FOREWORD

IN the twenty-two months covered by this volume, Jefferson spent most of his time at Monticello, where in his short-lived retirement from public office he described himself as completely absorbed in agriculture and a "monstrous farmer." He received orange trees, peas, wheat, vetch, grasses, and ideas from friends in America and Great Britain. In July 1796 he reported the "finest harvest" of wheat ever; the following month saw the first successful running of his Scottish threshing machine that was built by workers at Monticello. During this period Jefferson turned in earnest to the renovation of his residence. He anticipated that by summer 1796 the roof would be off and he would be living "under the tent of heaven." In fact the construction was always behind schedule as he entertained the many American and European visitors and family members who came to Monticello in 1796 and 1797. His two grandchildren, Anne Cary Randolph and Thomas Jefferson Randolph, frequently were in residence, sometimes with their mother and on occasion with both parents. Two significant family events occurred at Monticello: in October 1796 Martha Jefferson Randolph gave birth to another daughter, Ellen Wayles Randolph, and in the same month of the following year Mary Jefferson married John Wayles Eppes. Jefferson received the news of the proposed marriage "with inexpressible pleasure" and eagerly anticipated having both daughters and their families within close proximity of Monticello.

Although in the highly charged political context of this period Jefferson often was the target of attacks by Federalist newspaper editors, on two occasions in particular he was excoriated in the press for his writings. In May 1797 Noah Webster's New York *Minerva* published a portion of a private letter that a year earlier Jefferson had sent to his former neighbor Philip Mazzei. Vividly expressing Jefferson's profound disillusionment with the direction the nation and its political leaders had taken since the Revolution, the extract, widely reprinted, gave Federalists an opportunity to question Jefferson's loyalty to George Washington and the country and to doubt his fitness for public office. This famous letter plagued him for the rest of his life. Jefferson also came under attack by Luther Martin of Maryland, who beginning in the spring of 1797 addressed him in a series of letters in newspapers—some of which, like William Cobbett's anti-Jeffersonian *Porcupine's Gazette*, were fiercely partisan. Martin challenged Jefferson's treatment, in the *Notes on the State of Virginia*, of the famous speech of the Mingo Indian Logan and the role that Martin's father-in-law, Michael Cresap, was alleged to have played in the murder of Logan's family in 1774. Although he had a strong private reaction in each case,

Jefferson made no public response to the publication of the Mazzei letter or to Martin's attacks.

Losing by three electoral votes to John Adams in the presidential
election of 1796, Jefferson became vice president of the United States
in March 1797. His public duties called him to Philadelphia three times
in the course of the year. He made a short journey there to take the oath
of office in a one-day session of Congress. Inaugurated as president of
the American Philosophical Society on the same trip, an honor attesting
to his reputation as a preeminent patron of natural philosophy, he presided over a meeting at which his paper on the newly discovered fossils
of the megalonyx was presented. He reluctantly returned to the capital
for two months in the spring and early summer to preside over the Senate in the first full session of the Fifth Congress summoned by Adams to
deal with the country's worsening relations with France. He had only a
limited function in the Senate's business, but in a reversal of their earlier
roles he was a full reporter of domestic politics and foreign affairs to
James Madison in Virginia. Jefferson spent the summer and autumn at
home where, in addition to his attention to farming and architectural
renovation, he was keenly attentive to local and national politics. He
continued his close collaboration with Madison and James Monroe.
With the benefit of their advice, in the summer he drafted an important
petition for the Virginia House of Delegates that upheld the right of
representatives to communicate freely with their constituents. At the
end of the year Jefferson returned to Philadelphia for a stay that would
last six months. With a deepening dismay over the policies of the Adams
administration and what he saw to be a radical departure from the ideals
of the American revolutionary tradition, he increasingly was drawn into
the political affairs of the nation.

BARBARA OBERG

17 January 2001

ACKNOWLEDGMENTS

I<small>T</small> is the Editors' pleasant duty to record their gratitude to the many individuals who have assisted them in numerous ways as they prepared this volume for the press. Stephanie Longo helped in the transcription of documents and entering of editorial corrections. Assistant Editors Shane Blackman and F. Andrew McMichael assisted in reading proofs and preparing the index. Those who answered research queries or helped in other ways are Charles C. Gillispie, Anthony T. Grafton, William C. Jordan, Princeton University; also at Princeton, Karin A. Trainer, University Librarian, William Blair, Alfred L. Bush, Mary George, Sooni K. Johnson, Rosemary Little, and Susanne McNatt of Firestone Library; Timothy Connelly, J. Dane Hartgrove, Michael T. Meier of the National Historical Publications and Records Commission; James H. Hutson and his staff at the Manuscript Division of the Library of Congress, especially Fred Bauman, Jeffrey Flannery, Gerard W. Gawalt, and Mary Wolfskill; Rosemary Plakas of the Library of Congress Rare Book and Special Collections Division; Peter Drummey, Brenda M. Lawson, Virginia H. Smith, and others at the Massachusetts Historical Society; James Horn, Zanne MacDonald, Lucia C. Stanton, and Gaye Wilson of the Thomas Jefferson Foundation at Monticello; Michael Plunkett and the staff of the Special Collections Department at the University of Virginia Library; John S. Hopewell, Robert L. Scribner, and Minor T. Weisiger of the Library of Virginia; E. Lee Shepard of the Virginia Historical Society; Whitfield J. Bell, Jr., Robert Cox, Scott DeHaven, and Roy Goodman at the American Philosophical Society; Diana Peterson and Ann W. Upton of the Haverford College Library; Erika Piola of the Library Company of Philadelphia; Ted Daeschler of the Academy of Natural Sciences in Philadelphia; Verna L. Corwin and James L. Swauger of the Carnegie Museum of Natural History; Paul Romaine of the Gilder Lehrman Collection; staff members of the Historical Society of Pennsylvania and the New-York Historical Society; Melissa Malnati and Nancy Blum of the Bridgeman Art Library, New York; Arlene Shy and John C. Harriman of the William L. Clements Library; John Shy of the University of Michigan; Rebecca Cape of the Lilly Library, Indiana University; Douglas L. Wilson, Knox College; Chuck Hill of the Missouri Historical Society; Catherine Barnes of Philadelphia; our fellow editors of the Adams Papers at the Massachusetts Historical Society, the Papers of George Washington and the Papers of James Madison at the University of Virginia, the Papers of Benjamin Franklin at Yale University, the Papers of Robert Morris at Queens College of the City University of

ACKNOWLEDGMENTS

New York, the Papers of John Marshall at the College of William and Mary, the Documentary History of the First Federal Congress at The George Washington University, and the Documentary History of the Supreme Court. To these and other colleagues the Editors tender their cordial thanks.

GUIDE TO EDITORIAL APPARATUS

1. TEXTUAL DEVICES

The following devices are employed throughout the work to clarify the presentation of the text.

[. . .], [. . . .]	One or two words missing and not conjecturable.
[. . .]¹, [. . . .]¹	More than two words missing and not conjecturable; subjoined footnote estimates number of words missing.
[ ]	Number or part of a number missing or illegible.
[roman]	Conjectural reading for missing or illegible matter. A question mark follows when the reading is doubtful.
[*italic*]	Editorial comment inserted in the text.
⟨*italic*⟩	Matter deleted in the MS but restored in our text.

2. DESCRIPTIVE SYMBOLS

The following symbols are employed throughout the work to describe the various kinds of manuscript originals. When a series of versions is recorded, *the first to be recorded is the version used for the printed text.*

Dft	draft (usually a composition or rough draft; later drafts, when identifiable as such, are designated "2d Dft," &c.)
Dupl	duplicate
MS	manuscript (arbitrarily applied to most documents other than letters)
N	note, notes (memoranda, fragments, &c.)
PoC	polygraph copy
PrC	press copy
RC	recipient's copy
SC	stylograph copy
Tripl	triplicate

All manuscripts of the above types are assumed to be in the hand of the author of the document to which the descriptive symbol pertains. If not, that fact is stated. On the other hand, the following types of manuscripts are assumed *not* to be in the hand of the author, and exceptions will be noted:

FC   file copy (applied to all contemporary copies retained by the author or his agents)

Lb   letterbook (ordinarily used with FC and Tr to denote texts copied into bound volumes)

Tr   transcript (applied to all contemporary and later copies except file copies; period of transcription, unless clear by implication, will be given when known)

3. LOCATION SYMBOLS

The locations of documents printed in this edition from originals in private hands and from printed sources are recorded in self-explanatory form in the descriptive note following each document. The locations of documents printed from originals held by public and private institutions in the United States are recorded by means of the symbols used in the National Union Catalog in the Library of Congress; an explanation of how these symbols are formed is given in Vol. 1: xl. The symbols DLC and MHi by themselves stand for the collections of Jefferson Papers proper in these repositories; when texts are drawn from other collections held by these two institutions, the names of those collections will be added. Location symbols for documents held by institutions outside the United States are given in a subjoined list. The lists of symbols are limited to the institutions represented by documents printed or referred to in this volume.

CLU-C   University of California, Los Angeles, William Andrews Clark Memorial Library

CSmH   The Huntington Library, San Marino, California

CtY   Yale University Library

DLC   Library of Congress

DNA   The National Archives, with identifications of series (preceded by record group number) as follows:

        DL   Domestic Letters

        MTA   Miscellaneous Treasury Accounts

        PCC   Papers of the Continental Congress

DeHi   Historical Society of Delaware, Wilmington

InU-Li   Indiana University at Bloomington, Lilly Rare Books

ICN   Newberry Library, Chicago

MH   Harvard University, Cambridge

MHi   Massachusetts Historical Society, Boston

MdAN   United States Naval Academy Library, Annapolis, Maryland

MiU-C	William L. Clements Library, University of Michigan, Ann Arbor
MoSHi	Missouri Historical Society, St. Louis
NHi	New-York Historical Society, New York City
NN	New York Public Library
NNPM	Pierpont Morgan Library, New York City
NSyU	Syracuse University, New York
NcD	Duke University, Durham
NcU	University of North Carolina, Chapel Hill
NhPoS	Strawberry Banke, Portsmouth, New Hampshire
NjMoHP	Morristown National Historical Park, New Jersey
PHC	Haverford College Library, Pennsylvania
PHi	Historical Society of Pennsylvania, Philadelphia
PPAmP	American Philosophical Society, Philadelphia
PPRF	Rosenbach Foundation, Philadelphia
ScHi	South Carolina Historical Society, Charleston
TxU	University of Texas, Austin
Vi	Library of Virginia, Richmond
ViHi	Virginia Historical Society, Richmond
ViU	University of Virginia Library, Charlottesville
ViW	College of William and Mary Library, Williamsburg, Virginia
ViWC	Colonial Williamsburg, Inc., Williamsburg

The following symbol represents a repository located outside of the United States:

BNF	Biblioteca Nazionale, Florence, Italy

4. OTHER SYMBOLS AND ABBREVIATIONS

The following symbols and abbreviations are commonly employed in the annotation throughout the work.

Second Series   The topical series to be published as part of this edition, comprising those materials which are best suited to a topical rather than a chronological arrangement (see Vol. 1: xv-xvi)

TJ   Thomas Jefferson

TJ Editorial Files   Photoduplicates and other editorial materials in the office of *The Papers of Thomas Jefferson*, Princeton University Library

TJ Papers   Jefferson Papers (applied to a collection of manuscripts when the precise location of an undated, misdated, or otherwise problematic document must be furnished, and always preceded by the symbol for the institutional repository; thus "DLC: TJ Papers, 4: 628-9" represents a document in the Library of Congress, Jefferson Papers, volume 4, pages 628 and 629. Citations to volumes and folio numbers of the Jefferson Papers at the Library of Congress refer to the collection as it was arranged at the time the first microfilm edition was made in 1944-45. Access to the microfilm edition of the collection as it was rearranged under the Library's Presidential Papers Program is provided by the *Index to the Thomas Jefferson Papers* [Washington, D.C., 1976])

RG Record Group (used in designating the location of documents in the National Archives)

SJL Jefferson's "Summary Journal of Letters" written and received for the period 11 Nov. 1783 to 25 June 1826 (in DLC: TJ Papers). This register, kept in Jefferson's hand, has been checked against the TJ Editorial Files. It is to be assumed that all outgoing letters are recorded in SJL unless there is a note to the contrary. When the date of receipt of an incoming letter is recorded in SJL, it is incorporated in the notes. Information and discrepancies revealed in SJL but not found in the letter itself are also noted. Missing letters recorded in SJL are, where possible, accounted for in the notes to documents mentioning them or in related documents. A more detailed discussion of this register and its use in this edition appears in Vol. 6: vii-x

SJPL "Summary Journal of Public Letters," an incomplete list of letters and documents written by TJ from 16 Apr. 1784 to 31 Dec. 1793, with brief summaries, in an amanuensis's hand. This is supplemented by six pages in TJ's hand, compiled at a later date, listing private and confidential memorandums and notes as well as official reports and communications by and to him as Secretary of State, 11 Oct. 1789 to 31 Dec. 1793 (in DLC: TJ Papers, Epistolary Record, 514-59 and 209-11, respectively; see Vol. 22: ix-x). Since nearly all documents in the amanuensis's list are registered in SJL, while few in TJ's list are so recorded, it is to be assumed that all references to SJPL are to the list in TJ's hand unless there is a statement to the contrary

V Ecu

f Florin

£ Pound sterling or livre, depending upon context (in doubtful cases, a clarifying note will be given)

s Shilling or sou (also expressed as /)

d Penny or denier

₶ Livre Tournois

℞ Per (occasionally used for pro, pre)

5. SHORT TITLES

The following list includes only those short titles of works cited frequently, and therefore in very abbreviated form, throughout this edition. Since it is impossible to anticipate all the works to be cited in very abbreviated form, the list is accordingly revised from volume to volume.

Adams, *Diary*   L. H. Butterfield and others, eds., *Diary and Autobiography of John Adams*, Cambridge, Mass., 1961, 4 vols.

Adams, *Works*   Charles Francis Adams, ed., *The Works of John Adams*, Boston, 1850-56, 10 vols.

Ammon, *Monroe*   Harry Ammon, *James Monroe: The Quest for National Identity*, New York, 1971

ANB   John A. Garraty and Mark C. Carnes, eds., *American National Biography*, New York and Oxford, 1999, 24 vols.

Annals   *Annals of the Congress of the United States: The Debates and Proceedings in the Congress of the United States . . . Compiled from Authentic Materials*, Washington, D.C., Gales & Seaton, 1834-56, 42 vols. All editions are undependable and pagination varies from one printing to another. The first two volumes of the set cited here have "Compiled . . . by Joseph Gales, Senior" on the title page and bear the caption "Gales & Seatons History" on verso and "of Debates in Congress" on recto pages. The remaining volumes bear the caption "History of Congress" on both recto and verso pages. Those using the first two volumes with the latter caption will need to employ the date of the debate or the indexes of debates and speakers.

APS   American Philosophical Society

ASP   *American State Papers: Documents, Legislative and Executive, of the Congress of the United States*, Washington, D.C., Gales & Seaton, 1832-61, 38 vols.

Bear, *Family Letters*   Edwin M. Betts and James A. Bear, Jr., eds., *Family Letters of Thomas Jefferson*, Columbia, Mo., 1966

Beauvais de Préau, *Guerres de la révolution française*   Charles Théodore Beauvais de Préau, ed., *Guerres de la révolution française et du premier empire, par une société d'écrivains militaires et civils*, Paris, 1876, 13 vols.

Bemis, *Pinckney's Treaty*   Samuel Flagg Bemis, *Pinckney's Treaty: America's Advantage from Europe's Distress, 1783-1800*, rev. ed., New Haven, 1960

Berkeley, *Beckley*   Edmund Berkeley and Dorothy Smith Berkeley, *John Beckley: Zealous Partisan in a Nation Divided*, Philadelphia, 1973

Betts, *Farm Book*   Edwin M. Betts, ed., *Thomas Jefferson's Farm Book*, Princeton, 1953

Betts, *Garden Book*   Edwin M. Betts, ed., *Thomas Jefferson's Garden Book, 1766-1824*, Philadelphia, 1944

Biog. Dir. Cong.   *Biographical Directory of the United States Congress, 1774-1989*, Washington, D.C., 1989

Biographie universelle   *Biographie universelle, ancienne et moderne*, new ed., Paris, 1843-65, 45 vols.

Boyd, "Megalonyx"   Julian P. Boyd, "The Megalonyx, the Megatherium, and Thomas Jefferson's Lapse of Memory," *Proceedings of the American Philosophical Society*, CII, no. 5, 1958, 420-35

Brant, *Madison*   Irving Brant, *James Madison*, Indianapolis, 1941-61, 6 vols.

Brigham, *American Newspapers*   Clarence S. Brigham, *History and Bibliography of American Newspapers, 1690-1820*, Worcester, Mass., 1947, 2 vols.

Callender, *History*   James T. Callender, *The History of the United States for 1796; including a Variety of Interesting Particulars Relative to the Federal Government Previous to that Period*, Philadelphia, 1797

Chandler, *Campaigns of Napoleon*   David G. Chandler, *The Campaigns of Napoleon*, New York, 1966

Clarkson and Jett, *Luther Martin*   Paul S. Clarkson and R. Samuel Jett, *Luther Martin of Maryland*, Baltimore, 1970

Combs, *Jay Treaty*   Jerald A. Combs, *The Jay Treaty*, Berkeley, 1970

Cooke, *Coxe*   Jacob E. Cooke, *Tench Coxe and the Early Republic*, Chapel Hill, 1978

Cuvier, "Mégalonix"   Georges Cuvier, "Sur le Mégalonix, Animal de la famille des Paresseux . . . ," *Annales du muséum National d'Histoire Naturelle*, v, 1804, 358-75

CVSP   William P. Palmer and others, eds., *Calendar of Virginia State Papers . . . Preserved in the Capitol at Richmond*, Richmond, 1875-93, 11 vols.

DAB   Allen Johnson and Dumas Malone, eds., *Dictionary of American Biography*, New York, 1928-36, 20 vols.

DHRC   Merrill Jensen, John P. Kaminski, Gaspare J. Saladino, and others, eds., *The Documentary History of the Ratification of the Constitution*, Madison, Wis., 1976- , 14 vols.

DHSC   Maeva Marcus and others, eds., *The Documentary History of the Supreme Court of the United States 1789-1800*, New York, 1985- , 6 vols.

Dictionnaire   *Dictionnaire de biographie française*, Paris, 1993- , 18 vols.

DNB   Leslie Stephen and Sidney Lee, eds., *Dictionary of National Biography*, 2d ed., New York, 1908-09, 22 vols.

DSB   Charles C. Gillispie, ed., *Dictionary of Scientific Biography*, New York, 1970-80, 16 vols.

Durey, *Callender*   Michael Durey, *"With the Hammer of Truth": James Thomson Callender and America's Early National Heroes*, (Charlottesville, 1990)

Duvergier, *Lois*   Jean B. Duvergier, ed., *Collection Complete des Lois, Décrets, Ordonnances, Réglemens, avis du Conseil-d'État*, Paris, 1834-1908, 108 vols.

EG   Dickinson W. Adams and Ruth W. Lester, eds., *Jefferson's Extracts from the Gospels*, Princeton, 1983, *The Papers of Thomas Jefferson*, Second Series

Ehrman, *Pitt*   John Ehrman, *The Younger Pitt: The Reluctant Transition*, London, 1983

Elkins and McKitrick, *Age of Federalism*   Stanley Elkins and Eric McKitrick, *The Age of Federalism*, New York, 1993

Emsley, *British Society and the French Wars*   Clive Emsley, *British Society and the French Wars 1793-1815*, London, 1979

Evans   Charles Evans, Clifford K. Shipton, and Roger P. Bristol, comps., *American Bibliography: A Chronological Dictionary of all Books, Pamphlets and Periodical Publications Printed in the United States of America from . . . 1639 . . . to . . . 1820*, Chicago and Worcester, Mass., 1903-59, 14 vols.

Fitzpatrick, *Writings*   John C. Fitzpatrick, ed., *The Writings of George Washington*, Washington, D.C., 1931-44, 39 vols.

Ford   Paul Leicester Ford, ed., *The Writings of Thomas Jefferson*, Letterpress Edition, New York, 1892-99, 10 vols.

Freeman, *Washington*   Douglas Southall Freeman, *George Washington*, New York, 1948-57, 7 vols.; 7th volume by J. A. Carroll and M. W. Ashworth

Gaines, *Randolph*   William H. Gaines, Jr., *Thomas Mann Randolph: Jefferson's Son-in-Law*, Baton Rouge, 1966

Gibbs, *Memoirs*   George Gibbs, ed., *Memoirs of the Administration of Washington and John Adams, edited from the Papers of Oliver Wolcott, Secretary of the Treasury*, New York, 1846, 2 vols.

Goebel and Smith, *Law Practice of Hamilton*   Julius Goebel, Jr., and Joseph H. Smith, eds., *The Law Practice of Alexander Hamilton: Documents and Commentary*, New York, 1964-1981, 5 vols.

Greene, *American Science*   John C. Greene, *American Science in the Age of Jefferson*, Ames, Iowa, 1984

Hamilton, *Observations*   *Observations on Certain Documents Contained in No. V & VI of "The History of the United States for the Year 1796," in Which the Charge of Speculation Against Alexander Hamilton, Late Secretary of the Treasury, is Fully Refuted. Written by Himself*, Philadelphia, 1797

HAW   Henry A. Washington, ed., *The Writings of Thomas Jefferson*, New York, 1853-54, 9 vols.

Heitman, *Dictionary*   Francis B. Heitman, comp., *Historical Register and Dictionary of the United States Army . . .* , Washington, D.C., 1903, 2 vols.

Heitman, *Register*   Francis B. Heitman, *Historical Register of Officers of the Continental Army during the War of the Revolution, April, 1775, to December, 1793*, new ed., Washington, D.C., 1914

Hening   William Waller Hening, ed., *The Statutes at Large; Being a Collection of All the Laws of Virginia*, Richmond, 1809-23, 13 vols.

Hoefer, *Nouv. biog. générale*   J. C. F. Hoefer, *Nouvelle biographie générale depuis les temps les plus reculés jusqu'a nos jours*, Paris, 1855-66, 46 vols.

Imlay, *Topographical Description*   Gilbert Imlay, *A Topographical Description of the Western Territory of North America; containing a succinct Account of its Climate, Natural History, Population, Agriculture, Manners and Customs . . .*, London, 1792

Jackson, *Papers*   Harold D. Moser and others, eds., *The Papers of Andrew Jackson*, Knoxville, 1980- , 5 vols.

JAH   *Journal of American History*, 1964-

JCC   Worthington C. Ford and others, eds., *Journals of the Continental Congress, 1774-1789*, Washington, D.C., 1904-37, 34 vols.

Jefferson Correspondence, Bixby   Worthington C. Ford, ed., *Thomas Jefferson Correspondence Printed from the Originals in the Collections of William K. Bixby*, Boston, 1916

JEP   *Journal of the Executive Proceedings of the Senate of the United States . . . to the Termination of the Nineteenth Congress*, Washington, D.C., 1828

JHD   *Journal of the House of Delegates of the Commonwealth of Virginia* (cited by session and date of publication)

JHR   *Journal of the House of Representatives of the United States*, Washington, D.C., Gales & Seaton, 1826, 9 vols.

Johnston, *Memorials*   Frederick Johnston, *Memorials of Old Virginia Clerks*, Lynchburg, 1888

JS   *Journal of the Senate of the United States*, Washington, D.C., Gales, 1820-21, 5 vols.

Kimball, *Jefferson, Architect*   Fiske Kimball, *Thomas Jefferson, Architect*, Boston, 1916

King, *Life*   Charles R. King, ed. *The Life and Correspondence of Rufus King: Comprising His Letters, Private and Official, His Public Documents and His Speeches*, New York, 1894-1900, 6 vols.

Kline, *Burr*   Mary-Jo Kline, ed., *Political Correspondence and Public Papers of Aaron Burr*, Princeton, 1983, 2 vols.

Kline, *PAB*   Mary-Jo Kline and others, eds., *The Papers of Aaron Burr, 1756-1836*, microfilm edition in 27 reels, Glen Rock, N.J., 1978

Kurtz, *Presidency of John Adams*   Stephen G. Kurtz, *The Presidency of John Adams: The Collapse of Federalism, 1795-1800*, Philadelphia, 1957

L & B   Andrew A. Lipscomb and Albert E. Bergh, eds., *The Writings of Thomas Jefferson*, Washington, D.C., 1903-04, 20 vols.

La Rochefoucauld-Liancourt, *Voyage*   François Alexandre Frédéric, Duc de La Rochefoucauld-Liancout, *Voyage dans les États-Unis d'Amérique, fait en 1795, 1796 et 1797*, Paris, 1799, 8 vols.

LCB   Douglas L. Wilson, ed., *Jefferson's Literary Commonplace Book*, Princeton, 1989, *The Papers of Thomas Jefferson*, Second Series

Lefebvre, *Thermidorians*   Georges Lefebvre, *The Thermidorians and the Directory: Two Phases of the French Revolution*, trans. Robert Baldick, New York, 1964

Leonard, *General Assembly*   Cynthia Miller Leonard, comp., *The General Assembly of Virginia, July 30, 1619-January 11, 1978: A Bicentennial Register of Members*, Richmond, 1978

List of Patents   *A List of Patents granted by the United States from April 10, 1792, to December 31, 1836*, Washington, D.C., 1872

Lyons, *France Under the Directory*   Martyn Lyons, *France Under the Directory*, Cambridge, 1975

McColley, *Slavery*   Robert McColley, *Slavery and Jeffersonian Virginia*, Urbana, Ill., 1964

Madison, *Letters*   William C. Rives and Philip R. Fendall, eds., *Letters and Other Writings of James Madison . . . Published by Order of Congress*, Philadelphia, 1865, 4 vols.

Madison, *Papers*   William T. Hutchinson, Robert A. Rutland, J. C. A. Stagg, and others, eds., *The Papers of James Madison*, Chicago and Charlottesville, 1962-   , 26 vols.
    Sec. of State Ser., 4 vols.

Malone, *Jefferson*   Dumas Malone, *Jefferson and his Time*, Boston, 1948-81, 6 vols.

Marchione, *Mazzei: Writings*   Margherita Marchione, ed., *Philip Mazzei: Selected Writings and Correspondence*, Prato, Italy, 1983, 3 vols.

Marshall, *Papers*   Herbert A. Johnson, Charles T. Cullen, Charles F. Hobson, and others, eds., *The Papers of John Marshall*, Chapel Hill, 1974- , 8 vols.

Mason, *Papers*   Robert A. Rutland, ed., *The Papers of George Mason 1725-1792*, Chapel Hill, 1970, 3 vols.

MB   James A. Bear, Jr., and Lucia C. Stanton, eds., *Jefferson's Memorandum Books: Accounts, with Legal Records and Miscellany, 1767-1826*, Princeton, 1997, *The Papers of Thomas Jefferson*, Second Series

Melton, *First Impeachment*   Buckner F. Melton, Jr., *The First Impeachment: The Constitution's Framers and the Case of Senator William Blount*, Macon, GA, 1998

Merrill, *Jefferson's Nephews*   Boynton Merrill, Jr., *Jefferson's Nephews: A Frontier Tragedy*, Princeton, 1976

Miller, *Treaties*   Hunter Miller, ed., *Treaties and other International Acts of the United States of America*, Washington, D.C., 1931-48, 8 vols.

Monroe, *Writings*   Stanislas Murray Hamilton, ed., *The Writings of James Monroe*, New York, 1899, 7 vols.

Morris, *Papers*   E. James Ferguson, John Catanzariti, Elizabeth M. Nuxoll, Mary A. Y. Gallagher and others, eds., *The Papers of Robert Morris, 1781-1784*, Pittsburgh, 1973- , 8 vols.

MVHR   *Mississippi Valley Historical Review*, 1914-64

National State Papers: Adams   Martin P. Claussen, ed., *National State Papers of the United States, 1789-1817. Part II: Texts of Documents. Administration of John Adams, 1797-1801*, Wilmington, 1980, 24 vols.

Nichols, *Architectural Drawings*   Frederick Doveton Nichols, *Thomas Jefferson's Architectural Drawings, Compiled and with Commentary and a Check List*, Charlottesville, Virginia, 1978

Notes, ed. Peden   Thomas Jefferson, *Notes on the State of Virginia*, ed. William Peden, Chapel Hill, 1955

OED   Sir James Murray and others, eds., *A New English Dictionary on Historical Principles*, Oxford, 1888-1933

Palmer, *Democratic Revolution*   R. R. Palmer, *The Age of the Democratic Revolution: A Political History of Europe and America, 1760-1800*, Princeton, 1959-64, 2 vols.

Peale, *Papers*   Lillian B. Miller and others, eds., *The Selected Papers of Charles Willson Peale and His Family*, New Haven, 1983-96, 4 vols. in 5

Perkins, *First Rapprochement*   Bradford Perkins, *The First Rapprochement: England and the United States, 1795-1805*, Philadelphia, 1955; Berkeley, Los Angeles, and London, 1967

Peterson, *Jefferson*   Merrill D. Peterson, *Thomas Jefferson and the New Nation*, New York, 1970

PMHB   *The Pennsylvania Magazine of History and Biography*

Prince, *Federalists*   Carl E. Prince, *The Federalists and the Origins of the U.S. Civil Service*, New York, 1977

PW   Wilbur S. Howell, ed., *Jefferson's Parliamentary Writings*, Princeton, 1988, *The Papers of Thomas Jefferson*, Second Series

Randall, *Life*   Henry S. Randall, *The Life of Thomas Jefferson*, New York, 1858, 3 vols.

Randolph, *Domestic Life*   Sarah N. Randolph, *The Domestic Life of Thomas Jefferson, Compiled from Family Letters and Reminiscences by His Great-Granddaughter*, 3d ed., Cambridge, Mass., 1939

Rose, *Prologue to Democracy*   Lisle A. Rose, *Prologue to Democracy: The Federalists in the South, 1789-1800*, Lexington, Ky., 1968

Scott and Rothaus, *Historical Dictionary*   Samuel F. Scott and Barry Rothaus, eds., *Historical Dictionary of the French Revolution, 1789-1799*, Westport, Conn., 1985, 2 vols.

Seeber, "Critical Views,"   Edward D. Seeber, "Critical Views on Logan's Speech," *Journal of American Folklore*, LX, 1947, 130-46

Shackelford, *Jefferson's Adoptive Son*   George Green Shackelford, *Jefferson's Adoptive Son: The Life of William Short, 1759-1848*, Lexington, Ky., 1993

Shepherd, *Statutes*   Samuel Shepherd, ed., *The Statutes at Large of Virginia, from October Session 1792, to December Session 1806 . . .*, Richmond, 1835-36, 3 vols.

Sowerby   E. Millicent Sowerby, comp., *Catalogue of the Library of Thomas Jefferson*, Washington, D.C., 1952-59, 5 vols.

Stewart, *French Revolution*   John A. Stewart, *A Documentary Survey of the French Revolution*, New York, 1951

Stewart, *Opposition Press*   Donald H. Stewart, *The Opposition Press of the Federalist Period*, Albany, 1969

Syrett, *Hamilton*   Harold C. Syrett and others, eds., *The Papers of Alexander Hamilton*, New York, 1961-87, 27 vols.

Tagg, *Bache*   James Tagg, *Benjamin Franklin Bache and the Philadelphia Aurora*, Philadelphia, 1991

Terr. Papers   Clarence E. Carter and John Porter Bloom, eds., *The*

Territorial Papers of the United States, Washington, D.C., 1934-75, 28 vols.

TJR   Thomas Jefferson Randolph, ed., *Memoir, Correspondence, and Miscellanies, from the Papers of Thomas Jefferson*, Charlottesville, 1829, 4 vols.

TQHGM   L. G. Tyler, ed., *Tyler's Quarterly Historical and Genealogical Magazine*, Richmond, 1920-52, 34 vols. in 33

Tucker, *Life*   George Tucker, *The Life of Thomas Jefferson*, Philadelphia, 1837, 2 vols.

U.S. Statutes at Large   Richard Peters, ed., *The Public Statutes at Large of the United States . . . 1789 to March 3, 1845*, Boston, 1855-56, 8 vols.

Van Horne, *Latrobe*   John C. Van Horne, ed., *The Correspondence and Miscellaneous Papers of Benjamin Henry Latrobe*, New Haven, 1984-88, 3 vols.

VMHB   *Virginia Magazine of History and Biography*, 1893-

Washington, *Diaries*   Donald Jackson and Dorothy Twohig, eds., *The Diaries of George Washington*, Charlottesville, 1976-79, 6 vols.

Washington, *Papers*   W. W. Abbot, Dorothy Twohig, Philander D. Chase, and others, eds., *The Papers of George Washington*, Charlottesville, 1984-   , 39 vols.

    Pres. Ser., 1987-   , 9 vols.

    Ret. Ser., 1998-99, 4 vols.

White, *Federalists*   Leonard White, *The Federalists: A Study in Administrative History*, New York, 1948

White, *Middle Ground*   Richard White, *The Middle Ground: Indians, Empires, and Republics in the Great Lakes Region, 1650-1815*, Cambridge, 1991

WMQ   *William and Mary Quarterly*, 1892-

Woods, *Albemarle*   Edgar Woods, *Albemarle County in Virginia*, Charlottesville, 1901

Young, *Democratic Republicans*   Alfred F. Young, *The Democratic Republicans of New York: The Origins, 1763-1797*, Chapel Hill, 1967

CONTENTS

FOREWORD   vii
GUIDE TO EDITORIAL APPARATUS   xi
ILLUSTRATIONS   xxxvii
JEFFERSON CHRONOLOGY   2

1796

From Benjamin Rush, *1 March*   3
To James Monroe, *2 March*   4
From Robert Pollard, *3 March*   6
To James Madison, *6 March*   6
From James Madison, *6 March*   9
To Martha Jefferson Randolph, *6 March*   11
To Richard Harrison, *8 March*   11
Statement on Accounts as
      Minister Plenipotentiary in France, *8 March*   13
To Richard Harrison, *9 March*   24
From James Madison, *13 March*   25
To Thomas Mann Randolph, *13 March*   26
From Thomas Pinckney, *16 March*   27
From William Cabell, *17 March*   30
To Jean Antoine Gautier, *17 March*   30
To Richard Harrison, *17 March*   33
To William Blount, *19 March*   34
To William Branch Giles, *19 March*   35
To Thomas Mann Randolph, *19 March*   36
To Robert Brooke, [*20 March*]   37
From William Branch Giles, *20 March*   38
Memorandum to Richard Harrison, [*ca. 20 March*]   38
To John Pendleton, *20 March*   39
To James Madison, *21 March*   41
From James Madison, *21 March*   41
To James Monroe, *21 March*   41
To Benjamin Hawkins, *22 March*   42
To John Bowyer, *25 March*   44
From Patrick White, *25 March*   45
From William Branch Giles, *26 March*   45
To John Barnes, *27 March*   50

CONTENTS

To James Brown, *27 March*   50

To James Madison, *27 March*   51

To Thomas Mann Randolph, *27 March*   52

From Volney, *28 March*   53

From William Branch Giles, *31 March*   54

From James Madison, *4 April*   55

To Archibald Stuart, *5 April*   57

From John Adams, *6 April*   58

From William Branch Giles, *6 April*   60

To Volney, *10 April*   61

From James Madison, *11 April*   62

To Thomas Mann Randolph, *11 April*   63

From John Stuart, *11 April*   64

From Van Staphorst & Hubbard, *11 April*   65

Agreement with Randolph Jefferson, *17 April*   66

To James Madison, enclosing Extract of Madison's Notes on
    Debates in the Federal Convention and
    Extracts from Jefferson's Papers, with Comments, *17 April*   67

From Thomas Pinckney, *17 April*   69

From James Madison, *18 April*   70

From Tench Coxe, *22 April*   71

From Aaron Burr, *23 April*   72

From James Madison, *23 April*   72

Jefferson's Letter to Philip Mazzei   73

    I. Thomas Jefferson to Philip Mazzei, *24 April*   81

    II. Extract and Commentary Printed in the Paris *Moniteur*,
      [*25 January 1797*]   84

    III. Extract and Commentary Printed in the New York *Minerva*,
      [*2 May 1797*]   86

    IV. Italian Translation of Extract, *n.d.*   88

To James Madison, *24 April*   88

To Van Staphorst & Hubbard, *24 April*   90

To Thomas Mann Randolph, [*25 April*]   90

From Bushrod Washington, *26 April*   91

From Edward Rutledge, *30 April*   92

To James Lyle, *1 May*   93

From James Madison, *1 May*   93

From James Madison, *9 May*   95

To James Lyle, enclosing Deed of Mortgage of Slaves to
    Henderson, McCaul & Company, *12 May*   96

Deed of Mortgage of Slaves to Van Staphorst & Hubbard, *12 May*   98

To Francis Walker, *14 May*   99

CONTENTS

From Archibald Stuart, *15 May* 99
To Mann Page, [*16 May*] 100
From Alexandre Lerebours, *17 May* 101
From Patrick White, *19 May* 102
From William Strickland, *20 May* 102
From Van Staphorst & Hubbard, *21 May* 106
To John Barnes, 2[2] *May* 107
From James Madison, *22 May* 108
From William Thornton, *22 May* 110
From Volney, *22 May* 111
To James Brown, *23 May* 112
To Archibald Stuart, *26 May* 113
To John Stuart, *26 May* 113
From Sir John Sinclair, *28 May* 114
From William Strickland, *28 May* 115
From Joseph Marx, *29 May* 119
From James Madison, *30 May* 119
From Robert Pleasants, *1 June* 120
To Joseph Marx, *4 June* 121
To Charles Willson Peale, *5 June* 121
From Jean Antoine Gautier, *7 June* 122
To James Monroe, *12 June* 123
To John Barnes, *19 June* 125
To George Washington du Motier de Lafayette, [*19 June*] 126
To George Washington, *19 June* 127
From Richard Stith, *20 June* 130
From Jonathan Williams, *20 June* 130
To John Breckinridge, *21 June* 131
To Jean Baptiste Ducoigne, [*21 June*] 131
To Harry Innes, *21 June* 132
To Henri Peyroux de la Coudrèniere, *21 June* 132
To Isaac Shelby, *21 June* 134
To Archibald Stuart, *21 June* 134
From Tench Coxe, *22 June* 134
From Charles Willson Peale, *22 June* 136
To ———— Hite, *29 June* 137
To Archibald Stuart, *29 June* 138
To David Rittenhouse, *3 July* 138
To Jonathan Williams, *3 July* 139
To J. P. P. Derieux, [*4 July*] 141
From George Washington, *6 July* 141
To Madame de Chastellux, *10 July* 144

CONTENTS

To Tench Coxe, *10 July*   146
To James Monroe, *10 July*   147
From LaRochefoucauld-Liancourt, *11 July*   148
From Volney, *12 July*   150
From John Stuart, *13 July*   152
To Francis Willis, *15 July*   153
From John Guillemard, *18 July*   154
From Philip Turpin, *18 July*   155
From James Martin, [*20 July*]   156
To William Alexander, *26 July*   158
From George Wythe, *27 July*   158
From George Washington du Motier de Lafayette, *29 July*   159
From James Monroe, *30 July*   160
From Benjamin Smith Barton, *1 August*   165
To Francis Eppes, *4 August*   166
To John Barnes, *7 August*   167
To George Wythe, *8 August*   168
To Thomas Mann Randolph, *12 August*   168
From William Cocke, *17 August*   169
To Wilson Cary Nicholas, *19 August*   170
To Thomas Mann Randolph, *19 August*   170
From Archibald Stuart, *19 August*   171
From Wakelin Welch, enclosing
        Account with Robert Cary & Company, *22 August*   173
From Volney, *24 August*   174
From John Stuart, *25 August*   177
To Robert Pleasants, [*27 August*]   177
From George Washington, *28 August*   178
Questions on the Cow Pea, with Answers of Philip Tabb,
        [*after 30 August*]   179
From John Carey, *1 September*   180
From Benjamin Smith Barton, *5 September*   182
From Sir John Sinclair, *10 September*   183
To John Barnes, *11 September*   183
To Joseph Donath, *11 September*   184
From ——— Galvan, *21 September*   184
From John Garland Jefferson, *21 September*   185
From John Wayles Eppes, *25 September*   186
To John Barnes, *2 October*   186
To Joseph Donath, *2 October*   187
To William Booker, *4 October*   187
From William Booker, *7 October*   188

CONTENTS

To Bushrod Washington, *9 October*   189

From William Frederick Ast, *10 October*   190

To Benjamin Smith Barton, *10 October*   192

Documents Relating to the 1796 Campaign for Electors in Virginia   193

    I. Certificate of William Marshall, *10 October*   196

    II. Certificate of Joseph Jones Monroe and Thomas Bell,

      17 October   198

To William Cocke, *21 October*   199

From Van Staphorst & Hubbard, *21 October*   199

To James Currie, *22 October*   200

From Benjamin Smith Barton, *25 October*   200

From James Lyle, enclosing Statement of Interest and Payments

    on Bonds to Henderson, McCaul & Company, *25 October*   202

From William Fleming, *30 October*   204

To John Carey, *10 November*   205

To John Stuart, *10 November*   205

To John Barnes, *13 November*   206

From William Booker, *17 November*   207

From Jean Armand Tronchin, enclosing Tronchin's Memorandum

    on Recovering Foreign Debts in America, *17 November*   207

Deed of Mortgage of Slaves to Van Staphorst & Hubbard,

    21 November   209

To Peter Carr, *28 November*   210

To Thomas Mann Randolph, *28 November*   211

To John Barnes, *4 December*   212

To Joseph Donath, *4 December*   212

To Henry Banks, *5 December*   213

From James Madison, *5 December*   214

To Wilson Cary Nicholas, *5 December*   215

From John Wickham, *8 December*   217

From James Madison, *10 December*   218

To John Barnes, enclosing Power of Attorney to

    John Barnes for William Short, *11 December*   219

To Thomas A. Taylor, *11 December*   219

From Volney, *12 December*   220

To John Garland Jefferson, *17 December*   222

To James Madison, *17 December*   223

To Volney, [*17 December*]   224

From John Wayles Eppes, *19 December*   226

From James Madison, *19 December*   226

From James Madison, *25 December*   227

From Volney, *26 December*   229

CONTENTS

From Enoch Edwards, *27 December*   230
To Edward Rutledge, *27 December*   231
Jefferson's Letter to John Adams   234
     I. To John Adams, *28 December*   235
     II. Copy from Memory, *28 December*   236
From Volney, *29 December*   237
From Archibald Stuart, *31 December*   239
Declaration for the Mutual Assurance Society, [*1796 or later*]   239
Memorandum on Farming Operations, [*1796 or later*]   244
Notes on a Copying Process, [*1796*]   246

1797

Jefferson's Letter to James Madison   247
     I. To James Madison, *1 January*   247
     II. Copy from Memory, *1 January*   249
From Benjamin Rush, *4 January*   251
To Archibald Stuart, *4 January*   252
From the American Philosophical Society, *7 January*   254
To James Madison, *8 January*   255
From James Madison, *8 January*   255
To Volney, *8 January*   257
To Thomas Mann Randolph, *9 January*   260
From James Sullivan, *12 January*   262
From James Wood, *14 January*   262
From James Madison, *15 January*   263
To James Madison, *16 January*   266
From John Stuart, *16 January*   266
To Henry Tazewell, *16 January*   267
To John Wickham, *20 January*   268
To Enoch Edwards, *22 January*   269
To John Langdon, *22 January*   269
To James Madison, *22 January*   270
From James Madison, *22 January*   272
To Thomas Mann Randolph, *22 January*   273
To Benjamin Rush, *22 January*   275
To George Wythe, *22 January*   275
To the American Philosophical Society, *28 January*   276
To John Barnes, *28 January*   277
To John Marshall, *28 January*   278

CONTENTS

To James Wood, *28 January* — 279

From James Madison, *29 January* — 280

To James Madison, *30 January* — 280

From Henry Tazewell, *1 February* — 281

From George Wythe, *1 February* — 283

From Benjamin Rush, *4 February* — 284

From James Madison, *5 February* — 285

From Charles Willson Peale, *6 February* — 286

To Thomas Mann Randolph, *6 February* — 287

From Robert Pleasants, *8 February* — 287

To James Sullivan, *9 February* — 289

Memoir on the Megalonyx, [*10 February*] — 291

From James Madison, *11 February* — 304

From Timothy Pickering, *11 February* — 305

From Timothy Pickering, *11 February* — 306

To James Lyle, *12 February* — 306

From Timothy Pickering, *16 February* — 307

From Mary Jefferson, *27 February* — 308

To Martha Jefferson Randolph, *28 February* — 308

Notes on a Paragraph by John Henry, [*after 1 March*] — 309

From James Wood, *3 March* — 309

Address to the Senate, [*4 March*] — 310

From Madame de Chastellux, *5 March* — 312

From Enoch Edwards, [*6 March*] — 313

From Enoch Edwards, *9 March* — 313

To Mary Jefferson, *11 March* — 314

To Thomas Mann Randolph, *11 March* — 315

To William Short, *12 March* — 316

To Sir John Sinclair, *12 March* — 318

To William Strickland, *12 March* — 319

From Volney, *15 March* — 320

From Samuel Brown, *17 March* — 321

To Thomas Mann Randolph, *23 March* — 322

From Peregrine Fitzhugh, *25 March* — 323

To John Barnes, *26 March* — 324

From Timothy Pickering, *26 March* — 325

From John Trumbull, *26 March* — 325

From Elbridge Gerry, *27 March* — 326

To William Vans Murray, *27 March* — 327

To Martha Jefferson Randolph, *27 March* — 327

To Van Staphorst & Hubbard, enclosing
      Bond to Van Staphorst & Hubbard, *27 March* — 329

[xxix]

CONTENTS

To Van Staphorst & Hubbard, *28 March*   331

From William Short, *30 March*   332

From Martha Jefferson Randolph, *31 March*   334

From Willink, Van Staphorst & Hubbard, *31 March*   334

To James Wood, enclosing Notes on Plan of a Prison, and
       Table of Estimates, *31 March*   335

From Thomas Paine, *1 April*   340

To John Brown, *5 April*   345

To Peregrine Fitzhugh, *9 April*   346

From Alexandre Giroud, *9 April*   347

To Martha Jefferson Randolph, *9 April*   349

To Thomas Mann Randolph, *9 April*   349

To Elizabeth House Trist, *9 April*   350

To Volney, *9 April*   352

From Mann Page, *19 April*   353

From Jean François Paul Grand, *1 May*   354

From Pierre Auguste Adet, *4 May*   355

From Elbridge Gerry, *4 May*   355

From Edward Rutledge, *4 May*   356

From William Wirt, with Jefferson's Notes, *4 May*   358

From "Monitor," *7 May*   359

To Thomas Mann Randolph, *7 May*   360

From Antonia Reynon Carmichael, *8 May*   360

From Horatio Gates, *9 May*   361

To Elbridge Gerry, *13 May*   361

From Thomas Paine, *14 May*   366

From Thomas Bee, *16 May*   367

To Benjamin Smith Barton, *17 May*   367

From Stephen Cathalan, Jr., *17 May*   368

From Dugnani, *17 May*   370

To Thomas Bell, *18 May*   370

To James Madison, *18 May*   371

Richard O'Brien's Memorandum on Naval Protection, *18 May*   375

From John Oliver, *18 May*   377

To Martha Jefferson Randolph, *18 May*   379

From Peregrine Fitzhugh, *19 May*   380

From "A Native American," [*19 May*]   382

To Thomas Mann Randolph, *19 May*   385

From Edward Rutledge, *19 May*   386

From Elbridge Gerry, *22 May*   387

To Alexandre Giroud, *22 May*   387

To Allen Jones, *22 May*   388

CONTENTS

From Charles Louis Clérisseau, *23 May*   389

To Louis of Parma, *23 May*   389

The Senate to John Adams, [*23 May*]   392

John Adams to the Senate, [*24 May*]   396

To Angelica Schuyler Church, *24 May*   396

From Hugh Williamson, *24 May*   398

To Elbridge Gerry, *25 May*   398

To Mary Jefferson, *25 May*   399

From William Linn, *25 May*   400

To William Wardlaw, *25 May*   401

To Thomas Mann Randolph, *26 May*   402

From Elbridge Gerry, *28 May*   402

From Hugh Williamson, *28 May*   403

From Sebastian Bauman, *29 May*   403

To Thomas Pinckney, *29 May*   404

To Antonia Reynon Carmichael, *30 May*   406

To Horatio Gates, *30 May*   407

To John Oliver, *30 May*   408

To John Gibson, *31 May*   408

To James Madison, *1 June*   411

To Thomas Mann Randolph, *1 June*   413

To Dugald Stewart, [*2 June*]   415

To Peregrine Fitzhugh, *4 June*   415

To Wakelin Welch, *4 June*   419

Senate Resolution on Appointment of Charles C. Pinckney, [*5 June*]   420

From Tench Coxe, *7 June*   420

To James Madison, *8 June*   421

To Martha Jefferson Randolph, *8 June*   424

To French Strother, *8 June*   425

To Thomas Mann Randolph, *9 June*   426

From Thomas Bell, *12 June*   427

From Mary Jefferson, *12 June*   428

To John Moody, *13 June*   428

To Mary Jefferson, [*14 June*]   429

To Edward Stevens, *14 June*   431

To John Strode, *14 June*   432

To James Madison, *15 June*   433

From Pierre Malon, *15 June*   435

To Thomas Mann Randolph, *15 June*   436

To Aaron Burr, *17 June*   437

From John Gibson, *17 June*   440

To Henry Remson, *17 June*   441

CONTENTS

From Peregrine Fitzhugh, *20 June*   442

Book Dedication from Benjamin Smith Barton, *21 June*   445

From Aaron Burr, *21 June*   447

To Elbridge Gerry, *21 June*   448

From Sir John Sinclair, *21 June*   449

To James Madison, *22 June*   450

To Thomas Mann Randolph, *22 June*   451

To John Gibson, *24 June*   451

From Luther Martin, *24 June*   452

To Edward Rutledge, *24 June*   455

From Van Staphorst & Hubbard, *26 June*   457

To Andrew G. Fraunces, *27 June*   459

To Edmund Randolph, *27 June*   459

To Andrew G. Fraunces, *28 June*   460

To James Madison, *29 June*   461

To Thomas Mann Randolph, *29 June*   462

From La Rochefoucauld-Liancourt, *30 June*   462

To William Short, *30 June*   463

From Willem H. van Hasselt, *30 June*   465

To Thomas Mifflin, *1 July*   468

Account with John Francis, *3 July*   469

From Arthur Campbell, *4 July*   469

From Edmond Charles Genet, *4 July*   470

Senate Resolution on William Blount, *[4 July]*   472

To Volney, *5 July*   474

From Volney, *5 July*   474

From Elbridge Gerry, *6 July*   475

Suit against the Estate of William Ronald:
    Order and Report, *10 July*   476

From James Monroe, *12 July*   478

From Sir John Sinclair, *15 July*   480

From William Wirt, with Jefferson's Notes, *15 July*   481

To John Barnes, *[18] July*   481

From Volney, *19 July*   482

To James Madison, *24 July*   483

From John Barnes, *26 July*   484

To John Barnes, *31 July*   484

From Delamotte, *31 July*   485

Note on Diplomatic Appointments, *[July]*   486

From Thomas Bee, *1 August*   487

From James Madison, *2 August*   488

From St. George Tucker, *2 August*   488

CONTENTS

To James Madison, *3 August*   489

Petition to Virginia House of Delegates   491

    I. Petition to the Virginia House of Delegates,
       [*on or before 3 August*]   493

    II. Revised Petition to the Virginia House of Delegates,
       [*7 August-7 September*]   499

From James Madison, *5 August*   505

To Volney, *5 August*   507

From Citizens of Vincennes, *7 August*   507

From John F. Mercer, *9 August*   508

From John Barnes, *10 August*   509

To John Stuart, *15 August*   509

From William Strickland, *16 August*   510

From William Strickland, *18 August*   511

From Allen Jones, *20 August*   513

From Rufus King, *22 August*   514

From St. George Tucker, *22 August*   515

From James Madison, *24 August*   516

Notes on Alexander Hamilton, *24 August*   517

To Willem H. van Hasselt, *27 August*   518

To St. George Tucker, *28 August*   519

To Robert Lawson, *31 August*   520

To Benjamin Vaughan, *31 August*   521

To John Vaughan, *31 August*   521

To Arthur Campbell, *1 September*   522

To John Barnes, *2 September*   523

From Volney, *2 September*   523

To John F. Mercer, *5 September*   524

From James Monroe, *5 September*   524

To Archibald Stuart, *5 September*   525

From John Stuart, *6 September*   525

To James Monroe, *7 September*   526

To Alexander White, *10 September*   527

To John Vaughan, *11 September*   529

To Alexander White, *12 September*   530

From John Barnes, *14 September*   530

To John Barnes, *17 September*   531

To Francis Eppes, *24 September*   531

To John Barnes, [*25*] *September*   534

From Andrew Ellicott, *28 September*   534

From James Thomson Callender, *28 September*   536

From Arthur Campbell, *30 September*   538

CONTENTS

From Dugnani, *30 September*   538

Statement of Nailery Profits, *30 September*   540

From John Barnes, *3 October*   542

From John McQueen, *6 October*   543

To John Barnes, *8 October*   544

To John Barnes, enclosing Power of Attorney, *8 October*   544

To John Taylor, *8 October*   545

From Elizabeth Wayles Eppes, *10 October*   546

Marriage Settlement for John Wayles Eppes, *12 October*   547

Marriage Settlement for Mary Jefferson, *12 October*   549

Note on Spanish Expenditures, *13 October*   551

Notes on Conversations with
      John Adams and George Washington, *[after 13 October]*   551

From John Taylor, *14 October*   553

From Peregrine Fitzhugh, enclosing a Citizen to the *Rights of Man*
      and Peregrine Fitzhugh to the *Rights of Man*, *15 October*   555

From John Barnes, *19 October*   561

From James Madison, *20 October*   562

From James Monroe, *[22] October*   562

From James Madison, *25 October*   564

To James Monroe, *25 October*   564

From James Monroe, *[27 October]*   565

From Benjamin Galloway, *[October]*   566

Memorial of Charleston Merchants to the Senate, *2 November*   567

To William Bradford, *6 November*   568

From Thomas Mann Randolph, *6 November*   568

Memorial of Charleston Wharfholders to the Senate, *10 November*   570

From Paroy, *[before 10 November]*   570

From Edmund Randolph, *15 November*   572

From John Wayles Eppes, *[17 November]*   572

From John Taylor, *19 November*   573

From Edmund Randolph, *21 November*   574

Bond to Van Staphorst & Hubbard, *25 November*   574

To Henry Tazewell, *28 November*   575

From James Monroe, *[November]*   576

To Mary Jefferson Eppes, *2 December*   576

To George Jefferson, *2 December*   577

From James Monroe, *2 December*   578

From Mary Jefferson Eppes, *8 December*   579

From Arthur Campbell, *10 December*   580

From Luther Martin, *11 December*   581

To Thomas Mann Randolph, *14 December*   583

CONTENTS

From Oliver Wolcott, Jr., *15 December*   584

To Richard Richardson, *16 December*   585

To John Wayles Eppes, *21 December*   585

To Francis Walker, *21 December*   587

To John Taylor, *23 December*   588

John Henry to Henry Tazewell, *24 December*   590

From James Madison, *25 December*   591

Notes on Comments by John Adams and Robert Goodloe Harper,
    26 December   592

To James Monroe, *27 December*   593

Notes on a Conversation with Tench Coxe, [*27 December*]   596

To Martha Jefferson Randolph, *27 December*   596

From William Short, *27 December*   597

From George Jefferson, *30 December*   598

To John Gibson, *31 December*   599

To John Henry, *31 December*   600

To Henry Tazewell, *31 December*   604

Design for Chimney and Flues, [*1797*]   605

Notes on John Jay's Mission to Great Britain, [*1797 or after*]   605

APPENDIX: Notations by Jefferson on Senate Documents   633

INDEX   635

ILLUSTRATIONS

Following page 318

"THE PROVIDENTIAL DETECTION"

This engraving by an unidentified artist, with its unabashed depiction of Jefferson as an agent of evil, attests to the political legacy of the letter that he wrote to Philip Mazzei on 24 Apr. 1796, which was published the following year without Jefferson's authorization. With Satan lurking close at hand, Jefferson has here offered up on the "Altar to Gallic Despotism" writings by authors considered by the artist to be subversive of political order. Among them are Rousseau, Voltaire, Paine, William Godwin, Volney, and "Munro" (James Monroe, who published his version of events surrounding his diplomatic service in France, *A View of the Conduct of the Executive*, in 1797), as well as such newspapers as the *Aurora*. The American eagle, guided by the vigilant eye of Providence, protects the Constitution as the Mazzei letter floats from its startled author's hand. Bags of money around the altar, labeled for such French diplomatic gains as "Venice" and "Sardinia" as well as "American Spoliations," imply that France's exercise of power beyond its borders was based on a desire to fill its coffers and underwrite the expansion of revolution. The label on one bag refers to a scandal surrounding António de Araújo Azevedo, Portugal's minister to France, who reputedly distributed bribes to facilitate a treaty between the two nations. The revelation of that incident in the United States during the middle days of March 1798 provides a clue to the possible date of this engraving. In the beginning of that month Robert Goodloe Harper had cited the letter to Mazzei in a speech on the floor of the House of Representatives and condemned Jefferson as the "missionary" of revolutionary France. Significantly, there is no reference in this cartoon to the XYZ Affair, which one would expect to play a large role in any effort to slander Jefferson for his sympatic ties to a seemingly corrupt France. Although it became known in Philadelphia during the first week of March 1798 that the American envoys had failed to open negotiations with France, details, including the apparent demands for monetary payments, did not come to light until after the publication of dispatches a month later. Since several references in this picture presumably would have lessened in significance to an American audience as the XYZ scandal deepened, the engraving may have been made just before the eruption of that affair in the spring of 1798. A full two years after Jefferson had penned his frank missive to Mazzei it was apparently still vivid in the popular political imagination (Thomas C. Blaisdell, Jr., Peter Selz, and others, *The American Presidency in Political Cartoons: 1776-1976* [Salt Lake City, 1976], 42-3; Michel Poniatowski, *Talleyrand et le Directoire, 1796-1800* [Paris, 1982], 595-8; António Simões Rodrigues, ed., *História de Portugal em Datas* [Lisbon, 1996], 189; *Gazette of the United States*, 12 Mch. 1798; *Annals*, VII, 1192-3; TJ to Mann Page, 6 Mch., and to Madison, 6 Apr. 1798).
Courtesy of the Library Company of Philadelphia.

[xxxvii]

ILLUSTRATIONS

VOLNEY

Seventeen letters between Jefferson and Volney appear in this volume. Volney, already internationally known as an Enlightenment intellectual figure and as the author of *Voyage en Syrie et en Égypte* (1787) and *Les Ruines; ou, Méditation sur les Révolutions des Empires* (1791), arrived in the United States in October 1795. During his residence in America he sat for this oil portrait painted by Gilbert Stuart at Germantown, Pennsylvania. Volney and Jefferson, who had become acquainted in Europe, enjoyed discussing scientific and political topics of mutual interest, and in June 1796 Volney stopped at Monticello for perhaps two weeks before setting off for Kentucky and the Ohio Valley. Two years later, ready to return to France and feeling the effects of hardened sentiment toward his country in America, he embarked for home with other French citizens apprehensive of the pending alien acts. During his travels in North America he devoted particular attention to winds and climate, and he compiled the results of his observations as *Tableau du Climat et du Sol des États-Unis d'Amérique* (1803), published in English as *View of the Climate and Soil of the United States of America* (Lawrence Park, comp., *Gilbert Stuart: An Illustrated Descriptive List of His Works*, 4 vols. [New York, 1926], II, 779; Vol. 27: 390-1n; Volney to TJ, 12 July 1796; TJ to Madison, 3 May 1798; TJ to Monroe, 21 May 1798).

Courtesy of the Pennsylvania Academy of Fine Arts.

LA ROCHEFOUCAULD-LIANCOURT

Displaced, like Volney, by events in France, the political economist and social theorist the Duc de La Rochefoucauld-Liancourt traveled in the United States from 1794 to 1797. Like Volney, too, he visited Jefferson at Monticello. Although they traveled separately, the French wanderers' trips to Albemarle County coincided, both of them visiting in June 1796. La Rochefoucauld-Liancourt's account of his travels, which included observations of Monticello and its owner, appeared in both English and French editions in 1799 (see La Rochefoucauld-Liancourt to Jefferson, at 11 July 1796).

This small pencil portrait of the duc is from a portfolio of drawings by the English artist Ellen Wallace Sharples (1769-1849). She was in the United States with her husband James Sharples during La Rochefoucauld-Liancourt's American sojourn. Ellen Sharples executed some original portraits, but also assisted her husband, who had been her art instructor before their marriage, and made close copies of many of his works. She became an influential mentor to their daughter, Rolinda, who was also an artist (Delia Gaze, ed., *Dictionary of Women Artists*, 2 vols. [London, 1997], I, 58-9, II, 1262-4; Katharine McCook Knox, *The Sharples: Their Portraits of George Washington and his Contemporaries* [New Haven, 1930], 99-101).

Courtesy of Bristol City Museum and Art Gallery, UK/Bridgeman Art Library.

FLOOR PLAN OF MONTICELLO

The interior layout of Monticello appears here not as it existed in 1796, when Jefferson likely drew this plan, but as it was to become on completion of his ambitious renovation of the house. The original first floor, seen in the lower half of this diagram, had as its most prominent feature the octagonal room offset from the long axis that was formed by the flanking rooms. When Jefferson sketched Monticello and its dependencies on an insurance plat, he showed the house with that original floor plan (see it at the end of 1796 in this volume). But the long course of renovation then underway would expand the house considerably along its eastern side, adding the rooms that appear in the top half of the plan illustrated here and separating them from the original rooms by a "passage" through the middle of the house along its long axis. This transformation of the building created the distinctive entry "Hall," which with the octagonal room forms the central core of the first floor. Jefferson's reconceptualization of Monticello not only expanded the floor plan but gave the house its signature dome and silhouette.

He drew this plan in pencil and ink on a 9 x $11\frac{1}{2}$ inch sheet of paper ruled in inches and tenths. At the top he wrote: "This draught is merely to shew the joist holes, and is not to be depended on in any other part." In the lower right corner he noted, "the joist holes within the house are from the 40th. to the 42d joint above the capping," and "those on the Piazza are from the 45th. to the 47th joints, towit 5 courses of bricks or $15\frac{1}{2}$ I. higher." Those notations led Fiske Kimball, the great early authority on Jefferson's architecture, to conclude that Jefferson drew this plan in "the autumn of 1796, or soon after" (Kimball, *Jefferson, Architect*, 58-61, 164-5, plate 150; Nichols, *Architectural Drawings*, No. 135).

Courtesy of Massachusetts Historical Society.

THE "GREAT CLAW" OF THE MEGALONYX

Jefferson's paper on the Virginia fossils of the prehistoric sloth he named the megalonyx ("great claw"), printed in this volume at 10 Feb. 1797, appeared in the fourth volume of the *Transactions* of the American Philosophical Society published in 1799. The same volume contained a technical description of the specimens by Caspar Wistar, who had received medical training in Philadelphia and Scotland and devoted particular attention to anatomy both as a doctor in the Pennsylvania Hospital and as a professor at the University of Pennsylvania. His description of the megalonyx bones, like Jefferson's discussion of the animal's characteristics, was an early landmark in American paleontology. Wistar's paper was accompanied by two engravings made by James Akin. The one shown here, illustrating bones of the feet and the distinctive claws that gave the megalonyx its name, originated as chalk drawings by William S. Jacobs, a young Belgian who had studied medicine in Europe before emigrating to the U.S. in the mid-1790s. Working as a dissector at the University of Pennsylvania, he earned an M.D. degree from that institution in 1801. He became a member of the Philosophical Society in 1802 and was elected one of its curators early the following year. The drawings for the other engraving, not reproduced here, illustrated longer bones of the megalonyx and were by Titian Peale, the lesser-known of Charles Willson Peale's two sons of that name. Still in his teens when he drew the megalonyx specimens, he died in the yellow fever epidemic of 1798 before the *Transactions* volume appeared (ANB, s.v. "Wistar, Caspar"; Wyndham Miles, "William Stephen Jacobs," *Journal of Chemical Education*, XXIV [1947], 249-50; APS, *Proceedings*, XXII, pt. 3 [1884], 326, 330; DAB, s.v. "Peale, Titian Ramsay").

ILLUSTRATIONS

Akin (b. 1773), the engraver, was a South Carolinian who worked in the office of Secretary of State Timothy Pickering. Later, during the administrations of John Quincy Adams and Andrew Jackson, he created notable lithographed political cartoons. His earliest signed work of that genre, however, referred to American ambitions to obtain West Florida in 1804, and was one of the most savage caricatures ever drawn of Thomas Jefferson. Akin's harshly satirical "Prairie Dog" cartoon depicted the president as a miserable canine goaded by the French to cough up a stream of gold coins in exchange for Spanish territory (Maureen O'Brien Quimby, "The Political Art of James Akin," *Winterthur Portfolio*, VII [1972], 59-60, 67-8; David McNeely Stauffer, *American Engravers upon Copper and Steel*, 2 vols. [New York, 1907], I, 4-6).

Courtesy of the American Philosophical Society.

JOHN ADAMS

Adams stands here in a mezzotint by George Graham, an obscure engraver who used both mezzotint and stipple engraving techniques. Graham's Adams holds the Constitution in one hand, the temple of Fame visible in the far background. The picture's caption identifies Adams as president and says, "Hail! Noble Chief! Protector of the cause Of purest Freedom Founded on the Laws." Graham, whose career is traced only through his signed works, was in Philadelphia in 1797 and also worked in Boston and New York. This print was published by Dr. John Berkheanhead, possibly John L. Berkenhead, an organist and composer active in New England during Adams's presidency (David McNeely Stauffer, *American Engravers upon Copper and Steel*, 2 vols. [New York, 1907], I, 109, II, 196; George C. Groce and David H. Wallace, *The New-York Historical Society's Dictionary of Artists in America, 1564-1860* [New Haven, 1957], 268-9; Nicolas Slonimsky, ed., *Baker's Biographical Dictionary of Musicians*, 7th ed. [New York, 1984], 234; *The Boston Directory: Containing the Names of the Inhabitants* . . . [Boston, 1798], 20).

Courtesy of National Portrait Gallery.

THOMAS JEFFERSON

This portrait in pastels by English artist James Sharples pictures Jefferson early in his term as vice president. Sharples probably drew it from life, with the aid of a physiognotrace machine, in Philadelphia during Jefferson's residence there from May to July 1797. This was one of a number of likenesses of well-known Americans and visitors by Sharples, and several members of his talented family made similar portraits. Sharples used a fine brush to apply his own powdered pastels to paper (measuring in this case 7 x 9 inches). A duplicate of this portrait, probably by a member of the Sharples family, is in the National Park Service collection in Philadelphia (Alfred L. Bush, *The Life Portraits of Thomas Jefferson*, rev. ed. [Charlottesville, 1987], 25-7).

Courtesy of Bristol City Museum and Art Gallery, UK/Bridgeman Art Library.

BRITISH BOARD OF AGRICULTURE DIPLOMA

In September 1797 Jefferson learned that he had been admitted as a foreign honorary member of the Board of Agriculture and Internal Improvement, the organization chartered in Great Britain in 1793 to inform farmers on the best agricultural methods and encourage a spirit of industry and experiment. Signed by Sir John Sinclair, promoter and first president of the the board, this diploma depicts his initial interest in sheep and the improvement of wool production that widened to include a full range of agricultural pursuits. The engraver, Josiah Boydell, had studied under Benjamin West and was a prominent painter, exhibiting portraits and historical paintings at the Royal Academy between 1772 and 1799. Jefferson periodically received the board's publications and in return sent back to London communications on American agriculture and farm implements, including Thomas C. Martin's drill and a model and description of his own moldboard plow. Sinclair urged Jefferson and George Washington, who had become a foreign honorary member of the board in 1795, to support the establishment of a comparable organization in the United States (Rosalind Mitchison, "The Old Board of Agriculture (1793-1822)," *English Historical Review*, LXXIV [1959], 41-3; Fitzpatrick, *Writings*, XXXIV, 235; DNB, s.v. "Boydell, Josiah"; Sinclair to TJ, 21 June and 15 July 1797; Rufus King to TJ, 22 Aug. 1797; TJ to Sinclair, 23 Mch. 1798).

Courtesy of Massachusetts Historical Society.

Volume 29

1 March 1796 to 31 December 1797

JEFFERSON CHRONOLOGY

1743 · 1826

1743	Born at Shadwell, 13 Apr. (New Style).
1760	Entered the College of William and Mary.
1762	"quitted college."
1762-1767	Self-education and preparation for law.
1769-1774	Albemarle delegate to House of Burgesses.
1772	Married Martha Wayles Skelton, 1 Jan.
1775-1776	In Continental Congress.
1776	Drafted Declaration of Independence.
1776-1779	In Virginia House of Delegates.
1779	Submitted Bill for Establishing Religious Freedom.
1779-1781	Governor of Virginia.
1782	His wife died, 6 Sep.
1783-1784	In Continental Congress.
1784-1789	In France as Minister Plenipotentiary to negotiate commercial treaties and as Minister Plenipotentiary resident at Versailles.
1790-1793	Secretary of State of the United States.
1797-1801	Vice President of the United States.
1801-1809	President of the United States.
1814-1826	Established the University of Virginia.
1826	Died at Monticello, 4 July.

VOLUME 29

1 March 1796 to 31 December 1797

19 Mch. 1796	Tells William B. Giles that "demolitions" have begun at Monticello.
24 Apr.	Discusses state of American politics in private letter to Philip Mazzei.
May	Mortgages 150 of his slaves (and does so again in November).
June	La Rochefoucald-Liancourt and Volney visit Monticello.
19 Aug.	First operates his threshing machine at Monticello.
28 Aug.	Washington writes TJ the final letter of their correspondence.
Oct.	Ellen Wayles Randolph (second granddaughter of that name) born.
5 Dec.	Presidential electors meet in their states to cast votes.
28 Dec.	Writes Adams a congratulatory letter but leaves its delivery to Madison's discretion.
20 Feb. 1797	Leaves Monticello for Philadelphia, arriving late on 2 Mch.
3 Mch.	Installed as president of the American Philosophical Society.
4 Mch.	Inaugurated as vice president of the United States.
10 Mch.	Paper on the megalonyx read before the Philosophical Society.
13 Mch.	Leaves Philadelphia, arriving home on 20 Mch.
Apr.	Luther Martin's attacks on TJ first appear.
5 May	Leaves Monticello for first session of Fifth Congress, arriving 11 May and learning en route of the publication of his letter to Mazzei.
21 June	Urges Elbridge Gerry to accept appointment as an envoy to France.
4 July	Senate opens its investigation of William Blount.
6 July	Leaves Philadelphia, arriving at Monticello 11 July.
by 3 Aug.	Drafts petition to Virginia House of Delegates on grand jury presentment.
28 Sep.	James Thomson Callender asks for financial assistance.
30 Sep.	Completes statement on profits of nailery.
13 Oct.	Mary Jefferson marries John Wayles Eppes at Monticello.
4 Dec.	Departs from Monticello, arriving on 12 Dec. for "the real business" of the second session of Fifth Congress.
31 Dec.	Writes John Henry defending himself against Luther Martin.

THE PAPERS OF
THOMAS JEFFERSON

·《━━━━━━》·

From Benjamin Rush

DEAR SIR   Philadelphia March 1st 1796.

The bearer of this letter Mr. Weld a young Gentleman of amiable manners, and good education was introduced to me by a letter from an old Scotch friend now settled in Dublin. In travelling through the United States he could not be satisfied without paying his respects to Mr. Jefferson.

What strange events have happened in our city since your retirement from public life! The late honourable treaty with Spain has revived your name among your republican friends. Mr. Pinkney's Success as a negociator has been ascribed to information and instructions issued by our Executive, at a time when your influence was felt in the Councils of our Country.

We have been much struck lately by a public Acknowledgement from a late Officer of State, of our Obligations to Great Britain for many of the political institutions to which the United States owe their happiness. This Acknowledgement has led some of the Republicans to inquire into the *nature* and *number* of those institutions. Upon an investigation of them they are as follows. 1. Funding Systems, and perpetual debt. 2. A cruel and Absurd System of penal laws. 3. A cruel and Absurd code of laws with respect to Debtors. 4. Oppressive religious establishments. 5. Imposts and excise instead of an equal land tax. 6. Unequal distribution of property among the Children of the same family. 7. Innumerable perjuries from the Absurd mixture of Oaths with all our Revenue laws. Our Judicial System alone derives some merit from our descent from, and former connection with G. Britain, but it owes the obstinate Stability of most of its present imperfections, chiefly to the unfortunate Association of the evil with the good parts of it.

You drew up the Act of Independance of the United States. The wishes and prayers of thousands are, that you may live to realize that Act, by giving us the principles, and habits of an *independant* people. From my Dr Sir your sincere Old friend   BENJN RUSH

[3]

RC (DLC); endorsed by TJ as received 8 May 1796 and so recorded in SJL.

PAYING HIS RESPECTS: see note to Anthony Gerna to TJ, 2 Sep. 1795. OUR EXECUTIVE: Report on Negotiations with Spain, 18 Mch. 1792. LATE OFFICER OF STATE: Alexander Hamilton, who on 25 Feb. 1796 argued in the government's behalf in Hylton v. U.S. (see James Madison to TJ, 21 Feb. 1796). In a three-hour address before the Supreme Court and a large audience, Hamilton used British precedent to declare that the carriage tax was an excise, not a direct tax, and stated that "it is fair to seek the meaning of terms in the statutory language of that Country, from which our Jurisprudence is derived" (Goebel and Smith, *Law Practice of Hamilton*, IV, 355; *Gazette of the United States*, 26 Feb. 1796).

To James Monroe

DEAR SIR   Mar. 2. 96.

I wrote you two[1] letters in the course of the last twelvemonths to wit May 26. and Sep. 6. 95. and have recieved from you those of Sep. 7. 94. and June 23. 95. neither of which were late enough to inform me if either of mine had got to hand. In those I gave you all the details public and private which my situation enabled me to do. In the last I asked the delivery of a note to Frouillé for some books, particularly the sequel of the Encyclopedie, come out since he last furnished me. I hope these have got to hand.

The most remarkeable political occurrence with us has been the treaty with England, of which no man in the US. has had the effrontery to affirm that it was not a very bad one except A.H. under the signature of Camillus. It's most zealous defenders only pretend that it was better than war. As if war was not invited rather than avoided by unfounded demands. I have never known the public pulse beat so full and in such universal unison on any Subject since the declaration of Independence. The House of representatives of the US. has manifested it's disapprobation of the treaty. We are yet to learn whether they will exercise their constitutional right of refusing the means which depend on them for carrying it into execution. Should they be induced to lend their hand to it it will be hard swallowing with[2] their constituents, but will be swallowed[3] from the habits of order and obedience to the laws which so much distinguish our countrymen. The resignation or rather removal of R. you will have learnt. His vindication bears hard on the executive in the opinions of this quarter, and tho' it clears him in their judgment of the charge of bribery, it does not give them high ideas of his wisdom or steadiness.   The appointment of J. Rutledge to be C.J. seems to have been intended merely to establish a precedent against the descent of that office by seniority, and to keep five mouths always gaping for one sugar plumb: for it was immediately negatived, by the very votes

[4]

which so implicitly concur with the will of the executive. I may consign the appointment of Chace to the bench to your own knolege of him and reflections. McHenry Secy. at war, Charles Lee Atty. Genl. with Pickering and Wolcott by their devotion to genuine republicanism will shew to our citizens on what principles alone they can expect to rise.   The office of Secy. of State was offered to P.H. in order to draw him over and gain some popularity: but not till there was a moral certainty that he would not accept it. I presume you recieve the newspapers, and will have seen the amendments to the constitution proposed by the Virginia assembly. Their reception by some of the other assemblies has been such as to call for the sacrifice of all feeling rather than ruffle the harmony so necessary to the common good.   The finances are said to have been left by the late financier in the utmost derangement, and his tools are urging the funding the new debts they have contracted. Thus posterity is to be left to pay the ordinary expences of our government in time of peace.

As small news may escape the notice of your other correspondents, I shall give you what occurs to me. The James river canal is now conducted into the town of Richmond and full toll is exacted. 30. Doll. a share more however are necessary to complete it. The Patowmac and Norfolk canals are not in such forwardness. Mayo bridge, nearly destroyed by a flood, is reestablished. R. is settled again in Richmond in the business of the law.—Carter's lands on the back of yours and Mr. Short's have got into the hands of one of the sons, Ned, who is coming to live on them. The price of wheat is 13/ here the bushel, and corn 20/ the barrel, and not to be had indeed at any price. I have been desirous of planting some fruit trees for you that they may be growing during your absence. But Mr. Jones's visits to the neighborhood have been so rare and short that I have not had an opportunity of asking from him the inclosure and allotment of the piece of ground which seems proper for it. The season is now passing. Do not fail to send over the Abricot-peche. Bartram would recieve and plant it, and then furnish new plants.—Deaths are Zane, and Thos. Pleasants of 4. mile creek. Mr. Pendleton is also said to be all but gone. A remarkeable marriage is that of Capt. Alcock with the widow of Dr. Walker. Your brother and family well. Derieux living in Goochland under great sufferance, and hoping a renovation of the aid promised from his aunt. My sincere affections to Mrs. Monroe and to yourself. Adieu.

RC (DLC: Monroe Papers); unsigned; at foot of first page: "Colo. Monroe." PrC (DLC); endorsed in ink by TJ on verso.

DISAPPROBATION OF THE TREATY: a reference to the carefully hedged allusion to the Jay Treaty in the address of the House of Representatives to the president on 16 Dec. 1795, which TJ interpreted as a condemnation of the treaty (see note to William

Branch Giles to TJ, 9 Dec. 1795). R.: Edmund Randolph. P.H.: Patrick Henry. AMENDMENTS TO THE CONSTITUTION: see Madison to TJ, 31 Jan. 1796.

[1] Word interlined in place of "three."
[2] TJ first wrote "hardly swallowed by" and then altered it to read as above.
[3] Word interlined in place of "obeyed."

From Robert Pollard

SIR   Richmond March 3d. 1796

Your favor of the 29th last Month I received by post, and have Subscribed the Thirty dollars ℔ Share on each of Mr. Shorts shares in the James River Company, agreeably to Your instructions.

I send you under cover Deeds to Mr. Short for thirteen shares in said Company which I wish safe to hand & am Sir Your Most Obd Servt

ROBERT POLLARD

James Heron & Wife to   W Short. 6 Shares
Benjn Harrison jr to   do   6
Robert Pollard & Wife to   do   1
                                      ──
                                      13

RC (DLC: Short Papers); endorsed by TJ as received 11 Mch. 1796 and so recorded in SJL. Enclosures not found.

A 12 Dec. 1796 letter from Pollard to TJ, recorded in SJL as received 16 Dec. 1796, and TJ's 18 Dec. 1796 reply are both missing.

To James Madison

Mar. 6. 96.

I wrote you Feb. 21. since which I have received yours of the same day. Indeed mine of that date related only to a single article in yours of Jan. 31. and Feb. 7. I do not at all wonder at the condition in which the finances of the US. are found. Ham's object from the beginning was to throw them into forms which should be utterly undecypherable. I ever said he did not understand their condition himself, nor was able to give a clear view of the excess of our debts beyond our credits, nor whether we were diminishing or increasing the debt. My own opinion was that from the commencement of this government to the time I ceased to attend to the subject we had been increasing our debt about a million of D. annually. If Mr. Gallatin would undertake to reduce this chaos to order, present us with a clear view of our finances, and put them into a form as simple as they will admit, he will merit immortal honor. The accounts of the US. ought to be, and may be, made, as simple as those of a common farmer, and capable of being understood by common farmers.

[6]

Disapproving, as I do, of the unjustifiable largess to the daughters of the Ct. de Grasse, I will certainly not propose to rivet it by a second example on behalf of M. de Chastellux' son. It will only be done in the event of such a repetition of the precedent, as will give every one a right to share in the plunder.—It is indeed surprizing you have not yet recieved the British treaty in form. I presume you would never recieve it were not your co-operation on it necessary. But this will oblige the formal notification of it to you.—I thank you for your information respecting Lownes. There is one article still necessary to be known from Mr. Howell. Lownes began with credits of 90. days from the time of the departure of the nailrod from Philadelphia (not his delivery of it to the vessel: for that makes a difference sometimes of many weeks) but he afterwards reduced it to 60. days. What would be Mr. Howell's credits? I know that credits in Virginia startle a merchant in Philadelphia; but I presume that Mr. Howel could have confidence enough in me (tho' not personally known to him) to make a trial, and govern himself afterwards according to the result, and to the punctuality with which he would recieve his remittances. I wish to know this, tho' I am not yet decided to drop Lownes, on account of his being a good man, and I like much to be in the hands of good men. There is great pleasure in unlimited confidence. My consumption has now advanced from 3. to 4. tons a quarter. I call for a quarter's supply at once, so that the last quarter's supply is always paid for before the next is called for, or at the very time.—The Spanish treaty will have some disagreeable features, seeds of chicanery and eternal broils, instead of peace and friendship. At a period not long before that, they had been ready to sign one giving us vastly more than we had ever contemplated; particularly in our intercourse with their W. Indies.—I by no means think of declining the work we have spoken of. On the contrary, I wish with ardor to begin it, since the change of form into which I propose to put it: the first ideas had always oppressed me from a consciousness of my want both of talents and materials to execute it.—But it will be impossible for a year to come; and I am not certain whether, even after the present year, I shall not be obliged to put my farms under such direction as that I should be considered as not here as to them, while I should be here as to my papers. My salutations to Mrs. Madison: friendly esteem to Mr. Giles, Page &c.

P.S. Have you considered all the consequences of your proposition respecting post roads? I view it as a source of boundless patronage to the executive, jobbing to members of Congress and their friends, and a bottomless abyss of public money. You will begin by only appropriating the surplus of the post-office revenues: but the other revenues will soon be called in to their aid, and it will be a scene of eternal scramble among the members who can get the most money wasted in their state, and they will always get most who are meanest. We have thought hitherto that the roads of a state could not be so well administered even by the state legislature as by the magistracy of the county, on the spot. What will it be when a member of N.H. is to mark out a road for Georgia? Does the power to *establish* post roads given you by congress, mean that you shall *make* the roads, or only *select* from those already made those on which there shall be a post? If the term be equivocal, (and I really do not think it so) which is the safest construction? That which permits a majority of Congress to go to cutting down mountains and bridging of rivers, or the other which if too restricted may refer it to the states for amendment, securing still due measure and proportion among us, and providing some means of information to the members of Congress tantamount to that ocular inspection which even in our county determinations the magistrate finds can not be supplied by any other evidence? The fortification of harbours was liable to great objection. But national circumstances furnished some color. In this case there is none. The roads of America are the best in the world except those of France and England. But does the state of our population, the extent of our internal commerce, the want of sea and river navigation, call for such expence on roads here, or are our means adequate to it? Think of all this and a great deal more which your good judgment will suggest, and pardon my freedom.

RC (DLC: Madison Papers); unsigned; postscript on separate sheet. PrC (DLC); at foot of first page in ink: "James Madison."

WORK WE HAVE SPOKEN OF: this project was perhaps discussed in the letter from TJ to Madison, 24 Jan. 1796, which has not been found. In the letter he also requested Madison to send certain pamphlets and copies of correspondence of TJ and of John Jay (Madison to TJ, 7 Feb. 1796).

On 5 Feb. 1796, Madison introduced a resolution RESPECTING POST ROADS which authorized the president to locate the "route most proper for the transportation of the mail" between Maine and Georgia and lay before Congress the result, along "with an estimate of the expense of rendering such route fit." The cost of examining and surveying the route was to be covered by the SURPLUS OF THE POST-OFFICE REVENUES. Six days later the resolution was debated and Madison was appointed to the committee charged with reporting a bill, which was considered and adopted by the House in May 1796 but not passed by the Senate (*Annals*, v, 297, 314-5, 1406, 1415; JHR, II, 440, JS, II, 270).

From James Madison

Dear Sir   Philada. Mar. 6, 1796

I have received your's of   covering a letter to John Bringhurst which has been forwarded to him. There has not been time enough yet for an answer. The letter promised to myself, in yours, has not come [to]¹ hand. The delay can be sufficiently accounted for by the irregularities of the Southern Mails, particularly South of Baltimore.

The Senate have unanimously ratified the Algerine and Spanish Treaties. The latter was a bitter pill to some for two reasons; first as inviting additional emigrations to the Western Country: secondly, as jostling with the Mississippi article in the British Treaties. The Spanish article is in the words following: "It is likewise agreed that the western boundary of the United States which separates them from the Spanish Colony of Louisiana, is in the middle of the channel or bed of the river Mississippi from the Northern boundary of the said States, to the completion of the 31°. of latitude North of the Equator. And his C. Majesty has likewise agreed that the navigation of the said river in its whole breadth from its Source to the Ocean shall be free only to his subjects and the Citizens of the U. States, unless he should extend this privilege to the subjects of other powers by special Convention." Doubts were expressed by King in the Senate whether this could be construed into a harmony with the stipulations to G.B. and the pulse of the body felt on the subject with a view to a declaratory proviso to the ratification. It was concluded however not to risk the project, and to presume a construction that would avoid the inconsistency. It seems that Pinkney considered the article as admitting a construction reconcileable with the British article. It is also said that he was offered and refused a proposition expressing or implying our right to the navigation, but more directly clashing with the British Treaties.

The President laid the Treaty before the H. of Reps. on tuesday last about one OClock; and in the afternoon it appeared in a Proclamation in Brown's paper. I am well informed that its publication was concerted with the Printer prior to its communication to the House. Whether an original ratification was received as the ground of this proceeding, or the copy heretofore not deemed of sufficient formality has been viewed in a more favorable light I can not undertake to say. I suspect the latter to be the case. Perhaps also the ratification of the Spanish and Algerine Treaties, which contain some stipulations analogous to those complained of as unconstitutional in the British Treaty, may have had weight on the occasion. In general however the Spanish Treaty forms rather a contrast to the British, being more than reciprocal in its essential articles, and on the subject of contraband, and the freedom of goods in free ships, being perfectly satisfactory. A motion has been laid on the table by Mr. Livingston, calling on the President for the instructions to Jay &c. The policy of hazarding it is so questionable that he will probably let it sleep or withdraw it. Notice of direct propositions on the Treaty will probably be given tomorrow. The purport and form of them create much diversity of ideas among the opponents of the Treaty. The state of the business as it now presents itself, with the uncertainty of the particular way of thinking in several quarters of the House, make it truly difficult to decide on the course most acceptable to the body of anti-treaty members. The other side, of course have no difficulties of this sort to contend with.

The bill for the sale of the back lands makes progress tho' but slowly. Its fate is very uncertain. The proposed aid to the federal City will probably succeed in the event, under the patronage of the P. but in the mean time will no doubt be played off in favor of the Treaty.

The Court has not given judgment yet on the Carriage tax. It is said the Judges will be unanimous for its constitutionality. Hamilton and Lee advocated it at the Bar, against Campbell and Ingersoll. Bystanders speak highly of Campbell's argument, as well as of Ingersoll's. Lee did not shine, and the great effort of his coadjutor as I learn, was to raise a fog around the subject, and to inculcate a respect in the Court for preceding sanctions, in a doubtful case.

We are three month's without news from France, or even G. Britain. There is a report that one of the Sedition bills has passed the H. of Lords, and is not likely to pass the H. of Commons. There is a paragraph which says that Sweeden and Denmark have prohibited the exportation of Grain. Flour here is about 15 dolrs. and Wheat 20/. Adieu Yrs affy.

Js MADISON JR

RC (DLC: Madison Papers); at foot of first page: "Mr. Jefferson"; endorsed by TJ as received 18 Mch. 1796 and so recorded in SJL.

The missive COVERING A LETTER was TJ to Madison, 21 Feb. 1796.

President Washington LAID THE TREATY BEFORE THE H. OF REPS. on 1 Mch. 1796, the same day that the articles of the agreement, along with the proclamation signed by the president the previous day declaring that the treaty with Great Britain was in effect and should be observed by all accordingly, appeared in Andrew BROWN's *Philadelphia Gazette*. On 2 Mch. Edward LIV-INGSTON, Republican congressman from New York, introduced a resolution requesting the president to submit to the House of Representatives the INSTRUCTIONS TO JAY, along with correspondence and other papers relating to the negotiation of the treaty. From 7 to 24 Mch. 1796, the House daily debated its constitutional right in relation to treaties, especially the right to refuse to pass laws executing them, and on the final day passed the Livingston resolution by a vote of 62 to 37 and submitted it to the president (*Annals*, v, 400-1, 426-760). For a discussion of Washington's response, see Giles to TJ, 31 Mch. 1796.

BILL FOR THE SALE OF THE BACK LANDS:

on 6 Apr. 1796, the House passed legislation which established procedures for the survey and sale of public lands northwest of the Ohio River and above the mouth of the Kentucky River that had become available through the 1795 treaty of Greenville. Washington signed the act on 18 May 1796. The bill allowing the president to borrow up to $300,000 to complete the public buildings in the FEDERAL CITY passed the House on 31 Mch. and was approved by Washington on 6 May 1796 (JHR, II, 490-1, 497; U.S. Statutes at Large, I, 461, 464-9; Malcolm J. Rohrbough, *The Land Office Business: The Settlement and Administration of American Public Lands, 1789-1837* [New York, 1968], 17-19).

[1] Word supplied.

To Martha Jefferson Randolph

Monticello Mar. 6. 96.

Our neighborhood my dear daughter furnishes us with not one word of news to you, and I am so fatigued with writing for this post that I can only inform you we are all well, Jefferson robust as a beef, and all our desires alive to see you. My kisses to dear Anne, and best affection's to Mr. Randolph and yourself. Adieu my dear and love me as I do you.

Th:J.

RC (NNPM); addressed: "Mrs. Martha Randolph Varina Henrico"; stamped. PrC (MHi); endorsed in ink by TJ on verso.

To Richard Harrison

DEAR SIR   Monticello Mar. 8. 1796.

I now inclose you the explanations you desired on the subject of my accounts. As your letter of Sep. 28. 95. reduced to 4. heads the matters on which you wished explanations, I have accordingly brought into one view whatever had been said in other papers on those heads, with what was further necessary to be said; so that the papers now inclosed, together with my account of Oct. 12. 92. and the statement of the public account with Mr. Grand signed by me Feb. 21. 92. contain every thing requisite to the understanding this subject, and render it unnecessary to recur to any other papers written before or since.

My letter of Nov. 13. went on the mistaken supposition that the private account of Mr. Grand against me, referred to in your's of Sep. 28. was the antient one, which had been incorporated afterwards into the public one, and it explained properly the nature of that. But I found afterwards that the private account referred to in your letter was a late one, of which I then had no knolege. Consequently what I wrote in that letter is not at all pertinent to this, and therefore may be disregarded altogether, both the former and latter accounts being fully explained in the inclosed papers.

You will find upon the whole that the difficulties in the articles of charge have arisen from two sources only. 1. Mr. Grand's first attempt to keep separate accounts against the US. and myself, and the subsequent incorporation of the two into one. 2. The mutual loans between the funds of the US. and of Virginia, which confused the first accounts.[1] But the latter accounts set all this to rights;[2] and if you will attend to the latter alone, and reject the former, no error can be committed. I say this under the belief that the public account examined by me Feb. 21.[3] 92. was in the incorporated and corrected form; for I have no copy of that account by me, and therefore am not quite certain of it. I think it would be a security to the public if you would forward me a copy of that account, that I may be enabled to place you on sure ground. Grand's last form of account with Virginia I have examined minutely, and can affirm that it stands perfectly right, as that state is therein debited with all monies paid for it's use and with no others; and temporary loans by Mr. Grand's right hand to his left, replaced immediately after, are kept entirely out of sight.

Upon the whole I am in hopes you will now find the several heads of difficulty so fully explained as to leave no further obstacle to the Quietus which I am anxious to obtain, on account of my family, in case any accident should happen to me, if accident that can be called which at my time of life is within the order of nature. The articles of charge in your abstract are perfectly cleared.—The Period of my commission is ascertained by facts not before known to you.—You are so sensible that House-rent was habitually allowed by the former Congress, by whose rules you of course settle their accounts, that you seem to have entertained little difficultly as to that:[4]—and I am in hopes you will be equally sensible that Outfit, tho' not by that name, was yet allowed by them in another form to every resident Minister preceding me, and consequently that there can be no reason for witholding it from me. I have the honor to be with great esteem Dear Sir Your most obedt humble servt

TH: JEFFERSON

PrC (DLC); at foot of first page: "The Auditor of the US." Dft (DLC: TJ Papers, 100: 17111); dated "Mar. 1796"; written on both sides of a parallelogram-shaped sheet with Dft of TJ's second letter to Harrison of 9 Mch. 1796; heavily emended text with numerous stylistic variations, only the most important revisions being noted below. Enclosure: Statement on Accounts as Minister Plenipotentiary in France, 8 Mch. 1796, and enclosures.

MY ACCOUNT OF OCT. 12. 92.: see the account statement of 8 July 1792, to which TJ appended a final entry on 12 Oct. 1792 (Document I in a group of documents on the settlement of Jefferson's accounts as minister plenipotentiary in France, Vol. 24: 175-89).

[1] In Dft TJ here first wrote "which were in the same accounts produced false results."

[2] In Dft TJ here first wrote "But the latter form of accounts is perfect."

[3] Reworked from "22" in both Dft and PrC.

[4] In Dft TJ here first wrote "that it cannot be questioned."

Statement on Accounts as Minister Plenipotentiary in France

The Auditor in his letter of Sep. 28. 95. observes that nothing is requisite to a final settlement of my accounts as Min. Plenipy. of the US. but 1. an adjustment of certain articles of charge against me. 2. Outfit. 3. Houserent.[1] 4. the Period of my commission. I shall proceed therefore to give the necessary explanations on each of these heads.

1. ARTICLES OF CHARGE.[2] Some preliminary observations are necessary here.

My account, given in on oath to the Auditor, contains an exact statement of all the monies recieved by me for my own use as M.P. for the US. and he may be assured that no other articles of charge found in any other account, and omitted in this are chargeable to me personally, however they may be blended with my name. This account was signed Oct. 12. 92 and will be referred to by that date.

I also made out for the Auditor (on a view which he presented me of Mr. Grand's general account from July 10. 84. to July 15. 87.) a statement signed by me Feb. 21. 92. which may be considered as an Index for the Treasury, shewing to what person they are to charge every article of Mr. Grand's account during that period. This I was enabled to do with exactness from my knolege of the transactions, and from my notes and letters, except in a very few instances. Besides this, wherever sums had been paid on my orders I had made the orders shew for what purposes they were paid, or to whom chargeable. Since my making out this Index, Mr. Grand has sent me copies of my orders, and I presume has done the same to the Auditor. They corroborate the Index in every instance where that was explicit and compleat it in the few articles of doubt expressed. To this Index I shall refer by that name, or by it's date, and shall consider references to that, or to my account of Oct. 12. 92. as a sufficient explanation of any article, because it's explanation will be found there.

I have also lately recieved from Mr. Grand a continuation of his public account from July 15. 87. The only articles of it preceding my departure are

1787. Aug. 21. Petit 4000.ᵗᵗ for which see both my account and the Index under the proper date.

1788. May 24. 1789. May. 21. June 25. July 1. Aug. 16. five articles to Gateau & Duvivier, engravers for the medals. This little addition to the Index makes that a compleat information to the Auditor as to the persons to whom every article is to be charged which was paid by Mr. Grand during my time. I will observe also that the statement of Feb. 21. 92. contained a like explanation of such articles of the accounts of Willinks, Van Staphorst & Hubbard as are within my knolege.[3]

These observations premised, I proceed to explain the articles of charge against me in a paper sent me by the Auditor, called "an ABSTRACT from Mr. Grand's accounts against the US." containing, I presume, all the articles of charge wherein explanations are desired. I shall take it up therefore article by article.

'Amount of payments from Aug. 7. 84. to July 18. 85. debited
me in T. Barclay's books   64,000.ᵗᵗ

		ᵗᵗ	
1786. Feb. 15. Grand's charges as paid on account of salary		16,271–16	
paid on account of do.		23,625–	
paid for expences of office		10,587– 8–6	50,484–4–6
			114,484–4–6

Mr. Grand had been in the habit of setting apart Dr. Franklin's salary at the end of every quarter, of paying off his private bills, and of charging him a commission; thus in fact doing all his money business. He began a separate account with me, and I did not attend to it till Mr. Barclay first observed to me that Mr. Grand had a commission for recieving and paying the monies of the US. and that there was no reason for his taking from me, any more than any other creditor of the US. a second commission for the payments he made to me. This was the less reasonable as I was in the habit of paying my own bills, recieving the money from Mr. Grand in mass.[4] Upon this I desired him to change the form of his accounts, and not to keep a separate one for me. He had then proceeded on the old plan near two years (as I now find) and in the mean time had settled his account with Mr. Barclay as low down as the date of the 64,000.ᵗᵗ by which means that sum got into Mr. Barclay's accounts.   Hence have arisen two forms of rendering his accounts. In the first he has erected a private account against me, charging me all the monies he issued to me, in detail, and crediting me orders on the US., which, while this practice continued, were for the aggregate sums of 64,000.ᵗᵗ

16,271^{tt}–16   23,625.^{tt}⁵ and 10,587^{tt}–8–6 and in the concurrent account against the US. he debits them these aggregate sums, but does
not debit them the details. So that, under this form, the US. are charged
but once, as of right should be. I now send the Auditor one of these
accounts of the old form; where he will observe, in my private account,
from Aug. 20. 84. to July 18. 85. details making up Mr. Barclay's
64,000.^{tt} and from July 18. 85. downwards, other details making up a
little more than the 50,484^{tt}–4–6. My memory does not enable me to
explain the cause of this small difference,⁶ as not one of these details are
debited in the concurrent public account; but, instead thereof, the aggregate sums which cover them. But the second form of account, made
at my request, drops the private account against me altogether, incorpo-
rates it's details into the public account, and then omits the aggregate
sums. This I presume was the form of the account examined and explained in my statement of Feb. 21. [for I have not a copy of that account
but only of my statement from it.]⁷ In that are all the details from my
private account which were covered in the first forms of account by the
aggregates 64,000.^{tt} and 50,484^{tt}–4–6 and these aggregates are omitted. So that under this form also the US. are debited to Grand but once.
Then as to the application of that money, every article of it will be found
in my account of Oct. 12 at dates corresponding with those of Grand;
and in the Index of Feb. 21. page 3. will be seen that the 10,000^{tt} (part
of the 64,000^{tt}) was a temporary accomodation to the state of Virginia,
the principles of which are explained in the same page. I presume that
this suffices to shew that the US. having credit in my account of Oct. 12.
for the details composing these aggregates of 54,000^{tt} and 50,484–4–6
(the remaining 10,000.^{tt} repaid by Virginia,) they are not to charge
them to me a second time under the forms of the aggregates themselves:
and I may add that they will find no one of Grand's accounts wherein
they are charged with both the aggregates and the details.

'1786. Jan.16. to Marc. 5000.^{tt} ⎫ See these articles expressly credited
       Feb. 2. to do.   4000. ⎬ in my account of Oct. 12. and in the
           27. to do.   5000. ⎭ Index pa. 5. how it happened that
they were not thrown into the aggregate sums, with the other details of
the same period.

'1786. June 1. 4000.^{tt}—to 1787. Aug. 21. 1122^{tt}–14s–3d inclusive.
Every article is credited in my account of Oct. 12. except the quarterly
ones of 1875.^{tt} for house rent for which see Index page 1. and 2. under
the respective dates.

'11,085^{tt}–1–6 credited as repaid by me. How this arises see Index pa. 5.

[15]

I know not why it was called a repaiment by me. I rather view it as a technical entry, resulting from the first form of the accounts, and necessary to make them correspond in result with the second form.

18,392^{tt}–5–6 a late private account erected against me by Mr. Grand, and then transferred to the US. I send a copy of this to the Auditor and observe on the articles as follows.

159^{tt}–6 this is a just article of private charge against me. The US. are not concerned in it.

tt

1789. Oct. 12. Petit   2613– 2   }   These are just articles of pri-
      Nov. 30. Begouen   <u>3011– 8</u>   }   vate account against me. They
                  5624–10   }   were for expences incurred at

Havre previous to my embarcation. But on the 21st. of Oct. I sent Mr. Grand a bill on Willinks, V. Staph. & Hub. for 2687f–10 Bo. for the express purpose of covering the draught of 2613^{tt}–2 which I had already made, and the monies I either had recieved, or knew I must still call for from Begouen. I conjectured they would amount to 6000.^{tt} and as Mr. Grand had just before taken a bill of 2687f–10 Bo. equivalent to 6000.^{tt} cash, I sent him a second draught of exactly the same amount in florins, and credited the US. 6000.^{tt} as will be seen in my account under the date of Oct. 21. 1789. But I do not find that Mr. Grand has credited this 2d sum of 2687f–10 either in my private account or in the public one, and judge from present appearances that it has been omitted. The US. being credited for it in my account are no further concerned in the article but it remains to be settled between Mr. Grand and myself, and a balance results from it in my favor of 375^{tt}–10 against which he has to count the 159^{tt}–6 before mentioned[8] and perhaps [100] as hereafter mentioned.

'1790. May   27. Mr. Short for Langeac   1200.^{tt} } These articles being
      Aug. 20. Langeac   3000.   } a part of the general
      Nov. 17. do.   <u>1377</u>   } account of house-rent
                           5577   } are a debit against

the US. on the same ground with all the previous charges of houserent. They ought therefore to be credited to Mr. Grand as the former similar articles have been.[9]

'1792. Apr. 27. Cathalan 100.^{tt} I know nothing of this: but it is very possible it may have been for me. I will therefore have an explanation of it with Mr. Grand, and it need not enter into the accounts of the US.
'1793. May 25. Virginia 6931^{tt}–9s–6d. This is an article of [account between] Mr. Grand and the state of Virginia. I closed my gestion of their business at my departure from France, settled my accounts with

them on my arrival here, and obtained their quietus. Mr. Grand seems to have transferred the charge from them to me, that he might after-wards transfer it from me to the US. But neither the US. nor myself have any thing to do with it. However I will, on behalf of Mr. Grand take immediate measures with the Executive of Virginia to procure a settlement and discharge of the balance from them to him.　　On the whole, of this 18,392^{tt}–5–6. it appears that the US. taking to them-selves the 5577.^{tt} houserent, ought to reject all the other articles from their accounts, and leave them to be settled between Mr. Grand, the state of Virginia, and myself.

This finishes the explanations of the articles of the ABSTRACT, not a single one of which has been passed over. [10]

2. Outfit and 3. House rent. It will be necessary here to enter into some developement of the uncertain ground on which Congress first set out in the allowance to their ministers, of their progress, step by step, to the certainty to which they have at length reduced it, to shew in what stage of this process I was placed and what was under contemplation of the old Congress to have done in my special case. [11]

When they made[12] their first appointments, having themselves no ex-perience or knolege of the allowance usually made by other nations, and confiding in the discretion of their ministers, they left it to them to find what should be their expences, engaging to pay those expences and a handsome [allowance] besides for their services. [See their resolutions Sep. 28. 1776 and May 7. 1778.]. [13] The Ministers, on their arrival in Europe, had therefore to do as they saw others of their grade do. In Aug. 1779. Congress settle the allowance which they had promised for their *services* at £500 sterl. a year 'besides their expences.' And in Oct. 1779 they establish a fixed salary of £2500. sterl. for both the *services* and *expences* of their ministers. But what particular expences were to be considered as those of the Minister, and to be covered by this salary, were not specified, from the same want of information in Congress, which had obliged them from the beginning to go step by step only in fixing the allowances. The Ministers therefore, now as before, enquired into the usage established by other nations; in order to know what ex-pences were considered as those of the Minister, and what of the sover-eign. I find on the records a letter from Dr. Franklin, who was one of those earliest appointed, to Mr. Adams, dated June 11. 1781. and transmitted to Congress, wherein he gives this as the result of his enquiries. 'As we are all new [14] in these matters I consulted, when I was making up my accounts, one of the oldest foreign ministers here as to the custom in such cases. He informed me that it was not perfectly uniform with the ministers of all courts: but that in general where a salary was given for *service* and *expences*, the expences understood were merely those necessary to the man, such as house keeping, cloathing, and coach: but that the rent of the hotel in which he dwelt, the payment of couriers, the postage of letters, the salary of clerks, the stationary for his bureau, with the feasts and illuminations made on public occasions, were deemed expences of the Prince or State that appointed him, being for the service or honor of his prince or Nation; and either entirely, or in good part, expences that as a private man he would have been under no necessity of incurring. These therefore were to be charged in his accounts. He remarked that it was true the minister's house keeping, as well as his house, was usually, and in some sort necessarily more expensive than those of a private person. But this he said was considered in his salary to avoid trouble in his accounts: but that where the prince or state had not purchased or built a house for their Minister, which was sometimes the case, they always paid his house-rent.' On these principles then their accounts were kept. [15] At Paris the US. rented an hotel: at the Hague they resolved to buy one, which was done. See Resolution Dec. 27. 1782. On the 7th. of May 1784. they [reduced] the *salary* from £2500. sterl. to 9000. Dollars and on the 9th. of May they appointed me one of their ministers for negociating treaties. It is to be observed that [they] had never had occasion to consider at all the articles of *Outfit* to a Minister separately, because no appointment had taken place since Octob. 1779 when the *salary* was first fixed: and all the Ministers then resident in Europe, having at the time of their Outfit, been allowed their expences, these necessarily included the Outfit. My first appointment having been only for a special purpose, and not to reside in Europe, consequently not obliging me to take or furnish a house, I did not, on that appointment, claim an Outfit. When I was afterwards appointed to reside at Paris, as Minister there, I applied to my predecessor, Dr. Franklin, to know how I was to keep my accounts, who told me that the US. furnished the hotel, paid clerks, couriers, postage, stationary and court fees. I applied also to Mr. Barclay, who was authorized to settle all accounts of the US. in Europe; who gave me a copy of Dr. Franklin's account, as he had settled it, to be my guide. This contained an Outfit in fact, as has been beforementioned. I accordingly began an account of the cost of my furniture, carriage, horses, clothes &c. but finding that the details were numerous, minute, incapable from their nature of being vouched, that it was difficult to say where they should end, that a year's salary was allowed by most nations, and considerably more by some for this article, and that even this would be less than the actual amount of the particulars of my Outfit, I thought it better to charge it at once at a year's salary, presuming that Congress would rather at length fix a sum for that article also, as they had done for the salary. I wrote a private letter to Mr. Jay, then Secretary of foreign affairs, on this subject who laid it before Congress, and he informed me in his letter of Nov. 25. 1788. that 'they had referred it to a committee. Mr. Williamson of N. Carolina was chairman of it. They have not reported; but he says it was the opinion of the Committee that on consideration of these expences, you should be allowed, for two or three years, the salary of your predecessor, which exceeded yours.' Some members of that who are also of the present Congress, can vouch the same fact. [16] For want of a representation of 9. states, then necessary in money matters, they never could report during the old government, and so it [17] laid over for the new. The difference between the salary of my predecessor and myself was nearly £600. sterl. a year, which for three years would have nearly made up a year's salary, which I had proposed for the Outfit. July 1. 1790 the Congress [18] of the present government passed a general law, fixing the Outfit at a year's salary. This was not retrospective, and is only mentioned as shewing their sense that a year's salary was a reasonable allowance for Outfit.

From hence it appears that previous to the law lastmentioned, there was no complete and legal ascertainment of the principles on which the accounts of Ministers were to be settled. They were governed in some articles by fixed allowance; in others by the Usage of other nations, by precedents, or practice of their predecessors, and by the reason of the thing. Thus, in the present account, the article of salary till the 1st. of Aug. 1784. stands on the ground of the resolution of Congress of Oct. 4. 1779. and after that, on that of May 7. 1784. That of hotel-rent, couriers, postage, stationary, court fees, on usage and precedent, the hotel particularly being considered by practice as the permanent Office of the nation. That of Outfit, on usage and precedent, and on the proceedings of the committee of the old, [and] Congress of the new government. The rent of the hotel was paid by Mr. Grand for the most part when he had money, and at other times by myself and charged to the US. [19]

4. The PERIOD when my commission of Min. Pleny. terminated.

I left Europe in Oct. 1789. on a leave of absence previously obtained from the government, for 6. months (as well as I recollect the term.) I left it with a strong desire to return and see the end of a revolution which I then thought near it's close. On my way from Norfolk to my own house I recieved Dec. 11. the President's letters of Oct. 13. and Nov. 30. under the same inclosure, with a commission to be Secretary of state. In the letter of Oct. 13. are these expressions, which shewed he did not mean this as a recall, but to leave to my own choice to take the new, or continue under the old commission. 'Without being able to consult your inclination, or to derive any knowlege of your intentions from your letters either to myself or to any other of your friends, I was determined &c. to nominate you for the department of state &c. but, grateful as your acceptance of this commission would be to me, I am at the same time desirous to accomodate to your wishes, and I have therefore forborne to nominate your successor at the court of Versailles, until I should be informed of your determination.' In the letter of Nov. 30. he says 'I forward your commission to Virginia with a request to be made acquainted with your sentiments as soon as you shall find it convenient to communicate them to me.' I needed no time to make up my mind against a change of office; for that was bent on returning to my former station, with which I was acquainted, in preference to a new one of which I had fears and forebodings which gave me strong repugnance to it. I expressed, in my answer of Dec. 15. to the President my preference to return, only qualifying it with those expressions, which respect required of conforming to his will, and especially if his views were to any alteration in my former office. On the 6th. of Feb. I recieved another letter from the President dated Jan. 21. 1790. wherein he says 'I had the pleasure to recieve duly your letter of Dec. 15. but I thought proper to delay answering &c. until &c. [and] I now &c. of mentioning &c. the expediency of your deciding at as early a period as may consist with your convenience on the important subject before you. I feel such delicacy and embarrasment in consequence of the footing on which you have placed your final determination as to make it necessary for me to recur to the first ground on which I rested the matter.—In confidence therefore I will tell you plainly that I wish not to oppose your inclinations, and that after you shall have been made a little further acquainted with the light in which I view the office of Secretary of state, it must be at your option to determine relative to your acceptance of it, or *continuance in your office abroad*.—But in order that you may be the better prepared to make your ultimate decision on good grounds, I think it necessary to add one fact &c.—If you should finally determine to take upon yourself the duties of the department of state, it would be highly requisite for you to come on immediately &c. or in all events it would be essential that I should be informed of your conclusive option, so that if you return to France, another person may be nominated to fill the department of state.' Tho' my repugnance to the new office was still as great as ever, and really oppressive to my mind, I wrote to the President Feb. 14. that I would come on the [ensuing] week and undertake it, but I still retained the hope that when I should get to New York, I might find some opening to avoid it without giving dissatisfaction. In the course of my progress however to that place I found in the different societies I fell in with on the way that the public expected me to act in the new office, and that, should I decline it, I might incur reproaches which would give me more pain than the change of office. On my arrival at N. York therefore the 21st. of Mar. I declined making any effort to change the arrangement, but qualified into the new office;[20] and then, for the first time, wrote to Paris to put down my houshold, and wind up and [send home] my affairs. This was the first moment that I ceased entirely to hope I might go on to France, and the qualification was the first act which in my conception, determined my former commission. Assuredly if I had then pressed my return to France, it would have been yielded to, nor would a new commission have been thought necessary. The President's letter recieved Feb. [6]. clearly considered me as free to *continue* in my former commission, and consequently that it was not determined and the only doubt which could be raised would be whether this effect was produced by my letter of Feb. 14. or by my arrival and qualification at N. York.[21] The latter is my own opinion: but this is a small object to the public and not a great one to any individual.—These transactions being unknown to the Auditor, I have thought it necessary to state them to him specially, as it was on my own knolege of them that I had fixed the PERIOD of my salary.

There is more than common reason in the case against abridging the period of my commission. Congress allow three months from *notice* of the recall for the return home, an allowance which will never be found to cover the expence of return. This short allowance too goes[22] on the supposition that the person would be on the spot, so that his domestic establishment might be put down instantly. In confidence that I was to return to Paris,[23] I had left my servants, horses, and other current expences going on nearly as if I had been there, under the care of Mr. Short. He never recieved my letters notifying that all this was to be put down till June 12. The 3. months then which I should have had for getting every thing home, had I been on the spot, were within 10. days of expiring before the business began, and it was to be done in my absence to prodigious disadvantage and loss.[24] This circumstance brought my account into an arrear with the public which did not exist before, nor would otherwise have existed. To make good this, I was obliged to

[21]

borrow from Messrs. Van Staphorsts & Hubbard the two sums for which I take credit in my account, to wit

		D
1792. Jan. 29. order to V. Stap. & Hubbard	1004.54	
Oct. 12. do.	888.67	
	1893.21	

which sums I have still to pay them, and having no resource but my farms, which [were] not profitably managed in my absence, and are ignorantly so now,[25] I begin to percieve will be to be paid by the sale of some part of them. I do not mention this to obtain from the public any thing but what is right: but to justify my claiming, in my accounts, up to the strict line of right. I never desired any compensation for my time. I meant however to have kept my expences within the public allowance; and had done so, till this accidental protraction and increase of expence left me loser, on the whole mission, the sum beforementioned, and every defalcation now is to cut off exactly so much of a farm.[26] I hope that my aversion for this will not be mistaken for avarice.   TH: JEFFERSON

Mar. 8. 1796.

PrC (DLC: TJ Papers, 99: 17053-66); written entirely in TJ's hand on 14 numbered pages; badly faded, partly overwritten in ink by TJ, with bracketed words supplied from Dft except as noted; TJ's block printing shown as small capitals; endorsed by TJ in ink on verso: "Copy of Notes of Mar. 8. 96. sent to Auditor." Dft (same, 100: 17112-15); undated and unsigned; heavily emended text written on both sides of four parallelogram-shaped sheets, with the "preliminary observations" set down on a separate sheet (fol. 17113) and keyed for insertion in the body of the text (see note 2 below); with numerous variations in wording and punctuation not recorded here, the most important revisions and variations being noted below, including five places where TJ used "&c.—" to bridge passages that appear in expanded form in PrC and in variant form in the Explanatory Notes on Accounts printed under 8 July 1792 (see notes 12, 14-15, and 17-18 below); note by TJ at head of text: "rough draught of Notes of Mar. 8. 96. kept to help out the press copy where too faint"; with brackets inserted later by TJ to set off a passage for revision (see note below). Enclosure: Account of Grand & Cie. with TJ, 12 Oct. 1789 to 25 May 1793, being Enclosure No. 4 listed at

Grand & Cie. to TJ, 25 May 1793 (first letter). Other enclosure not found. Enclosed in TJ to Richard Harrison, 8 Mch. 1796.

THE AUDITOR: Richard Harrison. ACCOUNT ... SIGNED OCT. 12. 92: see preceding document and note. See also Explanatory Notes on Accounts, Document II in group of documents on Jefferson's French accounts, at 8 July 1792, Vol. 24: 194-9. STATEMENT SIGNED BY ME FEB. 21. 92.: Explanations of Ferdinand Grand's Accounts, 21 Feb. 1792. In several instances in Dft TJ initially designated the 12 Oct. 1792 document "statement No. 1" and that of 21 Feb. 1792 "statement No. 2." He subsequently altered those references in Dft to refer consistently to the 12 Oct. document by date and to that of 21 Feb. either by date or as the "Index."

MR. GRAND HAS SENT ME COPIES OF MY ORDERS: Grand & Cie. to TJ, 25 May 1793 (two letters), and enclosures. The CONTINUATION of Grand's PUBLIC ACCOUNT with TJ is listed as Enclosure No. 1 to the first of those letters. PAPER ... CALLED "AN ABSTRACT": the statement, not found, enclosed in Harrison to TJ, 28 Sep. 1795.

2687f–10 BO. FOR THE EXPRESS PUR-

POSE . . . IN MY FAVOR OF 375ᵗᵗ–10: for TJ's subsequent revision of this passage, see Memorandum to Richard Harrison, [ca. 20 Mch. 1796].

I WILL THEREFORE HAVE AN EXPLANATION OF IT WITH MR. GRAND: TJ to Jean Antoine Gautier, 17 Mch. 1796. I WILL . . . TAKE IMMEDIATE MEASURES WITH THE EXECUTIVE OF VIRGINIA: see TJ to Robert Brooke, and to John Pendleton, both 20 Mch.

THEIR RESOLUTIONS SEP. 28. 1776 AND MAY 7. 1778: in the first resolution the Continental Congress declared that its commissioners to the court of France "should live in such stile and manner . . . as they may find suitable and necessary to support the dignity of their public character." The resolution of May 1778 used similar language for commissioners to the courts of Spain, Tuscany, Vienna, and Berlin. AUG. 1779. CONGRESS SETTLE THE ALLOWANCE: a resolution of 6 Aug. 1779 set the annual allowance of a commissioner to a European nation at 11,428 livres tournois. OCT. 1779 THEY ESTABLISH A FIXED SALARY: a resolution of 4 Oct. 1779 established salaries for John Jay and John Adams, newly appointed ministers plenipotentiary to Spain and Great Britain (JCC, V, 833-4, XI, 473, XIV, 928, XV, 1143-5).

A LETTER FROM DR. FRANKLIN: Vol. 24: 198n. The salary fixed by the resolution of THE 7TH. OF MAY 1784. was effective 1 Aug. 1784 and applied to all ministers to foreign nations (JCC, XXVI, 354).

ON THE 9TH. OF MAY THEY APPOINTED ME: for a discussion of TJ's use of this date, see note to Document II in Editorial Note and group of documents on the settlement of Jefferson's accounts as minister plenipotentiary in France, at 8 July 1792. I WROTE A PRIVATE LETTER TO MR. JAY: TJ to Jay, 15 May 1788. For the GENERAL LAW passed by Congress on 1 July 1790, see TJ to Adams, 28 Feb. 1796. WROTE TO PARIS TO PUT DOWN MY HOUSEHOLD: TJ to William Short, 12 Mch. 1790.

¹ In Dft TJ originally listed house rent fourth, then interlined it to make it the third in the series.

² In Dft TJ wrote the extensive "preliminary observations" that follow—through the phrase "in a paper sent me"—on a separate sheet and keyed them for insertion here.

³ In Dft the text from "I have also lately recieved" to this point is heavily revised. Before TJ canceled and redrafted the paragraph it read: "⟨As I have no⟩ I think it of importance that the Auditor should send me a copy of Mr. Grand's general account from July 15. 87. to the end of 1789. that I may on an inspection of the articles inform him to what person and on what account each is to be debited. Copies of my orders indeed on Grand (if furnished him) may enable him to do this as to articles paid on them, but probably there are other articles not paid on my order, which my knolege of what was passing may enable me to explain."

⁴ Sentence interlined in Dft, which also has "more reasonable."

⁵ Dft lacks figures "16,271ᵗᵗ–16" and "23,625.ᵗᵗ"

⁶ Clause not in Dft.

⁷ Brackets in original.

⁸ In Dft paragraph ends here.

⁹ In Dft TJ originally wrote: "I think the Auditor should credit these articles to Mr. Grand, and let them abide the result of the General question between the US. and myself."

¹⁰ In PrC TJ left the remainder of the page blank and began the next paragraph on a new page.

¹¹ Preceding sixteen words inserted in Dft.

¹² In Dft text from this point to "of the sovereign" is lacking, represented by "&c.—."

¹³ Brackets in original.

¹⁴ In Dft text from this point to "always paid his house-rent" is lacking, represented by "&c.—."

¹⁵ In Dft text from this point to "who laid it before Congress" is lacking, represented by "&c.—." TJ canceled the following paragraph beginning on the next line: "⟨see⟩ enclose copy of a note of Mr. Remsen who was principal clerk in Mr. Jay's office stating this fact which tho' not signed (as it was informally given to me) is in his ⟨well known⟩ handwriting, ⟨and the fact can be otherwise proved if doubted.⟩ Mr. Remsen, who was chief clerk to Mr. Jay, stated the proceedings of this business to me in the following words (Mr. Jay having then left

the office) 'Mr. Jay with a letter &c.—increase of his salary.' Mr. Jay wrote me a private letter to the same effect, and other evidence of the intentions of Congress can be produced if necessary—July 1. 1790 &c."

[16] Preceding sentence interlined in Dft.

[17] In Dft preceding sixteen words are lacking and are represented by "&c.—."

[18] In Dft remainder of paragraph and entire next paragraph are lacking, represented by "&c.—." TJ wrote the text from "who laid it before Congress" to this point perpendicularly in the margin.

[19] In PrC TJ left the remainder of the page blank and began the next paragraph on a new page.

[20] Remainder of sentence interlined in Dft.

[21] Dft here reads "Mar. 21." and omits next nine words.

[22] Preceding eighteen words interlined in Dft.

[23] Preceding ten words interlined in Dft in place of "at once, and."

[24] Sentence interlined in Dft in place of a canceled sentence that read in part: "and I can say with truth that the return, with my family, and the bringing back my effects under the delay occasioned by the circumstances and the disadvantage of the winding up my affairs, packing and sending home my luggage cost me the double of the 3. months salary allowed for these objects."

[25] Preceding five words interlined in Dft in place of "on public affairs, nor are so now from that [very?] state of ignorance as to their management which a life spent in public employment has left me in myself."

[26] Preceding two words interlined in Dft in place of "my property [. . .]."

To Richard Harrison

DEAR SIR   Monticello Mar. 9. 96.

The letters and papers addressed to you by this post [are] public, and for the files of your office. But I cannot refrain indulging myself in a private line also. If you shall be satisfied by these papers that all the heads of difficulty are cleared away, I shall hope the matter will be finally settled by yourself. To me they appear to leave no difficulty, and the less, because mine being the last of those accounts, the precedent can have no consequence on any thing subsequent. If however you are still unsatisfied as to any one of these heads (and [from] the expressions of your letter I conjecture that if any difficulty [remains] it will be as to that of Outfit) then I would beseech you to decide on all those on which you are satisfied, that if I am obliged to [carry] the matter before Congress, it may be on a simple abstract question. No man upon earth has such mortal aversion,[1] as myself to be the subject of discussion, and therefore I wish to narrow the ground, if ground must still remain. Nothing but the accident of the change in the form of our government prevented my having the formal approbation of the charge of Outfit from the old Congress and a thing approved by the antient legislature, and [approved] by the present one cannot be doubtful in it's issue, tho it is [disagreeable in the process] to it. I am with very great esteem [Dr. Sir Your friend] & servt   TH: JEFFERSON

[24]

PrC (DLC); faded, with bracketed words supplied from Dft; at foot of text: "R. Harrison, Auditor of the US."; endorsed in ink by TJ on verso. Dft (DLC: TJ Papers, 100: 17111); undated and unsigned; written on parallelogram-shaped sheet with Dft of TJ to Harrison, 8 Mch. 1796; heavily emended text with numerous stylistic variations, the most significant being noted below.

On 9 Mch. TJ wrote another letter to Harrison in response to Harrison's 28 Sep. 1795 request for papers that remained in TJ's hands connected with the purchase of medals in France in accordance with resolutions of Congress (PrC in DLC; at foot of first page: "The Auditor of the US."; endorsed in ink by TJ on verso). The Dft, lacking dateline, salutation, complimentary close, signature, and first paragraph is printed as No. IV of a group of documents on notes on American medals struck in France, Vol. 16: 77-9. The first paragraph of the PrC reads "In complying with your desire of sending you the papers respecting the medals, I think it my duty at the same time to give you what information on the subject I can, which was the object indeed of my retaining the papers till now."

[1] Dft: "No mortal upon earth has such aversion."

From James Madison

DEAR SIR   Philada. Mar. 13. 1796.

Since my last by the last weekly mail, I have seen Mr. Rittenhouse on the subject of the Kitchen Stoves. He says that at Lancaster where they were invented and are best known, two only remain in use. They certainly save fuel; but are so much complicated in their operation, as to require particular care, and are liable to the objection of keeping the Kitchen excessively hot. Mrs. Rittenhouse intimated that, as several modes of Cookery, roasting boiling &c., were carried on at the same time, it often happened that one of the modes did not keep pace with the other. Mr. R. could not learn the price. He supposed, from the quantity of Iron, that it must be considerable.

We are at length embarked in the discussion of the Treaty, which was drawn in rather abruptly by a proposition calling on the President for papers. The point in debate is the Constitutional right of Congs. in relation to Treaties. There seems at present strong reason to conclude, that a majority will be firm in the doctrine that the House has a Constitutional right to refuse to pass laws for executing a Treaty, and that the Treaty power is limited by the enumerated powers. Whether the right ought in the present case to be exerted will be a distinct question on the merits of the Treaty, which have not yet come into discussion. I understand the Treaty Party expect success on this question, but despair on every other.

Nothing very late from Europe. The British armament is arriving in the W. Indies, which looks like a postponement of peace. It will augment the call on this Country for provisions, and of course the price. Flour is about 15. dolrs. here at present.

RC (DLC: Madison Papers); unsigned; endorsed by TJ as received 25 Mch. 1796 and so recorded in SJL.

To Thomas Mann Randolph

TH:J. TO TMR.   Monticello Mar. 13. 96.

All are well here: Jefferson particularly so. Almost immediately after the receipt of your order to pay Mr. Divers 120. D. and before I could give him notice, he went to Richmond, and returned only 3 days ago. I saw him yesterday and told him how long I had had your order to pay him that sum, which had been in constant readiness for him, and was still so. He appeared perfectly satisfied. I gave him his choice to recieve it here or in Richmond. He preferred the former and will call for it this week. Mr. Garland sheriff, has applied to me for your taxes, which he says it would be convenient for him to recieve in a few days. I told him I would pay them. Two of the persons from whom I have principally purchased corn (Mrs. Gilmer and F. Walker) prefer my paying the money to you for them. The sums are not yet exactly known; the former probably about £40. the latter perhaps double that. The money will be in readiness for you as soon as it's amount is known. I inclose you a note of Mr. Rives's on Brown, and a memorandum. We have never had an opportunity of sending your succory seed. I must trouble you again about Cobbs's affair. Our court did no business at the last session, so it lies over. This gave us another opportunity of trying to get the depositions of the Inspectors of Shockoe. We have given Cobbs notice to attend the last day of this month at Shockoe warehouse, at 12. oclock to take the deposition. I must trouble you to act for me. The commission and letter before forwarded to you on this subject will suffice.—A word on the subject of our breed of Shepherd's dogs. Every individual of old Grizzle's breed has proved so mischievous that we have been obliged to kill the whole except Damon who is kept chained; and we remark that not a single instance has been known of any such disposition in Bergere's family. On the contrary they are all remarkeably quiet, faithful, and abounding in the good qualities of the old bitch. This observation renders her breed extremely precious, and it now consists in two bitches and a dog here, and the dog (Sancho) which you have. We are collecting them at the top of the mountain, and I mention all this to you lest you should part with Sancho, in which case if any thing happens to Norman, the breed will be lost. It would therefore be desireable that your dog should return with you and remain with us till the breed is multiplied.—W. Nicholas is tolerably sure of being re-elected. Joseph Monroe and Colo. Jouett are canvassing for the other place of delegate at the ensuing election. I intend to be sick on that day, Nicholas being out of danger. My sister Carr, who is with us, and Maria join in love to my dear Martha and yourself. We wish to hear that your health is become firm. Adieu affectionately.

RC (DLC); endorsed by Randolph as received 19 Mch. 1796. Enclosures not found, but see note below.

TJ fulfilled Randolph's ORDER TO PAY MR. DIVERS. Randolph's TAXES were $20.17 (MB, II, 938-9).

I INCLOSE YOU A NOTE: according to SJL, TJ enclosed "Rives' ord. on Brown £215." in a letter to John Wickham of 13 Mch. 1796, which has not been found. For this transaction, see MB, II, 937.

COBBS'S AFFAIR: see TJ to Thomas Mann Randolph, 11 Apr. 1796.

As TJ anticipated, Wilson Cary NICHOLAS was reelected as a delegate to the Virginia Assembly. Joseph Jones MONROE, James Monroe's brother, defeated Robert JOUETT for the other Albemarle County seat (Leonard, *General Assembly*, 199, 203; Ammon, *Monroe*, 85).

From Thomas Pinckney

DEAR SIR   London 16 March 1796.

Your favor of the 8th. of September last reached London when I was on my return from Spain to England by which means I did not receive it till after my arrival in this Country: the letters inclosed for Mrs. Church and Mr. Mazzei were forwarded by Mr. Deas previous to my return.

You will receive herewith a letter from the hereditary Prince of Parma who married, during my residence in Spain, a daughter of his Catholic Majesty; he appears to be an amiable, liberal minded young Gentleman, and well informed for his time of life and station; being heir to a sovereign Prince and only 22 years of age. I inclose our correspondence on this subject and have to request that if the kind of intercourse wished for should not suit your convenience that you would be so obliging as to point out such an arrangement as may have the effect desired.

In the acrimonious extremes to which party matters appear to have been carried in our country your retreat is peculiarly enviable, and I hope shortly to be permitted to enjoy similar pursuits: I wished to have paid more attention to the subject of agriculture during my stay in Spain, but no one can better estimate than yourself how much my time must have been occupied during my short residence in that Country, as no one is better apprized of the obstacles to be removed before the treaty such as it is could be agreed upon: in my return however I took a circuitous route with a view to attend as much as I could in so rapid a journey to such objects of their culture and commerce on the eastern coast of Spain as I conceived might be beneficial to our country: and one object of their rural œconomy which I saw appears to me applicable to a topic you have mentioned in your letter namely that of treading out Grain—an operation universally practiced in the parts of Spain through which I travelled, the flail being there unknown; their autumnal weather is so serene and dry that they pursue this method in the most perfect security, an advantage I did not before know that you partook of in Virginia; but to the operation of the horses feet the Spaniards add a kind of sledge which is drawn by the animals employed in the operation; this sledge by them called a trillo is made of plank two inches and an half thick. It is about 5 feet long and nearly three wide and a little turned up in the fore part to facilitate its passing over the grain; in the under side are inserted sharp flints each about one inch and half in length, these are placed in rows parallel to the sides, the rows an inch and half distant from each other and the flints the same distance apart in the rows, and projecting half an inch from the under surface of the plank. The threshing floors are paved and the trillo is drawn lengthwise, the driver standing thereon, and this instrument performs the double operation of beating out the grain and at the same time cutting the straw small for feeding, for in Spain no hay is given to horses or mules, chopt straw and barley being the only provender. If it should be no object with you to have the straw chopt I should imagine another instrument I saw preferable to the trillo for your use, which is a wooden roller, in which are inserted many wooden pins or feet the exterior surface of the ends of which are about four by three inches and which being drawn over the grain in their revolutions stamp it out.

Another object of my attention which I think applicable to your husbandry consists of the receptacles in which in the southern parts of this country they have long been in the habit of preserving their grain—the whole art of which appears to be in keeping it dry and cool; these receptacles are made under ground of a conical shape, resembling a pear with the stalk end upwards. They are constructed of stone; the aperture about three feet wide the greatest diameter from 16 to 20 feet, and a little more in depth: two layers of dry wooden rails or rafters are laid transversely in the bottom, as in Ice-houses, in which is placed matting or well dried straw and the grain thereon, the sides also are lined with the same materials, and when filled the aperture to the cave the outward surface of which is placed about three feet below the level of the ground is well closed and covered with earth or other compact materials. I am assured that not only sound grain is perfectly preserved in these reservoirs but even that grain in a heated state has been recovered by being lodged therein: I need not add that a dry position and soil are always chosen for the site of these granaries. One article in the culture of rice to which I paid attention in the kingdom of Valencia appears applicable to the subject just mentioned as adapted to your culture of Wheat in Virginia; which is, that for the purpose of treading out the Rice they cut off the Ears alone, leaving no stalk or straw; might it not therefore answer for You to use the same method? Reaping by hand only the ears of your Wheat and leaving your straw to be mown down; the grain might then be more easily disengaged from the ear than when unincumbered by the straw: or the entire ears might be lodged in the subterraneous granaries without danger of the heat being sufficient to give birth to the weevil; and the wheat might be threshed and ground as it might suit your convenience.

You find my dear Sir, that I rely upon your being very seriously occupied in the agricultural line, or I should not have ventured to tresspass so much on your time with my speculations on that subject: and I have yet a few more thoughts on similar topics which I wish to submit to your Judgement, but which I am obliged to reserve for a future occasion, confining myself for the present to the expression of the sincere respect and affectionate Esteem with which I am Your obliged & obedient Servt

THOMAS PINCKNEY

RC (DLC); endorsed by TJ as received 3 June 1796 and so recorded in SJL. PrC (ScHi: Pinckney Family Papers). Enclosures: (1) Louis of Parma to TJ, 2 Nov. 1795. (2) Louis to Pinckney, [30 Oct. 1795], requesting the name of the director of the natural history collection in the United States so that they could correspond through the American minister to Spain and conduct exchanges that would enrich the collections of both, and regretting that the system of the Spanish court did not allow him to become better acquainted with foreign ministers such as Pinckney (Tr in DLC: TJ Papers, 99: 16957-8; in French; undated; in William A. Deas's hand; at head of text: "Copie"; at foot of text: "Recd 30th. Octr. 1795."). (3) Pinckney to Louis, Madrid, 31 Oct. 1795, directing him to TJ for the names of the directors of the several societies in the United States interested in natural history, and enclosing *Notes on the State of Virginia*, for its interesting account of that region's natural history; and that while he regretted the court system which prevented him from benefitting from the benevolence the prince wished to display to him, he would return home next summer grateful for the prince's kindnesses and ready and willing to be useful to him. (4) Louis to Pinckney, San Lorenzo, 2 Nov. 1795, stating that he was enclosing No. 1 for Pinckney either to mail at the first opportunity or to return with any defects noted; that he realizes the impertinence of disturbing such a distinguished man as TJ but hopes they can enter into a mutually beneficial exchange in the field of natural history; that he is greatly pleased by TJ's *Notes*; and that TJ may address his reply either to the American minister here or the minister who will be closest (Trs in DLC; in French; in Deas's hand; with "Copie" at the head of both texts). Missing Dupl enclosed in Pinckney to TJ, 17 Apr. 1796.

From William Cabell

SIR   Amherst March 17th. 1796.

Doctor Robert H. Rose son of Colo. Hugh Rose deceased and Mr. John Rose son of Mr. Charles Rose having signified to me their intention of going to the S. Western territory, with a view of residing there, and also a wish of obtaining from you letters of introduction to gentlemen of your acquaintance in that quarter, I take the liberty of writing you a few lines on the occasion. I have been long acquainted with both of the young gentlemen. They have made so considerable a progress in science, are of such amiable characters, and possess in so eminent a degree the powers of being useful and agreeable members of society, that I venture to say they will be found every way deserving of all the respect and consideration which may be shewn them by the judicious of any community. Any services which you may render them by way of letters, will be considered as an obligation conferred on Sir, Yr. Obt. Servant.   WILLIAM CABELL

RC (DLC); endorsed by TJ as received 19 Mch. 1796 and so recorded in SJL.

SJL records a missing letter from Cabell to TJ of 2 May 1795, recorded as received 5 May 1795, and missing letters from TJ to Cabell of 18 May 1795 and 8 Oct. 1796. A 17 May 1795 letter from TJ to JOHN ROSE and a 17 Mch. 1796 letter from Robert H. Rose to TJ, received from Geddes on 19 Mch. 1796, are also recorded in SJL but have not been found.

According to SJL, a missing letter to TJ of 18 Mch. 1796 from Cabell's youngest brother, Nicholas Cabell, was received 19 Mch. 1796 from Liberty Hall (Alexander Brown, *The Cabells and their Kin: A Memorial Volume of History, Biography, and Genealogy* [Boston, 1895], 72).

To Jean Antoine Gautier

DEAR SIR   Monticello in Virginia Mar: 17: 96.

The papers which you were so kind as to send me with some lately recieved from the Auditor of the US. have enabled me to take up the subject of your accounts with the US. with the state of Virginia, and with myself, and finally to place every article of your debets in the account of the party for whose use the money was paid. To you it matters not in what account you find your monies, if you find it all somewhere. I inclose you, on a single sheet of paper, the arrangement I have made, in which you will find every article of your debets. The account with Virginia was perfectly accurate. That erected against me after my departure, required corrections, which I shall proceed to explain by taking up that account article by article.

			₶		
1789.		Wine omitted	159–6		this is just & is properly chargeable to me.
			₶		
Oct. 12.		order favr. Petit	2613–2		this is just & properly charged
		cash from Begouen[1]	3011–8	5624–10	to me, but something further will be said on the subject presently.
			₶		
1790. May 27.		Short for Langeac	1200		just: but transferred from mine
Aug. 20.		Langeac	3000		to the account of the US. with
Nov. 17.		do.	1377	5577–	all the other charges of the same nature.
1792. Apr. 27.		Cathalan's draught		100.–	my knolege of Mr. Cathalan satisfies me this is right though I have no advice of the draught.
1793. May 25.		Balance of acct. of Virginia		6931–9–6	just, but carried back to the account of Virginia.

But my account has no credit for my letter of credit of Oct. 21. 1789. sent from Cowes, on Willinks, Van Staphorsts & Hubbard in favor of Grand & Co. for 2800.ƒ Bo. which was meant expressly to cover the 5624₶–10 to Petit and Begouen, and to leave a balance for future contingencies or account. I have always taken for granted that this draught got safe to hand, and that it was paid by Willinks &c. and debited by them to the US. I therefore credited it to the US. Your books and those of Willinks &c. will set this fact to rights.

[In order to prevent any confusion of one sum or] draught for another, I will here recapitulate all the draughts of that year made on Willinks &c. for my own use, with the sums I received from Mr. Grand for them.

1789. Feb.	2.	draught on Willinks &c. for	ƒ 2285– 5	₶ Bo. and recd. 5000. cash.
Mar.	2.		2725–	6000– do.
Apr.	1.		3179– 3	7000– do.
	14.		2731– 5	6000– do. paid to Langeac.
May	1.		2731– 5	6000– do. to myself.
June	2.		2700–	6000– do.
July	1.		2693–15	6000– do.
Aug.	1.		2687–10	6000– do.
Sep.	1.		2687–10	6000– do.
	24.		4031– 8	9000– do.
Cowes. Oct.	21.		2800–	5624–10 to wit. to Petit 2613– 2
				to Begouen 3011– 8
				5624–10
				balance undrawn 626– 8
				6250–18

Agreeable to these observations, I have carried into the account of Virginia it's own balance of 6931–9–6 into that of the US. the three articles to Langeac of 5577.^{tt} and left in my own account what was properly my own, from which a balance results to me of 367^{tt}–2. With respect to the account of the US. the Auditor will settle with you, without difficulty, agreeably to my statement, for the period and the articles comprehended in it. As to the state of Virginia, I now send to the Governor the account you inclosed to me, certifying it to be all just of my own knolege, except the article of 9000.^{tt} paid after my departure, and therefore unknown to me; and I sollicit from him an early discharge of the balance due to you; and I will not cease attending to it on your behalf till you recieve it. The balance due to me I shall probably desire to be transferred to the credit of the Virginia account, and perhaps answer to you the further sum of [1567^{tt}–1–6, making, with the balance beforementioned] 1934^{tt}–3–6 which I at present suppose [to be a balance] remaining in my hands after the paiments made by me for the state, so that the state will in that case have to remit you [4997–6] only. But if this arrangement takes place, it will be the subject of another letter to you. In the mean time pray favor me with information as to the draught of 2800.f. With every friendly disposition to your house, and very particular esteem & regard to yourself I am Dear Sir Your most obedt. servt.

TH: JEFFERSON

PrC (DLC); faded, with date overwritten in ink by TJ and with bracketed words supplied here from Dft; at foot of first page: "Mr. Gautier for Grand & Co."; endorsed in ink by TJ on verso. Dft (DLC: TJ Papers, 87: 14998); undated and unsigned; written on both sides of a parallelogram-shaped sheet. Enclosures: (1) "The US. to Grand & Co.," 17 Mch. 1796, containing a chronological list of debit entries from 10 July 1784 to 17 Nov. 1790 (PrC in same, 100:17078-9; consisting of the first two pages of a single sheet that was folded to make four pages in missing MS, with Enclosures Nos. 2-3 occupying the third and fourth pages; entirely in TJ's hand, and signed and dated by him). (2) "Virginia in account with Grand & Co.," 17 Mch. 1796, containing debit and credit entries from 18 July 1785 to 14 Dec. 1792 (PrC in same, 17080; consisting of one page entirely in TJ's hand, signed and dated by him; with note above his signature: "Certified to be just, except as to the article of Dec. 14. 92.

9000.^{tt} which being after I left France, I am uninformed of"). (3) "T. Jefferson in account with Grand & Co.," 17 Mch. 1796, containing debit and credit entries from 12 Oct. 1789 to 27 Apr. 1792 (PrC in same, 17081; consisting of one page entirely in TJ's hand, signed and dated by him, with overwriting in ink by TJ reflecting corrections to figures specified in Memorandum to Richard Harrison, [ca. 20 Mch. 1796]). The texts described by the Editors as Trs (in DLC: TJ Papers, 96: 16499) of Enclosures Nos. 2 and 4 listed at Grand & Cie.'s first letter to TJ of 25 May 1793 are actually Dfts of Enclosures Nos. 2-3 above. See also enclosures to TJ to Harrison, 17 Mch. 1796. Enclosed in TJ to Monroe, 21 Mch. 1796.

THE PAPERS WHICH YOU WERE SO KIND AS TO SEND ME: see Grand & Cie. to TJ, 25 May 1793 (two letters), 24 Mch. 1795, and 11 Sep. 1795, and their enclosures. SOME LATELY RECIEVED FROM THE AUDITOR OF

THE US.: a reference to the statement, not found, enclosed in Richard Harrison to TJ, 28 Sep. 1795. I NOW SEND TO THE GOVERNOR: TJ to Robert Brooke, 20 Mch. 1796.

[1] In Dft this entry is dated "Nov. 30."

To Richard Harrison

DEAR SIR   Monticello Mar. 17. 1796.

After forwarding to you my dispatches by the last post, I undertook for the use of Mr. Grand also, to make a proper statement of his debets against the US. against Virginia, and myself; ascribing every article of his charges to it's real party. As his whole accounts, while under my inspection are thus brought within the compass of a single sheet of paper, I thought it would be well to send you a copy of it, because, being unencumbered with the explanatory notes, it will be a more convenient manual for you for common use. The part relating to the US. contains nothing but what you will find in the former papers; but all is here brought together.

I thought it best too that you should possess his accounts with this state, and with myself; because it may be advantageous for you to know not only what he has a right to charge to the US. but also what he has not a right to charge to them, but should look for to the party in whose account I place it. I am satisfied at the same time that that house will have no hesitation to conform to this distribution of their accompts, and to settle with you in the form now inclosed, because it matters nothing to them if they find all their money in accounts with somebody.[1]

I must repeat that it would be very desireable to me to recieve from you a copy of the account of Mr. Grand against the US. which was the subject of my examination when I made out the Index of Feb. 21. 92. and it may be useful to your office also should you have occasion to apply to me for any future explanations. I am with great esteem & respect Dear Sir Your most obedt servt   TH: JEFFERSON

PrC (DLC); at foot of text: "The Auditor of the US." Dft (DLC: TJ Papers, 100: 17116); undated; written entirely in TJ's hand on a parallelogram-shaped sheet; with variations and emendations, the most important being noted below. Enclosures: (1) Variant text of Enclosure No. 1 listed at TJ to Jean Antoine Gautier, 17 Mch. 1796, in same format and otherwise identical except for note above TJ's signature: "The four preceding columns contain the articles of the account of Grand & Co. which are properly chargeable to the US during the time I was privy to that account, and indicate what particular person is responsible for each sum. Three articles are added subsequent to my departure, because they are within my knolege" (PrC in same, 17107-8). (2) Variant text of Enclosure No. 2 listed at TJ to Gautier, 17 Mch. 1796, in same format and otherwise identical except for note above TJ's signature: "The above articles are properly chargeable by Grand & Co. to the state of Virginia, as paid for their use" (same, 17109). (3) Another text of Enclosure No. 3 listed at TJ to Gautier, 17 Mch. 1796, with similar overwriting in ink by TJ reflecting corrections to figures specified in Memorandum to Harrison, [ca. 20 Mch. 1796] (same, 17110).

INDEX OF FEB. 21. 92.: see notes to Statement on Accounts as Minister Plenipotentiary in France, 8 Mch. 1796.

[1] Preceding sentence and first four words of following sentence are lacking in Dft.

To William Blount

DEAR SIR   Monticello Mar. 19. 96

Dr. Robert H. Rose and Mr. John Rose will have the honor of delivering you this letter. As they go to your government with a view of fixing themselves there, they have naturally a wish to enjoy there whatever advantages may justly result from a knoledge of their characters. They are of a county next adjoining to me, of an antient and respectable family of this state, are sons of two brothers with whom I have from my infancy been in habits of the most intimate friendship and affection, and as far as their age has given developement to their characters they stand themselves under the best personal reputations. With these titles I take the liberty of presenting them to your Excellency believing it as desireable to you to know the worthy as to the worthy to be known by you. The patronage of your office you will naturally extend to them; but I take the liberty of solliciting also for them the benefits of your advice and countenance which their ignorance of the country and circumstances in which they will be placed and your knolege of them, may render of high value to these gentlemen. To the gratification of fostering virtuous youth in virtuous enterprize is added that of the occasion it furnishes me of assuring you of the sentiments of high respect and esteem with which I have the honor to be your Excellency's most obedt. & most humble servt   TH: JEFFERSON

PrC (MHi); with day in dateline emended in ink; at foot of text: "H.E. Governor Blount"; endorsed in ink by TJ on verso.

YOUR OFFICE: Blount was governor of the "Territory of the United States South of the River Ohio," that is, the Southwest Territory.

SJL records a 17 Aug. 1796 letter from TJ to Blount recommending "R. Lewis" and a 17 Mch. 1797 letter from Blount to TJ, received from Alexandria on 10 Apr. 1798, both not found.

To William Branch Giles

TH:J. TO MR. GILES   Monticello Mar. 19. 96

I know not when I have recieved greater satisfaction than on reading the speech of Dr. Lieb in the Pennsylvania Assembly. He calls himself a new member. I congratulate honest republicanism on such an acquisition, and promise myself much from a career which begins on such elevated ground.—We are in suspense here to see the fate and effect of Mr. Pitt's bill against democratic societies. I wish extremely to get at the true history of this effort to suppress freedom of meeting, speaking, writing and printing. Your acquaintance with Sedgewick will enable you to do it. Pray get from him the outlines of the bill he intended to have brought in for this purpose. This will enable us to judge whether we have the merit of the invention: whether we were really before hand with the British minister on this subject: whether he took his hint from our proposition, or whether the concurrence in sentiment is merely the result of the general truth that great men will think alike, and act alike tho' without intercommunication. I am serious in desiring extremely the outlines of the bill intended for us.—From the debates on the subject of our seamen, I am afraid as much harm as good will be done by our endeavors to arm our seamen against impressment. It is proposed I observe to register them and give them certificates of citizenship to protect them from foreign impressment. But these certificates will be lost in a thousand ways. A sailor will neglect to take his certificate. He is wet twenty times in a voyage. If he goes ashore without it, he is impressed, if with it, he gets drunk, it is lost, stolen from him, taken from him, and then the want of it gives an authority to impress which does not exist now. After ten years' attention to the subject, I have never been able to devise any thing effectual but that the circumstance of an American bottom being made ipso facto a protection for a number of seamen proportioned to her tonnage: to oblige American captains when called on by foreign officers to parade the men on deck, which would shew whether they exceeded their quota, and allow the foreign officers to send 2. or 3. persons aboard and hunt for any suspected to be concealed. This Mr. Pinckney was instructed to insist upon with Great Britain, to accept of nothing short of it, and most especially not to agree that a certificate of citizenship should be requirable from our seamen: because it would be made a ground for the authorised impressment of them. I am still satisfied that such a protection will place them in a worse situation than they are at present. It is true the British minister has not shown a disposition to accede to my proposition: but it was not totally rejected: and if he still refuses, lay a duty of 1.d. sterl. a yard on British oznabrigs to make a fund for paying the expences of the agents you are obliged to employ to seek out our suffering seamen.—I congratulate you on the arrival of Mr. Ames and the British treaty. The newspapers had said they would arrive together.—We have had a fine winter. Wheat looks well. Corn is scarce and dear. 22/ here. 30/ in Amherst. Our blossoms are just opening. I have begun the demolitions of my house, and hope to get through it's re-edification in the course of the summer. But do not let this discorage you from calling on us if you wander this way in the summer. We shall have the eye of a brick-kiln to poke you into, or an Octagon to air you in. Adieu affectionately.

PrC (DLC); faded, with date overwritten in ink by TJ.

During a debate on the four amendments to the Constitution recently proposed and sent to the states by Virginia in reaction to the Jay Treaty, the radical Republican Dr. Michael Leib delivered a SPEECH to the Pennsylvania House of Representatives, published in the Philadelphia *Aurora* on 29 Feb., in which he strongly supported the Virginia proposals, upheld the right of the federal House of Representatives to withhold the appropriations necessary to execute the treaty, and denied the need for the United States to enter into any treaties with any foreign nation (*Dr. Leib's Patriotic Speech, Addressed to the House of Represen-*

tatives of Pennsylvania. February 24, 1796 . . . [New London, 1796]; Evans, No. 30684; see also Madison to TJ, 31 Jan. 1796). MR. PITT'S BILL, introduced into Parliament in November 1795 and passed into law the following month, was the Seditious Meetings and Assemblies Act, which imposed strict controls on public meetings in Great Britain (Ehrman, *Pitt*, 455-9). Contrary to TJ's wishes, Congress in May 1796 passed a law to protect OUR SEAMEN against impressment that, among other things, provided for issuing certificates of American citizenship to them (*Annals*, VI, 2919-21). MR. PINCKNEY WAS INSTRUCTED: see TJ to Thomas Pinckney, 11 June 1792 (second letter).

To Thomas Mann Randolph

TH:J. TO TMR.   Monticello Mar. 19. 96

Your's of the 16th. inst. from Richmd. came to hand last night. I believe it would be better to do without herrings till the new season, even if we could get them, considering the price. I have recieved no advice of any port wine having been sent to me by any body, and I never ordered any. If that delivered Mr. Brown be really addressed to me, you are welcome to it, and in every case to do with respect to it whatever I might rightfully do. If it has come to a mistaken address, I presume you will serve the owner by using it, and paying for it if you should be ever called on. But is it certainly Port? Perhaps it may be Sherry or Termo from my correspondents at Cadiz or Lisbon.—Wheat on the 6th. inst. was 2⅔ Doll. at Philadelphia. Yours I believe is not yet delivered to Fleming; nor is mine. Robertson tells me all are well at Edgehill. So are all here. We begin to look forward to the hour when we are to see you again. We have had remarkeable winds for 2. or 3. days past. This morning the mercury was at 26°. Our peach blossoms are just opening. Mr. Hornsby and family are arrived in our neighborhood. He and N. Lewis junr. set out in about a fortnight for Kentucky. Corn at 22/ here and 30/ in Amherst. Our love and kisses to our dear Martha and Anne. Adieu affectionately.

RC (DLC); endorsed by Randolph.

Randolph's letter OF THE 16TH. INST., recorded in SJL as received 18 Mch. 1796, has not been found.

To Robert Brooke

SIR   [Monticello Mar. 20. 96.][1]

I have lately recieved from Messrs. Grand & Co. the inclosed account of their transactions for the state of Virginia; which having all (except the last of them) taken place under my inspection, I have examined, and found them just, and so certified. It appears that a balance is thereon due to them from the state of 6931^{tt}–9–6. I have taken the liberty of putting under your cover a letter to the Auditor, which if you will be so good as to peruse before you order it's delivery to him, will explain to you an eventual reduction of the balance to *4997^{tt}–6*. Messrs. Grand & Co. are entitled to recieve the balance in *specie* livres, of which kind those were which were due to Houdon. As they have carried their whole balance into account against me, it will give me satisfaction to be able, when it shall suit your convenience, to inform them when and how they may expect paiment. I embrace with pleasure every occasion offered me of assuring you of the sentiments of sincere respect & esteem with which I have the honor to be your Excellency's most obedt & most humble servt   TH: JEFFERSON

RC (DLC); clipped dateline supplied from PrC; at foot of text: "Governor Brooke"; endorsed. PrC (same); faded, with overwriting in ink by TJ (see note 1 below); endorsed in ink by TJ on verso. Tr (Vi); in an unknown hand; lacks dateline; with note by Governor James Monroe at foot of text: "15. March 1802 Note. The original was sent by post to Mr. Jefferson on this day to enable him to adjust the account of the artist Houdon." Enclosures: (1) Enclosure No. 2 listed at Grand & Cie. to TJ, 25 May 1793 (first letter), bearing, as indi-

cated there, the following certification added in TJ's hand and signed by him:

"The state of Virginia authorised Dr. Franklin and myself to have a statue of Genl. Washington made. We agreed with Houdon to pay him for the marble and workmanship   24.000.^{tt} and also to defray his expences to and from Virginia for taking the model, and the insurance of his life for the benefit of his family.

The state authorised Mr. Barclay to have two marble busts of

M. de la Fayette made, one for themselves, the other for the city of Paris. They cost 3000^{tt} each They authorised him also to purchase arms and ammunition. Mr. Grand acted as their banker. All the articles charged by Mr. Grand in this account are for some of these purposes, and are known to me to be just except that of 9000.^{tt} which was after I left France and of course neither of my knolege or authority. If this be also right as I suppose it to be, the balance of 6931^{tt}–9–6 is justly due to Mr. Grand. Certified

6 000.^{tt}

under my hand this 20th day of March 1796. Th: Jefferson";

this certification appears also in the Tr. (2) TJ to John Pendleton, 20 Mch. 1796.

THE AUDITOR: John Pendleton. DUE TO HOUDON: a reference to the payment owed for the statue of Washington commissioned by the state of Virginia from Jean Antoine Houdon (see Vol. 8: xxvii).

[1] On PrC TJ overwrote a portion of the date—"17. 96."—in ink, then interlined "20" in place of "17."

From William Branch Giles

DEAR SIR   Philadelphia March 20th. *1796*

This letter will probably be presented to you by the Duke De Laincourt, who proposes by a circuitous rout to visit Monticello.

In announceing this Gentleman to you, I am perfectly satisfyed that your previous acquaintance with his history, his reputation and his connection, will render any other mention of him, than merely his name, wholly unnecessary. Be pleased to accept my most affectionate Respects &c.   WM. B. GILES

RC (DLC); at foot of text: "Mr. Jefferson"; endorsed by TJ as received 22 June 1796 and so recorded in SJL.

DUKE DE LAINCOURT: François Alexandre, Duc de La Rochefoucauld-Liancourt.

Memorandum to Richard Harrison

Monticello Mar. [. . .] [ca. 20 Mch. 1796]

Th: Jefferson having discovered that in his notes of Mar. 8. 96 he had copied the draught of Sep. 1. 89. in the date of Oct. 21. instead of the proper draught which was of 2800.f Bo. [and had] [. . .] and from thence had carried the same error into the [. . .] of the statement of accounts dated Mar. 17. begs the favor of Mr. Harrison to make the following corrections for him.

Notes of Mar. 8. 96. Strike the pen through the words which are here dashed out, and interline those here interlined, as follows.

2800f–

pa. 4. line 2d. from bottom. '⟨2687–10.⟩ Bo. for the express purpose of covering the draught of 2613^{tt}–2 ⟨*which I had already made*⟩ and the monies I ⟨*either*⟩ had recieved,[1] ⟨*or knew I must still call for*⟩ from Begouen. ⟨*I conjectured they would amount to 6000.*ᵗᵗ⟩ and as Mr. Grand

$$4031f-8 \qquad\qquad\qquad 9000.^{tt}$$

had just before taken a bill of ⟨*2687f–10*⟩ Bo. as equivalent to ⟨*6000.*ᵗᵗ⟩

at the same rate of exchange

cash, I, ⟨*sent him a second draught of exactly the same amount in florins*⟩

$$6250^{tt}-18$$

and⟩ credited the US. ⟨*6000*ᵗᵗ⟩ as will be seen in my account under the date of Oct. 21 1789. but I do not find that Mr. Grand has credited this

$$2800f-$$

⟨*2d.*⟩ sum of ⟨*2687–10*⟩ either in my private account or in the public one, and judge from present appearances that it has been omitted. The US. being credited for it in my account are no further concerned in the article; but it remains to be settled between Mr. Grand and myself, and

$$626^{tt}-8$$

a balance results from it in my favor of ⟨*375–10*⟩.

Grand's accounts stated and signed by me Mar. 17 1796. page. 4. instead of the Balance of 116ᵗᵗ–4 say 367ᵗᵗ–2 in the 1st. column. instead of 2687f–10 in the 2d. column say 2800f. instead of the amount 6000.ᵗᵗ in both columns, say 6250ᵗᵗ–18.

PrC (DLC: TJ Papers, 100: 17106); date assigned on the basis of TJ to Monroe, 21 Mch. 1796; faded; includes a passage from TJ's Statement on Accounts as Minister Plenipotentiary in France, 8 Mch. 1796, copied line for line from the PrC of that document with intended alterations marked as explained herein by TJ; with other emendations and one marginal note (see note 1 below); endorsed by TJ in ink on verso: "Harrison R." Dft (same, 99: 17067); undated and incomplete; written entirely in TJ's hand on two sides of a parallelogram-shaped slip; consists only of corrections to the statement of 8 Mch. 1796, with vertical marks to show locations of line breaks in that document.

GRAND'S ACCOUNTS STATED AND SIGNED BY ME: Enclosure No. 3 listed at TJ to Harrison, 17 Mch. 1796 (see also Enclosure No. 3 listed at TJ to Gautier of the same date).

[1] TJ wrote in the margin next to this word: "page 5."

To John Pendleton

SIR   Monticello Mar. 20. 1796.

Messrs. Grand & Co. having lately furnished certain papers which were necessary for the settlement of their account with the US. I undertook at the desire of the Auditor of the US. to examine so much of those accounts as arose under my inspection, to see that they stood right. My attention being thus recalled to the subject I had occasion to turn to the account I settled with you on my return to Virginia, and was never more astonished than to see that, according to this paper and to truth as far as I can see, a balance still remains in my hands of 1934ᵗᵗ–3–6. unless I should have otherwise accounted for it and as completely forgotten that as I had done the balance itself. But of this I have no vestige either in my memory or on paper, and therefore shall hold myself your debtor that sum, unless you know to the contrary what I do not. I account to myself for the lapse of memory thus. When I settled with you on my passage from Norfolk through Richmond, not meaning to undertake the office of Secretary of state, to which I had been nominated before my arrival, I counted certainly on returning to France, and of there paying away the residue of the money in my hands for the purposes of it's original destination, which were not then completed. When I went on to the Northward however, I was persuaded to undertake the new office, and entering instantly on it's duties, these gave me so complete occupation that my mind never recurred to the subject of my settlement with you. It remains now then to set it to rights.   I now inclose to the Governor the account of Grand & Co. against our state whereon a balance appears due to them from the state of   6931–9–6. I imagine it will simplify your accounts if I answer to Grand & Co. the 1934–3–6 balance remaining in my hands: so that a simple remittance of 4997–6–0 by the state to Grand & Co. will liquidate the whole transaction, both as to them and myself. If I am right in supposing myself your debtor, and this mode of settlement be approved I will, on your saying so, answer to Mr. Grand the amount in my hands, which will be the more convenient to me as a part of the sum is due to me from Grand & Co. being the balance of my private account with them.

I inclose you Houdon's account of his expences to and from America, which were under the eye and approbation of Doctr. Franklin till he left America, the Doctor furnishing him the money and drawing on me for reimbursement. I have the honor to be with great esteem Sir Your most obedt. and most humble servt   TH: JEFFERSON

RC (Vi); at foot of first page: "Mr. Pendleton, Auditor"; with calculation at foot of text by Pendleton showing balance of $1934.4. PrC (DLC); faded, with date overwritten in ink by TJ; endorsed by TJ in ink on verso. Enclosure not found. Enclosed in TJ to Robert Brooke, 20 Mch. 1796.

THE ACCOUNT I SETTLED WITH YOU ON MY RETURN TO VIRGINIA: Pendleton wrote a memorandum dated Auditor's Office, 28 Mch. 1796, which states: "It appears that Mr. Jefferson is indebted to the State (on an account he setled with the Auditor in Dec.

1789) 1934^{tt}–3–6. J.P wrote to him on this subject while he resided at Philadelphia [and] received for answer that his private Papers were all at Montecello and promising to settle the balance on his return to Virginia since which J.P has not reminded him of it. J.P wishes however that the deduction which Mr. Jefferson proposes of this sum from the Claim of Grand & Co. may be considered by the honorable Board as conditional for the present having a faint idea that Mr. Jefferson talked (at the time of the settlement above mentioned) of balancing the Account by Expences or Comml. for some

Public Agency; J.P will write to Mr. Jefferson now and have an explanation and final settlement with him. J. Pendleton" (MS in Vi; in Pendleton's hand; endorsed). However, no further correspondence between Pendleton and TJ has been found. For their earlier communication on the account, see TJ to Pendleton, 26 Feb. 1793.

To James Madison

Mar. 21. 1796.

Th: Jefferson presents his friendly respects to Mr. Madison and asks the favor of him to procure a safe conveyance for the inclosed letter to Colo. Monroe, which is of great importance public and private, as covering papers of consequence.

PrC (DLC); endorsed by TJ in ink on verso. Enclosure: TJ to Monroe, 21 Mch. 1796, and enclosures.

From James Madison

DEAR SIR   Philada March 21. 1796

At the desire of Mr. de Liancourt, I put into his hands this introduction to your remembrance of him as an acquaintance at Paris. He meditates a visit to the Southern States, and expects to have the pleasure of taking Monticello in his route, either in going or returning. I need add nothing to your knowledge of his respectability and virtues, I shall only say that the impression I have of both, induces me to concur cheerfully in the use he now makes of me. With the highest esteem & regard I am Dear Sir Yrs. affecly.   JS. MADISON JR

RC (PHi photostat); at foot of text: "Mr. Jefferson"; recorded in SJL as received 22 June 1796 "by Liancourt."

To James Monroe

DEAR SIR   Monticello Mar. 21. 96.

I wrote you on the 2d. inst. and now take the liberty of troubling you in order to have the inclosed letter to Mr. Gautier safely handed to him. I will thank you for information that it gets safely to hand, as it is of considerable importance to him, to the US. to the state of Virginia, and to myself, by conveying to him the final arrangement of the accounts of Grand & Co. with all those parties.

Mr. Jones happened fortunately to come into our neighborhood a few days after the date of my last, and ordered the proper ground to be inclosed and reserved for trees for you. My gardener is this day gone to plant such as we had, which will serve for a beginning. We shall engraft more for you this spring and plant them the next.

The British treaty has been formally at length laid before Congress. All America is atip-toe to see what the H. of Representatives will decide on it. We concieve the constitutional doctrine to be that tho' the P. and Senate have the general power of making treaties yet wherever they include in a treaty matters confided by the constitution to the three branches of legislature, an act of legislation will be requisite to confirm these articles, and that the H. of Repr. as one branch of the legislature are perfectly free to pass the act or to refuse it, governing themselves by their own judgment whether it is for the good of their constituents to let the treaty go into effect or not. On the precedent now to be set will depend the future construction of our constitution, and whether the powers of legislature shall be transferred from the P. Senate and H. of R. to the P. Senate and Piamingo or any other Indian, Algerine or other chief. It is fortunate that the first decision is to be in a case so palpably atrocious as to have been predetermined by all America.—The appointment of Elsworth C.J. and Chace one of the judges is doubtless communicated to you. My friendly respects to Mrs. Monroe. Adieu affectionately   TH: JEFFERSON

RC (DLC: Monroe Papers); at foot of text: "Colo. Monroe." PrC (DLC). Enclosure: TJ to Gautier, 17 Mch. 1796. Enclosed in TJ to Madison, 21 Mch. 1796.

To Benjamin Hawkins

DEAR SIR   Monticello Mar. 22. 96.

I am going to put you on a wild goose chace to find out the person to whom the inclosed letter is addressed. He moved to N. Carolina in 1782. and is settled somewhere up towards the mountains and not a great way from the Virginia line. This is all which his family here can tell me of him. A son of his here claims under him 100. acres of land which are in my possession, but he has no deed for it. For peace sake I have bought the son's claim, and it is important I should get from the father *a letter at least* confirming the right. But I have no means of finding him out, unless you can hunt him up, in which case you will render me a real service. He is probably an obscure planter, and very old man. He carried one son with him, one went to Georgia, and three remain here.

The vines you were so kind as to send me by Mr. Chiles were delivered to me alive. Every one budded after it was planted. Yet every one died immediately after. It was certainly not for want of care. Yours is unquestionably the most valuable collection in America; and I must keep it in view, and I pray you to do the same, to have a complete assortment of them, by the first opportunity which may occur. A direct one, in the proper season, cannot be hoped. We have no connection with Petersburgh, nor have I a single acquaintance there. But at Richmond Mr. Wythe would take pleasure in recieving and saving the cuttings for me. Would it be impracticable at the proper season to convey them to him thro' the medium of the stage, and under the care of some merchant or other coming in it from your neighborhood to Richmond?

I possess some valuable notes of the history of our country; particularly the debates of the old Congress on the confederation and some other subjects. I know that you took notes of what passed under your eye while in Senate and perhaps on other occasions, which I should consider as a precious deposit, and mark of great and confidential[1] friendship from you if you would give me a copy of them. I will give you in exchange a copy of mine. If you approve of this friendly intercommunication of information, the post is a very safe channel and they might come on from week to week as you can advance in copying.   I am now engaged in taking down the upper story of my house and building it on the ground, so as to spread all my rooms on one floor. We shall this summer therefore live under the tent of heaven. The next summer however we shall be able to tent you better, and I shall hope you will think our part of the country worth a visit. If you will make it during the months of August and September, we have then a good deal of agreeable society who take refuge from the country below during the sickly season, among these our hills, the most fertile soil, healthy and temperate climate in America. The mercury was never higher than 90°. here, and we abound in figs, which marks to you the limits of our heat and cold. A propos of figs. Of three very fine kinds I brought from France, one is the most delicious I ever tasted in any country. I had only one plant last year, but this spring have set out many cuttings. I have also a grape from Italy, of a brick dust colour coming about a fortnight later than the sweetwater and lasting till frost, the most valuable I ever knew. It deserves this character for it's flavor, it's quantity, and it's hardiness. I take it to be the Chasselas of Fontainebleau. I shall with pleasure avail myself of any means of conveying both these articles to you. Send me in a letter some seed of the Dionnea mascipula. Adieu. Your's affectionately

Th: Jefferson

PrC (DLC); at foot of first page in ink: "Hawkins Benj." Enclosure: TJ to William Spears, 22 Mch. 1796 (recorded in SJL as written to William "Spiers," but not found).

The 100. ACRES OF LAND were a portion of TJ's 400-acre Pouncey's tract. Peter Jefferson had willed one-fourth of the property to James Spears, but TJ had continuously paid taxes on the whole tract and Spears never took possession of his part. To resolve his title, TJ purchased the claim of Spears's grandson, John Spears, in February 1797. Two years later Richard Johnson—who had purchased from the son of TJ's tenant at Pouncey's a spurious deed originating with William Spears, James Spears's son— brought a chancery suit against TJ that resulted in 1804 in an affirmation of TJ's title (MB, II, 966, 1003n).

VALUABLE NOTES . . . ON THE CONFEDER- ATION: see Notes of Proceedings in the Continental Congress, [7 June-1 Aug. 1776], in Vol. 1: 320-7. TJ's proposal for an EXCHANGE of notes evidently went unanswered, for no reply from Hawkins has been found and none is recorded in SJL. Nor have any NOTES of debates kept by Hawkins during his 1789-95 term in the United States Senate been found in TJ's papers, although Hawkins did take notes (for an example, see enclosure to Hawkins to TJ, 3 Jan. 1792).

[1] Preceding two words interlined.

To John Bowyer

DEAR SIR   Monticello Mar. 25. 1796.

Your favor of Feb. 22. came to hand by our last post, and I thank you for the trouble you have taken to apprize me of an interest worth attending to, as well as the offer to act for me in what is to be done. Be so good as to make whatever bargain you think right with the person proposing to make saltpetre from my cave, and I confirm it. I have been told that the powder makers on your side of the mountain will give powder for saltpetre, pound for pound. Powder would be a more convenient article for me than saltpetre, as it happens in fact that I have a great job of blowing on hand in a mill race: so that if it can be exchanged on terms you approve, and lodged at Staunton, it would suit me. Mr. Samuel Clarke merchant at Staunton, who retails nails for me, would recieve and forward it. I embrace with pleasure this occasion of renewing our antient acquaintance, and I find from my feelings generally, that the more antient, the more valued. I am with great esteem Dear Sir Your friend & servt   TH: JEFFERSON

RC (ICN); at foot of text: "Colo. John Bowyer Rockbridge."

GREAT JOB OF BLOWING . . . A MILL RACE: see note to Inquest on Shadwell Dam, [18 Sep. 1795], and Bill to the High Court of Chancery, [24 Sep. 1795].

SJL records letters from TJ to Bowyer of 9 Sep. 1796 ("for H. Marks") and 31 Jan. 1799 (addressed to Bowyer at Lexington), and from Bowyer to TJ of 6 Feb. 1800, received from Rockbridge on 13 Feb. 1800 that have not been found.

From Patrick White

SIR   Petersburg. March 25th. 1796

I received yours of the 15th. informing me that by desire of M. Thomas Shippen of Philadelphia you had drawn on me at ten days sight for a balance due you by the late John Banister deceased. The principal I will pay to the holders of your draft, the Interest I am not Justifiable in paying as Administrator of the said deceaseds Estate not knowing whether or no there will be sufficient personal property to discharge the amount of the claims against said, if there is, as soon as they are discharged I am informed by my Attorney that I am justifiable in paying you the Interest. Indeed I am of opinion that Interest is but a small compensation for your friendship to Mr. Banister when in France. I am Respectfully Sir Yr. O Servt.   P. WHITE

FC (Lb in MiU-C); at head of text: "Thomas Jefferson esqr." Probably the letter of 20 Mch. 1796 recorded in SJL as received 10 Apr. 1796.

Patrick White, a merchant in Petersburg, Virginia, specialized in the grain and flour trade, first in partnership with Conway Whittle of Norfolk as White, Whittle & Co. and, after that firm was dissolved in 1794, as Patrick White & Co. During the 1790s he shipped produce, primarily tobacco, to his brother Dr. John Campbell White and the firm Campbell & Tenant in Belfast, Ireland, receiving Irish linens and nails in return. White corresponded with leading merchants along the Atlantic seaboard, including Archibald Gracie in New York and Oliver & Thompson in Baltimore. He served as administrator of the Banister estate at Battersea in 1796 (Patrick White Letterbook in unpublished description of collections at MiU-C; White to White & Tenant,

8 Dec. 1794, White to Oliver & Thompson, 17 Jan. 1795, White to John C. White, 19 Nov. 1795 and 6 May 1796, White to David Stewart & Sons, 3, 18 May and 7 Nov. 1796, White to Gracie, 7 Dec. 1796, White accounts with John C. White, 16 Dec. 1795-6 May 1796, all in Lb in MiU-C; *Virginia Gazette, & Petersburg Intelligencer*, 27 Dec. 1796; *Virginia Chronicle and Norfolk and Portsmouth General Advertiser*, 6 Oct. 1792, 14 Sep. 1793).

TJ's letter OF THE 15TH., recorded in SJL as "White   draught & lre of advice," has not been found.

For TJ's account with JOHN BANISTER, Jr., see TJ to John Dunbar, 15 Dec. 1789, and enclosure to TJ to Francis Eppes, 11 Mch. 1792. On 31 July 1796 TJ received notice that White had settled the debt, paying £63.3.8 into TJ's account with Charles Johnston & Co. on behalf of the Banister estate (MB, II, 944).

From William Branch Giles

DEAR SIR   Philadelphia *March 26th 1796*

I have permitted your much valued favor of the 31st. of December to remain unanswered until this time, because until now, no desicive event had occurred, by which a conjecture could be formed of the probable course, which the House of Representatives would take respecting the great question of the Brittish treaty, Because Europe afforded nothing interresting, and because I was unwilling to call your attention to the recital of trivial incidents.

You will observe from the accompanying paper that the day before yesterday a question was taken upon Mr. Livingston's motion request-ing the President to cause to be laid before the House of Representa-tives, the instructions to the late envoy extraordinaire and his correspon-dence with L. Granvile during the negotiation of the Brittish treaty &c. This incidental proposition gave rise to a discussion respecting the con-stitutional rights of the House of Representatives in checking the Treaty makeing power. The parties on both sides came forward and placed the fate of the proposition on that constitutional ground. The opposers of the resolution in their first onset, assumed a most authoratative tone, and without equivocation enthroned the treaty makeing power in a des-potism complete. They declared that the treaty makeing power was undefined in its nature, unlimited in its extent, and paramount in its authority. They then proceeded to denounce those who would not yield an assent to this doctrine, as rebels and traitors against the constituted authorities. For this doctrine and this language, at this time, we are probably indebted in some degree to the mockery displayed on the President's last Birth day, which has been construed into full evidence of what is called—*the counter current*. The partizans of despotism began to amuse themselves with a belief that the American mind had become so intoxicated with their clamors and their calumnies, that it was inca-pable of resisting the fetters prepared for it, and that the precious mo-ment of fixing them on, had arrived. But this candid avowal produceing rather a repulsive, than a submissive effect, attempts were ingeniously made by them in the more matured state of the debate, to level the High ground upon which this omnipotent treaty makeing power, was at first most firmly entrenched. It is easy to see that this doctrine totally dis-cards the utility of checks, and by means of the treaty makeing power completely Checkmates the whole constitution. It is proposed to have the debates upon this question printed in numbers by subscription; and as it is probable that you will not be able to see them in so satisfactory a shape in the any of the news papers I will take great pleasure in for-warding the numbers to you as they shall be printed. Since the vote of the house the treaty makeing party is in great trepidation for the ulti-mate fate of their favorite instrument, and would consent to a provision for carrying it into effect upon any conditions which the majority would prescribe, but the course of proceedure upon that question is yet unset-tled. I have always been of opinion since my first arrival here, that a vote would be obtained for effectuateing the treaty; and it is certain that some of the gentlemen who voted with the majority are now inclined to carry the treaty into effect. But I think the treaty more in Jeopardy now than I have done at any previous stage of the session for the following reasons amongst others. The majority upon the vote already passed is a very great one. The vote itself has united them in a common responsibility. Union is now necessary for their support. Their opinions are strongly against the contents of the treaty. The public mind will probably be with them upon the victory already obtained, and may afford some testimony of approbation before the discussion of the final question. European affairs will probably stand neutral. Under these circumstances, after declaring their right to examine the merits of the instrument, and upon the examination they find the treaty a bad one, they can hardly find any justification for carrying it into effect. But if its execution should not be denied, it is certain, that in makeing provision for effectuateing it, a reservation of every essential right of the House of Representatives will be made.

You must have remarked the proclamation accompanying the promulgation of the treaty. It is the more extraordinary as Congress were in session at the time and had received a promise at the opening of the session that the *subject* should be laid before them &c. You probably too have remarked the delay in makeing the communication. There are however some circumstances attending these transactions, of which you are not informed, and which may serve to show you some of the late improvements in the diplomatic agency. About six weeks before the communication was made, a copy of the exchanged ratifications was received from Mr. Deas charge De affairs at London, covered by a letter, which announced that when he applyed to L. Greenville for the purpose of exchangeing ratifications, he informed his Lordship, that the President did not intend by the ratification to sanction the provision order, to which his Lordship replyed, 'that was a distinct business,' and from the conversation Mr. Deas seems to have inferred that the provision order would be viewed as a *practical construction* of the treaty, and in consequence of this opinion requests instructions from the secretary of state as to the ground upon which he should place the subject in case of a renewal of the order. Upon the arrival of this copy it was expected that the *subject* would be laid before the House of Representatives, and clamors and distrusts began to be circulated by many of the members; but the time had not arrived when the communication was deemed expedient by the executive, or in other words the counter current was not then sufficiently strong—and no favorable auspices seemed to attend this Brittish practical construction. To prevent therefore the circulation of these distrusts &c., the segacious secretary of state addressed a private letter to the Speaker of the House of Representatives in his *private*

[47]

capacity, to be read at his lodgeings, and to enable him to satisfy *gentle-men individually* of the disposition of the President to comply with his promise of communication at the opening of the session; but that the P. did not deem the papers received sufficiently authentic to justify such a proceedure. The phraseology of the letter was not less remarkable than its object, for he assured Mr. Dayton that he would *not affront him so much as to ask his opinion as to the authenticity of the papers*; copies of which were inclosed. Notwithstanding this decisive course of proceedure upon the first arrival of these papers, a mere duplicate of the copies has since that time been deemed sufficiently authentic to authorise the same communication, and the promulgation of the treaty as the law of the land, with the proclamation injoining obedience to it. For as far as I have been informed the original ratification on the part of the British King is not yet arrived. These papers were submitted to the perusal of Mr. Madison and myself by the speaker the evening he received them and were taken from him early the next morning by the secretary of state in person.

I shall endeavour to forward herewith the treaty with Spain, which is universally approved of here and is in fact an excellent critical essay upon the treaty with Brittain. Presumeing upon your desire to see the spanish treaty I have been indeavouring to obtain a copy for you for some time past, but after having received the promise of a copy from one of the senators was at length disappointed. An incident has occurred which has put the public in possession of it. Amongst the various arts emplyed by the treaty makeing party to effect their object, a new one has been devised to operate upon the Western parts of the U.S. The British and Spanish treaties are united and the people are told that the execution of the one, is essentially dependent on the execution of the other, to this suggestion is added the importance of the surrender of the posts to the Western country. This artifice has so far succeeded as to cause a number of petitions to come forward from the western parts of Pensyvania praying the concurrence of the House of Representatives to pass all necessary laws to carry both of the treaties into effect. To effect this it became necessary to give the spanish treaty publicity, and with this view Mr. Ross is said to have transmitted a copy to Pittsburg which has been published in the paper of that place, and from thence is published in one of the daily papers here. So far however are these two treaties from harmoniseing, that it is suggested that both the governments of France and Spain have declared that they view the Missisippee article as militant with the similar article in the British treaty, and it is further said that the spanish minister has received instructions to make an intimation to that effect to our government. One thing is certain that in

consequence of the article in the British treaty, the U.S. have been compelled to receive the navigation of the Missicippe as a *concession* from
Spain, when the Spanish minister was willing to have admitted it as a
right. The spanish negotiation is said to have been very ably managed
and proves that the British exchequer had not monopolised all the talents of the U.S. The present session of Congress seems to be without
end. Our finances are now found to be extremely deranged—and all the
important business of the session is now before us. I never was so anxious to return to Virginia; and that anxiety must plead my excuse for
indulgeing myself in troubling you with so long a letter upon politicks.
I believe I shall elope as soon as the treaty question is settled, in which
event I propose to pay a visit to Monticello.

The Duke Liancourt proposes to make you a visit in five or six
weeks, he is now on his way by water to Charleston and proposes to
return by land. I have taken the liberty to give him a letter of annuncia-
tion. Be pleased to accept my most affectionate regards and present my
best respects to the Ladies of your Family &c.   WM. B. GILES

This letter has been so rapidly written that I have not stopped to mend
my pen.

RC (DLC); at foot of text: "Mr. Jefferson"; endorsed by TJ as received 10 Apr.
1796 and so recorded in SJL. Enclosure not
found, but see note below.

ACCOMPANYING PAPER: presumably *Claypoole's American Daily Advertiser*, 25 Mch.
1796, which contained news of the vote on
Livingston's MOTION (see Madison to TJ, 6
Mch. 1796). The MOCKERY of the PRESI-
DENT'S LAST BIRTH DAY was the unprecedented rejection by the House of Representatives on 22 Feb. 1796 of a motion to
adjourn so that it could pay its compliments
to Washington on this occasion (*Annals*, v,
355). DEBATES . . . PRINTED IN NUMBERS BY
SUBSCRIPTION: on 22 Mch. 1796 the *Aurora*
published a proposal for printing by subscription the House debates on the Jay
Treaty. The debates were distributed as
they became available from the printer as

half numbers, of forty pages, which allowed
congressmen to use their franking privilege
when sending them by post. On 15 June
1796 the first volume of 386 pages was offered to the public as *Debates in the House of
Representatives of the United States, During
the first Session of the Fourth Congress. Part
I. Upon the Constitutional Powers of the
House, With Respect to Treaties* (Philadelphia, 1796). The second volume of 362
pages, bearing the subtitle *Part II. Upon the
Subject of the British Treaty*, was offered for
the first time by the *Aurora* on 4 Oct. 1796.
See Sowerby, No. 3522. For a discussion of
the sources of these debates, see Madison,
Papers, XVI, 154-7n. PROVISION ORDER: see
note to James Monroe to TJ, 27 June 1795.
TO GIVE THE SPANISH TREATY PUBLICITY:
the 26 Mch. 1796 issue of *Claypoole's* published a text of Pinckney's Treaty.

To John Barnes

DEAR SIR   Monticello Mar. 27. 1796.

Since mine of Feb. 28. I have recieved your favors of Feb. 27. and Mar. 5. and 12. In consequence I now draw on you for 400. Doll. at 10. days sight in favor of Messrs. Charles Johnston & Co. These gentlemen having set up business in the brokerage line of every kind, undertaking among other things to recieve and forward goods for all persons, I shall make them in future the center of my affairs in Richmond. I will pray you therefore to address to them in future whatever comes to me from you; as I have long and with regret been troublesome to Colo. Gamble, who was extremely attentive and punctual and would take nothing for it. The hhd. of molasses is come safe to hand. I formerly advised you that if the boots from Starr had been sent, they had miscarried. I fear this is the fate also of the tea and the gongs, of which I hear nothing, and therefore recommend them to your enquiries. I am with great esteem Dr. Sir

PrC (MHi); unsigned; at foot of text: "Mr. John Barnes"; endorsed in ink by TJ on verso; letterpressed to same sheet as TJ's draft on Barnes for Johnston & Co., 27 Mch. 1796, in TJ's hand, of terms specified in letter above, at foot of text, in part: "Mr. John Barnes Merchant Philadelphia."

Barnes's FAVORS OF FEB. 27. AND MAR. 5. AND 12., recorded in SJL as received respectively on 12, 19, and 25 Mch. 1796, have not been found. I FORMERLY ADVISED YOU: TJ to Barnes, 17 Jan. 1796.

To James Brown

DEAR SIR   Monticello Mar. 27. 1796.

I have a workman of the name of David Watson, who has lived with me some time, and whose wife, Margaret Watson, is remaining in Scotland. He is extremely anxious to get her over as she is to come, and I am to indulge both. But I have no correspondent in that country, and on advising with Mr. Reeves, he encourages me to do, what I was before strongly disposed to, to ask your aid in bringing her over. She will require 5. guineas to be advanced to her there, and somebody to be responsible for the paiment of her passage at the port of delivery, which should be Richmond. The latter shall give no inconvenience, for I will lodge the money in Richmond in time to answer the call, and without fail, and will repay the former sum the moment it is known she [is fo]und and accepts the invitation to come. Will you then, Sir, be so [good as?] to undertake to help us in this business? That is to say, [deliver?] the inclosed letter to Mr. Rumley for Margaret Watson [have 5. gui]neas advanced to her there, if she agrees to come, and only say that you will pay her passage on her arrival in Richmond, which I will take care to keep off your hands. Presuming on your assistance in this, I inclose you the letter, desiring the Christian name to be attended to and not confounded with another of the same surname. Your favor herein will much oblige Dear Sir Your friend & servt   TH: JEFFERSON

RC (ViHi); part of five lines torn away; addressed: "James Brown esq. Richmond"; stamped; endorsed by Brown. Enclosure not found.

To James Madison

Mar. 27. 96.

Yours of the 13th. is recieved. I am enchanted with Mr. Gallatin's speech in Bache's paper of Mar. 14. It is worthy of being printed at the end of the Federalist, as the only rational commentary on the part of the constitution to which it relates. Not that there may not be objections, and difficult ones, to it, and which I shall be glad to see his answers to: but if they are never answered, they are more easily to be gulped down than those which lie to the doctrines of his opponents, which do in fact annihilate the whole of the powers given by the constitution to the legislature. According to the rule established by usage and common sense of construing one part of the instrument by another, the objects on which the P. and S. may exclusively act by treaty are much reduced, but the field on which they may act, with the sanction of the legislature, is large enough: and I see no harm in rendering their sanction necessary, and not much harm in annihilating the whole treaty making power, except as to making peace. If you decide in favor of your right to refuse cooperation in any case of treaty, I should wonder on what occasion it is to be used, if not on one where the rights, the interest, the honor and faith of our nation are so grossly sacrificed, where a faction has entered into conspiracy with the enemies of their country to chain down the legislature at the feet of both; where the whole mass of your constituents have condemned this work in the most unequivocal manner, and are looking to you as their last hope to save them from the effects of the avarice and corruption of the first agent, the revolutionary machinations of others, and the incomprehensible acquiescensce of the only honest man who has assented to it. I wish that his honesty and his political errors may not furnish a second occasion to exclaim 'curse on his virtues, they've undone his country.'—Cold weather. Mercury 26. in the morning. Corn fallen at Richmond to 20/—stationary here. Nicholas sure of his election. R. Jouett and Jo. Monroe in competition for the other vote of the county. Affections to Mrs. M. and yourself. Adieu.

RC (DLC: Madison Papers); unsigned; addressed: "James Madison Congress Philadelphia." PrC (DLC); faded, with date overwritten in ink by TJ.

MR. GALLATIN'S SPEECH: in his address before the House on 9 Mch. 1796, Pennsylvania Congressman Albert Gallatin supported Livingston's resolution calling upon the president to submit the documents relating to the Jay Treaty, arguing that "as far as a Treaty negotiated by the Executive embraced Legislative objects, so far it required the sanction of the Legislature" to make it the law of the land. "Unless it is allowed that either the power of the House over the purse-strings is a check, or the existing laws cannot be repealed by a Treaty, or that the special powers granted to Congress limit the general power of Treaty-making," Gallatin contended "there are no bounds to it, it must absorb all others, repeal all laws in contravention to it, and act without control" (Philadelphia *Aurora*, 14 Mch. 1796; *Annals*, v, 464-74).

ONLY HONEST MAN: Washington. CURSE ON HIS VIRTUES: Addison's *Cato*, Act IV, Sc. iv, l. 35.

To Thomas Mann Randolph

TH:J. TO TMR.   Monticello Mar. 27. [1796]

Your favor of the 20th. is received. It is not in my power to forward the land warrants for my certificates, as Clarke did not return them to me. I question if the surveyor returned them to him. I shall write to him by the next post, but you will be here before he can answer. He writes me that he put 300. ℔ tobacco of mine into a hhd. of yours. This may enter into our general account if you please at whatever price you sell at. Reeves has made me an offer which I believe I shall accept for my tobacco. I have prepared a writing conformably to it, which I shall propose to him for signature. The article respecting damage has not yet been mentioned to him. The rest is agreeable to what past. I inclose you a copy for your information should you not be able to do better with yours. You are perfectly free to settle with F. Walker in any way most convenient. Mrs. Gilmer's order will constitute a considerable balance to be paid by me to you, exclusive of F.W.'s. I am preparing to pay both sums, and can do it at short warning. Mrs. Gilmer's sum will be about £35. to £40. F.W. has not yet said what quantity of corn he can furnish me. But settle with him in that way most convenient to yourself, as it is perfectly equal to me which I make paiment to.—We have had some days of very cold weather. The last three mornings the thermometer has been 26. 26. and 29. Our peach blossoms are just opening and I fear are in danger.—I wish E.R. may be right as to your injunction. I do not readily see on what it can be regularly grounded, and have not so much confidence in his judgment as to be satisfied on the point. We are all well and hoping to see you soon. My love to my dear Martha. Adieu affectionately.

RC (DLC); partially dated; endorsed by Randolph as received 31 Mch. 1796. Enclosure not found.

Randolph's FAVOR of 20 Mch. 1796, recorded in SJL as received from Richmond five days later, has not been found.

I SHALL WRITE TO HIM: TJ to Bowling Clark, 27 Mch. 1796, recorded in SJL but not found. HE WRITES ME: probably Clark to TJ, 20 Mch. 1796, recorded in SJL as received six days later, also missing.
E.R.: Edmund Randolph.

From Volney

Philadelphie 28 Mars 1796.
MONSIEUR   fifth Street South, No. 69 opposite african church

Le tems que je M'étais proposé de passer en cette Ville tire désormais à Sa fin: je N'attends plus pour me mettre en route, que des Nouvelles de France que je ne prévois pas devoir changer mon plan, quoiqu'il paraisse qu'elles ayent changé Là Ma position. Mon dessein est de passer L'été dans la partie Montueuse, c'est à dire Salubre des etats du midi: il est bien évident qu'une des premieres et des plus intéressantes Visites que j'aurai L'avantage de faire Sera à Monticello. Je desirerais de Savoir dabord si en quittant philadelphie je ne pourrais pas Vous y être utile pour quelques commissions, et en second lieu si Vous comptez faire quelqu'absence qui M'empêchât de Vous rencontrer chez Vous dans le cours de Mai. Je puis recevoir ici jusques Vers la Mi-avril tous les ordres que Vous pourriez M'y donner, et je Me ferais un Veritable plaisir de les remplir. Passé cette epoque je commencerai Mon Voyage Vers Vos cantons sans faire de Station autre part qu'a Washington-City près Le docteur Thornton et Mr. Law. On Nous annonce un accomodement général en Europe: Malgré les doutes et les contradictions que L'on y oppose, j'y croirai jusqu'a L'ouverture positive de la campagne; puisqu'il me paraît constant que Le Systeme de Notre gouvernement est different de ce qu'il etait il y a un an. Au reste toute hypothèse est un Si vaste champ de conjectures et de reflexions qu'il N'y a que de longues Veillées qui puissent y suffire. C'est avec l'espoir d'en passer de bien instructives et de bien agréables pour Moi auprès de Vous que j'ai L'honneur d'être Monsieur Votre très humble et très Obeissant serviteur   C VOLNEY

RC (DLC); at foot of first page: "Mr. Jefferson"; endorsed by TJ as received 8 Apr. 1796 and so recorded in SJL.

From William Branch Giles

Dear sir   Philadelphia March 31st. 1796

I send you herewith a paper containing the Presidents refusal to comply with the call of the House of R. for the papers respecting the Brittish treaty. From your perfect acquaintance with the state of public affairs, and the views of parties, all comments upon this extraordinary production are rendered unnecessary; the language is too plain to be mistaken, and must press upon your mind a crowd of the most serious reflections.

The proper course to be pursued has not yet been settled. It is probable that the President's reply will be referred to a committee to prepare something in the nature of a manifesto, which will present to the public the reasons induceing the call on the part of the House. It is also probable that the House will refuse to act upon the treaty until the papers called for shall be placed upon the table.

These measures will require nerves, but we have no reasons to doubt of them from present appearances. Be pleased to make my best respects to the Ladies of your family and believe me to be your sincere friend &c.

WM. B. GILES

RC (DLC); at foot of text: "Mr. Thomas Jefferson"; endorsed by TJ as received 15 Apr. 1796 and so recorded in SJL.

I SEND YOU HEREWITH A PAPER: on 30 Mch. 1796, President Washington responded to the request by the House of Representatives for the documents surrounding the Jay Treaty negotiations with a written message rejecting the demands. It appeared in Philadelphia newspapers the next day (*Philadelphia Gazette* and Philadelphia *Aurora*, 31 Mch. 1796). In his REFUSAL TO COMPLY WITH THE CALL OF THE HOUSE, the president cited the importance of secrecy in diplomatic negotiations and argued that sharing the papers with the House would "establish a dangerous precedent." Calling upon his experience as a member of the Philadelphia Convention, he claimed to know "the principles on which the Constitution was formed," according to which treaty-making powers were "exclusively vested in the President, by and with the advice and consent of the Senate" and that every treaty so made and promulgated became the "law of the land." Finally, citing the closed journals of the Convention on deposit in the of-

fice of the Department of State, Washington noted that the body had "explicitly rejected" the proposition "that no Treaty should be binding on the United States which was not ratified by a Law" (Fitzpatrick, *Writings*, XXXV, 2-5).

The following day, the House considered the PROPER COURSE TO BE PURSUED and resolved, by a 55 to 37 vote, to refer the president's message to the committee of the whole, where treaty opponents planned to bring their reasons for differing with the president before the public. The debate began 6 Apr. 1796 with Thomas Blount of North Carolina offering two resolutions which were probably agreed upon at a meeting of House Republicans the previous Saturday evening. The first declared that the House had a right and duty to deliberate on any aspect of a treaty that required its action before being executed; and the second asserted that the House need not state reasons when applying to the executive for information. In a lengthy reponse to Washington's message, Madison supported the resolutions. They were passed the next day without further debate (*Annals*, V, 762-83; Beckley to Monroe, 2 Apr. 1796, Gerard

W. Gawalt, ed., *Justifying Jefferson: The Political Writings of John James Beckley* [Washington, 1995], 114). For a discussion of the House vote and for the debate on appropriations for the treaty, see Madison to TJ, 11, 18 Apr. 1796.

From James Madison

DEAR SIR   Philada. April 4. 1796

I have received yours of the 6th. Ult.; also your letters for Monroe, Mazzei and Van Staphorsts; and shall have a good conveyance for them in two or three days. I am in some doubt however whether it may not be best to detain those for Mazzei and V. untill you can add the information I am now able to furnish you from Dohrman. He has at length closed the business of Mazzei in a just and honorable manner, by allowing the N.Y. damages on the bills of 20 PerCt. and the N.Y. rate of interest of 7 PerCt. This mode of settlement after deducting the partial payments for which he has receipts, leaves a balance of 3087 dollars, which has been just paid into my hands, and will be disposed of as you shall direct. You will of course lose no time in writing to me on the subject.

I have not yet heard from Bringhurst on the subject of Sharpless. He has no doubt written to you, according to his promise. I have seen Mr. Howell, who says there would be no difficulty in allowing you the credit you desire, if his son should take the place of Lowns.

I was not unaware of the considerations you suggest with regard to the post roads; but do not consider my proposition as involving any dangerous consequences. It is limited to the choice of roads where that is presented, and to the opening them, in other cases, so far only as may be necessary for the transportation of the mail. This I think fairly within the object of the Constn. It had, in fact, become essential that something should be done, and something would have been attempted, on a worse principle. If the route shall be once fixt for the post road, the local authorities will probably undertake the improvement &c. of the roads; and individuals will go to work in providing the proper accomodations on them for general use.

The Newspapers will inform you that the call for the Treaty papers was carried by 62 against 37. You will find the answer of the President herewith inclosed. The absolute refusal was as unexpected, as the tone and tenor of the message are improper and indelicate. If you do not at once perceive the drift of the appeal to the Genl. Convention and its journal, recollect one of Camillus's last numbers, and read the latter part of Murray's speech. There is little doubt in my mind that the message came from N.Y. where it was seen that an experiment was to be made at the hazard of the P. to save the faction against the Reps. of the people. The effect of this reprehensible measure on the majority is not likely to correspond with the calculations of its authors. I think there will be sufficient firmness to face it with resolutions declaring the Const:l. powers of the House as to Treaties, and that in applying for papers, they are not obliged to state their reasons to the Executive. In order to preserve this firmness however, it is necessary to avoid as much as possible an overt rencontre with the Executive. The day after the message was received the bill guarantying the loan for the federal City, was carried thro' the H. of Reps. by a swimming majority.

I have letters from Monroe of the 12 and 20 Jany. The Truce with Austria was demanded by the latter, and was not likely to be renewed. A continuance of the war with England was counted on. The French Govt. was in regular and vigorous operation, and gaining daily more and more of the public confidence. A forced loan was going on for 25 Mil: Sterlg., 12 Mil. of which was receivable in assignats at 100 for one; the balance in Specie and produce. It is said that the British armament for the West Indies had suffered a *third* Coup de Vent, after leaving the channel, a *third* time.

According to my memory and that of others, the Journal of the Convention was by a vote deposited with the P. to be kept sacred untill called for by some competent authority. How can this be reconciled with the use he has made of it! Examine my notes if you please at the close of the business, and let me know what is said on the subject. You will perceive that the quotation is nothing to the purpose. Most of the majority would decide as the Convention did—because they think there may be some Treaties as a Mere Treaty of peace that would not require the Legislative power—a ratification by law also expresses a different idea from that entertained by the House of its agency. Adieu.

RC (DLC: Madison Papers); unsigned; at foot of text: "Mr. Jefferson"; endorsed by TJ as received 15 Apr. 1796 and so recorded in SJL. Enclosure: *Message from the President of the United States, Assigning the Reasons which Forbid his Compliance with the Resolution of the Twenty-Fourth Instant, Requesting "A Copy of the Instructions, Correspondence and other Documents, Relative to the Treaty Lately Concluded Between the United States and Great-Britain"* [Philadelphia, 1796]. See Evans, No. 31417.

YOUR LETTERS FOR MONROE, MAZZEI AND VAN STAPHORSTS: TJ to Monroe, 21 Mch. 1796, was enclosed in TJ's letter to Madison of the same date. To judge from SJL, TJ's letter to Philip Mazzei was probably a duplicate of that of 31 Jan. 1796 and his letter to Van Staphorst & Hubbard a duplicate of either that of 31 Jan. (not found) or 28 Feb. 1796. It is unclear whether TJ forwarded these letters to Madison with the Monroe letter on 21 Mch. 1796, or at an earlier date, but Madison found a CONVEYANCE for all three missives with his letter to Monroe of 7 Apr. 1796 (Madison, *Papers*, XVI, 303).

HE HAS NO DOUBT WRITTEN TO YOU: for the letter from John Bringhurst to TJ, see enclosure listed at Madison to TJ, 11 Apr. 1796.

ONE OF CAMILLUS'S LAST NUMBERS: in No. 38, the last of the essays defending Jay's Treaty signed "Camillus," Alexander Hamilton argued that although the records of the debates of the Constitutional Convention at Philadelphia were secret, all delegates understood that the Constitution conferred exclusive treaty-making power on the president and the Senate, a position that he argued was supported by publicized dissents on that subject at the time by George Mason, Elbridge Gerry, and Edmund Randolph. Hamilton appealed to all members of the Convention for confirmation of his assertion, particularly Madison and Abraham Baldwin, the only ones serving at that time in the House of Representatives. The SPEECH by the Maryland Federalist William Vans Murray on 23 Mch., which also contended that the power to make treaties was confined to the executive and the Senate, called upon Madison to expound on the convention's understanding of this issue and suggested that he "should almost feel at liberty to open the Journals of the Convention" in order to resolve the matter (Syrett, *Hamilton*, XVIII, 476-7n, XX, 22-5; *Annals*, V, 700-1). For the president's message and the response of the House, see note to Giles to TJ, 31 Mch. 1796. Hamilton's limited role in influencing Washington's response to the House is discussed in Freeman, *Washington*, VII, 354-5; see also Hamilton to Washington, 7 Mch. 1796, in Syrett, *Hamilton*, XX, 64-9n.

The LETTERS FROM MONROE OF THE 12 AND 20 JANY. are printed in Madison, *Papers*, XVI, 184-8, 195-8.

For TJ's use of Madison's NOTES, see Madison to TJ, 8 Nov. 1795.

To Archibald Stuart

DEAR SIR   Monticello Apr. 5. 96.

I am doomed to be a very troublesome acquaintance to you. I am now in want of a stone mason, one with whom I had agreed to begin my house within 3. weeks from this time having yesterday notified me that he cannot come. Mr. Cocke of this county tells me of a Mr. Felty Millar of your town a good workman and suitable on every account for my purposes. The object of this letter is to get you to engage this man for me. Mr. Cocke says he lately offered to come and work for him at 2/6 a perch. I should prefer hiring by the day, because it is the foundation of an addition to my dwelling house, which I have to do and which I wish to have great pains taken about. He supposes 7/6 a day equivalent to 2/6 a perch. However my necessity is such that I must have a workman, and therefore am only to try to get him as cheap as we can. I had in fact agreed to give the other man 9/ a day. I would wish him to be here ready to go to work on the 8th. of May, and could not admit of more than a week or a fortnight's delay beyond that: because after the foundation of stone, I have to go on with the brickwork, then the roof, and all within the limits of the summer. If he makes a difficulty of the distance, I will pay him for his time coming and going, rather than be disappointed. I lodge him and find provisions; but give no liquor. This is an absolute article, as I never saw work go on well if the workman had liquor. It is therefore a point which I never give up. I have about 140.

perch in the present job. The next year I have a large mill to build, which, if he gives satisfaction, he would probably be employed on. He might bring one assistant with him if he chuses. But this is not essential. I know you will recieve this during your district court and consequently in the midst of your business. Yet my necessities oblige me to pester you with it at so unseasonable a moment and so pressingly that it would be very desireable if I could recieve an answer by Monday's post, but at furthest by that of the week following.

You said in your last, that you apprehended my interference in the contest between Staunton and Charlottesville for the Academy. I have never put pen to paper on the subject, nor spoken of it but with one or two of my neighbors. My own suspicions are that both places may make themselves easy about it: and that the interests of George town will give New London the preference. But this is mere suspicion founded on private motives and therefore not to be mentioned as from me.—The money matter you mention has never entered my head, and I wish it to lie till it would be inconvenient to yourself or brother to keep it longer. Adieu Yours affectionately   TH: JEFFERSON

Pray tempt and persuade Millar by all possible motives to come.

RC (ViHi); addressed: "Archibald Stuart esq. Atty at law Staunton." PrC (MHi); lacks postscript; endorsed in ink by TJ on verso.

Letters from TJ to James Powell COCKE of 4 Feb. 1795, 4 Feb., 22 Mch. 1796, 14 May 1799, and 6 Jan. 1800, recorded in SJL, have not been found. Letters from Cocke to TJ of 6 Feb. 1795, 29 Jan., 5 Feb. 1796, 20 Jan. 1797, 3 June 1799, and 10 Feb. 1800, which according to SJL were received by TJ on 8 Feb. 1795, 31 Jan., 7 Feb. 1796, 20 Jan. 1797, 3 June 1799, and 18 Feb. 1800, respectively, are also missing. Stuart's LAST letter of 28 Feb. 1796, recorded in SJL as received 7 Mch. 1796, has not been found.

From John Adams

DEAR SIR   Philadelphia April 6. 1796

Since my Receipt of your favour of the 28 of February I have call'd on the Auditor and had some Conversation with him and with The Secretary of The Treasury and with The Secretary of State upon the Subject of Accounts and they think that some Regulation may be made by Congress which will reach the Cases without any formal Memorial on our Part and indeed without mentioning Names. The Secretary of The Treasury has it under Consideration: But if they finally determine that they cannot accomplish the object without our Interposition I will join you with all my Heart in an Application to Congress.

D'Ivernois is industrious and clever, but he is in Pay Pension or Employment of some kind or other under Mr. Pitt, and Some of his late Publications have a tang of the Cask from whence he draws his Wine. It is good to read all those Party Pamphlets and believe in none of them.

This is indeed as you say the Age of Experiments in Government. One Tryal has been fairly made in America and France, of Nedhams perfect Commonwealth, and at length given up. Holland is trying it again and if Britain should have a Revolution She will try it too. An hundred thousand Dutchmen guillotined or beknifed will convince Holland as soon as five hundred thousand Frenchmen and Women have convinced France. How many Hecatombs must be Slaughtered to convince John Bull I cannot calculate.

The Plural Executive in France is a new Attempt, borrowed from a conceit of De Mably in his posthumous Dialogue with Lord Stanhope. The Danger of Corruption and Intrigue in Elections is rather multiplied five fold, than diminished by this. And Jealousy, Emulation and Division among them are inevitable.

Corruption in Elections has heretofore destroyed all Elective Governments. What Regulations or Precautions may be devised to prevent it in future, I am content with you to leave to Posterity to consider. You and I Shall go to the Kingdom of the just or at least shall be released from the Republick of the Unjust, with Hearts pure and hands clean of all Corruption in Elections: so much I firmly believe. Those who shall introduce the foul Fiend on the Stage, after We are gone must exorcise him as they can. With great Esteem and regard I am, Sir your most obedient

JOHN ADAMS

RC (DLC); at foot of text: "Mr Jefferson"; endorsed by TJ as received 23 Apr. 1796 and so recorded in SJL.

NEDHAMS PERFECT COMMONWEALTH: a reference to tracts by the polemicist Marchamont Nedham, including *The Case of the Commonwealth of England, Stated* (London, 1650) and *The Excellencie of a Free State* (London, 1656), which upheld the cause of the Commonwealth government in England (Joseph Frank, *Cromwell's Press Agent: A Critical Biography of Marchamont Nedham, 1620-1678* [Lanham, Md., 1980], 74-100). TJ acquired a 1767 edition of the latter. See Sowerby, No. 2331.

DE MABLY IN HIS POSTHUMOUS DIALOGUE: Gabriel Bonnot de Mably, *Des Droits et des Devoirs du Citoyen* (Kehl, 1789), a work on political theory originally written in 1758. See Sowerby, No. 2402. Adams had known the abbé Mably, a philosophe whose works were frequently cited during the French Revolution, and evidently saw the Directory as the realization of Mably's call for a plural executive (Zoltán Haraszti, *John Adams and the Prophets of Progress* [Cambridge, Mass., 1952], 116, 118-19, 138, 229).

From William Branch Giles

DEAR SIR   Philadelphia April 6th. 1796

I sincerely thank you for your friendly favor of the 19th. Ultimo. I had written you two letters just previous to its receipt; in one of which I promised to forward you the several numbers of the debates upon the late call for papers by the House of R. as they should come into circulation, the first half of the first number made its appearance yesterday and according to promise I transmit it today. The President's refusal will be taken up in the House this day. Two declaratory resolutions are prepared—the one admitting the right of makeing treaties to be vested in the President and Senate, but asserting the right of the House, when called upon to make provision for carrying them into effect, to judge of the expediency or inexpediency of doing so, and declareing it to be its duty to act according to the result of its own judgement, &c.

The other declareing that when the House shall call for papers to which it has a constitutional right, The President has no right to judge of the purposes to which the House mean to apply them.

These resolutions will probably be carried by the same majority with the former resolution with the addition of Mr. Heister of Pensylvania and Mr. Crabb of Maryland, both of whom were absent upon the former vote. Mr. Duval has resigned and of course his vote will be counting; but his opinions are known to be desicively with the majority upon every treaty question.

No desicive conclusion has yet been made by the majority upon the question of finally executeing the treaty; but it will be their policy to be united upon every question, as every gentleman of that party is now sensible, that union is the only rock of salvation to republicanism. The weight of the President, twenty senators, funded gentry, British gentry, Land gentry, aristocratic gentry, military gentry and besides these a gregarious tribe of sycophants and run-mad speculators, will be found to be as much as the shoulders of the majority of the House will be able to bear; particularly when their activity and ingenuity in makeing divisions amongst the well meaning part of the community are taken into consideration.

I should be very much gratifyed in seeing your remarks upon all these important political novel[ties] and your anticipations of their probable consequence. If ever I should be able to leave this place, I shall avail myself of your polite invitation to the Brick kiln; for I can assure you that the society of Monticello is so pleasing to me that I would encounter any inconvenience for its enjoyment. Be pleased to make my best Respects to the Ladies and beleive me to be your affectionate friend &c.   Wm. B. Giles

RC (DLC); slightly torn; addressed: "Mr. Thomas Jefferson Monticello Virginia"; franked; endorsed by TJ as received 23 Apr. 1796 and so recorded in SJL.

I PROMISED TO FORWARD . . . NUMBERS OF

THE DEBATES: see Giles to TJ, 26 Mch. 1796.

For a discussion of the PRESIDENT'S REFUSAL and the TWO DECLARATORY RESOLUTIONS of the House of Representatives, see note to Giles to TJ, 31 Mch. 1796.

To Volney

DEAR SIR   April 10. 96. Monticello.

Your favor of [March] 28. came by our last post: and flatters me with the hope of seeing you here. I shall certainly be at home all the month of May, and very happy to recieve and possess you here. I shall have a great deal to learn from you of what passed in France after I left it. Initiated as I was into the mysteries of the revolution, I have much still to learn which the newspapers never knew. In return I will give you all the information relative to our agriculture &c. which you as a traveller may wish to receive. I regret that I am in a situation which will not leave us either in the quiet or comfort we might desire. My house, which had never been more than half finished, had during a war of 8. years and my subsequent absence of 10. years gone into almost total decay. I am now engaged in the repairing altering and finishing it. The noise, confusion and discomfort of the scene will require all your philosophy and patience. However your journey thro' the country from George town to this place will have prepared you in some degree for less comfortable lodgings than I shall be able to give you in your next year's visit. And for the present one you will endeavor to find comfort in a comparison of our covering with that of an Arabian tent, and in what Arabia and it's adust sands cannot shew, groves of poplars, towering mountains, rocks and rivers, blue skies[1] balsamic air yet pure and healthy; and count for something, the affectionate welcome of Dear Sir Your friend & servt

TH: JEFFERSON

PrC (DLC); faded; at foot of text: "M. de Volney."

YOUR FAVOR: Volney to TJ, 28 Mch. 1796.

[1] Preceding two words interlined.

From James Madison

DEAR SIR   Pha. Apl. 11. 1796.

Since my last the inclosed was received from J.B. The sample of rod must wait for a private conveyance.

Yours of the 27th. has been duly received. You already know that the call for papers was refused, and reasons assigned more extraordinary a great deal than the refusal. This measure of the Ex. produced two propositions asserting the right of the House to judge of the expediency of Treaties stipulating on legislative subjects, and declaring that it was not requisite in a call for papers to express the use to be made of them. It was expected that a long and obstinate discussion would have attended these defensive measures. Under that Idea I entered into a free, but respectful review of the fallacy of the reasons contained in the Message and the day being nearly spent the Committee rose and an adjournment succeeded. The next morning instead of a reply the question was called for and taken without a word of argument on the subject. The two resolutions were carried by 57 against 35, and six members, who not foreseeing the early call for the question had not taken their seats, soon appeared and desired to have their names added to the Majority. This was not permitted by the rules of the House; but the case is explained in the Newspapers. Today is fixed for taking up the Treaties. We shall separate the Spanish and other Treaties from the British, and proceed to make for them the necessary provisions. With respect to the latter, it seems at present probable, that it will be hung up on a recital of the vices of the Treaty itself, the want of information, and the perseverance in seizing our Ships and seamen, which ought to have the same influence on our decision whether viewed as consistent with or an infraction of the Treaty. An Embargo on Indian Corn is proposed, but has not been discussed. Nothing very material from Abroad. Bache is publishing the Treaty Debates in nos. for an 8o. vol: I inclose the 1st. no. under address to Mr. Carr. Adieu   J. M. JR

RC (DLC: Madison Papers); addressed: "Thomas Jefferson Charlottesville via Richmond Virginia"; franked and postmarked; endorsed by TJ as received 23 Apr. 1796 and so recorded in SJL. Enclosure: John Bringhurst to TJ, 5 Apr. 1796 (recorded in SJL as received from Wilmington 23 Apr. 1796, but not found).

For a discussion of the TWO RESOLUTIONS, see Giles to TJ, 31 Mch., 6 Apr. 1796. The SIX MEMBERS who missed the vote and wished THEIR NAMES ADDED TO THE MAJORITY were Richard Brent, Thomas Claiborne, and Anthony New of Virginia, James Gillespie and James Holland of North Carolina, and Christopher Greenup of Kentucky (Annals, v, 783). CASE IS EXPLAINED IN THE NEWSPAPERS: see Philadelphia Aurora, 8 Apr. 1796.

On 9 Apr. 1796, Gabriel Christie of Maryland introduced a resolution calling for an EMBARGO ON INDIAN CORN and corn meal, which two days later was expanded to include rye and rye meal, with proponents arguing that it was impolitic to export scarce produce "to feed foreign nations, which their own poor stood in need of." The committee to which the resolution was referred reported against the measure on 15 Apr. 1796, noting that the scarcity and demand were very limited geographically (*Annals*, v, 893-4, 904, 975).

TREATY DEBATES: see Giles to TJ, 26 Mch. 1796.

To Thomas Mann Randolph

TH:J. TO TMR.   Monticello Apr. 11. 96.

I did not write to you by the last post because I expected you would be on the road; but as I find this will reach you in time I will ask the favor of you to bring me the certificate from Byrd's warehouse relative to the 2. hhds. of tobacco T^{WC}. mentioned in your's of the 6th. inst. It will be extremely material to be brought on Cobbs by surprize, because they consider Colo. Bell's unsuccessful enquiries after these 2. hhds. *at Shockoe's* as proofs against us.—As I conjecture from your letter that you will come up by Watkins's, and of course by Elisha Lake's on the 3. notched road, if you can get Lake to tempt some waggoner to bring on my rope by offering an extraordinary bounty, I will be obliged to you. The other articles left there by Nat may wait till he can find an opportunity of forwarding them. Colo. Bell could never get a waggoner to undertake bringing them.—Reeves has declined taking my tobacco on the terms of the paper inclosed you, on account of the reference to the 60. days price, tho' he had not objected to that when first mentioned.

We have had a remarkeable drought. The ground is now got so hard, that we this day lay aside our ploughs as unable to break up the earth. It has also been very cold for these two days. The mercury was this morning at 35°. We are in dreadful confusion with the demolition of our walls, which is more tedious than I expected. The walls are so solid that 7. men get down but between 3. and 4000. bricks aday. They would make new ones as fast. The tumbling of brickbats keeps us in constant danger. We have as yet had but one accident of a man knocked down. We are all well Jefferson particularly so, and all anxious to see you, and our dear Martha and Anne. Adieu affectionately.

RC (DLC); endorsed by Randolph as received 15 Apr. 1796.

Randolph's letter of the 6TH INST., recorded in SJL as received from Varina 10 Apr. 1796, has not been found.

The suit brought by Thomas COBBS over two hogsheads of tobacco, lost after being carried to Richmond by TJ's slave Phill in 1786, came before the Albemarle County Court on 5 May 1795. Initially the court appointed Samuel Shelton and John Hudson to settle the suit with "their award to be the Judgment of the Court" but the order was set aside two days later. During the August term of court the case was brought before a jury that found in favor of Cobbs and awarded him almost £40 in damages, plus court costs. On the motion of TJ's attorney, the court set aside the award and agreed to a new trial. The court granted TJ's request for a continuance during the November 1795 term and also awarded him a commission to take a deposition "of Owen and Mosby Inspectors at Shockoe warehouse." At the second trial, held in May 1796, the jury once again found against TJ but assessed damages of only £22.16.6. On 6 June TJ settled with Robert Garland, Cobbs's attorney, paying the judgment plus court costs of £6.4.10. TJ also paid William Wirt five dollars for serving as his attorney in the suit (Albemarle County Court Order Book, 1793-95, Albemarle County Circuit Court Clerk's Office, Charlottesville, p. 361, 375, 435, 523, 526; same, 1795-98, p. 64; TJ to Nicholas Lewis, 11 Oct. 1791; TJ to John Wayles Eppes, 3 Sep. 1795; MB, II, 941-2).

From John Stuart

SIR   Greenbrier County 11th. April 1796.

Being informed you have retired from public Business and returned to your former Residence in Albemarle, and observing by your Notes your very curious desire for Examining into the antiquitys of our Country, I thought the Bones of a Tremendious animal of the Clawed kind lately found in a Cave by some Saltpetre manufacturers about five miles from my House might afford you some amusement, have therefore procured you such as were saved, (for before I was informed of them they were chiefly lossed). I donot remember to have seen any account in the History of our Country, or any other of such an animal which probabelly was of the Lion kind; I am induced to think so from a perfect figure of that animal carved upon a rock near the confluence of the Great Kenawha, which appears might been done many Centurys ago. The Claw I send must have been one of the Shortest for the man who owns the cave asures me he had one of the same kind that measured precisely eight Inches in Length. Other Bones of Human Creatures have been found here in Caves of a surpriseing size and uncommon kind some years ago, I should been happy to had it my power to have sent to you with these, but none are now to be got, if these should be worthy your observation it would give me much pleasure to hear Conjectures. And shall be Happy at all Times to communicate any thing from here you might desire to Know. And remain with very great respect Your Most Obe. Humbl. Servt.   JOHN STUART

RC (ViW); endorsed by TJ as received 12 May 1796 and so recorded in SJL.

John Stuart (1749-1823) was born in Augusta County and before the Revolution moved to the Greenbrier River, where he acquired large landholdings. Elected to the Virginia House of Delegates from Greenbrier County, 1778-79, he also served as county clerk, 1780-1807, was a lieutenant colonel of militia, and in 1788 was a delegate to the Virginia convention to ratify the

Constitution. On TJ's nomination, Stuart was elected to membership in the American Philosophical Society in April 1797. The Virginia Historical Society posthumously published his recollections of settlement on the frontier (Johnston, *Memorials*, 193-7; John Stuart, *Memoir of Indian Wars, and Other Occurrences* [Richmond, 1833]; Leonard, *General Assembly*, 129, 134; APS, *Proceedings*, XXII, pt. 3 [1884], 256; TJ to Stuart, 10 Nov. 1796).

YOUR NOTES: *Notes on the State of Virginia*. This letter was the first report to TJ of the discovery of the fossil BONES of the megalonyx; see Memoir on the Megalonyx, [10 Feb. 1797].

From Van Staphorst & Hubbard

SIR   Amsterdam 11 April 1796.

Since We addressed you the 27 January last; returning you with protests for non acceptance and non payment your remittance £39.17.10½ on Wm. Anderson, We have your esteemed favor of 31 of same month, covering another remittance for account of Mr. P. Mazzei, in Wm. Hodgson's Bill at 60 days sight on Robinson Sanderson & Rumney of Whitehaven payable in London, with Which We will do the needful to credit of said Gentleman to whom We forwarded an advice of the receipt thereof together with your letter for him. We are ever with regard and esteem Sir! Your mo: ob: hb: Servants

N & J VAN STAPHORST & HUBBARD

RC (DLC); at foot of text: "Thos. Jefferson Esqr. Monticello. Virginia"; endorsed by TJ as received 16 July 1796 and so recorded in SJL. Dupl, recorded in SJL as received 3 Sep. 1796, has not been found.

Two bills of exchange for Philip Mazzei had encountered delays in payment, and not until TJ received Van Staphorst & Hubbard's letter of 27 JANUARY in mid-May would he know that one of them, on William ANDERSON of London, had been refused and returned. Its issuer, Nathaniel Anderson, who was previously of Richmond, resided in Albemarle County, and TJ sought reimbursement of the amount of the bill plus the cost of the protest and interest. Anderson settled up by a series of transactions between 6 June and 15 Sep. 1796, including cash payments, beef and mutton that William Jones of Albemarle supplied to TJ for Anderson's credit, and the assumption of a part of the debt by John Steele, a stonemason who worked on the foundation at Monticello (notes of account with Nathaniel Anderson, 11 June 1794 to 15 Sep. 1796, MS in DLC: TJ Papers, 101:17269-70, entirely in TJ's hand, detailing costs and repayment of the protested bill with three different calculations of the amount due; bill of exchange, 11 June 1794, and copy bearing endorsement of protest, 14 Sep. 1795, in same, 100:17231-3; Jones's statement of account, 15 Sep. 1796, in same, 100: 17214; MB, II, 928-9, 941, 943-5; Vol. 28: 342, 500-501, 599-600). YOUR ESTEEMED FAVOR: see TJ to Philip Mazzei, 31 Jan. 1796.

Agreement with Randolph Jefferson

This indenture made on the 17th. day of April 1796. between [Ran]dolph Jefferson of the one part and Thomas Jefferson of the [other] part witnesseth that Whereas the said Randolph under the will of Peter Jefferson their father is siesed in feesimple in an undivided sixth part as tenant in common in a certain parcel of land in the county of Albemarle on the branches of Hardware river containing by estimation four hundred acres with a quarry of limestone thereon[1] and bounded as follows to wit beginning at Hudson's corner white oak, running thence on his line N. 53°. W. 217. poles, crossing two branches to a pine and a white oak thence on new lines N. 23°. E. 278. poles crossing four branches [to pointers of] small pines. S. 63°. E. 230. poles crossing two branches to pointers, S. 27°. W. 278. poles to a pine and N. 63°. W. 11. poles to the first station which said lands were granted Philip Mayo by patent bearing date the 1st. day of Sep. 1749. and by the said Philip were conveyed in feesimple to the said Peter Jefferson, Joshua Fry, Arthur Hopkins, Thomas Meriwether, Daniel Scott and William Stith to be held by them and their heirs without the benefit of survivorship by deed bearing date July the 2d. 1753. and recorded in the count[y court] of Albemarle, now the said Randolph in consideration of [the sum] of five shillings and of certain articles of houshold furniture to him now paid and delivered hath given granted bargained and sold unto the said Thomas Jefferson all his right title and estate in the said lands with it's appurtenances, to have and to hold the said lands and their appurtenances in the same proportion and estate heretofore held by the said Randolph to him the said Thomas and his heirs: in witness whereof the said Randolph hath here[to] set his hand and seal on the [day] and year first above written.

Signed sealed and delivered in presence of
JOHN NICHOLAS   RANDOLPH JEFFERSON
JOHN CARR
ALEXR. GARRETT

MS (Christie's, New York City, 1996); in TJ's hand, signed by Randolph Jefferson and witnessed by Nicholas, Carr, and Garrett; torn and stained, bracketed text being supplied from Tr; with subjoined attestation by Nicholas, dated Charlottesville, April 1796, that the indenture was produced in court and proved by the oaths of Nicholas, Carr and Garrett and ordered to be recorded; endorsed. Tr (ViU: Carr-Cary Papers); copy by Garrett, deputy county clerk; with minor variations; endorsed by TJ:

"Randolph Jefferson ⎫
to   ⎬ Deed
Th: Jefferson" ⎭

CERTAIN PARCEL OF LAND: see James Hopkins to TJ, 2 Jan. 1796.

SJL records letters that TJ wrote to his brother Randolph on 24 Aug. 1795, 9 May, 4 Sep., 3 Nov. 1796, 27 Oct. 1797, 8 Sep.,

17, 28 Oct. 1798, 4 Apr., 6 Nov. 1799, and 17 Aug. 1800, none of which has been found. Also listed in SJL, but missing, are letters Randolph Jefferson wrote to TJ on 19 and 30 Aug. 1795 (received 23 and 31 Aug.), [1?] May 1796 (received 8 May), 3 Sep. 1796 (incongruously recorded as received on 2 Sep. 1796), 6 Sep. and 27 Oct. 1798 (received on the dates they were written), 7 Apr. 1799 (received the same day), and 12 and 21 Aug. 1800 (received on 12 and 24 Aug. respectively). The brothers corresponded again in August and September 1802, TJ writing on 14 Aug., 2 Sep., and 7 Sep., and Randolph on 13 Aug. (received the following day) and 2 Sep. (received the same day). Those letters, recorded in SJL, have also not been located.

[1] Preceding six words interlined.

To James Madison

DEAR SIR   Apr. 17. 1796.

Yours of the 4th. came to hand the day before yesterday. I have turned to the Conventional history, and inclose you an exact copy of what is there on the subject you mentioned. I have also turned to my own papers, and send you some things extracted from them which shew that the recollection of the P. has not been accurate when he supposed his own opinion to have been uniformly that declared in his answer of Mar. 30. The records of the Senate will vouch this.   I happened at the same time with your letter to recieve one from Mazzei giving some directions as to his remittances. I have not time to decide and say by this post how Dohrman's paiment should be remitted according to his desire and existing circumstances, that is to say, whether by bill on Amsterdam to the V. Staphorsts, or by bill on London to himself. I will write to you definitively by next post.   We are experiencing a most distressing drought. The ground cannot now be broken with the plough. Our fruit is as yet safe, but the spring is cold and backward. Corn is at 25/ here, but greatly higher in some parts. Wheat 16/ at Richmond at 90. days. Tobacco 40/. My respects to Mrs. Madison. Adieu affectionately.

RC (DLC: Madison Papers); unsigned; at foot of text: "Mr. Madison." PrC (DLC).

RECOLLECTION OF THE P.: see note to Giles to TJ, 31 Mch. 1796.

For the missing letters from Philip MAZZEI of 26 Oct. 1795, see Document I of Jefferson's Letter to Philip Mazzei, 24 Apr. 1796.

I
Extract of Madison's Notes on
Debates in the Federal Convention

Extract verbatim from last page but one, and the last page.

'Mr. King suggested that the journals of the Convention should be either destroyed, or deposited in the custody of the President. He thought, if suffered to be made public, a bad use would be made of them by those who would wish to prevent the adoption of the constitution.

Mr. Wilson preferred the 2d. expedient. He had at one time liked the first best: but as false suggestions may be propagated, it should not be made impossible to contradict them.

A question was then put on depositing the journals and other papers of the Convention in the hands of the President, on which

N.H. ay. M. ay. Ct. ay. N.J. ay. Pena. ay. Del. ay. Md. no.† Virga. ay. N.C. ay. S.C. ay Georgia ay.   †This negative of Maryland was occasioned by the language of the instructions to the Deputies of that state, which required them to report to the state the *proceedings* of the Convention.

The President having asked what the convention meant should be done with the Journals &c. whether copies were to be allowed to the members if applied for, it was resolved nem: con: "that he retain the Journal and other papers subject to the order of the Congress, if ever formed under the constitution."

The members then proceeded to sign the instrument.' &c.

MS (DLC: Madison Papers); entirely in TJ's hand. PrC (DLC).

This debate on the disposition of the JOURNALS OF THE CONVENTION took place on 17 Sep. 1787 (Max Farrand, ed., *The Records of the Federal Convention of 1787*, 4 vols. [New Haven, 1911-37], II, 648).

II
Extracts from Jefferson's Papers,
with Comments

'In Senate Feb. 1. 1791.

The Committee to whom was referred that part of the speech of the Pr. of the US. at the opening of the session which relates to the commerce of the Mediterranean, and also the letter from the Secy. of state dated 20th. Jan. 1791. with the papers accompanying the same, reported, Whereupon

Resolved that the Senate do advise and consent that the Pr. of the US. take such measures as he may think necessary for the redemption of the citizens of the US. now in captivity at Algiers, provided the expence shall not exceed 40,000 Dols. and also that measures be taken to confirm the treaty now existing between the U.S. and the emperor of Marocco.'

The above is a copy of a resolution of Senate referred to me by the P. to prepare an answer to, and I find immediately following this among my papers a press copy from an original written fairly in my own hand ready for the P's signature and to be given in to the Senate the following answer.

'Gentlemen of the Senate.

I will proceed to take measures for the ransom of our citizens in captivity at Algiers, in conformity with your resolution of advice of the 1st. inst. so soon as the monies necessary shall be appropriated *by the legislature* and shall be in readiness.

The recognition of our treaty with the new Emperor of Marocco requires also previous appropriation and provision. The importance of this last to the liberty and property of our citizens induces me to urge it on your earliest attention.'

Tho' I have no memorandum of the delivery of this to the Senate yet I have not the least doubt it was given in to them and will be found among their records.

I find among my press copies, the following in my hand writing.

'The committee to report that the President does not think that circumstances will justify, in the present instance his entering into *absolute* engagements for the ransom of our captives in Algiers, nor calling for money from the treasury, nor raising it by loan, without previous authority from *both branches* of the legislature.' Apr. 9. 1792.

I do not recollect the occasion of the above paper with certainty. But I think there was a committee appointed by the Senate to confer with the P. on the subject of the ransom, and to advise what is there declined, and that a member of the committee advising privately with me as to the report they were to make to the house, I minuted down the above, as the substance of what I concieved to be the proper report after what had passed with the Pr. and gave the original to the member preserving the press copy. I think the member was either Mr. Izard or Mr. Butler; and have no doubt such a report will be found on the files of the Senate.

On the 8th. of May following, in consequence of Questions proposed by the Pr. to the Senate, they came to a resolution, on which a mission was founded.

MS (DLC: Madison Papers); entirely in TJ's hand. PrC (DLC).

For the 1 Feb. 1791 RESOLUTION OF SENATE REFERRED TO ME BY THE P. and for the ANSWER prepared by TJ for Washington, see Documents VII and VIII in Editorial Note and group of documents on the Mediterranean trade and Algerine captives, at 28 Dec. 1790.

The Senate committee conference WITH THE P. ON THE SUBJECT OF THE RANSOM OF American captives in Algiers, is treated in Washington to TJ, 10 Mch. 1792; Memorandum of Conference with the President on Treaty with Algiers, 11 Mch. 1792; and Memoranda of Consultations with the President, [11 Mch.–9 Apr. 1792].

From Thomas Pinckney

MY DEAR SIR   London 17th April 1796

The Chevalier de Irujo Minister Plenipotentiary from his Catholic Majesty to the United States purposing to embark for Norfolk I avail myself of the opportunity of inclosing to you a duplicate of my letter of the 16th. of the last Month, the original having been sent by a more circuitous route. Nothing new has occurred here since that date except the certainty of the war being to be continued between this Country and France.

Mr. and Mrs. Church whom I lately saw hearing that I was about to write to you requested to be recalled to your friendly recollection and with the intreaty that I may be continued therein I remain My dear Sir Your friend & Servant   THOMAS PINCKNEY

RC (DLC); endorsed by TJ; recorded in SJL as received 11 June 1796. PrC (ScHi: Pinckney Family Papers); at foot of text in ink: "Mr. Jefferson." Enclosure: missing Dupl of Pinckney to TJ, 16 Mch. 1796.

From James Madison

DEAR SIR   Philada. Apl. 18. 1796

My last requested your orders relating to Dohrman's payment to Me for Mazzei; and I impatiently wait for them.

Resolutions have passed for carrying into effect, the Spanish, Indian and Algerine Treaties. The British is now depending. I inclose the proposition in which the opponents of it, will unite. According to present calculation, this proposition will be carried by *nearly* the same majority as prevailed in the vote asserting the Rights of the House on the subject of Treaties. The debate is but just commenced. Those who at first were for a silent question, will probably now spin out time for the purpose of calling in the mercantile interference in behalf. You will see the expedient on foot in this City. The petition of the Merchants &c. will be signed by 7 or 800 as is said. An adverse petition will be signed by 3 or 4 times that number. In N.Y. and Boston it is hoped the counter petitioners will equally preponderate. Baltimore which was at first most opposed to the Treaty is become most generally reconciled to the execution. The hope of endimnification for past losses, and the fears for their floating speculations, which have been arranged on the idea that the Treaty would go into effect, bear down with that class all attention to the general and permanent good of the Country, and perhaps their own real and comprehensive interest. The Country also is under an operation for obtaining petitions for the Treaty. The Western Counties, have yielded a number; being dextrously alarmed for the Spanish Treaty as involved in the fate of the British. I expected to have sent you my observations on the Presidents Message, which the Printer told me should certainly be out this morning. He thought Mr. Iredell's charge and the eccho of the G. Jurey, entitled to priority.

RC (DLC: Madison Papers); unsigned; endorsed by TJ as received 30 Apr. 1796 and so recorded in SJL. Enclosure: *Mr. Maclay's Motion. 14th April 1796, Referred to a Committee of the whole House, on the state of the union* (Philadelphia, 1796), being a motion made in the House of Representatives by Samuel Maclay of Pennsylvania declaring that, with the information the House possessed, it was not "expedient at this time to concur in passing the laws necessary for carrying the said Treaty into effect" (see Evans, No. 31361).

On 14 and 15 Apr. 1796, the House of Representatives passed RESOLUTIONS for executing the SPANISH, INDIAN AND ALGERINE TREATIES and began considering appropriations for the BRITISH treaty, as provided in the resolution introduced by Connecticut Congressman James Hillhouse (JHR, II, 511-14; *Annals*, v, 951-76). Descriptions of the campaign of treaty advocates in April 1796 are included in Combs, *Jay Treaty*, 178-87; Young, *Democratic Republicans of New York*, 464-5; and Kurtz,

Presidency of John Adams, 51-67. The prediction of some Federalist senators that failure to appropriate funds to execute the Jay Treaty would lead to a dissolution of the government is recalled in Notes on a Conversation with Henry Tazewell, [1 Mch. 1798].

Madison's OBSERVATIONS on Washington's refusal to submit documents relating to the Jay Treaty, given in his speech before the House on 6 Apr. 1796, were printed in Andrew Brown's *Philadelphia Gazette* on 19 Apr. 1796, the same day Justice James IREDELL'S CHARGE to the Philadelphia grand jury of the United States Circuit Court of 12 Apr. 1796 and the grand jury's response of the same date were published in a supplement to Brown's newspaper. Iredell referred briefly to "the present momentous crisis" but declined to comment upon it. The grand jury declared that a great majority of the people in the Pennsylvania district wanted the British treaty to be carried into effect without delay and hoped that "no impediment may be thrown in its way by our representatives."

From Tench Coxe

DEAR SIR   Philada. April 22d. 1796—

Your two last letters for Europe, tho unacknowledged, have long since been carefully forwarded.

Peace does not appear to be at hand in Europe by our accounts to the 12th. of March. Belgium seems to be the principal cause. A just and safe disposition of that country for all the parties in the war *and for itself* appears to be a matter of great intrinsic difficulty. If France and England are not prevented from making another Campaign for it, I have no doubt they will each hazard one.

The continuance of the war, and the french dispositions against and the British anxiety for the Treaty with the U.S. bring us again into a situation of some hazard. It seems probable, that the House of Representatives will decline all legislation towards the execution of the Treaty— and appearances render it probable that the Supreme Court, on a case brought up, will coincide with the Senate and the President. Mr. Ellsworth was in the Senate, and the opinions of those who rest on him are with the President. To Mr. Wilson's Estate the miscarriage of the Treaty would be considered, as I presume, to be the most injurious of all possible Events. The Doctrines of some of the other Gentlemen upon the Treaty of Peace were unfavorable to the House, at least as important Symptoms of their opinions on the pending Question. My first impression was, prior to June, that a treaty superceded and repealed a law, but it appears to me more correct to say, that it is at least so far hypothetical as laws are opposed to it, and that they are to be removed before it can be a consummated law of the Land; I am convinced that the treaty making power has never been completely investigated in any Country. I am, dear Sir, with sincere good wishes Yr. very respectful Servant

TENCH COXE

RC (DLC); endorsed by TJ as received 14 May and so recorded in SJL.

TWO LAST LETTERS FOR EUROPE: TJ to Van Staphorst & Hubbard, 28 Feb. 1796, and another letter not identified.

From Aaron Burr

DR SIR   Philada. 23 Ap. 96

Mr. Guillemard an english gentleman of fortune and education, travelling from motives of Scientific Curiosity and amusement, will hand you this. I have thought you might regret that such a man should pass through your Country without being made known to you, and have therefore taken the liberty to introduce him to your Notice and acquaintance. What further apology may be necessary for this freedom, will be found in the character and manners of Mr. G. which are altogether amiable. I am very Respectfully Yr assured & Obt Sert

AARON BURR

RC (NNPM); at foot of text: "Mr. Jefferson." Recorded in SJL as received "by Guillemar" on 22 June 1796.

John GUILLEMARD visited Monticello with the Duc de La Rochefoucauld-Liancourt in June 1796 (see Guillemard to TJ, 18 July 1796).

From James Madison

DEAR SIR   Apl. 23. 1796

I inclose another number of the Debates on the Treaty. The subject is still going on in the House, as well as the press. The majority has melted, by changes and absence, to 8 or 9 votes. Whether these will continue firm is more than I can decide. Every possible exertion is made as usual on the other side. A sort of appeal has been made to the people, with an expectation that the mercantile force would triumph over the popular sentiment. In this city the majority of petitioners has appeared against the Mercantile party. We do not know the event of the experiment in N. York. Petitions on both sides are running thro' the adjoining States of Delaware, and N. Jersey. Among other extraordinary manoeuvres, the Insurance Companies here and in New Y. stopt business, in order to reduce prices and alarm the public. The Banks have been powerfully felt in the progress of the petitions in the Cities for the Treaty. Scarce a merchant or Trader but what depends on discounts, and at this moment there is a general pinch for money. Under such circumstances, a Bank Director soliciting subscriptions is like a Highwayman with a pistol demanding the purse. We hope the question will be taken tomorrow. But if carried against the Treaty, the game will be played over again in other forms. The Senate will either send it down by itself, or coupled with the Spanish Treaty or both. Nothing of importance from Europe. Adieu. Js. MADISON JR

RC (DLC: Madison Papers); endorsed by TJ as received 14 May 1796 and so recorded in SJL.

DEBATES ON THE TREATY: see Giles to TJ, 26 Mch. 1796.

Jefferson's Letter to Philip Mazzei

I. THOMAS JEFFERSON TO PHILIP MAZZEI,
24 APR. 1796

II. EXTRACT AND COMMENTARY PRINTED IN THE PARIS *MONITEUR*,
25 JAN. 1797

III. EXTRACT AND COMMENTARY PRINTED IN THE NEW YORK *MINERVA*,
2 MAY 1797

IV. ITALIAN TRANSLATION OF EXTRACT,
N.D.

EDITORIAL NOTE

On 24 Apr. 1796, Jefferson wrote a lengthy epistle to his former neighbor Philip Mazzei, who was by then living in Pisa (Document I). While the letter primarily discussed Mazzei's lingering business affairs in Virginia and relayed news of his old friends, a single paragraph transformed this piece of private correspondence into the notorious "Mazzei letter" that plagued Jefferson for the remainder of his life. Its publication on 25 Jan. 1797 in the Paris *Gazette Nationale ou Le Moniteur Universel* with four added paragraphs of commentary highly critical of American foreign policy (Document II) and subsequent appearances in American newspapers beginning in May 1797 thrust Jefferson into the very center of partisan controversy and made him the target of intense Federalist attack. A letter that he had written as a private citizen, at a time of deep discouragement over the Jay Treaty and general disenchantment with the direction of politics in America, was made public without his knowledge and in a context entirely different from that in which he had written it. By the time of its publication he had become the vice president of the United States and the recognized leader of the Republican opposition. The stinging criticisms that Jefferson had made of the Federalists in the spring of 1796 came back to haunt him on several occasions: in the summer and fall of 1797, during the second session of the Fifth Congress in early 1798, in the souring of his relations with George Washington, as a campaign issue in the election of 1800, and even as late as 1824 when he was still defending his judgments and blaming the furor on mistranslation and deliberate misinterpretation of his words, referring to the perverted text as "a pliant and fertile text of misrepresentation of my political principles." Observed Merrill Peterson, "No single writing from Jefferson's pen pursued him so remorselessly beyond the grave."[1]

The responsibility for moving the letter onto the public stage rests squarely with Mazzei, who shortly after receiving it eagerly copied (in English) the pertinent paragraph and sent it to at least two friends. One copy went to Giovanni Fabbroni, a young Florentine scholar whom Mazzei had hoped to entice to Virginia and with whom Jefferson had corresponded. Another was dispatched to the Dutch banker Jacob Van Staphorst, who rebuked Mazzei for his lack of "prudence and delicacy" in allowing the personal correspondence of a friend to be circulated without his permission. A third copy, as indicated by Mazzei's endorsement on the letter from Jefferson, must have gone to Giovanni Lorenzo Ferri de Saint-Constant, a writer who became acquainted with Mazzei in Holland, where Ferri served as a tutor for the children of the French ambassador. Mazzei presumably intended the paragraph for transmittal to the *Moniteur*, a newspaper with which he had had dealings in the past. It is not implausible that Ferri was also the translator of the paragraph into French, as he previously had translated writings by Mazzei.[2]

The translation into French evidently was made directly from the English, although Jefferson seems to have surmised that Mazzei had prepared an Italian translation and arranged for its printing in a Florence newspaper (TJ to Madison, 3 Aug. 1797, discussed below in this note). The Editors, however, have found no trace of an Italian publication and conclude that the letter's dateline of "Florence" merely indicates that the *Moniteur* received the piece from there. Mazzei apparently did translate it into Italian at some point, however, for on 26 June 1797 he dispatched a "draft of a translation" that he said he had made for "someone who does not understand English" to Paolo Garzoni, a member of a wealthy family in Lucca who occupied a series of diplomatic posts.[3] Although

---

[1] TJ to Martin Van Buren, 29 June, 1824; Merrill Peterson, *The Jefferson Image in the American Mind* (New York, 1960), 118.

[2] Marchione, *Mazzei: Writings*, III, 186-92, 194-6; *Dizionario Biografico degli Italiani*, 49 vols. to date (Rome, 1960-), XLVII, 166-8; see also above in this series, Vols. 1: 519-20, 9: 279, and 23: 533).

[3] Marchione, *Mazzei: Writings*, III, 198-9; Carlo Pellegrini and Francesco Giovanni, eds., *Un Patrizio Toscano alla Corte di Napoleone: Diari di Paolo Lodivico Garzoni* (Florence, 1994), 13-73.

no copy in Mazzei's hand of an Italian translation has been found, one in what appears to be a clerk's hand is in a collection of letters and other documents appended to the manuscript of his memoirs (Document IV). Those memoirs, with the miscellaneous appended documents, including the translation of Jefferson's letter, were first published thirty years after Mazzei's death. [4]

Three and a half months after the extract's appearance in France, the Federalist editor of the New York *Minerva*, Noah Webster, obtained a copy of the French newspaper from Epaphras Jones, a New York City merchant and ship owner who had recently returned from France. [5] Webster arranged to have the extract and the *Moniteur*'s subjoined paragraphs translated into English and printed in the 2 May issue of his newspaper (Document III). Subsequent mentions of it appeared in the *Minerva* on 3, 4, 6, 8, and 19 May. When Jones requested the return of his French newspaper, Webster made a copy for himself and had it certified by James Kent on 22 May. Webster also noted that Timothy Pickering, then secretary of state, "sent to me for the original paper, and had the letter in the original with a translation, if I mistake not, published in the *Gazette of the United States*" (NN: Webster Papers). After its publication there on 4 May, Pickering had his own copy prepared (MHi: Pickering Papers) and certified by his chief clerk for his files (on 3 June). Pickering returned the newspaper to Webster. The extract in the *Moniteur*, of unclear lineage, had by then become the official version of Jefferson's letter, from which all American subsequent versions derived.

Webster published Jefferson's letter—or, more accurately, an English translation of a French translation of a portion of it—along with the *Moniteur*'s subjoined paragraphs, and a footnote suggesting the French version contained a mistake. Several Federalist papers followed the lead of the *Minerva* and the *Gazette of the United States* in publishing the document, beginning with a 4 May printing in Philadelphia in William Cobbett's *Porcupine's Gazette*. Many of them reproduced everything from the *Minerva*, while some included only the actual paragraphs from Jefferson's letter and the *Moniteur*'s editorial additions. Letters to the editors and additional commentary often appeared in subsequent issues. The *Gazette of the United States* even published, on 31 May, the French version as it had appeared in the *Moniteur*, "there being some talk of inaccuracy in the translation." [6]

In a highly charged and partisan atmosphere, Vice President Jefferson became an easy target for Federalist criticism. His letter was used to justify the

---

[4] Capponi Collection, Mss. da riordinare, 238-9, Biblioteca Nazionale, Florence; Margherita Marchione and Barbara B. Oberg, eds., *Philip Mazzei: The Comprehensive Microform Edition of his Papers*, 9 reels (Millwood, N.Y., 1982), 4:1095-9; Margherita Marchione, ed., *Philip Mazzei: My Life and Wanderings*, trans. S. Eugene Scalia (Morristown, N.J., 1980), 13-14.

[5] For Jones, see *Annals*, IV, 971-2.

[6] Among the 1797 printings and commentary were the *Minerva*, 2, 3, 4, 6, 8, 19 May; *Porcupine's Gazette*, 4, 5, 9, 20, 22 May and 2 June; *Gazette of the United States*, 4, 5, 6, 8, 19, 20, 31 May; the Boston *Columbian Centinel*, 10, 13, 31 May; the Concord, N.H., *New Star*, 23 May; *Courier of New Hampshire*, 23, 30 May; the Keene, N.H., *Rising Sun*, 16 May; the Walpole, N.H., *Farmer's Weekly Museum*, 23 May; the Newburyport, Mass., *Impartial Herald*, 16 May; *The Herald; A Gazette for the Country*, 10 May, 14 June. For a general discussion of the publication of the letter in American newspapers, see also Malone, *Jefferson*, III, 302-6.

claim of President Adams and the Federalists that the Republicans were more loyal to France than they were to America, even "treasonable" and "traiterous" as Webster suggested. Jefferson was portrayed as the leader of a dangerous faction, the head of a French party. The New York *Herald; A Gazette for the Country* on 14 June warned against foreign attachments of any kind, associated Jefferson directly with a foreign interest, and observed that it "never had much doubt" that Jefferson had penned the letter. In August and September the *Gazette of the United States* reprinted from the *Virginia Gazette and General Advertiser* a series of articles by "Americanus" addressed to the "Citizens of America." Highly critical of Jefferson, the pieces analyzed relations between France and the United States, describing France's participation in the American Revolution as self-interested and dramatically announcing in the 23 Sep. issue that the French government's intention was to "overturn" the present American government and "place ourselves in the '*fraternal*,' or rather infernal, grip of France."[7]

Benjamin Bache's Philadelphia *Aurora* on 5 May 1797 was the first Republican newspaper to enter the fray on Jefferson's behalf.[8] Putting aside the question of the letter's authorship, which, Bache noted, he was "not competent to determine," the editor of the *Aurora* nonetheless judged the description of conflict and political parties the letter offered to be "substantially correct." Other sympathetic newspapers took a variety of approaches, not always consistent ones: the letter could not have been written by any well informed American because of a misstatement in the first sentence; Jefferson might not have been the author, and ought to be allowed to make a public statement to that effect; and finally, even if the author had expressed such thoughts, they merely reflected reality. The editor of the New York *Argus*, for example, inquired why Webster, who had his pen dipped, as usual, in the "*Sink Pot of Malignity*," could not wait for Jefferson's reply before judging. Whether Jefferson was the writer or not, the *Argus* proclaimed, the letter portrayed "in *real* colours, undeniable facts." It was the very accuracy of these facts, according to the Boston *Independent Chronicle and Universal Advertiser*, that caused the Federalists to "cry out."[9] Both Federalist and Republican newspapers challenged the vice president to deny explicitly that the letter was his or accept responsibility for it. This call reverberated across American newspapers from spring to fall of 1797. The *Gazette of the United States* began by noting on 5 May that if the letter was not by Jefferson, it was by someone who was "no stranger to the style and sentiments of the Vice President." By 31 May the paper pronounced Jefferson's silence "complete evidence" of his guilt. On 2 June *The Medley or New Bedford Marine Journal* published the letter with appended remarks and noted that it had refrained from earlier publication in order to give Jefferson a chance to disown it.

Jefferson learned of the letter's publication on 9 May 1797 at Bladensburg, Maryland, where he breakfasted on his way to Philadelphia to attend the special

[7] *Gazette of the United States*, 25 Aug. and 2, 7, 8, 23, and 26 Sep. 1797.

[8] Additional comment followed in the *Aurora* on 8, 12 May, and 7 June.

[9] See the *Argus*, 6 May; the *Independent Chronicle and Universal Advertiser*, 22 May. For another example of sympathetic press treatment, see the Newark, N.J., *Centinel of Freedom*, 17 May. The letter also appeared in a French language newspaper published in New York, the *Gazette Française*, on 8 May.

session of Congress recently summoned by Adams. Jefferson's extant correspondence, however, contains no mention of the affair until the summer, when in a letter of 12 July James Monroe urged him to acknowledge authorship, declaring that as a free man he was entitled to express his sentiments in a private letter, which had been made public without his knowledge or consent. Jefferson may have consulted with Monroe in Philadelphia, where the two attended a dinner party on 1 July, shortly after the American minister's return from France. When Jefferson conveyed Monroe's opinion to Madison in early August, Madison counseled just the reverse, although he said he would "converse with Col. Monroe" on the subject. Madison reasoned that it might be "ticklish" to "say publickly yes or no to the interrogatories of party spirit" and that an open avowal would force him into "disagreeable explanations, or tacit confessions." John Page later echoed Madison's sentiments, suggesting that if Jefferson "were the Author of *the* Letter to Mazzei" the language and "strong metaphorical Expressions" were suited to the "Taste and disposition" of the correspondent, and "not intended for public view." [10]

Jefferson's dilemma, as he explained it to Madison, was that he could not completely disown the publication because "the greatest part" was his in substance. It was in this letter to Madison that Jefferson first laid out the primary theme of his defense—that in reference to British influence he had written "forms," which had been incorrectly translated as "form," and that the substitution of the singular for the plural had greatly distorted his meaning. He also formulated what must have seemed a highly plausible hypothesis—that the letter had migrated from English to Italian to French, and then back to English. The similarity between Jefferson's explanation to Madison and Tench Coxe's description three years later of the letter's metamorphosis may indicate that the vice president had also consulted with Coxe before leaving Philadelphia for Monticello. [11] Jefferson maintained a determined public silence on the issue.

The letter was commonly interpreted by Federalists as a thinly disguised personal attack upon George Washington, whom the majority of his contemporaries were certain Jefferson saw as one of the prime "Samsons in the field and Solomons in the council." Jefferson in fact had criticized the former president in late 1794 and 1795 for pursuing a policy that favored Britain over France and for allowing himself to be the spokesman for a "faction of Monocrats" in his attacks on the democratic societies. Jefferson's assessment of the former president had, as Dumas Malone observed, "reached its historical nadir." Nonetheless, he refrained from attacking Washington's character or probity. As he wrote to William Branch Giles, Washington "errs as other men do, but errs with integrity." Relations between the two men were strained, however. Their final exchange of letters, properly polite and chiefly about agriculture, occurred after Jefferson had penned the letter to Mazzei, but before Washington learned of it. [12] When the letter did become public, the former president made no public response to the remarks. Almost thirty years later, Jefferson observed that

[10] Monroe to TJ, 12 July; TJ to Madison, 3 Aug. 1797, and Madison to TJ, 5 Aug. 1797; Page to TJ, 26 Apr. 1798.

[11] *Strictures upon the Letter imputed to Mr. Jefferson, Addressed to Mr. Mazzei* [Philadelphia, 1800]; Cooke, *Coxe*, 376n.

[12] TJ to Madison, 28 Dec., 1794; TJ to Giles, 31 Dec. 1795; TJ to Washington, 19 June 1796; and Washington to TJ, 6 July 1796; Malone, *Jefferson*, III, 268.

"there never passed a word, written or verbal, directly or indirectly, between Genl. Washington and myself, on the subject of that letter" and denied that Washington would ever "have degraded himself so far as to take to himself the imputation in that letter on the 'Samsons in combat.'" [13]

Although the "Mazzei letter" itself did not cause the severing of relations between these two distinguished Virginians, it did serve as the backdrop for and perhaps even an impetus toward the rupture. A letter from Jefferson's nephew Peter Carr dated 25 Sep. 1797, signing himself "John Langhorne" from Albemarle County and purporting to be the friend and sympathizer of Washington in resisting the "unmerited calumny" and "unjust aspersions" that had recently been flung at him, precipitated the final break. John Nicholas of Charlottesville informed Washington on 18 Nov. that Langhorne was really connected to some of his "greatest and bitterest enemies," and that living within "cannon shot of the very head-quarters of *Jacobinism*" and knowing the former president had been deceived "in the principles and *professions of friendship* of *certain characters* in *this quarter*," he thought it right to alert Washington. In a letter of 9 Dec. Nicholas made it explicit: Langhorne was the nephew of "your *very Sincere friend* Mr Jefferson." Carr's hope, it seemed clear, was to lure Washington into saying something negative about Jefferson or the Republicans that could be leaked to newspapers. On 22 Feb. 1798, Nicholas referred again to the insincerity of Jefferson's ("*that man's*") friendship and twice mentioned the letter to Mazzei. Although Washington maintained his discreet silence in public, his mention to Nicholas, after consulting with his nephew Bushrod Washington, of his shaken "belief in the sincerity of a friendship, which I had *conceived* was possessed for me," is an indication that the Mazzei incident, through the Langhorne episode, had touched him. Even after Washington's death, the *Gazette of the United States* on 13 Feb. 1800 found an excuse to recur to the letter: "At a time when America is overwhelmed with grief, when a whole country with the exception of a few individuals, is deploring the loss of the great and good WASHINGTON, whatever relates to him, naturally rushes upon our thoughts." The letter from Jefferson to Mazzei "some time ago cannot be forgotten," as "high wrought calumny on him who was their SAMSON in the field, and their SOLOMON in council." And in case the nation had forgotten the whole text of the letter, the *Gazette* reprinted it. [14]

Pointed allusions to the thoughts expressed in the letter surfaced in the second session of the Fifth Congress in 1798. The letter became a vehicle for praising the wisdom of Washington and the Federalists and criticizing dangerous opinions. Discussion on the foreign intercourse bill turned on whether the House had a role in deciding upon the size and cost of the foreign establishment or whether the executive had the exclusive authority to select his foreign ministers and establish their salaries. Connecticut Federalist Joshua Coit on 28 Feb. 1798 alluded to "certain opinions" held by many persons in the country that made it necessary for the president to inquire carefully into the views of individ-

[13] TJ to Martin Van Buren, 29 June 1824. TJ discussed the Mazzei affair in some detail in this lengthy letter to Van Buren after the New York senator sent to Jefferson Timothy Pickering's *A Review of the Correspondence* (1824), which Jefferson called an "elaborate Philippic."

[14] See Washington, *Papers, Ret. Ser.*, II, 128. For the rest of the Langhorne story, see same, I, 373-5, 409, 475-7, 491-2, 509-11, II, 99-102, 495-6, 514-15, 546-7.

uals who were to be appointed to office. As evidence for these disturbing opinions he read a paraphrase of Jefferson's letter, including the first of the *Moniteur*'s supplementary paragraphs, "said to be written by a person high in office in this Government." While Coit expressed his hope that no such sentiments were to be found in America, the evidence was "too strong that a sort of political enthusiasm existed, which seemed to take to itself exclusive republicanism" and held opinions "too much like those which he had cited." In a lengthy critique of the Republicans as the war party and defense of Washington's "system of national independence and fair neutrality," Robert Goodloe Harper on 2 Mch. attributed the Mazzei letter to Jefferson and cited it as an example of the vice president "stigmatizing" Washington's program as one of "ingratitude and injustice to France." Also echoing Jefferson's language, but using it in an implicit defense of him, Albert Gallatin on 1 Mch. delivered a sustained address that rebuked those who would consider "highly criminal" the very expression of the opinion "that there exists in America a Monarchico, Aristocratic Faction who would wish to impose upon us the substance of the British Government." Jefferson's position, in short, could not have been "a very pleasant one," as Theodore Sedgwick observed in a letter to fellow Federalist Rufus King. He noted that Jefferson, while presiding over the Senate, had "more than once" heard from the floor "Philipics pronounced against the author of the letter to Mazzei." Attacks in the Federalist press paralleled the jibes at Jefferson in the Congress. He was, claimed the *Gazette of the United States* in a sly allusion to his paleontological interests, a "great Mammoth of faction."[15]

In the year leading up to the election of 1800, references to the letter continued to appear in a variety of public forums by anti- and pro-Jefferson forces. At a banquet for Alexander Hamilton in Boston on 19 June 1800, a toast was proposed to "The Mechanics of the U.S. May they never act as the *Journeymen* of Jacobinism; nor as *Master-workmen* in the Mazzeian *Babel*." The editor of the *Aurora* on 6 July 1799 published a toast made to "the author of the declaration of independence, who prefers the activity of republicanism to the calm of despotism," language that explicitly echoed the phrases of Jefferson's letter. The *Gazette of the United States*, which reprinted the toast on 8 Aug., found the phrases "*highly obnoxious* and *rebellious*." "Brutus" in Georgia chided one Mr. H—y, whose fourth of July oration had strayed from the intended purpose of such addresses, calling to mind and perpetuating the independence of the United States, to a reviling of Jefferson, the "head of a French party in America," and "the greatest villain in existence." The evidence cited for Jefferson's wickedness was his authorship of the Mazzei letter. The letter, in short, could serve as a convenient touchstone for summing up everything that was objectionable about Jefferson's candidacy, and newspapers did not hesitate to cite it when politically useful. John Marshall, offering his "almost insuperable objections" to a Jefferson presidency, concluded that "the Morals of the Author of the letter to Mazzei cannot be pure."[16]

[15] *Annals*, VII, 1099-1101, 1138, 1192-4; King, *Life*, II, 311; *Gazette of the United States*, 28 Nov. 1798. See also the issues of 27 Jan., 7, 30 Mch., and 20 Dec.

[16] Syrett, *Hamilton*, XXIV, 581; *The Augusta Chronicle and Gazette of the State*, 13, 20 July 1799; Marshall, *Papers*, VI, 46. Marshall mentioned TJ's letter in the appendix to the final volume of his *Life of George Washington*, 5 vols. (Philadelphia, 1804-7), V, app., 36, and published it with extended commentary in the second edition, *Life* (2d ed. rev.;

As a result of the intensely personal attacks on him that the "Mazzei letter" prompted, Jefferson became considerably more circumspect in his correspondence. In the weeks immediately following the publication in the *Minerva* he warned his correspondents to take precautions so that the contents of his letters would not make their way into newspapers. The "hostile use" and the liberty of the press in "mutilating whatever they can get hold of," he said, necessitated his taking this step. The Frenchman Constantin François Chasseboeuf Volney, who visited and corresponded with Jefferson and Madison, in reassuring Madison that nothing he wrote him would find its way into the newspapers promised that he would "not be Mr. Mazzei." [17] Jefferson never chastised Mazzei for making public the contents of the letter or communicated to his former neighbor the serious consequences of his indiscretion. Yet although Jefferson's epistolary record notes the receipt of four letters that Mazzei wrote during 1797, Jefferson did not reply to his old friend until 29 Apr. 1800. [18] That letter, Jefferson observed, would be "short, contain private news only, nothing of politics, and without my name."

During his eight years as president Jefferson wrote to Mazzei infrequently, not nearly as often as Mazzei wrote him. [19] His first communication with the Tuscan after becoming chief executive, dated 17 Mch. 1801, was without a signature and would "hazard nothing but small and familiar matters." After a hiatus of more than three years and well into his first term as president, Jefferson apologized for his negligence but explained that he scarcely wrote "a letter to any friend beyond sea." He went on to observe that the pressure of public business had circumscribed his private correspondence and he worried as well about the probability of his "letters to miscarry, be opened and made ill use of." Cautious though he claimed to be about commenting on political subjects, however, Jefferson could not resist a brief reprise of the sentiments he had expressed to Mazzei on 24 Apr. 1796: "the great body of our country are perfectly returned to their antient principles, yet there remains a phalanx of old tories and monarchists more envenomed as all their hopes become more desperate" (TJ to Mazzei, 18 July 1804). Apparently feeling confident about the opinions of that great body of the country and the potential for his second term as president, Jefferson also sent Mazzei a copy of his second inaugural address, "an account of practice" on the "declaration of principles" that he had set forth in 1801 (TJ

---

2 vols, Philadelphia, 1832), ii, app., 23-32. Marshall was also responsible for rumors that along with portions of Washington's diary from the early 1790s an exchange of letters between Washington and TJ concerning the Mazzei incident had disappeared from Washington's papers, possibly while they were in the custody of Tobias Lear. TJ himself referred to it in his letter to Van Buren, 29 June 1824, discussed above. The editors of Marshall, *Papers*, give no particular credence to the charge against Lear: vi, 192-4. See also Malone, *Jefferson*, vi, 434-5.

[17] See, for example, TJ to Thomas Bell, 18 May 1797; TJ to Peregrine Fitzhugh, 4 June 1797; and TJ to John Moody, 13 June 1797; Madison, *Papers*, xvii, 30.

[18] SJL records letters from Mazzei of 5 Jan., 22 Feb., 21 Apr., and 8 Dec. 1797 that were received on 15 and 16 May, 13 Dec. 1797, and 25 Jan. 1799 that have not been found.

[19] Fewer than eight extant letters went to Mazzei from Jefferson and approximately forty-four went in the other direction. While Mazzei had always written more often to Jefferson than the American had directed letters to him, the imbalance had now become even greater.

to Mazzei, 10 Mch 1805). Whatever lessons Jefferson had learned from his letter of 24 Apr. 1796, he apparently still found it tempting to send some political news across the water and he saw no reason not to retain Mazzei's friendship.

I. Thomas Jefferson to Philip Mazzei

MY DEAR FRIEND   Monticello Apr. 24. 1796.

Your letter of Oct. 26. 1795. is just recieved and gives me the first information that the bills forwarded for you to V.S. & H. of Amsterdam on W. Anderson for £39.17.10$\frac{1}{2}$ and on George Barclay for £70.8.6. both of London have been protested. I immediately write to the drawers to secure the money if still unpaid. I wonder I have never had a letter from our friends of Amsterdam on that subject as well as acknoleging the subsequent remittances. Of these I have apprised you by triplicates, but for fear of miscarriage will just mention that on Sep. 8. I forwarded them Hodgden's bill on Robinson Saunderson & Rumney of Whitehaven for £300. and Jan. 31. that of the same on the same for £137.16.6. both received from Mr. Blair for your stock sold out.   I have now the pleasure to inform you that Dohrman has settled his account with you, has allowed the New York damages of 20. per cent. for the protest, and the New York interest of 7. per cent. and after deducting the partial payments for which he had receipts the balance was three thousand and eighty seven dollars, which sum he has paid into Mr. Madison's hands, and as he (Mr. Madison) is now in Philadelphia, I have desired him to invest the money in good bills on Amsterdam and remit them to the V. Staphorsts & Hubbard whom I consider as possessing your confidence as they do mine, beyond any house in London. The pyracies of that nation lately extended from the sea to the debts due from them to other nations, renders theirs an unsafe medium to do business through. I hope these remittances will place you at your ease, and I will endeavor to execute your wishes as to the settlement of the other small matters you mention: tho' from them I expect little. E.R. is bankrupt, or tantamount to it. Our friend M.P. is embarrassed, but having lately sold the fine lands he lives on, and being superlatively just and honorable I expect we may get whatever may be in his hands. Lomax is under greater difficulties with less means, so that I apprehend you have little more to expect from this country except the balance which will remain for Colle after deducting the little matter due to me, and what will be recovered by Anthony. This will be decided this summer.

I have written to you by triplicates with every remittance I sent to the V.S. & H. and always recapitulated in each letter the objects of the preceding ones. I inclosed in two of them some seeds of the squash as you desired. Send me in return some seeds of the winter vetch, I mean that kind which is sown in autumn and stands thro the cold of winter, furnishing a crop of green fodder in March. Put a few seeds in every letter you may write to me. In England only the spring vetch can be had. Pray fail not in this. I have it greatly at heart.[1]

The aspect of our politics has wonderfully changed since you left us. In place of that noble love of liberty and republican government which carried us triumphantly thro' the war, an Anglican, monarchical and aristocratical party has sprung up, whose avowed object is to draw over us the substance as they have already done the forms of the British government. The main body of our citizens however remain true to their republican principles, the whole landed interest is with them,[2] and so is a great mass of talents. Against us are the Executive, the Judiciary, two out of three branches of the legislature, all of the officers of the government, all who want to be officers, all timid men who prefer the calm of despotism to the boisterous sea of liberty, British merchants and Americans trading on British capitals, speculators and holders in the banks and public funds a contrivance invented for the purposes of corruption and for assimilating us in all things, to the rotten as well as the sound parts of the British model. It would give you a fever were I to name to you the apostates who have gone over to these heresies, men who were[3] Samsons in the field and Solomons in the council, but who have had their heads shorn by the harlot England. In short we are likely to preserve the liberty we have obtained only by unremitting labors and perils. But we shall preserve them, and our mass of weight and wealth on the good side is so great as to leave no danger that force will ever be attempted against us. We have only to awake and snap the Lilliputian cords with which they have been entangling us during the first sleep which succeeded our labors.—I will forward the testimonial of the death of Mrs. Mazzei which I can do the more incontrovertibly as she is buried in my grave yard, and I pass her grave daily. The formalities of the proof you require will occasion delay. John Page and his son Mann are well. The father remarried to a lady from N. York. Beverley Randolph e la sua consorte living and well. Their only child married to the 2d. son of T. M. Randolph. The eldest son you know married my eldest daughter, is an able learned and worthy character, but kept down by ill health. They have two children and still live with me. My younger daughter well. Colo. Innis is well, and a true republican still as are all those beforenamed. Colo. Monroe is our M.P. at Paris a most worthy patriot and honest man. These are the persons you enquire after. I begin to feel the effects of age. My health has suddenly broke down, with symptoms which give me to believe I shall not have much to encounter of the tedium vitae. While it remains however my heart will be warm in it's friendships and among these will always foster the affection with which I am Dear Sir Your friend & servt .... TH: JEFFERSON

RC (DLC: Miscellaneous Manuscripts); with two emendations noted below; endorsed by Mazzei as answered 5 Jan. 1797, beneath which he subjoined the following notes at a later date: "ò scritto poi ai 21 Aprile per il solo [affare] del Moniteur, ed ò incluso la lettera del Ferri. poi il 4 xbre 97. inclusa alla Casa V. in Amsterdana" (translation: I wrote on 21 April for the sole concern of the Moniteur, and I enclosed Ferri's letter. and then on 4 Dec. 97. enclosed to the house of V. in Amsterdam). PrC (DLC); with one change not found on RC (see note 2 below). Tr (DLC); consists of extract in TJ's hand of the first nine sentences of the third paragraph. Tr (MHi: Martin Van Buren Papers); consists of extract in TJ's hand of the first nine sentences of the third paragraph; at head of text: "Extract of a letter from Th: Jefferson to Philip Mazzei. April 24. 96"; enclosed in TJ to Van Buren, 29 June 1824. Tr (DLC: Monroe Papers); consists of incomplete extract in an unidentified hand of the first nine sentences of the third paragraph, parts of the seventh and eighth sentences and all of the ninth sentence being torn away; endorsed on verso by Monroe: "1809. Letter to Mr. Mezzai." Enclosed in TJ to Madison, 24 Apr. 1796.

Mazzei's LETTER of 26 Oct. 1795, erroneously recorded in SJL as a letter of 26 Oct. 1796, was received from Pisa on 15 Apr. 1796, but has not been found. For additional clues to its contents, see TJ to Mann Page, [16 May 1796]. A letter from Mazzei of 11 Apr., received from Pisa on 9 Sep. 1796, is also recorded in SJL but has not been found.

TJ did not receive the Van Staphorst & Hubbard firm's letters of 10 Oct. 1795, the first of which informed him that the BILLS applied to Mazzei's credit had been PROTESTED, until September 1796. I IMMEDIATELY WRITE TO THE DRAWERS: see TJ to

Van Staphorst & Hubbard, 24 Apr. 1796. For his letters to the Dutch firm on 8 SEP. 1795 and 31 JAN. 1796, which have not been located, see TJ's correspondence to Mazzei on those dates.

On his departure from Virginia in 1785 Mazzei had given John BLAIR and Edmund Randolph power of attorney to manage his affairs in Virginia (Mazzei to TJ, 26 Oct. 1785; enclosure to TJ to Mazzei, 5 Apr. 1790; TJ to Mazzei, 2 Aug. 1791). DOHRMAN HAS SETTLED HIS ACCOUNT: see Madison to TJ, 4 Apr. 1796. For TJ's request to Madison TO INVEST THE MONEY for Mazzei, see TJ to Madison, 24 Apr. 1796.

E.R.: Edmund Randolph. OUR FRIEND M.P.: Mann Page. Another Mann Page, mentioned by TJ later in this letter, was the son of the elder Mann's half brother, John Page (Richard C. M. Page, *Genealogy of the Page Family in Virginia* [New York, 1883], 63, 70-1). Acting in Mazzei's behalf TJ brought suit against Kemp Catlett, the purchaser of COLLE, Mazzei's property near Monticello, and did not receive final payment until 1805. ANTHONY Giannini's suit against TJ as Mazzei's agent was DECIDED in TJ's favor in August 1797; see MB, II, 937, 973, 1161; TJ to Mazzei, 30 May 1795; Thomas Mann Randolph, Jr., to TJ, 27 Feb. 1793; TJ to Charles Lilburne Lewis, 4 June 1793.

Mazzei's request for a TESTIMONIAL OF THE DEATH of his first wife in 1788 probably related to his marriage in 1796 to Antonia Antoni (ANB).

[1] Preceding sentence and possibly the one before it inserted by TJ at the end of the line.

[2] In ink on PrC TJ canceled "with them" and interlined "republican."

[3] TJ here canceled a passage reading, "lions in the field and councils when you were here."

II. Extract and Commentary Printed in the Paris *Moniteur*

[25 Jan. 1797]

Notre état politique a prodigieusement changé depuis que vous nous avez quitté. Au lieu de ce noble amour de la liberté et de ce gouvernement républicain, qui nous ont fait passer triomphans à travers les dangers de la guerre, un parti anglicain-monarchico-aristocratique s'est élevé. Son objet avoué est de nous imposer la substance, comme il nous a déjà donné les formes du gouvernement britannique; cependant le corps principal de nos citoyens reste fidele aux principes républicains. Tous les propriétaires fonciers sont pour ces principes, ainsi qu'une grande masse d'hommes à talens. Nous avons contre nous (républicains) le pouvoir exécutif, le pouvoir judiciaire, (deux des trois branches de la législature) tous les officiers du gouvernement, tous ceux qui aspirent à l'être, tous les hommes timides qui préferent le calme du despotisme à la mer orageuse de la liberté, les marchands bretons, et les américains qui trafiquent avec des capitaux bretons, les spéculateurs, les gens intéressés dans la banque et dans les fonds publics. (Etablissemens inventés dans des vues de corruption, et pour nous assimiler au modele britannique dans ses parties pourries.)

Je vous *donnerais la fievre* si je vous nommais les apostats qui ont embrassé ces hérésies, des hommes qui étaient des *Salomons* dans le conseil, et des *Samsons* dans les combats, mais dont la chevelure a été coupée par la *catin Angleterre.*

On voudrait nous ravir cette liberté que nous avons gagnée par tant de travaux et de dangers. Mais nous la conserverons; notre masse de poids et de richesse est trop grande pour que nous ayons à craindre qu'on tente d'employer la force contre nous. Il suffit que nous nous réveillons, et que nous rompions les liens lilliputiens dont ils nous ont garrottés pendant le premier sommeil qui a succédé à nos travaux. Il suffit que nous arrêtions les progres de ce système d'ingratitude et d'injustice envers la France de qui on voudrait nous aliéner pour nous rendre à l'influence britannique, etc.

Cette intéressante lettre, d'un des citoyens les plus vertueux et les plus éclairés des Etats-Unis, explique la conduite des Américains à l'égard de la France. Il est certain que de toutes les puissances neutres et amies, il n'en est aucune de qui la France fût en droit d'attendre plus d'intérêt et de secours que des Etats-Unis. Elle est leur véritable mere Patrie, puisqu'elle a assuré leur liberté et leur indépendance. En fils reconnaissans, loin de l'abandonner, ils devaient s'armer pour sa défense. Mais si des circonstances impérieuses les empêchaient de se déclarer ouvertement pour la République Française, ils devaient du moins faire des démonstrations, et laisser craindre à l'Angleterre que d'un moment à l'autre ils pourraient se déclarer. Cette crainte seule aurait suffi pour forcer le cabinet de Londres à faire la paix. Il est en effet évident que la guerre avec les Etats-Unis portait les coups les plus sensibles au commerce des Anglais, leur donnait des inquiétudes pour la conservation de leurs domaines du continent américain, et leur ôtait les moyens de faire la conquête des colonies françaises et hollandaises.

Aussi ingrat que mauvais politique, le congrès s'est hâté de rassurer les Anglais, afin qu'ils pussent poursuivre tranquillement leur *guerre d'extermination* contre la France, et envahir les colonies et le commerce d'Angleterre. Il envoya à Londres un ministre, M. Jay, connu par son attachement à l'Angleterre et par ses relations personnelles avec lord Grenville, et il conclut à la hâte un traité de commerce qui l'unissait à la Grande-Bretagne, plus qu'un traité d'alliance.

Un pareil traité, dans les circonstances où il a été fait, et par les suites qu'il devait avoir, est un acte d'hostilité envers la France. Le gouvernement français a pu enfin en témoigner le ressentiment de la Nation Française, et il l'a fait en rompant toute communication avec un allié ingrat et infidele, jusqu'à ce qu'il revienne à une conduite plus juste et plus bienveillante. La justice et la saine politique approuvent également cette démarche du gouvernement français. Il n'est pas douteux qu'elle donnera lieu, dans les Etats-Unis, à des discussions qui peuvent faire triompher le parti des bons républicains, des amis de la France.

Quelques écrivains, pour désapprouver cette mesure sage et nécessaire du directoire, soutiennent que dans les Etats-Unis, les Français n'ont pour partisans que *des démagogues qui voudraient renverser le gouvernement actuel.* Mais leurs impudens mensonges de persuadent personne, et ne prouvent seulement, ce qui n'est que trop évident, qu'ils se servent de la liberté de la presse pour servir les ennemis de la France.

Printed in the Paris *Gazette Nationale ou Le Moniteur Universel*, 25 Jan. 1797, being a translation of Document I above; at head of text: "*Florence, le* 1er *janvier. Lettre de M. Jefferson, ci-devant ministre des Etats-Unis en France, et secrétaire au département des affaires étrangeres, à un citoyen de Virginie.* Cette lettre (littéralement traduite) est adressée à M. Mazzei, auteur *des Recherches historiques et politiques sur les Etats-Unis d'Amérique,* demeurant en Toscane." Tr (MHi: Timothy Pickering Papers). Tr (NN).

III. Extract and Commentary Printed in the New York *Minerva*

[2 May 1797]

"Our political situation is prodigiously changed since you left us. Instead of that noble love of liberty, and that republican government, which carried us triumphantly thro the dangers of the war, an Anglo-Monarchico-Aristocratic party has arisen.—Their avowed object is to impose on us the *substance*, as they have already given us the *form*, of the British government. Nevertheless, the principal body of our citizens remain faithful to republican principles. All our proprietors of lands are friendly to those principles, as also the mass of men of talents. We have against us (republicans) the *Executive Power*, the *Judiciary Power*, (two of the three branches of our government) *all the officers of government, all who are seeking offices, all timid men who prefer the calm of despotism to the tempestuous sea of liberty, the British merchants and the Americans who trade on British capitals, the speculators, persons interested in the bank and the public funds.* [Establishments invented with views of corruption, and to assimilate us to the British model in its corrupt parts.]

"I should give you a fever, if I should name the apostates who have embraced these heresies; men who were Solomons in council, and Sampsons in combat, but whose hair has been cut off by the whore England. [In the original, par la catin Angleterre, probably alluding to the woman's cutting off the hair of Sampson, and his loss of strength thereby.]

"They would wrest from us that liberty which we have obtained by so much labor and peril; but we shall preserve it. Our mass of weight and riches is so powerful, that we have nothing to fear from any attempt against us by force. It is sufficient that we guard ourselves, and that *we break the lilliputian ties* by which they have bound us, in the first slumbers which succeeded our labors. It suffices that we arrest the progress of that system of ingratitude and injustice towards France, from which they would alienate us, to bring us under British influence, &c."

Thus far the letter; to which are subjoined, in the French paper, the following remarks:

"This interesting letter from one of the most virtuous and enlightened citizens of the United States, explains the conduct of the Americans in regard to France. It is certain that of all the neutral and friendly powers, there is none from which France had a right to expect more interest and succours than from the United States. *She is their true mother country, since she has assured to them their liberty and independence.*—Ungrateful children, instead of abandoning her, *they ought to have armed in her defense.* But if imperious circumstances had prevented them from openly declaring for the Republic of France, they ought at least to have made demonstrations and excited apprehensions in England, that at some moment or other they should declare themselves. This fear alone would have been sufficient to force the cabinet of London to make peace. It is clear that a war with the United States would strike a terrible blow at the commerce of the English, would give them uneasiness for the preservation of their possessions on the American continent, and deprive them of the means of conquering the French and Dutch colonies.

Equally ungrateful and impolitic, the Congress hastens to encourage the English, that they might pursue in tranquility their war of extermination against France and to invade the Colonies and the commerce of England.* They sent to London a minister, Mr. Jay, known by his attachment to England, and his personal relations to Lord Grenville, and he concluded suddenly a treaty of Commerce which united them with Great Britain, more than a treaty of alliance.

Such a treaty, under all the peculiar circumstances, and by the consequences, which it must produce, is *an act of hostility against France.* The French government in front has testified the resentment of the French nation, by breaking off communication with an *ungrateful and faithless ally,* untill she shall return to a more just and benevolent conduct. Justice and sound policy equally approve this measure of the French government. There is no doubt it will give rise, in the United States, to discussions which may afford a *triumph to the party of good republicans,* the *friends of France.*

Some writers, in disapprobation of this wise and necessary measure of the directory, maintain that in the United States, the French have for partizans only certain demagogues who aim to overthrow the existing government. But their imprudent falsehoods convince no one, and prove only what is too evident, that they use the liberty of the press, to serve the enemies of France."

[The foregoing letter wears all the external marks of authenticity. And yet it seems hardly possible an American could be capable of writing such a letter. As the letter is circulating in Europe, we deem it just, if a forgery, to give Mr. Jefferson an opportunity to disavow it.]

Printed in the New York *Minerva,* 2 May 1797; being a translation of Document II above; with brackets and quotation marks in original; at head of text: "Translated for the Minerva. From the Paris Monitor, of January 25. Florence, January 1. LETTER *From Mr. Jefferson, late Minister of the United States in France, and Secretary to the Department of Foreign Affairs, to a citizen of Virginia.* This letter, literally translated, is addressed to M. Mazzei, author of Researches, historical and political, upon the United States of America, now resident in Tuscany"; at foot of text: " ** There seems to be a mistake in the original in this passage, or we mistake the construction. Translator."*

IV. Italian Translation of Extract

Dopo che ci lasciaste il nostro aspetto politico ha cambiato sorprendentemente. In luogo di quel nobile amor di libertà e di governo repubblicano, che ci portò in trionfo tutto il tempo della guerra, è insorto un partito anglicano monarchico e aristocratico, il cui manifesto oggetto è di tirarci addosso la sostanza del governo inglese, come ce ne hanno già tirate le formalità. Il grosso però dei nostri concittadini resta fedele ai suoi principj repubblicani, e con questi sono tutti quei l'interesse dei quali è l'agricoltura, e una gran massa di talenti. Contro di noi abbiamo i membri del Potere Esecutivo, del Giudiciario e di due dei tre rami del legislativo; tutti quei che sono o bramano di essere in impieghi del Governo; tutti i pusillanimi che preferiscono la calma del dispotismo al burrascoso mare della libertà; i mercanti britanni e quei che trafficano con capitali britanni; gli speculatori e i capitalisti nelle banche e nei fondi pubblici, trappola inventata per corromperci e assomigliarci in tutto al modello inglese, nelle parti putride come nelle solide. Vi darei la febbre, se vi nominassi gli apostati che hanno adottato tali eresie; uomini che sono stati Sansoni in campo e Salomoni in consiglio, ma che hanno avuto la lor testa rasata dalla meretrice Inghilterra. Insomma conserveremo probabilmente la libertà che abbiamo acquisto, col solo mezzo d'incessanti fatiche e pericoli ma la conserveremo; e la nostra massa d'importanza e di ricchezza dalla parte sana è sì grande, da non dover temere che sia mai tentata la forza contro di noi. Basta che ci svegliamo e Strappiamo le corde lilliputiane, colle quali c'impastojno sul primo sonno che successe ai nostri sforzi.

Tr (BNF); consists of an undated translation in an unknown hand of the first nine sentences of the third paragraph of Document I above, possibly made later for use in Mazzei's memoirs; at head of text: "Articolo di Lettera di Tommaso Jefferson ad un so concittadino ed amico in Toscana 24 Aprile 1796" (translation: portion of the letter from Thomas Jefferson to one of his fellow-citizens and friend in Tuscany 24 April 1796). Printed in *Memorie della vita e delle peregrinazioni del fiorentino Filippo Mazzei*, 2 vols. (Lugano, 1845-46), II, 281-2.

To James Madison

Apr. 24. 96.

Yours of the 11th. is recieved, with the letter from Bringhurst. On consideration of all circumstances, I find that the advantages of taking iron from the manufacturer will be more than countervailed by disadvantages. I give up Sharpless therefore. Lownes I must abandon. Above a month ago I wrote to him for an additional ton of rod, merely to furnish a decent occasion to call for nearly that quantity still unfurnished tho paid for so long ago as October last. I find it is not furnished because it was paid for before hand. I therefore conclude to open dealings with Mr. Howel, to whom I have written the inclosed letter, which I have left open for your perusal, merely that understanding the ground of my application, you may have the goodness to call on him, and just make us as it were acquainted in the offset, which will start us with that degree of good understanding that might otherwise require a course of time and dealing to establish. This single office performed, I will give you no further trouble with the business.

With respect to Mazzei's money, I think it safest on the whole to remit it to the Van Staphorsts & Hubbard of Amsterdam, with whom Mazzei is on the best and most confidential terms. I will therefore ask the favor of you to invest it in bills on Amsterdam; not in London bills, as in a former remittance of bills on London payable to the V.S. & H. the drawee availed himself of Mr. Pitt's law forbidding paiment. I will write to V.S. & H. and also to Mazzei by this or the next post, to inform them of what we do, so that you need only put the bills under cover to V.S. & H. and refer them to the explanations they will recieve from me.—Nothing new in politics. We are withering under an unparraleled drought. Adieu affectionately.

P.S. I have written the letters to V.S. & H. and P.M. which I will pray you to have forwarded, for which purpose I inclose them.

RC (DLC: Madison Papers); unsigned; at foot of text: "Mr. Madison." PrC (DLC); lacks postscript. Enclosures: (1) TJ to Samuel Howell, Jr., 24 Apr. 1796 (recorded in SJL, but not found). (2) TJ to Van Staphorst & Hubbard, 24 Apr. 1796. (3) TJ to Philip Mazzei, 24 Apr. 1796.

TJ's letter to Caleb Lownes ABOVE A MONTH AGO was probably that recorded in SJL at 27 Mch. 1796, which has not been found. For TJ's payment to Lownes for three tons of nailrod in OCTOBER 1795, see Statement of Nailery Profits at 30 Sep. 1797.

Samuel HOWELL, Jr. & Company became TJ's major supplier for the nailery between May and Sep. 1796 with TJ purchasing six tons of nailrod and one-half ton of hoop iron from the company. Along with enclosure No. 1 listed above, SJL records that TJ wrote letters to Samuel Howell, Jr., son of the eminent Philadelphia merchant of the same name, on 22 May, 19 June, 13 Nov. 1796, and 26 Mch. 1797, but none have been found. Letters from Howell to TJ of 9 May, 15 June, 25 Nov. 1796, which according to SJL were received on 21 May, 2 July, and 4 Dec., respectively, are also missing. According to SJL TJ exchanged correspondence with George Howell of Philadelphia during this same period. Letters from this Howell to TJ of 16 May, 5, 28 July, 7 and 26 Sep., which according to SJL were received 3 June, 15 July, 6 Aug., 16 Sep., and 8 Oct., 1796, respectively, have not been found. Neither have letters from TJ to Howell of 17 July and 28 Aug. 1796. George Howell was perhaps the son of the the firms namesake who ultimately inherited his grandfather Samuel Howell's estate (Josiah Granville Leach, *Genealogical and Biographical Memorials of the Reading, Howell, Yerkes, Watts, Latham, and Elkins Families* [Philadelphia, 1898], 153, 159-63, 170-2, 180; Statement of Nailery Profits at 30 Sep. 1797).

To Van Staphorst & Hubbard

<small>GENTLEMEN</small>   Monticello in Virginia Apr. 24. 1796.

My letters to you covering remittances on behalf of Mr. Mazzei have been of May 27. and Sep. 8. 1795. and Jan. 31. 1796. By a letter from Mr. Mazzei I am advised that that of May 27. got safe to hand, but that the bills on Anderson of London for £39–17–10½ and George Barclay of the same place for £70–8–6 were refused paiment in consequence of the hostilities between Gr. Britain and the U. Netherlands. I shall in consequence immediately write to the drawers to redemand the money if it be still witheld.

I will just recapitulate that my letter of Sep. 8. covered Hodgeden's bill on Robinson &c. of Whitehaven for £300. and that of Jan. 31. covered a bill of the same on the same for £137–16 6.

I have now the pleasure to inform you that Dohrman has settled his account, the balance due from him to Mr. Mazzei three thousand and eighty seven dollars, which sum I have desired Mr. Madison (now in Philadelphia) to invest in good bills on Amsterdam and remit to you to be held subject to the order of Mr. Mazzei, which I hope he will be able to do, and to forward with this present letter. I shall be anxious to hear from you that it is safely recieved, as well as the remittances of Sep. 8. and Jan. 31.

I wrote to you Feb. 28. 96. on our separate affairs to which I beg leave to refer you and attend your answer, and am with great esteem Gentlemen Your friend & servt   TH: JEFFERSON

<small>PrC (DLC); at foot of text: "Messrs. Nichs. & Jac. V. Staphorst & Hubbard"; endorsed by TJ in ink on verso. Enclosed in TJ to Madison, 24 Apr. 1796.</small>

<small>LETTERS . . . COVERING REMITTANCES: see TJ to Philip Mazzei, 30 May, 8 Sep. 1795, and 31 Jan. 1796.</small>

To Thomas Mann Randolph

<small>TH:J. TO TMR.</small>   [25 Apr. 1796]

I have not written to you by the last posts expecting you would be on the road. Your last seems to suppose you may still recieve this at Richmond. The lad whom you mention to have eloped from Varina is at Edgehill. My groceries, and rope are arrived at Charlottesville. We had in the mean time fallen on an easy and quick method of taking down our columns, which was but the work of one day. I paid for you the other day the balance of a small note in the hands of T. Walker, which I presumed to be right, but reserved open for your correction. The money which I shall have to pay you for F. Walker and Mrs. Gilmer will be in Richmond where I expect it will be convenient for your purposes. It is partly there now in the hands of Charles Johnston, and can all be there at short warning.—We are experiencing the greatest drought remembered at this season. The oats and clover newly sown cannot sprout. The old clover instead of shooting up is growing white. It looks at this moment much like rain, tho rather cold as it has generally been through the spring. Wheat has suffered little yet. Corn will feel the effect because all ploughing has been suspended some time. It will gain somewhat however by taking the place of tobacco in the fields prepared for that, and which for want of plants must be otherwise applied. We are all well. Jefferson as robust and tanned as a sailor. Greatly delighted with the glass from Anne, which he kept near half an hour before he broke it. My love to my dear Martha. Adieu affectionately

P.S. Pray try if possible to know from whom we can get salt herrings as soon as they can be ready. My demand will be very great.

RC (DLC: TJ Papers, 104: 17905); undated, but assigned on basis of SJL and internal evidence.

Randolph's LAST letter of 18 Apr. 1796, recorded in SJL as received from Varina five days later, has not been found.

TJ paid $27.31, the amount of Randolph's NOTE IN THE HANDS of Thomas Walker, on 22 Apr. 1796. After he returned to Monticello, Randolph contested the payment, claiming that he had paid the debt on 7 Jan. 1795 (MB, II, 939; Randolph to Thomas Walker, 2 June 1796, in DLC: Rives Papers).

From Bushrod Washington

DEAR SIR   Richd April 26. 1796

I am Just setting off to Fredg. and have only time to enclose you with a N. Subpa., which please have delivered to the proper Shf. Your Letter respecting the other Suit, against Wayle's Exers. I received and shall attend to. With much respect I am Dear Sir Yr. Mo Ob Sert

B WASHINGTON

RC (MHi); endorsed by TJ as received 30 Apr. 1796 and so recorded in SJL.

YOUR LETTER: see note to Washington to TJ, 2 Nov. 1795.

From Edward Rutledge

Charleston April 30th. 1796.

Your Countryman, Mr. John Randolph, is on the wing for Virginia; and as he intends to pay you a Viset, in a short time after his Return, I have requested him to put this Letter into your Hands. I rejoice to see that, the popular branch of our Government have given a firm, and decided opposition, to one of the most unfortunate Treaties which ever was made, and I most sincerely wish they may adhere to their present apparent Resolution. True it is, that the people of America are placed in a predicament that, has left them nothing but a Choice of Evils; yet it is fortunate they have a Choice, and that they have the Liberty of preferring a temporary obstruction to their Commerce, and a suspension to their progress to Wealth; to the Abandonment of national Honor, and the establishment of principles, which will be permanently injurious. After saying so much, of this Treaty, would you beleive it possible, my Friend, that whilst I have reflected on the Subject, my *Mind*, not my *Tongue*, has some times been disposed to dart a Ray of Censure *on you*; feeling, as it does a Conviction, that no Instructions from your Office would have ever been sent, to warrant such a Treaty, or any influence so great, over the Mind of the President as to induce him to ratify it. But I sincerely believe, he unfortunately committed himself too far in the first Instance, and the Weight of Talent in favor of the Measure, (behind the Curtain,) were superior to those which were opposed to it. I say, behind the Curtain, because it is certain that the President did not approve it; that nothing was to be either hoped, or feared, from the Abilities of the present Secretaries; and that a third Person, was consulted. Had you remained at your post, you might have prevented the Mission; if not, you might have confined the Business of the Negociator, to that which was the ostensible Object; and had you failed on those points, you might have ultimately evinced the false Effects of such a Treaty. The time which you have employed, in studying the Interests of your Country, and the intimate Knowledge which you have acquired of those Interests, had well fitted you for the Office. But I am lamenting when it is too late, and will therefore quit the Subject for a private one.

I am much pleased with the Account which my Son has given me of you, and more than commonly satisfied with your reception of him. He is now on a tour to the Southern parts of this State, reviewing the Militia in the Character of Aid de Camp to his Uncle General Pinckney; but he has not been unmindful of your Commission. The Trees are in Boxes, and shall be sent at their proper Season. I shall be happy to think that I shall have placed any thing so immediately before your Eye, as to

[. . .] frequent recollection, one who esteem you, with the sin[. . .] very affectionate Fri[end]   ED: RUT[LEDGE]

RC (DLC); last page clipped; addressed: "The Honble. Thomas Jefferson Esquire"; endorsed by TJ as received 6 June 1796 and so recorded in SJL.

TREES ARE IN BOXES: see TJ to Rutledge, 30 Nov. 1795.

To James Lyle

DEAR SIR   Monticello May 1. 1796.

Finding that I cannot depend on the profits of my plantations for paying off the last bond to Kippen &c. I have come to a resolution to sell two tracts of land, the one in Bedford, the other here, and have given directions in Bedford accordingly. If they can be sold, they will effect the whole paiment. The sale will yet require some time, and the circumstances of our country always require credit you know. This renders it impossible for me to fix precise times of paiment of the balance; they shall be shortened as much as possible. In the mean time perhaps better seasons than we have had may enable me to do something from the ordinary resources of my plantations. I can only answer for sincere intentions and efforts to wipe off this old score honestly in the end, and as speedily as I shall be able. My peace as well as your interests urge me to this. I am with sincerity Dear Sir Your friend & servt

TH: JEFFERSON

PrC (MHi); at foot of text: "Mr. James Lyle"; endorsed in ink by TJ on verso.

BOND TO KIPPEN: see Notes on the Account with Richard Harvie & Company, 22 July 1795.

From James Madison

DEAR SIR   Philada. May 1. 1796

I have your favor of the 17 Apl. covering two Extracts one from your notes, the other from mine. The latter corresponds with the recollection which myself, and other members had expressed; and the former with that of Majr. Butler, and with the Journals of the Senate. The Report of the Committee to which you refer, can not be found, tho' Mr. B. says he knows one was made. This enquiry has been set on foot without your name.

The Treaty question was brought to a vote on friday in Committee of whole. Owing to the absence (*certainly* casual and momentary) of one member, and the illness of another, the Committee were divided 49 and 49. The Chairman (Muhlenberg) decided in the affirmative, saying that in the House it would be subject to modification which he wished. In the House yesterday, an Enemy of the Treaty moved a preamble, reciting "that altho' the Treaty was highly objectionable, yet considering all circumstances, particularly the duration for two years &c. and confiding in the efficacy of measures that might be taken for stopping the Spoliations and impressments &c." For this ingredient, which you will perceive the scope of, all who meant to persevere against the Treaty, with those who only yielded for the reasons expressed in it, ought to have united in voting, as making the pill a bitter one to the Treaty party, as well as less poisonous to the public interest. A few wrongheads however thought fit to separate, whereby the motion was lost by one vote. The main question was then carried in favor of the Treaty by 51 against 48. This revolution was foreseen, and might have been mitigated tho' not prevented, if sooner provided for. But some who were the first to give way to the crisis under its actual pressure, were most averse to prepare for it. The progress of this business throughout has to me been the most worrying and vexatious that I ever encountered; and the more so as the causes lay in the unsteadiness, the follies, the perverseness, and the defections among our friends, more than in the strength or dexterity, or malice of our opponents. It is impossible for me to detail these causes to you now. My consolation under them is in the effect they have in riveting my future purposes. Had the preamble condemning the Treaty on its merits, exercising the discretionary power of the House, and requiring from the Ex. a stoppage of the spoliations &c., been agreed to, I have reason to believe, the Treaty party would have felt it a compleat defeat. You will be informed by the newspapers of the means practised for stirring up petitions &c. in favor of the Treaty. The plan was laid in this City and circulated by a correspondence thro' the Towns every where. In the mean time the Banks, the British merchants, the insurance Companies were at work in influencing individuals, beating down the prices of produce, and sounding the tocksin of foreign war, and domestic convulsions. The success has been such as you would suppose. In several neighbouring districts the people have been so deluded as to constrain their Representatives to renounce their opposition to the Treaty. An appeal to the people on any pending measure, can never be more than an appeal to those in the neighbourhood of the Govt. and to the Banks, the merchants and the dependents and expectants of the Govt. at a distance. Adieu affy. J. M. Jᴿ

RC (DLC: Madison Papers); at foot of text: "Mr. Jefferson"; endorsed by TJ as received 14 May 1796 and so recorded in SJL.

When the TREATY QUESTION WAS BROUGHT TO A VOTE in the committee of the whole on 29 Apr. 1796, the temporary ABSENCE of Joseph B. Varnum of Massachusetts and the ILLNESS of John Patten of Delaware led to a tie that was broken by chairman Frederick A.C. Muhlenberg of Pennsylvania, who voted to approve the resolution calling for appropriations so it could be considered on the floor of the House. The next day Massachusetts Republican Henry Dearborn, AN ENEMY OF THE TREATY, introduced a PREAMBLE to the resolution which explained why the House was voting to carry the British treaty into effect even though it was "highly objectionable, and may prove injurious to the United States." By close votes the phrase was modified to say only that the treaty was "objectionable."

The preamble, which noted that the last 18 articles of the treaty were "to continue in force only during the present war, and two years thereafter" and expressed hope that the executive would take measures to bring a stop to the violation of neutral shipping rights and the impressment of seamen, was rejected by a vote of 49 to 50. The House then voted to pass the laws necessary to execute the treaty. On 6 May 1796 President Washington signed the acts for carrying all four treaties considered by the House during April into effect. The WRONGHEADS who voted against the preamble included Thomas Claiborne, John Heath, and Josiah Parker of Virginia, Nathan Bryan of North Carolina, and Thomas Sprigg of Maryland (JHR, II, 528-31, 542; *Annals*, v, 1280-92).

From James Madison

DEAR SIR   May 9. 1796

I have your letter on the subject of Mr. Howell and seen the old gentleman who interests himself in it. I think it probable you will find reason to be satisfied with the change you have made in your merchant. I have not yet been able to procure bills on Amsterdam for Van Staphorst. They can be got I am told, but not with so much ease or choice, as on London. I shall not intermit my attention to that object.

We have had a calm ever since the decision on the Treaty. Petitions however continue to arrive, chiefly in favor of the Treaty. The N. England States have been ready to rise in mass against the H. of Reps. Such have been the exertions and influence of Aristocracy, Anglicism, and mercantilism in that quarter, that Republicanism is perfectly overwhelmed, even in the Town of Boston. I hope it will prove but a transitory calamity; and that the discovery of the delusion, will ultimately work a salutary effect. The people have been every where made to believe that the object of the H. of Reps. in resisting the Treaty was—*War*; and have thence listened to the summons "to follow where Washington leads." Nothing late from abroad. We expect to adjourn about the 20 or 25 inst: Adieu Yrs. affy   Js. MADISON JR

We has just had a most plentiful rain after a drought nearly as severe as that with you.

RC (DLC: Madison Papers); addressed: "Thomas Jefferson Charlottesville via Rich-   mond Virginia"; franked and postmarked; endorsed by TJ as received from Philadelphia on 21 May 1796 and so recorded in SJL.

LETTER ON THE SUBJECT OF MR. HOWELL: TJ to Madison, 24 Apr. 1796.

A meeting held in BOSTON on 28 Apr. 1796 led to a pro-treaty memorial signed by 1,300 citizens and the appointment of a committee which drew up and sent a circular letter to every town in the state, declaring that if the House of Representatives persisted "in delaying their concurrence to give operation to the Treaty," peace would give way to "War! Horrid War!" Under these conditions, the memorialists exhorted, "it is impossible to doubt as to our choice—We cannot hesitate to follow where Washington leads" and choose peace and prosperity over war and distress (*Philadelphia Gazette*, 7 May 1796).

To James Lyle

DEAR SIR   Monticello May 12. 1796.

The present representative of Farrell & Jones has brought a suit against the executors of Mr. Wayles as *security* for the late R. Randolph on the foundation of a loose and equivocal expression in a letter neither meant as an engagement by Mr. Wayles nor understood as such by F. & J. I do not believe there is the smallest danger of it's being so understood by a court or jury, but as all things are possible and the sum so large that it would cripple my efforts to pay my real and honest debt to Henderson McCaul & Co. I inclose you a mortgage on a number of negroes sufficient to secure them effectually. I cannot pretend that the debt can be paid punctually at the instalments there provided for: on this head I shall count on the indulgence you have hitherto shewn by which both their debt and my fortune may in the long run be saved. You had better send the deed to your correspondent in Charlottesville where it may be proved by the witnesses or acknoleged by myself: and that without delaying a single post, as Mr. Hanson, if he gets his judgment will be upon us immediately. I am with great esteem Dear Sir Your affectionate friend & servt   TH: JEFFERSON

P.S. The sum not yet actually recieved is merely guessed at.

PrC (MHi); at foot of text: "Mr. James Lyle"; endorsed in ink by TJ on verso.

Although the enclosure printed below secured a financial obligation, TJ's primary motivation in drawing up this and several other instruments mortgaging most of his slaves in 1796 seems to have been to shield them from pending legal action for claims against the estate of his father-in-law, John Wayles. Virginia law—which defined slaves as personal property and allowed creditors to attach them for debt—prohibited slaveholders from using verbal conveyances, or even emancipation, to prevent slaves from being seized by creditors. TJ here employed an alternative tactic, giving mortgages to friendly creditors who were not likely to take his slaves (Shepherd, *Statutes*, I, 128-9; McColley, *Slavery*, 80-1; Malone, *Jefferson*, III, 179).

In addition to the 52 slaves here mortgaged to Henderson, McCaul & Company, TJ gave in collateral a total of 98 other slaves to William Short, Wakelyn Welch, Sr., Philip Mazzei, and the Dutch firm of

Van Staphorst & Hubbard. The deed of mortgage to Van Staphorst & Hubbard of 12 May 1796 and the present letter to Lyle with its enclosure are the only surviving texts of the May 1796 documents known to the Editors. TJ did not immediately inform all of the mortgagees of his action. According to SJL he wrote a letter to Short on 18 May 1796 that was to be "lodged with T.B.," and also wrote a letter of the same date to Thomas Bell, neither of which has been found. Only in 1800 did TJ tell Short of the mortgage indenture, which was still in Bell's keeping (TJ to Short, 13 Apr. 1800). Six months after drawing up the original mortgage documents, TJ drew up a new instrument conveying to Van Staphorst & Hubbard "his right and equity of redemption" in all 150 previously mortgaged slaves (see Deed of Mortgage of Slaves to Van Staphorst & Hubbard, 21 Nov. 1796). This second mortgage, the sole source of information about the missing agreements of May, nominally secured a new loan of $2,000 from Van Staphorst & Hubbard, but there is no evidence that TJ informed the firm of the mortgage, and he soon gave bonds to guarantee the loan—which suggests that the November mortgage, like those of May, was intended primarily to preserve his property in slaves against creditors (Van Staphorst & Hubbard to TJ, 21 May 1796; TJ to Van Staphorst & Hubbard, 27 Mch. 1797).

PRESENT REPRESENTATIVE OF FARRELL & JONES: Richard Hanson.

John Wayles's LOOSE AND EQUIVOCAL EXPRESSION, which concerned the consignment to him and Richard Randolph of 280 Africans transported to Virginia in the slave ship *The Prince of Wales*, appears in the first sentence of a letter Wayles wrote to the British firm of Farell & Jones on 14 May 1772—not, as the Editors mistakenly stated in Vol. 15: 649n, in Wayles's letter to John Thompson of 9 May 1770 (see Henry Skipwith to TJ, 7 Apr. 1791). For the conclusion of the case in Wayles's executors' favor, see TJ's letter to John Read of 25 June 1798. In Vol. 15, partly from a misreading of the date of TJ's letter to Lyle printed above, the Editors also conflated elements of three distinct lawsuits against the Wayles estate: the suit by Farell & Jones over the *Prince of Wales* consignment; another suit brought by the same firm concerning an obligation of John Randolph; and a third case, not involving Farell & Jones, over a bond to James Bivins (see editorial note and Documents I and VI of a group of documents on the debt to Farell & Jones, printed in Vol. 15: 647-9, 653; for the Bivins case, see List of Unretained Letters, [ca. 9 June 1794]).

CORRESPONDENT IN CHARLOTTESVILLE: possibly Richard Harvie (see Notes on the Account with Richard Harvie & Company, 22 July 1795).

ENCLOSURE

Deed of Mortgage of Slaves to Henderson, McCaul & Company

This indenture made on the 12th. day of May 1796. between Thomas Jefferson of Albemarle in Virginia of the one part, and Messrs. Henderson McCaul & Co. of Great Britain merchants and partners of the other part, witnesseth, that for the purpose of securing to the said Henderson McCaul & Co. several sums of money due to them from the said Thomas by several bonds amounting to about fifteen hundred pounds with interest, and in consideration that the said Henderson McCaul & Co. will forbear to demand by process in law, one third of the said debt till July 1797. one other third till July 1798. and one other third till July 1799, and for the further consideration of five shillings in hand paid to the said Thomas on their part, the said Thomas hath given, granted and conveyed to the said Henderson McCaul & Co. the following slaves to wit, Jame Hubbard and Cate his wife, and Armistead, Rachael, Burrel, Nace, Maria, Eve,

Philip, Sarah and Nancy their children, Will smith and Abbey his wife and Jesse, Sal, Lucy, Dick, Flora, Fanny, Edy and Armstead their children, Bess and Hal, Caesar and Cuffy her children, Suck and Cate, Daniel and Stephen her children, Hercules and Bet his wife and Austin, Gawen, Cate, Mary and Hercules their children, Hanah and Lucinda, Reuben and Solomon her children, Dick and Dinah his wife and John, Aggey, Moses, and Evans their children, all residing on the lands of the said Thomas called Poplar Forest in Bedford and Campbell, and Lucinda and Sarah, Sandy, and Sousy her children, residing on his lands called Lego in Albemarle, and Frank and Toby residing at Monticello in Albemarle, in all fifty two, to have and to hold the said slaves to them the said Henderson McCaul & Co. their heirs executors, and administrators. Provided that if the said Thomas shall pay to them, one third of the said debt and interest before July 1797. one other third before July 1798. and one other third before July 1799. or if the said Henderson McCaul & Co. should demand in law earlier paiment, then these presents to be void. In witness whereof the said Thomas hath hereto put his hand and seal on the day and year first above written.

PrC (MHi); unsigned, entirely in TJ's hand.

Deed of Mortgage of Slaves to Van Staphorst & Hubbard

This indenture made on the 12th. day of May 1796. between Thomas Jefferson of Virginia of the one part and Nicholas & Jacob Vanstaphorst & Hubbard of Amsterdam, bankers, of the other part, witnesseth that whereas the said Thomas is indebted to them in the two sums of one thousand and four dollars fifty four cents, and eight hundred and eighty eight dollars sixty seven cents making together eighteen hundred ninety three dollars twenty one cents for so much paid for him by them to the United states, for the purpose of securing the said whole sum lastmentioned, to them, and in consideration that they will forbear to demand by process in law one third of the said sum and interest till July 1797. one other third and interest till July 1798. and one other third and interest till July 1799. and for the further consideration of five shillings to him by them paid he the said Thomas hath given granted and conveyed to the said Nicholas & Jacob Van Staphorst & Hubbard the following slaves to wit, Ned and Jenny his wife and Ned, Fanny, Dick, Gill and Scilla their children, Rachael and Naney and Abram her children, old Betty and Val. residing at the lands of the said Thomas in Albemarle called Tufton, and Bagwell and Minerva his wife and Ursula, Mary and Virginia their children residing on his lands in Albemarle called Lego, in all seventeen to have and to hold the said slaves to the said Nicholas & Jacob Van Staphorst & Hubbard their heirs executors and administrators. Provided that if the said Thomas shall pay to the said Nicholas & Jacob Van Staphorst & Hubbard one third of the said debt and interest before July 1797. one [other] third before July 1798. and one other third before July 1799. or if they should demand in law earlier paiment then these presents to be void. In witness whereof the said Thomas hath hereto set his hand and seal the day first above written.

PrC (DLC); unsigned, entirely in TJ's hand; faded.

To Francis Walker

DEAR SIR   Monticello May 14. 1796

I now send you the nails desired, as is stated below. I must beg you, my dear Sir, to push the supply of corn as far as you possibly can. At the time I recieved your letter, I had an agent gone in quest of corn into the quarter you mention, to wit, Louisa and Orange; he returned having been able to get but 20. barrels, which is very far short of what will be necessary for our bread; for as to horses &c. I do not allow one grain to be given. I had found much repose to my mind in the extent of the supply expected from you. Not that I would encroach on the quantity necessary for yourself but only set up my necessities in opposition to those of any subsequent applicants. I am with sincere esteem Dear Sir Your friend & servt   TH: JEFFERSON

℔		£		
91 of VIs.	@ 11½d	4– 7–2½		(6/8½ per ₥)
80. of XVIs.	@ 9½d	3– 3–4		(15/10 per ₥)
		7–10–6½		
	cask	– 1		
		7–11–6½		

RC (DLC: Rives Papers); addressed: "Francis Walker esq. Castlehill."

Walker's LETTER of 12 May 1796, recorded in SJL as received the same day, has not been found.

From Archibald Stuart

DR SIR   Staunton 15th. May 1796

Your favor on the Subject of the Stone-Mason was received while at New-London. Immediately on my arrival at home I waited on him in hopes of being able to persude him to undertake your business but found it impracticable and should have written to you immediately to that effect had not Mr. Coalter Informed me he had done so. I then had recourse to a Mr. Jewell whom I could have recommended but found him engaged also.

I have Just returned from the court of Bath where I saw a Mr. Cavendish from Greenbrier who tells me that some people who were Makeing Salt-Petre in a large cave in that county have found a bone of the toe of some Animal eight or ten inches long and half as thick as his Wrist. That the end of it which went into the claw was as thick and almost as long as his finger. He has promised to send it to Me, as soon as I receive it shall forward it to you by the first safe Opportunity. The Frost has been so severe here as to Injure some of our forward rye and to kill the foliage in many places. I am with respect and esteem yr very H Servant

ARCHIBALD STUART

RC (ViW); at foot of text: "Thos Jefferson Esqr"; endorsed by TJ as received 20 May 1796 and so recorded in SJL.

YOUR FAVOR: TJ to Stuart, 5 Apr. 1796.

A letter from Stuart to TJ of 9 Apr., recorded in SJL as received 15 Apr. 1796, and another from John COALTER to TJ of 24 Apr., recorded in SJL as received 29 Apr. 1796, have not been found.

To Mann Page

TH: JEFFERSON TO MANN PAGE   Monticello [16 May 1796]

I am growing old, and am grown lazy, and particularly [in wri]ting letters. Yet, when any circumstance of business [orders] [. . .] to take up a pen for an old friend, I [. . .] feel the warmth [of earlier] years rekindle in my heart. While writing to you I am (in imagination) at Rosewell, 25 years old, in all the vigour of love and liberty. It is unpleasant that we should have been made, like our watches, to wear out by degrees, lose our teeth, and become unfit for our functions. A musical glass would have been a better type, sound, strong, and vibrating in all it's harmony till some accident shivers it to atoms.—But I am forgetting my business. I have just recieved a letter from our friend Mazzei, who is settled at Pisa and in want of common necessaries. He presses me to glean up some little matters he left here. He mentions a chair and horse left with you for sale, and something, he does not recollect what, with Mr. Lomax. If you have any thing in your hands, or can [. . .] from Mr. Lomax whatever he may have and place it in any hands in Richmond, I will have it remitted. In the application which I trouble you to make to Mr. Lomax (on account of your greater vicinity to him) pray convey to him my affectionate remembrance and respects, which neither time nor distance has lessened. I am full of business for this year. Besides the attention to my farms I am uncovering and repairing my house, which during my absence had gone much to decay. I make some alterations in it with a greater eye to convenience than I had when younger. Present my friendly respects to Mrs. Page. Adieu affectionately.

PrC (MHi) badly faded; date assigned on the basis of SJL and internal evidence (see note below); endorsed by TJ in ink: "Page Mann. probably 95."

This letter is almost certainly the missive to Page listed in SJL under 16 May 1796. The recently received LETTER FROM . . . MAZZEI, not found, is that of 26 Oct. 1795, TJ's reply to which dealt *inter alia* with Page (see TJ to Mazzei, 30 May 1795, 24 Apr. 1796).

From Alexandre Lerebours

Philadelphie 28 floreal an 4e. de
MONSIEUR   la République française (17 Mai 1796)

En traversant l'océan atlantique pour venir dans cette intéressante partie du nouveau monde, mon dessein était d'y propager les découvertes utiles de mon pays, et je vous prie d'accepter quelques mémoires et rapports que j'ai apportés de france concernant divers inventions et decouvertes dans les Sciences, les Arts-mécaniques et les métiers: La plupart de ces inventions ont été couronnées par les Sociétés savantes de Paris et ont mérité des recompenses nationales.

Je viens de recevoir de france plusieurs Journaux de Science et de littérature, et je me propose d'en faire une analyse que j'aurai soin de vous faire parvenir.

Je dois vous annoncer que nous avons en france un Tribunal de savans érigé, au nom du législateur, pour juger des inventions et découvertes, et decerner aux inventeurs les recompenses nationales. Les Savans qui composent ce tribunal sont pris dans les principales Sociétés savantes de Paris.

Autrefois les Ministres et les Rois prononçaient sur les ouvrages des Savans et des Philosophes; mais [on] conçoit aujourd'hui que c'était le comble du ridicule [et] de l'ignominie que de laisser l'ignorance, le Sceptre [en] main, juger, dans ses caprices souverains et pervers, les monumens du génie. J'ai l'honneur d'être très respectueusement, Monsieur, Votre très humble et très obéissant serviteur

ALEXANDRE LEREBOURS

RC (MoSHi: Jefferson Papers); second page torn; endorsed by TJ and recorded in SJL as received 4 July 1796. Enclosures not found.

Alexandre Lerebours of Paris was in the United States by 1794, for that year he ad-dressed a paper to the American Philosophical Society on recent discoveries and inventions in France and donated a group of pamphlets on the subject. He was elected to membership in the society on 15 Apr. 1796 (APS, *Proceedings*, XXII, pt. 3 [1884], 227, 238).

The JOURNAUX DE SCIENCE ET DE LITTÉRATURE may have included eight numbers of the *Journal des Arts et Manufactures publié sous la direction du bureau consultatif des arts et manufactures* that Lerebours presented to the American Philosophical Society in November 1796 (APS, *Proceedings*, XXII, pt. 3 [1885], 243). TRIBUNAL DE SAVANS: probably the National Institute of Arts and Sciences, established by a decree of 25 Oct. 1795, which replaced the Bureau de Consultation des Arts et Métiers and was to consist of 144 members in Paris, an equal number of associates residing elsewhere in the Republic, and 24 affiliated foreigners. Among other activities, it would award annual prizes for inventions and discoveries (Stewart, *French Revolution*, 638-41; R. R. Palmer, *The Improvement of Humanity: Education and the French Revolution* [Princeton, N.J., 1985], 235).

From Patrick White

SIR   Petersburg May 19th. 1796

I am favoured with yours of the 7th. which came to me by the hands of Messrs. Buchannan Dunlop & Co. the 14th. I never knew that John Banisters debt to you was partly a Bill of exchange and a note, as this is the case if you will forward them to your friends in Richmond with a Receipt in full for the debt he owed you I will pay your demand of Sixty three pounds three shillings and 8d. current money though you will please observe you charge interest on £34.2.4 from 1st. January 91 until the 5th. of the present month. I think with you that interest is but a trifling compensation for the service you rendered Mr. Banister in France yet I must in every Respect be governed by the Law in what I do as administrator to his Estate. I fear there will be a deficiency in his personal estate towards the payment of the different demands. I am wh. Respect &C.   P. W

FC (Lb in MiU-C); at head of text: "Thomas Jefferson Esquire"; recorded in SJL as received 27 May 1796.

TJ's letter OF THE 7TH. and another of 28 May 1796, both recorded in SJL, have not been found.

From William Strickland

DEAR SIR   London May 20th: 1796

Since my return home I have executed as fully as I have been able, tho not as compleatly as I could have wished the principal commission with which you charged me, that of procuring you the varieties of peas and vetches; those which I send you and of which some account is given in another paper which accompanies this are the sorts usually cultivated in this country, and all with which I am acquainted, tho I have heard that there are some other varieties cultivated in some parts of the country, possessing similar properties with these, propagated in the same manner and applied to the same purposes, but I rather suspect them to be the same plants bearing different names in different places; the whole of these form an essential article in the modern system of improved agriculture; they constitute one of the crops which succeed the very exhausting crops of grain, and that too in soils not sufficiently fertile to produce others of the intervening crops; they not only thereby prevent the too frequent recurrance of grain by which the soil is exhausted, but they seem to possess in themselves, either the power of restoring the agitating properties of the soil, or enable the soil more powerfully to attract from the atmosphere or otherwise to acquire those properties when coverd by their dense shade, than it would have were it exposed naked and bare to the influence of the atmosphere; Philosophy has not yet sufficiently accompanied agriculture to have ascertained how the earth regains the properties of which it has been deprived and the agriculturist is contented with the fact, without reasoning on the cause.

You pointed out to me some other kinds of Vetches which had been cultivated by Miller; but of them I can gain no intelligence; they are now known only to the Botanists; probably being found neither useful nor ornamental their cultivation ceased in this country soon after their introduction.

I send you along with the above mentiond seeds; a small parcel containing seeds of several of the vetch tribe, the native wild produce of this country; I gathered them some years since with a view of trying experiments with them for the purposes of Agriculture, and they still may possess the power of vegitation: while on the subject of vetches, I must remark to you; that in various parts of the mountains of Virginia particularly the Blue ridge, I observed several different plants, apparently of the Vetch tribe, and some probably perennial, growing spontaneously and very luxuriantly in the woods, one in particular with a Pink and white flower nearly as large as that of a cultivated Pea; these I should recommend to the attention of the American cultivator as the climate and soil would probably suit them better, than those from Europe; besides the *pea vine* which is no other than a vetch and which is highly nutricious to cattle, is known still to grow plentifully and spontaneously to the West of the mountains, and probably was formerly equally plentiful to the East of them, but it has there long since carried its own destruction in its own good qualities. This appears highly worthy of attention.

When at Monticello you shewd me the first field of Clover that had been sown in that part of Virginia, from observations I afterwards made I have no doubt of its thriving as well there, as elsewhere in America, and I see not why you should not equal the luxuriant crops of Pensylvania; but where the clover grows so vigorously it is necessary for some grass to be sown among it, to support its weight and keep it from lying too close to the ground; no other grass has hitherto been applied to the purpose in America than Timothy grass; but it does not answer it perfectly, not vegitating uniformly with the clover; the consequence of which is, that at hay time, either the clover must be cut too late to accommodate the timothy, or the latter too early in order that the clover may be cut when at its greatest perfection: after I left you I saw a single instance of the Meadow cocksfoot-grass (Dactylis gromerata) one of our best meadow grasses growing extremely luxuriantly; which appears to me likely every way to answer the purpose of Timothy, better than that grass, whether sown with Clover, or separately for pasturage; as it is not a grass the seed of which is separately collected and sown in this country, I have collected a few heads of it in the fields, and would have sent you more had I been able to procure them after the late period of my arrival in the Country; I recommend them to your care, and think they will reward you for what you bestow upon them.

Where the improvement of the agriculture of a country can go hand in hand, with the improvement of the morals of a people, and the increase of their happiness, there it must stand in its most exalted state, there it ought to be seen in the most favourable light by the Politician there it must meet with the countenance and support of every good man and every friend to his country; so is it at present circumstanced in your country: by the cultivation of Barley your lands would be greatly improved; and the morals and health of the people benefited by the beverage it produces exchanged for the noxious spirits to which they have at present unfortunately recourse; besides the labour of the year would be more equally and advantageously divided, the grain being sown in the spring; but it was a striking circumstance that while the government was wisely encouraging the Breweries, in opposition to the distilleries the country should be entirely ignorant of the grain by which alone they could prosper; I have reason to believe that a grain of Barley has never yet been sown on the Continent; the grain which is there sown, under that name, is not that from which our *malt-liquors* are made; it is here known under the name of *Bigg*, or Bigg-barley, is cultivated only on the Northern Mountains of this Island, and used only for the inferior purposes of feeding pigs or poultry, and is held to be of much too inferior a quality to Make into Malt, and of the five different grains of the species of Barley known to us, it is held to be by far the worst; I have therefore taken the liberty of sending a small quantity of the best species of Barley, (the Flat or Battledore Barley) and the one most likely to succeed with you; this grain is sown in *the spring*, on any rich cultivated soil; I recommend it strongly to your attention; and shall rejoice if[1] I prove the means of introducing into your country an wholesome and invigorating liquor.

I recollect seeing upon the Lawn of Monticello, a Larch tree, which appeard to thrive in the situation; I have therefore in order to fill the box sent a small bag of the cones; the timber is the best of all the resinous trees, the product of Europe; and the tree I think is likely to thrive on the North side of your Mountains or in shady situations among them; for the same reason I have also sent a few of the seeds of the Sycamore (Acer Pseudo platanus) an Umbrageous tree that may possibly shelter you from the scorching sun of Virginia.

You will find also in the box a few books, which possibly may prove worthy of your attention, some of them are voted to you by the Board of Agriculture, from whom I am requested to transmitt them to you; the labours of that Board are not yet sufficiently matured to come before the publick, but they are now engaged in perfecting an Agricultural survey of this Island which will communicate a mass of information from one part of it to another; and probably give to the world the best and most valuable information on the culture of the earth that ever yet has been before it.

Though this letter is meant to contain nothing but farming information, my intention being to write another, which I hope you may receive by an earlier conveyance, I will just mention that your map of Spanish America is safe in the hands of Mr: Faden, and that he wishes to keep it till about Christmas next, but will deliver it into any persons hands you order; or if you give no orders, into mine, and I will have it safely conveyed to you; he desires me to say that he hopes in about a twelvemonth to publish a map far more complete, than you would expect, he having obtaind some maps and information, unknown when you were last in Europe.

I have enquired after and seen the machine for ascertaining the resistance of Plows; and am told it answers well the purpose intended; the plan is extremely simple, consequently the price, which is five guineas is too great, but the inventors of machinery which will not have a general sale, expect and ought to be well paid, as much time is frequently bestowed upon perfecting a trifle. It is invented and sold by Winlaw, in Margaret Street, Cavendish square. I shall now conclude my long letter with informing you that I arrived in England in September last after a very short passage, and had the pleasure of finding all my family well;

that I shall ever remember with the greatest satisfaction my visit to America, and the civilities I received from yourself among so many other people, and rejoice in having it in my power to make any return for them. I beg my best Compliments to Mr: and Mrs: Randolph and Miss Jefferson, and am Dear Sir Yours very truly & sincerely

WM: STRICKLAND

Since writing the above I have procured two or three of the county surveys, in order to shew you the nature of the undertaking; they are not designed for the Public inspection; but printed for the Board and circulated in the districts to which they relate, in order to obtain, as you will immediately perceive on inspecting them, additional and more accurate information, which will then be published, and the whole afterwards digested and compressed, for the benefit of mankind, and will form an History of Agriculture at the close of the eighteenth century.

RC (DLC); addressed: "Thomas Jefferson Esqr Monticello Virginia"; endorsed by TJ as received "July 17" and recorded in SJL under 17 July 1797. Enclosures not found.

On Strickland and his visit with TJ WHEN AT MONTICELLO, see Notes on Conversations with William Strickland, May 1795.

TJ sent the MAP OF SPANISH AMERICA to London in Dec. 1786 to be placed in the hands of the English engraver William Faden. For its eventual publication, see note to TJ to William Stephens Smith, 10 Aug. 1786.

I HAVE PROCURED TWO OR THREE OF THE COUNTY SURVEYS: Sir John Sinclair, the first president of the British Board of Agriculture, undertook a systematic survey of agriculture in Great Britain, appointing surveyors to gather information from each county. The draft surveys were prepared with wide margins for remarks and additional observations. TJ received initial surveys of seven counties published between 1793 and 1795 (see Sowerby, Nos. 759-65). For problems encountered in compiling the surveys and an evaluation of the reports, see Rosalind Mitchison, "The Old Board of Agriculture (1793-1822)," *English Historical Review*, LXXIV (1959), 47-59. The county reports were completed by 1814, but the general HISTORY OF AGRICULTURE in England was not attempted by the Board (same, 49; Arthur Young, *General View of the Agriculture of the County of Sussex. With Observations on the Means of Its Improvement* [London, 1793], 5).

[1] MS: it.

From Van Staphorst & Hubbard

SIR   Amsterdam 21 May 1796.

Our last respects were of 11 Ultimo.

We have now to acknowledge receipt of your very esteemed favor of 28 February, applying for the Loan of One to Two Thousand Dollars, to meliorate your Farm, which request we deem a proof of your Friendship towards us, and of the confidence You place in our's for You.

The revolution in this Country, has caused money to be so scarce here, that We too can employ our Capitals, were they ten times greater than they are, more valuably than in simple Loans. Exclusive of this, our engagements and payments for the Government, are to an Amount, to compel us to decline advances. Wherefore it is highly gratifying to us, yours is of an extent still easily manageable for us. Such being the case, We most chearfully assent to your application, and inclose You a letter for Messrs. Harrison & Sterett of Philadelphia, desiring them to furnish you Two Thousand Dollars against your Bill on us for that sum, which they will take and remit us.

We forbear to acquaint Messrs. Harrison & Sterett of the nature of this Transaction, leaving entirely to your goodself, to forward us by duplicate or triplicate your Bond for the money at legal interest, reimbursable at the Terms, that will suit your Convenience.

As the Interest shall fall due Annually please pay it unto Messrs. Harrison & Sterett of Philadelphia, simply as so much money for our account, for which their receipt shall be of equal validity as our Own. Do us the justice to believe us with the most sincere esteem and regard Sir! Your very obed. hb. servants

N & J. VAN STAPHORST & HUBBARD

RC (DLC); in a clerk's hand, signed by the firm; at foot of first page: "Thos. Jefferson Esqr. Monticello. Virginia"; endorsed by TJ as received 26 Aug. 1796 and so recorded in SJL. A missing Dupl is recorded in SJL as received 9 Sep. 1796. Enclosure: Van Staphorst & Hubbard to Harrison & Sterett, 21 May 1796, requesting them to accept TJ's bill on Van Staphorst & Hubbard for $2,000 and debit their account accordingly (Dupl in DLC; in a clerk's hand, signed by the firm; note at head of text: "Duplicate"; addressed: "Messrs. Harrison & Sterett Philadelphia"; endorsed by TJ).

For TJ's BOND for the loan approved in this letter, see Deed of Mortgage of Slaves to Van Staphorst & Hubbard, 21 Nov. 1796; and TJ to Van Staphorst & Hubbard, 27 Mch. 1797.

SJL records eight letters from TJ to Harrison & Sterett between 28 Aug. and 13 Nov. 1796, including one on 24 Oct. for "draft for 2d. sum 1000. D.," and letters from Harrison & Sterett to TJ of 7 Sep. and 5 Nov. 1796, received on 16 Sep. and 25 Nov. 1796, respectively, that have not been found. TJ recorded two drafts on Van Staphorst & Hubbard, each to Harrison & Sterett for $1,000, in MB, II, 945, 947.

To John Barnes

DEAR SIR   Monticello May 2[2] 1796

On the 22d. of the last month I drew on you in favor of Robert Barclay for twenty seven dollars thirty one cents. The present serves to advise you that I have this day drawn on you for one hundred dollars in favor of Messrs. Samuel Howel junr. & Co.

Will you be able to give me any information by what conveyance were forwarded the boots, gongs and tea, so as to enable me to trace them? I am with great esteem Dr. Sir Your friend & servt

Th: Jefferson

PrC (CSmH); partly faded, with date completed from SJL; at foot of text: "Mr. John Barnes"; endorsed by TJ in ink on verso.

TJ had given Thomas Walker the order in favor of Robert Barclay as a payment due from Thomas Mann Randolph. The order of this day was for nailrod (MB, II, 939-40).

From James Madison

Dear Sir   Philada. May 22. 1796

Congress are hurrying through the remnant of business before them, and will probably adjourn about saturday next. Petitions in favor of the Treaty Still come in from distant places. The name of the President and the alarm of war, have had a greater effect, than were apprehended on one side, or expected on the other. A crisis which ought to have been so managed as to fortify the Republican cause, has left it in a very crippled condition; from which its recovery will be the more difficult as the elections in N.Y. Massachusetts and other States, where the prospects were favorable, have taken a wrong turn under the impressions of the moment. Nothing but auspicious contingences abroad or at home, can regain the lost ground. Peace in Europe would have a most salutary influence, and accounts just received from France revive in some degree the hope of it with the Emperor, which will hasten of course a peace with England. On the other hand, a scene rather gloomy is presented by a letter I have just received from Col. M. It is dated Feby. 27. The following extracts form the substance of it.

"About a fortnight past I was informed by *the*[1] *minister of foreign affairs that the government had at length resolved* how to act *with us in respect to our treaty with England* that *they considered it* as having *violated* or rather *annulled our treaty of alliance with them and taken part with the coalised powers that they had rather have a open enemy than a perfidious friend*—that it was *resolved to send an envoy extraordinary to the U.S. to discuss this business with us* and whose *powers would expire with the execution of the trust. I was astonished with the communication and alarmed with it's probable consequences. I told him it might probably lead to war* and *thereby separate us which was what our enemies wished*—that *it hasarded much and without a probable gain* that from the moment *a person of that character arrived their friends would seem to act under his banner* and which circumstance would *injure their character and lessen their efforts—in truth I did every thing in my power to prevent this measure* and in which I am now told by *the minister that I have succeeded* the *Directory having resolved to continue the ordinary course of representation only.* But thro' this *I hear strong sentiments will be conveyed—the whole of this is made known to the executive by me."*

"The forced loan was less productive than was expected, *and the embarrasment in the finance extreme.* Some *think another movement at hand but I see no evidence of it* at present. In all calculations on this subject *it ought to be recollected* that the *executive are sound and having the government in their hands are strong."*

"There are strong simptoms of an actual rupture between us and this country. The *minister the government preferd to have us as open rather than perfidious friends.*[2] Other proofs occur to shew that *this sentiment has gone deep into their councils."*

The "Minerva" of N.Y. lately announced, with an affected emphasis, a letter from Paris to N.Y. intimating that influencial persons in the U.S. were urging measures on France, which might force this Country to chuse war against England, as the only alternative for war against France. It is probable that categorical steps on the part of F. towards us are anticipated as the consequence of what has been effected by the British party here, and that much artifice will be practised by it to charge them in some unpopular form, on its Republican opponents.

Before I leave this I shall make up a parcel of pamphlets &c. for you to be forwarded to Richmond. The inclosed number of the Debates is a continuation which has been regular, I hope the preceding numbers have all arrived safe.

King is appointed Minister to London and
Humphreys to Madrid, Pinkney and Short retiring.
The vacancy at Lisbon not yet filled.

RC (DLC: Madison Papers); unsigned; at foot of text: "Mr. Jefferson"; includes extract of three paragraphs partly in code, being transcribed by Madison from Monroe's letter to him of 27 Feb. 1796, but containing minor coding anomalies introduced by Monroe and possibly words inadvertently omitted by him in the final paragraph (see note 2 below), with two coding errors corrected by Madison, the whole being deciphered interlinearly by TJ (see note 1 below); endorsed by TJ as received 3 June 1796 and so recorded in SJL. Monroe's letter to Madison (DLC: Madison Papers; written partly in Code No. 9 and deciphered interlinearly by Madison) is printed in Madison, *Papers*, XVI, 236-7.

Early in 1796 the French government hoped to arouse pro-French sentiment in America and force a repudiation of United States policy toward Great Britain. Accordingly, after the ratification and publication of the Jay Treaty, the Directory RESOLVED TO SEND AN ENVOY EXTRAORDINARY to protest the treaty. Monroe learned of the plans in a conversation with Charles Delacroix, minister of foreign affairs, on 15 Feb. 1796. At a meeting with Delacroix the next day and in a private letter to him of the 17th, Monroe argued that the proposed special mission could cause an outright breach between the two countries and that it might LEAD TO WAR. In a letter to Delacroix the following month, Monroe countered some of the Directory's complaints about the treaty. In June the appointment of Charles Vincent, director of fortifications at Saint-Domingue, to serve as envoy extraordinary was rescinded (Ammon, *Monroe*, 145-50; Alexander DeConde, *Entangling Alliance*: *Politics and Diplomacy under George Washington*, [Durham, N.C., 1958], 427-31; Albert Hall Bowman, *The Struggle for Neutrality: Franco-American Diplomacy During the Federalist Era* [Knoxville, 1974], 238-47).

THIS IS MADE KNOWN TO THE EXECUTIVE BY ME: see Monroe to Timothy Pickering, 16, 20 Feb. and 10 Mch. 1796, in Monroe, *Writings*, II, 454-60, 463-6.

The FORCED LOAN, decreed by the Directory in December 1795, was designed to bring 600 million francs into the treasury, but by the spring of 1796 the tax had yielded only a fraction of that amount (Lyons, *France Under the Directory*, 170; Lefebvre, *Thermidorians*, 265-6).

The extract from a LETTER FROM PARIS printed in the New York *Minerva*, 17 May 1796, was presumably that referred to in Gouverneur Morris to Alexander Hamilton, 4 Mch. 1796, but dated 15 Feb. rather than 14 Feb. 1796 (Syrett, *Hamilton*, XX, 59-60n). The informant asserted that "influential men" in the United States had encouraged the French government to take a strong stand against the execution of the Jay Treaty, "even to go so far, as to claim our guarantee of the French West Indies; placing before us the alternative of war with France or Great Britain."

INCLOSED NUMBER OF THE DEBATES: see Giles to TJ, 26 Mch. 1796.

[1] This and subsequent italicized words are written in code, the text being supplied from TJ's decipherment and verified by the Editors against Code No. 9.

[2] Preceding sentence thus encoded and deciphered. For the intended meaning, see the first enciphered sentence above.

From William Thornton

DEAR SIR   George Town May 22nd: 1796.

I should at all times rejoice in an opportunity of paying to you my particular respects, but more especially at the present time, as I am enabled to make my Devoirs through the medium of the celebrated Volney. He is too well known to you, not only personally, but by reputation, to allow me to say any thing in his behalf: I must, however, own, that my Selfishness induces me to wish I could have detained him longer, though by doing so I should delay those refined Gratifications, which, by intercourse, mutually await you. If the Duties of my Office would have suffered my Absence, I should have attended him with pleasure, for every Day would open a new Source of delight. I have conversed with him on the Establishment of a National University in this place, and am happy that he approves of the general plan. The particular Details I shall write as my Engagements will permit. The thought of incorporating in the University a Philosophical Society, upon an extensive Scale, and of having in its Bosom a Select Committee is much approved of by Mr. Volney. He mentioned the formation of one upon a similar plan in France, of which I had not before heard. The Account of that he will relate to you. Much may be done by a few persons labouring for the benefit of the World; indeed, a regenerated people may almost be expected from the exertions of Individuals: if, however, such Exertions should not succeed to the utmost extent, the Satisfaction of having done what is approved of by reflection is unspeakable; and whatever has a good tendency, though not immediately adopted, will finally be received with due attention. That Mr. Volney may have a pleasant Journey, and find you in good Health, is the sincere Wish of dear Sir, your affectionate & respectful Friend   WILLIAM THORNTON

RC (MoSHi: Jefferson Papers); at foot of text: "Thomas Jefferson"; endorsed by TJ as received 10 June 1796 and recorded in SJL as received on that date "by Volney." FC (DLC: Thornton Papers); in hand of Anna Maria Thornton; at foot of text: "Copy"; with minor variations.

SIMILAR PLAN IN FRANCE: the National Institute of Arts and Sciences (see Alexandre Lerebours to TJ, 17 May 1796).

From Volney

MONSIEUR   Georgetown 22 Mai 1796

Le lieu d'où je datte cette lettre Vous prouve que je suis deja bien rapproché de Vous, et je vais M'en rapprocher beaucoup davantage. Demain je pars pour remonter Le potomack et Le shenando et Me rendre par Staunton à Monticello. J'estime que ce Circuit Ne m'employera pas Moins de dix jours, ayant à Voir des forges et des Mines et voulant même faire une pointe a frederick town où je dois trouver un ancien collègue Etabli. Mr. Ross de Richmond a eu la complaisance de se charger de Ma legere Valise qu'il Vous adressera; en sorte que degagé de tout bagage je Marche Militairement partie à pied et partie a cheval Selon les occasions. On pretend que j'aurai à essuyer de grandes chaleurs; Mais c'est precisement une comparaison a faire avec La Syrie et L'Egypte; et je N'en goûterai que Mieux le plaisir de me reposer a Monticello. C'est en prenant ce lieu pour L'agreable point de Vue de Ma course actuelle que j'ai L'honneur de Vous offrir Mes Sentimens D'estime et d'attachement.   C: VOLNEY

RC (DLC); endorsed by TJ as a letter of 27 May 1796 received 3 June 1796, and so recorded in SJL.

To James Brown

Dear Sir Monticello May 23. 96.

Mr. Randolph tells me that a hogshead of my P. Forest tobacco has been lately sold by the inspectors as having remained there too long, and that you are kind enough to search into it in order to save the proceeds. It must of course have been of the following crops. To wit. of the growth of 1789. sold to Mr. Donald

of 1790. ⎱	shipped in 91. & 92. on my own acct. to Philadel-
of 1791 ⎰	phia by D. Hylton
of 1792	shipped to Mr. Brown on my acct.
of 1793 ⎱	sold to Mr. Brown.
of 1794 ⎰	

If it proves to be of 89. 93. or 94. the proceeds will belong to you because I was paid by the list from the Lynchburg warehouse. If of 90. 91. 92. it will belong to me.

I received your favor of May 3. Margaret Watson has no child, and I believe it is more than probable she will decline coming. But if she comes, the letter you were kind enough to inclose for her, directed her particularly to take a steerage passage, which a gardener I have who is not long since from Scotland, says is but £6. I omitted to mention a steerage passage to you, because it had not been spoken of, but the husband has shewn me the copy he retained of his letter, wherein it is expressly enjoined. It might not be amiss for you to limit your order to a steerage passage that she may not take it in the cabbin. I presume the whole advance will not exceed 11. or 12 guineas; if the tobacco abovementioned proves to be mine it may lie in your hands to countervail the advance. If not, I will place that sum in your hands before your friend in Scotland shall have advanced it.—The high price of waggonage, occasions me to leave a pipe of wine still trespassing on you. I am with great esteem Dr. Sir Your friend & servt   Th: Jefferson

RC (Mrs. Henry M. Sage, Albany, New York, 1954); addressed: "James Brown esq. Richmond"; stamped; endorsed by Brown.

Brown's favor of may 3, recorded in

SJL as received 10 May 1796, has not been found. For the letter enclosed for margaret watson, see TJ to Brown, 27 Mch. 1796. A letter from Watson to TJ of 27 June, recorded in SJL as received 22 Sep. 1797, has not been found.

To Archibald Stuart

DEAR SIR   Monticello May 26. 96.

Two or three days before the reciept of your favor of the 20th. I had recieved a letter from Mr. John Stuart of Greenbriar, accompanied with a leg bone and two joints of the toe of the animal mentioned in your letter. They are of a species not yet known most certainly, and the animal must have been as preeminent over the lion, as the big buffalo was over the elephant. The bones are too extraordinary in themselves, and too victorious an evidence against the pretended degeneracy of animal nature in our continent, not to excite the strongest desire to push the enquiry after all other remains of the same animal which any industry can recover for us. I will take the liberty therefore of hoping a continuance of your efforts through Mr. Cavendish or any other channel to procure what of the bones you can, and what information of them may be obtained. In hopes of further materials to make the first communication of the discovery as complete and exact as we can, I shall delay the preparing and forwarding the account of it for some time: and shall be happy to learn from you as soon as you can judge yourself whether any thing further may be expected. I am with great esteem Dear Sir Your affectionate friend & servt   TH: JEFFERSON

RC (ViHi); addressed: "Archibald Stuart esq. Staunton"; stamped; endorsed by Stuart. PrC (DLC); endorsed by TJ in ink on verso.

LETTER FROM MR. JOHN STUART: John Stuart to TJ, 11 Apr. 1796.

Drawing on oral traditions related to him by American Indians, TJ used the term BIG BUFFALO to refer to North American mammoths and mastodons, the fossil remains of which were not yet fully understood by scientists (Silvio A. Bedini, *Thomas Jefferson: Statesman of Science* [New York, 1990], 96-7; *Notes*, ed. Peden, 43-4).

To John Stuart

SIR   Monticello May 26. 96.

I have great acknolegements to make you for your favor of April 11. which came to hand a few days ago with the bones you were pleased also to send, towit the leg bone and two phalanges of the toe of the animal mentioned in your letter. One of these (the claw) was broke, but so that we could put it together. This animal is certainly hitherto unknown, and seems, from the dimensions of these bones, to have the same preeminence over the lion, which the big Buffalo or Mammoth has over the elephant. They furnish a victorious fact against the idle dreams of some

European philosophers who pretend[1] that animal nature in the new world is a degeneracy from that of the old. If the big buffalo [were] an Elephant, as Buffon would have us believe, it was surely an elephant improved, for it was of 4. or 5. times his size. So if his followers (in order to support their doctrine of a central heat in the earth) should chuse to consider the animal now discovered as a lion, they must admit it is a lion improved and not degenerated. I consider these bones as a great acquisition, and shall make a point of communicating the discovery and description of them to the learned on both sides of the Atlantic. I only defer it till I can learn whether a hope exists of finding any other of the bones, as I would wish that the first information should be exact and as complete as possible. Has there ever been any other remains of this species found any where? I must look to you, Sir, to complete the knowlege of this animal for us as you have begun it, by giving me all the further information you can, and sending what other bones can be got of it, and to be so good as to inform me by letter whether any thing more may be expected, that I may decide whether I ought to delay giving an account of it. I am with great esteem Sir your most obedt. servt.

TH: JEFFERSON

PrC (DLC); faded; at foot of text: "Mr. John Stuart Greenbriar"; endorsed in ink by TJ on verso.

[1] MS: "have pretend⟨ed⟩."

From Sir John Sinclair

Board of Agriculture Whitehall
May 28th. 1796.

DEAR SIR

I have much pleasure in transmitting to You a Copy of my last address to the Board of Agriculture, in which I have pointed out the progress of that Institution. It would give me additional Satisfaction to propose you as a foreign Honorary Member, But I think it would be better, if that Honor was Conferred in Consequence of Your favouring us with Some important Communication, to which you are So equal. I flatter myself, we may Still meet again once more in England, our last interview here is very present in my mind, and it would give me Concern, if we were not occasionally to renew our Correspondence, and intercourse. Believe me always with great truth and Regard. Dear Sir your faithful & obedient servant

JOHN SINCLAIR

RC (DLC); endorsed by TJ as received "Mar. 2." and recorded in SJL under 2 Mch. 1797. Enclosure: presumably *Sir* *John Sinclair's Address to the Board of Agriculture, on Tuesday, the Twenty-Fourth of May, 1796: Stating the Progress That Had*

Been Made by the Board, During the Third Session Since Its Establishment [London, 1796]. Sinclair enclosed the same work in a letter to George Washington of 30 May 1796 (DLC: Washington Papers).

From William Strickland

DEAR SIR   London May 28th: 1796

As soon as it was in my power after my return to England I set about procuring the different kinds of Peas and Vetches which are cultivated in this country and which I promised to send you; as they were to be obtaind from different and distant parts of the Kingdom they were not to be collected together at an earlier period than the present, which indeed is as early as is requisite as they could not have been sown before the next season; a box marked ⟨T.I.⟩V.IRGINIA. forming nearly a cube of fifteen or sixteen inches containing those seeds, some others which I thought might be useful to you, and some recent publications, I put yesterday into the hands of Mr: Alexander Donald (now residing at No: 5 Great Winchester Street, Broad Street) who took the charge of them and said he would have them conveyed to you by the first eligible opportunity. On the contents of the box it is not necessary for me here to enlarge, because should it arrive safe, you will find within it every necessary information, and should it not reach its destination, whatever might be said here would prove useless; I shall rejoice hereafter to hear that the contents of it, answer your and my expectation.

I have enquired of Faden respecting your map of Spanish America; he informs me that it is in his possession, and that he wishes to keep it till about Christmas next: but will deliver it up at any time to any one you may direct to receive it; and that if you direct no one to receive it, he will after that period sent it to me; he desires me to inform you that he expects his map to be out before this time twelve-month, and that you will find it far more compleat than you could have foreseen in consequence of some maps, hitherto unknown of, which he has received from Portugal and information he has obtaind from late travellers in the Spanish dominions. Should your map come into my possession I will carefully preserve it, till I receive your direction for its safe conveyance to you.

I have made enquiries about the machine for ascertaining the power required for the draft of Ploughs, and am informed by those who have tried it, that it answers well the purpose. It acts by means of a spring fixed on the swinging-tree by which the Plough is drawn; this spring being depressed by the force applied, shews by means of an index the number of ℔s: weight (or consequently proportion of strength) required to draw the plough, or any other body, to which it may be applied; the machine is very simple, and is the contrivance of and is sold by Winlaw, in Margaret Street, Cavendish Square; and the price of it is Five Guineas. I think I have now executed all the commissions with which you entrusted me, but in return for the civilities I received from you in America, shall never be happier than in being favour'd with your commands, whenever I can be of any service to you in this country.

In your *Notes on Virginia*, of which the world looks and wishes for a new and enlarged edition, because no one is so well qualified as yourself to afford an history of your country in all its branches, political, Philosophical, and Natural, notice is taken of several caverns in the Mountains from which issue strong currents of air; this is said to be very cold, tho' the temperature probably does not fall much below 60 degrees of Farenheits thermometer, the usual temperature of the water and consequently of the earth in the climate of Virginia, but which affords a sensation of greater cold, in consequence of the violence with which the current impinges upon the surface of the body. That air issues out of caverns into open day, has been observed in other countries, and may be accounted for, from the streams of air which are known to circulate within the bowels of the earth in these particular places meeting with a vent, and which being colder, are also heavier than the air without the earth and consequently rush forward to take its place; and therefore these currents of air are probably stronger, in proportion as the weather is hotter; but I was informed by a gentleman, whose authority and accuracy of observation I cannot doubt, that several caves have of late been discovered (and in consequence of the recent discovery I take the liberty of mentioning them to you as you may not have heard of them) on the North Branch of Cacapon (as I think it is called) a river flowing northward, from among the Mountains of Virginia into the Cohongaronta or Northern Branch of Potomack, which are there called the *Ice-caves*. The air issuing out of these is so intensely cold, that the insides of them are throughout the year incrusted with a coat of Ice; in some places observed to be several feet in thickness, any part of which being taken away is soon renewed by the dampness and frigorific powers of the atmosphere of the place. My informant had been at these caves and carefully examined them, not above ten days before he mentioned them to me, which was in the end of May last; and then found them in the state described.

This is a new Phanomenon of Nature and not easy to be accounted for. How should the air be so much colder than the earth in which it circulates and is pent up? or if of the same temperature with the earth, why should the earth here be much colder than the mean temperature of it elsewhere in the same latitude? Nitre is known to be productive of cold, and all the Mountains of Virginia to abound with it; but it has not hitherto been observed that in the caverns that produce it plentifully, the air has been colder than in other caverns not possessing this Salt and nitre seems alone scarcely cause sufficient for so singular an effect; I wished much to have ascertained the temperature of some of the caverns where the nitre is found, but it was not in my power to do it after I had received an account of the Ice-caves, much less was it in my power to visit these last, as I had already spent more time among the mountains than I had intended, and had I indulged my inclination for exploring all the wonders of that delightful region I should scarcely yet have crossed the Atlantic; to natives therefore must it be left to make the discoveries, and to me in future to be content with the account of them.

When in America I made several attempts to procure the seed of the Buffalo clover, which is said to abound in the Country west of the Mountains; but without effect; should it come in your way at any time to procure some of the seed, I should be greatly obliged to you for a very small quantity of it, it is described as a plant, the cultivation of which is worthy of being attempted. Bartram mentiond to me a singular shrub which he knew of as growing wild only in your neighbourhood, the fruit of which produced a pure oil; and which shrub if I recollect right I also mentiond to you; this may hereafter prove to America what the olive is to Europe; should you know this plant or be able to procure some of the seed of it, I should be glad to present some to my Botanical Friends here.

As to affairs in Europe it is as difficult as at any time heretofore to say what may be the result of their present situation; the French are following up their successes in Italy, of which at this moment they may be said to have made an absolute conquest; and are now in the heart of Milan from which the Austrians are fled; with Sardinia they have concluded a peace on their own terms; and on the Rhine the campain has not yet been opend probably as negotiations are carrying on with the Austrians who by Peace alone seem likely to regain their possessions in Italy, or perhaps divert greater evils; as to ourselves we are at peace at home, and relieved from the apprehensions of scarcity, which had been too hastily taken up in the last Autumn; grain and wheat in particular, tho this last bears an higher price than usual here, is cheaper than in almost any other country at this time, (about 9/6 ster: a Bushel, or $2\frac{1}{9}$ Doll: of your money); this has not been effected by foreign import, for at this price or even one considerably higher, no importation could be looked for; but from our own internal supply proving far greater than was expected, and probably nearly equal to the average produce, and consequently demand of the year; but the crop of 1795 was to make up for the deficient harvest of 1794, and which has been the chief cause of the present high price. The crop now on the ground has no future risks to run, and has every appearance of abundance; but notwithstanding these favourable circumstances we are involved in the evils of warfare; and tho in the progress of it we have nothing to dread from the arms of our opponents even should we be left to stand single against them, yet the expence of the opposition will be to them a victory; and our inability or disinclination to support greater burdens, must be productive of Peace; a fortunate circumstance for mankind that impotence should have power to act when principles that ought to prevail have lost their influence.

Remembering, as I always shall do, with pleasure the time I spent in America, the many civilities I received and liberal hospitality I experienced from yourself and so many others, the least return I can make is the offer of my services to yourself or any of your Friends, whether they be in this country or America, and to assure you that I shall never be happier than in receiving your commands and executing of them; I arrived in England in Septr: last after a very short passage, and had the pleasure to find all my family in perfect health; and as no one experienced any inconvenience from my absence, and I had every reason to be pleased with my visit to America I shall hereafter esteem the time I was there as the best spent year of my life. I beg you will make my best respects to Mr: and Mrs: Randolph and Miss Jefferson and mention my remembrance of the civilities I received to all who recollect me and believe me Dear Sir yours most sincerely & faithfully

WM: STRICKLAND

P:S: Pray remember me to Col: Cole when yo[u see] him; he desired me to make enquiries after Col: Lynn, who during the war had some time resided with him at Enniscorthy, but I am sorry to inform him that he died during my absence in America; but a Son, or Brother of his is alive and now a Col: in our service. My direction (if required) is W:S: at York. England.

RC (MiU-C); slightly torn; addressed: "Thomas Jefferson Esqr. Monticello near Charlottesville Virginia"; stamped and postmarked; endorsed by TJ as received "Oct. 14." and recorded in SJL under 14 Oct. 1796.

I WAS INFORMED BY A GENTLEMAN: Alexander White. The CACAPON River is a large tributary of the Potomac which flows in a northeasterly direction through Hardy, Hampshire, and Morgan counties in West Virginia. COHONGARONTA: Iroquoian name for the Potomac River west of the Blue Ridge mountains. The ICE-CAVES were located 30 miles from Winchester, Virginia (Strickland to TJ, 16 July 1798; Samuel Brown to TJ, 17 Mch. 1797; Hamill Kenny, *West Virginia Place Names: Their Origin and Meaning, Including the Nomenclature of the Streams and Mountains* [Piedmont, W. Va., 1945], 146; VMHB, XIII [1905], 129).

From Joseph Marx

SIR   Manchester May 29. 1796

By last Mail I recieved a Letter from Mr. B Bohlen of Philadelphia enclosing a Draft on You, from Jos Cerrachi favor G Meade 30 Days sight $1500. which I am requested to present for acceptance, not having an opportunity of personally presenting it, I should wish to be informed by return of Post, whether You intend to accept it, or should You decline doing it, I am requested to recieve the Bust sent by Mr. Cerrachi and forward it to Philadelphia. I am with due Respect, Sir Your very Hble Servt   JOS MARX

RC (ViW); at foot of text: "T. Jefferson Esq."; endorsed by TJ as received from Joseph "Mark" on 3 June 1796 and so recorded in SJL.

Originally from Hanover, Germany, Joseph Marx (1772-1840) was a merchant and investor in real estate as well as a founding member of Richmond's first synagogue (Joseph R. Rosenbloom, *A Biographical Dictionary of Early American Jews, Colonial Times through 1800* [Lexington, Ky., 1960], 109; Herbert T. Ezekiel and Gaston Lichtenstein, *The History of the Jews of Richmond from 1769 to 1917* [Richmond, 1917], 47-8, 105, 240, 303).

From James Madison

May 30th, 1796.

Congress will adjourn the day after to-morrow. News as late as April 8 from London; peace likely to take place between France and England; provisions falling much in price, both in F. and G.B. The moneyed distresses reviving in the latter, and great alarms for a terrible shock to the Banking and Mercantile Houses.

MS not found; text reprinted from Madison, *Letters*, II, 105. The missing RC is recorded in SJL as received 23 June 1796.

From Robert Pleasants

RESPECTED FRIEND   Richmond 6 mo. 1. 1796

Concieving the Instruction of black Children to be a duty we owe to that much degraded part of our fellow Creatures, and probably would tend to the spiritual and temporal advantage of that unhappy race, as well as to the Community at large, in fitting them for freedom, which at this enlightened day is generally acknowledged to be their right, I have much desired to see some sutable steps taken to promote such work; And believing thee to be a real friend to the cause of liberty, and endowed with ability and influence in regulating and promoting sutable plans for such a purpose, I take the liberty by my Friend Richard Dobs of sending thee a rough Essay for thy consideration, with a request, that should thou approve the subject, thou wilt please to make such alterations or amendments as may appear to thee more likely to answer the desired purpose, and to give it such other incouragement as thou may think right—I hope thou will excuse the freedom I have now taken, and believe me to be with sincere respect & Esteem Thy Friend

ROBERT PLEASANTS

RC (MiU-C); partially clipped at foot of text: "Thomas Jefferson Esqr"; endorsed by TJ as received "June 13" and so recorded in SJL. FC (Lb in PHC: Quaker Collection); in Pleasants's hand; with minor variations.

Robert Pleasants (1722-1801), a prominent Virginia Quaker merchant engaged in overseas and domestic trade, was the proprietor of a plantation at Curles Neck in Henrico County. A longtime advocate for abolition of the slave trade and for emancipation, he had been clerk of the Virginia Yearly Meeting of the Society of Friends, which successfully petitioned the legislature for an act to allow slaveowners to manumit their slaves. After passage of the law in 1782, Pleasants freed his own slaves at a reputed cost of £3,000 sterling. As executor of the estate of his father—whose will had provided for the emancipation of his slaves, but who died before enactment of the 1782 law—Pleasants filed a lawsuit, subsequently cited in other cases, that resulted in orders by the state's High Court of Chancery and Court of Appeals, 1799-1800, sanctioning the emancipation of the estate's approximately 430 slaves on the terms of the will. A founder of the Virginia Abolition Society organized in 1790, Pleasants op-

posed the deportation of freed bondsmen and women, and he took special interest in the establishment of free schools for black children, providing in his will for the creation of one such institution on his property (Betsy August, ed., "Robert Pleasants Letterbook, 1771-1773" [M.A. thesis, College of William and Mary, 1976], 3-5, 7-10, 22-3, 26-33; *Virginia: In the High Court of Chancery, March 16, 1798. Between Robert Pleasants . . . and Mary Logan . . .* [Richmond, 1800], Evans, No. 38963; Helen T. Catterall, ed., *Judicial Cases concerning American Slavery and the Negro*, 5 vols. [Washington, D.C., 1926-37], I, 105-6, 138, 165, 170, 237; Marquis de Chastellux, *Travels in North America in the Years 1780, 1781 and 1782*, trans. Howard C. Rice, Jr., 2 vols. [Chapel Hill, 1963], II, 596-7).

The enclosed ROUGH ESSAY may have been Pleasants's "Proposals for Establishing a free school for the Instruction of the Children of Blacks and people of Color," which he had evidently circulated around 1782 or earlier (Stephen B. Weeks, *Southern Quakers and Slavery: A Study in Institutional History* [Baltimore, 1896], 215).

A letter from Pleasants to TJ of 17 Mch. 1796, recorded in SJL as received from Curles on 10 Apr. 1796, has not been found.

To Joseph Marx

SIR   Monticello June 4. 1796.

I am favored with yours of May 29. Some time in the course of the last year I was informed by Mr. Meade that he held a draught of Mr. Ceracchi's on me for 1000 D. and desired to know if it was good. I explained to him, too much at length to be here repeated, how unfounded the draught was, and that I should not accept it. Nothing further therefore is now necessary than to repeat to you that I do not propose to accept the said bill,[1] nor claim the bust on which it is drawn. I am Sir Your very humble servt   TH: JEFFERSON

PrC (MHi); at foot of text: "Mr. Joseph   [1] Remainder of sentence inserted.
Mark"; endorsed by TJ in ink on verso.

To Charles Willson Peale

DEAR SIR   Monticello June 5. 1796.

I have recieved a proposition from Europe which may perhaps be turned to account for the enlargement of your Museum. The hereditary prince of Parma, a young man of letters, of 22. years of age, lately married to a daughter of the K. of Spain, is desirous of augmenting his cabinet of Natural history by an addition of all the American subjects of the 3 departments of nature[1] and will give those of Europe which can be procured or of which he has duplicates in exchange. Perhaps it would suit you to enter into this kind of commerce. If so, be so good as to inform me by letter how far you would chuse to enter into the exchange; I defer writing my answer to him till I hear from you. The intervention of the Spanish minister at Philadelphia would sometimes perhaps be used; sometimes perhaps my own; and shipments could be made to and from Genoa and Leghorn. I am with great esteem Dear Sir Your friend & servt   TH: JEFFERSON

RC (TxU); at foot of text: "Mr. Peale."   [1] Preceding five words and digit interlined.

PROPOSITION FROM EUROPE: Louis of
Parma to TJ, 2 Nov. 1795.

From Jean Antoine Gautier

Monsieur   Paris le 7e Juin 1796.

J'ai reçu avec un bien grand plaisir la lettre que vous m'avés fait l'honneur de m'écrire le 7e de 7bre de l'année dernière et qui a été fort retardée. Les personnes à qui vous me chargés de faire parvenir votre Souvenir, y sont infiniment Sensibles. Vous mettiés dans leur nombre notre excellent ami Mr. Le Veillard, ignorant sans doute qu'il a été une des malheureuses victimes du système de terreur qui a couvert la France de deuil en 1794. Son fils qui étoit passé à New-York pour un établissement de Commerce, y a succombé l'automne dernier à une Maladie trés courte. Madame et Mademlle. Le Veillard Se portent bien et Supportent tous ces malheurs avec beaucoup de force d'ame.

J'ai indiqué de Suite à Monsieur Monroe l'addresse de la Dame pour qui vous lui aviés fait passer une lettre.

J'espère, Monsieur, que la lettre de ma précédente Société du 11e. 7bre 1795 vous Sera parvenue avec l'expédition qu'elle contenoit de l'acte de dépot des assignats représentant le Solde du Compte des États-Unis montant à £48339: 15. assts. et celui de l'État de Virginie montant à £66000 assts. Mr. Short, Mr. Munroe et Mr. Skipwith en ont eu également des copies, contenant les Numéros des assignats déposés. D'après la nouvelle Loi et l'injonction faites par le Directoire aux Dépositaires d'assignats, ceux-ci vont être échangés contre des Mandats territoriaux Sur le pied de 30 assignats pour un en Mandat. Ces Mandats resteront également à la disposition de la Trésorerie des États-Unis, à la votre Monsieur et à celle de Mr. Short pour les £66000. de l'État de Virginie.

Je ne vois pas sans bien du regret qu'on ait laissé déprécier à ce point ces valeurs, malgré toutes nos lettres pour prier qu'on voulut bien en disposer.

Je profite de l'occasion de la personne qui veut bien se charger de cette lettre pour avoir l'honneur de vous addresser, Monsieur, un exemplaire d'un Ouvrage sur les États-unis en 2 volumes, rédigé par un de mes amis, Mr. Pictet, homme de mérite et infiniment attaché à la prospérité des États-Unis et à tout ce qui tient à l'Amérique. Son Ouvrage a été fort accueilli en Europe. Il est écrit dans un esprit qui doit plaire aux Américains. J'y joins une notice sur le respectable Mr. De Malesherbes dont la perte vous aura Surement causé les mêmes regrets qu'aux François. Pareilles pertes sont irréparables.

Les papiers publics et les autres publications qui parviennent Sans doute en Amérique, vous tiennent, Monsieur, au fait des Événemens de ce Pays. J'ai l'honneur de vous addresser deux brochures nouvelles relatives au nouveau Gouvernement de la France, elles sont écrites d'une Manière intéressante, l'une par Mr. Benjn. Constant, l'autre par Mr. Lézay de Marnesia. J'aurois beaucoup de plaisir à vous addresser, Monsieur, de tems à autres quelques envois pareils propres à vous intéresser.

Je connois votre philantropie éclairée et en particulier votre attachement pour la France. Puissent vos vœux pour le rétablissement de sa tranquillité et celui d'une paix générale être bientot exaucés. Veuillés agréer les Sentimens respectueux de dévouement avec lesquels j'ai l'honneur d'être Monsieur Votre très humble & très Obéissant Serviteur

J. A. GAUTIER

RC (DLC); at foot of first page: "Monsieur Thomas Jefferson à Monticello en Virginie"; endorsed by TJ as received 4 Nov. 1796 and so recorded in SJL.

PASSER UNE LETTRE: TJ to Madame de Tessé, 8 [i.e., 6] Sep. 1795. MA PRÉCÉDENTE SOCIÉTÉ: Grand & Cie.

By the beginning of Year IV in September 1795, French ASSIGNATS had depreciated to less than one percent of their face value. A law of 16 Mch. 1796 authorized a new form of paper money, the MANDATS TERRITORIAUX; these mortgage debentures plummeted in value so severely that by July they were refused for commercial transactions, and in February 1797 the government repudiated all paper currency as legal tender (Stewart, *French Revolution*,

658; Lyons, *France Under the Directory*, 72, 180-1; Lefebvre, *Thermidorians*, 266-8).

For the OUVRAGE of PICTET, see note to François D'Ivernois to TJ, 26 Feb. 1795. The NOTICE about Chrétien Guillaume de Lamoignon de Malesherbes, who was guillotined with his daughter and grandchildren in April 1794, has not been identified (Jean Tulard and others, *Histoire et dictionnaire de la Révolution française, 1789-1799* [Paris, 1987], 966). DEUX BROCHURES NOUVELLES: Benjamin Constant, *De la force du gouvernement actuel de la France et de la nécessité de s'y rallier* (Paris, 1796); and Adrien Lezay-Marnézia, *De la foiblesse d'un gouvernement qui commence, Et de la nécessité où il est de se rallier à la majorité nationale* (Paris, 1795-96).

To James Monroe

June 12. 1796.

The dreadful misfortune of poor Derieux, who has lost his house and all it's contents by fire occasions the present letter to cover one from him to his aunt. I send it open for your perusal. Be so good as to seal and send it. I hope she will if she has not done it already, send him some relief.

I recieved only 3. weeks ago your favor of Nov. 18. It had been 5. months on it's way to me. The season for engaging laborers to prepare for your buildings was then over. They are to be got only about the newyear's day. To this is added that the plan you promise to send is not come. It is perhaps not unfortunate that nothing was begun this year. Corn @ 25/ to 30/ a barrel would have rendered building this year extremely dear. It does so to me who had engaged in it before that circumstance was foreseen. If your plan arrives, I will consult with Mr. Jones, and according to the result of our consultation make preparations in the winter for the next year's work.

Congress have risen. You will have seen by their proceedings the truth of what I always observed to you, that one man outweighs them all in influence over the people who have supported his judgment against their own and that of their representatives. Republicanism must lie on it's oars, resign the vessel to it's pilot, and themselves to the course he thinks best for them.—I had always conjectured, from such facts as I could get hold of, that our public debt was increasing about a million of dollars a year. You will see by Gallatin's speeches that the thing is proved. You will see further that we are compleatly saddled and bridled, and that the bank is so firmly mounted on us that we must go where they will guide. They openly publish a resolution that the national property being increased in value they must by an increase of circulating medium furnish an adequate representation of it, and by further additions of active capital promote the enterprizes of our merchants. It is supposed that the paper in circulation in and around Philadelphia amounts to 20. millions of Doll. and that in the whole union to 100. millions. I think the last too high. All the imported commodities are raised about 50. per cent, by the depreciation of the money. Tobacco shares the rise because it has no competition abroad. Wheat has been extravagantly high from other causes. When these cease, it must fall to it's antient nominal[1] price notwithstanding the depreciation of that, because it must contend at market with foreign wheats. Lands have risen within the vortex of the paper, and as far out as that can influence. They are not risen at all here. On the contrary they are lower than they were 20. years ago. Those I had mentioned to you, to wit, Carter's and Colle were sold before your letter came. Colle @ two dollars the acre. Carter's had been offered me for two French crowns (13/2). Mechanics here get from a dollar to a dollar and a half a day, yet are much worse off than at old prices.

Volney is with me at present. He is on his way to the Illinois. Some late appointments judiciary and diplomatic you will have heard and stared at. The death of R. Jouett is the only small news in our neighborhood. Our best affections attend Mrs. Monroe, Eliza, and yourself. Adieu affectionately.

RC (DLC: Monroe Papers); unsigned. PrC (DLC); at foot of first page in ink: "Colo Monroe." Enclosure not found. Enclosed in TJ to Tench Coxe, 12 June 1796, presenting "his friendly respects" and requesting Coxe's "care of the inclosed letters with many apologies and thanks in the cases of the same nature which have occurred heretofore" (RC, Leslie A. Price, Mayville, New York, 1944; partly torn; addressed:

"Tenche Coxe esq. Commissioner of the revenue Philadelphia"; stamped; endorsed by Coxe).

The tavern of J. P. P. DERIEUX in Goochland County had recently burned at an estimated loss of over $1,500 (La Rochefoucauld-Liancourt, *Voyage*, v, 10).

ONE MAN: George Washington. Albert GALLATIN'S SPEECHES in the House of Representatives between 1 Apr. and 1 June 1796, which concerned loan payments due in the current year, demonstrated an excess of expenditures over receipts of $1,350,000 in 1794 and $1,500,000 in 1795. The repayment of funds advanced to the government by the BANK of the United States was one issue in the House debates on finances: Gallatin favored a partial payment of $1,200,000, rather than the $5,000,000 figure that was finally included in the autho-

rizing bill. In response to an inquiry from the committee of ways and means, the bank's board of directors on 21 Apr. 1796 had passed a RESOLUTION that called on the government to pay all outstanding obligations to the bank and provide for those coming due in the current year, justifying the request on the need to increase both CIRCULATING MEDIUM and investment CAPITAL (*Annals*, v, 846-9, 883-4, 914, 921-36, 1295, 1313, 1506-14).

An unsigned letter from Monroe of 7 May 1796 that resides in TJ's papers is actually a duplicate of a letter Monroe wrote to Madison. (Dupl in DLC; unsigned; written partly in Code No. 9; with encoding and other anomalies; endorsed by TJ; varies slightly in wording from the RC printed in Madison, *Papers*, XVI, 350-2).

[1] Word interlined.

To John Barnes

DEAR SIR   Monticello June 19. 96.

I wrote you May 22. advising you of a draught for 100.D. payable to Saml. Howell junr. & Co. The present serves to cover a power of attorney to recieve about 300.D. July 1. from the bank of the US. and to advise you that I have this day drawn on you for 300.D. payable to Samuel Howell & Co. July 2. which be pleased to honor on account of Dear Sir Your most obedt. servt   TH: JEFFERSON

PrC (MHi); at foot of text: "Mr. John Barnes"; endorsed by TJ in ink on verso. Enclosure not found, but see below.

The POWER OF ATTORNEY authorized Barnes to draw interest due to William Short on 1 July 1796; the draft for Howell was in payment for iron (MB, II, 942).

Letters from Barnes to TJ of 14 June 1796, from Howell to TJ of 15 June, both received on 2 July, and from TJ to Howell of 19 June are recorded in SJL but have not been found.

To George Washington du Motier de Lafayette

Dear Sir   Monticello [19 June 1796]

The enquiries of Congress were the first intimation which reached my retirement of your being in this country, and from Mr. Volney, now with me, I first learned where you are. I avail myself of the earliest moments of this information to express to you the satisfaction with which I learn that you are in a land of safety where you will meet in every person the friend of your worthy father and family. Among these I beg leave to mingle my own assurances of sincere attachment to him, and my desires to prove it by every service I can render you. I know indeed that you are already under too good a patronage to need any other, and that my distance and retirement render my affections unavailing to you. They exist nevertheless in all their purity and warmth towards your father and every one embraced by his love; and no one has wished with more anxiety to see him once more in the bosom of a nation who knowing his works and his worth desire to make him and his family for ever their own. You were perhaps too young to remember me personally when in Paris. But I pray you to remember that should any occasion offer wherein I can be useful to you, there is no one on whose friendship and zeal you may more confidently count. You will some day perhaps take a tour through these states. Should any thing in this part of them attract your curiosity it would be a circumstance of great gratification to me to recieve you here and to assure you in person of those sentiments of esteem and attachment with which I am Dear Sir Your friend & humble servt.   Th: Jefferson

RC (NNPM); undated, but supplied from PrC; at foot of text: "M. de la Fayette." PrC (DLC); dated in ink by TJ: "June 19. 96." Enclosed in TJ to George Washington, 19 June 1796.

George Washington Louis Gilbert du Motier de Lafayette (1779-1849) was the only son of the Marquis de Lafayette. After visiting the United States in 1795-97 (see below), he pursued a career as an officer in the French army, but finding his advancement slowed by antipathy between his father and Napoleon Bonaparte, he left the service in 1807. He subsequently entered politics, accompanied the marquis on his journey to the United States in 1824-25, and succeeded to his father's title in 1834

(Arnaud Chaffanjon, *La Fayette et sa descendance* [Paris, 1976], 163-71).

In 1795, while his father languished in an Austrian prison, George Washington Lafayette was sent by his mother to the United States with a tutor to reside under the care of his namesake, his father's old comrade in arms. The president, torn between his paternal feelings for his friend's son and his desire to maintain a neutral stance toward the conflict in Europe, privately extended his financial support to the young man through intermediaries. Lafayette avoided Philadelphia and was living incognito in New Jersey under the family name of Motier when, at the behest of Congressman Edward Livingston of New York, who had learned of Lafayette's visit, the House of

Representatives on 18 Mch. 1796 appointed a committee to make ENQUIRIES and, if the news was confirmed, to report appropriate measures for expressing "the grateful sense entertained by this country for the services of his father." This elicited a letter from the young Frenchman, who thanked the House for the honor but noted that as the recipient of the president's PA-TRONAGE, he did not require aid from Congress. In April the young man took up residence with the president's family until his departure from the United States in October 1797 (same, 166-7; *Annals*, v, 423, 798, 1202; Washington, *Diaries*, vi, 236-7, 261; Syrett, *Hamilton*, xix, 324-7, 455-8; Madison, *Papers*, xvi, 252).

To George Washington

DEAR SIR   Monticello June 19. 96.

In Bache's Aurora of the 9th. inst. which came here by the last post, a paper appears which, having been confided, as I presume, to but few hands, makes it truly wonderful how it should have got there. I cannot be satisfied as to my own part till I relieve my mind by declaring, and I attest every thing sacred and honorable to the declaration, that it has got there neither thro' me nor the paper confided to me. This has never been from under my own lock and key, or out of my own hands. No mortal ever knew from me that these questions had been proposed. Perhaps I ought to except one person who possesses all my confidence as he has possessed yours. I do not remember indeed that I communicated it even to him. But as I was in the habit of unlimited trust and counsel with him, it is possible I may have read it to him. No more: for the quire of which it makes a part was never in any hand but my own, nor was a word ever copied or taken down from it, by any body. I take on myself, without fear, any divulgation on his part. We both know him incapable of it. From myself then or my paper this publication has never been derived.   I have formerly mentioned to you that, from a very early period of my life, I had laid it down as a rule of conduct never to write a word for the public papers. From this I have never departed in a single instance: and on a late occasion when all the world seemed to be writing, besides a rigid adherence to my own rule, I can say with truth that not a line for the press was ever communicated to me by any other: except a single petition referred for my correction; which I did not correct however tho the contrary, as I have heard, was said in a public place, by one person through error, thro' malice by another. I learn that this last has thought it worth his while to try to sow tares between you and me, by representing me as still engaged in the bustle of politics, and in turbulence and intrigue against the government. I never believed for a moment that this could make any impression on you, or that your knolege of me would not overweigh the slander of an intriguer, dirtily employed in sifting the conversations of my table, where alone he could hear of me, and seeking to atone for his sins against you by sins against another who had never done him any other injury than that of declining his confidences. Political conversation I really dislike, and therefore avoid where I can without affectation. But when urged by others, I have never concieved that having been in public life requires me to bely my sentiments, nor even to conceal them. When I am led by conversation to express them, I do it with the same independance here which I have practised every where, and which is inseparable from my nature.—But enough of this miserable tergiversator, who ought indeed either to have been of more truth or less trusted by his country.

While on the subject of papers permit me to ask one from you. You remember the difference of opinion between Hamilton and Knox on the one part and myself on the other on the subject of firing on the Little Sarah, and that we had exchanged opinions and reasons in writing. On your arrival in Philadelphia I delivered you a copy of my reasons in the presence of Colo. Hamilton. On our withdrawing, he told me he had been so much engaged that he had not been able to prepare a copy of his and General Knox's for you, and that if I would send you the one he had given me he would replace it in a few days. I immediately sent it to you, wishing you should see both sides of the subject together. I often after applied to both the gentlemen but could never obtain another copy. I have often thought of asking this one or a copy of it back from you, but have not before written on subjects of this kind to you. Tho' I do not know that it will ever be of the least importance to me yet one loves to possess arms tho' they hope never to have occasion for them. They possess my paper in my own handwriting. It is just I should possess theirs. The only thing amiss is that they should have left me to seek a return of the paper, or a copy of it, from you.

I put away this disgusting dish of old fragments, and talk to you of my peas and clover. As to the latter article I have great encouragement from the friendly nature of our soil. I think I have had both the last and present year as good clover from common grounds which had brought several crops of wheat and corn without ever having been manured, as I ever saw in the lots around Philadelphia. I verily believe that a field of 34. acres sowed on wheat April was twelvemonth has given me a ton to the acre at it's first cutting this spring. The stalks extended measured $3\frac{1}{2}$ feet long very commonly. Another field a year older, and which yielded as well the last year, has sensibly fallen off this year. My exhausted fields bring a clover not high enough for hay, but I hope to make seed from it. Such as these however I shall hereafter put into peas in the broadcast, proposing that one of my sowings of wheat shall be after two years of clover, and the other after 2. years of peas. I am trying the white boiling pea of Europe (the Albany pea) this year till I can get the hog pea of England which is the most productive of all. But the true winter vetch is what we want extremely. I have tried this year the Caroline drill. It is absolutely perfect. Nothing can be more simple, nor perform it's office more perfectly for a single row. I shall try to make one to sow 4. rows at a time of wheat or peas at 12. I. distance. I have one of the Scotch threshing machines nearly finished. It is copied exactly from a model Mr. Pinckney sent me, only that I have put the whole works (except the horse wheel) into a single frame moveable from one field to another on the two axles of a waggon. It will be ready in time for the harvest which is coming on, which will give it a full trial. Our wheat and rye are generally fine, and the prices talked of bid fair to indemnify us for the poor crops of the two last years.

I take the liberty of putting under your cover a letter to the son of M. de la Fayette, not exactly knowing where to direct to him. With very affectionate compliments to Mrs. Washington I have the honor to be with great and sincere esteem and respect Dear Sir Your most obedt. & most humble servt   TH: JEFFERSON

RC (DLC: Washington Papers); at foot of first page: "The President of the US." PrC (DLC). Enclosure: TJ to George Washington du Motier de Lafayette, 19 June 1796.

With this letter, TJ initiated his last exchange with Washington (see Malone, *Jefferson*, III, 269-71).

On 9 June 1796 the Philadelphia *Aurora* printed a letter by "Paulding," one of 16 appearing between 24 May and 2 Sep. that sought to damage the president's reputation by presenting evidence that the administration was following a vitriolic, anti-French policy. The article included a PAPER consisting of 13 questions on neutrality and the alliance with France that Washington CONFIDED to his Cabinet on 18 Apr. 1793, just prior to the publication of the Proclamation of Neutrality (see Washington to the Cabinet, 18 Apr. 1793, and the enclosed questions; and Cabinet Opinion on Washington's Questions on Neutrality and the Alliance with France, [19 Apr. 1793]). See also James D. Tagg, "Benjamin Franklin Bache's Attack on George Washington,"

PMHB, C (1976), 216-18; and Stewart, *Opposition Press*, 229-30, 528, 735n.

PERSON WHO POSSESSES ALL MY CONFIDENCE: James Madison.

EXCEPT A SINGLE PETITION REFERRED FOR MY CORRECTION: TJ may have been recalling the petition that Madison addressed to the General Assembly of the Commonwealth of Virginia, 12 Oct. 1795, as part of the protest against the Jay Treaty. Madison began drafting the petition in early September, but he is thought to have revised it in early October, at approximately the same time he and Dolley Madison visited Monticello (Madison, *Papers*, XVI, XXVI, 66, 95-103). See also William Branch Giles to TJ, 29 Oct. 1795.

Henry Lee was almost certainly the INTRIGUER . . . SIFTING THE CONVERSATIONS OF MY TABLE. Lee had earlier reported to Washington that a "very respectable gentleman" had informed him of a conversation he had recently had with TJ at Monticello, noting that when he enquired whether Washington was "governed by British influence as was reported by many," TJ replied that there was no danger of Washing-

ton being biased as long as he was influenced by "wise advisers or advice which you
at present had" (Lee to Washington, 17
Aug. 1794, in DLC: Washington Papers;
Malone, *Jefferson*, III, 269-71n).

For the paper by HAMILTON AND KNOX on
the LITTLE SARAH that TJ had IMMEDI-
ATELY SENT to the president, see Enclosure
No. 2 listed at TJ to Washington, [11 July
1793].

From Richard Stith

HOND. SIR   Campbell County, June 20th. 1796

The change of Registers and the frequent alterations and additions
enacted in our Sessions of Assembly, I believe puzzles the Surveyors of
Land to keep up—as we have not right by Law, to a Book of each
Session, I remained ignorant of part of my duty—now, I hope that these
works have every Requisite attending them.

I have wrote the above lines lest I shou'd lose your opinion of me as
a Man of business: which good opinion, Sir, I am very unwilling to lose.
Am Sir your affectionate hble Servant   RICHARD STITH

I woudnt weary you with reading a long letter of my writing.

RC (ViU: McGregor Library); addressed: "Honble. Thomas Jefferson upon Parnassus
I mean Monticello"; endorsed by TJ as received 2 July 1796 and so recorded in SJL.

From Jonathan Williams

DEAR SIR   Mount Pleasant on schuylkill June 20. 1796.

Some time since I conveyed to you, through the medium of Mr.
Maddison, a transcript of my barometrical Journal over some of the
mountains in Virginia. As the philosophical Society are about publishing another Volume, and as the Committee of selection have put my
paper on the list for publication, I am extreemly desirous of receiving
your answer to my last, that I may avail myself of your friendly advice
whether to permit this publication or not. I found the calculated heights
of these mountains to be so much below the Ideas that travellers have
formed of them, that I had determined not to bring my Journal forward,
but the advice of such Friends as Dr. Rittenhouse and Mr. Patterson,
overcame my scruples; and I was much encouraged by a passage in your
Notes on Virginia, page 18, where you suppose the highest peak of
Otter to be about 4000 feet, "*from data, which may found a tolerable
conjecture.*"

I should be highly gratified to know what these data are, and
whether, by them, my calculations are supported or not; and if at the

same time you would enrich the proposed Volume by the result of your philosophical Observations during your late retirement, the Society would be highly sensible of your remembrance of the Object of its Institution. I am with great Respect & esteem Dear sir Your obedient Servant   JONA WILLIAMS

RC (MoSHi: Jefferson Papers); at foot of text: "Hon Mr. Jefferson"; endorsed by TJ as received 2 July 1796 and so recorded in SJL.

CONVEYED TO YOU: see Williams to TJ, 24 Jan. 1796, and enclosures.

To John Breckinridge

DEAR SIR   Monticello June 21. 96.

I take the liberty of introducing to you Mr. Volney the celebrated traveller, author, and member of the first national assembly of France. In all these characters his name will already have been familiar to you, and his worth as well as his being a traveller will readily obtain for him your attentions and good offices. To these claims let me add my own sollicitations, and assurances that you will find on an acquaintance with him that any services you can render him will be well placed. I am happy in this and every other occasion of assuring you of the sentiments of esteem with which I am Dear Sir Your friend & servt

TH: JEFFERSON

PrC (DLC); at foot of text: "Mr. Brackenridge"; recorded in SJL as written to John Breckinridge.

To Jean Baptiste Ducoigne

MY GOOD FRIEND & BROTHER
JOHN BAPTIST DE COIGNE   [21 June 1796]

This letter will be delivered you by Mr. Volney, my friend, [and a] countryman of old France. He proposes to go to your country and to be acquainted with you, because good people love to know one another. I therefore recommend him to you, and ask you to be his friend, to take ca[re of] him, and to render him all the services he needs while he is at Kaskaskia. [He] came to visit me at my own house in Virginia, where I had the pleasure of seeing you 15. years ago, when my name sake Jefferson was at his mother's breast. Now he is grown up to be a man, strong and young, and I am become old and infirm, or I should go to your country, as I have a gr[eat] friendship for our elder brothers the

Indians who first inhabited this country, and a very great one for you in particular. I wish you and them all peace and happiness, and never to be disturbed in your lands. Perhaps I may come some day yet and smoke the pipe of friendship with you and your friends. You told me your son would come to see me. I shall be very glad to recieve him here, and to be always his father and friend, for I am sure that your lessons and your example will make him always deserve it. My children too will make him very welcome and consider him as their brother, and their children and his will be always brothers and friends.

Farewell my good brother. Continue to esteem me always as I shall you, and shall always be your affectionate friend   TH: JEFFERSON

PrC (DLC); undated, but recorded in SJL under this date; faded.

To Harry Innes

DEAR SIR   Monticello June 21. 96.

Mr. Volney is so well known for his celebrated travels and other works, and as a member of the first national assembly of France that I need only name him to put him in possession of your attentions and kind offices. As he proposes to take Kentuckey in his way to the Illinois I have taken the liberty of introducing him to you well assured you will be pleased with an opportunity of becoming acquainted with a person of his worth and talents, and of rendering him those little services so useful and agreeable to a traveller. With very great esteem I am Dear Sir Your friend & servt   TH: JEFFERSON

PrC (DLC); at foot of text: "H. Innes esq."

To Henri Peyroux de la Coudrèniere

SIR   Monticello in Virginia June 21. 96

Retired to my estate and withdrawn from the bustle of public life I had not expected an occasion of recalling myself to your recollection. This however is furnished me by Mr. Volney whose name is already well known to you as the celebrated traveller into Egypt and Syria, author of some other very estimable publications, and a member of the first national assembly of France. These with his great personal worth and his character of a stranger will all be titles to your attentions, patronage and good offices should he pass over from the Illinois to St. Louis, as he expects. While making known to you a person of so much worth and celebrity, it is a great gratification to me to be brought again to your memory and to repeat assurances of the high esteem and respect with which I have the honor to be Sir, Your most obedt. & most humble servt   TH: JEFFERSON

PrC (DLC); at foot of text: "M. Peyroux de la Coudroniere Commandant de St. Louis."

Henri Peyroux de la Coudrèniere (b. ca. 1743), born and educated in France, was a strong advocate of emigration to Spanish Louisiana and in the mid 1780s served as an interpreter for Acadian families who were being settled there. He subsequently sought and received a commission as captain in the Spanish army and, in 1787, was appointed commandant at Ste. Genevieve, 45 miles south of St. Louis. In early 1792 Peyroux embarked on a trip to Philadelphia where he hoped to contact European immigrants and induce them to settle in upper Louisiana. There he met TJ and became acquainted with André Michaux, who reportedly recommended him to Edmond Charles Genet to aid in the projected French invasion of Spanish territory. When Peyroux returned to Louisiana in the summer of 1793 political opponents questioned his loyalty and succeeded in having him removed as commandant at Ste. Genevieve, although no formal charges were brought against him. In the late 1790s he became commandant at New Madrid, a position he held until 1803. TJ wrote to Peyroux that year requesting protection for Meriwether Lewis and the other members of the expedition. In 1805 Peyroux spent time in Philadelphia and presented a paper entitled "Essai sur la plus nouvelle des epoques de la nature suivi d'un tableau comparatif de la Basse Louisiane avec la Basse Egypte" before the American Philosophical Society. Two years later he published the essay in Annales Philosophiques, Politiques et Litteraires, the first, and only, volume of a journal which he attempted to establish in Philadelphia. In 1817 Peyroux remained committed to encouraging and aiding European emigration to Louisiana (Glenn R. Conrad, ed., A Dic-

tionary of Louisiana Biography, 2 vols. [New Orleans, 1988], II, 646-7; Carl J. Ekberg, Colonial Ste. Genevieve: An Adventure on the Mississippi Frontier [Gerald, Mo., 1985], 350-7, 461-2; A. P. Nasatir, ed., Before Lewis and Clark: Documents Illustrating the History of the Missouri, 1785-1804, 2 vols. [St. Louis, 1952], II, 598-99; Jose de la Pena y Camara, ed., Catalogo de Documentos del Archivo General de Indias Seccion V, Gobierno. Audiencia de Santo Domingo sobre la Epoca Espanola de Luisiana, 2 vols. [New Orleans, 1968], I, 44, II, 272, 277, 278; Ernest R. Liljegren, "Jacobinism in Spanish Louisiana, 1792-1797," Louisiana Historical Quarterly, XXII [1939], 85-7; APS, Proceedings, XXII, pt. 3 [1884], 368, 377-8; Donald Jackson, ed., Letters of the Lewis and Clark Expedition with Related Documents, 1783-1854 [Urbana, 1962], 104-5, 108-9, 133, 169; Peyroux to Albert Gallatin, [1817], in NHi: Gallatin Papers; TJ to Peyroux, 3 July 1803, 9 July 1807). For other publications by Peyroux, see Sowerby, Nos. 668, 1369, 1378, and Vol. 5: 668.

It is unclear when TJ obtained the following census information, which he attributed to Peyroux:

"Ste. Genevieve 1000. free persons
                  500. slaves
St. Louis.   2000. free persons
                        no slaves."

(MS in DLC: TJ Papers, 137: 23683; undated; entirely in TJ's hand; at head of text: "Don Enrique Peyroux de la Coudreniere cidevant Commandant de Ste. Genevieve en Louisiane"; endorsed by TJ on verso: "Louisiana").

In his travels Volney did not PASS OVER FROM THE ILLINOIS TO ST. LOUIS and there is no evidence that Peyroux received this letter (Volney to TJ, 24 Aug. 1796).

To Isaac Shelby

SIR   Monticello June 21. 96.

This will be delivered to you by Mr. Volney, well known in the literary world and a distinguished member of the first national assembly of France. As he proposes to take Kentuckey in his route Westward, I take the liberty of recommending him to your attentions and friendly offices. The esteem in which he is held both here and in Europe as well as his great personal merit and talents render him worthy of any services which his character as a stranger and a traveller may call for in the places where he shall pass. Your Excellency will therefore I hope pardon the liberty I take in giving him an opportunity of paying his respects to you and of solliciting your patronage of him while within your state, and accept the tribute of respect and esteem with which I have the honor to be Your Excellency's Most obedt. & most humble servt

TH: JEFFERSON

PrC (DLC); at foot of text: "Govr. Shelby."

To Archibald Stuart

DEAR SIR   Monticello June 21. 96.

The bearer hereof is Mr. Volney the celebrated traveller and author of several works highly esteemed in Europe. His name will also have been known to you among the worthies of the first National assembly of France. As he takes Staunton in his rout Westward I take the liberty of committing him to your good offices while there. He wishes to supply himself there with a cheap horse, just sufficient to bear him to Kentuckey. If you can guide him in his researches you will oblige me and serve him also who from his merit and talents is well worthy of your care of him. I am with great and sincere esteem Dr. Sir Your friend & servt.

TH: JEFFERSON

PrC (DLC); at foot of text: "Mr. Stuart."

From Tench Coxe

SIR   Philadelphia June 22d. 1796.

I have in my possession one of your letters inclosed to me on the 12th. instant, the other has been sent to Mr. Monroe. I presumed them to be duplicates. It will always give me pleasure Sir, to evince by attention to these little matters, my dispositions in regard to things of greater importance.

It seems Europe is not yet to have Peace. The french have opened the Campain on the side of Italy by a small action which ended favorably, and a great one in which they have taken the Austrian Generalissimo and 8000 prisoners, with further losses to the combined powers. It is probable the regeneration of Genoa will be the consequence, and troubles in Sardinia, Naples, and other parts of Italy, as also in Corsica. The Turks too will feel encouragement from this victory, and the dispositions to peace in the German Councils cannot fail to be increased. Money from England to the Italian and German powers will again be wanted and she is *really* not in a political or commercial condition to meet new demands. The disturbances of Europe, and her Colonies increase and multiply. Our chances of inconvenience are therefore continued; and if old causes of apprehension are diminished some new ones appear. Tis certain, that the french seem disposed to be less careful about inconveniencies to us from their measures against their principal Enemy, and that some bad leaves are in their hands from the book of precedent. Something has gone wrong in the Algerine affair, but as I know Nothing but from the acts of our Government, as published in the Gazettes, I am unable to say what it is, how it might have been prevented, or how it may be remedied.

I do not think we shall be involved in a rupture with any power, but I fear that we shall suffer considerable injury in 1796. The benefits resulting from some circumstances of the day may enable us to bear them, but many individual Sacrifices seem highly probable, in cases of property. In regard to political relations it seems to me pretty certain, that the US. will not have any power in a disposition effectually favorable towards them. I think a state of things rather better might have been accomplished, and might perhaps yet; but I do not perceive any ground to expect that we shall really put things into a more agreeable train. Being very retired in the Bosom of a large family and really, as to great public affairs, Spectator tantum, I may not be correct, but such are my impressions. With respectful consideration, I am, Sir Yr. mo. obedt. & humble Servant   TENCH COXE

RC (DLC); addressed: "Thomas Jefferson, Esqr Monticello near Charlottesville Virginia"; franked and stamped; endorsement by TJ torn, but recorded in SJL as received 2 July 1796.

TJ's letter to Coxe of the 12TH. INSTANT is noted at TJ to Monroe, 12 June 1796.

The *Philadelphia Gazette* of 22 June 1796 carried news from Paris of 25 Apr. describing FRENCH victories in ITALY under

Napoleon Bonaparte, in which the SMALL ACTION at Montenotte was the "prelude to successes still more brilliant" over the Piedmontese and Austrian forces. The report indicated that AUSTRIAN General Giovanni de Provera was among the 8000 PRISONERS taken. While the details of French victories in Italy were exaggerated (as newspaper reports from London were quick to suggest), Bonaparte did take Milan by the end of May 1796 (Lefebvre, *Thermidorians*, 316-19; Chandler, *Campaigns of Napoleon*, 63-76).

SPECTATOR TANTUM: "merely an observer."

From Charles Willson Peale

DEAR SIR   Museum June 22d. 1796.

The first object of my Life[1] is the inrichment of my Museum, In this view, I mean to continue my labours of preserving Duplicates of American Subjects for the purpose of exchanging them for those of other Countries, altho' I have been rather unfortunate in an attempt of this kind with Sweden—It is 6 years since I sent, by the recommendation of my friend Dr. Collin, some preserved Birds: This was repeated for 4 years but not a Single return has been made and I believe the Doctor is much hurt by this Negligence of his Countrymen.

I have it in my power to make an exchange of *Animals* generally—of Minerals a small number—but as to Vegetables I have not had time to pay much attention to them as yet; however by the help of Mr. Bartram and some others of my acquaintance in that line, The subjects wished for may be obtained. My third Son having the Talents of preserving the various Subjects of the Animal Kingdom, affords me considerable aid— from which I flatter myself that a reciprocal exchange will be made on our part.

I shall be happy if by my labours I can give Satisfaction where you are pleased to recommend me and accept my thanks for your obliging attention to the Interests of the Museum. I am with much respect and esteem Your friend   C. W. PEALE

RC (DLC); at foot of text: "Mr Jefferson"; endorsed by TJ as received 2 July 1796 and so recorded in SJL. FC (Lb in PPAmP: Peale-Sellers Papers); in Peale's hand; misdated 22 June 1786; the most important variation is recorded in note 1 below. Dft (Lb in same); at foot of text: "To Mr. Jefferson Virginia."

Peale had sent specimens to the Royal Academy of Science of SWEDEN in 1791. Similarly, ornithological specimens he sent to Louis of Parma early in 1799 did not result in any RECIPROCAL EXCHANGE (Lillian B. Miller and others, eds., *The Selected Papers of Charles Willson Peale and his Family*, 4 vols. in 5 [New Haven, 1983-96], I, 612-13, II, 149n, 236-8, 376n, 684; TJ to Louis of Parma, 25 Feb. 1799).

[1] Interlined here in FC: "which by no means excludes the Advantage of my family."

To ——— Hite

SIR   Monticello June. 29. 96.

The bearer hereof is the Duke de Liancourt one of the principal no-
blemen of France and one of the richest. All this he has lost in the revolutions of his country, retaining only his virtue and good sense which he
possesses in a high degree. He was president of the National assembly
of France in it's earliest stage and forced to fly from the proscriptions of
Marat. Being a stranger and desirous of acquiring some knolege of the
country he passes thro', he has asked from me to introduce him to some
person in or near Winchester. But I too am a stranger after so long an
absence from my country. Some apology then is necessary for my undertaking to present this gentleman to you. None is better than that it
is the general interest of our country that strangers of distinction passing thro' it should be made acquainted with it's best citizens and those
most qualified to give favorable impressions of it. He well deserves any
attentions you will be pleased to shew him. He would have had a letter
from Mr. Madison to you, as he was to have visited Mr. Madison at his
own house, being well acquainted with him. But the uncertainty
whether he has returned home, and a desire to see Staunton turns him
off the road at this place. I beg leave to add my acknolegements to his for
any civilities you will be pleased to shew him and to assure you of the
sentiments of esteem with which I am Sir Your most obedt & most
humble servt   TH: JEFFERSON

PrC (DLC); at foot of text: "Mr. Hite";
recorded in SJL as addressed to "Colo.
Hite."

The intended recipient of this letter was
probably Isaac Hite, Jr. (1758-1836), of
Frederick County, Virginia, even though
he was always addressed as "major" (his father, who was addressed as "colonel," had
died on 28 Sep. 1795). An officer of the Phi
Beta Kappa Society at the College of William and Mary before serving as an aide to
General Peter Muhlenburg at the siege of
Yorktown, Hite married Nelly Conway

Madison, sister of James Madison, in 1783,
settled a few miles from his father, who lived
at Long Meadows near Strasburg and Winchester, and, in the 1790s, built his own
mansion house, Belle Grove (Madison to
TJ, 5 Oct. 1794; T. K. Cartmell, *Shenan-
doah Valley Pioneers and Their Descendants:
A History of Frederick County, Virginia*
[Winchester, Va., 1909], 252-7; WMQ, 1st
ser., IV [1896], 213-14, 219-21, 245-6, x
[1902], 120-2, 2d ser., v [1925], 274-5).

This letter was not delivered (see La
Rochefoucauld-Liancourt to TJ, 11 July
1796).

To Archibald Stuart

Dear Sir Monticello June 29. 96.

The very contracted state of my acquaintance in my own country after so long an absence, and the general interest which prompts us to present strangers of distinction passing through it to the best men of our country, render me troublesome to you. The bearer hereof is the Duke de Liancourt of one of the most distinguished families of France, and of the wealthiest, till the events of his country deprived him of whatever could be lost. He retains nothing but an uncommon portion of worth and good sense. He was President of the national assembly in it's earliest stage. As he is anxious to know something of the circumstances of our country as he passes thro' it, I take the liberty of presenting him to you, for the benefit of any information he might wish to recieve relative to your part of it. He proposes to stay at Staunton one evening only. I am with great and constant esteem Dear Sir Your friend & servt

Th: Jefferson

PrC (DLC); at foot of text: "Archibald Stuart esq."

This letter was not delivered (see La Rochefoucauld-Liancourt to TJ, 11 July 1796).

To David Rittenhouse

Dear Sir Monticello July 3. 1796.

The inclosed letter has been misdirected to me. The services therein offered are for the Philosophical society and I therefore think it my duty, by a transmission of the letter to you, to put it in their power to avail themselves of them if they find occasion.

I think it proper to mention to you shortly at this moment a discovery in animal history of which I hope ere long to be enabled to give to the society a fuller account. Some makers of saltpetre, in digging up the floor of one of those caves beyond the blue ridge, with which you know the limestone country abounds, found some of the bones of an animal of the family of the lion, tyger, panther &c. but as preeminent over the lion in size as the Mammoth is over the elephant. I have now in my possession the principal bones of a leg, the claws, and other phalanges, and hope soon to recieve some others, as I have taken measures for obtaining what are not already lost or may still be found. One of the claw bones in my possession, without it's horny fang,[1] measures 7. inches long, and a larger one was found and has been lost. This phalange in the lion is under 2. inches, in length. It's bulk entitles it to give to our animal the name of the Great-claw, or Megalonyx. The leg bone does not indicate so vast an excess of size, over that of the lion, perhaps not more than a double or treble mass. But of this we shall be better able to judge when a fuller collection of the bones shall be made. The whole of them shall be deposited with the society. I am with very great esteem & respect Dr. Sir Your sincere friend & servt   TH: JEFFERSON

RC (PPAmP: Manuscript Communications—Natural History); at foot of text: "D. Rittenhouse. presidt. of the Amer. Phil. society"; endorsed by John Vaughan in part: "Communicated by Dr. Barton 19 Augt. 1796." PrC (DLC). Enclosure: Rodolph Vall-Travers to TJ, 16 Sep. 1795.

This letter, which Benjamin Smith Barton read to a meeting of the American Philosophical Society on 19 Aug. 1796, was the first notice of the discovery of the remains of the megalonyx received by the society (APS, *Proceedings*, XXII, pt. 3 [1884], 240-1).

[1] Word interlined in place "point."

To Jonathan Williams

DEAR SIR   Monticello July 3.[1] 1796.

I take shame to myself for having so long left unanswered your valuable favor on the subject of the mountains. But in truth I am become lazy as to every thing except agriculture. The preparations for harvest, and the length of the harvest itself which is not yet finished, would have excused the delay however at all times and under all dispositions. I examined with great satisfaction your barometrical estimate of the heights of our mountains, and with the more as they corroborated conjectures on this subject which I had made before. My estimates had made them a little higher than yours (I speak of the blue ridge.) Measuring with a very nice instrument the angle subtended vertically[2] by the highest mountain of the Blue ridge opposite to my own house from[3] a distance of about 18. miles South westward[4] I made the height about 2000. f. as well as I remember, for I can no longer find the notes I made. You make the South Side of the[5] mountain near Rockfish gap 1722.[6] f. above Woods's. You make the other side of the mountain 767[7] f. Mr. Thomas Lewis deceased an accurate man, with a good quadrant made the North side of the[8] highest mountain opposite my house something more (I think) than 1000. f. but the mountain estimated by him and myself is probably higher than that next Rockfish gap. I do not remember from what principles I estimated the peeks of Otter at 4000. f. But some late observations of judge Tucker's coincided very nearly with my estimate. Your measures confirm another opinion of mine that the blue ridge on it's South side is the highest ridge in our country compared with it's base. I think your observations on these mountains well worthy of being published, and hope you will not scruple to let them be communicated to the world. [9]—You wish me to present to the Philosophical society the result of my philosophical researches since my retirement. But my good Sir I have made researches into nothing but what is connected with agriculture. In this way I have a little matter to communicate, and will do it ere long. It is the form of a Mouldboard *of least resistance*. I had some years ago concieved the principles of it, and I explained them to Mr. Rittenhouse. I have since reduced the thing to practice and have reason to believe the theory fully confirmed. I only wish for one of those instruments used in England for measuring the force exerted in the draught of different ploughs &c. that I might compare the resistance of my mould board with that of others. But these instruments are not to be had here. In a letter of this date to Mr. Rittenhouse I mention a discovery in animal history very [10] signal indeed, of which I shall lay before the society the best account I can, as soon as I shall have recieved some other materials which are collecting for me.—I have seen with extreme indignation the blasphemies lately vended against the memory of the father of American philosophy. But his memory will be preserved and venerated as long as the thunders of heaven shall be heard or feared. With good wishes to all of his family and sentiments of great respect and esteem to yourself I am Dear Sir Your most obedt. & most humble servt

TH: JEFFERSON

RC (PPRF); addressed: "Jonathan Williams esq. Mount Pleasant near Philadelphia"; with reworked date and other emendations by TJ recorded in notes 1-5, 8, and 10 below; stamped; endorsed by Williams, who also evidently inserted square brackets and reworked two digits (see notes 6, 7, and 9 below) in preparing an extract for publication in APS, *Transactions*, IV (1799), 222, which contains minor variations of wording, punctuation, and capitalization. PrC (DLC); lacks later emendations, possibly by Williams, on RC.

YOUR VALUABLE FAVOR: Williams to TJ, 24 Jan. 1796. Regarding TJ's ESTIMATES of heights of Virginia mountains, see Williams to TJ, 20 June 1796.

The BLASPHEMIES uttered against Williams's great uncle, Benjamin Franklin, as the FATHER OF AMERICAN PHILOSOPHY came from the pen of William Cobbett, who mocked an address by the Society of United Irishmen in Dublin, on the occasion of Joseph Priestley's departure for America, that envisioned George Washington taking him by the hand and the spirit of Franklin looking down benevolently on "the first statesman of the age extending his *protection* to its first philosopher" on his arrival in the United States. Observing that Franklin could not possibly "look *down*" on that scene, for those who understood "the geography of the invisible world" generally believed that "Franklin's *shade*" had "taken a different route," Cobbett insisted that the address must have intended to say "that Washington would *look down upon him*, and Franklin *take him by the hand*" ("Peter Porcupine" [William Cobbett], *A Bone to Gnaw, for the Democrats; Containing . . . Observations on a Patriotic Pamphlet. Entitled, "Proceedings of the United Irishmen." . . . Part II*. [Philadelphia, 1795], 17-18). See Evans, No. 28434. Cobbett's real target was Benjamin Franklin Bache, his chief adversary in the partisan press wars (Tagg, *Bache*, 329).

[1] Digit reworked from "2."
[2] Word interlined.
[3] Word reworked from "at."
[4] Preceding two words interlined.
[5] Preceding four words interlined.
[6] Final digit reworked to "7", possibly by Williams.
[7] Final digit reworked to "8", possibly by Williams.
[8] Preceding four words interlined.
[9] Preceding nine sentences, which constitute the extract printed in APS, *Transactions*, are bracketed, possibly by Williams.
[10] TJ originally wrote "of very great" and then altered the passage to read as above.

To J. P. P. Derieux

[4 July 1796?]

[. . .][1] after [. . .][2] Loss by fire you [. . .] I procured 2. bed ticks, 3 pair sheets, and 6. blankets to ask your acceptance of towards replacing those you had lost. They were made up in a bale, and are now at Colo. Bell's who will forward them to you, or keep them till you pass on to Staunton as you shall direct. With my best respects to Mme. Derieux, I am Dear Sir Your friend & servt   Th: Jefferson

P.S. I was so pleased with the egg-plants brought by Peter, and his dressing them according to the directions you were so good as to give, that I must ask some seed, and advice how to cultivate them.

RC (Dabney S. Lancaster, Richmond, 1945); consists of mutilated fragment, being the lower half of one page; date tentatively conjectured from SJL and internal evidence; at foot of text: "Mr. Derieux."

LOSS BY FIRE: see TJ to James Monroe, 12 June 1796, and note.

According to SJL, TJ and Derieux exchanged 18 letters between 11 July 1796 and 22 Aug. 1799, none of which has been found.

[1] Estimated half page missing.
[2] Parts of two lines torn away here and below.

From George Washington

Dear Sir   Mount Vernon 6th July 1796

When I inform you, that your letter of the 19th. Ulto. went to Philadelphia and returned to this place, before it was received by me; it will be admitted, I am persuaded, as an apology for my not having acknowledged the receipt of it sooner.

If I had entertained any suspicions before, that the queries Which have been published in Bache's Paper proceeded from you, the assurances you have given of the contrary, would have removed them; but the truth is, I harboured none. I am at no loss to *conjecture* from what source they flowed; through what channel they were conveyed; and for what purpose they, and similar publications, appear. They were known to be in the hands of Mr. Parker, in the early part of the last Session of Congress; They were shewn about by Mr. Giles during the Cession—and they made their public exhibition about the close of it.

Percieving, and probably hearing, that no abuse in the Gazettes would induce me to take notice of anonymous publications, against me; those who were disposed to do me *such friendly offices*, have embraced without restraint[1] every opportunity to weaken the confidence of the People—and by having the *whole* game in their hands they have scrupled not to publish things that do not, as well as those which do exist; and to mutilate the latter, so as to make them subserve the purposes which they have in view.

As you have mentioned the subject yourself, it would not be frank, candid, or friendly to conceal, that your conduct has been represented as derogating from that opinion *I* had conceived you entertained of me. That to your particular friends and connexions, you have described, and they have announced[2] me, as a person under a dangerous influence; and that, if I would listen *more* to some *other* opinions all would be well. My answer invariably has been, that I had never discovered any thing in the conduct of Mr. Jefferson to raise suspicions, in my mind, of his insincerity; that if he would retrace my public conduct while he was in the Administration, abundant proofs would occur to him, that truth and right decisions, were the *sole* objects of my pursuit; that there were as many instances within his *own* knowledge of my having decided *against*, as in *favor of* the opinions of the person evidently alluded to; and moreover, that I was no believer in the infallibility of the politics, or measures of *any man living*. In short, that I was no party man myself, and the first wish of my heart was, if parties did exist, to reconcile them.

To this I may add, and very truly, that, until within the last year or two, I had no conception that Parties Would, or even could go, the length I have been Witness to; nor did I believe until lately, that it was within the bounds of probability—hardly within that of possibility, that while I was using my utmost exertions to establish a national character of our own, independent, as far as our obligations, and justice would permit, of every nation of the earth; and wished, by steering a steady course, to preserve this Country from the horrors of a desolating war, that I should be accused of being the enemy of one Nation, and subject to the influence of another; and to prove it, that every act of my Administration would be tortured, and the grossest, and most insiduous misrepresentations of them be made (by giving one side *only* of a subject, and that too in such exagerated, and indecent terms as could scarcely be applied to a Nero; a notorious defaulter; or even to a common pick-pocket). But enough of this; I have already gone farther in the expression of my feelings, than I intended.

The particulars of the case you mention (relative to the Little Sarah) is a good deal out of my recollection at present; and I have no public papers here to resort to. When I get back to Philadelphia (which, unless I am called there by something new, will not be 'till towards the last of August) I will examine my files.

It must be pleasing to a Cultivator, to possess land which will yield Clover kindly; for it is certainly a great Desiderata in Husbandry. My Soil, without very good dressings, does not produce it well: owing, I believe, to its stiffness; hardness at bottom; and retention of Water. A farmer, in my opinion, need never despair of raising Wheat to advantage, upon a Clover lay; with a single ploughing, agreeably to the Norfolk and Suffolk practice. By a misconception of my Manager last year, a field at one of my Farms which I intended should have been fallowed for Wheat, went untouched. Unwilling to have my crop of Wheat at that place so much reduced, as would have been occasioned by this omission, I directed, as soon as I returned from Philadelphia (about the middle of September) another field, not in the usual rotation, which had lain out two years, and well covered with mixed grasses, principally white clover, to be turned over with a good Bar-share; and the Wheat to be sown, and harrowed in at the tail of the Plough. It was done so accordingly, and was, by odds, the best Wheat I made this year. It exhibits an unequivocal proof to my Mind, of the great advantage of a Clover lay, for Wheat. Our Crops of this article, hereabouts, are more or less injured by what some call the Rot—others the Scab; occasioned, I believe, by high wind and beating rain when the grain is in blossom, and before the Farina has performed its duties.

Desirous of trying the field Peas of England, and the Winter Vetch, I sent last fall to Mr. Murray[3] of Liverpool for eight bushels of each sort. Of the Peas he sent me two kinds (a white and dark, but not having his letter by me, I am unable to give the names). They did not arrive until the latter end of April, when they ought to have been in the ground the beginning of March. They were sown however, but will yield no Seed; of course the experiment I intended to make, is lost. The Vetch is yet on hand for Autumn Seeding. That the Albany Peas will grow well with us, I know from my own experience: but they are subject to the same bug which perforates, and injures the Garden Peas, and which will do the same, I fear, to the imported Peas, of any sort, from England, in this climate, from the heat of it.

I do not know what is meant by, or to what uses the Caroline drill is applied. How does your Chicorium prosper? Four years since, I exterminated, all the Plants raised from Seed sent me by Mr. Young, and to get into it again, the Seed I purchased in Philadelphia last Winter, and what has been sent me by Mr. Murray this Spring, has cost me upwards of twelve pounds Sterling. This, it may be observed, is a left handed way to make money; but the first was occasioned by the manager I then had, who pretended to know it well in England, and pronounced it a noxious weed; the restoration of it, is indebted to Mr. Strickland and others (besides Mr. Young) who speak of it in exalted terms. I sowed mine broad-cast, some with, and some without grain. It has come up well, but there seems to be a serious struggle between *it* and the grass and weeds; the issue of which (as I can afford no relief to the former) is doubtful at present, and may be useful to know.

If you can bring a moveable threshing Machine, constructed upon simple principles to perfection, it will be among the most valuable institutions in this Country; for nothing is more wanting, and to be wished for on our farms. Mrs. Washington begs you to accept her best wishes— and with very great esteem and regard I am—Dear Sir Your obedient Hble Servt.   GO: WASHINGTON

RC (DLC); at foot of first page: "Thomas Jefferson Esqr."; with several emendations, the most important of which is noted below; endorsed by TJ as received 16 July 1796 and so recorded in SJL. FC (Lb in DLC: Washington Papers); only the most important variations are recorded below.

Washington apparently believed that Edmund Randolph, not TJ, was the SOURCE of the document (Freeman, *Washington*, VII, 391-2). Washington may have thought that the PERSON TJ had EVIDENTLY ALLUDED TO was Alexander Hamilton, but TJ was very likely describing Henry Lee (see TJ to Washington, 19 June 1796).

[1] Preceding two words interlined.
[2] FC: "denounced."
[3] "Maury" in FC here and below.

To Madame de Chastellux

DEAR MADAM   Monticello July 10. 96.

The letters of May 26. and Sep. 7. with which you honored me found me retired from business altogether and at a very great distance from the seat of government. I immediately forwarded to the President that which was directed to him, and I consulted with some of my friends who were in Congress to know whether that body had in any instance undertaken to provide for or assist any of the officers of the French army which had served in America. They assured me they had not, that in one case they had made some advances for the family of one of those officers (the Count de Grasse) who had taken refuge here in distress, but that they had grounded that on circumstances peculiar to the case, and excluding the general principle: that it was a prevalent opinion among them that they were not authorized to make a general provision by the words of the constitution which in the raising and applying money restrains them to very special purposes. As, from the circumstances of the revolution of France, it seemed probable that some of those officers, who had withdrawn to this country, might apply to Congress for aid, I desired my friends to attend to the case of y[our] son, and if any example of affording aid in a similar case sh[ould] take place, to notify it to me and I would put in a petition [in his na]me so as to give him the benefit of it. I have waited thr[ough] the whole session of Congress, and at it's close have repeated my enquiries and been assured that Congress have in no instance given reason to believe that they could be induced to take on themselves to give any aid whatever in these cases; that on the contrary they would certainly refuse it. Under these assurances I thought it most adviseable to offer no petition on the subject. It would have given me great pleasure to have been able to obtain for the family of my deceased friend, General Chastellux, the aids which unexpected events have occasioned them to want. But I have not been fortunate enough to succeed in my wishes. I had for him a very sincere esteem, which had commenced with our acquaintance here and had grown under a very intimate intercourse with him in France. His loss was one of the events which the most sensibly afflicted me while there: and his memory continues very dear to me. To this permit me to add that in the shorter acquaintance which I had had occasion to contract with you, I had observed in you those respectable qualities and dispositions which would have furnished new motives for any services I could render. Should any circumstance occur hereafter which may give me a better prospect of being useful to the family of my friend I will certainly avail myself of it, and give to you every proof of the sincerity of my affections to him and of the sentiments of attachment and respect with which I have the honor to be Madam Your most obedt & most humble servt   TH: JEFFERSON

PrC (DLC); faded; at foot of first page: "Madme. de Chastellux."

The 26 MAY 1795 letter from Madame de Chastellux was actually dated 6 May 1795 and enclosed a letter that TJ had FORWARDED TO THE PRESIDENT on 12 Sep. 1795. For her missing letter of 7 Sep. 1795, see TJ to James Madison, 3 Dec. 1795.

To Tench Coxe

DEAR SIR   Monticello July 10. 96.

Your favor of June 22. has been duly recieved, and I again avail my-self of the permission to trouble you with a letter for Europe which needs an unsuspicious conveyance. I rejoice at the victory obtained by the French over their enemies. I should have rejoiced much more how-ever to have seen them at peace with their continental antagonists, and the whole war reduced to a duel between them and the neighboring islanders. No man who is a friend to the freedom and independance of nations could have looked on such a duel with indifference as to it's event. But instead of being contracted, the bounds of war seem to be much enlarged: and our afflictions are destined to be prolonged. I see an interesting contest excited between Mr. Smith and Mr. Gallatin, and am glad that the H. of Representatives make it the occasion of deciding the question whether we are lessening our debt. That we are not how-ever, Mr. Smith seems to acknolege, unless we will allow him to count 4. millions before they are due to the treasury. I hope at any rate a clear statement of our situation, and honest and energetic endeavors to pay off our debts and be clear and independant.—We have had a very fine har-vest in this part of the country. The quality is as extraordinary as the quantity. Both however have been injured in other parts of the state, where earlier seasons threw their harvest into the forward rains. I am with great esteem Dear Sir Your most obedt. humble servt

TH: JEFFERSON

RC (CtY); addressed: "Tenche Coxe esq. Director of the public revenue Philadel-phia"; endorsed. PrC (DLC). Enclosure: TJ to James Monroe, 10 July 1796.

The INTERESTING CONTEST occurred in the House of Representatives on 1 June 1796, the last day of the first session of the Fourth Congress, when the South Carolina Federalist William Loughton Smith re-sponded to a lengthy discourse on Treasury Department receipts and expenditures made by Albert Gallatin on 12 Apr. 1796 in which the Pennsylvania Republican con-cluded that the national DEBT had increased by at least one million dollars during 1795 and that Congress was thereby "laying the foundation of that national curse—a grow-ing and perpetual Debt." In countering Gallatin's analysis, Smith credited four MIL-LIONS due from bonds for duties on im-ports. In his earlier presentation, Gallatin had challenged this procedure, noting that the bonds should not be included as receipts until they were DUE TO THE TREASURY and paid. The debate between Smith and Gal-latin was reported in the *Philadelphia Ga-zette*, 28-30 June 1796 (*Annals*, v, 921-36, 1499-1516).

To James Monroe

Your brother recieved a letter from you a few days since in which he says you mention having recieved but two from me since you left us. I have not been a very troublesome correspondent to you, I acknolege, but have written letters of the following dates to you, to wit 1794. Mar. 11. Apr. 24.—1795. May 26. Sep. 6.—1796. June 12. In this last I acknoleged the reciept of yours of Nov. 18. and mentioned that your plan was not yet come to hand, which with the difficulty and expence of getting laborers at this season would prevent beginning your works till the new year. I have been in daily expectation of hearing of the arrival of Mr. Short, having no news from him since his leaving Madrid for Paris. I am often asked when you will return. My answer is When Eliza is 14. years old. Longer than that you will be too wise to stay. Till then I presume you will retain a post which the public good requires to be filled by a republican. I put under your cover some letters from M. de Liancourt. I wish the present government could permit his return. He is an honest man, sincerely attached to his country, zealous against it's enemies, and very desirous of being permitted to live retired in the bosom of his family. My sincere affection for his connections at Rocheguyon, and most especially for Madame D'Anville would render it a peculiar felicity to me to be any ways instrumental in having him restored to them. I have no means however unless you can interpose without giving offence. If you can, I should be much pleased. The campaign of Congress is closed. Tho' the Anglomen have in the end got their treaty through, and so far, have triumphed over the cause of republicanism, yet it has been to them a dear bought victory. It has given the most radical shock to their party which it has ever recieved: and there is no doubt they would be glad to be replaced on the ground they possessed the instant before Jay's nomination extraordinary. They see that nothing can support them but the colossus of the President's merits with the people, and the moment he retires, that his successor, if a Monocrat, will be overborne by the republican sense of his constituents, if a republican, he will of course give fair play to that sense, and lead things into the channel of harmony between the governors and governed. In the mean time, patience.—Among your neighbors there is nothing new. Mr. Rittenhouse is lately dead. Governor Brooke has lost his lady. We have had the finest harvest ever known in this part of the country. Both the quantity and quality of our wheat are extraordinary. We got 15/ a bushel for the last crop, and hope two thirds of that at least for the present one.—Most assiduous court is paid to P.H. He has been offered every thing which they knew he would not accept. Some impression is thought to be made, but we do not believe it is radical. If they thought they could count upon him they would run him for their V.P. their first object being to produce a schism in this state. As it is they will run Mr. Pinckney, in which they regard his Southern position rather than his principles. Mr. J. and his advocate Camillus are compleatly treaty-foundered. We all join in love to Mrs. Monroe and Eliza, and accept for yourself assurances of sincere and affectionate friendship. Adieu.

RC (DLC: Monroe Papers); unsigned; at foot of first page: "Colo. Monroe." PrC (DLC).

COURT ... PAID TO P.H.: whether the fleeting consideration Federalists gave Patrick Henry as a vice-presidential candidate in 1796 was genuine or merely a ploy to draw off Republican support in Virginia, the plan did not advance very far, in large part because Henry—who had declined successive offers by the Washington administration to serve as envoy to Spain, secretary of state or in another cabinet position, or chief justice—showed little interest in public office (Norman K. Risjord, *Chesapeake Politics, 1781-1800* [New York, 1978], 464-7; Syrett, *Hamilton*, xx, 151-3, 158-9; Elkins and McKitrick, *Age of Federalism*, 524). MR. J.: John Jay. CAMILLUS: Alexander Hamilton (see note to TJ to James Madison, 3 Aug. 1795).

From La Rochefoucauld-Liancourt

Frederick town 11th Juillet 1792 [i.e. 1796]

Je ne veux pas m'eloigner de la Virginie, Monsieur, Sans vous remercier encor de votre obligeante reception. Les deux Lettres que vous avés eu la bonté de me donner ne m'ont ete malheureusement d'aucun usage. Mr. Steward etoit parti de Stanton avec Mr. de Volney. Et Mr. Hofman maitre du cabaret de Strasbourg m'a dit que le Clel. Hite n'etoit pas a Sa campagne, mais a une autre habitation beaucoup plus distante, et Sans famille. Quelque contrariete que j'aye eprouvé de ne pas voir un homme instruit a fond de cette partie du pays j'ay cru devoir de pas l'aller troubler dans Ses affaires. Je vous aurois renvoye vos deux Lettres Si le papier n'eut pas ete trop gros, et comme je pense qu'elles ne contenoient que des choses Obligeantes pour moi, Je les ay brulé. Les papiers publics vous auront apris le Succès des armées francoises en italie. Puissent elles en avoir de pareils dans Les West Indies. Permettes moy de presenter mon respectueux homage a Mrs. Randolph et Miss *Maria* et de me dire avec l'estime et la consideration qui vous sont dues Votre tres humble et tres obeissant serviteur LIANCOURT

RC (MoSHi: Jefferson Papers); endorsed by TJ as received 29 July 1796 and so recorded in SJL.

François Alexandre Frédéric, Duc de La Rochefoucauld-Liancourt (1747-1827), was a French philanthropist, author, and political figure who combined practical interests in technology and agriculture with an impulse for social reform. He was known as the Duc de Liancourt until 1792, when on the death of his cousin, the Duc de La Roche-Guyon et de La Rochefoucauld d'Enville, he became the seventh Duc de La Rochefoucauld. Liancourt traveled in England and Switzerland studying industry and agriculture and established a model farm on his estate to implement techniques he had observed abroad. He also built innovative cotton-spinning shops and founded a school of practical arts and crafts for the children of impoverished soldiers, which subsequently became a government institution, the École des Arts et Métiers. Liancourt held an honorary position at the court of Louis XVI. As a member of the Estates General he supported both popular liberty and the authority of the crown. Days before the fall of the Bastille, when the king characterized the situation in Paris as "une révolte," Liancourt reputedly answered, "Non, Sire, c'est une révolution." Immediately thereafter, he became the president of the National Assembly, where he proposed the abolition of the death penalty and championed other liberal causes. He fled to England in 1792 after plotting unsuccessfully to transport the king out of Paris to safety. From Britain, where he knew Arthur Young, La Rochefoucauld-Liancourt traveled to Philadelphia in 1794. During the next three years he journeyed from Canada to Georgia. He and TJ had not known one another well in France, and TJ approached the duc's visit to Monticello with caution (see TJ to James Madison, 3 Dec. 1795). The traveler found his host "somewhat cold and reserved" but possessing in general "a mild, easy and obliging temper." They talked of common acquaintances in France and La Rochefoucauld-Liancourt showed considerable interest in TJ's farming opera-

tions. Their subsequent correspondence was friendly though not copious. The duc's observations of America appeared in French and English editions in 1799 (*Travels through the United States of North America, the Country of the Iroquois, and Upper Canada ... with an Authentic Account of Lower Canada*, 2 vols. [London, 1799], II, 79; La Rochefoucauld-Liancourt, *Voyage*). See Sowerby, No. 4016. La Rochefoucauld-Liancourt left the United States late in 1797 to reside in Hamburg. In 1799 he returned to France, where under Napoleon he was restored to his privileges as a nobleman and took a seat in the Chamber of Peers. He played a prominent role in government councils on vaccination, prisons, hospitals, agriculture, and manufactures and held advisory positions with the Académie des Sciences and the Académie de Médecine (Hoefer, *Nouv. biog. générale*, XXIX, 650-4; Jean Dominique de La Rochefoucauld, Claudine Wolikow, and Guy Ikni, *Le Duc de La Rochefoucauld-Liancourt, 1747-1827: de Louis XV à Charles X, un Grand seigneur patriote et le mouvement populaire* [Paris, 1980], 41-2, 149, 211-16).

VOTRE OBLIGEANTE RECEPTION: La Rochefoucauld-Liancourt, in the company of the Englishman John Guillemard, had arrived at Monticello on 22 June 1796 and departed on the 29th (La Rochefoucauld-Liancourt, *Voyage*, v, 12-13, 38). DEUX LETTRES: TJ to Archibald Stuart and to ―――― Hite, both 29 June 1796.

LES WEST INDIES: news reached the United States in June that reinforcements for French troops in Saint-Domingue, comprising 2,000 soldiers and two battleships, had sailed from Brest in April (Philadelphia *Aurora*, 25 June 1796; Sir John W. Fortescue, *A History of the British Army*, 13 vols. in 14 [London, 1899-1930], IV, pt. 1, p. 471).

From Volney

Monsieur   Gallipolis 12 juillet 1796
J'arrivai avant-hier ici après 14 jours de Voyage à travers des Montagnes qui ne le cèdent à aucune de celles que j'ai vûes; L'on nous conte en Europe que les Montagnes d'amerique Sont de petite espece, abatardie comme les animaux: si les conteurs Veulent prendre la peine de traverser le pays de Kanahawa comme je l'ai fait, à pied, ils en reviendront sûrement désabusés de toutes ces rêveries Systématiques. Au reste Ma traversée a été favorisée d'incidens heureux qui M'en ont applani, très à propos deux ou trois fois, d'assez graves obstacles. Dabord si jeûsse différé, comme je le desirais, Mon depart de Monticello jusqu'au dimanche je manquais Mr. Steward à Staunton, et je perdais par ce premier anneau une chaine de recommandations et de ressources qui M'ont conduit jusqu'a greenbriar. Là elles ont fini, mais le hazard les a remplacé par des occasions qui M'ont Sauvé l'inconvenient de coucher dans les bois, et qui M'ont fait trouver, une heure après mon arrivée à la bouche de L'Elk un canot qui avait besoin d'un rameur; en sorte que j'ai eu l'avantage même d'être utile en Me Servant Moi même. Nous avions d'ailleurs fait chez Vous un calcul assez défectueux des distances et comme il est possible que d'autres Voyageurs reclament de Vous ces informations, je vais Vous en donner quelques détails.

De charlottes-ville a Staunton 45 Miles. Assez bon chemin, Même sur la montagne où la pente a été Menagée avec intelligence.

De Staunton a greenbriar . . . 101 Miles; fournis de distance en distance de Maisons et d'assez bonnes auberges. J'en Excepte celle de Warm spring qui Sans doute s'améliorera. Mais celle de heiskill a Staunton, et du Colonel Mathews à 31 Miles de là, peuvent le disputer aux Meilleures d'amérique: premiere journée, gorges et defiles pierreux, boueux, ennuyeux, et cependant j'avais beautems. Du colonel Mathews à Warm Spring 21 Miles; Montagnes dignes de la corse: il N'y Manque que des chevres et des stilets. De Warm Spring chez Morris 10 Miles encore Montagnes, et deux ou trois gués assez dangereux. De Morris à greenbriar 36 Miles; une forte branche de l'allegheni a traverser, plusieurs petits gués, une grande riviere, deux bonnes stations, Callahans, et Mr. Bowyer à Sulfur Spring. . . Heiskill donne à Staunton la Note imprimée de toutes les stations; ce qui est une idée à Mettre partout en pratique, il faudrait y joindre une ligne de route qui Marquat les *forks* où le Voyageur est embarrassé. Ce serait la perfection.

À greenbriar Mr. Edgar M'a ecrit Mon routier jusqu'ici; 168 Miles: savoir Robert Reynicks 8 Miles. pas Mauvaise route. High ballantines,

2 Miles; rudes Montagne. Ma Clungs 8 Miles, rudes Montagnes. Gililans 7 Miles, dont près de 5 en dangereux Marais. Young 34 Miles;
rudes et desertes Montagnes. Nulle Maison. Terrible journée. On pour-
rait la couper heureusement à 19 Miles où il y a un joli creek de bonne
eau: gililans tavern d'insouciance de paresse et de Malpropretés. Young
etabli depuis 8 Mois, sera une bonne Maison. Gauley river chez Deurtang; ce sera une bonne Maison. Mais le gauley est un gué detestable et
la montagne très rude surtout à l'ouest; je la regarde comme la fin du
massif dont Reynick's est le Commencement—Robert hugues 18 Miles
bon chemin: un sommet a franchir. La commence le Kanahawa; c'est
tout a coup un autre air, un autre climat, une autre Végétation: cela Sent
le pays chaud, le comtat D'avignon en y supposant les Monts de
Vivarais. Robert Morris 4 Miles. bonne Maison; bon chemin Mouth of
elk 17 Miles; route peu frayée Mais assez bonne. . Là on trouve assez de
secours en canots; Le fleuve a encore quatre ou cinq petits rapides, où
j'ai trouvé en eau basse 15 à 18 pouces d'eau seulement—les grandes
chutes commencent 30 Miles plus haut et continuent pendant un Es-
pace qui fait regarder cette Navigation comme impraticable. Ajoutez
que le fleuve dans son encaissement profond rejette l'idée de tout Canal
lateral. Je demeure convaincu que la jonction au james est a peu près
impossible. Mais lon peut infiniment ameliorer la route de terre.[a]
Désormais le tems [. . .] plutot le papier me manque pour Vous parler
de point pleasant [. . .] L'embouchure du Kanahawa. En deux Mots,
triangle entre deux rivieres, plateforme elevée de 60 pieds au dessus des
eaux, large d'un Mile, longue sans fin; bel aspect de Sol; 30 pauvres
log-houses: etablissement naissant—gallipolis; site Mal choisi. Rivage
élévé de 70 pieds; plateau et pourtant Marais. Mal Sain, Loghouses, et
cinq ans de procès, enfin terminé. En tout 83 lots de terre. J'ai trouvé ici
trois bateaux arrivés des illinois en le 2 jours; chargés en peaux. J'ai
obtenu tous les renseignemens. Je pars demain. Je me felicite de Navoir
point de cheval; car dechelle en Echelle je descendrai jusquau fort Massac. . Après ce poste ou plutot après Kaskaskias, je ne Vois pas par où
j'irai, Ni quand je pourrai Vous adresser une autre lettre et Vous réiterer
Mes sentimens. C. Volney

(a) Il y a passé les deux dernieres années plus de 600 Waggons d'émigrans.

RC (DLC); ellipses not enclosed in brackets are in original; final page torn; addressed: "Gallipolis—To Mr. Thomas Jefferson Charlotte'sville Monticello Virginia favoured By Mr Woodward"; stamped; endorsed by TJ as received 21 Aug. 1796 and so recorded in SJL.

In this letter describing his journey through the Virginia settlements to the Ohio River, Volney's comment that he arrived at Gallipolis two days earlier and after 14 JOURS DE VOYAGE suggests that he left Staunton ca. 26 June 1796. He apparently departed Monticello on 22 June, for on the previous day TJ wrote six letters of introduction for his guest; on 22 June a slave received two dollars "for exp. going with Volney"; and, as noted below, Volney wrote to TJ from Staunton on 23 June. The precise date of his arrival at Monticello is uncertain. According to his unpublished journal it was on 8 June 1796, but Volney's letter to William Thornton of the 13th implies a 5 June arrival and SJL records the receipt of Thornton's letter to TJ of 22 May 1796 "by Volney" on 10 June (MB, II, 942; Jean Gaulmier, *L'Idéologue Volney, 1757-1820: Contribution à l'Histoire de l'Orientalisme en France* [Geneva, 1980], 370; C. M. Harris, ed., *Papers of William Thornton* [Charlottesville, 1995-], I, 395).

CINQ ANS DE PROCÈS, ENFIN TERMINÉ: for the problem of disputed land titles at Gallipolis, see the Editorial Note to a group of documents on settlement in the Northwest Territory printed at 14 Dec. 1790; and Tobias Lear to TJ, 6 Mch. 1793. To secure ownership of the townsite they had occupied since 1790, the inhabitants purchased new titles from the Ohio Company in 1795, the year that Congress granted them an additional tract downriver (Theodore T. Belote, *The Scioto Speculation and the French Settlement at Gallipolis: A Study in Ohio Valley History* [Cincinnati, 1907], 58-9).

A letter from Volney to TJ of 23 June 1796, recorded in SJL as received from Staunton on 24 June 1796, has not been found.

From John Stuart

SIR   Greenbriar July 13th. 1796.

Your letter of 26th. May came to hand; and agreeable to your request I have sent you some more of the bones of the animal formerly sent, which is all could be procured, the most curious being taken away when they were first discovered, these I now send I took from the Cave myself, a gentleman from New York who was here accidenttly on business accompanyed me, we found one of the bones of the claw about Two Inches long which Mr. Hopkins took with him, if it was of the same animal of that I sent you, it must be the small claw that sticks to the leg above the foot; however the long bone I now send will enable you to Judge whether it is of the same animal or one of less size and as this appears to be the hind leg, and that you have of the foreleg, you can the better Judge his size, I was in some hopes the Head bones or teeth might be found, but so many large rocks are fallen from the Top of the cave these bones may ly covered. I have never heared of any bones of this kind being found any where before; but an account I had from two persons in the year 1769 when I first came to this Country (then inhabited only by a few Hunters) induces me to think such a Creature yet exists. The account I had as follows, and to which you will give what credit you may Judge it deserves.

George Wilson, and John Davis, informed they were lying on cheat River some time in the year 1765 in the nightime something approached their Camp with astonishing roaring and very much allarmed them, their dogs also srunk and lay down at their feet refuseing to bark, as it drew nerer its cry became in their Opinion as loud as thunder, and the Stomping seemed to make the ground shake, the darkness of the night prevented their seeing their enemy tho they stood long with their arms to defend themselves, they hoped to see its tracks in the morning, but in this they were disappointed, not a sign was to be found; Wilson gave me this account here; and Davis some years after in Kentuckey where he now lives. The former who was Lieut. Colo. to McCays Pennsylvania Regmt. died in New York in the late British War. Should you think proper to lay any farther commands on me they will be received with pleasure. I have the Honor to be your Obd. Humble Sevt.

JOHN STUART

RC (ViW); at foot of text: "Honbl. Thos. Jefferson"; endorsed by TJ as received 26 July 1796 and so recorded in SJL.

To Francis Willis

DEAR SIR   Monticello July 15. 96.

I was happy to recieve your favor by your son and happier to recieve him, and to learn that you are in good health. I find by his conversation that he has a fund of information which at his time of life must promise the best success: and should have thought him a valuable acquisition to our neighborhood. But the gr[ound?] had been occupied before the death even of Doctr. Gilmer, by a gentleman so much esteemed as to have got the better of all competition. We are now in consultation to find some other advantageous position for Doctr. Willis in this quarter of the country. The success as yet uncertain. He found me absorbed in my farming, for I am become a monstrous farmer. But my hills are too rough ever to please the eye, and as yet unreclaimed from the barbarous state in which the slovenly business of tobacco making had left them. They at least promise me enough to do as long as I can expect to retain the active dispositions of life.—It is too soon for us as yet to despair of a rendezvous but in the valley of Jehosaphat. I had rather flatter myself with seeing you here, or visiting you in Glocester. Among the reveries in which I indulge myself, one is to pass my winters in Norfolk or some such place, where I may find sun and society, the true comforts of that season. My vibrations would in that case certainly carry me through Gloucester. I make no calculations of time and chance upon this subject lest they should bring into question the practicability of the scheme. I had rather cherish the hope, whether well or ill founded, of assuring you some day in person of the sentiments of sincere and constant esteem with which I am, my dear Sir Your affectionate friend & servt

TH: JE[FFERSON]

P.S. Doctr. Willis promises to send me some of the cow-pea, a great desideratum in my plan of farming. I will sollicit your attention as well as his to it.

PrC (DLC); faded; signature partially clipped.

Willis's FAVOR of 26 June 1796, recorded in SJL as received 10 July 1796, has not been found.

From John Guillemard

SIR   York. in Pensylvania. July. 18. 1796

I thank you once more for the kindness with which you recieved me at your house. Wherever chance leads me I shall not very easily forget Mr. Jefferson. I beg to be remembered respectfully to your family Mr. and Mrs. Randolph and Miss Jefferson. I parted with the Duke de Liancourt at Winchester, but I hope to rejoin him at New York. I am an Englishman, not indeed by birth, by gratitude and privilege only, but such as only I should not be willing to part with. I know your prejudices only by hearsay. You have too good a heart as well as too formed an understanding to suffer me to see them. Your conduct is known in Europe. And that honorably as to your character. I confess I was desirous to be near a Man on whom so much vague Satire has been expended. You will excuse me for talking so much at random. I thank you for your hospitable entertainment. You shall hear no more of me. If, at any time, I can render you any[1] Service, you will oblige me by employing me. Any Letter will find me directed to Ascot Place, near Windsor, Berks.—or to St. Johns College in Oxford. I am sir with grateful respect Yours   J GUILLEMARD

If Mr. Volney returns to your house remember me to him, but I hope to see him in Philadelphia.

RC (DLC); endorsed by TJ as received 8 Aug. 1796 and so recorded in SJL.

John Lewis Guillemard (1764-1844), born in England of a Huguenot family, met the Duc de La Rochefoucauld-Liancourt in Philadelphia early in 1795 and subsequently accompanied him on his journeys in Canada and the United States. The recipient of B.A. and M.A. degrees from St. John's College of Oxford University, Guillemard in July 1797 was elected to membership in the American Philosophical Society. In Philadelphia from 1797 to 1799 he served as the final member, chosen by lot, of the five-person mixed commission established under Article 6 of the Jay Treaty to arbitrate British creditors' claims for payment of pre-Revolutionary debts. That commission failed to settle the claims, and in 1803 the British government appointed Guillemard and the two other British members of the group to act as a "domestic commission" to determine what claims would be paid under the Convention of 1802 between the United States and Great Britain. He was elected to the Royal Society in 1806 (*Notes and Records of the Royal Society of London*, III [1940-41], 95-6; Joseph J. Howard, ed., *Miscellanea Genealogica et*

Heraldica, n.s., 4 vols. [London, 1874-84], III, 388; François Alexandre Frédéric, Duc de La Rochefoucauld-Liancourt, *Journal de Voyage en Amérique et d'un Séjour a Philadelphie 1 Octobre 1794-18 Avril 1795*, ed. Jean Marchand [Paris and Baltimore, 1940], 92n, 93, 107; APS, *Proceedings*, XXII, pt. 3 [1885], 261; Perkins, *First Rapprochement*, 53, 117-19, 141; John Bassett Moore, ed., *International Adjudications, Modern Series, Volume III: Arbitration of*

Claims for Compensation for Losses and Damages Resulting from Lawful Impediments to the Recovery of Pre-War Debts [New York, 1931], 22, 359; Kenneth and Anna M. Roberts, trans. and eds., *Moreau de St. Mery's American Journey, 1793-1798* [Garden City, N.Y., 1947], 181, 254-5).

[1] Guillemard here interlined, and then canceled, "proper."

From Philip Turpin

DEAR SIR   Salisbury, July 18th 1796
The fact I mention'd to you relative to the Lion, is to be found in the Gent. & London Magazine for the Year 1783. It is an extract from a Work entitled Abrégé de l'Histoire générale des Voyages, M. de la Harpe, de l'Académie française.

'One resource of the Moors, when persued by the lion, is to take their Turban, and to move it before him in the shape of a Serpent. This sight is sufficient to compel him to accelerate his retreat. As it often happens that these people, when hunting, meet with lions, it is very remarkable, that their Horses, 'though famous for their swiftness, are seiz'd with so strong a terror, that they become motionless, and that the Dogs, not less timid, keep creeping at the feet of their master, or of his horse. The only expedient left to the Moors, is to alight, and to abandon a prey which they cannot defend. But if the Lion be too near, and they have not time to light a fire, the only means of terrifying him, they have no other resource than to lie down on the ground in a deep silence. The Lion, then, if not tormented by hunger, passes gravely on, as if satisfied with the respect thus paid to his presence.'

The Author mentions several other curious Circumstances relative to this Animal which are rather too lengthy to transcribe.

I feel myself much interested in your success in recovering some other remains of the Megalonex. It must be consider'd as a circumstance extremely fortunate for the lovers of natural history, that these curious bones should have fallen into the hands of a Person who knew something of their value, and that he should have transmitted them to one who is both able and willing to give an Account of them to the Public. Before you part with these curiosities, would it not be advisable to have a few castings of the claws in Lead or pewter?

I shall lodge the petrified Bone in my possession, with Mr. Johnson in Richmond, and get him to forward it to you by the first Opportunity.

As nothing relative to natural history can be uninteresting to you, I beg leave to inform you that about a twelve-month ago, an uncommon bird was caught in this neighbourhood. I did not see it myself, but was inform'd by those who did, that it was milk-white, with very red Eyes; and that it was about the size of the common Robbin. It followd a plough to pick up worms, on which it was so intent, and so gentle, that it suffer'd itself to be taken, and would readily eat out of the hand: it however died in the course of a few Days.

My neighbour Clarke, with the confidence natural to inventors is certain that his machine will go with sufficient force to turn a manufaturing mill. He observ'd (and wishes me to inform you) that the valves may be increas'd to almost any size, and that the Lever may be lengthen'd: and that whilst some of the valves are acted upon by the Current, the others may be made to revolve, if necessary, in still water: Further, that 'though the motion of the water Wheel might be slow, it would be forcible, and that it might be multiplied to the degree necessary for turning a mill. Should you wish to make a Trial of the Principle, in a saw-mill, Mr. Clarke appears dispos'd to render you any assistance in his Power.

Be pleas'd to present my respectful compliments to Mr. Randolph, and the Ladies; also to Mrs. Bolling, Mrs. Carr and other Relations. I am with great Esteem, Dr. Sir, yr sincere Frd. & hble. Ser.

P. TURPIN

RC (DLC); addressed: "Thos. Jefferson Esqr. Monticello"; endorsed by TJ as received 24 July 1796 but recorded in SJL as received 22 July 1796.

The playwright and literary critic Jean François DE LA HARPE was editor of the *Abrégé de l'Histoire générale des voyages, contenant ce qu'il y a de plus remarquable, de plus utile & de mieux avéré dans les pays où les voyageurs ont pénétré . . .* , 32 vols. and atlas (Paris, 1780-1801), an abridged version of a compilation by the Abbé Antoine François Prévost of information from Euro-pean explorations around the globe, published beginning in 1746 (Christopher Todd, *Voltaire's Disciple: Jean-François de la Harpe* [London, 1972], xiii-xiv, 24, 220n).

Letters from TJ to Turpin of 5 Oct. 1795 and 6 Mch. 1796, and from Turpin to TJ of 8 Nov. 1795, 7 Apr. 1796, and 29 Sep. 1799, received 11 Nov. 1795, 23 June 1796, and 2 Oct. 1799 respectively, are recorded in SJL but have not been found. See also note to TJ to Robert Pollard, 29 Feb. 1796.

From James Martin

[S]IR   Long Isla[nd 20 July 1796]

Having purchased near Jamaica on this Island the Whigs of the County nominated me to a task of which I enclose you the performance—it is not to a political but a Literary Character I present it, and not that it is calculated to stand your Criticism but that it may amuse a leisure hour—it was very numerously attended and had a good effect as to delivery if it fills up agreeably some of those listless Moments which even the best informed Mind cannot but feel in the Country my purpose in it will be complete.

Accept it as a proof of my high respect and a trifling return for the polite attention you honour'd me with upon my Arrival in philadelphia. Most obediently & faithfully yours   JAMES MARTIN

RC (ViW); salutation and dateline partly torn away; date assigned from SJL, which records it as a letter of 20 July 1796 received 14 July 1797. Enclosure: oration delivered by James Martin at Jamaica, Long Island, 4 July 1796, expressing antipathy for the monarchical form of government and for the influence which Great Britain still exercised in the United States; praise for France, which, inspired by the example of the United States, "fought and Conquered all the force which United Despotism could produce against" it; and concerns lest freedoms enjoyed by citizens of the United States be lost through corruption, such as that which occurred in Great Britain after the parliament was extended from three to seven years, noting especially the perils of the six-year terms of senators (MS in DLC: Rare Book and Special Collections Division; 24 p.; in Martin's hand, with title page in typeface: "Oration on the 4th of July, 1796 By James Martin"; endorsed in unknown hand: "James Martin, M.S. July 4th 1796"). See Sowerby, No. 3179.

James Martin (ca. 1753-1831), son of British artillery officer William and Anna Gordon Martin, was born and spent his early years in Boston before going to England for further schooling and to study law. He returned to Boston and was admitted to the bar in 1773 but then left for the British West Indies where he practiced his profession during the American Revolution. Upon his return to the United States in 1791, Martin laid the groundwork for a pro-

longed effort, in which he was ultimately successful, to reclaim property in Massachusetts confiscated from his parents during the war. In 1792 he became a member of the New York bar, practicing in Aaron Burr's law office and cultivating political ties with New York Republicans. He purchased an estate and resided at Jamaica, Long Island, New York, and also invested in lots in Washington, D.C. Through his acquaintance with Albert Gallatin, Martin obtained a position in the Treasury Department in 1813, reviewing cases filed for forfeitures. In 1815 he returned to his Long Island residence, where he spent the remainder of his life (Robert R. Livingston to Martin, 21 Jan. 1794, in NHi: Livingston Papers; Burr to Martin, 4 Jan. 1799, in NNPM; DHSC, VI, 199-211; Kline, *PAB*, 20: 187, 575, 592, 632; Benjamin H. Latrobe to Martin, 21 July 1810, in Van Horne, *Latrobe*, II, 881-3; Martin to TJ, 20 Aug. 1813; Martin to Gallatin, 12 Sep. 1815, in NHi: Gallatin Papers; *Letter from the Acting Secretary of the Treasury, Transmitting a Report of the Names of Clerks Employed in the Several Offices of the Treasury Department during the Year 1813...* [Washington, 1814]; Linda K. Kerber, *No Constitutional Right to be Ladies: Women and the Obligations of Citizenship* [New York, 1998], 3-7, 19-20).

See TJ to Benjamin Vaughan, 31 Aug. 1797, for TJ's mistaken response to this missive and TJ to Martin, 23 Feb. 1798, for his clarificatory reply.

To William Alexander

SIR   Monticello July 26. 96.

The large and constant remittances of cash which I am obliged to make to Philadelphia for nailrod for the supply of my nailery, constrain me to expect short paiments for the nails I furnish. I have lately even found it necessary to require ready money instead of the three months credit I formerly gave. I have therefore taken the liberty of drawing on you for £16–10–3 the amount of the nails I furnished you last September in favor of Mr. Samuel Clarke merchant of Staunton.

Mr. Monroe mentioned to me your directions to him to pay me the proceeds of a suit he brought for you in this county. But the delays of the Law leave it in the power of a debtor to lead a chace of years by the help of appeals, injunctions, replevins &c. inconsistent with the necessities of regular business. I am with respect Sir Your most obedt. servt

TH: JEFFERSON

1795. Sep. 29.

			£ s d
208. ℔ VIIId. nails	@ 11½d.		9–19–4
60. ℔ X.	@ 11d.		2–15–0
40. ℔ XVI.	@ 10d		1–13–4
50. ℔ XX.	@ 9½d		1–19–7
3. casks			3
			16–10–3

PrC (ViHi); at foot of text: "Mr. Wm. Alexander"; endorsed in ink by TJ on verso.

PAIMENTS FOR THE NAILS: in 1799 TJ received £13 on Alexander's "old nail acct." (MB, II, 1000).

From George Wythe

G WYTHE TO T JEFFERSON   27 of july, 1796.

Brend tells me he will finish the binding of your books in two or three weeks. The committee appointed to collect and publish the laws relating to land property, seeing your letter, in january, to me, declined proceding in the business, for the present, in hopes the general assembly may be persuaded by the reasons which you suggested to extend the work. Will you permit me to deliver a printed copy of the letter to every member? You say you will take the trouble of procuring a copy of the mss not sent to me. Adieu affectionately.

RC (DLC); endorsed by TJ as received 29 July 1796 and so recorded in SJL, which erroneously lists it as a letter of 21 July.

COMMITTEE APPOINTED TO COLLECT AND PUBLISH THE LAWS: see Wythe to TJ, 1 Jan. 1796. YOUR LETTER: TJ's second letter to Wythe of 16 Jan. 1796.

From George Washington du Motier de Lafayette

MONSIEUR   Mount Vernon 29 Juillet 1796

Si quelque chose en Amérique est capable d'adoucir le sentiment de mes peines, et de faire renaitre dans mon ame flêtrie par le découragement, quelque rayon d'espérance, c'est de voir, je ne dis pas seulement, qu'il est resté des amis à mon pere dans le malheur, mais quels amis lui sont restés! Connu, ou inconnu, je n'ai presque pas fait un pas sur cette terre de Liberté, sans y recueillir quelque portion de ce précieux patrimoine d'attachement, de bienveillance, et d'amitié, qu'il m'y avoit préparé dans de plus heureux temps, et qui l'y attend lui-même, s'il vit assez pour tromper les vœux des ennemis de son pays, au gré desquels il meurt trop lentement.

Je connois assez bien quelles consolations peuvent arriver jusqu'à lui, et de quelle espece de Jouissances son cœur est encore capable, pour pouvoir vous assurer que c'en seroit une des plus douces pour lui, de connoitre, au milieu de sa prison, et des supplices inventés contre lui par la haine coalitionnaire, les dispositions de l'Amérique à son égard. Tant qu'elles existeront, il lui sera impossible de croire que son étoile soit éteinte, et que le tombeau soit pour jamais fermé sur sa tête. Toujours il espérera que son tempéramment, plus heureusement que son bras, luttera contre la tyrannie, et que sa santé, par une heureuse obstination, ainsi que son ame, restera plus forte que ses maux. J'en ai pour garant ses propres lettres, dérobées par l'amitié courageuse à la vigilance de ses gardes, et où respire toujours ce sentiment de résistance à l'oppression qui ne l'a jamais abandonné, et ce pressentiment d'une délivrance, qu'il a constamment attendue de l'amitié des Etats-unis, et des anciens complices de ce que j'ai quelquefois entendu appeler, *sa sainte folie pour la liberté*: qu'on lui a tant reprochée, qui lui a déja tant coûté, sans ce qu'elle peut lui coûter encore.

Quoique bien jeune moi-même, lorsque vous étiez en France, je me rappelle parfaitement d'avoir eu souvent l'honneur de vous y voir. L'amitié qui régnoit entre mon pere et vous est également présente à ma mémoire et si j'avois pu l'oublier, ses lettres où je vois votre nom si souvent répété et son extrême confiance en vous aussi souvent exprimée, m'en auroient bientôt fait souvenir.

Le tendre interêt que vous lui conservez et celui que vous voulez bien me témoigner à moi-même, ne peuvent donc pas être des choses nouvelles ou imprévues pour moi: au contraire j'y ai toujours compté; et maintenant que ma mère et mes sœurs associées à ses étranges destinées partagent le poids de ses fers, j'y compte sans cesse encore; et s'il étoit possible que ses malheurs, et par conséquent les miens augmentassent encore, j'y compterois chaque jour davantage.

Cependant si souvent trompé dans l'espérance de le voir libre, puis-je faire autre chose, que de stériles efforts, pour remercier ses amis de n'avoir pas désespéré de sa délivrance? Si je ne puis faire plus, au moins je hâterai, j'accélérerai de tous mes vœux, le jour où, libres et réunis enfin, nous pourrons les remercier tous, en famille. J'ai l'honneur d'être, avec respect, Monsieur, Votre très-humble et très-obéissant serviteur,

G. W. Motier Lafayette

Un mal d'aventure à l'index, m'ayant privé pendant quelque tems de la faculté d'écrire, j'espère que vous m'excuserez de ne vous avoir pas répondu plutôt.

RC (DLC); at foot of text: "Mr. Jefferson. Monticello"; endorsed by TJ as received 6 Aug. 1796 and so recorded in SJL.

From James Monroe

Dear Sir   Paris July 30. 1796.

I have lately received your favors of the 2d. and 21. of March last and by which I find, to my surprise, that only two letters from me and those of the last year had reached you, tho' I had written one more of the last year and two of the present one.

Frouillé as I informed you in one of these was one of the victims of the reign of terror; Dr. Jemm is living and much gratified to find he has a place in your memory. The old Gentleman was somewhat afflicted with the hypocondria on my arrival, and which proceeded from the horrible abuses that were practic'd rather before that period; but he is now well, having breakfasted with me today, walking a league to do it, and desires to be affectionately remembered to you. I will procure for you the books you mention, but to execute that of the Encyclopedie it will be well for you to send me an account of what you have already received, as otherwise it may be difficult from the confusion which took place, even in those things, here at a certain time; I will also thank you to procure for me a like note of what I have, as I wish to send them at the same time for us both. I believe the work is now complete.

On this side of the water the scene has greatly changed for the better, in favor of republican government: for since the adoption of the New constitution liberty has as it were been rescued from the dust, where she was trampled under foot by the mob of Paris, whose leaders were perhaps in foreign pay, and restored to the elevated station she ought to hold, and where she is becoming as she ought to be, the idol of the country. France never bore, at any period of her history so commanding a position as she now bears, towards all the powers of Europe, nor did she ever approach it. Since the opening of the Campaign all Italy has in a great measure been subjugated. The Austrian army combined with the Sardinian and which protected Italy (by which I mean those powers in the coalition) was vanquished in the very opening of the campaign, in several severe actions, and finally driven thro' the Tyrol country out of Italy. After this, or rather after two or three defeats, Sardinia obtained peace, upon terms you have doubtless seen, and since all the other powers have done the same Naples excepted and who has now an Envoy here to obtain it. They have all paid money, yielded pictures, and in the instance of the pope, manuscripts of great value, and shut the Englh. from their ports. The French have likewise entered Leghorn, on the principle the Engh. held it as a deposit for supplies for Corsica &ca., and had likewise violated the neutrality of Tuscany against the French; and in pursuit of the Austrians who fled that way, they entered after them the Venetian territory. Thus you see the state of affairs in that quarter. Upon the Rhine too the French have been victorious, in several actions against the Imperial forces, driving them all on the other side, on which side, and some distance in the interior, the French armies now likewise are. They seem indeed to have gained a decided preponderance over their enemies here, tho' by no means in the degree they have in the other quarter; for the Austrian armies tho several times defeated, and seeking apparently to shun for the present a general action are nevertheless strong and united, protecting the country by their positions as well as by the forts which line the rivers emptying into the Rhine. It is often rumoured that negotiations are depending with the Emperor and in Paris, and which I think more than probable but yet know nothing certain on the subject. If the French should not be discomfited by some sudden reverse of fortune, and of which there is at present but little prospect, it cannot well be otherwise than that peace should be made soon with the Emperor, since he must now abandon all hope of recovering the Belgic &ca. and since it is to be presumed the French will insist on nothing beyond what they claimed in the commencment of the campaign. It is to be observed they have entered Frankfort and upon which city they have laid an imposition of 35. Millions of florins, a sum I presume beyond the ability of the place to pay it.

The general sentiment is to have no peace with Engld. for the present, and to which they are inclined as well in gratification of the resentment they bear that country for the trouble it has brought on this, as in the policy of keeping some employment for the immense force that will be on foot after the war on the Continent is closed. It seems to be the fixed determination of this government to inflict some great and rigorous punishment upon that nation if in its power, and with this view, and for the purpose of striking at the source of its prosperity all its treaties with the Italian powers are formed, and whereby Engld. will scarcely find admittance into any of their ports. This however is a delicate subject for me to write on, considering this letter passes thro' Engld., the bearer Dr. Edwards prefering that rout to the necessity of making a visit to Halifax or Bermuda, and which he would probably be forcd to do in case he sailed directly from a port of France. To him therefore I refer you for whatever is interesting in this or any other topic omitted here, and relating to French affairs and with which he is perfectly well acquainted.

In the interior relations the aspect is equally flattering as in the exterior. The financial system it is true, is bad, but yet not worse than it has been ever since my arrival. Their national domains is the great fund, and two or three times they have passed laws for throwing this away, but upon an idea the plan adopted was solid and would be productive: soon however it was discovered that these plans were visionary, and answered no end but to cede their property and[1] give discontent to the whole nation, a few land jobbers in each district excepted and some foreigners of the same respectable description, and whereupon they came back upon what they had done and remodified it. They seem to consider the ill success of the plan as a kind of breach of contract on the part of the purchasers, and therefore making it void ab initio. One thing however is to be observed that they never do the purchasers any real injustice, so far as to enable them to say they are made to pay even so much as a third of the value of the property: they only give them cause to make a great noise about publick faith &ca. and which you know none are so apt to make as those who have no faith at all. This government seems to have a horror of banks funding systems &ca. and therefore attempts every other resource in preference to those.

In other views the prospect is excellent. The party of discontented among those who were marshalled on the side of the revolution, diminishes daily and seems to be gradually reducing to those who dishonored it in the days of Robertspre. and his associates; men who were probably in the pay of foreign powers and employed to perpetrate those atrocities merely to make the revolution odious and thus oppose it, and who in consequence expect punishment from any established order of things. There are it is true some exceptions to this, and among men of principle who seem to fear the government will incline too much into the other scale, but at present I see no cause for such a suspicion. And on the side of royalty, its adherents likewise seem daily to diminish in number, and to be likewise declining to those, who are inflicted with a bias for that kind of government, which nothing can eradicate: upon whose minds no proof can work conviction. But the ranks of this corps throughout France has lessened, since this government was established, comparatively to nothing. Before this event the people of this country estimated the merits of republican government by those of the revolution, and therefore it is not surprising that many, and even among those who were ardent and active agents in putting it in motion, should have shrunk from it. Europe presented no example of republican government or of any other kind of free government, upon which they could dwell with pleasure, and therefore the revolution was their only standard. But since this government was established a new and more impressive example is before them, and which be assured has produc'd already a wonderful effect in reconciling the bulk of the people to it. I have this from many quarters and therefore confide in what I communicate.

This is a short sketch of the actual state of things here, according to the view I have of it, and which may be durable or fluctuating according as events yet depending may unfold themselves: for yet the scene of this great movment is not closed, nor can any one pronounce what its issue will be untill it is closed.

I rejoice that you pay attention to the improvement of my farm near you, since we look to it as to a place of comfort from the unquiet theatre on which we now stand: for to me and in more views than one it has been a very unquiet one indeed. But I think you can readily perceive why it is so, when you contemplate all the circumstances that apply to me, in regard to publick events since my arrival in the country: tis therefore unnecessary and unsafe to enter into them upon the present occasion. We never meant a long continuance here, and probably the term we had in view may yet be shortened. I wish therefore I could form a commencment of the house you suggested this fall or as soon as possible, and upon which head one of my letters was very minute: upon this I shall write you soon again.

I have done every thing in my power in favor of Mr. DeRieux but without effect. We have a small house next his aunt, and which we took to supervise the education of our child at St. Germains, as likewise that of Mr. Jones and a son of John Rutledge's who are at school there, in the hope too of seing the old Lady and entreating her to assist him. But she shuns me, as she would an officer of the peace from whom she expected a process of the revolutionary kind: and a visit which Mrs. M. made her sometime since in the hope of appeasing her fears, of importunate solicitation, was render'd very disagreeable, by her abruptly opening the subject, as soon as she entered and speaking of nothing else whilst she staid, but the impossibility of rendering any service to her nephew. Under these circumstances it will I fear be impossible to obtain any thing for him. I will however if possible. The order some time since enclosd for his uncle I still have, being unwilling to forward it, lest it should be paid in assignats or mandats, but I will attend to this object also in suitable time.

We are well and desire to be affectionately remembered to Mr. and Mrs. Randolph, Maria, and all our good neighbours. I thank you for information that my brother is well, and the more so because I never hear from him. With great and sincere esteem believe me sincerely your friend & servant   JAS. MONROE

I have just heard that I am charged with having become a speculator here, with other things still more exceptionable, and god knows what. I send therefore by this opportunity to Mr. Madison an ample refutation of these charges, advising that they be published if my friends think fit. He will probably see you on the occasion. I think I can ride any storm if I get safe to port from the sea upon which I am now embarked. Surely no man was ever in the hands of such a corps as I am at present. Augt. 6. 96.

RC (DLC); addressed: "Mr. Jefferson"; the most significant emendation is recorded below; endorsed by TJ as received 28 Oct. 1796 and so recorded in SJL.

For the ADOPTION OF THE NEW CONSTITUTION and the events of 13 Vendémiaire, see Monroe to TJ, 18 Nov. 1795. In a treaty signed with France on 15 May 1796, SARDINIA OBTAINED PEACE by renouncing all ties to the Coalition and allying itself with France. Sardinia maintained existing civil government while allowing free access by the French military (Stewart, French Revolution, 674-7). NAPLES agreed to a suspension of hostilities on 5 June 1796 and concluded a treaty of peace with France on 10 Oct. 1796 (Alexandre Jehan Henry de Clercq, ed., Recueil des traités de la France, 23 vols. in 24 [Paris, 1864-1917], I, 299, 303-6). The French government was so impressed by the PICTURES, statuary, and antiquities Napoleon Bonaparte sent to France from northern Italy that the Directory instructed other commanding generals to follow his example (Beauvais de Préau, *Guerres de la révolution française*, III, 516). ABANDON . . . THE BELGIC: a French decree of 1 Oct. 1795 had codified the "réunion" of Belgium and France (Duvergier, *Lois*, VIII, 300-1). The Directory levied an IMPOSITION of 8 million francs on the senate of Frankfurt Am Main following the capitulation of the city to the armée de Sambre-et-Meuse on 16 July 1796 (Beauvais de Préau, *Guerres de la révolution française*, III, 430-3, 515-16).

LAWS passed on 21 Nov. 1795 and 25 Apr. 1796 had suspended sales of the French *domaines nationaux*, then restored them as a means of backing the new currency, the *mandats territoriaux*. In addition, a proposal by prominent bankers in February 1796 to issue a circulating currency supported by large cessions of national property met approval in the Directory but was stopped by the Five Hundred (Duvergier, *Lois*, IX, 10, 83; Lefebvre, *Thermidorians*, 264, 266-7).

For the ORDER drawn on the UNCLE of J. P. P. Derieux, see TJ to Monroe, 6 Sep. 1795.

Although he confined the topic to his postscript, Monroe knew, several days before writing TJ, of rumors circulating in the United States that he was a SPECULATOR.

One allegation, which Madison was able to counter before he reported the accusations to Monroe, held that Monroe and Fulwar Skipwith, the American consul in Paris, had connived to buy a confiscated estate in France. Monroe assured Madison that the only property he had purchased there was the house in Paris he had needed for his own residence. Monroe and Skipwith were also accused of malfeasance in their handling of an American loan remittance that was destined for a bank in Amsterdam but had been stolen from the consulate in Paris. Monroe sent papers documenting his conduct to Madison and gave discretionary permission to publish his REFUTATION (Madison, *Papers*, XVI, 302-3, 379-80, 381-9). Unbeknownst to Monroe, however, on 8 July 1796 Washington had authorized his recall and begun the search for a replacement, not on the basis of the unsubstantiated rumors but because Monroe was considered to have been inadequate in representing the administration's policies. Timothy Pickering, alert to the approaching election, did not inform Monroe of his recall until 22 Aug. 1796, in a letter that Monroe did not receive until November (Ammon, *Monroe*, 150-3; Fitzpatrick, *Writings*, XXXV, 127-8; Madison, *Papers*, XVI, 449).

[1] Preceding four words interlined.

From Benjamin Smith Barton

SIR   Philadelphia, August 1st. 1796.

Mrs. Rittenhouse has received the letter (dated July 3d), which was directed to her excellent husband, and our friend. It came too late to be read by him, for he died on the 26th of the preceding month, with the calmness and the fortitude of a philosopher. You, who knew him well, will regret his loss. Even his country must feel it. We have lost one of the wisest and one of the best of our men.

The 4th vol. of the *Transactions* of our Philosophical Society is now in the press. About 150 pages are printed off. Your account of the bones lately discovered, will be very acceptable to us. It will be in time, if we receive it within the term of five or six weeks from this time.

I beg you to accept of the little memoir which I send.

Be so good as to let me know, to whom, in this place, I shall repay the money which you kindly lent to me, a considerable time since. I am, Sir, with very great respect, Your humble & obedient servant, &c.

BENJAMIN SMITH BARTON

RC (DLC). Recorded in SJL as received 30 Aug. 1796. Enclosure: Benjamin Smith Barton, *A Memoir Concerning the Fascinating Faculty which has been Ascribed to the Rattle-Snake, and other American Serpents* (Philadelphia, 1796). See Sowerby, No. 681.

ACCOUNT OF THE BONES: see Memoir on the Megalonyx, [10 Feb. 1797]. For the $60 TJ KINDLY LENT to Barton in 1792, see note to Barton to TJ, 12 Mch. 1793.

To Francis Eppes

DEAR SIR   Monticello Aug. 4. 1796.

I recieve with great satisfaction your information that we are likely to get Cary's claim against us settled on proper terms, and hasten to give my consent to any settlement you shall make, that it may recieve no delay from me. I had hoped indeed that a greater number of instalments would have been allowed us. Even Hanson gave us seven; a number which I would not ask from Mr. Welsh; but from my personal knolege of his very indulgent disposition towards us, and that all he cares about is, not the time when he shall recieve the money, but an assurance that he shall recieve it ultimately, I am persuaded he would consent without hesitation to more than three. I should have proposed five, and think Mr. Wickham will run no risque of displeasing his principal by fixing it at that number. Still I repeat that I will execute any agreement you shall make, and will send my bonds to Mr. Wickham as soon as I am informed of the sums and times allotted to me. I will give security too by a mortgage on negroes. It will be the first mortgage I ever gave, but had rather do it than that any body else should be made responsible for me. Mr. Wickam may say what number of slaves he thinks sufficient, and I will allot all those of some particular plantation or plantations to avoid the apprehensions of any unfair selection. I hope still that the money he is suing for us from R. Randolph's estate with the £1218–16–1 due from A. Cary's executors, will come in time to satisfy the bonds we shall give to Mr. Walsh.—With respect to the issuing execution for this last, I am content it shall be suspended till towards the meeting of the assembly; but not till they meet, lest they should renew the replevin law. It is impossible you should not become sensible on reflection that if an execution be not shortly levied we shall lose the debt. But this we will talk over when we meet, which you give me reason to hope will be in September, and here. I would have been to see you before this, but that a journey would be dangerous for my health which I lately begin to hope may with care be placed on a less discoraging footing. I must always except out of A. Cary's money so much as may replace what I paid Mr. Wickam for the estate. The balance only to go to him for Mr. Walsh. You did right in paying Jack £65. which I will consider as part of my reimbursement from the funds of the estate.—I am just finishing a threshing machine, which I hope will be at work within a week. If you come early in September it will probably be still at work at some of mine or Mr. Randolph's barns. If it were an untried thing I should not recommend it to your attention; but it's efficacy has been proved by so many years experience in G. Britain, and so generally that I do not apprehend a failure in it's performance: and it must be immensely interesting to you. Present my warm and never ceasing affections to Mrs. Eppes, and the blessings of an old man to all the young ones. To yourself every sentiment of sincere esteem and attachment from Dear Sir Your friend & servt   Th: Jefferson

RC (DLC); addressed: "Francis Eppes esq. at Eppington. to be delivered to the care of Mr. Dabney Richmond"; stamped.

The INFORMATION on the settlement of the CLAIM of Robert Cary & Company against the estate of John Wayles was probably included in the letter from Eppes to TJ of 25 July 1796, recorded in SJL as received 28 July 1796, but not found. SJL also records letters from Eppes to TJ of 28 Dec. 1795, received 16 Jan. 1796, and from TJ to Eppes of 10 Dec. 1795 and 1 Feb. 1796, which are now missing.

BONDS TO MR. WICKHAM: see TJ to John Wickham, 20 Jan. 1797. For previous plans to MORTGAGE slaves to Wakelin Welch, Sr., see TJ to James Lyle, 12 May 1796. Since 1786, TJ had coupled the payment of the debt to Cary & Company with Archibald

Cary's payment of a large sum he owed to the Wayles estate. After Cary's death in 1787, the Wayles executors received a judgment against CARY'S EXECUTORS, but the debt remained uncollected. In 1795 TJ paid Bushrod Washington for advice in the case (TJ to Francis Eppes, 22 Apr. 1786, 30 July 1787, 7 Apr. 1793; James Currie to TJ, 2 May 1787; TJ to James Brown, 20 Dec. 1792; MB, II, 934). The REPLEVIN LAW of 1787 allowed debtors upon execution of a judgment against them to give 12-month "replevy" bonds and have their property restored if commissioners, appointed under the law, agreed that the levied property would not sell for three-fourths of its value. In 1795 the legislature abolished the use of these bonds (Hening, XII, 457-60; Shepherd, *Statutes* I, 355-6; Marshall, *Papers*, V, 348n).

To John Barnes

DEAR SIR   Monticello Aug. 7. 96.

I recieved last night your favor of July 27. mentioning that Mr. Donath's arrival with my glass is hourly expected, and that you will *forward* it immediately. The object of the present is merely to desire it not to be *forwarded*, but only it's arrival *made known* to me, as I mean to have the sashes made and glazed with this glass in Philadelphia before it is forwarded. I thank you for your speedy attention to this enquiry and your information. The tea and gongs are safely recieved from Capt. Swail. Nothing is now missing but the boots and half boots from Mr. Starr, the shoes having got separated from them and come to hand immediately. I am with esteem Dear Sir Your most obedt. servt

TH: JEFFERSON

P.S. It will be very important for me to know from Mr. Donath whether the glass he brings for me 18. I. square as first ordered, or 18 I. by 12 I. according to the correction of that order.

PrC (MHi); at foot of text: "Mr. John Barnes"; endorsed by TJ in ink on verso.

Barnes's FAVOR of 27 July 1796, received

6 Aug., as well as Barnes to TJ of 28 June, received 8 July 1796, and TJ to Barnes of 17 July 1796 are recorded in SJL but have not been found.

To George Wythe

TH: JEFFERSON TO GEORGE WYTHE   Monticello Aug. 8. 96.

The object of my letter of January 16. was the preservation of the laws of this state still in existence; and it is one which I have had much at heart from an early period of my life. Of this, the industry I have used in making the collection is sufficient evidence. I consent therefore chearfully to your making any use of that letter which may promote it's object. I will take upon me any labor which may be desired in the superintendance of the work, so far as respects the Manuscripts or unprinted part of the laws, if the doing it in my own neighborhood be reconcileable with the plan which shall be adopted. Adieu affectionately.

PrC (DLC); endorsed in ink by TJ on verso.

MY LETTER OF JANUARY 16: TJ's second letter to Wythe of that date.

To Thomas Mann Randolph

TH:J. TO TMR.   Monticello Aug. 12. 96.

I received your favor from Staunton, and was happy to learn that your journey was agreeing with you. All here are well. Mr. and Mrs. D. Randolph left us the day before yesterday for the springs. Mr. Hurt yesterday, after putting our clocks into very good order. Robertson informs me he has got out about 500. bushels of wheat, and supposes himself half done. He goes on with his fallows at the same time with two ploughs and thinks the fallows and wheat treading will be finished about the same time, to wit, a fortnight hence, when all his force will be turned in to seeding. Our treading machine will be finished to day and will get to work early next week, so that by the next post I can inform you of it's success. It bids fair at present. The death of old Mrs. Alcock is the only news in our neighborhood. Another victory gained by the French in Italy over the Austrians gives hopes of a peace with the Emperor. That with Sardinia is made. So that there will remain to them only the English, whose armies in the W. Indies are dying by wholesale.—I shall be anxious to hear the further effect of your journey and of the waters, as the most interesting object of all our prayers is the reestablishment of your health, of which we should all have stronger hopes if you could trust more to nature and less to medecine. With the most sincere wishes for your recovery I bid you affectionately Adieu.

RC (DLC); endorsed by Randolph as received 19 Aug. 1796. PrC (CSmH).

Randolph's FAVOR of 28 July 1796, recorded in SJL as received FROM STAUNTON 2 Aug., has not been found. SJL also records a missing letter from Randolph to TJ, without date, that was received 2 May 1796.

RE-ESTABLISHMENT OF YOUR HEALTH: see note to TJ to Thomas Mann Randolph, 14 July 1794.

For the success of the FRENCH campaign in ITALY and her treaty with SARDINIA, see Monroe to TJ, 30 July 1796.

From William Cocke

SIR   Tennessee, Mulberry-grove August 17. 1796.

By your friend, Doctor Rose, I have the pleasure to inform you, that the people of this State, of every description, express a wish that you should be the next President of the United States, and Mr. Burr, Vice President.

I believe it is upwards of twenty years since I had the pleasure of seeing you; during which time, I have entertained a high respect as well for your person, as political sentiments, and shall be glad to receive a line from you, in return for which, I shall certainly give you the politics of this State, with such other information, as you may wish to have from this quarter. With respect, I am, Sir, Your real friend,

WILLIAM COCKE

RC (DLC); endorsed by TJ as received 15 Sep. 1796 and so recorded in SJL.

William Cocke (1748-1828), a legislator and Indian agent who was born in Amelia County, Virginia, had served with TJ in the Virginia House of Delegates in 1777-78. A man of the frontier, Cocke lived in Kentucky, where he became active in the politics of the short-lived colony of Transylvania. In the mid 1780s in the western counties of North Carolina he became a leader of the unsuccessful movement to establish the state of Franklin. After the reorganization of these counties into the Southwest Territory, Cocke served in the territorial legislature and the constitutional convention of 1796, which brought Tennessee into the Union in time to cast three electoral votes for TJ and Aaron Burr during the presidential election of that year. Cocke represented Tennessee in the Senate in 1796-97 and again from 1799 to 1805. Commended by General Andrew Jackson for his bravery in the Battle of Enitachopko during the Creek War in 1814, Cocke was subsequently appointed as United States agent to the Chick- asaws (DAB; Leonard, *General Assembly*, 127; Jackson, *Papers*, I, 60-1n, III, 408-9, 473; Samuel C. Williams, "The Admission of Tennessee into the Union" *Tennessee Historical Quarterly*, IV, [1945], 301-17).

To Wilson Cary Nicholas

DEAR SIR   Monticello Aug. 19. 96.

I now inclose you the draught you desired, which I have endeavored to arrange according to the ideas you expressed, of having the entry, not thro' a principal room as in Mr. Cocke's house, but at the cross passage. The notes which accompany the draught will explain it. I will add that it would be possible to contract the plan from front to back by giving less extent in that direction to the middle rooms, and making them encroach more on the passage, which would make them oblong octagons. But it would injure their shape and sacrifice the passage.

Should you part with a very good overseer I will thank you to send him to me writing very particularly his good and bad qualities. He must come before our court, as I have referred some other applicants to that epoch. I am with great esteem Dr. Sir Your friend & servt.

TH: JEFFERSON

RC (ViU: Nicholas Papers); addressed: "Wilson C. Nicholas esq. Warren"; stamped. Enclosures not found.

SJL records letters from Nicholas to TJ of 12 Feb. 1796, received 15 Feb., and from TJ to Nicholas of 15 Feb. 1796, neither of which has been found.

To Thomas Mann Randolph

TH:J. TO TMR.   Monticello Aug. 19. 96.

We are all well, and nothing new in our neighborhood. I have not heard from Edgehill this week. My threshing machine will only get to work this afternoon. Mr. W. Hylton senr. who called here on his way to the springs, tells me he has information in a letter from Sr. George Strickland that 2. steers will get out 120. bushels of wheat a day with it. This is encoraging. You will be astonished to find my buildings almost in the state you left them. Stephen Willis, on whom solely I depended, has been delayed by the fever and ague, and as yet is not arrived. This has already rendered imposssible the completion of my work this season. Add to this perpetual rains which give us only broken intervals for work. Patsy is removed into the Outchamber, the chamber being dismantled. P. Carr has taken rooms in Charlottesville. Adieu affectionately. Let us hear from you. No letter from you since your arrival at the sweet springs, tho perhaps this day's post may bring one.

RC (DLC); endorsed by Randolph.

NO LETTER FROM YOU: Randolph's letter

to TJ of 21 Aug. 1796, recorded in SJL as received from Sweet Springs eight days later, has not been found.

From Archibald Stuart

DR SIR   Staunton 19th. of August 1796

Having Occasion to be in Greenbriar last month I called upon My friend Colo. John Stuart with an intention to visit the cave where the bones of the American Lion were found, If possible to procure some more of his remains.

I found he had been there and procured some more bones which he promised to send you and had employed persons to Make farther search. The people who Made salt-petre at this cave gave him an account of a short part of a bone which they used as a support to one corner of their Hopper supposed to be from the thigh bone, about 18 Inches long and Split Nearly through the Centre, That the solid part of the Bone was 2 & $\frac{1}{2}$ Inches and the hollow $1\frac{1}{4}$ Inches = $6\frac{1}{4}$ Inches in diameter. This Bone was either covered in dirt or carried Away but as Stuart has offered a reward for it still hopes it will be recovered. I find many of these bones have been carryed through the County of Greenbriar and some into Augusta. The latter I hope to procure. From The disproportion which Appears in the bones found It has been conjectured that all of them do not belong to the Same Animal or perhaps this may be accounted for from our being ignorant of the proportion of the Animal. The following Accounts render it probable that this Animal Still exists in America. About the year 1765 George Wilson and John Davies report that they were hunting on Cheet river a branch of Monongahela, That one Night when in their Camp they heard from a great distance a tremendous Voice which became louder as it approached them untill it exceeded the loudest peals of Thunder they had ever heard. That the Animal walked round their camp untill near the Morning. That during that period they gave themselves up and expected certain destruction every moment. That Their dogs tho bold and faithful on ordinary occasions refused to bark and Could not be forced from the camp. That Before day he retired, at day break they heard his voice from a Knob on a high Mountain and in the Space of a Minute the same or a similar Voice was heard from the top of another Knob on the Same Mountain about one Mile distant from the place first mentioned. That from the Noise he Made in the night which the supposed was by

[171]

Stamping they expected to find the earth torn up in many places but to their great surprise found It was not even broken. A certain John Moorehead gave an Account similar to the Above. Moorehead and Wilson are dead, Davies is yet alive and resides in Woodford county in the State of Kentucky, and has always been reputed a man of truth. I farther add as a fact well ascertained That on a Rock on the bank of the Kanhawa the figures of many Animals most of Which are Known to be common in that Country have been carved out many years ago and among These that of the Lion and that from the rudeness of the execution it is clearly a work of the Natives. The bones we have been speaking of cannot be the bones of the Animal heard in the year 1765. They were found some distance underground. I am sorry I did not enquire into that fact particularly. I think two or three feet were Mentioned and Many of them had the appearance of Great Antiquity. From the Circumstances attending the discovery Mr. Cavendish Made this Observation to Me "That he began to apprehend this world was much older than was generally supposed." Some of the Best deer licks in Green briar and Which were formerly frequented by Buffaloe are Contiguous to the Cave where this Animals remains Were found.

Mr. Randolph when here had a Memo. from you to enquire whether V. Miller could be prevailed upon to go over and do some work for you in Septr. I have spoken with him on the Subject and received for answer that he can by no Means attend you that he has more work on hand than he can compleat in the Season.

The Executive have requested My Attention to the running of the Boundary line betwixt Virginia and Kentuckey; Upon examining I find The Act of Separation refers back to the division pointed out in the Act for establishing The County of Kentuckey. This Act is not in My possession and I do not Know that I can get it in This quarter. I must therefore beg the favor of you to lend Me yours. Mr. Monroe I expect will be oblidging enoug to bring it Over to our district Court. I once had thoughts of calling upon you on My way to New-London but lest I should find it inconvenient to do so I have made The above request. I am Dr Sir with respect and esteem your very humble sert

ARCHD STUART

RC (ViW); at foot of text: "Thos Jefferson Esqr"; endorsed by TJ as received 22 Aug. 1796 and so recorded in SJL.

For the initial presumption that the fossil BONES of the megalonyx were the remains of a gigantic AMERICAN LION, see John Stuart to TJ, 11 Apr. 1796; and TJ to Archibald Stuart, 26 May 1796. TJ's MEMO to

Thomas Mann Randolph has not been found; for his search for a stonemason, see his letter to Stuart of 5 Apr. 1796.

In July 1796, Governor Robert Brooke asked Stuart to serve as a commissioner for Virginia in the running of the BOUNDARY LINE with Kentucky (CVSP, VIII, 380, 386-7, 390-1). The ACT OF SEPARATION—the Virginia statute of December 1789 that authorized Kentucky statehood—confirmed the boundaries specified in the 1776 ACT by which Kentucky had been made a COUNTY (Hening, IX, 257-8, XIII, 18). For TJ's role in the passage of the earlier statute, see Editorial Note on the Fincastle County bills, at 15 Oct. 1776, Vol. 1: 564-9.

From Wakelin Welch

SR   London the 22 August 1796

The Death of my Father lays upon me the disagreeable Task of acquainting our Correspondents with the Event and (as his partner and Sole Executor) of Settling all his Concerns.

The Multiplicity of Accounts I have to prepare will be an Apology for my Abruptness.

I have inclosed your Account Current leaving a Balance due to the House of Robert Cary & Co. £132–17–8– which I will thank you to acknowledge by the first opportunity and to discharge as soon as possible.

The Affairs of the House will be transacted under the old Firm of Robert Cary & Co. and their office will be at No. 65 Houndsditch London. I am Sr your very humble Servant   for Robt Cary & Co
WAKE WELCH

RC (MoSHi: Jefferson Papers); in a clerk's hand, signed for the firm by Welch, who also added salutation and "Sr" in closing; at foot of text in Welch's hand: "Thomas Jefferson Esqr"; endorsed by TJ as received 20 May 1797 and so recorded in SJL.

ENCLOSURE

Account with Robert Cary & Company

Dr.			Thos. Jefferson Esqr. in accot. currt. with Robert Cary & Co.								Cr.		
1783							1786						
Feby	22	To Balance rendered under the City Seal	115	18	4		April	25	By Cash		40		
									By Interest of £40 fm 25 Apl 1786 to 22 Augt 1796 is 10 years 120ds		20	13	2
"	"	To Interest from this date to 22 Aug 1796 is 13½ yrs @ 5 prC	77	12	6								
							1796		By Balance due		132	17	8
							Augt	22	R Cary & Co.				
		£	193	10	10				£		193	10	10

Balance due Robert Cary & Co. one hundred & Thirty Two Pounds Seventeen Shillings & Eight pence

London 22d August 1796
Errors Excepted
for Robt Cary & C.
WAKE WELCH

MS (MoSHi: Jefferson Papers); in a clerk's hand, except for the firm's signature by Welch.

A receipt from William Reeves, London, 25 Apr. 1786, records TJ's payment of INTEREST OF £40 to Wakelin Welch, Sr., surviving partner of Cary, Moorey & Welch. On verso TJ recorded the following:

	£ s
"1774. Nov. 17.	85.1
1786. Apr. 1. balance includg.	
int. settled & sigd.	128.13.4
Apr. 25 By cash.	40
	88.13.4

> 1793. Aug. 26. balance includg.
> int. settled by
> Welch   112.13.4"

(MS in MoSHi: Jefferson Papers; with five lines heavily canceled between first and second entries in TJ's account; endorsed by TJ). For the antecedents, see TJ to Francis Eppes, 22 Apr. 1786. TJ made provisions for the payment of this private debt at the same time he provided bonds for the payment of the sum he owed to Welch as one of the executors of the Wayles estate (TJ to John Wickham, 20 Jan. 1797).

From Volney

MONSIEUR   Lexington, Kentucky, 24 aout—1796

Me Voici traversant Le Kentucky, sur Mon retour des deserts de L'ouest—qui ressemblent par trop à ceux de syrie et surtout de Diarbekr. L'echantillon de sol, de climat, de colonie française, et de tribus sauvages que j'ai Vu au poste Vincennes a suffi à Mes recherches; et les Nombreuses informations que j'y ai reçu M'ont prouvé que je perdrais à pousser jusqu'au Mississipi un tems précieux qu'avec Moins de fatigue et plus d'utilité je pouvais employer en une autre contrée. J'ai donc tourné le dos à la Monotone et immense prairie qui S'etend de L'ouabache et Même de White river jusqu'au Missouri, et Maintenant je dirige Ma route sur Cincinnati, et le Detroit pour descendre par le lac Erié à Niagara puis par L'ontario à oswego, delà a albani et probablement Boston. Cette direction me prive du plaisir de Vous revoir cette année Mais je n'ai pas le dessein de quitter L'amérique encore L'an suivant, et j'aurai tout le tems de Me dedommager avec plus de satisfaction pour Vous-même puisque je pourrai Vous rendre Compte d'un pays Moins à Votre portée.

Dès Ce Moment je puis Vous assurer que Votre procès du Mississipi est gagné. Les débordemens Se font d'avril en fin de juin. On peut les distinguer en trois périodes: un premier flot de la part de L'ohio occasionné par les pluyes et la fonte des Neiges à la fin d'avril. Un second flot de la part du Mississipi proprement dit, qui arrive en Mai—un troisieme flot de la part du Missouri qui arrive en juin. Il en resulte une echelle de latitude pour la source de ces fleuves qui indique celle du Missouri plus au Nord ou plus élevée que les deux autres. Le rapport d'un Voyageur américain qui a Vecu chez les Indiens de Techas (ou plutot tejas) Me confirme dans L'idée que le Missouri descend Nordouest de hautes Montagnes reculées Vers L'océan pacifique qu'elles doivent border à la Maniere des andes du perou. Rapidité, froideur, Masse de liquide, prouvent elevation de sol, Neiges abondantes, et haute Masse de Sol. C'est à la hardiesse des chasseurs à eclaircir ce problême. Tout Me porte à croire que le passage au Nord est un chimère. Je pense qu'avant dix ans nous saurons à quoi Nous en tenir. Présentement c'est une Veritable satisfaction pour Moi de Vous assurer que Vos informations ont été exactes sur L'ouabache et Sur bien d'autres points, et que Mr. Imlay finira par être rangé dans la classe des Voyageurs romanciers. J'ai Vû ici des personnes qui L'ont connu et Savent L'apprecier.

J'ai lieu de Me feliciter de Mes délais a acheter un cheval. Au Moment convenable jen ai aquis un aux rapides d'ohio qui se trouve très bon et à bon Marché. Il a fait Ma route D'ouabache, 240 Miles en 6 jours, et fera probablement de même les 400 Miles qui Me restent jusqu'au detroit. Un Américain Vient d'amener 50 chevaux sauvages de st. antonio, New Mexico; et Va les Vendre en ce pays. Il se propose d'en importer 500 L'an prochain. Il faut lui souhaiter du succès Mais y compter peu. Maintenant Mon embarras est de faire passer Ma Valise a philadelphie. Si Vous trouvez quelque Moyen qui Mérite Votre confiance je Vous serais très obligé de l'y adresser. Je compte être rendu en dece[mbre]. Je souhaite que la Saison N'ait point alteré Votre Santé Ni celle de Votre famille. Sur Ma route je N'entends parler que de fièvres et de Dyssenterie. L'abus des fruits Verds, du lait, de la Viande bœuf, des concombres cruds y contribue pour le moins autant que l'air. Toute balance faite des bonnes terres, des bonnes eaux, et du Climat les bords du potomac et du haut james N'ont rien à envier à ceux de L'ohio. Il est vrai que je puis porter ici un prejugé de Sentiment, puisque L'ohio Ne Me rappelle pas les Mêmes souvenirs que Le james et le potomack: Le livre juif a eu raison de dire: *lhomme ne vit pas Seulement de pain*; je Sens qu'il vit aussi de la parole, et de l'échange des idées. On peut posséder ici de Vastes terres, de Nombreux troupeaux; Mais tout cela laisse la tête bien Vuide, le cœur bien fade, et les jours bien longs. Par calcul fait, j'ai plus Vécu à Monticello dans quelques heures que je N'ai Vecu dans ces contrées en plusieurs jours. Il est donc tout simple que je préfère des côteaux, Même Maigres à la terre d'Egypte et D'ohio. Agréez les sentimens D'estime et D'attachement avec lesquels j'ai L'honneur D'être, Votre très humble serviteur   C. VOLNEY

RC (DLC); last page torn; addressed: "Mr Thomas jefferson Charlotte'sville Albemarle County Virginia"; endorsed by TJ as received 30 Sep. 1796 and so recorded in SJL.

Returning from a region touched on in *Notes on the State of Virginia* but never visited by TJ, Volney in this letter dealt with questions that he and his host had evidently discussed during the Frenchman's visit to

Monticello in June 1796. His discussions here of periods of high water on the MISSISSIPI, the unlikelihood of an easy water PASSAGE to the Pacific via the Missouri, and TJ's information about the OUABACHE (Wabash) and other rivers took issue with assertions—including harsh criticism of TJ and his *Notes*—made by Gilbert IMLAY in *A Topographical Description of the Western Territory of North America; containing a succinct Account of its Climate, Natural History, Population, Agriculture, Manners and Customs . . .* (London, 1792). Imlay, originally from New Jersey, had engaged in speculation in Kentucky in the mid-1780s, but left after failing to make good on land purchases. Little is known of his activities after shadowy dealings in England and France in the mid-1790s and a notorious affair with the writer Mary Wollstonecraft. On the heels of the *Topographical Description*, he published an epistolary novel about the western frontier, *The Emigrants* (London, 1793), which Volney may have had in mind when he consigned Imlay to the category of VOYAGEURS ROMANCIERS. Despite the book's guise as a series of letters written from Kentucky to an anonymous friend in England, Imlay was almost certainly not in America when he wrote the *Topographical Description*. Moreover, the title page depicted him as a "commissioner for laying out land in the back settlements," when he had actually only been a deputy surveyor of Jefferson County, Kentucky, and the book's introduction exaggerated his experience in the West by stating that he had grown to manhood on the frontier (Ralph Leslie Rusk, "The Adventures of Gilbert Imlay," *Indiana University Studies*, x, No. 57 [1923], 6-25). As a promotional work centered on Kentucky, however, the *Topographical Description* was widely disseminated. A second edition soon appeared (London, 1793), as well as an Irish edition (Dublin, 1793), a German translation (Vienna and Berlin, 1793), and an American edition (New York, 1793) containing a second volume with material from other sources, including John Filson's *The Discovery, Settlement, and Present State of Kentucky* (originally Wilmington, Del., 1784) and TJ's Report on Public Lands (enclosed in TJ to George Washington, 8 Nov. 1791). See Evans, No. 25648.

While Imlay made several uncontentious references to useful information to be found in the *Notes*, he caustically criticized TJ's lack of experience in the western regions: "He has written his notes on Virginia like a man of erudition, and considering that he never was in this country, he has given such an account of it as cannot be displeasing to an European. But, as in every thing which has characterized his political life, his judgment in this appears superficial, and his mind attached to the theory of its own fabrication" (Imlay, *Topographical Description*, 109). Imlay claimed that the *Notes* were incorrect about the time of year in which the Mississippi and its tributaries experienced high water, and he made general assertions about the navigability of rivers such as the Wabash that did not substantiate the detailed information in the *Notes*. He also drew the conclusion that some "ridges of hills," not "so high or so rugged as the Allegany mountain," formed the only obstacle between the upper Missouri River and the Pacific Ocean, contrary to TJ's statement in the *Notes*, reinforced by Volney in this letter, that the temperature and speed of the Missouri's current implied a significant elevation of land near the river's source (same, 105-7, 109-10; *Notes*, ed. Peden, 8-12). Imlay even more bluntly attacked TJ's depiction of African Americans in the *Notes*, saying that he was "ashamed" of the Virginian's "disgraceful prejudices" (Imlay, *Topographical Description*, 185). Perhaps to validate Kentucky's political institutions, which were derived from those of Virginia, he also found fault with TJ's critical analysis of the mother state's constitution and expressed regret that prominent individuals "who have acquired celebrity among the friends of freedom, should, by vainly circulating their crude sentiments, retard the progress of reason" (same, 168).

Imlay and TJ never exchanged views directly, and TJ is not known to have owned the *Topographical Description*. None of the notations made by TJ in his own copy of the *Notes on Virginia*—in the expectation, never realized in his lifetime, of thoroughly revising the work for a new edition—refers to Imlay's book or to the information provided in this letter by Volney (see *Notes*, ed. Peden, xx-xxi). In the end, Imlay's criticisms seem to have had little impact; Henri

Grégoire, in *De la Littérature des Nègres* (Paris, 1808), referred to differences between TJ and Imlay on race and the abilities of black writers, but did not develop the issue (see Sowerby, No. 1398).

From John Stuart

SIR   Augt. 25th. 1796

It is some time ago since I wrote you by Major Taylor, the Bones then mentioned I hoped would have Reached you nearly as soon as the Letter, but I unfortunately missed of the Waggoner—they are the same I now send by Mr. Silkniter. I am your Most Obd Humbl Servt.

JOHN STUART

RC (DLC); addressed: "Honbl. Thomas Jefferson Esqr"; endorsed by TJ.

Stuart last WROTE TJ on 13 July 1796. I NOW SEND BY MR. SILKNITER: TJ paid Jacob Silknitter for charcoal burning from 1795 to 1797 (MB, II, 925). According to SJL, TJ wrote letters to Silknitter on 30 Oct. 1794, 30 Oct. 1797, and 29 Aug. 1798, none of which has been found.

To Robert Pleasants

[27 Aug. 1796]

[. . .]¹ the establishment of the plan of emancipation if it should precede I am not prepared to decide. If it should precede, I would refer to your consideration whether the plan you propose is adequate to the object. I apprehend that private liberalities will never be equal but to local and partial effects. I venture therefore to suggest what alone can, in my opinion, accomplish the general object. Among the laws proposed in what was called the Revised code printed in 1784. was a bill entitled 'for the more general diffusion of knowledge.' This bill was much approved, [and] was taken from [the] bundle and printed for public consideration when it was first reported. I believe that it would now be [as] generally approved, and needs only to be brought into view again to be adopted. This might be effected by petitions from the several counties to the assembly to take that bill into consideration. Very small alterations² would make it embrace the object of your paper, it's effect would be general, and the means for carrying it on would be certain and permanent. Permit me therefore to suggest to you the substitution of that as a more general and certain means of providing for the instruction of the slaves, and more desireable as they would in the course of it be mixed with those of free condition. Whether, for their happiness, it should extend beyond those destined to be free, is questionable. Ignorance and despotism seem made for each other. I am, with perfect esteem Dear Sir Your friend & servt   TH: JEFFERSON

PrC (DLC: TJ Papers, 100: 17181); consists of last page only; undated, but assigned on the basis of SJL and Pleasants to TJ, 8 Feb. 1797; faded; with emendations, the most important of which is noted below.

This fragment is the conclusion of TJ's reply to Pleasants's letter of 1 June 1796. PLAN YOU PROPOSE: the "rough Essay" enclosed in Pleasants to TJ, 1 June 1796. As a member of a committee of revisors appointed in 1776 to overhaul Virginia's legal code, TJ had written an education BILL that proposed a three-tiered system of state-supported primary, grammar, and university education, the last two stages being progressively more selective. The bill was first presented to the House of Delegates in December 1778 and was one of several proposed revisions of statutes printed in 1784 for consideration by the Assembly (*Re-port of the Committee of Revisors Appointed by the General Assembly of Virginia in MDCCLXXVI* [Richmond, 1784]). See Sowerby, No. 1864. TJ soon came to regard the bill as the most important in the revisal of the laws, but the measure languished over the issue of funding the schools (Autobiography, in Ford, I, 66-7; and above in this series, Vol. 2: 526-35, for the legislative history of the bill). For the passage of a school bill in December 1796, see Pleasants to TJ, 8 Feb. 1797.

A letter from Pleasants to TJ of 13 June 1796, recorded in SJL as received the same day, has not been found.

[1] Estimated one or two pages missing.

[2] TJ originally wrote "very little alteration of it," then amended the passage to read as above.

From George Washington

DEAR SIR   Philadelphia 28th. Augt. 1796.

As soon as I returned to this City, and had waded through the Papers, and other matters which were laid before me on my arrival, and claimed my earliest attention I recollected the request in your letter of the 19th. of June, and herewith enclose copies of the Papers agreeably to that request. With great esteem & regard I am—Dear Sir Your Obedt Servt   GO: WASHINGTON

RC (DLC); at foot of text: "Thomas Jefferson Esqr"; endorsed by TJ as received 9 Sep. 1796 and so recorded in SJL. FC (Lb in DLC: Washington Papers). Enclosure: see Enclosure No. 2 listed at TJ to Washington, [11 July 1793].

Questions on the Cow Pea, with Answers of Philip Tabb

[after 30 Aug. 1796?]

Questions relative to the Cow-pea.

Answers.

1. Does dry or moist Land, rich or poor, suit it best?

1 Dry Land of a middle quality.

2. is it best in drills or broadcast.

2 hills better than either at least 4 feet distant

3. how much seed is sown to the acre in the broad-cast?

3 not known 2 or 3 plants enough to a hill.

4. what is the time of sowing, and particularly where it is to be followed by wheat?

4 from the 1st. to the 15 June, this Crop never followed by fall sowing here the growth being remarkably slow, till the latter end of Summer

5. what is the time of gathering?

5 from the middle of Sept. to the last of Novemr.

6. does it ripen generally together, or successively?

6 successively until stopt by the frost.

7. how is it gathered, by the hand, by the scythe or the sickle?

7 by hand or rather by Stock turned in to fatten.

8. what is it's produce according to the land and season?

8 Not ascertained probably from 15 to 20 Bushels the acre if alone it is rarely planted without Corn here.

9. is the haulm good fodder?

9 every part is good food for stock

10. is the grain given whole or ground?

10 whole in this country

11. what kinds of stock does it suit?

11 Horses Hoggs horned Cattle and Sheep

12. is it eatable by man also?

12 it is eatable but inferior to most of its species for that purpose.

MS (DLC); the first column and heading of the second being in TJ's hand, the remainder in Tabb's; undated, but conjecturally assigned on the basis of Tabb's letter quoted below.

TJ had apparently expressed interest in the cow pea when Dr. John Willis—a physician of Whitehall in Gloucester County, Virginia, who married Nelly Conway Madison, James Madison's niece—visited him at Monticello (TJ to Francis Willis, 15 July 1796; Madison *Papers*, xv, 378n). Willis evidently then inquired about the cow pea on TJ's behalf in a letter to Philip Tabb, a planter who resided at Toddsbury, the family estate in Gloucester County (WMQ, 1st ser., XIII [1905], 170). Tabb's reply to Willis, written on 30 Aug. 1796 from Toddsbury, eventually came to TJ's hands: "I received your favor of the 6th. Inst. per post and begg leave to assure you that I shall have pleasure in giving every proof in my power of a disposition to comply with Mr. Jefferson's request. I have for several years cultivated the pea you mention (the most general and perhaps proper name of which

is the Cow Pea). I am induced to think the growth of this grain peculiarly calculated for the reduced Corn Lands of our lower Country, the soil of which has a great proportion of sand. It is planted among the corn at the distance of about 6 or 8 feet frequently in the same hill; and 'tho put in early as may or 1st. June grows but slowly until the Corn begins to decline then rapidly. I think some fields near me has been much improved by this pea, and it is of considerable value by fatting different kinds of Stock both before and after the Corn crop is gathered—for rain does not spoil it in the pod when ripe as other Indian peas generally. I doubt whether this pea would grow as kindly on Mr. Jeffersons Lands as it does here. I think his has a redish soil and free from Sand but should he be disposed to make the experiment, I will endeavour to send a Bushell of Seed to any person he may think proper to appoint at Richmond and will then give any farther information in my power that may be wanted" (RC in DLC; addressed: "Doctr. John Willis Charlottesvile"; stamped; endorsed by TJ: "Peas Cow. Philip Tabb's lre").

From John Carey

September 1, 1796.
SIR
Falcon Court, Fleet Street, London.

It may appear presumptuous in me to address you, since I have not been honored with any reply to a letter which I took the liberty of writing to you about April, 1795. However, as that letter did not absolutely require an answer, and as, possibly, you may have sent an answer which miscarried, possibly, on the other hand, my letter may have never reached you, I venture to trouble you with a few lines on a subject, which, in my feeble judgment at least, appears entitled to some consideration. Not long since, I happened, in a coffee-house, to fall into conversation with a sensible, well-informed gentleman, an American, I believe, but, at least, well acquainted with American affairs, and with the characters of those who conduct them. Speaking of Genl. Washington, this gentleman mentioned his "*Official Letters*," and, without knowing my connexion with them, strongly condemned the editor for having "*suppressed a number of the most interesting passages, and presented the public with little better than the chaff.*" These, as nearly as I can recollect, were his words: and this he delivered, not as his own private opinion only, but as that of the most competent judges in America, mentioning, at the same time, some very respectable names, as coinciding with him in sentiment. I felt too deeply interested in the affair, to suffer it to pass over thus in general terms; and accordingly I endeavoured to bring him to particulars; when, to my very great surprise, he accurately repeated the substance of some very material passages which I had omitted, and pointed out, in one instance, the omission of an entire letter. I regret exceedingly that my astonishment at this extraordinary adventure deprived me of that presence of mind which might have enabled me to make some effort to discover who the gentleman was, in order the better to appreciate his opinion, and ascertain what degree of credit was due to his assertion respecting the opinions of those whose names he had quoted. But, in truth, I have ever entertained an extreme aversion to catechising strangers; and, since the casual rencontre abovementioned, I have never been able to meet with the gentleman again.   The purport, therefore, of the present letter is, to request, if it be not too high a degree of presumption to hope for such condescension on your part, that you, Sir, would be kind enough to honor me with your opinion on the subject, in order that I may not err on either side, through want or through excess of caution, in case I publish the continuation; which I wish to do as soon as I can render it convenient. Mr. Randolph, indeed, in a letter of June 23, 1795, was pleased to express himself as follows—(for I apprehend no impropriety in quoting his words, as the letter appears to be in Mr. Taylor's handwriting, and wears not the slightest feature of confidential secrecy)— *"My opinion upon the original propriety of the publication remains as it always was, in relation to the then circumstances. I acknowledge, however, that you have rendered that publication but little if at all exceptionable in my eye. The papers which are hereafter to appear, and the matter which you have retained to yourself, are not here spoken of."* This declaration, however, (as he did not then know what I had omitted) only assures me that there appeared no impropriety in what I had published, leaving me still uncertain whether the omissions were in every case proper and justifiable. But as I sent him, in November last, (in my answer to the above) a very minute list of the passages and letters omitted, with accurate references to the volume and page of the record where each might be found, it would at present be no difficult matter to determine whether I have in every instance acted properly. A hint on the subject from you, Sir, on whose judgment I place the most implicit reliance, would serve me as a guide in publishing the sequel, if I do but live to publish it. The delay, indeed, I poignantly regret, especially when I consider that we shall be inundated by such a deluge of French productions when once this disastrous war is brought to a period, as will swallow up all the curiosity and attention of European readers, and leave them nearly as indifferent to the events of the American contest, as to the transactions of the Antediluvians or Pre-adamites; a circumstance, which must of course operate as a material drawback on any advantages that I might hope to derive from the publication, which, by the way, has not yet reimbursed my original expenditure; though I attribute this rather to the delays of payment on the part of the booksellers, than to an actual want of sale.

To conclude, Sir, whether you condescend, or not, to honor me with your opinion and instructions on this subject, I hope and entreat that you will at least excuse my boldness in thus addressing you, and believe me to be (with very sincere respect, as well for your distinguished talents, as for your disinterested patriotism, and your well-known attachment to the cause of liberty, of all which, I hope your grateful country will not fail to shew a due sense on a proper occasion) Sir, Your much obliged, and most obedient humble servant,   JOHN CAREY

P:S: I hope, Sir, you have safely received a set of the "*Official Letters*," which I desired Mr. Rice (bookseller, philadelphia) to send to you immediately on receipt of the books. As I have not heard from him since their arrival in Philadelphia, I am of course, uncertain whether the intended set ever reached your hands.

RC (DLC); endorsed by TJ as received 4 Nov. 1796 and so recorded in SJL.

Carey's LETTER to TJ was dated 6 APRIL 1795. Edmund Randolph's LETTER to Carey of 23 JUNE 1795 is in DNA: RG 59, DL.

From Benjamin Smith Barton

SIR   Philadelphia, September 5th, 1796.

Sometime since, I wrote to you, in answer to the letter which you had written to my deceased uncle, Mr. Rittenhouse. At the same time, I did myself the pleasure to send to you a copy of my memoir, concerning the fascinating faculty which has been ascribed to different species of Serpents. As these went by a private hand, I am doubtful whether you have received them. In my letter, I requested that you would inform me to whom I should pay the money, which you kindly lent to me, a considerable time since. I have now to make the same request.

We are anxious to see your memoir concerning the bones which you mention to have been found in digging for nitre. I wish it could be sent soon, in which case it would be in time for the 4th vol. of the *Transac-*

tions, now in press. I do not imagine that this volume *can* be closed in less than four weeks from this date. We are slow in our motions. I am, Sir, with the greatest respect, your most humble and obedient servant, &c.   BENJAMIN SMITH BARTON

P.S. Be so kind as to make my compliments to Mr. Randolph. I have lately discovered, in the vicinity of this city, a new species of Dipus, or Jerboa. It is a very beautiful animal. I call it Dipus Americanus, in vol. 4th of the *Transactions*.

RC (DLC); endorsed by TJ as received 30 Sep. 1796 and so recorded in SJL.

Barton, who described the DIPUS AMERI-CANUS at a meeting of the American Philosophical Society on 2 Oct. 1795, published his report as "Some account of an American Species of Dipus, or Jerboa," APS, *Transac-*

tions, IV (1799), 114-24. A variety of meadow jumping mouse, the animal was subsequently renamed *Zapus hudsonius americanus* (APS, *Proceedings*, XXII, pt. 3 [1884], 234; E. Raymond Hall, *The Mammals of North America*, 2d ed., 2 vols. [New York, 1981], II, 841-2).

From Sir John Sinclair

Whitehall 10th. September 1796.
Sir John Sinclair presents his best compliments to Mr. Jefferson. Has the honour of sending him some of the papers printed by the Board of Agriculture of which he requests his acceptance, and should be happy to receive any communications upon Agricultural Subjects, with which Mr. Jefferson may have the goodness to favour the Board.

RC (MHi); in clerk's hand; endorsed by TJ as received 21 Jan. 1797 and so recorded in SJL. Enclosures not identified.

To John Barnes

DEAR SIR   Monticello Sep. 11. 96.
I have just recieved from Mr. Donath a letter announcing that he has brought my glass. The two inclosed letters are on that subject. Mr. Ingle was formerly a cabinetmaker. He is now I believe in some line of commerce. Not knowing his present address I take the liberty of putting his letter under your cover in hopes you will be so good as to find him out. Mr. Crosby knows him well. I am with esteem Dear Sir Your most obedt. servt   TH: JEFFERSON

PrC (MHi); endorsed by TJ in ink on verso, in part: "Barnes John." Enclosures: (1) TJ to Henry Ingle, 11 Sep. 1796 (see note to TJ to Sampson Crosby, 15 Sep. 1795). (2) TJ to Joseph Donath, 11 Sep. 1796.

To Joseph Donath

SIR   Monticello Sep. 11. 96.

I know not how it happened that your favor of Aug. 8. did not reach me till our last post. A letter by post generally comes in 9. days. I am extremely glad to hear of the arrival of my glass, and that it is of the size of 12. by 18. according to my second[1] order. If you will be pleased to forward me the bill of cost, I will immediately replenish my funds with Mr. Barnes, and desire him to pay for and recieve the glass. In the mean time I shall prepare and forward directions for the sashes and glazing. I am Sir Your very humble servt   TH: JEFFERSON

RC (PHi: Society Collection); addressed: "Mr. Joseph Donath Philadelphia"; endorsed by Donath as answered on 22 Sep. 1796. Enclosed in preceding document.

Donath's FAVOR of 8 Aug. 1796, recorded in SJL as received 9 Sep. 1796, has not been found.

[1] Word interlined in place of canceled "first."

From —— Galvan

MONSIEUR   charlott's ville 21e. Sepbre 1796.

Les égards que l'on doit au Merite et a un cytoyen comme vous, m'ont fait arretter aujourd'huy pour avoir L'honneur de vous assurer en personne de mon profond Respect; Jay eté malheureux en ne vous trouvant pas Chez vous ou jaurais volontiers demeurer a vous attendre, Si javais eté maitre de m'arretter aussy long tems que je l'eusse Désiré; mais mes jours de Marche Sont comptés, et J'ay des affaires dans la comté de Bottetourt qui me forcent a partir: permettez donc que je vous presente Les voeux les plus Sinceres pour la continuation d'une vie heureuse, qui Retiré du cahos de ces evenements incertains, ne peut que vous etre très agréable.

Un de mes amis Intime, Le colonel Jesse Ewell qui habite a Dumfries où je fais aussy ma Residence m'avait prié de vous faire agreer Lassurance de Son amitié Sincere et Ses Respectueux compliments; il est en fort Bonne Santé, et Sera Charmé d'apprendre que vous en possedez une pareille. En vous reïterant mon plus Sincere attachement Jay Lhonneur D'etre Monsieur Votre tres humble & tres obt. Serviteur

GALVAN

RC (DLC); endorsed by TJ as received 22 Sep. 1796 and so recorded in SJL.

The author of this letter was probably

Francis Galvan de Bernoux, evidently a resident of Dumfries, in Prince William County, Virginia, who in 1784 petitioned the Confederation Congress in hopes of receiving a military land warrant earned by his deceased brother, Major William Galvan. They had originally come to the United States from the West Indies, possibly Martinique, or France (Petition of Francis Galvan de Bernoux, 15 Mch. 1784, in DNA: RG 360, PCC; Morris, *Papers*, VI, 174n; Philip M. Hamer and others, eds., *The Papers of Henry Laurens*, 14 vols. [Columbia, S.C., 1968-   ], XIV, 40n).

From John Garland Jefferson

DEAR SIR   Petersburg September 21st. 1796.

Agreeable to your request I have examined the office of Lunenburg, and find that no conveyance was executed, by your father, or rather recorded in the Court of that County, between the year 1750. and 1757. I find from the Clerk of the County, that in 1752. Halifax was taken from Lunenburg, and Bedford in the year 1754. The Clerk supposes that the land in question, lies in the County of Halifax. He recollects a search having been once made in his office, with respect to land lying on the same Creek, on which yours lies. I mean to get an acquaintance of mine to make a search in Halifax from the year 1752 to 1757. In 1754 Bedford was taken from Halifax. If you can find out whether any conveyance was made from your father to any person between the last period and the present time in Bedford you may ascertain with certainty whether any conveyance was ever made. I feel the most sensible pleasure my dear Sir, in having in this one instance complied with a request made by you, and I shall feel still greater, if it is productive of any advantage to you. We have received information in this part of the world, that the President means to decline serving any longer as President. I rejoice at the news; because I consider him as a man dangerous to the liberties of this country. Misled himself, he lends his influence to others, and by his name gives a sanction to the most dangerous measures. For this reason I am glad he means to decline. Be pleased to give my best respects to your family, and believe me to be my dear Sir, with the most cordial esteem, Your most obt. servant   JNO G: JEFFERSON

RC (ViU: Carr-Cary Papers); at foot of first page: "Mr. Thomas Jefferson"; endorsed by TJ.

CLERK of LUNENBURG County: William Taylor (Johnston, *Memorials*, 242).

PRESIDENT MEANS TO DECLINE SERVING ANY LONGER: Washington submitted his Farewell Address to the cabinet on 15 Sep. 1796, and it appeared in David C. Claypoole's *American Daily Advertiser* four days later (Fitzpatrick, *Writings*, XXXV, 214-15n).

A missing letter from John Garland Jefferson to TJ of 6 Oct. 1795 is recorded in SJL as received 14 Oct. 1795.

From John Wayles Eppes

D<small>R</small> S<small>IR</small>   Monticello Sep. 25th. 1796.

To avoid the difficulties, which must ever attend personal applications, on subjects important and delicate, I have adopted the present
mode of addressing you. A stranger to forms, and following the impulse
of my feelings, I have ventured to indulge, and express, sentiments, for
a part of your family, which ought perhaps, to have received your previous sanction. Could I hope, that should time and future attentions render me agreeable, my wishes may be crowned with your approbation,
I should indeed be happy. A sincere, disinterested, affection, and an
anxious wish for the future happiness of your daughter, are the only
grounds, (moderate as they may appear) on which I have dared to entertain a hope that her decision may be yours. With sentiments of respect
and esteem I am Dr Sir yours &c   J<small>NO</small>: W: E<small>PPES</small>

RC (MHi); at foot of text: "Th Jefferson
Esqr."; endorsed by TJ as received 25 Sep.
1796 and so recorded in SJL.

HAPPINESS OF YOUR DAUGHTER: this is the
first letter dealing with the courtship and
engagement of Mary Jefferson to Eppes.

For the marriage arrangements, see Marriage Settlement for Mary Jefferson and
Marriage Settlement for John Wayles
Eppes, both 12 Oct. 1797. According to
SJL, TJ exchanged six letters with Eppes
between 9 Sep. 1795 and 2 June 1796, all of
which are missing.

To John Barnes

D<small>EAR</small> S<small>IR</small>   Monticello Oct. 2. 1796.

Your two favors of Sep. 18. and 20. are recieved, and I now inclose
letters to Mr. Donath and Mr. Ingles, all of which are left open for your
perusal and information. I inclose you also a draught for 300.D. on
Messrs. Harrison & Sterett which will enable you to answer that on you
in favor of Donath, and to meet the earlier demands of the sash-maker.
Further provision shall be made in due time for the whole of the work
now ordered, as well as for some further orders which will follow these
in a short time. I am with esteem Dear Sir Your friend & servt.

T<small>H</small>: J<small>EFFERSON</small>

PrC (MHi); at foot of text: "Mr. John
Barnes"; endorsed by TJ in ink on verso.
Enclosures: (1) TJ to Joseph Donath, 2
Oct. 1796. (2) TJ to Henry Ingle, 2 Oct.
1796 (see note to TJ to Sampson Crosby,
15 Sep. 1795). (3) TJ's draft on Harrison &
Sterett, 2 Oct. 1796, requesting them to pay

Barnes $300 at three days' sight (PrC in
MHi; at foot of text: "Messrs. Harrison &
Sterett Philadelphia").

Barnes's FAVORS to TJ of 18 and 20 Sep.
1796, both recorded in SJL as received 1
Oct. 1796, have not been found.

To Joseph Donath

SIR   Monticello Oct. 2. 1796.

Your favor of Sep. 22. came to hand two days ago, by which I observe you have laid by for me 7. boxes of 60. panes each of 12 by 18. I. glass, and 1. do. of 25. panes of 18. by 24. and wish to be informed if this was the amount of my order. My order was dated Oct. 20. 95. and was for 25. panes of 18. by 24. and

600. panes of 18. by 12 I. consequently there will be requisite in addition to the 420. panes of 18. by 12. I.

<u>180.</u> more to make up the 600.

As you mention that you are able to make up the whole order I inclose you a draught on Mr. J. Barnes for 199 D. 12 c. that is to say the 158.62 D. stated in your letter and 40.50 D. additional for the 180. panes deficient. Be pleased to deliver the glass to Mr. Barnes to whom I shall write on the subject.

I shall have occasion for about 200. panes 12. I. square of the same quality. Will you be able to furnish of that size? I am Sir Your very humble servt   TH: JEFFERSON

RC (ViU: McGregor Library); at foot of text: "Mr. Jos. Donath." Enclosure: TJ's draft on John Barnes, 2 Oct. 1796, requesting him to pay Donath $199.12 at ten days' sight (PrC in MHi; at foot of text: "Mr. John Barnes. Philadelphia"). Enclosed in TJ to Barnes, 2 Oct. 1796.

Donath's FAVOR of 22 Sep. 1796, recorded in SJL as received 1 Oct. 1796, has not been found.

To William Booker

SIR   Monticello Oct. 4. 96

I have this summer had a threshing machine made on the Scotch model, and have already got out a good part of my crop with it with great success. Hearing however that you had improved it by substituting whirls and bands for cogwheels and wallowers, I desired Colo. Coles to enquire whether your plan could be communicated. He did not see you, but Mr. Graham was kind enough to say I should have a drawing of it. This has encouraged me to send a workman and to ask your permission to let him examine it, and, on his return, make one for me. I understand you have either applied for a patent, or mean to do so. If it is not done, perhaps my experience in the Patent office may be of some service to you in preparing your petition, specification &c. I will either revise them for you or draw them originally if not done, on your furnishing materials, and the weekly post between Charlottesville and Richmond will furnish a ready conveyance for letters. If you will inform me by return of the bearer, Mr. Buck, what will be the price of your license to use your invention, I will have the price paid to you in Richmond if I build one. I am Sir Your very humble servt

TH: JEFFERSON

PrC (MHi); at foot of text: "Mr. Booker"; endorsed by TJ in ink on verso.

William Booker (d. 1802), an agricultural inventor from Goochland County, Virginia, received a patent for his machine for threshing wheat in 1797, shortly after which he moved to Richmond, where he built and sold his invention. He installed threshing machines at various estates, including George Washington's Union Farm in July 1797. Two years later, Washington engaged Booker to build a horse-powered grist mill by fixing it to a threshing machine (*List of Patents*, 13; *Virginia Argus*, 12 Jan. 1798; Washington to Booker, 26 June 1797, 3 Mch. 1799 in Washington, *Papers, Ret. Ser.*, I, 216-17, III, 404-5; Washington, *Diaries*, VI, 313, 356).

A letter from John COLES to TJ of 13 Nov. 1796, recorded in SJL as received on the same day, has not been found. According to SJL Coles and TJ exchanged six other letters between 24 Mch. 1794 and 2 Oct. 1800, all of which are missing.

From William Booker

SIR   Goochland County October 7. 1796

I Receiv.d yours of the fourth Instant by Mr. Buck. I have with pleasure Given him Every Information I am able respecting the Machine.

At present I am very unwell. As soon as I should be better in healh I will make a drawing of the machine and forward it by the post to charlottesville for you.

Mr. Graham told me Colo. Coles had apply.d to him and that he had promis.d him a drawing. But it has never been Since in my power to comply owing to my Indisposion and previous Engagements.

I feel much Indebted to you for your offering your assistance in procureing a patent. Had you been convenient, I should have Taken the Liberty to have Call.d on you at first.

I have got the assistance of some Gent. in Richmond, and have sent forward a model, at present I believe the buisiness is as forward as could be Expected if any difficulties Shoul arise by your permission I will Call on you.

Having not as yet obtained a patent I cannot Say what will be my price for using the machine but Shoul.d I Succeed the price Shall be Moderate. I am, with due respect your Most Obet. an very Humble Sevt   WM. BOOKER

RC (MHi); at foot of text: "Thomas Jefferson Esqr"; endorsed by TJ as received 11 Oct. 1796 and so recorded in SJL.

Upon his return to Monticello, John H. BUCK, whom TJ employed to build threshing machines, built one incorporating Booker's improvements (MB, II, 935, 946).

The INFORMATION Booker sent to TJ RESPECTING THE MACHINE probably included the following:

"A bill of Scantling, for a Threshing Machine to be worked by bands—

for a wheel thirty six feet Diameter
one Shaft   long. 16. Inches through
    hewd. 8 sqr
8. pieces for arms 19. feet Long 2 ½. by 9–
16. pieces for braces and Ties 13. feet long 2
    by 3

for the framing inside of a house or to Support the drum &C.
    4. pieces 16. feet Long 5. by 8
12. Do.   16   4. by 8

for Rolers bands beaters &c.
10. pieces of Tough. white oak. or any Strong hard wood 4. ½ feet long 4. Inches sqr.

2. wheels 4. feet Diameter made as a Common Cart or waggon wheel not Dished for the Drum

2. Do. for Turning the Rolers 3 feet 8. Inches Diameter as Strong as the Rim of a spinning will Will be sufficient, nuts 6 or 7. Inches through

one Do. 3. or 4. feet Diameter Some Stronger for Directing the band to the whirl"

(MS in MHi, in Booker's hand; undated).

To Bushrod Washington

DEAR SIR   Monticello Oct. 9. 96.

I now inclose you the record in the case of Dickenson v. Paulett and Marks. Mr. Marks, by purchasing all Paulett's right, stands completely in his shoes. His first wish is to obtain a confirmation of his right to the land. But if Dickenson notwithstanding his prevarications and delays of paiment shall be decreed to retain still an equitable right to the land on paying the purchase money, then, as he has by no means money at his command, the best thing for Mr. Marks would be that the day given Dickinson for paying up the money should be as short as possible, and that on failure, his right should be for ever foreclosed and Marks's title confirmed. I inclose you an order on Charles Johnston & Co. for five pounds as a fee in behalf of Mr. Marks, and am Dr. Sir Your most obedt. servt   TH: JEFFERSON

RC (PPAmP); at foot of text: "Bushrod Washington esq."; addressed: "Bushrod [. . .]"; endorsed by Washington: "Dickinson & Pawlett" and "Marks Ads Dickinson." The enclosed order for Washington's fee in this case involving TJ's brother-in-law, Hastings Marks, which TJ recorded as a "charge to Marks," has not been found (MB, II, 947).

SJL records letters from TJ to Washington of 4 June, 20 June, and 11 Sep. 1796, and from Washington to TJ of 10 June, an unspecified date in June, and 6 July 1796, received respectively 17 June, 8 July, and 16 July 1796, none of which has been found. Also noted in SJL, but missing, are letters from TJ to Washington of 24 Oct. 1796 on "R. Jeff's case," 6 Nov. 1796, 21

Jan., 16 and 30 Oct. 1797, and from Washington to TJ of 22 Nov. 1796, 22 Feb., 31 Oct., 5, 14, and 28 Nov. 1797, received respectively on 26 Nov. 1796, 21 Mch., 3, 10 Nov., and 13 Dec. 1797 (two letters).

From William Frederick Ast

SIR   Richmond, 10th October, 1796.

The Insurance having begun with those that have paid their premiums; I am therefore surprised that you have not yet sent in your declaration for assurance. By applying to your good self[1] he will get it made out for you.

A building not insured is no real property, because in a few hours it may be in ashes; you stand therefore at present in the precarious situation, that should you meet with an accident by fire, you might be a considerable loser: for a loss falls heavy upon *one*; but when it is divided amongst many each person's share becomes light. If the society was composed only of two, in case of a loss you would have to pay only the half, and would be better than if not insured, and as there are already better than four millions of dollars subscribed, you have of course four millions of chances to your *one*. We often see that individual houses burn, but the conflagration is never *general*: therefore *all* the houses in the State must be destroyed by fire, before you could lose as much as if you was at present to meet with an accident. The institution is on so liberal a footing, that I am astonished to find, that some people, should hesitate a moment to come into it; for if your neighbour's house was destroyed by fire, I am sure you would lend him your assistance to rebuild it; these are the principles of the institution; they all join to succour such of them as may be so unfortunate to lose their Buildings by fire; their contributions towards a loss are paid out of the interest of the premiums. The premiums average about three per cent. therefore we have to every hundred dollars insured three hundred cents in stock, which is immediately laid out in six per cents stock of the United States, and yields at the present prices near $7\frac{1}{2}$ per cent. interest, of course the premiums of each hundred dollars, insured yield $22\frac{1}{2}$ cents annual interest, supposing that $2\frac{1}{2}$ cents be absorbed by the expenses, then there remain 20 cents annual interest to each hundred dollars insured, which is one fifth per cent. of course there must out of every 500 houses annually one burn to absorb the interest, which is at the rate of 800 houses per annum in the state; and there must out of every thirty three houses one burn before you could be called upon for a second premium—which would be at the rate of twelve thousand houses in the state; and as in the course of 15 years past only about three hundred have burnt, there is no probability, that eight hundred houses should burn annually, nor that twelve thousand should burn in one year: therefore in all human probability these premiums *once* paid will insure the houses for *ever*.

As the premiums, which those that insure abroad have to pay *annually*, average, about one per cent; there being upwards of four millions of dollars subscribed here, therefore there must losses happen annually to the amount of forty thousand dollars and befal only the present subscribers (which is not likely as they are scattered all over the state) before they would have to pay as much as if they were insured abroad— and if all the state was insured abroad it would cost the people annually several millions of dollars, when by my plan we keep the money here to succour our unfortunate fellow-citizens and each person's contribution will only be a trifle.

You know that all the subscribers (of which you are one) have bound themselves; and the law obliges them to insure their property; therefore if we chuse it we can compel them to come forward: however as people begin now to understand it, we get daily more declarations in, and additional subscribers, so that we need not to force, but only acquaint, the people what they may do for their own good.

There is already a large sum of premiums received, by Mr. JAQUELIN AMBLER, Cashier-General, and laid out in six per cents stock of the United States, and daily more is receiving.

You will please to observe, that the Buildings which stand upwards of 20 feet from others pay only, when built of brick, $1\frac{1}{2}$ per cent. and if of wood $2\frac{1}{2}$ per cent. premium: but when they are contiguous to others, or situate on [Wharves], or hazardous work carried on therein, they pay more. *Health and Friendship.*   WILLIAM F. AST

RC (MHi); consisting of a printed form signed by Ast, with blanks for day in date-line and name in body of text (see note 1 below) completed by him; torn at foot; addressed: "Thomas Jefferson Esqr. Montecello"; stamped; postmarked; endorsed by TJ as received 14 Oct. 1796 and so recorded in SJL.

For Ast's INSURANCE company, see his letter to TJ, 1 Feb. 1795. DECLARATION FOR ASSURANCE: see TJ's Declaration for the Mutual Assurance Society, [1796].

[1] Preceding three words inserted in a blank by Ast, who also canceled "Mr." printed before the blank.

To Benjamin Smith Barton

Dear Sir   Monticello Oct. 10. 96.

Your favors should have been sooner acknoleged but that I have been in daily expectation of recieving some other bones of the newly discovered animal which would have enabled me to write to you more satisfactorily. There does exist somewhere a thigh-bone which has been seen by many and is believed to be still in the neighborhood where found. This with the bones I have would enable me to give the actual stature of the animal, instead of calculating it on the principle of ex pede Herculem. It will not be long before the diligence which is using for the collection of these bones will produce all which are to be recovered: but I do not flatter myself it will be done by the time at which you suppose the new volume of transactions will be ready. But as I know that that may be delayed, and am anxious this discovery should appear in it, I shall use all the diligence I can to forward it. It has been indeed the most tremendous of animals.

The little matter of money which you mention was never worth recollection. It was so little important that I do not remember what it was. But I had rather leave it in your hands to [be] a fund to furnish me now and then any good pamphlets which come out, and can be contrived to Richmond without postage. I will now draw on you for the odes of Jonathan Pindar which I see advertized by Mr. Bache.

I thank you for your paper on the fascination of the snake, and am persuaded you have resolved the problem truly. I had always ascribed their power over animals to antipathy and fear alone. I am satisfied that you justly add the effect of parental sollicitudes. We see daily proofs that the hawk has nearly the same power over the small birds which the snake has.

Be so good as to present my most friendly respects to Mrs. Rittenhouse and accept yourself assurances of the esteem with which I am Dear Sir Your most obedt. servt   TH: JEFFERSON

RC (PHi); addressed: "Doctr. Benjamin S. Barton Philadelphia"; stamped; endorsed by Barton as received 18 Oct. 1796 and answered. PrC (DLC).

BONES: the megalonyx. The ODES written by St. George Tucker under the pseudonym JONATHAN PINDAR are discussed in TJ to James Madison, 29 June 1793.

Documents Relating to the 1796 Campaign for Electors in Virginia

I. CERTIFICATE OF WILLIAM MARSHALL,
10 OCTOBER 1796

II. CERTIFICATE OF JOSEPH JONES MONROE
AND THOMAS BELL,
17 OCTOBER 1796

EDITORIAL NOTE

While Jefferson's correspondence makes no mention of the Virginia campaign for presidential electors in 1796, a group of documents pertaining to the election, including three letters, five depositions or certificates (two of which are printed below, the first dealing with Jefferson's indebtedness and the second with his relations with Aaron Burr), and a handbill are in his papers at the Library of Congress. None is addressed directly to Jefferson, nor has he endorsed them. All of the letters and Documents I and II have a number between four and twelve on the address sheet or at the bottom of the text indicating that they may have been part of a larger collection. The figures are perhaps in the hand of William A. Burwell, who served as the president's private secretary in 1804 and 1805 and may have numbered the documents at that time (Burwell to TJ, 15 Sep. 1805; TJ to Burwell, 20 Sep. 1805). A letter from John Beckley to Burwell of 28 June 1805 is numbered in the same way (RC in DLC). The three letters are addressed to Daniel Carroll Brent, who may also have collected the other election documents as he campaigned to be a Jefferson elector for the district consisting of Prince William, Stafford, and Fairfax counties against Federalist Charles Simms, an Alexandria lawyer who occasionally served as Washington's attorney. Both candidates were serving in the Virginia House of Delegates, Brent representing Stafford and Simms Fairfax county (Washington, *Papers, Pres. Ser.*, I, 419; Richmond *Enquirer*, 23 Aug. 1805; Malone, *Jefferson*, III, 279-81; Leonard, *General Assembly*, 172, 203, 205; *Biog. Dir. Cong.*).

This was one of several highly contested campaigns in the state. In an address dated 27 Sep. 1796 Simms publicized a charge that would haunt Jefferson for the remainder of his career; namely, that he had abandoned the office of governor of Virginia in 1781 when he resigned "at the moment of an invasion of the enemy, by which great confusion, loss, and distress accrued to the State in the destruction of public records." He also charged him with resigning as secretary of state at a time when the country was in peril, concluding that Jefferson displayed such a want of "firmness" that he was not fit to be trusted, "for no one can know how soon or from whence a storm may come." Simms defended John Adams against charges that he was a "friend to Monarchy and hereditary Titles" and made it clear that he would support the person who would continue the policies of the Washington administration: he would vote for fellow Virginian Patrick Henry and John Adams (*Columbian Mirror and Alexandria Gazette*, 29 Sep. 1796).

Virginia Republicans immediately collected documents to counter Simms's charges against Jefferson. Depositions by Archibald Blair, Daniel L. Hylton, and James Currie, the first two being dated 12 Oct. 1796 and the last undated but almost certainly from the same period, certifying the governor's concern for the public records, are printed as Document III of a group of notes and documents on the British invasions in 1781, above in this series at Vol. 4: 256-78. As the Editorial Note there indicates, Jefferson probably updated his diary and added memoranda of Benedict Arnold's invasion of Virginia at some point in 1796. See that collection for a full discussion of the enduring nature of these charges.

On 9 Oct. John Taylor responded to Brent's request for evidence to counter Simms's charges with an eight-page letter plus enclosures. Noting that he had served in the Virginia Assembly and militia during the war years, Taylor defended Jefferson's actions in 1781 and concluded that the government had abandoned Jefferson rather than the reverse. He rebutted Simms's "catalogue of Mr: Adams's merits," which included the signing of the Declaration of Independence, by noting that to "attribute Mr: Jeffersons resignation to fear, whilst Mr: Adams's concurrence in an instrument, which Mr: Jefferson had the additional hardihood to fabricate, is quoted as a decisive proof of bravery, seems to be an incorrect mode of reasoning." He quoted passages from *A Defence of the Constitutions of Government of the United States of America* to show the inconsistency of Adams's theories with the political system of the United States. But undoubtedly the postscript to Taylor's letter was of greatest political significance. At Brent's request, Taylor recounted, from notes that he had kept at the time, a conversation he had had in 1794 with Adams and New Hampshire Senator John Langdon. Their exchange stemmed from a difference of opinion over whether a democratic republican government could be established in France. Adams argued that the ignorance and corruption of Europe rendered it impossible. While he observed that America, a young country, could maintain popular government longer, Adams predicted that he would live to hear Taylor and other republicans acknowledge that "no government could long exist, or that no people could be happy, without an hereditary first magistrate, and an hereditary senate, or a senate for life" (RC in DLC; on address cover: "No 4th.").

John Mason, a merchant in Georgetown and son of George Mason, was running as an elector for Montgomery and Prince George counties in Maryland and wrote to Brent on 16 Oct. 1796 (*Columbian Mirror and Alexandria Gazette*, 17 Nov. 1796; Mason, *Papers*, I, lxxvii). His letter indicated that he had already received two documents regarding Jefferson's record as governor but he sought fuller information: the time of the British invasion, the actions of the Assembly, that body's subsequent thanks to Jefferson for his service, and the fate of the public records. He specifically asked, "Were any of the public Records taken and destroyed by the Enemy? If so, where were they destroyed—and if they had been removed by whose order, the governor's or a resolution of the assembly?" and requested Brent to send copies of records that would answer the questions. If he did not have documents, he should gather certificates from people assembled at the Dumfries District Court who could provide the answers and, if possible, convince men from "the other Side of the Question to join in exposing the truth." Mason also requested a certified copy of Taylor's 1794 conversation with Adams that Virginia congressman John Nicholas recently had read before the public, which would "do more good than any thing which has yet been spoken of." He urged Brent to send the documents by the next post without regard to postage costs (RC in DLC; on address cover: "No. 12th.").

Dated 17 Oct. 1796, Brent's response to Simms appeared in the *Columbian Mirror and Alexandria Gazette* in its entirety the following day. A mutilated handbill of it, "To the Freeholders of Prince William, Stafford, and Fairfax," is found in the Jefferson Papers at the Library of Congress. Brent declaimed that the vice president's political sentiments rendered him "dangerous and unfit for the Chief Magistracy in a Republican Government," noting that Adams looked to a monarchical form of government as the "standard of political perfection." And to refute Simms's charges that Jefferson had "badly administered and ultimately '*abandoned*' the government of Virginia," Brent observed that Jefferson had served out the term for which he was elected. Even if he had agreed to serve a third term, as the constitution allowed, "misdirected resentment" against his administration probably would have prevented his reappointment in June 1781. This "prejudice and indignation" against the governor, however, were of a "momentary duration." To prove this point, Brent printed certified extracts from the Virginia House of Delegates, including a 12 June 1781 resolution to inquire into the conduct of the governor and another of 12 Dec. 1781 thanking Jefferson "for his impartial, upright and attentive administration whilst in office," commending him for his "ability, rectitude, and integrity," and noting that by this public avowal they wished "to obviate and remove all unmerited censure." During the same session Jefferson was appointed a Virginia delegate to Congress. Brent went on to applaud Jefferson's correspondence as secretary of state, noting that the popular treaty with Spain was due in some measure to his correspondence with the ministers of that country. Finally, echoing Taylor's words, Brent questioned the logic of Simms's attributing "firmness" to Adams because he seconded and voted for the Declaration of Independence while denying the same quality to Jefferson even though he drew up the document and voted for it.

Brent's address did not end the campaign. Simms's war record was scrutinized by Virginia Republicans. On 27 Oct. 1796 "Firmness" publicized a 1779 resolution from the Continental Congress giving Simms, lieutenant colonel of the Second Virginia Regiment, a leave of absence to allow him to look after his land claims at a time when measures were being taken to prevent other officers from requesting leave in the midst of a campaign. In the very next issue of the newspaper, Simms responded with correspondence relating to his military career and on 1 Nov., several days before the election, he issued a major rebuttal to Brent's address. On election day, however, Brent defeated Simms by a large majority. When Adams appointed Simms to the collectorship at Alexandria in 1799, Republicans believed it was a reward for his spirited campaign (*Columbian Mirror and Alexandria Gazette*, 27, 29 Oct., 12 Nov. 1796; *Washington Gazette*, 9 Nov. 1796; Richmond *Enquirer*, 23 Aug. 1805; John Jay to TJ, 6 Sep. 1779; JEP, I, 326).

The northern Virginia counties of Loudoun and Fauquier made up another highly contested electoral district, where the Jefferson advocate Albert Russell, who had served four terms as a representative in the Virginia House of Delegates from Loudoun County, faced Federalist Leven Powell, a merchant and extensive holder of western lands who represented the same county for five terms in the House of Delegates. Early in the campaign, Powell used Aaron

Burr's visit to Monticello in 1795 to prove that Jefferson was an active foe of the present administration (see Document II). Throughout the contest Powell claimed that he would vote for the person who would most likely "preserve the *peace and happiness*" of the country and, like Simms, made support for the Washington administration his litmus test. He was the first to declare for the candidacy of Patrick Henry (*Columbian Mirror and Alexandria Gazette*, 8 Sep. 1796; Mason, *Papers*, I, lxxxviii; Leonard, *General Assembly*, 134, 165, 169, 173, 176, 180, 184, 188, 192; Rose, *Prologue to Democracy*, 130-2). Russell's address to the voters, dated 16 Sep., was relatively short. Remarking on Adams's "predeliction for Monarchy" he expressed support for Jefferson because of his "steady and uniform attachment to republican government" and noted that Powell's support of Henry would only divide the southern interest and promote the election of Adams (*Columbian Mirror and Alexandria Gazette*, 20 Sep. 1796). While this was Russell's only campaign document, other Republicans were circulating reports that his opponent was a "friend to Monarchy." This led to a published exchange between Virginia Senator Stevens Thomson Mason, identified as a major perpetrator of the rumors, and Powell. It also led to Powell's second address to the freeholders of Loudoun and Fauquier counties in which he explained his political theories by recalling conversations he had had with Mason and others. Powell defended his decision to vote for Henry, declaring that he had "as strong reasons to believe that Mr. Henry is a candidate as that Mr. Jefferson is." He continued: "I have not heard that either has offered; but I have heard, that both should say they would not serve, so that in this they stand equal." Powell concluded that if Henry refused to run he would vote for the person "least exceptionable." On 3 Nov., four days before the Virginia election, Henry wrote a letter in which he clearly declined to run for the presidency. Powell defeated Russell in the election by 287 votes and became the only Virginia elector to cast his vote for Adams. He went on to serve as a Virginia congressman from 1799 to 1801 (same, 8 Sep., 1, 25 Oct., 12, 15 Nov. 1796; Richard R. Beeman, *The Old Dominion and the New Nation, 1788-1801* [Lexington, Ky., 1972], 165-6; Rose, *Prologue to Democracy*, 157, 222, 288; *Biog. Dir. Cong.*).

I. Certificate of William Marshall

I William Marshall Clerk of the Court of the United States for the Middle Circuit in the Virginia District do hereby Certify, that there are no suits instituted in this Court against Mr. Jefferson except in the character of an executor, which are as follow: "John Wayles' executors" Francis Eppes, Thomas Jefferson and Henry Skipwith[1] executors of John Wayles deceased two suits, and Osgood Hanbury's Executor against the same, Given under my hand this 10th. of October 1796.

WILLIAM MARSHALL Clk

MS (DLC), entirely in Marshall's hand; on verso, in another hand, perhaps William Burwell's: "No. 6th."

William Marshall (1767-1816), a younger brother of John Marshall, established a successful law practice in Richmond and served as clerk of the United States circuit and district courts for Virginia (Marshall, *Papers*, I, 334, VII, 174, VIII, 137; DHSC, V, 319).

While it is not clear who requested this certificate or how it came to be in TJ's papers, the subject of TJ's debts appeared in printed form in September 1796 when "A Freeholder" from James City County challenged Richmond Federalist John Mayo's decision to vote for TJ as president if chosen elector. "Freeholder" had heard TJ was indebted on account of obligations that his late father-in-law had contracted prior to the Revolution. He asked, "Do you think that any man considerably indebted to the subjects of a foreign nation, ought to be President?" On 14 Oct. Mayo dismissed the accusation as a "palpable error." He added that even if the charge were just, he was certain that Jefferson would not "swerve from the strictest line of his duty as a public magistrate" (Richmond *Virginia Gazette, and General Advertiser*, 19 Oct. 1796; *Columbian Mirror and Alexandria Gazette*, 27 Oct. 1796). Although Brent had not taken up the question of TJ's financial affairs in his 17 Oct. address to the electorate, he was concerned enough about the issue to request information from Stevens T. Mason about a conversation reported to have taken place between his brother John T. Mason and John Marshall. Stevens T. Mason's response from Alexandria on 25 Oct. is found in TJ's papers (RC in DLC; on address cover: "No. 11th."). According to the account, Benjamin Stoddert, a Georgetown businessman who was chosen to head the Navy Department upon its creation in 1798, asserted in the presence of John T. Mason and John Mason, a cousin, that TJ was "sued in the federal Court of Virginia for British debts to a greater amount than his whole estate." When the Masons expressed their doubts concerning the veracity of the statement, Stoddert replied that the information had come from "Colo. Deakins who had it from Genl. Henry Lee of Virginia who said he had received his information from Genl. Marshall the Lawyer who had brought the suits against Mr. Jefferson." John T. Mason, who soon expected to see John Marshall at the Winchester District Court, was assigned the task of inquiring "into the truth of the tale." Marshall confirmed that "he had never brought or prosecuted a suit against Mr. Jefferson in any character, that he had never heard of Mr. Jeffersons owing a British debt, but that there had been considerable debts of that description due from the Estate of his Father in law Mr. Wayles." Marshall then referred to the settlement of the John Wayles debt to Farrell & Jones arranged at Monticello in 1790 for which TJ gave seven bonds for over £4,000 (see Editorial Note and Document XXV of a group of documents on the debt to Farell & Jones, printed above in this series at Vol. 15: 643-8, 674-6) and indicated that as far as he knew TJ had paid off the bonds or at least there had been no suits brought on them. He also referred indirectly to the *Prince of Wales* suit and agreed with TJ's opinion that the Wayles executors would not be held liable in the litigation (same; DAB, s.v. "Mason, George," "Mason, Stevens Thomson," "Stoddert, Benjamin"; Mason, *Papers*, III, 1211). For the *Prince of Wales* suit, which was one of the TWO SUITS before the United States Circuit Court, see TJ to John Read, 25 June 1798. The second suit was that of the John Randolph bond (see TJ to Francis Eppes, 28 Aug. 1794). The suit brought by OSGOOD HANBURY'S EXECUTOR John Lloyd is considered at Declaration of Hanbury's Executor against Wayles's Executors, [July 1798].

[1] Preceding name interlined in place of "Francis Eppes."

II. Certificate of Joseph Jones Monroe and Thomas Bell

We do hereby certify that at the time Mr. Burr visited Mr. Jefferson, there was no one then with him of any political character[1] as far as we know or believe—Living in his neighborhood, from the consequent intercourse, had there been any such meeting as Mr. Powell in his address contemplated we conceive we should not have been ignorant of it.

We have positive testimony before us (but from motives of delicacy, the author would not wish a public exhibition of it) that there was no persons present when Mr. Burr was at Monticello But some female relations of Mr. Jefferson—the gentleman of his family—Mr. John Eppes—and Mr. Wm. Hylton jr.

To these last mentiond gentlemen we beg leave to refer you for positive evidence

Albemarle Octr: 17th. 1796.

JO: JO: MONROE
THS. BELL

MS (DLC); in unknown hand; with one signifcant emendation (see note below); at foot of left margin, perhaps in William Burwell's hand: "No 5th."

Joseph Jones Monroe (b. 1771), a younger brother of James Monroe, lived in Albemarle county and practiced law in Charlottesville. He had studied at the University of Edinburgh from 1783 to 1789. He served as his brother's private secretary during the Monroe presidency until he moved to Missouri in 1820 (Madison, *Papers, Pres. Ser.*, IV, 153; Ammon, *Monroe*, 3, 85, 115, 405). For his election to the Virginia House of Delegates in April 1796, see TJ to Thomas Mann Randolph, 13 Mch. 1796.

The precise date of the visit to Monticello by BURR is unclear. In an 11 Oct. 1795 letter to his Senate colleague Henry Tazewell, Burr wrote from Richmond that a two-week illness on the road, from which he was still recovering, had consumed the time he had allotted for his visit to the state and would keep him from visiting Tazewell at his home near Williamsburg. He indicated that he had visited with Governor Robert Brooke, John Dawson, and John Taylor, who would provide Tazewell with the latest political news he had brought. Burr gave no indication that he would be visiting TJ be-

fore he left Virginia. TJ wrote Wilson Cary Nicholas on 19 Oct., however, that Burr had stayed one day at Monticello and had left "two or three days ago." This would indicate that Burr had just missed Madison who had visited Monticello from about 1 to 15 Oct. (Kline, *Burr*, I, 229; Madison, *Papers*, XVI, xxvi; Madison to TJ, 18 Oct. 1795).

In his address to the electorate dated 27 Sep., Leven Powell reiterated charges he had made earlier that month declaring that when Burr visited TJ he also met with other Virginians who like Burr were opposed to the Washington administration, and that they had agreed upon the "rash and violent measures brought forward in the last session of Congress" that Powell believed, if adopted, would have led the country into war with Great Britain. According to the rumor TJ not only planned and approved of the measures but "wrote to the different Southern members urging them to persevere in the line of conduct there agreed on." Powell noted that if any of TJ's letters appeared as proof of these charges, he most certainly could not vote for him. "A Friend to the present Administration of the Government" also referred to Burr's visit at Monticello, characterizing it as a meeting of Burr "and several members of congress from Virginia" to determine "the manner of attacking the British treaty after its ratification by the Senate and President" (*Columbian Mirror and Alexandria Gazette*, 1 Oct., 1 Nov. 1796). Powell's charges were repeated in the Boston *Columbian Centinel* by John Gardner in essays signed "Aurelius" which were later published separately as *Brief Consideration of the Important Services, and Distinguished Virtues and Talents, Which Recommend Mr. Adams for the Presi-* *dency of the United States* (Boston, 1796). While Powell and Gardner found no letters by TJ to support the charges, Federalist commentators identified his closest friends, Madison and John Taylor for example, as opponents of administration policies (*Columbian Mirror and Alexandria Gazette*, 25 Oct. 1796).

[1] Next seven words interlined.

To William Cocke

DEAR SIR   Monticello Oct. 21. 96.

The letter you were so good as to [write me of late?] came duly to hand, and I always learn with great pleasure that I am recollected with approbation by those with whom I [have served]. Our acquaintance commenced on a troubled ocean. We braved the storm like good sailors, never despairing of our [courage]. My [bark] has at length entered port less shattered than I expected, and I wish not to hazard it again. I have not the arrogance to say I would refuse the honorable office you mention to me; but I can say with truth that I had rather be thought worthy of it than to be appointed to it. [For] well I know that no man will ever bring out of that office the reputation which carries him into it. You are younger than I am and have many good years of service still due to your country. That they may be successfully employed and thankfully acknoleged is the sincere prayer of Dear Sir Your most obedt. humble servt   TH: JEFFERSON

PrC (DLC); faded and torn; at foot of text: "[Mr. C]ocke"; endorsed by TJ in ink on verso.   LETTER: Cocke to TJ, 17 Aug. 1796.

From Van Staphorst & Hubbard

SIR   Amsterdam 21 October 1796.

We had the pleasure the 21 May to address you on your particular affairs, in a manner that We flatter ourselves will have afforded you pleasure: since when We have received your very esteemed favor of 24 April, with the agreeable intelligence of Mr. Dohrman having settled his Account with Mr. Philip Mazzei for $3,087.$\frac{60}{100}$ the value of which has been remitted to us by Mr. James Yard of Philadelphia, in Pragers

& Co.'s draft at 90 days Sight on Widw. Levie Salomons & Sons for Hd. Cy. ƒ7,719. Which when in cash will be to the credit of Mr. Ph. Mazzei, whom We have already advised of the Receipt and Acceptance of the Bill.

Our former correspondence has informed you the good fate of all your different remittances for account of Mr. Mazzei, except the Bill £39.17.10½ on Wm. Anderson of London, which We returned to you the 27 January last, with protests for Non Acceptance and non payment. We are ever with great esteem and regard Sir! Your mo. ob. hb. servants

N & J. VAN STAPHORST & HUBBARD

RC (DLC); in a clerk's hand, signed by the firm; at foot of first page: "Thos. Jefferson Esq. Monticello. Virginia"; endorsed by TJ as received 18 Feb. 1797 and so recorded in SJL. A missing Dupl is recorded in SJL as received at Monticello on 21 Mch. 1797.

To James Currie

DEAR DOCTOR   Monticello Oct. 22. 1796

The return of Mr. Randolph's servant affords me the first opportunity of informing you that I mentioned the subject you desired to the gentleman who was to call on me. He is intelligent and close, and has his suspicions always about him. I was obliged therefore to avoid any direct proposition or question, and only prepare him by declaring my opinion in such a way as to avoid suspicion. He has my testimony of the talents of the person proposed, and so given as to weigh with him. But I have no means of conjecturing the part he may take but his acquiesence in the correspondence between the character I gave and the idea he had formed from other information. Wishing you success in all your undertakings and health and happiness I am with great esteem Dr. Sir Your friend & servt   TH: JEFFERSON

PrC (MHi); at foot of text: "Doctr. Currie." Not recorded in SJL.

According to SJL, TJ and Currie exchanged 16 letters between 3 Feb. 1794 and 16 May 1796, none of which has been found.

From Benjamin Smith Barton

DEAR SIR   Philadelphia, October 25th 1796.

Your letter has come safe to hand. I am extremely glad to learn, that[1] a number of the bones of the newly-discovered animal have been already discovered. I wish greatly to see your account of them. I find, by late inquiry, that the 4th vol. of the Transactions will not be published in less than two months.

As you request it, I shall retain the money (sixty dollars) lent to me, for the purpose which you mention. Several things, in the literary way, have made their appearance within the last year. These I shall not fail to transmit to you, by some safe conveyance. Have you seen a posthumous work, attributed to Condorcet, on the progress of the human mind? In many respects, it has, I think, great merit. Dr. Priestley has kindly lent to me the great work of Pallas, on the languages of all nations. This will enable me to discover what resemblances actually do subsist between the American languages and those of Northern-Asia. Of this great work, I have the first and second parts (two large quartos). As the empress has sent Mr. Pallas still farther north than Petersburgh, I fear the work will never be finished. He has not given any specimens of the languages of the American nations.

Some very interesting articles, which were taken out of an ancient tumulus, north of the Ohio, have been presented to the Philosophical Society. My account of, and conjectures concerning, these articles have been printed. I shall take the liberty of sending you a copy, by a safe conveyance.

Mrs. Rittenhouse requests me to present her compliments to you. I am, Dear Sir, with the greatest respect, Your most obedient & most humble servant, &c.   B. S. BARTON

RC (DLC); endorsed by TJ as received 4 Nov. 1796 and so recorded in SJL.

YOUR LETTER: TJ to Barton, 10 Oct. 1796. The POSTHUMOUS WORK was the Marquis de Condorcet's *Esquisse d'un tableau historique des progrès de l'esprit humain* (Paris, 1795), recently published in the United States as *Outlines of an Historical View of the Progress of the Human Mind: being a Posthumous Work of the late M. de Condorcet* (Philadelphia, 1796). See Sowerby, No. 1247.

The German-born scientist Peter Simon PALLAS, who spent most of his career working under the auspices of the Academy of Sciences at St. Petersburg, made significant contributions to geology, the classification of flora and fauna, and the systematic description of far-flung regions of the Russian empire (DSB). The great project of comparing and classifying linguistic families by rendering a list of 130 core words in each of

200 LANGUAGES was a personal project of the Russian EMPRESS, Catherine II. At her request, Pallas published the results of the study as *Sravnitel'nye slovari vsiekh iazykov i nariechii, sobrannye desnitseiu vsevysochaishei osoby*, 2 vols. (St. Petersburg, 1786-89), which also bore a Latin title and preface although the vocabularies themselves were all printed in the Cyrillic alphabet. George Washington, recruited for the enterprise by the Marquis de Lafayette, had obtained for Catherine translations of the word list in some American Indian languages, but the first edition of the book, as indicated by Barton, did not contain vocabulary from any AMERICAN NATIONS. Languages from the Americas and Africa were added to a second edition published in four volumes (St. Petersburg, 1790-91), also in the Cyrillic alphabet, which expanded the word list as well as the number of languages covered, but Catherine was so distressed by the scheme of classification and arrange-

ment introduced by her new compiler, Fedor Ivanovich de Mirievo, that she severely curtailed distribution of the second edition. TJ, like Barton, was interested in linguistic evidence that might provide clues to the origins of American Indians and compiled his own set of comparative word lists. He was evidently unaware of the expanded edition of the Russian work until 1806, when he learned of it from a published report by Volney and asked Levett Harris, the American consul in St. Petersburg, to find Pallas's book. Harris obtained both editions for TJ's library (Mary Ritchie Key, *Catherine the Great's Linguistic Contribution* [Carbondale, Ill., 1980], 51-2, 56-7, 60-70, 73-6; Volney, *Rapport fait à l'Academie celtique, sur l'ouvrage russe de M. le professeur Pallas* [Paris, 1805?]; TJ to Harris, 18 Apr. 1806,

28 Mch. 1807; Harris to TJ, 10 Aug., 15 Sep. 1806, 24 July 1807). See Sowerby, Nos. 4736-7.

Winthrop Sargent had sent the American Philosophical Society artifacts excavated from a burial mound at Cincinnati. Barton's ACCOUNT of the finds took the form of a letter to Joseph Priestley, 16 May 1796, which was printed that year and also subsequently in the society's *Transactions* (Winthrop Sargent and Benjamin Smith Barton, *Papers Relative to Certain American Antiquities* [Philadelphia, 1796]; APS, *Transactions*, IV [1799], 177-215; APS, *Proceedings*, XXII, pt. 3 [1884], 237, 239). See Evans, No. 30038.

[1] Barton here canceled "there is a probability that."

From James Lyle

DEAR SIR   Manchester Octr. 25th. 1796

I imagine you will be anxious to know how matters stand between you and our Company, and may not know what sums I have received from Mr. Christopher Clark your Attorney in Bedford &c., therefore I have sent this state, which contains all the payments enterd on our books, by it you will see your first and second bonds only are fully paid up. When you examine, our method of charging the Intrest I hope you will find it right, if any thing appear not so, you will please mention it. I shall be glad to hear from you and am with Esteem Dear Sir Your mo hue servt   JAMES LYLE

RC (ViU: Edgehill-Randolph Papers); subjoined to enclosure. Recorded in SJL as received 4 Nov. 1796.

TJ's agreement to pay his debt to Henderson, McCaul & COMPANY, the firm Lyle represented, by a series of six bonds falling

due in July of each year from 1790 to 1795 is discussed in the note to TJ to Lyle, 7 Mch. 1790. For TJ's request that CHRISTOPHER CLARK collect several debts for him and give Lyle the money received, see TJ to Clark, 5 Aug. 1794.

Statement of Interest and Payments on Bonds to Henderson, McCaul & Company

Statement of the Interest and payments on
Mr. Thomas Jefferson's, bonds to Henderson McCaul & Co.

1790		Sterling			Sterling		
March 4	To 1st. Bond of this date ℔ble 19th. July 1790 on Interest from 19th. April 1783	461	8	8			
	To Interest on this sum from 19th. April 1783 till 15th. Augt. 1789, 6 ys. 3 mos. 27 days	145	18	–			
		607	6	8			
	By a payment made to Mr. McCaul on 15th. August 1789	300	–	–			
		307	6	8			
July 19	To Interest on £307.6.8 from 15th. Augt. 1789 till 19th. July 1790 is 11 mos. 4 days	14	5	4			
		321	12	–			
	By Mr. Brown's Bill of Exchange	325	–	–			
	1st. Bond overpaid £	3	8	–			
	To 2d. Bond on Interest as the 1st., of same date, due 19th. July 1791				141	11	10
	To Interest on 2d. Bond from 19th. April 1783 till 19th. July 1790—is 7¼ years	51	6	5			
	balance of Interest due at this date £	47	18	5			
1794 Octr. 20	By Cash received of Mr. Christr. Clark £48.13.10 Curcy at 133⅓ ℔Ct. is	36	10	4½			
	Interest still due	11	8	–½			
1795 Janry. 5	To Interest on the amount of the 2d. bond from 19th. July 1790, the time of the last charge of Interest, till this date is 4 ys. 5 mos. 17 ds.	31	12	–			
		43	–	–½			
	By Cash recd. of Mr. Thos. M: Randolph £114.4.8 at 133⅓ ℔Ct. is Stg	85	13	6			
					42	13	5½
					98	18	4½
March 30	To Interest on this balance of the 2d. bond from 5th. Janry. till date—2 mos. 25 days				1	3	4
					100	1	8½
	By Cash recd. of Mr. Clark £49—a 133⅓ ℔Ct.				36	15	–
					63	6	8½
Octr. 5	To Interest on £63.6.8½ from 30th. March till this date—6 months 5 days				1	12	6
					64	19	2½
	By Cash recd. of Mr. Clark on accot. of Will: Milner's bond to you £120—a 133⅓ ℔Ct.				90	–	–
	2d. Bond overpaid £				25	0	9½

Octr. 5	By amount overpaid the 2d. Bond at this date, brought over	25	–	$9\frac{1}{2}$				
	To 3d. Bond on Interest as the others, of same date, due 19th. July 1792				136	15	–	
	To Interest on the 3d. Bond from 19th. April 1783 till this date 12 years 5 mos. 16 days	85	3	6				
	Interest still due £	60	2	$8\frac{1}{2}$				
Novr. 20	By Cash recd. of Mr. Brown for Robt. Snelson's order on him; on accot. of Kensolving's debt to you £20.–.2 is	15	–	$1\frac{1}{2}$				
	balance of last charge of Int. still due £	45	2	7				

MS (ViU: Edgehill-Randolph Papers); in a clerk's hand; endorsed by TJ: "Lyle James."

From William Fleming

Dr Sir   Blenhiem, 30th. Octr. 1796.

I herewith send you a geographical sketch of the several counties in the state of Kentucky, in which, I doubt not, there are many inaccuracies, as I had but little leisure to attend to the subject, and my means of information was often defective; especially with respect to the bearings of the different places attempted to be described. I was at eleven of their county courthouses, and at Danville, where one of their district courts is held; and what is stated from my own observation, I think, tolerably correct. This sketch will, for the present, serve to give you a general idea of the country, and when you receive a map, many of the errors may be corrected. I am, with great regard, dear sir Yr. obedt. servt:

Wm. Fleming

RC (DLC); subjoined to enclosure; addressed: "Thomas Jefferson, esquire Monte Ceillo"; endorsed by TJ and recorded in SJL as received 3 Nov. 1796. Enclosure: "Counties in the state of Kentucky, July 1796, in number nineteen"; describing the location, geography, and population of Bourbon, Clarke, Fayette, Woodford, Scott, Harrison, Campbell, Mason, Franklin, Logan, Green, Lincoln, Madison, Hardin, Jefferson, Shelby, Nelson, Washington, and Mercer; with Jefferson County receiving the fullest description, where the "local advantages are superior to most of the counties in the state" and the town of Louisville is "an excellent port for exportation which begins to attract the attention of the inhabitants" (MS in DLC; 6 p.; entirely in Fleming's hand).

To John Carey

DEAR SIR   Monticello Nov. 10. 96.

Your favor of Sep. 1. came to hand three [. . .]¹ [It] had been recieved in due time, but was not answered [. . .] [it did] not appear to require it, and I am so [involved?] in agriculture that like other farmers, I put off all letter-writing to wet days. These being few in our climate, and when they come, the improvement of a plough or a drill or some other implement, usurping the turn, letter-writing goes to the wall. This I hope will apologize for my omission to answer your first letter. With respect to the passages omitted in the official letters I am totally uninformed of their nature; for tho' I recieved from Mr. Rice the copy you were so kind as to send me, and for which I return you my thanks, yet, having gone over the letters in their MS. state, I have not read them as published; and indeed had I read them, it is not probable my memory would have enabled me to judge of the omissions. I am therefore prepared to give but one opinion, which is that the whole of the M.S.'S. examined and passed by myself, and the doubtful passages referred to the President and passed by him, were proper for publication. For tho' there were passages which might on publication create uneasiness in the minds of some, and were therefore referred by me to the President, yet I concurred fully in the opinion he pronounced that as these things were true they ought to be known. To render history what it ought to be the whole truth should be known. I am no friend to mystery and state secrets. They serve generally only to conceal the errors and rogueries of those who govern. I sincerely wish you may be able to prosecute your plan of publishing all the official letters of our war which may contribute to it's history. I am with sincere esteem Dear Sir Your friend & servt

TH: JEFFERSON

PrC (DLC); faded; at foot of text: "Mr. John Carey, Falcon court. Fleet street."   YOUR FIRST LETTER: Carey to TJ, 6 Apr. 1795.

¹ Estimated five words illegible.

To John Stuart

DEAR SIR   Monticello Nov. 10. 1796.

I have to acknolege the receipt of your last favor together with the bones of the Great-claw which accompanied it. My anxiety to obtain a thigh bone is such that I defer communicating what we have to the Philosophical society in the hope of adding that bone to the collection.

We should then be able to fix the stature of the animal without going into conjecture and calculation as we should possess a whole limb from the haunch bone to the claw inclusive. Whenever you announce to me that the recovery of a thigh bone is desperate, I shall make the communication to the Philosophical society. I think it happy that this incident will make known to them a person so worthy as yourself to be taken in to their body, and without whose attention to these extraordinary remains the world might have been deprived of the knolege of them. I cannot however help believing that this animal as well as the Mammoth are still existing. The annihilation of any species of existence is so unexampled in any parts of the economy of nature which we see, that we have a right to conclude, as to the parts we do not see, that the probabilities against such annihilation are stronger than those for it. In hopes of hearing from you as soon as you can form a conclusion satisfactory to yourself that the thigh bone will, or will not, be recovered, I remain with great respect & esteem Dr. Sir Your most obedt servt

Th: Jefferson

RC (Mrs. Charles W. Biggs, Lewisburg, West Virginia, 1950); addressed: "Colo. John Stuart Greenbriar"; stamped. PrC (DLC).

GREAT-CLAW: the megalonyx. PERSON SO WORTHY: see note to Stuart to TJ, 11 Apr. 1796, for Stuart's election to the American Philosophical Society.

To John Barnes

DEAR SIR   Monticello Nov. 13. 96.

Your two favors of Sep. 25. and Oct. 15. are duly recieved. It will be proper to have the sashes painted on the *outside*. Within a fortnight from this time it will be determined whether the walls of my house can be finished this autumn, and consequently whether I shall have occasion to call for any more sashes (other than those before called for) before next spring. I shall then furnish you with money for sashes and glass according to the extent of the call.

Mr. Peter Lott, a merchant of Charlottesville, chiefly in the grocery line, wanting a correspondent in Philadelphia to make his purchases there on commission on whose attention he can rely, I have recommended yourself to him, as I do him to you. He is the brother of the Lott late partner of Higbee in Philadelphia, who on his death left this gentleman his capital. He is industrious, oeconomical and of the purest integrity, and as his is a ready money business, the connection is a sure one. You cannot have a correspondent on whom you may more fully rely. He leaves his former one because he has not found him sufficiently punctual in his advices or the execution of his orders. I am with great esteem Dear Sir Your friend & servt   TH: JEFFERSON

PrC (MHi); at foot of text: "Mr. John Barnes"; endorsed by TJ in ink on verso.

Barnes's FAVORS OF SEP. 25. AND OCT. 15. 1796, recorded in SJL as received on 8 and

28 Oct. 1796, have not been found. SJL also records eleven missing letters exchanged by TJ and PETER LOTT between 12 June 1797 and 14 June 1798.

From William Booker

SIR   Goochland County Novr. 17. 1796
    Inclosed is a drawing of the threshing Machine I promised you by Mr. Buck. I hope your Liberallity will Excuse me, for the delay.
    My Situation has been Such as rendered it almost Impossible with any Tolarable Convenience to have done it Sooner.
    I have been but Little used to drawing. What blunders you See I trust you will Excuse. I hope however with it and the Information you got by Mr. Buck will be Sufficient to Shew you the principle after which I have no doubt you will Greatly Improve on it.
    I am Confident, it will suit this Country much better than Cog and rounds it being more Simple Less Expensive, and I think fully as opperative. I am with due Respt. your &c&c   WM. BOOKER

RC (DLC); endorsed by TJ as received 18 Nov. 1796 and so recorded in SJL. Enclosure not found.

From Jean Armand Tronchin

MONSIEUR   [La]vigny, par Rolle, Canton de Berne. le 17e. 9bre. 1796.
    Le vif intérêt que je prens à un ami, victime des événemens qui ont entrainés la ruine de ma malheureuse Patrie, me fait prendre la liberté, Monsieur, de recourir aux sentimens d'amitié dont vous m'hon[oriez] pendant nôtre séjour à Paris, pour tacher, au [moyen?] des lumières que je vous demande dans le M[émoire] cy joint, de sauver à cet ami le reste de sa fo[rtune qu'un] Débiteur de mauvaise foy lui a enlevé par sa res[idence aux] Etats Unis, où il a porté des sommes considérable[s qui] appartiennent légitimement à ses malheureux Cr[éanciers]. Tel est au moins le cri public et celui des gens instruits des affaires de ce Débiteur.
    N'étant mû que par l'intérêt de mon ami, c'est à celui là seul que je

m'attache. Il réclame environ Trente quatre Mille Livres de France, espèces métalliques. [Cette?] somme est minime, mais elle est considérable pour [le chef?] d'une nombreuse et respectable famille, qui de l'opulence est tombé dans un état qui approche de la misére sans qu'il y ait aucunement de sa faute.

Tous ces motifs sont bien puissans sur votre coeur, Monsieur, dont je connois la sensibilité et la justice; et seront la meilleure excuse que je puisse vous présenter de l'embarras que je prens la liberté de vous donner.

Cette occasion m'est bien précieuse, puisque je m'en promets le double avantage de rendre service à mon ami et d'avoir des nouvelles de votre santé à la quelle je prens l'intérêt le plus vif. J'ay l'honneur d'être avec les sentimens de la plus haute considération et de l'attachement le plus inviolable. Monsieur, Votre très humble et très Obeissant serviteur.

JN. ARMAND TRONCHIN
cy devant Ministre de la
République de Genève à la
Cour de france

RC (DLC); mutilated; at foot of first page: "Monsieur Jefferson"; endorsed by TJ as received 27 Dec. 1797 from "Lavigny par Rolle," and so recorded in SJL.

ENCLOSURE

Tronchin's Memorandum on
Recovering Foreign Debts in America

[17 Nov. 1796]

Mémoire

Quelques personnes, sans doute mal instruites, affectent de croire qu'un Débiteur qui a fui d'Europe en emportant avec lui les biens de ses créanciers, s'il a choisi son azile dans les Etats Unis d'Amérique, ne sauroit y être poursuivi, ni obligé à restitution: Ou ce qui revient au même, que les Tribunaux d'Amérique se refuseroient à mettre à exécution des Jugemens rendus en Europe contre ce Débiteur frauduleux, lors même qu'on produiroit aux Juges d'Amérique des Titres parés qui excluroient aucun doute sur la certitude de la dette et l'autorité des Juges d'Europe qui ont prononcé sur le titre qui la fonde; comme un protest s'il s'agit d'une lettre de change, et la [dite] prononciation du Juge qui s'en est ensuivie. Tous [ces] Actes düement vidimés et légalisés.

D'après cet exposé, on prend la liberté de deman[der:]

Si ce n'est pas sur une erreur, injurieuse au Gouvern[ement] Américain, qu'est fondée l'étrange assertion qu'un Débiteur Européen, réfugié en Amérique, peut y jouïr tranquillement de la fortune de ses créanciers légitimes d'Europe; et qu'il n'y a aucun moyen de le poursuivre tant qu'il [res]tera dans cet azile.

Si le contraire éxiste, ainsi que le bon sens, la justice et l'avantage des rélations commerciales entre tous les Etats, le persuadent à ceux qui connoissent la
loyauté et les sages loix qui gouvernent les Etats Unis. On demande si pour
entamer une action en Amerique, il faut envoyer les Titres originaux (exposés
à se perdre par un long trajet) ou si des copies düement vidimées et légalisées ne
les remplaceroient pas; et par qui et comment elles doivent l'être?

Si ces pièces n'acquerroient pas tout le degré d'authenticité convenable par la
légalisation du Ministre de france Résident à Genève; la Signature de ce Ministre, légalisée par celui des Rélations Extérieures du Gouvernement François; et
enfin cette signature légalisée par le Ministre des Etats Unis d'Amérique Résident à Paris.

On demande encore, de quelle maniére l'on doit constituer un Procureur
pour agir contre le Débiteur fugitif; et si l'on ne pourroit pas traiter avec ce
Procureur à tant pour cent du capital que ses poursuites arracheroit au
Débiteur: question que l'on fait pour éviter des répétitions de fraix dont on ne
sauroit présumer la valeur et qui pourroient être très onereux au malheureux
Créancier.

MS (DLC); entirely in Tronchin's hand; undated; mutilated.

Deed of Mortgage of Slaves to Van Staphorst & Hubbard

This deed made on the 21st. day of Nov. 1796. between Thomas
Jefferson of Albemarle in Virginia on the one part and Nicholas Van
Staphorst, Jacob Van Staphorst and   Hubbard of Amsterdam in
the United Netherlands merchants and partner. Witnesseth, that
whereas the said Thomas hath conveyed by deeds of mortgage fifty
seven negro slaves to William Short, fifty two other negro slaves to Henderson McCaul & Co., sixteen other slaves to Wakelyn Welsh, eight
other slaves to Philip Mazzei, and seventeen other slaves to the said Van
Staphorsts & Hubbard making in the whole one hundred and fifty
slaves specially named and described in the said deeds, whereupon
there remains to the said Thomas an equity of redemption on payment
of the sums of money due to the said mortgagees respectively and for
securing whereof the said mortgages were executed, and whereas the
said Van Staphorsts & Hubbard have now lately and since the dates of
the said deeds lent to the said Thomas the further sum of two thousand
dollars, now therefore for securing the same, and in consideration of the
further sum of five shillings to him in hand paid he hath given granted
and conveyed unto the said Nicholas and Jacob Van Staphorsts & Hubbard all his right and equity of redemption in the said hundred and fifty
negro slaves in full and absolute right and dominion. Provided never-

theless that if the said Thomas shall faithfully pay to the said Van Stap-horsts & Hubbard the said sum of two thousand dollars with lawful interest thereon, then these presents to become void. Witness his hand and seal the day and year above written TH: JEFFERSON

Signed
sealed and   RICHARD RICHARDSON
delivered in   RICHARD ADAMS
presence of

MS (DLC); in TJ's hand and signed by TJ, Richardson, and Adams.

Richardson and Adams were brickmasons who worked at Monticello during the summer and fall of 1796 (MB, II, 944, 945, 947, 949). For the earlier DEEDS OF MORTGAGE on TJ's SLAVES, see TJ to James Lyle, 12 May 1796, and enclosure; and Deed of Mortgage of Slaves to Van Staphorst & Hubbard, 12 May 1796.

To Peter Carr

DEAR SIR   Monticello Nov. 28. 96.

I sincerely congratulate you on the change which you expect shortly to make in your state of life. You may be assured in advance that the greatest source of human happiness is in the tender connubial connection of the two sexes. You have the better reason too to count on it from the character of the lady who unites her destiny with yours, and of whom fame has brought us so many good reports. Other prospects of benefit may also open themselves. The affections, present and future, arising from the union, may excite more powerfully to the active and useful exertion of the good talents which nature has given you, than considerations of meer personal interest have done, and that too when seemingly opposed to personal ease. Your friends will find in this new motives of satisfaction and sentiments of esteem for you still more pure and unmixed.

We shall flatter ourselves with the hope of seeing your new friend here, and shall endeavor to make her visits as comfortable as the shattered state of our castle will permit. I beg you to lay at her feet on my part the homage of my sincere respect and esteem, and repeat to you assurances of the continuance of the interest I feel in whatever concerns you, & of the sentiments of constant attachment with which I am Dear Sir Your's affectionately   TH: JEFFERSON

RC (MdAN); at foot of text: "P. Carr."

In a missing letter of 27 Nov. 1796, recorded in SJL as received the same day, Carr had evidently notified his uncle of his engagement to Hetty Smith, a sister of Republican Congressman Samuel Smith of Baltimore and of Robert Smith, later TJ's

Secretary of the Navy. The wedding took place on 6 June 1797 (VMHB, II, 223). A letter from Carr to TJ of 31 Oct. 1794 is recorded in SJL as received from "Union town" on 15 Nov. 1794, but has not been found.

To Thomas Mann Randolph

TH:J. TO TMR.   Monticello Nov. 28. 96.

It is so cold that the freezing of the ink on the point of my pen renders it difficult to write. We have had the thermometer at 12°. My works are arrested in a state entirely unfinished, and I fear we shall not be able to resume them. Clarke has sold our wheat in Bedford for 8/6 and the rise to the 1st. of June, with some other modifications. It appears to be a good sale. He preferred it to 10/6 certain which was offered him. I think he was right as there is little appearance of any intermission of the war.—I thank you for your letter of news, and am glad to see the republican preeminence in our assembly.—The paper you inclosed me presents a result entirely questionable according to my own ideas of the subject. The preponderance of the Mckain interest in the Western counties of Pensylvania is by no means as great as is there supposed. Few will believe the true dispositions of my mind on that subject. It is not the less true however that I do sincerely wish to be the second on that vote rather than the first. The considerations which induce this preference are solid, whether viewed with relation to interest, happiness, or reputation. Ambition is long since dead in my mind. Yet even a well-weighed ambition would take the same side.—My new threshing machine will be tried this week.—P. Carr is on the point of marriage.— All are well here, and join in the hope of your continuing so. Adieu.

RC (DLC); endorsed by Randolph. PrC (MHi); endorsed by TJ in ink on verso.

LETTER OF NEWS: probably Randolph to TJ of 23 Nov. 1796, recorded in SJL as received from Richmond three days later. Neither the letter nor the enclosed PAPER has been found.

The long-awaited presidential election results from Westmoreland and Fayette, Pennsylvania's WESTERN COUNTIES, did not arrive in Philadelphia until 24 Nov. 1796, six days after the date required by the election law. The returns gave Thomas McKean, who headed the list of the state's 15 Republican electoral candidates, the votes he needed to win in a very close race. Only two Federalists were among the 15 electors, but even they would have lost if the returns from Greene County had arrived soon enough to be included in the count. When the electors met in Harrisburg on 7 Dec. 1796, Samuel Miles, a Federalist, cast his vote for TJ. Thus Adams received only one electoral vote in Pennsylvania (Harry M. Tinkcom, *The Republicans and Federalists in Pennsylvania, 1790-1801* [Harrisburg, 1950], 167-72).

To John Barnes

DEAR SIR   Monticello Dec. 4. 1796.

The advance of the cold season has now determined that my walls are not to be finished this year, and consequently not to be covered in. I shall have no occasion therefore to order any more sashes till the next spring. Those already made, to wit, 12. sets of trebles and 6. pair of doubles I shall be obliged to you to forward to Richmond to the care of Mr. Johnston, retaining the boxes of glass 18. by 12. furnished by Mr. Donath, to be used in Philadelphia for the sashes hereafter to be ordered. Be so good as to pay Mr. Donath a small balance due him as you will see by the inclosed letter which I leave open for your perusal. Also to pay Mr. Mussi for 2. boxes of sweet oil forwarded to me. Mr. Trump was desired to apply to you for paiment of his work as fast as delivered. I now inclose you a draught on Messrs. Harrison & Sterett for a balance in their hands of 184. Dollars, and I draw on you this day in favor of Wm. Wardlaw or order for 70. Dollars at 10. days sight. Not knowing exactly the paiments to Mr. Trump, and some other of the items of our accounts I do not know whether I am a little under or a little over my mark in your books. If you will be so good as to send me a state of our affairs all shall be put to rights immediately. I am Dear Sir Your friend & servt.   TH: JEFFERSON

PrC (MHi); at foot of text: "Mr. John Barnes"; endorsed by TJ in ink on verso. Enclosures: (1) TJ to Joseph Donath, 4 Dec. 1796. (2) TJ's draft on Harrison & Sterett, 4 Dec. 1796, requesting them to pay Barnes $184 at three days' sight (PrC in MHi; at foot of text: "Messrs. Harrison & Sterett Merchts. Philadelphia").

A letter from TJ to Joseph MUSSI of this date was recorded in SJL but has not been found. Also on this day, TJ wrote a draft on

Barnes to pay William WARDLAW $70 as described above (PrC in MHi; at foot of text: "Mr. John Barnes Mercht."). Daniel TRUMP of Philadelphia, who later completed other woodworking for Monticello, wrote a letter to TJ of 24 Sep. 1796, recorded in SJL as received 8 Oct. 1796, that has not been found.

SJL records a letter from Barnes to TJ of 22 Nov. 1796 that was received on 4 Dec. 1796 but has not been found.

To Joseph Donath

SIR   Monticello Dec. 4. 1796.

I have recieved your favor of Oct. 19. and become sensible of the error in calculating the 180. panes as so many feet. It makes a difference, as I state it, of 20.D. 25c. which sum or whatever it may be Mr. Barnes will pay you on application in consequence of a letter I write him this day. With respect to the glass 14. by 12. instead of 12 I. square, I believe I must decline taking it, on account of the size, and it's not being 1 $\frac{1}{2}$ thick, as in the high situation of my house, the winds make a very stout quality of glass necessary. As we have failed to finish our walls this season and consequently cannot cover in, we have time till the spring or summer before this glass will be wanting, by which time you may perhaps be able to furnish me of the size and quality necessary. I am Sir Your very humble servt   TH: JEFFERSON

                         mills
180. panes = 270. feet @ .225 =   60.75
     remitted before   40.5
     balance short—remitted   20.25

PrC (ViU: McGregor Library); at foot of text: "Mr. Jos. Donath." Enclosed in TJ to John Barnes, 4 Dec. 1796.

No FAVOR from Donath of OCT. 19. has been found, but a missing letter from Donath to TJ of 14 Oct. is recorded in SJL as received 21 Oct. 1796.

To Henry Banks

SIR   Monticello Dec. 5 96
   Your favor of Nov. 20. has come to hand. I should be perfectly willing to do any thing which would accomodate you as to the land mortgaged to me, if the matter depended on myself alone. But it is extremely delicate for me to take any step without the consent of Mr. Hanson. He is in your neighborhood, and if you will be pleased to consult him, I will forward the patents to him or to any other person he shall direct, if a private conveyance can be found; for you are aware that they are too voluminous to go by post. I sincerely wish him to concur in any measures which will expedite the paiment of the money, till which takes place my mind is not at ease. I am Sir Your very humble servt
                                             TH: JEFFERSON

PrC (MHi); at foot of text: "Mr. Henry Banks"; endorsed by TJ in ink on verso.

Banks's FAVOR of 20 Nov. 1796, recorded in SJL as received on 25 Nov. 1796, has not been found. For the LAND MORTGAGED to TJ in the purchase of his Elk Hill plantation by Banks and Thomas A. Taylor, and for his assignment of proceeds from the transaction

to pay obligations for which Richard HANSON was the agent, see TJ to Banks, 15 Jan. 1795; and TJ to Taylor, 19 Feb. 1795.
   Recorded in SJL, but missing, are letters from Banks to TJ of 1 and 10 Apr. 1797, 31 May 1797, and 25 Oct. 1798, received on 21 Apr., 21 Apr., 31 May 1797, and 15 Nov. 1798 respectively, as well as a letter from TJ to Banks of 31 May 1797.

From James Madison

DEAR SIR   Philada. Decr. 5. 1796

It is not possible yet to calculate with any degree of certainty whether you are to be left by the Electors to enjoy the repose to which you are so much attached, or are to be summoned to the arduous trust which depends on their allotment. It is not improbable that Pinkney will step in between the two who have been treated as the principals in the question. It is even suspected that this turn has been secretly meditated from the beginning in a quarter where the *leading* zeal for Adams has been affected. This Jockeyship is accounted for by the enmity of Adams to Banks and funding systems which is now become public, and by an apprehension that he is too headstrong to be a fit puppet for the intriguers behind the skreen. It is to be hoped that P. may equally disappoint those who expect to make that use of him, if the appointment should in reallity light on him. We do not however absolutely despair that a choice better than either may still be made; and there is always the chance of a devolution of the business on the House of Reps. which will I believe decide it as it ought to be decided.

Adêts Note which you will have seen, is working all the evil with which it is pregnant. Those who rejoice at its indiscretions and are taking advantage of them, have the impudence to pretend that it is an electioneering manoeuvre, and that the French Govt. have been led to it by the opponents of the British Treaty. Unless the unhapy effect of it here and cause of it in France, be speedily obviated by wise councils and healing measures, the crisis will unquestionably be perverted into a perpetual alienation of the two Countries by the secret enemies of both. The immediate consequences of such an event may be distressing; but the permanent ones to the commercial and other great interests of this Country, form a long and melancholy catalogue. We know nothing of the policy meditated by the Executive on this occasion. The Speech will probably furnish some explanation of it. Yrs. always & affecy.

Js. MADISON JR.

RC (DLC: Madison Papers); endorsed by TJ as received 16 Dec. 1796 and so recorded in SJL.

The contention that Alexander Hamilton SECRETLY MEDITATED FROM THE BEGINNING to push Federalist vice-presidential candidate Thomas Pinckney for president rather than John Adams is explored in Kurtz, *Presidency of John Adams*, 98-113 and Elkins and McKitrick, *Age of Federalism*, 515-16, 523-8. According to

THIS JOCKEYSHIP, Hamiltonian Federalists worked to keep New Englanders in line behind Pinckney while counting on the fact that many southerners would refuse to support Adams, thus giving Pinckney the highest number of votes and the presidency.

The charge that John ADAMS was critical of BANKS AND FUNDING SYSTEMS became PUBLIC in Tench Coxe's tenth letter "To the Electors of the President of the United States," which he signed "A Federalist." Portraying Adams as "strongly opposed" to the nation's financial management as implemented by the Treasury Department, Coxe observed that "He has often spoken of the funding system as certainly to bring upon this country evils the most extreme" (*Gazette of the United States*, 30 Nov. 1796; Cooke, *Coxe*, 286, 289).

In a NOTE of 15 Nov., Pierre Auguste Adet, French minister to the United States, informed Secretary of State Timothy Pickering that the Directory had ordered him to suspend immediately his ministerial functions because it viewed the implementation of the Jay Treaty as a violation of the French-American treaty of 1778. Adet's exchange of notes with Pickering had begun two weeks earlier with his 27 Oct. announcement that according to the Directory's decree of 2 July France would henceforth "treat the flag of neutrals in the same manner as they shall suffer it to be treated by the English," thus subjecting American ships to French seizure. Adet had the notes to Pickering and a proclamation by the Directory calling upon French citizens in the United States to wear tricolored cockades if they wished to receive protection and services from the French government sent to Benjamin Bache's *Aurora* for publication (ASP, *Foreign Relations*, I, 576-88; Philadelphia *Aurora*, 31 Oct., 5, 18 Nov. 1796; Alexander DeConde, "Washington's Farewell, the French Alliance, and the Election of 1796," MVHR, XLIII [1957], 653-6).

Washington delivered the SPEECH, his annual message to Congress, on 7 Dec. 1796. In it he referred briefly to the "extensive injuries" which France was inflicting on United States commerce in the West Indies and to Adet's communications, but he postponed a full discussion until a later date. He reassured Congress that it was his "constant, sincere, and earnest wish . . . to maintain cordial harmony, and a perfect friendly understanding" with the French Republic. The president did not deliver his promised message on French-American relations until 19 Jan. 1797 (JHR, II, 607-10, 650).

To Wilson Cary Nicholas

DEAR SIR   Monticello Dec. 5. 96.

About the latter end of the last assembly I wrote to sollicit your endeavors to procure an act giving the character of citizens to Nicholas and Jacob Van Staphorst and Nicholas Hubbard merchants and bankers of Amsterdam. My letter got too late to your hands, and as you may not now have it with you I will state the subject again from the beginning.

On the failure of the revolution attempted in Holland in 1788 the leaders of the patriotic party were obliged to fly their country. They came chiefly to Paris, and consisted mostly of substantial merchants, bankers and lawyers. Of these, Jacob Van Staphorst was the principal, and was indeed destined for a principal office if the revolution had succeeded. At Paris their consultations were in what part of the world they should seek a new establishment. They had no difficulty in deciding on the United States, which occasioned their consulting me. On a view of all circumstances and advantages, Norfolk seemed likely to attract them. Just in this stage of the business the court of France took some measures which encouraged some of them to remain in Paris, others went elsewhere, some home, and so they got dispersed. On the commencement of the present revolution in the United Netherlands, the

Van Staphorsts, who had been increasing their business in the US. again turned their attention to this state and became desirous of having here a fixed resource in every event, and of being qualified to prepare an establishment. As I had been consulted before, and was personally acquainted with them they applied to me to use my endeavors to get them made citizens of this commonwealth; and this was the object of my former as it is of the present letter. I informed them of the accident which prevented the attempt at the last session, and I have lately recieved a letter from them solliciting a renewal of it. I have waited some time expecting the arrival of a petition for this purpose which they wrote me word they would send through their correspondents in Philadelphia, but as I do not know of it's arrival, and the present session may pass over before it does arrive I have thought it best not to await it longer. The general question Whether persons residing in foreign countries should be permitted to hold lands here admits of plausible arguments on both sides. Perhaps it is not easy to lay down general rules for the government of all cases, which may not in some of them produce inconvenience: and till this can be done, perhaps it is best for the legislature to keep in their own hands the dispensation of the rights of citizenship, governing themselves by their own discretion and the circumstances of every case. The idea of the present applicants was originally taken up with a view to a particular event. Perhaps even now it may in some degree be eventual. The short intercourse between Norfolk and St. Eustatius, where their chief commercial connections were, rendered such a change of residence scarcely a change of business. Having long contemplated the subject, and familiarized their minds to it, nothing is more possible than that, let events be what they will, it may lead to the commencement of an establishment there, and nothing but a collection of large capitalists is wanting to give to that place the immense advantages of it's natural position; to render it unnecessary for our merchants to go further to sell or buy. It is unnecessary to develope the benefits which would accrue from the rise of Norfolk; they must be obvious to every one. And I propose the present measure merely because it may prove the first step towards the acquisition of great advantages, and can at worst produce small inconvenience. If on a contemplation of the subject you view it as I do, I will ask the favor of you to endeavor to get an act passed declaring Nicholas Van Staphorst Jacob Vanstaphorst and Nicholas Hubbard of the city of Amsterdam citizens of this commonwealth. I think it would be best to clog it with no conditions inconsistent with their present citizenship but to leave the measure full and free to work it's own effect. I am with great esteem Dear Sir Your friend & servt   TH: JEFFERSON

RC (CSmH); at foot of first page: "W. C. Nicholas esqr."

SJL records no letters between TJ and Nicholas during the LATTER END OF THE LAST ASSEMBLY, which adjourned on 29 Dec. 1795 (Leonard, *General Assembly*, 199), but for a letter the preceding year on the subject of citizenship for NICHOLAS AND JACOB VAN STAPHORST, see TJ to Nicholas, 12 Dec. 1794. For the latest LETTER seeking a RENEWAL of the citizenship application, see Van Staphorst & Hubbard to TJ, 10 Oct. 1795.

From John Wickham

DEAR SIR   Richmond 8th. Decr. 1796.

I write to you at the Request of Mr. Eppes to inform You of a Settlement which he and Mr. Skipwith made with me of the Debt due from the Estate of Mr. Wayles to Mr. Welch.

This Adjustment took place on the 24th. Ulto. The principal Debt amounted to £1321–11–11. Stg. on the 30th. June 1775, on this Interest was calculated up to the Date of the Settlement, deducting 8 Years for the War, the aggregate Sum at $33\frac{1}{3}$ Exchange amounted to £2942–15 Current Money and was agreed to be divided into four Installments, $\frac{1}{4}$ payable with Interest from the Settlement, on the 1st. June 1798, and the other three fourths with Interest on the first of June in each Succeeding Year till the whole should be paid. In order to accommodate Mr. Skipwith and Mr. Eppes I consented to divide the Debt into three parts, and each of them gave Bond with the other as his Surety for one third payable at the periods above mentioned—The other third they informed me would be settled by You, and Mr. Eppes, at the same Time that he requested me to write to You, assured me he would lose no Time in informing You what had been done in this Business. In order more fully to explain the Terms of the Settlement I inclose You a Bond which, except that a blank is left for the Names of the Obligors, is an exact Transcript of those which have been executed by Mr. Skipwith and Mr. Eppes.

As it might well happen after so long an Extension of Credit, that Mr. Welch would have to look for payment from persons in whom he could not place so much Confidence as in yourself and the other Executors of Mr. Wayles, I thought it not unreasonable to ask a Security from Mr. Eppes and Mr. Skipwith, this they readily agreed to and became bound for each other. If You prefer paying off your part of the Debt in a short Time nothing but your own Undertaking will be wanted, but if the same Credit which is allowed the other Executors will be an accommodation You will of course take it on the same Terms that they have done.

The mode of your becoming bound for your proportion of the Debt

[217]

is submitted altogether to Yourself—Whenever You shall have fixed on it You will be pleased to execute the necessary writings and transmit them either to Mr. Waller or me. With great Respect I am Dear Sir Your obt: Servant   JNO: WICKHAM

RC (MHi); addressed: "Thomas Jefferson Esquire Monticello—By post to Charlottesville"; stamped and postmarked; endorsed by TJ as received 17 Dec. 1796 and so recorded in SJL. Enclosure not found.

John Wickham (1763-1839) studied law with George Wythe at the College of William and Mary and was admitted to the bar in 1786. Settling in Richmond in 1790, Wickham became a leading attorney, often serving as counsel for British creditors, while his close friend John Marshall frequently served as the attorney for Virginia debtors, as typified in the case of Ware v. Hylton in 1793. Wickham served as attorney for TJ and the Wayles executors in the suit against Richard Randolph's estate. In 1803, William Wirt characterized Wickham as displaying "a greater diversity of talents and acquirements than any other at the bar of Virginia." In his most famous case, he served as a defense attorney at Aaron Burr's trial for treason. In 1810, TJ unsuccessfully attempted to retain his services in the Batture case (DAB; Vol. 28: 99-100, 114-15, 290-1; TJ to Francis Eppes, 1 Aug. 1796; TJ to Wickham, 18 May 1810; Wickham to TJ, 16 and 22 May 1810; Marshall, *Papers*, v, 144, 267, 456; William Wirt, *Letters of the British Spy, Originally Published in the Virginia Argus, in August and September, 1803* [Richmond, 1803], 30-31; Imogene E. Brown, *American Aristides: A Biography of George Wythe* [East Brunswick, N.J., 1981], 213). For Wickham's experience in Virginia during the Revolution, see TJ to Charles Wall, 21 Dec. 1780.

According to SJL, TJ and Wickham exchanged six letters between 17 Jan. and 22 Sep. 1796, none of which has been found.

From James Madison

DEAR SIR   Decr. 10. 96

Exitus in dubio is still the Motto to the election. You *must* reconcile yourself to the secondary as well as the primary station, if that should be your lot. The prevailing idea is that Pinkney will have the greatest number of votes: and I think that Adams will be most likely to stand next. There are other calculations however less favaroble to both. The answer to the President's speech is in the hands of Ames, Sitgreaves Smith of Carola. Baldwin and myself—The form is not yet settled. There is a *hope* that it may be got into a form that will go down without altercation or division in the House. Yrs. sincerely   Js. M. JR

RC (DLC: Madison Papers); endorsed by TJ as received from Philadelphia 24 Dec. 1796 and so recorded in SJL.

EXITUS IN DUBIO: "His end is in doubt," Ovid, *Metamorphoses*, 12.522.

ANSWER TO THE PRESIDENT'S SPEECH: see Madison to TJ, 19 Dec. 1796.

To John Barnes

DEAR SIR   Monticello Dec. 11. 96.

I inclose you a power of Attorney to recieve a quarter's interest due on Mr. Short's stock. Be pleased to place one hundred dollars of this to the credit of Mr. Peter Lott with you, and to hold the residue subject to my draughts which will be made shortly. I am Dear Sir Your most obedt. servt   TH: JEFFERSON

PrC (CSmH); at foot of text: "Mr. John Barnes"; endorsed by TJ in ink on verso.

ENCLOSURE

Power of Attorney to John Barnes for William Short

Know all men by these presents that I Thomas Jefferson named in a certain letter of attorney from William Short of the state of Virginia, late one of the ministers of the US. abroad, to me, bearing date the 2d. day of April 1793. and now lodged in the bank of the US. by virtue of the power and authority thereby given me, do substitute and appoint John Barnes of Philadelphia as well my own as the true and lawful attorney and substitute of the said William Short named in the said letter of Attorney to recieve from the treasury or bank of the US. the interest which became due on the stock of different descriptions of the said Wm. Short registered in the proper office of the US. at the seat of government in Philadelphia from the 1st. day of July to the 1st. day of October last past amounting to three hundred and some odd dollars and becoming payable on the said 1st. day of October, hereby ratifying and confirming the paiment of the said interest to the said John Barnes and the discharge which he shall give for the same as done by virtue of the power of attorney aforesaid. In witness whereof I have hereunto set my hand and seal this 10th. day of December 1796.

TH: JEFFERSON

MS (MHi); entirely in TJ's hand; on verso, also in TJ's hand, are two attestations, the first signed by Thomas Bell confirming TJ's seal and signature on the document, the second signed by John Nicholas as clerk of Albemarle County certifying Bell's authority as a justice of the peace.

Barnes could not execute another power of attorney, sent by TJ on 17 Dec. 1796, because of some defect in its form, but it is not known if he encountered any difficulty in executing the above document (see TJ to Barnes, 28 Jan. 1797).

To Thomas A. Taylor

SIR   Monticello Dec. 11. 96.

I have recieved your last favor requesting that Mr. Banks's patents may be lodged with some friend in Richmond to facilitate his disposing of the lands. Mr. T. M. Randolph will leave this in about a week for Richmond. I will deliver them to him to be lodged with Mr. Hanson or otherwise disposed of as he shall direct. I wrote to Mr. Banks on this subject by the last post, but I did not then know that I should have so good and speedy an opportunity of conveying the patents to Richmond. I am Sir Your very humble servt.   TH: JEFFERSON

PrC (MHi); at foot of text: "Dr. T. A. Taylor"; endorsed in ink by TJ on verso.

Taylor's LAST FAVOR, recorded in SJL as written on "Nov. 31." and received on 10 Dec. 1796, has not been found. Also recorded in SJL, but missing, are twelve letters from Taylor to TJ, and six from TJ to Taylor, written between 23 Mch. 1797 and 25 July 1799.

From Volney

MONSIEUR   philadelphie 12 Xbre 1796

Je commence à me persuader que Vous N'avez point reçu une de mes Lettres, celle que j'eûs l'honneur de Vous adresser de lexington le 20 7bre. En vous y rendant compte de Mon Voyage Vers L'ouabache, au poste Canadien de Vincennes, et en Vous exposant les raisons qui M'empêchaient Malgré Mon desir, d'effectuer Mon retour par Monticello, je Vous priais de Vouloir bien Me faire passer Ma Valise par La premiere occasion Sûre que Vous auriez pour philadelphie, où j'esperais la rejoindre en decembre.

Madame Madison a qui je rendis Visite il y a deux jours, M'ayant dit que Vous attendiez de Mes Nouvelles, pour Me faire cet envoi, j'en conclus que Ma lettre de lexington S'est egarée. Je dois donc Vous reïterer Ma demande, quoique d'ailleurs je ne Veuille point Me désister de l'engagement de retourner à Monticello: Mais ne prévoyant point à quelle epoque je pourrai le remplir, et ayant besoin de quelques objets contenus dans cette Valise, je desire L'avoir ici dans Mes Mains avant de faire quelque Nouvelle course.

Celle que je Viens d'achever N'a pas laissé que d'être longue et penible: après être revenu de L'ouabache et avoir traversé le Kentuckey, je me dirigeai au Nord et Me rendis par Cincinnati et la ligne des forts, jusqu'a Votre Nouvelle possession de detroit. Il serait trop Long de Vous décrire cette partie de pays que les americains eux memes disent leur avoir été peu connue avant ce jour: surtout lorsque j'ignore Sur quelle partie Se porterait plus Specialement Votre intérêt: je me bornerai à Vous dire en Masse que de L'ohio aux lacs le sol est genéralement plat; que les eaux trouvent Si peu de pente qu'elles ne

savent par où S'ecouler; d'où resultent d'interminables detours, de per-
nicieux Marais, des Swamps aussi penibles que dangereux. Dans cent
ans quand toute cette Vaste foret Sera eclaircie et le Sol desseché, ce sera
une riche plaine telle que Notre flandre et La hollande, une pepiniere de
bestiaux pour tout le continent, et une habitation plus riche peut-être
que le Kentuckey: Mais en ce moment C'est une ennuyeuse et Sauvage
Solitude de bois et de prairie, où Malgré de bonnes tentes et une assez
bonne chère, toute Notre compagnie a pris la fievre en 15 jours: de
Maniere que de 26 personnes parties de Cincinnati, le Seul capitaine
sparks S'est Maintenu Sauf. Le Major Swan, et Moi qui resistâmes le
plus longtems passâmes un plus fort tribut en arrivant au detroit. Par
exception, au lieu de la fievre intermittente j'eûs une fievre bilieuse, qui
heureusement ceda en Six jours à deux Vigoureuses doses d'Emétique,
sans rien autre chose que la diete et L'eau, relevée ensuite, quand L'ap-
petit Vint, par le Vin de porto, et le beef Stek au Ketchap. Ma convales-
cence eût eté rapide, Sans Le lac Erié, où jessuyai 16 jours le Mal de
Mer sans compter l'un des plus eminens dangers de Naufrage, que de
Laveu de Notre capitaine on puisse Eprouver. Pendant 12 heures, Sur-
pris Sur Notre ancre, trop près d'une petite isle, par une tempete de
Nord ouest, Nous frappâmes de la quille plus de 60 fois le fond, et Nous
N'echappâmes au brisement de Notre: Sloop que par le Miracle d'une
construction excellente, et L'heureux incident de Netre point chargé.
Une fois pied à terre, le spectacle de Niagara M'a tout fait oublier. Ce
n'est pas Seulement la cataracte, c'est tout l'ensemble topographique du
terrein pendant 7 Miles qui est curieux à connaître. Aucun Voyageur
Ne me Semble l'avoir Saisi ou du Moins developpé. Depuis Niagara
jusqu'a Genesée c'est un desert, que je traversai à cheval Moyennant la
politesse du juge powell qui M'en prêta un et Me donna un guide. Il
M'avait fallu Vendre au detroit, le très bon cheval Kentuckois que
j'avais acheté. Au Genesée trouvant une route de charette qui traverse
une ligne d'etablissemens yankis fondés depuis 7 ans et déjà florissans,
je Me mis à pied—jusqu'au Mohawk, où Lhyver M'a obligé de prendre
La detestable Voye des Stages ouverts. Si jamais je publie des Mémoires, je traiterai ces Machines *brisereins* et donneuses de Rhumes de Maniere à ce qu'aucun Voyageur ne Soit tenté d'y Monter. Du reste, toute
rancune cessante, je suis arrivé Sain, Sauf, et très bien portant à philadelphie où je vais Me reposer cet hyver: j'entends reposer le corps, car
je me trouve arrieré en travaux d'esprit, et je me propose de Me remettre
au courant. Pour cet effet j'ai deja pris un plan de Vie aussi Solitaire qu'il
était dissipé L'an passé. En écoutant par passetems ce qu'on dit des
affaires d'Europe et Même d'amerique, je vais Mettre Mon portefeuille

en Ordre, et Si vous réimprimez Vos Notes de Virginie, j'aurai un Veritable plaisir à Vous en extraire ce qui Vous conviendra. Veuillez, Monsieur, Sur cet objet, comme Sur tout autre, M'indiquer Vos intentions, et Soyez persuadé de Mon desir constant de les remplir. Je recevrai ici toute lettre poste restante, Vû que je suis obligé Sous dix jours de changer de logement. On dit qu'outre Nos victoires d'italie, nos affaires intérieures Vont bien, que la Valeur de Nos biens fonds à doublé en Numéraire en 3 Mois: que l'on Vend à terme de 90 jours, chose inouïe depuis 3 ans. Malheureusement il parait que la paix N'aura point lieu, et il faudra faire au printems prochain une descente en angleterre: L'on S'en occupe très Sérieusement. La Nomination d'un Nouveau tiers de Notre legislature aura des conséquences très importantes Sur Notre esprit public. Ainsi le printems et leté prochain Nous promettent une Nouvelle Scène. Elle Sera très curieuse aussi en ce pays: le principal interet que j'y attache est de vous revoir quelque part que ce soit en aussi bonne santé et aussi heureux que Vous M'avez paru L'être à Monticello. Veuillez rappeller Mon souvenir à Votre famille et agréer Mes Sentimens D'attachement et D'estime   C. Volney

RC (DLC); endorsed by TJ as received 24 Dec. 1796 and so recorded in SJL.

No letter from Volney dated at LEXINGTON LE 20 7BRE 1796 has been found or was recorded in SJL. However, Volney's description of the letter suggests that he may have been thinking of the one he wrote to TJ on 24 Aug. 1796. See also TJ to Volney, 17 Dec. 1796.

To John Garland Jefferson

DEAR SIR   Monticello Dec. 17. 96.

At the time your favor of Nov. 11. came to hand I had not yet recieved an answer from Genl. Smith. It came some time after and I now inclose it to you. You will percieve that from a different construction of the same clause in the constitution in the superior and inferior courts, you would be refused in the former and admitted in the latter the first year. You would therefore not be merely idle the first year and might be making an acquaintance for your passage to the superior courts. I have no doubt that Tanissee is a good field for a man of industry, integrity and talents: and it is a good country to lay out advantageously the profits of business. I do not wonder therefore you prefer that to your present field. You are now at the time of life most capable of exertions, and you should make hay while the sun shines. As you advance in years it will become more and more disagreeable to be moving about. I sincerely wish you success in your undertaking, and shall always be happy to hear from you and to learn that you are doing well; being with sincere esteem Dear Sir Yours affectionately　　　　　　　　　　　TH: JEFFERSON

PrC (MHi); at foot of text: "J. Garland Jefferson"; endorsed in ink by TJ on verso. Enclosure not found.

J. G. Jefferson's FAVOR OF NOV. 11, recorded in SJL as received 18 Nov. 1796, has not been found.

To James Madison

TH:J. TO J.M.　　　　　　　　　　　　　　　Monticello Dec. 17. 96.

Your favor of the 5th. came to hand last night. The first wish of my heart was that you should have been proposed for the administration of the government. On your declining it I wish any body rather than myself: and there is nothing I so anxiously hope as that my name may come out either second or third. These would be indifferent to me; as the last would leave me at home the whole year, and the other two thirds of it. I have no expectation that the Eastern states will suffer themselves to be so much outwitted as to be made the tools for bringing in P. instead of A. I presume they will throw away their second vote. In this case it begins to appear possible that there may be an equal division where I had supposed the republican vote would have been considerably minor. It seems also possible that the Representatives may be divided. This is a difficulty from which the constitution has provided no issue. It is both my duty and inclination therefore to relieve the embarrasment should it happen: and in that case I pray you and authorize you fully to sollicit on my behalf that Mr. Adams may be preferred. He has always been my senior from the commencement of our public life, and the expression of the public will being equal, this circumstance ought to give him the preference. When so many motives will be operating to induce some of the members to change their vote, the addition of my wish may have some effect to preponderate the scale.　　　I am really anxious to see the speech. It must exhibit a very different picture of our foreign affairs from that presented in the Adieu, or it will little correspond with my views of them. I think they never wore so gloomy an aspect since the year 83. Let those come to the helm who think they can steer clear of the difficulties. I have no confidence in myself for the undertaking.

We have had the severest weather ever known in November. The thermometer was at 12°. here and in Goochland, and I suppose generally. It arrested my buildings very suddenly when eight days more would have completed my walls, and permitted us to cover in. The drought is excessive. From the middle of October to the middle of December not rain enough to lay the dust. A few days ago there fell a small rain, but the succeeding cold has probably prevented it from sprouting the grain sown during the drowth. Present me in friendly terms to Messrs. Giles, Venable, Page. Adieu affectionately.

P.S. I inclose a letter for Volney because I do not know where to address to him.

Pray send me Gallatin's view of the finances of the U.S. and Paine's letter to the President if within the compas of a conveyance by post.

RC (DLC: Madison Papers); addressed: "James Madison Congress Philadelphia"; franked. PrC (DLC); lacks final sentence of postscript. Enclosure: TJ to Volney, 17 Dec. 1796.

Madison used this letter to counter rumors that TJ would refuse to serve as vice president. He showed it to Benjamin Rush, who described it to John Adams. "In it," Adams reported to his wife on 1 Jan., TJ "tells Mr. Madison That he had been told there was a Possibility of a Tye between Mr. Adams and himself. If this should happen says he, I beg of you, to Use all your Influence to procure for me the Second Place, for Mr. Adams's Services have been longer more constant and more important than mine, and Something more in the complimentary strain about Qualifications &c." In closing Adams cautioned his wife: "These are confidential communications." But two days later, he informed her that TJ's letter "was yesterday in the mouth of every one. It is considered as Evidence of his Determination to accept—of his Friendship for me—And of his Modesty and Moderation" (John Adams to Abigail Adams, 1, 3, 5 Jan. 1797, MHi: Adams Papers; and see Rush to TJ, 4 Jan. 1797). On 9 Jan. 1797, Congressman Chauncey Goodrich sent fellow Connecticut Federalist Oliver Wolcott, Sr. an account of a letter from TJ that expressed "es-

teem" for Adams and satisfaction on his election. Goodrich continued that although he could not "vouch for the correctness of the publication," those who had seen the letter described the author as being "of meek humility" and "complimentary of the Vice-President." Theodore Sedgwick, Federalist senator from Massachusetts, fully described the letter which, he noted, "was disclosed, in confidence, within one or two days after the event of the election was certainly known." He summarized TJ's position on the election: first, he would prefer not to be a candidate for or elected president or vice president; second, if he were a competitor of Adams and the contest went to the House of Representatives, his own pretensions should be withdrawn in favor of those of his rival; and third, "(which he most dreads) that he may be elected President" (Goodrich to Oliver Wolcott, Sr., 9 Jan. 1797, in Gibbs, Memoirs, I, 417; Sedgwick to Rufus King, 12 Mch. 1797, in King, Life, II, 156-7).

Albert GALLATIN'S VIEW OF THE FINANCES, A Sketch of the Finances of the United States (New York, 1796), was published in November. It included an appendix with 19 tables, making the work over 200 pages long, too large to send by regular post. See Sowerby, No. 3523. PAINE'S LETTER TO THE PRESIDENT: see Madison to TJ, 10 Jan. 1796.

To Volney

DEAR SIR   Monticello. [Dec. 17.] 96

Your letters of [July 12th.] from Gallipolis and of Aug. [. . .] from Lexington were duly received, and [as I have seen?] by [the news]papers you have got no farther [than] [. . .], and [must] go to Boston according to the plan announced in your last, I presume this letter with the key of your valise will be in Philadelphia before you. By Mr. Randolph (my son in law) who was going to Richmond early in November I sent the valise, and he was to endeavor to find some person whom he knew going on in the stage to Philadelphia, and to get it carried under their care. One or two whom he knew and applied to having declined taking charge of them because they did not know their contents, he left them with Mr. Brown a merchant of Richmond, and went to his farm 12 miles lower, meaning when the members of Congress should be passing to get some one of them to take them. But during his absence Mr. Brown having to send a trunk with some things of his own to Philadelphia by sea, packed your valise in his trunk and sent it off. I have no doubt it is long since safely arrived at Philadelphia as the season has been fine: but it has run the risk of the sea contrary to all our wishes. Unfortunately Mr. Randolph has not brought me the address of Mr. Brown's correspondent in Philadelphia nor the name of the vessel. He is now setting out for Richmond and will supply this omission. In the mean time I know that Clow & Co. were formerly the correspondents of Brown. This firm was dissolved by the death of Clow, but any mercantile gentleman in Philadelphia will be able to tell you the names of the surviving partners of that firm, who probably are still the correspondents of Mr. Brown. Indeed most probably they will seek you out on your arrival at Philadelphia.

You have now seen, in the aboriginals of America, another edition of man. We wish much to know what impression it makes on an enlightened European to whom their peculiarities will be new and therefore more readily observed. Within a shade of the Indian, you have seen our own race with the habits of the Indian. I doubt whether you have found them precisely as M. de Crevecoeur has depictured them. But I am sure both varieties of the human character must have afforded much matter for the contemplation of a philosophic observer.

I hope you have preserved your health well amidst the enterprizes of your journey, which I think were too arduous for your physical constitution. Cherish well your health and life, as one in which all men are interested, and none more sincerely anxious for than Dear Sir Your friend & servt   TH: JEFFERSON

PrC (DLC); faded; at foot of first page: "Mr. Volney." Enclosed in TJ to James Madison, 17 Dec. 1796.

From John Wayles Eppes

DEAR SIR   Decr. 19th. 1796.

I have it now in my power to inform you that all obstacles to my happiness are removed, and that in every arrangement as to future residence, I shall be guided by yourself and Maria. I am with sincere regard yours   J. W. EPPES

RC (MHi); addressed: "Thomas Jefferson Esqr."; endorsed by TJ as received 19 Dec. 1796 and so recorded in SJL.

From James Madison

DEAR SIR   Philada. Decr. 19. 1796

The returns from N. Hampshire, Vermont, S.C. and Georga. are still to come in, and leave the event of the Election in some remaining uncertainty. It is but barely possible that Adams may fail of the highest number. It is highly probable, tho' not absolutely certain, that Pinkney will be third only on the list. You must prepare yourself therefore to be summoned to the place Mr. Adams now fills. I am aware of the objections arising from the inadequateness of the importance of the place to the sacrifices you would be willing to make to a greater prospect of fulfilling the patriotic wishes of your friends; and from the irksomeness of being at the head of a body whose sentiments are at present so little in unison with your own. But it is expected that as you had made up your mind to obey the call of your Country, you will let it decide on the particular place where your services are to be rendered. It may even be said, that as you submitted to the election knowing the contingency involved in it, you are bound to abide by the event whatever it may. On the whole it seems *essential* that you should not refuse the station which is likely to be your lot. There is reason to believe also that your neighbourhood to *adams*[1] may *have a valuable effect on his councils* particularly in *relation to our external system.* You know that *his feelings* will not *enslave him to the* example of *his predecessor.* It is certain that his *censures of our paper system* and the intrigues at *new York for setting P. above him* have fixed an *enmity with the British faction.* Nor should it pass for nothing, that the true *interest of new england* particularly requires reconciliation with France as the road to her commerce. *Add to the whole that he* is said to speak of *you now in friendly terms* and will no doubt be *soothed by your acceptance of a place subordinate to him.* It must be confessed however that all these calculations, are qualified by *his political principles* and *prejudices*. But they add weight to the *obligation from which you must*[2] not withdraw yourself.

You will see in the answer to the P.s speech, much *room for criticism*. You must, for the present, be *content to know that it resulted from a choice of evils*. His *reply to the* foreign *paragraph indicates a good* effect *on his mind*. Indeed *he cannot but wish to avoid entailing a war on his successor*. The *danger lies in the* fetters *he has put on himself* and *in the irritation* and *distrust of the French government*.

RC (DLC: Madison Papers); unsigned; written partly in code, with interlinear decipherment in TJ's hand (see note 1 below), including minor coding anomalies corrected by TJ; endorsed by TJ as received 31 Dec. 1796 and so recorded in SJL.

The 16 Dec. ANSWER of the House of Representatives to Washington's annual message to Congress noted concern over the disruption of friendly relations with the French Republic and echoed the president's expressed desire to preserve peace and restore harmony with that country. Expressing regret that Washington was about to retire, the House praised him expansively for his "wise, firm, and patriotic Administration." The concluding sentence noted that "For your country's sake—for the sake of Republican liberty—it is our earnest wish that your example may be the guide of your successors; and thus, after being the orna-

ment and safeguard of the present age, become the patrimony of our descendants." The House divided 54 to 24 against a motion to delete the last sentence and only 12 refused their consent to the final document. Madison, who had served on the committee to consider Washington's message, was not among them. Washington's REPLY to the FOREIGN PARAGRAPH in the House's address reiterated his regret at any interruption in our good understanding with France and pledged by "all honorable means" to preserve peace and to restore "harmony and affection" between the two nations (*Annals*, VI, 1611-17; JHR, II, 607-11, 615-20, 623).

[1] This and subsequent italicized words are written in code, the text being supplied from TJ's decipherment and verified by the Editors against Code No. 9.

[2] Encoded word underlined.

From James Madison

DEAR SIR   Philada. Decr. 25. 1796

I can not yet entirely remove the uncertainty in which my last left the election. Unless the Vermont election of which little has of late been said, should contain some fatal vice in it, Mr. Adams may be considered as the President elect. Nothing can deprive him of it but a general run of the votes in Georgia, Tenissee and Kentucky in favor of Mr. Pinkney, which is altogether contrary to the best information. It is not even probable that Mr. P. will be the second on the list, the secondary votes of N. Hampshire being now said to have been thrown away on Elseworth: and a greater number consequently required from the States abovementioned than will be likely to fall to his lot. We have nothing new from Europe. The prospect and projects in our foreign Depart-

ment are under a veil not a corner of which I have been able to lift. I fear
the distrust with which the French Govt. view the Executive here, and
the fetters which the President has suffered himself to put on, will be
obstacles to the reconciliation which he can not fail to desire. It is whis-
pered also that the Spanish Minister has intimated the probable dissatisfaction of his Court at the Explanatory Article of the British Treaty.
Nor can it be doubted, from the nature of the alliance between that and
France, that a common cause will be made in all the steps taken by the
latter with respect to this Country. In the mean time the British party
are busy in their calumnies for turning the blame of the present crisis
from themselves, on the pretended instigations of France, by americans
at Paris; and some of them are already bold eno' to talk of an alliance
with England as the resourse in case of an actual rupture with France.
The new President who ever he will be will have much in his power;
and it is important to make [1] as many circumstances as possible conspire
to lead him to a right use of it. There never was greater distress than at
this moment in the monied world. Failures and frauds occur daily; And
are so much connected with Banks that these Institutions are evidently
losing ground in the public opinion.

RC (DLC: Madison Papers); unsigned;
endorsed by TJ as received 7 Jan. 1797 and
so recorded in SJL.

On 26 Nov. 1796, Noah Webster's *Minerva* reported that the VERMONT ELECTION
was "invalid—being grounded only on a *Resolve* of the Legislature, not a law." The *Aurora* on 12 Dec. remarked that if the four
votes from Vermont for Adams were not
counted, the election could be thrown into
the House of Representatives, where TJ
would be elected president. On 28 Dec.
the *Minerva* admitted that the statement
was "ill-founded," but the *Aurora* continued to assert that as no direct word had been
received from Vermont, it was not clear
whether Adams or Jefferson would be president (Philadelphia *Aurora*, 28, 29 Dec.
1796).

The EXPLANATORY ARTICLE OF THE BRIT-
ISH TREATY, negotiated by Secretary of
State Pickering and British Consul General
Phineas Bond and approved by the Senate
on 9 May 1796, guaranteed British traders

free movement by land and water and the
right to engage in commerce throughout
the Northwest Territory, as required by Article 3 of the Jay Treaty, which appeared to
have been restricted by the Treaty of Greenville of 1795. Ratifications of the article
were exchanged in Philadelphia on 6 Oct.
and it appeared as a proclamation in Philadelphia newspapers early in November
(Miller, *Treaties*, II, 346-7; Philadelphia
Aurora, 11 Nov. 1796).

During a debate in the House of Representatives on 15 Dec. 1796, Fisher Ames alluded to newspaper accounts to prove that
the crisis in relations between the United
States and France was caused by AMERI-
CANS AT PARIS who were exciting "a spirit of
animosity against this country." He acquit-
ted the administration of responsibility in
case of war with France and blamed it on
"the intrigues carried on at Paris" (*Annals*,
VI, 1650).

[1] Remainder of text written in margin.

From Volney

Monsieur philadelphie 26 Xbre 1796

Dans une lettre que j'eûs L'honneur de Vous ecrire il y a environ dix jours, je Vous faisais part de Mon arrivée en cette Ville, et Vous priais de Me faire passer le portemanteau que javais laissé chez Vous. Votre obligeante prévoyance Vient de rendre inutile ce paragraphe de Ma longue Epître; après deux ou trois jours de recherche Mutuelle, Nous Nous sommes enfin rencontrés Mr. Emanuel Walker et Moi, et il M'a remis Mon porte-Manteau en aussi bon etat que je pouvais le desirer: Seulement la clef du cadenat Manquait, et il M'a dit Ne l'avoir point reçue: Si elle est, egarée c'est un petit Malheur dont je Suis tout consolé; Mais Si elle Se retrouve à Monticello je Serai bien aise tôt ou tard de la recouvrer. Du reste j'ai facilement ouvert Sans cette clef, en decoupant le cuir, et je jouis du Soin de propreté dans lequel j'ai trouvé Mon bagage.

Jai reçu de paris une lettre de L'eveque Gregoire, Membre de L'institut National par laquelle il Me Mande que le Naturaliste Dombey etait chargé de Vous faire passer un *Mètre* et un *grave* Echantillons Vérifiés de Nos Mesures Longues et cubiques. Dombey ayant eté pris par des Corsaires et conduit à L'Isle Montserrat où il est Mort, Ses effets ont eté dit on apportes à Newyork où lon croit quî ils sont deposés à la Douane: comme il devait y avoir une lettre d'envoy en avez-Vous jamais eu quelqu'avis? Ou bien Voulez-vous que je prie Le Colonel Burr d'en faire faire la recherche? J'attendrai un Mot de Votre part à cet egard. Au reste il paraît que Vous-meme Serez incessament en Mesure, puis que Vos amis comptent Vous Voir en Mars à philadelphie quoique ce ne soit pas de la maniere qu'ils L'ont désiré. Mais en cela Même il y a un Nouveau genre de Merite et de Vertu à Montrer, et Vous pourrez dire en Veritable ami des principes de L'egalité Republicaine, L'altè Non temo, è L'humile Non Sdegno.

(*clorinda N'el tasso*)

Moi qui Vous ai Vû jouir du bonheur champêtre, je Sens qu'il Vous en coutera de quitter Vos champs, Votre bâtisse, et L'utile clouterie; Mais Votre absence Ne Sera jamais longue, et outre le besoin d'un peu de Variété, Vous ne refuserez point un Sacrifice de plus en plus necessaire Sous bien des points de Vue; dailleurs Si Vous étiez bien embarrassé de trouver un œconome *overseer*, je pourrais Vous repondre d'un quî aurait au Moins le zele de L'attachement   C. Volney

Je ne suis point encore logé à demeure.

RC (DLC); below signature: "poste restante"; endorsed by TJ as received 7 Jan.
1797 and so recorded in SJL.

The ill-fated mission by Joseph DOMBEY
to bring the French standards of measure to
the United States is noted at Dombey to TJ,
1 May 1793. In the metric system established by French decree on 1 Aug. 1793, the
basic unit of weight was the GRAVE, defined
as the weight of a cubic decimeter of water
(Stewart, *French Revolution*, 506).

L'ALTÈ NON TEMO: "High or low, there is
no task I dread to call my own," as spoken by
the heroine Clorinda in Torquato Tasso's
Gerusalemme Liberata (1581), canto II,
stanza 46.

From Enoch Edwards

DEAR SIR   Philadelphia 27th Decr: 1796

When I arrived in Octr: last at N. York from France I forwarded on
a letter or two from Mr: Monroe to you—and I should have written to
you then as I promised him—but I really intended before I setled myself, to have taken a Trip into your State, and to have had the Pleasure
of seeing you at your own House.

I left Paris the 7th. of August in the Midst of their Success and Glory
as likewise the utmost Tranquillity—and every Prospect of Success
with thier Government as well as their Arms. The only thing that was
unpleasant about the time I left the Place was the Resentment which
that Government discovered towards Us on the Account of the Treaty.
Mr: Monroe as You must know entered into a Defence of it—so far as
to deny its being a direct Violation of our Treaty with them—this Defence I have a Copy of and intend to send it to you by Mr: Madison—
unless you should inform Me before he leaves Us that you have one.
You will see by it that our Freind Monroe is treated with as much Cru-
elty as has been possible. The Cry against him here is that he did not
reveal to the French Government certain Reasons assigned by our's for
its Conduct, early anough, When it will appear by the Correspondence
that he replied to their Complaints in less than a Week after he received
them, and in a Manner that does him the highest Honor both as to his
Talents and Patriotism.

I really suspect that the Directoire will not receive Mr: Pinckney—
but act as they did in the Case of the appointed Successor to Baron de
Staal—should that be the Case, We shall here have a great Noise about
it, much will be said about french Impudence, foreign Interference and
our Soverignty—more than if the English had taken a hundred of our
Seamen or sculped a thousand of our peaceable Citizens.

Mr: Monroe when he commited the Paper (with others) above mentioned into my Hands—submitted it entirely to my Discretion whether
to publish them or not. I think it right that some should be known to the

Publick but as it is likely we shall have him here soon, I have concluded to leave it untill he comes—perhaps the time also then may be quite as favorable as the present for heaving and giving Weight to Truth. With much Respect & Esteem I am your very obedt st.   ENO; EDWARDS

RC (DLC); addressed: "Thomas Jefferson Esqr. Virginia"; stamped and postmarked; endorsed by TJ as a letter from "John" Edwards received 21 Jan. 1797 and so recorded in SJL.

Edwards had FORWARDED James Monroe's letter to TJ of 30 July 1796. To explain his defense of the Jay TREATY to the Directory, Monroe sent Madison, by Edwards, copies of his correspondence with the French minister of foreign affairs, Charles Delacroix. In particular, Monroe's communications to Delacroix of 15 Mch. and 14 July 1796 were meant to answer French objections to the treaty (Madison, *Papers*, XVI, 387; Monroe, *Writings*, II, 467-82, III, 27-34).

Desirous of an American policy that would openly favor France over Great Britain, the Directory indeed refused to recognize Monroe's successor, Charles Cotesworth PINCKNEY, who arrived in Paris on 5 Dec. 1796. The following month the French government ordered Pinckney to leave the country, and early in February 1797 he went to Amsterdam to await instructions. When recalled in 1795, the BARON de Staël de Holstein, Sweden's ambassador to France, initially refused to leave Paris and influenced the Directory to block recognition of his replacement (Marvin R. Zahniser, *Charles Cotesworth Pinckney: Founding Father* [Chapel Hill, 1967], 141-9; Louis Antoine Leouzon le Duc, *Correspondance Diplomatique du Baron de Staël-Holstein* [Paris, 1881], 270).

To Edward Rutledge

MY DEAR SIR   Monticello Dec. 27. 1796.

I am afraid of being[1] a troublesome correspondent to you. I wish to obtain about 20. bushels of the Cowpea,[2] a red field pea commonly cultivated with you, and a principal article for the subsistence of your farms, which we have not yet introduced. I understand it is always to be had at Charleston, ready barreled for exportation: and the favor I ask of you is to engage some merchant of Charleston to ship me that quantity to Richmond consigned to the care of Chas. Johnston & Co. of that place who will recieve it and pay freight. Draw, if you please for the amount on John Barnes merchant of Philadelphia, South 3d. street, who will be instructed to honor *your* draught. I have supposed this the most ready channel of making a paiment in Charleston.[3]   I understand you have introduced the Lieth machine into your state for threshing your rice. I have used one this year for my wheat with perfect success. It was geered. A person of this state has made them more simple and cheap, by substituting bands and whirls instead of geer and they perform well, threshing $13\frac{1}{2}$ bushels of wheat an hour, which is as much as I did with mine which was geered. The improver has obtained a patent for his improvement, tho' I doubt the validity of it, as there is no new invention, but only a bringing together two things in full use before, to wit, the Lieth drum wheel or threshing wheel, and the band and whirl used for bolting and a thousand other things. I have made my Lieth machine portable from one barn to another, placing it on 4. waggon wheels, on which it always remains. It does not weigh a ton.

You have seen my name lately tacked to so much of eulogy and of abuse, that I dare say you hardly thought it meant for your old acquaintance of 76. In truth I did not know myself under the pens either of my friends or foes. It is unfortunate for our peace[4] that unmerited abuse wounds, while unmerited praise has not the power to heal. These are hard wages for the services of all the active and healthy years of one's life. I had retired after five and twenty years of constant occupation in public affairs[5] and total abandonment of my own. I retired much poorer than when I entered the public service,[6] and desired nothing but rest and oblivion. My name however was again brought forward, without concert[7] or expectation on my part (on my salvation I declare it.)[8] I do not as yet[9] know the result as a matter of[10] fact; for in my retired canton we have nothing later from Philadelphia than of the 2d week of this month. Yet I have never one moment[11] doubted the result. I knew it was impossible Mr. Adams should lose a vote North of the Delaware, and that the free and moral agency of the South would furnish him an abundant supplement. On principles of public respect I should not have refused: but I protest before my god that I shall, from the bottom of my heart, rejoice at escaping. I know well that no man will ever bring out of that office the reputation which carries him into it. The honey moon would be as short in that case as in any other, and it's moments of extasy would be ransomed by years of torment and hatred. I shall highly value indeed the share which I may have had in the late vote,[12] as an evidence of the share I hold in the esteem of my countrymen. But in this point of view a few votes more or less will be little sensible, and[13] in every other the minor will be preferred by me to the major vote. I have no ambition to govern men, no passion which would lead me to delight to ride in a storm. Flumina amo, sylvasque, inglorius. My attachment to my home has enabled me to make the calculation with rigor, perhaps with partiality to the issue which is to keep me there. The newspapers will permit me to plant my Cow-peas in hills or drills as I please (and my oranges by the bye when you send them) while our Eastern friend will be struggling with the storm which is gathering[14] over us, perhaps be shipwrecked in it. This is certainly not a moment to covet the helm.

I have often doubted[15] whether most to praise or to blame your line of conduct. If you had lent to your country the excellent talents you possess, on you would have fallen those torrents of abuse which have lately been poured forth on me. So far I praise the wisdom which has[16] descried and steered clear of a water-spout ahead. But now for the blame.[17] There is a debt of service due from every man[18] to his country, proportioned to the bounties which nature and fortune have measured to him. Counters will pay[19] this from the poor of spirit: but from you my friend, coin was due. There is no bankrupt law in heaven by which you may get off with shillings in the pound, with rendering to a single state what you owed to the whole confederacy. I think it was by the Roman law that a father was denied sepulture, unless his son would pay his debts. Happy for you and us, that you[20] have a son whom genius and education have qualified to pay yours. But as you have been a good father in every thing else, be so in this also. Come forward and pay your own debts.[21] Your friends the Mr. Pinckney's have at length undertaken their tour. My joy at this would be complete if you were in geer with them. I love to see honest men and honorable men at the helm, men who will not bend their politics to their purses, nor pursue measures by which they may profit, and then profit by their measures. Au diable les Bougres! I am at the end of my curse and bottom of my page, so God bless you and yours. Adieu affectionately.   TH: JEFFERSON

RC (Barney Balaban, New York City, 1946); with several emendations, only the most important of which is noted below (see note 7). PrC (DLC); at foot of first page in ink: "Rutledge Edwd." Dft (DLC: TJ Papers, 101: 17354, 17268); undated; consists of partial rough draft on three pages, the second being clipped along right margin; the most important emendations are noted below.

PERSON OF THIS STATE: William Booker.

FLUMINA AMO, SYLVASQUE, INGLORIUS: actually "flumina amem silvasque inglorious," "may I love the rivers and the woods, though fame be lost," Virgil, *Georgics*, 2.486. TJ has made Virgil's subjunctive voice into the indicative, "[though] inglorius, I love rivers and woods."

[1] Preceding three words lacking in Dft.
[2] Remainder of this and the following three sentences in Dft: "so much cultivated in your state and not yet introduced with us, tho' from what I learn it will be a valuable acquisition to our farms. I am told &c."
[3] For the remainder of this paragraph in Dft TJ wrote "Leith Machine."
[4] Preceding two words interlined in Dft in place of "us."
[5] Word interlined in Dft in place of "business."

[6] Sentence to this point lacking in Dft and previous sentence continues: "and ⟨asked⟩ desired nothing but ⟨more than⟩ tranquility and oblivion the rest of my days."
[7] Word reworked by TJ from "consultation." In Dft TJ wrote "My name was brought forward without ⟨consultation⟩ concert."
[8] In Dft TJ here canceled "on the first symptoms of it I entered into."
[9] Preceding two words interlined in Dft.
[10] In Dft preceding three words interlined in place of "absolute."
[11] Preceding two words interlined in Dft.
[12] Preceding word interlined in Dft in place of "election."
[13] Remainder of sentence in Dft: "therefore I say with truth I prefer the minor to the major vote." TJ then canceled the following clause: "My attachment to my home has."
[14] Dft: "which ⟨ever⟩ lowers."
[15] Dft here adds: "in my own mind."
[16] In Dft TJ here canceled "kept you out."
[17] Preceding four words interlined in Dft.
[18] Dft: "citizen."
[19] Dft: "do."
[20] Sentence to this point in Dft: "Happy for you ⟨that you⟩ to."
[21] Dft ends here.

Jefferson's Letter to John Adams

I. TO JOHN ADAMS,
28 DECEMBER 1796

II. COPY FROM MEMORY,
28 DECEMBER 1796

EDITORIAL NOTE

Anticipating an administration headed by John Adams with himself as vice president, Jefferson apparently hoped with this letter to restore a political relationship that had become frayed following the unintended publication in 1791 of his endorsement of Thomas Paine's *Rights of Man* and his implicit criticism of Adams's "political heresies" (see Editorial Note and documents at 26 Apr. 1791, Vol. 20: 277-80, 284-6, 302-3, 305-8, 310-12). Their differences had been left unresolved by their correspondence at the time—when Adams protested that their respective theoretical positions seemed much clearer to Jefferson than to him—but as the results of the election of 1796 became evident, Jefferson sought an accommodation with the presumed president-elect, one that emphasized the Virginian's condemnation of Alexander Hamilton rather than any supposed divisions that might still exist between Jefferson and Adams. Whatever Jefferson's intentions, Madison declined to forward the letter, although he had already begun to exhibit Jefferson's 17 Dec. 1796 letter to him in the capital as evidence of the prospective vice president's lack of enmity for the new administration (see the letters from Benjamin Rush, 4 Jan., and Madison, 15 Jan. 1797). For Jefferson's impressions of Adams's own March 1797 overture to him in Philadelphia, see Notes on Conversations with John Adams and George Washington, printed under 13 Oct. 1797.

In an unusual departure from his epistolary practices, Jefferson did not retain a press copy of this letter to Adams or the one to Madison of 1 Jan. 1797 in which he enclosed it for delivery. Instead, he recorded his recollection of their contents for his own letter file sometime—precisely when is unknown—after dispatching them to Madison. A few distinctive phrasings in the letter to Adams echo language Jefferson wrote to Edward Rutledge on 27 Dec. 1796, but his retained press copy and draft of that letter could have been of scant help in reconstructing in any detail the missive to Adams. He asked Madison to return the letter intended for Adams should he decide not to forward it, but Madison never did so, presuming that Jefferson had "no doubt" kept a copy. That Jefferson did not contradict this assertion may suggest that he had either already reconstructed the two letters, or had formed an intention to do so, by that date (Madison to TJ, 15 Jan. 1797; TJ to Madison, 30 Jan. 1797).

I. To John Adams

The public and the public papers have been much occupied lately in placing us in a point of opposition to each other. I trust with confidence that less of it has been felt by ourselves personally. In the retired canton where I am, I learn little of what is passing: pamphlets I see never; papers but a few; and the fewer the happier. Our latest intelligence from Philadelphia at present is of the 16th inst. but tho' at that date your election to the first magistracy seems not to have been known as a fact, yet with me it has never been doubted. I knew it impossible you should lose a vote North of the Delaware, and even if that of Pensylvania should be against you in the mass, yet that you would get enough South of that to place your succession out of danger. I have never one single[1] moment expected a different issue; and tho' I know I shall not be believed, yet it is not the less true that I have never wished it. My neighbors, as my compurgators, could aver that fact, because they see my occupations and my attachment to them. Indeed it is possible that you may be cheated of your succession by a trick worthy the subtlety of your arch-friend of New York, who has been able to make of your real friends tools to defeat their and your just wishes. Most probably he will be disappointed as to you; and my inclinations place me out of his reach. I leave to others the sublime delights of riding in the storm, better pleased with sound sleep and a warm birth below, with the society of neighbors, friends and fellow laborers of the earth, than of spies and sycophants. No one then will congratulate you with purer disinterestedness than myself. The share indeed which I may have had in the late vote, I shall still value highly, as an evidence of the share I have in the esteem of my fellow citizens. But while, in this point of view, a few votes[2] less would be little sensible, the difference in the effect of a few more[3] would be very sensible and oppressive to me. I have no ambition to govern men. It is a painful and thankless office. Since the day too on which you signed the treaty of Paris our horizon was never so overcast. I devoutly wish you may be able to shun for us this war by which our agriculture, commerce and credit will be destroyed. If you are, the glory will be all your own; and that your administration may be filled with glory and happiness to yourself and advantage to us is the sincere wish of one who tho', in the course of our voyage thro' life, various little incidents have happened or been contrived to separate us, retains still for you the solid esteem of the moments when we were working for our independance, and sentiments of respect and affectionate attachment.

Th: Jefferson

RC (NN: Emmet Collection); the most significant emendations are recorded below; addressed: "John Adams Vice President of the US. Philadelphia." Enclosed in TJ to Madison, 1 Jan. 1797.

Although Hamilton maintained that his energetic promotion of Thomas Pinckney as the Federalist candidate for vice president was meant to give the party "two chances against Mr. Jefferson," some of Adams's electors feared a TRICK engineered by Hamilton, Adams's supposed ARCH-FRIEND, and John Jay in the hope that Pinckney might tie Adams's electoral vote in the North and outdraw him in the South to win the presidency (Syrett, *Hamilton*, xx, 158, 376-7, 437-8, 465).

[1] Word interlined.
[2] TJ here canceled "more or."
[3] Preceding four words interlined.

II. Copy from Memory

Statement by memory of a letter written to J. Adams. Copy omitted to be retained.

DEAR SIR   Monticello Dec. 28. 96.

The public and the public papers have been much occupied lately in placing us in a point of opposition to each other. I confidently trust we have felt less of it ourselves. In the retired canton where I live we know little of what is passing. Pamphlets I see none: papers very few, and the fewer the happier. Our last information from Philada. is of the 16th. inst. At that date the issue of the late election seems not to have been known as a matter of fact. With me however it's issue was never doubted. I knew the impossibility of your losing a single vote North of the Delaware; and even if you should lose that of Pennsylva.[1] in the mass, you would get enough South of that to make your election sure. I never for a single moment expected any other issue, and tho' I shall not be believed, yet it is not the less true that I never wished any other. My neighbors, as my compurgators, could aver this fact, as seeing my occupations and my attachment to them. It is possible indeed that even you may be cheated of your succession by a trick worthy the subtlety of your arch-friend of New York who has been able to make of your real friends tools for defeating their and your just wishes. Probably however he will be disappointed as to you, and my inclinations put me out of his reach.[2] I leave to others the sublime delights of riding in the storm, better pleased with sound sleep and a warmer birth below it encircled with the society of neighbors, friends and fellow laborers of the earth, rather than with spies and sycophants.[3] Still I shall value highly the share I may have had in the late vote, as a measure of the share I hold in the esteem of my fellow-citizens. In this point of view a few votes less are but little sensible, while a few more would have been in their effect very sensible and oppressive to me. I have no ambition to govern men. It is a painful

[236]

and thankless office. And never, since the day you signed the treaty of Paris, has our horizon been so overcast. I devoutly wish you may be able to shun for us this war which will destroy our agriculture, commerce and credit. If you do, the glory will be all your own. And that your administration may be filled with glory and happiness to yourself and advantage to us, is the sincere prayer of one, who tho', in the course of our voyage, various little incidents have happened or been contrived to separate us, yet retains for you the solid esteem of the times when we were working for our independance, and sentiments of sincere respect and attachment.   TH: JEFFERSON

FC (DLC); entirely in TJ's hand; the most significant emendations are recorded below.

[1] TJ first wrote "Philadelphia."
[2] After this sentence TJ interlined and then canceled alternate wording for the passage that begins "Still I shall value" and runs through "a few more."
[3] TJ interlined the next two sentences and continued them into the margin.

From Volney

MONSIEUR   philadelphie 29 Xbre 1796

Votre lettre du 17 courant Me fut rendue hier Soir, et par un cas plaisant je Me trouve pour la troisieme fois atteint et convaincu de la precipitation française. Chez Vous, certain dimanche de juin deux heures d'attente M'eussent Sauvé 40 Miles de course après Ma Valise. Ici, cinq jours plus tard, je Ne Vous eûsse point inquiété par la demande que je Vous en faisais dans une premiere lettre. Aujourdhui enfin, deux jours de patience M'eussent empeché de Vous importuner pour la clef que je reçois dans Votre lettre. Il y a en ceci un peu de quoi Moraliser Nos têtes françaises, à l'avantage de la patience américaine: moi même j'avoue qu'en guerre défensive, Notre Vivacité Va Mal; aussi avons-Nous pris L'agressive; quant à Mon cas personnel qui N'est point de guerre, je ne puis M'en repentir, puisque Ma précipitation a eu pour objet de Vous Sauver un Souci; et que jaimerai toujours a être en avance dans tout ce qui tient à L'amitié.

Ma premiere lettre Vous a Expliqué Mes Motifs de Ne point aller cette année à Boston. Je dois Me feliciter de Mon retard, puisqu'il M'a Valu un article très obligeant dans le papier Nouvelle de cette Capitale de L'Est. Seulement j'ai peur pour Mon Compte, de la fable des bâtons flottans, et qu'après toutes ces grandes idées de Ma *philosophie*, l'on Ne s'appercoive que je suis un pauvre humain aussi faible que tant D'autres dont on Ne parle point. Il est Vrai qu'en cela Même je ressemblerais à beaucoup d'autres dont on parle; car graces à la capricieuse fortune, il y a dans ce Nouveau Monde comme dans L'ancien des Nuages eclatans de talent et de gloire qui Vûs de près, ne sont que du brouillard. *Cosi Va'l Mondo*: et comme entre les deux rôles philosophiques de rire et de pleurer, le Second porte aux obstructions Moi qui aime la Santé: je livre heraclite à qui Veut S'en ennuyer, et je tâche de Me désopiler la rate avec Démocrite.

La recette en devient nécessaire de plus en plus en cette Ville; car outre Lhabituelle gravité des *tea-parties*, l'on y éprouve en ce Moment un Surcroit de Serieux causé par les circonstances Mercantiles que Vous connaissez. Un peu de philosophie, cest a dire de Moderation dans le desir eût evité cette fâcheuse secousse des fortunes; Mais le Vent etait bon et chacun a forcé de Voiles; chacun S'en repent aujourdhui; et ce qu'il y a de consolant, c'est qu'aussitôt que l'orage Sera fini, tout le passé S'oubliera et l'on recommencera de plus belle. En ce Moment le commerce eprouve une Stagnation complette; la delaware au lieu de porter des Vaisseaux porte des patineurs; et S'il est vrai qu'à pitsbourg il y ait trois pieds de Neige, et quatre à presqu'isle, il y a tout lieu de Craindre que Nous soyons fermés jusqu'en Mars. Point de Nouvelles d'Europe. Les Vents de Nord West qui dominent, retiennent au large les Vaisseaux. Je suis curieux de Savoir quel degré de froid, et quel ciel Vous avez eu ces derniers tems à Monticello. Mes questions sur les Vents ne m'ont pas procuré une Seule lettre à la poste de philadelphie. J'ai ecrit au bureau de Boston: demain jécris à charlestown et je crains la Même disette: j'ai Neant-moins aquis par Moimême quelques resultats généraux, curieux Mais ils ne peuvent pas trouver place dans une lettre, Non plus que Mes [. . .] sur les Sauvages et sur Vos *settlers* des frontières. C'est un ample sujet de livre ou de conversation; et j'arrive à penser qu'il occupera avec interet quelques-unes de Vos Soirées de philadelphie ou Meme de Monticello. Agréez les Souhaits de bonne Santé et de Satisfaction que j'ai L'honneur de Vous adresser Moins comme l'etiquette de Noel que comme L'expression de L'attachement et de L'estime, de Votre très humble Serviteur   C. VOLNEY

RC (DLC); torn at seal; addressed: "To Mr. Thomas jefferson Charlotte's ville Virginia"; stamped and postmarked; endorsed by TJ as received 7 Jan. 1797 and so recorded in SJL.

ARTICLE TRÈS OBLIGEANT: in November and December 1796, the *Polar Star and Boston Daily Advertiser*, a newspaper that had begun publication in October, printed selections in English from Volney's work. On 2 Dec. the paper noted his current investigation of the American climate and called his research "the admiration of the learned and curious of every country."

In Aesop's FABLE of the camel and the BÂTONS FLOTTANS as popularized by La Fontaine, what is thought to be an approaching ship becomes on closer view a small boat, then a bale of goods, and finally some floating sticks (Jean de La Fontaine, *Fables: Psyché-Œuvres Diverses*, ed. Roger Delbiausse [Paris, 1947], 79).

From Archibald Stuart

Dr Sir   Staunton 31st. Decr. 1796.

Considering the attempts which will probably be made by some of the friends of Great Britain to widen our breach with France I feel an Inclination to forward a memorial to Congress from this quarter declaring our friendly disposition towards that Nation and that If we should be compelled to take part in the European War we prefer a union with France to that of Any Other power.

Lest however such a Measure should tend to embarrass the Government or be attended with evil consequences which I do not foresee I take the liberty of Asking your advice as to the propriety of the measure under my promise of Secrecy.   Out of your Large supply of Chinese Bells I am in hopes you can spare me one without incommoding yourselfe, I mean one of the highest price and to which you will add the expence of Carriage from Philadelphia here; If so the Money shall be remited to you through Mr. S. Clarke. Mr. Cavendish has not yet returned from the assembly. I am Dr Sir yrs. most sincerely

ARCHD STUART

RC (ViW); at foot of text: "Thos. Jefferson Esqr"; endorsed by TJ as received 2 Jan. 1797 and so recorded in SJL.

Declaration for the Mutual Assurance Society

[1796 or later]

Instructions.

IT must particularly be mentioned in the description of each plat, to wit: The dimensions of the Buildings intended to be insured, their situation and contiguity to other buildings or wharves, what the walls are built of, mentioning what part thereof is of brick, stone, or wood, that is how many feet of wood and how many feet of stone or brick, or if of wood and covered with thick plaster or lime, what the buildings are covered with, and for what use they are appropriated.

If the buildings are joined or are within twenty feet of others, it must be mentioned, and likewise what the walls of such buildings contiguous to them are built of, and what they are covered with. If they are situated so that on account of trees, or back buildings or other obstructions, the fire engines cannot play upon them from at least two sides, it must particularly be mentioned.

If a building is situated on a wharf or within one hundred feet thereof, or if buildings stand on dock yards or wharves where vessels are built, repaired, or caulked, it must particularly be mentioned.

If a house has wings or other additions to it, their dimensions, what the walls are built of, and what they are covered with, and the certified value of which must separately be mentioned in the same declaration of such house or building.

The valuation must be made in dollars.

Gun-Powder Mills or such great hazards, are not insurable, unless by special contract with the President and Directors, nor a risk on one building above twenty thousand dollars, nor a building under the value of one hundred dollars in ready money.

The full amount of the real value must be specified in the declarations, one fifth part thereof will be stricken off at the office.

If a person doth not chuse to insure four-fifths of the verified value, he must endorse the amount which he wants to ensure thereon.

A building is considered a house standing by itself, or between two whole party walls.

The declarations must be signed by the proprietor with christian and family names, mentioning his place of residence, day, month and year.

The valuations must be made by a majority of three respectable house-owners on oath or affirmation, as the case may require before a justice of the peace, and certify the same in writing under the declaration agreeably to the form annexed.

A separate declaration must be made of the buildings offered for insurance on each tenement. The dwelling-house, kitchen, stable, lumber-house, office and such like, may be in one declaration, but must be specified and valued each separately and described in the plat by A. B. &c.

No house will be considered as part of brick and part of stone, with one or more stories thereon, of wood; unless there be one complete story of brick or stone at least, eight feet above the surface of the earth, and the ceiling thereof plastered or arched, or one complete wall or walls, or gable ends of brick or stone, without any aperture.

The declarations so executed must be presented to Mr. WILLIAM F. AST, Principal Agent, at Richmond, and the premiums must be paid to JAQUELIN AMBLER, Esq. Cashier General at the said place.

Form of the Declarations for Assurance.

I the underwritten *Thomas Jefferson*[1] residing at *Monticello* in the county of *Albemarle* do hereby declare for Assurance in the Mutual Assurance Society against Fire on Buildings of the State of Virginia, established the 26th December, 1795, agreeable to the several acts of the General Assembly of this state, to wit:

My 6 *several* Buildings on *and near the summit of the hill* at *Monticello* now occupied by *myself* situated *in open ground*² in the county of *Albemarle aforesaid*. Their dimensions, situation and contiguity to other buildings or wharves, what the walls are built of, and what the buildings are covered with, are specified in the hereunto annexed description of the said Buildings on the plat, signed by me and the appraisers, and each valued by them as appears by their certificate here under, to wit:

The *dwelling house*	marked A. at	Dollars, say		Dollars
The *Outchamber*	do. B. at	do.		do.
The *joiner's shop*	do. C. at	do.		do.
The *smith's shop*	do. D. at	do.		do.
The *stone outhouse*	do. E. at	do.		do.
The *stable*	do. F. at	do.		do.³
say			Dollars in all.	

I do hereby declare and affirm that the above mentioned property is not, nor shall be insured elsewhere, without giving notice thereof, agreeably to the policy that may issue in my name, upon the filing of this declaration, and provided the whole sum do not exceed four-fifths of the verified value, and that I will abide by, observe, and adhere to the Constitution, Rules and Regulations as are already established, or may hereafter be established by a majority of the insured present in person, or by representatives, at a general Meeting to be agreed upon for the said Assurance Society. Witness my hand and seal at *Monticello aforesaid* the   day of   1796   TH: JEFFERSON

WE the underwritten, being each of us House-Owners, declare and affirm that we have examined the above mentioned Property of *Thomas Jefferson* and that we are of opinion that it would cost in cash   Dollars to build the same, and is now actually worth   Dollars in ready money, and will command the same as above specified to the best of our knowledge and belief.

Albemarle county   Sc.
The foregoing valuation *sworn to* in due form   Residing in before me, a Magistrate for the said *county* of *Albemarle*   Given under my hand this   day of   in the year 1796

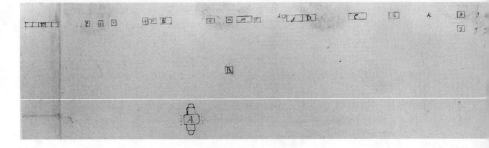

Plat of the buildings referred to in the above Declaration of Thomas Jefferson.

A. is the dwelling house 90. feet long 40. f. broad in the middle exclusive of porticos, two story high except the two bows at the ends, the walls entirely built of stone and brick, the floors above ground and the roof of wood.

B. is an Outchamber, with a kitchen below ground[4] 142 feet from the dwelling house. One story high, the walls of brick, the floor above ground and roof of wood. 20. f. square

C. is a joiner's shop, 57. feet by 18. feet, the underpinning and chimney of stone, the walls and roof of wood.

D. is a smith and nailer's shop 37. by 18. f. the walls and roof of wood.

E. is a stone outhouse 34. by 17. f. the floor of brick, the walls and chimney of stone, the roof of wood, one story high.

F. is a stable 105. feet long and 12. f. wide. One story high. All of wood. The following houses[5] are not included in the insurance, but as they are in a line with those ensured, and in their neighborhood they are described as follows.

g.g. are 2 coal sheds[6] of wood 20. by 15 f. and 22 f. apart, and it is proposed to build 4. others g.g.g.g about 25. f. apart for coal also. They are to contain about 8000. bushels of charcoal. From the nearest of them is 7 poles 15 links to

h. a sawpit where a considerable quantity of timber usually lies. From the pit is 47. feet to

i. a house 30 by $18\frac{1}{2}$ f. all of wood, the floor of earth, in which is stored plank and such things, it is used at times as a carpenter's shop, and sometimes a little fire is made on the floor. From this house is 56. feet to

C. the joiner's shop before mentioned, one of the ensured buildings. From C. is 98. f. to

D. the smith and nailers shop before mentioned, one of the ensured buildings.

j. is a shed to be added[7] to D. 50. feet by 18. f. for the nailers, to be built immediately, and making one building with D it is included in the valuation of D. as if it were already built, and is a part of the ensured property. This addition will extend to within 3. or 4 feet of k, a necessary house of wood 8. feet square. From k. it is 67. feet to

l. a house 16. by $10\frac{1}{2}$ feet, of wood, used as a storehouse for nailrod and other iron. From l. it is 8. feet to

m. a house $43\frac{1}{2}$ f. by 16. f. of wood, the floors of earth, used as a smoke house for meat, and a dairy. From m. it is 24 f. to

n. a wash house $16\frac{1}{2}$ f. square of wood, the chimney also wood, the floor earth. From n. it is 38. f. to

o. a servant's house $20\frac{1}{2}$ f. by 12. f. of wood, with a wooden chimney and earth floor. From o. it is 103. feet to

E. the stone out house before described, being part of the ensured property. From E. it is 7. feet to

p. a shed[8] 25. f. by $12\frac{1}{2}$ f. of wood, the floor of brick, used as a store house for joiner's work. From p. it is 3. f. to

q. a servant's house 14. f. by 17. f. of wood, with a wooden chimney, the floor of earth. From q. it is 75. feet to

r, which as well as s. and t. are servants houses of wood, with wooden chimnies, and earth floors, 12. by 14. feet, each and 27. feet apart from one another. From t. it is 85. feet to

F. the stable before described, being one of the ensured buildings.

This line of buildings from g. to F. is a strait one, and in it's nearest parts to A. and B. passes 227. feet from A. and 142. feet from B. The whole line i. to F. is shortly to be connected by a row of paling either touching or passing very near to every house between these points in the said line.

MS (MHi); unfinished and not sent; consisting of two sheets: a partially dated printed sheet bearing the instructions on recto and the form of declaration on verso, signed by TJ and sealed, with blanks in the declaration filled by William Frederick Ast and TJ reproduced in italics (see note 1 below); and an undated manuscript bearing the plat and description entirely in TJ's hand, pasted to foot of declaration; TJ's substantive emendations are recorded below; printed sheet endorsed by TJ: "Mutual insurance company. 1796." PrC (MHi); consists only of TJ's plat and its description; lacks some emendations (see notes 4-8 below). See Kimball, *Jefferson, Architect*, 61, 159, plate 136; Nichols, *Architectural Drawings*, No. 133.

This incomplete declaration, which TJ never sent to the Mutual Assurance Society, was the earlier of two such schedules of property that he undertook to complete for Ast's insurance company. TJ evidently received the printed form for this declaration prior to 10 Oct. 1796, judging from the reference to it in Ast's circular letter of that date, but it is not known precisely when he attempted to complete it. His plat depicts the outline of the main house at Monticello in its original form, as it was at the beginning of the lengthy sequence of alterations that commenced in 1796 and resulted, after some years' effort, in the form of the house as it is known today (for plans showing the original house in a form similar to that drawn by TJ on the plat, see Kimball, *Jefferson, Architect*, plates 32, 34; Nichols, *Architectural Drawings*, Nos. 57, 61). As TJ later explained to Ast, by the beginning of 1798 he had come to question the financial basis of the insurance plan, and he evidently stopped work on the declaration before completing the valuations of his buildings. His doubts were sufficiently assuaged by 1800, when he submitted another declaration and obtained fire insurance through the

society (TJ to Ast, 13 Sep. 1799; Declaration for the Mutual Assurance Society, 16 Aug. 1800). For descriptions of the slave quarters and other service buildings of Monticello's Mulberry Row that TJ located on this plat, see William M. Kelso, *Archaeology at Monticello: Artifacts of Everyday Life in the Plantation Community* [Charlottesville, 1997], 51-81.

[1] Name inserted in blank by Ast. Subsequent words in italics were inserted by TJ.

[2] TJ wrote the preceding three words across two blanks, canceling the word "between" printed before the first blank and the words "and that of" printed before the second.

[3] Below this line TJ canceled an identical line of printed text and blanks intended for use in listing a building designated "G."

[4] Remainder of sentence interlined by TJ, with figure reworked from "208." Number not amended in PrC.

[5] TJ evidently canceled this word and interlined "sheds" above, then erased the change and replaced it with the original word. Emendations not in PrC.

[6] Word interlined by TJ in place of "houses." Emendation not in PrC.

[7] Preceding five words overwritten and interlined by TJ in place of "an addition." Emendation not in PrC.

[8] Word interlined by TJ in place of "house." Emendation not in PrC.

Memorandum on Farming Operations

[1796 or later]

Preliminary observation. My farms are divided into 7 fields of 40. acres [each?]. In the center of each field is a granary of 2. rooms of $12\frac{1}{2}$ f. sq. each [1000. [. . .] contents][1] and an open passage between them of 12 sf. When there is wheat in the field, it is brought as fast as it is cut to this granary and stacked round it. The threshing machine is fixed in the passage, and as the wheat is got out, it is put with it's chaff into one room and there kept till the winter. The threshing machine being removed, the fan takes it's place, the wheat is passed thro it, and the clean grain thrown over into the other room. The winter of that year our cattle have a moveable shed fixed up at the same granary are fed with the straw and the manure is used in the same field the ensuing spring as will be explained. Many other conveniences result from having the little granary in the center of every field. In a large and hilly [farm] a great central [barn] is either useless or injurious. I permit no separate enclosures of my fields. Their limits are preserved by 2. rows of peach trees leaving a road between them. My fields are by this means protected from pasturage. My rotation in every field is as follows.

1. Wheat. This is after 2. years of clover. The clover turned in in autumn by [completely?] ploughing, the wheat sowed on that, and buried by a harrow drawn in the direction of the furrows.

As soon as the wheat is cut I propose (as soon as I can get the winter vetch) to turn in the stubble, sow vetch and cut it for green fodder in Feb. and March. Then turn in the stubble of that as a green dressing, and the ground is ready for

2. Corn & In alternate drills $4\frac{1}{2}$ feet apart. Put into the drills the long dung
Potatoes. which has been made from the straw of this field in the preceding winter.   In autumn sow vetch again to be cut for green fodder in Feb. and March as before. Then turn in the stubble for a green dressing, which prepares the ground for

3. Peas. In the broadcast, because in that way they stifle weeds, keep the ground cleaner than ploughing would, shade it from the sun, and leave it in better order. I am trying the white field pea of Europe. The gray will be better when I can get it. But as these peas are liable to the bug, some black eyed peas are tended for spring use. These are drilled instead of the other in those fields which have briars or other weeds which require the plough for extirpation. After cutting the peas and turning in the stubble, sow

4. Vetch, to raise a crop for seed. These 2. years of peas and vetch are instead of fallows, which are laborious, unproductive, and expose the ground naked to the sun. When the crop of vetch is taken off, turn in the stubble in time to rot, and then sow

5. Wheat. In the winter have another moveable cowshed at the granary of this field and convert the straw into dung, to remain a twelve-month rotting. In the spring sow red clover on the wheat. I use a box for sowing which saves $\frac{5}{8}$ of the seed. I do not cut my clover the same year in which it is sowed.

6. Clover. The 1st. year after that in which it is sowed gives the best crops. I select the weak spots where the clover is low and cut that for seed.

7. clover. In the spring of the 2d. year after that in which it was sowed put

on the dung (which has been rotting a twelvemonth) as a top dressing. In this way the clover gets the benefit of it in the first instance, and in autumn turn in the clover by one complete ploughing, and sow wheat to begin the rotation again, so that besides the clover root's, the wheat gets a secondary benefit from the dung which had been laid on the clover in the spring as a top dressing.

Having 2. cowsheds, to wit, 1. in each wheat field, enables one to divide the cattle, feeding the weak at one and the strong at another.

PrC (DLC: TJ Papers, 232: 41521-2); entirely in TJ's hand; undated, but no earlier than 1796, when the threshing machine was first used at Monticello; faded; one phrase enclosed by TJ in square brackets (see note below); endorsed by TJ in ink on verso: "Farming. Rotation."

[1] Outer brackets in original.

Notes on a Copying Process

[1796]

Un particulier de Hambourg dit avoir trouvé un procedé, pour prendre sur-le-champ à peu de frais, et en quelque endroit qu'on se trouve, copie de toute espece de manuscrit. Mais[1] desirant tirer quelque profit de sa decouverte, il ne la communiquera qu'aux personnes qui voudront payer cette communication 24. francs. On peut dès à present deposer ou faire parvenir cette somme, franc de port, chez le Cit. Coupery, notaire, rue Chabannais No. 18. le 12. Nivose prochain (1r. Janvier) 1797. Les souscripteurs recevront un petit memoire imprimé, dans lequel cette methode sera clairement expliquée. L'argent restera chez le notaire, jusqu'a ce que le memoire ait eté delivrée. Un certificat de douze negocians d'Hambourg et du Consul de France, atteste que les experiences qu'on a faîtes devant eux les ont complettement satîsfaits.

MS (DLC: TJ Papers, 104: 17912); written entirely in TJ's hand on a small sheet; undated, but assigned on the basis of internal evidence; endorsed: "Copying old writing."

The reference to 1 Jan. 1797 as LE 12.

NIVOSE PROCHAIN implies that this notice originated sometime in 1796, although TJ could have copied it from the source, which has not been identified, anytime thereafter.

[1] Following this word TJ canceled "tira."

Jefferson's Letter to James Madison

I. TO JAMES MADISON,
1 JANUARY 1797

II. COPY FROM MEMORY,
1 JANUARY 1797

EDITORIAL NOTE

Jefferson uncharacteristically failed to retain a press copy of this letter, making instead, as he did with the 28 Dec. letter to John Adams that he enclosed in this one, a "statement" of the contents based on recollection. It is not known if he indeed made the copy entirely from unaided memory, but if he drew on any draft or notes of the letter they have not been located. The effort he made to record these letters in detail reflects the importance he gave to reconstructing the language he had used to address Adams, the victor in the presidential contest, and to explain himself to Madison, his friend and trusted political advisor.

I. To James Madison

Jan. 1. 97.

Yours of Dec. 19. has come safely. The event of the election has never been a matter of doubt in my mind. I knew that the Eastern states were disciplined in the schools of their town meetings to sacrifice differences of opinion to the great object of operating in phalanx, and that the more free and moral agency practised in the other states would always make up the supplement of their weight. Indeed the vote comes much nearer an equality than I had expected. I know the difficulty of obtaining belief to one's declarations of a disinclination to honors, and that it is greatest with those who still remain in the world. But no arguments were wanting to reconcile me to a relinquishment of the first office or acquiescence under the second. As to the first it was impossible that a more solid unwillingness settled on full calculation, could have existed in any man's mind, short of the degree of absolute refusal. The only view on which I would have gone into it for a while was to put our vessel on her republican tack before she should be thrown too much to leeward of her true principles. As to the second, it is the only office in the world about which I am unable to decide in my own mind whether I had rather have it or not have it. Pride does not enter into the estimate; for I think with the Romans that the General of to-day should be a soldier tomorrow if necessary. I can particularly have no feelings which would revolt at a secondary position to Mr. Adams. I am his junior in life,[1] was his junior in Congress, his junior in the diplomatic line, his junior lately in our civil government. Before the receipt of your letter I had written the inclosed one to him. I had intended it some time, but had deferred it from time to time under the discoragement of a despair of making him believe I could be sincere in it. The papers by the last post not rendering it necessary to change any thing in the letter I inclose it open for your perusal, not only that you may possess the actual state of dispositions between us, but that if any thing should render the delivery of it ineligible in your opinion, you may return it to me. If Mr. Adams can be induced to administer the government on it's true principles, and to relinquish his bias to an English constitution, it is to be considered whether it would not be on the whole for the public good to come to a good understanding with him as to his future elections. He is perhaps the only sure barrier against Hamilton's getting in.

Since my last I have recieved a packet of books and pamphlets, the choiceness of which testifies that they come from you. The Incidents of Hamilton's insurrection is a curious work indeed. The hero of it exhibits himself in all the attitudes of a dexterous balance master.

The Political progress is a work of value and of a singular complexion. The eye of the author seems to be a natural achromatic, which divests every object of the glare of colour. The preceding work under the same title had the same merit. One is disgusted indeed with the ulcerated state which it presents[2] of the human mind: but to cure an ulcer we must go to it's bottom: and no writer has ever done this more radically than this one. The reflections into which he leads one are not flattering to our species. In truth I do not recollect in all the Animal kingdom a single species but man which is eternally and systematically engaged in the destruction of it's own species. What is called civilization seems to have no other effect on him than to teach him to pursue the principle of bellum omnium in omnia on a larger scale, and in place of the little contests of tribe against tribe, to engage all the quarters of the earth in the same work of destruction. When we add to this that as to the other species of animals, the lions and tygers are mere lambs compared with man as a destroyer, we must conclude that it is in man alone that Nature has been able to find a sufficient barrier against the too great multiplication of other animals and of man himself,[3] an equilibriating power against the fecundity of generation. My situation points my views chiefly to his wars in the physical world: yours perhaps exhibit him as equally warring in the Moral one. We both, I believe, join in wishing to see him softened. Adieu.

RC (DLC: Madison Papers); unsigned; with emendations, the most important of which are noted below.

EVENT OF THE ELECTION: TJ may have been the intended recipient of an undated fragment that Thomas Rodney of Delaware penned, evidently in the aftermath of the election of 1796: "I must confess My Own desire was to See You Succeed Washington but on Mentioning This I found the minds of Parties were fixed On Other Objects—Whereby you are left in the quiet Enjoyment of your felicity Untill Some more important Occasion calls you to the Official Post of painful Anxiety—In the Mean Time we Trust that Adams from &c." (Dft in DeHi: Rodney Family Papers). Rodney keyed the passage with an asterisk, apparently intending to insert it in the draft of a letter that, if he completed it, he may never have sent (for an instance in which Rodney wrote but did not post a letter to TJ, see Vol. 17: 547). Neither a letter from Rodney of appropriate date nor a reply from TJ is recorded in SJL.

INCIDENTS OF HAMILTON'S INSURREC-TION: Hugh Henry Brackenridge, *Incidents of the Insurrection in the Western Parts of Pennsylvania, in the Year 1794* (Philadelphia, 1795). See Sowerby, No. 530. For Madison's consideration, in 1829, of deleting this reference because of the "implied charge" that Hamilton had "a connection with the Insurrection" in Pennsylvania, see Madison, *Papers*, XVI, 442n.

POLITICAL PROGRESS: James T. Callender, *The Political Progress of Britain: or, an Impartial History of Abuses in the Government of the British Empire, in Europe, Asia, and America. From the Revolution, in 1688, to the Present Time: The Whole Tending to Prove the Ruinous Consequences of the Popular System of Taxation, War, and Conquest . . . Part Second* (Philadelphia, 1795). See Sowerby, Nos. 3184 and 3519. In this work, Callender took historians to task for vindicating "the system of war and conquest" and holding up "as patterns of excellence, incendiaries, who were remarkable for nothing but their crimes." He compared Britain with classical Rome, noting "What torrents of eloquence have been poured forth on the magnanimity and clemency of Julius Caesar, who butchered only twelve hundred thousand people, and whose portrait, as drawn by Suetonius, displays an accomplished model of every human vice! What volumes of execration have been discharged upon the ingratitude and rashness of Brutus, for depriving the world of so estimable a character! . . . Nor is modern England destitute of wonders, to rival the popularity and integrity of Julius Caesar" ([5]-6, 26). For the PRECEDING WORK UNDER THE SAME TITLE, see Tench Coxe to TJ, 7 July 1794.

BELLUM OMNIUM IN OMNIA: actually, "bellum omnium contra omnes," "the war of all against all" in Thomas Hobbes, *Elementa philosophica de Cive* (Amsterdam, 1669), preface. See Sowerby, No. 2388.

[1] Preceding five words interlined.
[2] Preceding three words interlined.
[3] TJ here canceled: "to produce."

II. Copy from Memory

Jan. 1. 97.   to James Madison.

Yours of Dec. 19. is safely recieved. I never entertained a doubt of the event of the election. I knew that the Eastern troops were trained in the schools of their town meetings to sacrifice little differences of opinion to the solid advantages of operating in Phalanx, and that the more free and moral agency of the other states would fully supply their deficiency. I had no expectation indeed that the vote would have approached so near an equality.[1] It is difficult to obtain full credit to declarations of disinclination to honors, and most so with those who still remain in the world. But never was there a more solid unwillingness, founded on rigorous calculation, formed in the mind of any man, short of peremptory refusal. No arguments therefore were necessary to reconcile me to a relinquishment of the first office or acceptance of the second. No motive could have induced me to undertake the first but that of putting our vessel upon her republican tack, and preventing her being driven too far to leeward of her true principles. And the second is the only office in the world about which I cannot decide in my own mind whether I had rather have it or not have it. Pride does not enter into the estimate. For I think with the Romans of old that the General of to-day should be a common souldier tomorrow if necessary. But as to Mr. Adams particularly, I could have no feelings which would revolt at being placed in a secondary station to him. I am his junior in life, I was his junior in Congress, his junior in the diplomatic line, and lately his junior in our civil government. I had written him the inclosed letter before the reciept of yours. I had intended it for some time but had put it off from time to time from the discouragement of despair to make him believe me sincere. As the information by the last post does not make it necessary to change any thing in the letter, I inclose it open for your perusal, as well that you may be possessed of the true state of dispositions between us, as that if there be any circumstance which might render it's delivery ineligible you may return it to me. If Mr. Adams could be induced to administer the government on it's true principles, quitting his bias for an English constitution, it would be worthy consideration whether it would not be for the public good, to come to a good understanding with him as to his future elections. He is the only sure barrier against Hamilton's getting in.

Since my last to you I have recieved a collection of pamphlets and books, the choiceness of which testifies that they come from you. The Incidents of Hamilton's insurrection is a curious work. The hero of it exhibits himself in all the attitudes of a dexterous balance-master.

The political progress is a work of value and of a singular complexion. The author's eye seems to be a natural achromatic, divesting every object of the glare of colour. The former work of the same title possessed the same kind of merit. They disgust one indeed by opening to our view the ulcerated state of the human mind. But to cure an ulcer you must go to the bottom of it, which no author does more radically than this. The reflections into which it leads us are not very flattering to the human species. In the whole Animal kingdom I recollect no family but Man, steadily and systematically employed in the destruction of itself. [2] Nor does what is called civilization produce any other effect than to teach him to pursue the principle of the[3] bellum omnium in omnia on a greater scale, and instead of the little contests between tribe and tribe, to comprehend all the quarters of the earth in the same work of destruction. If to this we add that as to other animals, the lions and tygers are mere lambs compared with Man as a destroyer, we must conclude that Nature has been able to find in Man alone a sufficient barrier against the too great multiplication of other animals and of Man himself, an equilibrating power against the fecundity of generation. Whilst in making these observations[4] my situation points my attention to the warfare of Man in the Physical world, yours may perhaps present him as equally[5] warring in the Moral one. Adieu.

The above is a statement from memory of a letter I wrote to J. Madison, and omitted to retain a copy.

FC (DLC); entirely in TJ's hand; with emendations, the most important of which are noted below.

[1] Sentence interlined.
[2] TJ originally wrote "his own species."

[3] TJ first wrote "to carry on the work of a" and then altered the passage to read as above.
[4] Preceding four words interlined.
[5] Word interlined.

From Benjamin Rush

My DEAR FRIEND   Philada: Jany: 4th. 1797.

I enclose you a humble tribute to the memory of our great republican and philosophical friend Mr. Rittenhouse. It is a feeble expression of respect for his Character compared with yours, in your defence of the genius of the Americans. Few such men have ever lived, or died in any Country.

Accept of my Congratulations upon your election to the Vice President's Chair of the United States, and upon your *escape* of the Office of President. In the present situation of our Country it would have been impossible for you to have preserved the Credit of republican principles, or your own character for integrity, had you succeeded to the *New York* Administration of our government. The Seeds of British Systems in every thing, have at last ripened. What a harvest of political evils[1] is before us!

It has given me great pleasure to hear of Mr. Adams's speaking with pleasure of the prospect of administring the government in a connection with you. He does you justice upon all occasions, And it is currently said, views the Attempt which originated in New York to prefer Mr. Pinckney to him, in its proper light.

The philosophical Society purpose to place you in the Chair vacated by the death of Mr. Rittenhouse. This will be done, in Consequence of your declaration in your letter to Mr. Madison that you will not refuse the Office of Vice President of the U States if elected to it. We shall expect you to preside in our Winter Meetings. From Dr. Sir your sincere Old friend   BENJN RUSH

RC (DLC); one emendation recorded in note below; endorsed by TJ as received 21 Jan. 1797 and so recorded in SJL. Enclosure: Benjamin Rush, *An Eulogium, intended to perpetuate the memory of David Rittenhouse, late President of the American Philosophical Society, delivered before the Society in the First Presbyterian Church* . . . *17th Dec. 1796* (Philadelphia, 1796). See Sowerby, No. 680.

As an example of American GENIUS, TJ in *Notes on the State of Virginia* had cited Rittenhouse's accomplishments in astronomy (*Notes*, ed. Peden, 64-5).

Rush had a long conversation with John ADAMS on 31 Dec. 1796 and expected to dine with him on the day the above letter was written. Rush recounted to Adams the contents of TJ's letter to Madison of 17 Dec. 1796, taken to be a DECLARATION concerning TJ's intentions toward the vice presidency, which Madison had shown to Rush in a chance encounter on the street (see note to that letter, and John Adams's correspondence with Abigail Adams cited there).

[1] Preceding three words interlined in place of a dash.

To Archibald Stuart

DEAR SIR   Monticello Jan. 4. 1797.

In answer to your favor of Dec. 31. and to the question whether adviseable to address the President on the subject of war against France, I shall speak explicitly, because I know I may do it safely to you. Such is the popularity of the President that the people will support him in whatever he will do, or will not do, without appealing to their own reason or to any thing but their feelings towards him: his mind had been so long used to unlimited applause that it could not brook contradiction, or even advice offered unasked. To advice, when asked, he is very open. I have long thought therefore it was best for the republican interest to soothe him by flattery where they could approve his measures, and to be silent where they disapprove, that they may not render him desperate as to their affections, and entirely[1] indifferent to their wishes; in short, to lie on their oars while he remains at the helm, and let the bark drift as[2] his will and a superintending providence shall direct. By his answer to the House of Representatives on the subject of the French war, and also by private information, it seems he is earnest that the war should be avoided, and to have the credit of leaving us in full peace. I think then it is best to leave him to his own movements, and not to risk the ruffling them by what he might[3] deem an improper interference with the constituted authorities. The rather too because we do not hear of any movement in any other quarter concurrent with what you suggest, and because it would scarcely reach him before his departure from office. As to the President elect, there is reason to believe that he (Mr. Adams I mean) is detached from Hamilton, and there is a possibility he may swerve from his politics[4] in a greater or less degree. Should the British faction attempt to urge him to the war by addresses[5] of support with life and fortune, as may happen, it would then[6] be adviseable to counteract their endeavors[7] by dissuasive addresses. At this moment therefore, and at our distance from the scene of information and influence, I should think it most adviseable to[8] be silent till we see what turn the new administration will[9] take. At the same time I mix so little with the world, that my opinion merits less attention than any body's else, and ought not to be weighed against your own good[10] judgment. If therefore I have given it freely, it is because you have desired it, and not because I think it worth your notice.

My information from Philadelphia confirms the opinion I gave you as to the event of the election. Mr. Adams will have a majority of three votes with respect to myself, and whether Mr. Pinckney will have a few[11] more or less than him seems uncertain. The votes of N.H., R.I. and Vermont had not come in, nor those of Georgia and the two Western states.

You shall recieve a gong by the first conveyance. It is but fair reciprocity to give me an opportunity of gratifying you sometimes, and to prove, by accepting this, that my repeated intrusions on you have not been too troublesome. It is a great satisfaction to know that the object will be acceptable to you. With every wish for your happiness I am dear Sir Your affectionate[12] friend & servt   TH: JEFFERSON

RC (ViHi); addressed: "Archibald Stewart Staunton"; stamped. PrC (DLC). Dft (DLC); with numerous emendations, the most important of which are noted below.

For Washington's ANSWER TO THE HOUSE OF REPRESENTATIVES, see Madison to TJ, 19 Dec. 1796.

[1] Word interlined in Dft.
[2] In Dft TJ first wrote "trust the vessel to drift where it" before altering the passage to read as above.
[3] Word interlined in Dft in place of "would."
[4] In Dft TJ first wrote "not pursue his

measures" before altering the passage to read as above. Sentence ends here in Dft.
[5] In Dft TJ first wrote " to sway him by addresses" before altering the passage to read as above.
[6] In Dft TJ here canceled "perhaps."
[7] Preceding three words interlined in Dft. in place of "strengthen his [disposition?]."
[8] In Dft TJ here canceled "lie still."
[9] Dft: "is likely to."
[10] Word interlined in Dft.
[11] Preceding two words interlined in Dft in place of "one or two."
[12] Word not in Dft.

From the American Philosophical Society

Sir   Philadelphia, Janry. 7th 1797.

We have the Pleasure of informing You, that, at the annual Election of Officers of the American Philosophical Society for promoting useful Knowledge, held at Philadelphia, on the 6th. Instant, You were chosen President of that respectable Institution.

The Society, Sir, cannot soon forget the Loss they sustained by the Death of the late worthy and ingenious D. Rittenhouse; but, after expressing their grief on this melancholy Occasion, they look forward with this consoling Reflection, That, in the same Chair, from which two American Philosophers have, successively, instructed *them*, and *the World*, a Third is now seated; by whose Genius and Knowledge, our National Name will preserve a distinguished Place in the Annals of Science.

Permit us, Sir, on this Occasion, to express our Satisfaction in this pleasing Event; and, in being the Organs by which the Society announce their Choice. We are, With sentiments of the highest Esteem & Respect Sir, Your obedient Servants,   Sam. Magaw
                                                       Jona Williams
                                                       W. Barton
                                                       John Bleakley
                                                       Secretaries of the American
                                                       Philosoph. Society

RC (MHi); in Magaw's hand, signed by each signatory; addressed: "Thomas Jefferson, Esq; Monticello via Richmond, Virginia"; stamped and postmarked; endorsed by TJ as received 21 Jan. 1797. FC (PPAmP: Ms. Minutes, 17 Feb. 1797); in Magaw's hand, using initials for signatures and omitting the underlining in text and the words "the highest" from the closing. This letter was printed in APS, *Proceedings*, XXII, pt. 3 [1884], 250, with same variations as FC; and in APS, *Transactions*, IV [1799], xi-xii, following RC but without underlining of words in text.

The Protestant Episcopal clergyman Samuel Magaw and attorneys William Barton and John Bleakley had been members of the American Philosophical Society since 1784, 1787, and 1789, respectively (APS, *Proceedings*, XXII, pt. 3 [1884], 121, 147, 172).

TWO AMERICAN PHILOSOPHERS: Benjamin Franklin, first elected to the presidency of the society in 1769, and David Rittenhouse, who succeeded Franklin in 1791 (same, 23, 187).

To James Madison

Jan. 8. 97.

Yours of Dec. 25. is safely recieved. I much fear the issue of the present dispositions of France and Spain. Whether it be in war or in the suppression of our commerce it will be very distressing and our commerce seems to be already sufficiently distressed through the wrongs of the belligerent nations and our own follies. It was impossible the bank and paper-mania should not produce great and extensive ruin. The President is fortunate to get off just as the bubble is bursting, leaving others to hold the bag. Yet, as his departure will mark the moment when the difficulties begin to work, you will see, that they will be ascribed to the new administration, and that he will have his usual good fortune of reaping credit from the good acts of others, and leaving to them that of his errors.—We apprehend our wheat is almost entirely killed: and many people are expecting to put something else in the ground. I have so little expectations from mine, that as much as I am an enemy to tobacco, I shall endeavor to make some for taxes and clothes. In the morning of the 23d. of Dec. my thermometer was 5°. below 0. and the 24th. it was at 0. On the 26th. of Nov. 22d. of Dec. and this morning it was at 12°. above 0. The last day of Dec. we had a snow $1\frac{1}{2}$ I. deep and the 4th. of this month one of 3. I. deep which is still on the ground. Adieu affectionately.

RC (DLC: Madison Papers); unsigned. Recorded in SJL at 7 Jan. 1797. PrC (DLC: TJ Papers, 101: 17278); dateline faded; at foot of text in ink: "J. Madison."

From James Madison

DEAR SIR Philada. Jany. 8. 1797

I have received your favor of the 17 ult. The election is not likely to terminate in the equilibrium of votes for which the Constitution has not provided. If the Vermont votes should be valid as is now generally supposed, Mr. Adams will have 71. and you 68. Pinkney being in the rear of both. It is to be hoped that the nicety and in truth the unpropitious casualty, of the choice of Mr. A. will lessen the evil of such an ostensible protest by this Country against Republicanism. Your acceptance of a share in the administration will not fail to aid this tendency. It is suggested to me that it will be necessary for you to be here before the adjournment of Congs. in order to be qualified. I have not examined the Constitution and the law on this subject. You will have the means of doing both and of deciding on the question. Altho' I am sensible of the inconveniency of such a trip at this season of the year, yet I see so many advantages likely to result from it that I can not help wishing it may be found necessary. If you can not qualify elsewhere, you must come of course, that the danger of an interregnum may be provided against. The expence would be no objection; and is besides balanced by the effect of the qualification in settling the date of the compensation.

The special communication from the President, on our affairs with France is not yet made. The gloom over them is in no respect diminished. Not a word from Monroe, or any other quarter, relating to his recall; or enabling us to judge on the question whether Pinkney will be received. We wait with anxiety for the light that will probably be thrown on the first point, by the expected communication.

The inclosed paper will give you the foreign news as it has first made its appearance here. A comparison of paragraphs renders the Italian part of it unfavorable to the French very improbable. There may nevertheless be some foundation for it. The French operations against our Trade seem to be better authenticated, as well as the renewal of the Algerine warfare. The abortive result of Lord Malmsbury's errand is also highly probable. I just understand that Spain declared war against G.B. on the 8th. of Ocr. Adieu

Gallatin's work is a book—and the letter of Payne to Genl. W. is not within the compass of our privilege. I sent it some time ago in parcels to Mr. Jones, and requested him to forward them to you.

RC (DLC: Madison Papers); unsigned; endorsed by TJ as received 21 Jan. 1797 and so recorded in SJL. Enclosure not found, but see note below.

VERMONT VOTES: see note to Madison to TJ, 25 Dec. 1796.

SPECIAL COMMUNICATION FROM THE PRESIDENT: see Madison to TJ, 22 Jan. 1797.

The PAPER enclosed by Madison was probably the *Philadelphia Gazette* of 7 Jan. 1797, which included news by way of Hamburg, Germany, which had first been translated and reported in the New York *Daily Advertiser* on 5 and 6 Jan. 1797. The *Philadelphia Gazette* included ITALIAN reports on the suspension of the truces the French Republic held with the Papacy and the Duke of Modena, and the commencement of an alliance between Pope Pius VI and the king of Naples. News from Paris, however, indi-

cated that the Council of Five Hundred had approved a treaty with Naples. This newspaper also carried news from Joseph Yznardi, the United States consul at Cadiz, that FRENCH OPERATIONS had commenced against American TRADE and a report from Baltimore which described the capture of American vessels indicating a RENEWAL OF THE ALGERINE WARFARE. Finally, the *Philadelphia Gazette* carried word of the failure of MALMSBURY'S ERRAND. This mission began in October 1796 when the noted diplomat James Harris, Lord Malmesbury, left for Paris with instructions from William Pitt to negotiate a peace settlement with France, with the condition that the Austrian Netherlands be restored to Emperor Francis II. The Directory refused to accept the condition and on 19 Dec. 1796 ordered the British dignitary to leave Paris. Malmesbury returned to France in July 1797 to resume negotiations at Lille, this time without the condition that had previously stalled negotiations, but the coup of 18 Fructidor (4 Sep. 1797) interrupted the proceedings and once again the British diplomat had to leave France without accomplishing his goal (DNB; *Diaries and Correspondence of James Harris, First Earl of Malmesbury*, ed. James Howard Harris, 2d. ed., 4 vols. [London: 1845], III, 336-52, 355; Emsley, *British Society and the French Wars*, 63-4; *Philadelphia Gazette*, 7, 10 Jan. 1797).

To Volney

DEAR SIR   Monticello Jan. 8. 97.

I recieved yesterday your two favors of Dec. 26. and 29. Your impatience to recieve your valise and it's key was natural. And it is we who have been to blame; Mr. Randolph for not taking information of the vessel and address to which your valise was committed, and myself for having waited till I heard of your being again immerged into the land of newspapers before I forwarded your key. However as you have at length got them safe, I claim absolution under the proverb that 'all is well which ends well.'

About the end of 1793. I recieved from Mr. Dombey (then at Lyons) a letter announcing his intention to come here. And in May 1794. I recieved one from a M. L'Epine dated from New York, and stating himself to be master of the brig Le Boon Capt. Brown, which had sailed from Havre with Mr. Dombey on board, who had sealed up his baggage and wrote my address on them, to save them in case of capture; and that when they were taken, the address did in fact protect them. He mentioned then the death of Mr. Dombey, and that he had delivered his baggage to the custom house at New York. I immediately wrote to Mr. L'Epine, disclaiming any right or interest in the packages under my address, and authorizing as far as depended on me the Consul at New York, or any person the representative of Mr. Dombey, to open the packages and dispose of them according to right. I inclosed this letter open to Mr. Randolph then Secretary of state, to get his interference for the liberation of the effects. It may have happened that he may have failed to forward the letter, or that M. L'Epine may have been gone before it reached New York. In any event I can do no more than repeat my disclaimer of any right to Mr. Dombey's effects, and add all the authority which I can give to yourself or to the Consul of France at New York to do with those effects whatever I might do. Certainly it would be a great gratification to me to recieve the Mètre and Grave committed to Mr. Dombey for me, and that you would be so good as to be the channel of my acknolegements to Bishop Gregoire or any one else to whom I should owe this favor.

You wish to know the state of the air here during the late cold spell, or rather the present one, for it is at this moment so cold that the ink freezes in my pen so that my letter will be scarcely legible. The following is copied from my diary.

		Sunrise	3. P.M.			Sunrise	3 aclock			Sunrise	3. P.M.	
Nov.	22.	60.	69.	Dec.	19.	50.	48.	Dec.	28.	18.	34	
	23.	32½	44		20.	19.			29.	30	39	
	24.	23	38		21.	24.			30	31	34	} a snow 1½
	25.	21.	35		22.	12.			31.	34.	39	} inch deep
	26.	12	26		23.	5. below 0.	11	Jan.	1.	30.	43	
	27.	15	29		24.	0.	20.		2.	28.	33	
	28.	18			25.	18.	32.		3.	23.	30	} a snow 3
	29.	25	36		26.	21.	30.		4.	23.	33	} Inches deep
	30.	22.	43.		27.	15	29.		5.	21	35	
									6.	27.	38	
									7.	25	22.	
									8.	12		

In the winter of 1779-80. the mercury in Farenheit's thermometer fell at Williamsburg once to 6°. above 0. In 83-84 I was at Annapolis without a thermometer and I do not know that there was one in that state. I heard from Virginia that the mercury was again down to 6°. In 1789-90. I was at Paris. The mercury there was as low as 13°. below 0. of Farenheit. These have been the most remarkably cold winters ever known in America. We are told however that in 1762[1] at Philadelphia it was 22°. below 0. In Dec. 93. it was 3°. below 0. there by my thermometer. On the 31st. of Jan. 96. it was at $1\frac{3}{4}$° above 0. at Monticello. I shall therefore have to change the maximum of our cold if ever I revise the Notes on Virginia, as 6°. above 0. was the greatest which had then ever been observed.

It seems possible, from what we hear of the votes at the late election that you may see me in [Philadelphia] about the [beginning of] March, exactly in that character which, if I were to re-appear at Philadelphia, I would prefer to all others. For I change the sentiment of Clorinda to 'L'altè temo, l'humile non sdegno.' I have no inclination to govern men. I should have no views of my own on doing [so,] and as to those of the governed, I had [rather that] their [disappointment] (which must always happen) should be granted to any other cause, real or supposed, than myself. I value the late vote highly; but it is only as the index of the place I hold in the esteem of my fellow-citizens. In this point of view the difference between 68. and 71. votes is little sensible, and still less that between the real vote which was 69. and 70. because one real elector in Pensylvania was excluded from voting by the miscarriage of the votes, and one who was not an elector was admitted to vote. My farm, my family, my books and my building give me much more pleasure than any public office would, and especially one which would keep me constantly from them. I had hoped when you were here to have finished the walls of my house in the autumn, and to have covered it early in winter. But we did not finish them at all. I have to resume the work therefore in the spring, and to take off the roof of the old part during the summer to cover the whole. This will render it necessary for me to make a very short stay at Philadelphia should the late vote have given me any public duty there. My visit there will be merely out of respect to the public, and to the new President.

I am sorry you have recieved so little information on the subject of our winds. I had once (before our revolution war) a project on the same subject. As I had then an extensive acquaintance over this state, I meant to have engaged some person in every county of it, giving them each a thermometer to observe that, and the winds twice a day for one year, to wit at sunrise and at 4. P.M. (the coldest and warmest point of the 24. hours) and to communicate their observations to me at the end of the year. I should then have selected the days in which it appeared that the winds blew to a center within the state, and have made a map of them, and seen how far they had analogy with the temperature of the air. I meant this to be merely a specimen to be communicated to the Philosopl. society at Philadelphia, in order to engage them, by means of their correspondents, to have the same thing done in every state, and through a series of years. By seising the days when the winds centered in any part of the United states, we might in time have come at some of the causes which determine the direction of the winds, which I suspect to be very various. But this long-winded project was prevented by the war which came upon us, and since that I have been far otherwise engaged. I am sure you will have viewed the subject from much higher ground, and I shall be happy to learn your views in some of the hours of delassement, which I hope we are yet to pass together. To this must be added your observations on the new characters of man which you have seen in your journey: as he is in all his shapes a curious animal, on whom no one is better qualified to judge than yourself, and no one will be more pleased to participate of your views of him than one who has the pleasure of offering you his sentiments of sincere respect & esteem.

TH: JEFFERSON

PrC (DLC); faded; the most significant emendation is recorded below; at foot of first page: "Mr. Volney."

Joseph DOMBEY had written to TJ on 1 May 1793, and the letter from Joseph

L'EPINE was dated 16 May 1794. TJ wrote to L'Epine and to Edmund Randolph on 28 May 1794.

COPIED FROM MY DIARY: TJ's meteorological observations for the dates tabulated in this letter are recorded in his weather memorandum book spanning the years 1776-1817 (DLC). In *Notes on the State of Virginia*, TJ considered a reading of 6° F. at Williamsburg in January 1780 to represent the extreme MAXIMUM OF OUR COLD re-corded in the state to that time (*Notes*, ed. Peden, 78).

¹ Figure interlined in place of "1769."

To Thomas Mann Randolph

TH:J. TO TMR.   Monticello Jan. 9. 97.

Yours of the 4th. inst. is duly recieved, and I rejoice that you got down without any accident from the cold, of which I had great apprehensions. The following is extracted from my diary to satisfy the wish you express to know what has been the degree of cold here.

		sunrise	3. P.M.				sunrise	
Dec.	19.	50°.	48.		Jan.	1.	30.	43
	20.	19.				2.	28.	33
	21.	24.				3.	23.	30.⎤ a snow
	22.	12				4.	23. a snow fog	33.⎦3.I. deep.
	23.	5. below 0.	11.			5.	21.	35.
	24.	0.	20.			6.	27.	38.
	25.	18.	32.			7.	25	22.
	26.	21.	30.			8.	12 blue birds.	25.
	27.	15.	29.			9.	10	
	28.	18.	34.					
	29	30.	39.					
	30.	31.	34.⎤ a snow					
	31.	34.	39.⎦ 1½ inch. deep					

My letters from Philadelphia inform me the snow is 3. feet deep at Pittsburg, and 4. feet at Presque isle. If so, we may expect a winter of perpetual cold. It is the general opinion here that the wheat is so much killed that it will not be worth reaping. Many propose to plant tobacco in their best wheat fields. I have determined to put tobacco into my new lands, that we may have something made. Our beeves did not arrive from Bedford till Thursday night (the 5th.). One of yours had become sullen at Lynchburg, and after nearly killing a man, chasing others, and refusing to move a step, he was left in the hands of Mr. Clarke, so that but one came here. On consultation therefore with Robinson we thought it best that both from Edgehill should go, that you might have your number. Wapping Joe and James, whom I had sent to work at Edgehill after Christmas were to set off on Saturday with the three. It having been found impossible to get the butter down from Lynchburg, the river being frozen and too low, Clarke sent 2. firkins on a horse, one for you and the other for us. Yours is here, and Robinson thinks that some body is to come up with your waggon and to return, who may carry it. Having heretofore experienced the possibility of the river's not being navigable from Lynchburg through the winter, so as to fail in getting my tobacco down, and believing it as probable now as it ever was, and at any rate that there will be a great throng of work and but a short season to do it in I have desired Clarke to induce watermen to take mine the very first trip, by some favor equivalent to an advanced price, but not in that form that it may not have effect on future prices. You will consider whether you had not better give him the same directions as to yours, as the delay of a year, and difference of price may be much more than equivalent to the premium.—Such are the distresses for money and bankruptcies in Philadelphia, and so critically timed that I begin to fear for the price of wheat, tho by the last price current it was 2.D. 15c. at New York. You must look sharp for the prices which shall be actually given and which will govern ours both here and in Bedford.

It seems probable from the papers that the 2d. call will fall on me—as between Mr. Adams and myself the vote has been little different from what I always expected. It stands as 68. and 71. but was in reality 69. and 70. It is fortunate Powell gave the vote he did because that has put the election out of question. Had his vote been otherwise, a very disagreeable question might have arisen, because the 15th. elector for Pensylvania, really elected attended and tendered his vote for me, which was refused, and one admitted to vote for Mr. Adams, who had not been really elected. This proceeded from the delay of the votes of Greene county and it would have been a dangerous question how far the Governor's proclamation declaring a man elected who was not elected, could give him a right to vote. For suppose a governor in the face of fact was to declare a whole set of men elected who had not even been voted for. We cannot concieve any law of the state could make that good which the constitution declares not so. I am sincerely rejoiced that the question is become useless, as well as that it is the 2d. and not the 1st. vote which falls on me; if any does. If it proves so on our ultimate information, I shall set out for Philadelphia Feb. 15. and be back about the middle of March.—Volney has safely recieved his baggage. We are all well here, except that Anne has a cold. My warmest love to my dear Martha. Adieu affectionately.

RC (DLC); addressed: "Thomas Mann Randolph at Varina near Richmond"; stamped; endorsed by Randolph as received 22 Jan. 1797. PrC (MHi); endorsed by TJ in ink on verso.

Randolph's letter OF THE 4TH INST., recorded in SJL as received from Varina 7 Jan. 1797, has not been found.

For Levin POWELL and his VOTE for Adams, see Editorial Note to documents relating to the 1796 campaign for electors in Virginia, at 10 Oct. 1796. DELAY OF THE VOTES OF GREENE COUNTY: see note to TJ to Thomas Mann Randolph, 28 Nov. 1796.

From James Sullivan

SIR   Boston 12th January 1797

This intrusion can do no hurt, if it can do no good. I ask leave to tell you, that your Friends in the New England States, who are many will be much disappointed if you should decline being Vice President. It is true that you have been abused. But this abuse came from a party, who are determined to abuse every one, who will not with them, bow, in adoration to the british monarchy. If the abuse, and calumny of these men can deprive the public of the services of those on whom they may confide with Safety, there will be an end of our free constitutions: and the Enemies of an Elective Republic will obtain a compleat Triumph. The motives for your Acceptance of the office, are the gratification of your friends, the mortification of your Enemies, and above all, the interest of your Country—I beleive, that you will suppose, What is really True, that I have no kind of inducement to trouble you in this way, but that of a wish for the public felicity. Did I think that your acceptance would be injurious to your own honour, or interest, I should interfere in the business—but this must be left to your own Judgment. I have the honor to be with great respect and friendship Your most humble servant   JAS SULLIVAN

RC (ViW); at foot of text: "His Excellency Mr Jefferson"; endorsed by TJ as received 3 Feb. 1797 and so recorded in SJL.

From James Wood

SIR   Richmond 14th January 1797.

I have the honor to enclose you an Authenticated Copy of a Resolution which passed the General Assembly at their late Session, respecting the boundary line between this Commonwealth and the State of Maryland; together with a Copy of the Resolution of the Legislature of Maryland On the same Subject. I pray you Sir, to have the goodness to Acknowledge the receipt of this dispatch as soon as Convenient. I have the honor to be with due Consideration & Respect. Sir Yr. Mo. Obt. servt.   JAMES WOOD

RC (DLC); addresssed: "Thomas Jefferson Esqr."; endorsed by TJ as received 21 Jan. and so recorded in SJL. FC (Vi: Executive Letterbook); at head of text: "To Thomas Jefferson, John Marshall, Edmund Randolph, Robert Brooke, Ludwell Lee, Bushrod Washington and John Taylor, Esquires, each." Enclosures: (1) Resolution of the Virginia House of Delegates, 26 Dec. 1796, that TJ and the six others listed as recipients of the FC be appointed commissioners to gather full information on Virginia's boundary with Maryland, any four of them to correspond with the commissioners appointed by that state, and report their findings to the next session of the General Assembly (MS in DLC; in hand of and attested as a true copy by Clerk of the House of Delegates John Stewart, including endorsement by Clerk of the Senate Humphrey Brooke recording that the Senate agreed to the resolution on 26 Dec. 1796). (2) Resolution of the Maryland House of Delegates, 21 Dec. 1795, appointing William Pinkney, William Cooke, and Philip Barton Key commissioners to meet with commissioners from Virginia and adjust by mutual agreement the western and southern boundaries of the state and settle any claims by either "to territory within the limits of the other," reporting to the next session of the General Assembly, the governor to transmit a copy of the resolution to the governor of Virginia (MS in same; in Stewart's hand, including endorsements by Clerk of the Maryland House of Delegates William Harwood and Clerk of the Maryland Senate Henry Warfield, the latter noting passage of the resolution by the Maryland Senate on 21 Dec. 1795, and attestation by Clerk Sam Coleman).

The lack of precise information about the location of the headwaters of the Potomac River and disagreement over whether the river's north or south branch should mark the border meant that the BOUNDARY LINE between Virginia and the western end of Maryland had never been determined. The Fairfax Stone, placed in 1746 by a surveying expedition that included Peter Jefferson, TJ's father, and established the western limits of the immense Fairfax grant in the Northern Neck of Virginia, was a primary reference point. Since neither the commissioners appointed by Maryland in 1795 nor others named in their place could serve, nothing came of the Virginia commissioners' appointments. Sporadic attempts at resolution continued through the nineteenth century, and the matter was settled by a Supreme Court decision in 1910 (Louis N. Whealton, *The Maryland and Virginia Boundary Controversy [1668-1894]* [New York, 1904], 19-34; Charles Morrison, *The Western Boundary of Maryland* [Parsons, West Virginia, 1976], 18, 21-6; Malone, *Jefferson*, I, 22-4).

From James Madison

DEAR SIR   Philada. Jany. 15. 1797.

The last mail brought me your favor of Jany. 1. inclosing an unsealed one for Mr. A. and submitting to my discretion the eligibility of delivering it. In exercising this delicate trust I have felt no small anxiety, arising by no means however from an apprehension that a free exercise of it could be in collision with your real purpose, but from a want of confidence in myself, and the importance of a wrong judgment in the case. After the best consideration I have been able to bestow, I have been led to suspend the delivery of the letter, till you should have an opportunity of deciding on the sufficiency or insufficiency of the following reasons. 1. It is certain that Mr. Adams, on his coming to this place, expressed to different persons a respectful cordiality towards you, and manifested a sensibility to the candid manner in which your friends had in general conducted the opposition to him. And it is equally known that your sentiments towards him personally have found their way to him in the most conciliating form. This being the state of things between you, it deserves to be considered whether the idea of bettering it is not outweighed by the possibility of changing it for the worse. 2. There is perhaps a general air on the letter which betrays the difficulty of your situation in writing it, and it is uncertain what the impression might be resulting from this appearance. 3 It is certain that Mr. A. is fully apprized of the trick aimed at by his pseudo-friends of N.Y: and there may be danger of his suspecting in memento's on that subject, a wish to make his resentment an instrument for avenging that of others. A hint of this kind was some time ago dropped by a judicious and sound man who lives under the same roof, with a wish that even the Newspapers might be Silent on that point. 4. May not what is said of "the sublime delights of riding in the storm &c." be misconstrued into a reflexion on those who have no distaste to the helm at the present crisis? You know the temper of Mr. A. better than I do: but I have always conceived it to be rather a ticklish one. 5. The tenderness due to the zealous and active promoters of your election, makes it doubtful whether their anxieties and exertions ought to be depreciated by any thing implying the unreasonableness of them. I know that some individuals who have deeply committed themselves, and probably incurred the political enmity at least of the P. elect, are already sore on this head. 6. Considering the probability that Mr. A.s course of administration may force an opposition to it from the Republican quarter, and the general uncertainty of the posture which our affairs may take, there may be real embarrassments from giving written possession to him, of the degree of compliment and confidence which your personal delicacy and friendship have suggested.

I have ventured to make these observations, because I am sure you will equally appreciate the motive and the matter of them; and because I do not view them as inconsistent with the duty and policy of cultivating Mr. Adam's favorable dispositions, and giving a fair start to his Executive career. As you have, no doubt, retained a copy of the letter I do not send it back as you request. It occurs however that, if the subject should not be changed in your view of it, by the reasons which influence mine, and the delivery of the letter be accordingly judged expedient, it may not be amiss to alter the date of it; either by writing the whole over again, or authorizing me to correct that part of it.

The special communication is still unmade. It is I am told to be extremely voluminous. I hope, under the sanction of the P.'s reply to our address, that it will be calculated rather to heal than irritate the wounded friendship of the two countries. Yet, I cannot look around at the men who counsel him, or look back at the snares into which he has hitherto been drawn without great apprehensions on this subject. Nothing from France subsequent to the arrival of Pinkney. The negociations for peace you will see are suspended. The accession of Spain to the war enforces the probability that its calamities are not likely yet to be terminated. The late News from the Rhine and from Italy are on the whole favorable to the French. The last battle was on the 27 Ocr. in the Hunspruck, and ended in a victory on their side. The House of Rep: are on direct taxes, which seem to be so much nauseated and feared by those who have created both the necessity and odium of them, that the project will miscarry. Hamilton, you will recollect assured the farmers that all the purposes of the Govt. could be answered without resorting to lands, Houses or stock on farms. This deceptive statement with other devices of his administration, is rising up in judgment against him and will very probably soon blast the prospects which his ambition and intrigues have contemplated. It is certain that he has lost ground in N.Y. of late; and his treachery to Adams, will open the eyes of N. England.

RC (DLC: Madison Papers); unsigned; endorsed by TJ as received 29 Jan. 1797 and so recorded in SJL.

For Madison's role in assuring that TJ's SENTIMENTS concerning Adams FOUND THEIR WAY TO HIM, see note to TJ to Madison, 17 Dec. 1796.

For the P.'s REPLY TO OUR ADDRESS, see note to Madison to TJ, 19 Dec. 1796.

The debate on DIRECT TAXES in the House of Representatives began on 12 Jan. 1797 when Federalist William L. Smith, chairman of the ways and means committee, reported on the need for additional revenues and—using, in part, a report on direct taxes submitted to the House by Secretary of the Treasury Wolcott on 14 Dec. 1796—introduced a resolution to raise the monies with a tax on land and slaves. The next day Robert Goodloe Harper submitted a counter-pro-

posal to raise revenues through an increase of indirect taxes. On 20 Jan., after a week-long debate, the House voted in favor of the direct tax resolution, and on 7 Feb. Smith brought in bills, as ordered, to lay a direct tax and to establish procedures for the assessment and collection of the new taxes. Madison's prediction that the PROJECT would MISCARRY was fulfilled, however, for the bills were not brought to a vote during the session. In the meantime the House continued to consider indirect taxes and on 18 Feb. passed resolutions calling for increased import duties on brown sugar, molasses, candy, bohea teas, and certain cotton goods. Two days later Harper brought the resolutions in as a bill, which on 25 Feb. 1797 passed the House by a 67 to 21 vote (*Annals*, VI, 1843-72, 1874-1913, 1915-42, 1963-5, 2031-8, 2168-2200, 2249-80; JHR, II, 616, 685, 704-5, 707-9, 719).

To James Madison

DEAR SIR   Jan. 16. 97. Monticello

The usual accidents of the winter, ice, floods, rains, have prevented the Orange post from coming to Charlottesville the last post-day, so that we have nothing from Philadelphia the last week. I see however by the Richmond papers a probability that the choice of V.P. has fallen on me. I have written the inclosed letter therefore to Mr. Tazewell as a private friend, and have left it open for your perusal. It will explain it's own object and I pray you and Mr. Tazewell to decide in your own discretion how it may best be used for it's object, so as to avoid the imputation of an indecent forwardness in me.

I observe doubts are still expressed as to the validity of the Vermont election. Surely in so great a case, substance and not form should prevail. I cannot suppose that the Vermont constitution has been strict in requiring particular forms of expressing the legislative will. As far as my disclaimer may have any effect, I pray you to declare it on every occasion foreseen or not foreseen by me, in favor of the choice of the people substantially expressed, and to prevent the phaenomenon of a Pseudo-president at so early a day. Adieu, Yours affectionately   TH: JEFFERSON

RC (DLC: Madison Papers); at foot of text: "Mr. Madison." PrC (DLC). Enclosure: TJ to Henry Tazewell, 16 Jan. 1797.

From John Stuart

SIR   Greenbrier January 16th. 1797

Your letter of the 10th. Novembr. I received by the post. I defered the answer in hopes of being able to gratify you with a part of the Thigh of the Animal you wished. Such was actually in the possession of the people at the Cave, but by some unaccountable neglect it is mislayed that it cannot be found again. This bone was about one foot in Length, one inch and a half thick to the Hollow, which was one inch and a Quarter wide. I seen the spot where it was found about 40 feet distant from where the great claws Lay. Should it be found hereafter, if it is in my power, I will not fail to convey it to you. I am very respectfully your Most Obd. Humbe Servt.   JOHN STUART

RC (ViW); endorsed by TJ as received 6   ANIMAL: the megalonyx.
Feb. 1797 and so recorded in SJL.

To Henry Tazewell

DEAR SIR   Monticello Jan. 16. 1797.

As far as the public papers are to be credited, I may suppose that the choice of Vice president has fallen on me. On this hypothesis I trouble you, and only pray, if it be wrong, that you will consider this letter as not written. I believe it belongs to the Senate to notify the V.P. of his election. I recollect to have heard that on the first election of President and Vice President gentlemen of considerable office were sent to notify the parties chosen. But this was the inauguration of our new government and ought not to be drawn into example. At the 2d election both gentlemen were on the spot and needed no messengers. On the present occasion the President will be on the spot, so that what is now to be done respects myself alone: and considering that the season of notification will always present one difficulty, that the distance in the present case adds a second, not inconsiderable, and may in future happen to be sometimes much more considerable, I hope the Senate will adopt that method of notification which will always be least troublesome and most certain. The channel of the post is certainly the least troublesome, is the most rapid, and considering also that it may be sent by duplicates and triplicates is unquestionably the most certain. Inclosed to the Postmaster of Charlottesville with an order to send it by express, no hazard can endanger the notification. Apprehending that, should there be a difference of opinion on this subject in the Senate, my ideas of self-respect might be supposed by some to require something more formal and inconvenient, I beg leave to avail myself of your friendship to declare, if a different proposition should make it necessary, that I consider the channel of the post office as the most eligible in every respect, and that it is to me the most desireable; which I take the liberty of expressing not with a view of encroaching on the respect due to that discretion which the Senate have a right to exercise on the occasion, but to render them the more free in the exercise of it by taking off whatsoever weight the supposition of a contrary desire in me might have in the mind of any member. I am with sincere respect Dear Sir Your friend & servt

TH: JEFFERSON

RC (facsimile in Paul C. Richards Catalogue No. 128, Feb. 1980); at foot of text: "Henry Tazewell." PrC (DLC). Enclosed in TJ to James Madison, 16 Jan. 1797.

To John Wickham

DEAR SIR   Monticello Jan. 20. 97.

You had a right to expect an earlier answer to your favor on the subject of my proportion of Mr. Wayles's debt to Mr. Welch. Yet I have not been wrong in delaying it; because it was not till now that I could take so certain a view of my resources as would enable me to settle times and sums to your satisfaction as well as my own. The alternative you proposed was the same instalments allowed the other gentlemen with security, or shorter ones without security. My repugnance to ask any one to be my security being invincible; I have preferred the latter alternative. The instalments stand comparatively thus.

Messrs. Eppes & Skipwith	Th:J
1798. June. 1. £245– 4–7	July 1. £300
1799. June 1. 245– 4–7	July 1. 300
1800. June 1. 245– 4–7	July 1. <u>381</u>
1801. June 1. <u>245– 4–7</u>	
980–18–4	£981.

I have taken three instalments instead of four, and substituted July 1. for June 1. because that day allows a much more advantageous term for the sale of our wheat and tobacco. I have accordingly executed and inclosed you three bonds for my part of Mr. Wayles debt, and have referred the interest to Dec. 1. 1796. as you did not mention the date of the settlement. Your letter was of Dec. 6. and Mr. Eppes's of Dec. 3. and it appeared to have been anterior to both.

I inclose a fourth bond for a particular debt of my own to Mr. Welch which according to his settlement of it, made it £112–13–4 sterl. including interest on the 26th. day of Aug. 93. This turned into currency at $33\frac{1}{3}$[. . .] is £150. I have taken another year for the paiment of that. I hope you are pressing for us the suit against Rich. Randolph's representatives for Bevins's money. I am with great esteem Dr. Sir Your most obedt. servt   TH: JEFFERSON

PrC (MHi); faded; at foot of text: "John Wickham esq."; endorsed in ink by TJ on verso. Enclosures not found.

Wickham's LETTER of 6 Dec. was actually dated 8 Dec. 1796. Francis EPPES's letter of 3 Dec. 1796, recorded in SJL as received one week later, has not been found.

For TJ's PARTICULAR DEBT, see Wakelin Welch to TJ, 22 Aug. 1796, and enclosure. For the resettlement of this account and the issuance of new bonds, see MB, II, 1258. PRESSING FOR US THE SUIT: see Bill in Chancery of Wayles's Executors against the Heirs of Richard Randolph, [on or before 2 Mch 1795].

To Enoch Edwards

DEAR SIR   Monticello Jan. 22. 97

I was yesterday gratified with the reciept of your favor of [Dec.] 27. which gave me the first information of your return from Europe. On the 28th. of Oct. I recieved a letter of July 30. from Colo. Monroe but did not know thro what channel it came. I should be glad to see the Defence of his conduct which you possess, tho no paper of that title is necessary for me. He was appointed to an office during pleasure[1] merely to get him out of the Senate and with an intention to sieze the first pretext for exercising the pleasure of recalling him. As I shall be at Philadelphia the first week in March, perhaps I may have an opportunity of seeing the paper there in Mr. Madison's hands. I think with you it will be best to publish nothing concerning Colo. Monroe till his return, that he may accomodate the complexion of his publication to times and circumstances. When you left America you had not a good opinion of the train of our affairs. I dare say you do not find that they have got into better train. It will never be easy to convince me that by a firm yet just conduct in 1793. we might not have obtained such a respect for our neutral rights from Great Britain, as that her violations of them and use of our means to wage her wars would not have furnished any pretence to the other party to do the same. War with both would have been avoided, commerce and navigation protected and enlarged. We shall now either be forced into a war, or have our commerce and navigation, at least, totally annihilated, and the produce of our farms for some years left to rot on our hands. A little time will unfold these things, and shew which class of opinions would have been most friendly to the firmness of our government and to the interests of those for whom it was made. I am with great respect Dear Sir Your most obedt. servt

TH: JEFFERSON

PrC (DLC); faded; at foot of text: "Dr.   [1] Preceding five words interlined.
John Edwards."

To John Langdon

DEAR SIR   Monticello Jan. 22. 97.

Your friendly letter of the 2d. inst. never came to hand till yesterday, and I feel myself indebted for the sollicitude you therein express for my undertaking the office to which you inform me I am called. I know not from what source an idea has spread itself, which I have found to be generally spread, that I would accept the office of President of the US. but not of Vice President. When I retired from the office I last held, no man in the union less expected, than I did, ever to have come forward again; and, whatever has been insinuated to the contrary, to no man in the union was the share which my name bore in the late contest, more unexpected than it was to me. If I had contemplated the thing before hand and suffered my will to enter into action at all on it, it would have been in a direction exactly the reverse of what has been imputed to me. But I had no right to a will on the subject, much less to controul that of the people of the US. in arranging us according to our capacities. Least of all could I have any feelings which would revolt at taking a station secondary to Mr. Adams. I have been secondary to him in every situation in which we ever acted together in public life for twenty years past. A contrary position would have been the novelty, and his the right of revolting at it. Be assured then, my dear Sir, that if I had had a fibre in my composition still looking after public office, it would have been gratified precisely by the very call you are pleased to announce to me, and no other. But in truth I wish for neither honors nor offices. I am happier at home than I can be elsewhere. Since however I am called out, an object of great anxiety to me is that those with whom I am to act, shutting their minds to the unfounded abuse of which I have been the subject, will view me with the same candor with which I shall certainly act. An acquaintance of many long years ensures to me your just support, as it does to you the sentiments of sincere respect and attachment with which I am Dear Sir Your friend & servt,   Th: Jefferson

RC (NhPoS: John Langdon Papers); at foot of text: "John Langdon"; endorsed by Langdon. PrC (DLC).

By the time TJ saw Langdon's FRIENDLY LETTER of 2 Jan. 1797, which was recorded in SJL as received 21 Jan. 1797 but has not been found, Madison had also confirmed the likelihood of his election to the OFFICE of the vice presidency (see Madison to TJ, 8 Jan. 1797).

To James Madison

Jan. 22. 97.

Yours of the 8th. came to hand yesterday. I was not aware of any necessity of going on to Philadelphia immediately, yet I had determined to do it, as a mark of respect to the public, and to do away the doubts which have spread that I should consider the second office as beneath my acceptance. The journey indeed for the month of February is a tremendous undertaking for me, who have not been seven miles from home since my resettlement. I will see you about the rising of Congress: and presume I need not stay there a week. Your letters written before the 7th. of Feb. will still find me here. My letters inform me that Mr. A. speaks of me with great friendship, and with satisfaction in the prospect of administering the government in concurrence[1] with me. I am glad of the first information, because tho' I saw that our antient friendship was affected by a little leaven produced partly by his constitution, partly by the contrivance of others, yet I never felt a diminution of confidence in his integrity, and retained a solid affection for him. His principles of government I knew to be changed, but conscientiously changed. As to my participating in the administration, if by that be meant the executive cabinet, both duty and inclination will shut that door to me. I cannot have a wish to see the scenes of 93. revived as to myself, and to descend daily into the arena like a gladiator to suffer martyrdom in every conflict. As to duty, the constitution will know me only as the member of a legislative body: and it's principle is that of a separation of legislative executive and judiciary functions, except in cases specified. If this principle be not expressed in direct terms, yet it is clearly the spirit of the constitution, and it ought to be so commented and acted on by every friend to free government. I sincerely deplore the situation of our affairs with France. War with them and consequent alliance with Great Britain will completely compass the object of the Executive from the commencement of the war between France and England, taken up by some of them from that moment, by others more latterly. I still however hope it will be avoided. I do not believe Mr. A. wishes war with France. Nor do I believe he will truckle to England as servilely as has been done. If he assumes this front at once and shews that he means to attend to self respect and national dignity with both the nations, perhaps the depredations of both on our commerce may be amicably arrested. I think he should begin first with those who first began with us, and by an example on them acquire a right to redemand the respect from which the other party has departed.—I suppose you are informed of the proceeding commenced by the legislature of Maryland to claim the South branch of Patowmac as their boundary, and thus, of Albemarle now the central county of the state, to make a frontier. As it is impossible upon any consistent principles and after such a length of undisturbed possession that they can expect to establish their claim, it can be ascribed to no other than an intention to irritate and divide, and there can be no doubt from what bow the shaft is shot. However let us cultivate Pennsylvania and we need not fear the universe. The assembly have named me among those who are to manage this controversy. But I am so averse to motion and contest, and the other members are so fully equal to the business that I cannot undertake to act in it. I wish you were added to them. Indeed I wish and hope you may consent to be added to our assembly itself. There is no post where you can render greater services without going out of your state. Let but this block stand firm on it's basis and Pennsylvania do the same, our union will be perpetual and our general government kept within the bounds and form of the constitution. Adieu affectionately.

RC (DLC: Madison Papers); unsigned; with emendations, only the most important of which is noted below; addressed: "James Madison Congress Philadelphia"; franked. PrC (DLC).

TJ did make one trip which took him more than SEVEN MILES FROM HOME when he traveled to Richmond to take care of financial affairs during the spring of 1794 (List of Unretained Letters, [ca. 9 June 1794]).

PROCEEDING COMMENCED BY THE LEGIS-LATURE OF MARYLAND: see James Wood to TJ, 14 Jan. 1797.

[1] Preceding two words interlined.

From James Madison

DEAR SIR   Philada. Jany. 22. 1797.

I have received yours of Jany. 8th. You will find by the papers that the communication on French affairs, has been at length made. Being ordered to be printed without being read, I have no direct knowledge of its character. Some of the Senate where it has been read in part, represent it as well fitted to convert into an incurable gangrine, the wound which the friendship between the two Republics has suffered. Adding this on our side to the spirit manifested in the language and the proceedings on the other, an awful scene appears to be opening upon us. The only chance to escape it lies in the President-Elect. You know the degree in which I appreciate it. I am extremely apprehensive that he may have been drawn into a sanction to this last step of the Executive, by a complimentary initiation into the business which is soon to devolve on him. This is however apprehension merely; no circumstance being known from Which the fact can be inferred. We hear nothing from Monroe or from Pinkney. It has got into the newspapers that an Envoy Extraordy. was to go to France, and that I was to be the person. I have no reason to suppose a shadow of truth in the former part of the story; and the latter is pure fiction. Doctr. Logan has put into my hands a copy of his Agricultural experiments for you which I will forward. A vote has passed in favor of a direct tax. The event is notwithstanding doubtful. The Eastern members, after creating the necessity for it, increasing the odium of it, and reproaching their Southern brethren with backwardness in supporting the Govt. are now sneaking out of the difficulty, and endeavoring whilst they get what they wish, to enjoy the popularity of having opposed it.

RC (DLC: Madison Papers); unsigned; endorsed by TJ as received 3 Feb. 1797 and so recorded in SJL.

President Washington presented his long-awaited COMMUNICATION ON FRENCH AFFAIRS to Congress on 19 Jan. 1797. While his message was brief and conciliatory, he enclosed other documents, the first being a long letter from Timothy Pickering to Charles C. Pinckney of 16 Jan. 1797, which Madison described as "corrosive." The Pickering letter, with accompanying documentation, reviewed relations between the United States and France since 1793 and served as an answer to the numerous complaints cited by Pierre Auguste Adet in his letter to Pickering of 15 Nov. 1796 (Annals, VI, 1914, 2713-69; ASP, Foreign Relations, I, 559-747; Madison to TJ, 5 Feb. 1797).

The New York *Minerva* of 19 Jan. 1797 reported that a letter from Philadelphia carried the news that Madison was appointed a special ENVOY to FRANCE and was soon to depart. The rumor spread to France where a Paris newspaper reported that Madison had arrived in the city on 2 Apr. 1797 (Brant, *Madison*, II, 450-1; Philadelphia *Aurora*, 15 June 1797). For John Adams's conversation with TJ on the desirability of gaining Madison's assent to participation in a mission to the French Republic, see Notes on Conversations with John Adams and George Washington, [after 13 Oct. 1797].

AGRICULTURAL EXPERIMENTS: George Logan, *Fourteen Agricultural Experiments, to Ascertain the best Rotation of Crops: Addressed to the "Philadelphia Agricultural Society"* (Philadelphia, 1797). See Sowerby, No. 717.

To Thomas Mann Randolph

TH:J. TO TMR.   Monticello Jan. 22. 97.

Yours of the 11th. came to hand yesterday. We are all well here. Anne's cold still continues, tho it gives no fever nor other inconvenience. Maria is also well notwithstanding a tumble thro' the floor into the cellar, from which she escaped miraculously without hurt. You ask for news, yet I think it impossible but you must get it from Richmond before you could from hence. The last Northern papers give reason to believe Ld. Malmesbury's mission will be fruitless. In spite of the most copious profusion of English lies I have ever yet seen, it appears that the French are eminently succesful on the Rhine, have good prospects in Italy, and have resumed possession of Corsica. Their depredations on our commerce wear indeed a most serious aspect. I hope Mr. Adams will be able to avert them. I really believe him disposed to do it and to arrest English violences. My letters inform me that he expresses all the feelings of antient friendship towards me, and a wish to conduct the government in concurrence with me. If by this would be meant my entering into the executive cabinet, that would be impossible. The constitution makes me the member of a legislative house, and forbids the confusion of legislative and executive functions except in the person of the President. I shall set out on the 15th. of February for Philadelphia as I am notified that the qualification must be during the session of Congress, and is desired to take place to prevent the danger of an interregnum were any accident to happen to Mr. Adams. I may set out a day sooner or later, according to the Fredericksburg stages, on which subject I must beg you to procure at the stage office Richmond, answers to the following questions.

What days of the week does the stage from Richmd. to Phila., reach Fredsburg.?

At what hour of the day?

In how many days from Richmond or Fredericksburg does it reach Philadelphia?

Answers to these questions are essential for my government and especially the last one; as I propose to go in the stage from Fredericksburg. It would kill my own horses to take such a journey at such a season. As I mean to get into Philadelphia under shadow of the stage and unpercieved to avoid any formal reception (which was practised on a former occasion) I do not let it be known that I go in the stage, and have announced a later arrival there than I mean actually to effect.—I expect Mr. Wythe will have a packet to send me by you. Will you be so good as to call on him for it? I must give you another trouble. To get for me an authentic copy of the late act of assembly 'concerning Nicholas and Jacob Van Staphorst and Nicholas Hubbard' with the Commonwealth seal to it. I would rather have the copy on parchment. I know not to whom to write for this or I would not trouble you about it. I will make out a power of attorney to Mr. Hanson to release the mortgage to Mr. Banks, and send it by this post if it can be executed before witnesses in time.—Maria and Anne send their love to you both. My warmest affections to Martha as well as to yourself. I shall be absent from home but four weeks. Adieu.

RC (DLC); endorsed by Randolph as received 26 Jan. 1797. PrC (MHi); endorsed by TJ in ink on verso.

Randolph's letter OF THE 11TH., recorded in SJL as received from Varina on 21 Jan. 1797, has not been found.

On 23 Dec. 1796, an ACT was passed by the Virginia ASSEMBLY granting NICHOLAS AND JACOB VAN STAPHORST AND NICHOLAS HUBBARD the right to own and dispose of land and, along with their wives and children, "to enjoy all the benefits, immunities, and privileges of citizens" of the commonwealth of Virginia "so far as they may, by this legislature, be constitutionally granted" (Shepherd, *Statutes*, II, 61).

To Benjamin Rush

DEAR SIR   Monticello Jan. 22. 97.

I recieved yesterday your kind favor of the 4th. inst. and the eulogium it covered on the subject of our late invaluable friend Rittenhouse, and I perused it with the avidity and approbation which the matter and manner of every thing from your pen has long taught me to feel. I thank you too for your congratulations on the public call on me to undertake the 2d. office in the US. but still more for the justice you do me in viewing as I do the *escape* from the first. I have no wish to meddle again in public affairs, being happier at home than I can be anywhere else. Still less do I wish to engage in an office where it would be impossible to satisfy either friends or foes, and least of all at a moment when the storm is about to burst which has been conjuring up for four years past. If I am to act however, a more tranquil and unoffending station could not have been found for me, nor one so analogous to the dispositions of my mind. It will give me philosophical evenings in the winter, and rural days in summer. I am indebted to the Philosophical society a communication of some bones of an animal of the lion kind, but of most exaggerated size. What are we to think of a creature whose claws were 8. Inches long, when those of the lion are not $1\frac{1}{2}$ I. Whose thigh bone was $6\frac{1}{4}$ I. diameter when that of the lion is not $1\frac{1}{4}$ I.? Were not these things within the jurisdiction of the rule and compass, and of ocular inspection, credit to them could not be obtained. I have been disappointed in getting the femur as yet, but shall bring on the bones I have, if I can, for the society, and have the pleasure of seeing you for a few days in the first week of March. I wish the usual delays of the publications of the society may admit the addition, to our new volume, of this interesting article, which it would be best to have first announced under the sanction of their authority. I am with sincere esteem Dear Sir Your friend & servt

TH: JEFFERSON

PrC (DLC); at foot of text: "Dr. Rush."

TJ here calculated the DIAMETER of the thigh bone of the megalonyx from information in Archibald Stuart's letter of 19 Aug. 1796 rather than the differing figures in John Stuart's letter of 16 Jan. 1797, which he had not yet received.

To George Wythe

TH: JEFFERSON TO G. WYTHE   Monticello Jan. 22. 97

It seems probable that I shall be called on to preside in a legislative chamber. It is now so long since I have acted in the legislative line that

I am entirely rusty in the Parliamentary rules of procedure. I know they have been more studied and are better known by you than by any man in America perhaps by any man living. I am in hopes that while enquiring into the subject you made notes on it. If any such remain in your hands, however informal, in books or in scraps of paper, and you will be so good as to trust me with them a little while, they shall be most faithfully returned. If they lie in small compass they might come by post without regard to expence. If voluminous Mr. Randolph will be passing through Richmond on his way from Varina to this place about the 10th. of Feb. and could give them a safe conveyance. Did the assembly do any thing for the preservation by publication of the laws? With great affection. Adieu.

PrC (DLC).

To the American Philosophical Society

GENTLEMEN   Monticello Jan. 28. 1797.

I have duly recieved your favor of the 7th. inst. informing me that the American Philosophical society have been pleased to name me their President. The suffrage of a body which comprehends whatever the American world has of distinction in philosophy and science in general is the most flattering incident of my life, and that to which I am the most sensible. My satisfaction would be complete were it not for the consciousness that it is far beyond my titles. I feel no qualification for this distinguished post but a sincere zeal for all the objects of our institution, and an ardent desire to see knowlege so disseminated through the mass of mankind that it may at length reach even the extremes of society, beggars and kings. I pray you, gentlemen, to testify for me to our body, my sense of their favor, and my dispositions to supply by zeal what I may be deficient in the other qualifications proper for their service, and to be assured that your testimony cannot go beyond my feelings.

Permit me to avail myself of this opportunity of expressing the sincere grief I feel for the loss of our beloved Rittenhouse. Genius, science, modesty, purity of morals, simplicity of manners, marked him as one of nature's best samples of the perfection she can cover under the human form. Surely no society, till ours, within the same compass of time ever had to deplore the loss of two such members as Franklin and Rittenhouse: Franklin, our Patriarch the ornament of our age and country,[1] whom Philosophy and Philanthropy announced the first of men, and whose name will be as[2] a star of the first magnitude in the firmament of heaven, when the memory of his companions of the way[3] will be lost in the abyss of time and space.[4] With the most affectionate attachment to their memory, and with sentiments of the highest respect to the society, and to yourselves personally I have the honor to be Gentlemen Your most obedient & most humble servt   TH: JEFFERSON

RC (DLC: William Thornton Papers); with emendations, recorded in notes below, made by TJ subsequent to receipt of the letter by American Philosophical Society (see below); addressed: "Messrs. Samuel Magaw Jonathan Williams William Barton John Bleakley Secretaries of the American Philosophical society Philadelphia"; endorsed by John Vaughan: "Thomas Jefferson's letter of Acceptance of The Presidentship of the Society. Monticello. 28 Jany. 1797 read: Feby. 10. 1797." PrC (DLC); incomplete, consisting of first page only; lacks emendations on RC. Tr (PPAmP: Archives); in Samuel Magaw's hand; lacks emendations on RC. Tr (PPAmP: Ms. Minutes, 17 Feb. 1797); in Magaw's hand; lacks emendations on RC. Printed in APS, *Proceedings*, XXII, pt. 3 [1884], 250-1,

which follows text of PrC; and APS, *Transactions*, IV [1799], xii-xiii, which follows the amended RC.

That the copies made by one of the Society's secretaries follow the text of TJ's letterpressed copy and not the altered RC suggests that TJ made the emendations on the RC sometime after the Society's receipt of the letter, perhaps in anticipation of its publication in the *Transactions*.

[1] Preceding seven words interlined.
[2] Word interlined in place of "like."
[3] Preceding five words interlined in place of "those who have surrounded and obscured him."
[4] Preceding two words inserted in space at end of sentence.

To John Barnes

DEAR SIR   Monticello Jan. 28. 97.

Your favor of the 2d. inst. came to hand only last night, having been delayed by the failure of the post two weeks successively, to come, perhaps on account of ice and bad weather. I am sorry a want of form in the power inclosed prevented your drawing Mr. Short's interest on the 1st. inst. and very thankful for your not suffering my bill to come back. The purpose as to Mr. Short was a very essential one, as it was to answer requisitions for his canal shares, liable to be sold on [the?] 2d. of Jan. if the requisition had not been paid. I now inclose you a new power of attorney modelled according to the one you inclosed me, which I hope will put you out of a state of advance for us. Should any nicety of form still render this insufficient (which I cannot foresee) I shall have the pleasure of seeing you in Philadelphia before you could apprise me of [it and?] receive an answer but I hope there will be no further difficulty. I do not understand the terms of the law you inclosed me [. . .][1] able to guess even what sum of dividends was due on the [. . .] however [I have made the power inclosed?] to all which [. . .][2] on that [. . .] [or] [. . .][3] any [prescribing?] times. Is it $3\frac{1}{2}$ per cent. per ann. or per quarter, or 6. per cent. per ann. or per quarter [that] is to be paid: such paiments per annum will never touch the principal, and such per quarter would pay it much sooner than 1818. yet the act does not say whether the dividends are to be quarterly or only annual. This you [can] explain to me when I see you. In the mean time I am with great esteem Dear Sir Your most obedt. servt   TH: JEFFERSON

PrC (CSmH); faded; at foot of text: "Mr. John Barnes"; endorsed by TJ in ink on verso. Enclosure not found.

Barnes's FAVOR of 2 Jan. 1797, recorded in SJL as received 27 Jan. 1797, has not been found. Also recorded in SJL but missing is a letter from TJ to Barnes of 17 Dec. 1796, which enclosed a POWER of attorney authorizing Barnes to receive INTEREST payable to William Short on 1 Jan. 1797 (MB, II, 950). The REQUISITIONS on Short's CANAL SHARES were for a loan by shareholders of the James River Company to fund completion of that project, which TJ had agreed to on Short's behalf. To meet that obligation, TJ wrote an order on Barnes, 25 Dec. 1796, for $300 in favor of Charles Johnston & Co. (same, 951; TJ to Short, 12 Mch. 1797). On 2 Jan. 1797 Robert Pollard, the canal company's treasurer, acknowledged receipt of £198 in principal and £5.9.1 in interest from Johnston & Co. as payment of two requisitions for the loan subscription on Short's 33 shares (MS in DLC: Short Papers, entirely in Pollard's hand and signed by him, endorsed by TJ).

The LAW TJ inquired about was probably "An Act in addition to an act intituled 'An act making further provision for the support of Public Credit, and for the redemption of the Public Debt,' " approved 28 Apr. 1796, under which holders of six percent funded stock of the United States, such as Short, would be paid quarterly dividends from 1796 through 1818, three of the dividends each year to be at $1\frac{1}{2}$ percent of the original capital, and the other dividend at $3\frac{1}{2}$ percent (U.S. Statutes at Large, I, 458-9).

A power of attorney from TJ to Barnes, dated 29 Jan. 1797 and described as authorizing Barnes to receive Short's "dividends on a certain certificate," has not been found (Robert F. Batchelder Catalog No. 13, April 1976, Lot 106). TJ wrote a draft on Barnes, 18 Dec. 1796, ordering payment of $200 to Johnston & Co. at ten days' sight (PrC in MHi; at foot of text: "Mr. John Barnes Mercht. Philadelphia S. 3d. street"; endorsed by TJ in ink on verso). SJL records a letter from TJ to Barnes of 18 Dec. 1796, and one written by Barnes to TJ on that date and received 31 Dec. 1796, neither of which has been found.

[1] Estimated two words illegible.
[2] Estimated three words illegible.
[3] Illegible word interlined.

To John Marshall

DEAR SIR   Monticello Jan. 28 [1797]

[In a letter of the 14th. inst. I] recieved [from the governor a resolution of the general assembly appointing a body of which I am named one, to correspond with certain Maryland Commissioners] on the dividing bounda[ries of the] two states. The periodical and long absences from the state which I must [incur, with the habitual state of my health] obliging me to avoid journies as much as possible, will I fear render me of little utility in this business. I feel however the less concern as the other names in the resolution leave nothing to desire as to the qualifications proper for it. I pray you therefore to proceed with them, without regarding my inability to attend your meetings. As soon as the points in question, and those on which the Commissioners of Maryland shall rest claims, shall be known, I will undertake to give a thorough examination to such documents as are in my possession, and to give you all the benefit which can be derived from them. Mr. Pendleton and Mr. Wythe are probably acquainted with facts on this subject. The papers of Colo Beverley, father of the gentleman [now living], those of Ld. Fairfax, of Mr. Mercer father of Mr. John Mercer, and especially those of the late Colo. George Mason, will be worthy examination. The last named [gen]tleman had probably committed notes [to paper] on the subject, as he was entirely intimate with it, and in expectation of such a claim. As I can only offer my services as a corresponding member, I pray you to use me freely in that way in all cases where I can be useful. Your name standing first on the list, I avail myself of your address for making this communication to all the gentlemen named, and as far as that circumstance might make it a duty to take measures for putting the business under way, you will be pleased to consider the duty as devolved on you. I am with great respect Dear Sir Your most obedt. servt.

TH: JEFFERSON

PrC (DLC); faded; at foot of text: "John Marshall."

Letters from TJ to Marshall of 9 July, 20, 29 Oct. 1795, and 11 Sep. 1796, and from Marshall to TJ of 1 Aug., 29 Oct., 2 Nov. 1795, and 26 Sep. 1796, received on 11 Aug., 3, 12 Nov. 1795, and 17 Oct. 1796 respectively, are recorded in SJL but have not been found.

To James Wood

SIR   Monticello Jan. 28. 97.

I have the honor to acknolege the receipt of your favor of the 14th. inst. covering a resolution of the General assembly authorising myself and others to correspond with the commissioners of Maryland on the subject of the boundaries dividing the two states. The long and periodical absences from this state which I shall be obliged to incur, together with the habitual state of my health unfriendly to much travelling, will render me I fear of little use to my collegues in this business. Upon this subject however I shall immediately explain myself to them, so that my necessary absences from their meetings may occasion no delay. I have the honor to be with great respect Sir Your most obedient & most humble servt   TH: JEFFERSON

RC (PHi); addressed: "Governor Wood Richmond"; endorsed by Wood.

EXPLAIN MYSELF TO THEM: see the preceding document.

From James Madison

DEAR SIR   Philada. Jany. 29. 1797.

Yours covering an unsealed letter to Mr. Tazewell came duly to hand, and will be turned to the use you wish. As you take the Philada. Gazette in which the Belligerent answer to Adêts note has been printed in toto, I refer to that for the posture and prospect of things with France. The British party since this overt patronage of their cause, no longer wear the mask. A war with France and an alliance with G.B. enter both into print and conversation; and no doubt can be entertained that a push will be made to screw up the P. to that point before he quits the office. The strides latterly made with so much inconsistency as well as weakness in that direction, prepare us for receiving every further step without surprise. No further[1] discovery has been made of the mind of the P. elect. I can not prevail on myself to augur much that is consoling from him. Nothing from abroad; nor more at home than you will gather from the Newspapers. Adieu Yrs Affy.

RC (DLC: Madison Papers); unsigned; endorsed by TJ as received 10 Feb. 1797 and so recorded in SJL.

TJ's COVERING letter to Madison and the UNSEALED LETTER to Henry TAZEWELL are of 16 Jan. 1797.
On 23 Jan. 1797, the *Philadelphia Gazette* printed Washington's address to Congress of 19 Jan. and the long enclosure from Timothy Pickering to Charles C. Pinckney, an ANSWER to Pierre Auguste Adet's NOTE of 15 Nov. 1796; see note to Madison to TJ, 22 Jan. 1797.

[1] Preceding word interlined by Madison.

To James Madison

Jan. 30. 97.

Your's of the 15th. came to hand yesterday. I am very thankful for the discretion you have exercised over the letter. That has happened to be the case which I knew to be possible, that the honest expressions of my feelings towards Mr. A. might be rendered[1] mal-a-propos from circumstances existing and known at the seat of government, but not seen by me in my retired situation. Mr. A. and myself were cordial friends from the beginning of the revolution. Since our return from Europe some little incidents have happened which were capable of affecting a jealous mind like his. The deviation from that line of politics on which we had been united, has not made me less sensible of the rectitude of his heart: and I wished him to know this, and also another truth that I am sincerely pleased at having escaped the late draught for the helm, and have not a wish which he stands in the way of. That he should be convinced of these truths is important to our mutual satisfaction, and perhaps to the harmony and good of the public service. But there was a difficulty in conveying them to him, and a possibility that the attempt might do mischief there or somewhere else, and I would not have hazarded the attempt if you had not been in place to decide upon it's expediency. It is now become unnecessary to repeat it, by a letter I have had occasion to write to Langdon in answer to one from him, in which I have said exactly the things which will be grateful to Mr. A. and no more. This I imagine will be shewn to him.

I have turned to the constitution and laws, and find nothing to warrant the opinion that I might not have been qualified here or wherever else I could meet with a Senator, every member of that body being authorised to administer the oath, without being confined to time or place, and consequently to make a record of it, and to deposit it with the records of the Senate. However I shall come on on the principle which had first determined me, respect to the public. I hope I shall be made a part of no ceremony whatever. I shall escape into the city as covertly as possible. If Govr. Mifflin should shew any symptoms of ceremony, pray contrive to parry them. We have now fine mild weather here. The thermometer is above the point which renders fires necessary. Adieu affectionately,

RC (DLC: Madison Papers); unsigned; only the most important emendation is noted below; addressed: "James Madison Congress Philadelphia"; franked. PrC (DLC).

DISCRETION YOU HAVE EXERCISED OVER THE LETTER: see TJ to John Adams, 28 Dec. 1796.

TJ's LETTER to John LANGDON is of 22 Jan. 1797.

[1] TJ first wrote "might not be a-propos" before reworking the passage to read as above.

From Henry Tazewell

DEAR SIR   Philadelphia 1st. February 1797.

Your Letter of the 16th. January was lately delivered to me by Mr. Madison. On examination, I found the proceedings on the two former Elections for President and V. President, had been as you stated them. When a proper occasion presented itself I intended to make the most adviseable use of your communication, as to the mode of notifying you of the appointment which should fall to your lot. But unexpectedly, the Senate this day appointed a Committee to meet another from the House of Representatives to report a Method of counting the Votes, and of notifying those concerned of their appointments. The names of those who were appointed on this Committee mark the measure as a thing of Concert: Sedgwick, Laurance, and Read. The House of Representatives have not yet acted on this subject. If a previous arrangement has been made, the speaker of that House will persue it—and you may easily conjecture of what kind the Report will be. Perhaps however as Mr. Adams is on the spot, if it can be contrived to make your wishes known to the Committee without hazard, they may be induced to adopt the plan of communication which you propose. This shall be attempted. If it fails, altho to oppose, will be less agreable, than originally to propose a mode of notification; yet my own inclination, backed by your wishes, will carry me as far as prudence will permit in an attempt to place it on the least exceptionable footing—I will however take no step which does not meet Mr. Madison's approbation. Under these circumstances suppose you were to set out for this place before any notification can reach you? You can be advised from hence at any place, of any fact, you may wish to know. By this means you can illude any disagreably ceremonious notification. It is extremely probable that the Senate will continue in Session longer than the 3d. of March. If you should be appointed the V. President, you can then take the necessary Oath—and enter on the duties of your office. The Newspapers of this Evening announce the arrival of some interesting intelligence from Europe. The manner, excites a belief that the communication is to the Executive—and conjecture says it contains an account of the failure of Malmsbury's Negotiation, and of the refusal to receive Mr. Pinkney as our Minister in France. These circumstances, if true, when added to a fact which I am told exists—that a French Vessel has lately captured an American East Indiaman, will increase our apprehensions of a War. Your friend & Servt

HENRY TAZEWELL

RC (DLC); endorsed by TJ as received 10 Feb. 1797 and so recorded in SJL.

Not until the electoral votes were counted on 8 Feb. 1797 did the Senate and House of Representatives actually begin to consider the MODE OF NOTIFYING TJ of his election. After two days of debate by both houses it was agreed that the Senate should take charge of the notification. A committee, consisting of Virginia Republican Stevens T. Mason and Federalists Theodore Sedgwick of Massachusetts and James Hillhouse of Connecticut, brought in a report that was adopted the same day requesting that the president of the United States be charged with transmitting the notification to the vice president elect and that the president of the Senate "make out and sign a certificate" in words agreed to by the Senate (JHR, II, 687, 689-90; JS, II, 321-3). For TJ's notification, see the two letters from Pickering to TJ of 11 Feb. 1797.

Tazewell's concern that the Senate committee appointed to develop the procedures for counting the electoral votes was a THING OF CONCERT probably stemmed from the composition of the committee: Sedgwick, John Laurance of New York, and Jacob Read of South Carolina, all Federalists.

Their appointments may have been decided at Senator William Bingham's residence, which, since his election in 1795, had evolved from a political gathering place for Federalists to the site of secret party caucuses (*Biog. Dir. Cong.*; Robert C. Alberts, *The Golden Voyage: The Life and Times of William Bingham, 1752-1804* [Boston, 1969], 262-3). By February 1797 these meetings were becoming public knowledge, for TJ—perhaps when he came to Philadelphia in early March to take the oath of office or when he returned to the city in May to preside over the Senate during the first session of Congress—received an extract of an undated letter between unidentified correspondents expressing concern over machinations in the choice of Bingham as president pro tempore of the Senate on 16 Feb., the day after President-elect John Adams relinquished his Senate duties. The correspondent conveyed the rumors circulating in his "part of the Country" that a number of senators were holding "clandestine consultations out of Doors." He had been informed that on 14 Feb., the day after Adams announced the date he would be leaving the Senate, Benjamin Goodhue of Massachusetts, Sedgwick, and Bingham invited "the federal part of the Senate" to a meeting at Bingham's house "to arrange measures for chusing a president of the Senate pro tempore." The invitation, so "derogatory to the honor of the Members of the Senate," was accepted by some, who met at the appointed hour and resolved to support the man who had the most votes. Upon counting the ballots it appeared that Sedgwick and Laurence each had a few votes and Bingham the majority. Bingham had thus gained his position "by this disgraceful combination." (Tr in DLC: TJ Papers, 96: 42162; being an extract in unknown hand; undated; at head of text, in a different hand: "Extract of a letter from a correspondence").

From George Wythe

G. WYTHE TO TH. JEFFERSON   1 of february, 1797.

I extracted, thirty years ago, from the journals of the british house of commons, the parliamentary rules of procedure, but left the copy of them among the papers belonging to the house of burgesses, among which a search for it at this day would be vain. Since 1775, I have thought so little of those rules that my memory doth not enable me to supply such of them as may deserve your attention.

Brend, notwithstanding his repeated promises, to bind your acts, had not begun the work when you gave me leave to publish your letter dated the 16 of january, in the last year. I then desired him not to procede without further orders; supposing you would not wish to have your copies bound, if the general assembly should consent to the complete edition proposed. A copy of that letter was delivered to every member of the legislature, the first day of the last session, or so soon as he came to town. Nothing however was done in the business. J. Marshall and some other members told me that they hoped the assembly would consent, at the next session, to the complete edition. Your copies are in my house, and shall be bound, if such be your desire. With unalterable affection, adieu.

RC (DLC); endorsed by TJ as received 14 Feb. 1797 and so recorded in SJL.

From Benjamin Rush

Dear Sir   Philadelphia 4th Feby: 1797.

Your Communication upon the Subject of the large Claws, and bones of the Lyon kind Animal, will arrive time en'o to have a place in the Volume of the transactions of the philosophical Society which is now in the press. I have Often been struck with the Analogy of things in the natural, moral and political world. The Animals whose stupendous remains we now and then pick up in our Country, were Once probably the tyrants of our forests, and have perhaps been extirpated by a Confederacy, and insurrection of beasts of less force indivudually than themselves. In like manner, may We not hope that kings will be extirpated from the face of the earth by a general insurrection of the reason and Virtue of man, and that the exhibition of crowns, Sceptres and maces, like the claws and bones of extinct Animals, shall be necessary to prove to posterity, that such canibals ever existed upon our globe?

Your Philadelphia friends will rejoice in taking you by the hand After the 3rd: of March. Dr. Priestley who will be in town at that time, longs for the pleasure of your Acquaintance. You will be Charmed with his extensive information, and amiable Simplicity of manners. I will give you a Specimen of his republicanism. "The time (said he to me) will I hope one day come, when *laws* shall govern so completely, that a man shall be a month in America without knowing who is President of the United States."

I am now preparing a paper for our Society in which I have Attempted to prove, that the black Color (as it is called) of the Negroes is the effect of a disease in the Skin of the Leprous kind. The inferences from it will be in favor of treating them with humanity, and justice, and of keeping up the existing prejudices against matrimonial connextions with them. Adieu. From Dr Sir your Sincere, and Affectionate friend

Benjn: Rush

RC (DLC); addressed: "Thomas Jefferson Esqr: Montecelli, Virginia"; endorsed by TJ as received 18 Feb. 1797 and so recorded in SJL.

The expected communication from TJ on the lyon kind animal was his Memoir on the Megalonyx, [10 Feb. 1797]. Rush presented his own paper to a special meeting of the American Philosophical Society on 14 July 1797 (aps, *Proceedings*, xxii, pt. 3 [1884], 260). Titled "Observations intended to favour a supposition that the Black Color (as it is called) of the Negroes is derived from the Leprosy," it was published in aps, *Transactions*, iv [1799], 289-97.

From James Madison

Dear Sir   Philada. Feby. 5. 1797

I have received yours of   giving notice that we shall have the pleasure of seeing you here soon, but that letters written before the 7th. would arrive before you leave home.

Nothing occurs to alleviate the crisis in our external affairs. The French continue to prey on our trade. The British too have not desisted. There are accounts that both of them are taking our East-India-men. This is an alarming symtom, there being 60 or 70 vessels from different parts of the U.S. engaged in that trade. Pickering's corrosive letter has not yet been fully printed so as to come before the H. of R. It is extremely difficult to decide on the best course to be taken. Silence may be construed into approbation. On the other hand it is not likely that any opportunity will be given for negativing an approving Resolution. And it is at least doubtful whether a vote of positive disapprobation in any form whatever could be safely risked in the House, or if passed whether the public opinion would not be brought to side with the Executive against it. It is moreover extremely difficult to shape any measure on the occasion so as to escape the charge either of censuring or advising without a proper warrant from the nature of our Constitutional relation to the Executive. Nor is it unworthy of consideration that there are formidable steps not yet taken by the P. which may be taken before the moment of his exit, which if taken might be efficacious, and which his successor without his sanction would not dare to take.

A bill for collecting the proposed taxes on land &c. is before the committee of ways and means. The difficulties of the subject, the shortness of the time, and the aversion of the Eastern people, render it uncertain whether it will pass or not at the present session. I suspect the policy of the Treasy. Department is to separate the preparatory arrangements, from the actual collection of the tax, and to provide for the former only at present, an expedient not unlikely to succeed, as it will smooth the way for the Eastern members. Some I find who do not disapprove of the plan of direct taxes, are unwilling to fortify the disposition to embroil us with France, by enlarging at the present juncture, our system of revenue.

I reserve for a verbal communication the indications by which we judge of the prospect from the accession of Mr. A. to the Helm. They are not I conceive very flattering.

I just learn that a British packet brings London accounts to Decr. 7. Nothing is as yet given out but that the negociations at Paris have ended in abortion. It is probable that, what is not given out, is not more favorable to G.B. I do not believe that any intelligence has been received from Monroe or Pinkney subsequent to the arrival of the latter. It is said that the Spaniards are fortifying at the Chickasaw Bluffs. If this be the case, it strengthens the apprehension that they regard the British Treaty with the explanatory article, as superseding the obligation or policy of their Treaty with us. Adieu

RC (DLC: Madison Papers); unsigned; endorsed by TJ as received 18 Feb. 1797 and so recorded in SJL. I HAVE RECEIVED YOURS: TJ to Madison, 22 Jan. 1797. PICKERING'S CORROSIVE LETTER: see note to Madison to TJ of the same date.

From Charles Willson Peale

DR. SIR   Museum Feby. 6. 1797.

Last June I received a Letter from you, respecting an exchange of the Subjects of Natural History, that the Hereditary Prince of Parma was desireous of making.

I answered your Letter in the same month (which I hope was received) and although I have had other avocations, such as Bridge building &c., yet I have made a beginning in this work and I have preserved such subjects as have occasionly offered, but in a short time, the returning Birds, will give me more ample imployment.

It is my intention to Make the best collections of the Animal kingdom generally, that I can possibly preserve, in the several seasons, as they advance, but I will not preserve any Subject that is not in good condition—therefore if I cannot obtain great numbers, at least they shall be such as will be approved off.

I am anxious to know, if this Gentleman wishes to have all the larger, as well as the smaller Animals, for although you say, he wants all the American subjects of the 3 kingdoms of Nature, yet like many Amateurs of Natural history in Europe, who have Cabinets, he may only desire the smaller and most beautiful parts of the Creation.

My Museum is becoming rich with subjects of every class, and although it cannot for many years to come, equal many of the Cabinets in Europe, yet I hope to see it in so complete order as to equal any of them, and perhaps it will by this means, be equally useful.

With the hope of getting the articles I want from the other quarters of the Globe, I will exert myself to have the Subjects of Natural History generally, of N. America to exchange for them, and my Children will continue, I hope, to promote the Interests of a Museum which I think

I have nearly made so good a foundation off, as will render it in some future day an honour to my Country. I am with much respect Dear Sir; your Friend   C W PEALE

RC (DLC); endorsed by TJ as received 18 Feb. 1797 and so recorded in SJL. Dft (Lb in PPAmP: Peale-Sellers Papers).

The LETTER concerning Louis of PARMA was TJ's missive to Peale, 5 June 1796, ANSWERED by Peale on the 22d.

To Thomas Mann Randolph

TH:J. TO TMR.   Monticello Feb. 6. 97.

All well here and in expectation of seeing you on Sunday next. Dr. Taylor has enjoined my judgments against him for delay. The pretext is that I have refused to execute a deed to him for Elkhill. But I never was so mistaken if I did not by his direction reacknolege the former deed before the clerks of the General court in Richmond on the 4th. of June 1794. or within a very few days after that. I write by this post to the clerk of the General court to send me a certificate of this, as it will enable me to have the injunction dissolved at once. Lest the clerk should not do it in the instant, and so miss the conveyance by post, will you be so good as to call on him and bring his certificate to me, or a certified copy of the deed which he pleases. I expect you will recieve this in Richmond, on your way up, and therefore omit loves to Martha and Jeff. Adieu affectionately.

RC (DLC); endorsed by Randolph as received 11 Feb. 1797. PrC (ViU: Edgehill-Randolph Papers); endorsed in ink by TJ on verso.

Evidence indicates that TJ did not EXECUTE A DEED to Thomas Augustus Taylor for ELKHILL until 5 Aug. 1799 (TJ to Daniel L. Hylton, 3 June 1792).

From Robert Pleasants

ESTEEMED FRIEND   Curles 2d. mo. 8. 1797.

I hope thou wilt excuse my not acknowledging before now thy acceptable favor of the 27th. Augt. last, on the subject of free schools. I am not insensible of the superior advantages which might reasonably be expected from Institutions of that sort, Established by law, and conducted in a proper Manner, but as I had no expectation at the time I wrote to thee, that such a law was likely to be obtained, I concluded it might at least be right to endeavour to do what might be practicable on a smaller Scale for the benifit of that oppressed and much neglected part of the human race among us; I was therefore much pleased to understand it had been the subject of thy consideration and endeavours, to promote so necessary a work on so extensive a plan; and from the incouragement thou gave of promoting applications to the Assembly, I took some pains to endeavour to get a sight of the Bill, which thou mentions to have been prepared, and to be found in the propos'd Code of 1784. with an intention (could I have found it) to have consulted some of the leading members of the Assembly, and to have done as thou recommended to bring the matter before the House; but I have never yet been able to find it, either in the printed Copy of those revised laws or in the hands of those who I thought most likely to have it so that nothing was done by way of Petition. I find however by the laws past the last Session, that the subject of free schools was taken up, and an Act is passed for that purpose, but Confined to free Children; and though those of Colour are not exempted from the benifit of such schools, yet I can't help fearing that the prevailing prejudices against that unfortunate race of people, will be an obstruction to an equal participation of the proposed benifit: It seems also doubtful, from the too general inattention to Institutions of a public nature, that this law may not be attended with all the good consequences which the importance of the subject requires. I am with great Esteem & respect Thy assured Friend.

ROBERT PLEASANTS

P.S. I have no doubt but thy statement of the little account with Ro. Pleasants & Co. is a right one, and am perfectly satisfied with it.

RC (MoSHi: Jefferson Papers); endorsed by TJ as received 14 Feb. 1797 and so recorded in SJL. FC (Lb in PHC: Quaker Collection); in Pleasants's hand; lacks postscript and has minor variations.

Not until December 1796 did the legislature approve an ACT providing for primary schools offering basic instruction in "reading, writing and common arithmetic" on the model of TJ's bill of 1778. Neither the bill nor the act refers directly to race, but instruction in both cases was CONFINED TO FREE CHILDREN. Though but a remnant of TJ's original proposals, little actually became of the 1796 act because it relied on local funding and left implementation to the discretion of county courts (Shepherd, *Statutes*, II, 3-5; Autobiography in Ford, I, 67).

The LITTLE ACCOUNT WITH RO. PLEASANTS & CO. has not been found, but was probably enclosed in a letter TJ wrote to Pleasants on 28 Aug. 1796, now missing but recorded in SJL with the notation "ord. Johnst. £3–2–10½." On that day TJ drew on Charles Johnston to pay Pleasants "for an old balance due" to the deceased Thomas Pleasants of Four Mile Creek in Henrico County, a son-in-law of Robert Pleasants who at one time had managed the latter's mercantile firm (Betsy August, "Robert Pleasants Letterbook, 1771-1773," [M.A. thesis, College of William and Mary, 1976], 7-8; MB, I, 413, II, 944).

To James Sullivan

Dear Sir   Monticello Feb. 9. 1797

I have many acknolegements to make for the friendly [anxiety you are pleased] to express in your letter of Jan. 12. for my undertaking the office to which I have been elected. The idea that I would accept the office of President, but not that of Vice President of the US. had not it's origin with me. I never thought of questioning the free exercise of the right of my fellow citizens to marshall those whom they call into their service according to their fitnesses; nor ever presumed that they were not the best[1] judges of these. Had I indulged a wish in what manner they should dispose of me, it would precisely have coincided with what they have done. Neither the splendor, nor the power, nor the difficulties, nor the fame, or defamation as may happen,[2] attached to the first magistracy[3] have any attractions for me. The helm of a free government is always arduous, and never was ours more so than at a moment when[4] two friendly people[5] are like to be committed in war by the ill temper of their administrations. I am so much attached to my domestic situation that I would not have wished to leave it at all. However if I am to be called from it,[6] the shortest absences, and most tranquil station suit me best.[7] I value highly indeed the part my fellow citizens gave me in their late vote, as an evidence of[8] their esteem, and I am happy in the information you are so kind as to give that many in the Eastern quarter entertain the same sentiment. Where a constitution, like ours, wears a mixed aspect[9] of monarchy and republicanism, it's citizens will naturally divide into two[10] classes of sentiment, according as their tone of body or mind, their habits, connections, and callings induce them to wish to strengthen either the monarchical or the republican features of the constitution.[11] Some will consider it as an elective monarchy which had better be made[12] hereditary, and therefore endeavor to lead towards that all the forms and principles of it's administration. Others will [view it] as an energetic republic, turning in all it's points on the pivot of free and frequent elect[ions]. The great body of our *native* citizens[13] are unquestionably of the republican sentiment.[14] Foreign education, and foreign connections of interest have produced some exceptions[15] in every part of the Union, North and South,[16] and perhaps [other circumstances] in your quarter better known to you,[17] may have thrown into the scale of exceptions a greater number of the rich. Still, there I believe, and here I am sure, the great mass is republican. Nor do any of the forms in which the public disposition has been pronounced in the last half dozen years evince the contrary. All of them, when traced to their true source, have only been evidences of the preponderant [18] popularity of a particular great [19] character. That influence once withdrawn [20] and our countrymen left to the operation of their own unbiassed good sense, I have no doubt we shall see a pretty rapid return of general harmony, and our citizens moving in phalanx [21] in the paths of regular liberty, [22] order, [23] and a sacro-sanct adherence to the constitution. Thus I think it will be if war with France can be avoided. But if that untoward event comes athwart us in our present point of deviation, nobody I believe can foresee into what port it will [24] drive us.

I am always glad of an opportunity of enquiring after my most antient and respected friend Mr. Samuel Adams. His principles, founded on the [immoveable basis] of equal right and reason, [25] have continued pure and unchanged. Permit me to place here my sincere veneration for him and wishes for his health and happiness, and to assure yourself of the sentiments of esteem and respect with which I am Dear Sir Your most obedt & most humble servt.   TH: JEFFERSON

PrC (DLC); faded, with missing words supplied in brackets from Dft; at foot of first page: "James Sullivan esq." Dft (DLC); includes numerous emendations, the most important of which are noted below.

[1] In Dft TJ first wrote "better" before reworking it to read as above.

[2] In Dft TJ began this sentence "Neither the abuse, nor the difficulties, nor the power nor splendor" before altering it to read as above.

[3] Word interlined in Dft in place of "office."

[4] In Dft TJ first wrote "and never was there a moment when ours was more so than at the present crisis when the administrations of" before altering the passage to read as above.

[5] In Dft TJ here canceled: "have got into such temper towards each other which threatens to."

[6] In Dft TJ first wrote "the shorter the times of absences and the ⟨less⟩ more tranquil the station assigned me, the more agreeable it is to me" before altering the remainder of the sentence to read as above.

[7] In Dft TJ reversed the order of the following two sentences.

[8] In Dft TJ first wrote "the place I hold in their esteem and am particularly pleased with your information that there are many in the eastern quarter of our [. . .] who think of me with approbation" before alter-

ing the remainder of this sentence to read as above.

[9] Here in Dft TJ interlined the preceding four words in place of "takes a middle position between."

[10] TJ here canceled "descriptions" in Dft.

[11] In Dft TJ wrote the following two sentences in the margin.

[12] In Dft TJ first wrote "they wish to make" before altering it to read "it would be better to make."

[13] In Dft TJ first wrote "of the people" before altering the clause to read as above.

[14] TJ here canceled in Dft: "I can say the whole body in the South, and I in the South it is every class, in the North I believe" before proceeding with the following sentence.

[15] In Dft TJ here canceled "[. . .] warped individuals from a communion of sentiment with their countrymen" before interlining the preceding three words.

[16] Dft: "South and North."

[17] In Dft TJ first wrote "of which you are a better judge than I am" before altering the passage to read as above.

[18] Preceding word interlined in Dft in place of "paramount."

[19] Preceding word interlined in Dft.

[20] In Dft TJ here canceled "I have no doubt we shall see."

[21] In Dft TJ interlined the preceding three words in place of "in mass following or drawing their government."

[22] In Dft TJ here canceled "equality and."

[23] In margin of Dft TJ canceled the following passage before interlining the remainder of the sentence: "sensible that when that compact is considered as blank paper, their general government loses it's only basis, [such] that ⟨when that⟩ those who like Peter in the tale of a tub deem every thing as authorised ⟨by that instrument⟩ which they can find in ⟨it⟩ that instrument in so many words, in so many syllables or so many letters, it is making it a blank paper."

[24] In Dft TJ here canceled "throw us."

[25] In Dft TJ first wrote "the basis of reason and justice" before altering the passage to read as above.

Memoir on the Megalonyx

[10 Feb. 1797]

To the American Philosophical society.[1]

In a letter of July 3. I informed our late most worthy President that some bones of a very large animal of the clawed-kind[2] had been recently discovered within this state, and promised a communication on the subject as soon as we could recover what were still recoverable of them.   It is well known that the substratum of the country beyond the Blue ridge is a lime-stone, abounding with large caverns, the earthy floors of which are highly impregnated with nitre; and that the inhabitants are in the habit of extracting the nitre from them. In digging the floor of one of these caves, belonging to Frederic Gromer[5] in the county of Greenbriar, the labourers, at the depth of 2. or 3. feet came to some bones, the size and form of which bespoke an animal unknown to them. The nitrous impregnation of the earth had served to preserve them till such a degree of petrification was brought on as had secured them from further decay.[6] The importance of the discovery was not known to those who made it. Yet it excited conversation in the neighborhood, and led persons[7] of vague curiosity to seek and take away the bones. It was fortunate for science that one of it's zealous and well informed friends, Colo. John Stewart, of that neighborhood, heard of the discovery, and, sensible from their description that they were of an animal not known, took measures without delay for saving those which still remained. He was kind enough to inform me of the incident, and to forward me the bones from time to time as they were recovered. To these I was enabled accidentally to add some others by the kindness of a Mr. Hopkins of New York, who had visited the cave. These bones are 1. a small fragment of the femur or thigh bone, being in fact only it's lower extremity, separated from the main bone at it's epiphysis,[8] so as to give us only the two condyles. But these are nearly entire.

2. a Radius, perfect.[9]

3. an Ulna or fore-arm, perfect, except that it is broke in two.

A Memoire On the Discovery of certain bones of an Animal[3] of the clawed[4] kind in the Western parts of Virginia.

[291]

4. three claws, and half a dozen other bones of the foot; but whether of a fore or hinder foot is not evident.

About a foot in length of the residue of the femur was found. It was split thro' the middle, and in that state was used as a support for one of the saltpetre vats. This piece was afterwards lost; but it's measures had been first taken as will be stated hereafter.

These bones only enable us to class the animal with the Unguiculated Quadrupeds, [10] and, of these, the lion being nearest to him in size, we will compare him with that animal of whose anatomy Monsr. Daubenton has furnished very accurate measures in his tables at the end of Buffon's natural history of the lion. These measures were taken as he* informs us from 'a large lion of Africa,' in which quarter the largest are †said to be produced. I shall select from his measures only those where we have the corresponding bones, converting them into our own inch and it's fractions, that the comparison may be more obvious: and to avoid the embarrasment of designating our animal always by circumlocution and description, I will venture to refer to him by the name of the Great-claw, or Megalonyx, to which he seems sufficiently entitled by the distinguished size of that member.

* Buffon XVIII. 38. of the Paris edition in 31. v. 12mo † 2. De Manet. 117.

	Megalonyx Inches	Lion Inches
length of the Ulna[11] or forearm	20.1	13.7
height of the Olecranum	3.5	1.85
breadth of the Ulna from the point of the Coronoide apophysis to the extremity of the Olecranum	9.55	
breadth of the Ulna at it's middle	3.8	
thickness at the same place	1.14	
circumference at the same place	6.7	
length of the Radius[12]	17.75	12.37
breadth of the radius at it's head[13]	2.65	1.38
circumference at it's middle[14]	7.4	3.62
breadth at it's lower extremity[15]	4.05	1.18
diameter of the lower extremity of the femur, to wit, at the base of the two condyles	4.2	2.65
transverse diameter of the larger condyle at it's base	3.	
circumference of both condyles at their base[16]	11.65	
diameter of the Middle of the femur[17]	4.25	1.15
hollow of the femur at the same place[18]	1.25	
thickness of the bone surrounding the hollow[19]	1.5	
length of the longest claw	7.5	1.41
length of the 2d. phalanx of the same	3.2	1.41

The largest of the bones of the foot[20] in my possession

	inches
it's greatest diameter, or breadth at the joint	2.45
it's smallest diameter, or thickness at the same place	2.28
it's circumference at the same place	7.1
it's circumference at the middle	5.3

	of the longest toe	Middle sized toe	Shortest toe
2d. phalanx, it's length	3.2	2.95	
greatest diameter at it's head or upper joint	1.84	2.05	
smallest diameter at the same place	1.4	1.54	
circumference at the same place	5.25	5.8	
3d. phalanx, it's length	*7.5	†5.9	3.5
greatest diameter at it's head or upper joint	2.7	2.	1.45
smallest diameter at the same place	.95	.9	.55
circumference at the same place	6.45	4.8	

* supposing $\frac{3}{4}$ I. of the point broken off.[21]

† supposing $\frac{1}{4}$ I. of the point broken off.[22]

Were we to estimate the size of our animal by a comparison with that of the lion on the principle of EX PEDE HERCULEM, by taking the longest claw of each as the module of their measure, it would give us a being out of the limits of nature. It is fortunate therefore that we have some of the larger bones of the limbs which may furnish a more certain estimate of his stature. Let us suppose then[23] that his dimensions of height, length and thickness, and of the principal members composing these, were of the same proportions with those of the lion. In the table of M. Daubenton, an Ulna of 13.78 inches belonged to a lion $42\frac{1}{2}$ inches high over the shoulders: then an Ulna of 20.1 inches bespeaks a Megalonyx of 5 f.–1.75 I. height.[24] And as Animals who have the same proportions of height, length and thickness, have their bulk or weight proportioned to the *cubes of any one of their dimensions, the cube of 42.5 I. is to 262. ℔ the height and weight of M. Daubenton's lion, as the cube of 61.75 inches to 803. ℔ the height and weight of the Megalonyx: which would prove him a little more than three times the size of the lion. I suppose that we should be safe in considering, on the authority of M. Daubenton, his lion as a large one. But let it pass as one only of the ordinary size; and that the Megalonyx whose bones happen to have been found was also of the ordinary size. It does †appear that there was dissected for the academy of sciences at Paris a lion of 4 f.–9$\frac{3}{8}$I. height. This individual would weigh 644. ℔. and would be in his species what a man of 8. feet height would be in ours. Such men have existed. A Megalonyx equally monstrous would be 7. feet high, and would weigh 2000. ℔. But the ordinary race, and not the monsters of it, are the object of our present enquiry.

* Buff. XXII. 121.

† Buff. XVIII. 15.

I have used the height alone of this animal to deduce his bulk, on the supposition that he might have been[25] formed in the proportions of the lion. But these were not his proportions. He was much thicker than the lion in proportion to his height, in his limbs certainly, and probably therefore in his body. The diameter of his radius at it's upper end is near twice as great as that of the lion, and at it's lower end more than thrice as great, which gives a mean proportion of $2\frac{1}{2}$ for 1.[26] The femur of the lion was less than $1\frac{1}{4}$ I. diameter. That of the Megalonyx is $4\frac{1}{4}$ I. which is more than three for one.[27] And as bodies of the same length and substance have their weights proportioned to the squares of their diameters, this excess of caliber compounded with the height would greatly aggravate the bulk of this animal. But when our subject has already carried us beyond the limits of nature hitherto known, it is safest to stop at the most moderate conclusions, and not to follow appearances through all the conjectures they would furnish, but leave these to be corroborated, or corrected by future discoveries. Let us only say then, what we may safely say, that he was *more* than three times as large as the lion: that he stood as preeminently at the head of the column of clawed animals[28] as the Mammoth stood[29] [at that of the elephant, rhinoceros, and hippopotamus: and that he may have been as formidable an antagonist to the mammoth as the lion to the elephant].

A difficult question now presents itself. What is become of the Great-claw? Some light may be thrown on this by asking another question. Do the wild animals of the first magnitude in any instance fix their dwellings in a thickly inhabited country? Such I mean as the Elephant, the Rhinoceros, the lion, the tyger?[30] As far as my reading and recollection serve me, I think they do not: but I hazard the opinion doubtingly because it is not the result of full[31] enquiry. Africa is chiefly inhabited along the margin of it's seas and rivers. The interior desart is the domain of the Elephant, the Rhinoceros, the lion, the tyger. Such individuals as have their haunts nearest the inhabited frontier, enter it occasionally and commit depredations when pressed by hunger: but the mass of their nation (if I may use the term) never approach the habitation of man, nor are within reach of it.[32] When our ancestors arrived here, the Indian population below the falls of the rivers was about the twentieth part of what it now is. In this state of things an animal resembling the lion[33] seems to have been known even in the lower country. Most of the accounts given by the earlier adventurers to this part of America, make a lion one of the animals of our forests. Sr. John Hawkins mentions this in 1564. Thomas Harriot, a man of learning and of distinguished candor, who resided in Virginia in 1587. does the same. So also does Bul-

Hakluyt 541. edition of 1589. id. 757. Smith's Hist. Virga. 10.

lock in his account of Virginia written about 1627. He says he drew his information from Pierce, Willoughby, Claiborne and others who had been here, and from his own father who had lived here 12. years. It does not appear whether the fact is stated on their own view or on information from the Indians. Probably the latter. The progress of the new population would soon drive off the larger animals, and the largest first. In the present interior of our continent there is surely space and range enough for elephants and lions, if in that climate they could subsist; and for mammoths and megalonyxes who may subsist there. [34] Our entire ignorance of the immense country to the West and North West, and of it's contents, does not authorize us to say what it does not contain. Moreover it is a fact well known, and always susceptible of verification, that on a rock on the bank of the Kanhawa near it's confluence with the Ohio, there are carvings of many animals of that country, and among these one which has always been considered as a perfect figure of a lion. And these are so rudely done as to leave no room to suspect a foreign hand. [35] This could not have been the smaller and [36] mane-less lion of Mexico and Peru, known also in Africa both in antient and modern times, tho' denied by M. de Buffon: because, like the greater African lion, he is a tropical animal. And his want of a mane would not satisfy the figure. This figure then [37] must have been taken from some other prototype, and that prototype must have resembled the lion sufficiently to satisfy the figure, [38] and was probably the Animal the description of which by the Indians made Hawkins Harriot and others conclude there were lions here. May we not presume that prototype to have been the Great claw? [39] Many traditions are in possession of our upper inhabitants, which themselves have heretofore considered as fables; but which have regained credit since the discovery of these bones. There has always been a story current that the first company of adventurers who went to seek an establishment in the county of Greenbriar the night of their arrival were alarmed at their camp by the terrible roarings of some animal unknown to them, that he went round and round their camp, that at times they [40] saw his eyes like two balls of fire, that their horses were so agonised with fear that they couched down on the earth, and their dogs crept in among them, not daring to bark. Their fires it was thought protected them, and the next morning they abandoned the country. This was little more than 30. years ago. [41]—In the year 1765. George Wilson and John Davis having gone to hunt on Cheat river, a branch of the Monongehela, heard one night at a distance from their camp a tremendous roaring which became louder and louder as it approached, till they thought it resembled thunder and even made the

Bullock pa. 5.

Arist. Anim. 9.4.
Plin. VIII. 16
Kolbe
Buff. XVIII. 18

earth tremble under them. The animal prowled round their camp a considerable time, during which their dogs tho on all other occasions fierce[42] crept to their feet, could not be excited from their camp nor even encouraged to bark. About daylight they heard the same sound repeated from the knob of a mountain about a mile off and within a minute it was answered by a similar voice from a neighboring knob. Colo. John Stuart had this account from Wilson in the year 1769. who was afterwards Lieutt. Colo. of a Pensva. regiment in the revolution war, and some years after from Davies who is now living in Kentuckey. These circumstances multiply the points of resemblance between this Animal and the lion. M. de la Harpe of the French academy in his abridgment of the General history of voiages speaking of the Moors, says 'it is remarkeable that when during their huntings they meet with lions, their horses, tho' famous for swiftness, are seized with such terror that they become motionless, and their dogs, equally frightened creep to the feet of their master or of his horse.' Mr. Sparrman in his Voyage to the cape of good hope chap. 11. says 'we could plainly discover by our animals when the lions, whether they roared or not, were observing us at a small distance. For in that case the hounds did not venture to bark, but crept quite close to the Hottentots; and our oxen and horses sighed deeply, frequently hanging back, and pulling slowly with all their might at the strong straps with which they were tied to the waggon. They also laid themselves down on the ground and stood up alternately, as if they did not know what to do with themselves, and even as if they were in the agonies of death.' He adds that 'when the lion roars, he puts his mouth to the ground, so that the sound is equally diffused to every quarter.' M. de Buffon [XVIII. 31.] describes the roaring of the lion as, by it's echos resembling thunder: and Sparrman c. 12. mentions that the eyes of the lion can be seen a considerable distance in the dark and that the Hottentots watch for his eyes for their government. The phosphoric appearance of the eye in the dark seems common to all animals of the Cat kind.[43] The terror excited by these animals is not confined to brutes alone. A person of the name of Draper had gone in the year 1770. to hunt on the Kanhawa. He had turned his horse loose with a bell on, and had not yet got out of hearing when his attention was recalled by the rapid ringing of the bell. Suspecting that Indians might be attempting to take off his horse he immediately returned to him, but before he arrived he was half eaten up. His dog scenting the trace of a wild beast, he followed him on it,[44] and soon came in sight of an animal of such enormous size, that tho one of our most daring hunters, and best marksmen he withdrew instantly and as silently as possible, checking and bringing off his dog.[45] He could recollect no more of

Marginal note: G'ent. & Lond. magazine for 1783.

the animal than his terrific bulk and that his general outlines were those of the Cat kind. He was familiar with our animal miscalled the panther, with our wolves and wild beasts generally [46] and would not have mistaken nor [47] shrunk from them.

In fine, the bones exist; therefore the animal has [48] existed. The movements of nature are in a never-ending circle. The animal species which has once been put into a train of motion, is still probably moving in that train. And if he be [49] still in being, there is no reason to disbelieve [50] the relations of honest men, applicable to him and to him alone. It would indeed be but conformable to the ordinary economy of nature to conjecture that she had opposed sufficient barriers to the too great multiplication of so powerful a destroyer. If lions and tygers multiplied as rabbets do, [51] all other animal nature would have been long ago destroyed, and themselves would have ultimately extinguished after eating out their pasture. It is probable then that the Great claw has at all times been the rarest of animals. Hence so little is known and so little remains of him. His existence however being at length discovered, enquiry will be excited, and further information of him will probably be obtained. [52]

The cosmogony of M. de Buffon supposes that the earth and all the other planets, primary and secondary, have been masses of melted matter struck off from the sun, by the incidence of a comet on it: that these have been cooling by degrees, first at the poles, and afterwards more and more towards their Equators; consequently that on our earth there has been a time when the temperature of the poles suited the constitution of the Elephant, the Rhinoceros and Hippopotamos: and in proportion as the remoter zones became successively too cold, these animals have retired more and more towards the Equatorial regions till now that they are reduced to the torrid zone as the ultimate stage of their existence. To support this theory he assumes the tusks of the Mammoth to 2. Epoq. have been those of an elephant, some of his teeth to have belonged to the 233. 234. hippopotamos, and his largest grinders to an animal much greater than either, and to have been deposited on the Missouri, the Ohio, the Holston when those latitudes were not yet too cold for the constitutions of these animals. He would of course then claim for the lion, now also reduced to the torrid zone and it's vicinities, the bones lately discovered; and consider them as an additional proof of his system; [53] and that there has been a time when our latitudes suited the lion as well as the other animals of that temperament. This is not the place to [54] [observe that we have all seen the teeth [55] of the Mammoth as well those ascribed to the Hippopotamos as those left to himself fixed in the same jaw and now in possession of Dr. Wistar one of the worthy Vicepresidents of our society [56] in the city of Philadelphia, nor to] examine all the other weak points of this system, in which indeed almost all are weak and untenable. But let us for a moment grant this with his former postulata, and ask how they will consist with another theory of his 'qu'il y a dans la combinaison des elemens et des autres causes physiques, quelque chose de contraire a l'aggrandissement de la nature vivante *dans ce nouveau monde*; qu'il y a des obstacles au developpement et peut-etre a la formation des grands germes.' XVIII. 145. He says that the Mammoth was

2. Ep. 223. an elephant, yet two or three [57] times as large as the elephants of Asia and Africa. That some of his teeth were those of a Hippopotamus, yet of a hippopotamus four [58] times as large as those of Africa [1. Epoq. 246. 2. Epoq. 232.] That the mammoth himself, for he still considers him as a distinct animal, 'was of a size superior to that of the largest elephants,—that he was the primary and greatest of all terrestrial animals' 2. Ep. 234. 235. We suppose him to claim the Megalonyx for a lion, yet certainly [59] a lion of more than 3 times the volume of the African. [60] I delivered to M. de Buffon the skeleton of our palmated elk called Ori-

1. Catesby. gnal or [61] Moose 7. feet high over the shoulders. [62] He is often consider-
Kalm I. 232. ably higher. I cannot find that the European elk is more than two thirds
II. 340. [63] of that height consequently not one third of the bulk of the American.

XXIX. 245 He acknoleges the palmated deer (daim) of America to be larger and stronger than that of the old world. He considers the round horned

XII. 91. 92. deer of these states and of Louisiana as the Roe and admits they
XXIX. 245. are of three times his size. Are we then from all this to draw a conclusion
V. Sup- the reverse of that of Monsr. de Buffon, that Nature, [64] has formed the
plem. 201. larger animals of America, like it's lakes, it's rivers and mountains on a greater and prouder scale than in the other hemisphere? Not at all. We are to conclude that she has formed some things large, and some things small on both sides of the earth for reasons which she has not enabled us to penetrate: and [65] that we ought not to shut our eyes upon one half of her facts and build systems on the other half. [66]

To return to our [67] Great claw, I deposit his bones with the Philosophical society as well in evidence of their existence [68] and of their dimensions as for their safe keeping and I shall think it [my] [69] duty to do the same by such others as I may be fortunate enough to obtain the recovery of hereafter. [70]

P.S. [71] After the preceding communication was ready to be delivered in
Monthly to the society, in a *periodical publication from London I met with an
Mag. Sep. account and drawing of the skeleton of an animal dug up near the river
1796. la Plata in Paraguay and now mounted in the cabinet of Natural history at Madrid. [72] The figure is not so done as to be relied on, and the account is only an abstract from that of Cuvier and Roumé. This skeleton is also

of the clawed kind, and[73] having only 4 teeth on each side above and below, all grinders,[74] is classed in this account in the family of unguiculated quadrupeds destitute of cutting teeth[75] and recieves the new denomination of Megatherium. Having nothing of our animal but the leg and foot bones, we have few points for a comparison between them. They resemble in their stature, that being 12 f.–9 I. long, and 6 f.–4$\frac{1}{2}$ I. high, and ours by computation 5 f.–1.75 I. high: in the colossal thickness of the thigh and leg bones also. They resemble too in having claws, but those of the figure appear very small and the verbal description does not satisfy us whether the claw-bone or only it's horny cover be large. They agree too in the circumstance of the two bones of the forearm being distinct and moveable on each other; which however is [believed][76] to be so common[77] as to form no mark of distinction. They differ in the following circumstances if our relations are to be trusted. The Megatherium is not of the cat form, as are the Lion, tyger and panther, but is said to have striking relations in all parts of it's body with[78] the Sloth (Bradypus) tatoo (Dasypus) pangolin (Manis) and the anteaters (Myrmecophaga and Orycteropus.)[79] According to analogy then it probably was not carnivorous, had not the phosphoric eye, nor leonine roar. But to solve satisfactorily[80] the question of identity the discovery of fore teeth, or of a jaw bone shewing it had or had not such teeth, must be waited for and hoped with patience. It may be better in the mean time to keep up even[81] the difference of name.

Dft (DLC: TJ Papers, 233: 41752-7); undated, but assigned from APS, *Transactions*, IV [1799], 258-9, which gives dates of 10 Feb. 1797 to the memoir and 10 Mch. 1797 to the postscript; consisting of a report written entirely in TJ's hand on both sides of five unnumbered sheets, possibly copied in whole or part from an earlier missing draft, and a postscript on a sixth sheet; heavily emended, the most significant changes being recorded in notes below; with one query written in margin (see note 54 below); brackets in original except where noted; TJ's block printing shown as small capitals; one passage and the location of one unkeyed insertion have been supplied from APS, *Transactions* (see notes 29 and 75 below); endorsed by TJ: "Megalonyx." Although no fair copy in TJ's hand has been found, variations between the Dft and the version printed by the American Philosophical Society suggest that one existed. Printed as "No. XXX. A Memoir on the Discovery of certain Bones of a Quadruped of the clawed Kind in the Western Parts of Virginia. By Thomas Jefferson, Esq.," in APS, *Transactions*, IV [1799], 246-60; contains datelines and signature lacking in Dft (see notes 70-1 below); with variations of capitalization, punctuation, abbreviations, paragraphing, and spelling not recorded; significant variations in wording are recorded in notes below; TJ's citations appear in printed version as footnotes keyed to text; at head of text: "Read March 10, 1797." See Sowerby, No. 3753.

With this paper TJ formally announced to the scientific world the discovery of fossilized skeletal remains of the mammal he called the megalonyx, now known to have been a form of extinct ground sloth of the Pleistocene epoch. The sequence of his work on the Dft is significant, given his late discovery of information he acknowledged in the postscript. Unfortunately, however, it is impossible to construct an exact chronology of his alterations to the manuscript.

Presumably TJ himself, on a fair copy since lost, furnished the 10 Feb. 1797 dateline that appears in APS, *Transactions*. It is unlikely that he began composition of this "memoire" before 6 Feb. 1797, for on that day he received John Stuart's letter of 16 Jan. announcing Stuart's failure to locate the substantially intact femur from which TJ had hoped to calculate the creature's size. In composing the memoir, TJ also drew on Stuart's letter for dimensions of that missing thigh bone—one foot long, four and a quarter inches in diameter—rather than using conflicting information from Archibald Stuart, which TJ relied on as late as 22 Jan. 1797 (see Archibald Stuart to TJ, 19 Aug. 1796; TJ to Benjamin Smith Barton, 10 Oct. 1796; John Stuart to TJ, 16 Jan. 1797; and TJ to Benjamin Rush, 22 Jan. 1797).

That nearly complete thigh bone, reported to TJ but never seen by him, was distinct from the SMALL FRAGMENT OF THE FEMUR he listed first among the megalonyx specimens described in the above memoir. The fragment proved elusive in its own way. As important as the femur was to TJ's deductions of the size of the megalonyx, his scientific contemporaries were unable to utilize even a piece of that bone in drawing conclusions about the animal. Perhaps due to uncertainty over its identification, Caspar WISTAR did not discuss the fragment mentioned in the memoir in a descriptive report he prepared on the megalonyx specimens (published, with illustrations from drawings by Titian Peale and Dr. W. S. Jacobs, as "No. LXXVI. A Description of the Bones deposited, by the President, in the Museum of the Society, and represented in the annexed plates," APS, *Transactions*, IV [1799], 526-31). After studying casts of the bones sent to Paris in 1802 by Charles Willson Peale, the French natural scientist Georges CUVIER—who in 1796, on the basis of information obtained in Spain by Philippe Rose Roume (ROUMÉ), had described the South American MEGATHERIUM—was unsure whether the piece had come from a femur or a humerus, and concentrated his analysis on other features (Cuvier, "Mégalonix," 359; Peale to Cuvier, 16 July 1802, in PPAmP: Peale-Sellers Papers; Boyd, "Megalonyx," 429).

TJ's initial misidentification of another bone, the radius, is reflected in his deletion from the Dft of references to the tibia (see notes 9 and 26-7 below). In his early analysis of the megalonyx remains he concluded that one bone was a tibia, a bone of the hind leg, for he would not otherwise have stated that the recovery of a complete thigh bone would mean that "we should possess a whole limb from the haunch bone to the claw inclusive" (TJ to John Stuart, 10 Nov. 1796). He maintained the notion that one of the fossils was a tibia as he penned the Dft, which originally made no mention of a radius. He subsequently revised his identification of the bone, and, in addition to substituting "radius" for "tibia" throughout, altered the sequence of entries in the table of measurements. Originally in the table he had placed entries for the "tibia" below those for the femur, thus grouping together what he thought were measurements of two long bones of the hind limb. After realizing that the supposed "tibia" was actually a radius, a bone of the forelimb, he revised the table to put those entries closer to the measurements of the bone's proper anatomical neighbor, the ulna (see notes 12-19 below).

According to his Memorandum Books, TJ left Monticello for Philadelphia on 20 Feb. and arrived in the capital late on 2 Mch. 1797. Although he possibly discovered the "tibia" error on his own and made those alterations to the Dft before his departure from Monticello, it seems likely that he only learned of his mistake when the fossils were seen in Philadelphia by a more expert anatomist such as Wistar. If so, TJ made the changes substituting the radius for the tibia in the period between his arrival in Philadelphia and the reading of the memoir to the Philosophical Society on 10 Mch. 1797. The society actually met on the evening of 3 Mch. with TJ, its newly elected president, in attendance, but after dealing with some other business adjourned for a week "on the account of a Communication to be made, before Mr. Jefferson leaves the City" (PPAmP: Ms. Minutes, 3 Mch. 1797). The minutes do not indicate whether the group originally expected to receive TJ's memoir on the 3d or, if so, whether the postponement was due to any need for him to revise the paper.

If he made a fair copy of the manuscript it stands to reason, but is not certain, that he did so before submitting the memoir to the society on the evening of 10 Mch., and that he did not alter the Dft after making the fair copy. Evidently sometime between his arrival on the 2d and the society's meeting on the 10th he saw in the September 1796 issue of the MONTHLY MAGAZINE the notice of Cuvier's description of the megatherium that impelled him to write the postscript (see Sowerby, No. 682). It has been suggested that he wrote the postscript not long before the society's 10 Mch. meeting and also made hurried changes to the Dft in light of the megatherium discovery, assigning the megalonyx to a general category of clawed animals rather than the family of large feline predators (Boyd, "Megalonyx," 425-6). Two months later, however, he continued to identify the creature as "a carnivorous animal" (TJ to Louis of Parma, 23 May 1797). The title of TJ's "memoire" is recorded in the society's minutes as "On the Discovery of certain Bones of a Quadruped of the   "—the blank suggesting that the issue of the beast's classification was not fully resolved at the time of the meeting. We may never know what taxonomic language appeared in the paper as Jonathan Williams, in his capacity as one of the society's secretaries, read it aloud to the group with TJ in the presiding chair (PPAmP: Ms. Minutes, 10 Mch. 1797).

Not all alterations to the Dft were necessarily late changes. For example, one set of emendations involved the removal of John Smith's observations from the anecdotal evidence TJ related in support of his contention that a gigantic predatory mammal still roamed North America (see notes 32 and 38 below). TJ was a close student of early Virginia history and, according to Sowerby, owned the books he cited on the subject. In this case, although he might have altered the passage relating to Smith after discussing his findings with others in Philadelphia, he could well have made those emendations as he prepared the Dft at Monticello in February. Barring discovery of new information, the various stages of the document's composition and revision remain enigmatic.

Although unmindful of the fact when he saw published accounts of the specimen in 1797, TJ had some years earlier been sent a description and sketch of the South American megatherium skeleton preserved in Spain (see William Carmichael to TJ, 26 Jan. 1789, and enclosure; and above in this series, Vol. 14: xxv-xxxiv).

In 1804 Cuvier, rejecting any association of the megalonyx with catlike meat eaters, demonstrated that both it and the megatherium were herbivores related to modern sloths. He also considered the two animals, because of a substantial difference in size, to be different species within the same genus, thus explicitly contradicting French geologist Barthélemy Faujas de Saint-Fond, who called both animals "mégalonix" and refused to classify them with the sloths. Cuvier's analysis therefore reinforced TJ's call for preserving the DIFFERENCE OF NAME pending further study. Wistar, too, in his report on the megalonyx bones, had noted apparent anatomical differences between the animals. However, by 1803 TJ himself believed that the megalonyx and the megatherium were probably the same, and when he became aware that Cuvier and Faujas were "rather at war" over classification of the beasts, he did not consider the arguments of the former to be conclusive. He applied Faujas's term "artificial" to Cuvier's taxonomy (Cuvier, "Mégalonix," 358-75; Cuvier, "Sur le Megatherium, Autre animal de la famille des Paresseux . . .," *Annales du Muséum National d'Histoire Naturelle*, 5 [1804], 376-87; TJ to Lacépède, 24 Feb. 1803; TJ to John Vaughan, 15 Aug. 1805). Nevertheless, modern paleontology, like Cuvier's work, makes a clear distinction between the animals, classifying the megalonyx and the megatherium in separate families of prehistoric ground sloths. To recognize TJ's role in publicizing the discovery, in 1822 another French scientist, Anselme Desmarest, labeled the Virginia specimen *Megalonyx jeffersonii*, the name by which the species is still known (Björn Kurtén and Elaine Anderson, *Pleistocene Mammals of North America* [New York, 1980], 135-8; Greene, *American Science*, 284).

[1] Line lacking in APS, *Transactions*.
[2] Preceding two words interlined in place of "family of the lion, tyger, panther &c."
[3] APS, *Transactions*: "a Quadruped."
[4] Word interlined in place of "Unguiculated."

[5] APS, *Transactions*: "Cromer."

[6] APS, *Transactions*: "The nitrous impregnation of the earth together with a small degree of petrification had probably been the means of their preservation."

[7] Word interlined in place of "children and others."

[8] Word interlined in place of "symphysis."

[9] Preceding two words written over erased "[Tibia] [. . .], perfect," with an estimated three illegible words in the middle of the erasure. In the next line, "an Ulna" is written over an illegible erasure.

[10] Sentence to this point interlined in place of "These bones, and particularly the claws, sufficiently characterize the animal to a species [. . .] of the same species with the lion, tyger, panther, etc."

[11] Here and at two other occurrences of the word in this table, TJ interlined "Ulna" in place of "Cubit."

[12] Line inserted in place of "diameter of the middle of the femur 4.25 1.15."

[13] Line inserted in place of "hollow of the femur at the same place [1.25]."

[14] Line inserted in place of "thickness of the bone surrounding the hollow [1.5]."

[15] Line inserted.

[16] Below this line TJ originally wrote an entry that read "length of the tibia or shank bone 17.75 12.37." He subsequently interlined "Radius" in place of "tibia" and canceled the entire line.

[17] TJ originally wrote "diameter of Radius." He wrote this entire line in place of "breadth of the tibia at it's head," followed by illegibly canceled measurements. He also illegibly canceled another pair of measurements below that line.

[18] Line inserted in place of "circumference at it's middle 7.4 3.62."

[19] Line inserted in place of "breadth at it's lower extremity," followed by illegibly canceled measurements that TJ evidently replaced with "4.05 1.18," which he also subsequently canceled. He also drew a bracket enclosing the canceled entries recorded in this and preceding three notes.

[20] Word interlined in place of "carpus or tarsus."

[21] APS, *Transactions*: "It is actually $6\frac{3}{4}$ inches long, but about $\frac{3}{4}$ inch appear to have been broken off."

[22] APS, *Transactions*: "Actually 5.65 but about $\frac{1}{4}$ inch is broken off."

[23] Word interlined. At the beginning of this sentence TJ canceled "from the general conformity of his bones with those of the lion."

[24] Both occurrences of "an Ulna" in this sentence are interlined in place of "a cubit."

[25] Preceding three words interlined in place of "was."

[26] Sentence interlined in place of canceled "M. Daubenton not having given us the diameter of the ⟨Cubit⟩ ulna of his lion, we can only compare the hinder limb." TJ also interlined and canceled "the tibia of the lion was 3.62 Inches in circumference at the middle. That of the Megalonyx [7.4] I. which is more than the double."

[27] Preceding two words interlined in place of "times as great." TJ interlined the next two sentences and the beginning of the succeeding sentence through "that he was" in place of canceled "as the tibia of the lion was 3.62 I. in circumference at the middle: that of the Megalonyx 7.4 I. which is more than the double. And as bones of the same length have their bulks proportioned to the squares of their diameters, this would lead to much stronger conclusions. It is possible however that the flesh of this animal might not exceed that of the lion in the same degree with his bones so that it is safest to conclude only in the general that he was considerably."

[28] Preceding two words interlined in place of "the lion, tyger and panther."

[29] Passage ends here at foot of a page; remainder of sentence supplied from APS, *Transactions*.

[30] TJ here canceled "I rather believe they do not."

[31] Word interlined. TJ originally wrote "actual research and enquiry into the subject."

[32] TJ interlined the next twelve sentences in place of the following passage, with his brackets enclosing the citation to John Smith's *History*: "in the interior country of our continent there is surely space and range enough for elephants and lions, if that climate suited them and for mammoths and megalonixes whom it does suit. Our entire ignorance of the immense ⟨space⟩ country to the West and N. West and of it's contents, does not authorize us to say what it does not contain. When capt. Smith who first effected the permanent settlement of our colony landed here in 1607

the Indian population below the falls of the rivers was about the twentieth part of what it now is: and the Indians having no flocks of domestic quadrupeds or fowls and little culture there was nothing to tempt the greater animals to remain among them or near them, while their perpetual hunting would be a cause for their retiring to a distance. Yet Capt. Smith [Hist. Virga. pa. 10.] mentions the lion among the game sometimes brought in and eaten by the Indians and speaks of a lion skin used as a mattres. Now certainly the animal we miscall a panther, or any other animal of our woods could not have been mistaken by capt. Smith for a lion. He had served many years in the [. . .] of the Turks in Europe and Asia, had been a very general traveller, and could not have been altogether unacquainted with the lion."

[33] TJ here canceled "(doubtless the Great claw)."

[34] TJ first wrote "to whom it is adapted," then altered the clause to read as above.

[35] TJ wrote the next two sentences as an insertion beginning on the line and continuing in the margin, probably adding the second sentence sometime after writing the first. He placed the citations at the edge of the margin alongside the insertion.

[36] TJ here canceled "injubate."

[37] TJ first began the sentence "But as there was no lion here, that" before altering it to read as above.

[38] Remainder of sentence interlined in place of "and sufficiently to impose on Capt. Smith."

[39] Preceding two words interlined in place of "Megalonyx."

[40] TJ first wrote "that they often," then altered the phrase to read as above.

[41] TJ first wrote "probably about between 30. and 40. years ago" before altering the passage to read as above.

[42] Preceding six words interlined.

[43] Sentence interlined.

[44] TJ first wrote "he perceiving the tract of a wild beast and following on it," then altered the passage to read as above.

[45] For the portion of the sentence following "marksmen," TJ first wrote and canceled "he lost the powers of his mind, and fled from irresistable instinct," then by successive changes altered the passage to read as above.

[46] Preceding eleven words interlined in place of "panthers, wolves and such animals."

[47] Preceding two words inserted in margin.

[48] TJ first wrote "must have," then altered the words to read as above.

[49] Preceding two words interlined in Dft in place of "it is."

[50] In place of sentence to this point, APS, *Transactions* reads: "For if one link in nature's chain might be lost, another and another might be lost, till this whole system of things should evanish by piece-meal; a conclusion not warranted by the local disappearance of one or two species of animals, and opposed by the thousands and thousands of instances of the renovating power constantly exercised by nature for the reproduction of all her subjects, animal, vegetable, and mineral. If this animal then has once existed, it is probable on this general view of the movements of nature that he still exists, and rendered still more probable by."

[51] APS, *Transactions* here adds "or eagles as pigeons."

[52] TJ evidently inserted this paragraph in space he left on the page during his initial drafting.

[53] In APS, *Transactions* sentence to this point reads: "Should the bones of our animal, which may hereafter be found, differ only in size from those of the lion, they may on this hypothesis be claimed for the lion, now also reduced to the torrid zone, and its vicinities, and may be considered as an additional proof of this system."

[54] Here in margin TJ wrote "qu. the fact?" In APS, *Transactions* remainder of sentence reads "discuss theories of the earth, nor to question the gratuitous allotment to different animals of teeth not differing in any circumstance."

[55] Word interlined in place of "grinders," which TJ had previously interlined in place of "teeth."

[56] TJ first wrote "one of our worthy members."

[57] Preceding three words interlined in place of a canceled word, possibly "six."

[58] Word interlined in place of a canceled word, possibly "nine."

[59] In APS, *Transactions* sentence to this point reads "If the bones of the megalonyx be ascribed to the lion, they must certainly have been of."

[60] TJ here wrote and canceled "He says that our Moose is a Renne."

[61] Preceding five words written in margin.

[62] TJ interlined the next four sentences in place of the following canceled passage: "The [Renne] is but of   feet. The American then is of   times the volume of the European. The animal which we miscall a panther, he calls a Cougar. I delivered to him the stuffed skin of one 2. or 3. times greater than the Cougar of   . He says that our deer is the Roe. Yet all who have seen ⟨the⟩ our deer ⟨of America⟩ and the Roe of Europe, and thousands have seen both, know that the former is of 3. or 4. times the bulk of the latter."

[63] APS, *Transactions* lacks citation to works by Catesby and Kalm.

[64] TJ here canceled "whatever she may have done as to smaller animals and objects."

[65] Preceding two words interlined in place of an illegible word and "discover."

[66] TJ originally continued this sentence with a semicolon and the following passage, which he subsequently canceled: "and that it is better to confess ignorance in things not made than to propagate error ⟨in things⟩ on subjects not made for our comprehension."

[67] TJ here canceled "Megalonyx."

[68] Having filled the sheet, TJ wrote the remainder of this sentence in the margin.

[69] Word torn, supplied from APS, *Transactions*.

[70] Here APS, *Transactions* adds a signature, "TH: JEFFERSON," and "Monticello, Feb. 10th, 1797."

[71] Here APS, *Transactions* adds: "March 10th, 1797."

[72] TJ here canceled "this [. . .] skeleton is also."

[73] TJ here canceled "wanting front."

[74] Remainder of sentence interlined in place of "falls into the linnaean class of   ."

[75] TJ wrote the preceding four words in the margin without keying their intended location. Placement of the phrase here follows APS, *Transactions*.

[76] Word supplied from APS, *Transactions*. Dft: "beloved."

[77] APS, *Transactions*: "usual."

[78] In APS, *Transactions* remainder of sentence reads "the bradypus, dasypus, pangolin, &c."

[79] TJ here canceled "it has not then probably the phosphoric eye. Probably also it is not carnivorous. The Leonine roar," then interlined and canceled "according to analogy then with this family it probably is not carniv."

[80] Word interlined.

[81] Word lacking in APS, *Transactions*.

From James Madison

DEAR SIR   Philada. Feby. 11. 1797

After several little turns in the mode of conveying you notice of your election, recurrence was had to the precedent of leaving the matter to the Senate, where on the casting vote of Mr. Adams, the notification was referred to the President of the U. States, in preference of the President of the Senate. You will see in the papers the state of the votes, and the manner of counting and proclaiming them. You will see also the intimation given by Mr. A. of the arrangement he has made for taking the oath of office. I understand he has given another intimation which excites some curiosity, and gives rise to several reflections which will occur to you: it is, that he means to take the advice of the Senate on his coming into office whether the offices held during pleasure are or are not vacated by the political demise of His predecessor?[1] This is the substance. I do not aim at or know the terms, of the question; of which previous notice is thus given that the members of the Senate may the better make up their opinions. What room is there for such a question at all? Must it not have been settled by precedent? On what principle is the Senate to be consulted? If this step be the result of deliberation and system, it seems to shew 1. that the maxims of the British Govt. are still uppermost in his mind. 2 That the practice of his predecessor are not laws to him, or that he considers a second election of the same person as a continuation of the same reign. 3 that the Senate is to be brought more into Executive agency than heretofore.

Accounts have been received of the arrival of Pinkney in France, but not at Paris. Nothing yet from Monroe since he knew of his recall. Every thing relating to that quarter remains in statu quo.

You will find in the inclosed papers that Buonaparte has nearly cut up another austrian army. It is to be hoped that its consequences may force the Emperor to a peace, and thro' him, Great Britain. Adieu.

This goes by Mr. Bloodworth son of the Senator from N. Carolina appointed to carry you notification of your appointment.

RC (DLC: Madison Papers); unsigned; endorsed by TJ as received 2 Mch. 1797 and so recorded in SJL. For enclosures, see below.

The MANNER OF COUNTING AND PROCLAIMING the electoral votes was described in a special supplement to the *Philadelphia Gazette* of 11 Feb., which gave an account of the joint meeting of Congress in the House of Representatives. As president of the Senate, Adams was in charge of the electoral count. The newspapers carried his address outlining the procedures to be followed and announced the results of the vote.

Probably one of the inclosed PAPERS was the *Philadelphia Gazette*, which delayed publication on 10 Feb. to include a letter from Napoleon Bonaparte to the French Directory of 1 Dec. 1796, announcing his victory over Austrian forces at the battle of Arcola, which he declared had "decided the fate of Italy."

THIS GOES BY MR. BLOODWORTH: for the plight of the dispatch and correspondence carried by Samuel Bloodworth, see Timothy Pickering to TJ, 16 Feb. 1797. Pickering had Virginia Congressman Samuel J. Cabell return this letter to Madison on 16 Feb. 1797, and, according to SJL, TJ did not receive it until he arrived in Philadelphia (Madison, *Papers*, XVI, 492-3).

[1] MS: "precedecessor."

From Timothy Pickering

Department of State
Philadelphia Feby. 11. 1797.

SIR

I have the honor to inform you, that pursuant to the request of the Senate communicated to him yesterday, the President of the United States has directed me to transmit to you the inclosed certificate, under the hand and seal of the present Vice-President, of your being elected, agreeably to the Constitution, Vice-President of the United States of America.

The bearer, Mr. Bloodworth, son of Timothy Bloodworth Esqr. Senator from North-Carolina, is specially charged with this dispatch. I have the honor to be with great respect sir, your most obt. servant,

TIMOTHY PICKERING

RC (DLC); at foot of text: "Thomas Jefferson Esquire"; endorsed by TJ as received 24 Feb. 1797 and so recorded in SJL. FC (Lb in DNA: RG 59, DL). Enclosure: Certificate of TJ's election, 10 Feb. 1797, signed by Adams as vice president of the United States and president of the Senate, notifying TJ that on 8 Feb. the Congress had convened, and in its presence the vice president had opened the certificates, counted the electoral votes, and determined TJ's election (MS in MHi, in clerk's hand except for signature by Adams, bearing seal).

From Timothy Pickering

Department of State
SIR   Philadelphia Feby. 11. 1797.

I have this day committed to Mr. Samuel Bloodworth, son of the Senator from North-Carolina, the original certificate of the President of the Senate, of your being elected Vice-President of the United States, which he is specially charged to deliver to you in person. But for the greater certainty of your receiving this notice, I have thought it expedient to convey to you a copy of the certificate by post: you will find it inclosed.

The House of Representatives referred the mode of communicating the notice of your election, to the Senate, who requested the President of the United States to cause the same to be transmitted to you, and by his direction Mr. Bloodworth has been employed as the bearer of the original certificate. I have the honor to be with great respect sir, your most obt. servant   TIMOTHY PICKERING

RC (DLC); at foot of text: "Thomas Jefferson Esquire"; endorsed by TJ. Recorded in SJL as received at Monticello, 21 Mch. 1797. PrC (MHi: Pickering Papers). For enclosure, see note to preceding document.

To James Lyle

DEAR SIR   Monticello Feb. 12. 1797.

Your favor of Oct. 25 came to hand in due time. Your [manner] of charging interest on my bonds is I believe the usual one. Being prepared for my departure to Philadelphia, I am not able to examine the particulars of the paiments. As far as my memory serves me I thought the overpaiment of the first bond by Mr. Donald's bill was a few pounds more than you make it. But I may misremember, or there may be a difference in the dates of the paiments. This is of no consequence, for as we agree in principles, and facts will speak for themselves, we can find no difficulty in our settlement. As soon as the Bedford bonds shall be completely collected and paid to you, I shall wish to have a settlement, and agree precisely as to the balance.

I should sooner have answered your letter, but I was anxious in the answer to say with some certainty when I shall wind up our affair altogether. I am now able to do this on tolerably sure grounds; and to say that I will pay you

> 1000. Dollars before the 1st. day of October of this year[1]
>
> 1000. Dollars before the 1st. day of Oct. of the next year
>
> 3000. Dollars before the 1st. day of July of the year after

the next, that is to say 1799. if so much shall be then due, and if more than that be due it shall be paid the year following, to wit in 1800. I hope the present year will bring to your hands all the Bedford collection. As soon as it is in I will thank you for a statement of all the receipts under that, and we will then immediately proceed to a settlement conclusive to that period. I am with affectionate esteem Dear Sir Your friend & servt   TH: JEFFERSON

PrC (MHi); faded; at foot of text: "Mr. James Lyle"; endorsed by TJ in ink on verso.

A letter from Lyle to TJ, recorded in SJL as written on 15 Apr. and received on 28 Apr. 1797, and one from TJ to Lyle of 30 Apr. 1797 have not been found.

[1] Preceding three words interlined in place of "next."

From Timothy Pickering

SIR   Department of State February 16. 1797.

On the 11th. instant I delivered the inclosed packet to Mr. Bloodworth, son of the Senator from North-Carolina, to deliver to you with his own hand. To-day it was returned to me by the father with the inclosed note. I also wrote you by the mail which left Philadelphia last monday, to communicate the copy of the certificate of your election to the office of vice-President of the United States, by way of precaution, lest any accident should prevent your receiving the original in due time by Mr. Bloodworth. Under these circumstances, and learning that you proposed leaving monticello about this time, it has been thought unnecessary now to forward the packet by a new messenger. I shall commit it to the mail of to-morrow, to meet you on your way. I have the honor to be &c.   TIMOTHY PICKERING

FC (Lb in DNA: RG 59, DL); above salutation: "Thomas Jefferson Esqr." Recorded in SJL as received at Georgetown, 24 Feb. 1797. Enclosures: (1) Timothy Bloodworth to Timothy Pickering, 16 Feb. 1797, informing the secretary of state that his son, Samuel Bloodworth, was confined by illness in Wilmington, Delaware, and was unable to deliver the dispatches, which were being returned to the secretary of state (RC in DLC). (2) Timothy Pickering to TJ, 11 Feb. 1797 (first letter), and enclosure.

From Mary Jefferson

Varina Feb. 27th. 1796 [i.e. 1797]

We arrived here, Dear Papa, last thursday without any accident and found my sister and her children in perfect health; she enjoying the satisfaction arising from the consciousness of fulfilling her duty to the utmost extent. But it is one she has always had. It would please you, I am sure, to see what an economist, what a manager she is become. The more I see of her the more I am sensible how much more deserving she is of you than I am, but my dear Papa suffer me to tell you that the love, the gratitude she has for you can never surpass mine; it would not be possible. * * * Adieu, dear Papa. It is one o'clock. The letters go off to-morrow by daylight and I only knew this night that I could write to you or I should have written to Sallie Cropper. Adieu dear Papa; believe me your most affectionate child.

Tr (ViU: Margaret and Olivia Taylor deposit); probably 19th-century transcript secured by Sarah Nicholas Randolph; misdated, with date assigned from TJ's reply of 11 Mch. 1797 and entry in SJL; at head of text: "Maria Jefferson to Thomas Jefferson." Recorded in SJL as received 7 Mch. 1797.

To Martha Jefferson Randolph

Chester-town Maryland Feb. 28. 1797.

I have got so far, my dear Martha, on my way to Philadelphia which place I shall not reach till the day after tomorrow. I have lost one day at Georgetown by the failure of the stages, and three days by having suffered myself to be persuaded at Baltimore to cross the bay and come by this route as quicker and pleasanter. After being forced back on the bay by bad weather in a first attempt to cross it, the second brought me over after a very rough passage, too late for the stage.—So far I am well, tho' much fatigued. I hope Mr. Randolph and Maria joined you long ago, and that you are all well. Tell Mr. Randolph that eleven dollars have been given in Baltimore and Philadelphia for the best James river tobacco, and that it is believed it will still rise considerably. It will be worth his while to have the making of his crab cyder well attended to hereafter, as I learn here that good cyder of the qualities commonly at market sell for a quarter of a dollar the bottle, wholesale, including in that the price of the bottle. Crab-cyder would probably command more. Wheat is at 2. dollars at Baltimore, and no immediate apprehensions of a fall. Present him my affections. My best love to yourself, Maria & the little ones. Adieu.

RC (NNPM); unsigned.

Notes on a Paragraph by John Henry

[after 1 Mch. 1797]

A paragraph written by Mr. Henry a Senator of the US. from Maryland, and inserted in Bache's paper about the 1st. of March 97. It is in his handwriting. It was[1] given by him to Mr. Hurt to copy and insert in the public papers. Mr. Hurt gave it to me.

MS (DLC); entirely in TJ's hand; undated and unsigned.

The PARAGRAPH in question from the *Aurora* has not been identified, nor is it known how long after its publication TJ made these notes. John Henry was a SENATOR until 10 Dec. 1797, when he resigned to serve as governor of Maryland, and he died on 16 Dec. 1798. Evidently the paragraph's courier was John HURT, a former military chaplain from Virginia (*Biog. Dir. Cong.*, 1174; Madison, *Papers*, XIII, 233, XVI, 8n, XVII, 388n; Hurt to TJ, 31 Aug. 1801).

[1] TJ here canceled "copied."

From James Wood

SIR   In Council 3d. March 1797.

I Contemplate with great pleasure the Change which is to take place in the penal Laws of the Commonwealth; and feel Much Anxiety that No time Shou'd be lost in bringing it into Complete Operation. The Law having Confided to the Executive, the purchase of a Sufficient Quantity of Land, and the direction of erecting the Necessary buildings for the Confinement and Accomodation of the Convicts; we feel Ourselves embarrassed from a want of Knowledge in Architecture, to fix upon the proper plan of a building to Answer the purposes of the Law. Our thoughts have turned On you, Sir, as best Qualified to give us Advice and Assistance in the Execution of this business. I do Myself the honor of enclosing the Act of Assembly, and take the liberty of Requesting the favor of you, to turn your thoughts to the Subject, and that you will have the goodness to Suggest to the Board, your Opinion as to the plan, as well as the Quantity of Land which you May deem Necessary for the purpose. I have the honor to be with due Consideration and Sincere esteem. Sir Yr most Obt. & Mo. hble Servt.   JAMES WOOD

RC (ViW); at foot of text: "Tho Jefferson Esq"; endorsed by TJ as received 24 Mch. 1797 and so recorded in SJL. FC (Vi: Executive Letterbook). Enclosure: see below.

The enclosed LAW was "An Act to amend the Penal Laws of this Commonwealth," passed 15 Dec. 1796, which specified prison terms rather than capital punishment for crimes other than first-degree murder. Prisoners were to labor in a penitentiary during their sentences, and each would spend a portion of the term in solitary confinement. The act authorized the governor to spend up to $30,000 for land and the construction of "a gaol and penitentiary house" large enough "to contain with convenience two hundred convicts at least" (Shepherd, *Statutes*, II, 5-14).

TJ's own "Bill for Proportioning Crimes and Punishments in Cases Heretofore Capital," part of the revisal of Virginia's laws that he, George Wythe, and Edmund Pendleton prepared in 1776-79, would not have ameliorated all of the harsh penalties of the pre-Revolutionary penal code. Nevertheless, TJ concluded that the reason for the bill's failure in the Assembly by one vote in 1786 was that it was, for its time, too innovative.

Having invested considerable effort in the bill and its underlying extensive legal citations, TJ believed that the 1796 measure that George Keith Taylor presented to the Assembly as an original creation was in fact based on TJ's proposed statute. TJ apparently regarded himself as the one who had introduced Virginia to the innovation of solitary confinement, in the form of a design for a prison he sent from Europe in 1786, before the state's lawmakers were ready to adopt such a progressive measure (see above in this series at Vol. 2: 492-507; TJ's summary of public services, [after 2 Sep. 1800], in DLC: TJ Papers, 219: 39161; and Autobiography in Ford, I, 60, 62-5).

Regarding TJ's PLAN OF A BUILDING for the new penitentiary, see his letter to Wood, 31 Mch. 1797, and enclosures. Three other architects also submitted proposals: George Hadfield, Maria Cosway's brother and the superintendent of the U.S. Capitol from 1795 to 1798; Samuel Dobie, who had supervised public construction in Richmond, including the state capitol built from TJ's design; and Benjamin H. Latrobe, whose plan for the penitentiary was adopted (Van Horne, *Latrobe*, I, 50n; Edmund Randolph to TJ, 12 July 1786).

Address to the Senate

GENTLEMEN OF THE SENATE   [4 Mch. 1797]

Entering on the duties of the office to which I am called, I feel it incumbent on me to apologize to this honourable house for the insufficient manner in which I[1] fear they may be discharged. At an earlier period of my life, and through some considerable portion of it, I have been a member of legislative bodies, and not altogether inattentive to the forms of their proceedings; but much time has elapsed since that,[2] other duties have occupied my mind, and in a great degree it has lost it's familiarity with this subject. I fear that the house will have but too frequent occasion to percieve the truth of this acknowledgment. If a diligent attention however will enable me to fulfill the functions now assigned me, I may promise that diligence and attention shall be sedulously[3] employed. For one portion of my duty I shall[4] engage with more confidence, because it will depend on my will and not on my capacity. The rules which are to govern the proceedings of this house, so far as they shall depend on me for their application, shall be applied with the most rigorous and inflexible impartiality, regarding neither persons, their views or principles, and seeing only the abstract proposition subject to my decision. If in forming that decision I concur with some and differ from others, as must of necessity happen, I shall rely on the liberality and candour of those from whom I differ to believe that I do it on pure motives.

I might here proceed, and with the greatest truth, to declare my zealous attachment to the constitution of the United States, that I consider the Union of these states as the first of blessings, and as the first of duties the preservation of that[5] constitution which secures it; but I suppose these declarations not pertinent to the occasion of entering into an office whose[6] primary business is merely to preside over the forms of this house, and no one more sincerely prays that no accident may call me to the higher and more important functions which the constitution eventually devolves on this office. These have been justly confided to the eminent character which has preceded me here, whose talents and integrity have been known and revered by me thro' a long course of years; have been the foundation of a[7] cordial and uninterrupted friendship between us; and I devoutly pray he may be long preserved for the government, the happiness, and prosperity of our common country.

MS (photostate in DNA: RG 46, Senate Records, 5th Cong., special sess.; original in Office of Senate Financial Clerk, 1938); entirely in TJ's hand; with several emendations, the most important of which are noted below; endorsed in clerk's hand: "The Speech of The Vice President at Commencing the Session of Senate of the U States 4th. March 1797."

William Bingham, president pro tempore of the United States Senate, administered the oath of office to TJ during the spe-

cial, one-day session of Congress on 4 Mch. TJ assumed his duties as president of the Senate by swearing eight new senators into office and then delivering the above address. Upon completion of his speech, the Senate removed to the chamber of the House of Representatives, where the presidential ceremonies began at noon (JEP, I, 233-8). For a description of the events of the day, see Malone, *Jefferson*, III, 296-8.

[1] Remainder of sentence interlined in place of "may fulfill it's functions."

From Madame de Chastellux

Paris march the 5th. 1797

I am at a loss my dear Sir to find words to express what I felt at the reception of your very friendly letter! So much kindness has filled my heart with gratitude and believe me when I assure you this Sentiment will last as long as my own existence. I can easily conclude from what you tell me that I can entertain little or no hopes of obtaining from Congress any kind of assistance for my Son: but what you are so good as to add affords in my opinion a real compensation, for I shall ever sett a much higher value upon a friend like you, than upon the gifts of fortune. Providence has hitherto given me the means of educating properly my darling boy: I have reason to flatter myself now, they will not be wanting in future, and when he is some years older I am conscious I shall not resist sending him to a Country his father loved and honoured. I Shall then apply to you again my dear Sir and request that you will grant your protection to your deceased friend's Son.

We all that know and respect you in this part of the world expected you would be elected President; it now seems you will not. We are perhaps from our situation and under many circumstances better judges than those who are upon the Spot, and look upon your not being chosen as a real misfortune to your Country, but as a happy event in regard to yourself.

I am constantly in Company with your venerable friend Madame d'Enville, and her interesting daughter, as also with Mr. Short; your name is often mentioned, and the Sentiments of affection and esteem you have inspired are of a nature that time has not the power of altering.

Mr. Monroe is so obliging as to take charge of my letter, I sincerely regret having seen so little of him and his amiable Wife, but I actually lead the life of a recluse. Within these some year's past, my circumstances are much changed tho' my situation has remained the Same: after having Shared in the prosperity of a Woman who is the honour of her Sex, I have since partaken of her miseries; they are however considerably lessened, since she has succeeded in procuring the liberty of her beloved Children, and know's they will be safe and happy in America;

any kind of attention you will be pleased to Shew them she will gratefully feel, and I am certain if you come acquainted with them, they will interest you personally for it is impossible to possess more virtues, and amiable qualities than are united in those three young Men. Accept again my dr. Sir of my sincere & grateful thanks & believe me as ever & for ever your very affectionate humble Ser.

PLUNKETT CHASTELLUX

RC (DLC); endorsed by TJ and recorded in SJL as received 29 June 1797 "by Colo. Monroe."

A WOMAN WHO IS THE HONOUR OF HER SEX: the Duchesse d'Orléans (see Madame de Chastellux to TJ, 6 May 1795). Her husband, although of liberal political tendencies at the beginning of the French Revolution, had been guillotined in 1793, and subsequently three of her BELOVED CHILDREN sought refuge in the United States.

Louis Philippe, who assumed the title of Duc d'Orléans on his father's death and in 1830 became king of France, arrived in Philadelphia in October 1796. His younger brothers, the Duc de Montpensier and the Comte de Beaujolais, joined him in February 1797, and the three traveled widely in North America before departing for England late in 1799 (Guy Antonetti, *Louis-Philippe* [Paris, 1994], 291-308; Scott and Rothaus, *Historical Dictionary*, II, 604-6).

From Enoch Edwards

DEAR SIR   Monday Morning [6 Mch. 1797]

I have received from our Freind Doctor Rush the Letter you did me the favor to write of the 22nd: of Jany: last—my Name is Enoch Edwards, and that was directed to John Edwards—which was the Reason of its laying with him so long.

I send you the Papers I mentioned from Mr: Monroe.

If you would do me the Favor to take breakfast with Me on Wednesday Morning, at 9 or 10 oClock (or your own hour) I will have some others here of a very curious Nature—and afterwards if agreable I will go to shew you the curious cooking Machines, I spoke to you about. I am very respectfully   ENO; EDWARDS

RC (MHi); undated, but endorsed by TJ as written and received on 6 Mch. 1797 and so recorded in SJL.

The PAPERS from James MONROE are discussed in Edwards's letter to TJ of 27 Dec. 1796.

From Enoch Edwards

DEAR SIR   9 March 97.

The best Receipt for the Sausage—is to send you one which I wish you to take home and try. In the Autumn at the time you kill Hogs—

take all the Skin off of the leaf Lard—and in every one wrap up as much sausage Meat—as will Make about the size and Shape of a neats Tongue (which can be done by a little Practice) [1]—it requires no sewing—just slap it over while wet and it will stick. Mrs: Edwards says the seasoning of the meat should be a little higher than that made for immediate Use and She always adds a small Quantity of Cloves to it.

She wishes She had a handsomer and larger One to send to You, but her's are in the County. All except this small One—which looks more like a [2] calfs Tongue than that of a Beef.

I send it with the string round it—and a stick passed thro' the top to shew our mode of hanging them up to dry.

Every Hog that is killed—instead of the Skin of the leaf lard being thrown away—as is common with the Cracklings, they will each make two of those sausage Tongues, which keeps the year round.

I will have the honor to call tomorrow and inclose those Papers to Genl: Washington—and have them unsealed for your perusal on the Way and to wish you an agreable Journey home. With great Respect I am your obedt st.   ENO; EDWARDS

RC (MHi); endorsed by TJ: "sausages."

The PAPERS TO GENL. WASHINGTON have not been found.

Letters from Edwards to TJ of June, 2 July 1797, and 10 May 1800, received respectively on 30 June, 3 July 1797, and 10 May 1800, as well as a letter written by TJ to Edwards on 27 Aug. 1797 are recorded in SJL but have not been found.

[1] Clause in parentheses interlined.
[2] Word interlined in place of "milk."

To Mary Jefferson

MY DEAR MARIA   Philadelphia Mar. 11. 97.

I recieved with great pleasure your letter from Varina, and though I never had a moment's doubt of your love for me, yet it gave me infinite delight to read the expressions of it. Indeed I had often and always read it in your affectionate and attentive conduct towards me. On my part, my love to your sister and yourself knows no bounds, and as I scarcely see any other object in life, so would I quit it with desire whenever my continuance in it shall become useless to you.—I heard, as I passed thro' Wilmington, that your acquaintance Miss Geddis was well, and not yet married. I have here met with another who was at Mrs. Pine's with you, Miss Mckain, who sings better than any body I have heard in America, and is otherwise well accomplished. I recieved a letter yesterday from Bruni, praying a seat *in my carriage* to some place in Virginia where she could get a passage by water which would shorten that to Varina. I am sincerely sorry not only that I have not my own carriage to offer her a seat, but that I had engaged with a party to take the whole of the mail-stage back, so that there was not a place left to offer her. I am obliged to apologize to her on this ground, but people under misfortune are suspicious, and I fear these little accidental checks may make her think them intentional. I leave this the day after tomorrow, and shall be at home on the 19th. or 20th. But, my dear, do not let my return hasten yours. I would rather you should stay where you are till it becomes disagreeable to you because I think it better for you to go more into society than the neighborhood of Monticello admits. My first letter from Monticello shall be to your sister. Present her my warmest love and be assured of it yourself. Adieu my dear daughter.

RC (ViU: Mary Kirk Moyer deposit); unsigned; addressed: "Maria Jefferson Varina." PrC (ViU: Edgehill-Randolph Papers); endorsed by TJ in ink on verso.

The LETTER TJ received from BRUNI (Madame de Salimberi), Martha Jefferson Randolph's friend and schoolmate at Paris from the West Indies, dated 1 Mch. 1797

and recorded in SJL as received from Wilmington nine days later, has not been found. TJ's response to Salimberi, recorded in SJL under 11 Mch., is also missing, as are letters from Salimberi to TJ of 2 and 13 June 1797, recorded in SJL as received on the same dates they were written (Martha Jefferson Randolph to TJ, 16 Jan. 1791; Barbier Demarais to TJ, 7 May 1791).

To Thomas Mann Randolph

Th:J. to TMR.   Philadelphia Mar. 11. 97.

Yours has been duly recieved, and the clover seed goes tomorrow in the schooner Industry, Capt. Green bound for Richmond. It is addressed to Chas. Johnston, and is in 3. casks containing $3\frac{1}{8}$ bushels each, of which 4. bushels are for yourself and the rest for me. It will be desireable to have it forwarded immediately, and of preference by waggon. I shall be at home the 19th. or 20th. and consequently in time to recieve it. It cost here only 10. Dollars per bushel. I have purchased the platting instruments for you, a neat little set, and shall take them on, but having nothing but a very small portmanteau it will not be in my power to take on a compass and chain. Therefore I conclude to defer that commission for November when I can find means of sending on to you such an article by somebody else. In the mean time you can use mine freely, as I never use it in the summer. I have ordered a thermometer for you from a most excellent hand here, on a construction very much recommended to me by Dr. Priestly as preferable to any thing he saw in Europe, because it shews what has been the maximum or minimum of cold during your absence. But I begin to fear it will not be ready, as I am now at Saturday night, and go off in the forenoon of Monday. I could have eleven dollars for my tobacco were it here. But if it were I would not take that, as it is confessedly on the rise. I shall order it on as soon as the March squalls are over. If you should chuse to adventure yours here, I have provided for it's being disposed of as mine, or otherwise as you shall direct, if you chuse to consign it to Barnes.—We receive information through three different channels (all private) that Mr. Pinckney is refused reception at Paris. One account adds that the French government has suspended all intercourse with us till satisfaction given them. This is less credited than the other part of the information. I hope and believe that the present administration will adopt friendly arrangements. My love to my ever dear Martha. Adieu affectionately.

RC (DLC); endorsed by Randolph as received 23 Mch. 1797. PrC (CSmH); endorsed by TJ in ink on verso.

YOURS HAS BEEN DULY RECEIVED: Randolph's letter to TJ of 27 Feb. 1797, recorded in SJL as received from Varina 7 Mch., has not been found. Randolph's letter to TJ of 25 Jan. 1797, recorded in SJL as received from Varina four days later, is also missing.

On 11 Mch., TJ bought PLATTING INSTRUMENTS for Randolph from William Richardson, a maker of mathematical and optical instruments in Philadelphia. TJ completed the transactions for the COMPASS (forty dollars) and the CHAIN upon his return to Philadelphia for the special session of Congress in May (MB, II, 891, 956, 964).

I HAVE ORDERED A THERMOMETER FOR YOU: TJ paid Joseph Gatty, a Philadelphia glassblower who specialized in weather instruments such as the maximum-and-minimum thermometer, twelve dollars for two thermometers, one for himself and one for Randolph in June 1797 (MB, II, 962).

To William Short

DEAR SIR   Philadelphia Mar. 12. 97.

I have recieved no letter from you since that which you wrote on your departure from Madrid. That gave me reason to believe you would come over early in the spring, and having been ever since in the daily expectation of your arrival I had suspended writing to you. Having come on here for a few days to qualify into office, and being now on my return again, I avail myself of the opportunity by Mr. Adet to write you a line on your affairs, but as I brought no papers with me, I can only give a very general view of them from memory. Your lands at Indian camp in Albemarle remain in the occupation of the same tenants and on the same rents. Not at all in the condition I approve permanently, but from an unwillingness to change into what you might chuse to change again on your arrival. You possess forty odd shares in the James river canal. This is now brought into the city of Richmond, and every thing is landed there. But some money having been still wanting to complete it, a contribution by way of loan was asked of such partners as were willing at an interest of 6. per cent. The object of the loan being to complete the value of the subject, and the loan bottomed on infallible security and at good interest, I subscribed for you, and have paid in (I think) about £200. Virga. currency. There remains still one or two more such paiments to be made when called for. The purchase money for these shares and lands have left you in the public funds 15,342.D. 18c. of sixpercents, and 11,256.D. 63c. of three per cents, on which small annual reimbursements are begun to be made. The interest which has been recieved has been immediately placed at an interest of 6. per cent on mortgage in hands which could be relied on for speedy reimbursement. It was for the establishment of a profitable work, which being now compleatly under way the borrower chuses to begin his repaiments in July and to complete them in a year from that time. When these paiments come in I shall be at a loss how to employ the money, whether in buying in stock, or re-lending on mortgage. I have hitherto gone on the idea you proposed and I much approved of having your property in different forms, to wit, land on rent, money in the funds, loans on mortgage. I consider the last as the surest for interest and principal. Ground rents in this place could not be bought when I first tried. They could now. But they are so liable to a loss of the capital by fire, that tho proposed by you I have not renewed endeavors to purchase them. The failures in the governmental remittances of your salary are irrecoverable if you are left to demand them of R. I am endeavoring to obtain justice from the government itself.—This is as complete an idea as I can give you by memory of your affairs, with which I am acquainted. The inclosed letter from your brother (whom I accidentally met here) will inform you of what was in his department. Mr. Skipwith and his family are well. A daughter of his is married to a Randolph of the Dungeoness family. Late deaths are Beverley Randolph, Frank Lee and his wife in the same week. Genl. Washington's retirement and Mr. Adams's succession to him will have been known to you. As I presume you are in habits of relation with Mesdames Danville and de la Rochefoucault, I pray you to tender them the homage of my respects, to assure them of my heartfelt sympathies in all their sufferings and that I shall ever recollect them with the same affections as if I were of their family. I have taken great pleasure in the acquaintance of M. de Liancourt here, as well because of his connection with them as for his own merit. Not knowing whether to expect next a letter from you, or yourself in person, I wait with impatience for that which is to happen, and in the mean time assure you that you may count without limits on my constant and affectionate attachment to you. The risk of capture by sea forbids me to put my signature to this, but you know my handwriting. Adieu affectionately.

RC (ViW); unsigned; addressed: "A Monsieur   Monsieur Short à Paris, chez le Ministre Plenipotentiaire, ou le Consul General des etats unis d'Amerique"; endorsed by Short. PrC (DLC: Short Papers); endorsed in ink by TJ. Enclosure not found.

THAT WHICH YOU WROTE ON YOUR DEPARTURE FROM MADRID: Short to TJ, 30 Sep. 1795. Short's certificates of investment in the PUBLIC FUNDS are listed in the enclosure to TJ's letter to Short of 23 Dec. 1793. A memorandum by John Barnes of an 8 Feb. 1797 entry in his waste book records REIMBURSEMENTS Short had received in the form of dividends on his certificates:

"6 ⅌Ct 15,342.18 @ 3½ ⅌Ct   536.97
3 ⅌Ct 11,256.63   ¾   84.42
                                 621.39
Entd. 8th feby. 1797.
Waste—394—JB" (MS in DLC: Short Papers; entirely in Barnes's hand; endorsed by TJ: "Short William. Barnes's note of reimbursement and interest received"). TJ recorded those reimbursements in MB, II, 955. For the payment of dividends in redemption of the public debt, see TJ to Barnes, 28 Jan. 1797.

LEFT TO DEMAND THEM OF R.: for a time Edmund Randolph, while secretary of state, had controlled Short's diplomatic salary (see Short to TJ, 29 Jan. and 2 Sep. 1795).

To Sir John Sinclair

DEAR SIR   Philadelphia Mar. 12. 97.

I take shame to myself at this late acknolegement of the receipt of so many of your favors: but the fact is that while I was here in my former office, it's unremitting duties obliged me to interdict to myself the pleasure of private correspondence. On return to my farms I felt myself, tho' an old man, yet too young a farmer to hazard any thing in the line which you are so firmly and usefully pursuing, a line as much more honourable than the occupation of an Alexander or a Marlborough, as the preservation of human life is more praiseworthy than it's destruction. I shall in the course of the present year be able to send you some farming implements of our invention which shall be worthy your acceptance. They are now preparing. Among these will be a drill which for sowing a single row I pronounce from experience to be perfect as far as it can be rendered so by cheapness, simplicity of materials and construction, ease of repair and the complete manner in which it opens the furrow, sows and covers it at one operation by a force scarcely greater than a strong man might perform. An ass would be the best animal for it. I rather hope it may be made to sow 3. or 4. rows at a time, and mean to try it, but I cannot affirm that it will. I came here for a few days only to qualify into a new office which will call and keep me here during the winter, and permit me to pass my summers at my own house in Virginia. Prob-

"The Providential Detection"

Volney

La Rochefoucauld-Liancourt

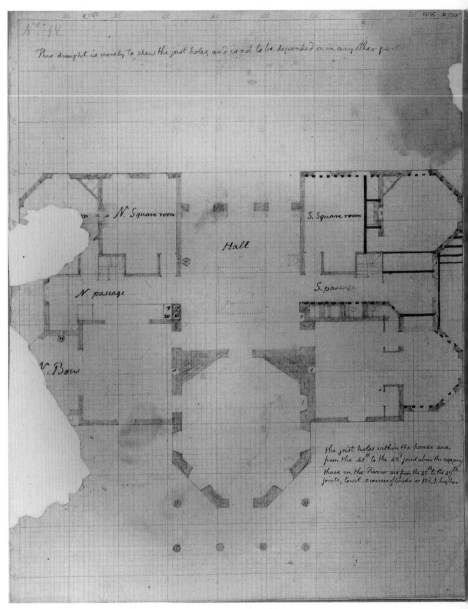

Floor Plan of Monticello

Plate II.

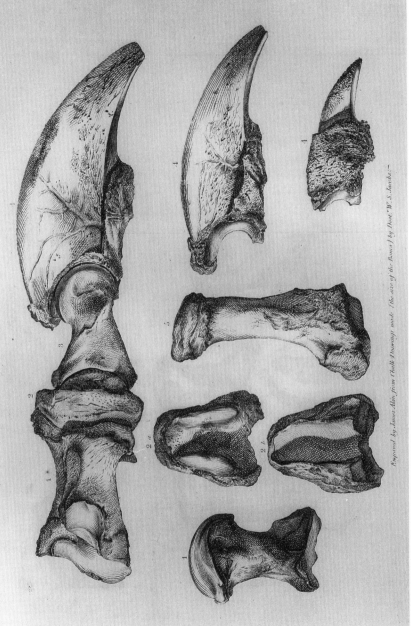

Engraved by James Akin, from Chalk Drawings made (the size of the Bones) by Docr. W. S. Jacobs.

The "Great Claw" of the Megalonyx

John Adams

Thomas Jefferson

Board of Agriculture
Whitehall, London, June 20th 1797.
The which day His Excellency Thomas Jefferson Vice Presid.t of the United States of America, was admitted a Foreign Honorary Member of the Board.
Signed by order of the Board. John Sinclair President

British Board of Agriculture Diploma

ably it will not be till my return here in October that I shall be able to forward the implements I propose for you. I must thank you for the many printed papers you have been so good as to send me from time to time, and above all for those on manure, wherein that interesting subject is better developed than ever was done before. Accept assurances of the constant and affectionate remembrance retained of you by Dear Sir your sincere friend & humble servant   TH: JEFFERSON

PrC (DLC); at foot of text in ink: "Sinclair Sr. John."

For the paper ON MANURE, see Sinclair to TJ, 15 July 1795.

To William Strickland

DEAR SIR   Philadelphia Mar. 12. 97.
    I have been longer in acknoleging the reciept of your favor of May 28. 96. than I would have been but for the constant expectation of procuring the seeds you desired (one kind of which was to be sent for to Kentuckey). This, the Buffalo clover, is in a packet which accompanies this letter: as also the wild pea which you wished to recieve, and I promised to send you. I have added some seeds of a plant I have never seen, but which we suppose to be a Vetch of some kind. It is known no where but at the antient settlement of Bermuda hundred and Varina. It comes up in the arable lands, produces a most heavy crop, lives thro the winter keeping the cattle and horses which feed on it fat without any other food, and as it was the 2d settlement made in Virginia, I suspect it to have been brought from Europe and to have preserved itself there. But this is mere conjecture. It grows abundantly in Mr. Randolph's farm at Varina, but he has never seen it in blossom so as to decide satisfactorily what it is. We propose to cultivate it this year in our orchards which suit it best as it grows well among trees and is perennial, and I send you some seeds for experiment also. The oil shrub of which Mr. Bartram spoke to you, grows near the medicinal springs at the foot of the Alleghaney. I have made many attempts to raise it at home both from the seed and plant, but without success. If I can ever succeed to establish the plants in my garden you shall be furnished with them. The seeds you were so kind as to deliver to Mr. Donald for me have never come to hand. Probably they have fallen into the hands of the sea-rovers who infest the ocean, and harrass in their peaceable pursuits those who are less mad and less unjust than themselves. I still retain much anxiety to get the *true winter* vetch. Mr. Young seems to doubt whether you possess it in England, because he has observed you have none which does

not suffer greatly by the cold. Our winters are more severe than yours, and still more likely to injure that plant, unless it be of the hardiest kind.—The ice-caves you mention are entirely singular, and never before heard of by me. I have enquired after them unsuccessfully as yet: and if you can recollect the name of your informer so as to give me a clue to get hold of, I shall thank you for it whenever you honor me with another letter: for I do not permit myself to believe that our correspondence is to end here. Those whose dispositions and qualifications inspire esteem, must add to their other virtues patience under the burthen even of esteem. Without embarrassing you with a regular correspondence, I must claim the permission of writing to you whenever occasion calls for it, and shall be always made happy by learning from yourself that you enjoy health and happiness in the bosom of healthy and happy friends. The time I had the happiness of possessing you at Monticello, tho short, was yet sufficient to impress that kind of remembrance which never dies.—I came here for a few days only to qualify into an office which will call and keep me here during the winter months, and permit me to pass my summers in my farms. Either there or here I shall be happy always to recieve the friends you may recommend, and render them all the attentions and services I can. Accept, I pray you, assurances of the sincere attachment & respect with which I am Dear Sir Your affectionate & humble servt   TH: JEFFERSON

PrC (DLC); at foot of first page in ink: "Strickland Wm."

From Volney

MONSIEUR   philadelphie 15 Mars 97

N'ayant pû avoir l'honneur de Vous revoir avant Votre depart, j'espère que Vous recevrez encore avant toute autre Voye, un Exemplaire de Ma reponse au dr. priestley que je joins ici. Si le français S'imprime comme jai lieu de le croire, Vous ne tarderez pas Non plus de l'avoir. C'est une affaire finie de Ma part. Le Saint-homme N'aura plus de Moi une Virgule. Avant trois Semaines je compte etre Sur le potowmack, et peut-etre cette course donnerat-elle lieu l'année prochaine à un Ouvrage plus utile et plus agreable que des disputes de thêologie. Ce sera pour Moi une grande tentation, que de Me voir si rapproché de Vous et de Mr. Madison Mais quand je considere Vos embarras de bâtisse, jai peine à croire que des Visites en ce Moment Soient auprès de Vous des témoignages d'amitié; et je me persuade plutot que d'en faire le Sacrifice pour cette année sera une Maniere plus delicate de Vous

indiquer les Sentimens avec les quels jai L'honneur d'etre, Monsieur
Votre très humble servitr.   C. VOLNEY

Comme je passerai quelques jours à federal city chez le dr. Thornton, toute lettre de Votre part Me parviendra là bien plus surement
quailleurs.

RC (DLC); at head of text: "Mr jefferson"; postscript on verso, with note at foot of
recto: "Tournez. S'il Vous plait"; endorsed
by TJ as received 31 Mch. 1797 and so recorded in SJL. Enclosure: Constantin
François Chasseboeuf, comte de Volney,
Volney's Answer to Doctor Priestley, on his
*pamphlet entitled, "Observations upon the in-
crease of infidelity, with animadversions
upon the writings of several modern unbeliev-
ers, and especially the Ruins of Mr. Volney
. . ."* (Philadelphia, 1797). See Sowerby,
No. 1679.

From Samuel Brown

SIR   Washington City March 17th. 1797—

I beleive I have obtained such information respecting the Freezing
Cave as will enable you to find it. It is thirty miles from Winchester, two
miles from the Road leading from that town to Romney, on the North
River of Cape Capon.

Mr. White, who gave Mr. Strickland an account of this curiosity,
says he has seen it and examined it with much attention. Impressed,
however, with an Idea, that the Ice was formed by some Mixture of Salt
petre, he does not appear to have been sufficiently careful in observing
those facts upon which a more rational Theory could be formed. The
Hill above the Cave is composed of loose stones thro which he says the
air and water pass without meeting with any earth or leaves which
could prevent their descent. From the mouth of the Cave (where the Ice
remains until August) there is a constant cold blast of wind issuing. He
was informed by the neighbours that when the Hill was covered with
snow this blast of cold air was not perceptable. This circumstance is
worthy of observation.

As it is your intention, soon to visit that part of the country I antici-
pate the pleasure of becoming better acquainted with the History and
Theory of that singular Phenomenon. With the greatest respect I am Sir
Yo. Mo. ob.   SAM BROWN

RC (DLC: TJ Papers, 72: 12488); endorsed by TJ as received 24 Mch. 1797 and
so recorded in SJL.

Samuel Brown (1769-1830) was born in
Rockbridge County, Virginia, the son of
Presbyterian clergyman John and Marga-
ret Preston Brown and younger brother of
James and John Brown, both of whom
served in the United States Senate. Gradu-
ating from Dickinson College in 1789,
Brown went on to study medicine, receiv-

ing a degree from the University of Aberdeen in Scotland. In 1797 he left the medical practice he had established in Bladensburg, Maryland, to join his brother James, first in Lexington, Kentucky, and then, in 1806, in New Orleans. Upon his marriage to Catherine Percy in 1809, Brown moved to Natchez, Mississippi, where he lived until his wife's death four years later, after which he moved to a plantation near Huntsville, Alabama, to raise his young family. In 1819 he rejoined the faculty of the medical school at Transylvania University, in Lexington, where he had taught from 1799 to 1806, remaining there until 1825 when he retired to Huntsville. Elected to membership in the American Philosophical Society in 1800, Brown sent the society papers and specimens, including saltpetre rock and mammoth bones from a Kentucky cave and minerals from Mexico. Brown's 1806 letter describing a cave in Madison County, Kentucky, with "observations on Nitre and Gun-Powder," was published by the Philosophical Society. Brown founded the Kappa Lambda Society of Hippocrates which began publication of *The North American Medical and Surgical Journal* in Philadelphia in 1826 (DAB; Samuel Brown to TJ, 10 Nov. 1805, 25 May 1813; APS, *Proceedings*, XXII, pt. 3 [1884], 299, 322, 344, 374, 379, 390, 401, 599; APS, *Transactions*, VI [1809], 235-47; Greene, *American Science* [Ames, Iowa, 1984], 122).

To Thomas Mann Randolph

TH:J. TO TMR.   Monticello Mar. 23. [1797]

I arrived at home on the 20th. inst. and found the cherry and peach trees in general blossom. They had begun about a week before that. This day our first dishes of asparagus and spinach came to table. This may enable you to compare climates. The price of wheat at Philadelphia and Baltimore was 2.13 D. at Alexandria and Dumfries 1.67 at Fredericksburg 1.16. The merchants of Philadelphia and Baltimore think wheat and flour will keep at their present prices the present season, notwithstanding the threatening aspect of affairs with France. I am the bearer of a diploma for you from the Amer. Phil. society, which I will deliver on your coming up; for I presume you will come to our election. There are two persons talked of besides Mr. Nicholas and yourself, but it is thought they will get few votes. Hening is one. I forget the name of the other, having never before heard it. He lives near Mr. Maury's. I think it probable you may recieve this in Richmd. on your way up. You will do well therefore to enquire after our clover and have it forwarded *by a waggon*, for it ought to be at Richmd. by this time. Will you be so good as to enquire the state of my pipe of wine at Brown's which I must send express for if no safe opportunity occurs. All are well at Edgehill. I shall write to my dear Martha by post, for this goes by an earlier accidental conveyance. My best love to her and Maria. The little ones I suppose have forgotten me. Adieu affectionately.

P.S. I find on further enquiry that the first cherry and peach blossoms here appeared on the 9th. inst. I passed Fredericksburg on the 18th. and the buds were not swelled.

RC (DLC); partially dated, with year supplied from SJL and internal evidence.

DIPLOMA FOR YOU: Randolph was elected to membership in the American Philosophi-cal Society on 18 Apr. 1794 (APS, *Proceedings*, XXII, pt. 3 [1884], 220).

For the ELECTION in Albemarle County, see TJ to Thomas Mann Randolph, 9 Apr. 1797.

From Peregrine Fitzhugh

Annapolis
DEAR SIR   March 25th. 1797—

Agreeably to my promise I cover you as many Grains of the Cumberland Corn as can be conveniently conveyed in a Letter and I hope they will reach you safe. I have also sealed up very carefully about a Pint of the same Corn and shall request our Friend John Mason to forward it to some Gentleman in Fredericksburg of whom I will give you notice in a P.S. to this Letter that you may direct any of your neighbours going to that Place to call for it unless a safe conveyance to you should sooner offer. This Corn tho it appears to have preserved its species has in a great degree lost its luxuriance from having been cultivated in a very poor Soil. I have little doubt however of its recovery with you and as little of its answering the purpose you wish it by coming in at the latter end of your roasting your Crops unless it should have got mixed with other Corn. You mentioned a valuable pea which you had brought to this Country from France. If on your way to Congress the ensuing fall it should not slip your memory and be not too troublesome to drop me a few Spoon-Fulls of them at Mr. Brydens Baltimore Town I shall consider it a singular Favor. Since I parted with you in Philadelphia I have not been free from those little occasional feuds peculiar to the wide difference of political Sentiments which unfortunately prevails in our Country. In some of these I have heard your friend Mr. Maddison vehemently charged with having tarnished his political career by a most glaring and palpable inconsistency of Conduct. It has been alledged that in the general Convention which gave birth to our present Government and Constitution he warmly opposed the principle of vesting the treaty making powers in the President and Senate to the utter exclusion of the representative branch as an abridgement of the Peoples priviladges equally dangerous and unnecessary that in the convention of his own state which adopted the Constitution he again urged the impolicy of the measure on similar Principles and that during the discussion of the british Treaty he as strenuously contended that the article did not give the President and Senate the right of making treaties perfectly independent of the Lower House. I found myself unable to contradict these charges without following the example which my adversaries were probably then setting me that of making round assertions without knowing or perhaps even caring whether they were founded in fact or not—I think I heard you say you had a correct sketch of all the arguments of any importance which took place in the Genl. Convention. If so and you should not deem it too troublesome I will thank you for putting it in my power to rescue a character I so much admire from the shade which is attempted to be cast upon it by his Enemies. I am so far on my return to my Partner and our large young Flock and anticipate a pleasure in the meeting of which you can readily form an Idea—I hope you found your Family well on your return and from the late favorable seasons a great change in the appearance of your Farm—I shall be happy to hear that the corn has got safe to you. A Letter by post directed to me near Hagers Town Washington County Maryland will find its way to me. I have the honor to be with every possible respect Dr Sir Yr. most obedt. & Humble Servant   PEREGNE. FITZHUGH

P.S. Being informed that a Person from this Town will go up in a few days to your House I shall hunt him out in the morning and lodge the Package of Corn with him—

RC (DLC); endorsed by TJ as received 31 Mch. 1797 and so recorded in SJL.

To John Barnes

DEAR SIR   Monticello Mar. 26. 97.
    I inclose a note for some more sashes to be made by Mr. Trump, as we have put up those he furnished before, and find them well made and according to directions. I would wish these now ordered to be made as early as possible so as that payment may not be due till the 1st. of July; for tho' I shall immediately order my tobacco to be sent on to you, yet it will not produce cash till July 1. I am desirous of sending you an invoice for some groceries and small things of about 2. or 300. Doll. value if they can be credited till July 1. but I will await your information on this head. Mr. Lott also wished to order on some supplies and applied to me for a draught but I informed him I should not be able to draw till July. I am with great esteem Dear Sir Your most obedt. servt
                                                     TH: JEFFERSON

P.S. I laid by, at John Bringhurst's a small paint box, and forgot afterwards to call for it. Will you be so good as to take it for me and pay the price which I think was about 7. Doll. It may be packed in a vacant interval with the sashes now ordered, or may come in a tight package of groceries whenever I [may] call for them.

PrC (MHi); faded; at foot of text: "Mr. John Barnes"; endorsed by TJ in ink on verso. Enclosure not found.

While in Philadelphia on 10 Mch. 1797, TJ signed a power of attorney authorizing Barnes "to recieve from the treasury of the US. all sums of money which may become due to me during this present year from the said treasury on account of salary as Vice-president of the United States" (MS in DNA: RG 217, MTA, No. 8766; consisting of a printed form with blanks filled by TJ and Notary Public Peter Lohra and some printed text canceled; signed by TJ, Lohra, and witnesses Jacob Hoffman and William Ming).

A letter from TJ to Barnes dated 27 Mch. 1797 is recorded in SJL but has not been found.

From Timothy Pickering

SIR

Department of State
Philadelphia March 26. 1797.

I have the honor to inclose a copy of the President's proclamation for convening the Congress of the United States at this city on the 15th of next May; and to be with great respect your most obt. servant

TIMOTHY PICKERING

RC (NNPM); at foot of text: "The Vice-President of the United States." FC (Lb in DNA: RG 59, DL). Recorded in SJL as received 8 Apr. 1797. Enclosure: Proclamation by President Adams countersigned by Pickering, 25 Mch. 1797, that "whereas an extraordinary occasion exists for convening Congress, and divers weighty matters claim their consideration," Congress will convene at Philadelphia on 15 May 1797 (*Annals*, VII, 49).

From John Trumbull

DEAR SIR

29 Berner's Street
London March 26th. 1797.

Our Friends Mr. and Mrs. Church with their Family, are on the point of embarking for America where they hope to pass the remainder of their time in a tranquillity of which Europe and especially this Country appears to have little to hope for many years to come.

Among the many friends whom they will find happy and impatient to receive them on their Return,[1] there are few whom Mrs. and Miss Church mention more frequently, and with more cordiality of Esteem than Mr. and the Miss Jeffersons. The happy Days[2] We passed in Paris, under your protecting roof, are the frequent subjects of our Conversation, and they look with much expectation of enjoyment to the Society soon to be regained, of Friends whom they remember with such well founded satisfaction.

The Situation in public Life to which you are again called to sacrifice the Enjoyments of Retirement and Domestic life,[3] (and on whose arduous Obligations and Duties, I know not whether to congratulate you or not,) will place you during a considerable part of the year, near this Family of your Friends: and much as I feel the severe Loss which my little Society in this place must suffer from their Absence, so cordially do I congratulate you on the acquisition which will be derived to your's from their Return.

I will say nothing on political Subjects, as Mr. Church's information is better[4] than mine, and conversation so much more satisfactory than Letters. With the best Wishes for the Happiness of yourself and Family in every situation of Life, I am with much Gratitude Dear Sir Your Obliged and faithful servant & friend   JNO: TRUMBULL

RC (DLC); endorsed by TJ as received 25 Aug. 1797 and so recorded in SJL. FC (DLC: John Trumbull letterbook); in Trumbull's hand; with several variations, the most important of which are noted below; notations in margin also in Trumbull's hand: "To Mr. Jefferson Vice President &c. &c." and "by Mr. Church in the Fair American Capt. Duplex."

[1] FC: "to welcome their Return."
[2] FC: "hours."
[3] FC: "Philosophic Retirement and Domestic Repose."
[4] This word is preceded by "so much" in FC.

From Elbridge Gerry

MY DEAR SIR   Cambridge 27th March 1797

Permit me, with great sincerity, to congratulate you on your appointment to the office of Vice-President of the United States. It was in my mind a very desirable object, and a wish which I ardently expressed at the meeting of the electors; but, as we were unanimously of opinion that Mr. Adams' pretensions to the chair were best, it was impossible to give you any votes without annulling an equal number for him; otherwise, you would certainly have had mine and I have reason to think several others', for Vice-President. The constitution, as it respects these elections, makes a lottery of them: and is, I think, imperfect. There was probably a plan laid, by coupling Mr. Pinckney with Mr. Adams, to secure so many votes on this list for the former, as with those for him on other lists, would bring him into the chair; but this was fortunately seen thro and defeated, and I flatter myself that the elections will eventually have an happy effect on the public mind, by the accomodating disposition of the P. and VP., their mutual friendship for each other, and the pursuit of a general system of moderation, exploding foreign influence of every kind, in every department of government. Being unconnected with parties, whose extremes I confess have been disagreable to me and [have detached me from] politics, I am a retired spectator, enjoying never[theless the] uncontrouled right of judging for myself, and of ex[pressing] independently to my friends, my ideas of the measures [springing] from public and of the artifices from private views. Thus cir[cum]stanced, give me leave to express my apprehensions that the consequence of this election will be repeat[ed stratagems, to] weaken or destroy the confidence of the P and VP in each other, from an assurance that if it continues to the end of the President's administration the VP will be his successor and perhaps from a dread of your political influence. Indeed I think such an operation has already commenced, and that you will discover it, but your mutual good sense will see thro the project and defeat it. Wishing you to possess a full share of the public confidence, which I am sure you have always merited, and with it much private happiness, I remain my dear Sir with every sentiment of esteem & respect, your friend & very hume Sert   E GERRY

RC (DLC); mutilated and stained, missing text supplied in brackets from Dupl; at foot of text: "His Exellency Mr. Jefferson"; endorsed by TJ and recorded in SJL as received 21 Apr. 1797. Dupl (same); subjoined to Gerry to TJ, 22 May 1797; with minor variations not recorded.

To William Vans Murray

DEAR SIR   Monticello Mar. 27. 97.

After congratulations on your appointment to represent us with the new Batavian republic, I take the liberty of solliciting your care of a letter to Messrs. Nicholas and Jacob Van Staphorst and Hubbard of Amsterdam, who will of course make themselves known to you on your arrival. I think you will find them of characters considerably and advantageously distinguished from the herd of money-machines you will find in that country. Wishing a safe and short voyage, pleasant breezes and clear skies to Mrs. Murray and yourself, I remain with great esteem and respect Dear Sir Your most obedt. servt   TH: JEFFERSON

PrC (DLC); at foot of text: "William V. Murray esq."; endorsed in ink by TJ on verso. Enclosures: TJ to Van Staphorst & Hubbard, 27 and 28 Mch. 1797.

To Martha Jefferson Randolph

MY DEAR MARTHA   Monticello Mar. 27. 97.

I wrote to Mr. Randolph two or three days ago, but I imagine he will recieve the letter at Richmond on his way up: for we expect he will of course come up this week. He has a more dangerous competitor in Billy Wood than had arisen before. But I hear little about it. I arrived in good health at home this day sennight. The mountain had then been in bloom ten days. I find that the natural productions of the spring are about a fortnight earlier here than at Fredericksburg. But where art and attention can do any thing, some one in a large collection of inhabitants, as in a town, will be before ordinary individuals whether of town or country. I have heard of you but once since I left home, and am impatient to know that you are all well. I have however so much confidence in the dose of health with which Monticello charges you in summer and autumn that I count on it's carrying you well through the winter. The difference between the health enjoyed at Varina and Presqu'isle is merely the effect of this. Therefore do not ascribe it to Varina and stay there too long. The bloom of Monticello is chilled by my solitude. It makes me wish the more that yourself and sister were here to enjoy it. I value the enjoiments of this life only in proportion as you participate them with me. All other attachments are weakening, and I approach the state of mind when nothing will hold me here but my love for yourself and sister and the tender connections you have added to me. I hope you will write to me: as nothing is so pleasing during your absence as these proofs of your love. Be assured my dear daughter that you possess mine in it's utmost limits. Kiss the dear little ones for me. I wish we had one of them here. Adieu affectionately.

I inclose you a letter I received in Philadelphia from Mde. Salimberi. As I came in a stage it was impossible to accomodate her. I wrote her the fact with such friendly expressions for us all as might tend to prevent her imputing it to unwillingness. Had it not been for the unroofing our house, I would have invited her to come here and spend the summer with you.

RC (NNPM); unsigned; with final paragraph on verso with instructions at bottom of first page to "turn over"; at foot of first page: "Mrs. Randolph." PrC (ViU: Edgehill-Randolph Papers); lacks final paragraph; endorsed in ink by TJ on verso. Enclosure: Madame de Salimberi to TJ, 1 Mch. 1797 (see note to TJ to Mary Jefferson, 11 Mch. 1797).

I WROTE: TJ to Thomas Mann Randolph, 23 Mch. 1797.

To Van Staphorst & Hubbard

ESTEEMED FRIENDS   Monticello in Virginia. Mar. 27. 97.

My last to you was of Apr. 24. 96. since which I have recieved your favors of the same year of Jan. 5. and 27. Apr. 11. May 21. and Oct. 21. For that of May 21. I am particularly to thank you, as well as for it's effects which came in due time to answer my object. I recieved the sum of two thousand dollars from Harrison & Sterett in the months of October and November, for which I gave them two draughts on you of one thousand dollars each, and for the same sums I now inclose you my obligations, the one for 1000. Doll. payable Oct. 1. 1800. the other for 1000. Doll. payable Nov. 1. 1801. with interest at 6. per cent. per annum from the dates at or about which the money was recieved. As you did not express any wish as to the time at which you would desire repaiment I filled them according to my own convenience; but shall be ready to shorten the term if desired. I would gladly have liquidated in a third obligation the balance I owed you on former dealings, but I have no accompt from you which enables me to do it. Be so good as to send me a statement of it, and I will send you a separate bond for it. I have thought it better not to hazard these papers during the winter. The equinoctial gales being soon to terminate I send this to Philadelphia in time I hope to reach our new minister to your government, Mr. Murray, before his departure.—You will hear of wonderful revolutions of fortune among the merchants and speculators of Philadelphia and New York. The banks may be considered as the primary source of this catastrophe. In order to increase their circulating paper and of course their profits, they issued it to every pretender in commerce, gave them thereby the appearance of capitals which these people did not possess, and a consequent credit, and facilities for overspeculating themselves which they greatly abused. Whilst the enormous sums of paper thus thrown into circulation banished all the precious metals, and raised all commodities to double and treble prices, the spirit of gambling in paper, in lands, in canal schemes, town lot schemes, manufacturing schemes and whatever could hit the madness of the day, spread like a contagion to our former good merchants. The slow and sure gains of useful commerce and navigation could no longer be waited for, scrip fortunes must be made in an instant, but in the height of their delirium, the baloon bursts, lets them drop from the clouds, and ends as such phrensies ought always to end and I pray to god may eternally end, in the prostration of gambling and encouragement of regular, honest and useful commerce and industry. A late visit of only ten days to Philadelphia gave me an opportunity of seeing the commencement of a scene of havoc among the race of speculators which in 1792. and 1793. I was sensible must come on sooner or later. It is later than I expected, yet earlier than it would have happened had it not been for the spoliations on our commerce begun by the English and now carrying on by the French. Some who have been connected with you have been deeply guilty in these scandalous scenes. It gave me great pleasure to see symptoms of a discontinuance of your connection as soon as their criminal temerity rendered them unworthy of it. Your early attachment and services to the US. have given me sincere wishes for the prosperity of your affairs, and if I can at any time serve them, I shall do it on motives which I deem virtuous. I am with great & sincere esteem Gentlemen Your most obedt. & most humble servt   TH: JEFFERSON

PrC (DLC); at foot of first page: "Messrs. Van Staphorsts & Hubbard"; endorsed by TJ in ink on verso. Enclosure: bond of TJ to Van Staphorst & Hubbard, 26 Mch. 1797, in the sum of $2,000 to secure payment, on or before 1 Oct. 1800, of $1,000 with interest at six percent per annum from 1 Oct. 1796 (PrC in same; entirely in TJ's hand and signed by him, not witnessed or attested). Other enclosure printed below. Enclosed in TJ to William Vans Murray, 27 Mch. 1797.

For the TWO DRAUGHTS on Van Staphorst & Hubbard to Harrison & Sterett, see note to Van Staphorst & Hubbard to TJ, 21 May 1796.

SOME WHO HAVE BEEN CONNECTED WITH

YOU HAVE BEEN DEEPLY GUILTY: in the 1780s, in partnership with other financial houses of Amsterdam, the Van Staphorst firm began speculative investments in America. Through its agent in the United States, Théophile Cazenove, the consortium invested heavily in such ventures as public securities, canal shares, and land, forming the Holland Land Company in 1796. The Dutch investors acquired several million acres in western New York and Pennsylvania in 1792-93, including large purchases from Robert Morris and James Wilson (Shaw Livermore, *Early American Land Companies: Their Influence on Corporate Development* [New York, 1939], 206-9; Paul Demund Evans, *The Holland Land Company* [Buffalo, 1924], 25-6, 31-4).

ENCLOSURE

Bond to Van Staphorst & Hubbard

Know all men by these presents that I Thomas Jefferson of Monticello in the county of Albemarle in Virginia am bound unto Nicholas and Jacob Van Staphorsts and Nicholas Hubbard of Amsterdam in the United Netherlands in the sum of two thousand Dollars of the United States of America, to the paiment whereof to themselves, their executors administrators or assigns, I bind myself, my heirs, executors and administrators. Witness my hand and seal this 26th. day of March 1797.

The Condition of the above obligation is such that if the above bounden Thomas, his heirs, executors or administrators shall pay to the said Nicholas and Jacob Van Staphorst and Nicholas Hubbard, their executors administrators or assigns on or before the first day of October which shall be in the year one thousand eight hundred and one the sum of one thousand dollars of like money with interest thereon at the rate of six per centum per annum from the first day of November which was in the year one thousand seven hundred and ninety six until such paiment shall be made, then this obligation to cease, but otherwise to remain in full force.   TH: JEFFERSON

Witness
DAVID WATSON

MS (DLC); entirely in TJ's hand; signed by TJ and Watson; also in TJ's hand are two attestations, the first signed by Thomas Bell and dated 27 Mch., acknowledging that TJ had appeared before him and was acting of his "own act and deed" and the second, signed by John Nicholas, clerk and keeper of the seal of the Albemarle County Court and dated 3 Apr., certifying that Bell was a justice of the peace for the county; endorsed; additional endorsement by LeRoy & Bayard & Co. of New York, 8 June 1818, acknowledging receipt of $2,387.69 in principal and interest, TJ's signature also being canceled by multiple strokes.

To Van Staphorst & Hubbard

ESTEEMED FRIENDS   Monticello in Virginia. Mar. 28. 97.

In a letter of yesterday's date I acknoleged the reciept of all yours which have come to hand since my last of Apr. 24. This is intended to answer yours of Oct. 10. 95. which never got to hand till Sep. 16. 96. Our legislature being then shortly to convene, I made timely applications to them, and obtained their act making you citizens of this state, which act duly authenticated I now inclose you, and hope it will get to hand safe, as the safe season for the seas is now approaching, and I shall endeavor to get it under the care of Mr. Murray who is going out as our Minister to your republic.   Should you ever be disposed to make a commercial establishment in the U.S. I hope our friend Jacob Van Staphorsts will recall to mind the advantages I so often pointed out to him in Norfolk, undoubtedly under way to become the greatest place in the US. and peculiarly convenient to your Eustatian connections. Without at all committing you, I held up to our legislature the hope I entertained myself that you would be tempted some day, or under certain events to do something at Norfolk. The contingency obtained the bill: and I shall be happy some time or other to see that I have not been mistaken in believing that this measure would eventually be interesting to the state as well as to yourselves. I am with great esteem Gentlemen Your friend & servt   TH: JEFFERSON

PrC (DLC); at foot of text: "Messrs. Van Staphorst & Hubbard"; endorsed by TJ in ink on verso. Enclosure: Act of Assembly, 23 Dec. 1796 (see TJ to Thomas Mann Randolph, 22 Jan. 1797). Enclosed in TJ to William Vans Murray, 27 Mch. 1797.

From William Short

MY DEAR SIR   Paris March 30. 1797

If I resume my pen once more to address you from this side of the Atlantic it is more that I may not let Colo. Monroe go without carrying some sign of life from me, than from any hope I retain of being able to add by it either to your instruction or amusement. You will recieve from him viva voce, all and every kind of information that I could give you of a public nature—and as to myself I hope to have so soon the pleasure of seeing you in person that I reserve for our interview every thing of that kind. Colo. Munro has just left this place for Bordeaux. I send this letter to overtake him there as he sat out sooner than I expected. I shall embark by the first vessel which shall sail in the month of May from Havre—or if there be none there I shall make use of the best opportunity which may present itself from any other port in France.[1] I had intended as I wrote you to have embarked last spring—but I did not recieve my letters of recreance[2] until the end of the summer—and I then yielded to the intreaty of friendship to prolong my stay here, added to my aversion to an autumnal or winter voyage. I have not written to you since my arrival in this country because I for a long time expected to have the pleasure of hearing from you conformably to my sollicitations from Spain of Sep. 2. 3. and 30. 1795.—and because as you did not write to me I thought it best to avoid repeating the trouble I gave you. The last and only letter I have received from you since you retired to Monticello was of May 25. 1795. It assured me that notwithstanding your silence your friendship for me was in [no] way diminished. I despair my dear Sir of conveying to you any idea of the heartfelt satisfaction I recieve from such assurances on your part. I feel sometimes that I have almost need of them after such long intervals of silence.

On the subject of the 9000 dollars I wrote you about, I know nothing further having never heard from E. Randolph and having only received a short answer from M. Pickering which said neither one thing or another. My desire will be when I shall be in America to place every thing I have in lands rented out at a sure and annual interest. On these subjects I shall I hope soon have the pleasure of conversing with you. M. Munro and Mr. Skipwith both offered to purchase my Indian camp at an advanced price—but I shall prefer adding to it if farmers can be found to rent it so as to yield an immediate profitable interest[3] on the purchase money.

I send you inclosed a few grains of a very esteemed kind of barley—called here *l'age de Siberie*. Its weight is to common barley as 41. to 32.—has several better qualities and particularly in its mixture with wheat, makes a fine bread, is more productive in the grain more easily cleaned &c. &c. I have thought it might be agreeable to you in your agricultural experiments. I get it from La Rocheguyon where I saw it growing this year in their potager. They have been cultivating it for some years past in order to multiply the seed which the Abbé Tessier furnished them from Rambouillet. On my mentioning to Mde. D'Enville my intention of sending you these grains she begs me to recall her to your recollection. She as well as her grandaughter have a real respect and attachment for you. The latter with her usual and incomparable modesty says she hardly supposes you recollect her. She assures me often there is no person whose friendship she would be more happy to cultivate.

I have made a valuable discovery in a bookseller here, who desires me to put him in correspondence with you. You may perhaps recollect a blind Chev. de Malthe at Mde. de Tessés. He is a man of science and honor and honesty and has adopted this business for a livelihood in which he succeeds perfectly. His[4] address is Charles Pougens, Libraire No. 246. Rue St. Thomas du Louvre—he understands English well[5] and you may therefore give him your commissions in that language if you chuse it. Adieu &c.

Dft (DLC: Short Papers); entirely in Short's hand, heavily emended, only the most important changes being reported in notes below; word in brackets supplied; at foot of text: "Mr. Jefferson &c." Recorded in SJL as received 29 June 1797 "by Colo. Monroe."

BARLEY never became a significant crop for TJ at Monticello (Barbara McEwan, *Thomas Jefferson: Farmer* [Jefferson, N.C., 1991], 64). Although not actually an ecclesiastic, the French agronomist Alexandre Henri TESSIER was called "abbé." He was educated as a physician, and beginning in the 1780s as director of the farms at RAMBOUILLET, an estate of Louis XVI which subsequently became a residence of Napoleon, he implemented numerous agricultural innovations, studied diseases of plants and animals, and introduced new varieties of crops and livestock, including most nota-
bly the merino sheep from Spain (*Biographie universelle*, XLI, 190-2; Jean Tulard, ed., *Dictionnaire Napoléon* [Paris, 1987], 1438). For the patronage once extended by the MDE. DE TESSÉ to Charles de POUGENS, see above in this series, Vol. 10: 158-9n.

[1] Short here canceled: "I shall prefer Havre, on account of its proximity and my having never been there."
[2] Word interlined in place of "recall."
[3] Short originally ended the sentence here, continuing and subsequently canceling: "This kind of vestment will be always agreeable."
[4] Word reworked from "He," and as first written the passage continued: "is much connected in friendship with your old acquaintance M. Gautier; who has now a separate house."
[5] Word interlined in place of "perfectly."

From Martha Jefferson Randolph

My Dearest Father   Varina March 31st. 1797

The first certain accounts we had of your arrival were conveyed by your letter to Mr. Randolph which would as you suposed have met on his way up had we not previously determined upon having the children innoculated. But every circumstance of season health &c. conspiring to make the present opportunity favorable Mr. Randolph thought no interest of his could excuse his letting it slip. I have often experienced that a mother's heart was of all things in nature the least subject to reason but never more fully than at present. The idea of exposing my children to such a disorder with out being able to accompany them alltho I have the certainty of their finding in their Father as tender and an infinitely more skill full nurse than my self, makes me perfectly miserable. I never look at them but my eyes fill with tears to think how soon we shall part and *perhaps* for ever. The anxiety I feel on their account my Dear Father does not prevent my feeling most sensibly for the solitude and gloom of your present situation. I never take a view of your solitary fire side but my heart swells. However as nothing detains us now but the children I hope soon [to][1] be restored to your paternal embraces and dispel by the presence of your children the cloud which obscures the beauties of spring, no where so enchanting as at Monticello. My Sister joins me [in] the tenderest love.[2] As the boys are waiting I am obliged to conclude with Dearest Father your most affectionate   M. Randolph

RC (MHi); endorsed by TJ as received 5 Apr. 1797 and so recorded in SJL.

Your letter: TJ to Thomas Mann Randolph, 23 Mch. [1797].

[1] Word supplied.

[2] Randolph first wrote "My Sister joins [. . .] the tenderest love with me and" before altering the sentence to read as above but neglecting to cancel "with."

From Willink, Van Staphorst & Hubbard

Sir   Amsterdam 31 March 1797.

Permit us to congratulate you, on your election to the high and honorable Office of Vice President of the United States, in the discharge of which We most sincerely and ardently wish you the Success that our personal knowledge and experience assure us your exertions, Zeal, and perseverance to promote the Honor, Interest, and Prosperity of your Country will most amply merit.

The warm part We take in the welfare of your Republic, as well as

our personal esteem and regard for you sir, all combine to fortify our hopes and desire, that you may enjoy perfect Health and Vigor, to meet and sustain the fatigues of your present elevated Station, and long live to taste in joy and tranquillity their happy fruits. With greatest respect We have the honor to be Sir! Your most obedient and very humble servants   WILHEM & JAN WILLINK
N & J. VAN STAPHORST & HUBBARD

RC (MoSHi: Jefferson Papers); in a clerk's hand, signed by both firms; at foot of text: "Dupl." and "The Honble. Thos. Jefferson Esqe. Vice President of the United States"; endorsed by TJ as received 28 June 1797 and so recorded in SJL.

To James Wood

SIR   Monticello Mar. 31. 97.

Your letter of the 3d. inst. did not get to Philadelphia till I had left it, and therefore came to hand here only this day week. I have bestowed on it's subject the earliest attention I could. When on a former occasion the Executive were pleased to apply to me (being then in France) for a plan of a Capitol, they at the same time desired one of a prison. An architect of Lyons had in 1761[1] proposed the idea of solitary confinement, and presented to that government an engraved plan for a prison on that idea. This was, as far as I know, the first proposition for this kind of punishment. It was *afterwards* as I believe, that a particular society adopted it in England. Pennsylvania is the 2d.[2] and ourselves the 3d.[3] instance of adoption. I recieved from the architect of Lyons (M. Bugniet) a copy of his plan, and sent it to our executive with the plans and models of the Capitol; and to adapt it to the smaller scale which suited us, I sketched a plan of a prison for us with solitary cells. These draughts probably still exist among the papers of the council. However lest they should not, as I retain the general idea in my mind, I have sketched it on paper and now inclose the sketch. But to accomodate 200. persons on this plan will cost 37,000 Doll. and 7000. D. more if it be surrounded by a fossé which I think very important for securing against escapes. I have drawn the plan however on this scale, but have added an estimate of the same plan reduced to 144. cells, which brings it to about 27,000. Doll. and to inclose it with a fossé would add about 5000 Doll. more. Cheap accomodations for 56. persons more might be provided in the two houses making part of the plan, and in barracks within the Area. I presume others have been invited to propose plans, and have no doubt some will chance to hit on something better. If not, and this should be adopted, I would wish to be advised of it, in order to propose some details for giving to the building a plain, decent appearance, and preventing an affectation of ornament which would be entirely misplaced on a building of this character. I have the honor to be with great respect, Sir, Your most obedt. & most humble servt   TH: JEFFERSON

RC (Vi: Executive Papers); addressed: "The Governor of Virginia Richmond"; franked; with emendations, only the most important being noted below; endorsed by Wood. PrC (DLC); endorsed on verso in ink by TJ. Enclosed plan not found; other enclosures printed below.

For the FORMER OCCASION on which TJ supplied plans for public buildings in Richmond, including one for a prison based on the plan of Pierre Gabriel BUGNIET, see his letter to James Buchanan and William Hay, 26 Jan. 1786.

The genealogy of solitary confinement, considered at the time to be a progressive reform, was not quite as direct as TJ understood it to be. The plan he saw in France was not the FIRST PROPOSITION of the idea, which had been suggested as early as 1701-02 in England and elsewhere, and in 1703 the Vatican had built a prison based on the concept. By the 1770s the notion was strongly advocated by reformers in England (Michael Ignatieff, *A Just Measure of Pain: The Penitentiary in the Industrial Revolution, 1750-1850* [New York, 1978], 53-4, 65-6). PENNSYLVANIA in 1790 authorized construction, at the Walnut Street prison in Philadelphia, of cells designed for solitary confinement, and in 1796 New York, New Jersey, and Virginia all followed that state

in reducing the number of capital offenses in their criminal codes and authorizing new penitentiaries. New York preceded Virginia in actual construction, but solitary confinement was not a primary feature of the New York facility. The Virginia act required inmates to spend a portion of their terms in solitude, so as TJ envisioned his design, Virginia could indeed claim to be the next INSTANCE OF ADOPTION after Pennsylvania (Adam Jay Hirsch, *The Rise of the Penitentiary: Prisons and Punishment in Early America* [New Haven, 1992], 59-60; Edward L. Ayers, *Vengeance and Justice: Crime and Punishment in the 19th-Century American South* [New York, 1984], 38; Norval Morris and David J. Rothman, eds., *The Oxford History of the Prison: The Practice of Punishment in Western Society* [New York, 1995], 114-15; W. David Lewis, *From Newgate to Dannemora: The Rise of the Penitentiary in New York, 1796-1848* [Ithaca, N.Y., 1965], 30-1).

A 3 Apr. letter from Wood to TJ and one from TJ to him of 30 Apr., both noted in SJL, have not been found.

[1] Preceding word and date interlined in place of "just then."
[2] Digit reworked from "3."
[3] Reworked from "4th."

ENCLOSURES

I

Notes on Plan of a Prison

Notes and Explanations

Fig. 1. The Ground plat of the building, which is an octagonal periphery of barracks, two stories high, within a single order, having before them a piazza, or arcade every arch of which corresponds to a lower and upper cell, which recieve their light and air through the arch and their own grated door. The cells are 8 f. wide, 10 f. long and 9. f. high in the clear, as directed by the act of assembly, the walls of rough stone 2. f. thick, except the arcade or inner front, the whole of which must be of brick, as well as the cross arches and vaults of the cells. The lower story is destined for the cells of rigorous confinement, the lower part of the arch having a venetian blind to exclude the sight while it admits air. The internal area is of 340. feet diameter. Being drawn on a ruled paper, every line of which is 2. feet, the dimensions of every part may be seen without particularly noting them.

A. is the jailer's house, the internal of which may be arranged ad libitum.

B. is the infirmary, the internal to be arranged ad libitum.

C. is a piazza, along which the watchman may perform his rounds every night, as the law directs. There must be cross arches of 60°.[1] from each of the pillars of the piazza to the front wall of the cells, in order that vaults of only 4. Inches thick[2] may be thrown from cross arch to cross arch to support a paved floor in the piazza on a level with the floor of the upper cells, which are destined for Penitentiary or milder confinement.

D. are the cells of rigorous confinement. To each must be a privy hole lined with plate iron, leading through the wall so that the matter may fall into the fossé. Above are the Penitentiary cells: the privies for which are in the 8. angles, as it is presumed these persons will be at liberty to go out of their cells. Every cell above and below to have an irongrated door, and an internal sash door which the prisoner may open or shut at pleasure. The steps to the upper cells must be placed so as best to answer the views of police entertained. The cells both above and below to be vaulted with an arch of 60°. of the thickness of a brick's length, the ends of the brick pointing downwards, and every course of them forming a distinct arch. Arches of 60°. are directed because they are stronger than half circles. The half circle is only to be used for the Arcades, for beauty.

E. is a fossé, 9. f. deep below the surface of the ground, and 18. f. wide, surrounding the whole.

F. is a bank 9. f. high, made of the earth thrown out of the fossé, faced with stone, and so presenting a perpendicular of 18. f. to a prisoner who has escaped from his cell. On the top of the bank plant trees.

g.h. shews the direction of the cross walls.

Fig. 2. is a section across the building. It shews the bank, fosse, upper and lower cells the vault which supports the upper floor of the piazza, and the level of the ground.

Fig. 3. is a section lengthwise through a cell and 2 half cells above and below, shewing their vaults of 60°.

Fig. 4. is the external front of an Arch and 2. half arches, shewing the grated doors through them.

Fig. 5. is an elevation of the side of the octagon having the jailer's house in it, and looking into the area.

The roof of the cells is to be covered with slate, so that there will be not a particle of wood in that part of the building but the joists, rafters and sheeting boards, and the sash doors. The whole of the cells are to be warmed by flue pipes leading from common fires in the manner a green house is warmed, and indeed as is usual in this country over the mountains, where all the rooms are sometimes warmed from a single fire.

The great size of the area (340. f.) will admit barracks to be set up for carrying on any kind of work. The entrance must be through the jailer's house by a draw bridge.

The law directs that 200. persons shall be accomodated, and at an expence of

30,000 Dollars. This cannot be done on this plan. If the 200. cells prepared in this draught are to be kept, it will cost more than that sum. If the sum of 30,000. D. be adhered to, the number of cells must (if this plan be preserved) be reduced to 10. of a side, 144. in the whole besides the jailer's house and infirmary, [3] and the fossé must be omitted. The internal area of the building will then be 245 instead of 340. feet.

I shall attempt an estimate of the cost on the scale here drawn as well as on the reduced scale (to wit of 10. instead of 14. cells of a side) but, it will be merely conjectural as I know nothing of the Richmond prices. I shall guess from what I know of prices at some other places, or from other circumstances.

There will be many details to be supplied by the workman; I have not descended into them, because less qualified to do it, and because it is probable that others have been invited to propose plans, and that some better ones will be proposed. Should this be adopted, I should be glad to be informed of it, that I may send a drawing of a plain neat cornice, and give some other directions respecting appearance.

MS (Vi: Executive Papers); entirely in TJ's hand, and meant to accompany his missing plan.

AS DIRECTED BY THE ACT OF ASSEMBLY: see James Wood to TJ, 3 Mch. 1797. TJ's references here to the specifications of the statute are accurate, except the act called for cells six feet wide, eight feet long, and nine feet high. ESTIMATE OF THE COST: see Enclosure II below.

[1] Preceding word and digits interlined.

[2] Preceding four words and digit interlined.

[3] TJ here changed a period to a comma and interlined the remainder of the paragraph.

II. Table of Estimates

Estimate		on the scale of 200. cells and 340. f. diam. of area		on the scale of 144. cells & 245. f. diam. of Area	
		Quantity	Dollars	Quantity	Dollars
Bricks.	Arcade 1120. feet running measure (for an internal area of 340. f. diam.)	386,000.		278,208	
	106. cross arches, of half a brick thick.	10,600		7,800	
	108. vaults at mid height of the Piazza, half a brick thick.	38,016		27,360	
	200. vaults of upper & lower cells. a brick length in thickness	216,000.		155,520	
	at 15. Doll. per thousand, as all the work is difficult.	650,616	9,759.	468,888.	7,032.
Stone work.	front wall of the cells. 1232. f. running measure				
	back wall of do. 1280.				
	106. cross walls. 1060				
	$3572. \times 2$ f. thickness & 23 f. height $= 164,312.$ cub. feet				
	which divided by 25. gives in perch	6 572. perch			
	add 3d. story of the 2. houses	342.		4,978	9,956
	at 2. Doll. the perch	6 914.	13,828		
	Fossé. below backwall 8 f. x 1280. and the outer wall 19. f. x 1440. x 2 = 75,200. cub. feet	3 008.	6,016.		
Digging.	cubic yards digging @ $\frac{1}{8}$ Doll. pr. yard	10,000. cub.yds	1,250		
Plaistering	Square yards.	10,000. sq.yards		7,200. sq yds	450.
Paving.	brickbats equivalent to whole bricks & laying them @ 5. D. pr. M	126,000. bricks	630.	90,000. bricks	3,456
Slating.	squares of 100. f. @ 12. D. the square (London price)	400. squares	4,800	288. squares	1,920.
Roof.	joists, rafters, sheeting & putting up @ $3\frac{1}{3}$ Doll. per hundred sq. feet	80,000. sq. feet	2,666	57,600. sq. f.	120.
Flooring.	plank floors @ $3\frac{1}{3}$ Doll. per square	50. squares	166.	36. squares	200
	15. pannel doors & 22. sash windows		277		
	200. sash doors @ $7\frac{1}{2}$ Doll.	200. doors	1 500.	144. doors	1 080.
	200 iron grated doors $6\frac{1}{2}$ by $2\frac{1}{2}$ f. 120. ℔ each @ $\frac{1}{8}$ Doll.	200. doors	3 000.	144. doors	2,160
	2000. f. of stove pipes + 300. f. of sheet iron tubes for privies	2 300. f.	575.	1 656 f.	414
			44,467.[1]		26,788.

If the smaller scale should be adopted, on returning to me the draught and this paper, I will furnish a new drawing on the scale adopted. It need occasion only one fortnight's delay. It would be well to accompany them with the notes and observations of intelligent workmen, that what is now defective may be known and supplied.

MS (Vi: Executive Papers); entirely in TJ's hand.

[1] TJ mistakenly placed this total at the foot of the first column.

From Thomas Paine

Havre de Grace April 1st—1797

I left Paris about ten days ago and came to this place, intending to take passage in the Dublin Packet for New York, but the Vessel being crouded I shall wait another opportunity. Mr. Monroe, whom I left at Paris, intended going by the way of Bordeaux. Four American Vessels have arrived since I have been here. 1 from Savannah, 1 from Charleston, 1 from Wilmington N.C.—and 1 from N.Y.—which are the only arrivals from America, for several [wee]ks past. American Vessels are not employed as Carriers by [Fran]ce; that trade, since Mr. Jay's *treaty of surrender*, is [gone into the?] hands of the Danes and Swedes. That neutral Ships [. . .] property must be a general principle, or not at all. Mr. [Jay?] [. . .] surrenders the principle, by treating it merely as a [. . .]; and that without perceiving, that through the Medium [. . .] second Article in the treaty of Commerce with france, ev[ery cir]cumstance is surrendered also. You can have but little conc[eption] how low the character of the American Government is sunk in Europe. The Neutral powers despise her for her meaness, and her desertion of a Common interest; England laughs at her imbecility, and France is enraged at her ingratitude, and Sly treachery. Such is the condition into which Mr. Washington's Administration has brought America, and what makes it worse is, that John Adams has not Character to do any good. Some of the American papers speak of Mr. Madison's coming as Envoy Extraordinary. As that Character is only temporary, and his reputation stands well here, he would, I believe,[1] be received, tho' it was refused to Mr. Pinckney, as a resident Minister. The recal of Mr. Monroe cut every thing asunder, for tho' here they were enraged at the American Government, they were not enraged at him. They had an esteem for him, and a good opinion of him; they would listen to him, and he could soften them; but to recall him and to send in his place the brother of the Man who was concerned in forming Jay's treaty was stupidity and insult both. If Mr. Madison should come you must not expect too much.

About the time this letter comes to hand you will hear that the Bank of England stopt payment on the 27 of Febru. and continues shut up. Several people who affected to laugh at my Decline and Fall of the English System of finance now see it in another light. That little Work was translated into french, and sent by the french Govermt. to all their foreign Agents and was also translated into German, low Dutch—Swedish and Italien. It demolished the credit of the English funds in those Countries, and caused a great [pu]lling out. It spread all over England, for it was sold as low as [. . .] Coppers, and at New-Castle at two. The farmers became [. . .] of Paper. They run upon the Country banks with the [. . .] Notes they took at Market. The Country Banks collected [. . .] as they could of the Bank of England, and run upon [. . .] for Cash—the people of London began to do the [same?] [. . .] the whole complicated Machine knocked up at once. [Every?] bank in England is now Stopt. For my own part I cannot see how it is possible the bank of England should ever open again. Were it to open tomorrow the run upon it would be so immense, they would be obliged to shut it immediately. They are now emitting 20 shilling and forty shilling Notes, and as it is easy to see that a shopkeeper will not give change in Cash for a twenty shilling Note they will be obliged to emit ten shilling, and five shilling Notes and so on. I much question if England has gained any thing by Trade for an hundred years past; that is, ever since the funding system began. She has pushed her Manufactures about the World, at great risk and often at loss, and the bustle it made gave her the opportunity of pushing forth a vast quantity of Paper at home, which the Commercial Idiots mistook for gain and Wealth; but now, she comes to wind up her affairs she finds she has not so much money as she had an hundred years ago. The quantity of Money at this time in England is less than it was at the revolution in 1688. It is not estimated now at more than twelve Millions sterling. It never was more than twenty and if the public papers speak truth, not less than ten Millions have sent out in foreign Subsidies, foreign loans, and Expeditions on the Continent. [2]

In france nothing is seen but Money. Paper is entirely gone. The quantity of Money in france must be great, since the whole of Trade and of Taxes is carried on entirely upon Money, and there is always a sufficiency of it whereever there is an Object to employ it [. . .]. Every article of provision (not foreign) is cheaper, better, and more abundant than before the [revolut]ion. Bread is two Coppers and an half per pound. Beef and Mutton eight Coppers. [3]

[. . .] Peace I am not able to give you any opinion upon it. It [seems to?] me to be at a greater distance than it did four or five Mo[nths] [. . .] two of the Coalized Powers, Austria and England, are now [. . .] is now defeated every where. Bonaparte carries [. . .] these last few days he has beaten the Arch-Duke C[harles] [. . .] taken five thousand prisoners, 1400 in one Action, and 3600 [in] another. The Government of England is in a State of Bankrupt [. . .] and her total downfal is probable. It will be a good thing when this happens, for it is the most mischievous, surly, [4] and ill willed Government in the World. In this state of things france is not in a hurry about peace; for of what use would be a peace that would be war again in a short time? Four times have the English

Government been running into War, or upon the brink of it, since the American War. Once on account of Holland; again on account of Russia, again on account of Nootka sound—and now to support the lubberly Junto, called Crowned-heads.

How America will scuffle through I know not. The Mean, ungrateful, and treacherous Conduct of her Administration, helped on by the political Ignorance of a Considerable body of her Merchants, have ruined her Character; and from being the favourite, she is become the Scoff of the World. It is very disagreeable to me to write truths of this kind; but it can do you no service to disbelieve them. For my own part, whereever I go, I curse the Conduct of the American Government to save the Character of the Country. I hope you will accept the Vice-presidency, were it only to keep an Eye upon John Adams, or he will commit some blunder that will make matters worse. He has a Natural disposition to blunder and to offend, and Mr. Secretary Pickering is of the same Cast. When John Adams was in Holland, he published a small Work in favour of republics as if purposely to offend France; and when he was in England he wrote in support of what he called the English Constitution as if to offend republics. He is a Man entirely under the Government of a bad [tem]per without having any thing Manly in his Manner of acting it. [. . .] Government of France appeared to be very unwilling to [. . .]nities with America. The injury which Governeer [Morris made?] was repaired by Mr. Monroe; and as they hated the Idea [. . .]ment between Republics, they enjoyed the return of con[fidence. When] Jay's treaty appeared, it is easy to suppose the impression it [made] [. . .]. They began to suspect that Mr. Monroe was sent for the purpose [of] amusing them while Jay was to act a contrary part in England. They waited however to see, if the President would ratify it. Then, what Notice Congress would take of it; and it was only till after the last chance was past that they broke out. They then told Mr. Monroe they had rather have the Government of America for an open Enemy than a treacherous friend. It is evident that if the two Treaties, that with France and that with England, could exist together, that France would be injured by the independance of America which cost her so much to support. Before that time the American flag was not a Neutral when England was at War, and if it is now to be a Neutral to protect English property and English Merchandize from Capture, whilst it gives no protection to those of France, it would be better to france that America was still under the English Government; for that Neutrality would be more benificial to England and more injurious to France than what America, considered merely in the Scale of Naval or Military power, could be to either. You ought not to be surprised if in the Issue of this business, France should demand reimbursement for the expence she was at in supporting the independance of America; for she feels herself most rascally treated for that support; and unless John Adams is watched his surly Manners and those of Timothy Pickering will give some new opportunity to provoke it. At the time the cringing treaty was formed with England, Timothy Pickering, as Secretary of State, wrote officially to Mr. Monroe, in an insulting Manner towards [Fran]ce. "The American Government, says Timothy, is the comp[etent] Guardian of every thing which concerns her National ho[nour, policy, or] interest, and it will not ask the opinion nor be [guided by the] Advice of any Nation." What are Ministers sent for, [. . .] and to Consult, especially between Nations supposed [. . .] alliance. The language of Timothy is the language of a Blow [. . .] and were it said directly to france, she might be provoked to [. . .]. There was a time when you were glad to ask our advice and [our] Money too, pay us what we have expended for you and get about your business. In the same letter Timothy calls those who oppose the English Treaty by the Name of *dissaffected persons*. "From the movements, says he, of *dissaffected persons* &c." You will observe that I write this part only to you. Should Mr. Monroe arrive while Congress is sitting it ought to call, or invite him, before them, to know the State of their affairs;[5] they will neither do Justice to the Country, to themselves, nor to him if they do not. It is only through the Medium of the house of representatives that the breach can be healed, and further Mischief avoided. Your Executive, John Adams, can do nothing but harm. You see that France has made every Power pay that insulted or injured her, yet those powers had not received former favours from her as America had done. The Ignorance in which your former executive has kept Congress and the Country, with respect to the State of their foreign Affairs, is equal to any assumption of the same kind, ever acted by any Despot.

For my own part I was always opposed, and ever shall be, to the plan of working government up to an Individual, and in all my publications I have written against it. In America, the place was made for the Man, and, at that time, it was not easy to prevent it. I hope it will be altered now, and my princi[pal mo]tive for wishing that you might be president, was, that [you might?] the better promote that alteration. The whole rep[. . .] is the president, and the part called the executive [. . .] a plurality, as in the french Constitution. Mr. Monroe has written quires of letters, to the secretary of State. He might [as] well have written them to the Sepulchre. An Individual President will never be any thing more than the Chief of a Party, and the conductor of its politics. All contrary information goes for nothing.

With respect to the Ships of Neutral Powers, (which makes the difficulty that America is now in) there were two Ways to have restrained if not totally to have prevented the depredation. The one was for the Neutral powers to have united for the protection of their own rights. Sweden and Denmark sent proposals to America for this purpose but no attention was paid to them. And as to Jay, he never held any communication with the Ministers of those powers when in England.

The other was, for France to have made a declaration to England, that if England Molested Neutral Ships coming to, or going from France, that France would take the Cargoes of all Neutral Ships going to or coming from England. England would then have seen that she would lose far more than she could gain. It was the forbearance of france that encouraged the depredations of England; for now that England sustains the reaction of her own politics, she seems disposed to let Neutral Ships pass. Had france made the Declaration at first, the Consequence would have been that either she would not have molested Neutral Ships, or she must have insured all Cargoes going and coming and sustained the loss of all. The Neutral Ships would not have been her [car]riers, nor traded with her, on any other Condition than being [insur]ed. I pressed the Minister De la Croix to make a declar[ation of this] kind to England when the british Agent, Malmsbury, [was in] Paris. I added, if you do not chuse to act upon the Dec[. . .] the effect of it. He wrote to me in answer that he would [. . .] all his possibles to have it done. I wish it had been done [at?] first; for it is the bold politics of France that must secure the Neutrality of the American flag since her government has surrendered it.

My health is much improved, but the Abscess in my side still continues but with very little pain. THOMAS PAINE

RC (DLC); mutilated; second set of closing quotation marks supplied; only the most significant emendations are recorded in notes below; endorsed by TJ as received 5 June 1797 and so recorded in SJL.

The cash reserves of the BANK OF ENGLAND had been depleted by advances to the government, and fears of a French-sponsored invasion had also drained specie from English banks. An Order in Council of 26 Feb. 1797, confirmed by Parliament in the Bank Restriction Act of 3 May, authorized the Bank of England to cease paying out gold. Intended as a short-term expedient, the measure, which caused notes of the Bank of England to replace specie in most

transactions, remained in effect for more than twenty years (Emsley, *British Society and the French Wars*, 57). THAT LITTLE WORK: Paine's pamphlet, *The Decline and Fall of the English System of Finance*, had been published in Paris and London in 1796. See Sowerby, No. 3188.

At Tarvis during March, Napoleon BONAPARTE, advancing through the Italian Alps, defeated three divisions of the Austrian army commanded by the ARCH-DUKE CHARLES and appeared to have opened the way for a final advance on Vienna (Chandler, *Campaigns of Napoleon*, 123-5).

John Adams's WORK IN FAVOUR OF REPUBLICS was *A Collection of State-Papers*, relative to the first acknowledgment of the sovereignty of the United States of America, printed in The Hague and London in 1782. His work IN SUPPORT OF WHAT HE CALLED THE ENGLISH CONSTITUTION was A Defence of the Constitutions of Government of the United States of America, published in London in 1787. See Sowerby, Nos. 3000, 3004.

Pickering's INSULTING MANNER TOWARDS FRANCE was displayed in his 12 Sep. 1795 letter to Monroe and concerned the French government's objections to the Jay Treaty. On the matter of the British definition of contraband, Pickering insisted that whether British pretensions ought to be resisted was a question for "the proper authorities of the United States to decide" (ASP, Foreign Relations, I, 597). DISSAFFECTED PERSONS: near the beginning of his letter Pickering noted, "it is proper that you should be possessed of the opinions of the Government, especially as it appears probable, from your letters, and from the movements of disaffected persons here, that unfavorable impressions upon the Government and people of France may be apprehended" (same, 596).

After learning that SWEDEN AND DENMARK had signed a convention on 27 Mch. 1794 to protect their commerce even to the extent of initiating reprisals, in July 1794 the majority of Washington's cabinet advised against joining such an alliance. That opinion was not announced, and in 1795 the Swedish government sent formal PROPOSALS to the United States, first through Pinckney in London and subsequently, after receiving no answer, through Monroe in France, who received only a noncommittal acknowledgment from Pickering. In May 1794, before the Washington administration had formed an opinion on the Scandinavian convention, the instructions given to John JAY for negotiating with Britain had authorized him, if "the situation of things with respect to Great Britain should dictate the necessity of taking the precaution of foreign cooperation upon this head," to meet with the Swedish, Danish, and Russian ministers in London to discuss the prospect of an alliance. However, the British government soon learned, by way of a conversation between George Hammond and Alexander Hamilton, that there was virtually no chance of the United States "entangling itself with European connexions" (Syrett, Hamilton, XVI, 327, 542-3, 548, 578-9; Monroe, Writings, II, 329-30).

[1] Preceding two words interlined.
[2] Paine here interlined and then canceled the three sentences identified as a subsequent interlineation in the following note.
[3] Preceding three sentences interlined.
[4] Word interlined.
[5] Preceding seven words and semicolon interlined.

To John Brown

DEAR SIR   Monticello April. 5. 97.

Tho' you thought you had made such progress in your plan that it could not be altered, yet I send you the one I mentioned, as you may perhaps draw some hints from it for the improvement of yours. The method of building houses 2, 3, or 4 stories high, first adopted in cities [where] ground is scarce, and thence without reason copied in the country where ground abounds, has for these 20. or 30. years been abandoned in Europe in all good houses newly built[1] in the country, and very often even in the cities. In Paris particularly all the new and good houses are of a single story. That is of the height of 16. or 18. f. generally, and the whole of it given to the rooms of entertainment; but in the parts where there are bedrooms they have two [tier] of them of from 8. to 10. f. high each, with a small private staircase. By these means great staircases are avoided, which are expensive and occupy a space which would make a good room in every story. Nor is a single storied house as expensive as those higher, when y[ou cre]dit them for the cellars and offices below and saving of partition walls,[2] and charge the higher ones [the thick]ening of the walls below, the expence of mounting materials so high, space for chimnies, great staircases &c. The wall of a single storied house should be[3] a brick and half thick from the water table upwards. A four storied house must have[4] the lower story 3. bricks thick, the second $2\frac{1}{2}$, the 3d 2. bricks and the fourth $1\frac{1}{2}$. a difference of 50. per cent. 4. rooms in a 4 storied house have 16. side walls, and in a one storied house 12 side walls, a difference of $33\frac{1}{3}$ per cent. But all this you can calculate yourself. As you left Philadelphia later than I did, I can communicate nothing new to you. Wishing you every felicity I am with great esteem Dr. Sir Your affectionate friend & servt

TH: JEFFERSON

PrC (DLC); faded and torn; significant emendations recorded in notes below; at foot of text: "John Brown"; endorsed by TJ in ink on verso. Enclosure not found.

Although claims have been made that "Liberty Hall," Brown's home in Frankfort, Kentucky, was actually built from TJ's design, the house as constructed had two stories and bore "none of the character of Jefferson's work" (Fiske Kimball, "Jefferson's Designs for Two Kentucky Houses," *Journal of the Society of Architectural Historians*, IX, No. 3 [1950], 14-16).

[1] Preceding two words interlined.
[2] Preceding five words interlined.
[3] TJ here interlined and then canceled "[2] bricks thick below the water table and."
[4] TJ here interlined and then canceled "[$3\frac{1}{2}$] bricks below the water table."

To Peregrine Fitzhugh

DEAR SIR   Monticello Apr. 9. 97.

Your favor of Mar. 25. came safely to hand with the grains of [corn it covered] for which accept my thanks. A nephew of mine, Mr. S. Carr who married a daughter of the Mr. Carr near Georgetown, setting out this day for that place, I have sent him some of the peas you [desired] which he will inclose under cover to you, and lodge in the care of Mr. John Thompson Mason. This letter goes separately by post, to notify you that you may call for them in time for the present season. I wish it were in my power to satisfy you with respect to the sentiments expressed by my friend Mr. Madison in the general convention. But the papers in my possession are under a seal which I have not broken yet, and wish not to break till I have time to give them a thorough perusal and consideration. Two things may be safely said. 1. when a man, whose life has been marked by it's candor, has given a latter opinion contrary to a former one, it is probably the result of further enquiry, reflection and conviction. This is a sound answer, if the contrariety of sentiment as to the treaty making power were really expressed by him on the former and latter occasion as was alledged to you. But 2. as no man weighs more maturely than Mr. Madison before he takes a side on any question, I do not expect he has changed either his opinion on that subject or the expressions of it, and therefore I presume the allegation founded in some misconception or misinformation.—I have just recieved a summons to *Congress* for the 15th. of next month. I am sorry for it, as every thing pacific could have been done without *Congress*, and I hope nothing is contemplated which is not pacific. I wish I may be as fortunate in my travelling companions as I was the last trip. I hope you found your father and family well. Present him, if you please, the respectful homage of one who knew him when too young probably to have been known by him and accept yourself assurances of the great esteem of Dear Sir Your most obedt. humble servt

TH: JEFFERSON

PrC (DLC); faded; at foot of text: "Peregrine Fitzhugh esq."

From Alexandre Giroud

Au Cap français le 20
Germinal an 5e de la République
francaise [i.e. 9 Apr. 1797].

Au Citoyen Jefferson, Vice Président du Gouvernement des Etats unis.

Giroud Ingénieur des Mines; Membre de l'Institut National de Paris.

Citoyen. Vous vous rappellerez peut-etre d'un francais qui vous fut presenté au Commencement de 1789, et à qui vous donnates des renseignements Sur une Succession provenant d'oglèthorpe Gouverneur jadis de la Géorgie. Ce francais c'est moi, et je Me rappelle avec plaisir les Moments que cette Affaire me fit passer auprès de vous.

Envoyé depuis un an environ par le Gouvernement francais, dans la Colonie de St. Domingue pour Entreprendre la description Minéralogique de Cette Isle, j'ai profité, dernierement, de l'envoy des frégates francaises commandées par le Brave Barney pour faire un voyage aux Etats unis. Je désirais vous y voir, et m'entretenir avec vous d'histoire naturelle Mais la fortune ne m'a pas bien servi, j'ai été obligé de repartir de Philadelphie, quelques jours avant votre arrivée dans cette ville.

Je profite d'une occasion favorable pour vous écrire, et vous adresser quelques Graines du Prima où Arbre à Pain. Cette Plante précieuse réussit parfaitement ici, où elle A été transportée des Isles des amis dans la mer du Sud. J'espère qu'elle réussira aussi dans les Etats Méridionaux de votre République. Puissé je apprendre un Jour que C'est moi qui aurai fait ce Beau présent à Votre patrie! Puisse, le verger du Philosophe et du Républicain de Monticello, etre dans 10 Ans, Couvert du Bel ombrage, et des fruits Alimenteux de cet arbre précieux. Je ne doute pas qu'avec quelques soins, Vous ne parveniez à le naturaliser dans la Virginie puisque le Célèbre Cook rapportte avoir trouvé l'arbre à Pain en plein rapport jusques dans la nouvelle Zélande, Sous une température plus froide que celle de Londres.

Je profiterai des occasions favorables qui pourront Se présenter pour vous faire par le Canal du Cn. franklin Bache de nouveaux envoys des graines du Prima et d'autres fruits précieux de l'Inde que nous possedons ici, et que nous devons Au Zèle des Philantropes, et des Botanistes pour multiplier, et répandre sur les divers points de la terre, les plantes utiles où agréables à l'homme. Salut Respect & fraternité,

GIROUD

RC (DLC); perpendicularly in margin: "Mon adresse, est. au Citoyen Giroud Ingénieur des Mines de la République francaise. chez le Citoyen Raymond, Commissaire du Directoire Exécutif. Au Cap francais. Isle St. Domingue"; endorsed by TJ as received 12 May 1797 and so recorded in SJL.

After the commencement of the French Revolution Alexandre Giroud (1761-1797), a member of a Grenoble family of printers and booksellers, held political office in the *département* of l'Isère, and, pursuing an interest in mineralogy and metallurgy, established an artillery foundry. In Paris in 1794 he was appointed an engineer of mines, in which capacity he taught metallurgy for the national agency of mines and also published several reports on mineralogical topics. In March 1796 he was named an associate of the National Institute, and that same month he left for Saint-Dominigue to act with a panel of commissioners appointed by the Directory. He began a geological investigation of the island, but died in September 1797 (*Dictionnaire*, XVI, 302).

While in France, TJ had addressed questions relating to inheritances from the estate of James Edward Oglethorpe (OGLÉTHORPE), the founder of the colony of Georgia (see TJ's Amplification of Subjects Discussed with Vergennes, [ca. 20 Dec. 1785]; TJ to the Governor of Georgia, 22 Dec. 1785; and the Report on Conversations with Vergennes enclosed in TJ to John Jay, 2 Jan. 1786).

For TJ's distribution of the seeds of the breadfruit or ARBRE À PAIN, see his letter to Allen Jones, 22 May 1797.

Another letter from Giroud to TJ, dated 28 Germinal [i.e. 17 Apr.] 1797 and recorded in SJL as received 24 May 1797 from "Cap Francois," has not been found.

To Martha Jefferson Randolph

Monticello Apr. 9. 97.

I recieved yours my dear Martha, of Mar. 31. four days ago. The inoculation at Richmond having stopped that post I send this by the way of Fredsbg. I entirely approve of your resolution to have the children inoculated. I had before been so much convinced of the expediency of the measure that I had taken it for granted before your letter informed me of it. I am called to Philadelphia to a meeting of Congress the 15th. of May and shall leave Monticello the 3d. or 4th. of that month. As Mr. Randolph informs me you would have quitted Varina and come up the beginning of this month but for the inoculation, would it not be best for you as soon as the children are quite recovered from the disease, to come up, you, Maria and Ellen and send the carriage back for Mr. Randolph and the children.[1] In this way I shall have the pleasure of seeing you certainly and him and the children probably before my departure and can make better arrangements for your accomodation during my absence. Still however let all this depend on your convenience. My love to Maria. Tell her I have made a new law, which is only *to answer letters.* It would have been her turn to have recieved a letter had she not lost it by not writing. Adieu most affectionately both of you.

RC (NNPM); unsigned; endorsed by Martha Randolph. Probably enclosed in TJ to Thomas Mann Randolph, 9 Apr. 1797.

[1] TJ here canceled "I think."

To Thomas Mann Randolph

Th:J. to TMR.   Monticello Apr. 9. 97.

Yours of Mar. 31. did not come to hand till the 5th. inst. It is a pity it had not been recieved before the election, as it gave much uneasiness and embarrasment to your friends to be unable to give any account of you. It made a serious impression even on the zealous; and I have this day written a circular letter, with the apologies your letter furnished, addressed to every militia captain for his company, which I hope will set the thing to rights. I am more anxious you should possess the affections of the people than that you should make any use of them. Their esteem will contribute much to your happiness: whether the offices they might confer would do so is another question.—I will take care for the clover box, as also for the mule-harnes. Will you be so good as to obtain information for me of the highest price which has been given for wheat since the 1st. day of March. I observe the price current for flour at Philadelphia was $9\frac{1}{2}$ Doll. March 27. which was 2 days after the President's proclamation was published for calling Congress, which shews that that circumstance did not lessen the price. I leave the inclosed open for your perusal, to save a repetition of the same things to you, for I have now been writing the whole day. Adieu affectionately.

RC (DLC); endorsed. PrC (ViU: Edgehill-Randolph Papers); endorsed by TJ in ink on verso. Enclosure: probably TJ to Martha Jefferson Randolph, 9 Apr. 1797.

Randolph's letter OF MAR. 31, recorded in SJL as received from Varina 5 Apr. 1797, has not been found. According to SJL, letters from Randolph to TJ of 5, 8, 11, 12 and 19 Apr. 1797, none of which has been found, were all received from Richmond on 21 Apr. 1797, except for that of 8 Apr.,

which was received from Richmond a week earlier.

Wilson Cary Nicholas and Francis Walker won the ELECTION held in Charlottesville on 3 Apr. for two delegates to represent Albemarle County in the House of the Virginia General Assembly. SJL indicates that TJ wrote a CIRCULAR LETTER to the captains of the MILITIA on 9 Apr. 1797, but it has not been found (Woods, *Albemarle*, 372-5; Gaines, *Randolph*, 40-1).

To Elizabeth House Trist

DEAR MADAM   Monticello Apr. 9. 97.

We feel too much interested here in the dispositions you expressed to become our neighbor, not to be attentive to any occasion which may favor it. A Mr. Lewis, my next door neighbor, having determined to remove to Kentuckey this fall offers his lands adjoining me for sale. The tract contains 700. acres, scarcely an acre of it but of first rate quality, tho' a part of what has been cleared has been too severely cropped. It is all however easily recoverable. The lands, like all in our neighborhood consist of hill and dale, except about 30. acres of good meadow. A bold creek (Moore's creek) runs through the middle of it, and furnishes a fine mill seat at it's entrance into the river. On one side the tract borders on Charlottesville, and on me on the other side. The farm on which he lives has about 300. acres cleared, with a dwelling house newly built by

himself on this plan containing 2. good rooms,

with garrets above, a cellar and a kitchen below; but finding the kitchen below not so agreeable, he built a separate one. The house is pleasantly situated on an eminence commanding a sublime prospect on the North, but too close under a mountain on the South. The soil capitally excellent for wheat, rye and red clover, consequently admitting the most approved husbandry. It is 2. miles from Charlottesville, $3\frac{1}{2}$ from the little town of Milton where our navigation begins, $3\frac{1}{2}$ from Colo. Monroe's,

$3\frac{1}{2}$ from where your old acquaintance (Martha) will perhaps settle, 1. mile from where another acquaintance may possibly be settled, and half a mile from Monticello. There is a second and smaller farm opened in the farther part of the tract. Mr. Lewis values his houses and mill seat at £750. to 800.£ our money, and the lands at £1300. asking £2100. or 7000. Doll. for the whole. This is rating the lands at 6D.–19c. the acre which is about 25. per cent higher than such lands have been usually sold at in this neighborhood. However their adjacency to Charlottesville admitting a part of the lands to be sold in lots at three or four pounds the acre, entitles them to more than the usual price. The lands can be entered on at seed-time of the next autumn. Should the features of this purchase be pleasing to yourself and my friend Browse, I would earnestly recommend to him to come on and see the lands, as I do not think such another situation likely to be offered soon. I do not know how to invite you for this summer, because about midsummer we take the roof off of the whole of our house, except two rooms where I shall stay myself, and my family will be obliged to go elsewhere for shelter.—I have been at home and alone ever since I returned from Philadelphia, my daughters being both at Mr. Randolph's farm below Richmond. He is at Richmond inoculating his two elder children, the mother being kept away by the suckling who being cutting teeth cannot be inoculated. I question whether they will come here till I shall be set out for Philadelphia, for I just learn that Congress is called there the 15th. of next month, when I shall expect the pleasure of seeing you there. Perhaps when I return may be time enough for Browse to come and reconnoitre the proposed purchase: as I do not yet hear that any body is treating for it. Ever since my return home I have been (as far as confinement by a rheumatism would permit me) in the enjoiment of our delicious spring. On the day I had the pleasure of seeing you in Philadelphia my peach and cherry trees blossomed, to wit, on the 9th. of March. I passed Fredericksburg 9. days after, and the buds were not opening. There is a great difference for the better between the climate of this place and Frederickbg and still more of Alexandria. Our cold season is a month shorter, the warm one that much longer, and both more temperate. Adieu à revoir. Your affectionate friend & servt   TH: JEFFERSON

RC (James H. Eddy, Charles B. Eddy, Jr., and John B. Eddy, New York City, 1948; photostat in NcU: Southern Historical Collection); at foot of first page: "Mrs. Trist." A later notation, in an unknown hand, indicates that the letter was directed to her at "Mulberry Court North 6th. Street Philadelphia."

A letter from Trist to TJ of 21 Apr. 1797, recorded in SJL as received from Philadelphia on 11 July, has not been found.

To Volney

Dear Sir   Monticello Apr. 9. 97.

Your favor of Mar. 15. came to hand a few days ago. It has been among the greatest of my regrets that I could scarcely see you while in Philadelphia. A thousand visits of ceremony, and some of sincerity, and all these to be returned filled up every moment of my time added to a little business. Since my return home I have been entirely alone, and much [con]fined by the rheumatism. Just now I recieve a summons to Philadelphia for the ensuing month, which I shall certainly obey if my rheumatism permits me. I am sorry for the summons, as every thing pacific could have been done without Congress, and I hope nothing is in contemplation which is not pacific. As far as my indisposition and solitude would permit I have been in the enjoiment of our delicious spring. The soft genial temperature of the season, just above the want of fire, enlivened by the reanimation of birds, flowers, the fields, forests and gardens, has been truly delightful and continues to be so. My peach and cherry trees blossomed on the 9th. of March which was the day I had the pleasure of meeting you on the street of Philadelphia as I returned from your lodgings. I passed Fredericksburg on the 18th. of Mar. whe[re not?] a blossom was opening. I think we are a fortnight forwarder than Fredericksburg, and the fine temperate [weather] of spring continues here about two months. Indeed my experience of the different parts of America convinces me that these mountains are the Eden of the US. for soil, climate, navigation and health. You have a little spring sometimes, but not much where you are: (Georgetown) there is more on the Eastern shore of Maryland, but none at Philadelphia or further North. There are fine autumns as far North as mid-Jersey, but none at New York, or very rarely, nor any further North. To-day my workmen assemble, and tomorrow begin their work. But they must suspend their works during my absence, as I am my own [architect], and my plan too little like what they have seen to trust them with it's execution in my absence. On my return we uncover all but the two middle rooms; and I am not without a hope that should your peregrinations lead you this way in September or October I may begin to enjoy in your society the pleasure I have so long wished of having a lodging for my friends with more comfort to them and satisfaction to myself. I thank you for your pamphlet. I esteem the Doctor, yet blame him as to you. It grieves me to see the time of genius wasted in polemics; and hope therefore the reply which I see published will not tempt you from the resolution you express of proceeding to more useful labours. I hope I shall see you in Georgetown, and certainly shall if the movements of the stage will permit it: for I prefer that conveyance to travelling with my own horses, because it gives me, what I have long been without, an opportunity of plunging into the mixed characters of my country, the most useful school we can enter into, and one which nothing else can supply the want of. I once intimately knew all the specimens of character which compose the aggregate mass of my fellow-citizens. But age, office, and literature have too long insulated me from them. I find that either their features or my optics have considerably changed in twenty years.— While at Georgetown I would recommend to you to get acquainted with Mr. John Thompson Mason a lawyer, and person of great worth and genius. I have myself but an acquaintance of two or three hours with him, which sufficed to accredit all the good things I had heard of him. Accept assurances of the sincere esteem with which I am Dear Sir affectionately Your friend & servt   TH: JEFFERSON

PrC (DLC); faded; at foot of first page: "Mr. Volney."

YOUR PAMPHLET: see Volney to TJ, 15 Mch. 1797.

From Mann Page

MY DEAR SIR   Mann's field April 19th. 1797

Mr. Hugh Mercer, the posthumous Son of the late Genl. Mercer, will do me the honour of forwarding this to you. I will shortly make known to you what have been his persuits in Science, and what is his Object in applying to you. His Education commenced with the Study of the Greek and Latin Languages, in which he made some Progress. His chief Attention has been to the Belles Lettres, in which he comprises Moral and Natural Philosophy and the first Principles of Mathematics together with Logic and Rhetoric. He has read but little of Law. Nor does he wish to make it a particular Study. His desire is, under your Advice to obtain that general Knowledge for which you are celebrated, to follow your Directions in every Instance, and implicitly to conform to your Will. In Return for so singular a Favour he will with Chearfulness become your Secretary and perform any Business which you may entrust to him. From what I know of him, and from his Professions of an absolute Conformity to good Manners, I beg leave to recommend him to you. You will, by receiving him, most probably well finish an Education which his Country worthily commenced.

I shall anxiously expect you at Mann's field on your Way to Congress. May Health and Happiness ever attend you. Your's most sincerely

RC (DLC); endorsed by TJ as received 29 Apr. 1797 and so recorded in SJL.

A letter from TJ to Page of 3 May 1797 is recorded in SJL but has not been found.

From Jean François Paul Grand

MONSIEUR LE VICE PRESIDENT

Lausanne, Canton
de Berne, en Suisse,
le pr. May 1797.

Je n'oublierai jamais les relations que nôtre maison et moi particulierement avons eu le bonheur d'entretenir avec vôtre Excellence, pendant Sa mission ministerielle à Paris, et je conserverai pour elle les Sentimens de vénération et d'attachement qu'elle m'a inspiré et qui lui Sont Si justement dûs.

D'après Cette façon de penser Vôtre Excellence permettra que je lui addresse mes félicitations Sur la place eminente de Vice President des Etats unis, à la quelle elle a été portée, et l'assurance de l'Interêt que je ne Cèsserai de prendre à ce qui la regarde, ainsi que mes Voeux pour Sa prosperité.

Je vis aujourdhui, en Suisse ma patrie, avec ma femme et mes enfans après la perte que j'ai eu le malheur de faire depuis 3 et 4 ans de mon Pere et de ma mère; et mes Interêts à Paris Se trouvent aujourdhui dans la maison de Corsange et ce. dont le chef est un ancien Interressé de la maison, et l'associé un de mes Parents, J'ose la recomander au Souvenir et Aux bontés de Vôtre Excellence, à la quelle Je Serois bien heureux de pouvoir quelques fois donner des preuves de ma très grande Considération et attachement. Je Suis avec les Sentimens les plus Respectueux Monsieur Le vice President Vôtre très humble & très obeissant serviteur

PAUL GRAND

Messrs. Corsange et ce. ont eu des relations Assés particulieres avec Mr. Munroe le Precedent Ministre des Etats unis a Paris.

RC (DLC); endorsed by TJ as received 13 Dec. 1797 and so recorded in SJL. Dupl and Tripl not found, but suggested by SJL, where entries at 8 and 22 Sep. 1797 each record the receipt of a letter from Grand written at Lausanne on 1 May 1797.

Jean François Paul Grand (1752-1829) retired to Lausanne, Switzerland, the family's ancestral locale, in 1794 after the death of his father, Ferdinand Grand of the Paris banking firm of Grand & Cie. (Société Générale Suisse d'Histoire, *Dictionnaire Historique et Biographique de la Suisse*, 7 vols. [Neuchatel, 1921-33], III, 518; Jean Antoine Gautier to TJ, 24 Mch. 1795; second letter of Grand & Cie. to TJ, 24 Mch. 1795).

A letter from Grand to TJ of 19 Feb. 1796, recorded in SJL as received from Lausanne on 22 July 1796, has not been found.

From Pierre Auguste Adet

Philadelphie Le 15 floréal An 5eme

MONSIEUR   de la République française, 4 mai 1797. v.s.

Agrées, mes remerciements pour Les choses obligeantes que renfermoit Le Billet que vous m'aves envoyé Lors de votre départ de cette ville. Si ma Carriere a été Semée, D'espines, Si en Remplissant Les volontés de mon gouvernement j'ai excité contre moi L'esprit de parti, Si je n'ai Rencontré que des desagréments dans un foule de circonstances, j'ai Esperé d'emporter avec moi L'estime des hommes Sans passions, Et celle des amis de La Liberté. Cette idée m'a toujours consolé, m'a fait regarder tout ceque j'ai eprouvé de desagréable, comme un moyen d'obtenir cette Estime, Et La certitude ou je Suis que vous ne me regardés pas indigne de la votre Est un ample dedommagement de ceque j'ai eu à Souffrir.

Je Regrette infiniment, que Les circonstances m'aient empeché de vous voir; je pense que j'aurois pu acquérir votre amitié. Elle m'eut Été infiniment précieuse! Et je Sens vivement combien elle m'eut été utile Dans Les circonstances ou La République française et Les Etats unis Se trouvent. Mais une pensée me tranquillise. Vous savés combien Les Ennemis de La liberté Seroient charmés S'ils allumoient La guerre entre nos deux pays. Tel a été jusqu'à ce moment—Le but de Leurs efforts. Vous ferés j'en Suis convaincu vos efforts pour éviter un pareil malheur. Mon pays ne Se verroit pas Sans un vif chagrin obligé de Rompre avec un peuple qu'il a toujours regardé comme une nation amie, comme le plus cher de Ses alliés. En vous exprimant ces Sentiments il est inutile de vous dire que toutes mes demarches tendront a éloigner de nos deux pays un fléau egalement contraires à nos interets respectifs. Et que tous mes voeux Sont pour le Retablissement de La Bonne harmonie qui a Subsisté jusqu'à ce jour Entre nos deux pays. Et pour votre Bonheur particulier. Agrées L'assurance de mon profond Respect.   P. A. ADET

RC (DLC); at foot of first page: "M. Jefferson. Esqre"; endorsed by TJ as received 13 May 1797 and so recorded in SJL.

The BILLET TJ sent Adet on his departure from Philadelphia is not recorded in SJL and has not been found.

From Elbridge Gerry

MY DEAR SIR   Cambridge 4th May 17[97]

On the 27th of March I had the pleasure of addressing a letter to yourself, and on the 4th of april another to Mr. Monroe, to your care;

but having no information of their being received, and having reason to apprehend that some of our post officers are guilty of mal practice and not to be trusted, I wish to be informed whether the letters have arrived, by a line directed to me at New York, where I intend to be soon, to the care of James Thompson or Samuel Osgood Esqrs. I remain my dear Sir with every sentiment of esteem & respect Your very hume Sert.

E GERRY

RC (DLC); damaged; at foot of text: "His Excellency Mr. Jefferson"; endorsed by TJ as received 12 May 1797 and so recorded in SJL.

Gerry's letter to Monroe of THE 4TH OF APRIL was apparently unaccompanied by any cover letter to TJ (see Gerry to TJ, 22 and 28 May 1797). No letter from Gerry to TJ of 4 Apr. 1797 has been found or was recorded in SJL.

From Edward Rutledge

MY DEAR SIR   Charleston May 4th: 1797.

My Nephew leaves me, in a few Hours, to take his Seat in Congress, and furnishes me with a direct opportunity of writing to you. He carries with him all the sincere Friendship which he has fondly cherished towards you, for a series of years, and with Him my warmest Wishes for your Enjoyment of all the Blessings of Life. You richly deserve them, my Friend, for a thousand good Reasons; but most of all for having consented, to fill the Station, which you now occupy. How have I rejoiced, and exulted, at your noble, dis-interested, and patriotic acceptance of the second office in our Government, when Talent, and Virtue, and Services, had given you a decided, and what ought to have been, an indisputable Title, to the first. But you acted like yourself: you remembered your Country, in the Hour of her distress; you forgot the Injuries of your Enemies; and you have put your Calumniators to Silence. Such is the Emanation of a great Soul, and the recollection of such Conduct will be the Source of perpetual Satisfaction; it will be more, it will diffuse Confidence, and enable you to pursue the Interests of our Country with redoubled Ardor.

Excuse, I beseech you, these effusions of affection; but the cruel, and undeserved Reproaches, by which you have been assailed, have given a keener Edge to my Sensibility, and I participate in the delight of every Action, which throws a Lustre around your Character. But let me Remind you, my good Sir, that it has long been an established point, that much, may justly be expected from Him, to whom, much has been given; we look confidently, then, to you, to relieve us from the distresses of a Situation, into which we have been plunged by Errors not your own. The Task is full of difficulty, but it is truly worthy of your Exertions. The Business, in its original, and primeval State, was God knows full bad enough, but the intervention of Mr: Pickering's diplomatic Talents, and above all, his last production, will greatly contribute to multiply your Troubles.

I know, full well, that it will border on the incompatible, truly, to preserve our Independence, in the full Sense of the Term, and obtain a Reconciliation, with the French Republic. Yet, both must be tried. The first, I feel will be sacredly preserved, amidst all your dislikes to former Measures, which have drawn us, into our present Condition; *you* will preserve it, because, if you were not actually the Father of Independence you were one of its earliest Apostles, and one of its sacred Sponsors. Upon this principle, bad as the Treaty with Great Britain really is, and justly deserving as it is, of detestation, yet having been unfortunately sanctioned by every branch of the federal Government, I would still adhere to it. But then you may ask, what is to be done? I answer, permit your Merchants to arm their Vessels for self defence; compleat your Frigates; fortify, as far as is well practicable, your Seaports, which are the primary Depot of your Revenue; and attempt to renew your Negociations with France. Not by sending new Ministers, but by sending, further Instructions, if necessary, to the Gentleman, who is at present, in Commission; whose Talents, and Integrity, and discretion, will do Credit to the Station that he fills. Before however, he enters France, it should certainly be known, whether a Minister will be received; and that, may be done thro' Mr. Noel, the French Minister at the Hague; if a more direct application cannot well be made. The new Election, a change in the Directory, a reverse of Fortune, or indeed the versatility of our Nature, may offer a favourable opportunity to negociate, and some Person, should I think be at Hand to profit of the occasion.

Your Peas, and Orange trees, are all packed, and only wait an opportunity. They have been ready a long while, but not one Vessel has cleared from this port, for Richmond, during the whole of the present year. But our Collector has undertaken to send them, thro' the officer at Norfolk: I will write you, the Mode of planting them, when they shall be sent, which will be in a few days. And now my dear Friend Adieu—continue to hold me, in your Esteem, & believe me ever yours most affectionately   ED: RUTLEDGE

P:S: I past the last Week on the Banks of Santee, with my friend Major Pinckney; who requested I would remember him to you, and ask, whether you ever received from him, a Letter, of which he sent a duplicate, enclosing one to you from the Prince of Parma.

RC (DLC); endorsed by TJ as received 15 May 1797 and so recorded in SJL.

MY NEPHEW: John Rutledge, Jr. For Timothy Pickering's LAST PRODUC-

TION, see Madison to TJ, 22 Jan. 1797. Thomas Pinckney's LETTER to TJ of 16 Mch. 1796 enclosed ONE from Louis, PRINCE OF PARMA to TJ of 2 Nov. 1795.

From William Wirt, with Jefferson's Notes

Pen. Park. May 4th. 1797

Mrs. Gilmer directs me to enquire whether you can furnish her with 20,000. 6 penny nails

10,000. 16 penny do.

200. 30. penny do.?

In what time they can be got ready? Or, if they be now ready, whether it would suit you to take a draught for the amount on Mr. James Brown of Richmond payable on sight, or to wait for the money until the post from Richmond to Charlottsville gets again in motion? Your answer by the bearer will oblige, Sir, Yours respectfully   WM. WIRT

[Notes by TJ:]

	℔	d	£
$7/3\frac{1}{2}$ per M	140. VI.	$12\frac{1}{2}$	7– 5–10
17/6	200. XVI.	$10\frac{1}{2}$	8–15–
	11. XXX 4. I. long @10d per ℔		9– 2
			16–10

ordered to be delivered May 10th.

	℔		£
July 15.	5. VIII	12d	0– 5– 0
	3. XXX	10d	0– 2– 6
18.	5. VIII	12d	0– 5– 0
			17– 2– 6

Aug. 2. by order on James Brown   17– 2– 6

RC (MHi); with subjoined notes by TJ; endorsed by TJ.

With no formal education beyond grammar school, William Wirt (1772-1834) earned recognition for his literary productions as well as his attainments as an attorney. A native of Maryland, he read law in a private office and first began to practice in Culpeper County, Virginia. In 1795 he married Mildred Gilmer of "Pen Park," the Gilmer family estate in Albemarle County. Her father died not long after, which accounts for Wirt's role, in the letter above, in ordering nails for his mother-in-law, Lucy Walker Gilmer. After the death of his wife in 1799 he relocated to Richmond, where he practiced law and was clerk of the House of Delegates, 1799-1802. He married, in 1802, Elizabeth Washington Gamble. In 1800 Wirt served as co-counsel for the defense in the sedition trial of James Thomson Callender. Seven years later he assisted in the prosecution of Aaron Burr. In 1817 Monroe appointed him attorney general of the United States, an office he held until 1829, arguing for the government in such landmark Supreme Court cases as McCulloch v. Maryland and the Dartmouth College case. In 1803 he established his literary reputation with the first installment of *The*

Letters of the British Spy. His other writings included *Sketches of the Life and Character of Patrick Henry*, published in 1817. Wirt gave the major oration in a memorial service held by the House of Representatives following the deaths of TJ and John Adams in 1826 (DAB; Leonard, *General Assembly*, 215, 219, 223).

Letters from TJ to Wirt of 5 Jan. and 2 Feb. 1796, one from Wirt to TJ incongruously recorded as written on 8 Jan. but received on 7 Jan. 1796, and another from Wirt written on 2 Feb. and received 3 Feb. 1796 are all recorded in SJL but have not been found.

From "Monitor"

SIR   Albemarle. May 7th. 1797

A report has reached Virga. that since your V. Presidency you made in the City of Philadelphia a declaration nearly in the following words viz "That war with France might be expected unless america made Compensation and Concessions for injuries alledged to have been received by the former: also resinded the British Treaty, and that your exertions would be to effect those measures before you would venture hostilities." This report is Stated to have come from a source not to be doubted. As your informant supposes, you yet to retain those honest feelings which every independant American should ever have—that you esteem Self Government preferable to a foreign yoke—that your partiality for France can never make you a traitor to your own Country, he will forbear Comments, sincerely wishing that your wisdom may enable you, to discard party Zeal, and as far as may on you depend, to effect such measures as shall eventuate in honor to yourself, and happiness to our Common Country. It is supposed that this report was fabricated by some Gallicans and Anti americans in order to give Strength to their party. Recollect my Dear Sir, that you have much reputation to lose— that the paths of dishonor are very unsafe—that you have solemnly Sworn to Support the Constitution of the United States, which is as good as to say, that your exertions shall be, to adhere "to a perfect union, establish justice, insure domestic tranquility, provide for the Common defence, promote the general Welfare and to secure the Blessings of liberty to ourselves and our posterity." It is the opinion of many that, the Counduct of the Virginia delegation will be a true index to your Views upon the presumption of their being shaped to your purpose—after

Some little time you may expect to receive the purport of this information thro the channel of a newspaper. I am your friend so long as I conceive you the friend of your Country　　　　　　　　MONITOR

RC (DLC); endorsed by TJ as received 16 May 1797 and so recorded in SJL.

To Thomas Mann Randolph

TH:J. TO TMR.　　　　　　　　　　Fredericksburg. May 7. 97.

Among the multiplicity of things I had to think of on my departure from home I omitted to speak with you on the subject of the cask of beer you were so kind as to put by for me at Hay's. I will thank you to have it bottled and sent up. At this moment C. Johnston has no money of mine in his hands. Therefore I have given Mr. Hay (whom I met with here) money for the bottles, and immediately on my arrival in Philadelphia I shall replenish Johnston's hands. I also forgot to ask the favor of you to get the box with the Mammoth tooth and bone forwarded by water to Philadelphia addressed to Mr. Barnes. I had ordered Johnny to give the box to you.—There is nothing new here. As soon as I learn any thing interesting you shall have it. Adieu affectionately.

RC (DLC); addressed: "Thomas Mann Randolph Richmond"; endorsed by Randolph as received 13 May 1797. Not recorded in SJL.

From Antonia Reynon Carmichael

MONSIEUR　　　　　　　　　　chester town ce 8 May 1797

Je profite de l'occasion de Monsieur Joseph Thompson pour vous faire parvenir ce petit paquets que j'ai trouvé dans les papiers de feu Monsieur Carmichael. J'avois chargé un Monsieur de cette Ville l'Eté passé qui alloit en Virginie de vouloir bien vous le remettre. Il s'en etoit chargé mais une Maladie lui est survenu quelques jours apres son depart. N'ayant pû continuer son voyage il me l'a fait rendre. Je l'ai porté a Philadelphia A mon dernier voyage croyant vous y trouver. Je suis fachée que ce ne Soit pas les œvres de Darien comme la crut Mr. Blake. S'il les a jamais vu a la maison certainement ils n'avoient été que pretéz parceque Je ne les ai pas trouvé dans mes caisses. Je me ferais un vrai plaisir de vous les offrir s'ils etoient dans ma possetions. J'ai eu l'honneur de vous ecrire que si les 12 gravures d'Hernan Cortes pouvoit vous être agreable Je connois une Personne qui me les cederoit. J'ai l'honneur d'Etre Monsieur Votre tres humble servante

veuve CARMICHAEL

RC (DLC); in an unidentified hand, signed by Carmichael; endorsed by TJ as received 25 May 1797 and so recorded in SJL. Enclosure: a manuscript, not found but evidently written by Antonio de Ulloa, on prospects for a canal at the Isthmus of Darien (see James Blake to TJ, 6 June 1795, and TJ to Blake, 29 Feb. 1796).

J'AI EU L'HONNEUR DE VOUS ECRIRE: Antonia Carmichael to TJ, 14 Oct. 1795.

From Horatio Gates

DEAR SIR   New York 9th. May 1797.

I have hitherto delayed acquainting You that Mr. Maddison had obliging forwarded my Letter Book. It was in as good order as you received it. As you should not have seen it, I Inclose you Mr: Erskines pamphlet on the Causes and Consequences of The War. It run through upwards of Twenty Edditions in a Fort night in London. Every True Whigg upon this Continent must adore the Man for the Wisdom of his Head, the uncorruptness of his Heart, and the Firmness with which he has delivered his Sentiments, to a deceived, and all but ruind Nation! All Eyes are turned to Congress to see what they will do, to bring Us out of the Scrape we have been led into with France. May the Friends of Freedom, and Independence, have reason to rejoice in the Important Event. To confirm the upright, to Convert the misled and to Fix the Wavering, I wish the pamphlet could be Republish'd in philadelphia; I think it would do Infinite Good to have the Members of Congress know its Contents; and the sooner, the better. Are we not to have the pleasure to see you before your return to Virginia? The Doors of Rose Hill are Open to receive You, whenever you will Oblige me, and my Mary, by reposing under our Roof. With the Sincerest Sentiments of Esteem, and Regard, I am Dear Sir Your Faithfull humble Servant

HORATIO GATES

RC (DLC); at foot of text: "Thomas Jefferson Esq."; endorsed by TJ as received in May and recorded in SJL as received at Philadelphia 11 May 1797. Enclosure: Thomas Erskine, A View of the Causes and Consequences of the Present War with France (London, 1797). See Sowerby, No. 2833.

In Jan. 1797, Madison made arrangements with Edward Livingston to return the LETTER BOOK that TJ had borrowed from Gates in 1793 (Madison, Papers, XVI, 467). For TJ's acquisition and use of the letterbook, see note to Gates to TJ, 19 July 1780.

To Elbridge Gerry

MY DEAR FRIEND   Philadelphia May 13. 1797.

Your favor of the 4th. inst. came to hand yesterday. That of the 4th. of Apr. with the one for Monroe has never been recieved. The first of the 27th. of March did not reach me till Apr. 21. when I was within a few days of setting out for this place, and I put off acknoleging it till I should come here. I entirely commend your dispositions towards Mr. Adams, knowing his worth as intimately, and esteeming it as much, as any one, and acknoleging the preference of his claims, if any I could have had, to the high office conferred on him. But in truth I had neither claims nor wishes on the subject, tho' I know it will be difficult to obtain belief of this. When I retired from this place and the office of Secretary of state, it was in the firmest contemplation of never more returning here. There had indeed been suggestions in the public papers that I was looking towards a succession to[1] the President's chair. But feeling a consciousness of their falsehood, and observing that the suggestions came[2] from hostile quarters, I considered them as intended merely to excite public odium against me. I never in my life[3] exchanged a word with any person on the subject till I found my name brought forward generally[4] in competition with that of Mr. Adams. Those with whom I then communicated could say, if it were necessary, whether I met the call with desire or even with a ready acquiescence, and whether from the moment of my first acquiescence I did not devoutly pray that the very thing might happen which has happened.[5] The second office of this government is honorable and easy. The first is but a splendid misery.[6] You express apprehensions that stratagems will be used to produce a misunderstanding between the President and myself. Tho' not a word having this tendency has ever been hazarded to me by any one, yet I consider as a certainty that nothing will be left untried to alienate him from me. These machinations will proceed from the Hamiltonians by whom he is surrounded,[7] and who are only a little less hostile to him than to me. It cannot but damp the pleasure of cordiality when we suspect that it is suspected. I cannot help fearing that it is impossible for Mr. Adams to believe that the state of my mind is what it really is; that he may think I view him as an obstacle in my way. I have no supernatural power to impress truth on the mind of another,[8] nor he any to discover that the estimate which he may form on a just view of the human mind as generally constituted, may not be just in it's application to a special constitution. This may be a source of private uneasiness to us. I honestly confess that it is so to me at this time. But neither of us are capable of letting it have effect on our public duties.[9] Those who may endeavor to separate us, are probably excited by the fear that I might have influence on the executive councils. But when they shall know that I consider my office as constitutionally confined to legislative functions, and that I could not take any part whatever in executive consultations, even were it proposed, their fears may perhaps subside, and their object be found not worth a machination. I do sincerely wish with you that we could take our stand on a ground perfectly neutral and independant towards all nations. It has been my constant object through public life; and with respect to the English and French particularly, I have too often expressed to the former my wishes, and made to them propositions verbally and in writing, officially and privately, to official and private characters, for them to doubt of my views, if they would be content with equality. [10] Of this they are in possession of several written and formal proofs, in my own handwriting. But they have wished a monopoly of commerce and influence with us. And they have in fact obtained it. When we take notice that theirs is the workshop to which we go for all we want, that with them center either immediately or ultimately all the labors of our hands and lands, [11] that to them belongs either openly or secretly the great mass of our navigation, that even the factorage of their affairs here is kept to themselves by factitious citizenships, that these foreign and [12] false citizens now constitute the great body of what are called [13] *our merchants*, fill our seaports, are planted in every little town and district of the interior country, sway every thing in the former place by their own votes and those of their dependants, [14] in the latter by their insinuations and the influence of their ledgers, [15] that they are advancing fast to a monopoly of our banks and public funds, and thereby placing our public finances under their controul, [16] that they have in their alliance the most influential characters in and out of office, when they have shewn that by all these bearings on the different branches of the government they can force it to proceed in any direction they dictate, and bend the interests of this country entirely to the will of another, [17] when all this I say is attended to, it is impossible for us to say we stand on independant ground, [18] impossible for a free [19] mind not to see and to groan under the bondage in which it is bound. [20] If any thing after this could excite surprise, it would be that [21] they have been able so far to throw dust into the eyes of our own citizens as to fix on those who wish merely to recover self-government the charge of subserving one foreign influence, because they resist submission to another. But they possess our printing presses, [22] a powerful engine in their government of us. At this very moment they would have drawn us into war on the side of England [23] had it not been for the failure of her bank. Such was their open and loud cry and that of their gazettes till this event.   After plunging us in all the broils of the European nations, there would remain but one act to close our tragedy, that is, to break up our union: and even this they have [24] ventured seriously and solemnly to propose and maintain by argument, [25] in a Connecticut paper. I have been happy however in believing, from the stifling of this effort that that dose was found too strong, and[26] excited as much repugnance there as it did horror in other parts of our country,[27] and that whatever follies we may be led into as to foreign nations, we shall never give up our union, the last anchor of our hope, and that alone which is to prevent this heavenly country from becoming an arena of gladiators. Much as I abhor war, and view it as the greatest scourge of mankind, and anxiously as I wish to keep out of the broils of Europe, I would yet go with my brethren into these rather than separate from them.[28] But I hope[29] we may still keep clear of them, notwithstanding our present thraldom, and that time may be given us to reflect[30] on the awful crisis we have passed through, and to find some means of shielding ourselves in future from foreign influence, commercial, political, or in whatever other form it may be attempted.[31] I can scarcely withold myself from joining in the wish of Silas Deane that there were an ocean of fire between us and the old world.   A perfect confidence that you are as much attached to peace and union as myself, that you equally prize independance of all nations and the blessings of self government, has induced me freely to unbosom myself to you, and let you see the light in which I have viewed what has been passing among us from the beginning of this war. And I shall be happy at all times in an intercommunication of sentiments with you, believing that the dispositions of the different parts of our country have been considerably misrepresented and misunderstood in each part as to the other,[32] and that nothing but good can result from an exchange of opinions and information[33] between those whose circumstances and morals admit no doubt of[34] the integrity of their views. I remain with constant & sincere esteem Dear Sir Your affectionate friend & servt

TH: JEFFERSON

RC (InU-Li); at foot of first page: "Elbridge Gerry"; with significant emendations recorded in notes 22 and 27 below. PrC (DLC); consists of first page only; lacks Gerry's name at foot. Dft (DLC: TJ Papers, 101: 17371, 102: 17543); consisting of TJ's heavily emended writing on both sides of two sheets, with damage causing loss of approximately one line each at bottom of recto and verso of the first sheet (see notes 8 and 21 below); the most significant changes and variations are recorded in notes below.

The hints of disunion IN A CONNECTICUT PAPER were contained in two pseudonymous letters which appeared in the *Connecticut Courant* in November and December 1796. The letters' author, "Pelham," suggested that the North should consider separating from the states south of the Potomac, citing differences between the regions and calling particular attention to the political advantage given to the South by the three-fifths clause of the United States Constitution, which counted that ratio of the slave population for purposes of representation. The suggestion elicited strong responses both in New England and IN OTHER PARTS OF OUR COUNTRY (Hartford *Connecticut Courant*, 21 Nov., 12 Dec. 1796; Stewart, *Opposition Press*, 348-50).

[1] Preceding five words interlined in Dft in place of "to be made a candidate for."
[2] In Dft TJ interlined preceding twelve words in place of "there was."
[3] Preceding three words interlined in Dft in place of "had a suggestion from any."
[4] In Dft TJ here canceled "as solely."

[5] In Dft TJ here canceled "that is to say that I ⟨*might*⟩ since my name was before the public I might ⟨*obtain*⟩ the minor vote might be mine, but so nearly equal to the major the vote might be such as to testify that my fellow citizens had been satisfied with my conduct, yet" and continued the sentence.

[6] In Dft TJ here canceled: "I had been ⟨*near enough to*⟩ intimate enough with it's condition to ⟨*know*⟩ have seen that."

[7] Remainder of sentence interlined in Dft.

[8] In Dft TJ here canceled "[. . .] and must [. . .] [meet] therefore with [acquiescence?] ⟨*this*⟩ a sentence which," and text from that cancellation to "just view" has evidently been lost at the bottom of the page.

[9] Word interlined in Dft in place of "interest."

[10] In Dft TJ first completed the sentence "to doubt it if they would have been content with it" before interlining "of my disposition towards them" in place of the first "it," and then altering the passage to read as above.

[11] In Dft TJ first wrote "the proceeds of every thing we make for exportation" before altering the passage to read as above.

[12] Preceding two words interlined in Dft.

[13] In Dft TJ interlined the preceding three words.

[14] In Dft TJ first wrote "their votes" before altering the passage to read as above.

[15] Preceding two words interlined in Dft in place of "credit they can give."

[16] In Dft TJ interlined the preceding nine words.

[17] Preceding thirteen words interlined in Dft, and after "entirely to" TJ first wrote and then canceled "⟨*their own*⟩ those of."

[18] In Dft TJ first ended the sentence here and continued with a passage, subsequently canceled, which read in part: "it is impossible and wonderful that."

[19] In Dft TJ first wrote "an unbiassed" before altering the phrase to read as above.

[20] In Dft TJ first wrote "in which we are" before interlining "it finds itself" and then altering the passage to read as above.

[21] Here in Dft TJ canceled "by their possession of [all or nearly] all the public," and interlined and canceled "almost every printing press in the Union." Remainder of sentence and following sentence are missing in Dft due to damage at bottom of

page, with the passages "so far to throw dust in the eyes of our own citizens to fix" and "[to] recover" visible as evident interlineations.

[22] Word written over "offices," erased.

[23] Word interlined in Dft in place of "Great Britain." This sentence begins the second sheet of the Dft, where TJ first wrote and then canceled with diagonal strokes the following passage: "⟨*are struggling. I shall never forget the prediction of the count de Vergennes that we shall exhibit the singular phaenomenon of a fruit rotten before it is [ripe], nor cease to join in the wish of Silas Deane*⟩ that there were an ocean of fire between us and the old world. Indeed my dear friend I am so disgusted with ⟨*this foreign bondage that*⟩ this entire subjection to a foreign power that ⟨*I feel myself unfit to take a part in the administration of a country*⟩ if it ⟨*should shall*⟩ were in the end to appear to be the wish of the body of my countrymen to remain in that vassalage. I ⟨*shall*⟩ should feel my unfitness to be an agent in their affairs, and seek in retirement that personal independance without which this world has nothing I value. I am confident you set the same store by it which I do: but perhaps your situation may not give you the same ⟨*view of our situation*⟩ conviction of it's existence. Entirely persuaded of the soundness of your views I shall always be happy whether in private or public to keep up an intercommunication with you, and ⟨*to continue*⟩ repeat to you through life assurances of the esteem with which I am my dear Sir Your sincere & affectionate friend & servt." Above this passage TJ inserted and canceled "at this very moment they would have drawn us into war on the side of Gr. Britain had."

[24] Here in Dft TJ canceled "dared."

[25] In Dft TJ interlined the preceding six words in place of "attempted."

[26] Preceding seven words interlined in Dft.

[27] Preceding two words written over "the Union." Dft: "the union."

[28] In Dft TJ first wrote "I would rather even join my brethren in European wars if that alone can save us from disuion among ourselves" before altering the sentence to read as above.

[29] In Dft TJ here canceled "that notwithstanding the present [report] of things."

[30] In Dft preceding sixteen words are an

interlineation in place of "ourselves at peace," which TJ interlined in place of "clear of all parties, and have time to reflect and to see."

[31] Preceding nine words interlined in Dft.

[32] Remainder of sentence interlined in Dft.

[33] Dft: "information and opinions," interlined in place of "views and sentiments."

[34] Preceding four words interlined in Dft in place of "can furnish the best security for."

From Thomas Paine

DEAR SIR   Havre May 14th. 97

I wrote to you by the Ship Dublin Packet—Capt. Clay, mentioning my intention to have returned to America by that Vessel, and to have suggested to some Member of the house of Representatives the propriety of calling Mr. Monroe before them to have enquired into the state of their Affairs in France. This might have laid the foundation for some resolves on their part that might have led to an accomodation with france, for that house is the only part of the American Governt. that have any reputation here. I apprised Mr. Monroe of my design and he wishes to be called up. You will have heard before this reaches you that the Emperor has been obliged to sue for peace and to consent to the establishment of the New Republic in Lombardy. How france will proceed with respect to England, I am not, at this distance from Paris, in the way of knowing, but am inclined to think she meditates a descent upon that Country, and a revolution in its Governt. If this should be the plan it will keep me in Europe at least another year.

As the british treaty has thrown the American Commerce into wretched Confusion, it is necessary to pay more attention to the appointment of Consuls in the ports of france than there was accasion to do in time of peace, especially as there is now no Minister and Mr. Skipwith; who stood well with the Governt. here, has resigned. Mr. Cutting, the Consul for Havre, does not reside at it. And the business is altogether in the hands of De la Motte, the Vice Consul, who, as a frenchman, cannot have the full authority proper for the office in the difficult state matters are now in. I do not mention this to the disadvantage of Mr. Cutting for no Man is more proper than himself if he thought it an object to attend to.

I know not if you are acquainted with Capt. Johnson of Massachusetts—he is a staunch Man, and one of the Oldest American Captains in the American Employ. He is now settled at Havre, and is a more proper Man for a Vice Consul than la Motte. You can learn his Character from Mr. Monroe. He has written to some of his friends to have the appointment, and if you can see an opportunity of throwing in a little service for him, you will do a good thing.

We have had several Reports of Mr. Madison's Coming. He would be well received as an individual—but as an Envoy of John Adams he could do nothing.   THOMAS PAINE

RC (DLC); addressed: "Thomas Jefferson Vice President Congress or Virginia Charlottesville"; postmarked and franked; endorsed by TJ as received 31 July 1797 and so recorded in SJL.

THE EMPEROR HAS BEEN OBLIGED TO SUE FOR PEACE: in April 1797, with Austrian forces seemingly unable to halt the advance of the French army toward Vienna, the Holy Roman Emperor Francis responded to Napoleon Bonaparte's offer of an armistice.

Under a preliminary peace agreement concluded at Leoben on 18 Apr. 1797, LOMBARDY and its primary city, Milan, previously part of the Hapsburg empire, were incorporated into the new, French-allied Cisalpine Republic, and in return Austria received control over Venice (Karl A. Roider, Jr., *Baron Thugut and Austria's Response to the French Revolution* [Princeton, 1987], 237-9, 244; Palmer, *Democratic Revolution*, II, 277, 305-6).

From Thomas Bee

Charleston May 16th. 97.

The President of the Agricultural Society of Charleston takes this opportunity of acknowledging the receipt, by the hands of Mr. Read, of a box containing specimens of rice, for the use of the Society. For this fresh proof of Mr. Jefferson's attention to the interests of the State of South Carolina, the President, in the name of the Society and in his own, begs to return Mr. Jefferson his and their best thanks, and to assure him that no pains will be spared to render his present as valuable as Mr. Jefferson hopes it will be. The Season for planting not being yet passed, it is probable that many satisfactory experiments will be made in the course of this year, the success of which shall be communicated to Mr. Jefferson as soon as possible after the Society have ascertained it.

RC (DLC); endorsed by TJ as received in June and recorded in SJL as received at Philadelphia, 3 June 1797, from "Agricul-turl. society Presidt. of (Thos. Bee)."

Reportedly TJ had sent to South Carolina almost "one hundred different kinds of rice" procured from the Philippines (*Philadelphia Gazette*, 17 May 1797).

To Benjamin Smith Barton

May 17. 97.

Th: Jefferson presents his friendly compliments to Dr. Barton and his thanks for his note of yesterday. He sets too high value on his esteem not to recieve every mark of it with sensibility. The subject of his piece is worthy of it's author and he is satisfied the execution also will do justice to the subject.

RC (PHi); addressed: "Doctr. Barton 86. North 5th. street." Not recorded in SJL.

Barton's NOTE OF YESTERDAY is not recorded in SJL and has not been found. The

PIECE was probably Barton's *New Views of the Origin of the Tribes and Nations of America* (see Book Dedication from Benjamin Smith Barton, 21 June 1797).

From Stephen Cathalan, Jr.

DEAR SIR   Marseilles the 17th. May 1797

I was favoured in due Time with your much Respected Letter of the 5th. last June, and Beg you to accept my Best thanks for the usefûll Information, you Gave me, for the Best means of Placing money in the united States;

Messrs. Mason & Fenwick placed the 1st. July Last Dard. 6000— for my own account in the Bank of the united States, with which they had only Twelve shares of Dard. 400—making Dard. 4800. This is a Proof that the Credit of that Banck is in the highest Reputation;

They Say that when I will Sale them again, I will Recover again my 6000 Ds. at a very Small Difference more or less; and that the dividend is about 4 pr. ct. every 6 months; I am then Satisfied, for the Present; Certainly lotts to Build houses in the Federative Town, or Lands in your neihbourg, would have been Prefferable, if Purchased with all the Security; but a Landholder who is not a Part of the year in his Lands, can't make the Benefit he would Draw, by his attendance and Industry.

You, my Dear sir—was Retired to the Care of your farms, occupied and delighted with agriculture, Resorting at times for amusement to the arts and Sciences &a. &a. with a Great Degrée of the Good Will of your fellow citizens! But the Americans Citizens, Long ere had Justly appreciated your Proffond knowledge in Political Concerns, and your Good patriotism for the wellfare and Improvment of your Country; They had found you was worth to Succeed in the Presidency, the Respected and Celebrated Georges Washington, and if by a *very Small* majority, they have not in the Last Election placed you at that Eminent Post; you have obtained and accepted the vice Presidency, and it has been proved that John Adams and Thos. Jefferson are equally worthy;

All my Family as well as I, we beg you to accept our Best Congratulations, and Compliments, on your Emminent appointment; asking the Continûation of your kind Sentiments and Protection towards me, begging you to ask this Protection of the President John Adams, assuring you both, that I will Continue in my Efforts, to fill the honourable office of this Consulate, as much as in my Power, to the Entire Satisfaction of our Government, and of the American Individuals;

My Father Tho' more than 80 years old, is enjoying a Good health, Going dayly on foot at a Small Country house I have Purchased on the Sea Coast in this Road; I have Sent my only Daughter to Paris, on the 9th. Inst. to be perfectioned in her Education in the Cy devant Couvent des Anglaises, for 2 or 3 years, I have been encourag'd to part with her, by the Dutchess of orleans, who has been So kind as to offer me to take Care of her, as if She was her mother; I hope that her Sons who are at Philadia. will have Presented to you their Respects, on your Arival; and my Recommendation to you, Sir, in their favour, would be now a very Small adition; as I am Confident, that they may have found in you, in the President, and all the Gentlemens in Philadilphia, Good hearts, Ready to Sofften in their own, the Sorrow of their kind of exile and of Being So distant from one of the most Respectable Mothers;

I would have, with Great Pleasure, taken the fair opportunity of our Captives in algiers, when I dispatched them to Philada. in November Last, to have paid a visit to U States, and presented them with their Compagnon. to our Govert. had not my Presence been necessary to the Service of my Consulate; in this District, and in deed as matters with the french Privateers in this Sea Stand, now, the appeals of the Prises made on our Vessels being before the Court of this Department, I must Remain here to follow these appeals; happy would I Be if I could Succeed! But till matters take a Better turn, I find prudent for our adventurers to Stop their Shipments this way; and I must Postpone my Project of Paying you my Respects in Philadelphia; meantime I have the honour to be with Respect Dear sir Your most obedt. Servt.

STEPHEN CATHALAN JUNR.

RC (DLC); at foot of first page: "Thos. Jefferson Esqr. Vice President of the united States Philadelphia"; endorsed by TJ as received 3 Nov. 1797 and so recorded in SJL.

TJ's MUCH RESPECTED LETTER of 5 June 1796 is recorded in SJL but has not been found. Regarding the SONS of the Duchesse d'Orléans, see Madame de Chastellux to TJ, 5 Mch. 1797, and note.

To ransom the surviving American CAPTIVES IN ALGIERS and implement the treaty concluded on 5 Sep. 1795, Congress, in a statute approved 6 May 1796, agreed to pay the dey and regency of Algiers $24,000 per annum for as long as the treaty remained in effect. Released in July 1796, sixty of the former prisoners returned to the United States the following February (Robert J. Allison, *The Crescent Obscured: The United States and the Muslim World, 1776-1815* [New York, 1995], 149-50; U.S. Statutes at Large, I, 460; Miller, *Treaties,* II, 313, 316).

Letters from Cathalan to TJ of 15 Apr. 1794 and 9 Feb. 1796, received from Marseilles on 25 Mch. 1795 and 3 June 1796 respectively, are recorded in SJL but have not been found.

From Dugnani

Monsieur   Rome ce 17. May 1797

Depuis Sept ans de Silence trouvez bon, que je me rapelle a votre Souvenir, et que Je vous prie de vouloir bien me donner de vos nouvelles, dont je suis impatient, car ni le tems, ni la distance pourra jamais me faire oublier l'amitié, dont vous m'avez honoré à Paris, ou diminuer les Sentimens d'estime, et d'attachement, que je vous ai voüé. Par les papiers publiques j'ai appris plusieures fois avec un plaisir extreme les marques de Confiance, et de la haute consideration, que vos concitoyens vous ont donné, mais il me sera bien doux de recevoir par vous même des details sur tout ce qui vous regarde, aussi bien, que votre charmante Famille.

Si cette lettre ne va pas egaré, et que j'aye le bonheur de recevoir la reponse, je vous prie de m'indiquer la voye plus prompte, et plus Sûre de vous faire parvenir en Suite les lettres. Agreez, Monsieur les assurances des Sentimens véritables de consideration, et d'attachement le plus tendre, avec lesquels j'ai l'honneur d'être, Votre tres humble, et tres affectioné Serviteur, et ami   Le Cardl. Dugnani

RC (DLC); at foot of first page: "Mr. Jefferson Secretaire du Congrès des Etats Unis d'amerique Boston"; endorsed by TJ as received 6 June 1798 and so recorded in SJL.

To Thomas Bell

Dear Sir   Philadelphia May 18. 97.

I inclose you a copy of the President's speech at the opening of Congress, from which you will see what were the objects in calling us together. When we first met our information from the members from all the parts of the union was that peace was the universal wish. Whether they will now raise their tone to that of the executive and embark in all the measures indicative of war and by taking a threatening posture provoke hostilities from the opposite party is far from being certain. There are many who think that not to support the Executive is to abandon government. As far as we can judge as yet the changes in the late election have been unfavorable to the republican interest. Still we hope they will neither make nor provoke war—there appears no probability of any embargo, general or special. The bankruptcy of the English bank is admitted to be complete, and nobody scarcely will venture to buy or draw bills lest they should be paid there in depreciated currency. They prefer remitting dollars for which they will get an advanced price: but this will drain us of our specie. Good James river tobacco here is $8\frac{1}{2}$ to 9.D. flour $8\frac{1}{2}$ to 9 D. wheat not saleable. The bankruptcies have been immense, but are rather at a stand. Be so good as to make known to our commercial friends of your place and Milton the above commercial intelligence. Adieu &c.   Th: J

P.S. Take care that nothing from my letter gets into the newspapers.

FC (DLC); entirely in TJ's hand; at foot of text: "Colo. Bell." Enclosure: see note below.

In the PRESIDENT'S SPEECH AT THE OPEN-ING OF CONGRESS, which TJ enclosed, Adams justified CALLING the special session to respond to the French government's refusal to receive the new United States minister to France, Charles Cotesworth Pinckney; to consider the Directory's leave-taking of James Monroe, in which Vicomte de Barras, the president of that body, expressed sentiments described by Adams as "dangerous to our Independence and Union" because they evinced "a disposition to separate the people of the United States from the Government"; and to respond to the decree passed by the Directory on 2 Mch. 1797, threatening the commerce of the United States with seizure. In the ad-

dress Adams proposed to "institute a fresh attempt at negociation" with France, but he also recommended a preparedness program including the establishment of a navy, the development of regulations for the arming of merchant vessels, the equipment of frigates "to take under convoy such merchant vessels as shall remain unarmed," the further fortification of major seaports, the formation of a provisional army, the reorganization of the militia, and finally, consultation with other neutral nations and consideration of the renewal of treaties with Prussia and Sweden (*Speech of the President of the United States, to Both Houses of Congress, on Tuesday, May 16th, 1797* [Philadelphia, 1797], 3-11).

According to SJL, TJ and Bell exchanged eight letters between 14 Mch. 1794 and 9 Apr. 1797, none of which has been found.

To James Madison

Philadelphia May 18. 97.

I was informed on my arrival here that Genl. Pinckney's dispatches had on their first receipt excited in the administration a great deal of passion: that councils were held from day to day, and their ill temper fixed at length in war; that under this impression Congress was called: that the tone of the party in general became high, and so continued till the news of the failure of the bank of England. This first gave it a check, and a great one and they have been cooling down ever since. The most intemperate only still asking permission to arm their vessels for their own defence, while the more prudent disapprove of putting it in the power of their brethren and leaving to their discretion to begin the war for us. The impression was too that the executive had for some time been repenting that they had called us, and wished the measure undone. All the members from North as well as South concurred in attesting that negociation or any thing rather than war was the wish of their constitutents. What was our surprise then at recieving the speech which will come to you by this post. I need make no observations to you on it. I believe there was not a member of either house, out of the secret, who was not much disappointed. However some had been prepared. The spirit of supporting the Executive was immediately given out in the lower house and is working there. The Senate admits of no fermentation. Tracy, Laurence and Livermore were appointed to draw an answer for them, Venable, Freeman, Rutledge, Griswald and   for the representatives. The former will be reported to day, and will be in time to be inclosed: the other not till tomorrow when the post will be gone. We hope this last will be in general terms, but this is not certain, a majority as is believed (of the committee) being for arming the merchantmen, finishing the frigates, fortifying harbors, and making all other military preparations, as an aid to negociation. How the majority of the house will be is very doubtful. If all were here, it is thought it would be decidedly pacific, but all are not here and will not be here. The division on the choice of a clerk was 41. for Condy, 40 for Beckley. Besides the loss of the ablest clerk in the US. and the outrage committed on the absent members, prevented by the suddenness of the call and their distance from being here on the 1st. day of the session, it excites a fear that the republican interest has lost by the new changes. It is said that three from Virginia separate from their brethren. The hope however is that as the Antirepublicans take the high ground of war, and their opponents are for every thing moderate, that the most moderate of those who came under contrary dispositions will join them. Langdon tells me there is a considerable change working in the minds of the people to the Eastward: that the idea that they have been decieved begins to gain ground, and that were the elections to be now made their result would be considerably different. This however is doubted and denied by others.   France has asked of Holland to send away our minister from them and to treat our commerce on the plan of their late decree. The Batavian government answered after due consideration that their commerce with us was now their chief commerce, that their money was in our funds, that if they broke off correspondence with us they should be without resources for themselves, for their own public and for France, and therefore declined doing it. France acquiesced. I have this from the President who had it from his son still at the Hague. I presume that France has made the same application to Spain. For *I know* that Spain has memorialized our Executive against the effect of the British treaty, as to the articles concerning neutral bottoms, contraband, and the Missisipi, has been pressing for an answer and has not yet been able to obtain one. It does not seem candid to have kept out of sight in the speech this discontent of Spain which is strongly and seriously pronounced and to have thereby left it to be imagined that France is the only power of whom we are in danger.—The failure of the bank of England, and the fear of having a paper tender there, has stopped buying bills of exchange. Specie is raked up from all quarters, and remitted for paiments at a disadvantage from risks &c of 20. per cent. The bankruptcies here have been immense. I heard a sensible man well acquainted with them conjecture that the aggregate of the clear losses on all these added together in all the states would be not less than 10. millions of Dollars. A heavy tax indeed, to which are to be added the maritime spoliations, and this tax falling on only a particular description of citizens.—Bills of lading are arrived to a merchant for goods shipped from Bordeaux for this place in a vessel in which *Monroe is coming passenger*. We hope hourly therefore to recieve him.—Innes is arrived, and that board going to work.

May. 19. The answer of the Senate is reported by the Committee. It is perfectly an echo and full as high toned as the speech. Amendments may and will be attempted but cannot be carried.—Note to me the day you recieve this that I may know whether I conjecture rightly what is our true post day here.

RC (DLC: Madison Papers); unsigned; with blank left by TJ for fifth member of the committee of the House of Representatives (see below); addressed: "James Madison junr. Orange." PrC (DLC). For enclosure, see note below.

Charles C. PINCKNEY'S DISPATCHES to the secretary of state from 20 Dec. 1796 through 8 Mch. 1797 were among eighteen documents and extracts referred to in Adams's address of 16 May and transmitted to Congress the following day (Pickering to TJ, 17 May 1797, in DNA: RG 46, Senate Records, 5th Cong., 1st sess.; *Annals*, VII, 64-7). For President Adams's SPEECH of 16 May at the opening of the special session of Congress, see the preceding document. Those from the House of Representatives appointed to DRAW AN ANSWER to the president's address were Abraham B. Venable of Virginia, Nathaniel Freeman, Jr., of Massachusetts, John Rutledge, Jr., of South Carolina, Roger Griswold of Connecticut, and John W. Kittera of Pennsylvania. TJ's hope that the House response would be in GENERAL TERMS was not realized. The report

submitted by the committee on 19 May stressed the impartial conduct of the United States in foreign affairs and assured the president of their "zealous co-operation in those measures which may appear necessary for our security or peace." On 22 May, the first day the report was considered by the House, Virginia Republican John Nicholas introduced an amendment that endorsed the president's plan for "a fresh attempt at negotiation," called for a "mutual spirit of conciliation," and advocated the removal of "inequalities" that might have arisen in relations between the United States and France due to the "operation" of treaties. The House debated it for a week. Robert Goodloe Harper opposed the amendment, arguing that France, once convinced of America's firm resolve to resist "encroachments and aggressions," would soon desist from them. On 29 May the House defeated the amendment by six votes. The next day Speaker Jonathan Dayton introduced an amendment approving of Adams's decision to renew negotiations with France and called for giving that nation treaty rights comparable to those of other countries. The Federalists argued against the latter clause, noting that the terms of the negotiations should "be left wholly to the President." The Dayton amendment passed by a five-vote margin on 31 May, but the following day Pennsylvania Federalist Samuel Sitgreaves introduced an alteration which canceled the clause urging equal treaty rights for France. This change was rejected by a 49 to 50 vote. Kittera then offered an alteration noting that since the negotiations were to be carried out in a "mutual" spirit of conciliation, France should be held responsible for injuries to neutral shipping suffered by the United States. Although Republicans feared that the French would view the phrase as an ultimatum which would subsequently defeat negotiations and lead to war, it passed on 2 June 1797. The controversial amendment as it was finally adopted by a 58 to 41 vote declared: "We therefore receive with the utmost satisfaction, your information that a fresh attempt at negotiation will be instituted, and we cherish the hope, that a mutual spirit of conciliation, and a disposition, on the part of France, to compensate for any injuries which may have been committed upon our neutral rights, and on the part of the United States to place France on grounds similar to those of other countries, in their relation and connection with us, if any inequalities shall be found to exist, will produce an accommodation compatible with engagements rights, duties, and honor, of the United States." After a Republican effort to strike out the sentence which reiterated Adams's assertion that the United States government had been "just and impartial to foreign nations" was defeated by a 45 to 53 vote, the amended address was passed and presented to the president on 3 June 1797 (JHR, III, 10-23; Annals, VII, 68-74, 191, 193, 199-200, 210-34).

It is not clear whether TJ actually enclosed the answer REPORTED by the Senate committee on 18 May 1797, because it was recommitted the next day and does not appear to have been printed. For the address, see the Senate to John Adams, 23 May 1797.

In the CHOICE OF A CLERK for the House of Representatives on 15 May, Federalists voted for Jonathan W. CONDY, a young law student, the candidate agreed upon the previous day at a caucus organized by William L. Smith. John BECKLEY had served as clerk of the House since the inception of the post (1 Apr. 1789) and was again elected to the postion in December 1801 (Annals, VII, 51-2; Biog. Dir. Cong.; Berkeley, Beckley, 154-6). For the partisan reaction to Condy's election, see Berkeley, Beckley, 156-8.

THREE FROM VIRGINIA SEPARATE FROM THEIR BRETHREN: Thomas Evans, James Machir, and Daniel Morgan were first-term congressmen elected in 1796 who voted with the Federalists (Biog. Dir. Cong.).

In the correspondence with his father of 3 Feb. 1797, John Quincy Adams's assessment of the demands of FRANCE and the reaction of HOLLAND was hypothetical and not as encouraging as presented here. The minister at the Hague noted that Dutch merchants and government officials agreed that United States COMMERCE and payments were "almost the only resources, the enjoyment of which is yet left them," but they feared and admitted they would "be *forced* to follow whatever France should dictate to them." In a letter to his father of 7 Feb. Adams predicted that if the French government ordered "this government to suspend all intercourse, commercial or political, or both, with the United States, they could not refuse the demand, although fully sensible that it would be a measure extremely odious to the people" (Worthington Chauncey Ford, ed., *Writings of John Quincy Adams*, 7 vols. [New York, 1913-17], II, 106, 108).

Spain's protests AGAINST THE EFFECT OF THE BRITISH TREATY were included in Spanish minister Carlos Martínez de Irujo's letter to Timothy Pickering of 6 May 1797 which, along with Pickering's ANSWER of 17 May, were among the documents transmitted to the Senate by the secretary of state on 17 May (Pickering to TJ, 17 May 1797; ASP, *Foreign Relations*, II, 14-17).

James INNES was a United States representative on the commission appointed under Article 6 of the Jay Treaty to consider claims of British subjects concerning debts owed them by United States citizens before the Treaty of Paris of 1783. The debt commission began its WORK in May 1797 (JEP, I, 204; Miller, *Treaties*, II, 249-50; Perkins, *First Rapprochement*, 53).

Richard O'Brien's Memorandum on Naval Protection

Requisite marine for the Protection of the Comerce of the United States to Protect, our trade against the Spoilations, of Foreign Corsairs and at all times to be in readiness, to act on any emergencie
As Viz
The 6 frigates on the original plan.
6 Ships of 24 Guns Each to mount 20 nine pounders & 4: Six Do.
6 Ships of 18 Six pounders As Sloops, of war.
6 Brigs, of 18 Six pounders
6 Schooners Mounting 18 to 14: foure pounders.
2 Sloops of 12 Guns Each —— — — — — — — .
These Vessels to be built, by Contract, the Could be built in 4: 5: or 6 Munths, to be live oak and Ceder, Composition bolts, and Coppered
The Could, when built, be, fitted and ready for Sea in 30 days, after the were launched, the whole of the Corsairs to be built, on the best plan for Sailing and Calculated for rowing—
For the Defence of the Coastes in the Summer time, and for the Speedy Conveyance, of troopes from one part of our extensive Coasts to the Other, is allso requisite, 4 Gallies, Carrying in the prow 2. 24 pounders, Stern Calculated for the Same with 50, or 80 Gun boats to be Calculated, for Carrying at the prow, an 18 pounder or 12 Do. these would be a terror, to frigates, Small Ships or privateers, aproaching adjacent to the Coasts of the U.S for if becalmed, the gallies and Gun boats would row up, and unavoidably must either take or destroy the enemie except, prevented, by A Suden Breese Springing up &c. the in Consequence makeing theire Escape—
NB. The Seamen belonging to Each State, Should be registired, the Coast Seamen allso, and the fishermen, and, the fresh water Sailors, and the Corsairs maned by Quotas from Each State, and Randevouses Opened for entering and recruiting for the Corsairs—[1]
NB. The 3d. of the Gun boats, Should be built as whale boats, well Calculated for rowing and Sailing to have a Brass, Six pounder in the bow—
If this list was to great, to have As Viz.

The 3 frigates fitted immediatly.

2 Ships, of 24 Guns	all to be built, by Contract
2 Sloops of war of 20 Guns Each.	in 4: 5. or 6 Munths time
3 Brigs, of 18 Guns, Each	and to be Coppered.
3 Schooners of 14 Guns Each	
12 whale boats with a 6 pounder Each	

When our peace is fully established, with all the Barbary States we Shall have in the meditteranian Seas from 3: to 500 Sail of Vessels, a part of our Corsairs, will all ways be requisite, to give Security to our meditteranian Comerce, to in Some respects, to keep the Barbary States in awe, to Make us respected by the Italian States, and to be in readiness, to annoy the Comerce of the Europian Nations, whom, Should attempt anything hostile to the american Comerce.

Being allways in readiness, with our Corsairs, we Should, not be liable to be insulted, we would Comand respect, and wherever in any part of the known Globe, where our Comerce leads, us there at times our Corsairs, Should be Seen, and without, Corsairs the U.S Can never have Any Security for her Comerce.

The Smaller, Corsairs would reconniter, gain intelligence be Serviceable as Packetts and Corriers, and all public, business, Should be done, by public Ships, and regular, and, approved, officers—

A Large and regular, Storeship is requisite for, Carrying our Stipulated, Maratime and Military Stores to the Barbary States. Said Ship Could, return with a Cargo, of Salt, annually on government account and would thereby defray Said Ships expences—

In the Barbary States, the Consuls of the U.S must hoist one american national Flag, as is Customary with all nations at peace with them good people, by the flag which the Consuls displays, and the Meditteranian pass, the Barbary States, knows, those, the are at peace with, but at present the U.S has So many different flags, or Colours, that the Barbary States will only know, the flag at peace with them, agreeable to the flag the Consul displays. Therefore it is requisite to have Some reform, in our Colours, we as one nation Should be known to all the world as one people and haveing one national flag.

To abolish the Eagle, in the present Colours generally worn would, be difficult, Some plan Should be Speedily adopted and Observed under Severe penalties.

Maratime Schools Should be established in the United States and the natives of this Country, Should be encouraged to be regularly bound to the Sea, we Should not be So, dependant, on foreign nations as we are at present.

A Country like the U.S with every thing necessary for Ship building, for establishing a Navy, with 4: or 5 Millions of, enterprizeing inhabitants, and haveing no Corsairs, must Certainly, be Considered by the nations of Europe, as an extraordinary, Circumstance—look at the Marine of the Dutch, whom has not 2 Milions of inhabitants, Sweden and Denmark both together, has not As Many inhabitants as the U.S but the have formidable Navies, and great regular Armies of troops.

From the Situation of the United States, relative to Europe, and the possesions of the Europian nations, whom has territory Joining on to the Territory of the U.S in Case of the war, with the British or Spaniards, or the french if the possess, Luisana or the floridas—it would be with those nations a privateering, war on the Seas—we Should embargo, our ports, necessiate those fleets of Corsairs, those Sea Robers to return to Europe, Starve thereby the west indies, and the Sooner, the negroes revolted, and the west india-islands, became independant, and Governed by the Blacks the better for this Country, we Should have a free trade, it would not be monapalized by the great, Europian nations.

The west indiees is So Situated, as allways to be dependant on the U.S for provisions, this Country has Much of the fate of them Islands at present in its power.

Our galliees and gun boats, Could pass, along Close to our Coastes in defiance to fleets of Corsairs, and Could get to the Bahamias unmolested, do, every damage to our enemies, Islands, or Could, be employed in the Baye of fundi River St. Laurence Missisippi Floridas and, Occasionally, Carried up our rivers, and into the lakes, there to Opperate, and Second the Efforts, of our troopes, and Effectually Strike terror to the enemiees of the United States. With all due respect, Submitted to the Government of the US. by theire Most Obt. Servt.

RD. O BRIEN

Philadelphia
May the 18th. 1797

MS (DLC); entirely in O'Brien's hand; with one insertion in margin (see note below); endorsed by TJ: "Barbary states."

Two days before O'Brien penned this document, the president discussed naval defense and the PROTECTION of American TRADE in his address to Congress (see TJ to Thomas Bell, 18 May 1797). THE 6 FRIGATES ON THE ORIGINAL PLAN: the "Act to provide a Naval Armament," approved 27 Mch. 1794, authorized construction of four vessels of 44 guns each and two more of 36 guns. Work on the ships was to cease in the event of peace with Algiers, a provision overridden by legislation of 20 Apr. 1796 that allowed completion of THE 3 FRIGATES that headed O'Brien's alternate plan above. A military and naval appropriations act of 3 Mch. 1797 had allocated $172,000 for the completion of the *United States*, the *Constitution*, and the *Constellation* (U.S. Statutes at Large, I, 350-1, 453-4, 509).

[1] O'Brien wrote the preceding paragraph perpendicularly in the margin.

From John Oliver

SIR   Bordentown May 18th 1797

Your writings and general Character, possessed me with an Idea, that you was a Lover of the Arts. This Idea and a New Invention, discovered and made by a Young man in this town, are the Cause of my present Intrusion.

This Young man more than 12 months since Conceived an Idea of making a certain Machine. His plan or rather his thoughts, he communicated to a Friend. This friend advised him to make it. He has been Ingaged Some months in making this Machine, and says it will be compleated in a short time.

This Machine, he and his friend, keeps a secret. No one here knows what it is or for what use Intended but them Selves.

Since he began the above mentioned Machine, He has at Intervals worked at and made a Self-movement, the Idea of which he had in his Mind some time previous to his Ingageing in the work of the former. When he made this Movement, he put it in his Chest and there it run for three months and a day, keeping it a Secret from his friend and every Other person.

At the end of the 3 months and a day, which was the 8th of this Inst:, He Exhibited his Movement to Mr. Allison Mr. Staughton and others, Who was pleased to Call it a perpetual motion. The next day Governor Howell came to see it, and said, That it gave him great pleasure to think that an American had made the grand discovery. Since that time a number of [Gentle]men has had the curiosity to view it.

The Works of this Movement, Are all out of Sight—they are Inclosed in a hollow Cylinder—the diameter about 11 Inches—the length much the same. The cylinder Turns on 2 pivots fixed in the centers of the Cylinder. Its Velocity, about one Revolution, in a second of time—its power Not yet accurately found. He says, He intends to make another One more pleasing to the Eye and more Accurate. The Cylindrical case of this first attempt he made by hand of white-pine. He says the Next shall be made of the American Wild-Cherry turned in a nice manner, But as he is now ingaged with his first Machine, he thinks he cannot compleat his Intensions in less than 3 months.

One Anecdote he related to me, which I take the liberty to mention. He had no scheme or draught on paper. His plan was in his Head. When he had put all his works together, *that he had thought of*, He found it was deficient in one thing—this thing he calls a Regulator. A regulator he made and apply'd it, But found it deficient. He soon perceived the deficiency and made a second regulator—this second he put in its place, and going to a nother part of his Shop to get Oil, to oil the works, which had not yet been done—on his return with the oil, he found his Machine in motion.

The secret still remains with himself—this Young man is very little aquainted with the World, and much less with Man wherefore I have recommended to him to Solicit your patronage and protection, And in his behalf hath made this Communication.

His Name—Robert Oliver—aged 24—was born and brought up in this Town—a Cabinet-maker by Trade, and is my Eldest Son. I am with Sincerity Your Well-wisher JNO. OLIVER

RC (MoSHi: Jefferson Papers); torn; at foot of text: "Thomas Jefferson Vice President"; endorsed by TJ as received 26 May 1797 and so recorded in SJL.

To Martha Jefferson Randolph

MY DEAR MARTHA   Philadelphia May 18. 1797.

I arrived here in good health on the 7th. day after my departure from home, without any intervening accident and am as well as when I left home. I recieved here the inclosed letter from Mr. Pintard our Consul at Madeira who sais it was given him by one of your old convent acquaintances settled there. I suppose the letter will inform you of more particulars. We yesterday recieved the President's speech. Till the answer shall be given in we cannot judge what work the legislature will now take in hand, nor consequently how long we shall be here. Opinions vary from 4. to 6. weeks. My next letter will give a better idea of the time of my return which will be within a week after the rising of Congress. Our affairs with France become more and more gloomy. Those of England every day more desperate. Nothing but their desperation prevents the stronger party in our government from making common cause with them. Prices of produce are at a stand. The current price of James river tobacco is 9. dollars. This information may be desireable to some of our mercantile neighbors. My love to my dear Maria. I write to Mr. Randolph on the presumption he is at Richmond. My affections are with yourself and Maria and my wishes to be with you. Continue to love me. Adieu.

RC (NNPM); unsigned; endorsed by Randolph. Enclosure: see note below.

The letter from John M. PINTARD to TJ of 28 Mch. 1797, recorded in SJL as received on 11 May, has not been found. The LETTER enclosed from one of Martha Randolph's OLD CONVENT ACQUAINTANCES has not been identified.

From Peregrine Fitzhugh

DEAR SIR   Cottage Washington County (Md) 19th. May 1797

I beg you to accept my thanks for your favor of the 9th. ulto. and for the peas which it notifies having been lodged for me with my friend John T. Mason. I shall receive them in a few days and will pay every attention to their Culture. I have lately met with some of the same species of Corn tho' in a much purer state than what I sent you but the Season being too far advanced to admit a chance of its reaching you in time I will have it carefully cultivated here and furnish you with seed from it in the ensuing fall or winter. We have frequent direct opportunities from hence to staunton which I think I heard you say was about 40 miles from your Seat, if you have any friend there to whom it could be directed I can upon a certainty have it lodged for you in time and it will very probably be in my power to accompany it with some of the large dutch white Clover seed of which I sowed about a pack this spring.

Your remarks on Mr. Maddisons *alledged* conduct in the Genl. and State Conventions and in Congress are perfectly satisfactory to me and would I think force conviction upon any rational or candid mind, but I have ever believed the allegations unfounded and that they were calculated to wound the republican Cause thro the riles of one of its Champions. While I sincerely lament your having been so soon drawn again from your domestic enjoyments on so long and tiresome a journey I cannot but confess that I anticipate the most salutary effects from the present meeting of Congress. What the disposition of the new President towards France may be I can form no judgment but on speculation— because we have seen the professions and Acts of the old Administration relative to that Government uniformly at variance—but it is a fact *too* well ascertained that all his immediate Counsellors and a majority of the honorable body over whom you preside have manifested a disposition favorable to the Interest of Britain and of course hostile to those of our Sister Republic. Upon the House of representatives then are we compell'd to rest our last hope and I feel a confidence that notwithstanding the few unfavorable changes which the late elections have produced, its complexion will be such as to encourage or if necessary influence a pacific disposition in the propos'd negotiations. This may probably induce a similar conduct on the part of France and secure us the enjoyment of a less interrupted Commerce which may be some consolation to us— but how are we to regain, or where seek an indemnity for the loss of our national Character? Having shown the World that we are capable of abandoning the sacred principles of honor justice and Gratitude—from motives of fear, avarice or whatever other ignoble passion, Let our Conduct now wear ever so much the appearance of candor, Let our measures towards France be ever so conciliatory—they will be regarded by all nations as the offspring of necessity and not an honorable conviction and we shall be allowed no credit for them. I hear that Mr. Ames has by his own desire been left out of the present Congress. *I* am glad of it. Tho he certainly ought not to have deserted his party till he had assisted them in getting their *Barque* out of the *breakers* but looking forward I presume to the loss of their chief support (the sanction of a *great Name*) he thought it advisable to retire also and he has meanly sneak'd out of difficulties into which he proudly strutted. I heartily wish the President was as well rid of his present *Body Guards*. He surely has as little to expect from their Wisdom or Talents as his Country has from their Patriotism. I recollect and will relate a little anecdote of one of them which if it does not add to *his* literary merit will at least make you smile. During our late War the Learned Secretary then Qr. Mr. Genl. of the army had occasion to issue an order relative to the disposition of Rations complained vehemently of the "uncommon *inundation* of women which the Camp had recently experienc'd." The expression caused a good deal of Laugh among the younger Officers (myself in the number) but we were at a loss to decide whether it was the effect of ignorance or whether our buckram Qr. Master did not actually fear a real inundation from the admission of so many additional Sourses in the Camp and that he might be *swept away* in the deluge. A few other orders of a similar Complexion very soon however removed our doubts on the subject. Have you seen a letter of instructions from one of your districts adress'd to Mr. New their representative. Our sentiments here perfectly coincide with those expressed in that Letter and we earnestly hope that Congress may make such principles the basis and such measures the result of their deliberations. We shall be in anxious suspense till we hear what you have done—if therefore you can find a leisure moment before you leave the City, a short communication of your sentiments on the present posture of Affairs and of the probable issue of your meeting would be very thankfully received. I have obeyed your Command relative to my Father. The old Gentleman whose intellect continues as strong as his republican principles are sound feels himself most gratified by your remembrance of him. He directs me to make a return of his affectionate and unfeign'd respects—to assure you of his warmest veneration for your private and political Character—and to add that he retains a perfect recollection of you, and that he shall consider it one of the most pleasing events of his life if chance should ever afford him an opportunity of embracing and paying his personal regards to you. Perhaps in some of your excurtions to and from the Seat of Government it might not be an unpleasant variety to take this County in your Route. At its proper season you would as a Farmer be delighted with the luxuriance of vegetation, and I can venture to assert that you would meet as many warm and respectable Friends here as perhaps in any other country Circle of the United States, and who would feel themselves highly gratified by your Presence among them. I need [not]¹ assure you of the pleasure I should feel on such an occasion. We are only 24 miles from Frederic Town thro which place runs a large Post Road delightful from thence to Philadelphia and an excellent line of Stages as I am informed establish'd on it. With earnest wishes for your Health & happiness & every possible respect I am Dr Sir Yr. Most obedt. & Hble Servant

PEREGNE FITZHUGH

P.S. About an hour after sealing up my Letter for the Post office I received a Paper containing the Presidents Speech. It pains me exceedingly as it breathes none of those conciliating sentiments towards the French republic which I had fondly cherished the Idea of. If from Speculation as in the beginning of this Letter I appeared to doubt the Presidents disposition towards France his Speech I think leaves us no room now towards it and we have now indeed no hope left but in the house of representatives.

RC (DLC); addressed: "Thomas Jefferson Esquire Vice President of the United States Philadelphia"; endorsed by TJ as received 27 May 1797 and so recorded in SJL.

LEARNED SECRETARY: Timothy Pickering.

On 11 Apr. 1797, the freeholders of Caroline County, Virginia, met and approved a LETTER OF INSTRUCTIONS to be presented to Anthony New, THEIR REPRESENTATIVE in Congress. Signed by Edmund Pendleton, the instructions called for negotiations rather than war with France and the establishment of a "substantial neutrality" that would give equal treaty rights to both England and France (Philadelphia *Aurora*, 21 Apr. 1797).

¹ Word supplied.

From "A Native American"

SIR [19 May 1797]

Your arrival at the seat of government immediately after the publication of a letter said to be written by you to your friend Mazzei in Italy, affords you a fair opportunity of doing away any bad impression respecting your character, which the falsely ascribing to you improper sentiments may hitherto have occasioned. For the honor of the American name I would wish the letter to be a Forgery, altho' I must confess, that your silence upon the subject, and the conduct of that party with which you appear, at present, to act, leaves but little probability of its not having proceeded from your pen. If it is not your production, an explicit disavowal of it appears incumbent on you, for several reasons.

1. Because it implies a contradiction of those sentiments respecting our excellent constitution, which you have formerly held, before a disappointed ambition threw you into the hands of a desperate faction, by whose means you expected, no doubt, to have filled the first office of our government.

2. Because it is a direct libel on the character of those men, whom the choice of a free people called to the exercise of the executive and judiciary powers of our government. And,

3. Because its publication in a country, from whose government and citizens we have met with every kind of injury and insult, has a tendency to encourage a continuance of such conduct in our allies, from a persuasion, that our internal situation would admit of its exercise with impunity.

You stated truly when you represented all our proprietors of land as friendly to republican principles, and if you had gone further and declared all our native citizens as faithful to the government they had formed, and disposed to defend their rights as an independent nation, from the insidious attacks of foreign foes, you would have run no risque of a contradiction. It is to be sure unfortunate for the *ancient dominion of Virginia*, that the names of the late secretary Randolph, Giles, Madison, Monroe and yourself are found in its rolls of citizens; but whilst she possesses the *beloved Washington*; and the memory of his great achievements and illustrious character is cherished by Americans, those names, like specks upon the sun's disk, will be but transiently observed, and detract but inconsiderably from her lustre. But it probably suited your purpose better to say, "Our political situation is prodigiously changed since you left us. Instead of that noble love of liberty, and that republican government, which carried us triumphantly through the dangers of the war, an anglo-monarchico-aristocratic party has arisen. Their avowed object is to impose on us the substance, as they have already given us the form, of the British government. Nevertheless the principal body of our citizens remain faithful to republican principles. All our proprietors of lands are friendly to those principles, as also the mass of men of talents. We have against us (republicans) the executive power, the judiciary power (two of the three branches of our government) all the officers of government, all who are seeking offices, all timid men, who prefer the calm of despotism to the tempestuous sea of liberty, the British merchants, and the Americans who trade on British capitals, the speculators, persons interested in the banks and public funds (establishments invented with views of corruption and to assimilate us to the British model in all its corrupt parts.)"

Supposing for an instant, what I can by no means admit, that such is the present situation of our country, is it, sir, the part of a friend to his country—is it the part of a citizen, who had been frequently intrusted with the management of public concerns, thus to expose the failings of his brethren—the weak and vulnerable part of his native land, to a prattling foreigner, whose self-consequence and pride, abstracted from any other motive, might induce him to make an improper use of this, at least, very imprudent confidence? We have not forgotten the fine theme, which the *precious confessions of your countryman Randolph* furnished to a former French minister, and we can readily conceive, that your letter, under the improving hand of an intriguing Italian, may prove the source of accumulating evils to the United States. Have we not repeatedly shewn our attachment to the cause of liberty and to France? Did we not exert every muscle—strain every nerve, to assist her in establishing her right to make her own form of government untrammelled by the will of other nations? And that too, when those who now basely fawn by her side, and ignominiously lick the dust from her feet, were foremost in their opposition to the regeneration of a numerous people. Did we not, for a long time, patiently bear with the cringing insolence of Genet—the impertinent suggestions of Fauchet—and the dark and insidious manœuvres of Adet, without shewing any intemperance of conduct at their behaviour, or ceasing our good offices to their nation, or their compatriots? True it is, sir, that the feeble attempts of a rising republic, without a navy or large standing army, could be of little service in battle, to either of the contending parties—of this, in the commencement of her struggle, France seemed fully sensible, and was aware of the advantage to be derived from our remaining neutral. And is it for this, we are charged by you with ingratitude and injustice, and are those men, whom you once thought *Solomons in council, and Sampsons in combat*, for this to be branded by you, with the name of *Apostates*?

But I am perhaps intruding upon your time, and taking up some moments which might be more profitably employed in attention to public affairs; I shall therefore close this letter, with a wish, that if the writing ascribed to you is spurious it may be disowned. In doing this, you will render a justice due to yourself, and oblige many of your fellow-citizens, but no one more than   A NATIVE AMERICAN

Text from *Gazette of the United States*, 19 May 1797; at head of text: "To Thomas Jefferson. Esquire, Vice-President of the United States and President of the Senate."

For the PUBLICATION OF A LETTER to Philip MAZZEI, see Editorial Note to Jefferson's Letter to Philip Mazzei, 24 April 1796. The author of another anonymous letter to TJ found TJ's silence "complete evidence of your guilt . . . considering you then as the avowed author of that indecent libel against the government and character of your country, I shall animadvert on it with that freedom which the magnitude of the subject requires." He went on to quote the appended paragraphs from the *Moniteur* that were translated in the *Minerva* (A Fellow Citizen to TJ, printed in *Porcupine's Gazette*, 2 June 1797).

For the PRECIOUS CONFESSIONS which Edmund Randolph was charged with having confided to French minister Jean Antoine Joseph Fauchet, see TJ to Monroe, 6 Sep. 1795.

To Thomas Mann Randolph

TH:J. TO TMR.   Philadelphia May 19. 97.

I inclose you a copy of the President's speech. Before that was delivered the dispositions of all the members from every quarter seemed averse from war. But that disposition appears to be changing, and those are taking the hue of the speech who wish the Executive to be the sole power in the government. The Republican interest has lost by the changes in the last election, particularly by those in our state. The struggle to keep us, while pretending to negociate for peace, from provoking war by putting ourselves into all it's attitudes will be arduous and doubtful. It would not be so doubtful if all were present; but many of the most distant[1] members are absent, and chiefly of those who are either peaceable or moderate.—Flour is from $8\frac{1}{2}$ to 9. Doll. Good James river tobacco $8\frac{1}{2}$ to 9 D. I have not yet been able to sell mine which I hold at 11. Dol. They admit that price has been given for the best hogsheads of old tobacco and tho' I have offered a credit equivalent to September (when it would be considered as old tobacco) yet I have not been able to engage. I think I shall keep it on hand till then rather than give up such a difference. Hereafter I will make my money engagements for September instead of July as there is a loss of 25. per cent in selling before September. I believe I could now sell for 10. or perhaps $10\frac{1}{2}$ Doll. on the credit I have offered of 2. 4. and 6 months, a third payable at each epoch, and the notes would be discountable 2. months before due. I have mentioned always in my propositions your tobacco if it should come, so that if you chuse it it shall go with mine. But I should wish your instructions how far such terms of paiment would suit you. I should have had less difficulty but that there is really none of the purchasers but Lieper I would trust so long. We all expect a session more or less short. I shall be happy to hear how your health is and that of the children, who I presume are still with you. I am impatient to meet you all at Monticello, and to exchange the turbulence and hatred of faction for the delights of domestic affection and tranquility. Adieu affectionately

P.S. There is not a single voice heard for embargo of any kind, so that the exporters may be tranquil on that subject.

RC (DLC); with several emendations only the most important of which is noted below; postscript written in the margin; endorsed by Randolph as received 25 May 1797. PrC (ViU: Edgehill-Randolph Papers); final line of text preceding postscript missing; endorsed by TJ in ink on verso. Enclosure: see note to TJ to Thomas Bell, 18 May 1797.

CHANGES IN THE LAST ELECTION: see note to TJ to Madison, 18 May 1797 for the three Virginia Federalists who were elected in 1796.

A letter from Randolph to TJ of 18 May 1797, recorded in SJL as received from Varina nine days later, has not been found.

[1] TJ first wrote "but so many Southern" before altering the passage to read as above.

From Edward Rutledge

MY DEAR SIR   Charleston May 19th: 1797.

Two days ago, I shipt your Peas, and Orange Trees on board a Vessel for Norfolk, and wrote by her to your Merchants in Richmond thro' the Collector of Norfolk. I am sorry to have delayed this Commission so long; but we have so little communication with Richmond that after waiting a considerable time in vain, I was obliged to adopt the expedient of sending them, in the Manner I have now done.

The Trees are small, and are packed in Matts, with a quantity of earth around them. I wish they may answer, tho' I doubt it, not only from the coldness of your Climate, but from your distance from the Sea; the latter is the Reason we assign for their not thriving in our interior Country: another Reason indeed may be found in the Laziness of our people.

The Pea is usually planted between the Corn, but in the same Row, with it. It is not planted until the Corn is at least two feet high, and our Month of planting is July; for the growth is quick, and the vine very Luxuriant. However you will make your experiments, and be govern'd by the Evi[dence.] We commonly put about as many into each hole, as would fill the bowl of a pipe. If the weevil shall seem to have injured the Grain; don't regard it; but plant it at all Ev[ents?] for appearances are not to be relied on in this Instance.

We are here, in a perfect Calm. Not one word of European News: and scarcely a conjecture whisper'd, of what will be done. I hope it will not be in the political, as it is in the natural hemisphere; if it should, we might look out for a terrible Storm. But we have one consolation in knowing that, if Palinurus should be asleep, my friend Æneas is on the watch—I expect to hear great things, and good things of you the[re?]

for the Fruit should be worthy of the Tree. With unabating friendship, I am my dear Sir, affectionately yours. ED: RUTLEDGE

RC (DLC); with several portions of words obscured by tape; endorsed by TJ as received 6 June 1797 and so recorded in SJL.

Since William Lindsay, the COLLECTOR OF NORFOLK, had recently died, Rutledge presumably worked through Daniel Bedin-ger, the Republican surveyor at Norfolk who had carried on the daily work at the custom house during Lindsay's long illness and continued to perform the duties after his death, hoping to receive the appointment as collector. When Adams chose Federalist Otway Byrd instead, Bedinger resigned his office (Prince, *The Federalists*, 107-11).

From Elbridge Gerry

MY DEAR SIR   New York 22d May 1797

Inclosed is a copy of a letter which I wrote to Mr. Monroe the 4th of april, to the care of yourself; and annexed is the copy of one to yourself of the 27th of march; both of which, I presume from their not being acknowledged, have been intercepted: and if this is the case, I wish to ascertain it. I have the honor to remain with the most perfect esteem & respect yours sincerely   E. GERRY

RC (DLC); at foot of text: "His Excellency Mr. Jefferson"; with Dupl of Gerry to TJ, 27 Mch. 1797, subjoined; endorsed by TJ as received 25 May 1797 and so recorded in SJL. Enclosure: Gerry to Monroe, 4 Apr. 1797 (DLC: Monroe Papers).

To Alexandre Giroud

SIR   Philadelphia May 22. 97.

I recieved at this place from Mr. Bache the letter of the 20th. Germinal with the seeds of the Bread tree which you were so kind as to send me. I am happy that the casual circumstance respecting Oglethorpe's affairs has led to this valuable present and I shall take immediate measures to improve the opportunity it gives us of introducing so precious a plant into our Southern states. The successive supplies of the same seeds which you are kind enough to give me expectations of recieving from you will in like manner be thankfully recieved, and distributed to those persons and places most likely to render the experiment successful. One service of this kind rendered to a nation is worth more to them than all the victories of the most splendid pages of their history, and becomes a source of exalted pleasure to those who have been instrumental to it. May that pleasure be yours, and your name be pronounced with gratitude by those who shall at some future day be tasting the sweets [1] of the blessing you are now² procuring them. With my thanks for this favor accept assurances of the sentiments of esteem & regard with which I am &c. &c.

FC (DLC); entirely in TJ's hand, unsigned; two emendations, both recorded below; at foot of text: "Mr. Giroud Ingenieur des mines de la republique Français chez le citoyen Raymond. Commissaire du Directoir executif au Cap Francois. Isle de St. Domingue."

THE LETTER OF THE 20TH. GERMINAL: Giroud to TJ, [9 Apr. 1797].

¹ Preceding three words interlined in place of "in the enjoiment."
² Word interlined.

To Allen Jones

Philada. May 22. 97.

I have lately recieved from a Mr. Giroud of St. Domingue [a] few seeds of the Bread tree, from plants growing there. [Our inform?]ation that Capt. Cook found that tree bearing fully in [New Zealand] in a colder temperature than that of London, [leaves?] little doubt it may be raised in our Southern states. Having only seven seeds, and desirous of [t]aking all the [. . .] possible for success, I send two to each of the states of Georgia, S. Carolina, and N. Carolina, reserving one for Virginia [and knowing?] your great attention to things of this nature, I cannot better dispose of those destined for N. Carolina than by putting them into the hands of [. . .]¹ [with the?] sentiment of public interest to [. . .]² plant to the productions of [this country?] [. . .] accordingly take the liberty of [. . .]³ by the first safe conveyance which offers from this place.

I avail myself with great pleasure of this occasion of [recall?]ing myself to your [recollection?] and of assuring you of the constant sentiments of esteem & respect with which I have the honor to be Sir Your most obedient and most humble [servt]   TH: JEFFERSON

PrC (DLC); badly faded, with dateline enhanced in ink by TJ; at foot of text, also enhanced in ink by TJ: "General Allen Jones Halifax. N. Carolina." Recorded under this date in SJL, but acknowledged as a letter of 23 May 1797 in Jones to TJ, 20 Aug. 1797.

Allen Jones (1739-1807) of Mount Gallant plantation, Northampton County, sat in the North Carolina House of Commons, 1773-75, and in all five of the provincial congresses that met from 1774 to 1776. He was elected to a number of terms in the state senate between 1777 and 1787, including

stints as speaker in 1778 and 1779, served in the Continental Congress, 1779-80, and saw active service during the war as a brigadier general of militia. During North Carolina's contentious ratification process he firmly supported the Federal Constitution (DAB).

TJ sent the seeds intended for GEORGIA and S. CAROLINA in a missing letter of this date to Thomas Bee (see Bee to TJ, 1 Aug. 1797).

¹ Estimated seven words illegible.
² Estimated six words illegible.
³ Estimated four words illegible.

From Charles Louis Clérisseau

MONSIEUR   a auteuil ce 23 Mai—1797

Je profite d'une ocasion tres favorable pour vous faire parvenir ces lignes qui vous prouveront que je conserve toujours les Sentiments les plus Sensibles pour une persone qui a bien voulû m'honorer de Sa confiance et qui a daigné estre Satisfait de mes productions en m'en donant les preuves les plus distingués.

Je prend la liberté de vous prier de vous resouvenir de moi. Je me trouverois tres honoré Si je pouvois vous estre de quelque utilité dans la partie des arts ce qui Seroit pour moi une preuve que vous daigné vous resouvenir de moi. Les circonstances facheuses dans les quels nous nous trouvons nous obligent de nous recomander a vos amis. Car etant obligé de tout vendre pour vivre attendue que l'on ne peut nous payer nos rentes et que les artistes Sont obligé de mourir de faim ou de quitter le pays. Et moi je suis proche destre obligé de vendre ma biblioteque. Qu'il me Soit donc permis de me recommader a vous et a vos amis pour m'eviter un tel Sacrifice. Je ne prendrois pas la liberté de vous parler ainsi Si je n'etois pas convaincû de l'amour que vous avez pour les arts, et la Satisfaction que vous aurié d'obliger celui qui est avec le plus profond respect Monsieur Votre tres humble tres obeissant Serviteur

CLERISSEAU

Si Vous avez quelques amateurs des arts qui vienent a paris je vous prie de me les adresser. Voila mon adresse Mr. Cle. architecte demeurant a auteuil prest de paris A paris.

RC (DLC); endorsed by TJ as received 30 Mch. 1798 and so recorded in SJL. Enclosed in William Short to TJ, 27 Dec. 1797.

To Louis of Parma

Philadelphia May 23. 97.

I recieved from your Royal[1] highness the letter with which you were pleased to honor me through the channel of Mr. Pinckney then our envoy extraordinary at the court of Spain, in which you expressed your wish to establish a correspondence with some person in the US. of America who might be able to furnish subjects of Natural history from this country in exchange for those of Europe. I have never myself undertaken[2] to form a cabinet of Natural history, nor consequently to make myself acquainted with the methods of preparing and preserving the different[3] subjects. My occupations in public life have been and still continue inconsistent with the attentions which would have been requisite to such an undertaking. However ardently then I wished I could myself have been the person who should gratify the laudable desires of your Royal[4] highness to enrich your cabinet with American subjects, yet I was sensible that the way to serve you was not to undertake what I should have executed very defectively, but to engage some person whose habits and occupations would enable him more completely to fulfill your wishes. As to the person to whom I should address myself there could be no doubt. Mr. Charles Wilson Peale a member of our philosophical society and inhabitant[5] of this city has for many years been engaged in forming a Cabinet[6] of Natural history, is constantly occupied in collecting and preparing new subjects, and does this with a skill unequalled by any other among us. To him therefore I ventured on behalf of your Royal highness to propose that he should enter into correspondence with the keeper of your cabinet, furnish you with such[7] subjects of the three kingdoms as should be called for from this region and recieve from yours in exchange such as your keeper could procure or spare. Mr. Peale readily acceded to the proposition limiting his undertaking very candidly by the following expressions in his letter. 'I have it in my power, sais he, to make an exchange of *Animal* subjects generally, of minerals a small number, but as to vegetables I have not had time to pay much attention to them as yet, however by the help of Mr. Bartram and some others of my acquaintance in that line, the subjects wished for may be obtained.' In addition to Mr. Peale I would observe that the Mr. Bartram he mentions is the owner and keeper of a Botanical garden in the neighborhood of this city, who provides and furnishes with great skill and at moderate prices such trees and shrubs of this country as the curious call for, and packs them so carefully as to preserve their vegetable powers through any length of voyage, within ordinary limits, and that should you wish to enrich your garden as well as your cabinet with American subjects, you may be well served through the medium of Mr. Peale as the single correspondent who can conveniently transact with Bartram whatever calls may be made on him. To relieve your Royal highness too from all doubt and embarrasment as to the expectations of Mr. Peale with respect to compensation, I will observe that he is a private citizen having no other fortune than his cabinet, and deriving the support of that as well as of his family from the profits made by shewing it to the curious, that by increasing it's subjects he increases the desire of seeing it, and consequently his profits arising therefrom; and hence will consider the subjects recieved in exchange *delivered here clear of expence* as full compensation for those he will deliver here *properly packed* to the minister of Spain or any other agent you shall appoint.[8] This throws on your R.H. the expences of transportation both of the subjects recieved and given in exchange, but he observes that neither his profits nor circumstances enable him to meet any pecuniary expences. You will be pleased therefore to decide for yourself whether the condition is more onerous than the object merits. Should the channel which I have opened for the fulfilment of your wishes meet your approbation, the person entrusted with the keeping of your cabinet may immediately commence his correspondence with Mr. Peale by sending a list of his wants in every line, which to the extent of Mr. Peale's opportunities will be speedily complied with. I willingly offer to your R.H. the continuance of my attentions to the[9] fulfilment of your wishes wherever I can be useful to you. Perhaps when we see how far your wants go beyond the faculties of Mr. Peale, I may be able to find some other who may make up his deficiencies.[10] In the mean time permit me to pay my personal tribute to science and to your R.H's dispositions to promote it, by depositing in your cabinet a tooth of the great animal called in Europe the Mammoth, of which we find remains in the interior and uninhabited parts of this country. Their great distance from us renders them rare and difficult to be obtained. This curiosity is now on it's way to this place, and will be put into the hands of the minister of his Catholic majesty for you, to be forwarded as you direct.

It is now incumbent on me to make some apology for the delay of this answer. I live far hence in the interior country and therefore was late in recieving your letter. The circumstance of distance too lengthened the negociation with Mr. Peale. I then wished to accompany my answer with the tooth beforementioned of the enormous quadruped which once inhabited this country, and with an account of a recent discovery of the remains of a carnivorous animal 4 or 5 times as large as the lion, found in the Western parts of Virginia; this account will make part of a volume of our Philosophical transactions now in the press, but not being yet printed and returning myself shortly from hence to my ordinary residence in Virginia, I have determined to make a subsequent mission of that and no longer to withold the acknolegements I owe you, and the homage of those sentiments of respect and attachment with which I have the honor to be your R.H's mo. ob. & mo. hble servt.

Dft (DLC); entirely in TJ's hand, unsigned; heavily emended, only the most important changes being recorded below; at foot of first page: "His R. Highness the hereditary prince of Parma."

THE LETTER WITH WHICH YOU WERE PLEASED TO HONOR ME: Louis of Parma to TJ, 2 Nov. 1795. I VENTURED . . . TO PROPOSE: TJ to Charles Willson Peale, 5 June 1796. EXPRESSIONS IN HIS LETTER: see Peale to TJ, 22 June 1796. The BOTANICAL GARDEN was Bartram's Garden on the Schuylkill River near Philadelphia, operated by the brothers John and William Bartram and first established by their father, John Bartram, in 1730 (Greene, *American Science*, 48-50). For the ACCOUNT OF A RECENT DISCOVERY, see TJ's Memoir on the Megalonyx, [10 Feb. 1797].

[1] Word interlined.

[2] Word interlined in place of "pretended."

[3] Preceding two words interlined in place of "the animal and vegetable."

[4] Word interlined.

[5] Preceding eight words interlined in place of "has rendered himself so eminent of this city has been a private citizen."

[6] Preceding three words interlined in place of "making a collection of subjects."

[7] TJ here canceled "American."

[8] Word interlined in place of "order."

[9] TJ here canceled "execution of your commands."

[10] Following this sentence TJ canceled "as a commencement of proof that."

The Senate to John Adams

SIR   [23 May 1797]

The Senate of the United States request you to accept their acknowledgments for the comprehensive and interesting detail you have given, in your speech to both Houses of Congress, on the existing state of the Union.

While we regret the necessity of the present meeting of the Legislature, we wish to express our entire approbation of your conduct in convening it on this momentous occasion.

The superintendance of our national faith, honour and dignity, being, in a great measure, constitutionally deposited with the Executive, we observe, with singular satisfaction, the vigilance, firmness and promptitude exhibited by you, in this critical state of our public affairs, and from thence derive an evidence and pledge of the rectitude and integrity of your administration. And we are sensible, it is an object of primary importance, that each branch of the government should adopt a language and system of conduct, which shall be cool, just and dispassionate; but firm, explicit and decided.

We are equally desirous, with you, to preserve peace and friendship with all nations, and are happy to be informed, that neither the honour or interests of the United States forbid advances for securing those desirable objects, by amicable negociation, with the French republic. This method of adjusting national differences, is not only the most mild, but the most rational and humane, and with governments disposed to be just, can seldom fail of success, when fairly, candidly and sincerely used. If we have committed errors, and can be made sensible of them, we agree with you, in opinion, that we ought to correct them, and compensate the injuries, which may have been consequent thereon, and we trust the French republic will be actuated by the same just and benevolent principles of national policy.

We do therefore most sincerely approve of your determination to promote and accelerate an accommodation of our existing differences with that republic by negociation, on terms compatible with the rights, duties, interests and honour of our nation. And you may rest assured of our most cordial co-operation so far as it may become necessary in this pursuit.

Peace and harmony with all nations is our sincere wish; but such being the lot of humanity that nations will not always reciprocate peaceable dispositions: it is our firm belief that, effectual measures of defence, will tend to inspire that national self-respect and confidence at *home*, which is the unfailing source of respectability *abroad*, to check aggression and prevent war.

While we are endeavouring to adjust our differences with the French republic by amicable negociation, the progress of the war in Europe, the depredations on our commerce, the personal injuries to our citizens and the general complexion of affairs, prove to us your vigilant care, in recommending to our attention, effectual measures of defence.

Those which you recommend, whether they relate to external defence, by permitting our citizens to arm for the purpose of repelling aggressions on their commercial rights, and by providing sea convoys, or to internal defence, by increasing the establishments of artillery and cavalry, by forming a provisional army, by revising the militia laws and fortifying, more completely, our ports and harbours, will meet our consideration under the influence of the same just regard for the security, interest and honour of our country, which dictated your recommendation.

Practices so unnatural and iniquitous, as those you state, of our own citizens, converting their property and personal exertions into the means of annoying our trade, and injuring their fellow-citizens, deserve legal severity commensurate with their turpitude.

Although the Senate believe, that the prosperity and happiness of our country does not depend on general and extensive political connexions with European nations, yet we can never lose sight of the propriety as well as necessity of enabling the Executive, by sufficient and liberal supplies, to maintain, and even extend our foreign intercourse, as exigencies may require, reposing full confidence in the Executive, in whom the constitution has placed the powers of negotiation.

We learn with sincere concern, that attempts are in operation to alienate the affections of our fellow-citizens from their government. Attempts so wicked, wherever they exist, cannot fail to excite our utmost abhorrence. A government chosen by the people for their own safety and happiness, and calculated to secure both, cannot lose their affections, so long as its administration pursues the principles upon which it was erected. And your resolution to observe a conduct just and impartial to all nations, a sacred regard to our national engagements, and not to impair the rights of our government, contains principles which cannot fail to secure to your administration the support of the National

Legislature, to render abortive every attempt to excite dangerous jealousies among us, and to convince the world that our government and your administration of it, cannot be separated from the affectionate support of every good citizen. And the Senate cannot suffer the present occasion to pass, without thus publicly and solemnly expressing their attachment to the constitution and government of their country, and as they hold themselves responsible to their constituents, their consciences and their God, it is their determination by all their exertions to repel every attempt to alienate the affections of the people from the government, so highly injurious to the honour, safety and independence of the United States.

We are happy, since our sentiments on the subject are in perfect unison with yours, in this public manner to declare, that we believe the conduct of the government has been just and impartial to foreign nations, and that those internal regulations which have been established for the preservation of peace, are in their nature proper, and have been fairly executed.

And we are equally happy, in possessing an entire confidence in your abilities and exertions in your station, to maintain untarnished, the honour, preserve the peace, and support the independence of our country; to acquire and establish which, in connexion with your fellow-citizens, has been the virtuous effort of a principal part of your life.

To aid you in the honourable and arduous exertions, as it is our duty, so it shall be our faithful endeavour. And we flatter ourselves, Sir, that the proceedings of the present session of Congress will manifest to the world, that although the United States love peace, they will be independent. That they are sincere in their declarations to be just to the French, and all other nations, and expect the same in return.

If a sense of justice, a love of moderation and peace, shall influence their councils, which we sincerely hope, we shall have just grounds to expect, peace and amity between the United States and all nations will be preserved.

But if we are so unfortunate, as to experience injuries from any foreign power, and the ordinary methods by which differences are amicably adjusted between nations shall be rejected, the *determination* "not to surrender in any manner the rights of the government," being so inseparably connected with the dignity, interest and independence of our country, shall, by us, be steadily and inviolably supported.

THOMAS JEFFERSON { Vice-President of the
United States and
President of the Senate.

FC (smooth journal in DNA: RG 46, Senate Records, 5th Cong., 1st sess.); under this date; in a clerk's hand. Printed in JS, II, 363-5.

Although a committee dominated by Federalists composed this communication, it was TJ's responsibility as president of the Senate to read the address to John Adams. Immediately after Adams delivered his message to Congress on 16 May, the Senate named three Federalists—Uriah Tracy of Connecticut, John Laurance of New York, and Samuel Livermore of New Hampshire—to prepare an answer, a draft of which was presented two days later. The committee report included only a brief consideration of negotiations with France, noting that the door "ought still to remain unclosed," and emphasized instead support for the specific defense measures advocated by Adams. It contrasted the impartial foreign policy of the United States with the injuries inflicted on the country by France, concluding that if "they will not hear, nor even receive our Ministers and neither listen to just terms of accommodation, nor offer us any but unconditional submission," appropriate action needed to be taken to maintain the rights of the United States (committee report of [18 May 1797] in DNA: RG 46, Senate Records, 5th Cong., 1st sess., in Tracy's hand and endorsed as "1st Draft" of report on president's message). TJ characterized the report as "perfectly an echo and full as high toned" as the president's speech (TJ to Madison, 18 May 1797).

The following day, however, the Senate recommitted the report and added Henry Tazewell and John Henry to the committee. The subsequent report of 20 May differed substantially from the first one. While there is no evidence that TJ influenced the composition of the revised report, how to respond to the president's address may have been discussed at the hotel where TJ and Henry resided. TJ credited Henry with objecting to the 18 May report and obtaining its recommittal, which led to "considerable alterations." TJ also had a close relationship with Tazewell and was known to communicate with him on Senate committee business (TJ to Madison, 1 June 1797; TJ to Tazewell, 27 Jan. 1798). The changes from the 16 May report included an expanded emphasis on AMICABLE NEGOTIATION WITH THE FRENCH REPUBLIC, a promise to consider the MEASURES OF DEFENCE advocated by Adams but without an enthusiastic endorsement of them, and an elimination of criticisms directed expressly at the French, including the insinuation that they were attempting to alienate the American people from their government, stressing instead that the government would retain the AFFECTIONS of the people as long as it was administered according the PRINCIPLES UPON WHICH IT WAS ERECTED. Senate Republicans also attempted to delete the paragraph that declared that the administration had been JUST AND IMPARTIAL TO FOREIGN NATIONS and had FAIRLY EXECUTED regulations established for the preservation of peace. On 23 May the Senate decided, by an 11 to 15 vote, to retain the paragraph, adopted the report, and made arrangements to present it to the president (committee report of 20 May 1797 in DNA: RG 46, Senate Records, 5th Cong., 1st sess., in a clerk's hand; Tazewell to Madison, 4 June, 1797 in Madison, *Papers*, XVII, 15; JS, II, 362-3).

On 24 May, TJ and the Senate went to the president's residence and, in the manner established during Washington's administration, TJ verbally delivered the Senate's address. While as vice president Adams had routinely left the seat of government before Congress adjourned, only once did he fail to arrive at the opening of a session in time to deliver the Senate's address. In contrast, this is the only instance in which TJ performed this function. Subsequently he arrived after the response had been given, allowing the president of the Senate pro tempore to carry out the duty (JS, I, 22-3, 104-5, 221, 331-2, 457, II, 9, 127, 197-8, 300-302, 365, 410-11, 562, III, 7-8, 109; TJ to Mary Jefferson Eppes, 1 Jan. 1799).

John Adams to the Senate

It would be an affectation in me, to dissemble, the pleasure I feel, on receiving this Kind Address.

My long experience of the Wisdom, Fortitude, and Patriotism of the Senate of the United States, enhances in my estimation, the Value of those obliging expressions of your approbation of my conduct, which are a generous reward for the past, and an affecting encouragement to constancy and perseverance, in future.

Our sentiments appear to be so entirely in Unison, that I cannot but believe them to be, the rational result of the understandings, and the natural feelings of the hearts, of Americans in general, on contemplating the present State of the nation. While such Principles and affections prevail, they will form an indissoluble bond of Union, and a sure pledge, that our Country has no essential Injury to apprehend from any portentous appearances abroad. In a humble reliance on divine providence, we may rest assured that while we reiterate with Sincerity, our endeavors to accomodate all our differences with France, the Independence of our Country cannot be diminished, its dignity degraded, or its glory tarnished, by any nation or combination of nations whether Friends or Enemies.   JOHN ADAMS.

RC (DNA: RG 46, Senate Records, 5th Cong. 1st sess.); in a clerk's hand, signed by Adams; endorsed: "Legis: 1st. Sess: 5th. Cong: Reply of the President of the United States to the Address of the Senate in answer to the Speech at the opening of the session. May 24th. 1797." Received by the Senate on 24 May 1797 and printed in its journal under that date (JS, II, 365).

To Angelica Schuyler Church

Dear Madam   Philadelphia May 24. 1797.

I learn through the newspapers your arrival at New York and hasten to welcome you to the bosom of your friends and native country. I feel[1] one anxiety the less for the fate of the rotten bark from which you have escaped, and sincerely congratulate you on that escape. I wish I could have welcomed you to a state of perfect calm: but[2] you will find that the agitations of Europe have reached even us, and that here, as there,[3] they are permitted to disturb social life: that we have not yet learnt to give[4] every thing to it's proper place, discord to our[5] senates, love and friendship to society. Your affections,[6] I am persuaded, will spread themselves over the whole family of the good, without enquiring by what hard names they are politically called.[7] You will preserve, from temper and[8] inclination, the happy privilege of the ladies, to leave to the rougher sex, and to the newspapers, their party squabbles and reproaches. A thorough disgust at these had withdrawn me from public life under an absolute determination to avoid whatever could disturb the tranquility of my mind. I have been recalled however by the only voice which I had not resolution to disregard.[9] Whether their will or my own will first carry me back[10] is not yet very certain.[11] A mutual consent is[12] perhaps the most probable.

Tho' you have taken so great a step, there is still a wide space between us. I shall entertain the hope that we may meet at this place, as on a middle ground. Perhaps you may find it not unpleasant in winter to get this much nearer the sun. But whether we meet or not, I shall for ever claim an esteem which continues to be very precious to me, and hope to be, at times, indulged with the mutual expression of it. What is become of our friends Cosway and de Corny? From the latter I have never heard. I had a letter from Madame Cosway about a year ago.[13] I must join others with me in my enquiries after[14] Catharine. Her friends at Monticello are well, and will be impatient to hear of her and from her. She must still permit an old man to love her. It will not stand in the way of any younger passion.[15] Make my respects and congratulations acceptable if you please to Mr. Church, and recieve yourself the homage as constant as it is sincere of Your's affectionately   TH: JEFFERSON

RC (ViU). Dft (DLC); with one significant variation (see note 10) and numerous emendations, the most important of which are noted below.

The Church family's ARRIVAL AT NEW YORK in the *Fair American* on 20 May 1797 was announced in the *Philadelphia Gazette*, 23 May 1797.

LETTER FROM MADAME COSWAY: Maria Cosway to TJ, 4 Dec. 1795.

[1] Word interlined in Dft in place of "shall have."

[2] Sentence to this point interlined in Dft.

[3] In Dft TJ first wrote "you will find however that we also have our agitations, and that here, as in the country you left" before altering the preceding passage to read as above.

[4] Word interlined in Dft in place of "confine."

[5] Word interlined in Dft in place of "the."

[6] Word interlined in Dft in place of "good will."

[7] In Dft TJ first wrote "by what names they are politically distinguished" before altering the passage to read as above.

[8] Preceding two words interlined in Dft.

[9] Word interlined in Dft in place of "withstand."

[10] In Dft TJ here wrote "to the calm from which I have been extracted."

[11] In Dft TJ here canceled "I shall flatter my self with the la[tter.] It is not improbable that both may."

[12] In Dft TJ first concluded the sentence with "not improbable" before altering it to read as above.

[13] In Dft TJ here canceled "Nor do I forget my young friend Catherine tho' she has probably forgotten her old one."

[14] In Dft TJ here canceled "Miss."

[15] Preceding sentence interlined in Dft.

From Hugh Williamson

DEAR SIR   Trenton 24th May 1797

This forenoon I was inform'd by a Letter from N York that Mr.
Apthorp is dead and to be buried tomorrow. The family extremely so-
licitous that I should come on without delay.

I shall from New York write a Letter to Mr. Caffery who wrote me
concerning the big Bones and after thanking him for his attention to my
former Request shall refer him to such Letter as he may receive from
some Officer of the Amer: Phil: Soc: By his Letter that is in the Hands
of Dr. Wister you will observe that he promises Attention to any Requests I or any other Gentleman may make touching that Subject. In
fact I had informed Mr. Jackson his Brother in Law, that it was for the
Amer: Philos: Society that I wished to have as much information as
possible on that Subject. A very trusty Man who lives at Nashville a few
Miles from the Bones is now in Philada. and proposes setting out next
Sunday. Mr. Wm. Blount knows him well and will hand him any Letters from any Officer of the Society. I am Dr Sir with the utmost Respect Yrs   HU WILLIAMSON

P:S I presume the Society will write in what manner they wish the
Bones to be put up and what Quantity sent.

RC (PPAmP: Manuscript Communications, Natural History); at foot of text:
"Honble Thos Jefferson"; endorsed by TJ
as received 25 May 1797; also endorsed by
an official of the American Philosophical
Society.

John CAFFERY of Tennessee had written
Williamson to report that his excavations for
salt near the Cumberland River had uncov-

ered the BONES of mammoths. At a special
meeting on 26 May 1797, the American
Philosophical Society accepted Caffery's
offer to send specimens, provided the expenses to the society did not exceed $100.
Caffery had contacted Williamson at the
suggestion of Andrew JACKSON (Jackson,
Papers, I, 132-3; APS, Proceedings, XXII, pt.
3 [1884], 258).

To Elbridge Gerry

DEAR SIR   Philadelphia May 25. 97

I this moment recieve your [favor] of the 22d. Nine days before that,
to wit, May 13. I had [written to you my last] letter acknoleging the
[receipt of yours] of May [4.] [. . .]¹ that that of Apr. 4. with the [one
for] Monroe [. . .]² hand. My letter was directed to yourself 'to the care
of Mr. Osgood New York.' from which I hoped it would be stopped
there as I did not superscribe the place of your residence. I [hope] you
will have got it ere now; and I shall be [. . .] [whether] you have, lest it

get into hands who [may make improper] use of it, and by pretended translations and [re-translations] make it say what they please. Should you not recieve it, I will send a duplicate. What stay do you make in New York? When 12. hours will bring you here, will nothing tempt you to visit us? Adieu Your's affectionately   Th: Jefferson

P.S. The letter to Monroe shall be taken care of and delivered the moment he arrives.

PrC (DLC); badly faded; at foot of text: "Elbridge Gerry esq."

[1] Estimated five words illegible.
[2] Estimated four words illegible.

To Mary Jefferson

My dear Maria   Philadelphia, *May 25th*, 1797.

I wrote to your sister the last week, since which I have been very slowly getting the better of my rheumatism, though very slowly indeed; being only able to walk a little stronger. I see by the newspapers that Mr. and Mrs. Church and their family are arrived at New York. I have not heard from them, and therefore am unable to say anything about your friend Kitty, or whether she be still Miss Kitty. The condition of England is so unsafe that every prudent person who can quit it, is right in doing so. James is returned to this place, and is not given up to drink as I had before been informed. He tells me his next trip will be to Spain. I am afraid his journeys will end in the moon. I have endeavored to persuade him to stay where he is and lay up money. We are not able yet to judge when Congress will rise. Opinions differ from two to six weeks. A few days will probably enable us to judge. I am anxious to hear that Mr. Randolph and the children have got home in good health; I wish also to hear that your sister and yourself continue in health; it is a circumstance on which the happiness of my life depends. I feel the desire of never separating from you grow daily stronger, for nothing can compensate with me the want of your society. My warmest affections to you both. Adieu, and continue to love me as I do you. Yours affectionately,
Th: Jefferson

MS not found; reprinted from Randall, *Life*, ii, 357.

From William Linn

SIR   New-York, May 25th. 1797.

I beg you to excuse the liberty I take in enclosing to you a list which has appeared in the newspapers of the names and numbers of the Indian tribes in North America. A circular address which accompanies it will inform you of the occasion of giving you this trouble. I have nothing to plead for interrupting your attention a moment to the affairs of the nation at this alarming and eventful period,[1] but that from your researches into this and other subjects interesting to a philosophic mind, you possess the best information.

Besides the names mentioned in the Address, and which are not found in your list, there are, in the treaty concluded at Greenville, Aug. 3d. 1795, the names of *Eelriver* and *Weeás*. I find that some to give the whole number of inhabitants, multiply the number of the warriors by six. This proportion is, perhaps, too great. You incline to fix the proportion to be as 3 to 10, and which, for any thing I have yet seen, is nearer the truth.

You will easily perceive that I have not yet read or thought much on this subject. Whatever communications your leisure will permit you make, or whatever directions you will please to give as to the sources of information, will be gratefully acknowledged by Your Obedient And humble servant   WM LINN

RC (DLC); at foot of text: "The enclosed papers on the other side"; endorsed by TJ as received 27 May 1797 and so recorded in SJL. Enclosures not identified, but see below.

The CIRCULAR ADDRESS was likely the printed address of the newly established New York Missionary Society, "To all them that love our Lord Jesus Christ in sincerity." Linn was a director of the society, which later adopted for use by its missionaries a printed form TJ created for recording American Indian vocabularies (*The Address and Constitution of the New-York Missionary Society* [New York, 1796], 3-10, 19; see

note to TJ to Linn, 5 Feb. 1798). YOUR LIST: TJ's listing of Native American tribes under Query XI of the *Notes on the State of Virginia* (*Notes*, ed. Peden, 103-7). Of the tribes subscribing to the GREENVILLE treaty, both the Weas and the people from the Eel River (in present-day Indiana) were components of the larger group often called the Miamis (ASP, *Indian Affairs*, I, 562, 582; William C. Sturtevant, gen. ed., *Handbook of North American Indians*, 11 vols. [Washington, 1978-98], xv, 681, 682, 689).

[1] Preceding six words interlined.

To William Wardlaw

DEAR SIR   Philadelphia May 25. 97.

[I have] your receipts for the [monies] [. . .]¹ cre[dited] [. . .] to bring with me a memorandum of the [. . .]² destined for Dr. Jackson, and he had recieved no letter [. . .]. But he conjectured the sum you wished paid to be 77.14.D. Should that added to 7.67 D. to Bache vary from what I recieved, it can enter into account between us, as I have not with me the book in which I noted what I recieved. We have nothing important the last week from Europe. Prices are here as when I wrote to Colo. Bell. The Senate has answered the President by an echo of his speech. The House of Representatives have not yet answered. The [. . .] part of the house is so nearly on a balance with that which has just awoke to our honour, dignity, independance, freedom of commerce &c. [. . .] accompanying negociation with a [threat] [. . .]³ [But] it is difficult to say whether the answer will breathe peace [. . .], or look towards war. If the former, the [session will be short, as there will be] nothing to do. If the latter it may be long, unless they find their measures cut short by the hazard of [. . .] [or] [. . .] the present taxes, less than which will not carry on a war; and not a dollar can be borrowed either here or in Europe. On this circumstance we [rest our] ultimate hope of preserving peace. The danger of having bills of exchange paid off in London in depreciated paper [. . .]⁴ bills. The merchants prefer remitting [. . .]⁵ they will get a premium. The banks are sensible that if our specie be expended they [will] be in great danger of being unable to pay their [own] paper [in specie when] called on, and that a small war will break them. Hence great alarm.—Take care nothing from me gets into the newspapers. I am Dear Sir [Your friend & servt]   TH: JEFFERSON

PrC (DLC); badly faded; at foot of text: "Dr. Wardlaw."

William Wardlaw, a physician who lived in Charlottesville, helped TJ give smallpox vaccinations at Monticello in 1801. He moved to Richmond by 1810 and established himself as a druggist (MB, II, 930n; Wardlaw to TJ, 1 Nov. 1810; *The Richmond Directory, Register and Almanac, for the Year 1819* [Richmond, 1819], 73).

TJ had received $85.17 from Wardlaw on 1 May 1797 for payments to the Philadelphia apothecary and physician Dr. David JACKSON and to Benjamin Franklin BACHE (MB, II, 935, 959, 961).

WHEN I WROTE TO COLO. BELL: TJ to Thomas Bell, 18 May 1797. THE SENATE HAS ANSWERED THE PRESIDENT: see the Senate to John Adams, 23 May.

Letters from Wardlaw to TJ of 16 Oct., 28 Dec. 1794, and 17 Jan. 1795, recorded in SJL as received on their respective dates, the first from Charlottesville, have not been found.

¹ Estimated three words illegible.
² Estimated three words illegible.
³ Estimated four words illegible.
⁴ Estimated five words illegible.
⁵ Estimated three words illegible.

To Thomas Mann Randolph

Tʜ:J. ᴛᴏ TMR.   Philadelphia May. 26. 97.

Nothing new has occurred this week, except that prices get duller. Embargo is also now beginning to be talked of, and I begin to fear I shall not get the price for my tobacco which I have held it at. Ten dollars may perhaps be yet had, tho' I have been afraid to ask the fact lest it should be thought a symptom of my falling. No judging yet when Congress will rise as the Representatives have not yet agreed on their answer. Adieu affectionately   Tʜ:J.

RC (DLC); recorded in SJL under 25 May 1797; endorsed by Randolph as received 1 June 1797.

From Elbridge Gerry

Dᴇᴀʀ Sɪʀ   New York 28th May 1797

On my return last evening from Mrs. Gerrys friends, on the Jersey side of North River, I received your letter of the 25th, and am happy to inform you, that you have received all my letters: it was mine to Mr. Monroe, which was dated the 4th of april. I was mortified to find, that before Mr. Osgood was informed of my intention to be here, he received your letter of the 13th of may and sent it forward, directed to me at Cambridge: on my arrival there, I will write to you respecting it.

I have every temptation and the strongest inclination, to pay my respects to the President and yourself, and to call on my other friends in Philadelphia; but Mrs. Gerry and myself have left six small children, under the care of the eldest, who is remarkably prudent for 10 years of age, and five domesticks; to pay a visit of a few days to her aged and infirm parents: and being just informed our second child has been unwell, we are anxious to return without delay. Be so obliging as to make particular enquiry for the letter to Mr. Monroe in Phila. and Virginia: it being directed "to your care" will authorize the measure. I will make a stir about it at Boston, for I will not be silent under the corruption of the post office. I have the honor to remain Dear Sir with the most perfect esteem & respect yours sincerely   E. Gᴇʀʀʏ

RC (DLC); at foot of text: "His Excellency Mr. Jefferson"; endorsed by TJ as received 30 May 1797 and so recorded in SJL. FC (MHi: Russell W. Knight Collection); entirely in Gerry's hand.

From Hugh Williamson

DEAR SIR   New York 28th May 1797

I had expected to inclose a Letter by the friday Mail for Mr. Caffery Nashville, Tennessee for I arrived here on Thursday PM but to write was impracticable. In a family of five young Ladies who had by a very short Illness lost a Parent, they too of much sensibility and delicate Constitutions, I found other attentions than writing Letters. I gave Mr. Cafferrys Letter to Dr. Wistar and wrote the Name on a slip of Paper which is lost, I don't remember his Christian Name. I intended to advise Mr. Caffery in sinking for Bones, when he should find one to dig all round carefully so as to be sure of reaching all the Bones of the same Animal, for they must lye nearly in their natural Positions unless Beasts of prey have pulled them away. And as many of the Bones of each Animal may have decayed I wished him to try to collect all that remained or 3 or 4 Animals but the Society as I presume have said all that was proper on that Head. If Williams a Merchant in Nashville is gone Mr. Blount will find some other conveyance for the inclosed. Be so good as inclose it with a proper Directions and Seal. Excuse this Trouble and be assured that I am with the utmost Respect Dr sir Your most obedt servt

                                                    HU WILLIAMSON

RC (PPAmP: Manuscript Communications, Natural History); addressed: "Honble Thomas Jefferson Vice Presdt of U:S: Philadelphia"; stamped and post-marked; endorsed by TJ as received 31 May 1797; also endorsed by an official of the American Philosophical Society. Enclosure not found.

From Sebastian Bauman

SIR   New York May 29th. 97

I have taken the liberty to inclose to you a pamphlet containing a statement of the cause of the resignation of all the Officers of the Regiment of Artillery of the City and County of New York, which I had the honor to command and which I hope will do away any unfavourable impressions our proceedings may have made in the mind of the public. I am Sir with great respect Your Obedt and very Humbe Servt

                                                    S. BAUMAN

RC (DLC); at foot of text: "Thomas Jefferson Esqr. Vice Presidt. of the United States"; endorsed by TJ as received 30 May 1797 and so recorded in SJL. Enclosure: see below.

Sebastian Bauman (d. 1803) had been the postmaster of New York City since 1789. As an artillery officer during the American Revolution he had risen in rank from captain of a New York company to major in the Continental artillery (Heitman, *Register*, 92; Robert J. Stets, comp., *Postmasters and Postoffices of the United States, 1782-1811* [Lake Oswego, Ore., 1994], 184; Bauman to TJ, 30 Apr. 1802).

The PAMPHLET, published in New York in 1797 and entitled *A Statement, Explanatory of the Resignation of the Officers of the Regiment of Artillery, of the City and County* *of New-York*, documented the officers' recent unanimous resignation to protest restrictions on the promotion of artillery officers that caused Bauman, the regiment's lieutenant colonel and commandant, to be passed over for promotion within the militia to the rank of brigadier. See Evans, No. 32568.

To Thomas Pinckney

DEAR SIR   Philadelphia May 29. 1797.

I recieved from you, before you left England, a letter inclosing one from the Prince of Parma. As I learnt soon after that you were shortly to return to America, I concluded to join my acknolegements of it with my congratulations on your arrival; and both have been delayed by a blameable spirit of procrastination for ever suggesting to our indolence that we need not[1] do to-day what may be done tomorrow. Accept them now in the sincerity of my heart. It is but lately I have answered the Prince's letter. It required some time to establish arrangements which might effect his purpose; and I wished also to forward a particular article or two of curiosity.

You have found on your return a higher style of political difference than you had left here. I fear this is inseparable from the different constitutions of the human mind, and that degree of freedom which permits unrestrained expression. Political dissension[2] is doubtless a less evil than the lethargy of despotism:[3] but still it is a great evil, and it would be as worthy the efforts of the patriot as of the philosopher, to exclude it's influence if possible, from social life. The good are rare enough at best. There is no reason to subdivide them[4] by artificial lines. But whether we shall ever be able so far to perfect the principles of society as that political opinions shall, in it's intercourse, be as inoffensive as those of philosophy, mechanics or any others, may well be doubted.[5] Foreign influence is the present and just object of public hue and cry, and, as often happens, the most guilty are foremost and loudest in the cry.[6] If those who are truly independant can so trim our vessel as to beat thro' the waves now agitating us,[7] they will merit a glory the greater as it seems less possible. When I contemplate the spirit which is driving us on here, and that beyond the water which will view us but as a mouthful the more, I have little hope of peace. I anticipate the burning of our seaports, havoc of our frontiers, houshold insurgency, with a long train of etceteras which it is enough for a man to have met once in his life.[8] The exchange which is to give us new neighbors in Louisiana (probably the present French armies, when disbanded)[9] has opened us to combinations of enemies on that side where we are most vulnerable.[10] War is not the best engine for us to resort to. Nature has given us one in our *commerce* which, if properly managed, will be a better instrument for obliging[11] the interested nations of Europe to treat us with justice. If the commercial regulations[12] had been adopted which our legislature were at one time proposing, we should at this moment have been standing on such an eminence of safety and respect as ages can never recover. But having wandered from that,[13] our object should now be to get back[14] with as little loss as possible;[15] and when peace shall be restored to the world, endeavor so to form our *commercial* regulations, as that justice from other nations shall be their mechanical result.[16]

I am very happy to assure you that the conduct of Genl. Pinckney has met universal approbation. It was marked with that coolness, dignity and good sense[17] which we expected from him. I am told the French government had taken up an uphappy idea that Monroe was recalled for the candor of his conduct in what related to the British treaty, and that Genl. Pinckney was sent as having other dispositions towards them. I learn further that some of their well informed citizens here are setting them right as to Genl. Pinckney's disposition, so well known to have been just towards them; and I sincerely hope not only that he may be employed as envoy extraordinary to them, but that their minds will be better prepared to recieve him. I candidly acknolege however that I do not think the speech and addresses of Congress[18] as conciliatory as the preceding irritations on both sides would have rendered wise. I shall be happy to hear from you at all times, to make myself useful to you whenever opportunity offers,[19] and to give every proof of the sincerity of the sentiments of esteem & respect with which I am Dear Sir Your most obedient & most humble servt   TH: JEFFERSON

PrC (DLC); with one significant emendation (see note 19 below); at foot of first page, clipped: "T[homas Pinckney]." Dft (DLC); with numerous emendations, the most important of which are noted below.

Pinckney's LETTER to TJ of 16 Mch. 1796 enclosed ONE to TJ from Louis, PRINCE OF PARMA of 2 Nov. 1795. TJ ANSWERED THE PRINCE'S LETTER on 23 May 1797.

For the COMMERCIAL REGULATIONS that Madison introduced in the House of Representatives on 3 Jan. 1794, which were based upon recommendations from TJ's commercial report, see Editorial Note on Report on Commerce, 16 Dec. 1793, in 27: 532-5.

[1] Preceding ten words interlined in Dft in place of "which never lets us."
[2] Preceding two words written in margin of Dft in place of "it."
[3] Preceding eight words interlined in Dft in place of "a great tho lesser evil."
[4] In Dft TJ first wrote "to divide them

then" before altering the clause to read as above.

[5] Preceding eight words interlined in Dft in place of "in [. . .] the intercourse of society."

[6] In Dft TJ here canceled "of stop thief. If the" and then interlined the first four words of the following sentence.

[7] In Dft TJ first wrote "can steer us clear of the present war now [hovering?] over us" before altering the preceding passage to read as above.

[8] In Dft TJ here canceled the following sentence: "So many steps of [a]mbition and injury have taken place on both sides that unless one or the other will stop and propose a parley blows must come [. . .]."

[9] Words in parentheses interlined in Dft.

[10] In Dft TJ here added "and defenseless" and then canceled the following: "For a few days past we have been hoping that [tho?] our honor [was] lost with the first insult, the [wrecks?] of it are surely not worth all these evils."

[11] In Dft TJ wrote "is a sufficient instrument of coercion for coercing" before altering the preceding passage to read as above.

[12] In Dft TJ first wrote "from which the late administration witheld tho legislature

had been adopting" before altering the following passage to read as above.

[13] In Dft TJ first wrote and canceled "Respect is for the present at least out of question with us safety and loss ⟨were⟩ are now to be weighed and to decide if we can now [keep?] ourselves" before interlining the beginning of this sentence as above.

[14] In Dft TJ wrote the preceding two words in place of "with draw."

[15] In Dft TJ here canceled "from the mistaken path in which we have been ever drawing."

[16] In Dft TJ here canceled the following sentences: "The recovery of respect will be a longer operation. ⟨Respect⟩ Honor is a plant of such slow growth that [where] once it has been killed to the root new seeds must be sown and time allowed for their development. They will thrive too the worse as their bed is tainted."

[17] Remainder of sentence interlined in Dft.

[18] Preceding two words interlined in Dft.

[19] TJ here canceled the first six words of the following passage, canceled here in Dft: "to assure you that the intrigues of which we have both been the subject have been to me as I trust they have to you as if they had never happened."

To Antonia Reynon Carmichael

MADAM   Philadelphia May 30. 1797.

I am to return you my thanks for the copy of the memoire you have been so good as to send me. It contains just and interesting observations on the importance of a navigation through the isthmus of Darien. The late Mr. Carmichael had hoped he could procure for us the copy of a survey of that isthmus said to exist in the archives of the Spanish government. But I imagine it is too carefully kept. My curiosity being entirely directed to this object the engravings which relate merely to Hernan Cortez would not be within my views. I shall be happy in every opportunity of renewing to you assurances of the sentiments of esteem & respect with which I have the honor to be Madam Your most obedt. & most humble servt   TH: JEFFERSON

PrC (DLC); at foot of text: "Carmichael."

The MEMOIRE on the ISTHMUS OF DARIEN was enclosed in Carmichael's letter of 8 May

1797. In regard to the SURVEY that William Carmichael had hoped to obtain, see his letter to TJ of 24 July 1788.

To Horatio Gates

DEAR GENERAL   Philadelphia May 30. 1797.

I thank you for the pamphlet of Erskine inclosed in your favor of the 9th. inst. and still more for the evidence which your letter afforded me of the health of your mind and I hope of body also. Erskine has been reprinted here and has done good. It has refreshed the memory of those who had been willing to forget how the war between France and England has been produced; and who ape-ing St. James's called it a defensive war on the part of England. I wish any events could induce us to cease to copy such a model and to assume the dignity of being original. They had their paper system, stockjobbing, speculations, public debt, monied interest &c. and all this was contrived for us. They raised their cry against jacobinism and revolutionists, we against democratic societies and antifederals. Their alarmists sounded insurrection, ours marched an army to look for one, but they could not find it. I wish the parallel may stop here: and that we may avoid instead of imitating a general bankruptcy and disastrous war. Congress, or rather the representatives have been a fortnight debating between a more or less irritating answer to the President's speech. The latter was lost yesterday by 48 against 51. or 52. It is believed however that when they come to propose measures leading directly to war, they will lose some of their numbers. Those who have no wish but for the peace of their country, and it's independance of all foreign influence, have a hard struggle indeed, overwhelmed by a cry as loud and imposing as if it were true, of being under French influence, and this raised by a faction composed of English subjects residing among us, or such as are English in all their relations and sentiments. However, patience will bring all to rights. And we shall both live to see the mask taken from their faces, and our citizens sensible on which side true liberty and independance are sought. Should any circumstance draw me further from home I shall with great cordiality pay my respects to you at Rose hill: and am not without a hope of meeting you here sometime. Here, there & every where I am with great & sincere esteem & respect, Dear General, Your affectionate friend & servt   TH: JEFFERSON

RC (MH: Frederick M. Dearborn Collection); at foot of text: "Genl. Gates." PrC (DLC).

For the ANSWER of the House of Representatives TO THE PRESIDENT'S SPEECH and for the amendment which was LOST YESTERDAY by a 46 to 52 vote, see note to TJ to Madison, 18 May 1797.

To John Oliver

S<small>IR</small> Philadelphia May 30. 1797

Tho strongly impressed myself against the possibility of forming a self moving machine, yet I do not place among impossibilities the invention of a machine whose moving power may be constantly renewed by some of the natural agents every where present, as air, gravity &c. If your son has invented any thing effectual in this way he will need no other patronage than the importance and value of his own discovery. When his invention shall be perfectly matured, and it's performance so certain as to prove itself by it's action and leave nothing to hypothesis, I presume he will bring it forward here to avail himself of it's advantages. Should I be here, I shall certainly be one of the forwardest to do justice to his invention, and contribute my mite to the public reputation he will deserve. The law will sufficiently secure to him the emoluments arising from it. Sincerely wishing his discoveries may fulfill expectation I am Sir Your most obedt. servt T<small>H</small>: J<small>EFFERSON</small>

PrC (DLC); in ink at foot of text: "John Oliver Bordentown."

To John Gibson

D<small>EAR</small> S<small>IR</small> Philadelphia May 31. 1797.

In my Notes on the state of Virginia I have given a translation of the celebrated speech of Logan to Ld. Dunmore with a statement of facts necessary to make it better understood. A Mr. Luther Martin of Maryland has lately come forward, denies the facts and also the authenticity of the speech. As far as my memory serves me we received the speech as a translation of yours, and tho' I do not recollect that I have heard the facts from yourself, yet I think I understood that you stated them substantially in the same way. I have to ask the favor of you to give me what information you can on this subject, as well respecting the speech as the facts stated by me. I do not mean to enter the newspapers with Mr. Martin. But if any mistake has been committed to the prejudice of Colo. Cresap, it shall be set to rights in a new edition of the book now about to be printed. The book is too large to send you by post, but I imagine you may find a copy of it in Pittsburgh so as to see in what manner the facts are stated. I should express my regrets at the trouble I have proposed to give you, but that I am persuaded you will with willingness give your help to place this transaction on solid ground. It affords me at the same time the satisfaction of recalling myself to your recollection

and of renewing to you assurances of the esteem with which I am Dear
Sir Your most obedt & most humble servt   TH: JEFFERSON

PrC (DLC); at foot of text: "Genl. Gibson."

This is the first of a series of letters TJ exchanged with various correspondents in 1797-98 concerning THE CELEBRATED SPEECH OF LOGAN, long a staple of oratorical instruction and a focus of sentimental feeling toward Native Americans. As a result of that correspondence TJ amended a passage in his *Notes on the State of Virginia*, but that change did not resolve all questions surrounding the oration. "Nothing Jefferson ever wrote," William Peden has asserted, "has evoked more controversy than the passage and its revision on the murder of Logan's family" (*Notes*, ed. Peden, 298). For assessments of TJ's role in this issue from very different perspectives, see Malone, *Jefferson*, III, 346-56, and Clarkson and Jett, *Luther Martin*, 171-88.

Otherwise called Soyechtowa or Tocaniadorogon, the man commonly known as Logan (d. 1780) had in recognition of his father's diplomatic relations with Pennsylvania adopted the name of the colony's longtime public official, James Logan. One of the Iroquoian Indians of the greater Ohio Valley who were called the Mingos, Logan in 1774 sent a short address to the governor of Virginia, the Earl of DUNMORE, at the conclusion of Dunmore's War, a brief but violent conflict between frontier militia and the Shawnees and their allies. Early the following year newspapers published Logan's declaration, which lamented the murder of members of his family at Yellow Creek by white frontiersmen on the eve of Dunmore's War, a crime that transformed his previously cordial relations with whites and compelled him to seek revenge. As TJ indicated in his letter to John Henry of 31 Dec. 1797, he learned of the speech in 1774 and wrote it down at that time. By including it in the *Notes on the State of Virginia* he gave it a wide circulation, and Logan's tragedy became a poetic theme during the early 1790s. The speech itself, along with TJ's accompanying STATEMENT OF FACTS, was reprinted from the *Notes* in various works (*Notes*, ed. Peden, 63; ANB, XIII, 836-7; Madison, *Papers*, I, 137-8n; Seeber, "Critical Views,"

130-1; Luther Martin to TJ, 24 June 1797).

TJ's query to Gibson was prompted by a letter of LUTHER MARTIN, the attorney general of Maryland, which was printed in William Cobbett's fiercely anti-Jeffersonian newspaper, *Porcupine's Gazette*, on 3 Apr. 1797, and a week later appeared in the Baltimore *Federal Gazette*, where TJ saw it (TJ to Henry, 31 Dec. 1797). Martin addressed the letter to James Fennell, a performer who had included Logan's speech in an oratorical program in Philadelphia. Logan had named COLO. CRESAP as the person responsible for the entrapment and slaughter of his relatives, and in the *Notes* TJ referred to the colonel—a title generally applied to Thomas Cresap of Old Town, Maryland, a prominent figure in the early western settlement of Virginia and Maryland—as "infamous for the many murders he had committed" against Indians (*Notes*, ed. Peden, 275). Martin's wife, recently deceased, was a daughter of Thomas Cresap's son, Captain Michael Cresap. Both Cresaps were dead by 1797, and Martin felt obliged to clear the family's name of the blot left by Logan and TJ. In his letter to Fennell, Martin stated that no Cresap played any part in the killing of members of Logan's family.

Moreover, Martin asserted "that no such specimen of *Indian* oratory was ever exhibited." Indeed, Logan did not speak directly to Dunmore, his address having been conveyed and translated by Gibson, who evidently was Logan's brother-in-law—Gibson's consort, Logan's sister, having been one of the victims at Yellow Creek, and their infant child almost killed (White, *Middle Ground*, 358; Reuben Gold Thwaites and Louise Phelps Kellogg, eds., *Documentary History of Dunmore's War: 1774* [Madison, Wis., 1905], 10-11). Martin suggested that whatever "fair flower of *aboriginal* eloquence" Logan's original oration may have presented, TJ gave it "the *embellishments* of *cultivation*." Disparaging the efforts of "philosophers," all of whom "are pretty much the same" in their efforts to prove their own hypotheses, Martin depicted TJ as so intent on the refutation of the Comte de Buffon's slanders against the Americas—"weighing the rats and the mice of the two worlds to prove that those of the *new* are not exceeded by those of the *old*"—that he would go to any lengths to aggrandize Logan's message to Dunmore as an example of native rhetoric. Martin called Logan's "story and speech" as presented by TJ a "*fiction*" (*Porcupine's Gazette*, 3 Apr. 1797; *Federal Gazette & Baltimore Daily Advertiser*, 10 Apr. 1797).

Martin subsequently penned a sequence of eight letters, the first dated 24 June 1797, all of which he nominally addressed to TJ but sent to newspapers for publication. TJ, averring that he would have replied to a direct query, ascribed a partisan motive to Martin's published attacks and refused to answer them (see TJ to Henry, 31 Dec. 1797; TJ to Samuel Brown, 25 Mch. 1798). The information he solicited from various sources did lead him to some revision of facts, although surely not to Martin's satisfaction. In 1800 TJ published *An Appendix to the Notes on Virginia Relative to the Murder of Logan's Family*, which printed statements that he had compiled on the affair (see *Notes*, ed. Peden, 226-58; Sowerby, No. 3225). The accounts from his informants indeed absolved "Colonel"—that is, Thomas—Cresap of any involvement in the murder of Logan's kin, much of the blame for which appeared to lie with one Daniel Greathouse. Nor was Captain Michael Cresap guilty of that outrage, although he was the leader of a group that had, in the belief that war had already broken out, killed other Native Americans not long before the Yellow Creek incident and had considered attacking the Mingos there (White, *Middle Ground*, 357). Although the evidence in the *Appendix* indicated that Michael Cresap was not involved in the actual killings at Yellow Creek, TJ gave fresh currency to a longstanding imputation that he bore responsibility for the events that precipitated the war. TJ proposed that in any NEW EDITION of the *Notes* he would revise the language introducing Logan's speech by deleting the passage about the "infamous" Colonel Cresap and substituting three sentences, which named Michael Cresap and Greathouse as leaders of parties involved in ambush killings of Indians but did not specifically ascribe the tragic killing of Logan's relatives to either man (see

Notes, ed. Peden, 62, 274-5, where the revised language appears in the text and the original passage, the one known to readers prior to 1800, is reported in a note). The *Appendix* left the wording of Logan's address, with its condemnation of "Colonel" Cresap, intact as it had appeared in the *Notes*. Readers, even with TJ's revised comments introducing the oration, would be likely to conclude that Michael Cresap, called by one military rank or another, led the killers at Yellow Creek. Concerning the charge, made long after TJ's death, that he suppressed evidence favorable to Cresap, see Malone, *Jefferson*, III 353-5; *Notes*, ed. Peden, 298-300; and Anthony F. C. Wallace, *Jefferson and the Indians: The Tragic Fate of the First Americans* (Cambridge, Mass., 1999), 6-11.

There were two printings of the *Appendix*, both dated 1800, the second of which included a declaration by John Sappington that had come to hand after the initial printing (see Evans, Nos. 37770, 37701). A revised edition of the *Notes on Virginia* did not appear during TJ's life, although as early as 1800 a printing of the work included the appendix on the Logan affair (see Evans, No. 37702).

As for the authenticity of Logan's speech itself, TJ believed any assertion that it was not of Logan's own composition must pass the test of rebutting not only Gibson's statements but "the general mass of evidence" (TJ to Benjamin Smith Barton, 21 Dec. 1806). While some critics, hoping to exonerate Cresap, still attempted to cast doubt on it, Logan's oration continued to be widely known in nineteenth-century America and, introduced by TJ's revised explanatory comments, formed a lesson in the famous McGuffey readers used by generations of schoolchildren (Seeber, "Critical Views," 130-46; Ray H. Sandefur, "Logan's Oration—How Authentic?," *Quarterly Journal of Speech*, XLVI [1960], 289-96; James H. O'Donnell, III, "Logan's Oration: A Case Study in Ethnographic Authentication," same, LXV [1979], 150-6; William H. McGuffey, *McGuffey's New Fifth Eclectic Reader: Selected and Original Exercises for Schools*, electrotype ed. [Cincinnati, 1866], 324-5).

To James Madison

Philadelphia June 1. [1797]

I wrote you on the 18th. of May. The address of the Senate was soon after that. The first draught was responsive to the speech and higher toned. Mr. Henry arrived the day it was reported. The addressers had not as yet their strength around them. They listened therefore to his objections, recommitted the paper added him and Tazewell to the committee, and it was reported with considerable alterations. But one great attack was made on it, which was to strike out the clause approving every thing heretofore done by the Executive. The clause was retained by a majority of four. They recieved a new accession of members, held a Caucus, took up all the points recommended in the speech, except the raising money, agreed the lists of every committee, and on Monday passed the resolutions and appointed the committees by an uniform vote of 17 to 11. (Mr. Henry was accidentally absent, Ross not then come.) Yesterday they took up the nomination of J. Q. Adams to Berlin which had been objected to as extending our diplomatic establishment. It was approved by 18 to 11. (Mr. Tatnall accidentally absent.) From these proceedings we are able to see that 18. on the one side and 10 on the other, with two wavering votes will decide every question. Schuyler is too ill to come this session, and Gunn is not yet come. Pinckney (the Genl.) John Marshall and Dana are nominated envoys extraordinary to France. Charles Lee consulted a member from Virginia to know whether Marshall would be agreeable. He named you as more likely to give satisfaction. The answer was 'nobody of Mr. Mad's way of thinking will be appointed.'

The Representatives have not yet got through their address. An amendment of Mr. Nicholas's which you will have seen in the papers was lost by a division of 46. to 52. A clause by Mr. Dayton expressing a wish that France might be put on an equal footing with other nations was inserted by 52. against 47.[1] This vote is most worthy of notice, because the moderation and justice of the proposition being unquestionable, it shews that there are 47. decided to go all lengths, to prevent accomodation. No other members are expected. The absent are two from Massachusets (not elected) one[2] from Tennessee (not elected) Benson from S.C. who never attends[3] and Burgess of N. Carolina. They have received a new orator from the district of Mr. Ames. He is the son of the Secretary of the Senate. They have an accession from S.C. also, that state being exactly divided in the H. of Repr. I learn the following facts which give me great concern. When the British treaty arrived at Charleston, a meeting as you know was called, a committee of 15. appointed of whom Genl. Pinckney was one. He did not attend. They waited for him, sent for him: he treated the mission with great hauteur, and disapproved of their meddling. In the course of subsequent altercations he declared that his brother T. Pinckney approved of every article of the treaty under the *existing circumstances*. And since that time the politics of Charleston have been assuming a different hue. Young Rutledge joining Smith and Harper is an ominous fact as to that whole interest.

Tobacco is at 9. Dollars here, flour very dull of sale. A great stagnation in Commerce generally. During the present uncertain state of things in England the merchants seem disposed to lie on their oars. It is impossible to conjecture the rising of Congress: as it will depend on the system they decide on, whether of preparation for war, or inaction.—In the vote of 46. to 52. Morgan, Machir, and Evans were of the majority, and Clay kept his seat, refusing to vote with either. In that of 47 to 52. Evans was the only one of our delegation who voted against putting France on an equal footing with other nations.—P.M. So far I had written in the morning. I now take up my pen to add that the address having been reported to the house, it was moved to disagree to so much of the amendment as went to the putting France on an equal footing with other nations; and Morgan and Machir turning tail (in consequence as is said of having been closeted last night by Charles Lee) the vote was 49. to 50. So the principle was saved by a single vote. They then moved to insert that compensation for spoliations shall be a sine qua non, and this will be decided tomorrow.

RC (DLC: Madison Papers, Rives Collection); partially dated; unsigned; with several emendations, the most important of which are noted below; addressed: "James Madison junr. near Orange Ct. House." PrC (DLC); with three alterations in ink (see note 1 below).

NEW ACCESSION OF MEMBERS: Elijah Paine of Vermont, Humphrey Marshall of Kentucky, and James Ross of Pennsylvania, all Federalists, took their Senate seats on 24, 26, and 29 May respectively (JS, II, 365-6). In a letter to Ralph Izard of 29 May, South Carolina representative William L. Smith reported on the Senate CAUCUS at which the Federalists AGREED to the LISTS OF EVERY COMMITTEE from which the minority Republicans were excluded to show that the Federalists had no confidence in them. When Theodore Sedgwick introduced RESOLUTIONS on 29 May to set up COMMITTEES to consider the proposals in the president's speech, the appointment of John Henry of Maryland, who had recently voted with the Republicans, was the only Federalist concession. The appointment may have been an attempt to influence Henry, whom Smith characterized as "a weak man" who was being corrupted by lodging at the Francis hotel with TJ and other Republicans (Ulrich B. Phillips, ed., "South Carolina Federalist Correspondence, 1789-1797," AHR, XIV [1909], 786-9; JS, II, 363, 366). ROSS NOT THEN COME: as noted above, Ross took his seat the day the committees were appointed and voted with the Federalists (JS, II, 366).

On 20 May President Adams submitted the NOMINATION of his son to serve as United States minister to Prussia. The Senate began debating the appointment on 23 May and a week later a resolution was introduced against the nomination, declaring it was "unnecessary to establish a permanent Minister at the Court of Prussia." On 31 May the Senate rejected the resolution and confirmed the nomination (JEP, I, 240-42).

For the nomination of the ENVOYS EXTRAORDINARY TO FRANCE, see Senate Resolution on Appointment of Charles C. Pinckney, [5 June 1797].

Isaac Parker and Stephen Bullock, both Federalists, were elected to the TWO seats FROM MASSACHUSETTS in the state elections in May 1797. Bullock took his seat on 9 June but the result of Parker's race was still unclear and he did not attend the session. Andrew Jackson, who was elected as the representative at large from Tennessee in October 1796, attended the last session of the Fourth Congress but not this one. Upon his election to the United States Senate in September, Jackson was succeeded in the

House by William C. C. Claiborne, who produced his credentials and took his seat on 23 Nov. (*Biog. Dir. Cong.*; JHR, III, 27; Philadelphia *Aurora*, 16 June 1797; Jackson, *Papers*, I, 98, 150). The NEW ORATOR FROM THE DISTRICT of Fisher Ames was Harrison Gray Otis, SON of Samuel A. Otis. South Carolina was EXACTLY DIVIDED IN THE HOUSE OF REPRESENTATIVES with John Rutledge, Jr., in most cases, joining Federalists William L. Smith and Robert Goodloe Harper, while Lemuel Benton, William Smith (of Spartan district) and Thomas Sumter voted with the Republicans (*Biog. Dir. Cong.*).

[1] Altered from "48" here, again in the following sentence, and in the final paragraph; altered in ink on PrC.
[2] Preceding word interlined in place of "two."
[3] Preceding three words interlined.

To Thomas Mann Randolph

TH:J. TO TMR.   Philadelphia. June 1. [1797]

Your's of May 24. is recieved, and I have directed the springs to be made according to your desire. Your other commissions shall also be executed with pleasure, and shall go with some things of mine in the course of this month. Your tobacco is not yet arrived. Mr. Johnston's express directions to ensure has induced us to do it: otherwise, considering the safety of the season I should have advised the contrary as being merely the throwing away 30. dollars, for Mr. Barnes concluded the insurance should be made on 1500.D. at 2. pr. cent. As yet I have no prospect of selling mine. Nine dollars can always be had: but I still rely on 10. or 11. by waiting. Lieper offers to take the tobacco and give me the price which shall be going in September, and as it would be unexampled that it should fall from this to September, I should do it were he not so difficult to settle a price with in this way.—The time of the rising of Congress cannot yet be foreseen. The conjectures are from a fortnight to six weeks according to the plan they shall adopt of inaction, or of preparation for war. On a motion yesterday for an amendment to the address of the Representatives expressing their desire that the French should be placed on as favorable a footing as other nations, it was carried by only 52. against 47.[1] Evans was of the 47.[2] You see from this the strength and spirit of a part of the house. They dare not avow they are for war, yet what else could a refusal of *equality* to France produce? Genl. Pinckney, John Marshal and Dana are appointed envoys extraordinary to France. John Quincy Adams Minister plenipotentiary to Berlin.—We have no important news from Europe. I begin to fear I shall not get home to harvest. I must pray you to notify this to Page and to George, and that they must make their own preparations. Indeed I must get you so far to interfere, as to settle with them whether they will chuse to carry on the harvest in one gang, or divide into two, each conducting their own. In this last case the hands I have usually thrown in must be equally divided between them. They may do this by drawing lots for the 1st. choice and then chusing alternately thro' the whole. Each will take a mule cart. Fleming & Mclanachen must be applied to to provide spirit, and they must make as small inroads as possible on our bacon. Their fish will enable them to do this, and I am in hopes they will have a plenty of peas and potatoes. There will be a difficulty as to the bricklayers. They should reserve for the harvest season that sort of work which will require the least attendance, and do with the least possible. What is absolutely necessary for them must be set apart before the division of the residue for the overseers takes place. The most indifferent hands for the harvest too should be allotted them.—To return to politics, the most afflicting circumstance when we attend to the division in the house of representatives, which we may consider for the most part as perfectly equal, is that it has been the changes in the Virginia elections which have occasioned it. Without that there would always have been a certain majority of half a dozen.—My love to my dear daughters, and kisses to the little ones. Adieu most affectionately.—P.M. So far I had written in the morning. The address having been reported to the House to-day, a motion was made to disagree to so much of the amendment as expressed a wish that the French might be placed on an equal footing with other nations, and Morgan and Machir, changing sides, the vote was 49. to 50. so the principle was saved by a single vote.

RC (DLC); partially dated; with several emendations, the most important of which are noted below; endorsed by Randolph. PrC (MHi); with two alterations in ink (see note 1 below); endorsed by TJ in ink on verso.

Randolph's letter of 24 MAY and another of 26 May, recorded in SJL as received from Richmond on 30 May and 1 June 1797 respectively, have not been found.

On 21 June, TJ paid $46.90 for Randolph's coach and chair SPRINGS (MB, II, 963). For the OTHER COMMISSIONS, see TJ to Randolph, 15 June 1797.

[1] Altered from "48" here and in the following sentence; altered in ink on PrC.
[2] Sentence interlined.

To Dugald Stewart

DEAR SIR   [Philadelphia June 2. 1797.]

It is as much as six years ago that I proposed to our Philosophical society to add the respect of your name to the list of their members, which was done at the first [ensuing] election. The diploma was to have been delivered to me to be transmitted you: but having soon after had occasion to be long absent from this place I desired it to be forwarded, as soon as made out, by the Secretaries. A presumption that it had been done prevented my making a particular enquiry till March last, when being called from Virginia, to which I had been retired for three or four years, to this place, and enquiring into it, I found that either the diploma had not been forwarded, or no evidence of it retained. We thought it safest to make out a new one, as, if a former had been transmitted, this would only [be a] duplicate.—We have little new to communicate to you in the line of science. The most remarkeable fact is a recent discovery, in the Western part of Virginia of the bones of an animal of the clawed kind, four or five times as large as the lion. This discovery having given us the first idea that such an animal had existed, we have begun to ask questions of the Indians concerning him, and so far as we have enquired, we have reason to believe the memory of the animal is preserved with more or less certainty among their traditions.

The fear of being drawn into a war with France occupies greatly our present attentions. We most sincerely wish to hear of peace in Europe. But I have little hope that even peace will bring us the wisdom to adopt those measures which are in our power for preventing our being again implicated in the broils of Europe. Ever happy when I can have occasion to satisfy my esteem and respect for you, I am in all the force of these sentiments Dear Sir Your affectionate friend & servt

TH: JEFFERSON

PrC (DLC); faded; at foot of text: "Mr. Dugald Stewart." Dft (same); undated and unsigned.

DIPLOMA: see TJ to Stewart, 10 Mch. 1793.

To Peregrine Fitzhugh

DEAR SIR   Philadelphia June 4. 1797.

I am favored with yours of May 19. and thank you for your intentions as to the corn and the large white clover, which if forwarded to Mr. Archibald Stuart at Staunton will find daily means of conveyance from thence to me. That indeed is the nearest post road between you and myself by 60. or 70. miles, the one by George town being very circuitous.

The representatives have at length got through their address. As you doubtless recieve the newspapers regularly from hence, you will have seen in them the address, and all the amendments made or proposed. [While mentioning newspapers, it is doing a good office to as distant places as yours and mine to observe that Bache has begun to publish his *Aurora* for his *country customers* on 3 sheets a week instead of six. You observe that the 1st. and 4th. pages are only of advertisements: the 2d. and 3d contain all the essays and news. He prints therefore his 2d and 3d pages of Monday's and Tuesday's papers on opposite sides of the same sheet, omitting the 1st. and 4th. so that we have the news pages of 2. papers on one. This costs but 5. instead of 8. dollars and saves half the postage. Smith begins in July to publish a *weekly* paper without advertisements, which will probably be a good one. Cary's paper is an excellent one, and Bradford's compiled by Loyd[1] perhaps the best in the city; but both of these are daily papers. Thinking this episode on newspapers might not be unacceptable in a position as distant as yours, I return to Congress and to politics.] You will percieve by the votes that the republican majority of the last congress has been much affected by the changes of the late election. Still however if all were here the majority would be on the same side, tho' a small one. They will now proceed to consider what is to be done. It is not easy nor safe to prophecy. But I find the expectation is that they will not permit the merchant vessels to arm, that they will leave the militia as it stands for the present season, vote further sums for going on with the fortifications and frigates, and prefer borrowing the money of the bank to the taking up the subject of taxation generally at this inconvenient season. In fact I consider the calling Congress so out of season as an experiment of the new administration, to see how far and in what line they could count on it's support. Nothing new had intervened between the late separation, and the summons, for Pinckney's non-reception was then known. It is visible from the complexion of the President's speech that he was disposed or perhaps advised[2] to proceed in a line which would endanger the peace of our country: and though the address is nearly responsive yet it would be too bold to proceed on so small a majority. The first unfavorable event, and even the necessary taxes, would restore preponderance to the scale of peace. The nomination of the envoys to France does not prove a thorough conversion to the pacific system. Our greatest security perhaps is in the impossibility of either borrowing or raising the money which would be necessary. I am suggesting an idea on the subject of taxation, which might perhaps facilitate much that business and reconcile all parties. That is to say, to lay a land tax leviable in 1799 &c. But if by the last day of 1798. any state brings it's *whole* quota into the federal treasury, the tax shall be suspended one year for that state. If by the end of the next year they bring another year's tax, it shall be suspended a 2d. year as to them, and so toties quoties for ever. If they fail, the federal collectors will go on of course to make their collection. In this way those who prefer excises may raise their quota by excises, and those who prefer land taxes may raise by land taxes, either on the federal plan, or on any other of their own which they like better. This would tend I think to make the general government popular, to render the state legislatures useful allies and associates instead of degraded rivals, and to mollify the harsh tone of government which has been assumed. I find the idea pleasing to most of those to whom I have suggested it. It will be objected to by those who are for a consolidation.—You mention the retirement of Mr. Ames. You will observe that he has sent us a successor, Mr. Otis as rhetorical as himself.—You have perhaps seen an attack made by a Mr. Luther Martin on the facts stated in the Notes on Virginia relative to Logan, his speech, the fate of his family, and the share Colo. Cresap had in their extermination. I do not mean to enter the field in the newspapers with Mr. Martin. But if any injury has been done Colo. Cresap in the statement I have given, it shall certainly be corrected whenever another edition of that work shall be printed. I have given it as I recieved it. I think you told me Cresap had lived in your neighborhood. Hence I have imagined you could in the ordinary course of conversations in the societies there, find the real truth of the whole transaction, and the genuine character and conduct of Cresap. If you will be so good as to keep this subject in your mind, to avail yourself of the opportunities of enquiry and evidence which may occur, and communicate the result to me, you will singularly oblige me.—The proceedings in the federal court of Virginia to overawe the communications between the people and their representatives excite great indignation. Probably a great fermentation will be produced[3] by it in that state. Indeed it is the common cause of the confederacy, as it is one of their courts which has taken the step. The charges of the federal judges have for a considerable time been inviting the Grand juries to become inquisitors on the freedom of speech, of writing and of principle of their fellow citizens. Perhaps the grand juries in the other states as well as in that of Virginia may think it incumbent in their next presentments to enter protestations against this perversion of their institution from a legal to a political engine, and even to present those concerned in it.—The hostile[4] use which is made of whatever can be laid hold of of mine, obliges me to caution the friends to whom I write, never to let my letters go out of their own hands, lest they should get into the newspapers. I pray you to present my most friendly respects to your father, and wishes for the continuance of his health and good faculties, and to accept yourself assurances of the esteem with which I am Dear Sir Your most obedt. & most humble servt

TH: JEFFERSON

RC (NcD); brackets supplied by TJ; with several emendations, the most important of which are noted below; at foot of first page: "Peregrine Fitzhugh esq." PrC (DLC).

On 23 June 1797, Uriah Forrest, who described Fitzhugh as "a democratic relation of mine," sent Adams an extract of this letter, which he had produced from memory after having read it twice. While Forrest noted that he was violating a confidence in sharing the contents, he justified his actions by arguing that he was fulfilling a duty he owed to his country and to Adams. He asserted that he extracted it "without exaggeration" and gave "it every degree of moderation it was susceptible of." In the extract Forrest reported on TJ's assertion that Adams had convened Congress "to try the strength of Government in the House of Representatives" to see "how far that House could be calculated" to support a war. Adams's speech indicated that he was not averse to war and the nomination of the envoys did not contradict this belief. War would not be risked at this time, however, because the majority for it was so small it "would be changed by the first unsuccessful event the first unpopular tax or when the taxes began to be felt." Forrest summarized TJ's tax plan, indicating that TJ believed it would raise the state governments "from their present degraded state" and check the "High tone of Government." He also noted TJ's criticism of the conduct of the grand jury at Richmond and of federal judges, who "courted Presentments" that were designed to check the freedom of speech, opinion, and writing, thus causing the courts to "become Political Machines for directing the Public Will and for answering Party Purposes." The extract concluded with TJ's summary of legislation to be considered during the session, his judgment that little would be accomplished, and a warning to take care lest the letter find its way into the newspapers (RC in MHi: Adams Papers).

The impact this extract of TJ's letter had upon Adams is evident in his reply to Forrest in which he noted that the enclosure was "a serious thing." He continued: "It will be a motive, in addition to many others, for me to be upon my guard. It is evidence of a mind, soured, yet seeking for popularity, and eaten to a honeycomb with ambition, yet weak, confused, uninformed, and ignorant. I have been long convinced that this ambition is so inconsiderate as to be capable of going great lengths" (Adams, *Works*, VIII, 546-7). For a description of the circumstances which led to the circulation of the contents of this letter, see Fitzhugh to TJ, 15 Oct. 1797. As Dumas Malone indicates in his discussion of this letter, there is no evidence that Fitzhugh or TJ was aware of Forrest's disclosure to Adams (Malone, *Jefferson*, III, 320-2).

TJ paid Samuel Harrison Smith three dollars to cover a year's subscription for his projected WEEKLY PAPER, which Smith did not begin publishing until 16 Nov. 1797 as *The Universal Gazette* (MB, II, 961). See Sowerby, No. 595.

For the ATTACK MADE by Luther Martin, see TJ to John Gibson, 31 May 1797.

On 22 May 1797, James Iredell, associate justice of the United States Supreme Court, delivered a charge to the grand jury IN THE FEDERAL COURT OF VIRGINIA, declaring that if a man loved his country he would respectfully submit to "any public authoritative decision" even if he disapproved of it. He declared that the jury had a responsibility to prosecute offenses against the United States in order to preserve the union, noting that if the country were disunited and allowed "differences of opinion to corrode into enmity" it would have the effect "of inviting some foreign nation to foment and take advantage" of the situation. The grand jury, under the foremanship of John Blair, a former associate justice of the Supreme Court, then proceeded to issue a presentment in which they charged that the circular letters of several members of the Fourth

Congress, particularly those of Samuel J. Cabell, were "a real evil" which with their "unfounded calumnies" threatened to separate the people from the government. In the letter to his constituents of 12 Jan. 1797, Cabell had reiterated French Minister Adet's charge that the United States government, particularly the executive branch, had shown partiality towards Great Britain to the "great injury of France," which culminated in the adoption of Jay's Treaty. Cabell also characterized the election of John Adams as an event "at which the patriotism of 76 and republicanism must sicken," contending that the preservation of peace and reconciliation with France were darkened by it. Cabell deprecated the idea of war with France and hoped "that the virtue, wisdom, and policy of our Executive" would lead to the adoption of measures designed to "restore the two Republics to their former love and friendship" (Noble E. Cunningham, Jr., ed., *Circular Letters of Congressmen to Their Constituents, 1789-1829*, 3 vols. [Chapel Hill, N.C., 1978], I, 67-70; DHSC, III, 173-8, 181). For the controversy resulting from Judge Iredell's charge to the grand jury and the grand jury's presentment, see DHSC, III, 149-51, 183-5, 187-220. For TJ's actions, see Petition to the Virginia House of Delegates, at 3 Aug. 1797.

[1] Preceding three words interlined.
[2] Preceding five words interlined in place of indecipherable word.
[3] Preceding word interlined in place of indecipherable word.
[4] Word interlined.

To Wakelin Welch

SIR   Philadelphia June 4. 1797.

Your favor of Aug. 22. never came to my hands till about a fortnight ago. In the meantime, that is to say about January or February last the subject of it had been included and settled in a general settlement of the debt of the late Mr. Wayles to Cary & Co. between Mr. Wickam acting for them and Mr. Wayles's executors, of which I have no doubt you recieved information in due time.   Your letter gave me the first news of the death of your late father. Permit me to place here my sincere regrets at this event, regrets founded on a great degree of personal esteem which I entertained for him. Accept yourself assurances of the regard with which I am Sir Your most obedt. & most humble servt

TH: JEFFERSON

PrC (MoSHi: Jefferson Papers); at foot of text: "Mr. Wakelyn Welch. Lon[don]"; endorsed by TJ in ink on verso.

For the GENERAL SETTLEMENT OF THE DEBT, see TJ to John Wickham, 20 Jan. 1797.

Senate Resolution on
Appointment of Charles C. Pinckney

[5 June 1797]

Resolved that the[1] Senate do advise and consent to the appointment of Chas. Cotesworth Pinckney as one of 3. envoys extraordinary and Min. Plenipotentiary with joint and several powers to the[2] republic of France.

MS (DNA: RG 46, Senate Records, 5th Cong., 1st sess.); entirely in TJ's hand; with emendations as noted below; conjoined with canceled passage at top of page in TJ's hand: "and encouraging the importation thereof," being a note on the Senate's consideration of "A Bill Prohibiting for a limited time, the exportation of Arms and Ammunition, and for encouraging the importation thereof," legislation passed earlier on 5 June, with the expanded title; endorsed in clerk's hand: "Statement of question on Nomination Ministers plenipo: Repub France June 5th 1797. L. 5th Con: 1 Sess." Printed in executive journal under this date (JEP, I, 243).

This was the first of three resolutions passed by the Senate on 5 June 1797, consenting to the appointments of Charles C. Pinckney, Francis Dana, and John Marshall, respectively, as ENVOYS EXTRAORDINARY to France as recommended by John Adams in his letter of nomination submitted to the Senate on 31 May. When Dana declined to serve, Adams on 20 June sent the nomination of his friend Elbridge Gerry to the Senate without consulting his cabinet, who had earlier opposed Gerry for the position. The debate on the appointment has not been preserved but Gallatin noted "The real reason of the opposition was that Gerry is a doubtful character, not British enough; but the ostensible pretence was that he was so obstinate that he would not make sufficient concessions." The Senate confirmed Gerry's appointment, with six dissenting Federalist votes, on 22 June (JEP, I, 241-5; Henry Adams, *The Life of Albert Gallatin* [Philadelphia, 1879], 185; Alexander DeConde, *The Quasi-War: The Politics and Diplomacy of the Undeclared War with France 1797-1801* [New York, 1966], 28-9).

[1] TJ first wrote "Resolved that it is the opinion" before altering the passage to read as above.

[2] TJ here canceled "French."

From Tench Coxe

June 7. 1797.

Mr. T. Coxe returns, with his best respects, the pamphlet Mr. Jefferson was so good as to lend him. It certainly has merit both for information, and reasoning. But Mr: Coxe would wish to see *An Enquiry into the means of Prosperity to the United States* well handled, before he would think it safe to settle finally the commercial course they ought to steer. Commerce would in his opinion be found to be

1st. a business in the hands of a part of our people, and of foreign *friends*, *rivals* and *indifferent persons*.

2dly. tho a valueable *auxiliary*, yet *no more*.

3dly. a means of prosperity[1] susceptable of serious perversions and abuses producing war—expence—loss of honest national[2] reputation—and sacrifices of principles not only of more importance but *indispensible*.

A work written with wisdom, knowledge and candor upon trade as it should be pursued by the United States would be invaluable. Perhaps nothing is so desireable to this Country except a work upon the nature and orthodoxy of representative Government.

RC (DLC); with two emendations as noted below; endorsed by TJ as received 7 June 1797 and so recorded in SJL.

The PAMPHLET which Coxe returned to TJ has not been identified.

[1] Preceding four words interlined.
[2] Preceding two words interlined.

To James Madison

Philadelphia June 8. 1797.

I wrote you last on the 1st. inst. You will have seen by the public papers that the amendment for putting France on an equal footing with other nations was clogged with another requiring compensation for spoliations. The objection to this was not that it ought not to be demanded, but that it ought not to be a sine qua non, and it was feared from the dispositions of the Executive that they would seize it's mention by the representatives as a pretext for making it a sine qua non. The representatives have voted a continuance of the fortifications, and a completion and manning of the three frigates. They will probably pass the bills recieved from the Senate prohibiting the exportation of arms and ammunition and for preventing our citizens from engaging in armed vessels. The Senate have also prepared or are proposing[1] bills for raising cavalry, raising a corps of artillerists, buying 9. more armed vessels, authorizing the Executive to employ them and the frigates as convoys for our commerce, and raising a great provisional army to be called into actual service only in the case of war. All these measures will pass the Senate by a majority of about 18. to 12. probably. That of permitting our merchant vessels to arm was rejected by the committee 3. to 2. Bingham who was of the committee stated to the Senate that he had taken pains to learn the sense of the merchants on this subject and that he had not found one in favor of the permission. Still a part of the Senate are for it, and do not consider it as laid aside. Smith and Harper brought on the same proposition yesterday (being the 5th. of Smith's resolutions) before the representatives. It was amended by changing the word *permitting* to restricting. Another amendment was proposed to add 'except[2] to the Mediterranean and E. Indies.' The day was spent in debate, and no question taken. I believe certainly the general permission will not be given. But what may be the fate of the 3d. 4th. 6th. 7th. and other resolutions is not very certain. We hope favorably.[3] The late victory of Buonaparte and panic of the British government has produced a sensible effect in damping the ardor of our heroes. However they might have been willing at first, partly from inclination, partly from devotion to the Executive, to have met hostilities from France, it is now thought they will not force that nail, but, doing of the most innocent things as much as may be necessary to veil the folly or the boldness of calling Congress, be willing to leave the more offensive measures till the issue of the negociation or their own next meeting. This is the most we can hope, and but for the late successes of France and desperate condition of England, it was more than we should have hoped.[4] For it is difficult to say whether the Republicans have a majority or not. The votes have been carried both ways by a difference of from 1. to 6. Our three renegadoes exactly make that difference. Clay proves to be as firm as a rock, having never separated but in the single instance I mentioned in my last letter, when I presume he must have been struck by some peculiar view of the question.—We expect the arrival of Paine daily. Of Monroe we hear nothing, except that he had not left Paris on the 1st. of April.

P.M. This day has been spent in the H. of Representatives in debating whether the restriction of the merchants from arming their vessels except when bound to the Mediterranean or E. Indies, should be taken off as to the W. Indies also. It was determined by 46. against 34. that the W. India vessels should not arm. This is considered as auguring favorably of the other resolutions. The Senate determined to-day 18. to 11.[5] that 9 vessels should be bought, armed &c. by the president. Their cost is estimated at 60,000.D. each. This was on the 2d. reading of the bill. These bills originated in the Senate and going under their sanction to the lower house, while in so vibratory a state, have a very mischievous effect. We expect to rise on Saturday the 17th. I have written for my horses to be at Fredsbg. on Sunday the 25th. and I may be with you perhaps on the 26th. or 27th. Adieu.

RC (DLC: Madison Papers); unsigned; addressed: "James Madison junr. near Orange Court house"; franked and postmarked. FC (DLC); entirely in TJ's hand; being a summary, with substantive exclusions recorded in notes below; at foot of text: "no copy retained. the above is the sum."

On 5 June 1797, William L. Smith presented ten resolutions for the consideration of the House of Representatives to provide for the defense of the country and implement the president's speech. The House immediately voted to appoint committees to bring in bills on the first two resolutions relating to the CONTINUANCE OF THE FORTIFICATIONS and the COMPLETION AND MANNING of the FRIGATES United States, Constitution, and Constellation. On 10 June, Edward Livingston brought in the fortifications bill, which provided "for the further defence of the ports and harbors of the United States." After extensive debate and amendment, the bill as adopted authorized states indebted to the federal government to credit state expenditures for fortifications to the settlement of their accounts if they ceded the land on which the fortifications were to be built to the United States. Passing the House by a 54 to 35 vote on 16 June, the bill allowed the expenditure of $115,000, a compromise between the $50,000 advocated by Republicans and the $200,000 desired by Federalists. The Senate passed the bill four days later and the president signed it on 23 June (*Annals*, VII, 298-324; JHR, III, 24, 28, 32-6; JS, II, 374, 376; U.S. Statutes at Large, I, 521-2). On 14 June, Josiah Parker reported a bill for the manning of the frigates but the measure was encompassed in the Senate bill for the protection of trade, which the House received the next day (JHR, III, 32, 35-6). For the eight remaining resolutions that Smith introduced on 5 June, see *Annals*, VII, 239.

On 30 May, Jacob Read introduced in the SENATE a bill that prohibited, for a limited time, the EXPORTATION OF ARMS AND AMMUNITION, and two days later Samuel Livermore reported one that prevented United States citizens FROM ENGAGING IN ARMED VESSELS and privateering against its own citizens or friendly nations, both of which were passed and sent to the House of Representatives on 5 June. The House approved the bills, with amendments, on 8 and 9 June, respectively. The Senate concurred with the amendments and Adams signed the legislation on 14 June 1797 (JS, II, 366-72; JHR, III, 26-7; U.S. Statutes at Large, I, 520-1).

Uriah Tracy headed the committee charged with drawing bills to augment the military. On 6 June, he reported a bill FOR RAISING CAVALRY that would have added four companies of mounted infantry to the two companies of light dragoons already in service ("A Bill For raising an additional corps of light dragoons," in DNA: RG 46, Senate Records, 5th Cong., 1st sess.). The Senate rejected the measure by a 15 to 13 vote after its second reading on 14 June (JS, II, 372). On 5 June Tracy proposed to raise A CORPS OF ARTILLERISTS, a bill that was passed by the Senate two days later by an 18 to 8 vote. The House rejected it by a wide

margin on 20 June (JS, II, 367-8; JHR, III, 38-9). For the history of the protection of trade bill, which called for the purchase of nine ARMED VESSELS, see TJ to Madison, 15 June 1797. Not until 19 June did Tracy propose giving the president the power, under certain conditions, to raise a PROVISIONAL ARMY consisting of up to 1,000 artillerists, 1,000 cavalry, and 13,000 infantry. The measure was defeated on its second reading three days later by a vote of 9 to 17 (JS, II, 373, 375; *National State Papers: Adams*, II, 7-9).

During this session of Congress, both Senate and House committees considered legislation on allowing MERCHANT VESSELS TO ARM. William BINGHAM served on the Senate committee appointed to establish a system of naval defense, which introduced a bill for the protection of trade on 6 June without a resolution for arming merchant vessels. The next day, however, Representatives SMITH and Robert Goodloe HARPER introduced the measure in the committee of the whole House, BEING THE 5TH. OF SMITH'S RESOLUTIONS. Vigorous debate ensued over whether merchant vessels of a neutral power had the right to arm for their own defense. New York Representative John Williams observed that it was important to establish restraints since it was well known that merchants were arming. Gallatin argued that passing legislation permitting the arming of neutral vessels "would be almost certain" to ignite a war with France. If merchant vessels were arming, he advised, it would be best for the government to remain silent. After extended discussion on whether to exempt merchant vessels in the MEDITERRANEAN AND E. INDIES trade from the restrictions or to extend the exemption to the West Indies also, attempts to bring a bill into the House were dropped. The Senate, however, continued to discuss the issue for the remainder of the month, until on 4 July they agreed to postpone consideration of the measure until the next session (JS, II, 372-4, 376-80, 384; *Annals*, VII, 253-83; Philadelphia *Aurora*, 9 June 1797).

The *Aurora* of 3 June took notice of Bonaparte's LATE VICTORY over the Austrians at Tarvis, which Paine also discussed along with the British financial PANIC in his letter of 1 Apr. above.

I HAVE WRITTEN FOR MY HORSES: see the following document.

¹ Preceding three words interlined.

² Preceding word interlined.

³ In FC TJ summarized the preceding seven sentences: "Smith and Harper proposed permit merchants to arm, yesterday."

⁴ Preceding sentence not included in FC.

⁵ Altered from "12."

To Martha Jefferson Randolph

MY DEAR MARTHA   Philadelphia June 8. 1797.

Yours of May 20 came to hand the 1st. inst. I imagine you recieved mine of May 18. about six days after the date of yours. It was written the first post-day after my arrival here. The commission you inclosed for Maria is executed, and the things are in the care of Mr. Boyce of Richmond, who is returning from hence with some goods of his own, and will deliver them to Mr. Johnston.—I recieve with inexpressible pleasure the information your letter contained. After your own happy establishment, which has given me an inestimable friend to whom I can leave the care of every thing I love, the only anxiety I had remaining was to see Maria also so associated as to ensure her happiness. She could not have been more so to my wishes, if I had had the whole earth free to have chosen a partner for her. I now see our fireside formed into a groupe, no one member of which has a fibre in their composition which can ever produce any jarring or jealousies among us. No irregular passions, no dangerous bias, which may render problematical the future fortunes and happiness of our descendants. We are quieted as to their condition for at least one generation more.   In order to keep us all together, instead of a present provision in Bedford, as in your case, I think to open and resettle the plantation of Pantops for them. When I look to the ineffable pleasures of my family society, I become more and more disgusted with the jealousies, the hatred, and the rancorous and malignant passions of this scene, and lament my having ever again been drawn into public view. Tranquility is now my object. I have seen enough of political honors to know that they are but splendid torments: and however one might be disposed to render services on which any of their fellow citizens should set a value; yet when as many would deprecate them as a public calamity, one may well entertain a modest doubt of their real importance, and feel the impulse of duty to be very weak. The real difficulty is that being once delivered into the hands of others, whose feelings are friendly to the individual and warm to the public cause, how to withdraw from them without leaving a dissatisfaction in their mind and an impression of pusillanimity with the public.

Congress, in all probability will rise on Saturday the 17th. inst. the day after you will recieve this. I shall leave Philadelphia Monday the 19th. pass a day at Georgetown and a day at Fredericksburg, at which place I wish my *chair* and horses to be Sunday evening the 25th. Of course they must set out Saturday morning the 24th. This gives me the chance of another post, as you will, the evening before that, recieve by the post a letter of a week later date than this, so that if any thing should happen within a week to delay the rising of Congress, I may still notify it and change the time of the departure of my horses. Jupiter must pursue the rout by Noel's to which he will come the first day, and by Chew's to Fredericksburg the next. I fix his rout because were any accident to get me along earlier, or him later, we might meet on the road. Not yet informed that Mr. Randolph is returned I have thought it safest to commit this article to my letter to you. The news of the day I shall write to him. My warmest love to yourself and Maria. Adieu affectionately.

Th: Jefferson

RC (NNPM); at foot of first page: "Mrs. Randolph." PrC (MHi); endorsed by TJ in ink on verso.

The letter of 20 May 1797 which CAME TO HAND THE 1ST INST., and another of an undetermined date in May, which accord-ing to SJL was received 13 June 1797, both arriving from Monticello, have not been found. The former letter evidently included INFORMATION on Mary Jefferson's plans to marry John Wayles Eppes.

BY NOEL'S: Sephemiah Noe's ordinary in Orange County (MB, II, 954, 966).

To French Strother

[Dear Sir]   Philadelphia June 8. 1797.

In compliance with the desire you expressed in the few short moments I had the pleasure of being with you at Fredericksburg, I shall give you some account of what is passing here. The President's speech you will have seen; and how far it's aspect was turned towards war. An opinion here is that the Executive had that in contemplation, and were not without expectation that the legislature might catch the flame. A powerful part of that has shewn a disposition to go all lengths with the Executive; and they have been able to persuade some of more moderate principles to go so far with them as to join them in a very sturdy address. They have voted the compleating and manning the three frigates, and going on with the fortifications. The Senate have gone much further. They have brought in bills for buying more armed vessels, sending them and the frigates out as convoys to our trade, raising more cavalry, more artillerists, and providing a great army, to come into actual service only if necessary. They have not decided whether they will permit the merchants to arm. The hope and belief is that the Representatives will concur in none of these measures: though their divisions hitherto have been so equal as to leave us under doubt and apprehension. The usual majorities have been from 1. to 6. votes, and these sometimes one way, sometimes the other. Three of the Virginia members dividing from their collegues occasion the whole difference. If they decline these measures, we shall rise about the 17th. inst. It appears that the dispositions of the French government towards us were of a very angry cast indeed: and this before Pickering's letter to Pinckney was known to them. We do not know what effect that may produce. We expect Paine every day in a vessel from Havre, and Colo. Monroe in one from Bordeaux. Tobacco keeps up to a high price and will still rise. Flour is dull at $7\frac{1}{2}$ Dollars. I am with great esteem Dear Sir Your friend & servt

Th: Jefferson

PrC (DLC); torn; at foot of text: "French Strother esq."

The ADDRESS of the House of Representatives in response to the president's message is discussed in TJ to Madison, 18 May 1797. For PICKERING'S LETTER TO PINCKNEY, see note to Madison to TJ, 22 Jan. 1797.

To Thomas Mann Randolph

Th:J. to TMR.   Philada June 9. 1797.

I have scarcely a moment left to write to you, having waited till the morning of the departure of the post to see Barnes in expectation I could inform you of the sale of our tobacco. Your's arrived yesterday. I had found it safest to sell for 10. Dol. as no more than $9\frac{1}{2}$ D. has been given for new tobacco and Lieper would not take it, as he formerly did, at the old tobacco price, giving a credit till Sep. Having therefore an offer yesterday of half a dollar above the highest market, and on such credit as will put the whole money into a negociable state in a short time I desired Barnes to conclude the bargain. I expect he has done it, and that in my next I shall be able to give you the particulars. The weather has been so fine, that I ventured to take on myself the contradiction of your orders to ensure, so that we have saved that 30. Dol. for you.—The legislature will probably pass bills prohibiting the exportation of arms and ammunition, and preventing our citizens from going on board armed vessels, and probably will do little more. We expect to rise the 17th. but of this I have written more particularly to Martha, lest you should not be at Monticello. Adieu affectionately.

RC (DLC). TJ kept a brief outline of the major points of this letter, entirely in his hand, on which he noted "June 9. 97. wrote to TMR. no copy. substce" (CSmH).

John Barnes brokered the sale of the TO-BACCO to William and Samuel Keith, merchants in the French trade, for ten dollars per hundredweight. TJ calculated, however, that with weight losses, freight charges, a commission, and other expenses, he netted only $8.75 (MB, II, 962; *Philadelphia Gazette*, 7 June 1797).

I HAVE WRITTEN MORE PARTICULARLY TO MARTHA: TJ to Martha Jefferson Randolph, 8 June 1797.

From Thomas Bell

DEAR SIR   Monday 12. June 97

Your favor of the 18th. Ult. came to hand the 10th. Inst. The delay was Owing to the Small pox in Fredriksburg and a Neglect of the post master not sending on to Richmond.

I am Sorry to see that there is a probability of Congress Sitting much longer than you expected and that the tone of the house looks rather hostile. Nicholases Amendment Spoke a Mildness which in our Situation, in my weak Opinion, we ought to Observe.

We have just heard of Marshal &c being appointed as Envoys. I hope they may be able to bring about a conciliation for War I dred as the greatest Curse that could befall our happy country.

The failure of the bank of England must materially effect the Merchantile world. And will it not effect our Own bank in case of a War— we are well assur.d that you will use your influence to keep us in peace. God send every one in office would do so. I din.d yesterday at the Mountain. The family are well. Majr. Randolph will write you himself therefore need say no more on that head.

We have generally had exesive dry Weather. Altho there have been partial rains—but in this Neighborhood we have had none since you left us that would give a Season for a collard plant. With due respect, I am your most Ob. Servt.   THS. BELL

note

Any confidential line I may at any time have the pleasure of receiving from you Shall never by me or my means be made publick. I see the unwarantable and Shamefull attacks at your Charactor from the moment you stepd into office. Such infernal Scoundrels ought to be consign.d to the Algerens or to the ——

RC (DLC); addressed: "Thomas Jefferson Vice President of the United States"; franked; endorsed by TJ as received 20 June 1797 and so recorded in SJL.

From Mary Jefferson

DEAR PAPA   Monticello June 12th 1797

Your letters to my sister and myself did not arrive here till the 9th. They were stopt in Fredericksburg by the sickness of the post boy, and were at last sent round by Richmond. We learnt with sorrow indeed[1] that you had again been tormented by your rheumatism, the consolation of seeing you when you are ill is the only one I know—and I never feel the distress of separation as much as then.[2] I have at last written to Sally Cropper and inclose the letter to you to direct to her in Acomac county, and if she will answer it will try for the future to keep up a more regular correspondance with her. Mr. Randolph and the children arriv'd here last tuesday all in perfect health Ann and Jefferson grown so much as to amaze us, Ann seems to promise more every day of resembling her mother. Her disposition is the same allready she will no doubt be worthy of her. We are alone at present. Mr. Hylton and a Mr. Lawrence with whom he is travelling left us to day after a visit of ten days. We have seen no one else and I hope we shall not for some time, solitude after such company as his is by no means unpleasant. I am not able to tell you whether Mr. Richardson is going on well, they to day, began to raise the walls of the hall, the other rooms are done. The garden has supplied us better with vegetables and fine lettuce than it has ever yet done although we have been so much in want of rain. But, I must finish my letter as they are waiting for it, the next we recieve from you I hope will let us know that you are recoverd and when to expect you. We wait in hopes of that in no small anxiety. Adieu Dear Papa I am your most affectionate daughter   M JEFFERSON

RC (MHi); with several emendations, the most important of which are noted below; minimal punctuation supplied; endorsed by TJ as received 20 June 1797 and so recorded in SJL. Enclosure not found.

LETTERS TO MY SISTER AND MYSELF: TJ to Martha Jefferson Randolph, 18 May, and TJ to Mary Jefferson, 25 May.

[1] Preceding two words interlined in place of three or four indecipherable words.

[2] Mary Jefferson first wrote "I never feel your absence more than" before altering the passage to read as above.

To John Moody

SIR   Philadelphia June 13 97

I might sooner have acknoleged the receipt of your favor of May 15. but I could not sooner have done it with any thing satisfactory on the subject it concerned. The first [offering?] of the session of Congress was rather [inau]spicious to those who consider war as among the greatest calamities to our country. Private conversation, public discussion, and thorough calculation, aided by the events of Europe, have nearly brought every one to the same sentiment, not only to wish for a continuance of peace, but to let no false sense of honor lead us to take a threatening attitude, which to a nation prompt in it's passions [and] flushed with victory might produce a blow from them. I rather believe that Congress will think it best to do little or nothing for the present to give fair play to the negociation proposed, and in the mean time lie on their oars till their next meeting in November. Still however both English and French spoliations continue in a high degree. Perhaps the prospects in Europe may deaden the [activity] of the former, and call home all their resources, but I see nothing to check the depredations of the French but the natural effect they begin to produce of starving themselves by deterring us from venturing to sea with provisions. This is the best general view I am able to give you of the probable course of things for the summer so far as they may be interesting to commerce.—The liberties which the presses take in mutilating whatever they can get hold of, obliges me to request every gentleman to whom I write to take care that nothing from me may be put within their power. I am Sir Your very humble servt   TH: JEFFERSON

PrC (DLC); badly faded; at foot of text: "Mr. John Moody Richmd."

John Moody (1746-1826), a Richmond merchant with the firm of Moody & Price in the late 1790s, was a Revolutionary War veteran with Republican sympathies. He unsuccessfully sought several patronage positions including that of Richmond postmaster in 1802 and a diplomatic post during the last months of the Monroe administration (Moody to TJ, 1 Dec. 1824 and 31 Jan. 1825; MB, II, 989; Madison, *Papers*, XVII,

198-9n; Madison, *Papers: Sec. of State Ser.*, II, 450; VMHB, XXXV [1927], 448; *Richmond Enquirer*, 3 Oct. 1826).

Moody's FAVOR of 15 May 1797, recorded in SJL as received five days later, has not been found. Letters from Moody to TJ of 31 Aug. 1796, 31 Dec. 1797, and 26 Jan. 1799, recorded in SJL as received 3 Sep. 1796, 9 Jan. 1798, and 3 Feb. 1799, respectively, are also missing. SJL also records a letter from TJ to Moody & Price, 21 Jan. 1797, which has not been found.

To Mary Jefferson

[14 June 1797]

I learn, my dear M. with inexpressible pleasure that an union of sentiment[1] is likely to bring on an union of destiny between yourself and a person for whom I have the highest esteem. A long acquaintance with him has[2] made his virtues familiar to me and convinced me that he possesses every quality necessary to make you happy and to make us all happy. This event in compleating the circle of our family has composed for us[3] such a group of good sense, good humor, liberality, and prudent care of our affairs, and that without a single member of a contrary character, as families are rarely blessed with.[4] It promises us long years of domestic concord and love, the best ingredient in human happiness, and I deem the composition of my family[5] the most precious of all the kindnesses of fortune. I propose, as in the case of your sister, that we shall all live together[6] as long as it is agreeable to you; but whenever inclination convenience or a curiosity to try new things shall give a wish to be separately established,[7] it must be at Pantops, which in the mean time while under your improvement will furnish to Mr. E. useful and profitable occupation as a farmer, and to you a[8] occasional rides to superintend the spinning house, dairy &c. You might even have a room there to be in comfort if business or variety should induce a short stay. From thence to Edgehill we can make a road on the dead level which shall make it as near as to Monticello.[9] But I should lose myself, my dear Maria, in these reveries as I always do when I think of yourself or your sister, did not the discordant noises,[10] the oppressive heats and other disagremens[11] of this place awaken me through the channel of every sense to very different scenes.[12] I long the more to be with you, and therefore see with the utmost impatience day after day drawn out here in useless debate, and[13] rhetorical declamation. Take care of your health my dear child for my happiness as well as your own and that of all those who love you. And all the world will love you if you continue good good humored, prudent and attentive to every body, as I am sure you will do from temper as well as reflection.[14] I embrace you my dear in all the warmth of my love,[15] and bid you affectionately adieu.

Dft (ViU: Edgehill-Randolph Papers); undated; unsigned; with numerous emendations, the most important of which are noted below; endorsed by TJ on verso "Jefferson Maria. June 14. 97." Tr (ViU: Margaret and Olivia Taylor deposit); probably 19th century transcript secured by Sarah Nicholas Randolph and made from the now missing RC; with some variations, one of which is noted below (see note 8) and minor changes in abbreviations, punctuation, and spelling; at head of text: "Thomas Jefferson to Maria Jefferson."

[1] Preceding four words interlined in place of "a mutual inclination."

[2] TJ here canceled "[developed?] to me."

[3] TJ first began this sentence "It completes the circle of our family and by composing it of members ⟨and former⟩ it has made up for us" before altering it to read as above.

[4] TJ first wrote "as no family can shew " before altering the passage to read as above.

[5] TJ here canceled "the happiest circumstance with which fortune."

[6] TJ here canceled "but whenever."

[7] TJ here canceled "as Mr. Eppes."

[8] TJ here canceled "daily ride." Preceding word lacking in Tr.

[9] TJ first wrote "shall be little more than 2 mile and a half" before altering the passage to read as above.

[10] TJ first wrote "the noises, the

stenches and" before altering the passage
to read as above.
    ¹¹ Preceding three words interlined.
    ¹² TJ first wrote "to a very different state
of things" before altering the passage to
read as above.

    ¹³ TJ here canceled "vain."
    ¹⁴ Preceding six words interlined.
    ¹⁵ TJ here canceled "for you."

To Edward Stevens

DEAR SIR   Philadelphia June 14. 97.

I recieved duly through your kindness the survey from Mr. Strode of
the road from Georgetown to Stevensburg. I propose on my passage
through George town to confer with the Bridge company and get them
to undertake having the road conducted from their bridge to the Culpeper line, after which I presume every county will go on with it till it
gets into the direct and proper road at Prince Edward courthouse. I
observe there are some little difficulties in your county, excited by an
inclination in some to draw it by their courthouse. I think it possible
that a winter road in that direction may become an object as an appendix
to the other. But the main object is to give us the benefit of a straight
road through the level country in such seasons of the year as it can be
used. I hope therefore that this may be accomodated.—Congress I think
will determine to trust to the event of their negociation, and to do little
at their present session, such is the complexion of their votes hitherto.
They spent most of their fire on the address, and are now rather more
temperate. The great events of Europe have not been without their influence on our debates. Buonaparte's victories, the peace of Austria,
bankruptcy of England and mutiny in her fleet, have been differently
felt here. British and French spoliations both continue as high as they
ever were. I hope myself, that as this must be the last campaign in Europe, we may rub through this summer without war, and in the interval
of peace try whether we cannot so arrange our commerce and navigation as to make them the instruments of preserving peace and justice to
us hereafter. Our people must consent to small occasional sacrifices, to
avoid the greater evil of war. I am with great esteem Dear Sir Your
friend & servt.   TH: JEFFERSON

PrC (DLC); at foot of text: "General
Stephens."

THE SURVEY FROM MR. STRODE: see the
following document. An April 1797 MU-

TINY of British sailors at Spithead, discontented over their pay and conditions of service, forced concessions from the government (Emsley, *British Society and the
French Wars*, 59).

To John Strode

DEAR SIR   Philadelphia June 14. 97.

I have to acknolege the receipt of your favor of May 7. together with the survey of the road from Georgetown to Stevensburgh. As I believe there will be no difficulty in getting the road established from it's entry into Culpeper till it gets into the established and direct road in Prince Edward, I propose to confer at Georgetown with some members of the Bridge company and get them to undertake to have the road opened to the Culpeper line.

We are in hopes of rising about Saturday the 24th. The immense events which are daily taking place in Europe render it impossible for Congress to know to what state of things to adapt their proceedings. I am in hopes therefore they will conclude it best to do almost nothing for the present, but await the event of their negociation with France, and hope the establishment of peace in Europe will give us leisure and opportunity to devise some means of preserving neutrality in all wars, yet of maintaining a due respect to our honour and our interests. It cannot be denied that these have been grossly trampled on by both the belligerent powers in the present war. I am with great esteem Dear Sir Your most obedt. servt   TH: JEFFERSON

PrC (DLC); at foot of text: "Mr. John Strode."

John Strode had, during the American Revolution, managed an arms factory near Fredericksburg. After the war he continued in iron founding and arms manufacture, and also owned several mills. When traveling in the 1790s and after, TJ would often stop over at Strode's Culpeper County residence, Fleetwood. Strode served in the Virginia House of Delegates, 1810-12 (MB, II, 834, 1229; Madison, *Papers*, XII, 248n; Raleigh Travers Green, *Genealogical and Historical Notes on Culpeper County, Virginia* [Culpeper, Va., 1900], pt. 2, 137; CVSP, VIII, 356-7).

Strode's FAVOR OF MAY 7. is recorded in SJL as received on 14 May 1797 but has not

been found. Also recorded in SJL but missing are twenty letters exchanged by TJ and Strode between 19 Sep. 1797 and 8 Oct. 1800.

On 17 June 1797, Gallatin laid a resolution on the table calling for the adjournment of Congress on SATURDAY, 24 June. Five days later the date was amended to the 28th and passed by the House by a 51 to 47 vote. On 27 June the Senate voted against the House's proposed date. Congress did not adjourn until 10 July but TJ left Philadelphia the morning of the 6th, arriving at Monticello five days later. Upon his departure, William Bradford of Rhode Island was elected president pro tempore of the Senate (*Annals*, VII, 333, 358-9; JHR, III, 42-3, 56; JS, II, 378, 386; MB, II, 965-6).

To James Madison

My last was of the 8th. inst. I had inclosed you separately a paper giving an account of Buonaparte's last great victory. Since that we recieve information that the preliminaries of peace were signed between France and Austria. Mr. Hammond will have arrived at Vienna too late to influence the terms. The victories lately obtained by the French on the Rhine were as splendid as Buonaparte's. The mutiny on board the English fleet, tho allayed for the present has impressed that country with terror. King has written letters to his friends recommending a pacific conduct towards France 'notwithstanding the continuance of her injustices.' Volney is convinced France will not make peace with England, because it is such an opportunity for sinking her as she never had and may not have again. Buonaparte's army would have to march 700. miles to Calais. Therefore it is imagined the armies of the Rhine will be destined for England.—The Senate yesterday rejected on it's 2d reading their own bill for raising 4. more companies of light dragoons by a vote of 15. to 13. Their cost would have been about 120,000 D. a year. To-day the bill for manning the frigates and buying 9. vessels @ about 60,000 D. each, comes to it's 3d. reading. Some flatter us we may throw it out. The trial will be in time to mention the issue herein. The bills for preventing our citizens from engaging in armed vessels of either party, and for prohibiting exportation of arms and ammunition have passed both houses. The fortification bill is before the Representatives still. It is thought by many that with all the mollifying clauses they can give it, it may perhaps be thrown out. They have a separate bill for manning the 3. frigates. But it's fate is uncertain. These are probably the ultimate measures which will be adopted, if even these be adopted. The folly of the convocation of Congress at so inconvenient a season and an expence of 60,000 D. is now palpable to every body: or rather it is palpable that war was the object, since, that being out of the question, it is evident there is nothing else. However nothing less than the miraculous string of events which have taken place, towit the victories of the Rhine and Italy, peace with Austria, bankruptcy of England, mutiny in her fleet, and King's writing letters recommending peace, could have[1] cooled the fury of the British faction. Even all that will not prevent considerable efforts still in both houses to shew our teeth to France.—We had hoped to have risen this week. It is now talked of for the 24th. but it is impossible yet to affix a time. I think I cannot omit being at our court (July 3.) whether Congress rises or not. If so, I shall be with you on the Friday or Saturday preceding. I have a couple of pamphlets for you, Utrum horum, and Paine's agrarian justice, being the only things since Erskine which have appeared worth notice. Besides Bache's paper there are 2. others now accomodated to country circulation. Gale's (successor of Oswald) twice a week, without advertisements at 4. Dollars. His debates in Congress are the same with Claypole's. Also Smith proposes to issue a paper once a week, of news only, and an additional sheet while Congress shall be in session, price 4. dollars.—The best daily papers now are Bradford's compiled by Loyd, and Markland & Cary's. Claypole's you know. Have you remarked the pieces signed Fabius? They are written by John Dickinson.

P.M. The bill before the Senate for equipping the 3 frigates and buying 9. vessels of not more than 20. guns has this day passed on it's 3d. reading by 16. against 13. The fortification bill before the representatives as amended in committee of the whole passed to it's 3d. reading by 48. against 41. Adieu affectionately with my best respects to Mrs. Madison.

RC (DLC: Madison Papers); unsigned; with several emendations, the most important of which is noted below; addressed: "James Madison junr. near Orange court house"; franked, stamped, and postmarked. PrC (DLC).

The PAPER on Napoleon Bonaparte's LAST GREAT VICTORY, which TJ previously sent to Madison, has not been identified but may have been the *Aurora* of 3 June or another newspaper carrying news of the battle at Tarvis (see TJ to Madison, 8 June). On 12 June, several Philadelphia newspapers brought out special issues with reports from Paris to 28 Apr. 1797 on the signing of the PRELIMINARIES OF PEACE at Leoben (see Paine to TJ, 14 May 1797), and the VICTORIES of the FRENCH ON THE RHINE (Philadelphia *Aurora*, 12, 13 June 1797; *Philadelphia Gazette*, 12, 13, 14 June 1797; Scott and Rothaus, *Historical Dictionary*, 465-6, 681-2, 773-4). According to the *Philadelphia Gazette* of 13 June, the victories were "unparalleled in the history of warlike operations."

KING HAS WRITTEN LETTERS TO HIS FRIENDS: Webster's *Minerva* of 12 June carried an extract of "A letter from a character of high respectability in an official station in England," dated 28 Apr., which the *Aurora* reprinted three days later with the correspondent identified as Rufus King, United States minister to Great Britain. He observed that the immense increase in taxes had "extended the wish for peace" throughout Great Britain. The United States, he advised, "must adhere to the pacific policy" that had kept the country out of war. King wrote in the same vein to Alexander Hamilton, 2 Apr., Oliver Wolcott, 14 Apr., and Timothy Pickering, 19 Apr. (Syrett, *Hamilton*, XXI, 8; Gibbs, *Memoirs*, I, 550-1; King, *Life*, II, 172-5).

On this day the Senate passed the bill for the protection of trade which provided for the MANNING of the three newly constructed FRIGATES and the purchase of nine VESSELS. The House of Representatives passed the measure nine days later but with amendments, including those which eliminated the nine vessels, forbade the president to use the frigates as convoys, and allowed the executive to increase the strength of revenue cutters. The Senate refused to accept several of these, and a House-Senate conference committee failed to reach a compromise. On 28 June the Senate reaffirmed its rejection of the amendment which limited the president in his use of frigates to protect trade, but withdrew opposition to the others (JS, II, 368-72, 379; JHR, III, 44-51, 54-7). When a motion was then made to amend one of the endorsed amendments, TJ raised a point of order requesting the sense of the Senate: "Is it in order in the present case, for the Senate to recede from their disagreement to an amendment of the H of R and agree to the same with an amendt.?" The Senate voted affirmatively on the question but then rejected the proposed change to the amendment (Rough Journal in DNA: RG 46, Senate Records, 5th Cong., 1st sess.). For TJ's handling of this question, see PW, 10-11. The bill was renamed "An Act providing a Naval Armament," as desired by the House, and on 29 June that body accepted the bill as agreed to by the Senate. Adams gave his approval on 1 July (JHR, III, 57-8; U.S. Statutes at Large, I, 523-5).

I HAVE A COUPLE OF PAMPHLETS FOR YOU: Dennis O'Bryen, *Utrum Horum? The government; or, the country?* (Dublin, 1796); and Thomas Paine, *Agrarian Justice, Opposed to Agrarian Law, and to Agrarian Monopoly . . .* (Philadelphia, 1797). See Sowerby, Nos. 2834 and 3187, respectively.

The first of fifteen PIECES SIGNED FABIUS appeared in Samuel H. Smith's *The New World* on 10 Apr. 1797 and was shortly thereafter reprinted in Bache's *Aurora.* Fearing that President Adams's unprecedented call of Congress into session would lead to war with France, Dickinson urged the country to remember the foundation of America's friendship with that country and their mutual love of liberty. Later in the year these essays were published as a pamphlet along with Dickinson's nine pieces in 1788 using the same pseudonym (*The Letters of Fabius, in 1788, on the Federal Constitution; and in 1797, on the Present Situation of Public Affairs* [Wilmington, Del., 1797], see Evans, No. 32042; Philadelphia *Aurora*, 21 Apr. 1797).

¹ TJ here canceled five or six illegible words.

From Pierre Malon

MONSIEUR   prince ton 15 juin 1797.

Le desir d'etre utile a mon Semblable m'avoit fait naitre l'idée de donner au public par la voie des journeaux le Secret de deux remedes precieux a l'humanité en general, mais plus precieux encore dans un Vaste pais ou la pluspart des habitants épars ne peuvent Se procurer aisement les Secours de la medecine; mais j'ai reflechi que la Classe que j'ai le plus en vue de Secourir, L'honnête ouvrier, ne S'amusant point a lire des gazettes, Seroit privé d'un Secours extremement important. J'ai donc Cru ne pouvoir emploier une voie mellieure que de vous l'envoier, pour que vous le rendiez public, Si vous le jugez Convenable, par les moiens que vous dictera Votre Sagesse et Celle de messieurs vos Confreres.

Une grande quantité d'ouvriers que j'emploiois en europe, que je pourvoiois dans leurs maladies, beaucoup d'honnetes indigents que j'aimois a Soulager m'ont valu quelque foible experience et la recherche de quelques remedes les plus efficaces, des voisins Compagnons respectables d'infortune, qui partagent avec moi les memes Sentiments, m'ont procuré la Connoissance d'autres non moins precieux que l'humanité Seule nous engage a donner au public, aucune vue d'interest ne nous guide, Soiez en Convaincu et l'unique grace que je vous demande que pour ma recompense je vous impose, S'il m'est permis d'user de Ce terme, est que vous ne prononciez mon nom ni au public ni a messieurs vos Confreres; pour en être Sur je me Serois dispensé de Signer ma lettre Si je n'avois point Cru qu'il fut utile que vous eussiez mon adresse dans le Cas ou vous pourriez avoir besoin de quelque détail.

Pardonnez, Monsieur, Si je vous interromp un instant dans vos importantes occupations, mais l'ami de Ses Concitoiens ne peut qu'applaudir au desir qu'on a de leur etre utile et en Cette faveur Sacrifier Sans peine quelques moments. Permettez que je Saisisse Cette occasion de vous assurer de la respectueuse Consideration avec la quelle je Suis Monsieur Votre tres humble et tres obeissant Serviteur

PRE MALON

RC (ViW); endorsed by TJ and recorded in SJL as a letter of 5 June received on 17 June 1797. Enclosure not found.

To Thomas Mann Randolph

TH:J. TO TMR.   Philadelphia June 15. 97.

It was expected the last week that we might have risen on Saturday next. Those expectations are now pushed off to Saturday the 24th. and perhaps it may be even later than that. I conclude however that instead of sending off my chair and horses on Saturday the 24th. as I had desired, they must set out on Wednesday the 28th. so as to be at Fredericksburg Thursday evening of the 29th. This will enable me to get to our court which I am very anxious to do. Jupiter must come by Noah's and Chew's, that we may meet in the road should any accident carry me on sooner.—Our tobacco is sold at 10. Dollars. The first paiment being at 60. days I will contrive to get it negociated so that you may command the sum you desired by the time you desired. I shall be with you in time to advise you how to draw.   I have got your thermometer, compass &c. oiled silk cloak, cotton shirting: so that nothing remains of your commissions unexecuted except the springs which are in hand.

The new victory of Buonaparte, the equally splendid victories on the Rhine, the peace made between France and Austria, mutiny of the British fleet, and King's letters to his friends here recommending a pacific conduct towards France 'notwithstanding the continuance of her injustices towards us' are the most remarkeable foreign events. The bills prohibiting the exportation of arms and ammunition and preventing our citizens from engaging in armed vessels, have past both houses. The bill of the Senate for raising cavalry was yesterday thrown out on it's 2d reading by a vote of 15. to 13. That for manning the 3. frigates and buying 9. other vessels comes to it's 3d. reading to-day. If not rejected by the Senate, it will be by the Representatives when it goes to them.

They have a separate bill of their own as to the frigates and some gallies. The fortification bill is now before the representatives. It's fate a little doubtful. All the other war measures will I think be rejected. The folly of the convocation of Congress at so inconvenient a season, and at an expence of 60,000 D. is now confessed. Or rather it is evident that war was the object; because events having driven even it's advocates from that ground, it is evident there is nothing else to do.

P.M. The Senate have this day passed the bill concerning the frigates and other vessels on it's 3d. reading by a vote of 15. to 13. The representatives by 48 to 41. have voted that the fortification bill as amended in committee shall be read a third time. Probably therefore it will pass. Adieu affectionately.

RC (DLC); endorsed by Randolph. PrC (MHi); endorsed by TJ in ink on verso.

For the THERMOMETER and COMPASS TJ purchased for Randolph, see TJ to Randolph, 11 Mch. 1797. TJ paid $23.50 for OILED SILK great coats for himself and Randolph (MB, II, 961, 965).

To Aaron Burr

DEAR SIR   Philadelphia June 17. 1797

The newspapers give so minutely what is passing in Congress that nothing of detail can be wanting for your information. Perhaps however some general view of our situation and prospects since you left us may not be unacceptable. At any rate it will give me an opportunity of recalling myself to your memory, and of evidencing my esteem for you.   You well know how strong a character of division had been impressed on the Senate by the British treaty. Common error, common censure,[1] and common efforts of defence[2] had formed the treaty majority into a common band which feared to separate even on other subjects. Towards the close of the last Congress however it had been hoped that their ties began to loosen, and their phalanx to separate a little. This hope was blasted at the very opening of the present session by the nature of the appeal which the President made to the nation; the occasion for which had confessedly sprung from the fatal British treaty. This circumstance rallied them again to their standard and hitherto we have had pretty regular treaty votes[3] on all questions of principle.[4] And indeed I fear that as long as the same individuals remain, so long we shall see traces of the same division.   In the H. of Representatives the Republican body has also lost strength. The non-attendance of 5. or 6. of that description has left the majority very equivocal indeed. A few individuals of no fixed system at all,[5] governed by the panic or the prowess of the moment, flap as the breeze blows against the republican or the aristocratic bodies,[6] and give to the one or the other a preponderance entirely accidental. Hence the dissimilar aspect of the address and of the proceedings subsequent to that. The inflammatory composition of the speech excited sensations of resentment which had slept under British injuries,[7] threw the wavering into the war scale, and produced the war address. Buonaparte's victories and those on the Rhine, the Austrian peace, British bankruptcy, mutiny of the seamen, and Mr. King's exhortations to pacific measures have cooled them down again, and[8] the scale of peace preponderates. The threatening propositions therefore, founded in the address, are abandoned one by one, and the cry begins now to be that we have been called together to do nothing. The truth is, there is nothing to do, the idea of war being scouted by the events of Europe: but this only proves that war was the object for which we were called. It proves that the Executive temper was for war; and that the convocation of the Representatives was an experiment on the temper of the nation, to see if it was in unison.[9] Efforts at negociation indeed were promised;[10] but such a promise was as difficult to withold as easy to render nugatory. If negociation alone had been meant, that might have been pursued without so much delay, and[11] without calling the Representatives:[12] and if strong and earnest negociation had been meant, the additional nomination would have been of persons strongly and earnestly attached to the alliance of 1778. War then was intended. Whether abandoned or not, we must judge from future indications and events; for the same secrecy and mystery is affected to be observed by the present, which marked the former administration. I had always hoped that the popularity of the late president being once withdrawn from active effect, the natural feelings[13] of the people towards liberty would restore the equilibrium between the Executive and Legislative departments which had been destroyed by the superior weight and effect of that popularity; and that their natural feelings of moral obligation would discountenance the ungrateful predilection of the Executive[14] in favor of Great Britain. But unfortunately the preceding measures had already alienated the nation who was the object of them, had excited reaction from them, and this reaction[15] has on the minds of our citizens an effect which supplies that of the Washington popularity. This effect was sensible on some of the late Congressional elections, and this it is which has lessened the republican majority in Congress. When it will be reinforced must depend on events, and these are so incalculable, that I consider the future character of our republic as in the air;[16] indeed it's future fortunes will be in the air if war is made on us by France, and if Louisiana becomes a Gallo-American colony. I have been much pleased to see a dawn of change in the spirit of your state. The late elections have indicated something which, at a distance, we do not understand. However, what with the English influence in the lower and the Patroon influence in the upper parts of your state, I presume little is to be hoped. If a prospect could be once opened upon us of the penetration of truth into the Eastern states, if the people there, who are unquestionably republican, could discover that they have been duped into the support of measures calculated to sap the very foundations of republicanism, we might still hope for salvation, and that it would come, as of old, from the East. But will that region ever awake to the true state of things? Can the middle, Southern and Western states hold on till they awake? These are painful and doubtful questions: and if, in assuring me of your health, you can give me a comfortable solution of them, it will relieve a mind devoted to the preservation of our republican [17] government in the true form and spirit in which it was established, but [18] almost oppressed with apprehensions [19] that fraud will at length affect what force could [20] not, and that what with currents and countercurrents, we shall in the end be driven back to the land from which we launched 20. years ago. Indeed, my dear Sir, we have been but as a sturdy fish on the hook of a dexterous angler, who letting us flounce till we have spent our force, brings us up at last.—I am tired of the scene, and this day sennight shall change it [21] for one where, to tranquility of mind, may be added pursuits of private utility, since none public are admitted by the state of things.—I am with great & sincere esteem Dear Sir Your friend & servt

TH: JEFFERSON

P.S. Since writing the above we recieve a report that the French Directory has proposed a declaration of war against the US. to the Council of antients, who have rejected it. Thus we see two nations, who love one another affectionately brought by the ill temper of their Executive administrations to the very brink of a necessity to embrue their hands in the blood of each other.

PrC (DLC); at foot of first page: "Colo. Burr"; postscript written perpendicularly in margin of last page. Dft (DLC); heavily emended, the most significant changes being recorded in notes below. Probably enclosed in TJ to Henry Remsen, 17 June 1797.

THE APPEAL WHICH THE PRESIDENT MADE TO THE NATION: Adams's message of 16 May 1797 (see TJ to Thomas Bell, 18

May 1797). Although results elsewhere in the state perhaps did not promise the same DAWN OF CHANGE, in New York City the May ELECTIONS for state senators and assemblymen appeared to signal a noteworthy Republican gain in strength. The city's Republican leadership had endorsed Burr and twelve others as candidates for the assembly. Their opponents presented not a Federalist slate of candidates, but rather a "coalition" or "Federal Republican" ticket, which initially included some of the Republicans but dropped them just before the election. Republicans decried the maneuver as a deception, but their candidates easily won the assembly seats and they interpreted the Federalist tactic as a concession to rising Republican power in the city (Kline, *Burr*, I, 316-17n; Philadelphia *Aurora*, 3 June 1797).

Rumors of a proposed French DECLARATION OF WAR, attributed to unspecified letters from Boston, appeared in Philadelphia newspapers but were unconfirmed by information from Boston or France (*Philadelphia Gazette*, 16, 17 June 1797; Philadelphia *Aurora*, 17 June 1797).

[1] Word interlined in Dft in place of "abuse, common danger."

[2] Preceding two words interlined in Dft in place of "to defend their measures."

[3] In Dft TJ here wrote and canceled "of about 17. to 11. on almost every," then interlined and canceled "of 19. to 11. and would be if all were here 21. to 11."

[4] Preceding two words interlined in Dft in place of "⟨when this unhappy⟩ we are to see this unfortunate."

[5] In Dft TJ interlined the following passage, to the word "republican," in place of "no clear object to guide them [. . .] between the."

[6] In Dft remainder of sentence, preceded by canceled text "makes the one or the other the greater vote," is interlined, all in place of "[. . .] the balance according to the caprice of the moment."

[7] Preceding seven words interlined in Dft in place of "[. . .] which the British kicks and cuffs had never been able to reach."

[8] Remainder of sentence interlined in Dft in place of "they threw themselves into the scale originally adverse to war measures."

[9] In Dft TJ first wrote "to see how far it would ⟨support⟩ enter into their ⟨vision⟩ spirit of a fruitless negociation nugatory" before reworking the passage to read as above.

[10] Remainder of sentence interlined in Dft in place of "to soothe but these could be weak or strong at their own will."

[11] Preceding five words interlined in Dft.

[12] Word interlined in Dft in place of "larger branch of the legislature, the call of this could only be for war. Of those who are still earnest for bullying measures, many."

[13] Word interlined in Dft in place of "dispositions."

[14] In Dft TJ first wrote "would force the government to discountenance the Executives predilection" before altering the passage to read as above.

[15] Preceding six words interlined in Dft in place of "them to begin to act against us, and their hostile action has the."

[16] Word "republic" interlined in Dft in place of "government." Remainder of sentence interlined in Dft, where TJ first wrote "French colony" for "Gallo-American colony."

[17] Word interlined in Dft.

[18] In Dft TJ interlined this word in place of "and sickening with."

[19] Word interlined in Dft in place of "fear."

[20] In Dft remainder of letter, including postscript, is written perpendicularly in the margin.

[21] In Dft TJ first wrote "and shall ⟨desert⟩ [leave] it this day sennight" before altering the passage to read as above.

From John Gibson

DEAR SIR   Pittsburg June 17th 1797.

I have Been honoured with your letter of the 31st. ulto., which I shoud have answered by the return of the same post, But coud not procure a Copy of Logan's Speech, Before the post set out. I have since seen one in the American Encyclopædia, the Extract of which is said to be taken from your notes, and is, to the best of my recollection, nearly the

Substance of Logans Speech as delivered by him to me, and which I afterwards communicated to Lord Dunmore.

In the year 1774, I accompanied Lord Dunmore on his Expedition against the Shawnese towns on our arrival within 15 miles of them, we were met by a flag, and a white Man of the name of Elliot, the Chiefs of the Shawnese sent a Message to his Lordship, and requested that he woud halt the Army, and send some person in who understood their Language. I accordingly at the request of Lord Dunmore, and the whole of the Officers with him went in, on my arrival in the town, Logan came into the house where I was sitting, and asked me to walk out with him; we went into a Copse of Woods, when after Shedding abundance of tears, he delivered the Speech nearly as you have related in your notes. Genl. Morgan who is now in the City, will recollect my delivering it to Lord Dunmore on my return to the Camp. Capt. Cressap was not present when Logans relations were killed, But he certainly was present, when the Shawnese Chief whose name was Ben, was wantonly murdered and with whom some more fell; and he Capt. Cressap may be ultimately considered as the Cause of the War of 1774.

Shoud you wish to have any further communication on the Subject please to inform me.

I am sorry to find that so little Attention has Been paid to the Indians in General by Goverment as they will be a powerful Enemy against us shoud a War with France, which God Forbid, take place.

Shoud any thing offer in the Indian or any other Department, in which I can serve my Country, I shall Esteem it as a favour of you to mention my Name. I have the Honour to be, Dear Sir. with much respect, your most Obedient, humble Servant   JNO. GIBSON

RC (DLC); endorsed by TJ as received 22 June 1797 and so recorded in SJL.

SEEN ONE IN THE AMERICAN ENCY-CLOPÆDIA: portions of the *Encyclopaedia; or, A Dictionary of Arts, Sciences, and Miscellaneous Literature*, printed by Thomas Dobson of Philadelphia, were published separately prior to the appearance of the larger work in 1798. Two sections written or revised by Jedidiah Morse, but without his name on the title page, were issued in 1790 as *The History of America*, in which Logan's oration, its wording identical to that in TJ's *Notes on the State of Virginia* and with prefatory text taken from the *Notes*, appeared on pages 75-6 (Evans, Nos. 22486, 22682).

To Henry Remsen

DEAR SIR   Philadelphia June 17. 1797.

It is so long since I have made any paiment for the New York papers that I am entirely ignorant what my arrears are, and I have been so much engaged here hitherto that I have failed to make enquiry of you. Pray be so good as to let me know, and to do it immediately as I shall not be here after the 23d. inst. If you could take the trouble of enquiring of Mr. Freneau also what I owe him you will oblige me, and I will remit all together.—I am sorry nothing could be effected on the subject you once wrote me on. My will was not wanting, but it depended on others.—We have disagreeable news as to the dispositions of the French directory. Pray God it may all blow over and give us time to place our foreign affairs under safer arrangements for the future. Not having entire confidence in the post office, I think it safer for the inclosed to be put under your cover and recommended to your care. I am with constant esteem Dr. Sir Your friend & servt   TH: JEFFERSON

RC (CtY); at foot of text: "Mr. Henry Remsen." Enclosure: probably TJ to Aaron Burr, 17 June 1797.

For TJ's arrangement with Remsen for NEW YORK PAPERS, especially *Greenleaf's New York Journal, & Patriotic Register*, see TJ to Remsen, 17 Dec. 1795. TJ remitted $20.67 to Remsen, which probably included payment for *The Time Piece, and Literary Companion*, a newspaper established in New York in March 1797 by Philip FRENEAU (MB, II, 964, 1014). See Sowerby, Nos. 541 and 560. A letter from Remsen to TJ of 20 June 1797, recorded in SJL as received two days later, has not been found, and one from TJ to Remsen of 28 June 1797 is also missing. A letter from Freneau to TJ of 21 June 1797, which according to SJL was received the following day, has not been found.

From Peregrine Fitzhugh

DEAR SIR   Cottage Washington County (Md) June 20th. 97

I have been duly favored with your Letter of the 4th. Inst. and beg you to accept my thanks for the various interesting communications which it contains. I shall certainly avail myself of the information which you have been polite enough to give me on the subject of News papers. Bache's we already have, to this I will add Smiths when he begins to publish. We receive as you surmise the proceedings of Congress regularly here and have lamented extreamely their unfavorable aspect towards our Sister Republic. From the opinion which you entertained of the political principles of Mr. Adams when I had the pleasure to see you and from the friendly sentiments which his *Virgin* speech breathed for France I was led to hope that the session of Congress would have been opened by a Speech of a very different complexion from that which was delivered. I would not have had it less firm but more ingenuous, temperate and dignified. I think the President especially under his peculiar situation ought to have contented himself with a fair and candid communication to the two houses of the business which had induced him to

convene them at so unseasonable a time and have submitted the propriety of the measures to be adopted to their deliberations and decisions.
Instead of this He appears from his Labored and inflammatory performance to have entered into the party against France with all the warmth
which a County Court advocate inspired by the receipt of one good Fee
and the expectation of another would shew for the cause of his Client. I
was pleased with the reply of your honorable Body which indeed was
unexpected. It breathes I think a perfectly pacific tho at the same time
a firm and manly spirit and is couched in such general terms and with
so much caution as cannot be disgusting even to the executive Directory
of France who perhaps like our own executive has shewn too much
violence on the occasion of our differences. The address of the representatives seems if any thing to exceed in warmth the Speech from the
Throne. It is certainly full of *indignation*. Nay such appears to be the
spirit among the members for encounter that unwilling to wait the approach of the common Enemy they have at least *shewn* a great eagerness
to begin the conflict with each other. It is however to be hoped that their
national like their individual indignation will evaporate in Smoke.
Nothing could have manifested more strongly the Party spirit of our
President than his nomination of the Envoys to the French republic, and
if the strength of the contending Powers of Europe were tolerably equal
it would not be difficult to proph[esy] into which scale our weight
would be thrown but the case being far otherwise Our Commissioners
may deem it prudent to hold out a pacific instead of an haughty and
indignant Tone and be induced to make a virtue of necessity. Hence
Buonaparte will have proven himself a more able Negotiator for us than
those whom we have entrusted with our business and we shall feel ourselves indebted to the brilliant successes of that General rather than to
any natural disposition of our Envoys for an amicable adjustment of our
unfortunate differences.   The mode of Taxation which you have
suggested is very pleasing to me and I have found it highly so to every
one with whom I have conversed on the subject—besides the many advantages you have enumerated It will possess the important one of en-
suring punctuality in the receipt of the reven[ues] as I take for granted
the States will have too much pride ever to suffer themselves to be punished for delinquency by having the nation[al] Tax gatherers let loose
upon them—it will likewise fully meet the objections of that part of our
Countrymen who advocated in the General Convention the Doctrine of
"no direct taxation without previous requisition." I have barely seen
Mr. Luther Martins attack on the facts stated in the Notes on Virginia.
Our circulation has been very partial for I believe it has never appeared
in any of the Maryland or any other Papers except Fenno. The only

excuse which even his own Friends attempt to offer for his scurrilous and contemptible performance is that he must have been in a state of drunkenness from which he is scarcely ever free. You may be assured of my particular attention to your request on Cresops subject and of receiving the result of my inquiries and information. I find it the general opinion here that the murder of Logans Family was committed by a Party headed not by old Colo. Cresop but his son Michael who afterwards marched to Boston at the head of a Rifle Company and died in '76 at New York. This Man was the Father and not the Grand Father of *Mr. Martins Childrens Mother*. The following short history of the above malencholy event has been related to me by a Colo. Francis Deakins a Man of great respectability with us and whose probity is undoubted. He says that in the year 74 he was out on the Frontiers of this state engaged in laying off a Manor for the then Lord Proprietor and in executing other surveys when a Party headed by the above Gentleman came to his Camp on their way to the Indian territory and remained with him some days that they appeared in a state of intoxication when they came, continued so during their stay and departed in a similar state vowing destruction to every Indian they should meet—that about ten days or a Fortnight after they left him he received accounts of the above horrid Massacre and a few days after while he was still surveying he thinks from three to five hundred Men Women and Children passed his Camp— some half naked all half starved and in great consternation flying from their homes to avoid the just resentment of the Indians and that he had never since heard it either doubted or denied that the murder was committed by Cresops Party.   I had read with a mixture of indignation and Contempt the proceedings of the Grand Jury of the Federal Court of Virginia. The aristocratic Party have for time past manifested a disposition to encroach on the liberty of the Yeomen of this Country but they have hitherto proceeded with great tenderness and caution. They have however got more bold and in this last attempt have laid their ax at the root of the Tree—for whenever it shall be recognized as a constitutional doctrine that every Man is to be branded as an enemy to his Country who shall dare to speak or write with freedom on Men and measures the fair Fabric which has been erected at so great an expence of blood and Treasure will be erased and the freedom and independance of these United States vanish like mists before the Morning Sun. I shall not fail to use my endeavors to impress the federal grand Jurors which may be summoned to the next Term with the propriety of entering protestations against such proceedings. I am told that the People of your State have shewn a proper spirit on the occasion and that the

Grand Jury thought it prudent to acknowledge that they had err'd and to express their Sorrow for having done so—this if true is the only atonement they could make and may serve as a caution to future Grand Juries. I was surprized to find the name of Blair who had generally been esteemed a Man of Virtue and Talent at the head of the list of those transgressors of Justice. The Caution which you give me shall be duly attended to. I have ever held it a duty never to let any Friends Letter be subj[ect] to the public view but with his desire or consent and I beg leave to assure you Sir that any communications with which you have already or may be pleased in future to honor me shall be [treated?] as sacred. I shall direct this letter to you not in your public character lest you should have left Philadelphia before it reaches that place—in which case it might possibly be opened by other persons. You observe we have now a line of Stages thro our Country from Philada. to Winchester— they pass within 4 miles of me and I am told the whole road and County from the seat of Govmt. are delightful. With every possible respect I have the honor to be Dear Sir Yr. most obedt. & most humble Servant

PEREGNE. FITZHUGH

RC (DLC); several words obscured by tape; endorsed by TJ as received 1 July 1797 and so recorded in SJL.

For the ADDRESS OF THE REPRESENTATIVES, see TJ to Madison, 18 May 1797.

Book Dedication from Benjamin Smith Barton

SIR   Philadelphia, June 21st. 1797.

If the following pages were more perfect, and of course more worthy of your notice, I should have taken additional pleasure in inscribing them to you. Even, however, in their present imperfect state, I flatter myself that you will receive them as a testimony of my high sense of your talents and virtues, and of your eminent services to your country. The only dedications I ever wrote were to two persons whom I greatly esteemed and loved: the last to a common friend*, whose virtues and science endeared him to his country, and whose removal from among us, we shall long have occasion to deplore.

These pages are, with peculiar propriety, inscribed to you. I know not that any person has paid so much attention to the subject which they involve: I know no one who places an higher value upon the question

* David Rittenhouse.

[445]

which I have ventured to discuss. Although, in the progress of my inquiry, I have differed from you, in one or two essential points, I cannot suppose that on that account the investigation of the question will be the less agreeable to you. I am confident, from my personal acquaintance with you, that you are anxious for the discovery of truth, and ardent to embrace it, in whatever form it may present itself. It is the jewel which all good and wise men are in pursuit of. It is the *punctum saliens* of science.

I regret, with you, Sir, the evanishment of so many of the tribes and nations of America. I regret, with you, the want of a zeal among our countrymen for collecting materials concerning the history of these people. I regret the want of the necessary endeavours to introduce among those of them who have escaped the ravages of time, [instead of the vices and the miseries of half-civilized nations] the true principles of social order; the arts which conduce to the dignity and the happiness of mankind, and a rational and lasting system of morals and religion. Let it not be said, that they are incapable of improvement. Such an assertion can only suit those speculative philosophers who retire to their closets inveloped in a thick atmosphere of prejudices, which the strongest lights of truth cannot pervade. Natural History, which opens the door to so much precious knowledge concerning mankind, teaches us, that the physical differences between nations are but inconsiderable, and history informs us, that civilization has been constantly preceded by barbarity and rudeness. It teaches us, a mortifying truth, that nations may relapse into rudeness again; all their proud monuments crumbled into dust, and themselves, now savages, subjects of contemplation among civilized nations and philosophers. In the immense scheme of nature, which the feeble mind of man cannot fully comprehend, it may be our lot to fall into rudeness once more. There are good reasons for conjecturing, that the ancestors of many of the savage tribes of America are the descendants of nations who had attained to a much higher degree of polish than themselves. My inquiries, at least, seem to render it certain, that the Americans are not, as some writers have supposed, specifically different from the Persians, and other improved nations of Asia. The inference from this discovery is interesting and important. We learn that the Americans are susceptible of improvement.

If civilization be a blessing; if man by relinquishing the condition of the savage or barbarian, assumes a more independent station in the range of human affairs; if in proportion to his advancement to improvement (I speak not of a vicious refinement), he is even fitting himself for the enjoyment of higher comforts, of unmeasured happiness elsewhere; it is surely worthy the attention of the good and wise to endeavour to extend the empire of civility and knowledge among the numerous nations who are scattered over the countries of America. Individuals have often laboured in this business: but it seems to be of sufficient importance to engage the attention of whole nations; and it is peculiarly worthy of the notice of the United-States, who have exhibited the august spectacle of a people relinquishing their dependance, and moving with an unparalleled rapidity to the attainment of knowledge, and of arts.

I know not, Sir, whether ever the government of our country will think the civilization of the Indians a matter of as much importance as I do: but I must confess, that I derive a portion of my happiness from supposing that they will. Should I be disappointed, I shall have no occasion to look back, with pain or remorse, to the times when I have indulged my feelings on the subject. I have the honour to be, with the greatest respect, Dear Sir, your most obedient and humble servant, and affectionate friend,   BENJAMIN SMITH BARTON

Text from Benjamin Smith Barton, *New Views of the Origin of the Tribes and Nations of America* (Philadelphia, 1797), iii-vii; at head of text: "To Thomas Jefferson, L.L.D. Vice-President of the United-States of America; President of the Senate; and President of the American Philosophical Society"; brackets in original. See Evans, No. 31777, and Sowerby, No. 3998.

In the work introduced by the above dedication, Barton sought to document affinities between American Indian languages and those of the Old World, particularly Asia. His essay discussed the use of linguistic evidence to trace the origins of Native Americans, followed by vocabulary lists translating into English 54 key words of selected languages. Both in its conceptual basis—using comparative word lists to find relationships between peoples—and for vocabularies of Old World languages, Barton's work drew on that of Peter Simon Pallas (see Barton to TJ, 25 Oct. 1796).

PUNCTUM SALIENS: jumping off point.

From Aaron Burr

N York 21 June 1797

I thank you my dear Sir, I thank you sincerely for your letter. The Moment requires free communication among those who adhere to the principles of our Revolution.

The Conduct of some individuals of the Treaty Majority has disappointed me a good deal. That of the executive something also, but much less. From the insidious professions Which were made in Feby. and March I had been led to hope that a more temperate System would have been adopted. All such expectations are now abandoned. The gauntlet

I see is thrown and the fruit of our War with Britain is again in Jeopardy. The prospect is afflicting, but we must not dispond. It would not be easy neither would it be discreet, to answer your enquiries or to communicate to you my ideas with satisfaction to either of us, in the compass of a Letter. I will endeavor to do it in person. Let me hope to meet you in Philadelphia on Sunday. Accept this Apology and be assured of my entire attachment & Esteem   A. BURR

RC (DLC); at foot of text: "Thos. Jefferson Esqr."; endorsed by TJ as received 23 June 1797 and so recorded in SJL.

YOUR LETTER: TJ to Burr, 17 June 1797.

To Elbridge Gerry

MY DEAR FRIEND   Philadelphia June 21. 97.

It was with infinite joy to me that you were yesterday announced to the Senate as envoy extraordinary jointly with Genl. Pinckney and Mr. Marshel to the French republic. It gave me certain assurance that there would be a preponderance in the mission sincerely disposed to be at peace with the French government and nation. Peace is undoubtedly at present the first object of our nation. Interest and honor are also national considerations. But interest, duly weighed, is in favor of peace even at the expence of spoliations past and future; and honor cannot now be an object. The insults and injuries committed on us by both the belligerent parties from the beginning of 1793. to this day, and still continuing by both,[1] cannot now be wiped off by engaging in war with one of them. As there is great reason to expect this is the last campaign in Europe, it would certainly be better for us to rub thro this year as we have done through the four preceding ones, and hope that on the restoration of peace we may be able to establish some plan for our foreign connections more likely to secure our peace, interest and honor in future. Our countrymen have divided themselves by such strong affections to the French and the English, that nothing will secure us internally but a divorce from both nations. And this must be the object of every real American, and it's attainment is practicable without much self-denial. But for this, peace is necessary. Be assured of this, my dear Sir, that if we engage in a war during our present passions and our present weakness in some quarters, that our union runs the greatest risk of not coming out of that war in the shape in which it enters it. My reliance for our preservation is in your acceptance of this mission. I know the tender circumstances which will oppose themselves to it. But it's duration will be short, and

[448]

it's reward long. You have it in your power by accepting and determining the character of the mission to secure the present peace and eternal union of your country. If you decline, on motives of private pain, a substitute may be named who has enlisted his passions in the present contest and by the preponderance of his vote in the mission may entail on us calamities, your share in which and your feelings will outweigh whatever pain a temporary absence from your family could give you. The sacrifice will be short, the remorse would be never-ending. Let me then my dear Sir conjure your acceptance, and that you will by this act, seal the mission with the confidence of all parties. Your nomination has given a spring to hope, which was dead before.—I leave this place in three days, and therefore shall not here have the pleasure of learning your determination. But it will reach me in my retirement and enrich the tranquility of that scene. It will add to the proofs which have convinced me that the man who loves his country on it's own account, and not merely for it's trappings of interest or power, can never be divorced from it; can never refuse to come forward when he finds that she is engaged in dangers which he has the means of warding off. Make then an effort, my friend, to renounce your domestic comforts for a few months, and reflect that to be a good husband and a good father at this moment you must be also a good citizen. With sincere wishes for your acceptance & success I am with unalterable esteem Dear Sir Your affectionate friend & servt   Th: Jefferson

RC (CtY); addressed: "Elbridge Gerry esq. Boston"; franked, stamped, and postmarked; endorsed by Gerry. PrC (DLC).

For Gerry's appointment as ENVOY EXTRAORDINARY, see note to Senate Resolution on Appointment of Charles C. Pinckney, [5 June 1797].

A letter from Gerry to TJ, written on 2 June 1797 and received from Cambridge, Massachusetts, on the 9th, is recorded in SJL but has not been found.

[1] Preceding two words interlined; emendation lacking in PrC.

From Sir John Sinclair

SIR

Board of Agriculture Whitehall
21. June 1797.

I have much pleasure in acquainting you, that at the last meeting of the Board of Agriculture, you were admitted a Foreign Honorary Member of that Board, an honour to which your zeal for the improvement of agriculture so justly entitles you, and which I have no doubt will prove an additional inducement, to your assisting the Board in bringing that most valuable Art to its highest state of perfection. Any communication from you will always be received by the Board with every proper attention. With esteem, I have the honour to be Your faithful and Obedient Servant

JOHN SINCLAIR
President

RC (DLC); in a clerk's hand, signed by Sinclair; at foot of text: "His Excellency Thomas Jefferson. &c &c &c"; endorsed by TJ as received 22 Sep. 1797 and so recorded in SJL.

TJ received a resolution of the British BOARD OF AGRICULTURE dated 20 June 1797, thanking him for his promise to send the Board a "Specimen of the Agricultural

Implements of America on an improved construction, which will be peculiarly acceptable" (printed form at DLC; with blanks filled by a clerk; signed by Sinclair; bearing seal; at foot of text in clerk's hand: "His Excellency Thomas Jefferson &c &c &c"). For TJ's diploma from the British Board of Agriculture, see enclosure listed at Rufus King to TJ, 22 Aug. 1797.

To James Madison

Philadelphia June 22. 97.

The Senate have this day rejected their own bill for raising a provisional army of 15,000. men. I think they will reject that for permitting private vessels to arm. The Representatives have thrown out the bill of the Senate for raising artillery. They yesterday put off one forbidding our citizens to serve in foreign vessels of war, till Nov. by a vote of 52. to 44. This day they came to a resolution proposing to the Senate to adjourn on Wednesday the 28th. by a majority of 4. Thus it is now perfectly understood that the convocation of Congress is substantially condemned by their several decisions that nothing is to be done. I may be with you somewhat later than I had expected. Say from the 1st. to the 4th.—Preliminaries of peace between Austria and France are signed.—Dana has declined the mission to France. Gerry is appointed in his room, being supported in Senate by the republican vote. 6. nays of the opposite description. No news of Monroe or Paine. Adieu à revoir.

RC (DLC: Madison Papers, Rives Collection); unsigned; at foot of text: "Mr. Madison." PrC (DLC).

On 16 June 1797, William L. Smith reported a bill prohibiting United States CITI-

ZENS from serving on FOREIGN VESSELS or entering the military of any foreign power. The House debated the bill on 20 and 21 June 1797 before deciding to postpone action on it until the next session (JHR, III, 36, 39-42; Annals, VII, 349-57).

To Thomas Mann Randolph

Th:J. to TMR.   Philadelphia June 22. 97.

The Senate have this day thrown out their own bill for raising 15,000 men as a provisional army. I think they will also reject the bill for permitting private ships to arm. The Representatives rejected the bill from the Senate for raising artillery, and have this day by resolution proposed to the Senate to adjourn on Wednesday the 28th. Under present appearances I may by possibility be 3. or 4. days later in getting home than I had expected. I still count however on being with you from the 2d. to the 6th. of July. A separate peace between Austria and France is signed preliminarily.—Dana has declined the mission to France and Gerry is appointed in his room: a good exchange.—My love to Martha and Maria. Salutations & Adieu affectionately.

RC (DLC); endorsed by Randolph as received 1 July 1797. PrC (MHi).

To John Gibson

Dear Sir   Philadelphia June 24 .97.

I have to thank you for your favor of the 17th inst. and the [infor]mation it contained, but have still to trouble you for an explanation [of a] passage in [which?] you say 'Capt Cressop was not present when [Logan's relations] were killed.' How then are we to understand that passage in Logan's speech which says 'Colo. Cressop the last year in cold blood and unprovoked killed all the relations of Logan, not sparing even my women and children.' I must trouble you once more for information as to this. I remember that the narration (which came I think from Ld. Dunmore on his return to Williamsburg) made Cressap the head of the party which destroyed Logan's family. But you must know this best.

Congress are negativing all the propositions which look towards a war with France, so that I hope that evil will be avoided. They propose to rise on the 28th.

Long acquainted with your merit I should certainly omit no opportunity of availing my country of it. Be so good as to direct your answer to me at Monticello near Charlottesville, and if you have any post line to Winchester it will come to me directly from thence. I am with great esteem Dear Sir Your most obedt. servt   Th: Jefferson

PrC (DLC); faded; at foot of text: "Genl. Gibson."

[451]

From Luther Martin

SIR   Baltimore, June 24th, 1797.

In your notes on Virginia, combating certain sentiments of the celebrated Buffon, you have given us an eulogium of the *North American savages*, and, to establish their eminence in oratory, have introduced the *speech* of Logan (whom *you* have dubbed a Mingo chief) to lord Dunmore, when governor of Virginia;—a morsel of eloquence, in your opinion, not to be excelled by *any* passage in the orations of Demosthenes, Cicero, or of any more eminent orator, if Europe has furnished more eminent. And, that your reader might be the better enabled to distinguish all its superiority of lustre, you have given him the following preliminary statement of incidents: "In the spring of the year 1774, (you say) a robbery and murder were committed on an inhabitant of the frontiers of Virginia, by two Indians of the Shawanese tribe. The neighbouring whites, according to their custom, undertook to punish this outrage in a summary way. Col. Cresap, a man *infamous* for the *many murders* he had committed on those much injured people, collected a party and proceeded down the Kanaway, in quest of Vengeance. Unfortunately, a canoe of women and children, with one man only, was seen coming from the opposite shore, unarmed, and unsuspecting an hostile attack from the whites. Cresap and his party concealed themselves on the bank of the river, and the moment the canoe reached the shore, singled out their objects, and at one fire killed every person in it. This happened to be the family of Logan, who had long been distinguished as the friend of the whites. This unworthy return provoked his vengeance. He accordingly signalized himself in the war which ensued. In the autumn of the same year, a decisive battle was fought, at the mouth of the Great Kanhaway, between the collected forces of the Shawanese, Mingoes and Delawares, and a detachment of the Virginia militia. The Indians were defeated and sued for peace. Logan, however, disdained to be seen among the suppliants. But lest the sincerity of a treaty should be distrusted, from which so distinguished a chief absented himself, he sent by a messenger the following speech to be delivered to Lord Dunmore."

This story and *that speech*, of Logan having been selected by Mr. Fennel in his readings and recitations, moral, critical, and entertaining, induced me to address to that gentleman a letter on the subject, which perhaps you may not have *seen*, for I know not whether you are in the habit of reading the news-papers; but that you may, if you please, have an *opportunity of seeing* it, permit me to refer you to the 26th number of Porcupine's Gazette, printed in the city of Philadelphia, in which paper a copy of my letter was published.

To the world at large, and to every individual interested, *you*, as an historian, *must* be considered *answerable*, that the *speech* of Logan is *genuine*, *unadulterated*, and not a *fiction*. And as, that the beauty and excellence of that speech might be the more clearly perceived, you thought good to enter into a detail of facts. To the world, and to every person interested, *you must*, as an historian, be considered answerable for the *truth* of those facts.

I *first* became acquainted with col. Cresap in the year 1772. I was then on a journey to Fort Pitt. Col. Cresap was at that time living at his seat by Old Town. He was *never* on the west side of the Allegany mountains from that day until his death. Nor was Logan's family killed on the Kanhaway, but at the mouth of Yellow Creek, on the east side of the Ohio river, and about forty or fifty miles above Fort Wheelan. And as you have so much mistook the *place* where the transactions happened, which, by the by, is a little remarkable in an *enlightened* historian, volunteering on events which happened in the state where he lived, and those too of so recent a date, it is not very improbable, that you have been equally mistaken in the *person*, or in the *title* of the person, whom you have fixed on as the principal personage in those transactions. Although the Cresaps all lived within a few hundred yards of your state, and the north branch of Potowmack, one of its boundaries ran through their possessions. I will therefore take no advantage of any error you may have made in the designatio personæ, but will give you full liberty to select, out of the *whole family*, the individual on whom you wish to fix the charge.

And now, Sir, to lay the proper foundation for the further investigation of this subject, permit me to request, and not only to request, but to *expect*, your answer to the following questions.

1st, From what document did you copy the speech of Logan; or from whom did you receive your information of that speech, and of its contents?

2d, What person was meant to be designated by the *title* and *name* of Col. Cresap, as used by *Logan* in his *speech*, and by *yourself*, in your *statement of the incidents* necessary for the better understanding that speech?

3d, Whence did you procure your information that Col. Cresap, or *any person of that name* was "infamous for the many murders he had committed on the much injured Indians?" When and where were those murders committed? and who of those "much injured people" were the victims?

It is not in the human heart to feel that I need an apology for proposing to you these questions; but, if an apology was wanting I have it:—In

[453]

two amiable daughters, a parent may at least be pardoned for thinking them such, who are directly descended from *that man*, whose character your pen, I hope from no worse motive than to support a philosophical hypothesis, has endeavoured to stigmatise with *indelible infamy!* a variety of circumstances have combined to give an *unmerited* celebrity, and extensiveness of diffusion to an *unfounded calumny*. This calumny *I will efface*.

The letter I have written on this subject to Mr. Fennel; the letter I now address to you, and *all* those which I shall hereafter address to you on the same subject, I shall transmit to the authors of the Annual Register in Great Britain, by them to be published; and to the Rev. Mr. Morse, to Mr. Lendrum, and to every other author, by whom the speech and story of Logan may have been copied from your *Notes*, will I also send *the same* to be hereafter inserted by them in a republication of their works.

If my directions are complied with, this will be delivered you immediately on the rising of Congress; for I would not wish to take off your attention one single moment from the concerns of the public, while Congress is in session. With *due* respect, I am, Sir, Your obedient servant, Luther Martin

Text from *Porcupine's Gazette*, 17 July 1797; subjoined to a letter from Martin to William Cobbett, 24 June 1797, which reads: "The letter of which I enclose you a copy, will be delivered to Mr. Jeferson immediately after the rising of congress. You will greatly oblige me by having the copy published, if possible, on the evening of the day when congress shall rise"; at head of text: "Copy"; addressed: "To the honourable Thomas Jefferson, Esq. Vice President of the United States."

More than once the prominent Maryland attorney Luther Martin (ca. 1748-1826) was a thorn in TJ's side. A native of New Jersey, Martin graduated from the College of New Jersey at Princeton in 1766. After teaching school in Maryland and Virginia he was admitted to the bar at Williamsburg in 1771 and commenced the practice of law in Somerset County, Maryland. In 1778 he became attorney general of Maryland, a position he held until 1805. A delegate to the Federal Convention in 1787, he did not sign the Constitution and vigorously opposed ratification. His marriage to Maria Cresap, who died in November 1796, led him in 1797-98 to challenge TJ's rendition, in the

Notes on the State of Virginia, of Logan's famous speech. He prominently aligned himself against TJ by acting as counsel for the defense during Samuel Chase's impeachment trial in 1805 and again in Aaron Burr's trial for treason in 1807. Serving again as attorney general of Maryland, 1818-20, he represented the state before the Supreme Court in the famous suit of McCulloch v. Maryland. Debilitated by broken health and alcoholism, in 1822 he was the beneficiary of a special license fee levied on attorneys in Maryland. He spent his last years in Burr's household. In 1807 a frustrated TJ, believing Martin to be complicit with Burr in some fashion, called him "this unprincipled and impudent federal bull-dog" (ANB; Clarkson and Jett, *Luther Martin*, 170, 206; TJ to George Hay, 19 June 1807).

THE SPEECH OF LOGAN and Martin's criticism of TJ's use of it are discussed in TJ to John Gibson, 31 May 1797. The above letter is the first that Martin addressed to TJ on the subject. After an interval of some months it was followed by others dated 11 Dec. 1797, 1, 8, 14 Jan., 3, 14, and 26 Feb. 1798. Martin sent each to *Porcupine's Gazette* and other newspapers (see, for example, the *Federal Gazette & Baltimore Daily*

Advertiser, 22 July 1797). In only one instance, that of 11 Dec. 1797, have the Editors found a manuscript version, and that letter is also the only one of the published series that is recorded in SJL. One from Martin to TJ of 20 July 1797, received from Baltimore on 31 July, is recorded in SJL but has not been found.

WHOM YOU HAVE DUBBED A MINGO CHIEF: Logan was a war leader but not a lineage chief with a leadership role in civil governance. His father, an Oneida chief, and an older brother had represented the Mingos in diplomatic relations with the colony of Pennsylvania (White, *Middle Ground*, 358; ANB, XIII, 836). In 1800 TJ altered the PRELIMINARY STATEMENT OF INCIDENTS, quoted by Martin above, with which he introduced Logan's address in the *Notes on the State of Virginia*; see note to TJ to John Gibson, 31 May 1797. FROM WHAT DOCUMENT DID YOU COPY THE SPEECH OF LOGAN:

see TJ to John Henry, 31 Dec. 1797. Concerning the TITLE AND NAME of the Cresap accused by Logan, see note to TJ to Gibson, 31 May 1797. DIRECTLY DESCENDED FROM THAT MAN: Martin had three surviving children, all daughters, who were grandchildren of Captain Michael Cresap and great-grandchildren of Colonel Thomas Cresap (Clarkson and Jett, *Luther Martin*, 57). ANNUAL REGISTER: Logan's speech and TJ's prefatory remarks to it were reprinted from the *Notes on Virginia*, not always with precise attribution, in *The Annual Register . . . For the Year 1787* (London, 1789), *American Universal Geography* of Jedidiah MORSE (Boston, 1793), and the *Concise and Impartial History of the American Revolution* of John LENDRUM (Boston, 1795). IMMEDIATELY ON THE RISING OF CONGRESS: for TJ's departure from Philadelphia prior to the adjournment of Congress, see note to TJ to John Strode, 14 June 1797.

To Edward Rutledge

MY DEAR SIR   Philadelphia June 24. 97.

I have to acknolege your two favors of May 4. and 19. and to thank you for your attention to the commissions for the peas and oranges, which I learn are arrived in Virginia.[1] Your draught I hope will soon follow on Mr. John Barnes merchant here, who, as I before advised you, is directed to answer it.

When Congress first met, the assemblage of facts presented in the President's speech with the multiplied accounts of spoliations by the French West Indians appeared, by sundry votes on the address, to incline a majority to put themselves into a posture of war. Under this influence the address was formed and it's spirit would probably have been pursued by corresponding measures, had the events of Europe been of an ordinary train. But this has been so extraordinary that numbers have gone over to those, who, from the first, feeling with sensibility the French insults, as they had felt those of England before, thought now, as they thought then, that war measures should be avoided and those of peace pursued. Their favorite engine, on the former occasion, was *commercial regulations*,[2] in preference to negociation, to war preparations and increase of debt. On the latter, as we have no commerce with France, the restriction of which could press on them, they wished for negociation. Those of the opposite sentiment had, on the former occasion, preferred negociation; but at the same time voted for great war-preparations and increase of debt: now also they were for negociation, war preparation and debt. The parties have in debate mutually charged each other with inconsistency, and with being governed by an attachment to this or that of the belligerent nations, rather than the dictates of reason and pure Americanism. But in truth both have been consistent: the same men having voted for war measures now who did before, and the same against them now who did before. The events of Europe coming to us in astonishing and rapid succession, to wit, the public bankruptcy of England, Buonaparte's successes, the successes in the Rhine, the Austrian peace, mutiny of the British fleet, Irish insurrection, a demand of 43. millions for the current services of the year,[3] and above all the warning voice, as is said,[4] of Mr. King to abandon all thought of connection with Great Britain, that she is going down irrecoverably, and will sink us also if we do not clear ourselves, have brought over several to the pacific party,[5] so as at present to give majorities against all threatening measures. They go on with their frigates and fortifications because they were going on with them before. They direct 80,000 of their militia to hold themselves in readiness for service. But they reject the propositions to raise cavalry, artillery and a provisional army, and to trust private ships with arms in the present combustible state of things. They believe the present is the last campaign of Europe and[6] wish to [rub?][7] through this fragment of a year as they have through the four preceding ones, opposing patience to insult, and interest to honor. They will therefore immediately adjourn. This is indeed a most humiliating state of things. But it commenced in 93. Causes have been adding to causes, and effects accumulating on effects, from that time to this. We had in 93. the most respectable[8] character in the universe. What the neutral nations think of us now I know not: but we are low indeed with the belligerents. Their kicks and cuffs prove their contempt.[9] If we weather the present storm[10] I hope we shall avail ourselves of the calm[11] of peace to place our foreign connections[12] under a new and different arrangement. We must make the interest of every nation stand surety for it's justice, and their own loss to follow injury to us, as effect follows it's cause. As to every thing except commerce, we ought to[13] divorce ourselves from them all. But this system would require time, temper, wisdom and occasional sacrifices of interest: and how far all of these will be ours, our children may see, but we shall not. The passions are too high at present to be cooled in our day. You and I have formerly seen warm debates and high political passions.[14] But gentlemen of different politics would then speak to each other, and separate the business of the senate from that of[15] society. It is not so now. Men who have been intimate all their lives cross the streets to avoid meeting, and turn their heads another way, lest they should be obliged to touch their hat. This may do for young men, with whom passion is enjoiment. But it is afflicting to peaceable minds. [16] Tranquility is the old man's milk. I go to enjoy it in a few days, and to exchange the roar and tumult of bulls and bears for the prattle of my grandchildren and senile rest. Be these yours, my dear friend, through long years, with every other blessing, and the attachment of friends as warm and sincere as [17] Your's affectionately

TH: JEFFERSON

PrC (DLC); at foot of first page: "E. Rutledge esq." Dft (DLC); with one significant variation (see note 2 below); with numerous emendations, the most important of which are noted below.

The House of Representatives passed the MILITIA bill on 20 June 1797 and the Senate concurred two days later (JHR, III, 38; JS, II, 375).

[1] In Dft TJ here continued the sentence and then canceled "where I shall my self join them in a few days."

[2] In Dft TJ wrote "restrictions."

[3] In Dft TJ wrote the passage from this point to "clear ourselves" in the margin.

[4] TJ interlined the preceding three words in Dft.

[5] In Dft TJ first wrote "to the moderate party a number of individuals" before altering the passage to read as above.

[6] TJ here canceled "hope" in Dft.

[7] Possibly "rule."

[8] Preceding two words interlined in Dft in place of "first."

[9] Sentence interlined in Dft.

[10] In Dft TJ wrote "If we escape the present danger" before altering the passage to read as above.

[11] Interlined in Dft in place of "leisure."

[12] In Dft TJ first wrote "on such arrangement as may make it the interest of other nations to be just to us, and that injustice shall bring on them loss as an immediate and necessary effect and that."

[13] Preceding two words interlined in Dft in place of "may."

[14] In Dft TJ first wrote "We have formerly seen ⟨high⟩ warm debates and great political differences" before altering the sentence to read as above.

[15] In Dft TJ interlined the preceding eight words in place of "politics and."

[16] In Dft TJ wrote "But it is too much for me" before altering the sentence to read as above.

[17] In Dft TJ first wrote "May these be yours ⟨with⟩ through long years, with every other blessing of life, and the affection of a thousand friends as warm and sincere as Dear Sir" before altering the closing to read as above.

From Van Staphorst & Hubbard

SIR   Amsterdam 26 June 1797.

We have before us your very esteemed favors of 27 and 28 March.

Accept our hearty thanks for your kind and friendly interference in procuring an Act aggregating us to the Citizenship of the State of Virginia, And be assured, We shall ever be happy on all occasions to testify our gratitude to You and to the State. As matters have turned out in this Country it is little probable We shall have occasion to avail ourselves of it: If We should, Your recommendation could not fail to fix our minds upon Norfolk, for our future residence, and whenever We can be useful to direct business to that port or to your State, We shall seize the opportunity eagerly and avail ourselves of it with Zeal and perseverance.

We have never been Gamblers in any of the Objects, which have caused the failure of many American Speculators. Our purchases of Stocks, Lands &c. have always been for permanent investments, or to derive profit from them, by the rise of property, naturally to be expected from the growing population and industry of your Country: such a commerce We deemed highly justifiable, and even advantageous to the United States, as furnishing the means to their Inhabitants, to anticipate the enjoyment of the prosperity they are susceptible of obtaining. All Stock jobbing, Purchases on Credit, Strained operations, and other things of this kind that have brought on the ruin of numerous families, at Same time they have tended to diminish the Love and attachment for Slow regular trade and industry, We reprobate so strongly as you can possibly do.

The condition You fix to any Services you can render us, insure us them to the fullest plenitude of our desire. Being incapable of asking what We deem indiscreet or improper, We shall always wish for a refusal, when We unknowingly might apply for whatever could be ranged under those denominations.

We are perfectly satisfied with the Bonds you have furnished us $1,000.—payable 1 October 1800.

1,000.—payable 1 October 1801 and not November as expressed in Your letter for the Monies paid you by Messrs. Harrison & Sterett of Philadelphia, against your Bills on us.

In pursuance of your desire, We inclose your account Current, the Balance whereon due by you to us, Hd. Cy. ƒ2,026.12.—We transfer to your debit in a new account.

Judging You may not have all your old papers by You, We have directed your account to be transcribed from the commencement of your opening one with us. Sincerely wishing You the enjoyment of Health Happiness and prosperity, We remain ever with greatest Esteem Sir! Your mo. ob. hb. servants

N. & J. VAN STAPHORST & HUBBARD

RC (DLC); in a clerk's hand, signed by the firm; at foot of first page: "The Honble. Thos. Jefferson Esqe."; endorsed by TJ as received 22 Sep. 1797 and so recorded in SJL. Dupl (same); in a clerk's hand, signed by the firm; at head of text: "(Dupl:) Orig: via New York ⅌. 3 friends. Grimes"; endorsed by TJ as received 13 Dec. 1797 and so recorded in SJL. Enclosure not identified, but likely the account described in note

to second letter of Van Staphorst & Hubbard to TJ of 10 Oct. 1795 (Vol. 28: 502n), which refers in its final entry to a balance of ƒ2,026.12 transferred to TJ's "Debit in new account."

A letter from Jacob Van Staphorst to TJ, dated 30 May 1797 and received from Paris on 13 Dec., is recorded in SJL but has not been found.

To Andrew G. Fraunces

SIR   Philadelphia, June 27, 1797.

It would have highly gratified me had it been in my power to furnish the relief you ask: but I am preparing for my departure and find, on winding up my affairs, that I shall not have one dollar to spare. It is therefore with sincere regret I have nothing better to tender than the sentiments of good will of Sir, Your most obedient servant,

TH. JEFFERSON

MS not found; reprinted from Hamilton, *Observations*, Appendix No. XLIV.

Andrew G. Fraunces, son of Samuel Fraunces, proprietor of Fraunces Tavern in New York City and Washington's steward while he was president, served as principal clerk of the Treasury Department from 1789 until 1793, when it is not clear whether he resigned or was dismissed. Shortly thereafter he charged Alexander Hamilton with speculation in government securities (Washington, *Papers: Pres. Ser.*, II, 438n, IV, 375-6n). For Fraunces's dispute with Hamilton and for the circumstances which led to Hamilton's publication of this and the subsequent letter from TJ to Fraunces of 28 June 1797, see Appendix on the first conflict in the cabinet, Vol. 18: 658-

9n, 687-8n. Later in the year a list of queries of Fraunces to Hamilton appeared in the newspapers which included the following regarding Hamilton's acquisition of TJ's letters: "Did you not in July last inveigle one of my letters from the vice president, of the 27th and 28th day of June last, when I, distracted from the sudden death of my infant, believing from your own words, that you, feeling the misery you had brought on me, and meant the exposure of them to Mr. Church only for my interest?" (*The Times. Alexandria Advertiser*, 27 Oct. 1797). See also John Barnes to TJ, 3 Oct. 1797.

Despite TJ's assertion that he had NOT ONE DOLLAR TO SPARE, entries in his financial memoranda for 26 and 28 June 1797 indicate that he gave Fraunces four dollars "in charity" on both days (MB, II, 964).

To Edmund Randolph

DEAR SIR   Philadelphia June 27. 97.

I have to acknolege the receipt of your two favors of May 26. and 29. which came to hand in due time and relieved my mind considerably, tho' it was not finally done. During the vacation we may perhaps be able to hunt up the letters which are wanting, and get this tornado, which has been threatening us, dissipated.

You have seen the speech and the address, so nothing need be said on them. The spirit of both has been so whittled down by Buonaparte's victories, the victories on the Rhine, the Austrian peace, Irish insurgency, English bankruptcy, insubordination of the fleet &c. that Congress is rejecting one by one the measures brought in on the principles of their own address. But nothing less than such miraculous events as have been pouring in on us from the first of our convening could have assuaged the fermentation produced in men's minds. In consequence of these events what was the majority at first, is by degrees become the minority, so that we may say that in the Representatives, moderation will govern. But nothing can establish firmly the republican principles of our government, but an establishment of them in England. France will be the apostle for this. We very much fear that Gerry will not accept the mission to Paris. The delays which have attended this measure have left a dangerous void in our endeavors to preserve peace, which can scarcely be reconciled to a wish to preserve it. I imagine we shall rise from the 1st. to the 3d. of July. I am Dear Sir Your friend & servt

TH: JEFFERSON

P.S. The interception of letters is becoming so notorious, that I am forming a resolution of declining correspondence with my friends through the channel of the post altogether.

PrC (DLC); at foot of text "E. Randolph."

Randolph's TWO FAVORS of 26 and 29 May, recorded in SJL as received 1 and 3 June 1797, respectively, have not been found. SJL records another nine letters exchanged with Randolph between 31 Jan. 1796 and 3 May 1797, all of which are missing.

To Andrew G. Fraunces

SIR   Philadelphia, June 28, 1797.

I know well that you were a clerk in the Treasury Department while I was in the office of Secretary of State; but as I had no relation with the interior affairs of that office, I had no opportunity of being acquainted with you personally, except the single occasion on which you called on me. The length of time you were in the office affords the best presumption in your favour, and the particular misunderstanding which happened to you with your principals may account for your not having obtained from them those certificates of character which I am not able to supply. I doubt not however that a knowledge of your conduct wherever you establish yourself will soon render all certificates unnecessary, and I sincerely wish you may obtain employment which may evince and reward good conduct. I am, Sir, Your very humble servant,

TH. JEFFERSON

MS not found; reprinted from Hamilton, *Observations*, Appendix No. XLV.

To James Madison

Philadelphia June 29. 97.

The day of adjournment walks before us like our shadow. We shall rise on the 3d. or 4th. of July. Consequently I shall be with you about the 8th. or 9th. The two houses have jointly given up the 9. small vessels. The Senate have rejected at the 3d reading their own bill authorizing the President to lay embargoes. They will probably reject a very unequal tax passed by the Repr. on the venders of wines and spirituous liquors (not in retail). They have past a bill for postponing their next meeting to the constitutional day; but whether the Repr. will concur is uncertain. The Repr. are cooking up a stamp tax which it is thought themselves will reject. The fate of the bill for private armaments is yet undecided in the Senate. The expences of the session are estimated at 80,000 Doll.—Monroe and family arrived here the day before yesterday, well. They will make a short visit to N. York and then set their faces homewards. My affectionate respects to Mrs. Madison, and salutations to yourself. Adieu.

RC (DLC: Madison Papers); unsigned. PrC (DLC); endorsed in ink by TJ on verso.

On 24 June, Senator Jacob Read introduced a bill AUTHORIZING THE PRESIDENT TO LAY EMBARGOES during the congressional recess. It was defeated by a vote of 12 to 15 three days later (JS, II, 376, 379). The VERY UNEQUAL TAX on wines and spirits was passed by the House and sent to the Senate on the 27th in a bill entitled "An act laying duties on licenses for selling foreign wines and foreign distilled spirituous liquors by retail." On 5 July, after several days of debate, the Senate passed the bill with amendments and sent it back to the House. After some discussion the next day, the House voted to postpone further action on the legislation until the fall session of Congress (JS II, 378-84, 386; JHR, III, 70-1).

On 28 June, the Senate passed a BILL FOR POSTPONING THEIR NEXT MEETING to the first Monday in December rather than the first Monday in November as approved in the previous session of Congress. After debate in the House the next day, the date was set for the second Monday in November, to which the Senate concurred (JS, II, 378-81; Annals, VII, 408; U.S. Statutes at Large, I, 507, 525).

The STAMP TAX, a "bill laying duties on stamped vellum, parchment, and paper," was introduced by William L. Smith, as chairman of the House ways and means committee, on 17 June. Following lengthy debates between 26 June and 3 July, the bill was passed by a 47 to 41 vote and sent to the Senate where it quickly passed without amendment, by a 20 to 7 vote. During the next session of Congress, the commencement date of this tax was postponed from 1 Jan. to 1 July 1798 (JS II, 382, 385; JHR, III, 36, 60-5; Annals, VII, 386-433; U.S. Statutes at Large, I, 527, 536).

To Thomas Mann Randolph

Th:J. to TMR.   Philadelphia June 29. 97

The day of adjournment walks before us like our shadow. It will not take place till the 3d. or 4th. of July. Consequently I shall not be at home till the 10th. or 11th.—Yours of the 19th. inst. came to hand on the 27th.   We still go on undoing what in the beginning of the session had been too ardently begun. A bill to authorize the President to lay embargoes, brought into the Senate, has been thrown out by themselves. A very unequal and oppressive tax on merchants selling wines and other liquors (not in retail) passed by the Representatives, will, I think, be rejected by the Senate. The Representatives are cooking up a stamp tax, which it is thought they will themselves reject. We have jointly given up the 9 small vessels which were to have been bought at an expence of half a million. The expences of this session are about 80,000.D.   Monroe and family arrived here on the 27th. They will make a short visit to N. York and then come on to Albemarle.—My love to my dear daughters and the little ones. Adieu affectionately

PrC (MHi).

Randolph's letter of the 19TH INST., recorded in SJL as received from Monticello on 27 June 1797, has not been found. Randolph's letter of 12 June 1797, recorded in SJL as received from Monticello eight days later, is also missing.

From La Rochefoucauld-Liancourt

N.Y. Le 30 Juin

Je recois avec une sensible reconnoissance, Monsieur, lavis que vous voulés bien me donner de L'arrivée du Colonel Munroe. Votre Obligeante lettre qui auroit du me parvenir hier ne m'est parvenue qu'aujourdhuy. Et j'avois esperé des hier Cette importante arrivée. J'ignorois toute fois Les agreables détails qui me Concernent et ils acquierent un prix de plus en me parvenant par vous. J'ay pris la liberté d'ecrire des hier au Colel. que je le priois de ne remettre mes lettres a personne, en suposant qu'il vint bientot a New yorck. Si cependant il differoit je seroi tres aise qu'il voulut bien Les Confier a Mr. Switzer un de mes amis qui doit partir de philadelphie pour se rendre icy lundy prochain.

Je pense que l'arrivée du Colo. Monroe va faire allonger bien des visages, et que nous serons promptement instruits de ce dont nous nous doutons si fort depuis longtems. J'espere autant que je le souhaite qu'il n'y aura pas de rupture entre les etats unis et la france. Mais a quelqu'extremite que puisse Conduire la deplorable Conduite de votre gouvernement, Je serai bien affligé que la france eut tu reellement Les premiers tords avec un pays que Les $\frac{99}{100}$emes des francois cherissoient et respectoient meme avant notre revolution.

Jay passé trois fois chéz vous avant mon depart, et nomement deux fois la veille. Javois meme chargé *francis* de vous temoigner mes regrets denepas vous voir avant mon depart. Je nose me flatter d'avoir le plaisir de vous revoir avant mon depart pour l'europe, ou chaque chose que j'en entends et chaqu'une de celles que je vois icy me déterminent irrevocablement daller en Automne. De la je seray votre meilleur Commissionaire en livres et je vous demande la permission de croire que vous m'autoriserés a vous ecrire. Je suis tres aise que mon petit homage ne vous ait pas semblé indigne de votre belle biblioteque. Recevés avec bonte l'assurance sincere de lestime profond et de lattachement avec Le quel Je Suis votre affectionné Serv

LIANCOURT

RC (MoSHi: Jefferson Papers); endorsed by TJ as received 3 July 1797 and so recorded in SJL.

TJ's LETTRE to La Rochefoucauld-Liancourt, recorded in SJL as written on 28 June 1797, has not been found. MON PETIT HOMAGE: probably La Rochefoucauld-Liancourt's pamphlet, *On the Prisons of Philadelphia. By an European* (1796), published at Philadelphia in both English and French by Moreau de St. Méry (see Evans, Nos. 30673, 30674).

To William Short

DEAR SIR   Philadelphia June 30. 1797.

Yours of Mar. 31. was delivered to me yesterday. I learn by that that my letters must have been unfortunate in their passage to you. I have no papers here which enable me to cite dates; but I know that I have written to you once or twice every year. There had been a longer interval indeed from the time of your leaving Madrid, because the last letter you wrote me thence (which is the last I have received till yesterday's) gave me constant reason to expect you here every day. In the first week of last March however, having heard nothing from you, and hearing then for the first time of a certainty that you were in Paris, I wrote to you from this place. That letter I imagine you would recieve towards the latter part of April. In that I gave you a general view of such of your affairs as are under my care, to wit, your shares in the James river canal, the remainder of your stock in the funds, and that the interest arising from that had been regularly put to interest secured by mortgage. I am not able to cite sums, not having my papers here. For some time past, portions of interest have been suffered to lie in the treasury to answer your immediate calls should you arrive here. Should you come, and to this port, apply to Mr. John Barnes merchant in South 3d. street in this place who is my agent, and will furnish whatever you may want, or should you arrive in any other port drop a line to him by post and he will immediately remit to you wherever you are. I shall leave a duplicate of[1] this in his hands to be delivered you here, if you come, and shall send this[2] to reach you in Paris if you continue there some time yet. The apprehensions that we may be engaged in this war, and the probable effects of that on stock in the funds, have induced me to endeavor much to find a mass of ground rents in this place, into which I would have converted the remains of your stock. But as yet no such property has been found at market, and as I shall leave this within a few days, and you give me reason to expect you within a month or so, your stock will lie in it's present form. Perhaps it may in the mean time gain in value, as the superior security of our funds is likely to draw demands on them from England and Holland. Your presence here would be advantageous to your landed property. The Indian camp lies in it's original state, which is by no means a desireable one for it to continue in; awaiting your orders. How far landed property here may be the best for you, as you will probably reside in another country, may be the subject of consultation when you come. If you arrive between this and December I shall be at Monticello, happy to recieve you there, and to accomodate you as far as the condition of my buildings will do it. Soon after my return the roof of the house will be taken off, and my family remove away till it shall be replaced. But I shall be there myself, and have some *gite* for a single friend. Should you arrive after the 1st. of December you will find me here for the winter.—With respect to the 9. ~~M~~. Dol. I have insisted to the proper officers that R. was not your agent here. Your authority to him to invest them in stock occasioned them to consider his receipt as your receipt. I satisfied them that I was your sole and full attorney, and they satisfied themselves on searching that no investiture in stock had actually been made. Had that been done, it could not have been got over. As it is, I have got them to acknolege in conversation that your right is good against the public. I therefore consider it as safe.[3] I thank you for the Siberian barley, which I will certainly endeavor to profit our country of. I am also obliged to you for the recommendation of Monsr. Pougens bookseller. Since the loss of poor Frouillée I have wished for a correspondent in that line, and shall with pleasure apply sometimes as you have recommended. Should you recieve this in France present me most affectionately to Madame D'Enville. I considered her friendship, while in France, as one of the most precious of my acquisitions, have ever cherished the remembrance of it with tenderness, and taken a lively part in all her interests and feelings. May heaven grant her the extension of live she would desire, with all the health of body and mind which the immutable laws of nature permit to the human frame. Make my respects acceptable to Madame de la Rochefoucault also, for whom I have ever entertained a very high degree of esteem. No body was impressed with a higher sense of her merit, and I paid it a sincere tribute of respect and attachment. Accept your self, my dear Sir, assurances of the high constant and unalterable attachment, and tenders of every service which can be rendered by Your affectionate friend & humble servant   TH: JEFFERSON

RC (ViW); at foot of first page: "Mr. Short"; endorsed by Short. PrC of Dupl (DLC: Short Papers); the most significant variations in wording are recorded in notes below; at head of text: "Duplicate"; at foot of first page: "Mr. Short"; endorsed by TJ in ink on verso. Recorded in SJL as an original sent to Paris and a Dupl held by John Barnes.

YOURS OF MAR. 31: Short's letter was actually dated 30 Mch. 1797. The LAST LETTER he wrote to TJ before leaving Madrid was that of 30 Sep. 1795. The letter that TJ recalled having written IN THE FIRST WEEK OF LAST MARCH was dated 12 Mch. 1797. On 22 June 1797 TJ signed a power of at-torney empowering JOHN BARNES to receive dividends paid for the period 1 Jan. to 30 June 1797 on Short's stock in the U.S. loan (MS in PHC; consisting of a printed form, signed and witnessed; endorsed by Comptroller of the Treasury John Steele).
R.: Edmund Randolph.

[1] Preceding three words lacking in PrC.
[2] PrC: "the original."
[3] Remainder of letter lacking in PrC, which reads instead: "—The residue of this letter sent to Paris is only relative to a reception of it there. To this duplicate therefore I shall here only add assurance of the great and unaltered esteem and attachment of Dear Sir Your sincere friend & servt."

From Willem H. van Hasselt

SIR   Charleston S:C: June 30 1797.
    The manner in which I go to adress meself to you hath I confess something extrordinary in it, and deviating from the common forms received by the world, will perhaps surprise you, and dispose you in my disadvantage, as being an utter Stranger to you: but Sir as necessity acknowledges no law, and the report I often heard of you as a Philosopher and a Citizen, I presume to take this step, and perhaps you are the only man in America certainly the first whom I would adress in this manner.
    Perhaps tho personally I am intirely unknown to you, my name you might have heard of or seen in some print. I came but in an advanced age in this Country, thus it is not to be Supposed that I can have made

great proficienties in the English Language, so that I must apologise for it as a Stranger, that you would not conclude that my education was equally bad as my language. I flatter me on the contrary that if my application in a language so meanly uttered does not draw upon it your reprobation, in a more elegant dress it might perhaps have reconciled your good Will. But ad rem.

I was born in Gilderland one of the states of the now Batavian Republicq, one of the first victims to the persecutions of the Prince of Orange, with my intimate friend John Derk van der Capellen tot den Poll, who died in the year 83 with a suspicion of being poisoned. I left Holland in August 81 and came over in the Ship South Carolina commanded by Commodore A: Gillon Capt. John Joyner. My education being not in the mercantile line, but in the way of one who was destined to occupy a place in government as a series of my ancestors had been. I receved my degrees as Juris utriusque Doctor at Leiden but the misfortunes of the times, intirely devoted to the republican party, driving me out of my country the little wrecks of my fortune which I had saved, and as I have Said not being educated as a Marchand, I was soon tricked out, and now I am reduced to loock for Shelter under your protection. As I never hired meself out, I Should be very auckward in proposing conditions; but I will try to expose to your vew my circumstances and the tendency of my wishes with what I think meself capable of performing.

I am already advanced to a certain age which you may call old but having no corruptions hanging upon me I enjoy a continued health, my choice and wish is for retirement and study, but as Agriculture was always my delight and I flatter meself I have made Some progresses in it my wish should be to be employed in it, however My Age would not allow me So much activity as is required in a Menager or overseer, at least in the State of south Car. I would wish for an occupation less laborious, and according to that less expensive to you.   I am informed that some where in the back part of Virginia you have Sir a fine country seat, which is and may be greatly improved. My wishes loock that way could you not Employ me there? My expectations of pay would be very moderate as I have no family, to be found in lodging table and plain dress would compass my whole prospect, and if I could I would only ask a reception.

Had you Childeren a little more than infants I should like to give them instructions and form them for society, where as I have seen the world from high to Low, teatchim them their moral duties, Moral and natural Philosophy modern languages as fransh and italian which by the bye I write and speak better than the English, Latin, German, or my own Country Language. I am tolerably well informed in the Theoretical and Practical principles of musicq and draw a little also.

Besides I must Sir inform you of one oddity, which for the worlds treasures I would not give up, tho it is not at all now a day in fashion, I mean I love my religion and am firmly attached to the protestant tenets.

I have staid with Mr. Thomas Middleton for about seven years, but what was the reason, whether he wanted to get rid of me or for other reasons I do not know he used me so ill at last notwithstanding the real Services I have done him out of friendship during those Seven years, without receiving a Shilling for it that I was obliged to quit him: But as people in such dispositions, cannot be Suspected of partiality in favor of the person whose Character we desire to investigate, chearfully I will appeal to him if you want information, as I defy any person in America to asperse with proofs my moral Character. The Gentlemen I am the most acquainted with and who know me best are the Middletons Pinckneys Izards Draytons Manigaulds &c. by whom you may easily get information, provided Sir that in case you find me true you would agree to my proposals. For if you will not I expect from your Generosity that without taking notice of any thing you will drop the matter at once only informing me in three words that you received my letter, that I might not trouble you over and over again in the uncertainty of the receipt of mine, else I know it would hurt me in the opinions of many wose tempers are not easily managed. Peace quietness and an occupation not exceeding my strength for the rest of my days is all what I wish for in an happy oblivion of the whole world that I might say with Seneca

> Sic cum transierint mei
> Nullo cum strepitu Dies,
> Plebejus moriar Senex.
> Illi mors gravis incubat,
> Qui notus nimis omnibus,
> Ignotus moritur sibi.

I was not so insignificant in my own country as I am here. My education was not neglected and my family in good repute. As I have said I had made some proficiency in sciences and Agriculture so I was chosen member of the Society of Arts and Scientes at Harlem and severall others the diplomata where of are still in keeping of Mr. Thomas Middleton, not thinking it worth my while to carry them all along with me and that I ever Should want them. That I was not despised in Holland the present President of the united states John Adams may witness who hath known me very well in Amsterdam. I begg Sir you would not attribute to any vanity the bringing on of these proofs of my caracter and circumstances, but as being in the necessity that you might not form disadvantageous ideas of me in taking Such an uncommon step, so that I may ground my hopes upon mine upon your circumstances that where the greatest part of your time you are occupied in the important affairs concerning the government of this extended country, you might be pleased, when you have leisure to visit your Seat with the idea of finding a Man there who thincks himself not unworthy of your confidance in the menagement of your afaires there and who in the same time would not be intirely destitute of those faculties required to support a rational conversation.

If these my hopes are not intirely vain, what ever may be your resolution I begg to favor me with a speedy answer. But as for the present my Abode is very unstable you will be pleased to adress your letter to me to the care of Florian Charles Mey Marchand in Charleston east Bay who transacts all my business and will forward it to me you will oblige Extremely Sir Your most obedient Humble Servant

W: H: van Hasselt

RC (MoSHi: Jefferson Papers); endorsed by TJ as received 4 Aug. 1797 and so recorded in SJL.

Willem H. van Hasselt (b.1732), a native of Zutphen in the Netherlands, received his law degree at Leiden in 1754. He later conducted experiments in raising silkworms on his estate near Voorst and published essays on the subject before immigrating to the United States in 1781, where he continued his work on the production of silk—in 1787 at Cedar Grove, Arthur Middleton's plantation on the Ashley River in South Carolina—without financial success. Baron van der Capellen, a Dutch sympathizer with the American cause during the Revolution, described his friend van Hasselt as "a man of good family" with a "lofty free intellect" who "deserves to be an American" (Carl E. Prince, et al., ed., *The Papers of William Livingston*, 5 vols. [Trenton and New Brunswick, N.J., 1979-1988], IV, 204; Pieter J. van Winter, *American Finance and Dutch Investment, 1780-1805: With an Epilogue to 1840*, rev. and trans. with the assistance of James C. Riley, 2 vols. [New York, 1977], I, 139-40, 188n; W. H. de Beaufort,

ed., *Brieven van en aan Joan Derck van der Capellen van de Poll* (Utrecht, 1879), 310-6; Philip C. Molhuysen, ed., *Nieuw Nederlandsch Biografisch Woordenboek*, 10 vols. [Leiden, 1911-1937], VIII, 707-8).

MY NAME YOU MIGHT HAVE . . . SEEN IN SOME PRINT: the South Carolina Society for Promoting and Improving Agriculture published a pamphlet entitled *Letters and Observations on Agriculture, &c. Addressed to, or Made by the South-Carolina Society for Promoting and Improving Agriculture, and other Rural Concerns* in Charleston in 1788 which included a lengthy extract of TJ's letter to William Drayton, 30 July 1787, and a letter from van Hasselt to the society describing his experiment in raising silkworms in South Carolina.

The lines of SENECA are from the tragedy *Thyestes*, verses 398-403:

So when my days have passed away
From noisy, restless tumult free,
May I, in meek obscurity
And full of years, decline in death
But death lies heavily on him
Who, though to all the world well known,
Is stranger to himself alone.

To Thomas Mifflin

DEAR SIR   July 1. 97.

The bearer hereof Mr. Blacon having some business with you desires me to give him a line of introduction. He was a good revolutionist of the first National convention, closely connected with La Fayette, a worthy and wealthy person[1] well known to me in France. On these grounds I take the liberty of presenting him to you. He will have with him a friend Mr. Sermaize whom I have not before known. I have the honor to be with great respect & esteem Dr. Sir Your most obedt. & most humble servt.   TH: JEFFERSON

RC (Herbert A. Strauss, Chicago, 1947); addressed: "Governor Mifflin Philadelphia handed by Mr. Blacon"; with one emendation noted below; endorsed by Mifflin and a clerk. Not recorded in SJL.

[1] Preceding five words interlined.

Account with John Francis

The Vice President

	To John Francis Dr.
To 7 Weeks & 5 days board at 26 dollars a week	200.55
To Wine porter &c	25.
	225.55

Phila. July 3d. 1797 Received payment of the above account in full
                                                                    JOHN FRANCIS

MS (MHi); entirely in Francis's hand; endorsed by TJ on verso. Not recorded in SJL.

John Francis was the owner of the hotel at 13 South Fourth Street in Philadelphia that served as TJ's residence while in the city during his years as vice president, as it had previously for John Adams. Two senators (John Brown of Kentucky and John Henry of Maryland) and seven representatives (Nathaniel Freeman, Jr., Thompson J. Skinner and Joseph B. Varnum of Massa-chusetts, Matthew Clay and Walter Jones of Virginia, William B. Grove of North Carolina, and Abraham Baldwin of Georgia) also lived at the Francis hotel in 1797 (MB, II, 955n; *Stephens's Philadelphia Directory, for 1796...* [Philadelphia, 1796], 65, 207-11; *A List of the Names, and Places of Residence, of the Members of the Senate and House of Representatives of the United States* [Philadelphia, 1797], Evans, No. 32975). Before TJ left Philadelphia he paid Francis an additional $9.50, for extending his stay two days and for postage (MB, II, 965).

From Arthur Campbell

SIR   Washington V. July 4th. 1797

Peace being happily restored on the Western Frontier, I had form'd the design of living in quiet, the remainder of my days, that is to decline writing, or almost thinking, of politics. But again we see our Country verging to an eventful crisis. I am fill'd with anxiety respecting her liberty, and independence, lest they are lost, and with them the happiness of so many Millions of the human race, and all this thro' the insidious manœvres of our old foe. This may justify all to break silence, to do more, to prepare to act. Altho I cannot help feeling indignation, at some of the measures of the French Directory, relative to the United States: yet I am a thousand times more apprehensive of the measures of the British Ministry: If they can dissolve our connection with France; we of course will have to throw ourselves into the arms of England. A Treaty of Alliance with that Nation may only be a prelude to a restoration of monarchy, a hateful monarchy! under one of the Boobys of that Island. To arouse, and arm the Citizens of America, under the ostensible pretext of being guarded against the unjust enterprizes of France, may be a wise and judicious measure, because it will give us confidence in our own prowess, and make us formidable in the eyes of G. Britain, consequently awe them to respect our independence. France can have no real interest to molest us: but as far as we discover a partiallity to her Rival. She will be peacable, and friendly, if we will generally reciprocate the same dispositions. The difference of language, and manners, and many other considerations, will forever prevent a union with France; with G. Britain it might be otherwise; late injuries, and resentments forgot: The Moses's and Joshua's, that conducted the People to the promised land, all gone to rest: Not a few perverse and stiff-necked Americans, may then murmur for the Onions and Garlic of old England. The assiduous endeavours of the Patriot, will be steadily exerted, to avert so direful an event. For my own part, I can yet shoot a Rifle well to the mark. I have three Sons that can excel me, and there is some hundreds that will follow us, and all take the field, with alacrity, rather then become dependant on any nation upon Earth.

Sir, the above is intended as a private communication, it is the effusions of the hour, and to no other could they be offered, with greater propriety, than to him, to whom, all the old Whigs look up with confidence. With every sentiment of Respect & Esteem I am Sir Your most obedient servt.   ARTHUR CAMPBELL

RC (DLC); endorsed by TJ as received 11 Aug. 1797 and so recorded in SJL.

From Edmond Charles Genet

Long Island, 4 July 1797. Stirred from his present tranquil life by a speech Giles made in Congress on 25 May, which blamed Genet for rude conduct toward the executive and for attempting to appeal directly to the American people, Genet responds not to Giles but to TJ, who has been his principal accuser and was the person through whom the government primarily dealt with him when he was minister plenipotentiary. He knows that TJ, as U.S. minister to France, himself meddled in the internal affairs of France by helping to incite the overthrow of the monarchy but then blocking any efforts to replace it with a genuine stable government of the people. He knows that TJ also corresponded with Mazzei and others whom Genet presumes played a role in the destruction of Poland. Recounting his posting to the U.S. and the subsequent events, he notes that very early on he became suspicious, from the attention given to the Proclamation of Neutrality, that the U.S. government did not really want a renewed relationship with France. With time TJ confided to Genet that Washington was under the influence of aristocrats and the British, and that supporters of republican France no longer had any voice in the government. For his part Genet was always candid about the interests and intentions of the French Republic and instructed his subordinates to say nothing that would even appear to constitute interference in internal political affairs. The expression of the sentiments of the American people, which took the form of support for the democratic societies, was spontaneous and not the result of any action by Genet. Nevertheless it frightened the executive, including TJ, who represented to Washington that Genet was circumventing him to appeal directly to the people. TJ probably did this to protect the administration's influence of office, and the speculative opportunities it presented, all of which seemed threatened by Genet's devotion to the cause of liberty. On his own initiative Genet managed to see Washington in person, but without any evident result, and through American influence on Robespierre, who sought to emulate in France the American model of a despotism nominally based on popular will, Genet was replaced by Citizen Fauchet. He would have been executed if Washington had complied with France's request for his arrest. Instead he withdrew to a quiet life of reflection and farming, and regrets that TJ did not do the same after playing his role in securing American independence. If TJ had done that, France might have had a peaceful transition of government from monarchy to democracy without regicide and terror, the French Republic would be powerful and respected in Europe without the loss of many lives, and the United States would not have earned itself the resentment of France, Spain, other nations, and even William Pitt, who despises the United States and draws closer to it only the better to destroy it. Genet believes that Adams has a good opportunity for successful negotiation with France, for although Adams has written in support of monarchy and aristocracy, the good republicans of France understand his position, which is not the deceptive and weak "demi Républicanisme" of the preceding administration. The accusation that Genet made a direct appeal to the American people and treated Washington with anything less than proper respect is an artifice and a lie. Genet met his downfall acting in France's behalf, yet also through the actions of the French government, and he believes that France and the United States together owe him reparations at least comparable to the outrages they inflicted on him.

FC (DLC: Genet Papers); 38 p.; in French, entirely in Genet's hand; dated at "Cornelias farm Long Island"; on title page preceding text of letter: "Lettre d'Edmond Charles Genet Ancien Ministre plenipotentiaire de la République francoise près les Etats unis, de l'academie des Sciences et de la Société de Médecine de Paris de la Société Royale des Antiquaires de Londres des Sociétés litteraires d'Upsal et de Stockholm &c. A Mr. Thomas Jefferson Ancien Secretaire d'Etat des Etats unis Vice Président des Etats unis et Président de la Société Philosophique de Philadelphie"; at head of title page: "copie au net"; with four appended notes, keyed to text, three of them containing extracts of documents mentioned in text; with emendations. 2d Dft (same); dated "le Juin 1797"; at head of text: "2e. minute"; with variations and emendations; lacks notes. Tr (NHi: Genet Family Papers); in DeWitt Clinton's hand, in English, being a translation of 2d Dft; dated June 1797; at head of text: "To Mr. Jefferson Translated by DeWitt Clinton"; with emendations. Translation of FC, with variations in paragraphing, printed in Minnigerode, *Genet*, 413-27.

TJ probably never saw this letter, for it is not recorded in SJL and there is no version in TJ's papers. Given its title page and notes, the document was intended for publication (Ammon, *Genet Mission*, 174). Genet's description in this letter is the only account of his call upon Washington, which probably took place on 16 July 1793 (Freeman, *Washington*, VII, 106n; Memorandum of Conversations with Edmond Charles Genet, 26 July 1793, above in this series, Vol. 26: 571-3).

Senate Resolution on William Blount

[4 July 1797]

That so much of the Presidents Message of yesterday and the papers accompanying the same[1] as relates to a letter purporting to have been written by Mr. Blount Esqe. a senator from the state of Tennisse be referred to a select commmittee to consider and report what in their opinion it is proper the senate should do thereon.

Resolved that the said Committee have power to send for persons papers and records relating to the subject committed to them.

MS (DNA: RG 46, Senate Records, 5th Cong., 1st sess.); probably in Theodore Sedgwick's hand, with emendation (see note below) and last sentence in TJ's hand; endorsed by Samuel A. Otis: "Committee of five to consider the Messg of P US respecting a letter signed Wm Blount July 4th 1797." For the final text of this resolution under this date, see JS, II, 383.

On 3 July 1797, President Adams sent a confidential MESSAGE with supporting PAPERS to both houses of Congress reporting that westerners, in association with the Cherokee and Creek Indians, were conspiring with the British to invade Spanish Florida and Louisiana. Among the documents was a letter from William BLOUNT to James Carey, a Cherokee nation interpreter, dated 21 Apr. 1797, in which the Tennessee senator, a former Federalist territorial governor who had broken with that party in 1796 when Federalist congressmen tried to block the admission of Tennessee into the Union, indicated that the "plan" would be carried out in the fall and that he would probably

"be at the head of the business on the part of the British." Blount predicted "if the Indians act their part, I have no doubt it will succeed" (ASP, *Foreign Relations*, II, 66-77; JS, II, 383; William H. Masterson, *William Blount* [Baton Rouge, 1954], 174-9, 292-8). Blount was absent from the Senate when the letter first was read aloud, but it was read again upon his return. When asked whether he had written it, Blount admitted corresponding with Carey but requested an opportunity to search his papers before replying. The following day a formal letter from Blount was laid before the Senate requesting more time to look through his correspondence and collect "other evidence to remove suspicion." The Senate responded by passing the resolution above and appointing James Ross, Richard Stockton, John Henry, Theodore Sedgwick, and Jacob Read to serve on the SELECT COMMITTEE, the first to be given investigative powers by that body. The next day Ross reported that while Blount had again requested more time to prepare his defense and obtain pertinent papers, the committee had received information that he intended to leave the city that morning and proceed by sea to North Carolina. They therefore resolved to have the president of the Senate exercise his authority "to compel the personal Attendance of William Blount" (MS in DNA: RG 46, Senate Records, 5th Cong., 1st sess.). In response, TJ wrote Blount from the Senate chamber: "You are hereby required to attend the Senate in your place without delay. By order of the Senate" and signed the letter "Th: Jefferson President of the Senate" (RC in same, addressed: "William Blount esquire of the Senate of the U.S.," endorsed by Otis: "Letter from the Vice President to Wm Blount, to attend Senate July 5th 1797"; Dft in same, in unknown hand, with signature, place, and date in TJ's hand, endorsed by Otis). Later that day TJ announced that James Mathers, doorkeeper of the Senate, had attempted to deliver the missive, but Blount could not be found (JS, II, 385). For the Tennessee senator's abortive attempt to flee, see Melton, *First Impeachment*, 109-10. On 6 July Blount informed the Senate that as he understood his attendance was desired, he would be in his seat at noon (RC in same; addressed: "The Vice President of the United States or the President Pr. Tem. of the Senate of the United States"). Since TJ departed for Monticello on that day, William Bradford, president of the Senate pro tempore, presided over the Blount proceedings during the remainder of the session.

Blount appeared in the Senate, indicated that he would answer the charges against him, and retained Alexander J. Dallas and Jared Ingersoll as counsel. In the meantime Samuel Sitgreaves introduced a resolution in the House calling for Blount's impeachment. In debate on 6 and 7 July, Virginia Republican John Nicholas called British Minister Robert Liston "equally culpable," a theme reiterated in the Republican press. Benjamin F. Bache's *Aurora* charged "that the British are fomenting divisions within the United States, and driving us into a war with Spain," and Republicans often referred to the episode as "Liston's plot," rather than "Blount's conspiracy" (Philadelphia *Aurora*, 20 July 1797; Madison to TJ, 25 Dec. 1797). On 7 July Sitgreaves appeared before the Senate, announced that the House had voted for impeachment, and requested

that Blount be "sequestered" or suspended from his Senate seat. The next day the Senate expelled Blount by a 25 to 1 vote—only Tazewell refused to support the resolution. The House appointed Sitgreaves, two other Federalists—James A. Bayard and Robert G. Harper—and Republicans John Dawson and Abraham Baldwin to investigate the "whole nature and extent of the offence" and prepare the articles of impeachment (JS, II, 383-92; JHR, III, 70-75; *Annals*, VII, 448-66; Melton, *First Impeachment*, 104-48).

The House committee spent the summer collecting evidence and writing a report, which after the convening of the new session of Congress was read before the House on 4 and 5 Dec. It produced, according to Dawson, "some long faces" because it concluded that "it was not a French plot with Mr. Jefferson at the bottom, as has been industriously circulated in the eastern states" (Madison, *Papers*, XVII, 58; *Report of the Committee of the House of Representatives of the United States, Appointed to Prepare and Report Articles of Impeachment against William Blount* [Philadelphia, 1798], in Sowerby, V, 207; *Annals*, VIII, 2319-416). On 25 Jan. 1798, Sitgreaves presented articles of impeachment to the House, charging that Blount intended to cooperate with Great Britain on an expedition against the Spanish possessions of Louisiana and Florida and that attempts had been made to engage the Creek and Cherokee Indians in the expedition, thereby corrupting relations between United States agents and the Indians. After agreeing to the articles four days later, the House on 30 Jan. began selecting by ballot the eleven managers who would conduct the proceedings. All of the members of the original investigative committee except Dawson were elected on the first day of balloting. Upon learning of Dawson's defeat, Baldwin refused to serve and the second day of voting saw the election of a complete slate of Federalists (JHR, III, 74, 149-56; Melton, *First Impeachment*, 161-2). The articles of impeachment were published as a pamphlet, *Further Report from the Committee, Appointed on the Eighth of July last, to Prepare and Report Articles of Impeachment against William Blount* [Philadelphia, 1798], cited in Sowerby, V, 207. For the ensuing actions in the Senate with TJ once again presiding, see TJ to Tazewell, 27

Jan. 1798; Sitgreaves to TJ, 6 Feb. 1798; Sitgreaves's address to the Senate, at 7 Feb. 1798; and Notes on the Framing of Oaths, [ca. 8-9 Feb. 1798]; and for the trial, which commenced on 17 Dec. 1798 in Blount's absence, and the subsequent dismissal of the case, see the Senate's resolution on the impeachment at 11 Jan. 1799.

Blount's later career is surveyed in Masterson, *William Blount*, 324-47. For an analysis of the weakness of the federal government in the region south of the Ohio River and Blount's desire to bring stability and economic development to Tennessee and the southwest, see Andrew R. L. Cayton, "'When Shall We Cease to Have Judases?' The Blount Conspiracy and the Limits of the 'Extended Republic,'" in Ronald Hoffman and Peter J. Albert, eds., *Launching the "Extended Republic": The Federalist Era* (Charlottesville, 1996), 156-89.

[1] Preceding six words interlined by TJ.

To Volney

TH: JEFFERSON TO MR. VOLNEY   July 5. 97.

I am really uneasy at your stay here, during the heats of the present season, and in your weak state. You mentioned that you were detained by business. Perhaps it may be some retardation of funds, or some other matter in which I can be serviceable to you. I am rarely rich in money, but probably can command such sums as might accomodate wants as moderate as yours. Be it this, or be it any thing else in my power, command me freely, and you will gratify me the more, as you can render me the more useful to you. Accept my friendly salutations.

FC (DLC); entirely in TJ's hand, and endorsed by him on verso: "Volney."

From Volney

VOLNEY À MONSIEUR JEFFERSON   philadelphie 5 juillet 1797

Je Suis aussi touché de Votre offre, en la considerant et quant au fonds et quant à la forme, que le peut être un cœur qui Connaît le Sentiment de L'amitié et le prix de la générosité. Je N'hesiterais pas de l'accepter, si j'étais dans le cas. Mais heureusement mon œconomie et ma prévoyance ne me laissent rien à desirer du coté de l'argent. Mon motif de rester ici porte sur d'autres causes, dont il Serait peut être bon que Nous traîtassions avant Votre départ: car il serait possible que Notre séparation fut longue: Voulez-Vous M'assigner une heure dans la Soirée depuis 6 heures.

RC (CtY); addressed: "Mr Thomas jefferson"; endorsed by TJ as received 5 July 1797 and so recorded in SJL.

From Elbridge Gerry

My dear Friend   Cambridge 6th July 1797

Your obliging letters of the 12th of may, and 21st of June, I have received; and have taken a step, by accepting the appointment to France, which it is difficult to justify to my family, under existing circumstances. Your information and opinion, which had great influence in this decission; the weighty considerations, that the appointment having been once declined, a second refusal might at home and abroad make disagreable impressions; and the critical state of our affairs, which, difficult as the enterprize is, requires the most vigorous effort of every friend to this country, have combined to form a determination, the result of which, as it respects the publick as well as the Envoys, is problematical; and may entail on the latter eulogiums or anathemas, according to light in which their conduct might be viewed by contending political parties. The public good shall nevertheless be my object, and if this should eventually be attained, I shall disregard personal considerations. It is impossible for me at this time, my dear friend, pressed as I am with attentions on all sides, and afflicted by an inflammation in my eyes, to do justice to your letters; in which is comprized a volume of politics—the declaration which you make, respecting your principles and veiws, is supported by the uniformity of your conduct and requires no collateral evidence. I do not conceive that the President has the least doubt of your disposition, in your proper department, to co-operate with him and support the dignity of his office; or the least apprehension, that you "veiw him as an obstacle in your way" to what you consider "splendid misery." There can be no doubt, I think, when he relinquishes the high office which he now fills, that you will be his successor; and a party, unfriendly to one or both of you, will naturally use every stratagem to interrupt your mutual *confidence*; for this would make the friends of each, the friends of both, and leave no doubts respecting your mutual support. But I sincerely hope that your friendship will never be interrupted; on the other hand, that it will be increased and confirmed: as the surest pledge of promoting the public welfare. When the great officers and departments of government act in unison, their example pervades the state, and often makes its impetus, which would be otherwise small, irresistable: such a line of conduct is dignified, and discourages opposition to the measures of government: it has great effect on the manners and morals of the people, which are sapped and contaminated by the influence of parties: and it is an effectual mean of counteracting the most virulent of all political poisons, foreign influence. Your opinions of this subject, of the monopoly of our commerce, on the peace interest and honor of our country, and on the consequences of a war are so perfectly coincident with my own as to leave no point of difference.

Nothing will afford me greater pleasure than to hear from you at Paris, and to receive every light which you can throw on the important objects of the mission. I cannot conclude, my dear Sir, without manifesting the satisfaction which I feel from your expressions of friendship and confidence, and assure you that with the highest esteem and respect I remain your affectionate friend & very hum Sert   E GERRY

RC (DLC); at foot of first page: "His Excellency Mr. Jefferson"; endorsed by TJ as received 21 July 1797 and so recorded in SJL.

THE 12TH OF MAY: Gerry mistook the date in referring to TJ's letter of 13 May 1797.

Suit against the Estate of William Ronald: Order and Report

In the Court of Chancery

Virginia:

Between

Thomas Jefferson   plt

and

William Bentley administrator of the goods, and chattels of William Ronald deceased, and Betsey Ronald and Nancy Ronald infants under the age of twenty one years and Co-heiresses of the said William Ronald by the said William Bentley their guardian   defendts.

This cause, by consent of parties, came on this thirteenth day of March in the year of our lord one thousand seven hundred and ninety seven, to be heard on the bill, answers, and exhibits, and was argued by counsil: on consideration whereof the court doth adjudge, order and decree that the surveyor of the County of Goochland, do on or before the first day of May next, go upon the land in the bill mentioned and lay off by metes and bounds six hundred acres thereof conformable to the description in the Indenture of mortgage among the exhibits made the twenty third day of May one thousand seven hundred and ninety, Between William Ronald of the one part, and Thomas Jefferson of the other part, so as to comprehend the mill seat, and return a fair plat thereof to the court; and the court doth further adjudge, order, and decree that unless the defendants or some of them do on or before the first day of June next pay unto the plaintiff seven hundred and seventeen pounds six shillings and eight pence of current money of Virginia, equal to the value of five hundred and thirty eight pounds sterling money of Great Britain with interest thereupon after the rate of five per centum per annum from the fifth day of October one thousand seven hundred and ninety, till payment and the costs of this suit, the said defendants Betsy Ronald, and Nancy Ronald and their heirs and all persons claiming under them, be from thenceforth barred and foreclosed of their equity and right to redeem the six hundred acres of land and mill seat so as aforesaid to be laid off, and in case of default in the payment of the said debt, Interest and costs at the time aforesaid that Thomas Bates, Joseph Watkins, James Pleasants and Thomas Royster Junr., or any two of them after giving ten days notice thereof in one or more of the Richmond News papers do expose to public sale by auction for ready money the said six hundred acres of land and mill seat with the appurtenances, and out of the proceeds of such sale pay to the plaintiff the said debt, interest and costs, and the surplus if any, after deducting the expences attending the said sale pay to the defendent William Bentley and make report thereof to the court: But liberty is reserved to the infant defendants to shew cause against this decree, at any time within six months after they shall have respectively attain their full ages: and the court doth further order the commissioners to convey the land and other premises to the purchaser or purchasers thereof at his or their costs in fee simple.

A Copy
Teste
PETER TINSLEY C C

Plts costs Clk $ 6.31
Lawyers fee & tax   17.66

In obedience to the within order, we the commissioners therein mentioned proceeded to expose to public sale on the premises, the six hundred acres of land on Beaverdam creek, including the mill seat, agreeably to a platt made out by the county surveyor to Colo. William Bentley, for the sum of nine hundred, sixty eight pounds current money. But he paid us no money; nor has any conveyance of the land been made by us. Given under our hands this 10th. of July 1797. £968.0.—

THOMAS F. BATES
JOSEPH WATKINS
JAMES PLEASANTS JR.
THO. ROYSTER

A Copy,
Teste,
P, TINSLEY, C,C,

[477]

D (MHi); entirely in Tinsley's hand; endorsed.

This chancery suit stemmed from TJ's sale to William Ronald, in October 1790, of 1,076 acres of land for £1,076 sterling. According to the sale agreement, Ronald was to make two equal payments, one of which was secured by SIX HUNDRED ACRES of land, including a MILL SEAT, in Goochland County. TJ applied the bonds toward his own debt to Farell & Jones, whose agent, Richard Hanson, instigated the effort to obtain payment from the estate of Ronald, who died in 1793. TJ did not receive final payment until 1822 (MB, I, 767-8, II, 1051, 1384; TJ to Hanson, 5 Apr. 1791 and 18 Oct. 1793; Hanson to TJ, 30 Apr. 1791; Agreement of Sale, [5-13 Oct. 1790], printed in Vol. 17: 569-70, where it is mistakenly captioned as a sale agreement for Elk Hill).

From James Monroe

DEAR SIR   New York July 12. 1797.

I arrived here two days since and sit out in return the day after to morrow for Phila. where I shall probably be a fortnight before I proceed on home. *Here* I have had an interview with the friend of Mr. or Mrs. R. each of us having a friend present, and which furnished no result, the business being adjourned over to Phila. *where* we meet the day after my return there in company with the other gentlemen Muhg. and Venable. The details of this interview are reserved till I see you. You may have some idea of them however when you recollect the previous good disposition of some of the parties for each other. The issue is quite incertain as to the mode of adjusting what is personal in the business.

I think you should acknowledge your letter to Mezzai, stating that it was a private one and brought to publick view without your knowledge or design: that the man to whom it was addressed had lived long as your neighbour, and was now in Pisa whither it was addressed: that you do think that the principles of our revolution and of republican government have been substantially swerved from of late in many respects, have often express'd this sentiment, which as a free man you had a right to express, in your publick places and in the walks of private life &ca according to the letter. That you declined saying any thing about it till you got home to examine how correct the letter was. This brings the question before the publick and raises the spirits of the honest part of the community.

13. I dine to day by invitation with a numerous and respectable assemblage of honest men.

You will doubtless exam and decide on the above suggestion soon and give me the result. You are fortunate in having our friend Madison near you. One thing I suggest for you both is, that by not denying it you have all the odium of having written it, and yet without taking a bold attitude which is necessary to encourage friends.

RC (DLC: Madison Papers); unsigned; endorsed by TJ as received 31 July 1797 and so recorded in SJL.

THE FRIEND OF MR. OR MRS. R.: Alexander Hamilton, whose adulterous relationship with Maria Reynolds and alleged connection to the financial speculations of her former husband, James Reynolds, had recently been made public by James Thomson Callender in pamphlets that he subsequently collected as *The History of the United States for 1796; including a Variety of Interesting Particulars Relative to the Federal Government Previous to that Period* (Philadelphia, 1797). See Sowerby, No. 3515. Hamilton hoped to discover Callender's source of detailed information about the Reynolds controversy (Monroe himself presumed it was John Beckley). He also wanted Monroe, a member of an ad hoc committee of three members of the House and Senate to whom he had made an explanation of the matter in December 1792, to state categorically that he accepted Hamilton's version of the events, which admitted adultery with Mrs. Reynolds but disclaimed involvement in any financial improprieties (Syrett, *Hamilton*, XXI, 121-3, 130-9; Notes on the Reynolds Affair, 17 Dec. 1792; note on the first conflict in the cabinet, above in this series in Vol. 18: 611-88). EACH OF US HAVING A FRIEND PRESENT: New York merchant David Gelston and Hamilton's brother-in-law, John Barker Church, were present at Monroe's lodgings in New York City on 11 July 1797 when an angry Hamilton confronted Monroe, who had delayed replying to a letter from the former Treasury secretary until he could confer with MUHG. AND VENABLE—Frederick A. C. Muhlenberg and Abraham B. Venable, who with Monroe had heard Hamilton's explanations in 1792 (Syrett, *Hamilton*, XXI, 146-8, 152, 157-62). According to Gelston's record of THE DETAILS OF THIS INTERVIEW, Hamilton refused to accept Monroe's denial of involvement in the fur-

nishing of papers to Callender, whereupon Monroe called him "a Scoundrel." "I will meet you like a Gentleman," Hamilton replied, to which Monroe rejoined, "I am ready get your pistols" (same, 161). Church and Gelston stepped in to cool the situation, but the threat of a duel lingered through a protracted written exchange between Hamilton and Monroe (same, 168-75, 176-7, 178-81, 184-7, 192-3, 200, 204-5, 208-9, 211-12).

Rather than communicate with Hamilton directly, Monroe soon used Aaron Burr as an intermediary—an oblique form of communication that Burr later in the year dubbed a "childish mode of writing." By mid-August 1797 Monroe assumed with Burr that there was "no prospect of a challenge" from Hamilton (same, 319n; Kline, *Burr*, I, 313). Nevertheless, that fall after the publication of Hamilton's pamphlet on the Reynolds affair (see TJ to James Madison, 24 July 1797), Monroe concluded that Hamilton had not exonerated him from involvement in supplying information to Callender. In letters to Burr and John Dawson that he enclosed in one to TJ of 2 Dec. 1797, Monroe rekindled the issue. Both TJ on 27 Dec. and Dawson, who consulted others in Philadelphia, advised Monroe to leave the matter alone. On 1 Jan. 1798, probably before he received that advice, Monroe wrote his rival a letter that has not been found but which provoked Hamilton to draft a reply calling unequivocally for a duel. Yet Hamilton did not send that letter, and there the matter ended (Syrett, *Hamilton*, XXI, 316-20, 346; Kline, *Burr*, I, 306-14, 320-1).

YOUR LETTER TO MEZZAI: Jefferson's Letter to Philip Mazzei, 24 Apr. 1796. A NUMEROUS AND RESPECTABLE ASSEMBLAGE: on 14 July 1797 Monroe attended a dinner of Republicans in New York that was presided over by Horatio Gates (New York *Daily Advertiser*, 15 July 1797; Ammon, *Monroe*, 159).

From Sir John Sinclair

SIR   Board of Agriculture Whitehall July 15th. 1797

I have the Honor to inclose a Copy of my address to The Board of Agriculture, delivered at the close of our late Session, from which you will perceive the present State of our Pursuits in the great Cause of Agriculture; I hope it will have the good fortune of meeting with your approbation.

I also have the pleasure of herewith sending the remainder of the Original Surveys according to the plan first undertaken which completes that part of our design.

I am persuaded that these Communications, though not so complete as they will yet Be rendered, will not be unacceptable to one, whose Zeal for Improvement is so well known, and universally acknowledged.

Any information upon these important Subjects from America, will be thankfully received by The Board. I have the honor to be, with great regard, Your faithful and obedient Servant   JOHN SINCLAIR

N.B. I hope that you approve of the establishment of a Board of Agriculture in America, and that we shall soon have the pleasure of hearing that it is constituted. A Sample of the virginia forward Wheat would be extremely acceptable.

RC (DLC); at foot of text: "His Excellency Thomas Jefferson &ca. &ca. &ca."; endorsed by TJ as received 9 Jan. 1798 and so recorded in SJL. Enclosure: *Sir John Sinclair's Address to the Board of Agriculture, on Tuesday the Twentieth of June, 1797: Stating the Progress That Had Been Made by the Board, During the Fourth Session Since Its Establishment* [London, 1797]. For other enclosures, see note below.

For a description of the ORIGINAL SURVEYS sent by Sinclair, see William Strickland to TJ, 20 May 1796. At Sinclair's urging, Washington had included in his annual message to Congress of 7 Dec. 1796 a recommendation to establish boards of AGRICULTURE in the United States "composed of proper characters, charged with collecting and diffusing information, and enabled by premiums, and small pecuniary aids, to encourage and assist a spirit of discovery and improvement" (Syrett, *Hamilton*, XX, 364; Fitzpatrick, *Writings*, XXXV, 315-16, 322). In correspondence in July 1797, Washington acknowledged that he had tried "in vain" to establish agricultural boards comparable to the one in Great Britain (Fitzpatrick, *Writings*, XXXV, 501).

From William Wirt, with Jefferson's Notes

DEAR SIR   Pen-Park. July 15. 1797.

In a day or two I will come up and settle with you for the nails which were furnished us some time ago—and at the same time for 500. 8d. and 50. 30d. do. if you will be so obliging as to have them sent by the bearer. Yr. obt. Servt.   WM. WIRT

[*Notes by TJ:*]

(500) 5 ℔ VIII d. 12d   0–5–0
 50. 3 ℔ XXX   10d.   0–2–6
                        0–7–6

RC (MHi); addressed: "Mr. Jefferson Monticello."

FURNISHED US SOME TIME AGO: see Wirt to TJ, 4 May 1797. Letters from Wirt to TJ, dated 11 Aug. and 1 Oct. 1797 and received on 11 Aug. and 2 Oct. 1797 respectively, are recorded in SJL but have not been found.

To John Barnes

DEAR SIR   Monticello July [18.] 1797

After parting with you at Philadelphia, I recollected that the box which Mr. Johnston was forwarding to you for me, went from this place and contained a large tooth and another bone of the Mammoth. I must ask the favor of you to open it and to take the tooth, have it packed in a box of exact size, to be directed to 'the Prince of Parma,' and delivered to the Chevalier Yrujo, Minister of Spain, to be forwarded. I have before spoken to the Minister concerning it, and have written to the Prince on the subject; so nothing more will be necessary, as to that. Be so good as to give the other bone houseroom till I come to Philadelphia.[1]

It will be necessary to discount the notes for the second moiety of paiments due for my tobacco which came to the discountable period on the 15th. inst. being then within 60. days of paiment. On this ground I have this day drawn on you in favor of Charles Johnston & Co. for five hundred dollars at 10. days sight. As an explanation of this draught, I inclose a state of our account according to my view of it which I believe is nearly correct. According to this, after paying the present draught of 500 Dol. there will remain a balance in my favor of about 131.41 without taking into account Mr. Short's dividend for the last two quarters.

No doubt you have some small debets against me not noted here nor known to me. I am with great esteem Dear Sir Your most obedt. servt

TH: JEFFERSON

PrC (ViU: Edgehill-Randolph Papers); faded; at foot of text: "Mr. Barnes"; endorsed in ink by TJ on verso. Enclosure not found.

HAVE WRITTEN TO THE PRINCE: TJ to Louis of Parma, 23 May 1797.

For Barnes's sale of TJ's TOBACCO, see TJ to Thomas Mann Randolph, 9 June 1797.

In Philadelphia on 1 June 1797, TJ wrote a promissory note stating that "Sixty days after date I promise to pay to the order of John Barnes, at the bank of the U. States (without defalcation) four hundred dollars, for value recieved" (MS in MHi; entirely in TJ's hand and signed by him, his signature subsequently canceled by short diagonal strokes; endorsed as paid on 31 July). A letter from Barnes to TJ of 6 Apr. 1797, received 21 Apr., and one from TJ to Barnes dated 9 Apr. are recorded in SJL but have not been found.

[1] Sentence interlined.

From Volney

MONSIEUR   federal city 19 juillet 1797

Le Surlendemain de Votre départ, le propriétaire du Vaisseau qui réunissait Mes Convenances s'etant decidé à Ne point l'expedier, je me decidai de mon côté à quitter philadelphie, et depuis cinq à Six jours je respire dans la *Ville-campagne* d'où je Vous ecris un air peut-etre aussi chaud Mais plus pur. Il N'est plus question de la fievre. Vous M'avez demandé Mon plan de Marche, le Voici. Le Manque de Vaisseaux, la convenance d'attendre des Nouvelles d'Europe, et diverses autres raisons Me font désormais remettre Mon passage j'usqu'à L'equinoxe. J'ai donc Six Semaines à Ma disposition et Mon desir est de les passer dans Votre Canton, partie près de Vous, partie près de Mr. Madison et Mr. Munroë: peut être Même irai-je jusqu'au pont Naturel, en profitant de l'invitation du Colonel Cabell. Maintenant il S'agit de Savoir à quelle epoque il Vous Sera le Moins genant de Me recevoir; la plus simple case Me suffira, comme Vous savez; Mais à son défaut, l'expedient de trouver une chambre à charlotte'sville peut tout arranger. Il Me Suffit d'y pouvoir disposer d'un domestique Male ou femelle une Seule heure par jour—rien Ne M'embarrassera: pas Meme la cuisine, car je nai poînt oublié Mon regime arabe; et de Mon gîte; tantot à cheval tantot à pied, je Vous importunerai presqu'autant que Si j'etais chez Vous. J'ai plus d'un interet à Vous aller Voir. Car outre l'inclination, j'ai encore l'objet de l'instruction qui pour divers articles de Mes recherches Ne peut Se remplir que chez Vous. Je me propose aussi de solliciter l'aide de Mr.

Madison, et je lui ecris par ce même courier pour M'entendre avec lui Sur le tems de Ses convenances. Je calculerai Ma Marche Sur Votre reponse et la Sienne. En attendant je recueille ici chez Mon Obligeant hote et ami le dr. thornton, des Notes et des dessins de ce local et de ses bâtimens, et je tire le parti que je peux de Ses livres peu Nombreux. Hier j'accompagnai le general Washington dans la Visite qu'il fit au capitole. Aujourd'hui il est allé a la grande-chute. Samedi jirai lui rendre Mes devoirs à Mount Vernon; du reste comme la Societé N'est plus agréable pour un français j'ai pris le parti de Vivre tout-à-faît retiré et j'ai profité de la premiere invîtation à diner, pour declarer Ma résolution de Ne Me rendre à aucune. Tout M'affermit dans L'idée de repasser en france: et la necessité Seule ou des accidens imprévus pourraient M'arrêter encore ici L'hyver prochain. L'etat des affaires publiques Noffre plus à un français que des dégoûts, et trouble pour trouble, j'ai une toute autre Existence une toute autre perspective en Europe que je puis jamais avoir dans les etats-unis. Toute lettre de Votre part Me Sera rendue, jespere, exactement a georgetown sur potowmack post office. Je desire que ce que l'on a publié ici [sur] la Maladie d'une de Mesdames Vos filles Soit aussi faux que [tant] d'autres articles. Je Vous Souhaite la Meilleure Santé, ainsi qu'a toute Votre aimable famille. Vous connaissez l'attachement sincere et l'estime distinguée de Votre très humble Serviteur　　　　　　　　　　　　　　　C Volney

RC (DLC); addressed: "Mr Thomas jefferson Vice president of the united States Charlotte'sville Virginia"; text partially obscured by seal; endorsed by TJ as received 31 July 1797 and so recorded in SJL.

To James Madison

Th:J. to J.M　　　　　　　　　　　　　　　　　Monticello July 24. 97.

In hopes that Mrs. Madison and yourself and Miss Madison will favor us with a visit when Colo. Monroe calls on you, I write this to inform you that I have had the Shadwell and Secretary's ford both well cleaned. If you come the lower road, the Shadwell ford is the proper one. It is a little deepened, but clear of stone and perfectly safe. If you come the upper road you will cross at the Secretary's ford, turning in at the gate on the road soon after you enter the three notched road. The draught up the mountain that way is steady, but uniform.—I see Hamilton has put a short piece into the papers in answer to Callender's publication, and promises shortly something more elaborate.—I am anxious to see you here soon, because in about three weeks we shall begin to unroof our house, when the family will be obliged to go elsewhere for shelter. My affectionate respects to the family. Adieu.

PrC (DLC).

For the SHORT PIECE which Alexander Hamilton put INTO THE PAPERS, see Hamilton to John Fenno, [6 July 1797], in Syrett, *Hamilton*, XXI, 149-50. It appeared in the *Gazette of the United States* on 8 July. For James T. CALLENDER'S PUBLICATION, see Monroe to TJ, 12 July 1797. Hamilton's MORE ELABORATE response in his pamphlet *Observations* was published in Philadelphia on 25 Aug. (Syrett, *Hamilton*, XXI, 215-85).

From John Barnes

DEAR SIR   Philadelphia 26th July 1797.

I am happy in being favored with yours of 18th—on Receipt of which, I opened the Box, and shall repack, the enormous tooth, Address, and deliver it, as directed. Annexed, you have Invoice of sash doors, as well your account up to this day, which on examining—*I trust and hope* will be found pretty Correct; though different—from yours's in some items—and mode of Statement: if any errors—pray Note them for my conformity.

Your draft favor C. Johnston & Co. for $500 shall be duly honored—with—or without a discount Obtained on the 2d Moiety of W. & S. Keiths—Notes. I am Dear Sir most respectfully. Your Obedt: H Servt:

JOHN BARNES

Good Tobacco scarse and risen.

RC (ViU: Edgehill-Randolph Papers); at foot of text: "Thomas Jefferson Esquire"; endorsed by TJ as received 4 Aug. 1797 and so recorded in SJL. Enclosures not found.

To John Barnes

DEAR SIR   Monticello July 31. 97.

Just after closing and sending away my letter of the 18th. Mr. Lott desired me to pay you for him 40. Dollars which I undertook to do. The last post day however escaped me without observing it: so that there has been a fortnight's delay not at all imputable to Mr. Lott. Be pleased now to debit my account and credit his by that sum, or perhaps it might be a dollar or two or some cents more, for I find I did not make a memorandum of it at the time and now quote it by memory: but you will know it as being the exact balance of his account then payable, and now to be transferred from him to me. I am Dear Sir Your most obedt. servt

TH: JEFFERSON

PrC (MHi); at foot of text: "Mr. Barnes"; endorsed by TJ in ink on verso.

On 17 July TJ promised Peter LOTT that he would pay Barnes $47.25 in his behalf. The same day TJ arranged to purchase corn from Mrs. Ann Key and used an order on Lott for $40.00 as partial payment (MB, II, 967).

A letter from Barnes to TJ, dated 22 Apr. and received 21 July 1797, is recorded in SJL but has not been found.

From Delamotte

MONSIEUR   Havre le [13] Therm. [5e.]
                                          31. Juillet 1797.

J'ai appris dans le tems Avec bien de l'interet votre Election et j'ai tout de Suite Compris par la nature des Suffrages, qu'il ne vous Seroit pas possible de vous refuser Au Vœu de vos Concitoyens. Lorsque les votes pour deux places éminentes Se portent Sur deux personnes Seulement, il est clair qu'elles n'ont pas la liberté de refuser et que ces personnes Sont destinées pour toujours à etre les très humbles Servantes de leur pays. Je vous Avouë que ci-devant je ne l'aurois pas Compris Ainsi j'aurois voulu qu'on fut toujours libre d'etre quelque chose ou rien, mais Aujourdhui je m'y fais et j'aurois été couroucé contre Mr. Barthelemy S'il Avoit refusé place Au directoire. Maintenant, Monsieur, je vous Souhaite du fond de mon Cœur toute la Satisfaction qui devroit etre le prix de votre dévouëment.

Je Souffre en Verité de l'embarras où Se trouve l'Amerique pour repondre à deux puissances qu'il faudroit qu'elle eut toutes deux pour Amies. J'esperois que nous allions faire la paix avec l'Angleterre et [. . .] les difficultés Avec l'Ameri[que] Seroient bien vite Arrangées, mais on n'espere plus en ce Moment la paix Avec l'Angleterre; les préliminaires Même de celle Avec l'empereur n'auront probablement point de Suite et alors vous Avés à craindre la continuation des Mêmes rigueurs de la part de notre gouvernement. Vous etes entre l'enclume et le marteau et vous Aurés fort à faire pour en Sortir. J'attends tous les jours Avec bien de l'impatience les Commissaires Ameriqs. Leur Arrivée pourroit faire changer cette Situation, et leur Succès dépend, dans mon Opinion, plus du Moment où ils Arriveront, que de toute autre chose. Tout change Si vite chés nous, que C'est chaque jour une Sçène Nouvelle. Lorsque les rigueurs Contre vous ont été déployées, il n'y avoit qu'une Volonté, c'etoit celle du directoire; aujourdhuy il y en a deux depuis la lutte qui S'est établie entre le directoire et le Corps legislatif. Les Atheletes, Sont en présence; ils ne Se sont point encore porté de Coups, ils cherchent l'un chez l'autre le Coté foible pour y frapper. À qui restera la Victoire? Le Corps legislatif est pour vous. L'evenement vous prouvera, je crois,

[485]

que Si vos Commissaires fussent Arrivés huit jours plustôt ou huit jours plus tard, ils Auroient fait tout differemment. Puissent-ils Arriver au bon moment pour bien faire. Vous etes placés trop loin pour la politique d'Aujourdhuy.

À tout évenement, Monsieur, Veuillés ne pas Negliger de faire prendre à tous les Navires des roles d'équipage Visés ou Certifiés par les *Naval officiers* Contenants l'Age et le lieu de Naissance ou de domicile de chaque homme embarqué, Comme le Veut l'Arreté du directoire du 12. Ventose dernier dont vous avés Sans doute Connoissance. Il me Semble que l'Amerique peut Se Conformer à cette formalité, Sans que cela implique Approbation de la Contravention au traité.

On a parlé du projet en Amerique de Mettre Un embargo Sur les Navires. Je verrois Avec plus de plaisir les Ameriquains Se mettre parfaitement en regle et Suivre leur Commerce pour regagner ce qu'on leur fait perdre. Si la paix Se fait, vous l'aurés aussi, Si la guerre continuë, il y aura encore bien de l'argent à gagner et on n'en Viendra jamais à Saisir les propriétés Américaines en france.

Mr. Provost vous donnera de Meilleurs détails que moi de la Situation Actuelle de nos affaires qui deviennent les votres. J'Ai l'honneur de vous Saluer, Monsieur, Avec la plus Sincere Affection et de vous Assurer du respect que je vous porte.   DELAMOTTE

RC (MoSHi: Jefferson Papers); corner mutilated; endorsed by TJ as received 3 Nov. 1797 and so recorded in SJL.

L'ARRETÉ DU DIRECTOIRE DU 12. VENTOSE DERNIER, approved 2 Mch. 1797, concerned neutral shipping and stated that the Jay Treaty necessitated the modification of certain articles of the 1778 TRAITÉ, the Treaty of Amity and Commerce between France and the United States. Under the new regulations, any American vessel that lacked a roster bearing prescribed information about its crew was a lawful prize (Duvergier, *Lois*, IX, 317).

Note on Diplomatic Appointments

1797. July. Murray is rewarded for his services by an appointment to Amsterdam; W. Smith of Charleston to Lisbon.

MS (DLC: TJ Papers, 102: 17461); entirely in TJ's hand; written as initial entry on same sheet as Notes on Alexander Hamilton, 24 Aug. 1797, a truncated version of Note on Spanish Expenditures, 13 Oct. 1797, and Notes on Conversations with John Adams and George Washington, [after 13 Oct. 1797].

Five previous editions of TJ's papers have included this document and other notes of meetings, conversations, and gossip that TJ compiled during his term as vice president and then as president with similar notes that he kept during his secretary of state years, which collectively have become known as the "Anas." TJ himself, however, applied this term only to materials pertaining to the secretary of state years that he gathered and bound together perhaps as early as 1800 in an effort to counteract John Marshall's upcoming history of George Washington's administration, which TJ surmised would be of a highly partisan character (Vol. 22: 33-8).

On 27 Feb. 1797, Washington nominated William Vans MURRAY, a Federalist leader in the House of Representatives from Maryland, to serve as resident minister of the United States to the Netherlands at AMSTERDAM. The Senate confirmed the appointment four days later. On 6 July, President Adams nominated William L. SMITH, Federalist leader of the House of Representatives from CHARLESTON, South Carolina, to serve as minister plenipotentiary at LISBON. The Senate confirmed the appointment by a 20 to 4 vote on 10 July 1797 (*Biog. Dir. Cong.*; JEP, I, 228, 248-9). Smith had been seeking a diplomatic appointment since the spring of 1795 (George C. Rogers, Jr., *Evolution of a Federalist: William Loughton Smith of Charleston (1758-1812)* [Columbia, S.C., 1962], 304-6).

From Thomas Bee

SIR   Charleston 1st. August. 1797

It is with pleasure I acknowledge the receipt of your favor of the 22d May received yesterday by Mr. Rutledge addressed to the President of the Agricultural Society accompanied with four Seeds of the Bread Fruit Tree, the greatest Attention will be paid to the raising this Fruit if they once Vegetate, but I am sorry to inform you that very few of the Seeds of the Rice which you sent by Mr. Read ever Sprouted, owing I imagine to their having been heated or damaged in the Voyage either to Europe or since, it being well ascertained by Experiment that the Seed of our Rice will grow and come to Perfection at the end of Seven or Eight Years after it has been gathered and carefully [preserved].

The Society are greatly obliged by your Attention both now and formerly, and if there is any way in which they can return the obligation it will afford them as well as Myself particular pleasure in doing so. Every Measure that can tend to add additional Blessings to the many our Country already enjoys, ought to be Attended to, and many no doubt may be acquired by proper Attention and It will give our Society great satisfaction to be the means of contributing thereto. I have the honor to be with Sentiments of great respect Sir Your most Obt & most humble Sert   THO BEE

President of the Agricultural Society

RC (DLC); at foot of text: "The Vice President of the U.S."; endorsed by TJ as received 25 Aug. 1797 and so recorded in SJL.

TJ's FAVOR of 22 May 1797 is recorded in SJL but has not been found.

For the SEEDS OF THE RICE previously SENT with Jacob Read, see Bee to TJ, 16 May 1797.

From James Madison

Dear Sir   Orange Augst. 2d. 1797

At the desire of Mr. Bringhurst I forward him to Monticello; and make use of the opportunity, the first that has offered, to return you the pamphlet you were so kind as to leave with me. I add to it a late Fredg. paper which has got hold of some important articles of later date than were brought by the last post, and which may therefore be new to you as they were to me. I have had nothing from Monroe since his letter by you. Dawson mentioned on the 10th. that he would be in Virga. in 14 days; but I see by the fête given him in New York that he was there about the middle of the month. I hope you have shared with us in the fine dose of rainey weather which has restored the verdure of the earth; and if followed by the ordinary course of the season, will save our crops of corn from any essential deficit. Mrs. M. joins in respects to the ladies, and the cordiality with which I remain Dear Sir, Yrs. affecly.

Js. Madison Jr

RC (DLC: Madison Papers); endorsed by TJ as received 2 Aug. 1797 and so recorded in SJL.

The pamphlet and Fredericksburg paper that Madison sent to TJ have not been identified. The letter from James Monroe to Madison, delivered by TJ during his visit with Madison on his return from Philadelphia on 10 and 11 July, has not been found. On 27 July, John dawson wrote Madison from Philadelphia informing him that Monroe would leave for Virginia "in about a week" (Madison, *Papers*, xvii, 32-3; mb, ii, 966). A letter written by Dawson at Orange Court House to TJ on 24 Apr. 1797, received 11 July, is recorded in SJL but has not been found. Also recorded in SJL but missing is a letter from Dawson at Richmond, written 18 Mch. and received 22 Mch. 1794.

From St. George Tucker

Dear Sir   Williamsburg. August 2d. 1797.

My worthy and intimate friend Dr. Barraud proposing to take an Excursion into the upper parts of the Country, the recollection of the pleasure I enjoyed at Monticello, two years ago, prompted me to recommend it to him to take it in his rout. Permit me to introduce him to your Acquaintance as one who possesses the most amiable qualities both to excite and secure Esteem and Friendship.

Doctor Barraud is kind enough to charge himself with the delivery of a pamphlet which I published last year, but which came to my hands but a few days ago. If the reception which it met with from some Individuals in the House of Delegates may be considered as determining its

Merits, I ought to blush to acknowledge myself the Author. Two other Copies for our mutual friend Monroe, and Mr. Madison of Orange, I have taken the Liberty to enclose, as presuming that your intercourse with those Gentlemen would procure them a Conveyance. With unfeigned Esteem, I remain, Dear Sir, Your most obedt. Servt.

S. G. TUCKER

RC (DLC); endorsed by TJ as received 16 Aug. 1797 and so recorded in SJL. Enclosure: see below.

In his PAMPHLET, *A Dissertation on Slavery: With a Proposal for the Gradual Abolition of It, in the State of Virginia* (Philadelphia, 1796), Tucker suggested a protracted schedule of abolition that would have required many people born into slavery to complete a period of servitude to the age of twenty-eight. His plan also proposed, as an undisguised inducement to voluntary emigration, severely restricted civil rights for free blacks. Tucker inscribed the pamphlet to the General Assembly, but even a cautious plan of abolition was so unpopular that when George Keith Taylor attempted to introduce the proposal, SOME INDIVIDUALS IN THE HOUSE OF DELEGATES voted against even admitting it to lie on the table (see Sowerby, No. 2818; McColley, *Slavery*, 135).

To James Madison

TH:J. TO J.M.   Monticello Aug. 3. 97.

I scribbled you a line on the 24th. Ult. It missed of the post and so went by a private hand. I perceive from yours by Mr. Bringhurst that you had not recieved it. In fact it was only an earnest exhortation to come here with Munroe, which I still hope you will do. In the mean time I inclose you a letter from him, and wish your opinion on it's principal subject. The variety of other topics, the day I was with you, kept out of sight the letter to Mazzei imputed to me in the papers, the general substance of which is mine, tho' the diction has been considerably varied in the course of it's translations from English into Italian, from Italian into French and from French into English. I first met with it at Bladensburgh, and for a moment concieved I must take the field of the public papers: I could not disavow it wholly, because the greatest part was mine in substance tho' not in form. I could not avow it as it stood because the form was not mine, and in one place the substance very materially falsified. This then would render explanations necessary; nay it would render proofs of the whole necessary, and draw me at length into a publication of all (even the secret) transactions of the administration while I was of it; and embroil me personally with every member of the Executive, with the Judiciary, and with others still. I soon decided in my own mind to be entirely silent. I consulted with several friends at Philadelphia, who, every one of them, were clearly against my avowing or disavowing, and some of them conjured me most earnestly to let nothing provoke me to it. I corrected in conversation with them a substantial misrepresentation in the copy published. The original has a sentiment *like* this (for I have it not before me) 'they are endeavoring to submit us to the substance as they already have to the *forms* of the British government.' Meaning by *forms*, the birth-days, levees, processions to parliament, inauguration pompositions &c. But the copy published says 'as they have already submitted us to the *form* of the British'¹ &c making me express hostility to the *form* of our government, that is to say to the constitution itself: for this is really the difference of the word *form*, used in the singular or plural in that phrase in the English language. Now it would be impossible for me to explain this publicly without bringing on a personal difference between Genl. Washington and myself, which nothing before the publication of this letter has ever done: it would embroil me also with all those with whom his character is still popular, that is to say nine tenths of the people of the US. And what good would be obtained by my avowing the letter with the necessary explanations? Very little indeed in my opinion to counterbalance a good deal of harm. From my silence in this instance it can never be inferred that I am afraid to own the general sentiments of the letter. If I am subject to either imputation it is to that of avowing such sentiments too frankly both in private and public, often when there is no necessity for it, merely because I disdain every thing like duplicity. Still however I am open to conviction. Think for me on the occasion and advise me what to do, and confer with Colo. Monroe on the subject.—Let me entreat you again to come with him. There are other important things to consult on. One will be his affair. Another is the subject of the petition now inclosed you to be proposed to our district on the late presentment of our representative by the Grand jury. The idea it brings forward is still confined to my own breast. It has never been mentioned to any mortal, because I first wish your opinion on the expediency of the measure. If you approve it, I shall propose to P. Carr or some other to father it, and to present it to the counties at their General muster. This will be in time for our assembly. The presentment going in the public papers just at the moment when Congress was together produced a great effect both on it's friends and foes in that body, very much to the disheartening and mortification of the latter. I wish this petition, if approved, to arrive there under the same circumstance to produce the counter-effect so wanting for their gratification. I could² have wished to recieve it from you again at our court on Monday, because P. Carr, and Wilson Nicholas will be there and might also be consulted and commence measures for putting it into motion. If you can return it then with your opinion and corrections[3] it will be of importance. Present me affectionately to Mrs. Madison and convey to her my intreaties to interpose her good offices and persuasives with you to bring her here, and before we uncover our house, which will yet be some weeks. Salutations & Adieu.

RC (DLC: Madison Papers); with several emendations, the most important of which are noted below. PrC (DLC); lacking one emendation (see note 3 below). Enclosure: Monroe to TJ, 12 July 1797. For second enclosure, see Editorial Note and Document I of group of documents on petition to Virginia House of Delegates printed immediately below.

YOURS BY MR. BRINGHURST: Madison to TJ, 2 Aug. 1797. SJL records two letters from John Bringhurst to TJ of 29 June 1797 and 27 Aug. 1798, received from Wilmington 30 June 1797 and 6 Sep. 1798 respectively, neither of which has been found. Letters from TJ to Bringhurst of 30 June 1797 and 27 Sep. 1798 are also missing.

For the controversy over TJ's LETTER TO MAZZEI, about which TJ sought the advice of Monroe and Madison, see Editorial Note on Jefferson's letter to Philip Mazzei, at 24 Apr. 1796.

For Monroe's AFFAIR, see Monroe to TJ, 12 July 1797.

For the PRESENTMENT of Virginia congressman Samuel Cabell BY THE GRAND JURY, see TJ to Peregrine Fitzhugh, 4 June 1797.

[1] Closing quotation mark supplied.
[2] Preceding two words reworked from "return."
[3] TJ interlined the preceding two words, which are lacking in PrC.

Petition to Virginia House of Delegates

I. PETITION TO THE VIRGINIA HOUSE OF DELEGATES,
[ON OR BEFORE 3 AUG. 1797]

II. REVISED PETITION TO THE VIRGINIA HOUSE OF DELEGATES,
[7 AUG.-7 SEP. 1797]

EDITORIAL NOTE

It is not clear when Jefferson decided to take it upon himself to respond to the grand jury presentment against Samuel J. Cabell (see TJ to Peregrine Fitzhugh, 4 June 1797), but he must have begun working on the draft of a petition to the Virginia House of Delegates soon after he returned to Monticello. Believing it was dangerous to let the attack on circular letters to constituents go unanswered, especially when Cabell represented Jefferson's own district, Jefferson constructed a defense of the right of representatives to communicate freely with their constituents and the natural right of citizens to correspond freely with other citizens. In his letter to Madison of 3 Aug., in which he enclosed the first state of the petition (Document I below), Jefferson asserted that he would speak of it to no one until Madison advised him on the "expediency of the measure." Jefferson encouraged him to respond quickly, however, indicating that he would show it to Peter Carr and Wilson Cary Nicholas at the 7 Aug. meeting of the Albemarle County Court if Madison approved of the document. Jefferson received Madison's encouraging response of 5 Aug. on the court day. The revised state of the petition (Document II below), transcribed in Paul L. Ford's ten-volume edition of Jefferson's papers from a manuscript which has not been found, incorporated some of the changes suggested by Madison on 5 Aug., including the use of "nominated" instead of "appointed" when referring to "officers" and "judges" in the paragraph beginning "That the grand jury is a part of the Judiciary"; the revision of the limitation on grand jurors from "such as resided within the American lines during the whole of the late revolutionary war" to "such as were citizens at the date of the treaty of peace which closed our revolutionary war" in the second to the last paragraph; and the use of "enumerated in the grant" instead of "expressly given" in the final paragraph. The revised state also included an alteration alluded to in a query from Monroe in his letter to Jefferson of 5 Sep., as to whether the petition should be sent to Congress rather than the state legislature. Adding the paragraph beginning "That independently of these considerations," Jefferson answered the question of jurisdiction by explaining that while the House of Representatives had the duty to uphold the rights of Cabell and its other members, the state had the responsibility to uphold the right of its citizens to freely correspond, a right which had not been alienated by the adoption of the United States Constitution. On 7 Sep. Jefferson wrote Monroe that the petition was not designed to punish "the breach of Mr. Cabell's privilege" but to punish the "wrong done to the citizens of our district."

The petition presented to the Virginia House of Delegates was probably in Monroe's hand. He completed it by the end of October, following Jefferson's instructions—given after he consulted with Madison and Nicholas—to omit the references to impeachment (Monroe to TJ, [27 Oct. 1797]). The paragraph that sought to restrict grand jurors to "native citizens of the United States" was also eliminated, fully incorporating the change urged by Madison in early August. Thus the final state of the petition as preserved in the *Journal of the House of Delegates of the Commonwealth of Virginia* left any measures to be taken against the jurors up to the state assembly (see notes to Document II below). Nicholas, one of the Albemarle County delegates, most likely brought the petition to Richmond where it was presented and read before the House of Delegates on 19 Dec. 1797. A committee of the whole House considered the petition on 26 and 27 Dec. and framed a resolution that was brought forward the following day. Describing the House of Delegates as the "grand inquest of the commonwealth" which had the right and duty "to oppose political error, or to call to account political criminality, by expressing an opinion, or presenting an impeachment," the resolution stated that the grand jury presentment had endangered the safety of the state and diminished the rights of the people by "subjecting representatives to censure, expense, or punishment, for communicating with their constituents." If the presentment were allowed to stand, constituents in the future would be ignorant of the conduct of their representatives, responsibility would be transferred from constituents to juries, the legislature would be dependent on the executive and judiciary, and free communication between citizen and citizen would be abolished. The House of Delegates therefore concluded that the presentment was a "violation of the fundamental principles of representation" because it subjected the "natural right of speaking and writing freely, to the censure and controul of Executive power" (JHD, Dec. 1797-Jan. 1798, 40-1, 59-62; Leonard, *General Assembly*, 207).

Three attempts, all unsuccessful, were made to amend the resolution. The first called upon Virginia congressmen to support legislation limiting grand juries to presentments against offences covered by the laws of Congress. The second argued that the House of Representatives, not the Virginia House of Delegates, was responsible for protecting the rights of congressmen. The third was a defense of the grand jury system, a "sacred political institution," against legislative and executive encroachments. The House went on to pass the original measure, 92-53, but adopted no punitive measures and failed to send it to the upper house for further action. The House agreed to insert the petition in it's journal and have one thousand copies, along with the House actions concerning it, printed for distribution (JHD, Dec. 1797-Jan. 1798, 61-4).

By using others to bring the petition forward, Jefferson attempted to keep his authorship quiet. He did not succeed. Federalist John Nicholas, Albemarle County clerk, learned of Jefferson's role in the measure and criticized him for secretly writing the petition while vice president, thus ignoring the separation of powers (Nicholas to George Washington, 22 Feb. 1798, in Washington, *Papers: Retir. Ser.*, II, 101-2). John Taylor, however, may not have been aware of Jefferson's role. While developing a political strategy for the meeting of the Assembly in 1798, he confided to Wilson Cary Nicholas on the ineffectiveness of resolutions and addresses brought forth by Republicans in previous years. "Even the masterly petition from your district," he observed, "about the grand jury presentment was called a 'party thing' and forgotten" (Taylor to Nicholas, 27 Oct. 1798, in ViU). This did not deter Jefferson. In 1798 he drafted another petition for presentation to the Virginia Assembly by which he sought to abolish the court's right to pick and exert power over the jurors (see petition enclosed in TJ to Madison, 26 Oct. 1798; Adrienne Koch and Harry Ammon, "The Virginia and Kentucky Resolutions: An Episode in Jefferson's and Madison's Defense of Civil Liberties," in WMQ, ser. 3, V [1948], 153-4).

I. Petition to the Virginia House of Delegates

[on or before 3 Aug. 1797]

To the Speaker and House of Delegates of the Commonwealth of Virginia

The Petition of the subscribers, inhabitants of the counties of Amherst, Albemarle, Fluvanna and Goochland sheweth

That by the constitution of this state, established from it's earliest settlement, the people thereof have possessed the right of being governed by laws to which they have consented by representatives chosen by themselves immediately:[1] that in order to give to the will of the people the influence it ought to have, and the information which may enable them to exercise it usefully, it was a part of the common law, adopted as the law of this land, that their representatives, in the discharge of their functions, should be free from the cognisance or coercion of it's co-ordinate branches Judiciary and Executive; and that their communications with their constituents should of right, as of duty also, be free, full,[2] and unawed by any:[3] that so necessary has this intercourse been deemed in the country from which they derive their descent and laws, that the communications between the Representative and Constituent are privileged there to pass free of expence through the channel of the public post, and that the proceedings of the legislature have been known to be arrested and suspended at times until the Representatives could go home to their several counties and confer with their constituents.

That when, at the epoch of Independance, the constitution was formed under which we are now governed as a commonwealth, so highly were the principles of representative government esteemed, that the legislature was made to consist of two branches, both of them chosen immediately by the citizens; and that general system of laws was continued which protected the relations between the representative and constituent, and guarded the functions of the former from the controul of the Judiciary and Executive branches:[4]

That when circumstances required that [the] antient confederation of this with the sister states, for the government of their common concerns,[5] should be improved into a more regular and effective form of general government, the same representative principle was preserved in the new legislature, one branch of which was to be chosen directly by the citizens of each state,[6] and the laws and principles remained unaltered which privilege the representative functions, whether to be exercised in the state or general government, against the cognisance and notice of the co-ordinate branches Executive and Judiciary; and for it's safe and convenient exercise, the intercommunication of the representative and constituent has been sanctioned and provided for through the channel of the public post, at the public expence:

That at the General partition of this commonwealth into districts, each of which were to chuse a representative to Congress, the counties of Amherst, Albemarle, Fluvanna and Goochland were laid off into one district: that at the elections held for the said district in the month of April in the years 1795. and 1797. the electors thereof made choice of Samuel Jordan Cabell of the county of Amherst to be their representative in the legislature of the General government:[7] that the said Samuel Jordan Cabell accepted the said office, repaired at the due periods to the legislature of the General government, exercised his functions there as became a worthy member, and as a good and dutiful representative was in the habit of corresponding with many of[8] his constituents, and of communicating to us by way of letter information of the public proceedings of asking and recieving our[9] opinions and advice, and of contributing as [far as depend]ed on him,[10] to preserve the transactions of the General government in [unison] with the principles and sentiments of his constituents: that while the said Saml. J. Cabell was in the exercise of his functions as a representative from this district, and was in the course of that correspondence which his duty and the will of his constituents imposed on him, the right of thus communicating with them, deemed sacred under all the forms in which [our government had] hitherto existed, never questioned or[11] infringed even by Royal judges or [governors, was] most dangerously and[12] [injuri]ously violated at a Circuit court of the General Government held at the city of Richmond for the district of Virginia in the month of   of this present year 1797:[13] that at the said court A.B. &c.   having been called upon to serve in the office of Grand jurors before the said court, were sworn to the duties of the said office in the usual forms of the law, the known limits of which duties are to make presentment of[14] those acts of individuals which the laws have declared to be crimes or misdemeanors: that departing out of the legal limits of their said office, and availing themselves of the sanction of it's cover, wickedly and contrary to their fidelity to destroy the rights of the people of this commonwealth, and the fundamental principles of representative government, they made a presentment of the act of the said Saml. J. Cabell in writing letters to his constituents in the following words, to wit, [here insert the presentment.][15]

That the Grand jury is a part of the Judiciary, not permanent indeed, but in office[16] pro hac vice, and responsible as other judges are for their actings and doings while in office: that for the Judiciary to interpose in the legislative department between the Constituent and his Representative, to controul them in the exercise of their functions or duties towards each other, to overawe the free correspondence which exists and ought to exist between them, to dictate what communication may pass between them,[17] and to punish all others, to put the Representative[18] into jeopardy of criminal prosecution, of vexation, expence, and punishment before the Judiciary, if his communications public or private do not exactly square with their ideas of fact or right, or with their[19] designs of wrong, is to put the legislative department under the feet of the Judiciary, is to leave us indeed the shadow, but to take away the substance of representation, which requires essentially that the Representative be as free as his Constituents would be, that the same interchange of sentiment be lawful between him and them as would be among themselves were they in the personal transaction of their own business; is to do away[20] the [influence of the] people over the proceedings [of their] representatives by excluding from their knolege [through fear] of punishment, all but [such] information or misinformation as may suit their own views; and is the more vitally dangerous when it is considered that Grand jurors are selected by officers appointed and holding their places at the will of the Executive, that they are exposed to influence from the judges who are appointed immediately by the Executive, and who, altho' holding permanently [21] their commissions as judges, yet from the career of additional office and emolument *actually* opened to them of late, whether *constitutionally* or not, are under all those motives, [22] which interest or ambition inspire, of courting the favor of that branch from which appointments flow; [23] that Grand juries are frequently composed in part of bystanders, often foreigners, of foreign attachments and interests and little knolege of the laws they are most improperly called to decide on, [24] of which description were some of the Grand jury in question; and finally is to give to the Judiciary, and through them to the Executive a compleat preponderance over the legislature, [25] rendering ineffectual that wise and cautious [26] distribution of powers made by the constitution between the three branches, and subordinating to the other two that branch [27] which most immediately depends on the people themselves, and is responsible to them at short periods.

Your petitioners further observe that tho' this crime may not be specifically defined and denominated by any particular statute, yet it is a crime, and of the highest and most alarming nature: that the Constitution of this Commonwealth, aware it would sometimes [28] happen that deep and dangerous crimes, pronounced [as such in] the heart of every friend to his country and it's free constitution, [29] would often escape the definitions of the law, and yet ought not to escape it's punishments, fearing at the same time to entrust such undescribed offences to the discretion of ordinary juries and judges, has reserved the same to the cognisance of the body of the Commonwealth acting by their representatives in General assembly, for which purpose provision is made by the constitution in the following words, to wit, 'the Governor, when he is out of office, and *others* offending against the state, either by mal-administration, corruption, *or other means* by which the safety [of the state may be endangered], shall be impeachable by the House of Delegates. Such impeachment to be prosecuted by the Attorney General or such other person or persons as the house may appoint in the General court, according to the laws of the land. If found guilty, he or they shall be either for ever disabled to hold any office under government, or removed from such offices pro tempore, or subjected to such pains or penalties as the law shall direct.'

Considering then the House of Delegates as the standing Inquest of the whole Commonwealth so established by the Constitution, that it's jurisdiction as such extends over all persons within it's limits, and that no pale, no sanctuary has been erected against their jurisdiction to protect offenders who have committed crimes against the laws of the Commonwealth within the same, that the crime committed by the said Grand jurors is of that high and extraordinary character for which the constitution has provided extraordinary procedure, that tho' the violation of right falls in the first instance on us your petitioners and the representative chosen immediately by us, yet in principle and consequence it extends to all our fellow citizens, whose safety is passed away whenever their representatives are placed, in the exercise of their functions, under the direction and coercion of either of the other departments of government: We your petitioners therefore pray that you will be pleased to take your constitutional cognisance of the premises and institute such proceedings for impeaching and punishing the said A.B. &c.[30] as may protect in future the Representatives of this Commonwealth in the exercise of their functions freely and independantly of the other departments of government, may guard that full intercourse between them and their constituents which the nature of their relations and the laws of the land establish, and may serve as a terror to others attempting[31] hereafter to subvert the fundamental principles of our constitution, to exclude the people from all direct influence over the government they have established by [reducing that] branch of the legislature which they chuse directly, to a subordination [under those branches] over whom they have but an indirect, distant and feeble controul.

And your petitioners further submit to the wisdom of the two houses of General assembly whether the safety of the citizens of this commonwealth in their persons, their property, their laws and government does not require that the capacity to act in the important office of a juror, grand or petty, civil or criminal, should be restrained in future (the single case of the medietas linguae excepted) to native citizens of the US. or such as resided within the American lines during the whole of the late revolutionary war, and whether the ignorance of our laws and natural partiality to the countries of their birth are not reasonable causes for declaring this to be one of the rights incommunicable to adoptive citizens.

We therefore your petitioners, relying with entire confidence on the wisdom and patriotism of our representatives in General assembly, cloathed preeminently with all the powers of the people which have not been[32] reserved to themselves, or expressly given to the General government, and stationed as centinels to observe with watchfulness and oppose with firmness[33] all movements tending to destroy the equilibrium of our excellent but complicated machine of government, invoke from you that redress of our violated rights which the freedom and safety of our common country calls for, and we, as in duty bound, shall ever pray &c.

PrC (DLC: TJ Papers, 232: 42022-7); undated; badly faded, with words in brackets supplied from Dft, except where noted (see note 15 below). Dft (same, 232: 42014-17); undated; with minor variations in punctuation, abbreviations, and wording, one being noted below (see note 16); with numerous emendations, only the most important of which are noted below. Enclosed in TJ to Madison, 3 Aug. 1797.

[1] In Dft TJ first wrote "laws made by a legislature one branch ⟨thereof⟩ of which that was chosen by the said inhabitants themselves directly" before altering the passage to read as above.

[2] In Dft TJ interlined the preceding nine words in place of "be free, uncontrouled and [in] frequent."

[3] In Dft TJ here canceled "other power, that information might be carried home to the [breast] of every citizen, and opportunity be thus given him to express to his representative his individual sense of measures, to have that influence on his judgment to which they were entitled."

[4] In Dft TJ first wrote "made a sacred [. . .] fundamental and important part, the rights duties and functions of each remained unimpaired and their correspondence privileged and kept sacred against the cognisance and [. . .] of the other coordinate branches" before altering the preceding clause to read as above.

[5] In Dft TJ first wrote "circumstances rendered it eligible for the happiness of our own and our sister states, that the confederation which had been formed in the earlier [. . .] moments of our revolution" before altering the preceding passage to read as above.

[6] In Dft TJ first wrote the passage from this point to "general government" as: "[and the] relations duties, rights privileges and functions between the represen-

tatives and constituent remained the same and the laws and principles on which they [rested] protecting [their] exercise of [their] functions and communication remained ⟨the same and thus⟩ unaltered and consequently privileged the [same and] sacred" before altering it to read as above.

[7] In Dft TJ here and in the next clause interlined the preceding two words in place of "US."

[8] Preceding two words interlined in Dft.

[9] In this passage and elsewhere in Dft TJ changed third person to first, altering "their" to "our," "they" to "we," and "them" to "us."

[10] Preceding three words interlined in Dft in place of "a single ⟨vote⟩ voice could do it."

[11] In Dft TJ first wrote "never violated or encroached or."

[12] Preceding two words interlined in Dft.

[13] In Dft TJ here canceled "before James Iredell   judge and Cyrus Griffin district judge, at which court John Blair &c."

[14] In Dft TJ here canceled "breaches those offenses public wrongs which."

[15] Brackets in original. Bracketed directive lacking in Dft.

[16] In Dft TJ here interlined "occasional only and in office."

[17] Preceding three words interlined in Dft in place of "be made."

[18] In Dft TJ first wrote "individuals" before interlining "of the legislature" and then altering the phrase to read as above.

[19] In Dft TJ here canceled "wicked."

[20] In Dft TJ wrote the passage from "is to leave" through "do away" in the margin in place of "is to poison free government in it's purest source of representation, is to mislead and invalidate."

[21] Word interlined in Dft.

[22] In Dft TJ here canceled "of subservience to the Executive."

[23] Preceding eleven words interlined in

Dft in place of "and are no longer to be considered as impartial and [. . .] between the Executive and people."

[24] Preceding three words interlined in Dft in place of "upon to execute."

[25] In Dft TJ inserted the remainder of the sentence in place of "and controul to the utter subversion of the constitution, and of the rights of the people."

[26] Word interlined in Dft in place of "⟨essential⟩ happy."

[27] Proceding seven words interlined in place of "to the suppression of that."

[28] Word interlined in Dft in place of "often."

[29] Preceding seven words interlined in Dft in place of "[. . .] freedom and his country."

[30] Dft: "J. Blair &c."

[31] Remainder of paragraph inserted in Dft in place of alternate wording that also included reference to the "most precious rights of the people."

[32] TJ here canceled "specially" in Dft.

[33] Preceding six words interlined in Dft.

II. Revised Petition to the Virginia House of Delegates

[7 Aug.-7 Sep. 1797]

The petition of the subscribers, inhabitants of the counties of Amherst, Albemarle, Fluvanna, and Goochland, sheweth:

That by the constitution of this State, established from its earliest settlement, the people thereof have professed the right of being governed by laws to which they have consented by representatives chosen by themselves immediately: that in order to give to the will of the people the influence it ought to have, and the information which may enable them to exercise it usefully, it was a part of the common law, adopted as the law of this land, that their representatives, in the discharge of their functions, should be free from the cognizance or coercion of the co-ordinate branches, Judiciary and Executive; and that their communications with their constituents should of right, as of duty also, be free, full, and unawed by any: that so necessary has this intercourse been deemed in the country from which they derive principally their descent and laws, that the correspondence between the representative and constituent is privileged there to pass free of expense through the channel of the public post, and that the proceedings of the legislature have been known to be arrested and suspended at times until the Representatives could go home to their several counties and confer with their constituents.

That when, at the epoch of Independence, the constitution was formed under which we are now governed as a commonwealth, so high were the principles of representative government esteemed, that the legislature was made to consist of two branches, both of them chosen immediately by the citizens;[1] and that general system of laws was continued which protected the relations between the representative and

[499]

constituent, and guarded the functions of the former from the control of the Judiciary and Executive branches.

That when circumstances required that the ancient confederation of this with the sister States, for the government of their common concerns, should be improved into a more regular and effective form of general government, the same representative principle was preserved in the new legislature, one branch of which was to be chosen directly by the citizens of each State, and the laws and principles remained unaltered which privileged the representative functions, whether to be exercised in the State or General Government, against the cognizance and notice of the co-ordinate branches, Executive and Judiciary; and for its safe and convenient exercise, the inter-communication of the representative and constituent has been sanctioned and provided for through the channel of the public post, at the public expense.

That at the General partition of this commonwealth into districts, each of which was to choose a representative to Congress, the counties of Amherst, Albemarle, Fluvanna, and Goochland, were laid off into one district: that at the elections held for the said district, in the month of April,[2] in the years 1795 and 1797, the electors thereof made choice of Samuel Jordan Cabell, of the county of Amherst, to be their representative in the legislature of the general government; that the said Samuel Jordan Cabell accepted the office, repaired at the due periods to the legislature of the General Government, exercised his functions there as became a worthy member, and as a good and dutiful representative was in the habit of corresponding with many of his constituents, and communicating to us, by way of letter, information of the public proceedings, of asking and receiving our opinions and advice, and of contributing, as far as might be with right, to preserve the transactions of the general government in unison with the principles and sentiments of his constituents: that while the said Samuel J. Cabell was in the exercise of his functions as a representative from this district, and was in the course of that correspondence which his duty and the will of his constituents imposed on him, the right of thus communicating with them, deemed sacred under all the forms in which our government has hitherto existed, never questioned or infringed even by Royal judges or governors, was openly and directly violated at a Circuit court of the General Government, held at the city of Richmond, for the district of Virginia, in the month of May[3] of this present year, 1797: that at the said court A, B, &c.,[4] some of whom were foreigners, having been called upon to serve in the office of grand jurors before the said court, were sworn to the duties of said office in the usual forms of the law, the known limits of which duties are to make presentment of those acts of individuals which the laws have declared to be crimes or misdemeanors: that departing out of the legal limits of their said office, and availing themselves of the sanction of its cover, wickedly and contrary to their fidelity to destroy the rights of the people of this commonwealth, and the fundamental principles of representative government, they made a presentment of the act of the said Samuel J. Cabell, in writing letters to his constituents in the following words, to wit: "We, of the grand jury of the United States, for the district of Virginia, present as a real evil, the circular letters of several members of the late Congress, and particularly letters with the signature of Samuel J. Cabell, endeavoring, at a time of real public danger, to disseminate unfounded calumnies against the happy government of the United States, and thereby to separate the people therefrom; and to increase or produce a foreign influence, ruinous to the peace, happiness, and independence of these United States."

That the grand jury is a part of the Judiciary, not permanent indeed, but in office, *pro hac vice* and responsible as other judges are for their actings and doings while in office: that for the Judiciary to interpose in the legislative department between the constituent and his representative, to control them in the exercise of their functions or duties towards each other, to overawe the free correspondence which exists and ought to exist between them, to dictate what communications may pass between them, and to punish all others, to put the representative into jeopardy of criminal prosecution, of vexation, expense, and punishment before the Judiciary, if his communications, public or private, do not exactly square with their ideas of fact or right, or with their designs of wrong, is to put the legislative department under the feet of the Judiciary, is to leave us, indeed, the shadow, but to take away the substance of representation, which requires essentially that the representative be as free as his constituents would be, that the same interchange of sentiment be lawful between him and them as would be lawful among themselves were they in the personal transaction of their own business; is to do away the influence of the people over the proceedings of their representatives by excluding from their knowledge, by the terror of punishment, all but such information or misinformation as may suit their own views; and is the more vitally dangerous when it is considered that grand jurors are selected by officers nominated and holding their places at the will of the Executive: that they are exposed to influence from the judges who are nominated immediately by the Executive, and who, although holding permanently their commissions as judges, yet from the career of additional office and emolument *actually*[5] opened to them of late, whether *constitutionally* or not, are under all those motives which interest or ambition inspire, of courting the favor of that branch from which appointments flow: that grand juries are frequently composed in part of by-standers, often foreigners, of foreign attachments and interests, and little knowledge of the laws they are most improperly called to decide on; and finally, is to give to the Judiciary, and through them to the Executive, a complete preponderance over the legislature, rendering ineffectual that wise and cautious distribution of powers made by the constitution between the three branches, and subordinating to the other two that branch which most immediately depends on the people themselves, and is responsible to them at short periods.

That independently of these considerations of a constitutional nature, the right of free correspondence between citizen and citizen on their joint interests, public or private, and under whatsoever laws these interests arise, is a natural right of every individual citizen, not the gift of municipal law, but among the objects for the protection of which municipal laws are instituted: that so far as the attempt to take away this natural right of free correspondence is an offence against the privileges of the legislative house, of which the said Samuel J. Cabell is a member, it is left to that house,[6] entrusted with the preservation of its own privileges, to vindicate its immunities against the encroachments and usurpations of a co-ordinate branch; but so far as it is an infraction of our individual rights as citizens by other citizens of our own State, the judicature of this commonwealth is solely[7] competent to its cognizance, no other possessing any powers of redress: that the commonwealth retains all judiciary cognisances not expressly alienated in the grant of powers to the United States as expressed in their constitution: that the constitution alienates only those enumerated in itself, or arising under laws or treaties of the United States made in conformity with its own tenor: but the right of free correspondence is not claimed under that constitution nor the laws or treaties derived from it, but as a natural right, placed originally under the protection of our municipal laws, and retained under the cognizance of our own courts.

Your petitioners further observe[8] that though this crime may not be specifically defined and denominated by any particular statute, yet it is a crime, and of the highest and most alarming nature; that the constitution of this commonwealth, aware it would sometimes happen that deep and dangerous crimes, pronounced as such in the heart of every friend to his country and its free constitution, would often escape the definitions of the law, and yet ought not to escape its punishments, fearing at the same time to entrust such undescribed offences to the discretion of ordinary juries and judges, has reserved the same to the cognizance of the body of the commonwealth acting by their representatives in general assembly, for which purpose provision is made by the constitution in the following words, to wit, "The Governor, when he is out of office, and *others* offending against the State, either by mal-administration, corruption, *or other means* by which the safety of the State may be endangered, shall be impeachable by the House of Delegates. Such impeachment to be prosecuted by the Attorney General or such other person or persons as the house may appoint in the general court, according to the laws of the land. If found guilty, he or they shall be either forever disabled to hold any office under government, or removed from such offices *pro tempore*, or subjected to such pains or penalties as the law shall direct."

Considering then the House of Delegates as the standing inquest of the whole commonwealth so established by the constitution, that its jurisdiction as such extends over all persons within its limits, and that no pale, no sanctuary has been erected against their jurisdiction to protect offenders who have committed crimes against the laws of the commonwealth and rights of its citizens: that the crime committed by the said grand jurors is of that high and extraordinary character for which the constitution has provided extraordinary procedure: that though the violation of right falls in the first instance on us, your petitioners[9] and the representative chosen immediately by us, yet in principle and consequence it extends to all our fellow-citizens, whose safety is passed away whenever their representatives are placed, in the exercise of their functions, under the direction and coercion of either of the other departments of government, and one of their most interesting rights is lost when that of a free communication of sentiment by speaking or writing is suppressed: We, your petitioners, therefore pray that you will be pleased to take your constitutional cognizance of the premises, and institute such proceedings for impeaching and punishing the said A, B, &c.,[10] as may secure to the citizens of this commonwealth their constitutional right: that their representatives shall in the exercise of their functions be free and independent of the other departments of government, may guard that full intercourse between them and their constituents which the nature of their relations and the laws of the land establish, may save to them the natural right of communicating their sentiments to one another by speaking and writing, and may serve as a terror to others attempting hereafter to subvert those rights and the fundamental principles of our constitution, to exclude the people from all direct influence over the government they have established by reducing that branch of the legislature which they choose directly, to a subordination under those over whom they have but an indirect, distant, and feeble control.

And your petitioners further submit to the wisdom of the two houses of assembly whether the safety of the citizens of this commonwealth in their persons, their property, their laws, and government, does not require that the capacity to act in the important office of a juror, grand or petty, civil or criminal, should be restrained in future to native citizens of the United States, or such as were citizens at the date of the treaty of peace which closed our revolutionary war, and whether the ignorance of our laws and natural partiality to the countries of their birth are not reasonable causes for declaring this to be one of the rights incommunicable in future to adoptive citizens. [11]

We, therefore, your petitioners, relying with entire confidence on the wisdom and patriotism of our representatives in General assembly, clothed preëminently with all the powers of the people which have not been reserved to themselves, or enumerated in the grant to the General Government delegated to maintain all their rights and relations not expressly and exclusively transferred to other jurisdictions, and stationed as sentinels to observe with watchfulness and oppose with firmness all movements tending to destroy the equilibrium of our excellent but complicated machine of government, invoke from you that redress of our violated rights which the freedom and safety of our common country calls for. We denounce to you a great crime, wicked in its purpose, and mortal in its consequences unless prevented, committed by citizens of this commonwealth against the body of their country. If we have erred in conceiving the redress provided by the law, we commit the subject [12] to the superior wisdom of this house to devise and pursue such proceedings as they shall think best; and we, as in duty bound, shall ever pray, &c.

MS not found; reprinted from Ford, VII, 158-64; dated [Aug. 1797], but see Editorial Note above; at head of text: "*To the Speaker and House of Delegates of the Commonwealth of Virginia, being a Protest against interference of Judiciary between Representative and Constituent.*" Printed in JHD, Dec. 1797-Jan. 1798, 61-2; with numerous variations in punctuation and capitalization; only the most important emendations, including the deletion of several paragraphs (see notes 8 and 11), are noted below; at head of text: "To the Speaker of the House of Delegates of Virginia."

[1] JHD: "people."

[2] JHD: "March."

[3] Word replaced by blank in JHD.

[4] JHD: "a grand jury having been called."

[5] Word lacking in JHD.

[6] Word and puncuation lacking in JHD.

[7] JHD: "safely."

[8] The remainder of this paragraph and the following paragraph through "extraordinary procedure" are lacking in JHD.

[9] Preceding two words lacking in JHD.

[10] JHD reads "pursue such steps" in place of the clause from "institute" to this point.

[11] Paragraph lacking in JHD.

[12] In JHD sentence to this point is lacking and previous sentence continues "viewing the subject in this light, we commit it."

From James Madison

Yours of the 3d. arrived safe yesterday. I will converse with Col. Monroe, as you desire, on the subject of his letter to you, and listen to all his reasons for the opinion he gives. My present conviction is opposed to it. I have viewed the subject pretty much in the light you do. I consider it moreover as a ticklish experiment to say publickly yes or no to the interrogatories of party spirit. It may bring on dilemmas, not to be particularly foreseen, of disagreeable explanations, or tacit confessions. Hitherto the Precedents have been the other way. The late President was silent for many years as to the letters imputed to him, and it would seem, deposited in the office of State only, the answer which the zeal of the Secretary communicated to the public. Mr. Adams has followed the example with respect to Callendar's charge, probably well founded, of advising the extermination of the Tories. Col. M. thinks that honest men would be encouraged by your owning and justifying the letter to Mazzei. I rather suspect it would be a gratification and triumph to their opponents; and that out of the unfixed part of the Community more converts would be gained by the popularity of Gen: Washington, than by the kind of proof that must be relied on against it.

Wishing to return the "Petition &c" to your Court as you recommend, I must be brief on that subject. It is certainly of great importance to set the public opinion right with regard to the functions of grand juries, and the dangerous abuse of them in the federal Courts: nor could a better occasion occur. If there be any doubts in the case, they must flow from the uncertainty of getting a numerous subscription, or of embarking the Legislature in the business. On these points the two gentlemen you mean to consult can judge much better than I can do. The Petition in its tenor, cannot certainly be mended. I have noted with a pencil, the passages which may perhaps be better guarded against cavil.

(1) The term "appoint," strictly taken includes the Senate, as well as, Executive.

(2) Is it true that the foreign members of the late Grand-jury, lie under *all* the defects ascribed to them? I am a stranger even to their names.

(3) "within the same" Does not impeachment extend to crimes committed *elsewhere*, by those amenable to our laws?

(4) "such as resided within the American lines during the *whole* war." Would not this apply to persons who came here during the war, and were faithful, to the end of it. Gallatin is an example. Would such a partial disfranchisement of persons already naturalized be a proper prec-

edent? The benefit of stating the evil to the public might be preserved and the difficulty avoided, by confining the remedy to future naturalizations, or by a general reference of it to the wisdom of the Legislature. This last may be a good expedient throughout the Petition, in case the assembly cannot be relied on to adopt the specific remedies prayed for.

(5) This change is, to avoid the term "expressly" which has been a subject of controversy, and rather decided against by the public opinion.

Your letter of the 24 has come to hand since mine by Mr. B. It is so much our inclination to comply with its invitations that you may be assured it will be done if any wise practicable. I have engagements, however, on hand of sundry kinds which forbid a promise to myself on that head. The situation of my health may be another obstacle. I was attacked the night before last, very severely by something like a cholera morbus or bilious cholic, of which, tho' much relieved, I still feel the effects, and it is not quite certain what turn the complaint may take. Adieu affecly,   Js. MADISON JR

RC (DLC: Madison Papers); endorsed by TJ as received 7 Aug. 1797 and so recorded in SJL.

HIS LETTER TO YOU: Monroe to TJ, 12 July 1797.

Washington remained SILENT concerning the LETTERS IMPUTED TO HIM that were published in London in 1777 and in New York in 1778. When the forged letters reappeared in pamphlet form in 1795 and 1796 and in the Philadelphia *Aurora*, Washington, on his final day in office, wrote a letter to Timothy Pickering, describing the forgeries and instructing him to deposit the letter in the State Department records. On 9 Mch. Pickering sent Washington's letter to the *Gazette of the United States* where it was published the next day and subsequently printed in other newspapers, including the *Aurora* on 11 Mch. (Fitzpatrick, *Writings*, xxxv, 350, 363-5, 414-16; *Letters from General Washington to Several of His Friends, in June and July, 1776* [Philadelphia, 1795]; *Epistles Domestic, Confidential, and Official, from General Washington, Written about the Commencement of the American Contest, When He Entered on the Command of the Army of the United States...* [New York, 1796], 1-66; Freeman, *Washington*, VII, 435-6).

James T. Callender's CHARGE was that John Adams, while in Amsterdam as minister to the Netherlands, wrote Lieutenant Governor Thomas Cushing of Massachusetts on 15 Dec. 1780, asserting that he had advocated fines, imprisonment, and hanging for those Americans who collaborated with the British. In the letter, which according to the account was found in a prize vessel and published in *The Annual Register for 1781*, Adams exclaimed that he would have hanged his own brother "if he had took a part with our enemy in this contest" (*The American Annual Register, or, Historical Memoirs of the United States, for the Year 1796* [Philadelphia, 1797], 234-5; *The Annual Register, or a View of the History, Politics, and Literature, For the Year 1781*, 2d ed. [London, 1791], pt. 1, 258-61). When Adams brought this letter to John Marshall's attention in early 1801 after it was once again published, Adams declared it to be a British forgery and insisted that he "never wrote any Letter in the least degree resembling it" to Cushing or to any one else. He asked Marshall to file his declaration and gave him permission to publish it if he thought fit (Marshall, *Papers*, VI, 76-7).

I HAVE NOTED WITH A PENCIL: see Petition to Virginia House of Delegates, at 3 Aug. 1797.

To Volney

Th. Jefferson to Mr. Volney   Monticello Aug. 5. 97.

Our post having failed to come as far as Charlottesville the last week delayed my reciept of yours of July 19. and consequently the answer to it one whole week. I consider it the more unfortunate as the period you have still to stay with us is flowing out. It is the wisest philosophy which directs us always to view circumstances under their most pleasing aspect. I will not consider therefore the change of destination in the vessel which was to have taken you away, as it is a disappointment to you, but as giving us a hope of seeing you here. And the sooner the better for the double reason of giving us more of your time, and that we are still in a condition to offer you a cover. It will probably be a month now, before we take off the roof of our house: consequently we can lodge you as before. It's inconveniences I felt and feel on your account, but your braving them will be a proof the more of your friendship. I shall hope therefore to see you soon, and that you will give me the first portion of your time, as Mr. Madison and Colo. Monroe will not be in the act of dismantling their dwelling. I rejoice that you have left your fever at Philadelphia. The place and the season gave me real uneasiness for you, as I know that strangers have frequently a severe initiation into the knolege of our climate. My daughters are well and have been constantly so. The inquietude you are so kind as to express on the rumor of their having been otherwise, proves your friendship, but also that Monticello has partaken of the libels heaped on it's master. We are never sick here. Hasten therefore to pass as much of the heats of August here as you can, and in the mean time accept my affectionate salutations & Adieu.—My respects to Doctr. Thornton.

PrC (DLC).

From Citizens of Vincennes

Sir   Vincennes August 7th. 1797

Altho' we have not the Honor of being acquainted with you, we trust our rights as Citizens Will not be the less regarded.

The enclosed memorials will express the Object of our desires. We beg leave however to observe, that we understand a Petition has Gone forward to Congress, praying all concessions Whatever heretofore Granted May be confirmed; These concessions all became forfeited by their being no actual improvements Made. That the object of the Said

Petition is founded in Speculation, and Should the Prayer of the Same be Granted Very Large and Extensive Bodies of Land of the United States Will be covered; the Small farms of your Memorialists Which they have toiled thro' a Savage War to Improve, Will be Swallowed up, and themselves Materially distressed.

We would farther request that you would have the Goodness to have one of the Enclosed memorials laid Before the Senate.

THE SUBSCRIBERS

RC (DNA: RG 46, Senate Records, 5th Cong., 2d sess.); in an unidentified hand; endorsed by a Senate clerk as a "Letter accompanying sundry memorials of the people of Vincennes." Enclosures: (1) Memorial, Vincennes to the vice president and Senate, 7 Aug. 1797, of fifteen men, seven widows, and the heirs of three other individuals, stating that beginning in 1784 they emigrated to Knox County, Northwest Territory, on the basis of promises by the commandant at Vincennes that each would receive "a reasonable Quantity of Land" in the vicinity of that settlement; that each memorialist had 400 acres of land surveyed; that through negligence of the clerk and malfeasance by the surveyor, no titles were issued as a result of those surveys; that the memorialists nevertheless cleared land and made improvements until forced to retire to Vincennes in 1786; that then for about two years the memorialists rented lands from "the ancient settlers" but also established outlying "Stations" which came under frequent attack by Indians; that in those attacks several of their number were killed, now represented by widows and heirs among the memorialists; that the memorialists never abandoned their claims to their improvements and returned to them after peace was made with the Indians of the Wabash in 1792; that the memorialists are heads of families, and if dispossessed of their improvements, their dependents "Must be reduced to Indigency and Want"; and the

memorialists pray that Congress will grant each of them 400 acres, the heirs and widows of those killed to receive "Such quantity as May Seem reasonable" (MS in same, in same hand as covering letter, signed by the memorialists, endorsed by Otis; printed in *Terr. Papers*, II, 620-1). (2) A similar memorial to the speaker and members of the House of Representatives (see *Terr. Papers*, II, 621n).

For settlements at Vincennes under inducements from French officials holding commissions from George Rogers Clark, see J. M. P. LeGras to TJ, 22 Mch. 1780; and TJ's report on lands at Vincennes, [14 Dec. 1790], Document II of a group of documents on the Northwest Territory, printed above in this series at Vol. 18: 186-7. In December 1797 several of the above memorialists joined others in a new petition addressed to the president and both houses of Congress. On 20 Feb. 1798 the Senate referred that petition to a committee along with two other appeals, one requesting permission to lay out lands on Kaskaskia Creek and another from Benjamin Reed of Vincennes, which asked for confirmation of land grants and may have been the petition declared above to be FOUNDED IN SPECULATION. The committee recommended that the governor of the Northwest Territory report to the Senate about the conflicting claims (*Terr. Papers*, II, 590, 621n, 634-6; *Annals*, VII, 504, 508, 516-17).

From John F. Mercer

DEAR SIR   Marlbro' Augt. 9. 97.

I have sent you small parcels of the two different kinds of wheat, I shew'd you when I saw you last.

No. 1. The Manyheaded wheat, commonly call'd Ægyptian—the triticum spica multiplici, a Smyrna wheat of Millar. This wheat is liable to rust, and shoud be sow'd early, any time after the 15th. Augt. It requires strong ground or it will not produce more heads than the common-sorts of wheat. It is mention'd as growing to great profit in So. America, by Ulloa.

No. 2. A great, white bearded Wheat. This I was told was brought into America lately by a Priest, who gave it to a M. Tubman a Catholic on the Eastern Shore of Maryland and call'd it *Sicilian Wheat*. This by repeated experiments by myself, must not be sow'd early—or it will joint and be Cut by the winter frost, in a great measure. If sown at all in the fall it shoud be about 10th. or 15th. October. But from information I was led to sow a little in the beginning (about 10th.) of March, and it came to perfection soon after that sown in the fall, so that it is certainly a Spring wheat. A little, might be tried 10th. Oct. and again from 10th. to 20th. February or as early as the weather will admit of spring sowing. Will you be so good as to make my Compliments to your daughters as those of an old friend and receive the assurances of the esteem & respect of Yr. friend & Servt. JOHN F. MERCER

RC (ViWC); endorsed by TJ as received 19 Aug. 1797 and so recorded in SJL.

From John Barnes

DEAR SIR   Philadelphia 10 Augst. 1797.

In conformity to your favor 31st. past, I have transposed—to your debt $47.25 and to Mr. Lott, Credit for said Amount, being the Ballancing Amount of said Gentleman's account rendered him—through you 30th June, at least, my Ledger tells me so; if not correct, I hope Mr. Lott, will please Notice it—and shall at all times be happy, in Rendering him, any services here, I am Dear Sir Most respectfully Your Obedt: H servt: JOHN BARNES

RC (ViU: Edgehill-Randolph Papers); at foot of text: "Thomas Jefferson Esqr: Monticello"; endorsed by TJ as received 18 Aug. 1797 and so recorded in SJL.

To John Stuart

DEAR SIR   Monticello Aug. 15. 97.

With great pleasure I forward to you the Diploma of the American Philosophical society adopting you into their body. The attention on your part to which they are indebted for the knowlege that such an animal has existed as the Great claw, or Megalonyx as we have named him, gives them reason to hope that the same attention continued will enrich us with other objects of science which your part of the country may yet perhaps furnish. On my arrival at Philadelphia, I met with an account published in Spain of the skelton of an enormous animal from Paraguay of the clawed kind, but not of the Lion class at all; indeed it is classed with the Sloth, Ant-eater &c. which are not of the carnivorous kinds. It was dug up 100. feet below the surface near the river La Plata. The skeleton is now mounted at Madrid, is 12. feet long and 6. feet high. There are several circumstances which lead to a supposition that our megalonyx may have been the same animal with this. There are others which still induce us to class him with the lion. Since this discovery has led to questioning the Indians as to this animal, we have recieved some of their traditions which confirm his classification with the lion. As soon as our 4th. volume of transactions, now in the press, shall be printed, I will furnish you with the account given in to the society. I take for granted that you have little hope of recovering any more of the bones. Those sent me are delivered to the society. I am with great esteem Dear Sir Your most obedt. servt   TH: JEFFERSON

RC (Frank C. Oltorf, 1969); at foot of text: "Colo. John Stuart." PrC (DLC). Enclosure: Certificate of membership in the American Philosophical Society for "John Stewart, of Greenbriar County, Virginia," 21 Apr. 1797 (MS, Mrs. Charles W. Biggs, Lewisburg, West Virginia, 1950; in a clerk's hand with ornamental lettering; signed by TJ as president of the society and by its vice presidents and secretaries; bearing seal).

THE ACCOUNT GIVEN IN TO THE SOCIETY: Memoir on the Megalonyx, [10 Feb. 1797].

From William Strickland

DEAR SIR   York Aug: 16th: 1797.

The largest bag contains, what I believe to be the true winter vetch, grown in this neighbourhood under my own inspection. The small bag is of Perennial Darnel grass, (Lolium perenne) commonly called Ryegrass; and the box is filled up with Trifolium agrarium, Hop trefoil, or Hop-Clover. The first I send according to your request; the two last merely to fill up the box with something that possibly may be useful. The ryegrass is much cultivated here; tho not a good grass is very valuable on account of producing early herbage and hardiness; it is frequently sown among the red clover, in the manner and for the purpose that Timothy is in America; I saw an instance of its being cultivated in America where it throve greatly. The Trefoil is also much cultivated, sown with a crop of grain after the manner of red clover; and frequently mixed with Ryegrass; The climate and soil of the United States being peculiarly favourable to the growth of the Trifolia I cannot but think that this species of it may prove a valuable acquisition and in the course of my tour I did not observe an instance of its cultivation or natural growth. It is more hardy than the red or white clover, and will grow on more barren land, and in more exposed situations. As I have written another letter which I apprehend you will receive by the same conveyance which brings you this; both being committed to the care of Mr: King, I shall here only add that I hope you may yet receive the box I formerly sent you, the loss of which I more particularly regret, as I am unable to make another collection of seeds the same as it contained, and that I am Dear Sir Your very faithful humble Servant

WM. STRICKLAND

P:S: I regret that having only lately returned into York I am unable to send you the vetches, so as to afford you any chance of sowing them in the Autumn of the present year.

RC (DLC); endorsed by TJ as received 6 Mch. 1798 and so recorded in SJL.

ANOTHER LETTER from Strickland to TJ of 18 Aug. 1797 (see below) was evidently sent by a different CONVEYANCE by Rufus KING. It arrived 9 Jan. 1798, almost two months before the above letter that accompanied the box with seed, which upon receipt TJ immediately forwarded to Virginia (TJ to Thomas Mann Randolph, 8 Mch. 1798). See also King to TJ, 22 Aug. 1797.

From William Strickland

DEAR SIR   York Aug: 18th: 1797

You will already have been informed by my letter of the fourth of June which I committed to the care of Mr: King before I left London of the receipt of yours dated the 12th: of March. Since my return home I have received a letter from Mr: Donald informing me that the box I committed to his care for you about the end of May 1796 lay in his possession several weeks before a safe conveyance offer'd itself, and that, tho' he cannot now inform me by what vessel it was sent, yet as all the vessels that sailed at that period are known to have arrived safe; and as the box was sent according to your direction, he hopes you will have received it long since; least however that should not have happend; and as you are desirous of possessing the winter vetch; I send you another venture, in a box which I send along with this letter to the care of Mr: King and which I hope may be attended by the wished for success both in its arrival and future cultivation. The seed I send you is the *true* winter vetch, or at least certainly the one we cultivate as such, as I saw it growing on the farm of a friend of mine in this neighbourhood the last winter; and from him I have just now procured it to send to You. If this plant will thrive, among the chilling fogs, the cold rains and varying frosts of the long winter of latitude 55; I cannot imagine why it should not thrive in your milder climate, your short, not more variable and never severe winter; but apprehensions may arise from the sudden and too violent heats that succeed; the plant is so valuable to us from producing early pasturage in the spring, and would be still more so to you, where it is less plentiful, that the attempt to cultivate it, is highly worthy of your attention. The winter vetch is usually sown after the wheat is cut; about the latter end of September, and thro winter shews scarcely any appearance of life; but shoots into vigorous growth with the first approach of warmth in the Spring; and in the southern counties will afford good pasturage in April; It is not unusual to sow a small quantity of rye with it, to support it in some degree and prevent it, should the crop be heavy, from lying too close to the ground.

In order that no space might be left unoccupied in the box I have filled it up with a bag of rye-grass seed, (the Lolium perenne) and the Hop-Trefoil or hop-Clover (trifolium agrarium) this latter I do not recollect to have seen growing either in cultivation or spontaneously in any part of the United States; It is here much cultivated, being sown either with red-clover, or ryegrass, when meant to stand for a single crop, or mixed with other grass seeds, when intended to produce permanent pasturage. Tho it may not in general produce as large a crop as Red Clover, yet being the hardiest of the genus, and growing on more barren grounds, and in more exposed situations, it is still of great value. The rye grass I once saw cultivated in America, and producing a more luxuriant crop than is usual in this country: it is not esteemed here a very good grass, being coarse when standing for hay; but is greatly cultivated, producing the first herbage for our sheep in the spring. These seeds are contained in a box about a foot square, marked on the top T.I. which I send from hence this day to the care of Mr: King, requesting him to put them in a way of being safely conveyed to You. I shall with great satisfaction hereafter learn that these seeds prove of the service to you that I wish; should it occur to you that I can be of any future use, I beg you will freely command me; it is the least return I can make for your kind attentions; and which I cannot but make with greatest pleasure to one, I have every reason to esteem and regard, and whose acquaintance I have reason to regret that I could not in person more intimately cultivate; entertaining, therefore such sentiments, and happy in standing also well in your estimation; I shall hope, that should occasion call for it our correspondence will not cease with this letter, as I am truly Dear Sir Yours very sincerely & faithfully   WM. STRICKLAND

RC (DLC); endorsed by TJ as received 9 Jan. 1798 and so recorded in SJL. Probably enclosed in Rufus King to TJ, 5 Sep. 1797 (recorded in SJL as received 9 Jan. 1798 but not found).

Strickland's LETTER OF THE FOURTH OF JUNE 1797 which he also COMMITTED TO THE CARE of King is not recorded in SJL and has not been found.

From Allen Jones

SIR   Mount Gallant Aug 20th. 1797

By Mr. Macon I was honoured with your favour of May 23d. Phila., also a tin box containing the seed of the bread tree mentioned in your letter, only that there were four instead of two Seeds. Accept my sincere thanks for this communication and be assured no attention shall be wanting on my part to render your benevolent intentions successful. If they could be raised for two or three years in a Greenhouse and then in the Spring of the Year turned into the full ground, I should make no doubt raising them, but I have no Greenhouse, and must therefore do the best I can without one. Whatever may be the issue, I am bound to acquaint you with the progress of this experiment to add this valuable plant to the list of our cultivated Vegetables. As I have long known your ardent wishes for the ease and happiness of your fellow Citizens, I have frequently asked the Gentlemen from your State whether the Teffe or Ensette had been raised, or any attempt made to do it at Monticello? The answer has always been in the Negative. This has surprized me as I knew you had Correspondents both in France and England; where I suppose these plants have been raised, as Mr. Bruce gave liberally of the seeds to both Kingdoms. Perhaps the Teffe is the most valuable acquisition that could be made for the lower parts of Virga. and the Southern States. As it is an annual and reaped like other small grain, there can be no doubt but it would grow any where in the Southern States, and as the Seed is protected by a Capsule I should hope it would escape the Weavil which renders the raising wheat so precarious. As to the Ensette I have not the same hopes, but think it might be cultivated probably as we do the Tannier, which I suppose the same plant that Cap. Cook found in the Islands of the South Sea, and called by the Natives Taro. This does not appear to me to be a name given it by the Natives, but by the Spaniards, and is a corruption of the word Arum of which this plant is a Species. Be this as it may it grows here in great vigour and is a valuable addition to our esculents. The roots are planted in April in hills three feet apart, they are sown twice or rather hilled twice and taken up in the fall and preserved like potatoes, and those who are accustomed to this root prefer them much to any kind of Potatoes. Our Success with this plant which is a native of the hottest parts of Africa induces me to think we might also raise the ensette. I hope we shall before long hear of Peace in Europe, and then the means of communication will be both frequent and safe, when I wish you would add to the favours you have already done the Public, the introduction of the Seeds of those two plants if to be had. Surely nothing can be so gratifying to an enlightened mind as adding to the felicity of your fellow Citizens by increasing the means of Subsistence. I shall make no apology for this long letter and the Hints in it, but that you have drawn it on yourself, by writing to an old man on his favourite Subject, and I verily believe we must have our hobby's as long as we live. Believe me with the most Sincere Respect & Esteem Sir Yr Mo. Ob. Hum. Sert.   ALLEN JONES

RC (MoSHi: Jefferson Papers); endorsed by TJ as received from "Mt. Gallant. N. Cara." 22 Sep. 1797 and so recorded in SJL.

TJ's FAVOUR to Jones was dated 22 May 1797.

From Rufus King

SIR   London, Aug. 22, 1797.

I have requested Capt. Newel of the Ship Cleopatra, who is bound to Philadelphia to take charge of a Diploma delivered to me for you by Sir John Sinclair, President of the Board of Agriculture.

I have just received from Mr. Strickland a letter for you; but as he informs me that the letter is to accompany a small box, containing an assortment of seeds which is also to be sent to my care, but which has not yet been received, I shall detain this letter to be sent with the box by a future opportunity. With perfect respect I have the honor to be, sir, Your obed. & faithful servt.,   RUFUS KING

MS not found; reprinted from King, *Life*, II, 213. Recorded in SJL as received 10 Nov. 1797. Enclosure: Diploma from British Board of Agriculture, 20 June 1797, acknowledging that TJ, vice president of the United States, was admitted as a "Foreign Honorary Member of the Board" (printed form at MHi; with blanks filled by a clerk; signed by Sinclair; bearing seal).

I HAVE JUST RECEIVED FROM MR. STRICKLAND A LETTER: see William Strickland to TJ, 16 Aug. 1797.

From St. George Tucker

Sir   Williamsburg, August 22. 1797.

I have doubted whether I should take the Liberty of addressing a
Letter to you on a subject which considered in an official light, should
certainly have been communicated to the Secretary of State. But having no acquaintance with that Gentleman, and being unable to produce
satisfactory affidavits of the Facts which I wish to communicate to the
Government, although perfectly satisfied of the truth of them in my
own Breast, I preferred giving you the trouble of perusing what I have
to say, being confident that if it merits the Attention of our Government I could not put it into a fairer Channel for full investigation: for
although the facts which I am about to state may not be capable of being
ascertained in a legal mode, yet others of a similar nature would very
probably come out if the Government should exert itself to make the
Enquiry.

Being call'd on some Business to Norfolk last week, I saw at an extreme distance four Ships said to be British Ships of War lying in
Lynhaven bay, where it was said by the passengers in the Boat they had
been lying a considerable time. It was mentioned as a thing notorious
that they frequently fired at vessels coming in from Sea and brought
them too, often under no other pretext than to enquire the news, and
with a degree of insolence scarcely to be credited had insulted those
which had not immediately obeyed their signals. One instance was
mentioned of a Brig belonging to Baltimore at[1] which they fired two
shot, and with the second actually struck her. This had before been told
me by Mr. John Hancock of princes Anne, who either is, or lately was
a Delegate in our Assembly and recieved the Information from a passenger on board. In Norfolk I had neither time nor Opportunity to make
any Enquiries on the subject, but on my return a Mr. Leiper, a young
Man a native of philadelphia I believe, whose residence perhaps is still
there, though from his Conversation he seemed to be pretty much at
Alexandria, mentioned that he had met with a Gentleman in Norfolk
who had just come passenger from Charleston. That after their Vessel,
which was an American had passed a considerable distance up the Bay
with American Colours flying,[2] one of the British Ships fired upon
them and brought them to, and obliged them to come under the ships
stern; the reason assigned for this Conduct was that they wanted to hear
if the Vessel had brought any news. The same Gentleman said this was
the second Instance within a few Weeks that he had been treated in the
same Manner, in the same place.

At Night we lodged at York. There Willet one of the Norfolk printers supped with us. I asked him why he never published any Accounts of such insolent and intollerable Conduct; that I doubted not he must have heard, as well as others, of these Transactions. He confessed he had, but that there was an unwillingness in the persons thus maltreated to appear in the papers in the Character of Informants, because they probably apprehended future ill treatment if they should lodge any information officially, or publish an Account in the papers which would immediately get to the hands of those named. He mentioned the Case of a New England Vessel which was fired upon and not bringing to immediately was by repeated shot compell'd to do it, and when she fell under the Ships Stern they pour'd a Volley of Musketry into the Vessel and made above a dozen shot holes in the Sails. This was told him by the Captain of the Vessel—he applied to him afterwards to make a formal protest, or Affidavit, which the other declined for the reasons above stated.

That facts like these should be known to our Government I presume will not be doubted. That in all the commercial towns there is a wilful suppression of them is I believe no less true; could I have accompanied this relation with authentic Documents I should not have given you this trouble, as I should in that Case have thought it my Duty immediately to transmit them to the Secretary of State, who might possibly disregard any Communication from a perfect Stranger, not accompanied by proper Vouchers. I am, Sir, with the greatest respect & esteem Your most obedt. Servt.   S. G. TUCKER

RC (DLC); at foot of text: "Thomas Jefferson Esqr. Vice-President of the United States"; endorsed by TJ as received 25 Aug. 1797 and so recorded in SJL.

[1] Preceding two words interlined in place of "Boston."
[2] Preceding four words interlined.

From James Madison

DEAR SIR   Augst. 24. 1797

The inclosed letter for Mr. B. came to my hands last week; but not till the opportunity by the then mail was lost. I hear nothing of Monroe but thro' the Newspapers containing his correspondence with Pickering. As that appears to have been closed on the 31st. of last month, I am in hourly expectation of seeing him. I am also without any late information with respect to the progress of the Committee on Blount's and Liston's Conspiracy. Dawson wrote me some time ago "that they were going on well, and that he had well grounded reasons, which he could not communicate by letter, to say, that they should bring in some large fish." It is much to be wished none of this description may escape; tho' to be feared that they will be most likely to do so. Mrs. M. offers her respects to the ladies, and joins in my inclinations to visit Monticello; but I am so compleatly plunged into necessary occupations of several kinds, that I can[not] positively decide that we shall have that pleasure. Yrs affecly.   Js. MADISON JR

RC (DLC: Madison Papers); with last digit of date apparently later misinterpreted as "1" and emended first to "4" and then to "5"; word in brackets supplied by Editors, remainder of sentence, closing, and signature written in margin; addressed: "[Tho]mas Jefferson Vice President of the United States Monticello"; franked; endorsed by TJ as received 25 Aug. 1797 and so recorded in SJL. Enclosure not found, but probably John Bringhurst (see Madison to TJ, 2 Aug. 1797).

On 4 Aug. the Philadelphia *Aurora* published Monroe's CORRESPONDENCE with Timothy PICKERING from 6 to 31 July 1797 regarding his recall as minister to France. For a discussion of the controversy, see the following document. I AM IN HOURLY EXPECTATION OF SEEING HIM: Monroe arrived at Montpelier about 30 Aug. (Madison, *Papers*, XVII, p. xxvii).

DAWSON WROTE ME SOME TIME AGO: see John Dawson to Madison, 27 July 1797, in same, 32. Dawson, the Virginia Republican who was elected to fill Madison's seat in Congress upon his retirement, was a member of the House committee meeting over the summer to collect evidence and bring in articles of impeachment against William Blount. In a letter to Madison of 13 Aug. 1797, Dawson stated that he believed the committee would be able to show the "criminality" of British minister Robert Liston and the "partiality" of Secretary of State Pickering in his efforts to protect Liston from implication in the conspiracy. During the first week in September, Dawson again wrote Madison noting that the result of the committee's enquiries would be "a bitter pill to the British minister, our Secretary of state and their faction" (same, 41-5).

Notes on Alexander Hamilton

Aug. 24. About the time of the British treaty, Hamilton and Taleyrand, bp. of Autun dined together, and Hamilton drank freely. Conversing on the treaty, Taleyrand says 'mais vraiment Monsr. Hamilton, ce n'est pas *bien honnete*, after making the Senate ratify the treaty to advise the Presidt. to reject it.' 'The treaty, said Hamilton is an execrable one, and Jay was an old woman for making it, but the whole credit of saving us from it must be given to the President.' After circumstances had led to a conclusion that the President also must ratify it, he said to the same Taleyrand, 'tho' the treaty is a most execrable one, yet when once we have come to a determination on it, we must carry it through thick and thin, right or wrong.' Taleyrand told this to Volney who told it to me.

There is a letter now appearing in the papers from Pickering to Monroe dated July 24[1] 97. which I am satisfied is written by Hamilton. He was in Philadelphia at that date.[2]

MS (DLC: TJ Papers, Vol. 102: 17461); entirely in TJ's hand, written on same sheet as Note on Diplomatic Appointments, July 1797, and Notes on Conversations with John Adams and George Washington, [after 13 Oct. 1797], and likely written at same sitting as the former; see also Note on Spanish Expenditures, 13 Oct. 1797.

HAMILTON AND TALEYRAND: French diplomat and politician Charles Maurice de Talleyrand-Périgord lived in exile in the United States, where he was on friendly terms with Alexander Hamilton, from April 1794 until June 1796 (John L. Earl III, "Talleyrand in Philadelphia, 1794-1796," PMHB, XCI [1967], 283, 286-7, 289, 298). The 24 July 1797 LETTER of Timothy PICKERING to James MONROE, one of a series of letters exchanged by the two during that month, concerned the administration's refusal to comply with Monroe's request for an explanation of his recall from France (Pickering to Monroe, 24 July 1797, DLC: Monroe Papers; Philadelphia *Aurora*, 4 Aug. 1797).

[1] Figure reworked.
[2] TJ added this sentence later.

To Willem H. van Hasselt

SIR   Monticello in Virginia Aug. 27. 97.

I have to acknolege the receipt of your favor of June 30. and feel myself indebted to the partiality which at so great a distance, has drawn your attention to me. It is with great sincerity I assure you that there are traits in your letter which interest me strongly in your favor, and increase the regret that my particular position does not permit me to avail myself of talents so well entitled to be employed. My fortune is entirely agricultural, consisting in farms which are under the management of persons who have been long in my employ, have behaved well, and are therefore entitled to be continued as long as I continue to occupy my farms myself. But in fact I mean shortly to tenant them out, in order to relieve myself from the attention they require.—My family consists of only two daughters, the one married and just beginning an infant family; the other marriageable; and consequently the business of education is past.—The office to which I have been called, takes me from home all the winter, during which time my daughters also go into the lower country to pass their winter, so that our house is shut up one half the year.—No commentaries on these circumstances are necessary with you to shew that they furnish me with no means of being useful to you. I trust with confidence however that qualifications as good as yours, with views as moderate, cannot fail of meeting employment advantageous and agreeable to yourself. In this hope I have only to add assurances that your confidence in my silence to others is not misplaced, and that I am with great respect Sir Your most obedt. & most humble servt

TH: JEFFERSON

PrC (MHi); at foot of text: "Mr. W. H. Van Hasselt"; endorsed in ink by TJ on verso.

To St. George Tucker

DEAR SIR   Monticello Aug. 28. 97.

I have to acknolege the receipt of your two favors of the 2d. and 22d. inst. and to thank you for the pamphlet covered by the former. You know my subscription to it's doctrines, and as to the mode of emancipation, I am satisfied that that must be a matter of compromise between the passions the prejudices, and the real difficulties which will each have their weight in that operation. Perhaps the first chapter of this history, which has begun in St. Domingo, and the next succeeding ones which will recount how all the whites were driven from all the other islands, may prepare our minds for a peaceable accomodation between justice, policy and necessity, and[1] furnish an answer to the difficult question Whither shall the coloured emigrants go? And the sooner we put some plan under way, the greater hope there is that it may be permitted to proceed peaceably to it's ultimate effect. But if something is not done, and soon done, we shall be the murderers of our own children. The 'Murmura, venturos nautis prodentia ventos' has already reached us; the revolutionary storm now sweeping the globe will be upon us, and happy if we make timely provision to give it an easy passage over our land. From the present state of things in Europe and America the day which begins our combustion must be near at hand, and only a single spark is wanting to make that day tomorrow. If we had begun sooner, we might probably have been allowed a lengthier operation to clear ourselves, but every day's delay lessens the time we may take for emancipation. Some people derive hope from the aid of the confederated states. But this is a delusion. There is but one state in the Union which will aid us sincerely if an insurrection begins; and that one may perhaps have it's own fire to quench at the same time.

The facts stated in yours of the 22d. were not identically known to me, but others like them were. From the general government no interference need be expected. Even the merchant and navigator, the immediate sufferers, are prevented by various motives from wishing to be redressed. I see nothing but a state procedure which can vindicate us

[519]

from the insult. It is in the power of any single magistrate, or of the attorney for the Commonwealth to lay hold of the commanding officer whenever he comes ashore for the breach of the peace, and to proceed against him by indictment. This is so plain an operation that no power can prevent it's being carried through with effect, but the want of will in the officers of the state.   I think that the matter of finances, which has set the people of Europe to thinking, is now advanced to that point with us, that the next step, and it is an unavoidable one, a land tax, will awaken our constituents, and call for inspection into past proceedings.—I am with great esteem Dear Sir Your friend & servt

TH: JEFFERSON

RC (O. O. Fisher, Detroit, 1950); addressed: "The honorable St. George Tucker Williamsburg"; with the most significant emendation recorded in note below; franked. PrC (DLC).

MURMURA, VENTUROS NAUTIS PRODENTIA VENTOS: "the breezes warning the sailors of the coming gale," Virgil, *Aeneid*, 10: 99.

[1] TJ here canceled "facilitate our."

To Robert Lawson

DEAR SIR   Monticello Aug. 31. 97.

I have to acknolege the receipt of your favor of June 27. and to assure you of my sincere dispositions to render you the service therein desired, in the best way in my power. This cannot be however to any effect during my absence from Philadelphia. But on my return to that place at the meeting of Congress I shall be able to interest those on behalf of your son whose applications at the war office will be favorably received. In the mean time as you mention your acquaintance with Genl. Wilkinson, it would be adviseable that a recommendation should originate with him, as he is at the head of the military, and particularly situated to be informed of the merits of your son: and if I am apprised when his recommendation comes to Philadelphia I will take measures to promote it's success.   I am happy in this occasion of recalling to memory antient times when we acted together in a virtuous cause, in hoping that you continue in good health, and subscribing myself Dear Sir Your most obedt. & most humble servt   TH: JEFFERSON

RC (Facsimile in Gary Hendershott Catalogue, Little Rock, Arkansas, March 1993, Sale 79); at foot of text: "Genl. Lawson."

Lawson's FAVOR of 27 June, received from Fayette, Kentucky, on 4 Aug., is recorded in SJL but has not been found.

To Benjamin Vaughan

DEAR SIR   Monticello Aug. 31. 97.
    I have to acknolege the reciept of your favor of July 20. and have read with great pleasure the piece it contained. I have just heard too of the publication of a pamphlet which I had expected with impatience, as I am sure it will convey to the world some truths which require some caution in their conveyance. The mind of the people is not prepared to recieve them abruptly. Your manner is well calculated to form the point of an entering wedge, and I am in hopes that the activity of your mind will render your residence among us an epoch which will be marked.   The season is now so far advanced that we can hardly expect that your curiosity may lead you to make a circuit thro' any considerable part of our states: but the ensuing summer may induce you to take some survey of them. Should your course lead this way I shall be happy in receiving and possessing you here whatever time you can spare to us. I am with sentiments of sincere esteem & respect Dear Sir Your most obedt. and most humble servt.   TH: JEFFERSON

PrC (DLC); at foot of text: "Mr. James Martin" (see below). Enclosed in TJ to John Vaughan, 31 Aug. 1797.

For TJ's erroneous supposition that Benjamin Vaughan had written to him as "James Martin," see the FAVOR of James Martin to TJ of 20 July 1796; TJ to John Vaughan, 11 Sep. 1797; and TJ to Martin, 23 Feb. 1798. TJ's mistake is easily explained, for Benjamin Vaughan, who generally published his writings anonymously or under a pseudonym, had begun to use the name John or Jean Martin as an alias in 1794, when, frightened by Home Office inquiries into correspondence between him and French-sponsored agents in Britain, he fled England for France. Living under the ficticious name in France and Switzerland, Vaughan used letters of recommendation from Monroe and Thomas Paine to obtain a French passport, then joined his family in New England during the summer of 1797. Perhaps compounding TJ's confusion was the fact that James Martin had written to him from Jamaica, Long Island, and by coincidence the Vaughan family had strong associations with the island of Jamaica, Benjamin Vaughan's birthplace (Craig C. Murray, *Benjamin Vaughan (1751-1835): The Life of an Anglo-American Intellectual* [New York, 1982], 336-41, 349-50, 361, 373, 381; George S. Rowell, "Benjamin Vaughan—Patriot, Scholar, Diplomat," *Magazine of History*, XXII [1916], 44, 51-2).

The PAMPHLET has not been identified.

To John Vaughan

DEAR SIR   Monticello Aug. 31. 97
    Not knowing how far the inclosed address may serve to give a certain conveyance to the letter, I have thought it safest to put it under your cover, not doubting that your communion with the person would en-

able you to procure it a sure passage to it's destination. I am with esteem Dear Sir Your friend & servt   TH: JEFFERSON

PrC (DLC); at foot of text: "Mr. John Vaughan." Enclosure: TJ to Benjamin Vaughan, 31 Aug. 1797.

To Arthur Campbell

DEAR SIR   Monticello Sep. 1. 97.

I have to acknolege the reciept of your favor of July 4. and to recognise in it the sentiments you have ever held, and worthy of the day on which it is dated. It is true that a party has risen up among us, or rather has come among us, which is endeavoring to separate us from all friendly connection with France, to unite our destinies with those of Great Britain, and to assimilate our government to theirs. Our lenity in permitting the return of the old tories gave the first body to this party, they have been increased by large importations of British merchants and factors, by American merchants dealing on British capital, and by stockdealers and banking companies, who by the aid of a paper system are enriching themselves to the ruin of our country, and swaying the government by their possession of the printing presses, which their wealth commands, and by other means not always honorable to the character of our countrymen. Hitherto their influence and their system has been irresistable, and they have raised up an Executive power which is too strong for the legislature. But I flatter myself they have passed their zenith. The people, while these things were doing, were lulled into rest and security from a cause which no longer exists. No prepossessions now will shut their ears to truth. They begin to see to what port their leaders were steering the vessel during their slumbers, and there is yet time to haul in, if we can avoid a war with France. All can be done peaceably, by the people confining their choice of Representatives and Senators to persons attached to republican government and the principles of 1776, not office hunters, but farmers whose interests are entirely agricultural. Such men are the true representatives of the great American interest, and are alone to be relied on for expressing the proper American sentiments. We owe gratitude to France, justice to England, good will to all, and subservience to none. All this must be brought about by the people, using their elective rights with prudence, and self-possession, and not suffering themselves to be duped by treacherous emissaries. It was by the sober sense of our citizens that we were safely and steadily conducted from monarchy to republicanism, and it is by the

[522]

same agency alone we can be kept from falling back. I am happy in this occasion of reviving the memory of old things, and of assuring you of the continuance of the esteem & respect of Dear Sir Your friend & servt

TH: JEFFERSON

PrC (DLC); at foot of first page: "Colo Arthur Campbell."

To John Barnes

DEAR SIR   Monticello Sep. 2. 1797.

I have to acknolege the reciept of your favors of July 26. and Aug. [10.] the former covering your account to July 24. balance in my favor 6[. . .] since which your's of Aug. 10. advises the acceptance of my draught in favor of [. . .] Lott for 47.25 which consequently leaves me in your hands only 14.36. This is exclusive of Mr. Short's dividends left in your hand for his purposes. Having now to pay for him a requisition of the James river Co. on his canal sh[ares] 330.D. I have this day drawn on you for that sum payable at 10. days [sight] to Chas. Johnston & Co. or order.

The chief difference between your account recieved in yours of July 26. and mine forwarded to you in my letter of July 18. arose from the excess of the bills of Trump, Stock and Ker above what I had conjectu[red]. Mr. Ker's was 15.D. more and Trump and Stock's 46.83 more. This last I suppose will be explained to me when I see his bill. I am with esteem Dear Sir Your most obedt. servt   TH: JEFFERSON

PrC (MHi); faded; at foot of text: "Mr. John Barnes."

From Volney

Chez Mr Madison 2 7bre.

Malgré la facilité et Même la brièveté du chemin de chez Vous ici, je Suis arrivé à une heure après Midi Si rôti, Si meurtri Si fatigué que j'ai à peine la force de Vous ecrire pour Vous remercier du bon Vieux guide et des deux chevaux qu'il remene[ra] demain en bon etat. Il est probable que je N'aurai point occasion de Vous ecrire plus amplement avant Mon retour à philadelphie. Votre affectionné Serviteur et ami

C. VOLNEY

RC (DLC); torn; addressed: "Mr Thomas jefferson Monticello"; endorsed by TJ as received 3 Sep. 1797 and so recorded in SJL.

To John F. Mercer

Dear Sir   Monticello Sep. 5. 1797.

I recieved safely your favor of Aug. 9. with the two packets of Smyrna and Sicilian wheat. The latter I shall value as well because it lengthens our fall sowing, as because it may be sown in the spring. And in a soil which does not suit oats (as is the case of ours) we want a good spring grain. The May wheat has been sufficiently tried to prove that it will not answer for general culture in this part of the country. In the lower country it does better.

We have now with us our friend Monroe. He is engaged [in] stating his conduct for the information of the public. As yet how[ever] he has done little, being too much occupied with re-arranging his houshold. His preliminary skirmish with the Secretary of [State] has of course bespoke a suspension of the public mind till he can lay his statement before them. Our Congressional district is forming under the present-ment of their representative by the G[rand] jury: and the question of a convention for forming a state constitution will probably be attended to in these parts. These are [the] news of our canton. Those of a more public nature you know before we do. My best respects to Mrs. Mercer and assurances to yourself of the affectionate esteem of Dr. Sir Your friend & servt   TH: JEFFERSON

PrC (DLC); torn at right margin; at foot of text: "John F. Mercer esq."

From James Monroe

DEAR SIR   Albemarle Sepr. 5. 1797.

I enclose the paper you were so good as commit to my care yesterday. I have perused it with attention and pleasure, and think its contents ought to be used so as to produce to the publick the beneficial effect likely to result from them. The only doubt which I entertain is as to the channel into which it is proposed to put the paper, whether for example, a state legislature can interfere in a question between a citizen of the U. States and his representative in Congress. It may be urged that the es-tablishment of the principle may lead to great extent, and even make all the members of the National Govt., by a code of crimes and punish-ments, amenable to state tribunals. I suggest this for your consideration, to which I beg to add whether it would not be better to address it to the Congress? I will endeavor to see you as soon as possible. Sincerely I am yr. friend & servant   JAS. MONROE

RC (DLC); endorsed by TJ as received 5 Sep. 1797 and so recorded in SJL. Enclosure: Petition to the Virginia House of Delegates, printed at 3 Aug. 1797.

YOU WERE SO GOOD AS COMMIT TO MY CARE YESTERDAY: Monroe and his wife had recently visited Monticello with James and Dolley Madison (Madison, *Papers*, XVII, 36n).

To Archibald Stuart

DEAR SIR   Monticello Sep. 5. 97.

I furnished to Wm. Alexander of Augusta in 1795. nails to the amount of £16–10–3. The year following I gave Mr. Saml. Clarke an order on him for the amount. He talked about some suit he had employed Joseph Monroe to bring for him in my county, the proceeds of which were to pay me. But lawsuits against others are not paiments to me; and in fact Joseph Monroe has removed into a distant part of the country with which we have no communication. I inclose you Alexander's original letter, and press copies of two I wrote him, the originals being in his hands. They contain the account. If you can collect the money from him with or without law, I shall be obliged to you: and you will be so good as to deduct from what he pays your fees of suit and commission for collecting. I am Dear Sir

RC (ViHi); unsigned; addressed: "Archibald Stuart esq. Staunton"; franked. Enclosures: see note below.

William ALEXANDER'S ORIGINAL LETTER

is not recorded in SJL and cannot be identified but the PRESS COPIES enclosed were probably TJ's last letters to Alexander of 29 Sep. 1795 and 26 July 1796, both of which contain information on the account.

From John Stuart

SIR   Greenbrier September 6th. 1797

Your favour of the 15th. ult. with the Diploma adopting me a member of the philosophical society came safe to hand—this Honour lays me under every obligation, and very greatful acknowledgments to you—be asured Sir, I shall be careful to enquire and deligent to communicate any thing that may fall in my way that I conceive will be interesting to the society. I fear no more of the bones of the Megalonyx will be got as I promised a reward for any that might be found in the cave. I was long in hopes the head bones or teeth would be got, which would more effectually proved his kind. I belive I before mentioned to you that there is a figure of a Lion carved on a rock on the Kenawha—which I presume is no small evidence that such an animmal had once an existance here,

Espesially as that figure with many others rudely cut bears every mark of very great antiquity. I have the Honor to be very respectfully Your Most. Obd. Humbe Servt.   JOHN STUART

RC (ViW); endorsed by TJ as received 20 Sep. 1797 and so recorded in SJL.

To James Monroe

TH:J. TO J. MONROE   Monticello Sep. 7. 97.

The doubt which you suggest as to our jurisdiction over the case of the grand jury v. Cabell, had occurred to me, and naturally occurs on first view of the question. But I knew that to send the petition to the H. of Represent. in Congress, would make bad worse, that a majority of that house would pass a vote of approbation. On examination of the question too it appeared to me that we could maintain the authority of our own government over it.

A right of free correspondence between citizen and citizen, on their joint interests, whether public or private, and under whatsoever laws these interests arise, (to wit, of the state, of Congress, of France, Spain or Turkey) is a natural right: it is not the gift of any municipal law either of England, of Virginia, or of Congress, but in common with all our other natural rights, is one of the objects for the protection of which society is formed and municipal laws established.

The courts of this commonwealth (and among them the General court as a court of impeachment) are originally competent to the cognisance of all infractions of the rights of one citizen by another citizen: and they still retain all their judiciary cognisances not expressly alienated by the federal constitution.

The federal constitution alienates from them all cases arising 1st. under that constitution, 2dly. under the laws of Congress, 3dly. under treaties &c. But this right of free correspondence, whether with a public representative in General assembly, in Congress, in France, in Spain, or with a private one charged with a pecuniary trust, or with a private friend the object of our esteem or any other, has not been given to us under 1st. the federal constitution, 2dly. any law of Congress, or 3dly. any treaty, but as before observed, by nature. It is therefore not alienated, but remains under the protection of our courts.

Were the question ever doubtful, it is no reason for abandoning it. The system of the General government is to sieze all doubtful ground. We must join in the scramble or get nothing. Where first occupancy is to give a right, he who lies still loses all. Besides it is not right for those who are only to act in a preliminary form, to let their own doubts preclude the judgment of the court of ultimate decision. We ought to let it go to the H. of delegates for their consideration, and they, unless the contrary be palpable, ought to let it go to the General court, who are ultimately to decide on it.

It is of immense consequence that the States retain as complete authority as possible over their own citizens. The withdrawing themselves under the shelter of a foreign jurisdiction, is so subversive of order and so pregnant of abuse, that it may not be amiss to consider how far a law of praemunire should be revived and modified against all citizens who attempt to[1] carry their causes before any other than the state courts in cases where those other courts have no right to their cognisance.[2] A plea to the jurisdiction of the courts of their state, or a reclamation of a foreign jurisdiction, if adjudged valid[3] would be safe, but if adjudged invalid, would be followed by the punishment of praemunire for the attempt.

Think further of the preceding part of this letter, and we will have further conference on it. Adieu.

P.S. Observe that it is not the breach of Mr. Cabell's privilege which we mean to punish: that might lie with Congress. It is the wrong done to the citizens of our district. Congress has no authority to punish that wrong. They can only take cognisance of it in vindication of their member.

RC (DLC: Monroe Papers); the most significant emendations are noted below. PrC (DLC).

[1] TJ here canceled a word, possibly "draw."
[2] Following this sentence TJ canceled "The risk of fai."
[3] Word interlined in place of "[sound]."

To Alexander White

DEAR SIR   Monticello Sep. 10. 97.

So many persons have of late found an interest or a passion gratified by imputing to me sayings and writings which I never said or wrote, or by endeavoring to draw me into newspapers to harrass me personally, that I have found it necessary for my quiet and my other pursuits to leave them in full possession of the field, and not to take the trouble of contradicting them even in private conversation. If I do it now it is out of respect to your application, made by private letter and not thro' the newspapers and under perfect assurance that what I write to you will not be permitted to get into a newspaper, while you are at full liberty to assert it in conversation under my authority.

I never gave an opinion that the government would not remove to the federal city; I never entertained that opinion; but on the contrary, whenever asked the question I have expressed my full confidence that they would remove there. Having had frequent occasion to declare this sentiment, I have endeavored to conjecture on what a contrary one could have been ascribed to me. I remember that in George town, where I passed a day in February, in conversation with several gentlemen on the preparations there for recieving the government an opinion was expressed by some, and not privately, that there would be few or no private buildings erected in Washington this summer, and that the prospect of their being a sufficient number, in time, was not flattering. This they grounded on the fact that the persons holding lots, from a view to increase their means of building, had converted their money, at low prices, into Morris and Nicholson's notes, then possessing a good degree of credit, and that having lost these by the failure of these gentlemen they were much less able to build than they would have been. I then observed, and I did it with a view to excite exertion, that if there should not be private houses in readiness sufficient for the accomodation of Congress and of the persons annexed to the government, it could not be expected that men should come there to lodge, like cattle, in the fields, and that it highly behoved those interested in the removal to use every exertion to provide accomodations. In this opinion I presume I shall be joined by yourself and every other. But delivered, as it was, only on the hypothesis of a fact stated by others, it could not authorize the assertion of an absolute opinion, separated from the statement of fact on which it was hypothetically grounded. I have seen no reason to believe that Congress have changed their purpose with respect to the removal. Every public indication from them, and every sentiment I have heard privately expressed by the members, convinces me they are steady in the purpose. Being on this subject, I will suggest to you, what I did privately at Georgetown to a particular person in confidence that it should be suggested to the managers. If, in event, it should happen that there should not be a sufficiency of private buildings erected within the proper time, would it not be better for the Commissioners to apply for a suspension of the removal for one year, than to leave it to the hazards which a contrary interest might otherwise bring on it? Of this however you have yet two summers to consider, and you have the best knolege of the circumstances on which a judgment may be formed whether private accomodations will be provided. As to the public buildings every one seems to agree that they will be in readiness.   I have for five or six years been encouraging the opening a direct road from the Southern part of this state, leading through this county to George town. The route proposed is from George town by Colo. Alexander's, Elk run church, Norman's ford, Stevensburg, the Raccoon ford, the Marquis's road, Martin Key's ford on the Rivanna, the mouth of Slate river, the High bridge on Appamattox, Prince Edward C.H. Charlotte C.H. Cole's ferry on Stanton, Dix's ferry on Dan, Guilford C.H. Salisbury, Creswell's ferry on Saluda, Ninety six's, Augusta. It is believed this road will shorten the distance along the continent 100. miles. It will be to open anew only from Georgetown to Prince Edward courthouse. An acutal survey has been made from Stevensburg to Georgetown, by which that much of the road will be shortened 20. miles and be all a dead level. The difficulty is to get it first through Fairfax and Prince William. The counties after that will very readily carry it on. We consider it as opening to us a direct road to the market of the federal city, for all the beef and mutton we could raise, for which we have no market at present. I am in possession of the survey and had thought of getting the Bridge Co. at Georgetown to undertake to get the road carried through Fairfax and Princewilliam, either by those counties or by themselves. But I have some apprehension that by pointing our road to the bridge, it might get out of the level country, and be carried over the hills which will be but a little above it. This would be inadmissible. Perhaps you could suggest some means of our getting over the obstacle of those two counties. I shall be very happy to concur in any measure which can effect all our purposes. I am with esteem Dr. Sir Your most obedt. servt

Th: Jefferson

PrC (DLC); at foot of first page: "Alexander White esq."

White's APPLICATION, MADE BY PRIVATE LETTER of 1 Sep. 1797, recorded in SJL as received one week later, has not been found. According to SJL, TJ exchanged thirteen letters with White between 18 Sep. 1797 and 10 Sep. 1800, all of which are missing.

To John Vaughan

Dear Sir   Monticello Sep. 11. 97.

I inclosed you by last post a letter meant for your brother. It was in answer to one I had recieved, signed James Martin. I begin now to suppose it possible that letter may not have come from your brother. If you have forwarded him mine, it is well as it is immaterial whether it goes to him or you send it back to me. But do not let it go to any hands but his or mine. Perhaps I may write you again on this subject. I am with esteem Dear Sir Your friend & servt   TH: JEFFERSON

PrC (DLC); at foot of text: "John Vaughan esq."

A LETTER MEANT FOR YOUR BROTHER: TJ to Benjamin Vaughan, 31 Aug. 1797.

A letter from John Vaughan to TJ, written on 29 Sep. 1797 and received from Philadelphia on 14 Oct. 1797, and a letter to TJ from another of Vaughan's brothers, William Vaughan, written on 7 Aug. 1797 and received from London on 25 Feb. 1798, are recorded in SJL but have not been found.

To Alexander White

DEAR SIR   Monticello Sep. 12. 97.

In my letter of the 10th. I mentioned that I had the original survey of a road from George town to Stevensburg. Since that I have had time to copy it on a reduced scale, and to forward the copy by a conveyance which will reach you perhaps as soon as that letter. You will be pleased to observe that the roads which pass directly from George town towards Norman's ford on the Rappahanock, traverse a country which is a dead level running in that direction. But any road which passes a little higher, (as that to Culpeper C.H.) engages with the hills making down from the South West and Bullrun ridge of mountains. For this reason we propose our road to be opened from George town directly to Norman's ford, and to lead it off from the bridge instead of George town would engage us in the hilly country. As we have this matter much at heart, and it will be interesting to your city also, as opening a long line of rich country to it, if you can put any spring in motion which will get it through Fairfax and Prince William, it will accomodate yourselves as well as[1] an extensive and thickly inhabited country. I am with esteem Dear Sir Your most obedt. servt   TH: JEFFERSON

RC (NSyU: Graeme O'Geran Presidential Autograph Collection); torn, with several words supplied from PrC; at foot of text: "Alexander White esq." PrC (DLC).

[1] Preceding four words interlined.

From John Barnes

SIR   Philada: 14th Sepr 1797—

Your favor 2d: received Yesterday, advise, your having drawn on me for $330: at 10 days on Mr. Shorts account will be duly honored. The excess of Messrs. Trumps and Stocks account you will find particulars of, in my Invoice 18th July with charges deducted $96.83. I most sincerely wish, I could say—the fever abates; if we are only so happy as to Arrest its progress, and wait patiently the certain effectual remedy, a frost—or two—(for nothing else, I fear will intirely eradicate its subtle poison).

So very great is the desertion of the City in general—that in 3d St. from Market to Chesnut—I can count Only 4 shops, Open—beside my Own; a street, I believe, as yet, intirely free from infection—tho' Melancholy, to View—is no small satisfaction, in point of safty—in 1793 We lost, 14 a 16, same Neighbourhood. I am Sir—most Respectfully—Your Obedt: H Servt.   JOHN BARNES

RC (ViU: Edgehill-Randolph Papers); at foot of text: "Thomas Jefferson Esqr: Monticello"; endorsed by TJ as received 22 Sep. 1797 and so recorded in SJL.

To John Barnes

DEAR SIR   Monticello Sep. 17. 97.

I wrote you on the 2d. inst. The present is merely to advise you that counting on your recieving a quarter's salary for me on the 1st. of the ensuing month, I have this day drawn on you in favor of Joseph Roberts Junr. for 446.D. 76c. payable Oct. 3. and that my buildings here will occasion me to draw on you for nearly the whole of the balance of salary almost immediately. I learn from Mr. Randolph that you continue in Philadelphia notwithstanding the prevalence of the fever there. I sincerely wish you may escape it, being with esteem Dr. Sir Your most obedt. servt   TH: JEFFERSON

PrC (MHi); at foot of text: "Mr. John Barnes."

In his financial memoranda TJ noted that the payment to JOSEPH ROBERTS JUNR. was for "amount of iron shipped me in July," and that his order for iron for the next quarter would be for three tons of rod and a quarter ton of hoops. TJ obtained nailrod from Roberts, a Philadelphia ironmonger, from 1797 until 1802 (MB, II, 964, 970). Eleven letters from TJ to Roberts and thirteen from Roberts to TJ, dated between 8 Apr. 1797 and 9 Jan. 1801, are recorded in SJL but have not been found.

To Francis Eppes

DEAR SIR   Monticello Sep. 24. 1797.

It is with sincere pleasure I learn that Wayles[1] and Maria have concluded to run their course of life together. From his prudence I presume[2] he has not proceeded thus far without knowing it would be agreeable to Mrs. Eppes and yourself. I have thought it right on this occasion to do precisely what I did on a former similar one. I have made what I gave to my daughter Randolph the measure of what I propose to give to Maria at present: with this difference, that, instead of lands at Poplar Forest, I propose my upper tract here of $819\frac{1}{2}$ acres, lying opposite to Monticello.[3] For this tract with thirty one negroes, corresponding almost[4] individually in value with the individuals given on the former occasion, I shall execute a deed expressing to be in consideration *of the marriage* and *of the advancement* he recieves from you,[5] considerations which being deemed *valuable* in law,[6] shelter them against all accidents. As you had before executed a conveyance to Wayles[7] for the Hundred, nothing would now remain to be done on your part, had not the occasion presented a ground for reexecuting it on higher considerations, to wit *of the marriage*, and *the advancement* Maria receives from me,[8] which render the conveyance firmer than that of *natural affection*, expressed in the former one. I have therefore prepared a deed which I inclose for this purpose. It is a surrender of the estate of the Hundred from Wayles to yourself, and a reconveyance to him at a single operation.—So far on the supposition that he keeps the Hundred. But he tells me you would not be averse to the exchanging Angola for that. This would certainly be a most important[9] object for him, not only as to present convenience, but in considering his future interests here and in Bedford. Angola would, with those, form a circuit practicable enough to be regularly attended while in one hand, and of convenient communication if given to different members of a future[10] family,[11] a circumstance of no small comfort in life. On this idea I have prepared a second deed, which is also inclosed, and is an Exchange of the two tracts between you, ingrafted on the considerations of marriage and advancement.[12] You will execute which you please. Any difference in value, if necessary, can be settled by yourself in some separate paper.[13] The deed on my part cannot be executed till I know which of these you prefer, as it must be grounded on that fact.   I have given lands here rather than in Bedford, because their inclinations concur with my wishes that they should live here. I consider them as equal in value to those I gave Martha; but whether they are or not, will make little odds, as on any future division of my property between them, I shall establish the principle of Hotchpot. In the mean time a plantation here will furnish him daily employment, which is necessary[14] to happiness, to health and profit. As I am at home eight months in the year, I shall wish them to[15] be here with me during that time; and the four winter months they can divide between their other friends and their affairs at Angola. This will put off the expence of building till it shall be convenient; and remove also to a distance[16] that of housekeeping,[17] so that they may begin the world square at an age when they will be disposed to keep themselves so.

I have been thus lengthy, because I thought it best to be explicit for your satisfaction on a subject which cannot but be interesting to you.

The ceremony of the marriage happens to come precisely when our house will be unroofed. I shall endeavor however to retard the uncovering one end if possible, till it is over. This will enable us to place Mrs. Eppes and yourself, and the younger members of the family[18] under cover, if you can be of the party, as I hope you will. Against another summer I hope I shall have good accomodations for you, and that the family intercourse may be revived on the[19] footing of old times.[20] Accept assurances of the sincere and[21] constant esteem of Dear Sir Your affectionate[22] friend & servt   TH: JEFFERSON

PrC (MHi); at foot of first page: "F. Eppes esq."; endorsed by TJ in ink on verso. Dft (ViU: Edgehill-Randolph Papers); with numerous emendations, the most important of which are noted below. Enclosures: (1) Marriage Settlement for John Wayles Eppes printed at 12 Oct. 1797. (2) Marriage Settlement for John Wayles Eppes, 1797, in which Francis and Elizabeth Eppes convey Angola, a tract of land of 3,419.75 acres in Cumberland County on the north side of the Appamattox River adjoining lands held by Henry and Anne Skipwith, being the whole of the lands held by Francis and Elizabeth Eppes "in that body from the late John Wayles father of the said Elizabeth," to their son upon marriage to Mary Jefferson in exchange for the Bermuda Hundred lands on the James River in Chesterfield County previously deeded to John Wayles Eppes by his parents, the exchange to be made upon payment of five shillings (MS in MHi, entirely in TJ's hand, incomplete, indented, partially dated, with unfilled blanks for day and month; Dft in CSmH).

For the legal rationale for REEXECUTING the deed by which John Wayles Eppes inherited his family's Bermuda Hundred tract to place it ON HIGHER CONSIDERATIONS of MARRIAGE, see note to the Bill in Chancery of Wayles's Executors against the Heirs of Richard Randolph, [on or before 2 Mch. 1795].

According to SJL, TJ exchanged six letters with Eppes between 6 Nov. 1796 and 21 June 1797, none of which has been found. Another six letters, exchanged between 28 Nov. 1797 and 10 Nov. 1800, are also missing.

[1] Word interlined in Dft in place of "[our?] Jack."

[2] Word interlined in Dft in place of "conclude."

[3] In Dft TJ here canceled "As I think their inclinations concurring with my wishes that they should fix here, I have supposed this better."

[4] Word interlined in Dft.

[5] Preceding eight words interlined in Dft, none of which are underlined.

[6] Preceding five words interlined in Dft and "valuable" is not underlined.

[7] Word interlined in Dft in place of "Jack."

[8] Preceding seven words interlined in Dft.

[9] Preceding two words interlined in Dft in place of "capital."

[10] Word interlined in Dft.

[11] Remainder of sentence interlined in Dft.

[12] Preceding two words interlined in Dft.

[13] Preceding sentence interlined in Dft.

[14] Remainder of sentence interlined in Dft.

[15] In Dft TJ first wrote "⟨live⟩ be with

me, and during" before altering the following passage to read as above.

[16] Preceding five words interlined in Dft.

[17] In Dft TJ first wrote "till the delirium shall be over to which young people are subject of having their house always full of company, the resort of constant company" before altering the remainder of the sentence to read as above.

[18] Preceding seven words interlined in Dft.

[19] In Dft TJ first wrote "old plan" before altering the remainder of the sentence to read as above.

[20] In Dft TJ here canceled "Present my affectionate invitations and respects to Mrs. Eppes, ⟨with my hopes of seeing her, as well as they younger members of the family, and⟩ and the younger members of the family with my expectations of seeing her and them as well as yourself."

[21] Preceding two words interlined in Dft.

[22] Word interlined in Dft.

To John Barnes

DEAR SIR   Monticello Sep. 25. 97.

Yours of the 14th. inst. is recieved. In mine by last post I advised you that, counting on your receiving a quarter's salary on the 1st. of Oct. I had drawn on you in favor of Joseph Roberts for 400 and some dollars payable Oct. 3. On the same ground I have this day drawn on you in favor of Charles Johnston & Co. for six hundred and fifty dollars payable Oct. 3. Be pleased also to credit Peter Lott 210. Dollars by me, and to debit my account therewith.

The fever now visiting Philadelphia is indeed a very serious calamity, and cannot but have serious effects on it's commerce and growth. The desertion of it's citizens will undoubtedly lessen the extent of the evil and shorten it's duration. No one more sincerly prays for it's cessation than myself; and that you may personally avoid it. I am Dear Sir Your most obedt. servt.   TH: JEFFERSON

P.S. Mr. Hamilton's pamphlet in answer to certain Documents in the History of the US. would be very acceptable by the post, if you can procure me a copy. It has not yet reached this place.

PrC (CSmH); faded; at foot of text in ink: "Barnes John."

HAMILTON'S PAMPHLET: see note to TJ to Madison, 24 July 1797.

From Andrew Ellicott

MY DEAR SIR   Natchez Septr. 25th. 1797

It is with real pleasure that I embrace this opportunity of congratulating you, on the elevated, and dignified station, which you hold by the voice of your country in our national legislature. It is an omen favourable to liberty, when science and legislation are combined.

The execution of the business which brought me into this country is yet delayed, and what the result will be I cannot pretend to determine: I can only say, that appearances are rather more favourable than they were some time ago.

The British have a considerable influence in this quarter, many of the inhabitants have an habitual prejudice for that nation, and government, and from some circumstances I am of the opinion, that Mr. Blunts intrigues have extended into this district and the Florida's. The British party are at this time very turbulent, in this quarter, and in daily expectation of hearing of an attack upon the spanish possessions on this side of the Mississippi. This party, in this district, I have reason to suspect are secretly encouraged in their factious conduct by the spaniards, not to aid Great Britain, (but to produce an apparent necessity for bringing more troops into this settlement to protect the quiet, and well disposed,) but in fact to oppose the U.S.

The British party in this district is headed by Col. Anty. Hutchins, who is certainly at this time in the pay of that nation. He is shortly going on to Congress with an address, or memorial, respecting this country. His business however plausible, is doubtless suspicious, and his intrigues to be guarded against. I have written more perticularly to Judge Tazewell concerning this man. It is certainly necessary for Congress to take some effective measures for securing this country, and quieting the minds of the inhabitants.

I have made a great number of Astronomical Observations since I left Philadelphia, which I shall arrange and publish on my return. The mouth of the Ohio I find has been laid down in our maps very errorniously: the latitude is 37°.0'.23" N. and longitude 5ʰ.55'.7" west from the Royal observatory at Greenwich. The latitude of the Town of Natchez is 31°.33'.46", and longitude 6ʰ.5' west.

That your exertions in the cause of liberty, and your scientific pursuits, may secure to you that fame, and happiness, to which I am sure you are entitled, is the undisguised wish of your Friend, and Hbl. Servt.

ANDW. ELLICOTT

RC (DLC); at foot of text: "Thomas Jefferson Esqr. President of the Senate and V.P.U.S"; endorsed by TJ as received 19 Dec. 1797 and so recorded in SJL.

THE BUSINESS WHICH BROUGHT ME INTO THIS COUNTRY: Ellicott had been in the Natchez region since February 1797, but his task of marking the boundary between the United States and Spanish territory in West Florida, as stipulated by Pinckney's Treaty, was delayed by Spain's reluctant evacuation of its posts on the Mississippi. The survey did not begin until the spring of 1798 (Catharine Van Cortlandt Mathews, *Andrew Ellicott: His Life and Letters* [New York, 1908], 149, 157-8; Bemis, *Pinckney's Treaty*, 294-5). When Anthony HUTCHINS sent his memorial to Congress, members of the American surveying party overtook his courier and relieved him of the paper, which evidently denounced Ellicott.

In February 1798 the House of Representatives received a memorial from Natchez District inhabitants with views differing from Hutchins's, asking Congress for a provisional government and for affirmation of Spanish land grants "notwithstanding any former British grants" (Arthur Preston Whitaker, *The Mississippi Question, 1795-1803: A Study in Trade, Politics, and Diplomacy* [New York, 1934], 64; *Annals*, VII, 960).

From James Thomson Callender

SIR   Philadelphia Septr. 28th. 1797.

I expect that your remaining numbers of the History of 1796 have come duly to hand. The other copy will be ready for you on your return to town.

I would not have intruded on you at this time about that; but am to request your indulgence for a few moments. I have begun another volume on American History; and it will be ready for the press in about a month. Having been in bad health, for a time, now better, having by the desertion of the town been reduced to some inconvenience, and having a small family, I laid my plan before M. Leiper and M. Dallas, who handsomely gave me most effectual assistance, till the time of printing and Selling the book.

In this dilemma, I recollected something that dropt from you, when I had the honour of seeing you at Francis's hotel. It related to Some assistance, in a pecuniary way, that you intended to make me, on finishing my next volume. Now, Sir, my design at present is to hint that, in the present dreadful situation of the town, if the matter in reserve could be made in *advance*, it would really treble the greatness of the favour. If it was a draft or Check for 5 or 10 dollars, say, it might be in favour of a third person, my name not being very proper to appear; vizt. "Mr. James Ronaldson," a particular friend of mine.

I hope in a few months to be (if I escape the fever) much less dependent than I have been upon my pen. Bookselling is at present in an entirely ruined State, otherwise my two last volumes would have put me far beyond the need of asking help. Your answer to me, *to be left at the Post office till called for*, will much oblige Sir Your very much obliged & humble Servant   JAS. THOMSON CALLENDER

P.S. Since the printing of Mr. Hamilton's *Observations* Bishop White has, in a public Company, declined to drink his health, assigning the pamphlet as a reason. If you have not seen it, no anticipation can equal the infamy of this piece. It is worth all that fifty of the best pens in

America Could have said against him, and the most pitiful part of the whole is his notice of you.

RC (DLC); endorsed by TJ as received 6 Oct. 1797 and so recorded in SJL.

James Thomson Callender (1758-1803), a native of Scotland, came to the United States in 1793 to escape prosecution for sedition when his authorship of the pamphlet *The Political Progress of Britain* became known. Settling in Philadelphia, Callender served as a stenographer recording the debates in the House of Representatives for Andrew Brown's *Philadelphia Gazette* from December 1793 to February 1796, when he was dismissed, having gained the enmity not only of Federalist congressmen but many Republicans as well. After a brief period in Baltimore, Callender returned to Philadelphia and became part of the circle of Republican propagandists, including John Beckley, James Carey, William Duane, Dr. James Reynolds, and Benjamin F. Bache. He was also befriended by Thomas Leiper, the wealthy Republican tobacco merchant and fellow emigré from Scotland, and lawyer Alexander J. Dallas. TJ and Callender probably met for the first time in June 1797 at Callender's publishers, Snowden and McCorkle, when TJ made his first recorded payment to Callender for the forthcoming *History of the United States for 1796*, the publication which made Callender a celebrity for the Republican cause. Between January 1794 and July 1798, Callender regularly wrote pieces for Bache's *Aurora* published under the heading "From a Correspondent." Bache being absent from Philadelphia, Callender probably had editorial charge of the newspaper in March 1798 when it advocated the publication of the dispatches from the American envoys to France. The communications included descriptions of French solicitation of bribes that, when read by the public, would lead to the XYZ affair and the subsequent passage of the alien and sedition acts. Upon passage of the Sedition Act, Callender fled to Virginia to avoid prosecution, staying for several months at Raspberry Plain, Steven T. Mason's home in Loudoun County, before moving to Petersburg. He began writing for the Republican Richmond *Examiner*

and in early 1800 published the first volume of *The Prospect Before Us*, an attack on the Adams administration that served as an important pamphlet in the presidential campaign. It also led to Callender's prosecution and conviction under the Sedition Act, with the partisan Federalist justice Samuel Chase presiding at the trial. Callender received a $200 fine and a jail sentence that ended with the expiration of the sedition law on 3 Mch. 1801. Writing from his jail cell, Callender became a martyr for the Republican cause. Upon TJ's election to the presidency, Callender expected some reward for his endeavours, such as the postmastership at Richmond with its $1,500 a year stipend. When an appointment was not forthcoming, he felt betrayed. In early 1802, in partnership with the Federalist newspaper editor Henry Pace, Callender began attacking the Republican establishment in Virginia in articles in the Richmond *Recorder*, culminating with his attacks on the president. One of these was the first accusation in print of TJ's liaison with Sally Hemings. In 1803 Callender once again experienced declining popularity and acrimoniously broke with Pace and the *Recorder*. On 17 July 1803, Callender's body was found in the James River. While accounts of his intoxication that day led to an official report of accidental drowning, a letter by Callender published several weeks later suggested that he had taken his own life (ANB; Durey, *Callender*, 51, 60-4, 74-8, 101, 106-7, 110-11, 143; Charles A. Jellison, "That Scoundrel Callender," in VMHB, LXVII [1959], 295-306; Madison, *Papers*, XV, 155; same, *Sec. of State Ser.*, I, 118-19; MB, 963, 1028; James M. Smith, *Freedom's Fetters: The Alien and Sedition Laws and American Civil Liberties* [Ithaca, 1956], 334-58; DHSC, III, 405, 435-6; Callender to TJ, 26 Oct. 1798).

Probably in response to Callender's request for SOME ASSISTANCE in ADVANCE of his publication of *Sketches of the History of America* (Philadelphia, 1798), TJ asked John Barnes, on 8 Oct., to pay him $20 for pamphlets (MB, II, 971). For Callender's dire financial state during the months ahead, see Durey, *Callender*, 104-6.

From Arthur Campbell

SIR Washington Sept. 30. 1797

Your favour of the first instant came safe to hand, by last Post. I have read it over and again, and will treasure up the ideas. We have but little of the party spirit in the Western Country when compared with the great Towns, but we have seen and felt too much. A jealousy must be awakened, and a resistance to foreign influence formed, or we may ere long repent our torpid state as a People. We have an enquiry to make. Will it, or not conduce to the revival of the spirit of 1776 the calling of a Convention to revise and amend the State Constitution?

Sober Men on this side the Blue-Ridge have their fears in setting matters afloat again on account of the probability of representation in the legislature being proportioned according to the number of *People* in the State, that is *black People* as well as White; The evils already experienced from that degraded species of population must afterwards be increased tenfold: Our Sons in that case might live to see like calamities come to pass in Virginia that have lately taken place in St. Domingo and instead of us progressing in moral and political improvment, and our national character become a safeguard to us, we would rapidly decline, and ere a century be past be as debased as the present Grecians, or the more feeble Gentoos of Hindostan.

You will excuse Sir, flights into futurity, love for our Country, and the happiness of posterity will be my apology. Accept my unfeigned Respects. ARTHUR CAMPBELL

RC (DLC); endorsed by TJ as received 3 Nov. 1797 and so recorded in SJL.

From Dugnani

MONSIEUR Rome ce 30. 7bre. 1797

Je me flatte, que cette lettre Sera plus heureuse d'autres, que je vous ai ecrit, et que enfin je parviendrai a me rappeller a votre Souvenir, et a vous exprimer mon desir d'avoir de vos nouvelles. Deux des vos Nationaux Americains elèves de la Propagande de Rome auront l'honneur de vous la presenter; leurs noms sont Raffael Smyth du Maryland, et Felix dougherty de Philadelfie; Ces jeunes hommes d'apres avoir fait leurs etudes iront rejoindre leurs familles, et comme j'espere, qu'ils seront de bons Citoyens, aussi je prends la liberté de vous les reccomander; et je vous serai bien reconnoissant, de ce, que vous aurez la bonté de faire pour eux.

Depuis que nous nous separâmes a Paris, Combien des choses sont arrivées dans l'Europe, et bien au dela de, qu'on pouvoit, s'y attendre! Ces années forment une Epoque, qui Sera a jamais memorable. Nous sommes dans ce moment a la Conclusion de la paix, ou de la Guerre; le Ciel voulut nous donner la paix, ce premier bien, qui est le Seul qui puisse nous faire jouir des autres.

Enfin, Monsieur, je vous prie de vouloir bien en bon ami agreer un essai des beaux-arts [dessiné], et d'être persuadé que quelle soit la distance, qui nous Separe, mes Voeux pour votre Satisfaction vous Suivront par tout, et que rien ne peut ajouter au sincere, et tendre attachement, que je vous ai voué. J'ai l'honneur d'etre, Monsieur, avec toute la Consideration, qui vous est düe Votre tres humble et tres Affectioné Serviteur, et Ami   LE CARDINAL DUGNANI

RC (DLC); at foot of first page: "Mr. Jefferson Vice-Presidt. des Etats Unis / Philadelphie"; endorsed by TJ as received 6 June 1798 and so recorded in SJL.

RAFFAEL SMYTH DU MARYLAND, ET FELIX DOUGHERTY DE PHILADELFIE: American Catholics expected much of Ralph Smith and Felix Dougherty, who were dispatched to Rome for study in 1787, when they were aged fourteen and thirteen respectively. However, on their return to the United States in 1798 both young men declined ordination, although Smith may have become a priest some years later (Thomas O'Brien Hanley, ed., *The John Carroll Papers*, 3 vols. [Notre Dame, Ind., 1976], I, 187, 255, 356, II, 249, III, 361).

Statement of Nailery Profits

Statement of annual disbursements and receipts on account of the Nailery.

1794.				D		D
May. 31.	To paid Caleb Lownes for 1. ton of nail rod			106.67		
		transportation		12.33		119.00
July. 1.	To do.	1. ton & transportn				119.00
Sep. 30.	To coal @ 2d. per bushel & 666. bushels for every ton is 18.50 per ton.					
	for 2. ton					37.
	To 3. pr. ct. on £49.2.11. to George					4.85
1795.						
Feb. 28.	To Lownes for nail rod 3. tons @ 105.33 =			316		
		transportn @ 16.D.		48		364.
July 1.	To Lownes nailrod	2. ton @ 105.		210		
		transprtn @ 16.D.		32		242.67
Sep. 30.	To coal for 5. ton of rod @ 18.50.					92.50
	To George & Isaac this year.					32.65
	Profit from beginning to this day					593.41
						1605.08

1794.					
May 21 Sep. 30	} By amount of sale of nails during this period £49.2.11 =	163.82	
Oct. 1 1795 Sep. 30	} By amount of sale of nails during this period £432.7.7 =	1441.26	1605.08

Oct.	To Lownes for nail rod 3. ton @ 112.	= 336.		
		transportation @ 16.	48	384.
Nov.	To Gamble for nailrod 1. ton @ 133.			
		transportn @ 8.33		141.33
1796.				
Apr.	To Gamble for nailrod ½ ton @	80.		
		transportn	4.16	84.16
May 13	To Howell for nailrod 3 ton @ 122.67 = 368.			
	hoops ½ ton @ 144.62 = 72.31			
	transportn @ 16.	56.		496.31
Sep. 24.	To Howell for nailrod 3. ton @ 138.67 = 416			
	transportn @ 16. = 48.			464.
30.	To coal for 11. ton of rod @ 18.50			203.50
	To George 2. p.c. on 2127.33.			42.54
	To Fleming & Mc.lanachan on their sales of	£ s d		
	this year	111– 2–1 5. per cent	18.52
	To T. Carr do.	48– 8–4	8.06
	To S. Clarke do.	254–18–4	42.50
	transportn to Staunton		42.50
	Profit from Oct. 1. 95. to Sep. 30. 96.		199.91
			2127.33

1795. Oct. 1. 1796. Sep. 30	} By amount of sales of nails during this period £638.4.	2127.33
		D
1797. Apr. 15.	To Roberts for nailrod 3. ton @ 133.33 = 400 transportn @ 16. 48	448.00
July	To Jordan for nailrod 1¾ton @ 142.33 = 249.08 transportn 9	258.08
Sep. 30.	To coal for 4¾ tons @ 18.50	87.87
	To George 2. p.c. on 1868.06	37.36

£   s   d

To Flem' & Mc.lan. on their sales of this year	47–11–4 @ 5. p.c.	7.93
To. T. Carr	80–90–0	13.40
To S. Clarke	234–18–6 ½	39.10
transportation to Staunton		39.10
PROFIT this year		937.22
		1868.06

1796. Oct. 1. 1797. Sep. 30	} By amount of sales of nails during this period	1868.06

Recapitulations from May 1794. to Sep. 30. 1797

Profits to Sep. 30. 1795.   593.41
        Sep. 30. 1796   199.91
        Sep. 30. 1797   937.22
                 1790.54 which on 22¾ ton of rod is 76.D pr. ton
                       profit.

Amount of sales to Sep. 30. 1794.   163.82
               Sep. 30. 1795   1441.26
               Sep. 30. 1796   2127.33
               Sep. 30. 1797. 1868.06
                     5600.47 which on 22 ¾ tons of rod is
                       244.17D received for the nails from
                       each ton of rod.

Analysis.   on every ton. George   5.   ⎫
            commn on sales   10.   ⎪
            coal   18.50 ⎬ 244.17
            transportn   16   ⎪
            profit   76   ⎪
            cost   118.67 ⎭

note the nailrod was all out Sep. 30. 97. which makes it a proper epoch for
    calculation[1]

MS (ViU); entirely in TJ's hand, with an additional entry in pencil (see note below); TJ's block printing shown in small capitals; written in a bound ledger that also contains personal accounts, 1767-1770, accounts of Nicholas Lewis as superintendent of TJ's properties, 1786-1792, TJ's index to those and other accounts of 1783-1792, and accounts, lists, and sketches made by members of the Randolph family in the 1840s and 1850s; this statement being immediately preceded in the ledger by eight pages of chronological accounts, 21 May 1794 through 27 Nov. 1795, entirely in TJ's hand, recording expenditures for nailrod and charcoal on the left (verso) side of each pair of facing leaves and receipts from sales of nails in pounds, shillings, and pence on the right (recto) pages, with heading on each verso page: "The Nailery," and with TJ's note below the final entry: "See a more summary statement in the following pages."

TJ paid Benjamin JORDAN $249.08 for nailrod on 21 July 1797. According to TJ's financial records this is the only time he used Jordan as a supplier for the nailery (MB, II, 967). Neither a letter from Jordan to TJ of 6

Jan., recorded in SJL as received the next day, nor letters from TJ to Jordan of 19 Jan. and 21 July 1797, recorded in SJL, have been found.

TJ kept another set of nailery accounts, in which he made a chronological record of nails "Bespoke" and "Delivered" from January 1796 to November 1800, noting the sizes, quantities, and price of the nails in each order. With those accounts are miscellaneous notes by TJ relating to nail production and his ledger of the daily production of different sizes of nails by each of the nailery's workers during the first six months of 1796 (CLU-C; entirely in TJ's hand).

[1] Below this statement TJ added in pencil an entry for 18 Oct. 1797: "To Roberts for nailrod $3\frac{1}{4}$ ton @ 128 = 416 transportn @ 16. 52"

From John Barnes

SIR   Philada: 3d: Octr: 1797.

I am this Instant favoured with yours, 25th Ulto: and Note your Additional draft, to the Order of Messrs. C. Johnston & Co: for $650. as well $210. to the Credit of Mr. P. Lott.

Very fortunately, the inclosed pamphlett, (which you request,) was some few days since, left with me—in the state you find it.✻ Mr. H— has assuredly, reduced his Consequence, to the most degrading and Contemptable point of view; And I am much pleased to find Mr. Monroe would not, humour his restless, unreasonable, and foolish Vanity, for under All circumstances, the several Gentlemens treatment towards him—was, throughout polite, and respectfull.

Such another piece of ridiculous folly: sure, never Man was guilty of—first, in Committing himself via his Dear—(dear indeed;) Maria; and than, to publish it, himself; as if, it were possible—by that means— to justify, his public Conduct, by a *simple* confession of his private ridiculous Amour, at the expence of both—his Reputation and future peace of mind; how it must, on Reflection, torture him, on poor Mrs. H. Account whose feelings on the Occasion—must be severely injured, if not expressed; how you came—(innocently) to be luged in—at the latter end of the fray, is yet to be explained; it seems, this poor Frauncis—to, whom you addressed the two letters in question—was met by Mr. H. on

✻ Mr. T. notes—

the Battery New York, and questioned respecting his situation and Circumstances—and withal Asked, who was his friend, and if he stood in Need of Assistance—his look, and condition plainly evinced the supposition—and Mr. H. Afforded him—a present relief. In the course of conversation F—informed Mr. H. he had waited upon you—in Philada. and to confirm it, produced your two letters, and withal added your promise of employment (at least so he expressed himself to me). Mr. H—immediately requested the persual of them, with a promise of Returning them. Imprudently F. Assented—and they still rest, with Mr. H. And by *this sorry Means* made Use of to *Grace*—as he suppose, his *ungracious* defence. In pity to F—s immediate wants—(Rather—than his Merits) I could not but Assist him; After a short breakfast he left me, and I have not seen him since—nothing but his extreme want, and expectation of seeing a worthless Brother, of his Here—(Absent) brought him—at this Crisis—to Town—and it is—more than probable, he will pay you another Visit on your Return—to Philada. I intimated too him the improbability of your employing him—and added, the very imprudent disclosier, of your letters—to *Mr. H.* could not but displease you.

We are still in the same very Anxious and unhappy situation, respecting the fever—as when I last wrote you: favoured however, with some cool refreshing showers—have and will, I hope—damp the Rage—tho. not, effectualy destroy, the Cause—which frost alone, must subdue. Most respectfully, I am Sir, Your Obedt: Hbl servt: JOHN BARNES

RC (Mrs. L. Carstairs Pierce, Bryn Mawr, Pa., 1950); at foot of text: "Thomas Jefferson Esquire—Monticello Virga."; endorsed by TJ as received 14 Oct. 1797 and so recorded in SJL. Enclosure: Hamilton, *Observations*, cited in note to Madison to TJ, 24 July 1797.

THIS POOR FRAUNCIS: see TJ to Andrew G. Fraunces, 27, 28 June 1797.

From John McQueen

SIR   St. Augustine Et. Florida 6th Octr. 1797.

By Captain Forrester I take the liberty of sending you a barrel of Oranges which I pray you to receive as a small acknowledgment for the civilities you were pleased to confer on me in the Year eighty six when I had the honour of seeing you at Paris. Am Sir With the highest respect Your most obliged and respectful servt.   JOHN MCQUEEN

RC (ViW); at foot of text: "Mr Jefferson"; endorsed by TJ as received 13 Dec. 1797 and so recorded in SJL.

THE CIVILITIES YOU WERE PLEASED TO CONFER ON ME: see TJ to McQueen, 16 Jan. 1786.

To John Barnes

DEAR SIR   Monticello Oct. 8. 97.

Your favor of Sep. 29. is at hand. The paiment to Mr. Bache is right. Myself and some of my neighbors have to pay for some of the pamphlets of Callendar, which they have desired me to do for them. Be so good therefore as to pay him twenty dollars on my account. He is to be found at the printing office of Snowden & Mckorkle No. 47. North 4th. street. If you will be so kind as to send a note there, he will call on you,[1] and will consider this act as a sufficient acknolegement of the receipt of his letter and attention to it's contents. It is probable I may write you on another subject by this post. Wishing yourself and fellow citizens safely thro' the dangers surrounding you I am Dear Sir Your most obedt. servt

TH: JEFFERSON

PrC (MHi); with one emendation noted below; endorsed by TJ in ink on verso.

Barnes's FAVOR OF SEP. 29., recorded in SJL as received on 6 Oct. 1797, has not been found. In MB under date of 6 Oct., TJ recorded that "J. Barnes has pd. Bache the currt. year of his paper for me 5.D" (MB, II, 971). For the payment for PAMPHLETS, see James Thomson Callender to TJ, 28 Sep. 1797.

[1] TJ here canceled "I will [write] you to."

To John Barnes

DEAR SIR   Monticello Oct. 8. 97.

Colo. James Monroe having immediate occasion for a sum of money in Philadelphia, I have concluded it better to let him have Mr. Short's quarter's dividends payable the 1st. instant, than to leave them lying in an unproductive state, on the expectation now beginning to be weak, of Mr. Short's arrival this autumn. I therefore inclose you a power of attorney to receive them, and as I do not know the exact amount I have not given a draught on you, but by this present, desire you to pay the amount whatever it is to Colo. Monroe's order. I have informed him it will be a few dollars over 300. He will accordingly authorize some person to call on you for the amount be it what it may, as soon as you shall have received it. I am with esteem Dear Sir Your most obedt. servt

TH: JEFFERSON

PrC (Thomas Jefferson Foundation, on deposit ViU); endorsed in ink on verso by TJ.

Monroe's IMMEDIATE OCCASION FOR A SUM OF MONEY IN PHILADELPHIA was a loan of $600 he made to Benjamin Franklin Bache to subsidize the publication of Monroe's vindication of his actions as minister to France (see Monroe to TJ, [22] Oct. 1797).

The book did not sell well, Bache was unable to repay the loan in its entirety, and in June 1798 TJ found means to help cover Monroe's obligation for the money drawn from William Short's income from public securities (Tagg, *Bache*, 327-8, 361; MB, II, 986).

Power of Attorney to John Barnes

Know all men by these presents that I Thomas Jefferson named in a certain letter of Attorney from William Short of the state of Virginia late one of the ministers of the US. abroad, bearing date the 2d. day of April 1793. and now lodged in the bank of the US. thereby constituting me his attorney with full powers to act for him in all cases as validly as he could do himself were he personally present, by virtue of the power thereby given me do make, constitute and appoint John Barnes of Philadelphia as well my own as the true and lawful attorney and substitute of the said William Short to recieve the dividends which were payable according to law on a certain certificate No. 2424. for 15,342. Dollars 18. cents bearing an interest of 6. per cent from the 1st. of Oct. 1793. and standing in the name of the said William Short, registered in the proper office of the US. at the seat of government in Philadelphia, on the 1st. day of this present month of October, and to do all lawful acts requisite for effecting the same; hereby ratifying and confirming the paiment so to be made to the said John Barnes and the discharge which he shall give for the same as done by virtue of the power of Attorney aforesaid. In witness whereof I have hereunto set my hand and seal this 8th. day of Octob. one thousand seven hundred and ninety seven.   TH: JEFFERSON

MS (PHC); entirely in TJ's hand; on verso are two attestations, the first signed and sealed by Thomas Bell and stating that TJ had appeared before him and acknowledged the power of attorney and the second signed and sealed by John Nicholas as clerk of Albemarle County certifying Bell's authority as justice of the peace; endorsed by Henry Kuhl: "There is but one witness— and according to precedent, the power otherwise requires admission"; endorsed by Comptroller John Steele as admitted, 18 Oct. 1797.

To John Taylor

TH:J: TO MR. TAYLOR   Monticello Oct. 8. 97.

We have heard much here of an improvement made in the Scotch threshing machine by Mr. Martin, and that you have seen and approved it. Being myself well acquainted with the original *geered* machine, and Booker's substitution of *whirls and bands* (as I have one of each kind) it will perhaps give you but a little trouble to give me so much of an explanation as will be necessary to make me understand Martin's. And let it apply if you please to the movements by horses or by hand.—I must ask the favor of you to get me one of the same drills you sent me before, made in the best manner, with a compleat set of bands and buckets, and packed in a box, in pieces, in the most compact manner the workman can do it, and forwarded to me at Philadelphia, as soon after the meeting of Congress as possible. It is for a friend, and to go still further, which renders this mode of packing necessary. For the amount when you will make it known I will either inclose you a bank bill from Philadelphia, or send it you in fine tea, or any thing else you please to order.—How did your turnep seed answer?—I have received from England, and also from Italy some seed of the winter vetch, a plant from which I expect a good deal. If it answers I will send you of the seed. I have also received all the good[1] kinds of field pea from England. But I count a great deal more on our Southern cow-pea.—If you wish any of them I will send you a part.[2] I have not yet seen Hamilton's pamphlet: but I understand that finding the straight between Scylla and Charybdis too narrow for his steerage, he has preferred running plump on one of them. In truth it seems to work very hard with him; and his willingness to plead guilty as to the adultery seems rather to have strengthened than weakened the suspicions that he was in truth guilty of the speculations. Present me respectfully and affectionately to my old friend and file-leader Mr. Pendleton, and accept yourself my friendly salutations & Adieux.

P.S. Your answer by the 1st. or 2d. post will find me here.

RC (MHi: Washburn Collection); with several emendations, the most important of which are noted below; addressed: "John Taylor esq. Caroline to be lodged at the Bowling green"; franked. PrC (MHi); endorsed by TJ in ink on verso.

Sir John Sinclair, president of the Board of Agriculture in London, was the FRIEND to whom TJ was sending Thomas C. Martin's drill (TJ to Sinclair, 23 Mch. 1798).

[1] Word interlined.
[2] Preceding sentence interlined.

From Elizabeth Wayles Eppes

DEAR SIR   Eppington Oct. 10 1797

The contents of your friendly letter gave me the highest satisfaction, and I long for the happy moment to call dear Maria my daughter, to say how much poor Betsy, and myself are disappoint'd at not being present requires a better pen than mine.

We look forward with the utmost pleasure for a happy meeting, and hope you will be able to visit us this month, we will then talk of their settling, you are too generous, I am sure not to let us have half their company. Yours affectionatly   EE

RC (MHi); endorsed by TJ as received 11 Oct. 1797 and so recorded in SJL.

YOUR FRIENDLY LETTER: TJ to Eppes, 25 Sep. 1797 (recorded in SJL, but not found). DISAPPOINTED AT NOT BEING PRESENT: the marriage between John Wayles Eppes and Mary Jefferson took place on 13 Oct. 1797, which TJ recorded without any other details ([John C. Wyllie, ed.], *Thomas Jefferson's Prayer Book* [Charlottesville, 1952], pl. IX; MB, II, 972). For Mary Jefferson's previous relationship with the Eppes family, see TJ to Elizabeth Wayles Eppes, 15 May 1791.

Marriage Settlement for John Wayles Eppes

This indenture made on the 12th. day of October[1] one thousand seven hundred and ninety seven between Francis Eppes and Elizabeth his wife on the first part, John Wayles Eppes their son on the second part, all of the county of Chesterfield, Thomas Jefferson on the third part and Mary Jefferson daughter of the said Thomas on the fourth part, witnesseth that Whereas the said Francis, being seised in feesimple in his own right of a certain tract of land at Bermuda hundred on the South side of James river in the county of Chesterfeild containing by estimation 750. acres and one other tract in Martin's swamp[2] adjoining to the lands of David Meade Randolph,[3] containing by estimation one hundred and thirty one[4] acres, in consideration of the natural love which he bore to his said son John Wayles Eppes, did, by deed indented, proved and recorded bearing date on the   day of April[5] one thousand seven hundred and   convey the same to him in feesimple, and thereof delivered possession;[6] and a marriage being now intended shortly to be had between the said John Wayles Eppes and the said Mary Jefferson, and the said Thomas[7] from natural love for his said daughter and for her advancement[8] and in consideration of the said marriage and of the advancement so heretofore made and by these presents confirmed on the part of the said Francis and Elizabeth his wife to the said John Wayles, hath conveyed or undertaken to convey before the said marriage to the said Mary in fee-simple a certain tract of land in the county of Albemarle on the North East side of the Rivanna river, called Pantops, containing by estimation[9] eight hundred and nineteen acres and one quarter;[10] heretofore the property of the Smiths, of which said tract the said Thomas is seised in feesimple, as also thirty one[11] slaves, with certain stock of horses cattle and hogs, and certain plantation utensils specified or to be specified in the said conveyance, and it being the desire of the parties interested, for their greater security, that the said John Wayles Eppes shall again convey the said lands at Bermuda Hundred and Martin's swamp[12] to the said Francis, in order that the said Francis and Elizabeth may reconvey the same to him in feesimple on more valuable, valid,[13] and beneficial considerations Now therefore this indenture witnesseth that the said John Wayles Eppes for the purpose aforesaid, and in consideration of the sum of five shillings to him in hand paid by the said Francis, hath given granted bargained and sold unto the said Francis the said tract of lands before described at Bermuda Hundred and Martin's swamp with their [14] appurtenances: To have and to hold the same to him and his heirs, for the sole use and purpose before expressed: And that the said Francis and Elizabeth his wife for the natural love they bear to the said John Wayles Eppes and his more certain [15] advancement, and in consideration of the marriage aforesaid and of the advancement given or to be given as aforesaid before the marriage by the said Thomas to the said Mary his daughter, and of the sum of five shillings to them the said Francis and Elizabeth in hand paid, do give grant bargain and sell to the said John Wayles Eppes the same tracts [16] of land at Bermuda Hundred and Martin's swamp before described with their appurtenances: To have and to hold the said tracts of land with it's appurtenances to him the said John Wayles Eppes and his heirs free of all incumbrances. In witness whereof the said Francis and Elizabeth his wife and the said John Wayles have hereto set their hands and seals on the day and year first beforementioned. [17]

Signed sealed and delivered
in presence of [18]
(the interlineations here noted)
    Richard Richardson
    Hugh Chisolm
    Matthew Toler.

PrC (ViU: Edgehill-Randolph Papers); entirely in TJ's hand; indented; with blanks filled and signatures supplied by TJ in ink (see notes 1, 4, 5, 11, and 18 below), except for one day of month and year which remain as blanks; other emendations by TJ in ink as noted below (see notes 2, 10, 12, 14, and 16). Dft (CSmH); partially dated, with blanks for day and month; lacks emendations in ink in PrC; with numerous emendations, the most important of which are noted below. Enclosed in TJ to Francis Eppes, 24 Sep. 1797.

[1] Preceding day and month entered in ink by TJ.

[2] Preceding twelve words interlined in ink by TJ.

[3] Preceding eight words interlined in Dft.

[4] Preceding five words entered in ink by TJ.

[5] Preceding word entered in ink by TJ. It appears as a dash in Dft.

[6] Preceding four words interlined in Dft.

[7] Word interlined.

[8] Preceding four words interlined in Dft.

[9] Preceding two words interlined in Dft.

[10] Preceding two words interlined in ink in place of "one half." Dft: "$\frac{1}{2}$."

[11] Preceding two words entered in ink by TJ.

[12] Preceding three words interlined in ink by TJ here and the two subsequent times they appear in the text.

[13] Word interlined in Dft.

[14] Word overwritten in ink by TJ replacing "it's" here and when it appears later in the same context.

[15] In Dft preceding two words interlined in place of "further."

[16] TJ added "s" in ink to this word at this point and again when it appears later in sentence.

[17] Dft ends here.

[18] Remainder of document completed in ink by TJ.

Marriage Settlement for Mary Jefferson

This indenture made on the twelfth day of October one thousand seven hundred and ninety seven between Thomas Jefferson of the one part, Mary Jefferson his daughter of the second part, both of Albemarle, Francis Eppes and Elizabeth his wife of the county of Chesterfeild[1] of the third part and John Wayles Eppes their son of the fourth part of the same county,[2] Witnesseth, that forasmuch as a marriage is intended shortly to be had between the said John Wayles Eppes and the said Mary Jefferson, and the said Francis Eppes and Elizabeth his wife[3] for the natural love which they bear to the said John Wayles Eppes and his advancement, and in consideration of the said marriage, and of the advancement made by these presents on the part of the said Thomas to the said Mary his daughter, have conveyed or undertaken to convey before the said marriage to the said John Wayles Eppes in feesimple a certain tract of land called Angola in the county of Cumberland on the North side of Appomattox river containing by estimation three thousand four hundred and nineteen and three quarter acres in exchange for a certain tract of land on the South side of James river[4] at Bermuda Hundred in the county of Chesterfeild,[5] heretofore conveyed by the said Francis to the said John Wayles Eppes in feesimple, and the said Francis hath also conveyed and confirmed or undertaken to convey or confirm before the said Marriage to the said John Wayles Eppes certain slaves[6] duly specified or to be specified before the marriage and whereof delivery hath been heretofore made or will be made before the 25th. day of December next. Now this indenture witnesseth that the said Thomas[7] for the natural love which he bears his said daughter and for her advancement, and in consideration of the said marriage and of the advancement so made or undertaken to be made before the marriage[8] by the said Francis and Elizabeth to the said John Wayles Eppes their son,[9] and for the further consideration of five shillings to him in hand paid hath given granted bargained and sold to the said Mary a certain tract of land whereof the said Thomas is now seised in feesimple, in the county of Albemarle on the North East side of the Rivanna river and adjacent thereto, called Pantops, containing by estimation eight hundred and nineteen and one quarter acres heretofore the property of the Smiths, and comprehended between the lands now held by the Keys, the said Rivanna river,[10] the tract of land of the said Thomas called Lego formerly the property of Edwin Hickman, and his newly patented lands;[11] and also the following slaves, to wit,[12] smith Isaac and Iris his wife and her two children Squire and Joyce, Lucinda and her four children Sarah, Sandy, Sousy, and

Barret, Judy and her three sons Tim, Austin, and York, Philip and his wife Thamer and her two children Rachael and Lucy[13] Scilla and her two children Nelly and Letty[14] Phyllis and her child Sophia, Sally, her sister Clarinda, and her brother Goliah, all three the children of Molly, Val, Martin son of Doll, Lucy and her child Zachary[15] Betsey the daughter of Mary and Melinda the daughter of Betty Brown being thirty one in number[16] together with the plantation tooles and[17] utensils heretofore appropriated to and used by the said slaves and also a proper stock[18] of horses cattle and hogs[19] for a farm of which said slaves and stock delivery shall be made on or before the 25st.[20] day of December next To have and to hold the said lands called Pantops with the said Slaves tooles utensils and stock to the said Mary and her heirs free of all encumbrance whatsoever—

In Witness whereof the said Thomas hath hereto set his hand and seal on the day and year first before mentioned   TH: JEFFERSON

Sealed and delivered in presents of }
Richard Richardson Hugh Chisholm ⎱
Matthew Toler   ⎰

Memorandum: that before the ensealing and delivery of these presents it was agreed that the lands at Bermuda Hundred instead of those called Angola should stand settled on the said John Wayles Eppes in fee and that this should be accepted instead of the Angola lands as one of the considerations of this deed acknowledged under my hand and seal at the date first before mentioned   TH: JEFFERSON

PrC (ViU: Edgehill-Randolph Papers); entirely in TJ's hand; indented; incomplete, with remainder of text, signatures, and memorandum supplied from Tr (see note 15 below); with day and month and two names (see notes 13 and 14 below) supplied in ink by TJ; with several emendations only the most important of which is noted below (see note 1). Dft (CSmH); partially dated, with dashes for day and month; lacks names of slaves (see notes 12 and 16 below), signatures, and memorandum; with numerous emendations, only the most important of which are noted below. Tr (Albemarle County Deed Book, No. 12, Albemarle County Circuit Court Clerk's Office, Charlottesville); in left margin: "Jefferson to Eppes} Deed Examined"; with later endorsement by Deputy Clerk Alexander Garrett noting that upon request a copy of the deed was sent to John Wayles Eppes on 15 Apr. 1812. Recorded on 4 Dec. 1797

(Albemarle County Court Order Book, in same).

[1] Preceding five words interlined in PrC and Dft.

[2] Preceding four words interlined in Dft.

[3] In Dft TJ first wrote "now for the advancement of their said son" before altering the following passage to read as above.

[4] Preceding seven words interlined in Dft.

[5] Preceding five words interlined in Dft.

[6] In Dft TJ here canceled "in the said conveyance specified or to be specified" and interlined the remainder of the sentence.

[7] In Dft TJ first wrote "for the advancement of the said M. his daughter" before altering the following passage to read as above.

[8] Preceding three words interlined in Dft.

9 Following passage interlined in Dft concluding with "to him paid."

10 Preceding four words interlined in Dft.

11 Preceding five words interlined in Dft.

12 TJ here placed a dash in Dft and did not include the names of the slaves.

13 Preceding name supplied by TJ in ink.

14 Preceding name supplied by TJ in ink.

15 PrC ends at this point with remainder of text from Tr.

16 Dft continues at this point.

17 Preceding two words interlined in Dft.

18 Interlined in Dft in place of "proportion."

19 In Dft TJ first wrote "for a plantation to be assigned to the said M. by the said T. in the presence of witnesses" before altering the following passage to read as above.

20 Preceding digit appears to have been reworked from "1" in Tr.

Note on Spanish Expenditures

Oct. 13. 97. Littlepage, who has been on one or two missions from Poland to Spain told that when Gardoqui returned from America, he settled with his court an account of secret service money of 600,000. Dollars. Ex relatione Colo. Monroe.

MS (DLC: TJ Papers, 102: 17495); in TJ's hand, on a fragment from which the remainder of the page, bearing a continuation of the text, has been clipped and is now missing. MS (same, 102: 17461); in TJ's hand, written between Notes on Alexander Hamilton, 24 Aug. [1797], and Notes on Conversations with John Adams and George Washington, [after 13 Oct. 1797]; consists of a note reading in its entirety, with TJ's opening bracket and a supplied closing bracket: "Oct. 13. Littlepage, who has been on one or two missions &c. [here insert from another paper]."

EX RELATIONE: "from the report of."

Notes on Conversations with John Adams and George Washington

[after 13 Oct. 1797]

Under date of May 10. 1797. ante is a memorandum to note in due time Mr. Adams's free conversation with me Mar. 3. 1797. at Mr. Madison's. It was as follows.

Mar. 2. 1797. I arrived at Philada. to qualify as V.P. and called instantly on Mr. Adams who lodged at Francis's in 4th. street. The next morning he returned my visit at Mr. Madison's where I lodged. He found me alone in my room, and, shutting the door himself, he said he was glad to find me alone for that he wished a free conversation with me. He entered immediately on an explanation of the situation of our affairs with France, and the danger of a rupture with that nation a rupture which would convulse the attachments of this country. That he was impressed with the necessity of an immediate mission to the Directory; that it would have been the first wish of his heart to have got me to go there, but that he supposed it was out of the question, as it did not seem justifiable for him to send away the person destined to take his place in case of accident to himself, nor decent to remove from competition one who was a rival in the public favor. That he had therefore concluded to send a mission which by it's dignity should satisfy France, and by it's selection from the three great divisions of the Continent should satisfy all parts of the US. In short that he had determined to join Gerry and Madison to Pinckney, and he wished me to consult Mr. Madison for him. I told him that as to myself I concurred in the opinion of the impropriety of my leaving the post assigned me, and that my inclinations moreover would never permit me to cross the Atlantic again: that I would as he desired consult Mr. Madison, but I feared it was desperate, as he had refused that mission on my leaving it in Genl. Washington's time, tho' it was kept open a twelvemonth for him. He said that if Mr. Madison should refuse, he would still appoint him and leave the responsibility on him.—I consulted Mr. Madison who declined as I expected. I think it was on Monday the 6th. of March, Mr. Adams and myself met at dinner at Genl. Washington's, and we happened in the evening to rise from table and come away together. As soon as we got into the street I told him the event of my negociation with Mr. Madison. He immediately said that on consultation some objections to that nomination had been raised which he had not contemplated, and was going on with excuses which evidently embarrassed him, when we came to 5th. street where our road separated, his being down Market street, mine off along 5th. and we took leave: and he never after that said one word to me on the subject, or ever consulted me as to any measures of the government. The opinion I formed at the time on this transaction was that Mr. A. in the first moments of the enthusiasm of the occasion (his inauguration) forgot party sentiments, and as he never acted on any system, but was always governed by the feeling of the moment, he thought for a moment to steer impartially between the parties; that Monday the 6th. of Mar. being the first time he had met his cabinet, on expressing ideas of this kind he had been at once diverted from them, and returned to his former party views.

A note under same date of May 10. The reason Genl. Washington assigned to me for having called such a body of Militia to the siege of Yorktown was, that by doubling with our own forces, the numbers of our French auxiliaries, the honour might more indisputably result to us.

MS (DLC: TJ Papers, 102: 17461); in TJ's hand, undated, but on same sheet with Note on Diplomatic Appointments, July 1797, Notes on Alexander Hamilton, 24 Aug. 1797, and following truncated version of Note on Spanish Expenditures, 13 Oct. 1797; continues on verso.

Adams's recollections of these conversations are noted in Freeman, *Washington*, VII, 440-2.

For Adams's nominations for the MISSION to France, see note to Senate Resolution on Appointment of Charles C. Pinckney, [5 June 1797].

From John Taylor

J TAYLOR TO THE VICE PRESIDENT   Caroline October 14. 1797.

A model of Martin's machine for seperating the grain of wheat from the straw, is now before me, and yet simple as it is, I have no hopes that my mechanical knowledge is equal to a description so perspicuous, as to enable you to erect one. For it probably bears a very distant analogy to the Scotch machine or to Booker's, neither of which had ever been seen by Mr: Martin, when he invented his.

But as Martin purposes to apply for a patent, you will gain a correct idea of the machine, if you will so far oblige me, as to become the patron of his application; because in that event, the model and description required by law, shall be sent in the same box which will cover the drill— that I have bespoke. I would not have adventured to trouble you in a trivial case; but I hoped, that an invention of such mighty expectation, emanating from a Virginian, would utter an apology for the request.

Mr: Martin's first machine is moved by water. The power which bestows upon it sufficient velocity, is 16 square inches of water, under a pressure of six feet, discharged upon a common tub mill wheel of two feet diameter. For the shaft of a little tub mill is used to set the machine in motion, by fixing a cog: wheel to it; the upper stone being previously removed; and the vast execution of the machine, enables him thus to accomplish all its ends, tho' he is a farmer of considerable property. The whole motion of the machine is derived from four cog: wheels, the largest of which is about 3 feet diameter; and a perpetual screw, cut in the axle of the roller. The roller is a light hollow tube, less than four feet long, and about two feet in diameter, upon which six beaters of wood, projecting about two inches, are nailed longitudinally. The upper hemisphere of this roller, bisecting it lengthwise, is cased with thin plank, because the beaters *turn the wheat upwards*, from the moment of its reception by the two rollers presently mentioned, and as this case confines it in passing over the large roller, each straw will receive between 40 and 50 violent strokes before it can escape. The wheat in straw is conducted by one breadth of brown linnen, 6 or 8 feet long, to the beaters, which linnen revolves upon light solid rollers, and two rollers (one of which serves the purpose of moving the linnen) receive the wheat between them, and by a gentle pressure keep it steady in its motion onward, until it receives many strokes. The upper of these rollers is moveable in a perpendicular direction. The machine will discharge the wheat as rapidly as two men, by their utmost efforts, can lay it on the linnen; a third man rakes away the straw, which is all the attendance necessary. The execution of this first assay is three bushells in seven minutes, extreamly well gotten out. And the same machine is, I am confident, capable of being occasionally altered into the best fan imaginable. The value of the workmanship cannot exceed 20 dollars—the whole machine is portable in a waggon—and its simplicity will almost defy accident, for it has no rope—chain—bandage or harness of any kind. The model to be sent will work by hand, but the description will comprise that which goes by water, and will contain several improvements lately invented, which I have not examined, and of which I do not therefore speak. To that which goes by hand, small rollers are subjoined, for the ends of the axle to run on, to lessen the friction. One attempt of an hand machine has been made; that may be worked in any house, and is competent to geting out 70 bushells a day. But another, having great improvements, is in forwardness, the execution of which will in Mr: Martin's opinion, amount to one third of that which goes by water.

The Sweedish turnip are not more hardy than, and hardly as Large as, the common; but a cubic inch of the Sweedish exceeds in weight the same quantity of superficies taken from the common—it retains its solidity better—and furnishes a later salad. Hence I have paid great attention to it, and this year sowed some acres—but the hard weather last fall, and the fly this, have almost robed me even of seed. So that I have again to begin upon a small scale.

A few of any species of pea or vetch, which you approve of, will be thankfully received. I have gotten a sort of pea from below, which produces the most luxuriant cover, I ever beheld; and would I think, plowed in, constitute a fine vegitable dressing. It may possibly be the southern cow pea. If it is not, I will send you a parcel. It is a late pea, and must of course be sown very early.

I have never seen Hamilton's pamphlett, but his idea of disproving one criminal charge, by confessing another, is at least novel, tho' it may not savour of his supposed acuteness. His speculations will only come to light, when his light is extinguished, and it may be a consolation to him perhaps, to reflect, that his children will enjoy them, and he will have escaped an impeachment before our earthly chief justice. Not knowing, he may not fear, the constitution above.

But I give up all for lost. The malady of all governments is monopoly. This is creeping and creeping into ours. Here is a sort of abstract of the american constitutions published by William Smith L.L.D, in which he dogmatically settles sundry important political questions. He tells us that triennial elections—encreasing the power of one man or a few in sundry modes—and of course diminishing that of the people, will be ameliorations of the federal and state constitutions. And this book circulates, unanswered, like gospel. Prosperity & happiness attend you!

RC (DLC); endorsed by TJ as received 21 Oct. 1797 and so recorded in SJL. Enclosure: William L. Smith, *A Comparative View of the Constitutions of the Several States with each Other, and with that of the United States: Exhibiting in Tables the Prominent Features of each Constitution, and Classing Together Their Most Important Provisions under the Several Heads of Administration; With Notes and Observations* (Philadelphia, 1796). See Evans, No. 31209.

From Peregrine Fitzhugh

DEAR SIR   Washington County (Md) Octr. 15th. 1797—

I took the Liberty of thanking you for your favor of the 4th. of June in a Long Letter directed to you at Philadelphia but having seen in the papers a few days after an account of your departure from thence for Virginia I had then my doubts and am still under an uncertainty whether it arrived in time to find you there or whether it ever got to your hands. As that Letter contained some communications relative to Cresops extermination of Logans Family as stated in the Notes on Virginia and may possibly have miscarried and as you appeared desirous of receiving every information which might tend in any degree to ascertain the correctness or error of that statement, I deem it not inexpedient to repeat what I there express'd on the subject and to add some further accounts, the result of my inquiries agreeably to your Wish. I wrote you that Colo. Francis Deakins a very respectable character in this State had informed me that some time in the year 74. he was on the Frontiers of this then Province laying off a Proprietors Manor and executing some other Surveys when *Capt.* Michael Cresop and his party called at his Camp on their way to the Ohio and remained there some days, that they were in a state of intoxication when they came, continued so during their Stay and left him in a similar State and vowing destruction to every Indian they should meet with—that some little time after their departure (perhaps ten days or a fortnight) he received intelligence of the above murder and a few days after while he was still surveying from 3 to 500 of the back Settlers consisting of Men Women and Children passed him some half naked and all half starved flying in confusion from their homes to avoid the just resentment of the Indians who had begun their retaliations and that he never had since heard it denied or even doubted that Cresop and his party committed the act. From the above it appears there has been an error in statement as to the Person that it was Capt. and not Colo. Cressop who headed the Party and the *Father* and not the Grand Father of Mr. Martins "Childrens Mother." I have now further to notify that Colo. Daniel Hughes one of the first Characters among us who has resided a great many years in this County and is well acquainted with the characters of old Colo. Cresop and his Son, assured me that shortly after the destruction of Logans Family he was informed by a respectable Friend Mr. Patric Allison that he was at the Station on the Ohio from whence issued Capt. Cresop and his Party the morning of the transaction, that Capt. Cresop pressed him to join the detachment which however he declined—that a few hours after they left the station he heard the firing which commenced the horrid business and in the evening received the particulars of it. Mr. Allison is now a resident of Kentucky near either Lexington or Washington and Colo. Hughes has not a doubt will confirm the above account if a Letter is address'd to him. Of the general conduct and character of both Colo. Cresap and his Son, Colo. Hughes just observed that he thought Mr. Martin had better have been silent on that subject for he believed the least said would be the most favorable to them. I am told that Martin has a certificate or affidavit, I cannot say with precision which from a Mr. Tomlinson of Alleghany County (Md.) *who was one of the* Party (on which he [bottoms] his attempts to exculpate his friends) purporting that Cresop was 60 miles from the scene of Action when the murder was committed. Such is the information I have as yet been able to obtain to this I can add that the general opinion seems to be that Cresop and his party did destroy Logans Family and that Mr. Martins publications have not when I have heard the subject mentioned made the smallest impression in favor of his cause. Should any further information occur I will with pleasure communicate it.

From the enclosed papers it is evident how necessary the caution at the conclusion of your last Letter was and with how much avidity *your good Friends the Artistocrats* grasp even at a Phantom when they think there is the smallest Chance of doing you an injury. A day or two after the receipt of your Letter I communicated its contents to my Father and consulted with him on the propriety of suffering them to go further; He was decidedly of opinion that it was neither your wish nor intention to have your sentiments kept from your republican Friends who [. . .] receive much pleasure from them—that a correspondence which had for its basis inviolable secrecy instead of being pleasing and instructive would become irksome and disagreeable and that your caution was intended merely to prevent any extracts from being suffered to be taken or get into the public papers—in company therefore some days after with Genl. Sprigg and a few other Gentlemen all your warm admirers I mentioned the contents of the Letter which afforded them much satisfaction but one of them repeating part of the substance again in Hagers Town it got to the Ears of one of the opposite party who stripping it of its zeal and d[. . .] it in false and exagerated colors forwarded it to Frederic and Geo. Towns the two hotbeds of Aristocracy in this state. Having occasion to visit the latter place shortly after I was informed of the report in circulation to wit that you had written me the President *had informed you* "he was clearly of opinion that War ought to be immediately declared against France and that he would certainly have done it if he and his party had not found the majority of Congress opposed to the Measure." It was my purpose to have this fals[ehood] effectually contradicted and I know that a bare denial of it by myself or any other republican would be given little credit to by the other party. I therefore thought it adviseable to shew that part of your Letter which touched on the subject to one of my Connexions in confidence and without seeming to have heard the report mentioned *nearly* the substance to two other Gentlemen (all however aristocrats) in order that they might contradict the calumny wherever they heard it and this had in a great degree the desired effect; [. . .] nearly two months after I was told that the enclosed Quere had appeared in a Frederic Paper and had been extracted by others. I immediately obtained it and gave th[ru?] the same channel the denial which is also covered and have since heard nothing [of] the subject. You have I doubt not had Hamiltons Pamphlet. Dreadful indeed have been the dilemmas into which the "spirit of Jacobinism" had driven this great and *virtuous* Man when all his wellknown talents and ingenuity could not furnish him with means of escape short of so great a Sacrifice when to shield his public, he [was?] himself compell'd to abandon to destruction his private character; nay to become the public recorder of his own infamy. Genl. Forest who married my Niece and myself [in?] our correspondence frequently direct political Squibs at each other. In a late [Letter] I asked him if he had seen the adulterous confessions of his Friend and whether he did not think them *nearly* equal to the precious confession of Mr. Randolph especially as the first was acknowledged and the latter merely supposed by Mr. Randolph's Enemies. Without giving a direct answer to the Question he endeavors to get over it by abusing the hearts of the "Citizen Minister and Displaced Clerk"[1] who (he says) knowing Mr. H.'s innocence of the charge of speculation had taken a disgraceful advantage to make him unhappy at home and subject to reproach abroad. He then rails with bitterness like his *fallen Angel* against the spirit of Jacobinism and in the progress of his Paroxism seems to have placed prudence and even consistency in the back Ground—and displays sentiments which would do honor to a despot or his Courtiers. After affecting to congratulate himself and all *other* friends to real Liberty and good government upon the low ebb into which the Leaders of the "Democratic Party" had dwindled he almost in the same breath says "I believe in my soul there is such a spirit of Jacobinism in our Country that if it be not immediately check'd by the interposition of virtuous, honest, wise Characters" (such I have written him I presumed as Mr. Forest, Mr. Jay, Mr. Webster Mr. Liston Mr. Porcupine Colo. Hamilton Mrs. Reynolds, Mr. A— his man Timothy, Mr. Wilcocks and Geo. 3d.) "will prove destructive of the happiness and prosperity of the United States." I have asked him what he meant by "the spirit of Jacobinism"? Whether it was the use in certain Citizens of their undoubted right to give their opinions freely upon the measures of their servants—whether he did not approve of a free country a free discussion of public measure or whether he did not with our President deplore that "revolutionary Spirit, that opposition to every species of Government which has been fashioned into a sort of Science in Europe &ca." which was clearly advocating the doctrine of Passive Obedience and non resistance to every species of Government—by what means he wished the restless spirit of which he complained check'd? Whether by emollient or corrosive medicines, whether by perswasion or by *Seditious Bills*—if the former I ventured to prophecy that the republicans would never suffer themselves to be lull'd into Slavery—if the latter, that the same Spirit which manifested itself in opposition to one Tyrant in 74. 5. and 6. would again burst forth and crush another. I expect by next post to have these Questions solved. I am sorry for the difference which appears to have taken place among the different branches of the French Government; it is more unfortunate at the moment of negotiation for a General Peace as it will probably if attended with no worse consequences retard that measure. Our last Accounts say that one popular General (Pichegru) is exhorting the soldiery and citizens of Paris to rouze and defend the Constitution by protecting the legislative Councils, while another General (Hoche) equally popular is moving to Paris with his army and threatening destruction to the enemies of the Executive Directory. I hope however that these accounts having gone thro the London [Prints?] may if not promotion be at least much exaggerated. As your opportunities of information must be far better than mine if you have received any intelligence more from [those] which I have stated I shall thank you for it and for your sentiments as to the state of that Country and the probable issue of their domestic misunderstandings. I derive a consolation from a belief that if they should unhappily arrive to the spilling of blood—they are strong enough to 1 or 200,000 men and still be more than a Match for all their Enemies—Buonaparte seems to be immersed in the business of regulating the concerns of the new republic's. He appears as absolute as ever Cæsar was but I hope not with Cæsars disposition and Views—if he has he will it is to be hoped without his successes meet his Fate.

We have experienced the most wonderful drowth that was ever known in this Country, having only had one Rain (this was a great one) to wet the Ground two inches since harvest—and scarcely a drop since We began to Seed. Our Grain must of course look dreadfully but in addition to the above we are laboring under the ravages of that destructive insect the Hessian Fly which made their appearance last fall and damaged us a little but are this season tearing up our Crops literally Root and branch. I hope it will be long before they reach your part of the Country if they ever do. We have had a succession of high Northerly Winds which with the Sun have parched our Grasses to mere Cynders. On Tuesday and Wednesday night [. . .] pretty severe Frosts. They caught my little Crop of butter corn $\frac{3}{4}$ths. in a perfect roasting Ear State and have very much injured it as also the Pumpkin Crop which was not quite secured. Mr. Beall a *Friend* of Hagers Town keeps a Waggon plying from thence to the S. Westward, thro Staunton and promised to give me notice when it would start. He this morning sent me word that it would start tomorrow and politely offered to have any Package for you carefully lodged with Mr. A. Steward [of] Staunton as you directed. I therefore forward some of the butter Corn which however had not time to make itself—but will answer well for seed in your Roasting [Ear] Crops. I also forward the most early kind perhaps in America and if you [. . .] not already of it you will find it an acquisition. I once planted some of it on the 30th. of May in my Garden and gathered from the produce Roasting Ears on [. . .] of the month of July—but the season was remarkable—and from the [lateness] of Planting they shot before they were 3 feet high—they are however vastly earlier than any other kind I ever knew and upon the Table a great delicacy.

My White dutch Clover has never got two inches above Ground nor shown a blossom—of course I fail in getting seed this season. I sow'd it with Oats in the spring which while they were in the Ground [Stifled] it and since there [has?] not been moisture enough to bring it forward. I have really tired myself with writing as I fear I shall you with reading this Scrawl. My Father [told?] me when I wrote to present you with his aff. respects—you will therefore be so good as to accept them and those of Dr. Sir Yr Most obedt & most Humble Servt

PEREGNE. FITZHUGH

I had almost forgot and should not have soon forgiven myself if I had, [to] tell you that your favor of the Peas got safe to hand but not till July. I however planted them in my Garden and had them regularly water'd—12 Hills 5 in each from whence I have saved 3 Pints of clean full grown Peas—these will furnish me with a good Patch the ensuing season. Accept my thanks for them.   P. F.

RC (DLC); frayed margin, with tape obscuring some text; at bottom of third page Fitzhugh wrote: "(my bad Eyes cause crooked lines)"; endorsed by TJ as received 6 Nov. 1797 and so recorded in SJL.

For Fitzhugh's LONG LETTER to TJ, see 20 June 1797.

The identity of the "Citizen" who sent the ENCLOSED QUERE (printed below) to the *Rights of Man*, a Fredericktown, Maryland, newspaper published by John Winter from 1794 to 1800, has not been established (Brigham, *American Newspapers*, I, 266). It is also unclear how extensively the "Quere" was EXTRACTED by other local newspapers

but a paraphrased version of it appeared in Noah Webster's *Minerva* on 2 Aug. 1797. While Fitzhugh was concerned with the gossip over this letter in Maryland, he did not realize that Uriah Forrest had sent an extract of it to President John Adams (see TJ to Fitzhugh, 4 June 1797).

PRECIOUS CONFESSION: for the controversy surrounding Edmund Randolph's resignation as secretary of state, see TJ to Monroe, 6 Sep. 1795, and TJ to Madison, 26 Nov. 1795.

CITIZEN MINISTER AND DISPLACED CLERK: James Monroe and John Beckley.

[1] Quotation mark supplied.

ENCLOSURES

I

A Citizen to the *Rights of Man*

A Quere.

Frederick, (Anniversary of Independence) '97.
Whether Mr. Jefferson did say, since he has taken his present position that "it was the intention of mr. Adams (the president!) and his party, on the call of congress, to declare war against France if there had been a respectable majority"—or, whether he had *indubitable* authority for it, if he did say so, is not satisfactorily ascertained. Report says, two gentlemen of respectability in George-Town, lately averred that major F— told them he had received a letter from Mr. Jefferson since he went to Philadelphia, containing the above sentiments.

Report also says, however, that a third gentleman, equally respectable, declared, when he heard it mentioned in company, that the letter was shewn him by mr. F—, *in confidence*, and that the above sentence was not in it; *but that it was an improper letter*.

As the solution of this question may be gratifying to the citizens at large, at the present interesting crisis, the investigation is humbly submitted to Peter Porcupine, *Mr. Bache*, and other critics.

It is supposed that the names of the within-mentioned gentlemen might readily be had if necessary.   CITIZEN

Printed in the *Federal Gazette & Baltimore Daily Advertiser*, 29 July 1797; at head of text: "From the Rights of Man"; along with a letter to "Messrs. Yundy & Brown," 26 July 1797, noting: "The contents of the inclosed Quere, taken from a Frederick paper, being of a very serious nature, you will, if you please, insert it in your widely-circulating Gazette, and you will oblige A Subscriber."

II
Peregrine Fitzhugh to
the *Rights of Man*

Septr. 15th. 1797

Mr. F— takes the Liberty of informing the Public that the report contained in a Quere published in this Paper of the 4th. of July last of Mr. Jeffersons having written him "that it was the intention of Mr. Adams and his party at the call of Congress to have declared war against France if there had been a greater majority" is without foundation and that the Gentlemen who are said to have averr'd that Mr. F. told them so if they did aver it must have grossly misapprehended him as their respectability precludes them from the suspicion of a designed misrepresentation. There is not a word in the Letter about Mr. Adams's Party or intentions nor does it express a sentiment which can be justly construed into disrespect for the President of the United States. Mr. F—'s never having seen the above quere till very lately will account for its not having been earlier noticed. It is hoped the Printers who have published the said Quere will in justice to Mr. Jefferson and Mr. F— be so obliging as to give this a place in their papers also.

MS (DLC); entirely in Fitzhugh's hand; at head of text: "For the Rights of Man."

From John Barnes

SIR   Philada. 19th Octr 1797.

Your two favours of the 8th: are at hand, and Mr. Callendar wrote to—as you desired. Your power of Attorney—though One Witness Only—was—by sending it, to Grays ferry, confirmed by the Comptrollar—and Colo. Monroes draft, shall meet my pointed Attention. From the late frosts, our Neighbours are daily returning to Town—too early I fear, from the continued indisposition of sundry persons especially to the Southward of the New Market, where New Cases still make their Appearance daily—and some few instances on persons returned. I am Sir Your most Obedt servt: JOHN BARNES

RC (ViU: Edgehill-Randolph Papers); at foot of text: "Thomas Jefferson Esqr: Monticello"; endorsed by TJ as received 27 Oct. 1797 and so recorded in SJL.

From James Madison

DEAR SIR   Octr. 20. 1797

I received the inclosed pamphlet from Col. Monroe with a request that it might be returned to you. The publication under all its characters is a curious specimen of the ingenious folly of its author. Next to the error of publishing at all, is that of forgetting that simplicity and candor are the only dress which prudence would put on innocence. Here we see every rhetorical artifice employed to excite the spirit of party to prop up his sinking reputation, and whilst the most exaggerated complaints are uttered against the unfair and virulent persecutions of himself, he deals out in every page the most malignant insinuations, against others. The one against you is a masterpiece of folly, because its impotence is in exact proportion to its venom. Along with the pamphlet is inclosed a letter which you will be good eno' to have delivered by an early opportunity. Yrs. Affecly   Js MADISON JR

RC (DLC: Madison Papers); endorsed by TJ as received 21 Oct. 1797 and so recorded in SJL. For enclosures, see note below.

The INCLOSED PAMPHLET was Alexander Hamilton's *Observations*, which Monroe had sent to Madison on 15 Oct. 1797, with the request that it be returned "by the post to Mr. Jeffn" (Madison, *Papers*, XVII, 50-51). For the INSINUATIONS against TJ, see TJ to Andrew G. Fraunces, 27 and 28 June 1797. The LETTER enclosed was perhaps that from Madison to Monroe of 19 Oct. 1797, printed in Madison, *Papers*, XVII, 53-4.

From James Monroe

DEAR SIR   Sunday—[i.e. 22] Octr. 1797.

I shall send Mr. Bache tomorrow about two thirds of my narrative and the residue by the next post. I have nothing from him by the last which gives cause to apprehend either that his people or himself are sick of the yellow fever. It becomes necessary that I give the publication a title, and therefore I wish your opinion upon that point. I subjoin one which is subject to your correction. You mentioned some time since the propriety of my discussing the question whether a minister was that of his country or the administration. It is a plain one, but yet I will thank you to put on paper what occurs to you on it, any time within a day or two and send it me.

There are letters of the Secry. of State which are omitted, such for example as that which I send, being rather a document accompanying one, than a letter. You will perceive it is lengthy and not applicable to the object of my publication. As also another respecting Mr. Fenwick, containing a charge against him of which some notice is taken in one of mine by way of reply. It was omitted as a personal thing from motives of delicacy to him. Would you publish both or either of these in the appendix? Skipwith's report to me is omitted also; would you instruct Bache to publish it in the appendix. The one I refer to is that published by Pickering with Mr. Adams's message to the last session of Congress. Yours respectfully   JAS. MONROE

"A view of the conduct of the administration in the managment of our foreign affairs for the years 1794. 5. and 6. by an appeal to the official instruction and correspondence of James Monroe late Minister p: of the U. States to the French republick, to which is prefix'd an introductory narrative by the said James M."

or

"A view of the conduct of the Executive of the U. States in the managment of the affairs of those States with foreign powers for the years 1794. &ca" as above.

RC (DLC); endorsed by TJ as a letter of October 1797 received 22 Oct. 1797 and so recorded in SJL; TJ at some point added, almost certainly in error, "probably 15." to his endorsement of the letter's date. Enclosure not found.

MY NARRATIVE: *A View of the Conduct of the Executive, in the Foreign Affairs of the United States, Connected with the Mission to the French Republic, During the Years 1794, 5, and 6. By James Monroe, Late Minister Plenipotentiary to the said Republic: Illustrated by his Instructions and Correspondence and other Authentic Documents* (Philadelphia, 1797), which consisted of Monroe's "View" of 64 pages followed by over 400 pages of documents. The work, which

Benjamin Franklin Bache published in mid-December 1797 and sold for the substantial price of $1.50, failed to persuade Monroe's opponents and provided his political allies with little new information (Tagg, *Bache*, 327-8; Ammon, *Monroe*, 167-9). See Evans, No. 32491; and Sowerby, No. 3524.

Edmund Randolph had written to Monroe, evidently on 30 July 1795, concerning an accusation that Joseph FENWICK had used his seal as United States consul at Bordeaux to cover French goods. Randolph's letter was printed in an appendix to Monroe's work under the erroneous date of 30 July 1797 (Monroe, *View*, 406-7; Monroe, *Writings*, II, 424-5). Fulwar SKIPWITH'S RE-PORT to Monroe in October 1794 concerned losses to American shipping at the hands of the French and was given to Congress by Timothy PICKERING in February 1797, not as one of the documents transmitted in conjunction with the president's MESSAGE in May (*Annals*, VI, 2770, 2774-7; TJ to Madison, 18 May 1797).

From James Madison

DEAR SIR   Orange Octr. 25. 97.

I am placed under circumstances which make it proper I should inform you that Mr. Knapp of Philada. is a candidate for the office of Treasr. to the Mint, vacated by the death of Dr. Way, and is particularly anxious that you should be possessed of that fact, and of the testimony I may be able to give as to his qualifications and character. During several of the last winters I spent in Phida. Mr. K. was a near neighbour, and a familiar intercourse prevailed between our families. I really believe him to be a worthy man, and the line of life he has been in supports the character he bears, of being skilful in the sort of business he aspires to. If you should be invited by any opportunity to say as much to the quarter from which appointments issue, it will be highly acceptable to Mr. K. and ought to be so to me. I have however intimated to him, that I did not expect that your opinion in any way would be asked, and that it would not be proper for you to give it unasked. It is astonishing that it does not occur in these cases that the patronage of those whose politics are adverse to the politics of the Administration is more likely to be of injury than service to the suiters for office.

We just have the pleasure of learning that an event has taken place in your family which calls for our joint and warmest congratulations, which we beg you to make acceptable to all to whom [they] are due. Yrs. truly   Js. M. JR

RC (DLC: Madison Papers); torn at seal; addressed: "Mr. Jefferson Monticello, Col. Monroe "; endorsed by TJ as received 27 Oct. 1797 and so recorded in SJL. Enclosed in Monroe to TJ, 27 Oct. 1797.

To James Monroe

TH:J. TO COLO. MONROE   [Monticello] Oct. 25. [97.]

I like your second title better than the first because it [is shorter.] I should like the following better than either. 'The Foreign affairs of the US. during the years 1794. 5. 6. laid before his fellow citizens by J.M. their late M.P. to the republic of France.' The reason of my preference is that it implies no inculpation of the Executive. Such an implication will determine prejudiced men against buying or reading the book. The following title would be better, but for one reason. 'An account of the foreign affairs of the US. during the years 1794. 5. 6. rendered to his fellow citizens by J.M. their late M.P. to the republic of France.' But that it would raise the old hue and cry against the attempt to separate the people from their government. For this reason it might be questionable whether the words 'laid before his fellow citizens' in the first title I propose, had not better be omitted. In that case the words 'a view of' should be premised, so as to make it 'a view of the Foreign affairs of the US. during &ca—by J.M.'[1] &c. Decide among them.

I should not be for publishing the long letters from the Secy. of state to Fauchet, and Hammond, because they were no part of your business and because they were already printed by the Executive. Perhaps it would be well to refer in a note to E.R.'s letter to you that it inclosed such and such letters which may be seen in such a publication, quoting the pages.— I rather think that to you relative to Fenwick ought to be published 1. because it is to you. 2. because it will shew how [vigorous] they were when the English interests were affected. 3. because it was a malversation in Fenwick if true, and ought to be published for the honor of the US. and warning to other Consuls.—Skipwith's report might be referred to as already printed.—As to the question Whether a Minister is that of his country or of G.W. or J.A. I do not think it will need a very formal discussion. A bare statement of it with a few such strong observations as will occur, currente calamo, will suffice. Still it is necessary to be stated, to bring indolent readers to reflection. Appearances might otherwise lead them astray. Adieu.

PrC (DLC); faded, with illegible text supplied in brackets from Ford, VII, 177-9.

CURRENTE CALAMO: "writing hastily."

[1] Quotation mark supplied.

From James Monroe

Friday—[27 Oct. 1797]

Jas. Monroe's best respects to Mr. Jefferson. He has lately been in Orange at Mr. Madisons, from whom he encloses him a letter. At Mr. Ms. he met Mr. Dawson lately from Richmond and who bade him inform Mr. Jefferson that if he takes the stage for Phila. from Fredbg. it will be necessary for him to be in the latter place on tuesday next to arrive in time for the commenc'ment of Congress, as it goes only three times a week: or indeed perhaps only twice—he adds the circumstance to view that it may be attended to more correctly than J.M. can inform. Mr. Dawson says that Mr. H. is given up wher'ever he has been, as an immoral man; and that the ease with which he acknowledges himself an adulterer inspires doubts that he was guilty of the other charge also. J.M. would ride up but that he has been much indisposed since his return. He will be glad to know when Mr. Jefferson sits out.　　　He was informed by Mr. Madison that a certain paper which himself and W. Nicholas left with him, was for the purpose of its being modified so as by omitting the prayer for impeachment, to avoid the objection which that trait in it exposed it to. J.M. supposed it was only to disguise the author, which could not be done without writing another, and which ought not to be done. Upon this principle J.M. after examining it to find such parts as might be altered upon the principle on which he supposed it was left with him, returned it unaltered to W.N. But as now advised he readily undertakes the modification, and if in possession of Mr. Jefferson will thank him for it—of which he will be pleased inform him as he shall write W.N. for it this evening in case it is not.

Will Mr. Jefferson with Mr. Randolph and Mr. Eppes with their Ladies come someday before his departure and dine with J.M. and family; and will sunday suit their convenience? Or what day will be more suitable?

RC (DLC); undated; endorsed by TJ as a letter of October 1797 received 27 Oct. 1797, and so recorded in SJL; TJ interlined "probably 20" in his endorsement, but see below. Enclosure: Madison to TJ, 25 Oct. 1797.

Although TJ surmised that Monroe wrote this letter on 20 Oct., on that day Monroe had not yet spoken with John DAWSON, whom he did not see until court day in Orange on the 23d (Madison, *Papers*, XVII, 50-1, 53-4). MR. H.: Alexander Hamilton. A CERTAIN PAPER: Petition to Virginia House of Delegates, printed at 3 Aug. 1797.

From Benjamin Galloway

[Oct. 1797]

Benjamin Galloway of Washington County and State of Maryland presentest his republican respects to Citizen Jefferson and begs leave to offer his perfect approbation of his Conduct and principles—if opportunity should suffer him, he will be happy to shake Mr. Jefferson by the Hand—he is an American, but at the same time, he would wish to be considered as a *Sans, Culotte*—　　　　　　　　　　B G

RC (MHi); undated; addressed: "Thomas Jefferson Esquire Monticello Al-bemarle County Virginia To the Care of Mr. Archd. Stewart Staunton"; endorsed by TJ as a letter of October 1797 received 6 Nov. 1797 and recorded in SJL under that date.

Around 1796, Benjamin Galloway (1752-1831), a native of Anne Arundel County, Maryland, had moved to Elizabeth Town (present Hagerstown) in Washington County. An attorney, planter, and landholder, he had previously served as a county justice, as a member of the Maryland assembly, and in 1778 as attorney general of the state. Considered an ardent Jeffersonian Republican, as late as 1823 he ran unsuccessfully for a seat in the Maryland House of Delegates (Edward C. Papenfuse and others, *A Biographical Dictionary of the Maryland Legislature, 1635-1789*, 2 vols. [Baltimore, 1979-85], I, 338-9; Carl N. Everstine, *The General Assembly of Maryland 1776-1850* [Charlottesville, Va., 1982], 357n).

Memorial of Charleston Merchants to the Senate

Charleston, 2 Nov. 1797. They represent that by the laws of South Carolina and by practice of long standing, the wharves onto which imported goods are unladen in the city of Charleston are privately owned and the proprietors of the wharves have collected fees for the weighing of merchandise. The present collector of the port refuses to recognize the wharfholders' agents as weighers. He insists, according to his construction of the 4 Aug. 1790 act for regulating the collection of duties, that customs officers weigh all landed goods. The proprietors of the wharves refuse to allow custom house officials to weigh merchandise on their wharves, and the collector requires that importers convey goods to locations away from the wharves for weighing. The memorialists represent that they are "burthened with the performance of duties and loaded with Expences not contemplated by any Law of the United States," suffer injury to their merchandise by exposure to the weather, and believe the present arrangement provides opportunities for fraud. Many of them became proprietors of stores and warehouses near the wharves in order to superintend the unloading, weighing, and storage of their goods and to avoid the expense and risk of transporting goods. They pray that the previous practice of weighing be sanctioned by law, or hope that they may obtain some other legislative relief.

MS (DNA: RG 46, Senate Records, 5th Cong., 2d sess.); 3 p.; signed by 104 individuals and firms; addressed: "To The Honorable Thomas Jefferson Esquire Vice President, and the Honorable the Members of the Senate of the United States"; endorsed by a clerk as received on 28 Dec. 1797.

The collector of customs at Charleston was James Simons, a merchant associated with a Federalist group that included Senator Jacob Read. Earlier in the year Simons had succeeded Isaac Holmes, whom the president had removed from the collectorship for failing to remit hundreds of thousands of dollars in customs duties. On 28 Dec. 1797 the Senate ordered the above memorial to lie on the table (Prince, *Federalists*, 127-30; JS, II, 417).

To William Bradford

Sɪʀ   Monticello Nov. 6. 1797.

To be present at the meeting of Congress would have required me to
set out on this day. But circumstances of necessity oblige me to ask of
the Senate the indulgence of some time, probably of about a fortnight.
Whether it be more or less I shall repair to my station the first moment
it is possible for me to do so. A knolege that in the mean time it is so
worthily filled, leaves me nothing to regret but the controul of those
circumstances which, in witholding me from my duties, impose them
on another. With these my apologies, permit me through you to present
the homage of my respect to the Senate, and be pleased to accept yourself assurance of the great and sincere esteem and respect with which I
have the honor to be Sir Your most obedt & most hble servt   Tʜ:J.

FC (DLC); at foot of text: "Govr. Bradford Presidt. p.t. of the Sen. of the US."; endorsed by TJ.

William Bradford (1729-1808) was born
in Massachusetts where he prepared for a
career in medicine. After moving to Bristol,
Rhode Island, he studied law and was admitted to the bar in 1767. Bradford served
as deputy governor of Rhode Island from
1775 to 1778 and regularly sat in the House
of Deputies of the Rhode Island General Assembly, where he was elected speaker in
1780 and frequently thereafter. A Federalist, Bradford represented that state in the
United States Senate from 1793 until he re-

signed in October 1797 (*Biog. Dir. Cong.*;
John Russell Bartlett, ed., *Records of the
Colony of Rhode Island and Providence
Plantations, in New England*, 10 vols.
[Providence, 1856-65; repr. New York,
1968], vi, 282, vii, 407, viii, 387, ix, 53,
383, 541, 690, x, 21, 93, 192, 428; js, ii, 10,
406). For his election as president pro tem-
pore of the Senate, see note to TJ to John
Strode, 15 June 1797.

While the second session of the Fifth congress commenced on 13 Nov., a quorum
did not attend until nine days later when the
senate elected Jacob Read to preside until
TJ arrived (js, ii, 405-6).

From Thomas Mann Randolph

Tʜ: M. Rᴀɴᴅᴏʟᴘʜ ᴛᴏ Tʜ: Jᴇꜰꜰᴇʀꜱᴏɴ   Dunginess Nov. 6: 97

I am greatly disappointed in being obliged to give up the attempt to
reach Monticello before you set out. On Saturday Morning I was in
Richmond ready to perform part of the journey that day but the rain
prevented me: on Sunday the sun shone and I sat out but was obliged to
put in at Cranches tavern two miles above Tuckahoe by a pretty smart
shower from which the oil cloth could not protect me as I sat in the chair
the wind blowing hard: I was detained there all day. This morning I
began my journey again and crossed the River to get firmer roads: I
reached this at half past eleven with the intention of advancing as far as
possible today and pushing the chair on in the night so as to insure its

reaching Mont'o. by your breakfast hour tomorrow: I feel myself too much indisposed to proceed having in a considerable degree a recurrence of my old nervous symptoms from what cause I cannot say: I have resolved to rest here a day or two and then proceed slowly on horseback. James will reach Mont'o. I hope early enough for you get to Mr. Madisons your first stage in general.

Geo: Jefferson has commenced business and is ready to transact your affairs in Richmond; with as much Zeal I will engage as ever you experienced and with sufficient judgement tho' his skill is yet small. The negroe clothing cannot be had cheaper on any credit in Richmond than 110—100 for cash: plains laid in at 18 to $19\frac{1}{2}$ D. sterling Cottons 22 to 27 the price of 20 ys. good German Osnaburgs may be had at 23 D. the Ell on a credit at Gamble & Temples: the British is abundant @$\frac{1}{2}$: every where.

I could not procure the copies you wanted of the acts of assembly: there were not enough printed even for the Counties. Mr: Wythe thinks the Assembly may yet see the value of an Edition of the laws from your collection of M.S. and sieze the opportunity you give them: he has added himself an M.S. copy of the acts of an extraordinary session of '92. He is convinced Brend will never bind them and has taken them home and skrewed down the box to avoid the importunities of the Delegates who eagerly use them tho' they cannot yet resolve on perpetuating them. I find that Currie the Book binder has taken to drink and is not fit I fear to be trusted. There is no other in Richmond.

If I can in any way whatever be of use to you in your albemarle or any other affairs I claim the service tho' I cannot help feeling that my frequent neglects and the weakness of my character should make me forfeit that honor.

Tell my Dear Martha that I shall hasten as much as I can without disabling myself from enjoying my family when I *do* meet it: the remembrance of the horrors of 94 and 95. makes me extremely cautious: I should shun them by embracing death if it could be done no other way. With most sincere affection   TH: M. RANDOLPH

RC (MHi); addressed: "Thomas Jefferson Monticello"; endorsed by TJ as received 8 Nov. 1797 and so recorded in SJL.

Memorial of Charleston Wharfholders
to the Senate

Charleston, 10 Nov. 1797. The owners and lessees of wharves in the city of Charleston represent that a compact among planters, merchants, and wharfholders to regulate the docking of vessels and the landing, weighing, and storage of goods in the city was codified by an act passed by the assembly of South Carolina on 12 Apr. 1768. That law specified rates for weighing merchandise, established penalties for neglect or abuse of the statute's provisions, and required owners of wharves to provide scale houses and weighmasters, who were bound by oath. Subsequent legislation continued these practices, and after the incorporation of the city of Charleston the municipal government took on the regulation of the harbor and wharves. A number of the memorialists purchased wharves "for very large prices, the essential right to weigh and to receive the compensation which was deemed very valuable, forming an important consideration in the price demanded by the Seller and paid by the purchaser." The memorialists maintain that the right to weigh goods landed on their wharves "is exclusively vested in them." That privilege, "being essential to this Kind of property, forms a part of their freehold and cannot be invaded or infringed without a violation of Rights founded in an Unbroken Custom" that predates the passage of any federal law. When the convention of South Carolina ratified the United States Constitution, "It could not be presumed, that they intended to surrender the private rights of individuals, founded on long usage and upon State Laws of many years existence." The wharfholders of Charleston have refused to allow the United States collector of customs to erect scales on the wharves, their private property, whereupon the collector has established locations in less accessible parts of the city for his officers to weigh imported merchandise. In addition, the memorialists claim that under the previous system the wharfholders' own best interests compelled them to appoint reputable weighers, whereas the collector's practice adds to the government's expense and creates opportunities for fraud. In conclusion the memorialists pray that the Senate will revise the law to "make it the duty of the Collector to conform to the Rights of your Memorialists."

MS (DNA: RG 46, Senate Records, 5th Cong., 2d sess.); 3 p.; at head of text: "To the Honorable Thomas Jefferson president, and the Members of the Senate of the United States"; signed by Christopher Gadsden and twenty other individuals and firms; endorsed by a clerk as received 12 Dec. 1797.

The Senate tabled this memorial on 12 Dec. (JS, II, 414).

From Paroy

A Belmont Prés Royan En Saintonge
MONSIEUR LE VICE PRESIDENT   [before 10 Nov. 1797]
Daignéz Excuser La Liberté que je Prends De me rappeller a votre Souvenir, et De vous Prier De me rendre Le Service ainsi qu'a toute ma famille De faire Parvenir Le Paquet çy-joint a mon frere. Ce Paquet

contient Des Papiers importants Comme Procuration, Certificat De
Residence, Lettre Du Ministre &c qui lui Sont absolument necessaires
pour rentrer En Possession De nos Biens qui Sont Séquestrés Entre Les
Mains De L'administration; J'ai Expedié Depuis un an plus De 25 Paquets a peu prés Pareils par la voie Des Batiments americains, quoi qu'ils
ayent eté Bien recommandés aux Capitaines, et que Plusieurs ayent eté
adressés a Des negotiants De Philadelphie ou D'autres Places de Commerce avec Priere De Les faire Parvenir Le plus Promptement et Le
plus Surement Possible a mon Malheureux frere au Cap; aucun De ces
Paquets ne lui est Parvenû, et il est toujours Dans Les Plus grandes
inquietudes Sur Le Sort De tout Ce qui lui Est cher En france, et faute
Des titres necessaires pour recouvrer nos Biens, il est Plongé Dans la
plus affreuse Détresse aprés avoir Echappé Comme par Miracle a tous
Les Dangers aux qu'els il a Eté Exposé, et Dont tant D'infortunés Co-
lons ont eté Les Déplorables victimes. J'etois Passé avec Lui et un autre
De mes freres a St. Domingue au Commencement de 1792. Aprés La
Catastrophe De La revolte Des negres qui a Detruit La Partie Du nord
et occasionnée La ruine de toute notre fortune Composée De Deux Su-
creries et de trois Caffeteries. Ma Santé m'avoit forcé De Les quitter et
De revenir En france a La fin De La même année, j'aurois Bien Desiré
qu'ils Eussent pris Le même Parti, je n'aurois pas Eu Le Malheur De
Perdre L'ainé Des Deux qui a eté massacré 18 mois aprés, nous ne
L'avons appris que L'année Derniere par Le Cadet qui aprés plus De
Deux ans De Silence a Enfin pû nous faire Savoir De Ses nouvelles.

Si je ne connoissois pas La Bonté et La Sensibilité De votre ame,
Monsieur, je n'aurois pas osé vous Prier De vous charger Du Soin De
faire Parvenir Ce Paquet a mon Malheureux frere, quoi qu'il Soit Bien
interessant pour lui et pour nous qu'il Le reçoive Le plus Promptement
Possible, il L'est Encore plus qu'il Le reçoive Surement, ainsi je vous
Prie De vouloir Bien Le recommander au Capitaine Dont Le Batiment
Sera Destiné pour Le Cap françois, m'en rapportant Entierement a
votre Prudence pour choisir La Circonstance La plus favorable, et La
voie La plus Sure, au reste Ce Paquet ne contient que Des Papiers qui
ont raport a nos interets Particuliers, et nullement a ce qui regarde La
Politique.

Depuis La Derniere fois que j'ai Eu L'honneur De vous voir a Paris
et Dans ma famille, Monsieur, et que vous avéz quitté notre continent,
il S'est Passé De grands Evenements qui Pourront Servir De Leçon a
La Posterité, Puisse votre heureuse et Sage Nation continuer a Se
Préserver Des mêmes orages! Je fais Les mêmes voeux pour que
L'union et L'harmonie qui ont toujours regnés Entre nos Deux nations
ne Soient jamais troublés. Je ne Perdrai jamais Le Souvenir Du Sejour
que j'ai fait pendant La guerre Derniere En Virginie et a Boston, et

Particulierement De toutes Les Bontés que j'ai recûs chéz vous a Williamsbourg. J'ai appris avec La plus vive Satisfaction La justice que vous avéz recûe De vos Concitoyens En vous Elevant a la Place Eminente que vous occupéz, et Dont je vous fais mes Sinceres Compliments. Je ne Désespere pas D'avoir Encore Le Bonheur De vous voir, mes interets me mettant Dans Le Cas De faire par la Suite Des voyages a St. Domingue, je Pourrai Sans me Détourner Beaucoup passer par La nouvelle Angleterre, et il me Sera Bien Doux De vous renouveller De vive voix Les assurances Des Sentiments D'attachement et De veneration, ainsi que Du Respect avec le qu'el je Suis Monsieur Le vice President Votre trés humble et trés Obeissant Serviteur.

PAROY
Ancien Captne De Vaisseaux

RC (MHi); undated; endorsed by TJ as received on 10 Nov. 1797 and so recorded in SJL. Enclosures not found.

The writer, likely a member of a Paroy family that owned extensive properties in ST. DOMINGUE, had been captain of the frigate Cérès in De Grasse's fleet in 1781-82 (Jean-Jacques Antier, L'Amiral de Grasse: Héros de l'Indépendance américaine [Paris, 1965], 402; Étienne Charavay, ed., Mémoires du Comte de Paroy [Paris, 1895], iv, x-xi).

From Edmund Randolph

Novr. 15. 1797.

E. Randolph informs his friend Mr. Jefferson, that he shall by the mail of tuesday next, put into his hands such documents, as have been promised by him respecting Mr. Short's affair.

RC (DLC: Short Papers); endorsed by TJ as received 13 Dec. 1797 and so recorded in SJL.

Letters from Randolph to TJ of 12 July and 6 Aug. 1797, recorded in SJL as received 14 July and 7 Aug. 1797, respectively, have not been found. SJL also records a letter from TJ to Randolph, 16 Oct. 1797, which is missing.

From John Wayles Eppes

DEAR SIR   Mrs. Paines Friday morning. [17 Nov. 1797]

The badness of the roads prevented our reaching Millers last Evening. We arrived here at an early hour after being overset once without receiving the smallest injury. The Carriage went down so gradually that the glass windows which were up received no injury.

Marias foot improves with traveling. She walked last evening conveniently without her stick. She is well this morning in good spirits and recovered from the fatigue of her journey. She sends her love to all at Monticello and begs you will request her sister to forward her shawl and veil by the first opportunity. Be kind enough to present my love &c. to Mr. and Mrs. R and to accept for yourself my best wishes. I am yours affectionately   JNO W EPPES

RC (ViU); partially dated; at foot of text: "Th: Jefferson"; includes calculations by TJ at bottom of page; endorsed by TJ as received 18 Nov. 1797 and so recorded in SJL.

From John Taylor

JNO. TAYLOR TO
THE VICE PRESIDENT   Virginia—Carolina—Novr. 19. 1797

Herewith I have forwarded to you the drill you requested, packed into a crate basket, in a secure manner. This machine is an improvement upon that heretofore sent you, in having cups cut into iron rollers, instead of being fixed to bands. The effect, is perfect regularity in the sheding of the grain, because no change will be produced by the quantity in the box—because these cups must fill with exactness, because no grain received by them will fall into the box—and because a spring is so contrived, as to strike every cup before it deposits its contents. Further, in lieu of a rake, two moveable lateral pieces, having iron ferrels, by sliding them into the proper position, will cover the grain with great neatness. The price is ten dollars.

In the same basket is the threshing machine, described in my last letter; and in this I have taken the liberty of inclosing the papers necessary to support an application for a patent, because I know not a warmer patron of the arts, beneficial to mankind; and because you have been so good as not to forbid me to do so. If however my request is improper, Colo. New of the house of representatives (whose constituent the inventor is) will do all he can to cure my mistake. This model has iron beaters, in place of wooden, because as their surface may be diminished, the resistance of the air will be lessened, and of course the same power will bestow greater velocity and more execution upon the machine; an effect very important, when it is worked by hand.

It is necessary to advance thirty dollars previous to an application. Of this, the price of the drill may constitute a part—and the residue I will place in your hands in a few days, by a bill on philadelphia. Be happy

RC (DLC); endorsed by TJ as received 13 Dec. 1797 and so recorded in SJL.

On 21 Dec. 1797, TJ deposited the patent fee of THIRTY DOLLARS for Thomas C. Martin at the Treasury Department. Martin received the patent for his water-powered threshing machine on 3 June 1798 (MB, II, 976).

From Edmund Randolph

DEAR SIR   Richmond November 21. 1797

While I supposed, that every thing was completed by Mr. Morris relative to Mr. Short's money, for which he (Mr. M.) gave me his note for stock in 1794, I have been deceived. Immediately I obtained from Mr. Lyons and Mr: Pendleton, who hold six per cent stock the inclosed assumpsit for £2,000 within thirty pounds; which you will find satisfactory; as it is certain. I am the absolute owner of the inclosed decree, not as administrator only, but in my own right. 'Till this moment I thought I had the decree of the 19th. of March 1795; but I must send it by the next mail. The papers sent shew, that judgment was obtained in 1767 by one Johnston against Royle on a bill of Speaker Robinson's, on which Royle was an indorser for £788.5.7. Sterling with interest 'till paid. Royle paid it, and Robinson's administrators endeavoured to postpone it to debts of the first dignity. A bill was filed against them to give it its true dignity, and, as a second resource, the scire facias was prepared, as is now [seen] by the inclosed; but it was never used; as Mr. Wythe decided and the administrators acquiesced in the decision; namely for the above Sum at 25 per cent and twenty years interest thus: £ 788. 5. 7. twenty[1]

years interest on which	788. 5. 7
	£1576.11. 2 Sterling
25 per cent	394. 2. 9
	£1970.13.11

I have arranged the balance in an equally sure way, and equally agreeable to Mr. Short; being for stock. You shall hear from me again the beginning of next week. I am dear sir yr. obliged friend

EDM: RANDOLPH

RC (DLC: Short Papers); with emendations, the most important of which is noted below; endorsed by TJ as received 13 Dec. 1797 and so recorded in SJL. Enclosures not found.

[1] Word overwritten by Randolph, probably in place of "sterling."

Bond to Van Staphorst & Hubbard

Know all men by these presents that I Thomas Jefferson of Monticello Albemarle county Virginia am held and firmly bound [unto] Nicholas and Jacob Van Staphorst and Nicholas Hubbard bankers and partners of the city of Amsterdam in the republic of the United Netherlands in the sum of five thousand six hundred florins currency of the said republic, to the paiment whereof I hereby bind myself my heirs executors and administrators. In witness whereof I have hereto set my hand and seal this twenty fifth day of November one thousand seven hundred and ninety seven.

The Condition of the above obligation is such that if the above bound Thomas his heirs executors or administrators shall pay or cause to be paid, on or before the 25th. day of December one thousand eight hundred and two, to the said Nicholas and Jacob Vanstaphorst and Nicholas Hubbard their executors administrators or assigns the sum of two thousand eight hundred florins with interest thereon at the rate of six per centum per annum from the 25th. day of December in this present year, then this obligation to be void: otherwise to remain in full force.

PrC (DLC); entirely in TJ's hand; faded.

TJ calculated THE SUM OF TWO THOUSAND EIGHT HUNDRED FLORINS he owed the Van Staphorst & Hubbard firm as of 25 Dec. 1797 in a "Statement of my 3d. bond to Messrs. V. Staph. & Hub.," which listed his remittances to the firm, drafts upon them, and accruals of interest owed beginning on 16 May 1792, and which also noted that the bond was payable 25 Dec. 1802 with interest to begin on 25 Dec 1797 (MS in DLC: TJ Papers, 102: 17506; entirely in TJ's hand; undated). He copied that statement, with differently worded entries, at the foot of a letter he wrote to the firm on 30 Apr. 1798, the date on which he actually sent them the bond. He did not record the bond in his financial memoranda (see MB, II, 997).

To Henry Tazewell

DEAR SIR   Monticello Nov. 28. 97.

In a letter addressed to the President p.t. of the Senate at the commencement of the session, I expressed the regret occasioned me by a detention from the place of my duty, and hoped sooner to have been on my way to it. The first cause which kept me[1] was an accident to one of my daughters, who fell out of a door. As soon as she was well enough to be removed, I was taken with a cold myself and a consequent indisposition, caught during a spell of eight days continual snows and rains. Our rivers too were raised by these; but they are now subsiding so that within a day or two they may be forded without danger. There are four of these within my two first days journies which have neither bridges nor boats. In the mean time I am so far reestablished that I shall set out within two days from this time. I presume according to the usual course of things that the addresses, appointing committees, settling the subjects of bills &ca will have filled up the session so far, and that I shall still be in place by the time the real business comes on.—Should you have an opportunity I will thank you to desire Mr. Francis to have my rooms *immediately* in readiness, as I shall be there, without an accident, nearly as soon as this letter. I am with sincere esteem Dear Sir Your friend & servt   TH: JEFFERSON

RC (NjMoHP: Lloyd W. Smith Collection); with emendation as noted below; addressed: "Henry Tazewell of the Senate of the US. at Philadelphia"; franked. PrC (DLC).

LETTER ADDRESSED TO THE PRESIDENT P.T. OF THE SENATE: TJ to William Bradford, 6 Nov. 1797.

[1] Preceding two words written over what appears to be "detained me."

From James Monroe

DEAR SIR   [Nov. 1797]

I have a letter from Mr. Bache with the printed documents complete all but a page or two, and 12. pages of "the view &c." I enclose a note to correct by way of erratum an important omission of almost a line in the latter. He tells me the late explosion at Paris has produced a wonderful effect on our rascals at home, who he thinks were in harmony with those there. I have no doubt that the stronger the attack upon them is, hinting a belief of bribery (I mean by the members in debate) the better: for yet the republican cause has never had a chance. Be assured the people are ready to back those who go most forward. I repeat my best wishes for your happiness. Remember me to Mr. M. and Lady. Mr. Barnes has paid the money. If I can place funds I shall begin soon to trouble you about windows [&ca] as my cabbin castle goes on.

RC (DLC); undated and unsigned; damaged; addressed: "Mr. Jefferson"; endorsement by TJ, obscured by tape: "Nov. [qu]."

THE PRINTED DOCUMENTS COMPLETE: see Monroe to TJ, [22] Oct. 1797. THE LATE EXPLOSION AT PARIS: the events of 18 Fructidor. Monroe's CABBIN CASTLE was

the house he built on his plantation, later known as the Highlands, adjacent to Monticello. Until the relatively modest dwelling, which was meant to be a precursor to a larger house, was ready for occupancy in December 1799, Monroe and his family lived in Charlottesville (Ammon, *Monroe*, 163-4).

To Mary Jefferson Eppes

MY DEAR MARIA   Monticello Dec. 2. 97.

You will be surprised at receiving a letter from me dated here at this time. But a series of bad weather having suspended our works many days, has caused my detention. I have for some time had my trunk packed and issued my last orders, and been only waiting for it to cease raining. But it still rains. I have a bad prospect of rivers and roads before me. Your sister removed to Belmont about three days ago. The weather ever since has kept us entirely asunder. If tomorrow permits my departure I shall be in Philadelphia in [about] a week from this time. You shall hear from me there, should it be only to provoke answers to my letters assuring me of your health, of Mr. Eppes's and the good family of Eppington. I received his letter from Mrs. Payne's which gave us great comfort: but we have apprehended much that you did not get to Eppington before the bad weather set in. Tell Mr. Eppes that I leave orders for a sufficient force to begin and finish his house during the week after the Christmas holidays; so that his people may come safely after New-year's day. The overseer at Shadwell will furnish them provisions. Present my affections to him, and the family, and continue to love me as you are tenderly beloved by Your's affectionately

TH: JEFFERSON

PrC (CSmH); torn; at foot of text: "Mrs. Maria Eppes"; endorsed by TJ in ink on verso.

LETTER FROM MRS. PAYNE'S: John Wayles Eppes to TJ, [17 Nov. 1797].

To George Jefferson

DEAR SIR   Monticello Dec. 2. 97.

I perceive, by an advertisement of yours in the public papers that you have commenced business in the Commission line. I have heretofore employed in the transaction of my business at Richmond, Mr. Charles Johnston, who has executed it with the greatest punctuality [and attention]. Rendering to him a just tribute on every occasion I feel myself bound on several grounds to transfer the mite of my employ to you, but most especially on that of your personal worth of which I have received honorable testimony from many. My business in Richmond consists chiefly in the lodging there my crops of tobacco to be shipped, sold, or delivered to my order as may happen: in receiving and forwarding to me by the Milton boats about 120. faggots of nail rod from Philadelphia every three months; in negotiating from time to time bills on Philadelphia, which tho drawn on John Barnes my agent there, are in fact bills on the Treasury; in receiving and forwarding to me packages which come addressed to me from Philadelphia, Europe, &c. [preferring] water transportation for heavy goods, and in being the [. . .]¹ for me in that quarter. [. . .] have [. . .]² for me. I [wish] you may find the profits [. . .].³ [I shall] set out for Philadelphia the moment the weather will permit, having been detained for some time by rains and high waters: and it is still raining. I am with great esteem Dear Sir Your friend & Servt   TH: JEFFERSON

PrC (MHi); with part of several lines torn away; at foot of text: "Mr. George Jefferson"; endorsed by TJ in ink on verso.

George Jefferson (1748-1812), grandson of TJ's uncle Field Jefferson, started in the commission business as George Jefferson & Co. in Richmond in 1797, specializing in flour and other produce. By May 1800, the firm was known as Gibson & Jefferson, with partner Patrick Gibson carrying on the business after President James Madison appointed Jefferson to serve as consul at Lisbon in 1811 (Virginia Argus, 3

Nov. 1797; MB, II, 975, 1019; JEP, II, 173; VMHB, XXIII [1915], 79, 175; TQHGM, VII [1926], 50-1; George Jefferson to TJ, 24 Oct. and 25 Nov. 1811). For a description of Jefferson's illness and death as he returned from Lisbon on board the ship Diana, see Patrick Gibson to TJ, 3 Aug. 1812.

For George Jefferson's ADVERTISEMENT on commencing BUSINESS, see Richmond Virginia Argus, 3 Nov. 1797.

¹ Estimated six words torn away.
² Estimated five words torn away.
³ Estimated six words torn away.

From James Monroe

DEAR SIR   Decr. 2. 1797.

I enclose you a letter for Mr. Dawson, one for Mr. [Gates,] one for Mr. Knox, and one for Colo. Burr. The last [is] left open for the inspection of Mr. Madison. That to Mr. Knox, you will be so good as put in the post office as soon as you arrive in Phila. I sincerely wish you peace and comfort thro the winter. The latter you may have in some respect— but the former I think you will not have. However tis possible a decided majority on the [port] side may give our country repose and safety, [and] of course extend those blessings to those who des[ire?] them. Very sincerely I wish you well.   JAS. MONROE

RC (DLC); right edge damaged; addressed: "Mr. Jefferson"; endorsed by TJ. Recorded in SJL as received on 2 Dec. 1797. Enclosures: (1) Monroe to John Dawson, 27 Nov. 1797, not found, but date and contents inferred from other correspondence, requesting Dawson to act for Monroe in arranging a resolution of Monroe's dispute with Alexander Hamilton and possibly enclosing a letter to Hamilton (see below; Syrett, Hamilton, XXI, 317n, 318n). (2) Monroe to Burr, 1 Dec. 1797, perhaps never delivered (see below), expressing dissatisfaction with Hamilton's response to Monroe's last communication in August and requesting Burr to act for Monroe in presenting an enclosed letter to Hamilton

should Burr consider it necessary (printed in Kline, Burr, I, 318-19). Other enclosures not found.

Although John DAWSON spoke to COLO. BURR "in general terms" about Monroe's situation, Dawson and TJ evidently did not give Burr the letter that Monroe had LEFT OPEN FOR THE INSPECTION OF MR. MADISON. Monroe may have enclosed a letter to Hamilton in his letter to Dawson as well as in that to Burr. In the draft of one to Hamilton dated 27 Nov., Monroe wrote: "In my judgment you ought either to have been satisfied with the explanations I gave you, or to have invited me to the field. There seemed to be no intermediate ground for a man of honor to take; yet you found one." That language was absent from a finished version of the letter dated 2 Dec. In both versions Monroe said that "I did not mean to become an aggressor nor was it justly inferable. It was however not my intention to decline that issue if sought by you in any mode whatever, either by challenge invitation or advance." The 27 Nov. draft appointed Burr to arrange any confrontation with Hamilton, while the 2 Dec. version named Dawson in that capacity. On 10 Dec. an impatient Monroe wrote Dawson again on the subject and enclosed a letter for Hamilton similar to the 27 Nov. draft, leaving blanks for the date and for the insertion of either Dawson's or Burr's name as Monroe's representative (Syrett, *Hamilton*, xxi, 316-20).

From Mary Jefferson Eppes

DEAR PAPA   Chestnut Grove December the 8th 1797

The fortnight that I spent at Eppington was so taken up in recieving and returning visits, that it was out of my power while there, to write to you. After a safe Journy down, we arrived in perfect health all, my ancle so much mended that I had no further use for my stick, and except a great weakness which I still feel when I attempt to exert it, it is quite well. We left them yesterday, all well except Betsy Eppes, who came here with us on her way to Petersburg, where she is gone with her brother to have a tooth drawn which the doctors suppose occasion the swelling in her jaw. I found my aunt suffering with hers, tho much easier than it has been, she is well otherwise. My uncle Bolling is much as usual, in a state of constant intemperance allmost, he is happy only with his glass in his hand, he behaves tho' much better to my aunt than he did, and appears to desire a reconciliation with her, and I think could she hide her resentment of his past behaviour to her, she might render her situation much more comfortable[1] than it is. I shall return to Eppington in a day or two, where I shall spend the time that is not taken up in visiting Mr. Eppes relations; and where, as much happiness as I can feel, seperated from you and my dearest sister I experience, in the kind attentions, and affectionate behaviour, of the whole family and which to merit will be my endeavour through life. Adieu My Dear Papa. My Aunt has sent to me to join the company which is here. Adieu once more. Your most affectionate daughter   M E

I have enclosed the size of the christal of my watch and must beg you to get one for I have not been able to find one large enough in Petersburg or Richmond.

RC (Mrs. Nicholas P. T. Burke, Boston, 1947); with several emendations, the most important of which is noted below. Recorded in SJL as received 21 Dec. 1797. Enclosure not found.

[1] Word interlined in place of "tolerable."

From Arthur Campbell

Sir Washington Decr. 10. 1797

I take the liberty to send you some political items received from Correspondents that may amuse you in a leisure moment. They may only be the effusions of the writers on hearing of so important an event.

May not all our fears of a war with France now evanish. Let republicans in America also take an erect attitude. Let them loudly proclaim their principles, and unite their voices with their friends and Allies across the Atlantic. This will conciliate, it will enable us to renew and improve the Alliance, to meet again as Brothers.

The occurrence is an important and critical one. The Executive, the Legislature, can make the first movement, and I auger that *We the People* will press fast after them in our Ranks. This will do more than half the Work of our Commissioners, at least it will introduce them to our Brethren, with eclat. When so received we trust they have both hearts and minds to improve an advantageous situation for the good, the lasting good of their Country. Please place these sentiments, to the account of an effusion, that your better judgment can appreciate, and use as you think proper. I am Sir, with the greatest Respect, Your most obedient servant

Arthur Campbell

RC (DLC); endorsed by TJ as received 5 Jan. 1798 and so recorded in SJL. Enclosures: (1) Extract "From an eminent Lawyer," 27 Nov. 1797, expressing a mixture of pleasure and terror at events in France, a wish that war between France and England would continue, a hope for "the destruction of the Royalists, Emigrants and Priests," and an apprehension that France would pursue an "invasion of Ireland, and harsh measures against America." (2) Extract "From Doctor — an old Whig," 2 Dec. 1797, predicting that only licentiousness can ruin France, "Knowledge and temperance" securing republics, and that after the storm, calm will prevail and France "yet be free." (3) Extract "From an Old Military Character," 1 Dec., 1797, noting the division in America between those leaning to the old order tending to monarchy and those

cherishing a republican form of government wanting freedom and independence, and trusting the Americans to follow closely after the French, to "trudge on steadily, making slow, but sure progress, in political attainments, and a knowledge of the Rights and Duties of Man"; and praising the "late *epoch* of the French Revolution" as one exceeding "all others in brilliancy" where republican principles will be established to withstand all future shocks, a peace with the Emperor will be concluded, France, Spain, and Holland will gain naval superiority, and the sun of the British monarchy set, "never to rise again" (MSS in DLC: TJ Papers, 102: 17510-12; in Campbell's hand; at head of text: "Extracts from Correspondents").

so important an event: the Fructidor coup of 4 Sep. 1797.

From Luther Martin

SIR   Baltimore 11th. December 1797

My first address to you was placed by me in the hands of a friend in Philadelphia, to be delivered to you immediately after the then Session of Congress should Terminate.

Your Departure before that Period prevented your receiving it as soon as I wished, and obliged me to transmit by the Mail to you in Virginia the printed Copy.

I take it for granted you receivd that Copy, and also that you have seen in the publick Papers my Letter to Mr. Fennell and that to yourself of which I sent you the Copy; And taking these facts for granted, I now again pay my respects to you.

You, Sir, are the avowd Author of the Notes upon Virginia. That work is publishd with your Name; And in it you have calumniated a family with which I am connected; The Individuals of which I respect and esteem, and to one of whom my Children owe their Birth. A Family, Sir, which, tho' it hath not furnished America with Philosophers, Writers of Notes upon Virginia, Ambassadors to France, Secretaries of State, or Vice Presidents of the Union, yet dares place its name in Competition with that of Jefferson. That work was also published by you when Mr. Michael Cresap had been dead more than seven years, and when Colo. Cresap borne down by the hand of Time, blind and deaf was sinking into his Grave.

I have in the most publick manner called on you to designate the Individual to whom you meant to apply the Calumny, and the Authority on which you published it. The Propriety of my so doing no person can question. I have waited sufficiently long for your Answer; but that you have not thought proper to give me. You have preserved obstinate, stubborn Silence. Was I much more your Enemy than I am, I could not have wished you to have acted differently. It is precisely the part the least honorable to your head or to your heart.

One of two things only with propriety could you have done; either justified your Publication; or acknowledged your Error.

That the first was not in your power *I know*. And for the last I did not believe you to possess sufficient Candor.

For your Silence the Publick expects a reason. It already condemns you. Come forward when you will; Assign [any] reason you choose, I pledge myself to [shew] its futility. One thing I will frank[ly] acknowledge; avail yourself of it as you please. I might, and had *I very highly* esteemed you, it is probable I should, have entered on a Discussion of this Subject in a manner less offensive; But even you, Sir, must admit that I have shewn as much attention to your feelings, as you thought decent to shew to the feelings of the Cresaps; and I am sure you can not be so lost to every Sentiment of Justice but that you must join with the publick Voice in acknowledging that from *me* you are not entitled to more.

That I should address this Letter to you immediately on your Arrival at Congress may by some be thought extraordinary or perhaps censurable; but finding on a former Occasion I appreciated your Publick Services beyond even your own Ideas, I have now changed my Conduct, and as I formerly waited for Congress to rise, I have now not only waited for Congress to meet, but also for you to meet the Congress; and during its session, I mean to take the Liberty, Sir, of keeping up a Correspondence with you through the medium of the publick Papers, until I effect the Object I have under taken, that of effacing from the name of Cresap the Stain you have attempted to fix thereon. Whether in so doing I shall sully your own the World will determine.

You have refused to inform me which of the Cresaps you intended to transmit to posterity as the infamous Murderer[1] of the family of that all-accomplished Orator, *your* Mingo Chief. You have thereby rendered my Undertaking more complex. However as I well know of that family there were but two persons, to either of whom your charge could be meant to be applied; To the Vindication of those two shall my future Letters be confined; The one Colonel Thomas Cresap, who, tho' when the British invaded Virginia he was more than one hundred years of age, I am confident had he been Governor of that State, would not have fled from the Seat of his Government at least without an attempt to defend it. The other Mr. Michael Cresap, his youngest Son, whose Life, had Heaven spared it to his family and to his *Country*, would I am well satisfied have prevented me the necessity of this Investigation, for, Sir, in that case I sacredly beleive neither the Story nor the Speech[2] of Logan would in their *present form* have graced the pages of the Notes on Virginia. I am Sir with *due* respect Your very Obedt Servt

LUTHER MARTIN

RC (DLC); second page damaged; endorsed by TJ as received 14 Dec. 1797 and so recorded in SJL. Printed in *Porcupine's Gazette*, 14 Dec. 1797; at head of text: "COPY"; at foot of text: "To the Hon. Thomas Jefferson"; the most significant variations are noted below.

MY FIRST ADDRESS TO YOU: Martin to TJ, 24 June 1797.

[1] In *Porcupine's Gazette* the preceding two words are in italics.

[2] This word and "Story" in the same sentence are in italics in *Porcupine's Gazette*.

To Thomas Mann Randolph

Th: Jefferson to T M Randolph   Philadelphia. Dec. 14. 97.

I arrived here on the 8th. day of my journey from Belmont, having suffered much with the severity of the weather, and taken moreover a violent cold which still indisposes me. Not so much however as to prevent my attendance on business, and it is going off. The Senate had as yet only a single bill before them, so that I found myself in place in time for business. They have since received and passed a law from the Representatives for suspending the stamp act till July. A law is also on the carpet for continuing the currency of foreign coin. The same motive which occasioned the postponement of the Stamp act, to wit, the approach of the elections, will occasion a postponement also of the land tax. Flour here is 9. to 10. dollars; wheat $1\frac{1}{2}$ dollar. I have a letter from the first merchant at Cowes informing me that in consequence of the bad weather during harvest, the quality as well as quantity of their wheat will be low: that wheat had risen from 6/6 sterl. to 8/ and 9/ and probably would get up to 10/ sterl. the bushel: and that we may count on 8/6 at least through the whole season. You will see the extract in Bache's paper, wherein I had it inserted for the information of both the merchant and farmer, and it may not be amiss to let our neighbors of both descriptions know that the extract is genuine, from me, and to be relied on. We have nothing late from Europe more than is in the newspapers. Colo. Monroe's pamphlet has not yet appeared but soon will. A great explosion in commerce is hourly expected. Great fall of prices in labor and at the markets has already taken place. The market here is now lower than it has been for four years past. It is expected that every thing will soon be down at old prices. My love to my dear Martha, and kiss the little ones for me. Adieu affectionately.

RC (DLC); endorsed by Randolph as received 1 Jan. 1798. PrC (CSmH); faded, with salutation and dateline overwritten by TJ: "TMR Dec. 16. 97" and recorded in SJL under that date.

The SINGLE BILL BEFORE the Senate when TJ arrived was that introduced by North Carolina Senator Timothy Bloodworth on 8 Dec. 1797, calling for Congress to consent to acts passed by his state which provided for a health officer and harbormaster at Wilmington. The bill was never reported out of committee, but in April 1798 a similar one was passed by the House and sent to the Senate where it was rejected on 16 Apr. (JS, II, 414, 469, 473).

The bill FOR SUSPENDING THE STAMP ACT until 1 July 1798, which was sent by the House to the Senate on 13 Dec. 1797, was passed by the Senate the next day (JS, II, 414-5). For the history of the legislation, see TJ to Madison, 29 June 1797.

On 21 Dec. 1797, the House passed and sent the Senate a bill for CONTINUING THE CURRENCY OF FOREIGN COIN by suspending the second section of the act of 1793 which required that foreign coins, except for Spanish milled dollars, cease to be used as legal tender three years after the United States Mint commenced the coinage of gold and silver. After Theodore Sedgwick and the committee considering the bill on 2 Jan. 1798 recommended the suspension for gold coins only, a debate and vote ensued that threatened passage of any bill. After an amendment by Humphrey Marshall of Pennsylvania on 17 Jan. proposing the repeal of the 1793 act altogether was defeated, the bill calling for the coverage of both gold and silver foreign coins passed by a 17 to 9 vote. Six days later, the House agreed to several minor amendments introduced by the Senate (JS, II, 416-8, 423-6; JHR, III, 146; U.S. Statutes at Large, I, 301; TJ to Madison, 3 Jan. 1798).

FIRST MERCHANT AT COWES: a letter from Thomas Auldjo to TJ of 19 Sep. 1797, which according to SJL was received from Cowes on 13 Dec. 1797, has not been found. An EXTRACT of it which was printed in BACHE's *Aurora* on 15 Dec. 1797, under the heading "Extract of a letter from a merchant of distinction in England to his friend in this city, dated 19 Sep. 1797," appeared as follows: "Our harvest is now nearly over in the Southern counties of England, but the weather has been so unfavourable that a great deal of wheat is much injured, and the whole has been so badly saved, that the quality must prove very indifferent, our prices have consequently risen very much, and old wheat, which about 5 weeks ago was at one dollar and twenty five cents (counting in your money) to one dollar and thirty six cents per bushel now sells as high as two dollars and eleven cents, and may get up to two dollars and twenty two cents (say 10/ sterling). It is impossible to say whether prices will continue so high during the winter and spring, but I think you may fairly expect to get 8/6, say one dollar and eighty nine cents per bushel for all the wheat that may come in good order from your side of the water."

From Oliver Wolcott, Jr.

Treasury Department

SIR   December 15th. 1797

I have the honour to transmit herewith, a Report on the Petition of William Imlay Commissioner of Loans for the State of Connecticut, which was refered to me by order of the Senate on the 5th. instant. I have the honour to be very respectfully Sir Your obedient Servant

OLIV WOLCOTT JR

RC (DNA: RG 46, Senate Records, 5th Cong., 2d. sess.); in a clerk's hand, signed by Wolcott; at foot of text: "The Honble. The President of the Senate"; endorsed in a clerk's hand: "Letter from the Secretary for the department of Treasury with Report on petition of Wm Imlay 1797." Enclosure: Report by Wolcott on petition of William Imlay, 15 Dec. 1797, supporting Imlay's request for reimbursement for $155.76, the sum paid for a third clerk, which exceeded the amount of $800 for two clerks as allowed by congressional acts of 3 Mch. 1795 and 30 May 1796, the extra clerk being necessary to carry out the legislation which authorized "the transfer of Stock standing in the Books of his Office to the credit of the State" (MS in same; in a clerk's hand, signed by Wolcott; endorsed by clerks).

On 5 Dec. 1797, James Hillhouse of Connecticut laid Imlay's PETITION before the Senate, immediately after which it was agreed that the secretary of the treasury should submit a report on it. TJ delivered Wolcott's report to the Senate on 18 Dec., where, on the same day, it was read and referred to a committee. Two days later, Uriah Tracy brought in a bill recommending that Imlay receive the full amount claimed. The Senate passed "An act for the relief of William Imlay" on 22 Dec., but the House of Representatives did not concur with it until 11 May 1798 (JS, II, 413, 416-7; JHR, III, 291).

To Richard Richardson

SIR   Philadelphia Dec. 16. 97.
Within a day or two after my arrival here, I called on Mr. Traquair, the Stonecutter, to whom I meant to apply for you. I explained to him your character and motives for wishing to pass a winter in learning to cut stone. He approved much of your motives, and immediately entered cordially into the desire to serve and aid you. On the subject of giving you board for your work he said he did not know whether it would be in his power to lodge you, as his house was small and his wife had a day or two before brought him his eighth child, but he promised to consult his wife and let me know. I have not seen him since; but I am so perfectly satisfied that if he cannot board you, he will nevertheless give you all the instruction in his power and employ you solely with a view to your instruction, that you may safely come on [immediately?] after the Christmas holidays; and in the mean time I will make the best bargain for you that I can. You may take the stage at Fredericksburg, and on the 5th. day you will be here. Enquire for me at Francis's hotel, South 4th. street between Market and Chesnut. I am Sir Your humble servt
                                              TH: JEFFERSON

RC (Joseph Rubinfine, West Palm Beach, Florida, 1990); torn; at foot of text: "Mr. Richard Richardson."

Richard Richardson (b. ca. 1775), a Virginia native, began working as a bricklayer at Monticello in 1796. At TJ's prompting he went to Philadelphia in early 1798, where he studied stonecutting and plastering for several months, after which he returned to Monticello, where he was regularly employed through 1800, during the last year as an overseer. In June 1801, after learning that his services would no longer be needed there, he received news from TJ that Joseph Richardson, his uncle, had left him an estate in Jamaica, which he promptly proceeded to claim. He visited the United States in 1804 but returned to his sugar plantation in Jamaica the same year. TJ last heard from Richardson in a letter of 27 July 1809, at which time he invited his brother George to visit him and outlined plans to return to the United States (TJ to Richardson, 8 Jan. and 1 June 1801, and enclosure; Richardson to TJ, 20 July 1801, 5 Aug. 1804; TJ to Dudley Richardson, 2 Nov. 1809; TJ to George Richardson, 15 July 1823; MB, II, 945; Jack McLaughlin, *Jefferson and Monticello: The Biography of a Builder* [New York, 1988], 336-7).

Letters from Richardson to TJ of 28 Dec. 1796 and 26 Jan. 1797, recorded in SJL as received on 23 and 29 Jan. 1797 respectively, have not been found. SJL records a letter from TJ to Richardson of 11 Mch. 1797, which is also missing.

To John Wayles Eppes

TH:J. TO J. W. EPPES   Philadelphia Dec. 21. 97.
Presuming that you get the newspapers I shall not repeat the public news which they detail. The great victory obtained by the English over

the Dutch fleet is placed beyond doubt, they have taken 9 out of 16.   As to the proceedings of Congress, they have passed a bill putting off the commencement of the Stamp act till July next. The land tax will not be taken up this session. It is suspected that the approaching elections have had as much influence in both these measures, as the condition of the treasury, which is said to be better than was expected. Congress therefore have absolutely nothing to do, but to wait for news from our Parisian envoys. If that is of a peaceable aspect I know nothing which ought to keep us long from home. And that it will be of peaceable aspect there is solid reason to expect, notwithstanding the newspaper paragraphs of a contrary import, fabricated to give a hostile impulse to Congress. We learn from Norfolk that Barny is made judge of admiralty in the French West Indies, and has forbidden the capture of any American vessels except going to rebel ports. This looks as if they wished to distinguish between real American vessels, and English ones under American papers. They suppose and probably that Barny will be able to distinguish them.—I send according to your desire Paine's letter. In my next I will inclose another pamphlet on the same subject. Monroe's book appears this day. It is of near 500. pages, consequently too large to go by [post.] Bache will send on 2. or 300 copies to Richmond.—I have put on board Stratton's schooner an anvil, vice and beak iron for George, proposing as soon as he receives them, that Isaac shall take those he has. We had hoped 2 or 3 days ago that the vessels here would have got out. But the weather has now set in so as to render it doubtful whether they are not shut up for the winter. If so, it will be February before these things get on. You would do well to employ Isaac in the mean time in preparing coal for his year's work. He should have about 2000. bushels laid in. Nor will it be amiss to cord his wood in order to excite him to an emulation in burning it well. I am in hopes you or Mr. Randolph will prepare for the road-contract. It is very interesting to us all. Tell my dear Maria I received her letter of the 8th. from Chesnut grove this day. I will write to her next. In the mean time convey to her the warmest expressions of my love. Present me affectionately to Mr. and Mrs. Eppes and to all the younger ones. Adieu with sincere affections.

P.S. I am entirely at a loss to what post office to direct your letters, I have conjectured you have most intercourse with Petersburg.

PrC (DLC). Enclosure: Paine, *Letter to Washington* (see Madison to TJ, 10 Jan. 1796).

Reports of the GREAT VICTORY OBTAINED BY THE ENGLISH OVER THE DUTCH FLEET in the battle of 11 Oct. 1797 off the coast of Holland "to the leeward of the Texel" were carried in Philadelphia newspapers, including the Philadelphia *Aurora* of 20 and 21

Dec. 1797 and the 20 Dec. 1797 supplement of the *Philadelphia Gazette.* On 21 Dec. the *Aurora* also included PARAGRAPHS from New York indicating that France had declared war against the United States and had issued "orders to capture all American vessels." At the same time the newspapers carried several reports FROM NORFOLK to members of Congress indicating that Joshua Barney, the Revolutionary War naval officer from Baltimore who began serving in the French Navy in 1796, had been appointed chief JUDGE OF ADMIRALTY IN THE FRENCH WEST INDIES and that "he had already issued a proclamation forbidding the capture of American vessels bound to any British port whatever, except such as are stiled 'Rebel ports.' " One Norfolk correspondent described Barney as "an honest man, who will doubtless do justice to every one of our REAL countrymen who may fall in his way" (*Philadelphia Gazette,* 21 and 22 Dec. 1797; Philadelphia *Aurora,* 22 Dec. 1797; DAB). On 26 Dec. the *Philadelphia Gazette* carried word that the report of Barney's appointment was incorrect. For Barney's difficulties with the French and the British authorities after he left Norfolk for Saint-Domingue in August 1797, see Hulbert Footner, *Sailor of Fortune: The Life and Adventures of Commodore Barney, U.S.N.* (New York, 1940), 220-4.

A letter from Eppes to TJ of 21 Nov. 1797, recorded in SJL as received 13 Dec. 1797, has not been found.

To Francis Walker

DEAR SIR   Philadelphia Dec. 21. 1797.

Mr. William Davenport desired me to pay you for him, one hundred dollars which I engaged to do soon after my arrival at this place. Besides this there were two quarters of one of the beeves you sent him (I believe the first) which I took and was to answer to you. You will see below a statement of that, which after deducting the amount of some nails, leaves a balance of 23/6 due on my account. I therefore inclose you an order on George Jefferson & Co. for 103.D. 92 c. Should you have debited the whole of that beef to Davenport, you will be so good as to credit him by me (besides the 100.D.) £3–13–4.

to wit.   220 ℔. of beef @ 4d.   is £3–13–4
    Cr. by 52. ℔ Xd. nails @ 11½d.   £2–19–10
    balance now remitted 3.92   <u>1– 3– 6</u>   3–13–4

The land tax will not now be taken up by Congress. It is agreed therefore that we have literally nothing to do but to wait for information from our commissioners at Paris. If that is peaceable, as there is good reason to believe (notwithstanding the fabricated paragraphs in the newspapers) I see nothing which ought to hinder us from being soon at home. The question of a naval armament must of course be discussed, because recommended in the speech. But I see no reason to believe that any change of opinion in Congress has taken place since their decision against it in the summer session. I am with great esteem Dear Sir Your friend & servt   TH: JEFFERSON

PrC (DLC: Rives Papers); addressed: "Francis Walker esq. of the General assembly of Virginia now at Richmond"; franked, stamped, and postmarked. Enclosure not found.

The president's address to Congress on 23 Nov. 1797 stressed the importance of commerce to the national welfare and advocated NAVAL ARMAMENT, noting "while pride, ambition, avarice, and violence, have been so long unrestrained, there remains no reasonable ground on which to raise an expectation that a commerce without protection or defence will not be plundered" (JS, II, 407-8). For the discussion of the naval establishment and the arming of merchant vessels in CONGRESS during the SUMMER SESSION, see TJ to Madison, 8 and 15

June 1797. On 26 Dec., when the House of Representatives began to consider regulating the arming of merchant vessels, John Nicholas successfully moved to postpone consideration of the proposed bill until 5 Feb. 1798. The Senate did not consider the issue of the protection of commerce until after President Adams reported on the reception of the American envoys to France (Annals, VII, 764-74; JS, II, 456-8).

Letters from Walker to TJ of 26 May, 6 June, 21 Oct., 21 Nov. 1796, 19 Apr. 1797, and 17 Oct. 1799, recorded in SJL as received 26 May, 7 June, 21 Oct., 22 Nov. 1796, 21 Apr. 1797, and 17 Oct. 1799 respectively, have not been found. SJL also records letters from TJ to Walker of 17 May and 21 Nov. 1796 which are missing.

To John Taylor

DEAR SIR   Philadelphia Dec. 23. 97.

Your favor of Novemb. — did not come to my hands till Dec. 13. It had awaited my arrival here: and the ordinary affairs of business and ceremony prevented my applying to the patent office till Dec. 21. I then paid at the treasury the 20. Doll. bill you inclosed adding 10. Dollars, the price of the drill, as you had mentioned. The petition and description are lodged in the patent office. But a drawing is indispensably required by the law, and none came. Nor is the model yet come to hand. I have received a letter from Messrs. Monroe & Roe that the vessel being unable to come up on account of the ice, the crate was landed and put into their care, and they ask my directions. But they give no date of time or place to their letter, and my enquiries here to find out who they are and where they reside have been hitherto fruitless. I have taken measures to find whether they live at Wilmington, Marcus Hook &c and trust I shall find them, as they reside some where on the Delaware. As soon as the model arrives I will make a drawing from that which shall be lodged in the patent office and will compleat the title. I inclose you the treasurer's receipt for the 30. Dollars.

Our stamp act is put off till July next. The land tax will also be put off. The approach of the elections may have had it's weight on both these measures. The affluence of the treasury has rendered it possible to go on a year longer without a land tax. The questions about beginning a navy, and permitting our merchants (alias the English merchants) to arm and begin the war for us, must of course be discussed, because the speech has recommended these measures. But I see no reason to apprehend any change in the opinion of Congress on these points since the summer session. These therefore and Blount's impeachment will serve to give us an appearance of business for some time. For in honest truth I believe every man here acknoleges we have nothing to do: that there is literally nothing which the public good requires us to act upon. As we are together, I think myself we ought not to separate till we hear from our envoys at Paris. And I think we may expect by the last of January not only to hear from them, but to see what is likely to be the aspect of our affairs with France. If peaceable, I know no reason why we should not go home immediately, and economise something on the daily expences of our session, which in truth are enormous. The French Consul here tells me he has a letter from his government mentioning that they expect our envoys and that they will be well recieved. A pamphlet written by Fauchet is come here. I have not read it. But I understand that the sum of it is that our Executive are the enemies of France, our citizens generally friendly, but that the mutual interests of both countries requires a continuance of friendly intercourse between the two republics.—A bill suspending for 3. years the law respecting foreign coins has passed the representatives with some difficulty and may possibly fail in the Senate. Whether from real fears for the mint or what other grounds I know not. But if it fails we are left almost without a coin for legal tenders. As you are in session it behoves you to see that your laws fixing the value of foreign coin and making them a tender are on a proper footing. By the constitution Congress may *regulate the value of foreign coin*, but if they do not do it, the old power revives to the states, the constitution only forbidding them to *make any thing but gold and silver coin a tender in payment of debts.* This construction is admitted here by persons not disposed to give to the states more powers than they are entitled to. Adieu affectionately   Th: Jefferson

RC (MHi: Washburn Collection); addressed: "John Taylor of the assembly of Virginia now at Richmond." PrC (DLC). Enclosure not found.

YOUR FAVOR: Taylor to TJ, 19 Nov. 1797.

According to SJL, TJ RECEIVED A LETTER from Munro & Roe on 13 Dec. 1797, but it has not been found. SJL records letters from TJ to Munro & Roe of 23 Feb. and 25 Mch. 1798 which also are missing.

FRENCH CONSUL Philippe de Létombe re-

ceived a letter from Talleyrand of 29 Sep. 1797 which, according to a report in the *Philadelphia Gazette* of 1 Jan. 1798, noted that the United States commissioners at Paris had been "cordially received by the French government,—that the negotiation would be commenced as soon as possible— and that he had no doubt of an amiable adjustment of affairs between the two countries."

A PAMPHLET WRITTEN BY FAUCHET: Joseph Fauchet, *Coup d'oeil sur l'état actuel des nos rapports politiques avec les États-Unis de l'Amérique Septentrionale* (Paris, 1797), which depicted the actions of the United States government as contributing to strained relations with France, was printed by Benjamin Franklin Bache as *A Sketch of the Present State of our Political Relations with the United States of North-America* (Philadelphia, 1797). See Evans, No. 32115.

On 19 Jan. 1798 the Virginia Assembly passed legislation FIXING THE VALUE of certain gold and silver FOREIGN coins and declaring them legal tender within the commonwealth (Shepherd, *Statutes*, II, 84).

John Henry to Henry Tazewell

DEAR SIR   Annapolis Decr. 24. 1797.

In Mr. Jeffersons Notes on Virginia it is stated (I have not the Book by me) that the Family of Logan were murdered by one of the Cresops. Mr. Martin the Attorney General of Maryland married into that family. He has heretofore and also within the last two weeks addressed a letter or letters to Mr. Jefferson upon this subject. He has likewise stated to me in a conversation which I had with him at my own request, that he now has in his possession documents which will shew that the passage in the Notes is incorrect.

As the feelings of Mr. Martin and his friends have been wounded by this part of the Notes, I am anxious that there should be an understanding upon this subject and their Minds made easy.

I can see no good reason why Mr. Jefferson should not give some speedy assurance directly to Mr. Martin or to some of his friends that the correction shall take place.

Altho in the Great Concerns of our Country we have differed as to the course which it was best to pursue; yet there has never been a time when I had not the highest respect and Esteem for the Character of Mr. Jefferson and of late having resided under the same roof with him, and been an eye witness of his deportment both public and private; I am free to declare that his Virtues have endeared him to me.

To lessen the Number of his Enemies and to assuage the accrimoney of those which he now has, are objects which I have much at heart.

I have the disposition to say much upon this subject, but a future occasion may be imbraced with more propriety.

I however now, from a strong and sincere desire to quiet the Mind of my friend Mr. Martin, as well as for other considerations, entreat you to press upon Mr. Jefferson the propriety of not adding unnecessarily to the Number of his Enemies. They are already numerous and bitter enough God knows.

Whatever he does upon the subject Matter of this letter, I know will be strongly marked with that Sincerity Candour and simplicity which has so eminently distinguished his character.

I will thank you for any communication respecting our public affairs. I am dear Sir with Sentiments of respect & Esteem Yr hbe Servt.

JNO. HENRY

RC (DLC); endorsed by TJ: "Henry Govr of Maryland. 97. Dec. 24."

That Henry Tazewell was the recipient of this letter and passed it on to TJ is established by TJ's direct reply to Henry on 31 Dec. 1797 and his letter to Tazewell of the same date.

From James Madison

DEAR SIR   Orange Decr. 25. 1797

I have let Col. Monroe know that you was furnished with a draught on a House in Philada. for 250 drs. and finding that it would be convenient to him, have authorised him to draw on you for that sum. I have also given him a draught on Genl. Moylan, of which the inclosed is a letter of advice. I reserve the note of Bailey towards covering the advance made by you, unless it should be otherwise settled by Col. Monroe and yourself, as he intimated a desire that it might be. Perhaps it would save delay and trouble to Mr. B. if you should find a convenient opportunity to drop a hint to his friend Van Cortland that the note was in your hand; as it is more than probable he may be the channel of taking it up.

According to the bill of nails given in by the Workman I shall want from your nailory,[1] 50,000 sixes, 3,000. eights, 20,000 tens, 5,000 twentys. and 12,000 flooring Brads. I shall also want 50,000. fours for lathing, 4,000 sprigs sixes, and 3,000 do. eights. You can inform me whether these are also made at your shops, or whether it would be better to get them in Philada. I shall write as you suggested to Col. Bell; but it may not be amiss for you to confirm the orders for having the supply prepared for me, according to the above list.

We have had a great proportion of cold weather since you passed us. The Thermometer however has not been lower than 10°. It was at this point, on the morning of the 21st. instant. The drought also is equal to the cold. Within the last 31 days the fall of water has been but $1\frac{1}{4}$ inches only. Of snow there has been none. This cold and dry spell succeeding the dry fall and late seeding, gives to the Wheat fields the worst of appearances.

You will not expect political occurrences from this quarter. The objects of enquiry here are Liston's Plot—the envoyship to France, and

Monroe's publication. The delay of this last occasions some surprize. I observe that the President, has laid hold of the late endemic at the seat of Government as an occasion for getting the prerogative of prorouging the Legislature. Fortunately the Constitution has provided an important barrier in this case, by requiring a session at least within every year. But still the power may in unforeseen emergencies, be made an instrument of party or of usurpation; and it is to be hoped will not therefore be granted. I have not examined it in a constitutional view, but that also merits attention. Ambition is so vigilant, and where it has a model always in view as in the present case, is so prompt in seizing its advantages, that it can not be too closely watched, or too vigorously checked.

When you do me the favor to write, let your letters leave Philada. in the mail of friday morning. They will then come without any halt. Adieu.

RC (DLC: Madison Papers); torn; unsigned; with TJ's notes in margin (see note below); endorsed by TJ as received 2 Jan. 1798 and so recorded in SJL. Enclosure not found, but see below.

In a letter of 17 Dec. 1797, Madison informed MONROE of the financial document he had delivered to TJ for Monroe's use. He also enclosed a DRAUGHT on Stephen MOYLAN for $200. The NOTE of Theodorus BAILEY for $1,250 was a payment for land Bailey had purchased from Madison. For these transactions and a discussion of the financial dealings between Madison, Monroe, and TJ, see Madison, *Papers*, XVII, 61-4.

In his address at the opening of Congress on 23 Nov., President Adams cited the late yellow fever epidemic at the SEAT OF GOVERNMENT as a reason to consider "a power to postpone the meeting of Congress, without passing the time fixed by the Con-

stitution." Legislation passed in 1794 allowed the president to change the meeting place of Congress in case of "contagious sickness," but Adams noted that that alternative would be inconvenient and expensive. The Senate appointed a committee to consider amending the act of 1794, but after hearing the report read by Timothy Bloodworth on 6 Dec. no further action was taken (JS, II, 407, 412-14). For a summary of legislative action on this measure in the House of Representatives, see Madison, *Papers*, XVII, 64.

[1] Here in the margin TJ wrote:

"℔
350 VI.
30. VIII
260. X
125. XX
240. XVI
1005."

Notes on Comments by John Adams and Robert Goodloe Harper

1797.
Dec. 26. Langdon tells me that at the 2d. election of Pr. and V.P. of US. when there was a considerable vote given to Clinton in opposition to Mr. Adams, he took occasion to remark it in conversa-

tion in the Senate chamber with Mr. A. who gritting his teeth said 'Damn 'em' 'Damn 'em' 'Damn 'em' you see that an elective government will not do.'—He also tells me that Mr. A. in a late conversation said 'Republicanism must be disgraced, Sir.' The Chevalr. Yruho called on him at Braintree, and conversing on French affairs, and Yruho expressing his belief of their stability in opposition to Mr. Adams's, the latter lifting up and shaking his finger at him said 'I'll tell you what, the French republic will not last 3. months.' This I had from Yruho.

Harper lately in a large company was saying that the best thing the friends of the French could do was to pray for the restoration of their monarch, then says a bystander 'the best thing we could do I suppose would be to pray for the establishment of a monarch in the US.' 'Our people says Harper are not yet ripe for it, but it is the best thing we can come to and we shall come to it.' Something like this was said in presence of Findlay.[1]

MS (DLC: TJ Papers, 102: 17524); entirely in TJ's hand, written on same sheet as Notes on a Conversation with Tench Coxe, 27 Dec. 1797, with beginning of Notes on the Formation of the Federal Government, 5 Jan. 1798, written on verso; later notation by TJ (see note below).

The comments by HARPER LATELY IN A LARGE COMPANY were printed in slightly different form by James T. Callender in his *Sketches of the History of America*, 52n, where they were attributed to a conversation in the Pennsylvania State House on 23 Dec. 1797 at which unnamed congressmen were present. In March 1798 the anecdote was reprinted by the *New York Argus* from Callender's work, and the Philadelphia *Au-*

rora of 21 Mch. 1798 carried a letter from Harper proclaiming the statement "an absolute falsehood from beginning to end." Harper admitted that "I have often said and now repeat, that the abolition of monarchy in France was, in my opinion, a misfortune to that country; but it is absolutely false that I ever expressed a sentiment respecting the American government, like that attributed to me in the above paragraph."

[1] Sentence possibly added later. In the space between this sentence and the Notes on a Conversation with Tench Coxe of 27 Dec. 1797, TJ interlined: "1798. Mar. He now denies it in the public papers tho it can be proved by several members."

To James Monroe

DEAR SIR   Philadelphia. Dec. 27. 97.

I communicated to Mr. M. the evening I was with him the papers you sent by me for Mr. D. He was clearly of opinion nothing further ought to be done. D. was decisively of the same opinion. This being the case then there was no ground for consulting L. or B. and accordingly nothing has been said to them.   Your book was later coming out than was to have been wished: however it works irresistably. It would be very gratifying to you to hear the unqualified eulogies both on the matter and manner by all who are not hostile to it from principle. A pamphlet, written by Fauchet (and now reprinting here) reinforces the views you have presented of the duplicity of the administration here. The republican party in the H. of representatives is stronger than it's antagonist party in all strong questions. To-day on a question to put off the bill for permitting private vessels to arm, it was put off to the 1st. Monday of Feb. by 40. to 37. and on a motion to reconsider was confirmed by 44. to 38. We have half a dozen members absent, who if here would give decisive preponderance. Two of these are of our state, Giles and Cabell. The stamp act is put off to July, and the Land tax will not be touched this session. Before the next the elections will be over. We have therefore literally nothing to do, but to await intelligence from our envoys at Paris, and as soon as we learn that our affairs there will be of peaceable aspect (as there is reason to expect) I see nothing which ought to keep us here. The questions about building a navy, to be sure must be discussed out of respect to the speech: but it will only be to reject them. A bill has passed the Representatives giving three years longer currency to foreign coins. It is in danger in the Senate. The effect of stopping the currency of gold and silver is to force bank-paper through all the states. However I presume the state legislatures will exercise their acknoleged right of regulating the value of foreign coins, when not regulated by Congress, and their exclusive right of declaring them a tender. The Marquis Fayette was expected in the ship John from Hamburgh. She is cast away in this river. 70 passengers were said to be got ashore, and the rest still remaining on the wreck. But we do not know that he was actually a passenger. Some late elections have been remarkeable. Loyd of Maryland in the place of Henry by a majority of 1. against Winder the republican candidate. Chipman senator for Vermont by a majority of 1. against I. Smith the republican candidate. Tichenor chosen governor of Vermont by a small majority against the republican candidate. Governor Robertson of that state writes that the people there are fast coming over to a sound understanding of the state of our affairs. The same is said of some other of the N. England states. In this state that spirit rises very steadily. The republicans have a firm majority of about 6. in the H. of representatives here, a circumstance which has not been seen for some years. Even their Senate is purifying. The contest for the government will be between Mc.kean and Ross, and probably will be an extreme hard one. In N. York it will be the same between Livingston and Jay, who is becoming unpopular with his own party. We are anxious to see how the N. York representatives are. The dismission of Tenche Coxe from office without any reason assigned is considered as one of the bold acts of the President. Tant mieux.—As soon as Fauchet's pamphlet appears I will send you a copy. Your book so far has sold rapidly. I received from Mr. Madison paper for 500.D. for you, which will be paid in the course of a few weeks. I shall desire Barnes to receive and hold it subject to your order. Present me respectfully to Mrs. Monroe and accept assurances of my sincere friendship. Adieu.

RC (DLC: Madison Papers, Rives Collection); unsigned; addressed: "Colo. Monroe near Charlottesville"; franked. PrC (DLC).

MR. M. was James Madison. Monroe wanted him to see at least one of the enclosures that Monroe SENT to TJ on 2 Dec. MR. D.: John Dawson. While TJ asserted that THERE WAS NO GROUND FOR CONSULTING L. OR B., Dawson reported to Monroe on 24 Dec. that after speaking with TJ he had in fact spoken with Edward Livingston and Aaron Burr about Monroe's conflict with Hamilton (Syrett, *Hamilton*, XXI, 319).

The MOTION TO RECONSIDER the postponement of the bill on the arming of merchant vessels, introduced when some members said they had voted incorrectly out of confusion over the proposed dates, occurred on 26 Dec. (ANNALS, VII, 764-74).

The MARQUIS de Lafayette had expected to travel to the United States on THE SHIP JOHN FROM HAMBURGH, but changed his plans before the ship sailed. The vessel, which had its home port at Boston, ran upon a shoal in Delaware Bay on 22 Dec. 1797 and became trapped by ice (Philadelphia *Aurora*, 26-28, 30 Dec. 1797).

James Lloyd was named United States senator by the legislature of MARYLAND to replace John HENRY, who had resigned earlier in December after his election as governor (*Biog. Dir. Cong.*, 1381, 1174). Similarly, Nathaniel CHIPMAN became SENATOR FOR VERMONT to succeed Isaac TICHENOR, whom the assembly had CHOSEN GOVERNOR after none of a field of candidates received a majority of the popular vote. The chief REPUBLICAN CANDIDATE for that office was former governor and senator Moses Robinson—evidently the GOVERNOR ROBERTSON of the above letter—who had vigorously opposed the Jay Treaty (Walter Hill Crockett, *Vermont: The Green Mountain State*, 5 vols. [New York, 1921-23], II, 565, 567, 568, V, 47; *Rutland Herald*, 16 Oct. 1797).

The president's removal of Tench COXE as commissioner of the revenue on 23 Dec. 1797 WITHOUT ANY REASON ASSIGNED was interpreted as the product of Coxe's open criticism of Adams prior to the election of 1796, and followed an acrid exchange of correspondence between Coxe and Oliver Wolcott (Cooke, *Coxe*, 286-90, 302-7).

Retained copies of four letters written by Monroe to an unnamed recipient on 25 Dec. 1797, 1 June, 15 Nov., and 16 Nov. 1798, now in his papers at DLC, were printed in Monroe, *Writings*, III, 89-92, 123-5, 139-47, 148-54, with TJ as the inferred recipient. However, the letters are not recorded in SJL, neither recipient's copies with endorsements by TJ nor replies by him to any of the four are known to exist, the letters are not mentioned in other correspondence between TJ and Monroe, and TJ is not known to have written to Monroe on 14 Dec. 1797 and 22 May 1798, as the recipient of the letters in question must have done. Another letter written by Monroe on 1 June 1798 that was definitely to TJ refers to an enclosure addressed to John Dawson. A mention of Spotsylvania County in the letter of 15 Nov. and, in that of 16 Nov. 1798, a reference to the recipient as a Republican "heretofore less prominent," support the conclusion that Dawson was the recipient of the four letters.

Notes on a Conversation
with Tench Coxe

[27 Dec. 1797]

27.   Tenche Coxe tells me that a little before Hamilton went out of office, or just as he was going out, taking with him his last conversation, and among other things, on the subject of their differences, 'for my part, says he, I avow myself a Monarchist; I have no objection to a trial being made of this thing of a republic, but' &c.

MS (DLC: TJ Papers, 102: 17524); entirely in TJ's hand; written on same sheet as Notes on Comments by John Adams and Robert Goodloe Harper, 26 Dec. 1797, and an incomplete entry, with date missing, beginning "[. . .] the following fact[:] When the British treaty was on the carpet, and it's fate [. . .]," with up to one-half page missing, and with Notes on the Formation of the Federal Government, 5 Jan. 1798, on verso; closing quotation mark supplied.

To Martha Jefferson Randolph

MY DEAR MARTHA   Philadelphia Dec. 27. 97.

I am at length got well of a terrible cold, which I think must have proceeded from the intense cold of the day I left Belmont. It became very bad by the time I got to Baltimore, and has been worse here. However it is now entirely passed off. We are here lounging our time away, doing nothing, and having nothing to do. It gives me great regret to be passing my time so uselessly when it could have been so importantly employed at home. I cannot but believe that we shall become ashamed of staying here, and go home in February or March at furthest. Nor are we relieved by the pleasures of society here. For partly from bankruptcies partly from party dissensions society is torn up by the roots. I envy those who stay at home, enjoying the society of their friendly neighbors, blessed with their firesides, and employed in doing something every day which looks usefully to futurity. I expect you will of course charge me before my departure with the procuring you such articles of convenience here as you can get best here. I shall be sending some things for myself in the spring. Tell Mr. Randolph I shall be glad from time to time to exchange meteorological diaries with him, that we may have a comparative view of the climates of this place and ours. I received a letter from Maria last week. She had got quite well of her sprain and was then at the Chesnut grove. However I suppose you hear from one another more directly than through me. Let me also hear from you, as your welfare, Mr. Randolph's and the little ones are the things nearest my heart. Do not let them forget me. Adieu my dear Martha affectionately.

RC (NNPM); unsigned.   LETTER FROM MARIA: Mary Jefferson
                                    Eppes to TJ, 8 Dec. 1797.

From William Short

Jefferson. Dec. 27. Acknowlege his of March. 12. and June 30. 97—successive causes of delay of my departure for Ame.—death of an old lady—gratitude of the young one for the expressions of his letter—have passed most of my time here in the country—in calm and study—an extensive library here. The affair of the 9. m. dol.—the last letter from S. of S. of July 17. 96.—never received any letter from Mr. R. of any other than a public nature—he was not therefore my private agent—beg Jff. to press the conclusion of this affair—and if necessary to recur to Mr. R's letters in the Dep. of State from Nov. 94. Drew on our bankers last spring for the quarter's salary for return—but this has nothing in common with the 9. m. doll.—my hope that my salary will be allowed until I received the letter of recreance, notwithstanding an expression in a former letter to the S. of S. from Madrid. Wish Ind. camp to be tenanted out if possible—desire to place all I have disponible in this way—shall be one of my pursuits on my arrival in America—suppose the farther north, the better the chance for tenants—prefer his neighborhood if tenants to be found—do not intend to acquire slaves—consider land rent at 5 p ct. equal to funds at 6. p. ct. Desire that my cash may be employed as he may judge best—but employed—and that Barnes, may constantly apply the interest as it accrues—as I shall have with me for my immediate expences—know nothing from my brother of my western lands—ignorant of the [acreage] a tract—consider property every where as in an unhinged state, and therefore wish to attend to the little I have (disposed generally to see en [noir]—combat this disposition but it is too often confirmed by my experience). Have never received Colo. Skipwith's account—although faithfully promised for the winter of 90. Inclose a letter for my brother, and one from Cleresseat, which had been accidentally long detained by me—Pougens, and his wish to send his editions to the U.S. for sale. (Sib. barley—wish that the Agents of the U.S. should be instructed to collect in the several countries where they be, what may be useful to be introduced into the agriculture and manuf. of the U.S.—this might be more useful than their political speculations, or the treaties they have or may make. Mention that concluded in Spain—did not approve it—have been silent since its conclusion and why— a well intentioned man—[. . .]— advised me to publish something in America, as he was sure it was generally thought there I had been recalled. A long time since I have so much dwelt on such subjects—have divorced with public affairs since leaving Spain)—have not seen our 3. commissioners (for 5. or 6. years back—it seems to me "we have done these things &c." The pleasure I expect in talking over with him past scenes. The pain of appearing in some degree a stranger to my country by my long absence—my love not diminished). My fixed intention to embark in the spring—but wish him to [send] a line or two.

FC (DLC: Short Papers); entirely in Short's hand; part of an epistolary record by Short recording his letters to TJ and others from 26 Dec. 1797 to 9 Oct. 1798, written on a sheet folded to make a notebook of eight narrow pages; endorsement by Short, in margin at head of text, indicating that this letter was answered. Enclosures: (1) William Short to Peyton Short, 26 Dec. 1797, concerning the delay of his planned departure from Europe, the state of correspondence between them, and his desire for information about his western lands (MS in same; consists of a summary written in same epistolary record as the letter above). (2) Charles Louis Clérisseau to TJ, 23 May

1797. (3) Charles de Pougens to TJ, recorded in SJL as written on 14 Dec. 1797 and received from Paris on 30 Mch. 1798, but not found. Recorded in SJL as received from La Roche-Guyon on 30 Mch. 1798.

DEATH OF AN OLD LADY: the recent decease of Madame d'Enville. Her daughter-in-law and Short's love interest, the Duchesse Alexandrine de La Rochefoucauld, WAS THE YOUNG ONE to whom TJ had also sent regards in his letter to Short of 30 June 1797 (Shackelford, *Jefferson's Adoptive Son*, 129).

S. OF S.: secretary of state. MR. R.: Edmund Randolph.

From George Jefferson

DEAR SIR   Richmond Decr. 30th. 1797.

I have to acknowledge the receipt of your letter of the 21st. instant enclosing Mr. John Barnes's draft on Mr. Joseph Boyce at three days sight for $200., which is accepted, and which shall be applied as you direct.

In making this first acknowledgment Sir, I cannot refrain from making another—I cannot refrain from endeavouring to convey to you by words some faint idea of the obligations I feel myself under to you; and that, not on my own account alone. In doing this I find myself much at a loss; for it has been but seldom that my gratitude has had cause of excitement: when it has, I have ever been desirous to evince by other means than words, my sense of the obligation—but to you at present, I have no other mode—indeed perhaps I never shall; for even admitting I may be more attentive to the business which your extreme goodness prompts you to put into my hands, than ever any one was to that of another, I shall only be performing a duty, for which *I am hired*.

In the performance of that duty though, to you at least, I must be bold to say, I will never be deficient.

With this resolution, and a determination to seize with avidity any opportunity of serving you which may ever present itself to my poor ability, I must endeavour to be content.

But I am forgetting myself—my great desire to extricate myself in some small degree from the debt of gratitude I owe you, induces me to make promises which I can never be called upon to fulfil.

I ought to reflect too that those who take most pleasure in conferring favors, are least desirous of receiving promises of a return. I will therefore only add that I am with the utmost sincerity, Your truly devoted friend & servt.   GEO. JEFFERSON

For the future government of your friend Mr. Barnes I will inform you, that Mr. Boyce *to my knowledge* is far from being punctual; and in my opinion, is not to be relied upon in any respect.   G.J.

RC (MHi); addressed: "Thomas Jefferson esquire Philadelphia"; franked, stamped, and postmarked; endorsed by TJ as received 6 Jan. 1798 and so recorded in SJL.

TJ's LETTER OF THE 21ST. Dec. 1797 is recorded in SJL but has not been found.

To John Gibson

DEAR SIR   Philadelphia Dec. 31. 97

I took the liberty the last summer of writing to you from hence making some enquiries on the subject of Logan's speech and the murder of his family, and you were kind enough in your answer, among other things, to correct the title of Cresap, who is said to have headed the party by observing that he was a Captain and not a Colonel. I troubled you with a second letter asking if you could explain to me how Logan came to call him Colonel. If you have favored me with an answer to this, it has miscarried. I therefore trouble you again on the subject, and as the transaction must have been familiar to you, I will ask the favor of you to give me the names and residence of any persons now living who you [. . .] were of Cresap's party, or who can prove his participation in this [. . .] [either] by direct evidence or from circumstances, or who can otherwise throw light on the fact. A Mr. Martin of Baltimore has questioned the whole transaction, suggesting Logan's speech to be not genuine, and denying that either Colo. or Capt. Cresap had any hand in the murder of his family. I do not intend to enter into any newspaper contest with Mr. Martin; but in the first republication of the Notes on Virginia to correct the statement where it is wrong and support it where it is right. My distance from the place where witnesses of the transaction reside is so great that it will be a lengthy and imperfect operation in my hands. Any aid you can give me in it will be most thankfully recieved. I avail myself with great pleasure of every occasion of recalling myself to your recollection and of assuring you of the sentiments of esteem & attachment with which I am Dr. Sir Your most obedt. humble servt

Th: Jefferson

PrC (MHi); faded; at foot of text: "Genl. Gibson"; mistakenly recorded in SJL as a letter to George Gibson.

TJ's letter of LAST SUMMER was that of 31 May 1797, to which Gibson penned an ANSWER on 17 June.

To John Henry

Dear Sir   Philadelphia Dec. 31. 1797.

Mr. Tazewell has communicated to me the enquiries you have been so kind as to make relative to a passage in the Notes on Virginia, which has lately excited some newspaper publications. I feel with great sensibility the interest you take in this business and with pleasure go into explanations with one whose objects I know to be truth and justice alone. Had Mr. Martin thought proper to suggest to me that doubts might be entertained of the transaction respecting Logan, as stated in the Notes on Virginia, and to enquire on what grounds that statement was founded, I should have felt myself obliged by the enquiry, have informed him candidly of the grounds, and cordially have co-operated in every means of investigating the fact, and correcting whatsoever in it should be found to have been erroneous. But he chose to step at once into the newspapers, and in his publications there, and the letters he wrote to me, adopted a style which forbade the respect of an answer. Sensible however that no act of his could absolve me from the justice due to others, as soon as I found that the story of Logan could be doubted, I determined to enquire into it as accurately as the testimony remaining after a lapse of twenty odd years would permit, and that the result should be made known[1] either in the first new edition which should be printed of the Notes on Virginia, or by publishing an Appendix. I thought that so far as that work had contributed to impeach the memory of Cresap, by handing on an erroneous charge, it was proper it should be made the vehicle of retribution. Not that I was at all the author of the injury. I had only concurred with thousands and thousands of others in believing a transaction on authority which merited respect. For the story of Logan is only repeated in the Notes on Virginia precisely as it had been current more than a dozen years before they were published. When Ld. Dunmore returned from the expedition against the Indians in 1774. he and his officers brought the speech of Logan, and related the circumstances of it. These were so affecting, and the speech itself so fine a morsel of eloquence that it became the theme of every conversation, in Williamsburg particularly, and generally indeed wheresoever any of the officers resided or resorted. I learned it in Williamsburg; I believe at Lord Dunmore's; and I find in my pocket book of that year (1774.) an entry of the narrative as taken from the mouth of some person whose name however is not noted, nor recollected, precisely in the words stated in the Notes on Virginia. The speech was published in the Virginia gazette of that time: (I have it myself in the volume of gazettes of that year:) and though it was the translation made by the common Interpreter, and[2] in a style by no means elegant, yet it was so admired,[3] that it flew thro' all the public papers of the continent, and thro' the magazines and other periodical publications of Great Britain; and those who were boys at that day will now attest that the speech of Logan used to be given them as a school-exercise for repetition. It was not till about 13. or 14. years after the newspaper publications that the Notes on Virginia were published in America. Combating in these the contumelious theory of certain European writers, whose celebrity gave currency and weight to their opinions, that our country from the combined effects of soil and climate, degenerated animal nature, in the general, and particularly the moral faculties of man, I considered the speech of Logan as an apt proof of the contrary, and used it as such: and I copied verbatim the narrative I had taken down in 1774. and the speech as it had been given us in a better translation by Ld. Dunmore. I knew nothing of the Cresaps, and could not possibly have a motive to do them an injury with design. I repeated what thousands had done before, on as good authority as we have for most of the facts we learn through life, and such as to this moment I have seen no reason to doubt. That any body questioned it, was never suspected by me till I saw the letter of Mr. Martin in the Baltimore paper. I endeavored then to recollect who among my cotemporaries, of the same circle of society, and consequently of the same recollections, might still be alive. Three and twenty years of death and dispersion had left very few. I remembered however that General Gibson was still living and knew that he had been the translater of the speech. I wrote to him immediately. He, in answer, declares to me that he was the very person sent by Ld. Dunmore to the Indian town, that after he had delivered his message there, Logan took him out to a neighboring wood, sat down with him, and rehearsing with tears the catastrophe of his family, gave him that speech for Ld. Dunmore; that he carried it to Ld. Dunmore, translated it for him, has turned to it in the Encyclopedia, as taken from the Notes on Virginia, and finds that it was his translation I had used, with only two or three verbal variations of no importance. These I suppose had arisen[4] in the course of successive copies. I cite General Gibson's letter by memory, not having it with me; but I am sure I cite it substantially right. It establishes unquestionably that the speech of Logan is genuine: and that being established, it is Logan himself who is author of all the important facts. 'Colo. Cresap, says he, in cold blood and unprovoked, murdered all the relations of Logan, not sparing even my women and children. There runs not a drop of my blood in the veins of any living creature.' The person, and the fact, in all it's material circumstances, are here given by Logan himself. Genl. Gibson indeed says that the title was mistaken: that Cresap was a Captain, and not a Colonel. This was Logan's mistake. He also observes that it was on a water of the Kanhaway,[5] and not on the Kanhaway itself that his family was killed. This is an error which has crept into the traditionary account: but surely of little moment in the moral view of the subject. The material question is Was Logan's family murdered, and by whom? That it was murdered, has not I believe been denied. That it was by one of the Cresaps, Logan affirms. This is a question which concerns the memories of Logan and Cresap; to the issue of which I am as indifferent as if I had never heard the name of either. I have begun and shall continue to enquire into the evidence, additional to Logan's, on which the fact was founded. Little indeed can now be heard of, and that little dispersed and distant. If it shall appear on enquiry that Logan has been wrong in charging Cresap with the murder of his family, I will do justice to the memory of Cresap, as far as I have contributed to the injury by[6] believing and repeating what others had believed and repeated before me. If on the other hand, I find that Logan was right in his charge, I will vindicate as far as my suffrage may go,[7] the truth of a Chief, whose talents and misfortunes have attached to him the respect and commiseration of the world.[8]

I have gone, my dear Sir, into this lengthy detail to satisfy a mind, in the candour and rectitude of which I have the highest confidence. So far as you may incline to use the communication for rectifying the judgments of those who are willing to see things truly as they are, you are free to use it. But I pray that no confidence which you may repose in any one may induce you to let it go out of your hands so as to get into a newspaper. Against a contest in that field I am entirely decided.   I feel extraordinary gratification indeed[9] in addressing this letter to you, with whom shades of difference in political sentiment have not prevented the interchange of good opinion, nor cut off the friendly offices of society and good correspondence. This political tolerance is the more valued by me who consider social harmony as the first of human felicities, and the happiest moments those which are given to the effusions of the heart. Accept them sincerely, I pray you from one who has the honor to be,[10] with sentiments of high respect[11] and attachment Dear Sir Your most obedient & most humble servt Th: JEFFERSON

Dupl (DLC); entirely in TJ's hand; at foot of first page: "Governor Henry of Maryland"; below signature: "(Copy)"; with the most significant emendations recorded below. PrC of Dupl (DLC: TJ Papers, 102: 17533-5); lacks some changes to Dupl, as recorded in notes below. PrC of RC (same, 102: 17528-30); incomplete (see notes 10 and 11 below); significant variations and emendations are recorded below. Printed for private circulation in 1798, following Dupl (see below; Evans, No. 48485). Printed in *An Appendix to the Notes on Virginia Relative to the Murder of Logan's Family* (Philadelphia, 1800), following Dupl, with two significant variations recorded in notes 2 and 5 below (in *Notes*, ed. Peden, 226-9; Sowerby, No. 3225). Enclosed in TJ to Henry Tazewell, 31 Dec. 1797, and in a letter from Tazewell to Henry of 2 Jan. 1798 (see below).

Since TJ never replied to Luther Martin directly, the letter above was an important part of his response to Martin's attacks concerning the circumstances of Logan's lamentation. TJ soon had the letter set in type to facilitate his private distribution of it, paying Benjamin Franklin Bache $5.50 for the printing job on 12 Jan. 1798 (MB, II, 977; TJ to Samuel Brown, 25 Mch. 1798). According to an article in the *Richmond Examiner* that was reprinted by other newspapers during June 1799, TJ's injunctions against publication were taken seriously by those people who received the printed copies. However, prompted by an attack on TJ in the *Lynchburg Weekly Gazette*, the Richmond paper expressed dismay over "frequent and reproachful allusions to the *uncontradicted* libels of Luther Martin," and intimated that TJ's political cause would benefit if his friends could be armed with more ammunition from his own pen. Ac-

knowledging that the step was "contrary to the desire of the vice-president," the *Examiner* published a lengthy extract from one of the privately printed copies of the letter (*Greenleaf's New York Journal & Patriotic Register*, June 15, 1799). When TJ, abiding by his declared intention for handling any revision of the Logan affair, published his appendix to the *Notes on Virginia* in 1800, he included the letter to Henry as an explanatory introduction to his new evidence on the subject.

THE ENQUIRIES YOU HAVE BEEN SO KIND AS TO MAKE: Henry to Henry Tazewell, 24 Dec. 1797. In a letter of 13 Mch. 1798 written to Tazewell and passed on to TJ, Henry explained that soon after he assumed office as governor of Maryland, Martin's charges prompted him to stand up for TJ's character and abilities. He found, however, that in the local political climate his "acknowledgment of a personal Amity with such a Man as Mr. Jefferson" was thought so offensive that most of the legislators who had unanimously appointed him governor only days before would almost certainly have reversed themselves and removed him from office had it been in their power to do so. Acknowledging receipt of TJ's letter covered by one from Tazewell on 2 Jan. 1798, Henry asked Tazewell to convey his respects to TJ, noting: "As occasions offer I make use of his letter and shall continue to do so. He may rest assured that it shall not go out of my hands" (DLC; endorsed by Tazewell and TJ).

If Logan's declaration BECAME THE THEME OF EVERY CONVERSATION, it likely did so early in 1775, when Madison took it down from an unidentified source and sent it to William Bradford of Philadelphia, through whom it was quickly published in the *Pennsylvania Journal* and subsequently elsewhere (Madison, *Papers*, I, 136-8). Reports from the frontier published in Virginia in 1774 had described Michael Cresap as threatening to kill any Indians he encountered on the Ohio River and as "the Perpetrator of the first Offence" that caused events to spiral out of control. No doubt contributing to later confusion, one account called him a colonel and another mistakenly named him as a leader of the killers at Yellow Creek, where Logan's kin were slain (*Virginia Gazette*, Purdie & Dixon, 2 June 1774, Rind, 14 July 1774).

The version of the speech that Madison conveyed to Bradford differed in minor aspects from the one TJ recorded in his POCKET BOOK in 1775 (MB, I, 385-6). Logan's SPEECH WAS PUBLISHED IN THE VIRGINIA GAZETTE of Dixon and Hunter on 4 Feb. 1775, differing somewhat in its phrasing but containing essentially the same sentences in the same order, and with much of the same wording, as Madison's text and the version in TJ's memoranda.

LETTER OF MR. MARTIN IN THE BALTIMORE PAPER: to James Fennell; see TJ to John Gibson, 31 May 1797.

I WROTE TO HIM IMMEDIATELY: TJ to John Gibson, 31 May 1797, to which Gibson wrote an ANSWER on 17 June 1797.

MURDERED ALL THE RELATIONS OF LOGAN: in the three versions from 1775—Madison's, TJ's, and that in the *Virginia Gazette*—Logan said that Cresap had "cut off" the members of his family, whereas in the *Notes on Virginia* TJ employed the less ambiguous term "murdered" (*Notes*, ed. Peden, 63).

[1] Word interlined in place of "publick." Emendation not in PrCs.
[2] Preceding ten words lacking in *Appendix*.
[3] Preceding five words not in PrC of RC.
[4] PrC of RC: "happened."
[5] *Appendix*: "on the Ohio."
[6] Preceding five words interlined in place of "concurred in." Emendation not in PrCs.
[7] Word interlined in place of "weigh." Emendation not in PrCs.
[8] Here in PrC of RC TJ drew a dash and continued the paragraph.
[9] Word interlined; emendation not in PrCs.
[10] Preceding five words lacking in PrC of RC.
[11] Text of PrC of RC ends here.

To Henry Tazewell

TH:J. TO MR. TAZEWELL   Dec. 31. 97.

I found that my statement would be too long to give you the trouble of copying in the form of a narrative from yourself as had been at first proposed. I therefore wrote it in a letter directly to Mr. Henry himself. Indeed I thought it a proper respect for the candid views with which he seemed to ask explanations. While it is in your hands make what use of it you judge expedient by permitting it's perusal by Mr. Blount, Mr. Beckley and any others you think proper. When you forward it, be so good as to put a wafer in it, and inclose it in your letter. Health and happiness. Adieu.

RC (ViU); addressed: "Mr. Tazewell at mr Beckley's Chesnut street." Enclosure: TJ to John Henry, 31 Dec. 1797.

Design for Chimney and Flues

[1797]

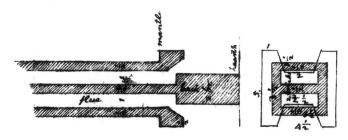

the base of the chimney is $6\frac{1}{2}$ bricks wide and 5. deep
the hearth is 4. br. wide in front, 2. bricks wide in back, & $1\frac{1}{2}$ brick deep
the back 2. bricks thick.
the opening of the chimney 32. Inches high.

the flues are each 1. brick by $2\frac{1}{2}$
the external of the flues is $3\frac{1}{2}$ bricks square

all the figures express measures in bricks.

MS (DLC); entirely in TJ's hand; undated, being assigned on the basis of an endorsement on verso in an unidentified hand: "Plan of Rumford Chimney 1797" (and see below). See Nichols, *Architectural Drawings*, No. 434.

Although an American edition of the *Essays* of Count Rumford (Benjamin Thompson), which included descriptions of shallow fireplaces similar to those depicted by TJ above, was not published until 1798, remodeling notes for Monticello that TJ evidently began in November 1796 contained drawings and dimensions for "Count Rumford's fire places in the square rooms" (remodeling notebook in MHi, No. 149b in Kimball, *Jefferson, Architect*, 162; Nichols, *Architectural Drawings*, No. 147b; see also Sowerby, No. 1182). A letter from TJ to Wilson Cary Nicholas on 2 May 1799 included diagrams and specifications of Rumford-style fireplaces.

Notes on John Jay's Mission to Great Britain

[1797 or after]

1794. Apr. 19. Commn. of Envoy Extr. to his Britannic majesty to John Jay. To hold the *said office* during pleasure.
May. 5. letter from the Pres. to the King
6. do. to the Queen.

Full powers concerning 1. inexecution or infraction of the
Armistice of Jan. 20. 83. or
treaty of Sep. 3. 83.

2. Instructions to British ships of
war &c of June 8. 93. and Nov.
6. 93, and Jan. 8. 94. Compensation &c

3. General commerce

3. full powers, for each of the above objects separately

Instructions to Mr. Jay.

Sir.   Philadelphia May 6. 1794.

The mission upon which you are about to enter as envoy extraordinary to the court of London has been dictated by considerations of an
interesting and pressing nature. You will doubtless avail yourself of
these to convince Mr. Pinckney our minister in ordinary there of the
necessity of this measure and will thus prevent any wound to his sensibility. He may be assured that it is the impression which will naturally
accompany this demonstration of the public sentiment, and not the
smallest abatement of confidence in him which has recommended a
special appointment, nor will any of his usual functions be suspended
except so far as they may be embraced in the present commission. It
would be unnecessary to add, but for the sake of manifesting this fact
and removing difficulties which may arise in your own breast that you
will communicate with him without reserve. §. A full persuasion is
entertained that throughout the whole negociation, you will make the
following it's general objects. To keep alive in the mind of the Brit.
minister that opinion which the solemnity of a special mission must
naturally inspire of the strong agitations excited in the people of the
US. by the disturbed condition of things between them and Gr. Br. To
repel war, for which we are not disposed, and unto which the necessity
of vindicating our honor and our property may, but can alone drive us.
To prevent the Br. Ministry, should they be resolved on war from carrying with them the British nation and at the same time to assert with
dignity and firmness our rights and our title to reparation for past injuries. §. One of the causes of your mission being the vexations and spoliations committed on our commerce by the authority of instructions
from the British Govmt. you will receive from the Secy. of state the
following documents viz. The instructions of the 8th. June 93. 6. Nov.
93. and 8. Jany. 94. The Secy. of state's letter to Mr. Pinckney, on the
7. Sep. 93. Mr. Hammond's letter to the Secy. of state on the 12th.
Sep. 93. Mr. Pinckney's note and memorial to Ld. Grenville, Mr.

Hamm.'s 2d letter to the Sec. of state 11. Apr. 94. The Sec. of state's answer on the 1st. instant. A list and sketch of the cases upon which complaints have been made to our government and the instructions given to N. C. Higginson who has been lately sent as agent to the Brit. islands in the W. Indies. §. These several papers develope the source of our discontent on this head, the representations which have been offered, the answers which have been rendered, and the situation of the business at this moment. §. You will perceive that one of the principles upon which compensation is demanded for the injuries under the instructions of 8. Jun. 93. is, that provisions, except in the instance of a seige blockade or investment are not to be ranked among contraband. To a country remote as the US. are from Europe and it's troubles it will be of infinite advantage, to obtain the establishment of this doctrine. §. Upon the instructions of 6. Nov. 93. Mr. Pinckney has made a representation, and perhaps a Memorial to Ld. Grenville, both of which you will procure from Mr. Pinckney. The matter of these instructions fills up the measure of depredation. They were unknown publicly in Engld. until the 26th. Dec. 93. There is good reason to suppose that they were communicated to the ships of war before they were published, and that in consequence of a private notification of them, a considerable number of new privateers were fitted out. The terms 'legal adjudication' in spite of the explanation on the 8. Jany. 94. was most probably intended to be construed away or not according to events, and many vessels have been condemned under them. §. Compensation for all the injuries sustained and captures will be strenuously pressed by you. The documents which the agent in the W. Indies is directed to transmit to London will place these matters in the proper legal train to be heard on appeal. It cannot be doubted that the Brit. ministry will insist that before we complain to them, their tribunals in the last resort must have refused justice. This is true in general. But peculiarities distinguish the present from past cases. Where the error complained of consists solely in the misapplication of the law it may be corrected by a superior court. But where the error consists in the law itself it can be corrected only by the law maker, who in this instance was the king, or it must be compensated by the government. The principle therefore may be discussed and settled without delay, and even if you should be told to wait until the result of the appeals shall appear it may be safely said to be almost certain that some one judgment in the W. Indies will be confirmed, and this will be sufficient to bring the
[*Page 2:*]
principle in question with the British ministry. §. Should the principle be adjusted as we wish and have a right to expect, it may be adviseable

to employ some person to examine the proper office in London for such vessels as may have been originally tried or appealed upon and finally condemned. You will also reserve an opportunity for new claims of which we may all be ignorant for some time to come. And if you should be compelled to leave the business in it's legal course you are at liberty to procure professional aid at the expence of the US. § Whenever matters shall be brought to such a point as that nothing remains for settlement but the items of compensation, this may be entrusted to any skilful and confidential person whom you may appoint. §. You will mention with due stress the general irritation of the US. at the vexations, spoliations, captures &c. And being on the field of negociation you will be more able to judge than can be prescribed now, how far you may state the difficulty which may occur in restraining the violence of some of our exasperated citizens. §. If the Brit. ministry should hint at any supposed predilection in the US. for the French nation as warranting the whole or any part of these instructions, you will stop the progress of this subject as being irrelevant to the question in hand. It is a circumstance which the British nation have no right to object to us, because we are free in our affections, and independant in our government. But it may be safely answered upon the authority of the correspondence between the Secy. of state and Mr. Hammond that our neutrality has been scrupulously

II.   observed. §. 2. A 2d cause of your mission, but not inferior in dignity to the preceding, though subsequent in order is to draw to a conclusion all points of difference between the US. and Gr. Br. concerning the treaty of peace. §. You will therefore be furnished with copies of the negociation upon the inexecution and infractions of that treaty and will resume that business. Except in this negociation you have been personally conversant with the whole of the transactions connected with the treaty of peace. You were a minister at it's formation, the Secy. of foreign affairs when the sentiments of the Congress under the Confedn. were announced through your office and as chief justice you have been witness to what has passed in our courts, and know the real state of our laws with respect to British debts. It will be superfluous therefore to add more to you than to express a wish that these debts and the interest claimed upon them and all things relating to them be put out right in a diplomatic discussion, as being certainly of a judicial nature, to be decided by our courts. And if this cannot be accomplished that you support the doctrines of government with arguments proper for the occasion, and with that attention to your former public opinions which self respect will justify, without relaxing the pretensions which have been hitherto maintained. §. In this negociation as to the treaty of peace we have been amused by transferring the discussions concerning it's inexecution and infractions from one side of the Atlantic to another. In the meantime one of the consequences of holding the posts has been much bloodshed on our frontiers by the Indians and much expence. The British government having denied &c [as in Callender's Hist. US. for 1796. page 173. l. 8. to l. 23. as corrected in my copy,] the words 'interfered with by the other.' §. It may be observed here as comprehending both of the foregoing points that the US. testify their sincere love of peace, by being nearly in a state of war, and yet anxious to obviate absolute war by friendly advances, and if the desire of G.B. to be in harmony with the US. be equally sincere she will readily discover what kind of sensations will at length arise when their trade is plundered, their resources wasted in an Indian war, many of their citizens exposed to the cruelties of the savages, their rights by treaty denied, and those of Gr. Br. enforced in our courts. But you will consider the inexecution and infraction of the treaty as standing on distinct grounds from the vexations and spoliations, so that no adjustment of the former is to be influenced by the latter. §. 3. It is referred to your discretion whether in case the two III. preceding points should be so accomodated as to promise the continuance of tranquility between the US. and G.B. the subject of a Commerical treaty may not be listened to by you, or even broken to the British ministry. If it should, let these be the general objects. 1. Reciprocity in navigation &c [as in Callender 174. l. 6. to 175. 26. to the words 'beyond 15. years' as corrected in my copy.]¹ §. 4. This enumeration presents generally the objects which it is desireable to comprize in a commercial treaty; not that it is expected that one can be effected with so great a latitude of advantages. §. If to the actual footing of our commerce and navigation in the Brit. European dominions, could be added the privilege of carrying directly from the US. to the Brit. W.I. in our own bottoms generally, or of certain defined burthens, the articles which by the act of parl. 28. G. 3. c. 6. may be carried thither in Brit. bottoms and of bringing from thence directly to the US. in our bottoms of like discription the articles which, by the same act may be brought from thence to the US. in Brit. bottoms, this would afford an acceptable basis of treaty for a term not exceeding 15. years, and it would be adviseable to conclude a treaty on that basis. But such a treaty instead of the usual clause concerning ratification must contain the following. 'This treaty shall be obligatory' &c [as in Callender pa. 176. l. 16. to line 30. 'a formal conclusion' then 'Some of the other points' &c as in Callendar 177. l. 3. to l. 19. 'valuable ingredient' then 'you will have no difficulty' &c as in Callender 178. l. 18. to 179 l. 7. 'fit for enquiry.' then 'Such are the outlines' &c as in Callender 180. l. 33. to 181. l. 16. 'foregoing prohibition' as corrected in my copy.]² §. Besides the papers and docu-

ments mentioned in the former parts of these instructions you have recieved your commision as Envoy Extraordy., letters of credence to the
K. and Q. of Engld. the latter of which being without superscription
you will address as may appear proper and deliver or not as you find to
be right on such occasions: 4 sets of powers, one general, comprehending all the points to be negociated with G.B. the other 3 special for each
separate point in order that you may be prepared to exhibit your authority altogether or by detachment as may be most convenient. Copies of
Ld. Dorchester's speech to the Indns. the authenticity of which, tho not
absolutely ascertained is believed, and of certain affidavits respecting
the Brit. interference with our Indians—and a cypher. §. You are too
well acquainted with the nature of the great functions which you are
called to exercise to render it necessary for me to add the earnest wish
of the Pres. of the US. that your communications to the Secy. of state
should be frequent and full and that you should correspond with our
ministers abroad upon any interesting occasion which may demand it.
For the latter of these purposes you will avail yourself of Mr. Pinckney's
cyphers. §. Your expences will be paid together with the allowance of
1350.D. per annum for a Secretary. §. On your return you will be
pleased to deliver into the Secy. of State's office such papers as you may
possess of importance sufficient to be filed there, and will prepare a
general report of all your transactions. §. Not doubting that you will
execute this trust in a manner honorable to yourself and salutary to the
US. I beg leave to offer you my sincere wishes for your health and safe
return. Edmund Randolph. Secy. of state.

1794.   May 27. E.R. to J. Jay. A letter of 4. pages. Nothing interesting
except that Hammd. seems catching at
materials for a manifesto, as if he foresaw
a rupture, and this paragraph 'We take
for granted that the nature of the subject,
the opinions expressed to you by the
Presidt. the instructions which were delivered to you and indeed your own judgment and inclination rendered it unnecessary to use any very pointed prohibition
of a surrender of the posts or any part of
our territory to G.B. upon any consideration. The interesting magnitude of the
business will therefore be my apology for
mentioning the decided and irrevocable
sense of the Presidt. relative to this affair.'

May. 28.	do. to do.	Covering documents.
29.	do. to do.	do.
June. 8.	do. to do.	Documents on spoliations.
9.	do. to do.	do.

'almouth. June 9. J. Jay to E.R. That he arrived the day before. Had immediately notified Ld. Grenville and Mr. Pinckney. Received Aug. 16.

London. June 23. do. to do. Arrived here 15th. Received by Ld. Grenville the 18th. Another interview the 20th. The topics generally touched on. Friendly appearances. Wishes no irritating news from America. Does not regard preparations for war of that nature. They ought to go on even in state of peace. Received Aug. 2.

26. do. to do. The minister has appointed tomorrow for conference. Appearances continue favorable. Received Aug. 28.

[Page 3:]

1794. July 6. J. Jay to E.R. (Received Sep. 20.) States conference of June 27. still of a general nature. Ld. Grenville had seen none of the cases of spoliations. Jay promised to procure some. Dr. Nicholl's opinion that the Admiralty &c. would maintain the principle that where France had not permitted a trade to her islands before the war, and only opened her ports during the war, as an expedient to protect their property against Brit.[3] captors, that neutral nations had no right to afford that occasional protection. That Gr. Br. acted on this principle in the war before last, but not in the last because France opened her colonial ports before the commencement of hostilities. She did not do this before the present hostilities. Ld. Dorchester's speech not defended by any body.

July 9. E.R. to J. Jay. To explain complaint of Hammd. and Govr. of Bermuda, about a vessel sent out by Fauchet during embargo under

		pretence of carrying dispatches (a like indulgence having been allowed Cong. ministers) and captured with 150. barrels powder on board.
July 9.	J. Jay to E.R.	Received Sep. 20. Nothing material.
July 10.	E.R. to J. Jay.	Complains of Mr. Ham.'s irascible disposition.
July 12.	J. Jay to E.R.	Agreed to forbid hostilities on our frontier, and keep things in statu quo.
16.	do. to do.	Received Sep. 19. Same subject.
18.	E.R. to J. Jay.	Sends more spoliation cases.
30.	J. Jay to E.R.	Received Oct. 7. Nothing done yet.
30.	E.R. to J. Jay.	On the reports that the British aid the Indians.
31.	J. Jay to E.R.	Received Oct. 7. Has had conference this morning on subject of spoliations.
Aug. 2.	do. to do.	Received Oct. 7. Ld. Grenville's answer giving expectation of compensation, distant but ultimate.
July 30.		His memorial to Ld. Grenville on spoliations and impressment of our seamen.
Aug. 1.		Ld. Grenv.'s answer. In general agreeing to do justice on both points.
8.	Jay to E.R.	Received Oct. 13. Hopes in a fortnight to give him agreeable details.
9.	do. to do.	Received Oct. 13. Incloses order of king and council of Aug. 6. relative to appeals.
11.	E.R. to Jay.	Spoliations. Pensva. insurrection. Richmond expedition against a vessel arming in Jas. river.
15.	do. to do.	Spoliation.
18.	do. to do.	Hammond's letters seem to admit Dorchester's speech genuine. Affair of fort Recovery.
21.	Jay to E.R.	Received Oct. 11. We are endeavoring to mature and digest a final settlement.
23.	do. to do.	He heard yesterday that Mr. Monroe had arrived at Paris.
30.	E.R. to Jay.	Complaints of Simcoe's proceedings, and of Hamd. having intermitted visits to the Pres. 2. months and gone to N.Y. without taking leave.

Sep. 5. do. to do. Western insurrection. Affair of Sodus.

12. do. to do. do. Ld. Dorchester and Simcoe.

13. Jay to E.R. Received Nov. 11. States conference. The carrying away negroes justified by Ld. G. On this could not agree. As to 1st. violation of treaty, Ld. G. insists the treaty not conclusive till *exchange* of ratifications, which was May. 84. but before this, states had past laws violating it. In short he convinced Mr. Jay that his construction was right. Proceeded then to try reciprocal concessions. After conference he sends to Ld. G. a project of a treaty which in fact was the basis of the treaty

see Jay's projet pretty fully pa. 4. [4]

which took place, containing almost every proposition we have complained of except the navigation of the Missisipi except also the renunciation of free bottom free goods, and contraband[5] and no provision for our sailors. It appears then that the restriction on cotton of US. moved from Jay himself. [6]

see this pretty fully pa. 4. [7]

Ld. Grenv.'s modifications of Jay's projet dated Aug. 30. It adds stipulation for Indns. to pass freely, and duty free. A curtail of boundary in our N. Western corner. Navigation of Missisipi. It is remarkeable he omits Jay's proposition that in case of war between Gr. B. and US. neither shall arm privateers against the other.

see his commercial projet pretty fully. pa. 4. [8]

His projet of treaty of commerce. He reduces Jay's 100. ton vessels for W.I. to 70. ton.

see these remarks more fully pa. 5. [9]

Jay's remarks to Ld. Grenville. He mentions a fact, that at the treaty of peace the Amer. minister offered the Brit. minister his choice of 2 lines, from Connecticut river at the 45th. degree along that degree to the Missisipi, or the line which was established. The Brit. minister chose the latter. He makes several proper re-

see these Notes pa. 5. No.
1. to 18.[11]

see these observations
Sep. 8. pa. 5.[13]

marks on Ld. G.'s projet, in subsequent Notes he[10] adds 'there should be an article against the impressment of each other's people.'

Ld. G.'s Observations.[12] He adds the Contraband and corn article, which he says was 'to meet the object which was this morning suggested in conversation.' He says also that in conformity to what was mentioned by Mr. Jay he has used the words of *Vattel*. As to the article about impressment he says 'he sees no reason whatever to object to this article.'

Sep. 14.	Jay to E.R.	Received Nov. 11.
17.	E.R. to Jay.	
18.	Jay to E.R.	Received Nov. 26.
20.	E.R. to Jay.	
Oct. 2.	Jay to E.R.	Received Nov. 29.
11.	E.R. to Jay.	
20.	do. to do.	
29.	do. to do.	

Nothing important.

29.   Jay to E.R.   Received Jan. 10. 95. That they have agreed to incorporate the 2. projets viz, settlement and commercial. Propositions for new line in N.W. corner suspended. Survey to be made. Foreign tonnage objected. His letter of Oct. 27. to Ld. G. expressing sense of Pres. on his gracious reception. Mr. Jay undertook the incorporation of the 2. projets.

Nov. 3.   E.R. to J. Jay.   On evidence of British debts in Virginia.
7.   do. to do.   Congress meeting.
8.   do. to do.   Spoliations.
* 19.   Jay to E.R.   Incloses treaty. He thinks the 3d. article favorable. Difficult to obtain. The 6th. he says was a sine qua non. It concerns Brit. debts. He proposed it in his original projet. The 10th. art. (against sequestering debts and property in funds) he thinks

* It is remarkeable that while in the copies of all the other letters from Jay to E.R. sent to the Senate, the date of their receipt [is no]ted, that circumstance [is] omitted as to this one.

will be useful, because the credit of some of the states has suffered from their being favorable to sequestration.

see this lettre of Nov. 19. fully pa. 6. 7.

The 12th. art. is of short duration, but if we meet the disposition of this country to good humour and cordiality he is much inclined to believe it will be renewed. The 13th. art. (E. Indies) he says is a manifestation and proof of good will towards us. 18th. respecting contraband and provisions. He says that Britain should not admit principles which would impeach the propriety of her conduct in seizing provisions bound to France, and enemy's property on board neutral vessels does not appear to me extraordinary. The 19th. about privateers taken from treaty between Gr. Br. and France, and that for treating natives commanding privateers as pirates was partly taken from ours with Holland. 'The prohibition to sell prizes in our ports had it's use, and we have no reason to regret that your instructions to me admitted of it.'

General remark that his letters are full of encomiums on the candour, liberality, good humour, cordiality, conciliatory disposition, friendliness, delicacy &c &c &c of the government of Engld. and particularly Ld. G.

[*Page 4:*]

Particulars of the report in the letter of Sep. 13. more minutely stated than in the preceding pages for beginning of it see pa. 6.[14]

Jay's original projet. Preamble agrees to merge all complaints and claims in the following articles. Confirmation of treaty of peace. St. Croix to be settled by Commrs. Missisipi to be surveyed and closing line established by Commrs. *His Majesty* shall withdraw troops from posts of US. by June 1. 95. Settlers and traders within the precincts to enjoy their property, and become citizens of the US. or sell and remove within 2 years. Spoliations to be compensated by government where cannot be done in judiciary way. And whereas British debts have *probably* been prejudiced and rendered more precarious by the *lawful imped-*

iments which after the peace *did* for some time exist, agreed that US. shall make reparation where cannot be obtained judicially. And for this purpose Commrs. to settle. US. may carry in vessels of 100 tuns or under whatever Brit. vessels may carry from US. paying there such tonnage as Brit. pay in US. and same duties as Brit. vessels pay there. And may bring away from said islands all articles and on same duties which Brit. may. Provided they land in US. and no W. India productions or manufactures to be transported in American vessels either from Brit. islands or from US. to other parts of world; except rum made of molasses. All other Brit. ports (not within chartered companies) to be open to citizens of US. paying for their vessels and cargoes same duties as Brit. pay. Both on importation and exportation except a tonnage equivalent to the foreign tonnage of US. And reciprocally all the ports of US. without exception shall be open to British on same terms. The trade between US. and B.W. Indies to be considered as regulated by the preceding (12th.) article and therefore excluded from operation of the following articles all productions and manufactures of Brit. dominions or US. may be imported in vessels of either party paying equal and like duties. That these duties may be made reciprocal, additional articles shall be negociated and added to this convention as soon as may be. When either party is at war and the other at peace, prizes taken from the belligerent shall not be sold in ports of the neutral party. If war between G.B. and US. they shall not arm privateers against each other, and merchants have 9. months to withdraw, and not liable to capture on return. Brit. or Americans now holding lands in dominions of the other, shall continue to hold according to the nature and tenure of their estates and titles therein and may grant sell and devise as if they were natives, and neither they nor heirs &c so far as respects the lands or legal remedies incident thereto shall be regarded as aliens. Neither debts nor property in funds or banks of either party shall in event of war be sequestered or confiscated, except that during the war payment may be suspended.

Ld. Grenv.'s projet. He says he proceeds on the foundation of Mr. Jay's, making occasional variations. 1. Troops from posts to be withdrawn by 1st. June 96. Settlers and traders within the precincts to enjoy property
1. and be protected *so long* as they think *proper* to remain and may with-
ˣ2 draw and sell lands &c. Shall allways be free to his ˣ*Maj.'s* subjects and
*3 **Indns. to Southward and Westward* of lakes to pass and repass with goods and to commerce within or without jurisdiction of posts as heretofore without hindrance from *officers* or citizens of US. The waters carrying places and roads adjacent to lakes or communicating with them shall be free to his Maj.'s subjects and Indns. for that purpose, and
4. no *duty* to be levied. Art. 2. The boundary of the St. Croix to be deter-

mined by Commrs. in *London*. The boundary towards the Missisipi to 5.
run from lake Huron to the Northward of the isle Philippeaux in L.
Superior, thence to the bottom of West bay in the said lake thence due
W. to the river of the Red lake or Eastern branch of the Missisipi and
down it to the Main river Misipi. [or 2dly. through L. Superior and
from thence to the water communication between the said lake of the
Woods, to the point where the said water communication shall be inter-
sected by a line running due N. from the mouth of the river St. Croix
which falls into the Misipi. below the falls of St. Anthony, and that the
boundary line shall proceed from such point of intersection in a due
Southwardly course along the said line to the Misipi.] and that as well
on the said branch [or 2dly. the said water communication] as on the
Misipi. where it *bounds the territory of the US.* the navigation shall be 6
free to both parties and his *Maj.'s subjects* shall *always* be admitted to 7
enter freely into the bays ports and creeks on the *American* side and to
land and dwell for commerce, and ratifies and confirms this boundary
and the others in treaty of peace. Art. 3. Alledged that by operation of
lawful impediments debts are impaired in their security and *value* and 8
that relief cannot be obtained judicially, where relief cannot be had for
whatever reason, the U.S. will satisfy, and for this purpose commrs. &c 9.
and the Commrs. to take into consideration and to determine all claims
on account of principal or interest in respect of the said debts and to
decide respecting the same according to the merits of the several cases
[as in the actual treaty to the words 'see cause to require.'] Then fixes
board to consist of 3 at least, viz 1 on each side and the 5th. 'the award
of the said commrs.' &c [as in Art. 6. of treaty to 'may be directed.'] Art.
4. Same as Art. 7 of treaty to the words 'Brit. govmt. to the said com-
plainants' then 'that for the purpose' &c as in same Art. of treaty substantially to the words 'taken by vessels originally armed in ports of the
said states' the *US*. will make full satisfaction for such loss or damage, 12
to be assertained by commrs. as before mentioned. Art. 5. With respect
to the Neutral commerce which one party may carry on with the *European* enemies of the other, the belligerent shall observe to the other the
principles which they observe towards the most favored neutral nation
of Europe. Art. 6. As in 17. of treaty omitting 'and if any property'
&c—to 'and it is agreed.' Art. 7. When one of the parties is at war and
the other at peace, the neutral shall not suffer prizes made on the other
to be brought into or sold in it's ports, and if brought the master and
crew and passengers shall be set at liberty and the prize to depart. Saving previous treaties; but in *all cases to which these do not apply* this
article to be in force, and neither party will make any future treaty in 15
derogation of this article. Art. 8. In substance as the 21st. of treaty,

except that Ld. G.'s does not make it *piracy*, but only says the transgressor shall be severely punished by laws 'to be provided.' Then it goes on substantially (but rather more in detail) as Art. 22. of treaty. Art. 9. Same as latter part of Art. 25. of treaty from the words 'Neither of the said parties shall permit' &c but instead of 'the party whose territorial &c—or merchant vessels' it is 'both parties shall employ their *united*

17. *force* to obtain reparation of the damage thereby occasioned.' Art. 10. Verbatim as had been proposed in Jay's projet [not fully copied above] to wit 'if it should unfortunately happen that a war should break out between G.B. and the U.S. all merchants and others residing in the 2 countries respectively shall be allowed 9. months to retire with their effects and shall be protected from capture in their way home. Provided always that this favor is not to extend to those who shall act contrary to the established laws. The treaty here varies remarkeably from Ld. G.'s projet. [15] And it is further agreed that neither *debts due* from *individuals* of the one nation, to individuals of the other, nor shares or monies which

18 they may have in the *public funds* or in the public or private banks &c exactly as Art. 10. of treaty. Art. 11. Same as Art. 9. of treaty and verbatim as in Jay's 1st. projet.

Ld. Grenv.'s COMMERCIAL PROJET. Art. 1. Precisely as Art. 14. of treaty except that after 'commerce and navigation' Ld. G. inserts 'and a free admission of all ships belonging to either party whether the same be ships of war or merchant vessels.' Art. 2. Same as Art. 16. of treaty except that Ld. Grenv. required that Consuls 'should be of the nation on whose behalf they are appointed and not otherwise' and had not the provision of the treaty for punishing or sending away a consul acting improperly. Art. 3. and 4. In substance as Art. 15. of treaty from beginning to 'any other foreign country' except Ld. G. proposed that they should pay same tonnage as natives. Art. 5. This article (instead of 'nor shall any prohibition &c—to all other nations') is in these words. 'No new prohibition shall be laid in any of the territories or dominions aforesaid, by one of the contracting parties on the importation of any article being of the growth produce or manufacture of the territories or dominions of the other, nor shall articles being of the growth produce or manufacture of any other country be prohibited to be imported into the dominions of one of the contracting parties by the vessels of the other, except such articles only as are now so prohibited.' Art. 6. Same as Art. 12. of treaty from beginning to 'reasonable seastores excepted.' Except some changes in the 1st. paragraph concerning our foreign tonnage duty, and in 3d paragraph, Ld. G. has it 'the US. will prohibit the carrying any W. India productions or manufactures' and the treaty has

it 'any molasses, sugar, coffee, cocoa or cotton.' The paragraph beginning 'Provided also' and ending 'or exported in American vessels' is not
in Ld. G.'s projet. Then it proceeds as in the Treaty 'it is agreed' &c to
'advantage and extension of commerce.' The rest of the paragraph in the
treaty 'and the said parties'—'inserted on those subjects.' is not in Ld.
G.'s projet. Art. 7. Answers to Art. 28. of treaty but is very different. It
is thus 'this treaty and all the matters therein contained except the 6th.
article shall continue to be in force for 12. years from the day of the
exchange of ratification. And if during the continuance of this treaty
there shall arise on either side any complaint of the infraction of any
article thereof, it is agreed that neither the whole treaty nor any article
thereof shall on that account be suspended until representation shall
have been made to the government by the minister of the party com-
plaining, and even if redress shall not then be obtained, 4. months notice
shall be given previous to such suspension.'
[*Page 5:*]
1794. Sep. 4. Jay's REMARKS on the 2d Art. of Ld. Grenv.'s projet respecting
the N. Western boundary. As to the 1st. reason urged that a
West line from the Lake of the Woods will pass above the
source of the Missipi., he observes that this is entirely unknown
and therefore proper to be examined by survey. As to the 2d.
reason, that the treaty of peace gave the navigation of the
Misipi. to both parties and shews an intention that each should
border on a navigable part. He sais 'a right freely to navigate a
bay, a straight, a sound or a river is perfect without, and does
not *necessarily* presuppose the dominion and property of lands
adjacent to it.' He argues that it was always known that the La.
of the Woods was so far North that a due W. line from that
would pass far above the falls of St. Anthony which interrupt
the *navigation* of the Misipi. So it was not intended the English
territory should come to a navigable part. How far navigable
above those falls is unknown. He then mentions the fact of the
2. lines before stated to have been offered to the British minister
and his choice of the Northern water line. So it was the navigation of that water line which was aimed to be kept uninterrupted, as it would have been had the 45th. degree been taken.
He adds that the stipulation for the navigation of the Misipi.
was an *after-thought* and gave occasion to a new and subsequent
article to wit the 8th. No connection was introduced between
that right and the boundaries, no facility stipulated for a communication between Canada and the navigable part of Misipi.

The 1st. line proposed by Ld. G. would include 35,575 square miles and the 2d. 32,400 besides the country between the Red-lake river and the Misipi.

Sep. 5. Ld. Grenv.'s Observations [more fully than the previous extracts]. The boundary in the treaty is a due West line from the *La. of the Woods* to the *Misipi*. That it shall strike the *Misipi.* is as much required as that it shall strike the *La. of the Wood*. However he agrees to the survey. [The true argument is this. The line required by treaty has 4. characteristics. 1. That it shall strike the *L. of the Woods*. 2. The *Misipi*. 3. Be *a line*, singular, not several lines. 4. *East and West*. All these are impossible. If an E. and W. line be proposed from the L. of the Woods and a meridian from that to the head of Misipi. or an E. and W. line from the head of the Misipi. and a meridian to the La. of the Woods, these will have but 2. of the characteristics, for there will be a N. and S. line and 2. lines. And in either way one of the parties will lose territory. Let *a line* then be run from the head of the *Misipi.* to the *La. of the woods*. This has 3. of the 4. characteristics, and divides diagonally the territory in dispute so as to give a part to each. This is my own thought, not suggested by either of these negociators.]

Mr. Jay's Notes on Ld. G.'s projet. 1. In what capacity are they so to remain? As Brit. subjects or Amer. citizens. If the first, a time to make their election should be assigned. 2. If his Maj.'s subjects are to pass into the Amer. territories for the purposes of Indn. trade, ought not Amer. citizens to be permitted to pass into his Maj.'s territories for the like purpose? If the Amer. Indns. are to have the privilege of trading with Canada, ought not the Canada Indns. to be privileged to trade with the US? 4. If goods for Indn. trade shall be introduced duty free by Brit. traders, how is the introduction of other goods with them to be prevented? And for this privilege, operating a loss to the Amer. revenue, what reciprocal benefit is to be allowed? 5. Why should the Commrs. for ascertaining the river St. Croix, meet and decide in London? Is it not probable that actual views and surveys, and the testimony and examination of witnesses on the spot will be necessary? 6. Why confine the mutual navigation of the Misipi. to where the same *bounds the territory of the US*? 7. Why should *perpetual* commercial privileges be granted to Gr. Br. on the *Misipi.* &c when she declines granting *perpetual* commercial privileges to the US. *anywhere*? 8. This preamble connected with the silence of the treaty as to the negroes carried away implies that the US. have been aggressors. It also unnecessarily impeaches their judicial proceedings. 9. On no principle ought more to be asked than that the US. indemnify creditors for losses and damages caused by the impediments mentioned. 10. The word *had* is not sufficiently definite, the object being not only sentence, decree or judgment but payment and satisfaction. 11. Sterling money fluctuates according to exchange. This should be *fixed*. 12. Why not place these captures on the footing with the others, and charge the US. only in cases where justice and complete compensation cannot be had from judicial proceedings. 13. Why provide only for neutral commerce with *European* enemies? The whole of this article is so indefinite as to be useless. 14. What are or shall be deemed *contraband* in the sense of this article? 15. As the US. have permitted the French to sell prizes in the US. should not the restriction not to do it in future commence at the expiration of the present war? 16. There should be an article against the impressment of each others people. 17. This United force should be confined to the *moment* of aggression. 18. The *confiscation* of debts &c. This Article should be in the *treaty of commerce*.

Sep. 6. He sais he waited on Ld. Grenv. Discussed these points. He promised to consider. Manifested every disposition to accomodate. 'We may not finally be able to agree. If we should not, it would in my opinion occasion *mutual* regret, for I do believe that the greater part of the Cabinet, and particularly Ld. G. are really disposed and desirous not only to settle all differences amicably, but also to establish permanent peace, good humor and friendship between the 2 countries.'

Sep. 8. Ld. Grenv.'s Observations, with 'a Note of 2. alterations in the Commercial projet in consequence of the conversation of yesterday.' 1. Add in the 1st. Art. after the words 'property thereof' these 'and such of them as shall continue to reside there for the purposes' &c as in Art. 2. of treaty to 'evacuation.' 2. 3. 4. Reserved for further examination. 5. The meeting of the Commrs. respecting the river St. Croix is proposed to be in London, because it is supposed that the great mass of evidence on the subject is here. A power may be given to them, either to direct a local survey, or to adjourn to America, but it seems very unlikely that this would become necessary. 6. No idea was entertained of confining the mutual navigation of the Misipi. to that part of the river where it bounds the territory of the US. That qualification was intended only to have reference to the free admission of Brit. merchants and ships into the bays ports and creeks of the US. on the Misipi., nor would it have been proposed at all to repeat in this article what is so distinctly stipulated in the treaty of peace respecting the free navigation of the Misipi., except for the purpose of expressly extending that stipulation to every part of the waters now proposed to form a part of the boundary. 7. The right of admission into ports &c for the purposes of trade and the general liberty of commerce spoken of in this article, are not considered as commercial privileges, such as are usually made the subject of temporary regulation by special treaties of commerce. Gr. Br. by no means declines to give the same rights permanently to America, as with respect to those parts of her dominions which are open to foreign commerce. These rights are indeed now generally acknoleged to be incident to a state of amity and good correspondence, and if it is proposed to particularize them as with respect to the Misipi., this is done only with the view of removing the possibility of such doubts as were formerly raised here upon the subject. 8. On the fullest reconsideration of this preamble Ld. G. sees no ground to think it liable to the objection made by Mr. Jay, particularly when compared with the preamble proposed for the 4th. art. The proceedings in both articles are grounded on the allegations of individuals. The truth of those allegations is referred to the decision of the Commrs. Ld. G.'s opinion with respect to the prior aggression of the US. as well as his reasons for that opinion are well known to Mr. Jay. But he has no wish to introduce into the proposed treaties any discussion of that point. He is therefore very ready to consider any form of words which Mr. Jay may suggest for those articles as better suited to the two objects to which they are directed. Those of justice to individuals, and conciliation between the governments, and this applies equally to the remarks No. 9. and 10. 11. The substitution of the word *specie* as suggested by Mr. Jay seems fully to meet the object here mentioned. 12. What Mr. Jay here desires was intended to be done, and was indeed concieved to be implied in the general words at the end of the article. But Ld. G. sees no objection to the insertion of express words for the purpose. 13. Ld. G. explained to Mr. Jay this morning the reason of the insertion of the word *European* in the place here referred to. The subject is connected with the larger consideration to which their conversation led, and from the further discussion of which Ld. Grenville is inclined to hope that mutual advantage may arise. Mr. Jay will observe that the subject to which his remark No. 15. applies is one instance among many which might be brought to shew that this article would not be inefficient. 14. To meet the object which was this morning suggested in conversation on this article Ld. G. would propose the adoption of the following additional article to come in immediately after the 8th. Ld. G. has in conformity to what was mentioned by Mr. Jay used the words of *Vattel*. 'In order to regulate what is in future to be esteemed contraband' &c as in 18. of treaty to end of paragraph 'to an enemy' except that the word 'horses' before 'horse furniture' in Ld. G.'s note is omitted in treaty.[16] 'And whereas corn grain or provisions can be considered as contraband in certain cases only, namely when there is an expectation of reducing the enemy by the want thereof it is agreed that in all such cases the said articles shall not be confiscated but that the captors or in their default the government' &c as in 2d. paragraph of 18th. art. to end of it 'such detention.' 15. It seems by no means unreasonable that the effect of this stipulation should be extended to the existing war, as a natural consequence of the good understanding to be established by this negociation, and by the removal of all existing differences. And it would tend to prevent so many occasions of acrimony and dispute on both sides that Ld. G. thinks it highly desireable to maintain this article in it's present form. 16. Ld. G. sees no reason whatever to object to this article. 17. This remark seems also perfectly just and will be best met by omitting the concluding part of this article. 18. 'Ld. G. rather thinks this Art. ought to be permanent for the mutual interest of both countries. But he is content to leave this point to the decision of Mr. Jay who is much too enlightened not to see the effect which a contrary conduct to that here prescribed must produce as with respect to America.' COMMERCIAL PROJET. Art. 2. Omit these words 'the same being of the nation on whose behalf they shall be so appointed and not otherwise' and insert in lieu thereof 'the same being first approved by the government of the country in which they shall be so appointed to reside.' 3d. The last sentence to run thus 'by which the vessels of the one party shall pay in the ports of the other any higher or other duties than shall be paid in similar circumstances by the vessels of the foreign nation the most favored in that respect, or any higher or other duties than shall be paid in similar cases by the vessels of the party itself into whose ports they shall come.'

Jay proceeds in his letter to E.R. [viz of Sep. 13. 94] 'thus Sir I have given you a very particular and correct account of the negociation. Many observations and explanatory remarks might be added. I might also inform you that I had strenuously urged the justice of compensation for the detention of the posts, and that I consider the privilege of trading to the W. Indies as providing for claims of that kind. On this privilege and the probability of it's being revived after the expiration of the term assigned for it's duration I could enlarge. But not necessary &c.

[*Page 6:*]

The following is the preceding part of the letter or report of Sep. 13. and ought to have come in between pa. 3. and 4.

After a few preliminary sentences in the letter, he states that a number of informal conversations took place &c. The enquiry naturally led to the fact which constituted the 1st. violation of the treaty of peace. The carrying away the negroes contrary to the 7th. Art. of the treaty of peace was insisted on as being the *first* aggression. It was answered this meant that would not carry away any *negroes or other property* of the Amer. inhabitants or in other words that the evacuation should be made without depredation. That no alteration in the actual state of property was intended to be operated. That every slave like every horse which escaped or strayed from within the Amer. lines, and came into possession of the British army, became by the laws and rights of war *British* property, and therefore ceasing to be *American* property, it's exportation was not inhibited. That to extend it to negroes who had come to them under the faith of proclamations, and to whom, according to promise, liberty had been given was to give it an *odious* construction contrary to the established rules for construing treaties. To this he replied the several considerations from a report he once made to Congress on this subject. That on this point the negociators could not agree. Then urged that from the documents recited and stated in Mr. Jefferson's letter to Mr. Hammond the posts were not evacuated within reasonable time, nor ever ordered to be evacuated. Answered the provisional articles were signed at Paris Nov. 30. 82. These were to constitute the treaty, but not till terms should be concluded between Gr. Br. and Fr. The treaty of peace was not concluded till Sep. 3. 83. Not ratified in Amer. till Jan. 14. 84. Ratification not received in Lond. till May 28. 84. nor exchanged till the end of that month. That according to the Laws of Nations treaties do not oblige the parties to begin to execute them till they have received their whole form, i.e. till ratification and exchange of ratifications. That therefore Gr. Br. was not obliged to give orders for evacuation till May 84. which could not arrive at Quebec till July 84. That therefore allegations of infraction prior to July 13. 84. are unfounded. That in the interval between the arrival and publication in America of the provisional articles and July 84. violations of the treaty had taken place in the US. That reason and the practice of nations warrant during a suspension of hostilities *only* such measures as result from a continuance of the *status quo*, until the final exchange of ratifications. That in opposition to this new legislative acts had passed in the interval, evidently calculated to be beforehanded with the treaty, and to prevent it's full operation in certain points when it should be ratified and take effect. That these acts were the first violations and justified detention of the posts till the injuries caused by their operation should be compensated. Jay admitted the proposition that Gr. Br. was not obliged to evacuate till ratifications exchanged and that certain legislative acts had passed inconsistent with the treaty: but that it does not thence naturally follow that those acts were without justice even as relative to the treaty, for precedent violations on the part of Gr. Br. would justify subsequent retaliation on the part of the US. Here again the affair of the negroes emerged and was insisted on and answered as before. He confesses that this answer made an impression on his mind and induced him to suspect that his former opinion on that head might not be well founded. They therefore abandoned the question of the 1st. aggression. After free conversations on various points and returning home he prepared the outlines for a convention and treaty of commerce and inclosed to Ld. Grenville. [To wit the same which are before stated pa. 4.[17] and called Jay's original projet. Note from the top of this page to this place being inserted at the head of pa. 4.[18] makes this abstract of the whole letter or report of Sep. 13. pretty complete and full.]

Jay's letter of Nov. 19. 'Sir. The long expected treaty accompanies this letter. A probability of soon concluding it has caused the packet to be detained more than a week. The difficulties which retarded it's accomplishment frequently had the appearance of being insurmountable. They have at last yielded to modifications of the articles, in which they existed and to that mutual disposition to agreement which reconciled Ld. G. and myself to an unusual degree of trouble and application. They who have levelled uneven grounds know how little of the work afterwards appears. § Since the building is finished it cannot be very important to describe the scaffolding or go into all the details which respected the business. Explanatory remarks on certain articles might be useful by casting light on governing principles, which in some instances are not so obvious as to be distinctly seen on the 1st. view. Feeling the want of leisure and relaxation, I cannot undertake it in this moment of haste. I must confine myself to a few cursory observations and hope allowances will be made for inaccuracies and omissions. My opinion of the treaty is apparent from my having signed it. I have no reason to believe or conjecture that one more favorable to us is attainable. Perhaps it is not very much to be regretted that all our differences are merged in this treaty, without having been decided. Disagreeable imputations are thereby avoided and the door of conciliation is fairly and widely opened by the *essential* justice done, and the conveniences granted to each other by the parties. The term limited for the evacuation of the posts could not be restricted to a more early day. That point has been pressed. The reasons which caused an inflexible adherence to that term I am persuaded were these. Viz. that the traders have spread thro' the Indn. nations goods to a great amount. That the returns for those goods cannot be drawn into Canada at an earlier period: that the impression which the surrender of all the posts to Amer. garrisons will make on the minds of the Indns. cannot be foreseen. On a former occasion it was intimated to them (not very delicately) that they had been forsaken and given up to the US. That the protection promised on our part, however sincere, and however in other respects competent, cannot entirely prevent those embarrasments which, without our fault, may be occasioned by the war. That for these reasons the traders ought to have time to conclude their adventures which were calculated on the existing state of things. They will afterwards calculate on the new state of things; but that in the mean time the care of government should not be withdrawn from them. §. The 3d. art. will I presume appear to you in a favorable light. A number of reasons which in my judgment are solid support it. I think they will on consideration become obvious. It was proposed and urged that the commercial intercourse opened by this article ought to be exempted from all duties whatever on either side. The inconveniences which we should experience from such a measure were stated and examined. It was finally agreed to subject it to native duties. In this compromise, which I consider as being exactly right, that difficulty terminated. But for this compromise the whole article would have failed and every expectation of an amicable settlement been frustrated. A continuance of trade with the Indns. was a decided ultimatum. Much time and paper and many conferences were employed in producing this article. That part of it which respects the ports and places on the Eastn. side of the Misipi. if considered in connection with the   article in the treaty of peace, and with the article in this treaty which directs a survey of that river to be made, will I think appear unexceptionable. § In discussing the question about the river St. Croix before the Commrs. I apprehend the old French claims will be revived. We must adhere to Mitchell's map. The V. President perfectly understands this business. § The 6th. art. was a *sine qua non*, and is intended as well as calculated to afford that justice and equity which judicial proceedings may on trial be found incapable of affording. That the Commrs. may do exactly what is right, they are to determine according to the merits of the several cases, having a due regard to all the circumstances and as justice and equity shall appear to them to require. §. It is very much to be regretted that a more summary method than the one indicated in the 7th. art. could not have been devised and agreed upon for settling the capture cases. Every other plan was perplexed with difficulties which frustrated it. Permit me to hint the expediency of aiding the claimants by employing a gentleman at the public expence to oversee and manage the causes of such of them as cannot conveniently have agents of their own here. And whether in some cases pecuniary assistance might not be proper. I do not consider myself at liberty to make such an appointment, nor to enter into any such pecuniary engagements. It would probably be more easy to find a proper person on your side of the water than on this. Here there are few fit for the business &c. [about 12. lines respecting an agent.]

You will find in the 8th. Art. a stipulation which in effect refers the manner of paying the Commrs. very much to our election. I prefer paying them *jointly*. The objection to it is that the English pay high. I have always doubted the policy of being *Penny wise*. §. The Ld. Chancellor has prepared an Art. respecting the mutual admission of evidence &c which we have not had time fully to consider and decide upon. It contains a clause to abolish *alienism* between the 2 countries. His Ldp.'s conduct and conversation indicate the most friendly disposition towards us. A copy of his article shall be sent, and I wish to recieve precise instructions on that head. §. The credit of some of the states having to my knolege suffered by appearances of their being favorable to the idea of sequestrating British debts on certain occasions, the 10th. art. will be useful. Persons wishing to invest their property in our funds and banks, have frequently applied to me to be informed whether they might do it without risk of confiscation or sequestration. My answer has been uniform, to wit, that in my opinion such measures would be improper, and therefore that in my opinion they would not be adopted. Some pressed me for assurances, but I have declined giving any. § The 12th. art. admitting our vessels of 70. tons and under into the British islands in the W. Indies, affords occasion for several explanatory remarks. It became connected with a proposed stipulation for the abolition of all alien duties of every kind between the 2 countries. This proposition was pressed but strong objections opposed my agreeing to it. A satisfactory statement of the negociation on this point would be prolix. At present I cannot form a very concise one, for that would not require less time. The selection and arrangement necessary in making abridgments cannot be hastily performed. The duration of this article is short, but if we meet the disposition of this country to good humor and cordiality I am much inclined to believe it will be renewed. The duration of the treaty is connected with the renewal of that article, and an opportunity will then offer for discussing and settling many important matters. § The article which opens the Brit. ports in the E. Indies to our vessels and cargoes needs no comment. It is a manifestation and proof of good will towards us. §. The questions about the cases in which alone provisions become contraband, and the question whether and how far neutral ships protect enemy's property have been the subjects of much trouble and many fruitless discussions. That Britain at this period and involved in war should not admit principles which would impeach the propriety of her conduct in seizing provisions bound to France, and enemy's property on board of neutral vessels does not appear to me extraordinary. The articles as they now stand secure compensation for seizures and leave us at liberty to decide whether they were made in such cases as to be warranted by the *existing* law of nations. As to the principles we contend for, you will find them saved in the conclusion of the 12th. article, from which it will appear that we still adhere to them.

[*Page 7:*]

The articles about privateers were taken from the treaty of commerce between Gr. Br. and France, and the one for treating natives commanding privateers as pirates in certain cases was partly taken from ours with Holland. § The prohibition to sell prizes in our ports had it's use: and we have no reason to regret that your instructions to me admitted of it. § Various articles which have no place in this treaty have from time to time been under consideration, but did not meet with mutual approbation and consent. § I must draw this letter to a conclusion. Ld. G. is anxious to dismiss the packet as soon as possible. §. There is reason to hope that occasions for complaint on either side will be carefully avoided. Let us be just and friendly to all nations. § I ought not to omit mentioning the acknolegements due from me to Mr. Pinckney &c. §. It is desirable that I should have the earliest advice of the ratification &c. §. I had almost forgotten to mention that on finishing and agreeing to the draught of the treaty I suggested to Ld. G. as a measure that would be very acceptable to our country the interposition of his Maj. with Algiers and other states of Barbary that may be hostile to us. This idea was favorably received and it is my opinion that this court would in good earnest undertake that business, in case nothing should occur to impeach the sincerity of that mutual reconciliation which it is to be hoped will now take place. § It will give you pleasure to hear that great reserve and delicacy has been observed respecting our concerns with France. The stipulation in favor of existing treaties was agreed to without hesitation. Not an expectation nor even a wish has been expressed that our conduct towards France should be otherwise than fair and friendly. In a word: I do not know how the negociation could have been conducted on their part with more delicacy, friendliness, and propriety than it has been from first to last. I have the honor to be &c'

John Jay

MS (DLC: TJ Papers, 97: 16629-32); entirely in TJ's hand, undated, but assigned on the basis of internal evidence (see below); consisting of close writing, heavily abbreviated, filling both sides of three sheets and part of one side of a fourth; to clarify internal page references, the Editors have indicated page breaks and corrected errors in TJ's page references (see notes 4, 7-8, and 17-18 below); significant emendations are recorded in notes below; author's footnote written in margin, keyed by an asterisk; TJ's block printing shown as small capitals; brackets in text are TJ's except as noted and in TJ's footnote, where mutilated text is supplied in brackets; brackets in textual notes below are the Editors'; several quotation marks supplied.

TJ made these notes from a set of documents that President Washington transmitted to the Senate with the Jay Treaty on 8 June 1795. TJ's notes follow the documents sequentially, then at the fourth page of the MS he returned to some of the papers in order to give them fuller treatment. It is evident from this arrangement of the notes, from the internal cross-references added to p. 3, and from the explanatory notations at the heads of p. 4 and 6, that TJ composed the above notes in at least two sittings: one that produced the overview encompassed on p. 1-3 of the MS and another that resulted in the additional detailed précis on p. 4-7.

The sequence of the notes is as follows:

(1) Brief notes of John Jay's commission as envoy extraordinary to Great Britain, his letters of introduction to the king and queen, and four documents specifying his powers (p. 1 of MS).

(2) A transcription of Edmund Randolph's 6 May 1794 letter of instructions to Jay, TJ using the symbol § to indicate paragraph breaks within the letter (p. 1-2 of MS).

(3) Notes of letters exchanged by Randolph and Jay, 27 May-19 Nov. 1794, this record incorporating, in addition to the letters, enclosures of 30 July and 1 Aug. 1794 that were covered by Jay's letter of 2 Aug. 1794, and also a set of documents that was copied within Jay's letter of 13 Sep. 1794 and consisted of his and Grenville's original "projets" of treaties and their subsequent written exchanges (p. 2-3 of MS).

(4) More extensive notes and extracts from the following papers incorporated within Jay's letter of 13 Sep. 1794: Jay's original proposals or "projet" (of 6 Aug. 1794; see ASP, Foreign Relations, I, 486); Grenville's projet treating issues that lingered from the 1783 treaty, TJ reproducing the marginal numbers by which Jay keyed his "Notes" relating to this projet (see below), the numbers 10-11, 13-14, and 16 being skipped because for those articles TJ referred to the final treaty rather than minuting Grenville's projet in detail; a separate "Commercial projet" by Grenville concerning matters of trade (Grenville's two projets both being dated 30 Aug. 1794; ASP, Foreign Relations, I, 487); Jay's "remarks" of 4 Sep. 1794 on Grenville's projet concerning the boundary; Grenville's "Observations" of 5 Sep. 1794 on the boundary issue, TJ's notes here containing his own commentary enclosed in brackets; Jay's "Notes," consisting of a series of numbered questions and comments referring to Grenville's first projet and keyed by numbers Jay placed in the margin of that document (see above); Jay's comments on his 6 Sep. 1794 meeting with Grenville; two more sets of "Observations" by Grenville, received by Jay on 8 Sep. 1794, the first consisting of a numbered

series of responses to Jay's numbered "Notes," the second set referring to two articles of Grenville's "Commercial projet"; an extract from Jay's letter of 13 Sep. 1794 (p. 4-5 of MS).

(5) Extensive notes on the letter of 13 Sep. 1794 (p. 6 of MS).

(6) A transcription, with the symbol § signifying paragraph breaks, of Jay's letter to Randolph of 19 Nov. 1794.

Although in the above notes TJ did not explain under what circumstances he studied the record of Jay's diplomatic mission, he almost certainly examined the papers in the Senate's files, and probably did so during his tenure as vice president. Immediately upon receipt of the papers from the president in June 1795 the Senate had laid "an injunction of secrecy" on them, and only in 1832 was the complete series of documents published (JEP, I, 178; ASP, *Foreign Relations*, I, 470-504). Randolph may have called TJ's attention to the contents of the documents (see Notes of a Conversation with Edmund Randolph, [after 1795], in Vol. 28: 568-9). That TJ saw the papers in the Senate's files is indicated by the footnote he added to the third page of his notes, where he refers to endorsements on the Senate's copies of the documents. Moreover, his notes cover only those documents Washington transmitted to the Senate in June 1795, making no mention of other papers that were not given to that body (see ASP, *Foreign Relations*, I, 501). In all likelihood TJ penned these extensive notes during his vice presidency, when he had access to the Senate's files (but not those of the Department of State, as he would have during his presidency), when Jay's treaty was a source of political friction in the United States, and when the details of the negotiation with Great Britain were still largely unknown outside the Senate and the inner circle of Washington's administration.

TJ's references to notations he had made in CALLENDER'S HIST. US. FOR 1796 provide a further clue to the dating of these notes. James Thomson Callender's anonymous work, *The History of the United States for 1796*, was published in Philadelphia on 27 July 1797 (Durey, *Callender*, 199; Syrett, *Hamilton*, XXI, 121-2n). The book, which had appeared in the preceding weeks as a series of pamphlets, gained most notoriety as an exposé of Alexander Hamilton's liaison with Maria Reynolds. It also included extracts of Jay's instructions as envoy to Britain in 1794, and Callender, who did not reveal his source for the instructions, accused Jay of violating them in forming the treaty (Callender, *History*, 170, 172-85). It is the book and not the pamphlets that TJ cites in his notes above, for he makes no reference to the numbers by which the pamphlets were identified, and his citations to pages and lines match those of the book. The copy of the *History* in which he CORRECTED Callender's extracts has not survived, but one can infer in general terms the extent to which he marked any changes: in Callender's book the passages cited by TJ in the above notes contain minor variations from the official version of the instructions, and there are two places where Callender, in bridging between extracts, omitted text as long as a clause or a sentence. Although in June 1797 he paid for multiple copies of Callender's work, probably to help subsidize its publication, TJ left Philadelphia for Monticello three weeks before the appearance of the book. His earliest subsequent opportunity to consult the documentation of Jay's mission in the Senate files came on his return to the capital in December of that year (MB, II, 963, 965, 975). Therefore, since his markings in Callender's book preceded the above notes on Jay's mission, the notes were probably composed no earlier than late 1797, during that or a subsequent stay by TJ in Philadelphia.

LD. DORCHESTER'S SPEECH TO THE INDNS.: see note to Madison to TJ, 25 May 1794. RICHMOND EXPEDITION AGAINST A VESSEL ARMING IN JAS. RIVER: in July 1794 John Marshall led militia detachments from Richmond and Petersburg to Smithfield, Virginia, after the militia of Isle of Wight County failed to turn out in support of David Meade Randolph, who as federal marshal acting in response to a complaint from the British consul at Norfolk had seized the ship *Unicorn*, thought to be fitting out as a French privateer. Writing to Jay in the 11 Aug. 1794 letter summarized above by TJ, Edmund Randolph cited the incident as "evidence of our unchangeable neutrality" (ASP, *Foreign Relations*, I, 482; CVSP, VII, 213, 240-7; Marshall, *Papers*, II, 273-9). FORT RECOVERY, a base of operations in Anthony Wayne's campaign against the Indians of the Great Lakes region, was the target of a two-day attack at the end of June 1794. In his letter of 18 Aug. 1794 Randolph cited evidence "that the British were associated with the Indians in the affair of Fort Recovery" (ASP, *Foreign Relations*, I, 483; Richard H. Kohn, *Eagle and Sword: The Federalists and the Creation of the Military Establishment in America, 1783-1802* [New York, 1975], 156). For the advance to the Maumee River of British troops under orders from John Graves SIMCOE, governor of Upper Canada, see note to Madison to TJ, 25 May 1794. The American government was alarmed in August 1794 by a report of an "insolent demand" by Simcoe that Americans abandon their settlement at SODUS, New York (ASP, *Foreign Relations*, I, 484).

VIZ 1 ON EACH SIDE AND THE 5TH: both Grenville's "projet" and the finished treaty provided for two commissioners selected by each side, with a final member of the panel to be chosen by the other four. One member from each nation plus that mutually selected fifth commissioner would constitute a quorum (same, 488, 521).

TJ's transcription of JAY'S LETTER OF NOV. 19 on p. 6-7 of the document printed above is complete except for the omission of: ABOUT 12 LINES RESPECTING AN AGENT for handling capture claims; a passage expanding on THE ACKNOLEGEMENTS DUE to Thomas PINCKNEY; and, following a request for THE EARLIEST ADVICE OF THE RATIFICATION, Jay's comments on his own health, which he said prevented him from making the winter voyage to bring the treaty to the United States in person (same, 503, 504).

[1] Opening bracket supplied.
[2] Opening bracket supplied.
[3] TJ here canceled "cruisers."
[4] Sentence and brace inserted; TJ mistakenly wrote "pa. 3."
[5] Preceding 11 words interlined in place of "[and the Georgia] cotton."
[6] Sentence interlined.
[7] Sentence and brace inserted; TJ mistakenly wrote "pa. 3."
[8] Sentence and brace inserted; TJ mistakenly wrote "pa. 3."
[9] Digit reworked from "[4]"; sentence and brace inserted.
[10] Preceding four words interlined in place of "[remarks]."
[11] Sentence inserted.
[12] Word interlined in place of "remarks."
[13] Sentence inserted.
[14] Sentence interlined.
[15] Sentence interlined.
[16] TJ here canceled " 'And whereas it frequently happens."
[17] TJ mistakenly wrote "pa. 3."
[18] TJ mistakenly wrote "pa. 3."

Appendix
Notations by Jefferson on Senate Documents

E D I T O R I A L   N O T E

As vice president of the United States, Jefferson's primary responsibility was to preside over the Senate. In his opening address to that body on 4 Mch. 1797 he observed that although he had spent a considerable time in legislative bodies earlier in his life, lack of recent experience had left him unfamiliar with legislative procedings. He was, he lamented to George Wythe, "entirely rusty in the Parliamentary rules of procedure." With his official duties relatively light—his post was "honorable and easy," as he wrote to Elbridge Gerry—he had time to remedy this deficiency by turning to his earlier "Parliamentary Pocket-Book" for guidance (he later referred to it as his "pillar"). He also began work on a manuscript that in 1801 was printed as *A Manual of Parliamentary Practice* (TJ to Wythe, 22 Jan. 1797; TJ to Gerry, 13 May, 1797; PW, 6-10, 16).

Although Jefferson did not take an active legislative role in the Senate's proceedings, he sometimes did make notes on documents that came before that body. These markings, which reflect less his own thought or opinion than his recording of the deliberations of the senators, give some indication of Jefferson's involvement in day-to-day proceedings of the Senate.

For examples of extensive emendations by Jefferson on Senate documents, see the resolutions printed above at 5 June and 4 July 1797. The following list enumerates other motions, bills, committee reports, and acts that came before the Fifth Congress in 1797 and received some written comment by the vice president. The Editors have grouped Jefferson's markings on the documents into three categories: "emendation" indicates that Jefferson recorded changes to a bill or motion, from a word or two to several sentences; "notation" means that brief information on action taken by the Senate appears in Jefferson's hand, most often as "agreed" in the margin of the text of the document, or, for example, in the first document cited below the notation, "moved by Mr. Sedgwick"; and "endorsement" indicates that Jefferson provided one or more entries in the docketing or clerical endorsement that gives a history of the document. Jefferson's is usually only one of several hands making notations or endorsements on Senate documents, indicating that in addition to presiding he may have filled a clerical role on occasions when clerk Samuel A. Otis and his assistants were away. The docketing provides inclusive dates for a document; in the absence of such endorsements we have derived the dates from the printed *Journal of the Senate*. If the document marked by Jefferson was a motion or bill printed for the Senate's consideration, that fact is also noted in the description below.

All the documents listed below are from Senate Records, DNA: RG 46, 5th Congress. The first session ran from 15 May to 10 July 1797 and the second session began on 13 Nov.

Motion for a committee relative to the building and equipping cruisers, 29 May 1797; notation by TJ. Printed in JS, II, 366.

Bill Prohibiting for a limited time, the exportation of Arms and Ammunition, [2-5 June 1797]; emendations by TJ.

Bill for raising an additional corps of light dragoons, [ca. 6-14 June 1797]; printed; emendations by TJ.

Bill Providing for the protection of the trade of the United States, 7-28 June 1797; printed; emendations by TJ.

Act in addition to an Act, intituled, "An Act concerning the registering and recording of ships and vessels," [ca. 19-22 June 1797]; printed; emendations by TJ.

Act Directing the appointment of agents, in relation to the sixth article of the treaty of amity, commerce and navigation, between the United States, and Great-Britain, [ca. 20-26 June 1797]; printed; notation and emendations by TJ on separate sheet pasted to printed act.

Bill to prevent the arming of private ships, except in certain cases, and under certain regulations, [ca. 17 June-4 July 1797]; printed with printed committee report conjoined; notations and endorsement by TJ.

Act laying duties on licences for selling foreign wines and foreign distilled spirituous liquors by retail, [ca. 28 June-4 July 1797]; printed; emendations by TJ.

Bill for confirming the titles to certain holders of lands, in the south-western part of the United States, [ca. 30 June-10 July 1797]; printed; emendations and endorsement by TJ.

Committee report on bill laying duties on licences for selling foreign wines and foreign distilled spirituous liquors by retail, [4 July 1797]; printed; notations by TJ.

Committee report on North and Vesey's Bill, 28 Dec. 1797; notation by TJ.

INDEX

abolition: Va. laws on, 96n, 120n;
Tucker's proposals for, 488-9, 519
Abolition Society, Virginia, 120n
Abram (Abraham, TJ's slave): TJ mortgages, 98
Abrégé de l'Histoire générale des voyages,
contenant ce qu'il y a de plus remarquable,
de plus utile & de mieux avéré dans les
pays où les voyageurs ont pénétré (Jean
François de La Harpe): cited by TJ,
155, 156n, 296
Acer pseudoplatanus (sycamore): seeds of,
sent to TJ, 105
Adams, Abigail: correspondence with husband, 224n, 252n

ADAMS, JOHN: letter to, 235-7; letter from,
58-9; letter to cited, 23n; address from
Senate, 392-5; address to Senate, 396

Diplomatic Career
expenditures, accounts, 17-18, 58; and
Franklin, 17-18; minister to Britain,
23n; in Amsterdam, 467; and forged
letter on treatment of Tories, 506n;
and boundary with British possessions, 626-7

Election of 1796
election results, viii, 211, 218, 226-7,
228n, 234-7, 255, 261; characterized
as friend of monarchy, 193-6; support
for, 193-9, 232, 253, 326; and Hamilton's intrigues, 214, 223, 226, 251,
265, 326; as opponent of banks and
funding system, 214-15, 226; supported by TJ as president elect, 223-
4, 234-7, 247-8, 250, 270; comments
on support for Clinton, 592-3

Opinions
on D'Ivernois, Mably, 58-9; on France,
59, 593; on republicanism, democra-
cies, 59, 593; on banks, 214-15; on
elective government, 592-3

Personal Affairs
correspondence with A. Adams, 224n,
252n; and Wirt, 359n

Portraits
mezzotint by Graham, xl, 318 (illus.)

President
convenes Congress, viii, 76-7, 325, 350,
392, 416, 418n, 435n; and TJ's letter
to Mazzei, 76; TJ urges to avoid war,

235, 237; and relations with France,
316, 340, 342-3, 367, 370-1, 371n,
373-4n, 380, 382, 394-5, 396, 416,
418-19n, 425, 442-3, 551-3, 557,
560; sends correspondence, papers to
Congress, 325, 472, 563-4; relations
with Gerry, 326-7, 402, 415; Paine
criticizes, 340, 342-3, 367; public regard for, 368-9; and sons of Duchesse
d'Orléans, 369; May 1797 address to
Congress, 370-1, 372, 373n, 379,
382, 385, 392, 395n, 401, 405, 407,
411, 416, 425, 431, 438, 442-3, 455,
459; and French influence in Netherlands, 372; recommends naval defense, 377n, 594; appointments,
387n, 486-7; and unity of sentiment
with Senate, 396; and appointment of
envoys to France, 420n, 443; signs
legislation, 423n; and legislation,
434-5n; and authority to lay embargoes, 461, 462; Genet praises, 471;
petitioned by Vincennes claimants,
508n; relations with Cabinet, 552;
and U.S. ministers abroad, 565;
Nov. 1797 address to Congress, 587-
9, 592; on convening Congress during epidemics, 592; removes Coxe,
595

President Elect
attitude toward France, Britain, 272,
273; desires Madison on mission to
France, 273n; Madison's views on,
280, 285; and notification of election
to office, 282; relinquishes Senate duties, 283n; seeks advice on transition
to new administration, 304-5; succeeds Washington, 317

Relations with Jefferson
defeats TJ for presidency, 226-7; political differences, 234, 362-3; TJ's conciliatory letter to, 234-7; distorted by
press, 235; TJ expresses esteem, respect for, 235, 237, 259, 270, 311,
362; cordiality after election, 251,
252n, 263-4, 271, 273, 280-1; Gerry
on, 326-7, 475; and TJ's letter to
P. Fitzhugh, 418n, 560; consults with
TJ on mission to France, 551-2

Vice President
and TJ's notification of election, 282n,
304, 305-6; counts electoral votes,

ADAMS, JOHN (*cont.*)
305n, 306n; resides at Francis's hotel, 469n; response to publication of forged letter, 505

Writings
Defence of the Constitutions of Government of the United States of America, 194, 342, 345n; *Collection of State-Papers,* 342, 344-5n

Adams, John Quincy: reports on French influence at the Hague, 372, 374n; appointed minister to Prussia, 411, 412-13n, 414

Adams, Richard (brickmason): witnesses mortgage, 210

Adams, Samuel: TJ praises, 290

Adams administration: and France's refusal to receive C. C. Pinckney, 371; and appointments, 564

Addison, Joseph: *Cato,* 52n

Adet, Pierre Auguste: letter from, 355; and French opposition to Jay Treaty, 214-15; addresses French complaints against U.S., 273n, 280; returns to France, 316, 355; wishes good relations with TJ, U.S., 355; letter to cited, 355n; and U.S. policy, 384, 419n

Aeneid (Virgil): quoted, 519; mentioned, 386

Aesop: fable of floating sticks, 237, 238n

Africa: languages, 201n

Aggey (Aggy, TJ's slave): TJ mortgages, 98

Agrarian Justice, Opposed to Agrarian Law, and to Agrarian Monopoly (Thomas Paine): TJ sends to Madison, 434, 435n

agriculture: La Rochefoucauld-Liancourt's innovations, 149n; research in France, 333; S.C. Agricultural Society, 367, 487; grasses, clovers, and legumes grown in the U.S. and Britain, 510-12. *See also* Great Britain: Agriculture

Akin, James: megalonyx engravings, xxxix, 318 (illus.); caricature of TJ, xl

Albany, N.Y.: Volney to visit, 174

Albemarle Co., Va.: suits in county court, 26, 63-4n, 158; elects delegates to Va. General Assembly, 27, 52, 322-3, 327-8, 349, 350n; price of corn in, 37, 51-2, 67; crops and weather in, 43; land prices, 124; wheat grown in, 146, 147, 350; physicians in, 153; prospects for mill seat on Moore's Creek, 350-1; TJ

plans to attend court, 436; and TJ's grand jury petition, 490, 491-504, 524; roads in, 586

Alcock, Elizabeth Gregory Thornton Walker, 5, 169

Alcock, Weston, 5

alcohol: brewed v. distilled, 104-5; supply of, for harvest, 414; tax proposed on, 461, 462

Alexander (the Great), 318

Alexander, William: letter to, 158; orders nails from TJ, 158, 525; letter from cited, 525n

Alexandria, Va.: wheat prices at, 322; climate at, compared to Monticello, 351

Algiers: U.S. treaty with, 9, 62, 70-1, 95n, 369n; ransom of U.S. captives in, 68-9, 369; U.S. relations with, 135, 256; and construction of U.S. frigates, 377n; potential British intercession with, 628-9

alien acts: passage of, 537n

Allegheny Mountains: plants at foot of, 319

Allison, Burgess, 378

Allison, Patrick: recounts attack on Logan's kin, 556

Ambler, Jacquelin, 191, 240

American Minerva (New York): and TJ's letter to Mazzei, vii, 75-6, 80, 86-7, 385n; publishes letter from Paris, 109-10. *See also* Webster, Noah

American Philosophical Society: letter to, 276-7; letter from, 254; elects TJ president, viii, 252, 254, 276-7; elects members, 65n, 101n, 154n, 206, 322, 323n, 415, 509-10, 525; books presented to, 102n; papers by members, 130, 133n, 140, 322n; TJ announces megalonyx discovery to, 138-9; publishes TJ's megalonyx report, 165, 182-3, 200-2, 205-6, 275, 284, 391, 510; seeks, receives specimens, 201, 202n, 398, 403; officers, 254; and TJ's plan to record, study winds, 259; publishes TJ's letter, 277n; TJ's report on the megalonyx, 291-304; TJ presides over, 300-1n. *See also* Rittenhouse, David

American Revolution: France's participation in, 76; lands confiscated during, 157n; J. Carey's publication of letters from, 180-2, 205; T. Pickering's role in, 381; principles of jeopardized, 447-8

American Universal Geography (Jedidiah Morse): prints Logan's speech, 455n

"Americanus" (pseudonym): publishes articles in *Va. Gazette* criticizing Jefferson, 76

Ames, Fisher: and Jay Treaty, 36; as member of House committee, 218; views on relations with France, 228n; retires from Congress, 381, 411, 413n, 417

Amherst Co., Va.: price of corn in, 36, 37; and TJ's grand jury petition, 490, 491-504, 524

Amis, Iles de. *See* Tonga

Amsterdam: and American financial transactions, 89, 95, 165n; C. C. Pinckney goes to, 231n; Adams in, 467

"Anas": described, 486-7n

Anderson, Nathaniel: and Mazzei's finances, 65n; TJ's account with, 65n

Anderson, William (London merchant): and Mazzei's finances, 65, 81, 90, 200

Andes Mountains: Volney alludes to, 175

Anglicans: and Jay Treaty, 95

Angola (Eppes estate, Cumberland Co., Va.): and marriage settlement of J. W. Eppes, 532-3, 549-50

Annales Philosophiques, Politiques et Litteraires: Peyroux publishes essay in, 133n

Annual Register . . . For the Year 1787 (London): prints Logan's speech, 454, 455n

anteaters: associated with megatherium, 299, 510

Anville, Madame d'. *See* Enville, Louise Elisabeth de La Rochefoucauld, Duchesse d'

Appendix to the Notes on Virginia Relative to the Murder of Logan's Family: publication of, 410n; as revision of *Notes on Virginia*, 455n, 600; prints documents, 603n. *See also* Logan (Mingo Indian)

Appomattox River: and proposed road from Georgetown to Ga., 529; lands on, 533n, 549

apricots: possible introduction of French variety, 5

Apthorpe, Charles Ward, 398, 403

Arcola: French victory in battle of, 305n

Argus (New York): publishes TJ's letter to Mazzei, 76; reports comments by Harper, 593n

Aristotle: *History of Animals*, 295

Arnold, Benedict, 194

artisans: cabinetmaker, 379; in Philadelphia, 523. *See also* Monticello: brickmasons, stonemasons

Asia: and comparative study of languages, 201-2, 446-7

asparagus: grown at Monticello, 322

asses: and farm implements, 318

Ast, William Frederick: letter from, 190-1; fire insurance program, 190-1, 239-44

auditor. *See* Harrison, Richard; Pendleton, John

Augusta, Ga.: as terminus of proposed road from Georgetown, 529

Augusta Chronicle and Gazette of the State (Ga.): and TJ's letter to Mazzei, 79n

Auldjo, Thomas: letter from quoted, 583-4; letter from cited, 584n

"Aurelius" (John Gardner), 199n

Aurora (Philadelphia): criticized, xxxvii; and TJ's letter to Mazzei, 76, 79; and election of 1796, 228n; publishes political correspondence, 309, 440n, 517n, 593n; TJ subscribes to, 442, 544; prints forged Washington letters, 506n. *See also* Bache, Benjamin Franklin

Austin (TJ's slave): TJ mortgages, 98; in marriage settlement of Mary Jefferson, 550

Austria: truce with France, 56; War of First Coalition, 117, 169, 341, 422, 423n; opposes France along Rhine and in Italy, 135-6, 161; Archduke Charles defeated by Bonaparte, 341, 344n; and peace of Leoben, 367n, 431, 433, 434n, 436, 438, 450, 451, 459, 558

Avignon, France: Volney compares Kanawha River region to, 151

Azevedo, António de Araújo: and Portuguese-French diplomacy, xxxvii

Bache, Benjamin Franklin: prints speeches, papers, 51, 215n, 435n; publishes debates on Jay Treaty, 62-3; as publisher of *Aurora*, 76, 79, 309, 442; publishes Washington's questions to Cabinet on neutrality, 127, 129n, 141-2; as Cobbett's adversary, 140n; advertises "Jonathan Pindar" odes, 192; forwards items from Saint-Domingue, 348, 387; and financial transactions, 401, 544; publishes country edition of *Aurora*, 416, 434; and Callender, 537n; publishes Monroe's *View*, 544-5n, 562-3, 576, 586; and TJ's correspondence with P. Fitzhugh, 561; on situation in France, 576; prints TJ's extract of letter, 583-4; prints TJ's letter to J. Henry, 603n. *See also Aurora* (Philadelphia)

INDEX

Bache's Philadelphia Aurora: country edition of the *Aurora*, 416, 434
bacon: in diet during harvest, 414
Bagwell (TJ's slave): TJ mortgages, 98
Bahama islands, W.I.: within range of U.S. coastal gunboats, 377
Bailey, Theodorus: buys land from Madison, 591, 592n
Baldwin, Abraham: at Constitutional Convention, 57n; as member of House committee, 218; resides at Francis's hotel, 469n; investigates charges against Blount, 473n
Ballantine, Hugh, 150-1
Baltimore, Md.: response to Jay Treaty, 70; transportation at, 308-9; price of wheat and tobacco at, 309, 322
Banister, John, 102
Banister, John, Jr.: TJ's account with, 45n; debt owed TJ by estate of, 102
Bank of England: ceases specie payments, 340-1, 344n, 370-1, 373, 379, 427, 431, 433, 438, 459
Bank of the United States: role in U.S. public finance, 124, 125n; Cathalan invests in, 368; influence of war on, 427; and TJ's transactions, 482n, 545
bankruptcies: in Philadelphia, 261
banks: favor Jay Treaty, 73, 94; Adams's views on, 214-15; public opinion of, 228; blamed for economic distress, 255; and financial speculation, 329; and British influence in U.S., 363; and paper money, metals, 401, 594
Banks, Henry: letter to, 213; mortgages Greenbrier lands to TJ, 213, 219-20; letters from cited, 213n; letter to cited, 213n; purchases Elk Hill, 274
Barbary States: relations with U.S., 376, 377n
Barclay, George, & Co.: and Mazzei's finances, 81, 90
Barclay, Robert: order in favor of, 107, 108n
Barclay, Thomas: and TJ's French accounts, 14-15, 18; makes purchases for Va., 37-8n
barley: used for feed in Spain, 28; for breweries, 104-5; varieties compared, 104-5; Short sends variety from France, 332-3, 464, 597-8
Barnes, John: letters to, 50, 107-8, 125, 167-8, 183, 186, 206-7, 212, 219, 277-8, 324-5, 481-2, 484-5, 523, 531, 534, 544-5; letters from, 484, 509, 530-1,

542-3, 561-2; letters to cited, 50n, 278n, 325n, 482n; handles TJ's financial transactions, 125, 186, 219, 231, 324-5, 455, 481-2, 484-5, 509, 523, 530-1, 534, 542, 577, 598-9; letters from cited, 125n, 278n, 482n, 485n, 544n; fills orders for TJ, 184, 187, 212-13, 324; draft on cited, 187n; powers of attorney, 219, 277-8, 465n, 544-5, 561; and Short's affairs, 219, 277-8, 318n, 464, 481, 523, 530, 544-5, 597; and TJ's tobacco, 316, 413, 426-7; and mammoth tooth, 360, 481, 484; promissory note to, 482n; and A. Hamilton, 534, 542-3; and payments to Callender, 537n, 544, 561; and funds for Monroe, 544-5, 576, 595; pays for newspapers, pamphlets, 544
Barney, Capt. Joshua: commands French squadron, 347; and possible appointment to W.I., 586, 587n
Barras, Paul François Jean Nicolas, Vicomte de, 371n
Barraud, Philip, 488-9
Barrett (b. 1795, TJ's slave): in marriage settlement of Mary Jefferson, 550
Barthélemy, François, 485
Barton, Benjamin Smith: letters to, 192, 367-8; letters from, 165-6, 182-3, 200-2; reads TJ's letter to APS, 139n; debt to TJ, 165-6, 182, 192, 201; essay on snakes, 165, 166n, 182, 192; and natural history, 165-6; to send pamphlets, 192, 201; describes Ohio artifacts, 201, 202n; studies American Indians, languages, 201-2, 367-8, 445-7; dedicates book to TJ, 367-8, 445-7; ideas of progress, civilization, 446-7
Barton, William: secretary of APS, 254, 276-7
Bartram, John, 391n
Bartram, John, Jr., 391n
Bartram, William: and French apricots, 5; converses with Strickland, 117; collection of botanical specimens, 136, 390, 391n; and oil shrub, 319
Bartram's Garden (Philadelphia), 390, 391n
Batavian Republic: Adams assesses, 59; and British restrictions on Dutch firms, 89, 90; political turmoil in, 215; appointment of U.S. minister to Amsterdam, 327, 486-7; U.S. representation in, 327; British policy toward, 342; relations with U.S and France, 372, 374n; naval strength, 376; potential invest-

ment in U.S. funds, 464; British defeat Dutch fleet, 585-6
Bates, Thomas, 477
Bauman, Sebastian: letter from, 403-4; identified, 403-4n; dispute over militia rank, 403-4
Bayard, James A., 473n
Beall, Mr., 559
Beaujolais, Louis Charles d'Orléans, Comte de: travels in U.S., 312-13, 369
Beckley, John: defeated as clerk of House of Representatives, 372, 374n; and Callender, 479n, 537n; and charges against A. Hamilton, 558, 560n; and TJ's letter to J. Henry, 604
bedding: TJ supplies Derieux with, 141
Bedford. See Poplar Forest (TJ's estate)
Bedford Co., Va.: TJ's transactions in, 93, 202-4, 307; search for P. Jefferson's land records at, 185; and marriage settlements of TJ's daughters, 424, 532
Bedinger, Daniel: and E. Rutledge's shipment to TJ, 357, 386, 387n
Bee, Thomas: letters from, 367, 487; thanks TJ for gifts to Agricultural Society, 367, 487; letter to cited, 487n
beef: in payment of protested bill, 65n; beefsteak with ketchup, 221; price of, in France, 341; Federal District as potential market for, 529; TJ takes portion of from Davenport, 587
beer: morality improved by use of brewed rather than distilled liquor, 104-5; bottled for TJ, 360
Begouën, Desmeaux & Cie.: in TJ's French accounts, 16, 31, 39
Belgium: and War of First Coalition, 71; brought under French control, 161-2, 165n
Bell, Thomas: letter to, 370-1; letter from, 427; and Cobbs suit, 63; and TJ's slave mortgages, 97n; and Derieux's affairs, 141; attests to documents, 219n, 331n, 545n; TJ sends political and financial news to, 371, 401; letters from cited, 371n; letters to cited, 371n; dines at Monticello, 427; urges TJ to keep out of war with France, 427; and Madison's order for nails, 591
Belle Grove (Frederick Co., Va.): Hite's residence at, 137n
Ben (Shawnee Indian): murder of, 441
Bentley, William, 476-7
Benton (Benson), Lemuel, 411, 413n
Berkenhead (Berkheanhead), John L.: publishes Adams portrait, xl

Berlin: U.S. diplomats in, 23n
Bermuda: British prize court, 162; and French shipping violation, 611-12
Bermuda Hundred (Eppes estate, Chesterfield Co., Va.): in marriage settlement of J. W. Eppes, 532-3, 547-8, 549, 550
Bermuda Hundred (Randolph estate): vetch grows at, 319
Bern, Switzerland: and private claims on funds in U.S., 207-9; Tronchin's residence, 207
Bernoux. See Galvan de Bernoux, Francis
Bess (TJ's slave): TJ mortgages, 98
Bet (Island Betty, TJ's slave): TJ mortgages, 98
Betsey (TJ's slave): in marriage settlement of Mary Jefferson, 550
Betty (TJ's slave): TJ mortgages, 98
Beverley, Robert (d. 1800), 279
Beverley, William (ca. 1698-1756), 279
Bible: Volney quotes Old Testament, 175
"big buffalo." See mammoth
Bingham, William: chosen president pro tempore of Senate, 283n; hosts Federalist Party caucuses, 283n; administers oath of office to TJ, 311n; opposes arming of merchant vessels, 421, 423n
birds: unusual bird described, 156; hawks, 192; bluebirds at Monticello, 260
Bivins, James: R. Randolph bond to, 97n, 268
blacks: education of, 120, 177-8, 287-8; in Notes on Virginia, 176-7n; Rush associates blackness with leprosy, 284; rights of, in Va., 489n; TJ on future prospects of, 519; and legislative representation, 538
Blacons, Henri François Lucrecius d'Armand de Forest, Marquis de, 468-9
Blair, Archibald, 194
Blair, John (1732-1800): and Mazzei's finances, 81; given power of attorney for Mazzei, 83n; and grand jury presentment, 418n, 445, 498-9n
Blake, James, 360
Bleakley, John: secretary of APS, 254, 276-7
Bloodworth, Samuel: and TJ's official notification of election, 305, 306, 307-8
Bloodworth, Timothy: in Senate, 305, 306, 583n, 592n; and TJ's official notification of election, 307-8
Blount, Thomas: and Jay Treaty, 54n; and TJ's letter to J. Henry, 604

Blount, William: letter to, 34; TJ recommends R. H., J. Rose to, 34; letter from cited, 34n; letter to cited, 34n; conveys letters for APS, 398, 403; expelled by Senate, 472-3n; and plans to invade Spanish territory, 472-4, 535; Senate resolution on, 472-4; correspondence with TJ and Senate quoted, 473n; impeachment of, 473n, 516-17, 589, 591
Blue Ridge Mountains: vetch observed in, 103; and ice caves, 116-17, 119n
Bohlen, Bohl, 119
Bolling, John, 579
Bolling, Mary Jefferson (Mrs. John Bolling, TJ's sister): regards sent to, 156; relationship with husband, 579
Bonaparte, Napoleon: Italian campaign, 117, 135-6, 146, 148, 161, 169, 222, 265, 273, 305, 341, 422, 423n, 431, 433, 434n, 436, 438, 456, 459; and Lafayette, 126n; and La Rochefoucauld-Liancourt, 149n; and artworks of subjugated territories, 161, 164-5; estate at Rambouillet, 333n; forces Emperor Francis to terms, 367n; influence on U.S. negotiations with France, 443; P. Fitzhugh's assessment of, 559
Bond, Phineas, 228n
Bone to Gnaw, for the Democrats; Containing . . . Observations on a Patriotic Pamphlet (William Cobbett), 140n
Booker, William: letter to, 187-8; letters from, 188-9, 207; identified, 188n; threshing machines of, 187-8, 189n, 207, 231, 545, 553
Boon (ship), 257
Bordeaux, France: Monroe embarks from, 332, 340; accusations against consul at, 563n, 565
Boston: response to Jay Treaty, 70, 95-6; Volney expects to visit, 174, 225, 237; Volney seeks meteorological information from, 238
Bowyer, John: letter to, 44; business dealings with TJ, 44; letter from cited, 44n; letters to cited, 44n
Bowyer's (inn, western Va.), 150
Boyce, Joseph: cares for TJ's shipment, 424; draft on, 598; G. Jefferson's assessment of, 599
Boydell, Josiah: engraver, xli
Brackenridge, Hugh Henry: *Incidents of the Insurrection*, 248-50
Bradford, Thomas: TJ praises newspaper of, 416, 434
Bradford, William: letter to, 568; identi-

fied, 568n; as Senate president pro tempore, 432n, 568, 575-6; presides over Blount proceedings, 473n
Bradford, William (Philadelphia printer): publishes Logan's speech, 603-4n
breadfruit: TJ receives, distributes seeds of, 347-8, 387-8, 487, 513
Breckinridge, John: letter to, 131; introduced to Volney, 131
Brend, Thomas: binds TJ's collection of Va. laws, 158, 283, 569
Brent, Daniel Carroll: as candidate for elector in 1796, 193-5, 197n
Brent, Richard, 62n
bricklayers. *See* Monticello: brickmasons, stonemasons
bricks: and renovation of Monticello, 63
Bridge Company (Georgetown): and proposed road, 529
Bringhurst, John: corresponds with TJ, 9, 56n, 88; provides information on Sharpless, 55; letters from cited, 62, 491n; TJ purchases paint from, 324; visits TJ, 488, 516; carries letter, 489, 506; letters to cited, 491n
Brooke, Humphrey, 263n
Brooke, Mary Ritchie (Mrs. Robert Brooke), 147
Brooke, Robert: letter to, 37-8; and TJ's French accounts, 17, 32, 37-8, 40; death of wife, 147; and Va. boundaries, 172, 263n, 271-2, 278-9; Burr visits, 198n
Brown, Andrew: publishes documents on Jay Treaty, 9-10; prints Madison's address, 70-1; and Callender, 537n. *See also Philadelphia Gazette*
Brown, Betty (TJ's slave): daughter of, in marriage settlement of Mary Jefferson, 550
Brown, Catherine Percy, 322n
Brown, James: letters to, 50-1, 112; TJ's account with, 26, 27n, 112, 203; and TJ's wine order, 36, 322; asked to deliver letter for TJ, 50-1, 112; letter to cited, 112n; Snelson's order on, 204; forwards Volney's valise, 225; drafts on, 358
Brown, James (1766-1835), 321-2n
Brown, John (clerk of General Court of Va.): and publication of Va. laws, 158-9
Brown, John (Ky.): letter to, 345-6; in U.S. Senate, 321n; TJ offers architectural advice, 345-6; "Liberty Hall" residence, 346n; stays at Francis's hotel, 469n
Brown, Margaret Preston, 321n

Brown, Nathaniel William, 257
Brown, Samuel: letter from, 321-2; identified, 321-2n; describes ice caves, 321
Bruce, James, 513
Bruni. *See* Salimberi, Madame de
Brutus: characterized by historians, 249n
"Brutus" (pseudonym): criticizes TJ's letter to Mazzei, 79
Bryan, Nathan, 95n
Bryden, James (Baltimore tavern keeper), 323
Buchanan, Dunlop & Co.: delivers TJ's letter, 102
Buchanan, James: and TJ's prison designs, 336n
Buck, John H.: builds threshing machine for TJ, 187-9, 207
Buffon, Georges Louis Leclerc, Comte de: TJ criticizes, 113-14; TJ cites works of, 292, 293, 295, 296, 297-8; theories of, 295, 297-8, 409-10n, 452, 601; TJ uses Logan speech to refute, 601
Bugniet, Pierre Gabriel, 335, 336n
Bulkeley, John, & Son: as TJ's wine supplier in Lisbon, 36
Bullock, Stephen, 413n
Bullock, William: TJ cites *Virginia*, 294-5
Burges, Dempsey, 411
Burr, Aaron: letter to, 437-40; letters from, 72, 447-8; introduces Guillemard to TJ, 72; and election of 1796, 169, 193, 195-6, 198-9, 439; visits Monticello, 195-6, 198-9; tried for treason, 218n; and units of measure sent from France, 229; defended by Wirt, 359n; discusses Jay Treaty, U.S.-British relations, 437-9, 447-8; and L. Martin, 454n; and Monroe-Hamilton conflict, 479n, 578-9, 593, 595n
Burwell, William A.: as TJ's private secretary, 193
Butler, Pierce, 69, 93
butter: shipment of, 260-1
Byrd, Otway, 387n
Byrd's warehouse: and Cobbs suit, 63

Cabell, Nicholas: letter from cited, 30n
Cabell, Samuel J.: returns Madison's letter, 305n; criticizes government in letter to constituents, 419n; and grand jury presentment, 419n, 490-1, 524; and TJ's grand jury petition, 526-7; effect of absence from House, 594
Cabell, William: letter from, 30; requests letters for R. H., J. Rose, 30; letters from

cited, 30n; letters to cited, 30n; and Volney, 482
Cacapon River: ice caves on, 116-7, 118n, 321
Caesar (TJ's slave): TJ mortgages, 98
Caesar, Julius: characterized by Callender, 249n; Bonaparte compared to, 559
Caffery, John: and recovery of mammoth fossils, 398, 403
Callahan's (inn, western Va.), 150
Callender, James Thomson: letter from, 536-7; identified, 537n; *Political Progress of Britain*, 248-51; sedition trial, 359n; exposes Hamilton's affair, 479n, 630n; *History of the United States for 1796*, 479n, 483-4, 534, 536, 609, 630n; charges against Adams, 505; seeks, receives financial assistance from TJ, 536, 544, 561, 630n; *Sketches of the History of America*, 536, 593n; pamphlets by, 537n; publishes comments by Harper, 593n
"Camillus" (Alexander Hamilton): and Jay Treaty, 4, 55-7, 148
Campbell, Alexander, 10
Campbell, Arthur: letter to, 522-3; letters from, 469-70, 538, 580; worries about American politics, liberty, 469-70, 522, 538, 580; forwards political items, 580
Campbell & Tenant (Belfast firm), 45n
Canada: within range of U.S. coastal gunboats, 377. *See also* Jay Treaty: boundary issue
candy: duties on, 265n
Capellen tot den Poll, Joan Derk van der, 466
capital: and financial speculation, 329-30, 458
Carey, James: TJ praises newspaper of, 416, 434; and Blount conspiracy, 472; and Callender, 537n
Carey, John: letter to, 205; letter from, 180-2; *Official Letters to the Honorable American Congress*, 180-2, 205
Carmichael, Antonia Reynon: letter to, 406; letter from, 360-1; sends Ulloa manuscript, 360-1, 406
Carmichael, William: sends information about megatherium, 301n; papers of, 360, 406
Caroline Co., Va.: and U.S. relations with France, 381, 382n
Carr, Mr., 62
Carr, Eleanor (Nelly, Mrs. Samuel Carr), 346
Carr, John (b.1753), 66

Carr, John Overton, 346
Carr, Martha Jefferson (Mrs. Dabney Carr, TJ's sister): visits Monticello, 27; regards sent to, 156
Carr, Peter (TJ's nephew): letter to, 210-11; and TJ's letter to Mazzei, 78; stays in Charlottesville, 170; letters from cited, 210-11n; marriage of, 210-11; and TJ's grand jury petition, 490, 492, 505
Carr, Samuel (TJ's nephew), 346
Carr, Thomas, 540-1
carriages, 572
carriage tax: Hamilton's argument in Hylton v. U.S., 4n; argued before Supreme Court, 10
Carter, Edward (d. 1792): estate of, 5, 124
Carter, Edward (Ned), 5
Cary, Archibald: debt to Wayles estate, 166-7
Cary, Moorey & Welch: and TJ's debt to W. Welch, 174n
Cary, Robert & Co.: and settlement of Wayles estate debt, 166-7, 419; TJ's account with, 173-4
Case of the Commonwealth of England, Stated (Marchamont Nedham), 59
Cate (b. 1788, Bet's daughter, TJ's slave): TJ mortgages, 98
Cate (b. 1788, Suck's daughter, TJ's slave): TJ mortgages, 98
Catesby, Mark: TJ cites Natural History, 298, 304n
Cathalan, Eulalie (Stephen Cathalan, Jr.'s daughter), 369
Cathalan, Stephen, Jr.: letter from, 368-9; in TJ's French accounts, 16, 31; business affairs, family, 368-9; as consul at Marseilles, 369; letters from cited, 369n; letter to cited, 369n
Cathalan, Stephen, Sr., 369
Catherine II (the Great), Empress of Russia: sponsors comparative study of languages, 201-2
Catholic Church: American students in Rome, 538-9
Catlett, Kemp, 83n
Cato (Joseph Addison): quoted, 52n
cattle: feed for, 103, 179, 319; and TJ's farming operations, 170, 244-6; raised by TJ and T. M. Randolph, 260; given to Mary Jefferson, 547, 550. See also beef
Cavendish, William Hunter: and megalonyx discovery, 100, 113, 172; as member of Va. assembly, 239

Cazenove, Théophile, 330n
Centinel of Freedom (Newark, N.J.): publishes TJ's letter to Mazzei, 76n
Ceracchi, Giuseppe: bust of TJ, 119, 121
Cérès (ship), 572n
charcoal: used at Monticello, 177, 242, 540-2, 586
Charles, Archduke of Austria: defeated by Bonaparte, 341, 344n
Charles IV, King of Spain: and navigation of the Mississippi, 9; mentioned, 121
Charleston, S.C.: Volney seeks meteorological information on, 238; and trade with France, 340; response to Jay Treaty, 411-12; merchants', wharfholders' memorials to Senate, 567, 570
Charlotte Court House (Va.): site on proposed road from Georgetown to Ga., 529
Charlotte Sophia, Queen of Great Britain: and Jay's commission as envoy, 605, 610, 629n
Charlottesville, Va.: and possible location of school at, 58; distance from Staunton, 150; postal service, 266, 507; price of lands near, 351; dry weather at, 427
Chase, Samuel: appointment to Supreme Court, 5, 42, 124; L. Martin defends, 454n; presides at Callender's trial, 537n
Chastellux, Alfred Louis Jean Philippe, Comte de: education, support of, 7, 145, 312
Chastellux, François Jean de Beauvoir, Marquis de: financial support for family of, 7, 144-5, 312; TJ's regard for, 145
Chastellux, Marie Joséphine Charlotte Brigitte Plunkett, Marquise de: letter to, 144-5; letter from, 312-13; seeks compensation for son, 7; pension application, 144-5, 312-13; and Duchesse d'Orléans, 312-13
Cheat River: in early hunters' accounts, 152-3, 171, 295
Cherokees: and plans to invade Spanish territory, 472-3n
Chesterfield Co., Va., 533n
Chew, Joseph: TJ stops at ordinary run by, 425, 436
Chickasaw Bluffs: Spanish fortifications at, 286
Chickasaw Indians: U.S. agent to, 170n
children: Eliza Monroe's maturation in France, 147, 164; C. Gerry supervises siblings, household, 402; illness of, 402. See also Randolph, Anne Cary (TJ's granddaughter); Randolph, Ellen

Wayles, II (TJ's granddaughter);
Randolph, Thomas Jefferson (TJ's grandson)
Chiles, Micajah: delivers vines for B. Hawkins, 42-3
Chipman, Nathaniel, 594, 595n
Chisholm, Hugh, 548, 550
Christie, Gabriel, 62n
Christmas: Volney mentions, 238
Church, Angelica Schuyler (Mrs. John Barker Church): letter to, 396-7; letter for sent care of T. Pinckney, 27; sends regards to TJ, 70; returns to U.S., 325-6; arrives in N.Y., 396-7, 399
Church, Catherine (Kitty): returns to U.S., 325-6, 399; TJ's affection for, 397
Church, John Barker: sends regards to TJ, 70; returns to U.S., 325-6, 399; TJ sends regards to, 397; and Monroe-Hamilton conflict, 479n
Cicero, Marcus Tullius: oratory of, 452
cider: price of, 309
Cincinnati: Volney visits, 174, 220
ciphers, 610
Cisalpine Republic: formed, 366, 367n
"Citizen" (pseudonym): query to *Rights of Man*, 560-1
citizenship, U.S.: and jury service, 497, 504, 505-6
civil liberties: threats to, 35-6, 417, 444-5, 537n; TJ's defense of, 491-504; and freedom to discuss public measures, 558
Claiborne, Thomas, 62n, 95n
Claiborne, William: information on colonial Va., 295
Claiborne, William C. C., 413n
Clarinda (TJ's slave): in marriage settlement of Mary Jefferson, 550
Clark, Bowling: and TJ's crops, livestock, 52, 211, 260-1; and TJ's Poplar Forest lands, 52; letter from cited, 53n; letter to cited, 53n
Clark, Christopher: collects bonds for TJ, 202-4
Clark, George Rogers, 508n
Clarke, John, 156
Clarke, Samuel: to forward powder, 44; and TJ's financial transactions, 158, 239, 525; and nailery statement, 540-1
Clay, Capt. (master of *Dublin Packet*), 366
Clay, Matthew: abstains from vote, 412; votes with Republicans, 422; resides at Francis's hotel, 469n
Claypoole's American Daily Advertiser (Philadelphia): prints Pinckney Treaty, 49n; carries congressional debates, 434

Cleopatra (ship): and TJ's diploma, 514
Clérisseau, Charles Louis: letter from, 389; seeks position, patronage, 389; Short forwards correspondence, 597
Clinton, DeWitt, 472n
Clinton, George, 592
clocks: repaired at Monticello, 168
Clorinda (character in Tasso's *Gerusalemme Liberata*), 229, 230n, 258
cloth, clothing: TJ purchases, 436; price of, for slaves, 569
clover: hurt by drought, 91; grasses sown with, 103-4; thrives for TJ, 128-9; Washington reports on growing of, 143; in TJ's crop rotation plan, 245-6; red, grown in Albemarle Co., Va., 350; described, 510-11, 512
clover seed: for Strickland, 117, 319; TJ purchases, 315, 322, 349; dutch white, 380, 415, 559-60; hop trefoil or hop clover sent to TJ, 510-12
Clow & Co. (Philadelphia), 225
Coalter, John: writes TJ about stonemason, 100; letter from cited, 100n
Cobbett, William: publishes L. Martin's attacks on TJ, vii, 409n, 452, 454n; publishes TJ's letter to Mazzei, 75; mocks Franklin, 140; as Bache's adversary, 140n; *Bone to Gnaw*, 140n; and Federalist politics, 558, 561. See also *Porcupine's Gazette*
Cobbs, Thomas: suit against TJ, 26-7, 63-4
cockades: tricolored, worn by French citizens in U.S., 215n
Cocke, Mr., 170
Cocke, James Powell: recommends F. Millar, 57; letters from cited, 58n; letters to cited, 58n
Cocke, William: letter to, 199; letter from, 169-70; identified, 169-70n; and election of 1796, 169, 199
cocoa: and Article 12 of Jay Treaty, 619
coffee: and Article 12 of Jay Treaty, 619
coinage: legislation on foreign, 583-4, 589-90, 594
Coit, Joshua, 78-9
Coleman, Sam, 263n
Coles, John (Enniscorthy): Strickland sends respects to, 118; and Booker's threshing machine, 187, 188; letters from cited, 188n; letters to cited, 188n
Cole's ferry, Roanoke (Staunton) River: site on proposed road from Georgetown to Ga., 529

Colle (Mazzei's Va. estate): recovery of money for, 81; purchased by Catlett, 83n, 124

Collection of State-Papers, relative to the first acknowledgment of the sovereignty of the United States of America (John Adams): Paine criticizes, 342, 344-5n

Collin, Nicholas, 136

Columbian Centinel (Boston): publishes TJ's letter to Mazzei, 75n

Comparative View of the Constitutions of the Several States with each Other, and with that of the United States (William L. Smith): J. Taylor's remarks on, 555

compasses: TJ purchases, 315, 316n

Concise and Impartial History of the American Revolution (John Lendrum): prints Logan's speech, 455n

Condorcet, Marie Jean Antoine Nicolas de Caritat, Marquis de: *Esquisse d'un tableau*, 201

Condy, Jonathan Williams, 372, 374n

Congress, Continental: TJ's notes on the debates of, 43; and leaves for military personnel, 195

Connecticut: at Constitutional Convention, 68

Connecticut Courant (Hartford): prints disunionist letters, 363, 364n

Constant, Benjamin: *De la force du gouvernement*, 123

Constellation (U.S. frigate), 422n

Constitution (U.S. frigate), 422n

Constitutional Convention: journals of, 54n, 56-7, 67-8, 93; and treaty-making powers, 55-7, 323-4, 346-7, 380; Madison's notes on, 56-7, 67-8, 93, 324, 346-7; debate on taxes, 443

Constitution of the United States: Va. proposes amendments to, 5, 36n; and taxation, finance, 10, 55; and treaties, 25, 46, 51-2, 54n; and separation of powers, 60, 285, 304-5, 492-3; and electoral votes, 255, 261; on oath of office for vice president, 255-6, 281; and role of vice president, 271, 273-4; aspects of monarchy and republicanism in, 289-90; TJ's attachment to, 311; preamble quoted, 359; three-fifths clause and southern political power, 364n; and rights of citizens to correspond freely, 492; W. L. Smith's pamphlet on, 555; South Carolina and, 570; on legal tender, 589; requires yearly meeting of Congress, 592

constitutions, state: W. L. Smith's pamphlet on, 555

Cook, Capt. James: finds breadfruit in New Zealand, 348, 388, 513

Cooke, William: Md. boundary commissioner, 263n, 278-9

corn: price of, 5, 36, 37, 51-2, 67, 123; scarcity of, 5; purchased by TJ, 26, 52, 485n; proposed embargo on, 62-3; as crop, 91, 128, 488; TJ's supply of, 99; planting of, related to peas, 179-80, 386; in TJ's crop rotation plan, 245; seed sent to TJ, 323-4, 346, 380, 415; raised by P. Fitzhugh, 559; and definitions of contraband, 623

Corsange, Pierre Claude Etienne, 354

Corsange & Cie.: relations with Monroe, 354

Corsica: and French campaign in Italy, 135, 161; Volney likens Va. mountains to, 150; taken by France, 273

Cortés (Cortez), Hernán: engravings of, 360, 406

Cosway, Maria Hadfield (Mrs. Richard Cosway), 397

cotton, cotton goods: duties on, 265n; and Article 12 of Jay Treaty, 613, 619, 631n

cougars: and megalonyx, 297, 299, 303n, 304n

Coup d'oeil sur l'état actuel des nos rapports politiques avec les États-Unis de l'Amérique Septentrionale (Joseph Fauchet): arrives in Philadelphia, 589-90; printed in English by Bache, 590n; TJ comments on, 594, 595

Coupery, Citizen (Paris notary), 246

Courier of New Hampshire (Concord, N.H.): publishes TJ's letter to Mazzei, 75n

Cowes, England: and TJ's French accounts, 31

Coxe, Tench: letter to, 146; letters from, 71-2, 134-6, 420-1; forwards letters for TJ, 71, 134-5, 146; on Jay Treaty, 71-2; and TJ's letter to Mazzei, 77; *Strictures upon the Letter*, 77n; letter to cited, 124-5n; and election of 1796, 214-15n; publishes letters signed "A Federalist," 214-15n; on commerce, economy of U.S., 420-1; removal from commissionership, 595; correspondence with Wolcott, 595; criticizes Adams, 595n; on Hamilton's politics, 596

Crabb, Jeremiah, 60

Cranch's tavern: T. M. Randolph stops at, 568

Creek Indians: and plans to invade Spanish territory, 472-3n

Cresap, Michael: and deaths of Logan's kin, vii, 408-10, 441, 444, 451, 555-6, 581-2, 590-1, 599-600, 600-4; L. Martin's father-in-law, vii, 409n, 444, 453-4, 455n, 556; and attacks on Indians, 410n, 441, 452, 453, 604n; TJ's depiction of, 410n

Cresap, Thomas: and Logan's speech, 408-10, 416, 590-1, 599-600, 600-2; uninvolved in murder of Logan's kin, 410n, 444, 453, 556; defended by L. Martin, 453-4, 581-2; relationship to L. Martin's children, 455n

Creswell's ferry (Saluda River): site on proposed road from Georgetown to Ga., 529

Crèvecoeur, Michel Guillaume St. John de: on inhabitants of frontier, 225

Cromer. See Gromer, Frederick

Cropper, Sarah Corbin: as Mary Jefferson's friend, 308, 428

Crosby, Sampson, 183

Cuffy (TJ's slave): TJ mortgages, 98

Culpeper Co., Va.: TJ proposes road to, 431, 432

Culpeper Court House: and road from Georgetown, 530

Cumberland Co., Va.: lands in, 533n

Cumberland River: and mammoth remains, 398n

Curles Neck (Pleasants estate), 120n

currency: depreciation of, and prices, 124; estimates of circulating, 124, 125n; glut of paper, 329-30; in Britain, 340-1, 344n, 370-1, 373; supplanted by specie in France, 341; bill to use foreign coins as, 583-4, 589-90, 594

Currie, Mr. (Richmond bookbinder), 569

Currie, James: letter to, 200; and election of 1796, 194; letters from cited, 200n; letters to cited, 200n

Cushing, Thomas, 506n

customs duties: procedures for collection, at Charleston, 567, 570

Cutting, Nathaniel, 366

Cuvier, Georges: describes megatherium, 298-9, 301n; studies megalonyx, 300n; classifies megalonyx, megatherium, 301n

Dactylis gromerata (meadow cocksfoot or orchard grass): sent to TJ by Strickland, 104

Daily Advertiser (Philadelphia): TJ praises, 416, 434

Dallas, Alexander J.: as Blount's attorney, 473n; assists and befriends Callender, 536, 537n

Dana, Francis: appointed envoy to France, 411, 414, 420n, 427; declines appointment, 450, 451

Daniel (TJ's slave): TJ mortgages, 98

Danville, Ky.: district court at, 204

Darien. See Panama

Dartmouth College case, 359n

Daubenton, Louis Jean Marie: data on lions, 292-3, 302n

Davenport, William: asks TJ to pay F. Walker, 587

Davis (Davies), John: recollection associated with megalonyx, 152-3, 171-2, 295-6

Dawson, John: Burr visits, 198n; and Blount investigation, 473n, 516-17; and Monroe-Hamilton conflict, 479n, 565-6, 578-9, 593, 595n; letters from cited, 488n; and Monroe, 488, 595n; letters to Madison quoted, 517n

Dayton, Jonathan: and Jay Treaty, 47-8; and business in House of Representatives, 282; on U.S. relations with France, 373-4n, 411; and House reply to president's address, 411

Deakins, Francis: and election of 1796, 197n; recounts attack on Logan's kin, 444, 555-6

Deane, Silas: on U.S. and Europe, 364, 365n

Dearborn, Henry, 94-5

Deas, William A.: forwards letters, 27; and Jay Treaty, 47

Debates in the House of Representatives of the United States, During the first Session of the Fourth Congress: publication of, 46, 49n; sent to TJ, 60-1, 72-3, 109-10

Declaration of Independence: TJ's authorship of mentioned, 79; and election of 1796 in Va., 194-5. See also Independence Day

Decline and Fall of the English System of Finance (Thomas Paine): increasing popularity of, 340-1, 344n

deer: sizes of American, Old World varieties, 298, 304n

Defence of the Constitutions of Government of the United States of America (John Adams): cited in election of 1796 in Va., 194; Paine criticizes, 342, 345n

Delacroix de Constant, Charles: correspondence with Monroe, 108-10, 231n; Paine seeks to influence, 344

*De la foiblesse d'un gouvernement qui com-
mence, Et de la nécessité où il est de se ral-
lier à la majorité nationale* (Adrien
Lezay-Marnézia), 123
*De la force du gouvernement actuel de la
France et de la nécessité de s'y rallier*
(Benjamin Constant), 123
De la Littérature des Nègres (Henri
Grégoire): and TJ's racial views,
176-7n
Delamotte, F. C. A.: letter from, 485-6; as
vice consul at Le Havre, 366; reports on
situation in France, 485-6
Delaware (Lenni Lenape) Indians: and
Dunmore's War, 452
Delaware: at Constitutional Convention,
68; and Jay Treaty, 73
Delaware River: as political divide, 235,
236; blocked by ice, 238, 595n
Demanet, Abbé: TJ cites *Nouvelle His-
toire*, 292
democratic societies: and British sedition
act, 35-6; denunciation of, 407
Democritus, 238
Demosthenes, 452
Denmark: and exportation of grain, 10;
trades with France, 340; and U.S. neu-
trality, 345n; naval strength, 376
Derieux, Justin Pierre Plumard: letter to,
141; misfortunes of, 5; loses possessions
in fire, 123, 125n, 141; letters from
cited, 141n; letters to cited, 141n; Mon-
roe tries to assist, 164
Derieux, Maria Margarita Martin (Mme
Justin Pierre Plumard Derieux), 141
Description du Cap de Bonne-Esperance
(Peter Kolb): cited by TJ, 295
Des Droits et des Devoirs du Citoyen
(Gabriel Bonnot de Mably): cited by
Adams, 59
Desmarest, Anselme: names *Megalonyx
jeffersonii*, 301n
Detroit: Volney visits, 174, 220-1
Deurtang's (inn, western Va.), 151
Dick (b. 1767, TJ's slave): TJ mortgages,
98
Dick (b. 1790, TJ's slave): TJ mortgages,
98
Dickenson v. Paulett: case of, 189
Dickinson, John: as author of letters
signed "Fabius," 434; fears war with
France, 435n
Dinah (TJ's slave): TJ mortgages, 98
dionnea mascipula: TJ requests seed of,
43
dipus americanus: Barton describes, 183

*Discovery, Settlement, and Present State of
Kentucky* (John Filson), 176n
*Dissertation on Slavery: With a Proposal for
the Gradual Abolition of It, in the State of
Virginia* (St. George Tucker): rejected
by House of Delegates, 489n
D'Ivernois, François, 58-9
Divers, George: receives payment from
T. M. Randolph, 26, 27n
Dix's ferry (Dan River): site on proposed
road from Georgetown to Ga., 529
Dobie, Samuel, 310n
Dobs, Richard, 120
Dobson, Thomas: *Encyclopaedia*, 441n
dogs: shepherd, TJ characterizes, 26-7
Dohrman, Arnold Henry: and Mazzei's
business affairs, 55, 67, 70, 81, 90, 199-
200
Doll (TJ's slave): son of, in marriage set-
tlement of Mary Jefferson, 550
Dombey, Joseph: brings French units of
measure to U.S., 229-30, 257, 259n;
death of, 229
Donald, Alexander: tobacco sold to, 112;
forwards items to TJ, 115, 319, 511;
and TJ's financial transactions, 307
Donath, Joseph: letters to, 184, 187, 212-
13; TJ orders glass from, 167, 183, 184,
186, 187, 212-13; letters from cited,
184n, 187n, 213n
Dorchester, Lord (Sir Guy Carleton): inflammatory speech to Indians, 610-13,
626
Dougherty, Felix, 538-9
Draper, John: recollection associated with
megalonyx, 296-7
Drayton family: as reference for van Hasselt, 467
Duane, William, 537n
Dublin Packet (ship), 340, 366
Ducoigne, Jean Baptiste: letter to, 131-2;
introduced to Volney, 131-2
Ducoigne, Jefferson: invited to visit Monticello, 131
Dugnani, Antonio: letters from, 370, 538-
9; revives correspondence with TJ,
370; recommends Catholic students,
538-9
Dumfries, Va.: TJ known at, 184; wheat
prices at, 322
Dunbar, John, 45n
Dungeness (Randolph estate): T. M. Randolph stops at, 568
Dunmore, John Murray, fourth Earl of:
and Logan's speech, 408, 409-10n, 441,
451, 452, 601-2

Dunmore's War, 409-10n, 441, 452
Duvall, Gabriel, 60
Duvivier, Pierre Simon Benjamin: engraves medals, 14

eastern states: and election of 1796, 223, 247, 249, 289; aversion to land tax in, 285; changing political opinion in, 372; and future of republicanism in, 439; efforts to connect TJ with Blount conspiracy in, 473n
East Indies: seizure of U.S. ships in, 285, 421-2, 423n
East Indies, British: opened to U.S. trade, 628
École des Arts et Métiers, 149n
Edgar, Mr. (Greenbrier Co., Va.), 150
Edgehill (Randolph estate): farm manager at, 36, 168, 260-1; slaves at, 90, 260; absence of news from, 170; conditions at, 260, 322; TJ hopes Randolphs will settle at, 351; TJ proposes road to Pantops, 430
education: of blacks in Va., 120, 287-8; of Americans in Paris, 164; TJ's education bill, 177-8, 287-8
Edwards, Enoch: letter to, 269; letters from, 230-1, 313-14; carries letters, 162, 230, 231n; entrusted with discretion to publish Monroe documents, 230-1, 269, 313; reports on affairs in France, 230-1, 269; sends recipes, information on cooking, 313-14; bears papers for Washington, 314; letters from cited, 314n; letter to cited, 314n
Edwards, Frances Gordon (Mrs. Enoch Edwards), 314
Eel River Indians, 400
eggplant: TJ seeks seeds, information on, 141
Egypt: Volney's experience in, xxxviii, 111, 132, 175
election of 1796: Adams's victory in, viii, 247-50, 255; in Tenn., 169, 199; in Va., 193-9; in Pa., 211, 261-2; intrigues against Adams, 214-15, 223, 226, 235-6, 251, 264, 326; closeness of presidential race, 223-4, 226, 227-8; in Vt., 228n; distribution of Federalist support in, 232, 235-6, 253; dissemination of results, 235, 236, 258; Hamilton's role, 235-6, 362; Federalist tactics in New England, 262; as will of the people, 289; electoral votes counted, 304, 305n; decreases number of Republicans in Con-

gress, 416; impact of Washington's popularity in, 438
election of 1800: and TJ's letter to Mazzei, 74, 79; Callender's *Prospect Before Us* and, 537n
Elementa philosophica de Cive (Thomas Hobbes): quoted by TJ, 249n
elephants: compared to mammoths, 113-14, 138, 294; habitat of, as analogy for megalonyx, 294, 295, 297-8; Buffon on, 297-8
Elk Hill (TJ's estate): purchase of by Banks, T. Taylor, 213n, 219-20, 287
Elk River, 150, 151
Elk Run Church (Fauquier Co., Va.): site on proposed road from Georgetown to Ga., 529
Ellicott, Andrew: letter from, 534-6; and British influence on frontier, 534-6; boundary survey, 535-6; conflict with Hutchins, 535-6
Elliott, Matthew, 441
Ellsworth, Oliver: appointment as chief justice, 42, 124; and Jay Treaty, 71; and election of 1796, 227
embargo: on grains, proposed, 62-3; recommended in event of war, 377; and Congress, 386, 402; president's authority to lay, 461, 462
Emigrants (Gilbert Imlay), 176n
Encyclopaedia; or, A Dictionary of Arts, Sciences, and Miscellaneous Literature (Thomas Dobson): prints Logan's speech, 440-1, 602
Encyclopédie Méthodique: TJ orders volumes of, 4, 160-1
ensette (ensete, abyssinian banana), 513
Enville, Louise Elisabeth de La Rochefoucauld, Duchesse d': friendship with TJ, 147, 312, 317, 333, 464-5; death of, 597, 598n
envoys to France. *See* France: U.S. relations with: U.S. envoys to
Epoques de la nature (Comte de Buffon): cited by TJ, 297-8
Eppes, Betsy: invited to Monticello, 533, 546; tooth extracted, 579
Eppes, Elizabeth Wayles (Mrs. Francis Eppes, TJ's sister-in-law): letter from, 546-7; TJ's affection for, 167, 586; marriage of son and Mary Jefferson, 531-3, 546-50; letter to cited, 546-7n
Eppes, Francis (TJ's brother-in-law): letters to, 166-7, 531-4; letters to cited, 45n, 167n, 533n; and Wayles estate, 166-7, 196n, 217, 268, 419; letters from

Eppes, Francis (*cont.*)
cited, 167n, 268, 533n; marriage of son
and Mary Jefferson, 531-3, 547-50;
gives slaves to J. W. Eppes, 549; TJ
sends respects to, 586
Eppes, John Wayles: letter to, 585-7; letters from, 186, 226, 572-3; courts, mar-
ries Mary Jefferson, vii, 186, 226, 425n,
531-3, 546-7, 549-50; and TJ's accounts, 167; letters from cited, 186n,
587n; letters to cited, 186n; and Burr's
visit to Monticello, 198; TJ approves
of marriage plans, 424, 429-30; marriage settlement, 532, 533n, 547-8;
Monroe extends invitation to, 566;
travels from Monticello to Eppington, 572; TJ provides house for, 577;
visits relatives, 579; and road contract,
586
Eppes, Mary Jefferson (Mrs. John Wayles
Eppes). *See* Jefferson, Mary (Maria,
Polly, TJ's daughter)
Eppes family: invited to Monticello, 533;
TJ sends regards to, 577; kindness to
Mary Jefferson, 579; TJ's affection for,
586
Erie, Lake, 174, 221
Erskine, Thomas: praised by H. Gates,
361; *View of the Causes and Conse-
quences of the Present War with France*,
361, 407, 434
*Esquisse d'un tableau historique des progrès
de l'esprit humain* (Marquis de Con-
dorcet), 201
Ethis de Corny, Anne Mangeot (Mme
Ethis de Corny), 397
*Eulogium, intended to perpetuate the mem-
ory of David Rittenhouse* (Benjamin
Rush): sent to TJ, 251, 252n, 275
Europe: absence of news from, 25, 73, 95,
227, 414; prospects for peace in, 108;
hinderances to establishment of republi-
can governments in, 194; and War of
First Coalition, 393, 396; events in,
decrease prospect of U.S. war with
France, 429
Evans, Thomas: as Federalist congress-
man from Va., 372, 374n, 422; votes on
U.S. policy with France, 412, 413
Evans (TJ's slave): TJ mortgages, 98
Ewell, Jesse, 184
Examiner (Richmond): and Callender,
537n; and L. Martin's attacks on TJ,
603n
Excellencie of a Free State (Marchamont
Nedham), 59

Fabbroni, Giovanni, 74
"Fabius." *See* Dickinson, John
Faden, William: map of South America by,
105-6, 115
Fair American (ship), 397n
Fairfax, Thomas, sixth Lord, 279
Fairfax Co., Va.: campaign for presidential
elector in, 193, 195; and proposed road
from Georgetown to Ga., 529, 530
Fairfax Stone: and Va.-Md. boundary,
263n
Fanny (TJ's slave): TJ mortgages, 98
Farell & Jones: and Wayles estate, 96-7,
197n; TJ's debt to, 478n. *See also* Hanson, Richard
farmers: fear taxes on land, 265; encroach-
ment on liberties of yeomen, 444; TJ
provides information for, 583-4
Farmer's Weekly Museum (Walpole,
N.H.): publishes TJ's letter to Mazzei,
75n
farm implements: Caroline drill by
T. Martin, 129, 143-4, 318, 545-6, 553,
573, 588; and farm animals, 170, 545;
TJ's interest in, 205; TJ sends to Britain, 318, 450n, 545-6. *See also* plow,
moldboard; threshing machines
Fauchet, Jean Antoine Joseph: and U.S.
internal affairs, 384, 385n; replaces
Genet, 471; and Monroe's recall, 565;
Coup d'oeil sur l'état actuel, 589-90, 594,
595; British complaint against, 611-12
Faujas de Saint-Fond, Barthélemy, 301n
Fauquier Co., Va.: campaign for presiden-
tial elector in, 195-6
Fayette Co., Pa.: 1796 election results
from, 211
Federal District: federal aid for, 10-11, 56;
investment in land in, 157n, 368;
Volney visits, 483; location of government at, 528-9; potential market for Va.
products, 529; and proposed road from
Georgetown to Ga., 529
*Federal Gazette & Baltimore Daily Adver-
tiser* (Baltimore): publishes L. Martin's
attacks on TJ, 409n, 454-5n, 601
"Federalist." *See* Coxe, Tench
Federalist Papers: TJ suggests addition to,
51
Federalists: and TJ's letter to Mazzei, vii,
73-88; and Jay Treaty, 25, 46, 48, 51,
60, 71n, 94, 147; as British faction, 109,
228, 407, 433; and P. Henry, 147-8;
and election of 1796, 193-9, 211, 214,
223-4, 226; geographical distribution
of, 235-6; tactics in New England, 262;

and Monroe, 269; and U.S. relations with France, 280, 370, 372, 373-4n; caucuses by, 283n, 411, 412n; attack Madison's reputation, 323-4, 380; "Hamiltonians" as wing of, 362; Washington as supporter of, 381; control appointments to Senate committees, 411, 412n; as war party, 413-14; and appointment of Gerry, 420n, 450; influence of events in Europe on, 422; and expenditures for fortifications, 423n; encroach on liberties of yeomen, 444; and Tenn. statehood, 472n; and Blount impeachment, 473n; and diplomatic appointments, 486-7; and Callender, 537n; denoted as aristocrats, 556-7; and newspaper attacks on TJ, 556; in S.C., 567n

Fennell, James: performs Logan's speech, 409n, 452, 454, 581

Fenno, John: publishes L. Martin's attacks on TJ, 443; prints piece by Hamilton, 484n. See also *Gazette of the United States* (Philadelphia)

Fenwick, Joseph, 563, 565

Fenwick, Mason & Co., 368

Ferdinand IV, King of Naples, 256n

Ferri de Saint-Constant, Giovanni Lorenzo, 74

Filson, John: *Discovery, Settlement, and Present State*, 176n

Findley, William, 593

fireplaces: Count Rumford's designs for, 605n

fires: residential, in Va., 123, 125n, 141; insurance against, 190-1, 239-44

fish: high price of herring, 36; TJ orders herring, 91; in diet during harvest, 414

Fitzhugh, Elizabeth Chew (Mrs. Peregrine Fitzhugh), 324

Fitzhugh, Peregrine: letters to, 346-7, 415-19; letters from, 323-4, 380-2, 442-5, 555-61; exchanges seeds with TJ, 323-4, 346, 380, 415, 559-60; and Madison's views on treaty-making powers, 323-4, 346-7; criticizes Adams's advisors, 380-1; on U.S relations with France, 380-2; provides information on Cresaps and death of Logan's kin, 416, 444, 555-6; shares contents of TJ's letter, 418n, 556-7, 560-1; letter to the *Rights of Man*, 561

Fitzhugh, William: TJ sends respects to, 347, 381, 418; encourages son to show TJ's letter to Republican friends, 556-7; sends respects to TJ, 560

flags: on U.S. consulates in Mediterranean, 376

Flanders: Volney compares Ohio to, 221

Fleming, John, 36

Fleming, William: letter from, 204; describes counties of Ky., 204

Fleming & McClenahan: and supplies for Monticello, 414; sell nails from Monticello, 540-1

Florida, East: oranges from, 543

Florida, West: boundary with U.S., 535

Floridas: within range of U.S. coastal gunboats, 377; plans to invade, 472-3n

flour: price of, 10, 26, 350, 371, 385, 426, 583; sale of, 412

Fluvanna Co., Va.: and TJ's grand jury petition, 490, 491-504, 524

Forrest, Rebecca Plater (Mrs. Uriah Forrest), 557

Forrest, Uriah: sends president extract of TJ's letter to P. Fitzhugh, 418n, 560n; and Hamilton's *Observations*, 557-8

Forrester, Simon, 543

Fort Recovery, Northwest Terr.: Indians attack, 612, 630-1n

Fourteen Agricultural Experiments, to ascertain the best rotation of crops (George Logan): sent to TJ, 272, 273n

Fourth of July. *See* Independence Day

FRANCE

Agriculture
pea seeds from, 323; research in, 333

Army
potential disbanding of, 405

Constitution
Volney notes change in, 53; pamphlets on new government, 123; prospects for, 161; Paine cites, 343

Directory
Adams skeptical of, 59; response to Jay Treaty, 109-10, 215n; taxes under, 110n; and paper currency, 122, 123n; and loot from subjugated territories, 161, 164-5n; and foreign diplomatic appointments, 230-1; refuses to receive C. C. Pinckney, 230, 231n, 340; change in composition of, 357; and declaration of war against U.S., 439; disagreeable disposition of, 442; measures of, criticized in U.S., 470; in competition with legislative councils, 485; arreté of 12 Ventose, 486

FRANCE (*cont.*)

Economy
forced loan in, 56, 109-10; falling price of provisions in, 119; funding system, currency, 122, 123n, 162, 165n; strength of, 222, 341; specie, paper currency in circulation, 341

Foreign Relations
alleged corruption of, xxxvii; and Jay Treaty, 71, 357; with Geneva, 208, 209; with Spain, 228, 372; dissemination of Paine's *Decline and Fall*, 340; with Batavian republic, 372, 374n; and establishment of republican principles, 460; treaty of commerce with Britain, 615, 628

Internal Improvements
roads, 8

Italian Campaign
auspicious beginning of, 117, 135-6, 146, 148, 161, 222; art, antiquities taken from subjugated territories, 161, 164-5n; French successes in, 169, 265, 273, 305, 341, 422, 423n, 431, 433, 434n, 436, 438, 456, 459

National Assembly
members of, 131-2, 134, 137

National Institute of Arts and Sciences
established, 102n; philosophical society within, 110-11; and Dombey's mission, 229; members, 347, 348n

Politics and Government
TJ welcomes information about, 61; Gautier sends pamphlets on, 122-3; bright prospects of, 163, 230; elections, 222; legislative councils in power struggle with Directory, 485; Adams criticizes, 593; Harper criticizes Republic, 593. *See also* French Revolution

Public Opinion
resentment of Jay Treaty, 230; against U.S., 340; regard for Monroe, 340

Rhine Campaign
anticipated, 117; French successes in, 161, 265, 273, 433, 434n, 436, 456, 459

Society
in state of vigor and increasing public confidence, 56; unsuitable place for young American woman, 147; char-acteristics of people, 237; Royal Academy of Sciences, 293; penal institutions and solitary confinement, 335, 336n

U.S. Relations with
prospects for war, possibilities of peace, viii, 135, 227, 239, 271, 272-3, 289-90, 342-3, 355, 359-60, 361, 379, 381-2, 392-3, 395n, 396, 407, 415, 418-19n, 421-3, 429, 433, 435n, 441, 442, 462-3, 522, 557, 580, 587n; Jay and Pinckney treaties compared, 48; and American party politics, 76, 455-6, 580; during American Revolution, 76; and Jay Treaty, 108-10, 214-15, 230, 340, 342, 345n, 405, 486n, 629; and Washington's sentiments, 142, 553; and Independence Day orations, 156-7; and treaty of amity and commerce, 215n, 340, 342, 486; distrusts U.S. executive branch, 227-8; refusal to receive C. C. Pinckney, 230, 231n, 316, 340; TJ's thoughts on, 235, 237, 252, 255, 426, 438-9, 448-9, 586, 594; commences attack on U.S. trade, 256, 273; U.S. envoys to, 256, 265, 342, 411, 414, 416, 420, 427, 443, 448-9, 450, 460, 475-6, 485-6, 552, 580, 586, 589, 591-2, 594, 598; interference with U.S. shipping, 282, 285, 330, 369, 371n, 429, 431, 448, 563-4n; previous French support of U.S. resented, 342-3; and Pickering, 343, 345n; and U.S. neutrality, 344, 363, 485, 611; appointment of U.S. consuls to, 366-7; and U.S. relations with Netherlands, 372, 374n; and equal treaty rights, 373-4n, 411-12, 413-14, 421; and spoliation claims, 374, 421; West Indies and possible war, 377; influence in U.S. internal affairs, 383-4, 393-5; effects of Pickering letter, 426; and American Indians, 441; and Adams's address of May 1797, 442-3; Genet and, 470-2; and Blount conspiracy, 473n; French travelers uncomfortable in U.S., 483; and competition between legislative councils, Directory, 485-6; distance affects communication, decisions, 485-6; U.S. ship rosters required, 486; Adams considers sending mission to, 551-2; *Unicorn* affair, 612, 630n

War of First Coalition
prospects for peace, 53, 71, 108, 119, 415; on Austrian and British fronts,

FRANCE (*cont.*)
56; Britain as primary foe, 70, 146, 162; prospects for peace fade, 135, 222, 341-2; reinforcements for Saint-Domingue, 148, 149n; preparations for conquest of Britain, 222, 344n, 366, 433; failure of British peace mission, 256-7, 273, 282, 285-6; and neutral shipping, 344; peace at Leoben, 367n, 431, 433, 434n, 436, 438, 450, 451, 459, 558; causes of, 407; French agents in Britain, 521n

Francis II, Holy Roman Emperor: prospects of peace with France, 108, 161-2, 169; and restoration of Austrian Netherlands, 256n; forced to seek peace, 305; agrees to armistice, 366, 367n, 485. *See also* Holy Roman Empire

Francis, John: identified, 469n; Liancourt sends message by, 463; account with, 469; prepares rooms for TJ, 576

Francis's hotel: residents at, 412n, 469n; TJ stays at, 412n, 469, 536, 576, 585; Callender visits TJ at, 536; TJ visits Adams at, 551

Frank (TJ's slave): TJ mortgages, 98

Frankfurt Am Main: surrendered to French, 162, 165n

Franklin, Benjamin: diplomatic expenditures, 14, 17-18; letter to Adams quoted, 17-18; and Houdon statue of Washington, 37n, 40; Cobbett mocks, 140; TJ praises, 140, 276-7; and American science, 254

Fraunces, Andrew G.: letters to, 459, 460; identified, 459n; and Hamilton's *Observations*, 459, 459n, 460, 542-3, 562n; seeks aid from TJ, 459, 460

Frederick, Md.: as Federalist stronghold, 557

Fredericksburg, Va.: stagecoaches to Philadelphia, 274, 565; fruit trees at, 322; wheat prices at, 322; shipments to TJ from, 323; spring at, 328, 351; TJ visits, 425, 436; delays in mail at, 427, 428

Freeman, Nathaniel, Jr.: appointed to House committee, 372, 373n; resides at Francis's hotel, 469n

French Revolution: Adams assesses, 59; executions, 123n, 160, 313n; displaces military officers who served in America, 145; displaces artists, 389; Fructidor, 558-9, 576, 580

Freneau, Philip: TJ pays for newspaper of, 442; letter from cited, 442n

Friendly Islands. *See* Tonga

Friends, Society of, 120

Froullé, Jean François: TJ orders books from, 4; death of, 160, 464

fruit trees: establishment of Monroe's orchard, 5, 41-2; in blossom at Monticello, 322, 351; orange, E. Rutledge sends to TJ, 357, 386, 455

Fry, Joshua, 66

Gadsden, Christopher: signs wharfholders' memorial, 570n

Gales, Joseph, 434

Gallatin, Albert: encouraged to bring order to U.S. finances, 6; and Jay Treaty, 51-2; TJ praises speech by, 51; and TJ's letter to Mazzei, 79; speeches on public debt and expenditures, 124, 125n; debates W. L. Smith, 146; obtains position for J. Martin, 157n; *Sketch of the Finances of the United States*, 224, 256n; on Gerry's appointment, 420n; opposes arming of merchant vessels, 423n; calls for Congress to adjourn, 432n; and TJ's grand jury petition, 505

Gallipolis, Northwest Terr.: Volney describes, 150, 151; disputed land titles, 151, 152n

Galloway, Benjamin: letter from, 566-7; identified, 567n; sends praise, 566-7

Galvan, William, 185n

Galvan de Bernoux, Francis: letter from, 184-5; identified, 184-5n; calls at Monticello, 184-5

Gamble, Elizabeth Washington, 359n

Gamble, Robert: business dealings with TJ, 50, 540

Gamble & Temple, 569

Gardner, John ("Aurelius"), 199n

Gardoqui, Diego de, 551

Garland, Edward, 26

Garland, Robert, 64n

Garrett, Alexander: endorses documents, 66, 550n

Garzoni, Paolo, 74

Gates, Horatio: letter to, 407; letter from, 361; invites TJ to Rose Hill, 361; TJ returns correspondence, 361; sends Erskine pamphlet to TJ, 361n; presides over Republican dinner, 479n; and Monroe-Hamilton conflict, 578

Gates, Mary Vallance (Mrs. Horatio Gates), 361

Gatteaux, Nicolas Marie, 14

Gatty, Joseph, 315-16

Gauley River, 151

Gautier, Jean Antoine: letter to, 30-3;

Gautier, Jean Antoine (*cont.*)
letter from, 122-3; accounts with U.S., Va., 30-3; and TJ's French accounts, 30-3, 41; and Grand & Cie., 122; friendship with Pougens, 333n

Gawen (TJ's slave): TJ mortgages, 98

Gazette Française (New York), 76n

Gazette Nationale ou Le Moniteur Universel (Paris): publishes TJ's letter to Mazzei, 73-4, 75, 84-5, 385n

Gazette of the United States (Philadelphia): publishes TJ's letter to Mazzei, 75-9; prints Washington letter, 506n. *See also* Fenno, John

Geddis, Miss, 314

Gelston, David, 479n

Gem, Richard, 160

Generall Historie of Virginia (Capt. John Smith): TJ utilizes, 294, 301n, 302-3n

Genesee, N.Y.: Volney visits, 221

Genet, Edmond Charles: and French plan to liberate Louisiana, 133n; interferes in U.S. internal affairs, 384; criticizes TJ, 470-2; letter from summarized, 470-2

Geneva: citizens' claims on funds in U.S., 207-9; relations with France, 208, 209

Genoa: port for northern Italy, 121; and French campaign in Italy, 135

Gentleman's and London Magazine, 155, 296

George (1730-1799, TJ's slave): prepares for harvest at Monticello, 414

George (1759-1799, TJ's slave): works in nailery, 540-1; TJ sends blacksmith's equipment to, 586

George III, King of Great Britain: and ratification of Jay Treaty, 48; and Federalist politics, 558; and Jay's commission as envoy, 605, 610, 629n; and U.S. complaints about orders in council, 607

Georgetown, Md.: stagecoaches at, 308; Volney visits, 352-3; TJ visits, 425, 528; survey for road to Stevensburg, Va., 431, 432, 529, 530; as Federalist stronghold, 557

Georgia: post road between Me. and, 8n; vote at Constitutional Convention, 68; and election of 1796, 226, 227; and Oglethorpe estate, 347, 348n; TJ sends breadfruit to, 388

Georgics (Virgil): quoted, 233n

Gerry, Ann Thompson (Mrs. Elbridge Gerry), 402

Gerry, Catharine, 402

Gerry, Elbridge: letters to, 361-6, 398-9, 448-9; letters from, 326-7, 355-6, 387, 402, 475-6; at Constitutional Convention, 57n; and partisan politics, 326-7, 361-6; relations with Adams, 326-7, 402, 475; relations with Monroe, 355-6, 361, 387, 398-9, 402; suspects interception of mail, 355-6, 387, 398-9, 402; relationship with TJ, 365n, 448-9, 587; family of, 402; as envoy to France, 420n, 448-9, 450, 451, 460, 475-6, 552, 580, 586, 589, 591, 594, 598; letter from cited, 449n; and TJ's view of the vice presidency, 633

Gerry, Eleanor Stanford, 402

Gerusalemme Liberata (Torquato Tasso): Volney quotes, 229, 230n; TJ adapts quote from, 258

Giannini, Antonio: and Mazzei's finances, 81, 83n

Gibson, John: letters to, 408-10, 451, 599-600; letter from, 440-1; and Logan affair, 408-10, 440-1, 451, 599-600, 601-2; translates Logan's speech, 408, 409n, 441, 602; ties to Logan's family, 409n; seeks government position, 441

Gibson, Patrick, 578n

Giles, William Branch: letter to, 35-6; letters from, 38, 45-49, 54-5, 60-1; TJ sends respects to, 7, 224; and visit to Monticello, 36, 49, 60; introduces La Rochefoucauld-Liancourt, 38; and politics of Jay Treaty, 45-9, 54, 60; sends *Debates* to TJ, 60; and TJ's letter to Mazzei, 77; obtains Washington document, 142; as tarnish on Va.'s reputation, 383; criticizes Genet, 470; effect of absence from House, 594

Gililan's (inn, western Va.): Volney criticizes, 151

Gill (TJ's slave): TJ mortgages, 98

Gillespie, James, 62n

Gillon, Alexander: sails from Holland to America, 466

Gilmer, Dr. George, 153

Gilmer, Lucy Walker (Mrs. George Gilmer): TJ purchases corn from, 26, 52, 91; orders nails, 358; "Pen Park" estate, 358

Giroud, Alexandre: letter to, 387-8; letter from, 347-8; identified, 348n; acquaintance with TJ, 347-8; sends breadfruit seeds, 347-8, 387-8; letter from cited, 348n

glass: TJ orders, 184, 187, 212-13

Godoy Alvarez de Faria, Manuel, Duque de la Alcudia, 48-9

Godwin, William, xxxvii

Goliah (TJ's slave): in marriage settlement of Mary Jefferson, 550
gongs: Chinese, A. Stuart orders from TJ,
239, 253
Goochland Co., Va.: cold weather at, 223;
property in secures debt, 476-8; and TJ's
grand jury petition, 490, 491-504, 524
Goodhue, Benjamin, 283n
Goodrich, Chauncey, 224n
Gracie, Archibald, 45n
Graham, Mr., 187, 188
Graham, George: portrait of Adams, xl,
318 (illus.)
grain: export of, 10; treading and storage
of in Spain, 28; exhausts soil, 103; hurt
by drought, 224, 559; in Jay Treaty negotiations, 614, 623, 628
Grand, Ferdinand: death of, 354. *See also*
Grand & Cie.
Grand, Jean François Paul: letter from,
354; identified, 354n; congratulates TJ
on vice presidency, 354; family of, 354;
letter from cited, 354n
Grand, Mme Jean François Paul, 354
Grand, Marie Silvestre (Mme Ferdinand
Grand), 354
Grand & Cie.: accounts of U.S. with, 11-
24, 32n, 33-4, 39; TJ's accounts with,
11-24, 31, 33-4, 39, 41; Va. accounts
with, 12, 15, 16-17, 33-4, 37-8, 39-41;
and U.S. assignats, 122
grapes: imported from Italy, 43
Grasse, François Joseph Paul de, Comte
de Grasse and Marquis de Grasse-Tilly:
U.S. grant to family of, 4-5, 7, 14n; fleet
of, 572n
grasses: seed sent to TJ, vii; meadow
cocksfoot or orchard, recommended by
Strickland, 104; timothy, sown with
clover, 104; descriptions of, 510-12; rye
grass or darnel grass seed sent to TJ,
510-12; in Md., 559

GREAT BRITAIN

Agriculture
Board of Agriculture diploma for TJ, xl-
xli, 318 (illus.), 449-50, 514; publications of British Board sent to TJ, 105-
6, 114, 183, 480; threshing machines
in, 167, 170; seeds from sent to TJ,
546; poor wheat harvest in, 583-4

Army
and Napoleonic campaigns, 456

Economy
and War of First Coalition, 117-18; distressed state of, 119, 422, 423n, 456;
Bank of England suspends specie payments, 340-1, 344n, 370-1, 373, 379,
401, 427, 431, 433, 438, 459; Paine
on expansion of, 341; needs capital in
U.S., 464; high price of wheat, 583-4

Foreign Relations
and Jay Treaty, 71; Spain declares war
against, 256, 265; bellicose tendencies of British government, 341-2;
treaty of commerce with France, 615,
628

House of Commons
and rules of procedure, 283

Internal Improvements
roads, 8

Laws
as antecedent to American jurisprudence, 4n

Navy
mutiny at Spithead, 431, 433, 436, 438,
456, 459; defeats Dutch fleet, 585-6

Parliament
sedition bills in, 10; Bank Restriction
Act, 344n; ministers of, criticized,
470

Politics and Government
Adams on prospects of revolution, 59;
forms of British government and TJ's
letter to Mazzei, 82; compared to classical Rome, 249n; Paine expects collapse of government, 341; actions
against pro-French sentiment in, 407,
521n

Public Opinion
popularity of Paine's *Decline and Fall*,
340-1; scorns U.S., 340

Society
penal institutions and solitary confinement, 335, 336n; unsafe to reside in,
399

U.S. Relations with
Republicans mock British institutions,
3; and impressment of sailors, 35,
612, 613, 614, 621, 623; orders in
council, 47, 606, 612; and influence
upon Washington administration,
142; claims commissions, 154n;
and Independence Day orations, 156-
7; and U.S.-French relations, 239,
271, 485, 629; TJ on, 269, 448-9;

GREAT BRITAIN (*cont.*)
interference with U.S. shipping, 285, 330, 429, 431, 448, 515-16, 519-20; and Hamilton's communication with Hammond, 345n; British policy detrimental to U.S. neutrality, 363-4; role of West Indies in event of war, 377; influence of British economy on, 379, 412; executive and Senate said to favor interests of, 380; and American party politics, 438, 455-6; and establishment of republican principles in, 460; possible treaty of alliance, 470, 522; Genet on, 471; southwestern frontier, 472-3n, 535-6; British courts and U.S. complaints, 607, 615; and seizure of *Unicorn*, 612, 630n; boundary issue, 613, 614, 615, 616-17, 619-22, 626-7; and privateers, 613, 615, 616, 628; and Algiers, 628-9. *See also* Jay Treaty

War of First Coalition
in West Indies, 25-6, 56, 169; as France's primary foe, 70, 146, 162, 433; prospects for peace, 71, 108, 119, 305, 341, 415; subsidizes, loses allies, 135, 161; prospects of French invasion, 222, 344n, 366; TJ's views on, 252-3; failure of peace mission, 256-7, 273, 282, 285-6; and neutral shipping, 344; public reaction to, 361; causes of, 407

Great Claw. *See* megalonyx
Greathouse, Daniel: and murder of Logan's kin, 410n
Great Lakes: and deployment of U.S. coastal gunboats, 377
Green, Capt. (*Industry*), 315
Greenbrier Co., Va.: site of megalonyx discovery, 64, 152, 266, 291, 295; Volney travels through, 150; lands in, mortgaged to TJ, 213, 219-20
Greene Co., Pa.: and election of 1796, 211, 261-2
Greenleaf, Thomas (editor, *Argus*): publishes TJ's letter to Mazzei, 76
Greenleaf's New York Journal, & Patriotic Register (New York): TJ subscribes to, 442n
Greenup, Christopher, 62n
Grégoire, Henri: *De la Littérature des Nègres*, 176-7n; and TJ's racial views, 176-7n; and Dombey's mission, 229, 257
Grenville, William Wyndham, Lord: ne-

gotiation of Jay Treaty, 46-7, 605-31; offers commercial treaty, 613, 614, 618-19, 623, 629n; offers treaty to resolve standing issues, 616-18, 629n; Jay comments on, 621, 625
Griffin, Cyrus: and TJ's grand jury petition, 498n
Grimes, Capt. (master of *Three Friends*), 458n
Griswold, Roger, 372, 373n
groceries: shipment of, 90; purchased by TJ, 324
Gromer, Frederick: and megalonyx discovery, 291
Grove, William B., 469n
Guilford Court House, N.C.: site on proposed road from Georgetown to Ga., 529
Guillemard, John: letter from, 154-5; identified, 154-5n; visits Monticello, 72, 154; travels with La Rochefoucauld-Liancourt, 149n, 154-5
Gunn, James, 411
gunpowder, 44, 240

Hadfield, George, 310n
Hakluyt, Richard: TJ cites *Principall Navigations*, 294
Hal (TJ's slave): TJ mortgages, 98
Halifax, Nova Scotia: British prize court, 162
Halifax Co., Va.: search for P. Jefferson's land records at, 185
Hamburg: copying process invented by citizen of, 246; Lafayette rumored to arrive from, 594, 595n
Hamilton, Alexander: and Hylton v. U.S., 3, 4n, 10; "Camillus" essays by, 4, 55-7, 148; and public finances, 5-6, 265; and TJ, 5, 142, 144n, 234, 362, 542-3; on Jay Treaty, 55-7, 517; banquet honoring (1800), 79; and pro-French sentiment in U.S., 110n; opinion on *Little Sarah*, 128, 130n, 178; and election of 1796, 214, 226, 235-6; and Whiskey Insurrection, 248-50; relations with Adams, 253, 264-5; correspondence with Hammond, 345n; R. King writes, 434n; *Observations*, 459, 460, 483-4, 534, 536-7, 542-3, 546, 554-5, 557-8, 562; dispute with A. Fraunces, 459n, 542-3; dispute with Monroe, 478-9, 490-1, 542, 562, 566, 578-9, 593, 595n; Reynolds affair, 478-9, 542-3, 566, 630n; responds to Callender's

charges, 483-4; criticizes Jay, 517; friendly with Talleyrand, 517-18; and Pickering, 518; calls himself a monarchist, 596

Hamilton, Elizabeth Schuyler (Mrs. Alexander Hamilton), 542

Hamilton, Henry (governor of Bermuda), 611

Hammond, George: and negotiations on impressment of U.S. seamen, 35-6; Hamilton transmits information to, 345n; on mission to Vienna, 433; correspondence with secretary of state, 565, 606-7, 608; and Monroe's recall, 565; as British minister, 610, 611, 612; characterized, 612; TJ's letter of 5 Sep. 1793, 624

Hanah (TJ's slave): TJ mortgages, 98

Hanbury, Osgood, 196-7

Hancock, John (Princess Anne Co.), 515

Hanson, Richard: as agent of Farell & Jones, 96-7; suits against Wayles estate, 96-7, 166; TJ's payments to, 213, 220; and TJ's power of attorney, 274; and suit against Ronald estate, 478n

Harper, Robert Goodloe: condemns TJ, xxxvii; and TJ's letter to Mazzei, 79; favors indirect taxes, 265n; on U.S. relations with France, 373n; as Federalist, 412, 413n; promotes defense measures, 421, 423n; investigates charges against Blount, 473n; on monarchy, 593; TJ notes comments by, 593

Harriot (Hariot), Thomas: cited by TJ, 294-5

Harris, James, first Earl of Malmesbury: failure of peace mission to France, 256-7, 273, 282; negotiation with France, 344

Harris, Levett, 202n

Harrison, Benjamin, Jr., 6

Harrison, Richard: letters to, 11-13, 24-5, 33-4; and settlement of TJ's accounts, 11-25, 30, 32, 33-4, 38-9; letter to cited, 25n; memorandum to, 38-9; Adams consults, 58

Harrison & Sterett (Van Staphorst & Hubbard's agent): handle loan to TJ, 107, 186, 212, 329, 458; letters from cited, 107n; letters to cited, 107n

Harvie, Richard, & Co., 96, 97n

Harwood, William, 263n

Hawkins, Benjamin: letter to, 42-4; TJ asks for information on Continental Congress, 42-3; sends vines to TJ, 43

Hawkins, Sir John, 294-5

hawks: mesmerize prey, 192

hay: and agriculture in Spain, 28

Hay, Mr.: bottles beer for TJ, 360

Hay, William: and TJ's prison designs, 336n

Heath, John, 95n

Heiskell (Heiskill), Mr. (innkeeper, Staunton), 150

Hemings, James: plans trip to Spain, 399; TJ sees in Philadelphia, 399

Hemings, John: gives box to T. M. Randolph, 360

Hemings, Peter: prepares eggplant for TJ, 141

Hemings, Sally: and Callender's charges, 537n

Henderson, McCaul & Co.: TJ indebted to, 96-8, 202-4, 306-7; TJ mortgages slaves to, 96-8, 209. *See also* Lyle, James

Hening, William Waller, 322

Henry, John: letter to, 600-4; sends paragraph to *Aurora*, 309; in Senate, 395n, 411; and TJ's account of Logan's speech, 409n, 590-1, 600-4; characterized, 412n; resides at Francis's hotel, 469n; investigates charges against Blount, 472n; letter to Tazewell, 590-1; relationship with TJ, 590-1, 602-3, 604; resigns from Senate, 594, 595n; TJ prints, distributes letter to, 603n

Henry, Patrick: asked to serve in Washington's administration, 5, 147-8; and election of 1796, 147-8, 193, 196

Heracleitus, 238

Herald; A Gazette for the Country (New York): publishes TJ's letter to Mazzei, 75n, 76

Hercules (b. 1794, TJ's slave): TJ mortgages, 98

Hercules (ca. 1733-1807, TJ's slave): TJ mortgages, 98

Heron, James, 6

Heron, Sarah Taylor (Mrs. James Heron), 6

Hessian fly: destroys crops in Md., 559

Hickman, Edwin, 549

Hiester, Daniel, 60

Higginson, Nathaniel C., 607

Hillhouse, James: and Jay Treaty, 71n; committee appointment, 282n; and Imlay's petition, 584n

hippopotamuses: compared to mammoths, 294; Buffon ascribes mammoth teeth to, 297-8; habitat, as analogy for megalonyx, 297-8

Histoire Naturelle, générale et particulière (Comte de Buffon): cited by TJ, 292, 293, 295, 296, 298

historians: criticized by Callender, 249n

History of America (Jedidiah Morse): prints Logan's speech, 441n

History of Animals (Aristotle): cited by TJ, 295

History of the United States for 1796; including a Variety of Interesting Particulars Relative to the Federal Government Previous to that Period (James T. Callender): publication of, 479n, 536, 630n; Hamilton responds to charges in, 483-4, 534; TJ obtains, utilizes, 536, 537n, 609, 630n; TJ subsidizes, 630n

Hite, Isaac, Jr.: letter to, 137; identified, 137n; mentioned, 148

Hite, Isaac, Sr., 137n

Hite, Nelly Conway Madison (Mrs. Isaac Hite, Jr.), 137n

Hix, Judy (TJ's slave): in marriage settlement of Mary Jefferson, 550

Hobbs, Thomas: *Elementa philosophica de Cive*, 249n

Hobby, William J., 79

Hoche, Louis Lazare, 558

Hodgson (Hogden), William: and Mazzei's finances, 65, 81, 90

Hoffman, Jacob, 325n

Hofman, Mr. (Strasburg, Va.): tavern keeper, 148

hogs: feed for, 179; used for sausage, 313-14; given to Mary Jefferson, 547, 550

Holland, James, 62n

Holland Land Company: and Dutch speculations in U.S., 330n

Holmes, Isaac: and E. Rutledge's shipment to TJ, 357; removed from Charleston collectorship, 567n

Holy Roman Empire: and War of First Coalition, 135, 161; and peace of Leoben, 366, 367n

hominids: bones of, reported in saltpetre caves, 64

Hopkins, Arthur, 66

Hopkins, James: letter from cited, 66n

Hopkins, Samuel (N.Y.): and megalonyx discovery, 152, 291

Hornsby, Joseph, 37

horses: in Spain, 28; feed for, 99, 179, 319; sold in Ky., 175, 221; of Tex., 175; for TJ, 422, 423n, 425, 436; and farm implements, 545; given to Mary Jefferson, 547, 550; as contraband, 623

Houdon, Jean Antoine: Washington statue for Va., 37-8, 40

houses: taxes on, 265

Howell, George: letters from cited, 89n; letters to cited, 89n

Howell, Richard (governor of N.J.): views perpetual motion device, 378

Howell, Samuel, Jr.: supplies TJ with nailrod, 7, 55, 89, 95-6, 540; letters from cited, 89n, 125n; letters to cited, 89n, 125n

Howell, Samuel, Jr., & Co.: financial transactions with TJ, 107, 125

Howell, Samuel, Sr.: and nailrod suppliers, 55, 95; as Philadelphia merchant, 89n

Hubbard, Armistead (TJ's slave): TJ mortgages, 97

Hubbard, Burrel (TJ's slave): TJ mortgages, 97

Hubbard, Cate (TJ's slave): TJ mortgages, 97

Hubbard, Eve (TJ's slave): TJ mortgages, 97

Hubbard, Jame (b. 1743, TJ's slave): TJ mortgages, 97

Hubbard, Maria (TJ's slave): TJ mortgages, 97

Hubbard, Nace (TJ's slave): TJ mortgages, 97

Hubbard, Nancy (TJ's slave): TJ mortgages, 98

Hubbard, Nicholas: and slave mortgages, 209-10. *See also* Van Staphorst & Hubbard; Willink, Van Staphorst & Hubbard

Hubbard, Philip (TJ's slave): TJ mortgages, 98

Hubbard, Rachael (TJ's slave): TJ mortgages, 97

Hubbard, Sarah (TJ's slave): TJ mortgages, 98

Hudson, John, 63n

Hughes, Daniel: provides information on Cresaps, 556

Hughes (Hugues), Robert, 151

Humphreys, David, 109

Hunsrück: battle in, 265

Hurt, Mr.: repairs clocks at Monticello, 168

Hurt, John, 309

Hutchins, Anthony, 535-6

Hylton, Daniel L.: ships tobacco for TJ, 112; and election of 1796, 194

Hylton, William, Jr.: and Burr's visit to Monticello, 198

Hylton, William, Sr.: and threshing machines, 170; visits Monticello, 428

Illinois: Volney plans to visit, 124, 132, 151; peltry trade of, 151
Imlay, Gilbert: contradicts *Notes on Virginia*, 174-7; Volney criticizes, 175; criticizes TJ's racial views, 176-7n; writings, 176n
Imlay, William, 584
Impartial Herald (Newburyport, Mass.): publishes TJ's letter to Mazzei, 75n
impeachment: and TJ's grand jury petition, 492, 505; TJ recommends, of jurors, 496-7, 502-3. *See also* Blount, William
impressment: measures to protect American seamen against, 35; of seamen by Britain, 612, 613, 614, 621, 623
Incidents of the Insurrection in the Western Parts of Pennsylvania, in the Year 1794 (Hugh Henry Brackenridge): TJ's views on, 248-50
Independence Day: Fourth of July oration and TJ's letter to Mazzei, 79; J. Martin delivers oration at Jamaica, Long Island, 156-7, 521
Independent Chronicle and Universal Advertiser (Boston): publishes TJ's letter to Mazzei, 76
Indians: of Texas, 174; burial mound artifacts, 201, 202n; languages, 201-2, 367-8, 400n, 445-7; and character of whites on frontier, 225, 238, 259; numbers of, 294, 400; and evidence of megalonyx, large carnivores, 295, 415; in Kanawha R. region, 296; domestication of animals, 303n; and Christian missionary activity, 400; in *Notes on Virginia*, 400; tribal identities, 400; and war along U.S. frontiers, 400, 609, 612, 630-1n; oratorical skills, as subject of dispute, 409-10n, 452-5; sentimental depictions of, 409n; as threat to U.S. in case of war with France, 441; and Eastern Hemisphere cultures, 446; and European notions of progress, 446-7; of Wabash R. region, 508n; British incite, 610, 611, 612, 613, 626, 630-1n; and Jay Treaty, 613, 616, 620. *See also* Creek Indians; Delaware (Lenni Lenape) Indians; Logan (Mingo Indian); Mingo Indians; Shawnee Indians
Industry (schooner), 315

Ingersoll, Jared: and Hylton v. U.S., 10; as Blount's attorney, 473n
Innes, Harry: letter to, 132; introduced to Volney, 132
Innes (Innis), James: reported to be a true republican, 82; serves on Jay Treaty commission, 373, 374n
insurance: fire, Ast's plan for, 190-1; fire, TJ's declaration for, 239-44; on tobacco, 413, 426
insurance companies: favor Jay Treaty, 73, 94
Iredell, James: charge to grand jury, 70-1, 418-19n; and TJ's grand jury petition, 498n
Ireland: political turmoil in, 456, 459; possible invasion of by France, 580
Iris (b. 1775, TJ's slave): in marriage settlement of Mary Jefferson, 549
Irujo, Carlos Fernando Martínez de: carries letter for T. Pinckney, 69-70; to assist Louis of Parma, 121, 390-1, 481; and Jay Treaty, 228, 372-3, 374n; reports comment by Adams, 593
Isaac (TJ's slave): works in nailery, 540
Italy: TJ's grape from, 43; War of First Coalition, 117, 169, 256, 305; and U.S. naval strength, 376; TJ receives winter vetch seed from, 546. *See also* France: Italian Campaign
Izard, Ralph: as member of Senate committee, 69; and congressional politics, 412n
Izard family: as reference for van Hasselt, 467

Jackson, Andrew: and Battle of Enitachopko, 170n; and mammoth fossils, 398; as congressman, 413n
Jackson, David, 401
Jacobs, William S.: draws megalonyx specimens, xxxix, 300n
James (Randolph slave): works at Edgehill, 260; travels with T. M. Randolph, 569
James River: difficulty of connecting with western rivers, 151; climate and health by, 175; cold weather interrupts shipping on, 260-1; lands on, 533n, 547-8, 549; mentioned, 568
James River Company: canal reaches Richmond, 5; Short's shares in, 6, 316-17, 463, 523; Pollard's handling of shares of, 278n; borrows from partners, 317
Jaudenes, Josef de, 195

Jay, John: correspondence of, 8n, 610-31; commission, instructions as envoy, 10, 605-10, 629n, 630n; as secretary of foreign affairs, 19, 23-4n; letter to cited, 23n; as minister to Spain, 23n; letter from cited, 24n; reputation associated with treaty, 148; and Hamilton, 236n, 517; Paine criticizes, 340; ignores neutral powers, 344; and Federalist politics, 558; as likely candidate for governor, 594; and treaty of peace with Britain, 608; assesses treaty, 626; and relations with Algiers, 628-9; and U.S. relations with France, 629; health, 631n

Jay Treaty: in House of Representatives, 4, 5n, 7, 9-10, 42, 45-9, 51, 54, 55-7, 62-3, 70-1, 93-5; public response to, 4, 36n, 70-1, 72-3, 94; TJ's views on, 4, 42; and U.S. spoliation claims, 6, 607-8, 611, 612, 614, 627, 631n; and Pinckney's Treaty, 9-10, 48-9, 286; and northwest posts, 48, 609, 610, 612, 615, 616, 624-5, 626; description of supporters of, 60; Supreme Court and, 71-2; and American politics, 74, 147, 198-9n, 343, 345n; pressures for implementation of, 94; petitions for, against, 95-6, 108, 129n; legislation for execution of, 95n; and U.S. relations with France, 108-10, 359, 405; and claims of British creditors, 154n, 373, 608, 614, 615-16, 617, 618, 621, 623, 627, 631n; resented in France, 214-15, 230, 340, 342, 345n, 419n; explanatory article to, 228; Monroe justifies to French government, 230, 231n; and debate on treaty-making powers, 323; Paine on, 340; and neutral nations, 344, 345n, 613, 617, 621, 622-3, 628; definitions of contraband, 345n, 614, 615, 621, 623, 628; and Hamilton's communication with Hammond, 345n; E. Rutledge discusses, 357; effects on commerce, 366; Spain's response to, 372, 374n; Charleston's response to, 411-12; in Senate, 437, 614n, 629n, 630n; support for in Congress, 447; ratification of, 517; negotiation of, 605-31; Jay's instructions for commercial treaty, 609; and impressment of sailors, 612, 613, 614, 621, 623; boundary issue, 613, 614, 615, 616-17, 619-22, 626-7; Jay's proposals to Grenville, 613, 615-16; and privateers, 613, 615, 616, 628; Jay explains provisions of, 614-15, 625-9; and sequestration of debts, 618, 621, 627;

and East Indies, 628; mentioned, 36, 596n. See also Grenville, William Wyndham Lord; Peace Treaty, Definitive (1783); West Indies, British
Jefferson, Field, 578n
Jefferson, George: letter to, 577-8; letter from, 598-9; identified, 578n; handles TJ's business affairs in Richmond, 569, 577-8, 598-9; letter to cited, 599n
Jefferson, George, & Co., 587
Jefferson, Isaac (1775-ca.1849, TJ's slave): in marriage settlement of Mary Jefferson, 549; blacksmith's equipment for, 586
Jefferson, John Garland: letter to, 222-3; letter from, 185; searches land records for TJ, 185; letters from cited, 185n, 222n; considers moving to Tenn., 222-3
Jefferson, Mary (Maria, Polly, TJ's daughter): letters to, 314-15, 399, 429-31, 576-7; letters from, 308, 428, 579; courtship, marriage to J. W. Eppes, vii, 186, 226, 424, 425n, 429-30, 531-3, 546-51, 564; affection for sister and family, 27, 274, 308; regards sent to, 49, 54, 61, 106, 118, 148, 154, 156, 164, 488, 509, 517; and visitors at Monticello, 131-2, 428; accident at Monticello, 273, 572-3, 575, 579, 596; at Varina, 308, 351; TJ's affection for, 309, 314, 322, 328, 379, 414, 425, 430, 451, 462; friendships, 314, 325-6, 397, 399; affection for TJ, 334; correspondence with TJ, 349, 586; and trip to Monticello, 349; TJ's purchases for, 424, 579; rumored to be ill, 483, 507; Monroe extends invitation to, 566; travels to Eppington, 577, 579; mentioned, 518
Jefferson, Peter (TJ's father): will of, 43n, 66; and land records, 66, 185; survey of Fairfax grant, 263n
Jefferson, Randolph (TJ's brother): agreement with, 66-7; land transaction with TJ, 66; letters to cited, 66-7n; letters from cited, 67n

JEFFERSON, THOMAS

Agriculture
builds threshing machine, vii, 129, 167, 168-9, 170, 187-9, 207, 211, 231-2; exchanges ideas, seeds with various people, vii-viii, 61, 82, 465-8, 518-19; corresponds with British Board of Agriculture, receives diploma, xl-xli, 318 (illus.), 449-50; designs moldboard plow, xli, 140; foresees placing

INDEX

JEFFERSON, THOMAS (*cont.*)
  farms under direction of others, 7;
  crop rotation plan, 128-9, 245-6; experiments with crops, 128-9; devotion to, 139; works to restore farms,
  153; Questions on the Cow Pea, 179-
  80; to plant cow peas and orange
  trees, 231, 232, 455; sends farm implements to Britain, 318-19, 450n,
  545-6; exchanges seeds with P. Fitzhugh, 322-3, 346, 380, 415, 559-60;
  receives, distributes breadfruit seeds,
  347-8, 387-8, 487; sends rice to
  Charleston, 367, 487; exchanges
  ideas, seeds with Strickland, 510-12,
  514; says he plans to tenant out his
  farms, 518; and markets for beef and
  mutton, 529. *See also* clover; clover
  seed; corn; Monticello; Taylor, John
  (of Caroline); tobacco; wheat

  Architecture
  renovation of Monticello, vii-viii,
  xxxviii-xxxix, 318 (illus.), 352; consulted on residential designs, 170,
  345-6; design for Va. penitentiary,
  309-10, 335-9; designs Va. Capitol,
  310n, 335; designs unfamiliar to
  workmen, 352; acquaintance with
  Clérisseau, 389; Design for Chimney
  and Flues, 605

  Business and Financial Affairs
  account with James Brown, 26, 27n,
  112, 203; and Cobbs suit, 26-7, 63-4;
  search for land records, 42, 185; Banister estate's debt to, 45n, 102; land
  transactions, 52, 66, 213, 219-20,
  287; arranges work on house, 57-8;
  debt to Kippen & Co., 93; intends to
  sell land, 93; debt to Henderson,
  McCaul & Co., 96, 97-8, 202-4, 306-
  7; debt owed by Barton, 165-6, 182,
  192, 201; seeks overseer, 170; debt to
  W. Welch, 173, 268; and Ast's insurance plan, 190-1, 239-44; collects
  bonds in Bedford Co., 202-4, 307;
  Kinsolving's debt to, 204; arrangements with R. Hanson, 213, 220; refuses to ask anyone to serve as his security, 268; settlements of accounts,
  288; advises Cathalan, 368; with
  E. Randolph, 459; suit against Ronald
  estate, 476-8; requests A. Stuart's
  help in collecting payments, 525; uses
  vice presidential salary for Monticello
  renovation, 531; accounts, ledgers de-

  scribed, 541-2n; transfers business in
  Richmond to G. Jefferson, 577, 598-
  9; with Madison and Monroe, 591,
  592n. *See also* Barnes, John; Short,
  William; Van Staphorst & Hubbard;
  Wayles estate

  Character
  described, 149n; Guillemard praises,
  154; reputation in Europe, 154; as
  issue in election of 1796, 193-5; attacks on, 427; called a philosopher
  and a citizen, 465

  Correspondence
  Madison obtains copies of, 8n; fatigued
  from writing, 11; the "Mazzei letter,"
  73-88; sends Mazzei Second Inaugural Address, 80-1; urges correspondents to keep his letters out of newspapers, 80, 371, 417-18, 429, 445,
  527-8, 556-7; copies letters from
  memory, 234-7, 249-51; fails to retain
  press copies, 234, 247; expects letter
  to be shown to Adams, 281; with-
  holds signature from letters, 318;
  Gerry suspects interception of mails,
  387, 398-9; extracts, queries on TJ's
  letter to P. Fitzhugh, 418, 557, 560-
  1; fears interception of letters, 442,
  445, 460, 529-30; in Hamilton's *Observations*, 459, 460, 542-3, 562;
  places extract of letter in *Aurora*, 583-
  4; and Monroe's letters to Dawson,
  595n

  Educational Theories
  and education of blacks, 120, 177-8; Bill
  for the More General Diffusion of
  Knowledge, 177-8, 287-8

  Election of 1796
  elected vice president, viii, 255-6, 261;
  and campaign for electors in Va., 193-
  9; as a reluctant candidate, 199, 264;
  and electoral votes, 211, 258, 261,
  266; urged to accept vice presidency,
  218, 226-7, 229, 262, 269-70, 342;
  endorses Adams as president elect,
  223-4, 234-7, 247-8, 250, 270; news
  of election results, 227-8; supporters'
  expectations, 229; seeks accommodation with Adams, 234-7, 362-3; receives congratulations on vice presidency, 251, 326-7, 334-5, 368-9,
  370, 485, 534; supplies information
  to A. Stuart, 253; on acceptance of office of vice president, 258, 289, 362;

JEFFERSON, THOMAS (*cont.*)
expectations of friends in France, 312;
praised by E. Rutledge for patriotism,
356-7; discusses effect of Washington's popularity on, 438-9

Governor of Virginia
and British invasions of 1781, 193-4;
acquaintance with Paroy, 570-2;
mocked by L. Martin, 582

Health
TJ on decline of, 83; hopes for improvement of, 166-7; rheumatism, 351,
352, 399, 428; indisposed with a cold,
575, 583, 596

House of Delegates
service with W. Cocke in, 199

Law
collects and preserves Va. laws, 158,
168, 276, 283, 569; Dickenson v.
Paulett, 189; seeks rules of parliamentary procedure, 275-6, 283, 633; marriage settlements, 532-3; Marriage
Settlement for John Wayles Eppes,
547-8; Marriage Settlement for Mary
Jefferson, 549-51

Library
Encyclopédie, 4, 160-1; requests books,
pamphlets, 4, 160-1, 192, 201, 224;
books and pamphlets sent to, 46, 49n,
60, 105-6, 114-15, 182, 183, 205,
248-50, 256, 319, 361, 480; Pinckney Treaty sent to, 48; lends Faden's
map of South America, 105-6, 115;
lends Va. statutes, 172; obtains works
on languages, 202n; Pougens as
source for books, 333, 464; La
Rochefoucauld-Liancourt to buy
books for, 463

Minister to France
settlement of accounts, 11-25, 33-4, 37-
9; departure from France, 19; balance
owed to Va., 39-40; entertains
friends, 325; and Oglethorpe estate,
347, 348n, 387; and French politics,
470-1

Nailery
nailrod and iron stock for, 7, 62, 88-9,
531, 540-2, 577; and suppliers of nailrod, 7, 55, 88-9, 95; sale of nails, 99,
158, 358, 481, 525, 540-2, 587; importance to TJ, 229; buildings described, 242-3; Statement of Nailery

Profits, 540-2; workers at, 540-1;
accounts described, 542n; nails
ordered by Madison, 591, 592n

Opinions
on Gallatin, 6; on public finance, taxation, 6, 520, 594; opposes federal support for postal roads, 7-8; on Pinckney
Treaty, 7; opposes citizenship certificates for U.S. seamen, 35-6; on treaty-
making powers, 51; on Washington,
51, 252-3; on changes in American
politics, 73-88, 456-7; on Madison,
127, 129n, 223, 346-7, 380; on relations with France, Britain, 146, 269,
290, 448-9; on France as residence for
Eliza Monroe, 147; on use of medicine, 169; on ignorance and despotism, 178; favors publication of official
letters and state documents, 205; on
marriage, 210; on candidacy for president, 211, 223, 235-6, 247-8, 250,
275, 362; on Crèvecoeur's depictions
of frontier inhabitants, 225; on political ambition, 232-3, 235, 236-7, 258;
on politics and public life, 233; on
Adams, 234, 271, 280-1, 352, 552;
on prospects of war, 235, 237, 269,
431, 432; on nature of man, 248-51,
259; on Rittenhouse, Franklin, 251,
252n, 276-7; on distaste for popular
dissatisfaction, 258; on following the
will of the people in elections, 266;
opposes ceremony, 267, 274, 281; on
conflict in Washington's cabinet, 271;
on foreign influence in U.S., 289; on
mortgages as investment, 317; on
farming as an occupation, 318, 522-3;
on financial speculations, 329-30; on
convening of Congress, 347, 416,
418n; on his isolation from the public,
353; on presidency as "splendid misery," 362; on Britain's influence over
U.S., 363-4; on need for U.S. neutrality, independence from European en-
tanglements, 363-4, 415; war with
France preferable to U.S. disunion,
364; on defeat of Beckley as House
clerk, 372; on political tolerance, social harmony, 396-7, 603; on role of
women, 397; on political divisions,
404-5; on Jay Treaty, 405, 437-8;
compares U.S. and British policies,
407; on federal courts and grand
juries, 418-19n, 496, 502, 505-6;
on war policies of executive and

INDEX

JEFFERSON, THOMAS (*cont.*)

legislative branches, 438; on future of republicanism in America, 439; on sacrifice and public service, 449; says foreign connections should have a new arrangement, 456-7; on prospects of emancipation, insurrection, 519; says executive has become too strong, 522; on natural right of free correspondence, 526-7; on opening roads in Va., 529, 530

Personal Affairs

courtship and marriage of Mary Jefferson, vii, 186, 226, 424, 429-30, 547-8; interest in history, historical records, 7, 361; gathers information on kitchen stoves, 25; cares for T. M. Randolph's business affairs, purchase orders, 26-7, 413, 414n, 436-7; plans to be absent at election for Albemarle Co. delegates, 27; recommends R. H. Rose and J. Rose, 34; and wine orders, 36, 322, 469; orders rope, 63, 90; groceries for, 90, 324; refuses bill for Ceracchi bust, 121; introduces Volney, 131-4; introduces Liancourt, 137, 138; aids Derieux, 141; forwards Volney's valise, 175, 220, 224-5, 229, 237, 257; advises J. G. Jefferson, 222-3; notes document copying process, 246; sausage recipe from E. Edwards, 313-14; affection for family, 314, 399; desires to keep family near Monticello, 328, 334, 430, 532-3; and smallpox inoculations for grandchildren, 349; urges Trists to settle near Monticello, 350-1; and Wirt, 359n; orders beer, 360; sends news to Va. merchants, 370-1, 379, 386, 428-9, 583; evaluates Philadelphia newspapers, 416, 434, 442; values family tranquility, 424; orders newspapers, 441-2; lacks confidence in post office, 442; news of Mary's trip to Eppington, 572-3; fears grandchildren will forget him, 597

Political Theories

respect due from officeholder to electorate, 259, 270; on monarchical and republican aspects of U.S. Constitution, 289; on state involvement in collection of federal taxes, 416-17, 418n, 443; as advocate of separation of powers, 493-504; on autonomy of states, 525-6

Politics

criticized as ally of France, xxxvii; seeks information on sedition acts, 35; as author of "Mazzei letter," 73-88, 382-5, 488-90, 505; and plans for measures against Jay Treaty in House, 198-9n; distrusts Hamilton, 234, 362, 517-18, 542-3; gathers gossip, intelligence, 309, 517-18, 551, 592-3, 596; apologizes for T. M. Randolph's nonattendance at election, 349; sends political news to H. Gates, 407; refuses to respond to charges in newspapers, 410n, 416, 527-8, 600; analyzes congressional actions, 411-12, 586, 588; and defense preparations in Congress, 421-2; on party division in House of Representatives, 422; criticizes special session of Congress, 433, 450, 461, 462; and appointment of Gerry, 450; and Adams, 475, 560-1; aids Bache, Callender, 536, 544, 561, 630n; and publication of Monroe's *View*, 544-5, 561, 562-3, 564-5; receives praise, 566-7; relationship with J. Henry, 590-1, 602-3

Portraits

political cartoons, xxxvii, xl; by J. Sharples, xl, 318 (illus.); bust by Ceracchi, 119, 121

Public Service

appointed to Va.-Md. boundary commission, 262-3, 271-2, 278-9; laments return to public life, 424

Religion

refers to valley of Jehosaphat, 153; prays for restoration of T. M. Randolph's health, 169

Retirement

shuns everything but agriculture, vii, 139; seeks papers on *Little Sarah*, 128, 143, 178; postpones letter writing, 205; prefers private life, 232, 258-9, 270, 275, 289; says he has no desire to govern, 232, 258; reads few newspapers, no pamphlets, 235, 236; did not seek return to public life, 362; says tranquility is the old man's milk, 457

Scientific Interests

and Buffon, 113-14, 292-3, 295-8, 409-10n, 601; and fossil remains, 113; on theory of degeneracy, 113; and J. Williams's barometric observations,

JEFFERSON, THOMAS (*cont.*)

130-1, 139-40; measurements of elevations, 139; dispute with Imlay, 174-7; and trans-Mississippi west, 174-7; comparative studies of languages, 201-2, 367-8, 400n, 445-7; and theories of extinction, 206, 294-8, 303n; Indians, frontier whites as human types, 225, 238, 259; France sends official units of measure, 229-30, 257; records weather data, winds, 258, 259-60, 596; criticizes Cuvier's taxonomy, 301n; early information on megatherium, 301n; purchases scientific instruments, 315-16, 436-7; sends tooth and bone of mammoth, 360, 391; and Oliver's perpetual motion invention, 377-9, 408; does not collect natural history specimens, 389-90; and Ellicott's observations, 535. *See also* American Philosophical Society; Louis of Parma; megalonyx; *Notes on the State of Virginia*

Secretary of State
influence on Pinckney Treaty, 3, 4n, 195; appointed, 20-1, 40; and public opinion, 21; and negotiations on impressment of U.S. seamen, 35-6; keeps records for personal use, 67-9, 93; questions on neutrality and the French alliance, 127, 129n, 141-2; seeks papers on *Little Sarah*, 128, 143, 178; Fraunces's position during TJ's tenure as, 460; and British evacuation of northwest posts, 624; letter to Hammond of 5 Sep. 1793, 624

Slaveholder
mortgages slaves, 96-9, 166-7, 209-10; gives slaves to Mary Jefferson, 532, 547, 549-50; instructions to improve work habits, 586. *See also* slaves

Travels
between Monticello and Philadelphia, vii; says he dreams of spending winters in Norfolk, 153; to Philadelphia, 261, 270-1, 274, 300n, 308-9, 379, 575, 576-8, 583; to Richmond, 272n; from Philadelphia, 314-15, 422, 425, 432, 436, 459, 461, 462; visits Madison, 569

Vice President
fulfills duties in Senate, viii, 311, 583, 633-4; takes oath of office in Philadel-phia, viii, 255-6, 261, 270-1, 274, 281, 282, 318, 320; views on office of vice president, viii, 271, 273-4, 311, 362, 633; and official notification of election, 266, 267, 281-2, 304, 305-6, 307-8; Address to the Senate, 310-12, 633; receives official papers, 325; salary payments to, 325n, 531, 534; Gerry on Adams-TJ relationship, 326-7; occupied by callers, 352; criticized as pro-French, 359-60; depicts work in Senate, 362, 430, 596; O'Brien's suggestions on naval defense, 375-7; signs and delivers address to Adams, 392-5; aversion to ceremony, 395n; delays attending sessions, 395n, 568, 575-6; resides at Francis's hotel, 412n, 469, 536, 576, 585; on prospects of war with France, 429; raises point of order in Senate, 434-5n; presides over Blount's impeachment trial, 473-4n; on Adams's diplomatic appointments, 486-7; learns of British harassment of ships, 515-16, 519-20; and patronage, 520; on removal to Federal District, 528-9; and appointments, 564; delivers Wolcott's report on Imlay's petition, 584n; awaits news from envoys at Paris, 586, 589; on expense of congressional sessions, 589; makes notations on Senate documents, 633-4

Writings
Petition to Virginia House of Delegates, viii, 490, 491-504, 505-6, 524-5, 526-7, 566; Statement on Accounts as Minister Plenipotentiary in France, 13-24; Agreement with Randolph Jefferson, 66-7; Deed of Mortgage of Slaves to Henderson, McCaul & Co., 97-8; Deed of Mortgage of Slaves to Van Staphorst & Hubbard, 98-9, 209-10; Imlay utilizes Report on Public Lands, 176n; Declaration for the Mutual Assurance Society, 239-44; Memorandum on Farming Operations, 244-6; Notes on a Copying Process, 246; Memoir on the Megalonyx, 291-304; Notes on a Paragraph by John Henry, 309; Address to the Senate, 310-12; Bill for Proportioning Crimes and Punishments, 310n; Notes on Plan of a Prison, 336-8; Table of Estimates, 339; and "Anas," 486-7n; Note on Diplomatic

JEFFERSON, THOMAS (*cont.*)
  Appointments, 486-7; Notes on Alexander Hamilton, 517-18; Note on Spanish Expenditures, 551; Notes on Conversations with John Adams and George Washington, 551-3; Notes on Comments by John Adams and Robert Goodloe Harper, 592-3; Notes on a Conversation with Tench Coxe, 596; first record of Logan's speech, 601, 604n; prints, distributes letter to J. Henry, 603n; Notes on John Jay's Mission to Great Britain, 605-31; *Manual of Parliamentary Practice*, 633; "Parliamentary Pocket-Book," 633. *See also* Declaration of Independence; Logan (Mingo Indian); *Notes on the State of Virginia*

Jefferson Co., Ky.: described, 204n
Jemm, Dr. *See* Gem, Richard
Jenny (TJ's slave): TJ mortgages, 98
Jewell, Joseph, 100
Jews: in Richmond, 119n
Joe (Randolph slave): works at Edgehill, 260
John (TJ's slave): TJ mortgages, 98
John (ship): wrecks, 594, 595n
Johnson, Capt. (Mass.), 366-7
Johnson, Richard, 44n
Johnston, Mr., 574
Johnston, Charles: TJ's account with, 91, 360; conveys natural history specimens, 155, 481; and shipments to TJ, 212, 315, 386, 424; and TJ's transactions, 288n, 481, 484, 523, 534, 542; and tobacco insurance, 413; and TJ's business affairs in Richmond, 577
Johnston, Charles, & Co.: TJ's account, transactions with, 45n, 189, 231, 278n; TJ to make center of affairs, 50
"Jonathan Pindar": pseudonym used by St. G. Tucker, 192
Jones, Allen: letter to, 388; letter from, 513-14; identified, 388n; corresponds with TJ on breadfruit, 388, 513-14
Jones, Epaphras, 75
Jones, Joseph: and Monroe's business affairs, property, 5, 41-2, 124; son attends school at St. Germain, 164; forwards books to TJ, 256
Jones, Joseph, Jr., 164
Jones, Walter, 469n
Jones, William, 65n
Jordan, Benjamin: supplies nailrod, 541-

2; letter from cited, 542n; letters to cited, 542n
Jouett, Robert: as candidate for Va. General Assembly, 27, 52; death of, 124
Journal des Arts et Manufactures (France): presented to APS, 102n
Joyce (b. 1796, TJ's slave): in marriage settlement of Mary Jefferson, 549
Joyner, John: sails from Holland to America, 466
Jupiter (TJ's slave): brings chair and horses to TJ in Fredericksburg, 425, 436
juries, grand: of U.S. Circuit Court in Philadephia, 70-1; as threat to civil liberties, 417, 418n; charged with prosecuting offenses against U.S., 418n; influences on, 444-5; and petition against S. Cabell, 491-504; TJ suggests limitations on service on, 492, 497, 503-4; abuses of system, 505-6

Kalm, Peter: TJ cites *Travels*, 298, 304n
Kanawha River: petroglyphs near, 64, 172, 295, 525-6; Volney describes region of, 150-1; and oral accounts associated with megalonyx, 296; and Dunmore's War, 452-3, 602
Kaskaskia: Volney to visit, 131, 151; land titles, 508n
Keith, Samuel: buys TJ's tobacco, 427n, 484
Keith, William: buys TJ's tobacco, 427n, 484
Kent, James, 75
Kentucky: Volney's travels through, 132, 134, 174, 220; boundary with Va., 172-3; counties described by Fleming, 204; potential of, compared to Ohio, 221; and election of 1796, 227, 253; Buffalo clover seed from, 319; caves in, 322n
Kerr, James: performs work for TJ, 523
Key, Ann: TJ purchases corn from, 485n
Key, James, 549
Key, Joshua, 549
Key, Philip Barton: and Va.-Md. boundary, 263n, 278-9
Key, Walter, 549
Key's ford (Rivanna River): site on proposed road from Georgetown to Ga., 529
King, Rufus: letter from, 514; considers Pinckney and Jay treaties, 9; and journals of Constitutional Convention, 68;

King, Rufus (*cont.*)
and TJ's letter to Mazzei, 79; appointed minister to London, 109; recommends pacific policy towards France, 433, 434n, 436, 438; warns against connections with Britain, 456; forwards letters and parcels to TJ, 511, 512, 514
Kinsolving, James: and debt to TJ, 204
Kippen & Co.: TJ's bond to, 93
Kittera, John Wilkes, 373n
Knapp, John, 564
Knox, Henry: opinion on *Little Sarah*, 128, 130n, 178; and Monroe-Hamilton conflict, 578
Kolb, Peter: *Description du Cap de Bonne-Esperance*, 295
Kuhl, Henry: endorses document, 545n

labor: shortage of, in Albemarle Co., 123; mechanics' wages, 124
Lafayette, Anastasie Louise Pauline du Motier de (Anastasie, daughter of the Marquis de Lafayette), 160
Lafayette, George Washington Louis Gilbert du Motier de: letter to, 126-7; letter from, 159-60; identified, 126-7n; Congress offers to aid, 126-7; Washington assists, 126-7; TJ writes, 129; residence in U.S., 159-60
Lafayette, Marie Adrienne Françoise de Noaille, Marquise de: sends son to U.S., 126-7n; mentioned, 160
Lafayette, Marie Antoinette Virginie du Motier de (Virginie, daughter of the Marquis de Lafayette), 160
Lafayette, Marie Joseph Paul Yves Roch Gilbert du Motier, Marquis de: Va. commissions busts of, 38n; TJ's regard for, 126, 159-60; imprisoned by Austrians, 126n; Americans' regard for, 159-60; and War of First Coalition, 159-60; aids Russian linguistic study, 201n; and Blacons, 468; rumored arrival in U.S., 594, 595n
La Harpe, Jean François de: *Abrégé de l'Histoire générale*, 155, 156n, 296
Lake, Elisha: forwards TJ's rope, 63
Lake of the Woods: and U.S. boundary with British possessions, 617, 619-20
Lancaster, Pa.: kitchen stoves in, 25
lands: paper money affects price of, 124; as investment, 368; speculation, claims at Vincennes, 507-8. *See also* taxes: federal, proposed on land
Langdon, John: letter to, 269-70; and conversation with Adams, 194; urges TJ to accept vice presidency, 269-70; letter from cited, 270n; TJ writes, 281; provides political intelligence, 372, 592
Langeac, Auguste Louis Joseph Fidèle Armand de Lespinasse, Comte de: in TJ's French accounts, 16, 31-2
Langhorne, John, 78
languages: comparative study of, 201-2, 367-8, 400n, 445-7
Lansdowne, William Petty, first Marquis of (Earl of Shelburne), 613
La Rochefoucauld, Alexandrine Charlotte Sophie de Rohan-Chabot, Duchesse de: regard for TJ, 312, 333, 597; TJ sends respects to, 317, 465; relations with Short, 598n
La Rochefoucauld d'Enville, Louis Alexandre, Duc de La Roche Guyon et de, 149n
La Rochefoucauld-Liancourt, François Alexandre Frédéric, Duc de: letters from, 148-9, 462-3; identified, 148-9n; portrait by E. Sharples, xxxviii, 318 (illus.); travels in U.S., xxxviii, 49, 137, 148-9; visits Monticello, xxxviii, 38, 72n, 148-9; introduced to TJ, 41; TJ introduces, 137, 138; prospects of return to France, 147, 463; TJ comments on, 147, 317; describes TJ, 149n; *Travels*, 149n; and French-U.S. relations, 462-3; and Monroe, 462-3; letter to cited, 463n; *On the Prisons of Philadelphia*, 463n
La Roche-Guyon (Rocheguyon), France: horticulture at, 333; Short visits, 598n
Latrobe, Benjamin Henry, 310n
Laurance, John: appointed to Senate committee, 282, 372, 395n; and Senate vote, 283n
Law, Thomas, 53
Lawrence, Mr.: visits Monticello, 428
Lawson, Robert: letter to, 520; seeks army commission for son, 520; letter from cited, 520n
Lear, Tobias, 80n
Lee, Charles: appointment to cabinet, 5; and Hylton v. U.S., 10; and appointment of envoys to France, 411; influences Va. congressmen, 412
Lee, Francis Lightfoot, 317
Lee, Henry: as political intriguer, 127-8, 129-30n, 144n; and election of 1796, 197n
Lee, Ludwell: and Va.-Md. boundary, 263n, 271-2, 278-9

Lee, Rebecca Tayloe, 317

Leghorn (Livorno), Italy: port for northern Italy, 121; French take control of, 161

Lego (TJ's estate): slaves at, 98; adjoins Pantops, 549

legumes: for improvement of soil, 102-3

Le Havre, France: Short's expected port of departure, 332, 333n; Paine at, 340; U.S. consulship at, 366-7

Leib, Dr. Michael: TJ praises, 35; supports Va. amendments to U.S. constitution, 36n

Leiper, Mr. (Alexandria, Va.), 515

Leiper, Thomas: buys tobacco, 385, 413, 426; assists and befriends Callender, 536, 537n

Lendrum, John: publishes Logan's speech, 454, 455n

Lenni Lenape. *See* Delaware (Lenni Lenape) Indians

Leoben: articles of peace signed at, 367n, 431, 433, 434n, 436, 438, 450, 451, 459, 558

L'Epine, Joseph, 257, 259n

leprosy: Rush associates disease with blacks' skin color, 284

Lerebours, Alexandre: letter from, 101-2; and French science, technology, 101-2

Leroy & Bayard & Co. (N.Y.), 330n

Létombe, Philippe André Joseph de, 589

Letter to George Washington (Thomas Paine): TJ requests copy of, 224; sent to TJ, 256; forwarded to J. W. Eppes, 586

Letty (TJ's slave): in marriage settlement of Mary Jefferson, 550

Le Veillard, Geneviève, 122

Le Veillard, Geneviève Elisabeth Belamy, 122

Le Veillard, Louis, 122

Le Veillard, Louis Guillaume: victim of Reign of Terror, 122

Lewis, Meriwether, 133n

Lewis, Nicholas: manages TJ's affairs, 541n

Lewis, Nicholas Meriwether: moves to Ky., 37, 350-1

Lewis, Thomas, 139

Lexington, Ky.: Volney visits, 174

Lezay-Marnézia, Adrien: *De la foiblesse*, 123

Liancourt. *See* La Rochefoucauld-Liancourt, François Alexandre Frédéric, Duc de

lieth machine. *See* threshing machines

Life of George Washington (John Marshall): and TJ's letter to Mazzei, 79-80n; and TJ's compilation of the "Anas," 487n

Lindsay, William, 387n

Linn, William: letter from, 400; and missionary activity, 400

lions: megalonyx associated with, 64, 113-14, 138-9, 155, 171, 172, 275, 284, 296, 297-8, 299, 525; size compared to megalonyx, 292-4; habitat, as analogy for megalonyx, 294, 295; historical accounts of American, 294-5, 303n; African, 295, 296; of Mexico and Peru, 295; as examples of predators, 297

Liston, Robert: and Blount conspiracy, 473n, 516-17, 591; and Federalist politics, 558

Littlepage, Lewis, 551

Little Sarah (ship): Cabinet opinions on, 128, 130n, 143, 178

Livermore, Samuel: appointed to Senate committee, 372, 395n; introduces defense measure, 423n

Livingston, Edward: and Jay Treaty, 10, 46, 52n; proposes to aid Lafayette's son, 126-7n; returns correspondence to H. Gates, 361n; and fortification bill, 422-3n; and Monroe-Hamilton conflict, 593, 595n; as likely candidate for governor, 594

Lloyd, James, 594, 595n

Lloyd, John, 196-7

Lloyd, Thomas: as compiler of congressional debates, 416, 434

Logan (Mingo Indian): publication, circulation of speech of, vii, 409-10n, 441n, 454, 455n, 601, 603-4n; address to Dunmore, 408-10, 440-1, 451, 452-5, 599-604; relatives killed at Yellow Creek, 409-10n, 444, 452, 453, 555-6, 581-2, 590-1, 599-600, 604n; accuses Cresap, 416, 451; as Mingo leader, 455n

Logan, George: *Fourteen Agricultural Experiments, to ascertain the best rotation of crops*, 272, 273n

Logan, James, 409n

Lohra, Peter, 325n

lolium perenne: rye grass seed sent to TJ, 510-11, 512. *See also* grasses

Lomax, Thomas: and Mazzei, 81, 100

Lombardy: incorporated in Cisalpine Republic, 366, 367n

London: bills on, 89, 95

Lott, Peter: wants correspondent in Philadelphia, 206; financial transactions with, 219, 324, 484-5, 509, 523, 534, 542

Loudoun Co., Va.: campaign for presidential elector in, 195-6

Louis XVI, King of France: La Rochefoucauld-Liancourt in court of, 149n; estate at Rambouillet, 333n

Louisiana: encouragement of emigration to, 133n; politics in, 133n; TJ's concern about French designs on, 438-9; plans to invade, 472-3n

Louis of Parma: letter to, 389-92; T. Pinckney describes, 27; sent *Notes on the State of Virginia*, 29n; seeks natural history specimens, 121, 136, 286-7, 389-92; T. Pinckney forwards letter from, 357-8, 404; TJ sends tooth of mammoth to, 391, 481, 484

Louisville, Ky.: described, 204n

Lownes, Caleb: characterized by TJ, 7; supplies TJ with nailrod, 7, 55, 88, 540; letter to cited, 89n

Lucinda (TJ's slave): TJ mortgages, 98; in marriage settlement of Mary Jefferson, 549

Lucy (daughter of Thamar, TJ's slave): in marriage settlement of Mary Jefferson, 550

Lucy (TJ's slave): in marriage settlement of Mary Jefferson, 550

Lunenburg Co., Va.: search for P. Jefferson's land records at, 185

Lyle, James: letters to, 93, 96-7, 306-7; letter from, 202; and TJ's bond to Kippen & Co., 93; and TJ's debt to Henderson, McCaul & Co., 96, 202-4, 306-7; letter from cited, 307n; letter to cited, 307n

Lynchburg Weekly Gazette: and L. Martin's attacks on TJ, 603n

Lynn, Col., 118

Lyons, France: prison at, 335, 336n; mentioned, 257

Lyons, Peter, 574

Mably, Gabriel Bonnot de: cited by Adams, 59; *Des Droits et des Devoirs du Citoyen*, 59

McCaul, Alexander: and TJ's debt to Henderson, McCaul & Co., 203

McClung's (inn, western Va.), 151

McCulloch v. Maryland, 359n, 454n

McGuffey readers: include Logan oration, TJ commentary, 410n

McHenry, James: appointment to cabinet, 5; as advisor to Adams, 380-1

Machir, James: as Federalist congressman from Va., 372, 374n, 422; votes on U.S. policy with France, 412, 414

Mackay (McKay, McCay), Eneas, 153

McKean, Sarah, 314

McKean, Thomas: and election of 1796, 211; as likely candidate for governor, 594

Mckorkle. *See* Snowdon & McCorkle (Mckorkle)

Maclay, Samuel: *Mr. Maclay's Motion. 14th April 1796*, 71n

Macon, Nathaniel, 513

McQueen, John: letter from, 543; sends oranges, recalls old favor, 543

Madison, Dolley Payne Todd: TJ sends respects to, 7, 52, 67, 434, 461; visits Monticello, 129n, 525n; Volney visits, 220; invited to Monticello, 483, 490, 506, 517; sends regards to TJ's daughters, 488; sends congratulations on Mary Jefferson's marriage, 564; Monroe sends regards, 576

Madison, Frances Taylor: invited to Monticello, 483

MADISON, JAMES: letters to, 6-8, 41, 51-2, 67, 88-9, 223-4, 247-51, 255, 266, 270-2, 280-1, 371-4, 411-13, 421-4, 433-5, 450, 461, 483-4, 489-91; letters from, 9-11, 25-6, 41, 55-7, 62-3, 70-1, 72-3, 93-5, 95-6, 108-10, 119, 214-15, 218, 226-7, 227-8, 255-7, 263-5, 272-3, 280, 285-6, 304-5, 488, 505-6, 516-17, 562, 564, 591-2; letter to cited, 8n; letter from Monroe cited, 125n

Congress
supports federal aid for postal roads, 7-8, 55; describes treaties, bills, and political maneuvers in, 9-10, 25, 55-6, 62-3, 70-1, 72-3, 93-6, 108, 228, 265, 272-3, 285-6; and Jay Treaty papers, 48, 54n; and House response to president's message, 218, 227n; views on taxes, 265; and TJ's notification as vice president, 282; resolutions on TJ's Report on Commerce, 405n

Opinions
on Washington's refusal to send Jay Treaty papers to House, 55-6, 62; on Adams, 226-7, 263-4, 285, 304-5; on land tax, 285; on Hamilton's *Observations*, 562; fears usurpation of power by the executive, 592

MADISON, JAMES (*cont.*)

Personal Affairs

and Mazzei's business affairs, 81, 90; and Liancourt, 137; relationship with Monroe, 164, 165n, 488, 516, 517n, 576, 595; friendship with Volney, 320, 482-3, 507, 523; financial dealings with TJ and Monroe, 591, 592n; records, disseminates Logan's speech, 603-4n

Politics

shows TJ's letter of 17 Dec. 1796 to B. Rush, 224n; assists Monroe, 230-1, 269; and stand on treaty-making powers, 322-3, 346-7, 380; as tarnish on Va.'s reputation, 383; Federalists oppose appointment as envoy to France, 411, 552; and Tucker's abolition proposal, 489; and appointments, 564; confers with Monroe, 565-6; and Monroe-Hamilton conflict, 578, 593, 595n

President

appointments, 578n

Public Service

rumors of appointment as envoy to France, 272, 273n, 340, 367; declines mission to France, 551-2

Relations with Jefferson

TJ sends reports on Congress, viii, 371-3, 411-12, 421-2, 433-4, 450, 461; and TJ's grand jury petition, viii, 491-2, 505-6, 566; gathers information on iron merchants, 7, 88-9; urges TJ not to abandon historical task, 7; forwards books, pamphlets, newspapers to TJ, 8n, 72, 109, 248, 250, 256, 272, 305, 488; transmits letters, papers, 9, 130, 224, 280, 281, 361; gathers information on kitchen stoves, 25; forwards letters, 41, 55, 56n, 89, 266, 361, 516; sends introduction, 41; conveys news from Monroe, 56, 108-9; and TJ's letter to Mazzei, 77, 80, 478, 489-90, 491n, 505; executes commissions for TJ, 95; sends news from London newspapers, 119; TJ's trust and confidence in, 127, 129n; invited to, visits Monticello, 129n, 198n, 483, 489-91, 506, 525n; identified as TJ's friend, 199n; conveys news on relations with France, 214, 272, 280, 285; sends news on election of 1796, 214, 226, 227, 255; urges

TJ to accept vice presidency, 218, 226-7; requested to forward TJ's letter to Adams, 234, 248, 250, 263-4, 280; and TJ's posture toward Adams, 252, 270n; urges TJ to take oath in Philadelphia, 255-6; urged to run for Va. assembly, 272; news on arrangements for change of administrations, 304-5; TJ defends against political attacks, 346-7, 380; TJ plans to visit, 422, 433, 450, 461, 569; TJ sends newspapers and pamphlets to, 433-5; TJ forwards correspondence with Monroe, 488, 562; sends news of Blount investigation, 516-17; consulted on mission to France, 551-2; returns pamphlet, 562; recommends Knapp, 564; sends congratulations on Mary Jefferson's marriage, 564; orders nails, 591

Writings

notes on debates at the Federal Convention, 56-7, 67-8, 93, 324, 346-7; address on Jay Treaty papers, 70-1; petition against Jay Treaty, 127, 129n

Madison family: TJ sends respects to, 484

Magaw, Samuel: secretary of APS, 254, 276-7

Maine: post road between Ga. and, 8n

Malesherbes, Chrétien Guillaume de Lamoigner de: execution of, 122, 123n

Malmesbury, Lord. *See* Harris, James, first Earl of Malmesbury

Malon, Pierre: letter from, 435-6; medical remedies, 435-6

Malta, Knights of, 333

mammoth: called "big buffalo," 113-14; size compared to elephant, 113-14, 138, 294; Turpin sends bone to TJ, 155, 481; TJ believes it not extinct, 206; probable habitat of, 295; Buffon on, 297-8; TJ ships tooth and bone to Philadelphia, 360; tooth sent to Louis of Parma, 391, 481, 484; bones of found in Tenn., 398, 403

Manigault family: as reference for van Hasselt, 467

Manual of Parliamentary Practice (Thomas Jefferson): TJ begins work on, 633

manure: and TJ's crop rotation plan, 245-6; Board of Agriculture's report on, 319

Map of the British Colonies in North America (John Mitchell), 626

maps: of South America, 105-6, 115

Marat, Jean Paul, 137
Marc (TJ's valet de chambre): and TJ's French accounts, 15
María Luisa, Infanta of Spain, 121
maritime academies, 376
Markland, John: TJ praises newspaper of, 434
Marks, Hastings (TJ's brother-in-law), 189
Marlborough, John Churchill, Duke of, 318
Marquis's road (Albemarle Co., Va.): site on proposed road from Georgetown to Ga., 529
Marseilles, France: consulship at, 369; French prize court at, 369
Marshall, Humphrey: takes seat in Senate, 411, 412n; and foreign coinage, 584n
Marshall, John: letter to, 278-9; *Life of George Washington*, 79-80n, 487n; and TJ's letter to Mazzei, 79; and publication of Va. laws, 158-9, 283; as brother of William Marshall, 196n; and election of 1796, 197n; as attorney for Va. debtors, 218n; and Va.-Md. boundary, 263n, 271-2, 278-9; letters from cited, 279n; letters to cited, 279n; as envoy to France, 411, 414, 420n, 427, 448, 580, 586, 587, 589, 591, 594, 598; Adams consults, 506n; commands militia, 630n
Marshall, William: identified, 196-7n; certificate of, 196-7; and suits against TJ, 196-7
Martin, Anna Gordon, 157n
Martin, James: letter from, 156-7; identified, 157n; Independence Day oration by, 156-7, 521; TJ confuses with B. Vaughan, 521, 529-30
Martin, Luther: letters from, 452-5, 581-2; identified, 454n; challenges TJ's account of Logan speech, vii-viii, 408-10, 416, 418n, 443-4, 452-5, 556, 581-2, 590-1, 599-604; description, characterization of, 443-4, 454n; and Burr, 454n; letter from cited, 455n; letter to Cobbett quoted, 455n
Martin, Maria Cresap (Mrs. Luther Martin): relationship to T. and M. Cresap, 409n, 444, 453-4, 455n, 556; mentioned, 581
Martin, Thomas C.: threshing machine and drill by, xli, 318, 545, 553-4, 573, 588
Martin, William, 157n
Martin (b. 1777, TJ's slave): in marriage settlement of Mary Jefferson, 550

Martinique, W.I., 185n
Martin's swamp (Chesterfield Co., Va.): in marriage settlement of J. W. Eppes, 547-8
Marx, Joseph: letter to, 121; letter from, 119; identified, 119n; and Ceracchi bust of TJ, 119, 121
Mary (b. 1788, TJ's slave): TJ mortgages, 98
Mary (b. 1792, TJ's slave): TJ mortgages, 98
Mary (TJ's slave): daughter of, in marriage settlement of Mary Jefferson, 550
Maryland: and disposition of journals of Constitutional Convention, 68; and election of 1796, 194-5; boundary with Va., 262-3, 271-2, 278-9; General Assembly, 262-3; political views in, 322; subsidizes L. Martin, 454n; crops in, 559; senators from, 594, 595n
Mason, George: at Constitutional Convention, 57n; papers relating to Va.-Md. boundary, 279
Mason, John, 194-5
Mason, John Thomson: and election of 1796, 197n; and P. Fitzhugh, 323, 346, 380; TJ recommends to Volney, 353
Mason, Stevens Thomson: and election of 1796, 196, 197n; committee appointment, 282n; assists Callender, 537n
Mason & Fenwick. *See* Fenwick, Mason & Co.
Massac, Fort (Illinois): Volney to visit, 151
Massachusetts: vote at Constitutional Convention, 68; and Jay Treaty, 108; and election of congressmen, 411, 413n
Mathers, James, 473n
Mathews, Sampson, 150
Maury, Matthew, 322
Maury (Murray), James, 143-4
Mayo, John, 197n
Mayo, Philip, 66
Mayo River: bridge rebuilt on, 5
Mazzei, Marie Hautefeuille "Petronilla" Martin (Mrs. Philip Mazzei): buried at Monticello, 82, 83n
Mazzei, Philip: letter to, 81-3; and TJ's criticism of U.S. politics, vii-viii, 82, 489-90, 491n; TJ's letter of 24 Apr. 1796, xxxvii, 73-88, 382-5, 505; letter enclosed for, 27; claim against Dohrman, 55, 199-200; TJ's correspondence with, 55-6; finances of, 65, 67, 70, 73, 81-3, 83n, 89, 90, 95, 100; Madison and

TJ's 24 Apr. 1796 letter, 77, 80, 478, 489-90, 491n, 505; Monroe advises TJ about letter to, 77, 478; letters from cited, 80n, 83n, 101n; and TJ's interest in agriculture, 82; letters to cited, 83n; *Recherches historiques et politiques sur les États-Unis de l'Amérique Septentrionale*, 85n, 87n; TJ mortgages slaves to, 96n, 209; Genet criticizes, 471

Meade, George: and bill for Ceracchi bust of TJ, 119, 121

medals: engraved in France, 14, 25n

medicine: TJ's views on use of, 169; unidentified remedies, 435-6

Mediterranean: and arming of U.S. private vessels for trade in, 421-2, 423n

Medley or New Bedford Marine Journal (Mass.): publishes TJ's letter to Mazzei, 76

megalonyx: TJ announces discovery to APS, viii, 138-9, 140, 275; diagrams of specimens, xxxix, 318 (illus.); associated with lions, cats, 64, 113, 155, 171, 172, 275, 284, 296, 299, 301n, 391, 415, 510, 525-6; J. Stuart sends fossils, information, 64-5, 113-14, 152-3, 171, 177, 205-6; petroglyphs associated with, 64, 172, 295; TJ's interest in, alluded to in Federalist press, 79; A. Stuart sends information about, 100; named by TJ, 139, 292; hunters' accounts associated with, 152-3, 171-2, 295-7; APS publishes TJ's report on, 165, 182-3, 200-2, 205-6, 284, 299n, 391, 510; skeleton incomplete, 171, 192, 205-6, 266, 510, 525; estimation of size of, 192, 206, 275, 293-4, 298, 299, 415; question of extinction or survival of, 206, 294-8, 303n; bones described, 291-3; TJ's report to APS, 291-304; size compared to lion, 292-4; probable numbers of, 297; compared to megatherium, sloths, 298-9, 301n, 510; TJ deposits specimens, information with APS, 298; as Pleistocene sloth, 299n; *Megalonyx jeffersonii*, 301n; scientific classification, 301n; and Native American oral traditions, 415, 510

megatherium: and classification of megalonyx, 298-9, 301n, 510; Cuvier, Roume describe, 298-9, 300n, 301n; information sent by Carmichael, 301n

Melinda (b. 1787, TJ's slave): in marriage settlement of Mary Jefferson, 550

Memoir Concerning the Fascinating Faculty which has been Ascribed to the Rattle-Snake, and other American Serpents (Benjamin Smith Barton), 165, 166n, 182, 192

Mercer, Gen. Hugh, 353

Mercer, Hugh (son of Gen. Mercer), 353

Mercer, John, 279

Mercer, John Francis: letter to, 524; letter from, 508-9; and Va.-Md. boundary, 279; sends wheat to TJ, 508-9, 524

Mercer, Sophia Sprigg (Mrs. John F. Mercer), 524

merchants, U.S.: and Jay Treaty, 70, 72-3, 94; and speculative frenzy, 329-30; Paine denounces, 342; as agents of British influence, 363; TJ sends political and commercial news to Va. merchants, 370-1, 379, 386, 428-9, 583-4; and arming of vessels, 371, 421, 423n; and specie, currency, 401; and tax on wine and liquor, 461, 462; memorials from Charleston merchants, 567, 570

Merchants' Daily Advertiser (Philadelphia): TJ praises, 416, 434

Meriwether, Thomas, 66

Message from the President of the United States, Assigning the Reasons which Forbid his Compliance with the Resolution of the Twenty-Fourth Instant (George Washington): sent to TJ, 55-6

Metamorphoses (Ovid): TJ quotes from, 218n

metric system: French standards, 229-30

Mexico: lions of, 295

Mey, Florian Charles (Charleston merchant), 468

Miami Indians, 400n

mice: Barton describes variety of, 183

Michaux, André, 133n

middle states: future of republicanism in, 439

Middleton, Thomas, 467

Mifflin, Thomas: letter to, 468-9; and election of 1796, 261; welcomes TJ, 281; receives Blacons, 468-9

Milan: Bonaparte captures, 136n; incorporated in Cisalpine Republic, 367n

Miles, Samuel, 211

militia: reorganization of, 371n, 393, 416; dispute over rank in N.Y., 403-4; Congress passes act for, 456, 457n. *See also* Virginia: Militia

Millar, Felty: and possible work for TJ, 57, 99, 172

Miller (Millar), Philip: cultivates vetches, 103; description of wheat, 509

Miller, Valentine. *See* Millar, Felty

Miller's ordinary: as stop between Monticello and Eppington, 573

Milliner (Milner), William: debt to TJ, 203

mills: mortgage on Goochland Co. millseat, 476-8

Minerva (TJ's slave): TJ mortgages, 98

Minerva. See American Minerva (New York)

Ming, William, 325n

Mingo Indians: identified, 409n; and Dunmore's War, 452; leadership positions among, 455n

Mint, U.S.: seeks new director, 564; and foreign coinage, 583-4n, 589

Mirievo, Fedor Ivanovich de, 202n

Mississippi River: and Jay and Pinckney treaties, 48-9, 372; dispute over flood stages of, 174, 176n; within range of U.S. coastal gunboats, 377; in Jay Treaty negotiations, 613, 615, 617, 619-20, 621-2, 626

Missouri River: and Mississippi River flood stages, 174; speculative connection to Pacific Ocean, 174-5, 176n

Mitchell, John, 626

Mohawk River: Volney crosses, 221

molasses: duties on, 265n; in Jay Treaty, 616, 619

Molly (TJ's slave): children of, in marriage settlement of Mary Jefferson, 550

monarchy: and U.S. Constitution, 289; Harper on, 593

Moniteur. See Gazette Nationale ou Le Moniteur Universel (Paris)

"Monitor" (pseudonym): letter from, 359-60; accuses TJ of pro-French sentiments, 359-60

Monongahela River, 171, 295

monopoly: as malady of all governments, 555

Monroe, Eliza: TJ sends regards to, 124, 148; as young woman in France, 147; attends St. Germain school, 164

Monroe, Elizabeth Kortright (Mrs. James Monroe): TJ sends regards to, 5, 124, 148, 595; and Mme Plumard de Bellanger, 164; visits Monticello, 525n; mentioned, 312

Monroe, James: letters to, 4-6, 41-2, 123-5, 147-8, 526-7, 564-5, 593-5; letters from, 160-5, 478-9, 524-5, 562-4, 565-6, 576, 578-9; and TJ's grand jury petition, viii, 492, 524-5, 526-7, 565-6; publishes *View*, xxxvii, 562-5, 576, 583, 586, 592, 593-4, 595; Albemarle Co.

property, 5, 123-4, 163-4, 350, 576; orchard, 5, 41-2; 1802 endorsement on document, 37n; forwards correspondence, 41, 122, 123, 312, 565; TJ's correspondence with, 41, 55-6, 230, 595n; corresponds with Madison, 56-7, 108-9, 125n; and TJ's letter to Mazzei, 77, 478, 489-90, 491n, 505; TJ gives Mazzei news of, 82-3; and French reaction to Jay Treaty, 108-10; and U.S. deposits in France, 122; Coxe forwards letters to, 134; sends, receives news from France, 147-8, 160-5, 593-5; orders *Encyclopédie*, 161; on situation in France, 161, 576; accused of financial improprieties, 164, 165n; defends Jay Treaty to French, 230, 231n, 269, 405; entrusts E. Edwards with discretion to publish papers, 230-1, 269, 313; absence of news from, 256, 272, 286, 305, 422, 450; Federalists' motives toward, 269; returns to U.S., 332, 340, 343, 366, 373, 426, 461, 462, 478, 488; relations with French government, 340, 342, 371n; and Congress, 343, 366; correspondence with secretary of state, 343, 345n, 516, 517n, 518, 563-4, 565; forwards Swedish proposal of alliance, 345n; relations with Corsange & Cie., 354; relations with Gerry, 355-6, 361, 387, 398-9, 402; TJ forwards letters to, 355-6, 361, 562n; and consulships in France, 366; as tarnish on Va.'s reputation, 383; patronage appointments as president, 429n; and La Rochefoucauld-Liancourt, 462-3; attends N.Y. Republican dinner, 478, 479n; dispute with Hamilton, 478-9, 490-1, 542, 558, 560n, 562, 566, 578-9, 593, 595n; and Volney, 482, 507; visits Montpelier, 483, 517n; relationship with Madison, 488, 565-6, 576, 595; and Tucker's abolition proposal, 489; visits Monticello, 489-90, 524, 525n; defends conduct, asks explanation of recall, 518n, 524; assists B. Vaughan, 521n; and Short, 544-5, 561; and subsidy for *View*, 544-5, 561, 576, 595; as conduit for political intelligence, 551; *View* described, 563n; financial affairs with TJ and Madison, 591, 592n; correspondence with Dawson, 595n; Jay reports on, 612

Monroe, Joseph Jones: identified, 198n; elected to Va. General Assembly, 27, 52; practices law, 158, 525; certificate of, 198-9; offers to buy Short's land, 332; mentioned, 5, 147, 164, 172

Montenotte: French victory at, 136n

Monthly Magazine (London): describes megatherium, 298, 301n

Monticello: renovation and expansion of, vii-viii, xxxviii-xxxix, 318 (illus.), 36, 43, 61, 100-1, 170, 211, 223, 351, 352, 428, 484, 491, 533, 605n; various visitors to, vii, 27, 49, 129n, 153, 168, 184, 320, 428, 524, 525n; La Rochefoucauld-Liancourt visits, xxxviii, 38, 49, 148-9, 154; Volney visits, xxxviii, 111, 126, 148, 151-2n, 154, 175-6n; insurance plat, xxxix, 242; slaves at (*see* Jefferson, Thomas: Slaveholder; slaves); corn for, 26, 52; dogs at, 26-7; invitations to visit, 36, 60, 131, 210, 483, 489-91, 506, 517, 533, 546; spring at, 36, 322, 328, 334, 351; peach trees bloom at, 37, 52, 322, 351; trees at, 37, 52, 105; weather at, 37, 43, 258, 281; gardener assists with Monroe's orchard, 42; cold weather at, 51, 52, 63, 67, 91, 255, 260; brickmasons, stonemasons, 57, 65n, 99-100, 172, 210n, 414, 585; drought at, 63, 67, 89, 91, 224, 428; progress of construction, 63, 90, 213, 259, 352; Mazzei's wife buried at, 82; crops at, 91, 128-9, 513; Strickland sends seeds to, 102-5; clover sown at, 103-4; sashes for, 167, 184, 186, 206, 212, 324, 484, 523; clocks repaired at, 168; rain at, 170, 575, 576-8; glass for renovation, expansion of, 184, 187, 212-13; Burr visits, 198-9; importance to TJ, 229; insurance declaration, description of buildings, 239-44; slave dwellings, 243; and TJ's farming operations, 244-6; snow at, 255, 260, 575, 576-8; beef and butter for, 260-1; healthy climate of, 328, 507; TJ enjoys grandchildren at, 328; smallpox vaccinations, 401n; preparations for harvest at, 414; dinner guests at, 427; garden at, 428; roofing of, 464, 507; roads to, 483; construction costs, 531; fireplaces and chimneys, 605

Montpelier: weather at, 488, 591

Montpensier, Antoine Philippe d'Orléans, Duc de: travels in U.S., 312-13, 369

Montserrat, W.I.: and privateers' operations, 229

Moody, John: letter to, 428-9; identified, 429n; seeks news on commerce, 429; letters from cited, 429n

Moody & Price: letter to cited, 429n

Moorehead, John, 172

Moors: and lions, 155

moose: compared to European elk, 298

Moreau de St. Méry, Médéric Louis Elie, 463n

Morgan, Daniel: as Federalist congressman from Va., 372, 374n, 422; votes on U.S. policy with France, 412, 414; and Logan's speech, 441

Morris, Gouverneur: on pro-French sentiment in U.S., 110n; as minister to France, 342; and Short's salary, 574

Morris, Robert: and Holland Land Company, 330n; financial failure of, 528

Morris, Robert (innkeeper, western Va.), 151

Morris's (inn, western Va.), 150

Morse, Jedidiah: and publication of Logan's speech, 441n, 454, 455n; *American Universal Geography*, 455n

Moses (TJ's slave): TJ mortgages, 98

Moylan, Stephen, 591, 592n

Mr. Maclay's Motion. 14th April 1796 (Samuel Maclay): sent to TJ, 71n

Muhlenberg, Frederick Augustus Conrad, 94, 95n, 478-9

Muhlenburg, Peter, 137n

Mulay al Yazid (Emperor of Morocco), 68-9

mules: in Spain, 28

Munro (Monroe) & Roe: care for goods sent to TJ, 588; letter from cited, 589n; letters to cited, 589n

Murray, Charlotte Hughins, 327

Murray, William Vans: letter to, 327; and Jay Treaty, 55, 57n; appointed U.S. minister to Netherlands, 327, 486-7; carries letters for TJ, 327, 329, 331

Mussi, Joseph, 212

mutton: in payment of protested bill, 65n; price of, in France, 341; Federal District as potential market for, 529

Mutual Assurance Society: and TJ's insurance, 190-1, 239-44; investment of premiums, 191; form of declaration, 239-41

nailrod. *See* Jefferson, Thomas: Nailery

Naney (Nanny, TJ's slave): TJ mortgages, 98

Naples: and French campaign in Italy, 135; negotiates peace with France, 161, 164n

Nat (T. M. Randolph's slave): and supplies for TJ, 63

Natchez: factional disputes at, 535-6; latitude, longitude of, 535

National Institute of Arts and Sciences. *See* France: National Institute of Arts and Sciences

"Native American" (pseudonym): letter from, 382-5; and TJ's letter to Mazzei, 382-4

Natural Bridge, Va.: Volney may visit, 482

natural history: of Virginia, 29n; birds, 156, 260; snakes, 165, 166n, 182, 192; meadow mice, 183; hawks, 192; man as most destructive species, 248, 250-1; Rush on animal and human insurrections, 284; preferred habitats of large animals, 294-5; theories of extinction, 297-8, 303n; sizes of Old World, American animals, 298; classification of species, 301n. *See also* Barton, Benjamin Smith; Buffon, Georges Louis Leclerc, Comte de; Jefferson, Thomas: Scientific Interests; Louis of Parma; megalonyx; Peale, Charles Willson

Natural History (Pliny): TJ cites, 295

Natural History of Carolina, Florida, and the Bahama Islands (Mark Catesby): cited by TJ, 298, 304n

Ned (1760-1818?, TJ's slave): TJ mortgages, 98

Ned (b. 1786, TJ's slave): TJ mortgages, 98

Nedham, Marchamont, 59

Nelly (b. 1796, TJ's slave): in marriage settlement of Mary Jefferson, 550

Nero: referred to by Washington, 143

Netherlands: Volney compares Ohio to, 221; treaty of amity and commerce with U.S., 615, 628. *See also* Batavian Republic

Netherlands, Austrian: and War of First Coalition, 256-7n

neutrality: French threaten seizure of U.S. vessels, 215n; of Denmark and Sweden, 344, 345n; and Jay Treaty, 344, 345n, 613, 617, 621, 622-3, 628; League of Armed Neutrality, 344, 345n; TJ on need for American, 363-4, 415; U.S. consults with neutral nations, 371n; Proclamation of Neutrality, 471; U.S., and *Unicorn* affair, 612, 630n

New, Anthony: misses vote on Jay Treaty, 62n; instructions from constituents, 381, 382n; and patent for threshing machine, 573

Newel, Capt., 514

New England: and Jay Treaty, 95; and U.S. relations with France, 226; and election of 1796, 262; Hamilton's influence in, 265

New Hampshire: at Constitutional Convention, 68; and election of 1796, 226, 227

New Jersey: at Constitutional Convention, 68; and Jay Treaty, 73; penal system, 336n

New London, Va., 58, 172

newspapers: and publication of TJ's letter to Mazzei, 73-88; TJ warns to keep his correspondence out of, 80, 371, 417-18, 429, 445, 527-8, 556-7; TJ refuses to write for, 127, 416; Washington refuses to respond to anonymous publications, 142; British influence over, 363; TJ evaluates, 416; attacks on TJ in, 427; TJ's relations with, 429; TJ's subscription to New York, 441-2; anti-French bias of London, 559

New Star (Concord, N.H.): publishes TJ's letter to Mazzei, 75n

New Views of the Origin of the Tribes and Nations of America (Benjamin Smith Barton): dedicated to TJ, 367-8, 445-7

New York: and Jay Treaty, 108; Republicans in, 156-7, 594; Hamilton's influence in, 265; penal system, 336n; English influence on election of 1796 in, 439

New York City: response to Jay Treaty, 70, 73; price of wheat at, 261; election of 1796, 264, 439n; and financial speculation, 329; and trade with France, 340; artillery regiment, 403-4; TJ's subscription to newspapers in, 441-2; Republican dinner for Monroe in, 478, 479n, 488

New York Missionary Society, 400n

New Zealand: Cook finds breadfruit in, 348, 388

Niagara: Volney visits, 174, 221; described, 221

Nicholas, John (brother of W. C. Nicholas): and election of 1796, 194-5; on U.S. relations with France, 373n; and House reply to president's address, 411, 427; and charges against Blount, 473n; moves to postpone naval armament legislation, 588n

Nicholas, John, Jr. (clerk of Albemarle County Court): attestations by, 66, 219n, 330n, 545n; and TJ's letter to

Mazzei, 78; and TJ's grand jury petition, 493

Nicholas, Wilson Cary: letters to, 170, 215-17; election to Va. General Assembly, 27, 52, 322, 350n; TJ sends house design to, 170; letters from cited, 170n; letter to cited, 170n; and Burr's visit to Monticello, 198n; and TJ's grand jury petition, 490, 492-3, 505, 566

Nicholl, John, 611

Nicholson, John, 528

niter: and ice caves, 117

Noe, Sephemiah: TJ stops at ordinary run by, 425, 436

Noël, Jean François, 357

Nolan, Philip, 175

Nootka Sound: and British foreign policy, 342

Norfolk, Va.: TJ disembarks from France at (1789), 19, 40; TJ imagines winters in, 153; as developing commercial center, 215-16; as potential residence for Van Staphorsts, 331, 457-8; British harass vessels near, 515-16, 519-20; *Unicorn* affair, 630n

Norfolk Canal Company, 5

Norman's ford (Rappahannock River): site on proposed road from Georgetown to Ga., 529, 530

North Carolina: vote at Constitutional Convention, 68; TJ sends breadfruit to, 388; sites on proposed road from Georgetown to Ga., 529

northern states: support for Adams in, 232; in election of 1796, 235-6, 253; growing Republican strength in, 289-90, 594, 595n; lack of fine spring, fall seasons in, 352; misrepresented, misunderstood in south, 364; wish to avoid war with France, 371-2

Northwest Territory: procedures for survey and sale of lands in, 10-11; posts in, 48; free movement of British traders in, 228n; land claims in, 507-8. *See also* Gallipolis, Northwest Terr.; Kaskaskia; Vincennes

Notes on the State of Virginia: and Logan's speech, vii, 408-10, 416, 440-1, 443, 452-5, 555, 581-2, 590-1, 600-4; T. Pinckney encloses to Louis of Parma, 29n; Strickland comments on, 116; cited by J. Williams, 130; Imlay disputes statements in, 174-7; depiction of blacks in, 176-7n; potential revision of, 222, 258, 408, 410n, 416, 600; praises Rittenhouse, 251, 252n; and TJ's

weather records, 258, 260n; on Native American tribes, 400. See also *Appendix to the Notes on Virginia Relative to the Murder of Logan's Family*; Logan (Mingo Indian)

Nouvelle Histoire de l'Afrique Françoise (Abbé Demanet): cited by TJ, 292

oats: as crop, 91; soil at Monticello unsuitable for, 524; seeded with clover, 559-60

O'Brien, Richard: memorandum on naval protection, 375-7

O'Bryen, Dennis: *Utrum Horum? The government; or, the country?*, 433-4, 435n

"Observations intended to favour a supposition that the Black Color (as it is called) of the Negroes is derived from the Leprosy" (Benjamin Rush), 284n

Observations on Agriculture, &c. Addressed to, or Made by the South-Carolina Society for Promoting and Improving Agriculture, and other Rural Concerns (S.C. Society for Promoting Agriculture): includes extract of TJ letter, 468n

Observations on Certain Documents Contained in No. V & VI of "The History of the United States for the Year 1796" (Alexander Hamilton): includes TJ's correspondence with Fraunces, 459, 460; publication of, 483-4; TJ obtains copy of, 534, 542-3; views on, 536-7; TJ's remarks on, 546; comments on, 554-5, 557-8, 562

Official Letters to the Honorable American Congress (John Carey): criticized for omissions, 180-2, 205; sent to TJ, 182

Oglethorpe, Gen. James Edward, 347, 348n, 387

Ohio: artifacts from, 201, 202n; Volney describes, 220-1; potential of, compared to Ky., 221

Ohio Company, 152n

Ohio River: and Mississippi River flood stages, 174

Ohio Valley: climate and health, 175

oil shrub: TJ attempts to grow, 319

Oliver, John: letter to, 408; letter from, 377-9; son's inventions, 377-9, 408

Oliver, Robert (Bordentown, N.J.): claims invention of perpetual motion device, 377-9, 408

Oliver & Thompson, 45n

Ontario, Lake, 174

On the Prisons of Philadelphia (Duc de La Rochefoucauld-Liancourt), 463n

Orange Co., Va.: winter weather interrupts postal service in, 266

oranges: sent to TJ from East Florida, 543

orange trees: TJ receives from Rutledge, vii, 357, 386, 455

Orléans, Antoine Philippe d'. *See* Montpensier, Antoine Philippe d'Orléans, Duc de

Orléans, Louis Charles d'. *See* Beaujolais, Louis Charles d'Orléans, Comte de

Orléans, Louise Marie Adélaide de Bourbon, Duchesse d', 312-13, 369

Orléans, Louis Philippe, Duc d': travels in U.S., 312-13, 369

Orléans, Louis Philippe Joseph, Duc d': guillotined, 313n

Osgood, Samuel (N.Y.): and Gerry's correspondence, 356, 398, 402

osnaburgs (osnabrigs): retaliatory duties on British, 36; price of, in Richmond, 569

Oswald, Eleazer, 434

Oswego, N.Y., 174

Otis, Harrison Gray: takes seat in House of Representatives, 411, 413n; as orator, 417

Otis, Samuel A.: as father of congressman, 411, 413n; as clerk of Senate, 633

Otter, Peaks of (Va.): altitude of, 139

Ottoman Empire: and French campaign in Italy, 135

Ouabache. *See* Wabash River

Outlines of an Historical View of the Progress of the Human Mind (Marquis de Condorcet), 201

Outlines of the Fifteenth Chapter of the Proposed General Report from the Board of Agriculture, on the Subject of Manures (Robert Somerville): sent to TJ, 319

Ovid: *Metamorphoses*, 218n

Owen & Mosby (tobacco inspectors), 26, 64n

Pace, Henry, 537n

Pacific Ocean: Missouri River as prospective connection to, 174-5, 176n

Page, John: TJ sends respects to, 7, 224; reported well, 82

Page, Mann: letter to, 100-1; letter from, 353; and Mazzei, 81, 100; invites TJ to visit, 353; recommends H. Mercer, 353

Page, Mann (the younger), 82

Page, Margaret Lowther (Mrs. John Page), 82

Page, Mary Tayloe (Mrs. Mann Page), 101

Page, William, 414, 577

Paine, Elijah, 411, 412n

Paine, Thomas: letters from, 340-5, 366-7; political views, xxxvii; *Letter to George Washington*, 224, 256, 586; *Rights of Man*, 234; comments on situation in England, France, 340-5; *Decline and Fall*, 340-1, 344n; on U.S. presidency, 343; on appointment of consuls in France, 366-7; expected in U.S., 422, 426; news from Europe, 423n; *Agrarian Justice*, 434, 435; absence of news from, 450; assists B. Vaughan, 521n

Pallas, Peter Simon: identified, 201-2n; comparative study of languages, 201-2, 447n

Panama: TJ's interest in Isthmus of, 360-1, 406

panthers. *See* cougars

Pantops (Albemarle Co., Va.): in marriage settlement of Mary Jefferson, 424, 430, 532, 547-8, 549

Paraguay: site of megatherium discovery, 298, 510

Paris: bust of Lafayette given by Va., 38n; as haven for bankers and political refugees from Netherlands, 215; Americans in, and U.S. relations with France, 228; weather, 258; residential designs, 345-6; English convent in, 369

Parker, Isaac, 413n

Parker, Josiah: and Jay Treaty, 95n; obtains Washington document, 142; introduces defense measure, 423n

Parma, Prince of. *See* Louis of Parma

Paroy, Capt.: letter from, 570-2; sends papers for brother, 570-2; commander of *Cérès*, 572n

patents: sought by Booker for threshing machine, 187-8; and protection of inventions, 408; sought by T. Martin for threshing machine, 553-4, 573, 588

patronage: and postal roads, 7-8; influence of, 94; and Monroe administration, 429n; and TJ's vice presidency, 520

Patten, John, 94-5

Patterson, Robert, 130

"Paulding" (pseudonym): seeks to damage Washington's reputation, 129n

Payne's (Mrs. Paines) ordinary: J. W. and M. J. Eppes stop at, 572, 577

Peace Treaty, Definitive (1783): as watershed in U.S. history, 235, 237; and Jay Treaty negotiations, 606, 608-9, 613, 615, 624-5, 626, 629n; boundary provisions of, 616-17; dates of ratification, 624-5

peach trees: bloom at Monticello, 37, 52, 322, 351; used as boundary for fields, 245

Peale, Charles Willson: letter to, 121; letters from, 136, 286-7; exchanges of specimens, 121, 136, 286-7, 390-1; museum, 121, 136, 286-7; engineering activities, 286; and study of megalonyx, 300n

Peale, Titian Ramsey (1780-1798): draws megalonyx specimens, xxxix, 300n; skilled taxidermist, 136

peas: sent by Rutledge, vii, 386, 455; sent by Strickland, vii, 102, 115; and vetches, 103; and TJ's crop-rotation plan, 128-9, 154, 245; Washington procures seed from England, 143; TJ's queries on cow peas, 179-80; grown in S.C., 231; sent by TJ, 319, 346, 380, 560; seed from France, 323; in diet during harvest, 414; field and cow peas, 546; grown by J. Taylor, 554

Peirce (Pierce), William, 295

"Pelham" (pseudonym): urges separation of northern, southern states, 364n

penal institutions: in Va., 309-10, 335-9; solitary confinement, 310n, 335-6; TJ and reform of, 310n; in Britain and Europe, 335, 336n; in Pa., 335, 336n, 463n; in U.S., 335, 336n; specifications of TJ's plan for penitentiary, 336-9; La Rochefoucauld-Liancourt pamphlet, 463n

Pendleton, Edmund: in poor health, 5; and Va.-Md. boundary, 279; and revisal of Va. laws, 310n; and U.S. relations with France, 382n; TJ sends respects to, 546; and Short's salary, 574

Pendleton, John: letter to, 39-41; as auditor of Va., 37; and settlement of TJ's accounts, 39-41

Pennsylvania: considers Va. amendments to U.S. constitution, 35-6; support for Jay and Pinckney treaties in western, 48; vote at Constitutional Convention, 68; support for Jay Treaty in, 70-1; clover in, 104; and election of 1796, 211, 235-6, 258, 261-2; and Va.-Md. boundary dispute, 271-2; penal system, 335, 336n, 463n; growing Republican strength in, 594

Pennsylvania Journal (Philadelphia): publishes Logan's speech, 603n

Persia: as analogy for American Indian cultures, 446

Peru: lions of, 295

Petit, Adrien: and TJ's French accounts, 14, 16, 31

petroglyphs: associated with megalonyx, 64, 172, 295

Peyroux de la Coudrèniere, Henri: letter to, 132-3; identified, 133n; introduced to Volney, 132-3

Philadelphia: price of wheat and flour at, 10, 26, 36, 322, 350, 371, 385, 426, 583; response to Jay Treaty, 70, 73, 94; weather at, 95, 258; sashes for Monticello built at, 167, 184, 186, 206, 212, 324, 484, 523; glass for Monticello from, 184, 187, 212-13; as center of information, 221; economic distress in, 238, 261, 583; stagecoaches from Va. to, 274, 445; price of tobacco at, 309, 316, 371, 379, 385, 402, 412, 413; as market for tobacco, 324, 481, 484; and financial speculation, 329-30; prisons at, 336n, 463n; lack of spring season at, 352; bankruptcies in, 371, 373; prices stagnant, falling at, 371, 379, 402, 412; Bartram's Garden, 390, 391n; politics disturbs social life in, 396-7, 456-7; TJ criticizes society in, 430, 596; as source for iron and nailrod, 531; yellow fever in, 531, 534, 536, 543, 544, 562, 592; TJ's business affairs in, 577; harbor freezes over, 586, 588

Philadelphia Gazette: carries foreign news, 256-7, 305; publishes letters on French affairs, 280; prints letters that rumor war, 440n. See also Brown, Andrew

Philip (TJ's slave): in marriage settlement of Mary Jefferson, 550

Philippines: TJ receives, distributes rice from, 367n, 487

Phill (TJ's slave): and loss of tobacco, 63n

Phyllis (TJ's slave): in marriage settlement of Mary Jefferson, 550

physiognotrace machine: used by J. Sharples, xl

Piamingo (Chickasaw Indian), 42

Pichegru, Jean Charles, 558

Pickering, Timothy: letters from, 305-6, 307-8, 325; employs Akin, xl; appointment to cabinet, 5, 124; and Jay Treaty, 47-8, 228n, 374n; and diplomats' accounts, 58; and TJ's letter to Mazzei, 75, 78n; and Monroe, 109-10, 165n,

Pickering, Timothy (*cont.*)
343, 345n, 516, 517n, 518, 524; and relations with France, 215n, 373n; addresses U.S. complaints against France,
273n, 280, 285; sends TJ notification of
election, 305-6, 307-8; sends papers,
325; and Short's salary, 332; Paine criticizes, 342, 343; offends French, 343,
345n; and Swedish proposal of alliance,
345n; E. Rutledge criticizes, 357; as advisor to Adams, 380-1, 382n; stories of,
as quartermaster general, 381; correspondence with C. C. Pinckney, 426;
R. King writes, 434n; submits Washington letter to the press, 505, 506n;
Tucker avoids communicating with,
515-16; and Blount conspiracy, 517n;
and Hamilton's influence, 518; and Federalist politics, 558; publishes official papers, 563-4
Pictet de Rochemont, Charles: *Tableau*,
122
Pinckney, Charles: and visit from
H. M. Rutledge, 92
Pinckney, Charles Cotesworth: France rebuffs as minister, 230, 231n, 256, 265,
282, 316, 340, 371, 416; absence of
news from, 272, 286, 587, 589, 594,
598; letter from Pickering, 273n, 280n,
426; arrives in France, 305; and Jay
Treaty, 340, 412; and U.S. relations
with France, 357, 373n, 405; as envoy
to France, with Gerry and Marshall,
411, 413n, 414, 420, 427, 448, 552,
580, 586, 591
Pinckney, Thomas: letter to, 404-6; letters
from, 27-9, 69-70; successful negotiation with Spain, 3; and Jay Treaty, 9,
340, 412, 606-7, 610, 611, 628, 631n;
describes agriculture in Spain, 27-9; describes Louis of Parma, 27; letters from
cited, 29n; letters to cited, 29n; and negotiations on impressment of U.S. seamen, 35-6; reports on war between
France and England, 70; resigns diplomatic appointment, 109; sends TJ
model of threshing machine, 129; and
election of 1796, 148, 214, 218, 223,
226, 227, 235-6, 251, 253, 255, 326; as
minister in London, 345n; forwards letter from Louis of Parma, 357-8, 404;
and Louis of Parma, 389; TJ discusses
politics, Jay Treaty with, 404-5
Pinckney family: take turn in public service, 233; as reference for van Hasselt,
467

Pinckney Treaty: and TJ, 3, 7, 195; described, 9-10; and Jay Treaty, 9-10, 48-
9, 70, 73; publication of, 48; considered
in House of Representatives, 62; implementation of, 70-1, 95n, 286; fulfill-
ment of terms of, 535n; Short criticizes,
598
Pine, Mary (Mrs. Robert Edge Pine), 314
Pinkney, William: and Va.-Md. boundary,
263n, 278-9
Pintard, John M.: forwards letter, 379; letter from cited, 379n
Pitt, William: and efforts to suppress civil
liberties, 35; and D'Ivernois, 59; and
British restrictions on Dutch firms, 89;
seeks peace with France, 256n; policy
toward U.S., 471
Pittsburgh, Pa.: heavy snows reported at,
238, 260
Pius VI, Pope, 256n
Pleasants, James, 477
Pleasants, Robert: letter to, 177-8; letters
from, 120, 287-8; identified, 120n; and
education of blacks, 120, 177-8, 287-8;
and emancipation, 120n, 177-8; letters
from cited, 120n, 178n; letter to cited,
288n
Pleasants, Robert, & Co.: TJ's account
with, 288
Pleasants, Thomas, Jr. (of Four Mile
Creek), 5, 288n
Pliny: *Natural History*, 295
plow, moldboard: TJ designs, xli, 140;
and instrument for measurement of re-
sistance, 105, 115-16, 140
Plumard, M., 164
Plumard de Bellanger, Mme: and
Derieux's entreaties, 5, 123, 164
Point Pleasant, Va.: Volney describes, 151
Poland: partitioned, 471; Littlepage visits,
551
Polar Star and Boston Daily Advertiser
(Boston): praises Volney, 237, 238n
Political Progress of Britain (James T. Cal-
lender): TJ's views on, 248-51; labeled
seditious in Britain, 537n
Pollard, Mary (Mrs. Robert Pollard), 6
Pollard, Robert: letter from, 6; and Short's
business affairs, 6, 278n; letter from
cited, 6n
Poplar Forest (TJ's estate): slaves at, 98;
in marriage settlement of Martha Jeffer-
son Randolph, 532. *See also* Clark,
Bowling
Porcupine's Gazette (Philadelphia): pub-
lishes L. Martin's attacks on TJ, vii,

409n, 452, 454n, 582n; publishes TJ's letter to Mazzei, 75; and queries on TJ's correspondence with P. Fitzhugh, 561. *See also* Cobbett, William

Portugal: relations with France, xxxvii; U.S diplomatic post in, 109, 486-7; information for map from, 115

postal roads: federal monies for, 7-8, 55; from Md. to Philadelphia, 382; from Staunton, Va. to Washington Co., Md., 415-16

postal service: irregularity of mail south of Baltimore, 9; winter weather interrupts, 266; and notification of TJ's election, 267, 306, 307-8; Gerry distrusts, 387, 398-9; in Va., 427, 428; TJ distrusts, 442, 445, 460, 529-30; and franking privilege, 494, 499-500

potatoes: in TJ's crop rotation plan, 245; in diet during harvest, 414

Potomac Canal Company, 5

Potomac River: as Cohongaronta River, 116, 118-19n; tributaries of, 116, 118n; climate and health, 175; and Va.-Md. boundary, 263n, 453; as national political divide, 364n; Washington visits falls of, 483

Pougens, Charles: Paris bookseller, 333, 464; letters from cited, 597, 598n; plan to sell books in U.S., 597

poultry: feed for, 104

Pouncey's tract (TJ property): TJ's claim to part of, 42, 43-4n

Powell, Leven: as candidate for elector in 1796, 195-6, 198-9; casts electoral vote for Adams, 261

Powell, William Dummer, 221

Pragers & Co., 199-200

Presque Isle, Pa.: snow at, 238, 260

Prévost, Abbé Antoine François, 6n, 15

Priestley, Joseph: commended by United Irishmen, 140n; removes to U.S., 140n; and study of languages, 201; and American Indian artifacts, 202n; quoted, 284; wishes to see TJ, 284; recommends thermometer, 315; dispute with Volney, 320-1, 352

Prince Edward Co., Va.: TJ proposes road to, 431, 432

Prince Edward Court House, Va.: site on proposed road from Georgetown to Ga., 529

Prince of Wales case: and Wayles estate, 97n, 196-7; J. Marshall's opinion on, 197n

Princeton, N.J., 435-6

Prince William Co., Va.: residents acquainted with TJ, 184; campaign for presidential elector in, 193, 195; and proposed road from Georgetown to Ga., 529, 530

Principall Navigations (Richard Hakluyt): cited by TJ, 294

prisons. *See* penal institutions

privateers: bill to prevent U.S. citizens from serving on, 421, 423n, 426, 433, 436

Proclamation of Neutrality: Washington's questions to Cabinet on, 127, 129n, 141-2

Propaganda Fide, College of (Rome): American students at, 538-9

Prospect Before Us (James T. Callender): and presidential campaign of 1800, 537n

Provera, Giovanni, Marquis de, 135, 136n

"Providential Detection" (cartoon), xxxvii, 318 (illus.)

Provost, William, 486

Prussia: and renewal of treaty with U.S., 371n; appointment of U.S. minister to Berlin, 411, 412-13n, 414

public lands: bill for sale of, 10-11

pumpkins: as crop, 559

quartermaster general (U.S.): role of T. Pickering as, 381

Raccoon ford: site on proposed road from Georgetown to Ga., 529

Rachael (b. 1790, TJ's slave): in marriage settlement of Mary Jefferson, 550

Rachael (TJ's slave): TJ mortgages, 98

Rambouillet, France: experimental farms at, 333

Randolph, Mr.: servant of, 200

Randolph, Anne Cary (TJ's granddaughter): visits Monticello, vii, 349; TJ's affection for, 11, 37, 63, 309, 328, 414, 457, 462, 583, 597; sends gift to brother, 91; health of, 261, 273, 308, 399; affection for parents, 274; separation from TJ, 322; smallpox inoculation, 334, 349, 351, 385; growth of, 428; resembles mother, 428; mentioned, 82

Randolph, Beverley (d. 1797), 82, 317

Randolph, David Meade: visits Monticello, 168; lands adjoining Martin's swamp, 547; as U.S. marshal, 630n

Randolph, Edmund: letter to, 459-60; letters from, 572, 574; resignation, 4,
560n; practices law in Richmond, 5; and
T. M. Randolph's legal affairs, 52-3; at
Constitutional Convention, 57n; and
Mazzei's finances, 81, 83n; and publication of Washington's correspondence,
141-2, 144n, 181; and Dombey's papers, 257, 259n; and Va.-Md. boundary, 263n, 271-2, 278-9; and Short's salary, 317, 318n, 332, 464, 572, 597; as
tarnish on Va.'s reputation, 383; relations with Fauchet, 384, 385n, 557-8,
565; TJ shares political views with,
459; letters from cited, 460n, 572n; letters to cited, 460n, 572n; and Monroe,
563-4, 565; correspondence with Hammond, 565, 606-8; correspondence with
Jay, 606-31
Randolph, Ellen Wayles, II (TJ's granddaughter): birth of, vii; and trip to Monticello, vii, 349; health of, 308; TJ's affection for, 309, 328, 414, 457, 462,
583, 597; separation from TJ, 322; cuts
teeth, 351
Randolph, John (d. 1784), 97n, 196-7
Randolph, Lucy Bolling (Mrs. William
Randolph), 82
Randolph, Martha Cocke (Mrs. Beverley
Randolph), 82
Randolph, Martha Jefferson (Patsy, Mrs.
Thomas Mann Randolph, TJ's daughter): letters to, 11, 308-9, 327-8, 349,
379, 424-5, 596-7; letter from, 334;
gives birth to daughter, vii; and trip
to Monticello, vii, 170, 334, 349; TJ's
affection for, 11, 27, 37, 53, 63, 91, 261,
274, 287, 314, 316, 328, 399, 414,
425, 430, 451, 462, 583; regards sent
to, 49, 54, 61, 106, 118, 148, 154, 156,
164, 488, 509, 517; and Jefferson
Ducoigne, 132; and Mary Jefferson,
308, 573, 579; at Varina, 308, 351;
friendships, 314-15, 325-6, 328, 379,
397; TJ says he will write to, 322; fails
to write, 328; anxiety over children's
smallpox inoculation, 334; TJ sends financial, mercantile news to, 379; letters
from cited, 425n; TJ seeks to keep her
near Monticello, 430; rumored to be ill,
483, 507; marriage settlement, 532;
Monroe extends invitation to, 566; and
T. M. Randolph's health, 569; at
Belmont, 577; TJ offers to purchase
goods in Philadelphia for, 596; mentioned, 82, 518

Randolph, Mary (Mrs. David M. Randolph, sister of Thomas Mann
Randolph), 168
Randolph, Mary Skipwith, 317
Randolph, Richard (d. 1786): and Wayles
estate, 96, 97n; suit against heirs of, 166,
218n, 268, 533n
Randolph, Thomas Jefferson (TJ's grandson): at Monticello, vii, 11, 26, 63, 349;
health of, 11, 91, 308, 399, 428; TJ's
affection for, 287, 309, 328, 414, 457,
462, 583, 597; separation from TJ, 322;
smallpox inoculation, 334, 349, 351,
385; mentioned, 82
Randolph, Thomas, Jr. (of Dungeness),
317
Randolph, Thomas Mann (TJ's son-in-
law): letters to, 26-7, 36-7, 52-3, 63-4,
90-1, 168-9, 170-1, 211, 260-2, 273-4,
287, 315-16, 322-3, 349-50, 360, 385-
6, 402, 413-14, 426-7, 436-7, 451, 462,
583-4; letter from, 568-9; TJ's affection
for, 11, 424, 597; and Cobbs suit, 26-7,
63-4; health of, 27, 169, 385, 399, 428,
569; executes business for TJ, 36, 52,
172, 203, 220, 276, 287, 322, 360, 414,
569; letters from cited, 37n, 53n, 91n,
169n, 171n, 211n, 261n, 350n, 386n,
414n, 462n; legal, business affairs of,
52-3, 90-1, 108n; Strickland sends respects to, 106, 118; and sale of tobacco,
112, 385, 413, 426, 436; regards sent
to, 154, 156, 164, 183, 573; and threshing machine, 167; visits Sweet Springs,
171; memorandum to cited, 172; and
Burr's visit to Monticello, 198; supervises Volney's valise, 225, 257; travels
to, from Varina, 276, 309, 351; makes
cider, 309; TJ purchases goods for, 315-
16, 436-7; as candidate for Va. General
Assembly, 322, 327-8, 349; elected
member of APS, 322-3; forwards clover
seed, 322; takes children for smallpox
inoculation, 334, 349, 351; TJ writes,
379, 425; at Monticello, 427, 428; TJ
plans to visit, 451; provides information,
531; Monroe extends invitation to, 566;
travels from Richmond to Monticello,
568-9; and road contract, 586; and
weather diaries, 596; mentioned, 82
Randolph, William, 82
Raymond, Julien (French commissioner in
Saint-Domingue), 348n, 388n
Read, Jacob: committee appointment,
282; carries rice seed to S.C., 367, 487;
introduces bills, 423n, 461n; and

INDEX

Charleston customs dispute, 567n; as Senate president pro tempore, 568

Recherches historiques et politiques sur les États-Unis de l'Amérique Septentrionale (Philip Mazzei): and TJ's letter to Mazzei, 85n, 87n

Recorder (Richmond): and Callender, 537n

Reed, Benjamin, 508n

Reeves, William: and TJ's accounts, 174n

Remsen, Henry: letter to, 441-2; clerk to Jay, 23-4n; TJ orders newspapers from, 441-2; letter from cited, 442n; letter to cited, 442n

Renick (Reynick), Robert, 150, 151

republicanism: and election of 1796, 255; TJ's views on, 289-90; land owners as friendly to, 383; TJ laments decline of, 439; establishment of principles of, 460; and the principles of 1776, 522; and party divisions, 580; Adams on, 593

Republicans: mock British institutions, 3; and Jay Treaty, 46-7, 54n, 60, 108; and TJ's letter to Mazzei, 73-8, 382-3; accused of Jacobinism, pro-French sentiments, 76, 78-9, 407, 557-8; as pro-French, 109-10, 359; in N.Y., 156-7, 478, 479n, 594; and campaign for electors in Va., 193-9; and election of 1796, 211, 223, 416; in Pa., 211, 594; and Washington's popularity, 252-3; and TJ's reluctance as a candidate, 264; in Congress, 370, 372, 385, 412n, 422, 426, 594; and U.S. relations with France, 374n; political attacks on leaders of, 380; and expenditures for fortifications, 423n; ineffectiveness of, in Va. assembly, 493; and Callender, 537n; support for TJ in Md., 557; as defenders of civil liberties, 558; urged to proclaim their principles loudly, 580; in New England, 594, 595n

Reuben (TJ's slave): TJ mortgages, 98

Review of the Correspondence (Timothy Pickering): and TJ's letter to Mazzei, 78n

Reynolds, James, 478-9

Reynolds, Dr. James, 537n

Reynolds, Maria Lewis (Mrs. James Reynolds): and Hamilton, 478-9, 542, 630n; and Federalist politics, 558

rheumatism: TJ suffers from, 351, 399, 428

Rhine Valley: military campaigns in, 161, 265, 273, 456, 459

rhinoceroses: compared to mammoths, 294; habitat of, as analogy for megalonyx, 294, 297-8

rice: grown in Spain, 29; lieth machine for threshing, 231-2; TJ receives, distributes seed from Philippines, 367, 487

Rice, Henry: forwards books to TJ, 182, 205

Richardson, George, 585n

Richardson, Joseph, 585n

Richardson, Richard: letter to, 585; identified, 585n; witnesses documents, 210, 548, 550; and renovations at Monticello, 428; to receive training in stonecutting, 585; letters from cited, 585n; letter to cited, 585n

Richardson, William, 316n

Richmond, Va.: James River Canal reaches, 5; price of corn at, 51-2; price of commodities at, 67; Jews in, 119n; TJ's business affairs in, 272n, 577; stagecoaches to Philadelphia, 274; state capitol, 310n, 335, 336n; inoculation for smallpox at, 349, 351; price of clothing for slaves in, 569; militia seizes *Unicorn*, 612, 630n

Rights of Man (Frederick, Md.): prints Fitzhugh's response, 557, 561; prints query from a "Citizen," 557, 560-1

Rights of Man (Thomas Paine): and Adams-TJ estrangement, 234

Rising Sun (Keene, N.H.): publishes TJ's letter to Mazzei, 75n

Rittenhouse, David: letter to, 138-9; and kitchen stoves, 25; advises J. Williams, 130; TJ announces megalonyx discovery to, 138-9, 140, 291; TJ describes moldboard plow to, 140; death of, 147, 165, 182; as exemplar of American genius, 251, 252n; Rush pays tribute to, 251-2, 275; TJ succeeds as president of APS, 252, 254; TJ praises, 275; B. S. Barton's regard for, 445

Rittenhouse, Hannah Jacobs (Mrs. David Rittenhouse): on kitchen stoves, 25; and death of husband, 165; TJ sends regards to, 192; sends regards, 201

Rivanna River: and route for road from Georgetown, 529; lands on, 547, 549

Rives (Reeves), Robert: and TJ's accounts, 26, 27n; TJ consults with, 50; and TJ's tobacco, 52, 63

roads: local versus federal support for postal, 7-8, 55; in Britain, France, 8; across mountains of western Va., 150-1; TJ proposes building of, 430, 431, 432,

roads (*cont.*)
529, 530; from Georgetown through southern Va. to Ga., 529; contracts for in Albemarle Co., 586. *See also* postal roads
Roberts, Joseph, Jr.: supplies nailrod, 531, 534, 541, 542n; letters from cited, 531n; letters to cited, 531n
Robertson (Robinson), Mr.: cares for T. M. Randolph's affairs at Edgehill, 36, 168, 260-1
Robespierre, Maximilien François Marie Isidore de: as leader of Terror, 163; and Genet, 471
Robinson, John, 574
Robinson (Robertson), Moses, 594, 595n
Robinson, Saunderson (Sanderson) & Rumney: and Mazzei's finances, 65, 81, 90
Rockfish gap, Va., 139
Rocky Mountains: existence of inferred by Volney, TJ, 174-5, 176n
Rodney, Thomas: and election of 1796, 249n; letter from quoted, 249n
Rome, Romans: classical, used as an example by TJ, 247, 250; classical, references to, 249n; Americans study for priesthood in, 538-9
Ronald, Betsey, 476-7
Ronald, Nancy, 476-7
Ronald, William: TJ sues estate of, 476-8
Ronaldson, James, 536
rope: for TJ, 63, 90
Rose, Charles, 30
Rose, Hugh, 30
Rose, John: TJ asked to recommend, 30, 34; letter to cited, 30n
Rose, Robert H.: TJ asked to recommend, 30, 34; letter to cited, 30n; and election of 1796, 169
Rose Hill, N.Y.: TJ's invitation to, 361, 407
Ross, David, 111
Ross, James: and publication of Pinckney Treaty, 48; takes seat in Senate, 411, 412n; investigates charges against Blount, 472-3n; as likely candidate for governor, 594
Roume, Philippe Rose, 298-9, 300n
Rousseau, Jean Jacques, xxxvii
Royal Society of London, 154n
Royle (Royal) v. Robinson Administrators, 574
Royster, Thomas, 477
Ruines; ou, Méditation sur les Révolutions

des Empires (Constantin François Chasseboeuf Volney), xxxviii
rum: in Jay Treaty, 616
Rumford, Count. *See* Thompson, Benjamin (Count Rumford)
Rumley, Mr., 51
Rush, Benjamin: letter to, 275; letters from, 3-4, 251-2, 284; political commentary, 3-4, 251-2, 284; and election of 1796, 224n; reports on TJ's letter to Madison, 224n; Rittenhouse *Eulogium*, 251, 252n, 275; and TJ's election to APS presidency, 275; notes analogies between nature and politics, 284; theories on dark skin color, 284; forwards correspondence for TJ, 313
Russell, Albert, 195-6
Russia: and comparative studies of languages, 201-2; British policy toward, 342; and U.S. neutrality, 345n
Rutledge, Edward: letters to, 231-3, 455-7; letters from, 92-3, 356-8, 386-7; on Jay Treaty, 92, 357; sends cow peas and orange trees, 92, 231, 357, 386, 455; TJ discusses politics with, 232-3; praises TJ, 356-7; on news from Europe, 386-7; mentioned, 234
Rutledge, Henry Middleton: on tour of S.C., 92; TJ praises, 233
Rutledge, John (1739-1800): Supreme Court nomination, 4-5; son attends St. Germain school, 164
Rutledge, John, Jr.: carries letter to TJ, 356; appointed to House committee, 372, 373n; joins Federalists, 412, 413n; carries breadfruit seeds to S.C., 487
Rutledge, States, 164
rye: embargo proposed on, 63n; as crop at Monticello, 129; grown in Albemarle Co., Va., 350

Saint Croix River: and U.S. boundary, 615, 616-17, 620, 621, 626-7
Saint-Domingue, W.I.: reinforcements for, 148, 149n; geological survey of, 347, 348n; effects of slave insurrection in, 519, 538, 570-2; and Paroy family, 570-2
St. Germain-en-Laye, France: Americans attend school at, 164
St. John's College (Oxford University), 154
St. Louis: Volney plans to travel to, 132-3; census information on, 133n
St. Petersburg, Russia, 201

Ste. Genevieve: census information on, 133n

Salimberi, Madame de (Bruni): plans trip to Varina, 314-15; letters from cited, 315n; letter to cited, 315n; as M. J. Randolph's friend, 328

Salisbury, N.C.: on proposed road from Georgetown to Ga., 529

Sally (daughter of Molly, TJ's slave): in marriage settlement of Mary Jefferson, 550

Salomons, Levi: firm of widow and sons of (London), 200

salt: mined in Tenn., 398n

saltpetre: extraction of, 64, 171, 291; to be made, 100; and ice caves, 321-2

San Antonio, Texas, 175

Sandy (b. 1789, TJ's slave): TJ mortgages, 98; in marriage settlement of Mary Jefferson, 549

Sappington, John, 410n

Sarah (b. 1786, TJ's slave): TJ mortgages, 98; in marriage settlement of Mary Jefferson, 549

Sardinia: and French foreign relations, xxxvii; treaty with France, 117, 161, 164n, 169; and French campaign in Italy, 135; and War of First Coalition, 161

Sargent, Winthrop, 202n

sausage: recipe for, 313-14

Savannah, Ga.: and trade with France, 340

Schuyler, Philip J., 411

Scilla (TJ's slave): TJ mortgages, 98; in marriage settlement of Mary Jefferson, 550

Scott, Daniel, 66

seamen, U.S.: certificates of citizenship for, 35-6

seaports: fortification of harbors, 8, 371n, 393, 416, 421, 422-3n, 425, 433-4, 437

Second Inaugural Address (Thomas Jefferson), 80-1

Secretary's ford (Rivanna River): TJ clears, 483

Sedgwick, Theodore: and sedition act, 35; and TJ's letter to Mazzei, 79; and election of 1796, 224n; committee appointment, 282; attends Federalist caucus, 283n; introduces resolutions, 412n; investigates charges against Blount, 472n; and foreign coinage, 583-4n

sedition acts: TJ seeks information on, 35-6; Callender's prosecution under, 537n

seeds: of varieties of squash, 82; sycamore, sent to TJ, 105; of eggplant, 141; TJ

sends to Strickland, 319; of breadfruit, 347-8, 387-8, 487, 513; rice from Philippines, 367, 487. See also clover seed; grasses; peas; vetch

Seneca: quoted, 467-8

Sermaize, M., 469

Shadwell ford (Rivanna River): TJ clears, 483

Sharples, Ellen Wallace: as portraitist, xxxviii, 318 (illus.)

Sharples, James: executes portraits, xxxviii; portrait of TJ, xl, 318 (illus.)

Sharples, Rolinda, xxxviii

Sharpless, Jonathan: and nailrod for TJ, 55, 88

Shawnee Indians: and Dunmore's War, 409n, 441, 452

sheep: feed for, 179, 512; merino, 333n; markets for mutton, 529

Shelburne, Earl of. See Lansdowne, William Petty, first Marquis of (Earl of Shelburne)

Shelby, Isaac: letter to, 134; introduced to Volney, 134

Shelton, Samuel, 63n

Shockoe warehouse, 26, 63-4

Short, Peyton: correspondence with W. Short, 317, 597, 598n

Short, William: letters to, 316-18, 463-5; letters from, 332-3, 597-8; Albemarle Co. property, 5; business affairs, 6, 219, 277-8, 316-18, 332-3, 463-5, 597-8; and TJ's French accounts, 16, 21, 31; letter to cited, 23n; TJ mortgages slaves to, 96-7n, 209; leaves Spain, 109, 147, 463; and U.S. deposits in France, 122; powers of attorney, 125n, 219, 465n, 544-5, 561; canal shares of, 277, 316-17, 463, 523; relations with Duchesse de La Rochefoucauld, 312; Indian Camp Quarter, 316, 332, 464, 597; tenants, 316, 332, 597; correspondence with brother, 317, 597, 598n; salary due to, 317, 318n, 332, 464, 572, 574, 597; U.S. securities, 317, 318n, 463-4, 465n, 481, 523, 530, 544-5; expects to return to U.S., 332, 597-8; funds advanced for Monroe, 544-5, 561; forwards letters, 597; rejects use of slave labor, 597

Silknitter, Jacob: charcoal burner, 177; letters to cited, 177n

Simcoe, John Graves: intimidation of American settlements, 612-13, 631n

Simms, Charles: as candidate for elector in 1796, 193-6; appointed collector at Alexandria, 195

Simons, James: collector at Charleston, 567, 570

Sinclair, Sir John: letter to, 318-19; letters from, 114-15, 183, 449-50, 480; and TJ's diploma, xli, 450n, 514; sends publications, surveys to TJ, 106n, 114-15, 183, 480; praised as farmer, 318; TJ sends farm implements to, 450n, 546; urges establishment of board of agriculture in U.S., 480

Sir John Sinclair's Address to the Board of Agriculture, on Tuesday the Twentieth of June, 1797, 480

Sir John Sinclair's Address to the Board of Agriculture, on Tuesday, the Twenty-Fourth of May, 1796, 114-15

Sitgreaves, Samuel: as member of House committee, 218; on U.S. relations with France, 374n; and impeachment of Blount, 473n

Sketches of the History of America (James T. Callender): financial assistance during work on, 536, 537n; and comments by Harper, 593n

Sketch of the Finances of the United States (Albert Gallatin): TJ requests, receives copy of, 224, 256

Sketch of the Present State of our Political Relations with the United States of North-America (Joseph Fauchet): published by Bache, 590n

Skinner, Thompson J., 469n

Skipwith, Anne Wayles (Mrs. Henry Skipwith, TJ's sister-in-law), 533n

Skipwith, Fulwar: and U.S. deposits in France, 122; accused of financial improprieties, 165n; resignation, 366; reports losses to shipping, 563-4, 565

Skipwith, Henry: and Wayles estate, 196n, 217, 268, 419; offers to buy Short's land, 332; lands of, 533n; and Short's business affairs, 597; mentioned, 317

Skipwith, Mary. *See* Randolph, Mary Skipwith

Slate River (Buckingham Co., Va.): site on proposed road from Georgetown to Ga., 529

slavery: Va. laws on, 96n, 120n; Quakers and, 120n; and three-fifths clause of Constitution, 364n; potential revolts in West Indies, 377; Tucker proposes gradual abolition, 488-9; TJ foresees potential slave revolt, 519. *See also* Saint-Domingue, W.I.

slaves: travel without permission, 90;

dwellings, 243; federal tax considered on, 265n; diet of, during harvest, 414; given to J. W. Eppes, 549; clothing for, 569; and work habits, 586; Short does not wish to own, use, 597; taken or freed by British during Revolution, 613, 620-1, 622, 624-5. *See also* Jefferson, Thomas: Slaveholder

sloths: associated with megatherium, 299, 510. *See also* megalonyx; megatherium

smallpox: inoculations, 334, 349, 351, 385, 401n; in Va., 427, 428

Smith, Abbey (Abby, TJ's slave): TJ mortgages, 98

Smith, Armstead (TJ's slave): TJ mortgages, 98

Smith, Daniel, 222

Smith, Dick (TJ's slave): TJ mortgages, 98

Smith, Edy (TJ's slave): TJ mortgages, 98

Smith, Fanny (TJ's slave): TJ mortgages, 98

Smith, Flora (TJ's slave): TJ mortgages, 98

Smith, Hetty: engaged to Peter Carr, 210-11

Smith, Israel, 594

Smith, Jesse (TJ's slave): TJ mortgages, 98

Smith, John: land in Albemarle Co., Va., 547, 549

Smith, Capt. John (1579-1632): *Generall Historie of Virginia*, 294; TJ's use as source, 301n, 302-3n; on American lions, 303n

Smith, Larkin: land in Albemarle Co., Va., 547, 549

Smith, Lucy (TJ's slave): TJ mortgages, 98

Smith, Philip: land in Albemarle Co., Va., 547, 549

Smith, Ralph, 538-9

Smith, Robert, 210-11n

Smith, Sal (TJ's slave): TJ mortgages, 98

Smith, Samuel, 210n

Smith, Samuel Harrison: plans for weekly newspaper, 416, 434, 442; prints letters signed "Fabius," 435n. See also *Universal Gazette* (Philadelphia)

Smith, Thomas: land in Albemarle Co., Va., 547, 549

Smith, Will (TJ's slave): TJ mortgages, 98

Smith, William, 413n

Smith, William Loughton: debates Gallatin, 146; and Adams's speech, 218; and taxes, 265n, 461n; as Federalist, 412, 413n; reports on congressional politics, 412n; promotes defense measures, 421-3, 450; on Americans serving in foreign military, 450n; as U.S. minister at Lisbon, 486-7; *Comparative View of the Constitutions of the Several States*, 555

snakes: thought to mesmerize prey, 165, 166n, 182, 192

Snelson, Robert: and Kinsolving's debt, 204

Snowden & McCorkle (McKorkle): and Callender, 537n, 544

Sodus, N.Y.: British intimidation of, 613, 631n

soil: exhaustion of, 103

Solomon (TJ's slave): TJ mortgages, 98

"Some account of an American Species of Dipus, or Jerboa" (Benjamin Smith Barton), 183n

Somerville, Robert: *Outlines of the Fifteenth Chapter of the Proposed General Report from the Board of Agriculture, on the Subject of Manures*, 319

Sophia (b. 1796, TJ's slave): in marriage settlement of Mary Jefferson, 550

Sousy (b. 1793, TJ's slave): TJ mortgages, 98; in marriage settlement of Mary Jefferson, 549

South America: maps of, 105-6, 115; megatherium discovery, 298, 301n, 510

South Carolina: vote at Constitutional Convention, 68; and election of 1796, 226; agricultural society in, 367, 468n, 487; TJ sends breadfruit, rice to, 367, 388, 487; politics in, 411-12; cultivation of rice in, 487; sites on proposed road from Georgetown to Ga., 529; politics and Charleston customs dispute, 567, 570; relationship to U.S., 570

South Carolina (ship): carries van Hasselt to America, 466

South Carolina Society for Promoting and Improving Agriculture: publishes extract of TJ's letter, 468n

southern states: and election of 1796, 232, 235-6, 253; republican sentiment in, 289-90, 439; misrepresented, misunderstood in north, 364; political advantage given by three-fifths clause, 364n; wish to avoid war with France, 371-2

Southwest Territory, 30, 34n

Soyechtowa. *See* Logan (Mingo Indian)

Spain: U.S. diplomats in, 23n; farming methods in, 27, 29; relations with France, 228, 372; relations with U.S., 255, 471, 598; declares war against Britain, 256, 265; and study of megatherium, 298-9, 300n, 301n, 510; role of West Indies in event of war with U.S., 377; U.S.-West Florida boundary, 535-6; secret service expenditures in America, 551. *See also* Louis of Parma; Pinckney Treaty

Sparks, Richard, 221

Sparrman, Anders: *Voyage*, 296

Spears, James, 43n

Spears, John: TJ purchases claim of, 43n; mentioned, 44n

Spears, William: letter to cited, 43n; mentioned, 44n

specie: replaced by paper currency, 329-30, 401; Bank of England suspends payments in, 340-1, 344n, 401; abundant in France, 341; flows from U.S. to Britain, 370-1, 373; and bill extending currency of foreign coins, 583-4, 589-90, 594; in Jay Treaty, 621, 622

spinach: grown at Monticello, 322

Spithead, England: mutiny of British sailors at, 431n, 433, 436, 438, 456, 459

Sprigg, Richard, Jr.: and TJ's letter to P. Fitzhugh, 557

Sprigg, Thomas, 95n

Squire (b. 1793, TJ's slave): in marriage settlement of Mary Jefferson, 549

Sravnitel'nye slovari vsiekh iazykov i nariechii, sobrannye desnitseiu vsevysochaishei osoby (Peter Simon Pallas), 201n

Staël de Holstein, Eric Magnus, Baron de, 230-1

Stafford Co., Va.: campaign for presidential elector in, 193, 195

stagecoaches: Volney abhors open stages, 221; TJ travels by, 274, 308-9, 314-15, 352-3; as means of contact with public, 353; to Philadelphia, 565

Stanhope, Philip (second Earl of Stanhope), 59

Starr, James, 50, 168

State, U.S. Department of: flags flown over consulates, 376

Statement, Explanatory of the Resignation of the Officers of the Regiment of Artillery, of the City and County of New-York, 404n states: and power to regulate value of foreign coinage, 589-90

Staughton, William, 378

Staunton, Va.: as possible location of school, 58; Volney, La Rochefoucauld-Liancourt pass through, 111, 148, 150, 152n; distance from Charlottesville, 150; and communication with Washington Co., Md., 380, 415-16; as market for TJ's nails, 540-1

Steele, John (comptroller of treasury): endorses documents, 465n, 545n, 561

Steele, John (stonemason): works at Monticello, 65n

Stephen (TJ's slave): TJ mortgages, 98

Stevens (Stephens), Edward: letter to, 431; sends Strode's survey to TJ, 431

Stevensburg, Va.: site on proposed road from Georgetown to Ga., 431, 432, 529, 530

Stewart, David, & Sons, 45n

Stewart, Dugald: letter to, 415; and natural science, 415

Stewart, John, 263n

Stith, Richard: letter from, 130; as surveyor, 52, 130

Stith, William, 66

Stock, John: performs work for TJ, 523, 530

stocks, six percent, 574

Stockton, Richard, 472n

Stoddert, Benjamin, 197n

stonemasons. See Monticello: brickmasons, stonemasons

stoves: kitchen, invented in Lancaster, Pa., 25

Stratton, Capt. Henry, 586

straw: used for feeding in Spain, 28

Strickland, Sir George, 170

Strickland, William: letter to, 319-20; letters from, 102-6, 115-19, 510-11, 511-13; exchanges seeds with TJ, 102-5, 115, 117, 319, 510-12, 514; sends publications to TJ, 105-6, 115; seeks information on ice caves, 116-17, 320, 321; on costs of war as impetus to peace, 117-18; praises succory, 144; letter from cited, 513n

Strictures upon the Letter imputed to Mr. Jefferson, Addressed to Mr. Mazzei (Tench Coxe), 77n

Strode, John: letter to, 432; identified, 432n; surveys road, 431, 432; letters from cited, 432n; letters to cited, 432n

Strother, French: letter to, 425-6; TJ sends political news to, 425-6

Stuart (Stewart), Archibald: letters to, 57-8, 113, 134, 138, 252-3, 525; letters from, 99-100, 171-3, 239; letters from cited, 58n, 100n; searches for stonemason, 99-100; sends information about megalonyx, 100, 275n, 300n; asked to assist Volney, 134, 148, 150; asked to assist La Rochefoucauld-Liancourt, 138; and Va.-Ky. boundary, 172; orders gongs, 239, 253; proposes memorial to Congress on relations with France, 239; TJ discusses politics, French war with, 252-3; forwards seed to TJ, 415; cares for TJ's shipments, 559; forwards correspondence, 566n

Stuart, Gilbert: portrait of Volney, xxxviii.) 318 (illus.)

Stuart (Stewart), John: letters to, 113-14, 205-6, 509-10; letters from, 64-5, 152-3, 177, 266, 525-6; identified, 64-5n; sends megalonyx fossils, information, 64-5, 113-14, 152-3, 155, 171, 177, 205-6, 266, 275n, 291, 296, 300n, 509-10, 525-6; letter from cited, 113n; election to APS, 206, 509-10, 525

succory: for T. M. Randolph, 27; Washington grows, 144

Suck (b. 1771, TJ's slave): TJ mortgages, 98

Suetonius Tranquillus, Gaius: on Julius Caesar, 249n

sugar: and Article 12 of Jay Treaty, 619

sugar, brown: duties on, 265n

Sullivan, James: letter to, 289-91; letter from, 262; urges TJ to accept vice presidency, 262

Sumter, Thomas, 413n

Superior, Lake: and U.S. boundary with British possessions, 617

surveying instruments: TJ purchases, 315, 316n, 436-7

Swaile (Swail), James, 168

Swan, Caleb, 221

Sweden: and exportation of grain, 10; Royal Academy of Science, 136; recall of Baron de Staël, 230-1; trades with France, 340; relations with U.S., 345n, 371n; naval strength, 376

Sweet Springs (Greenbrier Co.): T. M. Randolph visits, 171

Switzer, Mr., 462

Syria: Volney travels in, xxxviii, 61, 111, 132, 482; Volney compares western prairies to, 174

T., Mr.: and Hamilton's *Observations*, 542

Tabb, Philip: answers TJ's questions on the cow pea, 179-80

Tableau de la Situation Actuelle des États-Unis d'Amérique (Charles Pictet de Rochemont): Gautier sends to TJ, 122

Tableau du Climat et du Sol des États-Unis d'Amérique (Constantin François Chasseboeuf Volney), xxxviii

Talleyrand-Périgord, Charles Maurice de (Bishop of Autun): gossips about Hamilton, 517; in U.S., 518n; and reception of U.S envoys in Paris, 589

tannier (taro, esculenta): possible cultivation of, in Va., 513-14

Tarvis: French victory at, 341, 344n, 423n, 433

Tasso, Torquato: Volney quotes *Gerusalemme Liberata*, 229, 230n; TJ adapts Volney's quote from, 258

Tattnall, Josiah, 411

taxes: payment of T. M. Randolph's, 26-7; TJ grows tobacco to pay, 255; federal, proposed on land, 265, 272, 285, 520, 583, 586, 588, 594; federal, proposed on slaves, 265; TJ's proposal on, 416-17, 418n, 443; federal, proposed on wine and liquor, 461, 462; Stamp Act (1797), 461, 462, 583, 586, 588, 594

Taylor, Maj., 177

Taylor, George, Jr., 181

Taylor, George Keith: and revision of Va. penal laws, 310n; and Tucker's abolition proposal, 489n

Taylor, John (of Caroline): letters to, 545-6, 588-90; letters from, 553-5, 573; and election of 1796, 194; Burr visits, 198n; as TJ's friend, 199n; and Va.-Md. boundary, 263n, 271-2, 278-9; and TJ's grand jury petition, 493; and T. Martin's threshing machine, 553-4, 573, 588; exchanges seeds with TJ, 554; sends farm implements, 573; attends Va. General Assembly, 589

Taylor, Thomas Augustus: letter to, 219-20; and purchase of Elk Hill, 213n, 219-20, 287; letters from cited, 220n; letters to cited, 220n

Taylor, William, 185

Tazewell, Henry: letters to, 267, 575-6, 604; letter from, 281-3; and Jay Treaty, 71n; Burr fails to visit, 198n; TJ writes, 266, 280; on TJ's notification as vice president, 267, 281-2; appointed to Senate committee, 395n, 411; votes against Blount's expulsion, 473n; and Ellicott,

535; and TJ's Senate duties, 575-6; and TJ's account of Logan's speech, 590-1, 600, 603n; and TJ's correspondence with J. Henry, 590-1, 604

teas: duties on bohea, 265n; as payment, 546

teffe (teff, African cereal grass), 513

Tennessee: and election of 1796, 169, 227, 253; practice of law in, 222; mammoth remains in, 398, 403; and election of congressman, 411; and admission into Union, 472n

Tessé, Adrienne Catherine de Noailles, Comtesse de: TJ corresponds with, 122; and Pougens, 333

Tessier, Henri Alexandre, 333

Texas: Americans in, 174-5

Thamar (TJ's slave): in marriage settlement of Mary Jefferson, 550

thermometers: TJ purchases, 315-16, 436-7

Thompson, Benjamin (Count Rumford), 605n

Thompson, Mrs. James, 402

Thompson, James (N.Y.), 356, 402

Thompson, Joseph, 360

Thornton, William: letter from, 110-11; ties to Volney, 53, 152n, 321, 483, 507; and plans for a university, 110-11

Three Friends (ship), 458n

threshing machines: built, used by TJ, 129, 167, 168-9, 170, 187-8, 211, 231-2, 244; Washington's views on, 144; bill of scantling for, 189n; improvement of, 207; leith machine, 231-2; T. Martin's, 545, 553-4, 573, 588

Thyestes (Seneca): quoted, 467-8

Tichenor, Isaac, 594, 595n

tigers: habitat, as analogy for megalonyx, 294; as examples of predators, 297, 299

Tim (TJ's slave): in marriage settlement of Mary Jefferson, 550

timber: of larch tree, 105

Time Piece, and Literary Companion: TJ subscribes to, 442n

Tinsley, Peter, 477-8

tobacco: sale of TJ's, 52, 63, 255, 260, 261, 268, 316, 385, 402, 413, 426-7, 436, 484, 577; price of, 67, 124, 309, 371, 379, 385, 402, 412, 413, 426; as crop, 91, 153; for payment of TJ's accounts, 324, 481; price of insurance on, 413

Toby (TJ's slave): TJ mortgages, 98

Tocaniadorogon. *See* Logan (Mingo Indian)

Toler, Matthew, 548, 550
Tomlinson, Benjamin, 556
Tonga: source of breadfruit seeds, 348
tools and utensils: given to Mary Jefferson, 547, 550
Topographical Description of the Western Territory of North America (Gilbert Imlay): criticizes TJ, 176n
Tories: during the American Revolution, 505, 506n
toys: and TJ's grandchildren, 91
Tracy, Uriah: appointed to Senate committee, 372, 395n; introduces defense measures, 423n; and Imlay's petition, 584n
traders, British: rights in Northwest Terr., 228n
Traquair, James (stonecutter), 585
Travels into North America (Peter Kalm): cited by TJ, 298, 304n
Travels through the United States of North America, the Country of the Iroquois, and Upper Canada (François Alexandre Frédéric, Duc de La Rochefoucauld-Liancourt), 149n
Treasury, U.S. Department of the: land tax policy, 285; affluence of, allows postponement of taxes, 586, 588
Treaty of Greenville: U.S. acquisition of lands under, 11n; considered in House of Representatives, 62, 70-1, 95n; and British traders in Northwest Terr., 228n
trees: at Monticello, 105
trifolium agrarium: clover seed sent to TJ, 510-12; described by Strickland, 512. *See also* clover seed
Trist, Elizabeth House: letter to, 350-1; considers buying lands near Monticello, 350-1; letter from cited, 351n
Trist, Hore Browse, 351
triticum spica multiplici: wheat sent to TJ, 509. *See also* wheat
Tronchin, Jean Armand: letter from, 207-8; and foreign creditors' recovery of funds in U.S., 207-9
Trumbull, John: letter from, 325-6; and TJ's return to public life, 325-6
Trump, Daniel: makes sashes for TJ, 212, 324, 523, 530
Tubman, M., 509
Tuckahoe (Randolph estate), 568
Tucker, St. George: letter to, 519-20; letters from, 488-9, 515-16; scientific pursuits, 139; "Jonathan Pindar" odes, 192; abolition proposal, 488-9, 519; *Disserta-*

tion on Slavery, 489n; reports British harassment of ships, 515-16
Tufton (TJ estate): slaves at, 98
Turkey: Volney compares western prairies to, 174
turnips, 546, 554
Turpin, Philip (TJ's cousin): letter from, 155-6; and natural history, technology, 155-6; sends mammoth bone, 155, 481; letters from cited, 156n; letters to cited, 156n
Tuscany: U.S. diplomats in, 23n; and French campaign in Italy, 161

Ulloa, Antonio de: manuscript on Panama, 360-1, 406; and wheat in S. America, 509
Unicorn (ship): seizure of, 612, 630n
United Irishmen, Society of, 140n

UNITED STATES: France sends official units of measure, 229-30, 257

Army
proposal for provisional army, 371n, 421, 423n, 450, 451; Senate supports expansion of, 393; and Whiskey Insurrection, 407; artillerists, 421, 423n, 450, 451; cavalry, 421, 423n, 433, 436; applications for commissions, 520

Cabinet
TJ on conflict in Washington's, 271; opposes Gerry's appointment, 420n

Congress, Fourth
(4 Mch. 1795-3 Mch. 1797)
and compensation of families of Revolutionary War officers from France, 7, 144-5, 312; and postal roads, 7-8; and act for survey and sale of public lands, 10-11; seems endless, 49; adjournment of, 95, 108, 119; Gallipolis land grant, 152n; counts electoral votes, 281-2, 304, 305n, 306n; to notify president and vice president of election to office, 281-2, 306; and treaty-making power, 323; ransom to Algiers, 369n; authorizes, funds construction of frigates, 377n; and letters to constituents, 418-19n; avoiding war measures, 441

Congress, Fifth
(4 Mch. 1797-3 Mch. 1799)
and TJ's letter to Mazzei, 74, 78-9; special session of, 76-7, 347, 351, 402;

INDEX

UNITED STATES (*cont.*)
relations with France, 272, 361, 370-1, 380, 385, 429, 455, 557, 586; and inauguration day, 311n; convening of, 325, 352; and arming of merchant vessels, 371n, 372, 416, 421-2, 450, 451, 461, 588-9, 594, 595n; and reorganization of militia, 371n, 393, 416, 456, 457n; act to provide for the defense of ports and harbors, 372, 421, 422-3n, 425, 433-4, 437; bill for protection of trade (act providing a naval armament), 377n, 421-2, 423n, 425-6, 433-5, 436-7, 461, 462; response to Adams's May 1797 address to, 379, 405, 431, 438; talks of embargo, 386, 402, 461, 462; and defense measures, 416, 418n, 459-60; political divisions in, 416; prefers borrowing to raising taxes, 416; act prohibiting exportation of arms and ammunition, 421, 423n, 426, 433, 436; artillery bill, 421, 423n, 450, 451; bill to prevent U.S. citizens from engaging in armed vessels (act to prevent citizens of the United States from privateering), 421, 423n, 426, 433, 436; delays in adjournment of, 422, 425, 432n, 433, 436, 450, 451, 460, 461, 462; impact of European events on, 432, 459-60; newspapers report fully on, 437; TJ estimates cost of convening, 437; support for Jay Treaty in, 447; bill for convening fall session, 461; proposes tax on wine and liquor, 461, 462; and stamp act, 461, 462, 583, 586, 588; and grand jury presentment against S. Cabell, 490; memorial from Vincennes, 507-8; power of, in relation to executive, 522; on removal to Federal District, 528-9; and governance of Natchez region, 535-6; receives documents with president's May 1797 message, 563-4; bill for officers at port at Wilmington, N.C., 583; and bill giving currency to foreign coins, 583-4, 589, 594; and land tax, 583, 586, 587, 588; and Imlay's petition, 584; and naval buildup, 587-8, 588-9; and Blount impeachment, 589; convening of during epidemics, 592; little business in, 596

Courts
and foreigners' claims on funds in U.S., 208-9; influenced by politics, 417, 418n; influence on selection of jurors,

505-6; opened to suits of British creditors, 608, 615-16

Description
as refuge from European upheavals, 312-13; and loss of national character, 380-1

Economy
investments in government securities, 191, 464; economic failures and distress, 228, 255, 329-30, 458; drainage of specie to Britain, 370-1; impact of bankruptcies and seizures of U.S. vessels, 373; impact of failure of Bank of England, 373; commercial stagnation, 412; Coxe on, 420-1; relationship of American merchants and British capital, 522. *See also* Philadelphia

Executive
and treaties, 42; excessive power, influence of, 60, 370, 385, 522, 592; and authority over foreign establishment, 78; on official notification of election of office, 267; combines legislative and executive functions, 274; and treaty-making power, 323; role of presidency, 343; policy toward neutral powers, 344, 345n; and power to negotiate with foreign nations, 393; and power to purchase vessels and employ convoys, 421-2, 434-5n; and power to raise provisional army, 421, 423n; and relations with France, 421-1

Government
policies follow British model, 407; and extension of diplomatic establishment, 411, 413n; right of citizens and their representatives to communicate freely, 491-504

House of Representatives
and Jay Treaty, 4, 5-6n, 7, 9-10, 25, 36n, 45-9, 51-2, 55-7, 60, 62, 71, 72-3, 93-6; *Debates in the House of Representatives*, 46, 49n, 60-1, 72-3, 109-10; refuses to adjourn for Washington's birthday, 46, 49n; call for Jay Treaty Papers, and president's refusal, 54, 55-6, 60-1, 62; passes aid for Federal District, 56; and appropriations for treaties, 62, 70-1; considers embargo on corn and rye, 62-3; consulted on ransom for U.S. captives in Algiers, 69; *Mr. Maclay's Motion.*

UNITED STATES (*cont.*)

14th April 1796, 71n; and debate on
foreign intercourse bill, 78-9; Gallatin's speeches on finance, 124, 125n;
and Bank of the U.S., 125n; considers
aid for Lafayette's son, 126-7; Smith-
Gallatin debate, 146; and policy toward France, 164-5, 252, 285, 366;
and election of 1796, 214, 223-4,
228n; response to Washington's Dec.
1796 address, 218, 227; considers
taxes, 265, 272-3, 285; and Monroe, 343, 366; role in foreign policy,
343; elect Condy as clerk, 372; response to Adams's May 1797 address
to, 372, 373n, 401, 402, 407, 411-12,
413-14, 416, 421, 425, 427, 438,
443; and Madison's resolutions on Report on Commerce, 405; party divisions in, 414, 422, 426; Republican
presence in, 437, 594; bill prohibiting
U.S. citizens from serving on foreign
vessels, 450; and Blount investigation, impeachment, 473n, 516-17;
and privilege of members to correspond freely with constituents, 491-
504; and TJ's grand jury petition,
524, 526-7

Navy

construction, manning of frigates for,
371n, 372, 375, 377n, 416, 421, 422-
3n, 425-6, 433, 434-5n; establishment of, 371n; O'Brien's suggestions
for naval defense, 375-7; and Barbary
States, 376; Dutch, Scandinavian examples, 376; and Italian states, 376;
to assert U.S. independence from Europe, 377; and convoys, 393, 421,
425, 434-5n; Congress considers aug-
mentation of, 421-2, 423n, 433-5,
436-7, 461, 462; Adams advocates increases in, 587-9; as political issue,
594

Politics

consideration of taxes postponed during
elections, 583

Public Finance

TJ on Hamilton's financial program, 5;
TJ on public debt, 6, 124; TJ's accounts in France, 11-12, 30-4; congressional action on diplomats' expenditures, 12, 17, 19, 23n, 24, 58;
assignats on deposit, 122; Gallatin's
speeches on, 124, 125n; debts and expenditures, 146; funding system and
American politics, 214-15; and redemption of the public debt, 277-8;
and pending war, 401; follows British
model, 407; and TJ's tax plan, 416-
17, 418n, 443. *See also* taxes

Public Opinion

on Jay Treaty, 4, 42; Washington's popularity, 124, 147, 290; on banks, 228;
strong divisions over France, Britain,
230, 448-9; British influence, 363-4;
proposed separation of northern,
southern states, 363-4; regional political positions misrepresented, 364;
wishes peace with France, 370; and
Genet, 471; French travelers uncomfortable in U.S., 483; and taxation,
financial policies, 520

Senate

rejects Rutledge nomination, 4-5; and
treaties, 9, 42, 54n, 60; TJ requests
Hawkins's notes on, 43; records of,
67-9, 93; on U.S. captives in Algiers,
68-9; and Jay Treaty, 71, 73, 342,
437, 517, 614n, 629n, 630n; and six-
year term for senators, 157n; approves
Explanatory Article to Jay Treaty,
228n; to notify president and vice
president of election to office, 267;
administer oath of office to vice president, 281; consulted on transfer of
power to new administration, 304-5;
and TJ's notification as vice president, 304; TJ's address to, 310-12;
replies to Adams's May 1797 address,
372, 373, 374n, 392-5, 401, 411,
443, 459; address to John Adams,
392-5; supports negotiations with
France, 394-5; address from John
Adams, 396; unity of sentiment with
president, 396; Federalist control of,
411, 412n; and J. Q. Adams's appointment, 411, 412-13n; confirms
diplomatic appointments, 420, 448,
450, 487n; resolution on appointment
of C. C. Pinckney, 420; bill for provisional army, 421, 423n, 450, 451; bill
for raising cavalry, 421, 423n, 433,
436; TJ depicts work in, 430; considers authorizing president to lay embargo, 461, 462; resolution on
Blount, 472-4; appoints first investigative committee, 472n; Blount's impeachment trial, 473-4n; memorials
from Charleston merchants, wharf-

UNITED STATES (*cont.*)
holders, 567, 570; delay in TJ's attendance, 568, 575-6; elections of senators, 594, 595n; TJ presides over,
633-4

Supreme Court
and carriage tax, 4n, 10; appointment of
Chase, 5, 42, 124; Ellsworth as chief
justice, 42, 124; and Va.-Md. boundary, 263n; counsel in McCulloch v.
Maryland, 359n, 454n; Dartmouth
College case, 359n

United States (U.S. frigate), 422n
Universal Gazette (Philadelphia): TJ en-
dorses, subscribes to, 416, 418n. *See
also* Smith, Samuel Harrison
Ursula (TJ's slave): TJ mortgages, 98
*Utrum Horum? The government; or, the
country?* (Dennis O'Bryen): TJ sends to
Madison, 433-4, 435n

Val (TJ's slave): TJ mortgages, 98; in
marriage settlement of Mary Jefferson,
550
Valencia: culture of rice in, 29
Vall-Travers, Rodolph, 138, 139n
Van Buren, Martin, 74n, 78n
Van Cortlandt, Philip, 591
van Hasselt, Willem H.: letter to, 518-19;
letter from, 465-8; identified, 468n;
seeks employment as tutor, 465-8,
518-19
Van Staphorst, Jacob: and TJ's letter to
Mazzei, 74; and slave mortgages, 209-
10; potential relocation to Va., 331; letter from cited, 458n
Van Staphorst, Nicolaas: and slave mortgages, 209-10
Van Staphorst & Hubbard: letters to, 90,
329-30, 331; letters from, 65, 106-7,
199-200, 457-8; make loan to TJ in
France, 22; and Mazzei's finances, 55,
65, 67, 81-2, 89, 90, 95; TJ's correspondence with, 55-6; letters to cited,
83n; TJ mortgages slaves to, 96-7n, 98-
9, 209-10; TJ borrows from, 97n, 106-
7, 329-31, 458, 574-5; made citizens of
Va., 215-17, 274, 331, 457-8; TJ comments on, 327; and Dutch speculations
in U.S., 330, 458; TJ's bonds to, 330-1,
458, 574-5. *See also* Willink, Van Staphorst & Hubbard
Varina (Randolph estate): slaves at, 90;
Randolphs travel to, from, 276, 309,

351; Mary Jefferson visits, 308, 309,
351; vetch grows at, 319; compared to
Monticello, 328; TJ's family at, 351
Varnum, Joseph B.: and vote on Jay
Treaty, 93-5; resides at Francis's hotel,
469n
Vatican, 336
Vattel, Emmerich de: cited in Jay Treaty
negotiations, 614, 623
Vaughan, Benjamin: letter to, 521; TJ
mistakes for J. Martin, 521, 529-30;
Home Office investigates, 521n; pseudo-
nyms of, 521n
Vaughan, John: letters to, 521-2, 529-30;
as officer of APS, 139n, 277n; and
B. Vaughan's identity, 521-2, 529-30;
letter from cited, 530n
Vaughan, William: letter from cited, 530n
Venable, Abraham B.: TJ sends respects
to, 224; appointed to House committee,
372, 373n; and Monroe-Hamilton conflict, 478-9
Venice: and France, xxxvii, 161; Austria
attains control over, 367n
Vergennes, Charles Gravier, Comte de,
365n
Vermont: and election of 1796, 226, 227,
228n, 255-6, 266, 594, 595n
vetch, spring: only variety available in
England, 82
vetch, winter: TJ exchanges seed of, with
Strickland, vii, 102-3, 115, 319-20,
510-11; TJ seeks, 82, 129; seed from
England and Italy, 143, 320, 546; in
TJ's crop rotation plan, 245; description
of, on T. M. Randolph's farms, 319;
Strickland's description of, 512; seed for
J. Taylor, 554
Vienna: U.S. diplomats in, 23n; French
threaten, 367n
*View of the Causes and Consequences of the
Present War with France* (Thomas Er-
skine): sent to TJ, 361; reprinted in
U.S., 407; deemed worthy of notice,
434
*View of the Climate and Soil of the United
States of America* (Constantin François
Chasseboeuf Volney), xxxviii
View of the Conduct of the Executive (James
Monroe). *See* Monroe, James
Vincennes: Volney visits, 174, 220; land
claims, 507-8; letter, memorials from
citizens of, 507-8
Vincent, Charles, 110n
Vindication of Mr. Randolph's Resignation
(Edmund Randolph): TJ discusses, 4

Virgil: *Georgics*, 233n; *Aeneid*, 386, 519
Virginia (TJ's slave): TJ mortgages, 98

VIRGINIA

Agriculture
compared to Spanish, 27-9; abundant
Albemarle Co. harvest, 146, 147; harvest harmed by rains, 146; TJ sends
breadfruit to, 348, 388, 513; varieties
of plants for, 513-14

Constitution
TJ's analysis of criticized, 176n; separation of powers under, 493-4, 499-500;
potential revision of, 524, 538

Courts
and emancipation, 120n; and Wayles estate, 196-7; and land transactions,
287; presentment against S. Cabell,
417, 418-19n, 444-5, 490-1, 491-
504, 524; chancery suits, 476-8;
and British harassment of vessels,
519-20; and protection of natural
rights, 526; and TJ's grand jury petition, 526-7

Description
and ice caves, 116-19, 320, 321; elevations of mountains, 138-9; boundaries
of, 172-3, 262-3, 271-2, 278-9

Economy
insurance rates, premiums, 190-1; investments in U.S. securities, 191;
claims of British creditors, 614

Education and Science
TJ's education bill, 177-8, 287-8

Elections
campaign for presidential electors in
1796, 193-9

Federal Convention
vote on journals, 68; debates on ratification of U.S. Constitution, 323, 380

General Assembly
and TJ's grand jury petition, viii, 524-5,
526-7; and amendments to U.S. Constitution, 5, 36n; election of delegates
to, 27, 52, 322-3, 327-8, 349, 350n;
and Jay Treaty, 129n; and replevin
law, 166; education bills, 177-8, 287-
8; and citizenship for Van Staphorsts,
Hubbard, 215-17, 274, 331, 457-8;
resolution on Md. boundary, 262-3,
278-9; appoints boundary commis-

sion, 271; rebuffs abolition proposal,
488-9; ineffectiveness of Republicans
in, 493; fixes value of foreign coinage,
590n

House of Burgesses
papers of, 283

House of Delegates
and TJ's grand jury petition, viii, 490,
491-504, 505-6, 524; resolutions on
TJ's conduct as governor, 195; impeachment powers, 496-7, 502-3

Laws
on slaves, slavery, 96n, 120n; and land
surveyors, 130; preservation, publication of, 158, 168, 276, 283, 569; replevin law, 166-7; establishing Ky. as
county, 172-3; and Ky. statehood,
172-3; and education of blacks, 177-
8, 287-8; revisals of, 177-8, 287-8; revision of penal, 309-10, 335, 336,
336n, 337-8

Militia
TJ writes captains of, 349, 350n; Dun-
more's War, 409-10n, 441, 452; and
Unicorn affair, 612, 630n

Politics
abolitionism in, 120n, 488-9; design,
construction of state capitol, 310n,
335; and TJ's influence on congressional delegation, 359-60; and party
alignments in House of Representatives, 372, 374n, 385-6, 412, 414,
422, 426; public figures characterized, 383; impact of Saint-Domingue
revolt on, 538

Public Finance
accounts with Grand & Cie., 12, 15, 16-
17, 33-4, 37-8, 39-41; collection of
taxes in, 26-7; accounts with Gautier,
30-3; balance due from TJ, 39-40;
assignats on deposit, 122; estimated
penitentiary costs, 337-9

Society
Houdon statue of Washington, 37-8;
design of new penitentiary, 309-10,
335-9; smallpox, and delay of post,
427, 428; TJ on racial problems,
prospects of black insurrection, 519

Weather
healthy climate in, 43; record low temperatures, 258, 260n; at Williams-

VIRGINIA (*cont.*)
burg, 258, 260n; TJ's plan to record winds, 259; causes delays in postal service, 266; at Montpelier, 488, 591. *See also* Monticello

Virginia, Governor of. *See* Brooke, Robert; Dunmore, John Murray, fourth Earl of; Wood, James

Virginia Argus (Richmond): G. Jefferson advertises in, 577-8

Virginia Chronicle and Norfolk and Portsmouth General Advertiser (Norfolk), 45n

Virginia Gazette, and Petersburg Intelligencer (Petersburg), 45n

Virginia Gazette (Dixon and Hunter): publishes Logan's speech, 601, 604n

Virginia Gazette and General Advertiser (Richmond): publishes TJ's letter to Mazzei, 76

Virginia Impartially Examined (William Bullock): cited by TJ, 294-5

Vivarais, France: mountains compared to western Va.'s, 151

Volney, Constantin François Chasseboeuf: letters to, 61, 224-5, 257-60, 352-3, 474, 507; letters from, 53, 111, 150-2, 174-7, 220-2, 229-30, 237-8, 320-1, 474, 482-3, 523; political views, xxxvii; portrait by G. Stuart, xxxviii, 318 (illus.); travels, xxxviii, 53, 61, 134, 148, 150-2, 174-7, 220-2, 224-5, 482-3; visits Monticello, xxxviii, 61, 111, 124, 126, 148, 151-2n, 175-6n, 482, 507, 523; works by, xxxviii; and TJ's letter to Mazzei, 80; converses with Thornton about university, 110-11; introduced by TJ, 131-3, 134; letter from cited, 152n; Guillemard sends regards to, 154; baggage of, 175, 220, 224-5, 229, 237, 257, 261; and linguistic studies, 202n; friendship with TJ, 224, 352-3, 474; reports Dombey's death, 229-30, 257; on French haste, American patience, 237; noticed by Boston newspaper, 237, 238n; sends news from Philadelphia, 237-8; collects meteorological data, 238, 257-60, 352; on Indians, frontier whites, 238, 259; dispute with Priestley, 320-1, 352; friendship with Madison, 320, 482-3, 507, 523; predicts continuation of war between Britain and France, 433; and Monroe, 482, 507; postpones return to France, 482-3; conveys gossip, 517

Volney's Answer to Doctor Priestley (Constantin François Chasseboeuf Volney), 320-1, 352

Voltaire, François Marie Arouet, xxxvii

Voyage en Syrie et en Égypte (Constantin François Chasseboeuf Volney), xxxviii

Voyage to the Cape of Good Hope (Anders Sparrman): cited, quoted by TJ, 296

Wabash (Ouabache) River: Volney travels to, 174, 175, 220; Imlay challenges TJ's statements about, 175, 176n; Indians of region near, 508n

Walker, Emanuel, 229

Walker, Francis: letters to, 99, 587-8; TJ purchases corn from, 26, 52, 91, 99; TJ sends nails to, 99; letters from cited, 99n, 588n; elected to Va. House of Delegates, 350n; letters to cited, 588n

Walker, Thomas: and T. M. Randolph's business affairs, 90-1, 108n

Waller, Benjamin Carter, 218

Wapping (Randolph slave): works at Edgehill, 260

war: and Jay Treaty, 95-6, 108-10; and the destructiveness of man, 248-51; high costs of, 416, 418n

Wardlaw, William: letter to, 401; financial transactions, 212, 401; letters from cited, 401n

Warfield, Henry, 263n

Warm Springs, Va.: Volney travels through, 150

Washington, Bushrod: letter to, 189-90; letter from, 91; and TJ's letter to Mazzei, 78; letters from cited, 91n, 189-90n; and publication of Va. laws, 158-9; as TJ's attorney, 167n, 189; letters to cited, 189-90n; and Va.-Md. boundary, 263n, 271-2, 278-9

WASHINGTON, GEORGE: letter to, 127-30; letters from, 141-4, 178; and journals of Constitutional Convention, 68; invoked by Society of United Irishmen, 140n

Agriculture
recognized by British Board of Agriculture, xli; and publications from Sinclair, 115; reports on crops and farm practices at Mt. Vernon, 143-4; installs threshing machines, 188n

American Revolutionary War
correspondence from Revolution published by J. Carey, 180-2, 205; and seige of Yorktown, 553

INDEX

WASHINGTON, GEORGE (*cont.*)

Opinions
on anti-administration sentiments in the press, 141-2; on danger of political parties, 142-3

Personal Affairs
statue by Houdon, 37-8; aids Lafayette's son, 126-7; collects linguistic information, 201n; papers from E. Edwards, 314; Volney visits, 483

President
and Pinckney Treaty, 3; cabinet appointments, 5; and Jay Treaty, 9-10, 25, 46-8, 52n, 54, 55-7, 60-1, 62, 70-1, 108, 342, 517, 614; supports aid for Federal District, 10-11; signs acts, 11n, 95n; appoints TJ secretary of state, 20-1; celebration of birthday, 46, 49n; *Message from the President of the United States, Assigning the Reasons which Forbid his Compliance with the Resolution of the Twenty-Fourth Instant*, 54, 55-6, 60-1; and treaty-making powers, 54n, 67-9; statement on U.S. captives in Algiers, 68-9; public veneration for, 93-6, 124, 147, 252, 290, 368, 381, 383, 438; accused of anti-French sentiment, 127, 129n, 141-2; questions on neutrality and the French alliance, 127, 129n, 141-2; seeks steady course to prevent war, 142, 227; and Mme de Chastellux's application, 144-5; and presidential succession, 147, 249n; recalls Monroe from France, 165n, 564-5; characterized as dangerous to country's liberties, 185; Farewell Address, 185, 223; 1796 annual address, 214-15, 218, 223, 227; and relations with France, 215n, 223, 228, 252-3, 280, 285; and Paine, 224, 256, 340, 342, 343, 586; influence on Adams, 226; praised by House of Representatives, 227n; delays address on relations with France, 256, 264-5; sends correspondence and papers to Congress, 272-3, 629n; communications from Europe, 282; and TJ's notification of election as vice president, 282n, 304, 305, 306; retirement, 317; and Genet, 470-2; recommends establishment of board of agriculture, 480; response to publication of forged letters, 505, 506n;

and appointment of minister to France, 552; hosts dinner, 552; and Jay's commission, instructions as envoy, 605, 610

Relations with Jefferson
and TJ's letter to Mazzei, vii, 74, 77-9, 82, 84, 86, 88, 490, 505; TJ quotes letters of, 20-1; TJ criticizes, 51-2, 124, 255; publications in *Aurora* undermine friendship, 127-8, 129-30n, 142-3; papers on *Little Sarah*, 128, 143, 178; accepts TJ's word on publication in newspaper, 141-2

Washington, Martha Dandridge Custis: regards to, from, 129, 144

Washington administration: Federalists seek to continue policies of, 193, 196; opposition to, 198-9n; Madison's criticism of, 265; and U.S. relations with Britain and France, 380; and TJ's letter to Mazzei, 489

Washington City. *See* Federal District

Washington Co., Md.: TJ invited to visit, 381-2; communications with Staunton, Va., 415-16

Watkins, Joseph, 477

Watson, David: and passage for Mrs. Watson, 50, 112; letter from cited, 112n; witnesses document, 331

Watson, Margaret, 50-1, 112

Way, Nicholas, 564

Wayles, John: as security for R. Randolph bond, 96; lands of, 533n

Wayles estate: suit against, 91; claims against, 96-7, 166-7, 197n, 217-18, 268, 419; and case of J. Randolph's bond, 196-7; and *Prince of Wales* case, 196-7; chancery suit against R. Randolph's heirs, 533n

Wayne, Anthony, 630n

Wea (Weeás) Indians, 400

weather: in Spain, 28; Volney collects data on, 238, 257-60, 352; coldest winters, 258; TJ's plan to record, study winds, 259; drought in Md., 559. *See also* Albemarle Co., Va.; Jefferson, Thomas: Scientific Interests; Monticello; Virginia: Weather

Webster, Noah: prints TJ's letter to Mazzei, vii, 75-6, 86-7; and election of 1796, 228n; prints extract of R. King letter, 434n; and Federalist politics, 558; prints charges against TJ, 560n. See also *American Minerva*

Wedderburn, Alexander, Baron Loughborough (Lord Chancellor of Great Britain), 62

weevil: and granaries of wheat, 29; attacks peas, 386

Welch (Welsh), Wakelin, Jr.: letter to, 419; letter from, 173; and TJ's debt to Cary & Co., 173; and settlement of Wayles estate debt, 217-18, 419

Welch (Welsh), Wakelin, Sr.: TJ mortgages slaves to, 96n, 209; and settlement of Wayles estate debt, 166-7, 268; death of, 173, 419; TJ's debt to, 268

Weld, Isaac, 3

West, Benjamin, xli

western states: future of republicanism in, 439

West Indies: French seizure of U.S. vessels in, 215n; as element in U.S. policy, 377; prospect of U.S. support for slave revolts in, 377; and arming of U.S. private vessels for trade in, 422, 423n

West Indies, British: and negotiation of Jay Treaty, 607, 613, 616, 618-19, 624, 627-8; seizure of American shipping, 607

West Indies, French: British expeditionary force against, 25-6, 56, 169; U.S. guarantees French control of, 110n; spoliations in, 455; and seizure of American vessels, 586, 587n; restrictions of trade, 611

West Indies, Spanish: and Pinckney Treaty, 7

Westmoreland Co., Pa.: 1796 election results from, 211

West Virginia: Potomac River in, 116, 118-19n

wheat: harvested by TJ, vii, 168, 170, 244; price of in various American cities, 5, 10, 36, 67, 124, 147, 261, 309, 322, 349-50, 371, 583; scarcity, 5; sold by TJ, 36, 211, 268; effects of drought, cold on, 91, 255, 260, 591; price of, in Britain, 117-18; competition of foreign wheat, 124; and TJ's crop-rotation plan, 128-9, 245-6; Washington reports on growing of, 143; grown in Albemarle Co., 146, 147, 350; TJ uses lieth machine for threshing, 231-2; Sinclair writes about, 480, 512; descriptions of Smyrna and Sicilian, 508-9, 524

Wheeling (Wheelan), Fort, 453

Whiskey Insurrection: Brackenridge's book on, 248-50; compared with insurrection in Britain, 407; and negotiation of Jay Treaty, 612, 613

White, Alexander: letters to, 527-9, 530; provides information on ice caves, 116, 118n, 321; seeks TJ's views on removal to Federal District, 527-9; and road from Georgetown to Ga., 529, 530; letters from cited, 529n; letters to cited, 529n

White, John Campbell, 45n

White, Patrick: letters from, 45, 102; identified, 45n; as administrator of Banister's estate, 45, 102; letters to cited, 102n

White, Whittle & Co., 45n

White, William, 536

White River, 174

Whittle, Conway, 45n

Wickham, John: letter to, 268; letter from, 217-18; identified, 218n; letters to cited, 27n, 218n; and publication of Va. laws, 158-9; as counsel in Wayles estate suits, 166, 268; and settlement of Wayles estate debt, 166-7, 217-18, 268, 419; letters from cited, 218n

Wilcocks, Mr., 558

Wilkinson, James, 520

Willett (Willet), Charles (Norfolk printer), 516

William and Mary, College of, 137n

Williams, Mr. (Nashville, Tenn.), 398, 403

Williams, John, 423n

Williams, Jonathan: letter to, 139-41; letter from, 130-1; barometric measurements of altitude, 130-1, 139-40; seeks TJ's advice, 130-1; relationship to Franklin, 140n; as secretary of APS, 254, 276-7; reads TJ's megalonyx report to APS, 301n

Williamsburg, Va.: coldest temperatures at, 258, 260n

Williamson, Hugh: letters from, 398, 403; in Confederation Congress, 19; and natural history, 398, 403

William V, Prince of Orange (stadtholder of Netherlands), 466

Willink, Van Staphorst & Hubbard: letter from, 334-5; and TJ's French accounts, 14, 31; congratulate TJ, 334-5. See also Van Staphorst & Hubbard

Willis, Francis: letter to, 153-4; TJ hopes to visit, 153; letter from cited, 154n

Willis, Dr. John: TJ's assessment of, 153; and queries on the cow pea, 154, 180n; correspondence with P. Tabb quoted, 180n

Willis, Nelly Conway Madison (Mrs. John Willis), 180n

Willis, Stephen: and renovation of Monticello, 170

Willoughby, Thomas, 295

Wilmington, N.C.: and trade with France, 340; officers for port at, 583n

Wilson, George: recollection associated with megalonyx, 152-3, 171-2, 295-6

Wilson, James: and journals of Constitutional Convention, 68; and Jay Treaty, 71-2; and Holland Land Company, 330n

Winchester, Va.: ice caves near, 116-7, 119n, 321; La Rochefoucauld-Liancourt visits, 154; and post to Charlottesville, 441; stagecoaches to Philadelphia, 445

Winder, William, 594

wine: in TJ's accounts, 31, 469; for TJ, 36, 322; port, drunk by Volney, 221; taxes proposed on, 461, 462

Winlaw, William, 105, 116

Winter, John, 560n

Wirt, Elizabeth Washington Gamble (Mrs. William Wirt): marriage, 359n

Wirt, Mildred Gilmer (Mrs. William Wirt): marriage, death of, 358-9n

Wirt, William: letters from, 358-9, 481; identified, 358-9n; and Cobbs suit, 64n; characterizes Wickham, 218n; orders nails, 358-9, 481; attorney for Callender, Burr, 359n; letters from cited, 359n, 481n; letters to cited, 359n; memorial oration for TJ, Adams, 359n; writings, 359n

Wise, John: and TJ's grand jury petition, 493, 504n

Wistar, Caspar: describes megalonyx specimens, xxxix, 300n, 301n; natural history specimens, 297, 398, 403

Wolcott, Oliver, Jr.: letter from, 584; appointment to cabinet, 5; and diplomats' accounts, 58; reports on direct taxes, 265n; as advisor to Adams, 380-1; R. King writes, 434n; transmits report on Imlay's petition, 584; and removal of Coxe, 595n

Wolcott, Oliver, Sr., 224n

Wollstonecraft, Mary, 176n

wolves: on Appalachian frontier, 297

women: Hannah Rittenhouse's comments on cookery, 25; and politics, 198; musical accomplishments of Sarah McKean, 314; as partners to husbands, 324; as camp followers during American Revolution, 381; TJ's view on role of, 397

Wood, James: letters to, 279, 335-6; letters from, 262-3, 309-10; and Va.-Md. boundary, 262-3, 278-9; and revision of Va. penitentiary system, 309-10, 335-6; letter from cited, 336n; letter to cited, 336n

Woods, William: as candidate for Va. General Assembly, 322, 327-8

Woodward, Augustus B.: visits Monticello, 151n

Wythe, George: letters to, 168, 275-6; letters from, 158-9, 283; would save vines for TJ, 43; and TJ's collection of Va. laws, 158, 168, 569; as law professor, 218n; TJ asks about parliamentary procedure, 274, 275-6, 283, 633; and Va.-Md. boundary, 279; and revisal of Va. laws, 310n; decision of, 574

XYZ Affair: and alien and sedition acts, 537n; mentioned, xxxvii

Yard, James (Philadelphia), 199

Yellow Creek. See Logan (Mingo Indian)

yellow fever: in Philadelphia, 531, 534, 536, 543, 544, 562, 592

York (TJ's slave): in marriage settlement of Mary Jefferson, 550

Yorktown, Va.: seige of, during Am. Revolution, 553

Young, Arthur: praises cichoreum (succory), 144; acquainted with La Rochefoucauld-Liancourt, 149n; and winter vetch, 319-20

Young's (inn, western Va.), 151

Yznardi, Joseph, Jr.: as TJ's wine supplier in Cadiz, 36; and French attacks on U.S. trade, 256n

Zachary (TJ's slave): in marriage settlement of Mary Jefferson, 550

Zane, Isaac, 5

A comprehensive index of Volumes 1-20 of the
First Series has been issued as Volume 21.
Each subsequent volume has its own index,
as does each volume or set of volumes
in the Second Series.

DATE DUE

GAYLORD		PRINTED IN U.S.A.